THE COLLINGRIDGE

ENCYCLOPEDIA OF
GARDENING

THE COLLINGRIDGE
ENCYCLOPEDIA OF GARDENING

ARTHUR HELLYER

MBE, VMH, FLS

Line drawings by Norman Barber

CHARTWELL
BOOKS INC.

CONTENTS

Introduction 5

About Names and Abbreviations 6

Associating Plants 8

Garden Plants 25

Index of Common Names and Synonyms 211

Garden Design 217

Fruits and Vegetables 231

Garden Management 253

ACKNOWLEDGEMENTS
We would like to thank the
following for providing the photographs used in
this book: Pat Brindley, Kenneth Scowen,
and the Harry Smith Horticultural
Photographic Collection

Published by Chartwell Books Inc.,
A Division of Book Sales Inc.,
110 Enterprise Avenue, Secaucus
New Jersey 07094

Printed in England by
Butler and Tanner Ltd., Frome, Somerset
Filmset in England by Tradespools Ltd., Frome, Somerset
Set in 9 on 10pt Monophoto Ehrhardt

INTRODUCTION

The germ of this book was really born 46 years ago when I joined the staff of *Amateur Gardening* as an assistant to the editor, A. J. Macself, and was immediately told to get on with the revision of *Sanders' Encyclopaedia of Gardening*. It was a task far beyond my capability at the time but it introduced me to the peculiar world of the encyclopedists who must compress within an arbitrary space imposed by the economics of publishing a vast amount of information about the subject of their choice, and it made me want to do something of the kind myself.

In due course the new edition appeared, to be followed by numerous reprints, and yet another revision in 1948, by which time I was editor and other people worked on the encyclopedia under my direction. But still I was not happy with the result and resolved that one day, if fortune favoured me, I would attempt to build an entirely new encyclopedia upon the Sanders' base, but not one that simply set out to bring the old matter up to date.

Times had changed since T. W. Sanders first serialized his great work in *Amateur Gardening* in the closing years of the 19th century. Then, gardening was still mainly the hobby of the well-to-do, and most owners employed professional gardeners to do much or all the work for them. Gardens were less numerous but, on average, far larger, labour and fuel were cheap and greenhouses could be maintained at temperatures which seem ridiculously extravagant today.

Science had as yet made scarcely any impact on gardening practice and, in fact, Sanders had omitted all reference to the routine operations of the garden and to chemicals which might need to be used in it, presumably because these would be well known to the professionals who managed them. As a result he had produced what was in effect not so much an encyclopedia of gardening as an encyclopedia of garden plants. Then, for economy of space, illustrations had not been included, either in the original serialization or in any of the subsequent volumes founded on it.

The second of these omissions I was able to rectify in 1953 with a companion volume to Sanders' encyclopedia, *The Encyclopaedia of Plant Portraits*, and by that time I was also at work on a third book in the same format, *The Encyclopaedia of Garden Work and Terms*, which was published in 1954. As a last stage on this particular road the three volumes were bound together and offered as *The Gardeners' Golden Treasury*.

This combined volume was very successful but I was still far from content. The book was an obvious hybrid, it was too big, contained too many plants which had been unobtainable for years if, in fact, they ever had been grown in gardens, and its information about the cultivation of individual species was still pretty firmly based in the pre-scientific period. What I still hankered after was an encyclopedia in the admirably concise Sanders' manner, but dealing with plants, cultivation and garden management in a completely contemporary way.

The opportunity arose three years ago when the Hamlyn Group proposed the publication of a single volume garden reference book to be known as *The Collingridge Encyclopedia of Gardening*, and asked me if I would like to prepare the copy. I accepted with alacrity though I knew that it would be a formidable task. That it has been possible to complete it in such a comparatively short time is due to the generous help I have received from a number of people. In particular I am indebted to Susanne Mitchell, who not only typed a large part of the copy, a task requiring great concentration and endurance, but diligently read it and the subsequent printers' proofs, pointed out omissions, duplications and contradictions and made countless useful suggestions, and supervised the choice and preparation of all the illustrations.

My wife assisted me in the preparation of the copy, read all the proofs and checked all the genera and families to ensure they conformed with the authorities followed.

I am grateful also to Kenneth Midgley for producing an account of garden designing with which I find myself in complete agreement and for providing such admirably clear plans and sketches to illustrate it.

Then there is the artist, Norman Barber, who has drawn the many line illustrations in the text, the photographers who have contributed the beautiful pictures reproduced in the colour section and the designer, Bryan Dunn, who has put the whole work together and made what appears to me such a very attractive book.

Finally, I must thank Robert Pearson, editor of gardening books to the Hamlyn Group, who conceived the idea of the book and has never lost faith in it despite the steadily mounting costs imposed by inflation and whose total support has made the work so much easier than it would otherwise have been.

Arthur Hellyer

ABOUT NAMES & ABBREVIATIONS

Any serious encyclopedia of plants must make use of a binomial system of nomenclature since no other is sufficiently concise or so readily permits the grouping of plants of a kind under one shared name, so enabling an orderly alphabetical sequence with no unnecessary repetition. Since the only system of this kind that has ever been devised for plants is that used by botanists, gardeners have been glad to make use of it, though not always with a clear idea of what they were about. What is overlooked most often is that in this matter of plant names the needs of botanists and those of gardeners are not always alike and are sometimes diametrically opposed. Gardeners require names that are stable, remaining as nearly as possible the same at all times and in all places. Botanists need (and have devised for themselves) a system of nomenclature which is sufficiently flexible to express changing ideas about the relationships between plants based on new information about them or different interpretations of existing information. As knowledge grows so the names alter and since quite different botanists see the facts in different ways several names may compete simultaneously for the same plant, each expressing an individual view about its true place in the evolutionary order.

It is absurd for gardeners to complain that botanists are monkeying about with the names. It is their system devised for their purposes and they protect themselves against the confusion which it would otherwise produce by always quoting the authority for every name they use. Thus *Pharbitis purpurea* Voigt, *Ipomoea purpurea* Roth, and *Convolvulus purpureus* L. are all names for the same plant – the lovely twining annual which gardeners often call Morning Glory. The first name was given by a botanist named Johann Otto Voigt, who lived between 1798 and 1843, the second by Albrecht Wilhelm Roth, 1757 to 1834, and the third by the father of modern botany and inventor of the binomial system, the great Carolus Linnaeus (or Carl von Linné) whose life span was from 1707 to 1778. If any doubt should arise as to whether these three were really naming identical plants their original descriptions can be consulted, and, if necessary, re-assessed.

All this is far too complex for gardeners who, as a rule, are little concerned with the finer points of relationship, but simply want names as a means of intelligible communication. What would be ideal for them would be standardized plant names based on the binomial system and approved by national (or better still international) authorities, but not subject to the changes and uncertainties of botanical classification. It really would not be very difficult to do this, but, though at least one start has been made, the work stopped for lack of money and nothing has yet materialized. So the most useful thing that any gardening encyclopedist can do is to select one authority for all or at least most of the names he uses. This is what I have done in this book, my chosen guide being the Royal Horticultural Society's *Dictionary of Gardening* from which I have only departed when I had strong reason to believe that to adhere to it would cause unnecessary confusion or would be misleading. The Morning Glory already quoted is such a case of departure, for the R.H.S. uses the name *Pharbitis purpurea*, which has never caught on with gardeners, whereas the present fashion among botanists seems to be to return all species of *Pharbitis* to *Ipomoea*, a name which is much used in gardens. It would, therefore, seem silly to ask gardeners to change from a familiar to an unfamiliar name which botanists are in process of abandoning.

To give readers the widest possible scope for associating names they know or have heard with those used in this book I have also included many alternatives, treating these as synonyms. In doing so I make no judgement about their botanical status since this would be quite outside the scope or competence of this work.

The binomial system just described covers the genera and the species in which botanists group plants. These, with the varieties which are often selected and maintained in gardens, are all that the gardener needs to know in order to obtain the plants he requires or to discuss them intelligibly with other gardeners. Indeed, often the generic and varietal name are themselves sufficient, since under the international rules for naming horticultural plants the same varietal name cannot be given to two different varieties in the same genus. The gardener who asks for *Forsythia* Lynwood or *Buddleia* Royal Red therefore makes as precise a request as another who gives the full name *Forsythia intermedia* Lynwood and *Buddleia davidii* Royal Red, and this kind of horticultural abbreviation has much to commend it for many horticultural purposes.

But botanists do more than group plants in species and genera. They also build them up into much larger assemblages of related kinds, attempting in so doing to illustrate the evolutionary process. There is no practical need for gardeners to be conversant with such large scale systems of classification, but many like to do so as a matter of interest, and so in this encyclopedia I have included the family to which each genus belongs after the name of the genus itself. Since there are several rival systems of classification it has been necessary to make a choice between them (some encyclopedias quote two or more of them, but this seems to me to be confusing for all but the most botanically sophisticated readers who will in any case know where to get the information elsewhere). Since this is a purely botanical and not at all a horticultural matter I have not chosen the R.H.S. dictionary as my guide but *A Dictionary of the Flowering Plants and Ferns* by J. C. Willis, in its 8th edition revised by H. K. Airy Shaw of the Royal Botanic Gardens, Kew.

A few other matters may require some explanation. Since flowering times are usually controlled by temperature and day length they can vary considerably from place to place. I have, therefore, used seasons rather than months to indicate them, but for those who seek something more precise I would define my seasons for much of Britain as follows:

SPRING   March to May
SUMMER   June to August
AUTUMN   September to November
WINTER   December to February

It follows that for the same areas 'early spring' could be read as March, 'mid-spring' as April, 'late spring' as May, and so on round the year. But in the extreme South-west spring comes early, autumn continues late and winter is almost non-existent, while the reverse holds true for the coldest parts of the North and East where spring comes later, autumn arrives early, summer is curtailed and winter prolonged.

To avoid needless repetition I have used some short cuts in the cultural notes, particularly in describing the treatment of plants under glass. Thus I have frequently referred to John Innes potting composts or equivalents. Fuller particulars about these will be found in the final section of this book under the heading 'Composts'. In recommending composts for orchids I have usually specified 'fibre' rather than 'osmunda fibre' because the latter has become scarce, expensive and in some places unobtainable. Fibre can be interpreted as any long-lasting, fibrous material including the roots of polypodium as well as osmunda ferns and also such popular and relatively cheap substitutes as bark chippings or pounded bark.

I have also used the phrase 'normal watering' where a plant grown under glass needs to be watered fairly freely while in growth from spring to autumn, but only moderately in winter.

The terms 'cold greenhouse', 'cool greenhouse', 'intermediate greenhouse', and 'warm greenhouse' often appear as abbreviated descriptions of temperature regimes where these do not depart from the norm covered by these terms. These norms are defined on page 312.

Finally, on the difficult question of metrication, I have used centigrade (Celsius) temperatures throughout the book as these are now generally accepted in many parts of the world. However, I include here a simple conversion chart to the Fahrenheit scale. For further details see Thermometers on pages 399 to 400.

Centigrade	Fahrenheit (approx.)
− 10	14
− 5	23
0	32
5	40
7	45
10	50
13	55
15	59
18	65
20	68
25	77
27	80
30	86

Measurements of length are given in Imperial units as I believe these are likely to remain the most easily recognizable for most readers for some time. A guide for converting these to metric units is given below.

inches	cms (approx.)	feet	metres (approx.)
2	5	3	1
4	10	6½	2
6	15	10	3
8	20	13	4
10	25	16	5
12	30	20	6
18	45	30	9
		40	12
		50	15
		100	30
		150	48

ASSOCIATING PLANTS

The idea that it matters greatly which plants go with which – since in association they may make or mar each other's beauty – is relatively new and even today is by no means fully appreciated. To many professional garden architects design is still mainly a matter of form and volume, of a correct balance between masses and voids, lights and shades; all of which are matters which can be more readily achieved by architectural means and a strictly limited range of plants, than by making full use of the enormous range of plant material now available. Many would go further and declare that they neither had any great knowledge of plants nor desired to acquire it since too many plants would simply confuse design, and that in any case exotic plants, being alien to the British landscape, appear incongruous in it.

To plant lovers this seems perverse since to them gardens are primarily places in which to grow and enjoy plants, the more, and more diverse, the better. Yet without design a plantsman's garden can become a rather muddled collection, interesting for its contents, but meaningless as an artistic creation.

Clearly for the gardener it is necessary to reconcile these two approaches and it is astonishing how little has been written about such an important matter. One must still turn back to the books of Gertrude Jekyll, many of them written 70 years and more ago, for the best guidance in the use of plants, and it was the partnership between this sensitive artist and plant lover and the architect Edwin Lutyens which turned those ideas into practice. It is greatly to be regretted that so few of the gardens which Lutyens designed and Jekyll planted have survived in their original form, and it is of the nature of gardening that in the passage of time it is the plants, not the architectural designs, that have suffered most.

Yet though there are few authentic Jekyll gardens to serve as guides today, others have made gardens following similar principles of firm underlying pattern, often with quite elaborate architectural features, overlaid with a rich mantle of plants which softens and sometimes almost completely conceals the formal lines below, yet is an integral part of the whole conception. The gardens of Hidcote Manor in Gloucestershire, made by Major Lawrence Johnston in the early years of the century, and those of Sissinghurst Castle in Kent, made by Vita Sackville-West and her husband, Sir Harold Nicholson,

from about 1930 until their deaths in the 1960s, are two of the most famous and admired examples of this kind. Both are beautifully maintained by the National Trust and open to the public for much of the year. There are many more, some smaller and less well known, but showing the same sensitivity in the use of plants to embellish design and create an ever-changing series of pictures through the year.

Gardens such as these not only require a wide knowledge of plants, their needs, growth rates, foliage, colour and time of flowering, but also an artist's eye in associating the material that is available to best advantage and assessing the impact which each plant will make upon its neighbours either by contrast, harmony or simply by making an effective background.

Stimulus to this kind of clever planting has also come from the increase of interest in flower arranging. Many of those who practise this, either as a hobby or a profession, are constantly looking for new and interesting flowers and foliage and learning how to use them effectively. Some have gone on to apply this knowledge to the use of these same plants in their own gardens and these in turn have given inspiration to other garden makers.

It is the purpose of this colour section to illustrate just a few of the many kinds of plant groupings which can be used effectively and the type of settings in which plants look their best. The possible combinations are limitless and it is unlikely that all those shown here were completely premeditated or turned out quite right at the first attempt. Some may have done so, more were probably arrived at by a process of trial and error, and some may simply have been happy accidents which surprised as much as they delighted their creators.

Gardening is like that, since plants behave differently in different places and even in successive years, so that it is rarely possible to work entirely by rule of thumb.

Perennial plants, a term which is used here to include trees and shrubs as well as the herbaceous kinds, also have an awkward habit of growing larger and larger, which means that they require constant oversight to keep everything in scale. This explains why gardens in which plants play the key role so often deteriorate rapidly when their owners depart and they are no longer managed, pruned, coaxed and renewed with the skill which created them. It also explains why this kind of garden making so completely captivates those who fall under its spell.

Paths and Paving

1 | 2
3 | 4

Choice of the correct paving material is important for two reasons, one practical, the other aesthetic. Paths and terraces must not only be durable and convenient to walk on at all seasons of the year, but also, because they are a permanent and sometimes dominant feature of the scene, they must contribute to its mood and character.

Random stone paving, such as that shown in the overall picture on these two pages, is essentially rustic in appearance and hard wearing in character, but it is not the easiest of surfaces to walk on and it can be a very bumpy one over which to wheel a heavily laden barrow. It is an ideal paving material for gardens laid out in the cottage style and it looks good in a kitchen garden, but loses points on the score of convenience.

Brick [1] is a dual-purpose material, equally suitable for a dignified or a natural setting. It can be laid in a variety of ways and patterns and it wears just as well as stone paving but it can become very slippery in wet weather. For this reason it is to be avoided for steeply sloping surfaces.

Delightful effects can be obtained by combining two or more materials [2], as in this cobbled path edged with roughly shaped paving slabs. But paths such as this, especially if heavily stocked with carpeting and tufted plants, are decorative features of the garden chosen as much for their appearance as for utility and are not suitable for constant use.

Much the same applies to stepping stones [3], which can provide a useful means of reducing wear on lawns and look delightful in the right place, but should be regarded as suitable for occasional use only.

In formal settings, and also for steps, no paving surpasses rectangular slabs, either of natural or reconstituted stone [4], which can be used alone or, as here, in combination with brick or other materials.

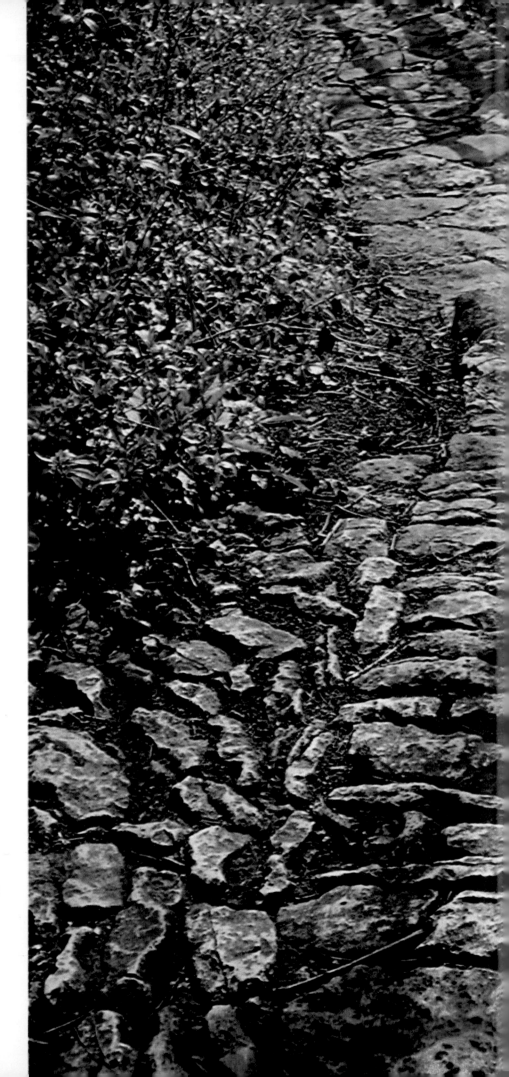

Rock Gardens and Walls

Many rock plants are quite small and so it is possible to enjoy a considerable variety in a relatively small space. Many also succeed just as well in raised beds or walls as in rock gardens and these are methods of culture which often fit very conveniently into the design of a garden. The first picture shows such a wall built of unmortared Cotswold stone and gay in spring with aubrieta, perennial candytuft and small brooms.

Another possibility is the scree bed [2], which can be either quite flat, as here, or made on a slope with or without some rocks outcropping from it. The essential feature of the scree is that it consists very largely of stone chippings so that drainage is perfect and many alpines, otherwise difficult to cultivate, thrive. Here a lovely form of *Iris reticulata* named Joyce is obviously enjoying the conditions.

Below [3] is a good example of a rock garden made with sandstone. Note the way in which the large blocks of stone have been well bedded into the soil and arranged to form a series of fairly level terraces or steps, such as might occur in any natural outcrop of this kind. The alpine daisy, *Anacyclus depressus*, is in the background with a hybrid lewisia established in a vertical crevice in the middle and a ramonda sheltering behind it.

Old stone troughs [4] make excellent containers for rock plants and can be used effectively as ornaments in almost any garden. This fine example contains *Chiastophyllum oppositifolium*, *Sedum spathulifolium* Cappa Blanca and *Saxifraga aizoon*,

as well as sempervivums, achilleas and other small plants.

Large rock gardens fit well into natural or semi-wild settings such as this [5], but can involve a lot of work since most weeding must be done by hand and grass edgings can be a problem. But the effect, when well planted, can be tremendous.

Pools and Water Gardens

1 3
2 4

Even a tiny stream or rivulet can be converted into a notable garden feature by widening its banks, possibly altering its course, and constructing small dams at fairly frequent intervals to maintain an adequate water level even when the flow is at its lowest. In this charming example [1] the banks are planted with kingcups, drumstick primulas, daffodils, tulips, hyacinths and violas.

This pool [2] is associated with a rock garden and has become a natural and convincing extension of it. In the foreground are the solidly architectural leaves of a variegated hosta, while in the water itself several aquatic irises have been established as well as coppery-orange mimulus. Candelabra primulas make a strong splash of colour in the background.

Water can be used effectively in the most sophisticated surroundings, as in this little courtyard [3]. Here there is a deliberate contrast between 'natural' effects in the foreground where trollius thrives among the rocks and kingcups flower in the water, and the artificiality of the brick plant troughs with their bedded out hydrangeas and coleus. Note the handsome foliage and feathery crimson flower spikes of *Rheum palmatum tanguticum* beyond the flag-paved bridge.

Finally in this garden [4] water is the main feature, used in a romantic way to suggest cascades feeding a large pool surrounded by a profusion of plants. Though the model for this charming garden is natural, the setting is artificial and no attempt has been made to conceal this either in the overall design or the treatment of individual details. It is rather as though a beautiful landscape picture had been hung on the wall of a well-furnished room.

14

Foliage Associations

Effects contrived with foliage usually last much longer than those made with flowers. For example, the leaves of *Rodgersia podophylla* [1] will emerge in April and remain until October, and the peeling bark of *Acer griseum* will be decorative all the year.

The white-striped leaves of *Hosta undulata* are the central feature of this town garden group [2], with the variegated form of *Sedum sieboldii* in front, the lime-green flowers of *Alchemilla mollis* behind and the contrasted foliage shapes and colours of *Helleborus foetidus* and *Tiarella* *cordifolia* in the foreground.

Picture [3] shows a little garden planted entirely in shades of yellow, orange and green. Plants used include golden elder, the yellow-tipped form of Pfitzer's juniper, hostas, *Ligularia* Grallagh Gold and the rose Frühlingsgold.

In this winter scene [4] the orange-yellow stems of golden willow are contrasted with the silver grey of

lavender cotton (santolina).

A blue and grey border [5] which makes good use of lavenders, ballota, lavender cotton, atriplex, rue, and *Sisyrinchium striatum*.

Rich autumn colour [6] is provided by *Parrotia persica* in the foreground of this garden glade with *Acer palmatum* in the distance.

Flower
Associations

Since many plants flower for only a few weeks, considerable care is needed in devising effective flower associations to ensure that all varieties chosen for any group do bloom at the same time.

The scene in the first picture is planned for June and relies in the main on the tall, bearded irises in numerous varieties and colours contrasted with the deep-coloured form of red valerian (*Centranthus ruber*) in the foreground, and some early flowering pink and red climbing roses on the arches beyond. There would be little to follow here in late summer and indeed irises are not good mixers.

Below is a late spring association with doronicum and pansies providing much of the colour, assisted by May-flowering tulips and double-flowered *Kerria japonica* on the fence with some late blooms of the scarlet Japanese quince (*Chaenomeles speciosa*). The pansies will continue well into the summer but the other flowers will not.

The border [3] will make a longer display because the antirrhinums, zinnias and ageratum used will remain in flower for months, though the phlox, perennial sunflower, boltonia and delphinium will not keep pace with them. However it would be easy to interplant with Michaelmas daisies and other late-flowering perennials to extend the season.

Heathers [4] can be selected to flower most months of the year and flower colour can be supplemented by the foliage colour of golden and coppery leaved varieties. Double-flowered varieties, such as *Calluna vulgaris* H. E. Beale in the foreground, last in bloom particularly well. Other heathers shown here are white forms of ling (*C. vulgaris*), the compact crimson-flowered *Erica vagans* Mrs D. F. Maxwell and a crimson bell heather (*E. cinerea*) in the background.

(continued overleaf)

18

Many annuals [5] have a particularly long flowering season and even when they have not it is usually fairly easy to raise two batches, one to follow the other. However, there would be no need to take even this precaution with the lobelia and French and African marigolds used in these gay beds. The fluffy hare's tail grass, *Lagurus ovatus*, provides a pleasant foil for the rather stolid marigolds.

Flowering trees and shrubs can be associated in equally clever ways as in this garden [6], in which rose and yellow azaleas and a purple rhododendron are grouped beneath laburnums.

A much more complex association has been attempted in this early summer border [above], in which perennials of many kinds are displayed against a brick wall well clothed with roses and *Vitis coignetiae*. Among the plants used are veronica, peony, bearded iris, pyrethrum, *Stachys lanata*, oriental poppies, aquilegia and eremurus, not yet fully in bloom.

Containers

1 | 2
3 | 4

Plants in containers are particularly useful around the house and in patios and courtyards. Beds have been kept to a minimum in the small bungalow garden [1] where most of the colour comes from window boxes and a large tub planted with pelargoniums, marguerites, marigolds and lobelia.

Zonal and ivy-leaved pelargonium combined [2] provide an economical means of stocking a sunny window box. The ivy-leaved variety with cream-edged leaves is L'Elegante.

Below [3], container plants are so cleverly combined with plants in a bed that it is hard to see where one begins and the other ends. Plants include petunias, coleus, pelargoniums, fuchsias, lobelia, nasturtium, annual alyssum and a small, grey-leaved conifer.

The metal stand [4] is itself decorative and gives scope for a constantly changing display of pot–grown plants – at this moment pelargoniums, petunias, nemesias, alyssum and lobelia.

21

Bulbs

1 | 2 | 3 4 5

Bulbs have the great merit that, provided one starts with good, well-developed specimens, they are almost certain to make a good display the first year since the flowers are likely to be already formed in embryo within the bulb and waiting only for moisture, warmth and light to emerge and develop.

This is true of the crown imperial, *Fritillaria imperialis* [1], one of the most statuesque of bulbous plants but not, unfortunately, always an easy one to maintain in good condition. The clusters of bell-shaped flowers, carried high on stout stems and surmounted by a curious top-knot of leaves, may be yellow, orange or tawny red. This fritillaria thrives in rich soil and, if doing well, should be left undisturbed until obviously overcrowded.

Totally different in character is the deceptively fragile-looking *Crocus tomasinianus* [2]. It is, in fact, a robust and easy plant to grow and one that usually multiplies rapidly whether

planted in a rock garden or, as here, naturalized in short grass.

Daffodils of all kinds are also easy plants to grow either in cultivated beds or naturalized in grass [3]. They look their best grown naturally in generous drifts as here, either in the open or under widely spaced trees, such as the ornamental cherries with which they are associated here.

There are lilies for sun or shade, some easily grown, others more difficult and requiring special soil or treatment, but none more beautiful or accommodating than the regal lily, *Lilium regale* [4]. It will grow in most fertile soils, even those containing some lime or chalk, and it often spreads quite rapidly by self-sown seedlings.

Erythroniums are small bulbs for semi-shady places in rock gardens or beside woodland paths. Some are known as dog's-tooth violets, but this charming American species, *E. revolutum* [5], is called the trout lily.

Climbers

Well-clothed walls are as essential to the garden scene as properly stocked borders and there is the same scope for skill in association between plants of contrasting yet mutually compatible character.

This sunny wall at Sissinghurst Castle [1] has just such an association starting at the left with *Magnolia grandiflora*, followed by an evergreen ceanothus and then pink and crimson climbing roses. Note also the purple pansies in a terracotta container, a typical Sissinghurst touch.

Large-flowered clematis are never happier than when climbing into other stouter plants as here [2], where *Clematis* Ville de Lyon finds support from honeysuckle and *Euonymus fortunei* Silver Queen.

Madame Grégoire Staechelin [3] is one of the most opulent of climbing roses and though it crowds most of its flowering into one early summer display it usually follows this with a handsome crop of crimson hips.

GARDEN PLANTS

ABELIA – *Caprifoliaceae*. Hardy or slightly tender evergreen and deciduous flowering shrubs. Good maritime subjects.

Soil, ordinary, well drained for most kinds but lime free for *A. serrata*. Position, warm, sunny, or *A. floribunda* in a frost-proof greenhouse in winter but outdoors in summer.

Plant in spring or early autumn. Prune, if necessary, in spring.

Increase by layering in spring; by cuttings of firm shoots in a cold frame or under mist in summer.

Recommended kinds are *A. chinensis*, white, fragrant, summer, early autumn, to 6 ft., deciduous, China; *floribunda*, rosy purple, early summer, to 6 ft., evergreen, Mexico; *grandiflora*, pink, summer, autumn, to 6 ft., semi-evergreen, hybrid between *chinensis* and *uniflora*; *schumannii*, pink, late summer, autumn, to 5 ft., deciduous, China; *serrata*, white tinged pink or orange, late spring, early summer, 3 to 4 ft., deciduous, Japan; *triflora*, white and pink, fragrant, early summer, to 12 ft., deciduous, Himalaya.

ABELIOPHYLLUM – *Oleaceae*. Hardy deciduous shrub.

Soil, ordinary, well drained. Position, sheltered, sunny. Prune fairly hard after flowering.

Increase by summer cuttings or by layering in spring or autumn.

The only species is *A. distichum*, white, late winter, to 3 ft., Korea.

ABIES (Fir) – *Pinaceae*. Hardy coniferous evergreen trees of pyramidal habit.

Soil, good, deep, not liable to dry out badly. Mostly unsuitable for shallow chalk though *A. cephalonica* and *pinsapo* are exceptions.

Increase by seeds kept for three months at temp. 4°C. and then sown in a frame or outdoors.

Recommended kinds are *A. alba* (syn. *pectinata*), Silver Fir, 100 to 150 ft., Central and S. Europe; *amabilis*, Pacific Silver Fir, 60 to 100 ft., British Columbia; *balsamea*, Balsam Fir, Balm of Gilead, 60 to 80 ft., Canada, and var. *hudsonia*, dwarf; *bracteata*, 100 to 150 ft., California; *cephalonica*, Grecian Fir, 80 to 120 ft., Greece; *cilicica*, 60 to 80 ft., Asia Minor; *concolor*, Colorado Fir, 80 to 130 ft., Colorado, New Mexico, Arizona, vars. *compacta*, low rounded bush, *lowiana*, narrower habit, *violacea*, effective glaucous form; *delavayi*, 50 to 80 ft., China; *grandis*, Giant Fir, 100 to 300 ft., California; *homolepis* (syn. *brachyphylla*), Nikko Fir, 80 to 100 ft., Japan; *koreana*, 30 to 60 ft., Korea; *lasiocarpa*, Alpine Fir, 60 to 100 ft., Western N. America, var. *arizonica*, Corkbark Fir, slow growing, grey foliage; *magnifica*, Red Fir, 100 to 180 ft., N. W. America; *nordmanniana*, Caucasian Fir, 100 to 200 ft., Caucasus; *numidica*, Algerian Fir,

70 to 100 ft., Algeria; *pindrow*, 80 to 100 ft., Himalaya; *pinsapo*, Spanish Fir, 60 to 100 ft., Spain, var. *glauca*, grey leaved; *procera* (syn. *nobilis*), Noble Fir, 100 to 200 ft., Western U.S.A.; *sachalinensis*, 130 ft., N. Japan; *spectabilis* (syn. *webbiana*), 80 to 150 ft., Himalaya; *veitchii*, 50 to 70 ft., Japan; *vilmorinii*, 50 to 80 ft., hybrid.

ABUTILON – *Malvaceae*. Slightly tender shrubs or sub-shrubs, grown both for foliage and flower.

Soil, good, loamy. Position, warm, sunny, or in a cool greenhouse. Garden varieties and *A. striatum thompsonii* are used for summer bedding. Cut out winter-damaged stems in spring.

Increase by seeds sown in a greenhouse or frame in spring, grow young plants in pots until finally planted; by cuttings in sandy soil in summer.

Abutilon striatum thompsonii

Recommended kinds include garden varieties with bell-shaped flowers in various colours produced all the year, and the following species: *A. megapotamicum*, yellow and scarlet, summer, early autumn, 4 to 8 ft., Brazil; *striatum*, orange-red, all year round, 6 to 10 ft., Brazil, and var. *thompsonii*, leaves yellow mottled; *vitifolium*, blue, mauve, white, summer, downy vine-like leaves, 10 to 25 ft., sometimes short lived, Chile.

ACACIA (Wattle) – *Leguminosae*. Slightly tender, evergreen flowering shrubs or small trees. All species recommended are of Australian origin and yellow flowered, but there are also African species.

Soil, well drained, most kinds dislike lime but *A. longifolia* and *rhetinodes* are tolerant. Position, warm, sunny places or in a frost-proof greenhouse. Prune after flowering to maintain shape.

Increase by seeds sown in spring; by cuttings of half-ripened shoots inserted in sandy peat in a frame in summer; some kinds by suckers in autumn or early spring.

Recommended kinds are *A. armata*, Kangaroo Thorn, spring, 6 to 10 ft.; *baileyana*, late winter, early spring, 15 to 20 ft.; *dealbata*, Silver Wattle, Mimosa, late winter,

Acacia verticillata

early spring, 20 to 50 ft.; *drummondii*, spring, 10 ft.; *longifolia*, Sydney Golden Wattle, late winter, spring, 15 to 30 ft.; *melanoxylon*, Blackwood Acacia, spring, 20 to 30 ft., one of the hardiest, Australia and Tasmania; *pendula*, Weeping Myall, spring, grey foliage, pendulous branches, 15 to 20 ft.; *pravissima*, spring, 10 to 20 ft.; *rhetinodes*, all year, 15 to 20 ft.; *riceana*, spring, 20 to 30 ft., Tasmania; *verticillata*, spring, 15 to 30 ft.

See also Albizia and Robinia.

ACAENA – *Rosaceae*. Hardy, trailing, low-growing evergreen perennials with ornamental foliage and burrs but insignificant flowers. Cultivated kinds mostly native to New Zealand.

Soil, ordinary, reasonably well drained. Position, open or semi-shaded, as ground cover or in paving.

Increase by seeds sown in spring; by division of roots in spring or autumn.

Recommended kinds are *A. buchananii*, silvery green foliage, red burrs; *microphylla*, crimson burrs, var. *inermis*, khaki-coloured loose mats; *novae-zelandiae*, New Zealand Burr, trailing, bronze foliage, red-purple burrs.

ACALYPHA (Copper-leaf) – *Euphorbiaceae*. Tender evergreen plants with attractive foliage.

Compost, equal parts leafmould, peat, loam and sand. Pot and prune in late winter. Temperatures, summer 20°C. or more, winter 15 to 18°C. Increase by cuttings in a temperature of 25°C. in spring.

Recommended kinds include *A. hispida*, Red-hot Cat-tail, or Chenille Plant, 6 to 10 ft., New Guinea, which is the only kind with notable flowers. Others grown solely for foliage are *godseffiana*, 1 to 3 ft., New Guinea; *wilkesiana* (syn. *tricolor*), 3 to 4 ft., Fiji, and vars. *macafeana*, *macrophylla*, *marginata*, *musaica*, *obovata* and *triumphans*.

ACANTHOLIMON (Prickly Thrift) – *Plumbaginaceae.* Hardy evergreen perennials, flowering in summer.

Soil, ordinary, well drained. Position, full sun in a rock garden or warm wall. Plant in spring.

Increase by cuttings in a frame in late summer, or by seeds sown in spring or early summer.

Recommended kinds are *A. androsaceum*, pink, 6 in., S. Europe; *creticum*, pink, 3 in., Crete; *glumaceum*, rose, 6 to 9 in., Armenia, the easiest and commonest; *venustum*, deep pink, 6 in., Asia Minor.

ACANTHOPANAX – *Araliaceae.* Hardy, ornamental-leaved deciduous shrubs formerly included in the genus *Aralia.* Ivy-like fruits and, usually, prickly stems.

Soil, rich well-drained loam. Position, warm, sheltered. Plant in spring or autumn.

Increase by seed sown in temp. 15 to 18°C. in spring; by cuttings of ripened shoots in autumn; by suckers at any time.

Recommended kinds are *A. henryi*, 8 ft., finely toothed compound leaves, China; *sieboldianus* (syn. *pentaphyllus*), 8 ft., elegant foliage, Japan, var. *variegatus*, leaves edged creamy white; *simonii*, 4 ft., attractive compound leaves, yellow spines, China.

ACANTHUS (Bear's Breech) – *Acanthaceae.* Hardy herbaceous perennials with ornamental foliage. All produce stiff spikes of flowers in summer.

Soil, ordinary. Position, sun or partial shade. Plant in spring or autumn.

Increase by root cuttings in winter; by seeds sown in light soil in spring, or by division of roots in spring or autumn.

Recommended kinds are *A. longifolius*, purple, 3 to 4 ft., Dalmatia; *mollis*, white, rose, lilac, 3 to 4 ft., S. Europe, var. *latifolius*, larger and hardier form; *spinosus*, purple, leaves spiny, 3 to 4 ft., S. Europe.

ACER (Maple) – *Aceraceae.* A large genus of hardy ornamental trees, including a few shrubby species, notably the Japanese Maple, *A. palmatum*, and its varieties. Most are deciduous. All have typical winged fruits (samarae). The majority have five-lobed palmate leaves which assume attractive autumn tints.

Soil, reasonably good. Position, sun or semi-shade; Japanese kinds in sheltered places and well-drained soil. Plant in autumn or late winter.

Increase by seeds sown in a sheltered position as soon as ripe or stratified for three months at 4°C. and then sown; by grafting in spring; by budding in summer for choice Japanese and variegated kinds; by layering in autumn.

Recommended kinds are *A. campestre*, Field Maple, to 30 ft., Britain, var. *variegatum*, leaves white and yellow, 20 ft.; *capillipes*, 35 ft., marbled bark, Japan; *cap-padocicum* (syn. *laetum*), to 50 ft.; *circinatum*, Vine Maple, leaves scarlet in autumn, 5 ft., N. W. America; *davidii*, 30 to 40 ft., striated bark, China; *ginnala*, 10 to 15 ft., China, Japan, Manchuria; *griseum*, 40 ft., dark-coloured peeling bark revealing orange younger layers beneath, magnificent autumn tints, China; *grosseri*, 20 to 30 ft., striated bark, China; *hersii*, similar to the last; *japonicum*, 20 ft., Japan, and its vars. *aureum*, golden-leaved, *laciniatum* finely-cut leaves, and *vitifolium*, vine-leaved; *negundo*, Box Elder, 40 to 70 ft., N. America, and vars. *auratum*, yellow leaves and *variegatum*, green and white leaves; *nikoense*, 40 ft., slow-growing, intense autumn colouring,

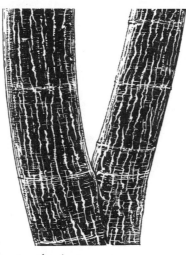

Acer pensylvanicum

Japan; *palmatum*, 10 to 20 ft., Japan, and vars. *aureum, atropurpureum, dissectum, heptalobum* (and numerous sub-varieties), *roseomarginatum* and *senkaki*, Coral Bark Maple; *pensylvanicum*, Snake Bark Maple, 30 ft., white-striated stems, N. America; *platanoides*, Norway Maple, 50 ft., Europe, and its vars. *aureo-variegatum*, Crimson King, *laciniatum, rubrum*, Schwedleri; *pseudoplatanus*, Sycamore, 100 ft., Central Europe, and vars. *albo-variegatum, brilliantissimum*, slow growing, *corstorphinense, leopoldii*, Prinz Handjery, slow growing, *worleei*, foliage rich yellow; *rubrum*, Red Maple, 80 to 100 ft., scarlet flowers, Canada; *saccharinum*, Silver Maple, 80 to 100 ft., Eastern N. America; *saccharum*, Sugar Maple, 100 ft., maple sugar is produced from the sap of this tree, N. America, var. *monumentale* (Temple's Upright), narrow erect growth.

ACHILLEA (Yarrow) – *Compositae.* Hardy herbaceous perennials and rock plants.

Soil, ordinary, well drained. Position, dwarf species on sunny rock gardens, tall ones in open borders. Plant in spring or autumn.

Increase by seeds sown in spring in sandy soil under glass; by division of roots in autumn or spring.

Recommended kinds are *A. ageratifolia*, close mounds, silvery leaves and stems, white, summer, Greece; *ageratum*, Sweet Maudlin, Sweet Nancy, white, summer, 6 in., Greece; *clavennae*, white, summer, 6 in., Austria; *clypeolata*, white-tomentose, yellow, 1 to 1½ ft., summer, Balkans; *filipendulina* (syn. *eupatorium*), yellow, summer, 3 to 5 ft., Caucasus; *lewisii*, creamy yellow, 4 in., summer, hybrid between *clavennae* and *tomentosa*; *millefolium*, Milfoil, white, summer, 1 to 3 ft., Europe (Britain), and var. *rosea*, rose; Moonshine, pale yellow, summer, 2 ft., hybrid between *clypeolata* and *taygetea*; *ptarmica*, Sneezewort, white, 2 ft., summer, Europe (Britain), and several double-flowered varieties such as Perry's White and The Pearl; *sibirica* (syn. *mongolica*), narrow leaves, large white flower heads on long stems, to 3 ft., Mongolia; *taygetea*, pale yellow, summer, early autumn, 18 in., Middle East; *tomentosa*, yellow, summer, 6 to 8 in., Europe and N. Asia; *umbellata*, white, summer, 4 in., Greece.

ACHIMENES – *Gesneriaceae.* Tender, weak-stemmed, tuberous-rooted, deciduous perennials, needing a temperature of 15 to 18°C.

Grow in a compost of two parts peat and loam, one part leafmould and sand. Pot tubers successively in late winter and spring, 1 in. apart, 2 in. deep, in pots, pans or baskets. Water moderately at first, freely when in growth. After flowering, gradually withhold water from the roots, and when foliage dies place pots on their sides in a greenhouse, letting them remain there till it is time to replant.

Increase by seeds sown in early spring in light soil at 21 to 27°C.; by cuttings of young shoots and leaves from new growth in spring in a warm propagator; by division of rhizomes when repotting in late winter.

Recommended kinds are *A. coccinea*, scarlet, summer, 1 ft., W. Indies; *grandiflora* (syn. *patens*), crimson, summer and autumn, 1½ ft., Mexico; *heterophylla*, scarlet and yellow, summer, 1 ft., Brazil; *longiflora*, violet, summer, 1 ft., Mexico, and vars. *alba* and *major*. A number of hybrids and varieties will be found in trade lists.

Achimenes (hybrid)

ACIDANTHERA – *Iridaceae*. More or less tender cormous plants with flowers like those of gladiolus.

Acidanthera bicolor can be treated like gladiolus, planted outside in spring and lifted in late autumn, but in cold places is best potted in early to mid-spring in equal parts sandy loam and leafmould or peat and started in a greenhouse, and then planted out in early summer. Lift and store in autumn.

Position, sunny and warm or in pots in a cool greenhouse. Water freely during the growing period, little at other times.

Acidanthera bicolor murieliae

Recommended kinds are *A. bicolor*, white and purple, 1 to 1½ ft., Abyssinia, var. *murieliae* (syn. *Gladiolus murieliae*), white, blotched crimson, fragrant, 3 ft., late summer, autumn, Abyssinia; *candida*, white, 1 to 1½ ft., Eastern Tropical Africa.

ACONITUM (Aconite) – *Ranunculaceae*. Hardy herbaceous perennials, containing strong poisons. The flowers are hooded and foliage delphinium-like.

Soil, ordinary. Position, sunny or partly shaded. *A. volubile* is a climber suitable for growing on pillars, arbours, etc. Plant in spring or autumn.

Increase by division of roots in autumn or spring; by seeds sown in spring out of doors or under glass.

Recommended kinds are *A. cammarum*, various shades of purple, sometimes with white, summer, 2 to 5 ft., hybrid between *napellus* and *variegatum*, and vars. *bicolor*, purple and white, 3 ft., Bressingham Spire, violet-blue, 3 ft., Spark's Variety, deep violet-blue, 5 ft.; *carmichaelii* (syn. *fischeri*), pale purple-blue, autumn, 4 ft., China, var. *wilsonii*, 6 ft., deep blue-purple; *lycoctonum*, Wolf's Bane, Badger's Bane, yellow, summer, 6 ft., Europe, Siberia; *napellus*, Monkshood, blue, summer, 4 to 6 ft., Europe, Asia, var. *album*, white, *carneum*, flesh-colour, *pyramidale*, late flowering, and *roseum*, pink; *variegatum*, blue and white, summer, 3 to

5 ft., Europe; *volubile*, dark blue, autumn, to 12 ft., climbing, Central Asia.

ACORUS – *Araceae*. Hardy aquatics with tufts of narrow leaves. *A. calamus* is fragrant in all its parts.

Soil, heavy loam. Position, margins of ponds or streams or in damp soil in any open situation; *A. gramineus* var. *pusillus* may be grown in aquariums. Plant in spring. Increase by division in spring.

Recommended kinds are *A. calamus*, Sweet Flag, 3 ft., foliage resembling a flag iris, North Temperate Regions, var. *variegatus*, leaves striped cream and green, 2 ft.; *gramineus*, 1 ft., grassy, Japan, vars. *pusillus*, 3 in., *variegatus*, 1 ft., leaves variegated with yellow.

ACTAEA (Baneberry) – *Ranunculaceae*. Hardy herbaceous perennials with showy but poisonous berries.

Soil, moist, lime-free loam. Position, shady. Plant in spring or autumn.

Increase by seeds sown out of doors in spring; by division of roots in spring.

Recommended kinds are *A. alba* (syn. *pachypoda*), white, late spring, early summer, berries white, 1 to 1½ ft., N. America; *rubra*, white, late spring, early summer, berries red, N. America; *spicata*, Herb Christopher, white, late spring, early summer, black berries, 1½ to 2 ft., Europe (Britain), Asia.

ACTINIDIA – *Actinidiaceae*. Hardy deciduous and mostly rampant twining shrubs. Flowers, frequently unisexual, produced in early summer. Fruit, gooseberry-like berry. All species from E. Asia.

Grow in ordinary soil on walls, trellis or tree stumps. Plant in spring or autumn. Shorten stems not required for extension to 6 in. during summer, and in winter cut out old stems where they can be replaced by younger growth.

Increase by seeds sown in pots in a cold frame in spring; by layering shoots in autumn; by cuttings of half-ripened shoots in a propagator.

Recommended kinds are *A. arguta*, very vigorous, reaching the tops of tall trees, white fragrant flowers, yellow berries; *chinensis*, Chinese Gooseberry, vigorous growths and fruit covered with reddish hairs; *kolomikta*, 6 ft., foliage variegated white and pink, best in a warm sunny place and calcareous soil; *melandera*, very vigorous, white flowers, purplish-brown fruits; *polygama*, 10 ft., silver-variegated; *purpurea*, sweet-flavoured purple berries, vigorous.

ADA – *Orchidaceae*. Epiphytic orchids allied to *Odontoglossum* but with small, brightly coloured flowers.

Compost, three parts osmunda fibre and one part chopped sphagnum moss. Position, pots in shade. Repot when new growth

begins. Water fairly freely during season of growth, moderately afterwards; no resting period. Grow in an intermediate house, minimum winter temp. 10°C.

Increase by division at potting time.

Recommended kinds are *A. aurantiaca*, orange, winter, 1 ft., Colombia; *lehmanni*, cinnabar orange, lip whitish, early summer, leaves grey-marked, Colombia.

ADIANTUM (Maidenhair Fern) – *Adiantaceae*. Tender and hardy ferns.

Compost for pot plants two parts peat or beech or oak leafmould, one part loam, and one part coarse sand or well-broken charcoal. Pot in spring. Water normally. Position, shady at all times, in an intermediate or warm greenhouse, minimum temp. 13°C. for very tender kinds, or cool greenhouse, minimum 7°C. for slightly tender kinds. Plant hardy kinds in spring outdoors in a shady place in soil to which plenty of peat or leafmould has been added.

Increase by spores sown on fine sandy peat, kept moist and shaded in a propagator with temperature appropriate to the species; by division in spring.

Recommended very tender kinds are *A. caudatum*, pendent, Tropics; *concinnum*, 1 to 1½ ft., Mexico, Brazil; *cristatum*, 1½ to 3 ft., W. Indies; *cuneatum*, 9 to 18 in., Brazil, and vars. *dissectum*, *elegans*, *gracillimum*, *grandiceps*, etc.; *curvatum*, fronds forked, Brazil; *dolabriforme*, pendent, Brazil, Panama; *macrophyllum*, 1 ft., Tropical America; *moorei*, 1 ft., Peru, and var. *plumosum*, plumed fronds; *tenerum*, to 3 ft., W. Indies, and var. *farleyense*, 3 ft., waved fronds, Barbados; *tinctum*, 6 to 12 in., Tropical America, and var. *wagneri* (syn. *decorum*), 12 to 15 in., Colombia, Peru; *trapeziforme*, 2 to 4 ft., Tropical America, and var. *sanctae-catharinae*, deeply cut lobes.

Adiantum cuneatum

Recommended slightly tender kinds are *A. aethiopicum*, 1 to 1½ ft., Africa, Australia, New Zealand; *affine* (syn. *cunninghamii*), 1 ft., New Zealand; *capillus-veneris*, 3 to 12 in., Tropical and Warm Temperate Zones, (Britain), nearly hardy, and numerous varieties; *excisum*, to 1 ft., Chile, Panama, Mexico, and var. *multifidum*, deeply cut;

formosum, to 2 ft., Australia, New Zealand; *hispidulum* (syn. *pubescens*), fronds forked at base, Old World; *venustum*, 2 ft., Himalaya, nearly hardy; *williamsii*, Golden Maidenhair, 1 ft., Peru.

The best hardy kind is *A. pedatum*, 1 to 3 ft., N. America.

ADONIS (Pheasant's Eye) – *Ranunculaceae*. Hardy annuals and herbaceous perennials with ferny foliage and showy flowers.

Soil, fairly rich, well drained, likes lime. Position, open sunny border for annuals, rock garden for perennials. Plant perennial kinds in autumn or spring.

Increase annuals by seeds sown shallowly in spring; perennials by seeds sown under glass directly they are ripe, and by division of roots in spring or autumn.

Recommended kinds are *A. aestivalis*, Pheasant's Eye, crimson, summer, 1 ft., annual, S. Europe; *amurensis*, yellow, early spring, 1 ft., perennial, Japan, China; *autumnalis*, Red Chamomile, scarlet, early spring to summer, 1 ft., annual, Europe (Britain); *pyrenaica*, yellow, summer, 1 ft., perennial, Pyrenees; *vernalis*, yellow, spring, 1½ ft., Europe.

AECHMEA – *Bromeliaceae*. Tender evergreen plants, with ornamental leaves in stiff rosettes and heads of flowers encased in coloured bracts.

Aechmea fasciata

Compost, equal parts of fibrous loam, peat, sand, and osmunda fibre. Pot in spring. Water normally keeping the hollow or 'vase' in the centre of the rosette constantly full of water. Good drainage is essential. Position, intermediate or warm greenhouse, minimum winter temp. 13°C., well shaded and humid in summer.

Increase by offshoots inserted in small pots in spring.

Recommended kinds are *A. fasciata* (syn. *rhodocyanea*), rose and blue, summer, 1½ ft., Brazil; *fulgens*, scarlet, summer, 1½ ft., French Guiana, var. *discolor*, leaves purplish underneath, Brazil; *macrantha*, red, autumn, 1 ft., leaves purple, Mexico; *mariae-reginae*, violet and crimson, summer, 2 ft., Costa Rica; *marmorata*, pink and blue, summer, 1 ft., Brazil.

AEONIUM – *Crassulaceae*. Rather tender succulent plants making large rosettes of fleshy leaves; once included in the genus *Sempervivum* but now kept distinct.

Compost, equal parts loam, leafmould and coarse sand or grit. Position, well-drained pots or pans in a sunny part of a cool greenhouse or window or in a warm sunny rock garden in places where there is little or no frost. Pot or plant in spring. Water moderately from spring to autumn, keep nearly dry in winter. No shading or syringing required. Minimum temperature under glass 5°C. but outdoors most species will survive two or three degrees of frost, especially if kept dry.

Increase by seeds sown in spring in temp. 15 to 18°C.; by cuttings of shoots or leaves inserted in sand in spring or summer; or by division in spring.

Recommended kinds are *A. arboreum*, yellow, to 3 ft., rosettes 6 in. diameter, Morocco, vars. *variegatum*, leaves variegated, *foliis purpureis*, leaves dark purple; *haworthii*, pale yellow and pink, spring, 2 ft., Canary Islands; *tabuliforme*, pale yellow, summer, to 1 ft. or more, Canary Islands.

AERIDES – *Orchidaceae*. Epiphytic orchids. Most species have beautiful flowers. Stems arching, sometimes branching. Leaves distichous, persistent. Flowers, often fragrant, in axillary spikes, sometimes branched, often drooping from the upper portions of the stems.

Compost, equal parts of osmunda fibre, chopped sphagnum moss, liberally mixed with broken brick in very well-drained pots, or teak baskets. Shade lightly in summer. Grow in an intermediate or warm greenhouse, minimum winter temp. 13°C. Syringe freely in summer and water freely in spring and summer but sparingly in winter, just sufficiently to keep the sphagnum moss green.

Increase by removing stems or offsets with roots in spring, potting individually and keeping for a few weeks in a warm propagator until well established.

Recommended kinds are *A. crispum*, white, rose flushed, lip rose-purple, summer, 9 to 10 in. India; *falcatum*, racemes 1 to 1½ ft. long, sepals and petals creamy white crimson tipped, mid-lobe of lip deep purple, spring and summer, Burma; *japonicum*, white or greenish white marked red, lip with purple spots and ridge, dwarf, fragrant, summer, Japan; *lawrenceae*, wax like, fragrant, white, crimson-purple, large, summer, early autumn, 1½ ft., Philippines; *multiflorum*, white, flushed or spotted purple, summer or early autumn, 1 ft., India; *odoratum* (syn. *suavissimum*), fragrant, white and lilac-magenta, summer or early autumn, 8 to 12 in., India, China; *quinquevulnerum*, white and purple, summer, 15 in., Philippines; *vandarum*, white or rose, scented, late winter, early spring, 9 in., Himalaya.

AESCHYNANTHUS – *Gesneriaceae*. Tender, trailing, evergreen flowering plants. Sometimes known as trichosporum.

Compost, equal parts fibrous peat, sphagnum moss, and charcoal. Position, hanging baskets or pots. Pot in spring. Water freely in summer, sparingly in winter. Grow in an intermediate or warm greenhouse, minimum temp. 13°C. Maintain a moist atmosphere in summer and shade from direct sunshine.

Aeschynanthus speciosus

Increase by cuttings of firm shoots inserted in pots of the compost already described in a warm propagator in spring.

Recommended kinds are *A. boschianus*, scarlet, summer, Sumatra; *fulgens*, scarlet and yellow, autumn, 1 ft., E. Indies; *grandiflorus*, scarlet, summer, 3 to 5 ft., India; *lobbianus*, scarlet and purple, early summer, 1 ft., Java; *marmoratus*, green, spotted brown, summer, 2 ft., habitat unknown; *pulcher*, scarlet and yellow, early summer, 2 ft., Java; *speciosus*, orange, summer, Java.

AESCULUS (Horse Chestnut, Buckeye) – *Hippocastanaceae*. Hardy, deciduous flowering trees and shrubs suitable for ordinary soils and open sunny places. Plant in autumn or late winter. Cut out dead wood in late winter or spring.

Increase by seeds sown 3 in. deep in the open as soon as ripe or stratified immediately for three months at 4°C. and then sown; by layering in late winter; and by grafting choice varieties in spring or budding in summer.

Recommended kinds are *A. californica*, white, summer, 20 to 30 ft., California; *carnea*, Red Horse Chestnut, rose, early summer, 30 to 50 ft., hybrid, vars. *briotii*, best red form, *plantierensis*, seedless form, pink flowers; *glabra*, cream, late spring, 30 ft., U.S.A.; *hippocastanum*, Horse Chestnut, white, late spring, 60 to 100 ft., S. E. Europe, and its var. *baumannii*, double flowered; *indica*, white, blotched yellow and rose, summer, up to 100 ft., Himalaya; *octandra* (syn. *flava*), Yellow Buckeye, Sweet Buckeye, yellow, late spring, 30 to 60 ft., Southeast U.S.A.; *parviflora*, Dwarf Buckeye, 10 ft., spreading, white, late summer, U.S.A.; *pavia*, Red Buckeye, red, summer, 10 to 20 ft., U.S.A.; *splendens*, handsome 12 ft. shrub, scarlet, late spring, U.S.A.; *turbinata*, Japanese Horse Chestnut, creamy, summer, to 100 ft., Japan.

AETHIONEMA (Stone Cress) – *Cruciferae*. Hardy evergreen perennials subshrubby in habit and with heads of flowers similar to candytuft (iberis).

Soil, ordinary, light. Position, sunny, well-drained rock garden, raised bed or unmortared terrace wall. Plant in spring or autumn.

Increase by cuttings of shoots inserted in sandy soil in a frame in summer; or by seeds sown in a cool greenhouse or frame in spring.

Recommended kinds are *A. armenum*, pink, summer, 4 to 5 in., Turkey, and var. Warley Rose, deeper rose; *coridifolium*, Lebanon Candytuft, pink, summer, 6 to 8 in., Turkey, Cilicia; *grandiflorum* (syn. *pulchellum*), rose-pink, summer, 10 to 18 in., Iraq, Iran; *iberideum*, white, spring, 6 in. Turkey; *oppositifolium*, pink or lilac, late spring, early summer, 2 in., Turkey, Lebanon.

AGAPANTHUS – *Alliaceae*. Slightly tender, fleshy-rooted evergreen and deciduous herbaceous plants from S. Africa. Deciduous kinds are, in general, hardier than evergreen species.

Soil, ordinary. Position, sunny, warm, well-drained border or cool greenhouse. Plant in spring.

Increase by division of plants in spring; or by seeds sown in spring.

Recommended kinds are *A. africanus* (syn. *umbellatus*), evergreen, blue, summer, 2 to 3 ft., and var. *albus*, white; *campanulatus*, deciduous, deep blue, summer, 1½ to 2 ft.; *caulescens*, deciduous, lilac-blue, summer, 2½ to 4 ft.; *comptonii*, evergreen, blue, late summer, 2 ft.; *inapertus*, deciduous, violet-blue or white, late summer, 1 to 3 ft.; *praecox*, evergreen, pale blue or white, early summer, 2 to 3 ft.

AGASTACHE – *Labiatae*. Hardy herbaceous perennial with aromatic leaves and narrow spikes of magenta flowers. Sometimes listed as brittonastrum.

Soil, ordinary, well drained. Position, open, sunny. Plant in spring or early autumn.

Increase by division in spring; or by seeds sown outdoors or under glass in spring.

The best species is *A. mexicana*, magenta, summer, 2 to 2½ ft., Mexico.

AGAVE – *Agavaceae*. Tender evergreen flowering plants. Leaves usually stiff and spiny in large rosettes. Flowers, yellowish

green or red, borne in short spikes on bare stems. In some cases the rosette dies after flowering.

Compost, John Innes potting compost No. 2 plus one-sixth its bulk of coarse sand. Position, pots or tubs in a cool or intermediate greenhouse, minimum winter temp. 7°C.; may be stood outside in summer. *A. americana* can be grown outdoors in sunny sheltered places in nearly frost-free gardens. Water moderately in spring or summer, little afterwards. Good drainage essential.

Increase by offsets inserted in sandy soil in spring or summer.

Recommended kinds are *A. americana*, American Aloe, Century Plant, 6 to 25 ft., Tropical America, and its vars. *medio-picta*, leaves yellow, edged green, and *variegata*, leaves dark green and yellow; *attenuata*, 6 to 8 ft., Mexico; *filifera*, 6 to 8 ft., Mexico; *franzosinii*, 8 to 40 ft., blue-grey leaves, origin uncertain; *lophantha*, 12 to 15 ft., Mexico, and var. *lechequilla*, (syn. *poselgeri*), blue-green; *potatorum*, 12 ft., Mexico; *sisalana*, Sisal Hemp, 15 to 20 ft., origin uncertain; *striata*, 12 ft., leaves striped grey and green, Mexico; *stricta* (syns. *A. hystrix*, *Bonapartea hystrix*, *Yucca hystrix*), 10 to 12 ft., Mexico, and var. *glauca*, glaucous leaved; *victoriae-reginae*, 10 to 12 ft., leaves dark green, grey or white edged, Mexico. There are many other species.

AGERATUM (Floss-flower) – *Compositae*. Slightly tender herbaceous perennials grown as annuals. Flowers in small fluffy clusters like little balls.

Soil, ordinary. Position, sunny. Sow in spring in temp. 15 to 18°C. and harden off for planting outdoors in late spring or early summer. Can also be increased by cuttings of young non-flowering shoots in a warm propagator in spring or summer.

Recommended kinds are *A. houstonianum* (syns. *caeruleum* and *mexicanum*), blue, summer, 1½ to 2 ft., Mexico. Numerous varieties or hybrids, including dwarfs (6 in.), white, rose and purple, are available.

AGLAONEMA – *Araceae*. Tender perennials with arum-like flowers and variegated leaves.

Compost, John Innes potting compost No. 2 or equivalent. Position, well-drained pots in an intermediate or warm greenhouse, minimum winter temperature 15°C., or in a warm room. Shade from direct sunshine. Water freely when growing in spring and summer, little afterwards. Syringe foliage daily. Feed fairly frequently in summer. Repot annually in spring.

Increase by division in spring.

Recommended kinds are *A. commutatum*, white, summer, 9 in., leaves green and silvery, Malaysia, Philippines; *costatum*, green, summer, 6 in., leaves dark green and white, Malaysia; *modestum* (syn. *acutispathum*), green, summer, 1 to 1½ ft., leaves green,

Aglaonema (hybrid)

Philippines, China; *oblongifolium*, green and white, summer, 1 to 3 ft., leaves green, Malaysia, Borneo, and var. *curtisii*, leaves variegated with white; *pictum*, cream, summer, 1 to 2 ft., leaves in various shades of green and grey, Malaysia, Borneo, Sumatra; *robelinii*, leaves in two shades of green, 1 ft., Malaysia; *treubii*, white, summer, 1 ft., Indonesia.

AICHRYSON – *Crassulaceae*. Slightly tender succulent perennials allied to *Aeonium* and *Sempervivum*.

Compost, John Innes potting compost No. 2 with some extra sand. Position, cool or intermediate greenhouse or frost-proof room. Can be grown in full sun but will put up with some shade. Water freely in spring and summer, sparingly at other times. Minimum winter temp. 7°C. Pot in spring.

Increase by cuttings in sandy soil in spring or summer.

The best kind is *A. domesticum variegatum*, yellow, early summer, 6 to 12 in., leaves green and white, sub-shrubby, garden origin probably a hybrid.

AILANTHUS – *Simaroubaceae*. Handsome, hardy deciduous trees with ornamental foliage. Male and female flowers borne on separate trees, the male flowers have an unpleasant smell.

Soil, light, rich. Position, sunny and open. Very good in towns and industrial areas. Plant in autumn or late winter. Can be pruned almost to ground level each year in late winter for production of extra large leaves.

Increase by inserting portions of roots in pots of light soil in late winter, keep in a propagator until growth starts and transplant the following spring; or by seeds sown in spring.

The best kinds are *A. altissima* (syn. *glandulosa*), Tree of Heaven, leaves pinnate, 30 to 60 ft., China, and vars. *erythrocarpa*, fruits bright red, *pendulifolia*, leaves large and drooping.

AIRA (Hair Grass) – *Gramineae*. Hardy annual ornamental grass with fine leaves and loose sprays of very small flowers.

Soil, ordinary. Sow seeds in spring where plants are required. Position, open. May be grown in pots in the cold greenhouse.

The best kind is *A. capillaris* (syn. *elegans*), 12 to 18 in., S. Europe, var. *pulchella*, awned florets.

AJUGA (Bugle) – *Labiatae*. Hardy perennials creeping in habit and useful as ground cover. The flowers, in short spikes, are produced in early summer.

Soil, ordinary. Position, sunny or shady. Plant in spring or autumn.

Increase by division of roots in spring or autumn.

Recommended kinds are *A. genevensis*, blue, 6 in., non-trailing, Europe; *reptans*, blue, 6 in., Britain, and vars. *atropurpurea*, purple leaves, *multicolor*, leaves green, bronze, yellow and pink, and *variegata*, leaves variegated, cream.

AKEBIA – *Lardizabalaceae*. Hardy, twining semi-evergreen shrubs from China and Japan.

Suitable for most soils and sunny or partially shady places. The sausage-shaped purple fruits are quite decorative but are only likely to be produced in warm, sunny places. Plant in autumn or spring. Prune out weak or dead shoots in winter.

Increase by cuttings inserted in sandy soil in gentle heat; by layers in autumn; or by seeds sown as soon as ripe.

Recommended kinds are *A. trifoliata* (syn. *lobata*), purple flowers in spring followed by pale violet-tinted fruits; *quinata*, deep maroon, fragrant, spring.

ALBIZIA (Pink Siris Tree, Nemu Tree or Silk Tree) – *Leguminosae*. Slightly tender, deciduous acacia-like shrubs or small trees suitable for warm, sunny places and light well-drained soils.

Increase by seeds sown in warmth in spring or by root cuttings in late winter or early spring. In cold places albizias may be trained against sunny walls or grown in cool sunny greenhouses.

Recommended kinds are *A. julibrissin*, pink, summer, to 30 ft., Asia; *lophantha*, yellow, spring, 10 to 20 ft., Australia.

ALCHEMILLA (Lady's Mantle) – *Rosaceae*. Hardy herbaceous perennials with palmately-lobed or divided leaves and small greenish or yellowish flowers in clusters.

Soil, ordinary, well drained. Position, sunny, front of border or as ground cover. Plant in spring or autumn.

Increase by division at planting time; or by seeds sown in spring outdoors or in a frame.

Recommended kinds are *A. alpina*, flowers green, early summer, foliage silvery, 6 in., Europe (Britain); *mollis*, greenish yellow, leaves green, softly downy, summer, 9 in., Asia Minor; *vulgaris*, greenish yellow, leaves more or less downy, summer, Europe (Britain).

ALISMA (Water Plantain) – *Alismataceae*. Hardy aquatic perennials with sprays of small white or pink flowers.

Soil, loam. Position, shallow water or bog. Plant in spring.

Increase by division; or by seeds sown in shallow pans of loam and charcoal barely covered with water.

Recommended kinds are *A. gramineum*, foliage ribbon like when grown submerged, oblong above water, palest pink, summer, 6 to 12 in., Europe; *lanceolatum*, pink, summer, leaves lance shaped, 2 to 3 ft., Europe (Britain), W. Asia, N. Africa; *plantago-aquatica*, rose, summer, leaves large, plantain like, 2 to 3 ft., Europe (Britain).

ALLEMANDA – *Apocynaceae*. Tender evergreen climbing plants with showy, funnel-shaped flowers.

Compost, fairly rich, John Innes potting compost No. 2 or equivalent. Position, pots, tubs, or a prepared border; shoots to be trained close to the roof. Pot or plant in early spring; water normally, shade in summer from strong sunshine. Grow in an intermediate or warm greenhouse, minimum winter temp. 13°C. Prune shoots in late winter to within one joint of the main branch.

Allemanda cathartica

Increase by cuttings of shoots of previous year's growth, 3 in. long, inserted in a warm propagator in spring. *A. violacea* succeeds best when grafted on to the more vigorous *A. cathartica* or one of its varieties.

Recommended kinds are *A. cathartica*, yellow, summer, to 10 ft., Brazil, and vars. *grandiflora*, flowers to 4½ in. across, *hendersonii* (syn. *A. hendersonii*), leathery leaves, large flowers, *nobilis*, magnolia-like fragrance, *schottii*, yellow with dark-striped throat, *williamsii*, yellow with reddish brown throat, more bushy in habit; *nerifolia*, yellow, summer, to 3 ft., Brazil; *violacea*, lavender, summer, 6 to 8 ft., Brazil.

ALLIUM – *Alliaceae*. Hardy and slightly tender bulbs, many with a strong onion or garlic odour. Hardy flowering species need ordinary, well-drained soil and a sunny position. Plant in autumn covering bulbs to twice their diameter with soil.

Increase by offsets or seeds in rich gritty soil in spring.

In cool climates the smaller and more delicate species such as *A. acuminatum, amabile, cyaneum, cyathophorum* var. *farreri, oreophilum* and *subhirsutum* are best grown in pans in a cool greenhouse. *A. neapolitanum* can be forced. Plant dormant bulbs almost touching in open compost and plunge pots or pans in ashes till growth begins. Remove to a cold frame till growth is well advanced. Flower in a cold greenhouse or force *A. neapolitanum* in temp. 15°C. Water freely when growing, dry off after flowering. Increase by offsets removed at potting time or by seeds sown in spring.

Recommended kinds are *A. acuminatum*, lilac, summer, 6 to 9 in., N. W. America; *aflatunense*, purple, early summer, 2½ to 3 ft., Iran; *albopilosum*, lilac, summer, 1½ ft., Central Asia; *amabile*, magenta, 4 to 8 in., China; *atropurpureum*, dark red, summer, 3 ft., E. Europe; *beesianum*, blue, 1 ft., W. China; *bidwelliae* (syn. *campanulatum*), pink, summer, 8 in., California; *breweri*, violet-purple, summer, 3 in., California; *bulgaricum* (syn. *siculum dioscoridis*), Honey Garlic, whitish, late spring, 3 ft., S. E. Europe; *caeruleum* (syn. *azureum*), deep blue, 1 to 3 ft., W. Siberia, Central Asia; *caesium*, dark blue, summer, 1 to 3 ft., W. Siberia, Central Asia; *cernuum*, rose or purple, summer, 1 to 1½ ft., N. America, and var. *oxyphilum*, white or pale pink, late summer, 10 to 12 in., Virginia; *cyaneum*, bright blue, late summer, 6 in., N. W. China; *cyrillii*, lilac, summer, 2 to 3 ft., S. Europe; *denudatum* (syn. *albidum*), creamy white, summer, 6 to 12 in., Caucasus, E. Europe; *farreri*, reddish purple, summer, 6 to 12 in., N. W. China; *flavum*, sulphur yellow, summer, 1 ft., S. Europe; *giganteum*, lilac, summer, 4 to 5 ft., Central Asia; *karataviense*, white, lilac, late spring, 9 in., Central Asia; *macranthum*, purple, summer, E. Himalaya, China; *mairei* (syn. *yunnanense*), pale rose, autumn, 4 to 8 in., W. China; *moly*, bright yellow, summer, 1 to 1½ ft., S. W. Europe; *narcissiflorum* (syn. *pedemontanum*), red-purple, summer, 9 in., Alps; *neapolitanum*, white, spring, 1 ft., S. Europe; *ochroleucum*, yellowish white, late summer, 1 ft., Central Europe; *oreophilum*, rose, late spring, 6 in., Caucasus, Central Asia, and var. *ostrowskianum*, light rose; *paradoxum*, white, spring, 1 ft., Caucasus; *pendulinum*, white, spring, 6 to 9 in., S. Europe; *pulchellum*, reddish violet, summer, 1 to 1½ ft., Mediterranean, and var. *album*; *ramosum* (syn. *odorum*), white and rose, summer, 2 ft., Central Asia; *rosenbachianum*, rose-purple, late spring, 2 to 2½ ft., Central Asia; *roseum*, light rose, summer, 1 to 1½ ft., S. Europe, var. *bulbiferum*, common in gardens; *schubertii*, rose, summer, 1 ft., W. and

Central Asia; *scorzonerifolium*, bright yellow, summer, 6 to 9 in., Spain, Portugal; *siculum*, green and dull pink, spring, 3 ft., S. Europe; *sphaerocephalum*, dark red, late summer, 1½ to 2½ ft., Europe (Britain); *triquetrum*, white with a green line, spring, 9 to 12 in., S. Europe, N. Africa; *unifolium*, rose, summer, 1 to 1½ ft., California; *ursinum*, Ramsons, white, late spring, 1 ft., Europe (Britain); *victorialis*, white, late spring, 1 to 2 ft., Alps; *zebdanense*, white, spring, 1½ ft., Syria.

ALNUS (Alder) – *Betulaceae*. Hardy deciduous trees and shrubs producing catkins before the leaves.

Soil, ordinary, moist, preferably acid or neutral though the kinds recommended will tolerate some lime or chalk. Position, open or partially shady. Plant in autumn or late winter.

Increase by seed, that of *A. glutinosa* sown in a frame or greenhouse as soon as ripe, other kinds stratified for three months at 4°C. and then sown outdoors or under glass; or by cuttings of firm wood taken after leaf fall and inserted in the open ground.

Recommended kinds are *A. cordata*, Italian Alder, 30 to 40 ft., Corsica and Italy; *glutinosa*, Common Alder, 50 to 60 ft., Europe (Britain), N. Africa and Asia, and vars. *aurea*, golden leaved, *laciniata*, cut leaved and *pyramidalis*, narrow conical habit; *hirsuta*, Manchurian Alder, 30 to 40 ft., Manchuria and Japan; *incana*, Grey Alder, 20 to 50 ft., North Temperate Zone, and vars. *aurea*, yellow leaves, red catkins, *laciniata*, cut leaved, and *pendula*, weeping. There are others but these are of no special interest.

ALOCASIA – *Araceae*. Tender perennials with ornamental foliage, usually arrow or heart shaped.

Compost, equal parts peat, sphagnum moss, fibrous loam, with a little silver sand and charcoal. Pot in early spring keeping the base of the plant above the rim of pot; good drainage is essential. Position, pots in a warm greenhouse, winter minimum temp. 15°C., shade in spring and summer. Water normally. Maintain a moist atmosphere at all times.

Increase by division of rhizomes in spring.
Recommended kinds are *A. argyraea*, leaves silvery above, to 1½ ft. long, Tropical Asia; *cuprea*, leaves bronze-purple, to 1½ ft. long, Malaysia; *gigas*, leaves dark green, deeply cut, to 5 ft. long, hybrid; *indica*, 4 to 6 ft., leaves dark green, to 15 in. long, Malaysia, and vars. *metallica*, leaves purplish, and *variegata*, leaves dark green, veins lighter green or grey on white; *korthalsii* (syn. *thibautiana*), leaves veined white and purple beneath, to 14 in. long, Borneo; *lowii*, leaves with pale veins, purple beneath, to 1½ ft. long, Borneo; *macrorhiza*, to 15 ft., leaves to 2 ft. long, Tropical Asia, and var. *varie-*

gata, leaves mottled with white; *sanderiana*, leaves purple beneath, white veins, to 1½ ft. long, Philippines; *zebrina*, leaves green, midrib and leaf stalk banded with white, Philippines.

ALOE – *Liliaceae*. Rather tender, evergreen, succulent plants with fleshy and more or less prickly or spiny leaves and red or yellow flowers borne on slender spikes.

Compost, two parts loam, one part peat and coarse sand. Position, pots or tubs in a sunny frost-proof greenhouse or out of doors in a warm, sunny place in reasonably frost-free areas. The hardiest species will survive a few degrees of frost for short periods. Plant or pot in spring. Water moderately in spring and summer, little in autumn and winter. No shade required except for *A. humilis*.

Increase by seeds sown in sandy soil in temp. 18 to 21°C. in spring; by rooted suckers removed in spring; or by cuttings in summer.

Aloë variegata

Recommended kinds are *A. arborescens*, red, spring, 10 to 12 ft., Nyasaland, S. Africa, Rhodesia; *aristata*, orange, summer, 6 to 8 in., S. Africa; *ciliaris*, red and green, spring and summer, climbing or sprawling, S. Africa; *ferox*, orange, spring, 10 ft., S. Africa; *humilis*, red tipped green, winter, S. Africa; *succotrina*, scarlet, spring, 3 to 4 ft., S. Africa; *variegata*, Partridge Breasted Aloe, red, spring, 1 ft., leaves banded with white, S. Africa.

ALONSOA (Mask Flower) – *Scrophulariaceae*. Tender perennials with red, tubular, two-lipped flowers carried upside down. In gardens they are nearly always grown as annuals.

Sow seeds in temp. 15 to 18°C. in spring and harden off for planting outdoors when danger of frost is over; or, in warm places, sow outdoors where plants are to flower; alternatively, grow throughout in pots in a sunny greenhouse. Plant in light, fairly rich

soil and a sunny position. Discard after flowering.

Recommended kinds are *A. acutifolia* (syn. *myrtifolia*), scarlet, to 3 ft., summer, Peru, and var. *alba*, white; *warscewiczii*, scarlet, summer, 1½ to 2 ft., Peru.

ALOPECURUS (Meadow Foxtail) – *Gramineae*. Hardy perennial grasses with flowers in close spikes.

Soil, any reasonably good, light, well drained. Position, full sun.

Increase by seeds sown when ripe in sandy soil, or by division in spring.

The best ornamental kinds are *A. pratensis aureus*, 1 to 2 ft., leaves yellow; *pratensis aureo-variegatus*, leaves striped yellow, Europe (Britain).

ALSTROEMERIA (Peruvian Lily) – *Alstroemeriaceae*. Hardy and slightly tender fleshy rooted perennials with showy flowers.

Soil, deep, reasonably fertile, well drained. Position, warm and sunny, or pots or borders in a sunny frost-proof greenhouse or frame. Plant or pot in spring. Outdoors cover roots with 5 to 6 in. of soil. *A. aurantiaca*, the hardiest kind, will survive quite severe frost when so planted.

Increase by seed sown in temp. 15 to 18°C. in spring, transplanting seedlings singly to small pots and planting out from there; or by division of roots in spring.

Recommended kinds are *A. aurantiaca*, orange and red, summer, 2 to 3 ft., Chile; *campaniflora* (syn. *Bomarea campaniflora*), green, summer, 2 to 3 ft., Brazil; *chilensis*, red or pink, summer, 2 to 3 ft., Chile; *haemantha*, red, green and purple, also white, summer, 2 to 3 ft., Chile; *ligtu*, pale lilac or red and purple, 1½ to 2 ft., Chile; *pelegrina*, lilac, red and purple, summer, 1 ft., Chile, and var. *alba*, Lily of the Incas, pure white; *pulchella* (syn. *psittacina*), red, green and brown, summer, 2 to 3 ft., Brazil; *versicolor*, yellow and purple, summer, 1 ft., Peru; *violacea*, violet-mauve, summer, 1 to 2 ft., Chile. There are hybrids of several species, including *A. ligtu*, with flowers in shades of buff, pink, salmon, flame, orange and purple.

ALTERNANTHERA (Joy Weed) – *Amaranthaceae*. Tender perennials grown primarily for their small highly coloured leaves and much used in carpet bedding.

Soil, ordinary. Position, sunny beds outdoors in summer, or as long as there is no danger of frost. In autumn and winter pots or boxes in an intermediate greenhouse, minimum temp. 13°C.

Increase by cuttings inserted in sandy soil in a warm propagator in spring or summer; or by division in warmth in spring.

Recommended kinds are *A. amoena*, leaves green, red and orange, 3 in., Brazil; *bettzickiana*, olive green and yellow or red leaves, 6 in., Brazil; *versicolor*, leaves coppery red, cerise, yellow and green, 3 in., Brazil. There are many garden varieties some of which have been given names but there is much confusion about them.

ALTHAEA (Hollyhock) – *Malvaceae*. Hardy perennial plants usually of short duration and often treated as annuals or biennials.

Soil, ordinary, well drained, moist for *A. officinalis*. Position, sunny. Plant in spring, early summer or autumn.

Increase by seeds sown outdoors or in a frame in late spring. Transplant seedlings 6 in. apart and replant in flowering positions in autumn or spring. Some strains of hollyhock can be treated as annuals, seeds being sown in late winter or early spring in temp. 15 to 18°C. and seedlings planted out in late spring.

Recommended kinds are *A. ficifolia*, Figleaved Hollyhock, yellow or orange, summer, 6 ft., Siberia; *officinalis*, Marsh Mallow, rose, summer, 3 to 4 ft., Europe (Britain); *rosea*, Hollyhock, pink, red, crimson, yellow or white, 5 to 6 ft., summer, China, single- and double-flowered varieties.

ALYSSUM (Madwort) – *Cruciferae*. Hardy annuals, perennials and sub-shrubs mostly with grey foliage. The summer bedding plant known as Sweet Alyssum is now classified in the genus *Lobularia*.

Soil, ordinary, well drained. Position, an open sunny border or rock garden. Plant in spring or autumn.

Increase by seeds sown in spring under glass or outdoors in summer as soon as ripe; or by cuttings of firm young growth inserted in a propagator in spring or summer.

Recommended kinds are *A. alpestre*, yellow, spring and early summer, 3 in., Europe; *argenteum*, yellow, summer, 1 ft., woody at base, Europe; *idaeum*, soft yellow, late spring, prostrate, Crete; *montanum*, yellow, fragrant, summer, 2 to 4 in., Europe; *saxatile*, Gold Dust, yellow, spring and early summer, 1 ft., shrubby, Central and S. Europe, and vars. *citrinum*, lemon yellow, *compactum*, 6 in., *flore pleno*, double; *serpyllifolium*, yellow, early summer, prostrate, S. W. Europe; *spinosum*, white, summer, 4 to 6 in., woody and spiny, S. Europe and N. Africa, and var. *roseum*, pink; *wulfenianum*, golden yellow, summer, 3 in., S. Europe.

AMARANTHUS – *Amaranthaceae*. Slightly tender annuals, some of which are grown for their long, catkin-like flower trails and some for their brightly coloured foliage.

Soil, ordinary. Position, sunny. Sow in spring, either in a greenhouse in a temperature of 15 to 18°C., seedlings to be planted out when there is no danger of frost, or sow directly outdoors when danger of serious frost is over.

Recommended kinds are *A. caudatus*,

Love-lies-bleeding, Velvet Flower, crimson-purple or greenish yellow, summer, 3 to 4 ft., Tropics; *hybridus* var. *hypochondriacus*, Prince's Feather, crimson, summer, 4 to 5 ft., Tropical America; *tricolor*, leaves green, crimson and yellow, Tropics, the most tender kind commonly cultivated.

AMARYLLIS – *Amaryllidaceae*. Slightly tender bulb.

Soil, sandy loam, enriched with leaf-mould and manure. Position, well-drained, warm, sunny, minimum winter temp. −6°C. Plant bulbs 9 in. deep and 12 in. apart in summer. Water freely in dry weather whilst growing. Mulch with decayed manure in spring.

Amaryllis belladonna

Increase by offsets or from seed.

The only species is *A. belladonna* (also known as *Callicore rosea*), Belladonna Lily, rose-red, fragrant, 18 in., Cape Province, various colour forms. The flowers appear before the new leaves.

AMELANCHIER – *Rosaceae*. Hardy deciduous spring-flowering trees and shrubs. The small white flowers are very freely produced but are short lived. Leaves usually colour well before they fall in the autumn.

Soil, ordinary, well drained but not dry; preferably lime free. Position, open. Plant in autumn or late winter. Remove suckers from standard trees.

Increase by seeds sown outdoors as soon as ripe or stratified for four months at 4°C. and then sown outdoors or under glass; by cuttings of firm young growth in a propagator in summer; by grafting on to seedlings in spring; and some kinds by division or removal of suckers with roots in autumn. Suckers from grafted trees will reproduce the stock not the scion.

Recommended kinds are *A. alnifolia*, 10 to 20 ft., N. W. America; *canadensis* (syn. *oblongifolia*), June Berry, Shadbush, Serviceberry, 30 to 50 ft., N. America; *florida*, to 30 ft., N. America; *laevis*, 30 to 40 ft.,

N. America; *lamarckii* (syn. *grandiflora*), 15 to 25 ft., hybrid; *ovalis* (syn. *vulgaris*), Snowy Mespilus, 15 to 20 ft., Europe; *stolonifera*, 4 to 5 ft., N. America.

See also Aronia.

ANACYCLUS (Mount Atlas Daisy) – *Compositae*. Perennial rock-garden plants like very choice and neat daisies.

Soil, light, sandy, gritty loam or scree mixture. Position, full sun.

Increase by seeds sown in a cold frame in light, gritty soil in early spring; as the seeds are difficult to identify, the whole seedhead should be rubbed up and sown chaff and all.

The best kind is *A. depressus*, white, backs of petals crimson, spring and summer, prostrate, N. Africa.

ANAGALLIS (Pimpernel) – *Primulaceae*. Hardy trailing annuals and perennials.

Soil, reasonably fertile. Position, sunny for annuals; moist and boggy places for *A. tenella*.

Increase annuals by seeds sown in spring where plants are to flower; perennials by division of roots in spring.

Recommended kinds are *A. linifolia* (syn. *grandiflora*), blue, summer, prostrate, W. Mediterranean, and vars. *carnea*, pink, *coccinea*, scarlet, *monellii*, large blue, all perennials in nature but cultivated as annuals; *tenella*, rosy, summer, prostrate, Europe (Britain), perennial.

ANANAS – *Bromeliaceae*. Tender evergreen plants, bearing the well-known pineapple fruits. Some kinds are cultivated as ornamental plants for their decorative foliage.

Grow in moderately rich soil with plenty of peat. Minimum temp. 15°C. Normal watering, and full exposure to sun desirable. A moist atmosphere is most essential in spring and summer, and a slightly dry one in winter. When fruit begins to ripen withhold water. Feed fruiting plants freely. Plants come into bearing when two years old.

Increase by suckers, or crowns of fruit inserted in small pots in temp. 25 to 28°C. in spring.

Recommended kinds are *A. comosus*, Pineapple, 3 ft., Tropical America, and its var. *variegatus*, leaves edged with cream.

ANAPHALIS – *Compositae*. Hardy perennials with 'everlasting' flowers.

Soil, ordinary, well-drained. Position, sunny. Plant in spring.

Increase by division in spring; or by seeds sown outdoors or under glass in spring.

Recommended kinds are *A. cinnamomea*, white flowers and foliage, cinnamon scented, late summer, 1 to 2 ft., China, Japan; *margaritacea*, Pearly Everlasting, white, late summer, 1½ to 2 ft., grey leaves, N. America; *nubigena*, white, late summer, 1 to 1½ ft., grey-green leaves, China, Tibet; *tripli-nervis*, 1 to 1½ ft., white, downy leaves, Himalaya.

ANCHUSA (Alkanet, Bugloss) – *Boragin-aceae*. Hardy annuals, biennials and perennials often of rather short duration. The plant formerly known as *A. myosotidiflora* is now classified as *Brunnera macrophylla*.

Soil, ordinary, well drained. Position, sunny. Plant in spring or autumn.

Anchusa azurea

Increase by seeds sown outdoors or in a frame in spring; by root cuttings in winter; some kinds by division in spring; annuals by seeds sown in spring where plants are to bloom.

Recommended kinds are *A. angustissima* (sometimes erroneously called *caespitosa*), blue, late spring and summer, 15 in., Asia Minor; *azurea* (syn. *italica*), blue, early summer, 3 to 4 ft., Caucasus; *capensis*, annual or biennial, blue, summer 1 to 1½ ft., S. Africa.

ANDROMEDA – *Ericaceae*. Small hardy evergreen flowering shrubs, suitable for damp rock gardens or peat gardens. Soil, lime free, peaty and moist. Position, open or partially shaded. Plant in autumn or spring. No pruning required except to cut away dead wood.

Increase by layering shoots in spring; or by seeds sown in peaty soil in spring.

Recommended kinds are *A. glaucophylla* (syn. *polifolia angustifolia*), pink, spring and early summer, 1 ft., N. E. America; *poli-folia*, Bog Rosemary, pink, spring and early summer, 1 ft., North Temperate Regions (Britain), and vars. *compacta* and *major*.

See Pieris, Leucothoë and Zenobia for other species formerly included in this genus.

ANDROSACE (Rock Jasmine) – *Primula-ceae*. Hardy perennial alpine plants making cushions or carpets of soft, rosetted leaves.

Soil, sandy loam and leafmould with sharp grit added generously. Position, open,

sunny or slightly shaded, in a rock garden or raised rock bed. Plant in spring. For the more difficult kinds, which are best suited for alpine house or cold frame cultivation, use a compost of loam, leafmould, sand, and sharp grit in equal proportions.

Increase by seeds sown in sandy gritty soil in pans in spring; by cuttings in sandy soil in frames in spring; or by division of roots in spring.

Recommended kinds are *A. carnea*, pink, spring, 3 in., Europe, var. *laggeri*, more densely tufted; *chamaejasme*, white, late spring, 3 in., Europe and N. America; *ciliata*, rose-pink, spring, 2 in., Pyrenees; *helvetica*, pink fading to white, late spring, dense mound 2 to 3 in. high, Europe; *imbricata*, white, spring, dense mound 2 to 3 in. high, Alps; *lactea*, white, yellow-eyed, late spring, 6 in., Switzerland; *lanuginosa*, rose, summer, 6 in., Himalaya, var. *leichtlinii*, white, crimson-eyed; *pyrenaica*, white, spring, dense mound 2 to 3 in. high, Pyrenees; *sarmentosa*, rose, late spring, early summer, 3 to 4 in., Himalaya, vars. *chumbyi*, more tufted and downy, *watkinsii*, smaller and neater; *sempervivoides*, pink with red eye, spring, 3 in., Himalaya; *villosa*, white, pink eyed, late spring, 3 in., Europe, var. *arach-noidea*, white, yellow-eyed, 1 in., E. Europe.

ANEMONE (Windflower) – *Ranuncula-ceae*. Hardy herbaceous and hardy or slightly tender tuberous-rooted perennials. Certain species formerly included here have been placed in the genus *Hepatica*, and others in *Pulsatilla*.

Soil, ordinary for Japanese anemones, open textured with plenty of leafmould or peat for *A. apennina*, *blanda* and *nemorosa*, rather rich for *coronaria*, *fulgens*, *hortensis*, *pavonina*, and garden varieties and hybrids derived from them.

Position, sunny or shady for most, but *A. coronaria*, *fulgens*, *hortensis*, *pavonina* and derivatives are best in fairly warm places.

Garden varieties of these can be grown in frames for winter or early spring flowers.

Plant fibrous-rooted kinds in spring or autumn but the Japanese anemones dislike disturbance and are best left alone until really overcrowded. Plant *A. apennina*, *blanda*, and *nemorosa* in autumn, 2 to 3 in. deep, and leave undisturbed for years. Plant *A. coronaria*, *fulgens*, *pavonina* and derivatives in autumn or spring according to the time at which flowers are required. They can be lifted annually when the foliage has died down and stored dry until replanting time.

Increase by seeds sown in spring outdoors or under glass; by division of roots of fibrous-rooted kinds in spring or autumn; by the natural multiplication of tubers of tuberous-rooted kinds.

Recommended fibrous-rooted Japanese anemones are *A. hupehensis*, pink, late summer and autumn, 2 ft., China and var. *japonica* (syn. *A. japonica*), rose, double, late summer and autumn, 21 to 24 in., China; *hybrida* (syn. *elegans*), pink, late summer and autumn, 3 to 4 ft., hybrid between *hupehen-sis japonica* and *vitifolia*, and numerous garden varieties ranging in colour from white to rose, 2 to 5 ft., single, semi-double and double; *vitifolia*, white, late summer and autumn, 2 ft., Burma, China, slightly tender.

Recommended tuberous-rooted kinds are *A. apennina*, blue, pink or white, early spring, 6 in., S. Europe, and var. *plena*, double; *blanda*, blue, pink, rose or white, early spring, 6 in., Asia Minor, and var. *scythinica*, blue and white; *coronaria*, Poppy Anemone, red, pink, blue, white, spring or summer, 18 in., Europe, Asia, and numerous varieties such as De Caen, large single, St Brigid, double, etc; *fulgens*, scarlet, spring, 1 ft., hybrid between *pavonina* and *horten-sis*; *hortensis*, violet or rose, spring, 8 to 12 in., Mediterranean region, Asia Minor; *nemorosa*, Wood Anemone, white, early

Anemone hupehensis (left) St Brigid anemone (right)

spring, 6 in., Europe (Britain), and vars. *alba*, white, *allenii*, pale blue, *rosea*, white and pink, *rubra*, white becoming rose, *rubra plena*, similar to the last but double; *pavonina*, carmine, purple-red, white, spring, 9 to 15 in., Mediterranean region.

ANEMONOPSIS – *Ranunculaceae*. Hardy herbaceous perennial related to anemone. Clusters of flowers with petal-like bracts.

Soil, deep rich loam. Position, well-drained and partially shaded border. Plant in spring or autumn.

Increase by division of roots in spring; by seeds sown under glass in spring.

The only species is *A. macrophylla*, lilac and purple, summer, 2 to 3 ft., Japan.

ANGELICA – *Umbelliferae*. The most useful garden kind is a handsome hardy perennial herb used for flavouring confectionery and liqueurs. The root is candied for cake decoration. If permitted to flower and seed it usually dies, and is often treated as a biennial, but if the flowers are removed annually it can continue for years.

Soil, deep moist loam. Position, lightly shaded.

Increase by seeds sown in spring or as soon as ripe where plants are to remain. When seedlings are 3 in. high, thin them to 6 in. apart. When happily established, angelica usually maintains itself by self-sown seedlings.

The best species is *A. archangelica*, green flowers in large flat heads, summer, leaves large, compound, shining green, 4 to 5 ft., Europe.

ANGRAECUM – *Orchidaceae*. Tender epiphytic orchids, flowers fragrant in some species.

Compost, three parts fibre to one part sphagnum moss. Position, in suspended baskets or well-drained pans in a warm greenhouse. Shade in spring and summer. Water freely from spring to autumn, moderately in winter. Maintain a very moist atmosphere. Only repot in spring every third or fourth year.

The stems being short in many species, and basal growths very rarely emitted, propagation can seldom be effected with the majority. The climbing species, which should be trained against bark, are readily propagated by severing the stems with three or four nodes below the stem roots and allowing the division to remain on the bark till growth is seen.

Recommended kinds are *A. bilobum*, white and pink, autumn, winter, 8 to 10 in., Tropical Africa; *distichum*, white, variable flowering time, 6 in., W. Africa; *eburneum*, greenish white, winter, 18 in., Madagascar; *eichlerianum*, green and white, summer, autumn, scandent, W. Africa; *falcatum*, white, summer, 4 in., Japan; *sesquipedale*, ivory white, winter, spring, 3 ft., Madagascar.

ANGULOA (Cradle Orchid) – *Orchidaceae*. Terrestrial orchids with large, fragrant, tulip-shaped flowers borne singly.

Compost, equal parts fibre, sphagnum moss and peat.

Position, pots in a shady part of a cool or intermediate house. Pot when new growth begins. Water freely from spring to early autumn, very seldom afterwards. The resting period is usually in winter. The leaves should never be syringed but a moist atmosphere is necessary in spring and summer.

Increase by division of large plants when repotting. When five bulbs or more are present, the rhizome may be severed behind the fourth bulb and the fifth then often produces a growth which can be repotted and grown on.

Recommended kinds are *A. clowesii*, yellow, spring, 18 in., Colombia; *ruckeri*, green, yellow and crimson, late spring, early summer, 18 in., Colombia, var. *sanguinea*, crimson colour deeper and on a larger area; *uniflora*, white and pink, early summer, 2 to 3 ft., Colombia.

ANIGOZANTHOS (Kangaroo Paw) – *Amaryllidaceae*. Slightly tender evergreen perennials with sword-shaped leaves and curving tubular flowers. All are natives of Western Australia.

Compost, one part loam, two parts peat, and two parts coarse sand. Pot in spring.

Position, cool greenhouse fully exposed to light, minimum winter temp. 7°C. (but in warm countries some kinds will survive a little frost). Water normally.

Increase by division of the roots in spring; by seeds sown in temp. 13 to 15°C. in spring or as soon as ripe.

Anigozanthos manglesii

Recommended kinds are *A. flavidus*, greenish yellow and red, summer, 5 ft.; *manglesii*, green and red, summer, 3 ft.; *pulcherrimus*, yellow and white, late spring, 2 to 3 ft.; *rufus*, purple and white, late spring, 2 to 3 ft.; *viridis*, bright green, summer, 2 ft.

ANNONA – *Annonaceae*. Tender fragrant-leaved evergreen shrubs with edible fruits.

Compost, John Innes potting compost No. 2 or equivalent. Pot in spring.

Position, light and sunny, intermediate or warm greenhouse, minimum winter temp. 13°C. Water normally. Syringe daily in spring and summer. Shade from bright sunshine.

Increase by seeds sown in spring in temp. 18 to 20°C.; or by cuttings of firm shoots in moist sand in a warm propagator in summer.

Recommended kinds are *A. cherimola*, Cherimoyer, brown and yellow, summer, 12 to 18 ft., Peru; *muricata*, Sour Sop, green and yellow, summer, 10 ft., Tropical America; *reticulata*, Custard Apple, Bullock's Heart, yellow and brown, summer, 15 to 18 ft., Tropical America; *squamosa*, Sweet Sop, greenish yellow and purple, summer, 15 to 20 ft., Tropical America.

ANOECTOCHILUS (Jewel Orchid) – *Orchidaceae*. Tender terrestrial and epiphytic orchids grown primarily for their foliage, the flowers being of minor interest and often unpleasant smelling.

Grow in a warm house in equal parts peat and sand with a little sphagnum moss in well-drained pans. Keep in a moist, still atmosphere free of draughts. Shade from all direct sunshine. Water fairly freely throughout the year. Plants do well in a Wardian case or propagator. Stronger plants are obtained if the flower buds are removed.

All the species which produce stem roots should be propagated in spring and summer. Cut the stems below the roots, near the plant base. If available, a propagator with bottom heat should be used. *A. discolor* and similar swollen-stemmed forms may be increased by division of the rhizomes in early spring. Usually two or three swollen stems may be obtained on the same piece of rhizome; single pieces with a portion of the rhizome and a growth will succeed.

Recommended kinds are *A. argyroneurus*, leaves olive, veins silvery, Java; *discolor*, leaves green, red, white, China; *regalis*, green leaves netted with yellow, Ceylon.

ANTENNARIA – *Compositae*. Hardy herbaceous perennials with silvery white leaves; useful for edgings to borders or for clothing dry spots.

Soil, ordinary, gritty, well drained, preferably rather acid. Position, sunny. Plant in spring or autumn. Increase by division of roots in spring.

The best species is *A. dioica*, white or pale pink, 3 in., Europe (Britain), and var. *rosea*, deep pink.

ANTHEMIS – *Compositae*. Hardy perennials with fully cut, strongly scented foliage and daisy flowers. Flowers of the Common Chamomile, *A. nobilis*, are used for making chamomile tea.

Soil, ordinary, well drained. Position, sunny borders for tall species, rock gardens for dwarf ones. Plant in spring or autumn, Common Chamomile to be planted 2 ft. apart in rows 2½ ft. apart in spring. Gather flowers when fully expanded. Common Chamomile can also be planted 6 to 9 in. apart and clipped occasionally in late spring and summer to form fragrant lawns.

Increase by division in spring; by seeds sown outdoors in spring; by cuttings of young growth in spring.

Recommended kinds are *A. biebersteiniana*, yellow, leaves filigree silver, summer, 1 ft., Caucasus; *cupaniana*, white, summer and early autumn, 1 ft., Italy; *nobilis*, Common Chamomile, white, summer, 1 ft., Europe (Britain); *sancti-johannis*, orange-yellow, summer, 2 to 3 ft., Bulgaria; *tinctoria*, Dyer's or Ox-eye Chamomile, yellow, summer, 2 to 3 ft., Europe (Britain), and var. E. C. Buxton, lemon yellow.

ANTHERICUM – *Liliaceae*. Hardy herbaceous perennials with tufts of narrow, grassy leaves and erect, spike-like racemes of white flowers.

Soil, light, rich. Position, open, sunny or lightly shaded. Plant in spring or autumn.

Increase by seeds sown in light soil in a frame in spring; by division of roots in spring.

Recommended kinds are *A. liliago*, St Bernard Lily, white, early summer, 1 to 1½ ft., S. Europe, var. *major*, a superior form; *ramosum*, white, early summer, 2 ft., Europe.

See the genera *Paradisea* and *Chlorophytum* for other species formerly included in this genus.

ANTHOLYZA – *Iridaceae*. Slightly tender herbaceous perennials making corms. Flowers narrowly funnel shaped in dense spikes. Species formerly included here are to be found in the genera *Chasmanthe* and *Curtonus*.

Soil, light, sandy. Position, pots or borders in a cool greenhouse. Plant in autumn. Lift when leaves become brown, dry and store in a cool place till planting time.

Increase by offsets; or by seeds sown in slight heat in spring.

The only species cultivated is *A. ringens* (syn. *Babiana ringens*), crimson and greenish yellow, summer, 1 to 1½ ft., the upper part of the flower stalk flowerless and in its native habitat serves as a perch for sunbirds which suck the nectar and pollinate the curiously shaped blooms, S. Africa.

ANTHURIUM (Flamingo Plant, Tail Flower)– *Araceae*. Tender evergreen flowering plants with small, yellow or white flowers crowded on a slender spadix backed by a showy spathe.

Compost, John Innes potting compost No. 1 plus one-quarter its bulk of osmunda

Anthurium andreanum

fibre or coarse peat. Pot in spring, keeping crowns above the compost. Place plenty of drainage in the pots. Position, intermediate or warm greenhouse, minimum winter temp. 13°C., or *A. scherzerianum* in a warm, well-lighted room. Water normally. Maintain a moist atmosphere especially for *A. andreanum*. Shade from direct sunshine in spring and summer.

Increase by division of roots in late winter; by seeds sown in temp. 24 to 26°C. in spring.

Recommended kinds are *A. andreanum*, scarlet, spring to autumn, 2 ft., Colombia, and vars. *album*, white, *amoenum*, rose-red, *rhodochlorum*, rose and green; *crystallinum*, green, summer, 2 ft., grown for its large heart-shaped leaves, deep green, white veined, Colombia; *scherzerianum*, scarlet, Guatemala, and numerous varieties including *album*, white, *rothschildianum*, creamy white, spotted crimson, *wardianum*, scarlet, with extra large bracts.

ANTIRRHINUM (Snapdragon) – *Scrophulariaceae*. Hardy perennial plants with tubular flowers conspicuously lobed at the mouth. Some species are grown as annuals for summer bedding. Some authors place *A. asarina* in a separate genus as *Asarina procumbens*.

Soil, ordinary. Position, warm dry borders, rock gardens or walls for dwarf species, sunny open borders for bedding varieties. Plant permanent kinds in spring; bedding varieties in late spring or early summer.

Increase by seed, that of bedding varieties being sown in late winter or early spring in a temp. 15 to 18°C., and seedlings hardened off for planting out when danger of severe frost is over; that of permanent kinds in a cool greenhouse or frame in spring or summer as soon as ripe; also by cuttings in spring or summer in a frame or propagator.

Recommended kinds are *A. asarina*, pale yellow, summer, trailing, S. W. Europe; *glutinosum*, cream and yellow, summer, prostrate, Spain; *majus*, Common Snapdragon, pink, red, crimson, orange, yellow, cream, white and mauve, 6 to 36 in.

summer, Mediterranean region; *molle*, white and yellow, prostrate, summer, Pyrenees. The bedding antirrhinums have been developed mainly from *majus* but also through hybridization with other species, notably *glutinosum* and *molle*, to increase the range, height and form. Flowers with open instead of lobed funnels have also been produced, and double forms.

APHELANDRA – *Acanthaceae*. Tender, evergreen shrubs with showy flowers in close spikes and ornamental leaves.

Compost, John Innes potting compost No. 2 or equivalent. Position, intermediate or warm greenhouse, minimum winter temp. 13°C. Water normally. Shade only lightly in summer. Maintain a moist atmosphere in spring and summer. Feed fortnightly in summer with weak liquid fertilizer. Shorten stems after flowering to improve habit. Plants can also be grown in warm rooms but rarely flower freely under such conditions because of lack of light.

Increase by cuttings of firm young shoots inserted in sandy soil in a warm propagator in spring or summer.

Recommended kinds are *A. aurantiaca*, orange, winter, 3 ft., Mexico, and var. *roezlii*, leaves white veined; *fascinator*, scarlet, autumn, 1½ ft., leaves green and white above, purple beneath, Colombia; *nitens*, bright

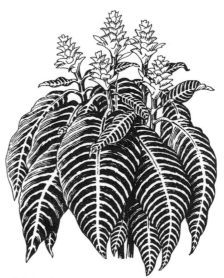

Aphelandra squarrosa louisae

red, spring and summer, 2 to 3 ft., Colombia, and var. *sinitzinii*, leaves white veined; *squarrosa*, yellow, late spring, early summer, 2 ft., Brazil, and vars. *louisae* and *leopoldii*, leaves white veined; *tetragona*, scarlet, summer, 3 ft., W. Indies, S. America.

APONOGETON – *Aponogetonaceae*. Hardy and tender aquatics, annuals and perennials. Leaves submerged or floating, and forked or single spiked flowers floating or standing above water.

Soil, heavy loam enriched with bonemeal. Position, sunny ponds or lakes with from 6 in. to 2 ft. of water for most kinds but no more than 9 in. for *A. krauseanus* or 2 in. for *A. leptostachyus abyssinicus*; or tubs in frost-proof greenhouses for tender species. *A. fenestralis* in a deep tub in shade and temp. 15 to 24°C. Plant in late spring or early summer in pans, sinking these into the water.

Increase by division at planting time, or by seeds sown directly after gathering in sifted loam and charcoal in shallow pans and kept very wet.

Recommended kinds are *A. distachyus*, Cape Pondweed, Water Hawthorn, white, forked, fragrant flowers all summer, floating strap-like leaves, hardy, Africa, Australia; *fenestralis*, Madagascar Lace Plant, leaves skeletonized to a lattice pattern, submerged, very beautiful, twin spikes, white flowers, tender, Madagascar; *krauseanus*, sulphur twin spikes above water, summer, scented, hardy, Africa, Australia; *leptostachyus* var. *abyssinicus*, forked spikes, mauve, annual, tender, Abyssinia; *ulvaceus*, submerged, foliage like Hart's-tongue Fern, flowers sulphur, tender, Madagascar.

APOROCACTUS – *Cactaceae*. Tender succulent perennials with slender prostrate or pendulous stems.

Compost, two parts turfy loam, one part coarse sand and broken brick. Position, well-drained pots or pans in a sunny greenhouse or window, minimum temp. 10°C. Pot as required, water sparingly.

Increase by seeds sown in well-drained pots or pans in temp. 15 to 18°C. in spring; by cuttings in sand in spring or summer.

The best kind is *A. flagelliformis*, Rat's Tail Cactus, red or pink, Peru.

AQUILEGIA (Columbine) – *Ranunculaceae*. Hardy perennial plants with spurred (rarely spurless) flowers and elegant compound leaves. Graceful plants for the border or rock garden, often short lived but readily increasing by seed.

Soil, sandy loam enriched with leafmould. Position, sunny or brightly shaded. Plant in spring or autumn.

Increase by seeds sown in sandy soil in a frame in spring or in an open border in spring or as soon as ripe; by division of roots in spring.

Recommended kinds are *A. alpina*, powder blue, late spring, 1 ft., Europe; *bertolonii*, deep blue, late spring and early summer, 6 in., Europe; *caerulea*, Colorado Columbine, blue, summer, 1 to 1½ ft., America; *canadensis*, red and yellow, spring and early summer, 1 to 2 ft., N. America, var. *nana*, 6 to 9 in.; *chrysantha*, soft yellow, late spring and summer, 2 ft., America; *discolor*, blue and white, late spring, 4 in., Spain; *flabellata*, pale purple or white, summer, 1 to 1½ ft., Japan, var. *nana-alba*, white, 6 to 9 in.; *formosa* (syn. *arctica*), red

Aquilegia bertolonii

and yellow, late spring and summer, 3 ft., N. America; *glandulosa*, blue and white, late spring and early summer, 8 to 12 in., Siberia, and var. *jucunda*, shorter wider flowers; *hybrida*, various colours, late spring, early summer, 1½ to 3 ft., garden hybrids of complex parentage, some long spurred, some short spurred; *longissima*, long spurred, yellow, late spring, early summer, 2 to 3 ft., America; *pyrenaica*, blue, late spring, early summer, 9 in., Europe; *scopulorum*, blue, early summer, 6 in., America; *skinneri*, red and yellow, late spring and summer, 2 to 3 ft., Mexico; *vulgaris*, Common Columbine, various, single and double, summer, 1½ to 2½ ft., Europe (Britain).

ARABIS (Wall Cress, Rock Cress) – *Cruciferae*. Hardy perennial trailing or cushion-forming plants.

Soil, ordinary. Position, as edgings to well-drained borders, on sunny rock gardens, banks and unmortared terrace walls, for carpeting beds of spring-flowering bulbs, etc. Plant in spring or autumn.

Increase by seeds sown out of doors or in a frame in spring or as soon as ripe; by cuttings inserted in a propagator in summer; by division of roots in autumn.

Recommended kinds are *A. albida* (syn. *caucasica*), white, spring, trailing, S.E. Europe, Iran, and vars. *flore pleno*, double, *rosabella*, pink, compact, *variegata*, leaves variegated pale yellow, *plena variegata*, similar to the last but double flowered; *aubrietioides*, rose, summer, 6 in., Asia Minor; *blepharophylla*, bright red, late spring, 4 in., cushion forming, California, suitable for an alpine house; *ferdinandi-coburgii*, white, early summer, 2 to 3 in., cushion forming, Macedonia; *procurrens*, white, spring, creeping, Europe.

ARALIA – *Araliaceae*. Hardy or tender herbs, shrubs or trees with ornamental foliage.

Soil, light well-drained loam. Position, shady borders for herbaceous species, warm

and sunny for shrubby or tree-like species. Plant in autumn or spring. Remove dead or frost-damaged growth in spring. In cold places aralias may be grown in cool greenhouses but they take up a lot of room.

Increase by seeds stratified as soon as ripe at 20 to 25°C. for about four months, then at 5°C. for three months and then sown in a temp. 15 to 18°C.; by root cuttings in winter; by rooted suckers dug up carefully in autumn or late winter.

Recommended kinds are *A. cachemirica*, white, summer, 6 ft., herbaceous, Kashmir; *chinensis*, Chinese Angelica Tree, to 20 ft., spiny, China; *cordata* (syn. *edulis*), white, summer, 4 to 6 ft., young blanched shoots edible, herbaceous, Japan; *elata*, Japanese Angelica Tree, to 45 ft., Manchuria; *nudicaulis*, Wild Sarsaparilla, greenish, summer, 3 to 4 ft., herbaceous, N. America; *racemosa*, American Spikenard, greenish white, summer, herbaceous, N. America; *spinosa*, Devil's Walking Stick, Hercules' Club, to 25 ft., very spiny, N. America.

ARAUCARIA – *Araucariaceae*. Hardy and slightly tender evergreen coniferous trees, notable for their stiff, symmetrical habit which is particularly marked in young specimens.

Soil, deep, rich, rather moist loam. Position, sheltered. Plant in spring or autumn.

Araucaria excelsa

Tender kinds can be grown in a compost of two parts loam, one part leafmould, and one part coarse sand in well-drained pots or tubs in a sunny house. Repot in spring when necessary. Avoid overcrowding; give plenty of room. Temperature, spring to autumn 15 to 20°C., winter 5 to 10°C. Requires plenty of air in summer.

Increase by cuttings of tips of young shoots inserted in sandy loam in a warm greenhouse in summer; by seeds sown 1 in. deep in light soil in temp. 18°C. in spring.

Recommended tender species are *A. bidwillii*, Bunya-bunya Tree, 100 to 150 ft.,

Queensland; *columnaris* (syn. *cookii*), 150 to 200 ft., New Caledonia; *cunninghamii*, Moreton Bay Pine, 150 to 200 ft., Queensland; *excelsa*, Norfolk Island Pine, 100 to 120 ft., Norfolk Island, and vars. *glauca* and *robusta*; *rulei*, 50 ft., New Caledonia. Heights are for trees in the wild. Pot- or tub-grown specimens can be kept relatively small for many years by root restriction.

The hardy species recommended is *A. araucana* (syn. *imbricata*), Chile Pine, Monkey Puzzle, 50 to 100 ft., Chile, var. *aurea*, golden-tinted foliage.

ARBUTUS – *Ericaceae*. Hardy or slightly tender evergreen trees. Small white urn-shaped flowers in spring followed by strawberry-like fruits ripening in winter. Plant in spring or autumn in sun or partial shade. *A. andrachne* in lime-free soil but *hybrida* and *unedo* are lime tolerant.

Arbutus unedo

Increase by seeds sown 1 in. deep in well-drained pans of sandy peat in a cold frame in spring; or by grafting on seedling stocks of *A. unedo* in heat during spring.

Recommended kinds are *A. andrachne*, 12 to 14 ft., Levant, rather tender, especially when young; *hybrida* (syn. *andrachnoides*), 20 to 30 ft.; *menziesii*, Madrona, 50 to 80 ft., with peeling bark revealing cinnamon stems, N. America; *unedo*, Strawberry Tree, 20 to 30 ft., Europe, including Ireland, var. *rubra*, a good deep-pink-flowered form.

ARCTOSTAPHYLOS (Bearberry) – *Ericaceae*. Hardy and slightly tender evergreen shrubs.

Soil, peat, leafmould and loam. Position, warm and sunny. Plant in spring or autumn.

Increase by cuttings inserted in gritty soil in summer or autumn; by seeds sown in spring.

Recommended kinds are *A. manzanita*, red stems, grey foliage and pink flowers in spring, 10 ft., California, will stand only a few degrees of frost; *uva-ursi*, pink, spring, succeeded by red berries, evergreen, trailing, useful as ground cover, hardy, Northern Hemisphere.

ARCTOTIS – *Compositae*. Slightly tender annuals and perennials with daisy-type flowers. All kinds described here are native of S. Africa. Soil, ordinary, well drained. Position, warm, sunny. Sow seeds of annuals in spring in temp. 15 to 18°C. and harden off seedlings for planting outdoors when there is no danger of frost. Alternatively, grow throughout in pots in a sunny greenhouse, discard after flowering. Perennial kinds can be grown in the same way but can be retained through the winter in a frost-proof greenhouse.

Increase by seed as described; perennial kinds also by cuttings of side shoots inserted in sandy soil in a frame in early summer.

Recommended kinds are *A. acaulis* (syn. *scapigera*), orange-carmine, summer, 6 in., perennial, S. Africa; *breviscapa*, orange, summer, 6 in., S. Africa; *grandis* (syns. *stoechadifolia* and *venusta*), African Daisy, white, lavender-blue reverse, summer, 2 ft., annual, Africa.

ARDISIA (Spear Flower) – *Myrsinaceae*. Tender berry-bearing evergreen shrubs.

Soil, John Innes potting compost No. 2 or equivalent. Pot or plant in spring in a cool or intermediate greenhouse, minimum winter temp. 7°C. Water normally. Shade lightly in summer. Ventilate freely while plants are in flower to assist pollination.

Ardisia crispa

Prune straggly shoots in late winter to maintain neat, well-branched plants.

Increase by seeds sown in temp. 18 to 21°C. in spring; by cuttings of side shoots in a warm propagator in spring or summer.

The best species is *A. crispa* (syn. *crenulata*), white, early summer, followed by red berries, 3 to 4 ft., Malaysia, China.

ARENARIA (Sandwort) – *Caryophyllaceae*. Hardy herbaceous perennials and rock garden plants, creeping or mat forming and some making good ground cover for small bulbs.

Soil, ordinary, well drained. Position, sunny or shady; *A. balearica* prefers shade. Plant in spring or autumn.

Increase by division of roots in spring or autumn.

Recommended kinds are *A. balearica*, white, late spring, early summer, mat forming, Balearic Isles; *caespitosa* (syn. *Minuartia verna caespitosa*), white, late spring, cushion forming, Europe, and var. *aurea*, yellow-green leaves; *laricifolia* (syn. *Alsine laricifolia*), white, early summer, prostrate, Europe; *ledebouriana*, white, ash-grey leaves, summer, Alps; *montana*, white, late spring, early summer, to 12 in., sprawling, Spain; *purpurascens*, soft purple, summer, 2 in., cushion forming, Pyrenees; *tetraquetra*, white, early summer, 3 to 4 in., Spain.

ARGEMONE – *Papaveraceae*. Hardy annuals and perennials with poppy-like flowers. All are usually grown as annuals.

Soil, sandy. Position, sunny, warm. Sow outdoors in spring where plants are to flower and thin seedlings to 9 in.

Argemone grandiflora

Recommended kinds are *A. grandiflora*, white, summer, 2 to 3 ft., Mexico; *mexicana*, Mexican Poppy, Prickly Poppy, yellow or orange, summer, 2 ft., Mexico, and var. *ochroleuca*, cream; *platyceras*, white or purple, summer, 2 to 4 ft., N. and S. America.

ARISAEMA – *Araceae*. Tender and hardy tuberous-rooted perennials. Flowers, arum like in shape.

Culture of tender kinds: John Innes potting compost No. 1 or equivalent. Position, cool or intermediate greenhouse, minimum winter temp. 7°C. Pot in spring. Water freely spring to early autumn but keep dry in winter. Shade from direct sunshine.

Culture of hardy kinds: Soil, ordinary, well mixed with peat or leafmould. Position shady. Topdress with peat or leafmould after new growth begins. Plant in spring.

Increase by seeds sown in peat or leafmould and loam in a frame or greenhouse in spring or as soon as ripe; or by division of the tuberous roots.

Recommended tender kinds are *A. concinnum*, green or purple and white, early summer, 1 to 2 ft., Himalaya; *speciosum*, white, spring, 1 to 2 ft., Himalaya; *tortuosum*, purple and green, late spring, early summer, 1 to 3 ft., India.

Recommended hardy kinds are *A. candidissimum*, white, sometimes pale pink, summer, 1½ ft., W. China; *dracontium*, green, early summer, 1 to 1½ ft., Eastern U.S.A.; *griffithii*, brown, violet and green, spring, 1 to 1½ ft., Sikkim; *ringens*, white and green, spring, 2 ft., Japan; *sikokianum*, brown, cream and white, spring, early summer, 2 ft., Japan; *triphyllum*, Jack-in-the-Pulpit, green and brown, summer, 2 ft., U.S.A.

ARISARUM – *Araceae*. Hardy, tuberous-rooted perennials.

Soil, cool, light, enriched with leafmould. Position, semi-shade or north aspect. Increase by division of roots in spring.

The best species is *A. proboscideum*, Mousetail Plant, flowers resemble long-tailed brown mice half-hidden in round green leaves, early summer, 6 in., Italy.

ARISTOLOCHIA (Birthwort) – *Aristolochiaceae*. Tender and hardy climbing or herbaceous plants, with curiously shaped tubular flowers.

Soil, reasonably fertile, well drained; John Innes potting compost No. 2 or equivalent for pot-grown plants. Position, sunny borders for herbaceous species; warm sunny walls, pergolas, trellises, etc., for climbing kinds. Plant in autumn or spring.

Increase herbaceous kinds by division in spring; climbing kinds by cuttings in summer in a propagator, heated for tender species; by root cuttings in winter in a frame, temp. 15 to 18°C. for tender species; all kinds by seeds stratified for three months at 4°C. and then sown in a temp. of 15 to 18°C. (18 to 21°C. for tender kinds).

Recommended tender climbers are *A. elegans*, Calico Flower, green, white and purple, 8 to 10 ft., Brazil; *grandiflora* (syn. *gigas*), Pelican Flower, purple spotted, early summer, 8 to 10 ft., W. Indies, Central and S. America, and var. *sturtevantii*, which

is better than the type species; *sempervirens* (syn. *altissima*), yellowish purple, late spring, early summer, 8 to 10 ft., Crete, N. Africa, will survive a few degrees of frost.

The best hardy herbaceous species is *A. clematitis*, yellow, 2 to 3 ft., Europe (Britain).

Recommended hardy climbing kinds are *A. macrophylla* (syns. *durior* and *sipho*), Dutchman's Pipe, yellowish-brown, early summer, 15 to 30 ft., Eastern U.S.A.; *tomentosa*, yellow and purple, summer, downy foliage, 10 to 15 ft., South-eastern U.S.A.

ARMERIA (Thrift) – *Plumbaginaceae*. Dwarf perennials with narrow leaves in tufts or basal rosettes and globular heads of flowers.

Soil, sandy loam. Position, sunny edging to borders or rock gardens, excellent for dry and exposed places. Unaffected by salt spray. Plant in autumn or spring.

Increase by seeds sown in sandy soil in spring, or division of roots in early autumn or spring.

Recommended kinds are *A. caespitosa* (syn. *juniperifolia*), compact hummocks, white to pink, late spring, Spain; *maritima*, Lady's Pincushion, Common Thrift, Sea Pink, pink, spring and summer, 6 in., Europe (Britain), vars. *alba*, white, *laucheana*, carmine; *mauritanica*, glowing carmine, 2 to 3 ft., summer, Spain and Portugal; *plantaginea*, Jersey Thrift, pink, summer, 1 to 2 ft., Europe (Jersey), and var. Bees Ruby, larger, ruby-red flower heads; *pseud-armeria* (syn. *cephalotes*), rose-pink, summer, 1 ft., Europe.

ARNEBIA – *Boraginaceae*. Hardy perennials and rather tender annuals with trumpet-shaped flowers in clusters.

Soil, ordinary, well drained. Position, sunny, warm, even rather dry. Sow seeds of annuals in light soil in frames or a cool house in early spring and plant out seedlings when danger of frost is past. Plant perennial species in spring or autumn.

Increase perennial species by seeds or division in spring.

Recommended kinds are *A. cornuta*, yellow spotted with purple, summer, 1½ to 2 ft., annual, Afghanistan; *echioides* (syn. *Echioides longiflorum*), Prophet Flower, yellow and purple, late spring, early summer, to 1 ft., perennial, Armenia.

ARNICA – *Compositae*. Hardy herbaceous perennials with medicinal uses.

Soil, light, gritty, with some peat or leafmould. Position, sunny. Plant in autumn or spring.

Increase by division of roots in spring.

The best species is *A. montana*, Mountain Tobacco, yellow, summer, 1 ft., Europe.

ARONIA (Chokeberry) – *Rosaceae*. Deciduous shrubs with coloured autumn foliage

and fruits. Sometimes included in *Amelanchier*.

Soil, ordinary, well drained. Position, sunny. Plant in autumn or late winter.

Increase by seeds stratified for three months at 4°C. and then sown outdoors or under glass; by cuttings in summer in a propagator; by division in autumn or late winter.

Recommended kinds are *A. arbutifolia*, Red Chokeberry, white or pale pink, late spring, pear-shaped red fruits, 5 to 10 ft., Eastern N. America; *melanocarpa*, Black Chokeberry, white, late spring, black fruits, 1½ to 5 ft., spreading by suckers, Eastern N. America; *prunifolia* (syn. *floribunda*), Purple Chokeberry, white, late spring, purplish-black fruits, to 12 ft., Eastern N. America.

ARTEMISIA – *Compositae*. Hardy sub-shrubs and herbaceous perennials, with grey or silvery and fragrant foliage. Of those commonly grown in gardens only *A. lactiflora*, with panicles of milk-white flowers, has beauty of flower. The rest are grown as foliage plants.

Soil, ordinary, well drained for most kinds but *A. lactiflora* will thrive in heavier, moister soil. Position, sunny. Plant in spring or autumn.

Increase shrubby and herbaceous species by cuttings inserted in a frame in summer; by division in spring or autumn for herbaceous species; by seeds sown outdoors in spring for all species.

Recommended shrubby kinds are *A. abrotanum*, Southernwood, Lad's Love, or Old Man, finely divided grey aromatic leaves, 2 to 4 ft., Europe; *arborescens*, finely divided silvery leaves, 3 ft., S. Europe; *tridentata*, silvery grey, strongly fragrant leaves, 6 to 8 ft., America.

Recommended herbaceous kinds are *A. absinthium*, Wormwood, finely divided, silky, white leaves, 3 ft., Europe; *frigida*, finely divided silvery leaves, 1 to 1½ ft., N. America, Siberia; *gnaphalodes*, grey leaves, 1 to 2 ft., N. America; *lactiflora*, cream, late summer, early autumn, green leaves, 5 ft., China; *ludoviciana*, grey leaves, 2 ft., N. America; *pedemontana*, silver-grey, finely divided foliage, 4 to 6 in., Europe; *schmidtiana*, finely divided silvery leaves, 2 ft., Japan, and var. *nana*, 6 in.; *stelleriana*, Old Woman, Dusty Miller, Beech Wormwood, white woolly leaves, 2 ft., N. E. Asia and Eastern N. America.

ARUM – *Araceae*. Hardy or tender tuberous-rooted perennials.

Soil for the hardy species, good but not dry. Position, partially shaded shrub borders or in grass. Plant in autumn or spring.

The more tender species need to be frost free in winter. In pots in a cool greenhouse use a compost of two parts loam, one part decayed manure, and one part sand. Plant or pot in autumn. Water freely whilst growing but keep nearly dry when foliage dies.

Increase by offsets in autumn or from seed sown in spring.

Recommended hardy species include *A. italicum*, Italian Arum, creamy white, spring, 1 to 1½ ft., grown for its white-veined leaves produced in autumn, S. Europe; *maculatum*, Cuckoo Pint, Lords and Ladies, yellowish green, spotted purple, 6 in., Britain.

Slightly tender species include *A. creticum*, spathe yellow, late spring, 1 ft., Crete; *palaestinum* (syn. *sanctum*), yellow and deep purple, late spring, 2 ft., Syria.

ARUNCUS (Goat's Beard) – *Rosaceae*. Hardy perennial with plumy panicles of creamy white flowers. At one time included in *Spiraea*.

Soil, moist, rich. Position, partial shade. Plant in spring or autumn.

Increase by seeds sown in spring; by division in spring or autumn.

Aruncus sylvester

Recommended kinds are *A. sylvester* (syn. *Spiraea aruncus*), creamy white, summer, 4 to 6 ft., North Temperate Regions, var. *kneiffii*, finely dissected foliage.

ARUNDINARIA – *Gramineae*. Hardy shrubby grasses commonly known as bamboo. They are grown for their canes and elegant foliage.

Soil, good, not too heavy and of reasonable depth. Position, sheltered from cold winds, dry root conditions are disliked. Increase by division.

Recommended kinds are *A. anceps*, to 10 ft., spreads rapidly, Himalaya; *fastuosa* to 20 ft., very strong canes, Japan; *gigantea*, Southern Cane, Cane Reed, 10 to 15 ft., slightly tender, needs a sheltered place, N. America; *humilis*, 2 to 5 ft., good ground cover, Japan; *japonica* (syns. *Pseudosasa japonica* and *Bambusa metake*), 10 to 15 ft.,

Japan; *murieliae*, 9 to 12 ft., arching, China; *nitida*, 9 to 12 ft., purple canes, China; *pumila*, 1 to 2 ft., purple canes, spreading, Japan; *simonii*, 12 to 15 ft., Japan; *vagans*, 1 to 2 ft., runs underground, Japan; *variegata*, 2 to 3 ft., leaves striped with white, Japan; *viridistriata*, 3 to 6 ft., leaves striped with yellow, Japan.

See also Sasa.

ARUNDO – *Gramineae*. Very tall hardy perennial grasses.

Soil, good, rather moist loam. Position, sheltered in isolated groups especially near water. Plant in spring.

Increase by division of roots in spring.

The best kind is *A. donax*, Giant Reed, reddish changing to white, summer, 12 ft., S. Europe, var. *variegata*, leaves striped with white, 3 ft.

ASCLEPIAS (Milkweed) – *Asclepiadaceae*. Hardy and tender herbaceous perennials.

Soil, rich, light lime-free loam. Position, sunny and moist. Plant in spring or autumn. *A. curassavica* in pots in a greenhouse with minimum winter temp. 7°C. Keep rather dry in winter and cut back fairly hard in early spring.

Increase by division of roots in spring or autumn; also by seeds sown in temp. 18 to 21°C. in spring.

Recommended kinds are *A. curassavica*, Blood Flower, scarlet and orange, summer and early autumn, 3 ft., tender, Tropical America, and var. *aurea*, orange-yellow; *incarnata*, rose-purple, summer, 4 to 5 ft., U.S.A.; *tuberosa*, Butterfly Milkweed, Pleurisy Root, Swallow-wort, orange, summer, 2 to 3 ft., U.S.A.

ASPARAGUS – *Liliaceae*. Slightly tender climbing foliage plants.

Asparagus plumosus

Compost, John Innes potting compost No. 2 or equivalent. Position, pots, hanging baskets, tubs or beds in a cool greenhouse, minimum winter temp. 7°C., stems of climbers trained up the roof or back walls;

trailing kinds on the edge of the staging, in pots or baskets suspended from the roof. Pot or plant in spring. Water and syringe freely during the summer, moderately at other seasons. Apply weak liquid fertilizer occasionally to established plants.

Increase by seeds sown in temp. 15 to 18°C. in spring; by division in spring. Pot seedlings in John Innes potting compost No. 1 or equivalent and only move into a richer compost when ready for 5-in. (or larger) pots.

Recommended kinds are *A. medeoloides* (syns. *A. asparagoides* and *Myrsiphyllum asparagoides*), Smilax, 6 to 10 ft., branching vine, S. Africa, and vars. *aureus*, leaves pale yellowish green, and *myrtifolius*, Baby Smilax, smaller leaves; *plumosus*, Asparagus Fern, 4 to 10 ft., S. Africa, and vars. *nanus*, dwarf, and *tenuissimus*, wiry stemmed, all used in floristry; *sprengeri*, climbing to 6 ft., Natal; *verticillatus*, 10 ft., S. Africa, and vars. *compactus*, 1 to 1½ ft., and *variegatus*, leaves variegated.

ASPERULA – *Rubiaceae*. Hardy herbaceous perennials and annuals with small flowers in clusters.

' Soil, light, well drained. Position, sunny rock gardens, raised beds or edgings to borders, *A. odorata* in semi-shade or woodland. Plant perennial kinds in spring or autumn.

Sow seeds of annual kinds in spring where plants are to flower. Increase perennial species by division of roots in spring and seeds sown in open borders or under glass in spring.

Recommended perennial kinds are *A. gussonii*, pale pink, summer, 2 in., tufted habit, Sicily; *hirta*, white becoming pink, late spring, 3 in., hummock forming, Pyrenees; *lilaciflora caespitosa*, light carmine, summer, 2 in., carpeting, E. Mediterranean; *odorata* (syn. *Galium odoratum*), Sweet Woodruff, white, late spring, early summer, 9 in., leaves sweet scented when dried, Europe (Britain); *suberosa*, pink, summer, 3 in., grey downy leaves, Greece.

The best annual is *A. orientalis* (syn. *azurea*), lavender-blue, summer, fragrant, 1 ft., Caucasus.

ASPHODELINE – *Liliaceae*. Hardy herbaceous perennials with flowers in slender erect racemes.

Soil, ordinary. Position, open, sunny or shady. Plant in spring or autumn.

Increase by division of roots in spring or autumn.

The best species is *A. lutea* (syn. *Asphodelus luteus*), Asphodel, King's Spear, yellow, summer, 3 to 4 ft., Mediterranean region, var. *flore-pleno*, flowers double.

ASPHODELUS (Asphodel) – *Liliaceae*. Hardy herbaceous perennials with flowers in narrow racemes or broader panicles.

Soil, ordinary, well drained. Position, shady or open borders. Plant in autumn or spring.

Increase by division of roots in spring or autumn; by seeds sown in a frame in spring.

Recommended kinds are *A. cerasiferus*, White Asphodel, white, late spring, early summer, 3 to 4 ft., S. Europe; *liburnicus*, yellow, summer, 3 to 4 ft., S. E. Europe; *ramosus*, Silver Rod, white, early summer, 4 to 5 ft., S. Europe.

ASPIDISTRA – *Liliaceae.* Tender evergreen plants. Leaves large, green or variegated with cream.

Compost, two parts loam, one part each of peat and sand. Repot in spring. Water normally. Will grow in very shady places and make excellent house plants. Sponge leaves with water occasionally to keep them clean. Minimum temp. 7°C.

Increase by division of roots in early spring.

Recommended kinds are *A. elatior* (syn. *lurida*), Parlour Palm, leaves green, 1 to 2 ft., China, var. *variegata*, leaves striped cream.

ASPLENIUM (Spleenwort) – *Aspleniaceae.* Tender and hardy ferns. Height varies from 6 in. to 4 ft. Fronds very variable in form.

Asplenium bulbiferum

The tender kinds make good pot plants in a compost of two parts peat or leafmould, one part medium loam and one part coarse sand. Pot in early spring. Water normally. Temperature for warm house kinds 18°C. minimum in winter, rising to 20 to 25°C. in summer; for cool house kinds minimum in winter 7°C. rising to 13 to 18°C. in summer.

Grow hardy kinds in equal parts peat, loam, leafmould and sand, plus old mortar rubble or broken chalk for *A. ruta-muraria*. Position, old walls, rock gardens; moist shady borders for Lady Ferns.

Increase tender species by spores sown in sandy peat at any time in temp. 20 to 25°C.; hardy species by spores when ripe in a frame or unheated greenhouse, or by division in spring; *A. bulbiferum* by pegging mature leaves to the soil without severing

them from the plant and allowing the little plantlets which form along the fronds to grow. Later these plantlets can be lifted carefully and potted individually.

The best warm greenhouse kind is *A. nidus*, Bird's Nest Fern, undivided green fronds 2 ft. or more long, Asia, Polynesia, and var. *australasicum*, midrib usually black.

The best cool greenhouse kind is *A. bulbiferum*, much divided fronds to 2 ft. long, Australia, New Zealand.

Recommended hardy kinds are *A. adiantum nigrum*, Black Spleenwort, French Fern, fronds 1 ft. long, Temperate Zones (Britain); *ruta-muraria*, Wall Rue, fronds to 3 in. long, Europe; *trichomanes*, Maidenhair Spleenwort, fronds to 1 ft. long, N. America, Europe, Asia.

ASTER (Starwort, Michaelmas Daisy) – *Compositae.* Hardy herbaceous perennials with daisy flowers freely produced in summer and autumn. See Callistephus for China Aster; Solidaster for *A. hybridus luteus*.

Soil, good, ordinary. Position, open, sunny or partially shady. Plant in spring or autumn. Lift, divide and replant when overcrowded, every year for some of the vigorous growing large-flowered varieties of *novaeangliae* and *novi-belgii*.

Increase by division in autumn or spring; species also by seeds sown out of doors or under glass in spring.

Recommended kinds are *A. acris* (syn. *sedifolius*), light blue, late summer, 3 ft., S. Europe, and var. *nanus*, 1½ ft.; *alpinus*, blue-purple, late spring, early summer, 6 in., Europe, and vars. *albus*, white, *roseus*, rosy mauve; *amellus*, violet-blue, late summer, 2 ft., Italy and numerous varieties from light lavender and pinkish mauve to reddish purple; *cordifolius*, mauve, late summer, early autumn, to 5 ft., N. America; *diplostephioides*, blue-purple, late spring to early summer, 6 to 18 in., China, Tibet; *ericoides*, white sometimes tinged pink, autumn, 1 to 3 ft., Canada, U.S.A., and varieties with blue and pink flowers; *farreri*, violet-blue, summer, 1½ ft., China, Tibet; *frikartii*, lavender-blue, late summer and autumn, 2 to 3 ft., hybrid between *amellus* and *thompsonii*; *grandiflorus*, violet-purple, autumn, 3 to 4 ft., Eastern U.S.A.; *novae-angliae*, purple, autumn, 3 to 5 ft., N. America, and varieties, some with pink or carmine flowers; *novi-belgii*, blue-violet, autumn, 3 to 5 ft., N. America, and numerous varieties white, pink, lavender to crimson and deep blue-purple and from 6 in. to 6 ft., single, semi-double and double; *pappei*, see Felicia; *paniculatus*, white or pale lilac, autumn, 3 to 8 ft., N. America; *subcaeruleus*, lavender, late spring, early summer, 6 to 12 in., India; *thomsonii*, lavender, late summer to early autumn, 2 ft., Himalaya; *tradescantii*, white, autumn, 2 to 5 ft., N. America; *yunnanensis*, lilac-blue, summer, 9 to 12 in., China.

ASTERANTHERA – *Gesneriaceae.* Slightly tender evergreen climber clinging by aerial roots.

Soil, lime-free peat and loam. Position, shady woodland or wall. Plant in spring. Can be used as ground cover. Will withstand a few degrees of frost but is unsuitable for cold places.

Increase by layering in spring or summer; by seeds sown in temp. 15 to 18°C. in spring.

The only kind is *A. ovata*, scarlet, late summer, autumn, Chile.

ASTILBE (False Goatsbeard) – *Saxifragaceae.* Hardy herbaceous perennials with finely divided leaves and plumy sprays of small flowers. They are sometimes incorrectly called spiraea.

Soil, loamy, rather moist. Position, shady borders or margins of lakes or ponds. Plant in spring or autumn. Plenty of water is required in dry weather.

Can be forced under glass, for which purpose use John Innes potting compost No. 2 or equivalent. Pot strong roots in early autumn. Place pots in a frame till about midwinter, then introduce to a temperature of 7 to 10°C. for a week or so, then transfer to 15 to 18°C. Water freely when growth begins. Apply weak liquid manure when flower spikes show. After flowering, harden off in a frame and then plant out in the garden.

Increase by division in spring or autumn.

Recommended kinds are *A. arendsii*, white to red, summer, 2½ to 5 ft., hybrids between *astilboides*, *davidii*, *japonica* and *thunbergii*, of which many named varieties will be found in catalogues; *astilboides*, white, early summer, 2 to 3 ft., Japan; *chinensis*, white, and pink, late summer, 2 ft., China, and var. *pumila*, purple, dwarf; *crispa*, white, pink, red, summer, 6 to 12 in., hybrid probably between *simplicifolia* and *arendsii*; *davidii*, magenta, late summer, 4 to 6 ft., China; *japonica*, white, late spring, 2 ft., Japan; *lemoinei*, white or rose, summer, 2 to 3 ft., hybrid between *astilboides* and *thunbergii*; *rivularis*, white, late summer, early autumn, 5 to 6 ft., Himalaya; *rosea*, pink, late spring, 1 to 2 ft., hybrid between *chinensis* and *japonica*; *simplicifolia*, white, summer, 1 ft., Japan, and varieties with pink flowers or bronze leaves; *thunbergii*, white, late spring, 1 to 2 ft., Japan.

ASTRANTIA (Masterwort) – *Umbelliferae.* Hardy herbaceous perennials with tight clusters of flowers surrounded by starry bracts.

Soil, ordinary, slightly moist. Position, shady borders or margins of woodland walks. Plant in spring or autumn.

Increase by seeds sown in sandy loam in a frame in spring; by division of roots in spring or autumn.

Recommended kinds are *A. biebersteinii*, silvery lilac, late spring, 2 ft., Caucasus; *carniolica*, pale lilac-pink, late spring, early summer, 1 ft., E. Europe; and var. *rubra*,

Astrantia major

deeper rose-pink and green; *major*, pink and greenish white, early summer, 2 ft., Europe; *maxima* (syn. *helleborifolia*), rose, summer, 2 ft., Caucasus; *minor*, white, tinted green, late spring, early summer, 6 to 9 in., Europe.

ATHYRIUM – *Polypodiaceae*. Hardy ferns with foliage similar to *Asplenium* with which genus this is sometimes united.

Culture and propagation as for asplenium, but *A. goringianum* preferably in a frost-free greenhouse.

Recommended kinds are *A. alpestre*, to 3 ft., N. Europe (Britain), Asia; *filix-femina*, Lady Fern, to 3 ft., North Temperate Zone (Britain), India, Java, Tropical America, Peru, Argentina, and numerous varieties; *goeringianum*, pendulous, Japan, and var. *pictum*, fronds, green, purple and grey.

ATRIPLEX (Salt Bush) – *Chenopodiaceae*. Hardy annuals, perennials and shrubs. *A. hortensis*, which is occasionally grown as a substitute for spinach, has coloured-leaved varieties used for border decoration. *A. halimus* is a grey-leaved shrub, sometimes used for hedging with tamarisk.

Grow *A. hortensis* in ordinary soil and an open sunny position. Sow seeds thinly in spring where plants are to grow and thin out seedlings to 8 to 12 in.

Grow shrubby species in light sandy soil near the sea. They are suitable for hedges or windbreaks. Plant in autumn. Trim into shape in spring.

Increase by cuttings in summer.

Recommended annual species are *A. hortensis*, Orach, 3 to 5 ft., Central Asia, and vars. *atrosanguinea*, *cupreata*, *rosea*, with red foliage.

Recommended shrubby kinds are *A. canescens*, Grey Sage Bush, leaves light grey, 5 to 6 ft., N. W. America; *halimus*, Tree Purslane, silvery grey leaves, 6 to 8 ft., S. Europe.

AUBRIETA (Purple Rock Cress) – *Cruciferae*. Hardy trailing evergreen perennials. Former spelling aubrietia.

Soil, ordinary, loves lime. Position, sunny border, rock garden, banks or walls. Plant in spring or autumn. Plants will benefit from a severe trimming after flowering.

Increase by cuttings (small) in sandy soil in a propagator in summer; by seeds sown in sandy soil in spring; by division of the roots in spring. Seeds of named garden varieties will not come true to type.

The best species is *A. deltoidea*, lavender blue or mauve, trailing, S. Europe, of which there are numerous varieties ranging in colour from pale lavender and pink to deep violet-purple and crimson, some with double flowers.

AUCUBA – *Cornaceae*. Hardy evergreen shrubs. Male and female flowers produced on separate bushes. Female aucubas bear red berries freely in winter if a male plant is grown close to them, or if a branch of male blossom is placed on the female plant when in bloom. May be used for pot culture in cool greenhouses or windows in winter.

Soil, ordinary. Position, open or in shade; used as a town shrub and as a good screen beneath dense trees. Plant in spring and autumn.

Increase by seeds sown in a cold frame in autumn; by cuttings inserted in sandy soil in a sheltered border or cold frame in late summer or autumn.

Recommended kinds are *A. japonica*, Spotted Laurel, Variegated Laurel, 6 to 10 ft., Japan, and vars. *crassifolia*, male, thick dark green leaves, *crotonifolia*, male, leaves heavily blotched with yellow, *fructu-albo*, female, leaves spotted yellow, fruits pale yellow, Gold Dust, female, leaves blotched yellow, fruits red, *salicifolia*, female, narrow green leaves, red fruits, *variegata* (syn. *maculata*), female, leaves spotted yellow, fruits red.

AVENA (Oat) – *Gramineae*. Hardy, mostly annual grasses. One species is grown for ornament; the awns are susceptible to change of weather and appear animated.

Sow seeds outdoors in spring in ordinary soil and an open place. The inflorescences can be gathered when fully developed and dried for winter decoration.

The best kind is *A. sterilis*, Animated Oat, 2 ft., Mediterranean region.

AZARA – *Flacourtiaceae*. Fairly tender evergreen shrubs with ornamental leaves and small fragrant yellow flowers. All are natives of Chile.

Soil, ordinary. Position, warm and sheltered or in a cool greenhouse. Plant in spring or autumn.

Increase by cuttings inserted in sandy soil in summer in a propagator.

Recommended kinds are *A. dentata*, late

spring, 10 to 12 ft.; *lanceolata*, to 15 ft.; *microphylla*, early spring, strongly vanilla scented, to 15 ft., var. *variegata*, leaves heavily variegated with cream; *petiolaris* (syn. *gilliesii*), 20 to 25 ft., early spring.

AZOLLA (Fairy Moss) – *Azollaceae*. Hardy, floating aquatic perennials with delicate fern-like foliage.

Grow in shallow ponds or in indoor aquariums. Require no soil, plants float on the surface of the water. Can become a weed by spreading too fast. Increase by division.

Recommended kinds are *A. caroliniana*, pale green turning red in autumn, lacy, North, Central and South America; *filiculoides*, larger fronds, pale green tinted rose, Western S. America.

BABIANA (Baboon Root) – *Iridaceae*. Slightly tender cormous plants, occasionally fragrant, from S. Africa. Showy, funnel-shaped flowers in spikes.

Soil, light, well drained. Position, sunny, warm border or frost-proof greenhouse in pots of John Innes potting compost No. 1 or equivalent with a little extra sand. Plant or pot in autumn. Under glass place corms 4 in. deep and 2 in. apart. Water moderately from the time the corms begin to grow until the flowers fade, then gradually withhold it, keeping pots dry until growth restarts in autumn.

Increase by offsets at planting time; seeds sown in temp. 15 to 18°C. in spring.

Recommended kinds are *B. plicata*, blue, late spring, early summer; *pulchra*, blue or yellow and purple, early spring, 9 in.; *tubulosa*, cream and red, spring, 6 in.; *stricta*, blue-purple, early spring, 6 to 8 in., and var. *sulphurea*, light yellow.

BACCHARIS – *Compositae*. Hardy deciduous and evergreen shrubs useful in maritime districts because of their ability to withstand salt spray. Male and female flowers are produced on separate bushes but are rather inconspicuous.

Soil, ordinary, well drained. Position, open and sunny. Plant in autumn.

Increase by cuttings of young shoots in summer.

Recommended kinds are *B. halimifolia*, Tree-groundsel, deciduous, white, autumn, 6 to 12 ft., Eastern N. America; *patagonica*, evergreen, yellowish white, spring, 8 to 10 ft., Magellan Straits.

BALLOTA – *Labiatae*. Slightly tender perennials or sub-shrubs grown for their white woolly foliage. Soil, ordinary, well drained. Position, sunny, warm, even dry. Some protection may be required in winter especially in damp places, since a combination of damp and cold will destroy the plants. Plant in spring.

Increase by cuttings in sandy soil in a frame in summer.

Ballota pseudodictamnus

The best species is *B. pseudodictamnus*, sprawling sub-shrub to 2 ft., Crete.

BAMBUSA (Bamboo) – *Gramineae*. Tall woody grasses. All are tender, the hardy bamboos belonging to allied genera such as *Arundinaria*, *Phyllostachys* and *Sasa*.

Grow in a compost of equal parts loam, leafmould and sand in large pots or tubs in a cool greenhouse. Water freely in spring and summer, then moderately.

Increase by seeds sown in sandy soil in heat in spring; by cuttings of rhizomes in heat in spring; by division in spring.

Recommended species are *B. arundinacea*, 10 to 50 ft., India; *glaucescens* (syn. *multiplex*), Hedge Bamboo, 10 to 50 ft., China, Japan, and numerous garden varieties; *vulgaris*, Feathery Bamboo, to 50 ft., Tropical Asia.

BANKSIA (Australian Honeysuckle) – *Proteaceae*. Tender evergreen shrubs or trees with flowers in crowded cone-like heads. All are natives of Australia.

Compost of equal parts peat, lime-free loam and sand. Pot in spring in well-drained pots or plant in well-drained borders in a cool greenhouse or outdoors in very warm sunny places. Some species will survive several degrees of frost if growth is well ripened in autumn. Water carefully in winter, moderately in summer.

Increase by cuttings of firm shoots in well-drained pots of sandy soil in summer in a propagator, temp. 15 to 18°C.; also by seeds sown in sandy soil in spring in a similar temperature.

Recommended kinds are *B. collina*, honey brown and purple, winter, 6 ft.; *grandis*, yellowish green, early spring, 30 to 40 ft.; *integrifolia*, greenish yellow, autumn; *occidentalis*, brownish red, winter, 5 to 8 ft.; *serrata*, bluish grey, winter, to 20 ft.

BAPTISIA (False Indigo) – *Leguminosae*. Hardy herbaceous perennials and shrubs.

Soil, ordinary loamy. Position, sunny, well drained. Plant in spring or autumn.

Increase by seeds sown in sandy soil in a frame or outdoors in spring; by division in spring.

Recommended kinds are *B. australis*, deep blue, late spring, early summer, 3 to 4 ft., Eastern U.S.A.; *tinctoria*, yellow, summer, 3 to 4 ft., Eastern U.S.A.

BAUHINIA (Butterfly or Orchid Tree) – *Leguminosae*. Tender evergreen shrubs or small trees with very showy orchid-like flowers.

Compost, equal parts of peat and loam, one-sixth part of sand. Pot firmly in early spring. Position, light, sunny, moist in summer. Water normally. Minimum winter temperature for hardiest kinds 7°C., but most need warm house treatment.

Increase by cuttings inserted in sandy peat in a warm propagator in summer.

Recommended kinds are *B. blakeana*, reddish purple, autumn to spring, to 20 ft., China; *galpinii* (syn. *punctata*), red, summer and autumn, 6 to 10 ft., Natal; *variegata*, rosy purple, spring, 6 to 20 ft., China, India, one of the hardiest, and var. *candida*, white.

BEGONIA – *Begoniaceae*. Tender, fibrous- and tuberous-rooted perennials. Some are grown for flowers and others for ornamental foliage.

Culture of winter-flowering kinds: Compost, John Innes potting compost No. 1 or equivalent. Position, pots in an intermediate or warm greenhouse, minimum winter temp. 13°C. Best grown from cuttings taken afresh each spring. Pot rooted cuttings in 3-in. pots and move on to 4-in. and later 6-in. pots. Water freely in summer, maintain a fairly moist atmosphere and shade from direct sunshine. After flowering water sparingly for a few weeks, then cut back plants and water more freely to induce young growth to be taken as cuttings. The semi-tuberous-rooted kinds need particularly careful watering in winter as roots may decay in over-wet soil.

Culture of tuberous-rooted kinds: Compost, John Innes potting compost No. 2 or equivalent. Position, in cool greenhouse or outdoors in sunny or partially shady

Double-flowered tuberous-rooted begonia

places in summer when there is no danger of frost. Start tubers in late winter or early spring in moist peat in temp. 15°C. and pot in John Innes potting compost No. 1 as soon as two or three leaves have formed. Pot on as necessary in John Innes potting compost No. 2. Water freely in spring and summer but gradually reduce water in autumn and keep quite dry in winter. Feed weekly in summer with weak liquid fertilizer. Shade from direct sunshine. Ventilate freely in summer. Support flower stems of erect kinds individually. Grow pendulous kinds in baskets suspended from the rafters. For outdoor culture start tubers similarly but later, harden off and plant out in rich soil in partial shade when danger of frost has passed. Lift tubers in autumn, place in boxes to ripen off, then store as advised for pot tubers.

Culture of fibrous-rooted kinds: Compost, John Innes potting compost No. 2 or equivalent. Position, cool or intermediate greenhouse, minimum winter temp. 7°C. Water normally. Shade in summer and maintain a fairly moist atmosphere. Pot in spring. *B. semperflorens* is widely grown as a summer bedding plant for which purpose it is treated as a half-hardy annual. Seeds are sown in spring in John Innes seed compost or equivalent in temp. 15 to 18°C. and seedlings are transplanted into trays of John Innes potting compost No. 1 or

Begonia masoniana

Lorraine begonia

equivalent and hardened off for planting outdoors in late spring or summer in good fertile soil and a sunny or partially shady place. Water freely in dry weather, discard after flowering.

Culture of Begonia rex and others grown solely for foliage: Compost, John Innes potting compost No. 2. Position, cool or intermediate greenhouse in pots or beds. Shade at all times. Water freely in spring and summer, moderately in autumn, sparingly in winter. Feed in summer with weak liquid fertilizer. Pot or plant in spring.

Increase all kinds by seeds sown in late winter or spring in temp. 15 to 18°C.; fibrous-rooted kinds by cuttings in a propagator in summer; winter-flowering kinds by cuttings in a warm propagator in spring; *B. socotrana* by bulbils removed from base of plant in spring; tuberous-rooted kinds by careful division of the tubers after they have been started into growth; fibrous-rooted kinds by division in spring.

The best tuberous-rooted kinds are hybrids derived from various species including *B. boliviensis*, scarlet, summer, 2 ft., Bolivia; *clarkei*, rose, summer, Peru; *davisii*, red, summer, Peru; *pearcei*, yellow, summer, 1 ft., Bolivia; *rosaeflora*, rose, summer, Peru; *veitchii*, red, summer, Peru.

The hybrids are very variable, white, pink, red, crimson, yellow and orange in colour, single, semi-double, and fully double, with small, medium or large flowers, upright or pendulous in habit. Other useful tuberous-rooted kinds are *B. dregei*, white, summer, 1 to 3 ft., S. Africa; *evansiana*, pink, summer, autumn, 1 to 2 ft., nearly hardy, China, Japan, Malaysia; *sutherlandii*, orange, summer, 1 to 2 ft., nearly hardy, Natal.

Recommended fibrous-rooted kinds are *B. coccinea*, scarlet, summer, 4 to 7 ft., Brazil; *corallina*, red, spring, 4 to 7 ft., Brazil; *fuchsioides*, scarlet, most of the year, 2 to 3 ft., Mexico; *haageana*, pink, summer, autumn, 2 ft., Brazil; *lucerna*, pink, all the year, 2 to 4 ft., hybrid; *manicata*, pink, winter, spring, 1 to 1½ ft., Mexico; *metallica*, white and pink, summer, autumn, 3 to 4 ft.,

Bahia; *semperflorens*, white, pink, red, spring to autumn, 9 to 15 in., Brazil.

Recommended kinds to grow mainly for foliage are *B. albo-picta*, leaves white spotted, 4 ft., Brazil; *daedalea*, leaves covered with red hairs becoming brown, 1 ft., Mexico; *feastii*, leaves red beneath edged with white hairs, 9 in., hybrid, and var. *bunchii*, leaf edges frilled; *masoniana*, Iron Cross, leaves green and black, 9 in., S. E. Asia; *rex*, leaves variously marked and blotched with green, shades of purple, and silver, 1 ft., Assam.

Recommended winter-flowering kinds are the Lorraine group, red, pink, white, 1 to 1½ ft., hybrids between *dregei* and *socotrana*; Gloire de Sceaux, pink, 1½ ft., hybrid between *subpeltata* and *socotrana*; Hiemalis group, pink, carmine, yellow, orange, white, single- and double-flowered, to 2 ft., hybrids between *socotrana* and various tuberous-rooted species; *socotrana*, rose, 1 to 1½ ft., Socotra.

BELLIS (Daisy) – *Compositae*. Hardy herbaceous perennials.

Soil, ordinary. Position, sunny or shady. Plant in spring or autumn.

Increase by division in early summer; by seeds sown outdoors in late spring or early summer. The large double-flowered forms of *B. perennis* are usually treated as biennials being raised annually from seed, seedlings planted a few inches apart in a nursery bed as soon as they can be handled and transplanted to flowering beds in the autumn. After flowering plants are discarded.

Recommended kinds are *B. perennis flore-pleno*, white, pink or red, spring, 3 to 6 in., garden forms of the wild daisy of Europe (Britain) and Asia Minor.

BELLIUM (False Daisy) – *Compositae*. Hardy or slightly tender perennials, resembling small neat daisies.

Soil, sandy loam. Position, warm, sunny, rock garden or border. Plant in spring.

Increase by division of plants in spring; by seeds sown as for bellis.

The best kind is *B. bellidioides*, white, summer, 3 in., Mediterranean region.

Beloperone guttata

BELOPERONE – *Acanthaceae*. Tender evergreen shrubs with curling spikes of flowers surrounded by coloured bracts.

Soil, John Innes potting compost No. 1 or equivalent. Position, cool or intermediate greenhouse, minimum winter temp. 7°C. Water normally. Shading unnecessary.

Increase by cuttings inserted in sandy soil in a propagator in summer.

The best kind is *B. guttata*, Shrimp Plant, white spotted purple, bracts shrimp pink or greenish yellow, all year in a sufficiently warm temperature, 1 to 3 ft., Mexico.

BERBERIDOPSIS (Coral Plant) – *Flacourtiaceae*. Rather tender evergreen climbing shrub.

Soil, lime-free loam, fairly moist in summer but porous and not waterlogged in winter. Position, sheltered, warm, and moderately shady or in a shady frost-proof greenhouse. In spring prune straggly shoots only. Requires training.

Increase by seeds sown in well-drained pots of sandy soil, in temp. 12 to 15°C. in spring; by cuttings of young shoots in similar soil and temperature; by layering shoots in the open in autumn.

The only species is *B. corallina*, crimson, summer, 10 to 15 ft., Chile.

BERBERIS (Barberry) – *Berberidaceae*. An extensive family of beautiful and easily-grown shrubs, evergreen and deciduous, the former grown mainly for beauty of flower and the latter for autumn colouring and fruits. Berries of the common barberry, *B. vulgaris*, make excellent preserve. Many species make good hedges. Some species formerly included in this genus have been transferred to *Mahonia*.

Soil, any well drained. Position, anywhere except in dense shade, preferably sunny, and thriving on dry sandy or chalky formations. Plant deciduous species in autumn or late winter; evergreen species require care, spring or early autumn being the best times, but preferably these should be container grown until planted out. Deciduous species are better for an occasional thinning out of older, darker coloured wood in winter; evergreen species require no pruning but if overgrown or used as hedges can be trimmed immediately after flowering.

Increase by seeds sown in a sheltered border in late autumn, but the resultant plants may show considerable variation; by cuttings of firm young shoots in sandy soil in summer or early autumn; by layering shoots in spring.

Over 170 hardy species are known in cultivation, mostly highly ornamental, and there are also many garden varieties.

Recommended deciduous kinds are *B. aggregata*, yellow, summer, red berries, good autumn colour, 4 to 5 ft., W. China; *chitria*, yellow, summer, dark red berries,

Berberis rubrostilla (left) *Berberis darwinii* (right)

10 to 12 ft., Himalaya; *concinna*, yellow, summer, large red berries, 3 ft., Sikkim; *dictyophylla*, yellow, summer, large red berries, white bloom on stems, 6 ft., W. China; *jamesiana*, yellow, summer, coral-red berries, 10 to 12 ft., W. China; *koreana*, yellow, summer, red berries, good autumn colour, 6 ft., Korea; *polyantha*, yellow, summer, red berries, good autumn colour, 5 ft., W. China; *rubrostilla*, yellow, summer, coral-red berries, 4 ft., hybrid; *thunbergii*, yellow, summer, deep red berries, fine autumn colour, Japan, and numerous varieties including *atropurpurea*, reddish purple foliage; *vulgaris*, Common Barberry, yellow, summer, egg-shaped red berries, Europe (Britain), and var. *atropurpurea*, reddish purple leaves; *wilsoniae*, yellow, summer, coral-red berries, 3 to 4 ft., W. China.

Recommended evergreen kinds are *B. buxifolia*, yellow, spring, bluish-purple berries, 6 ft., only semi-evergreen in cold places, Magellan Straits, and var. *nana*, 2 ft.; *candidula*, yellow, late spring, 2 to 3 ft., W. China; *darwinii*, orange, spring, bluish black berries, 8 to 10 ft., Chile; *gagnepainii*, yellow, late spring, bluish black fruits, 6 ft., W. China; *hookeri*, yellow, spring, black berries, 3 to 5 ft., W. China; *julianae*, yellow, spring, bluish black berries, 6 to 9 ft., China; *linearifolia*, orange-red, early spring, bluish black berries, 4 to 6 ft., Argentina; *lologensis*, orange-yellow, spring, bluish black berries, 6 ft., hybrid; *pruinosa*, pale yellow, spring, black berries with white bloom, 6 ft., W. China; *sargentiana*, pale yellow, early spring, bluish black berries, 5 to 6 ft., W. China; *stenophylla*, yellow, sweetly scented, spring, 8 ft., hybrid, and dwarf varieties such as *coccinea*, *corallina*, *gracilis* and *nana*; *verruculosa*, yellow, spring, 5 to 6 ft., W. China.

BERGENIA – *Saxifragaceae*. Hardy perennial plants with large, more or less evergreen foliage, some richly coloured in winter and short, stout panicles of flowers mostly in early spring and subject to frost damage. Formerly known as saxifraga and megasea.

Soil, ordinary, reasonably rich, rather moist. Position, borders or woodlands in sun or light shade.

Increase by division in spring or autumn; by seeds sown out of doors or under glass in spring.

Recommended kinds are *B. ciliata*, white flushed pink, early spring, 9 to 12 in., Himalaya, and var. *ligulata* (syn. *B. ligulata*), leaf edge fringed; *cordifolia*, pink, spring, 15 in., Siberia, and var. *purpurea*, deep reddish purple, taller panicles; *crassifolia*, rose-purple, early spring, 1½ ft., Siberia, Korea; *purpurascens*, (syn. *beesiana*, and *delavayi*), purplish red, early spring, 15 in., Himalaya, China, Burma; *schmidtii*, rose-pink, early spring, 15 in., hybrid between *ciliata* and *crassifolia*, and numerous garden varieties; *smithii*, pink or reddish purple, early spring, 1 to 2 ft., hybrid between *cordifolia* and *purpurascens*, and numerous garden varieties; *stracheyi*, white fading to pink, spring, 9 to 12 in., Afghanistan, Himalaya.

BERKHEYA (South African Thistle) – *Compositae*. Ornamental thistle-like herbaceous perennials.

Soil, ordinary, well drained. Position, hot and sunny.

Increase by seeds sown in spring in temp. 15 to 18°C.

Recommended kinds are *B. grandiflora* (syn. *ilicifolia*), yellow, summer, 2 ft., S. Africa; *macrocephala*, yellow, summer, 4 ft., S. Africa.

BESCHORNERIA – *Agavaceae*. Slightly tender shrubs with rosettes of sword-shaped leaves and flowers in long sinuous spikes.

Soil, ordinary, well drained, do not mind chalk. Position, warm, sunny. Plant in spring.

Increase by seeds sown in temp. 15 to 18°C. in spring; by offsets removed in spring.

The best kind is *B. yuccoides*, green, red bracts, early summer, 4 to 6 ft., Mexico.

BETULA (Birch) – *Betulaceae*. Hardy ornamental deciduous trees and shrubs, many valued for their decorative bark and elegant habit. They succeed in most soils and will grow on chalk though not so freely as on moderately acid soils. Position, open or partially shaded. The common Silver Birch and its varieties do well in towns. Plant in autumn or late winter.

Increase by seeds sown on the surface of sandy soil as soon as ripe, seeds to be simply pressed in, not covered, transplant seedlings when one year old; by layering shoots of dwarf birches in autumn; by grafting garden varieties of Silver Birch on to young stock of the type plant.

Recommended kinds are *B. albo-sinensis*, orange-red bark, 50 to 60 ft., China; *caerulea-grandis*, silver trunk, large foliage, 30 ft., N. America; *davurica*, reddish peeling bark, 40 to 60 ft., N. E. Asia; *ermanii*, pinkish white bark, to 60 ft., N. E. Asia; *humilis*, 8 to 10 ft., Europe, Asia; *koehnei*, white bark, hybrid between *pendula* and *papyrifera*; *lenta*, Sweet or Cherry Birch, 40 to 70 ft., shining purple bark, N. E. America; *lutea*, Yellow Birch, yellow bark, 90 ft., N. E. America; *nigra*, River Birch, 60 ft., a fine species with shaggy cream-coloured trunk, grows well near water, N. E. America; *papyrifera*, Paper Birch, white trunk to 60 ft., bark used for making canoes, N. America; *pendula*, Silver Birch, best forms have white bark, 50 ft., Europe (Britain), vars. *dalecarlica*, Swedish Birch, cut leaves, slender weeping habit, *fastigiata*, slender upright habit, *purpurea*, leaves purple, *tristis*, tall, slender, weeping, *youngii*, the best weeping form for small gardens; *platyphylla* (syn. *mandschurica*), white peeling bark, 60 ft., N. E. Asia; *populifolia*, Grey Birch, ashen bark, 30 ft., N. E. America; *pubescens*, Common White Birch, reddish white bark, 50 ft., Europe (Britain), better for damp places than *B. pendula*; *utilis*, Himalayan Birch, coppery brown peeling bark, 40 to 60 ft., Himalaya.

BILLARDIERA (Apple Berry) – *Pittosporaceae*. Slightly tender evergreen twining shrub.

Soil, good ordinary, well drained. Position, warm, sheltered but sunny, or a cool greenhouse. Plant in spring. Prune away all weak or dead shoots in spring.

Increase by cuttings inserted in sandy soil in a temp. 15 to 18°C. in summer; also by seeds sown in a similar temperature in spring.

The only species grown is *B. longiflora*, creamy white to purple, succeeded by blue edible berries, summer, 6 ft., Tasmania.

BILLBERGIA – *Bromeliaceae*. Tender, flowering epiphytic evergreen plants.

Compost, equal parts lime-free loam, peat and sand. Pot in spring. Good drainage essential. Grow in a cool or intermediate greenhouse, minimum winter temp. 7°C. Shade lightly in summer. Water freely from

Billbergia nutans

spring to autumn, sparingly in winter. *B. nutans* makes a good room plant near a window.

Increase by offshoots in spring or summer.

Recommended kinds are *B. decora*, green and red, winter, 1 ft., Brazil; *nutans*, yellowish green with blue margins, summer, 1½ ft., Brazil; *windii*, greenish yellow and red, summer, 1 ft., hybrid between *decora* and *nutans*; *zebrina*, green and salmon, leaves banded with white, 1½ ft., Brazil.

BLECHNUM – *Blechnaceae*. Tender and hardy evergreen ferns. The genus formerly known as *Lomaria* is included here.

Culture of tender species: Compost, equal parts loam, leafmould, peat and sand. Pot in spring. Position, cool or intermediate greenhouse, minimum winter temp. 7°C. Water normally. Shade from direct sunshine, syringe freely in spring and summer. Some kinds, such as *B. gibbum*, make good house plants.

Culture of hardy species: Soil, two parts sandy peat and one part loam with some crushed chalk or limestone. Position, shady. Plant in spring. Water freely in dry weather. Protect *B. penna marina* in very severe weather.

Increase by spores sown on fine sandy peat in well-drained pans in temp. 15 to 18°C.; dwarf species by division in spring.

Recommended tender kinds are *B. gibbum* (syn. *Lomaria gibba*), to 5 ft., New Caledonia, and vars. *bellii*, fronds forked, *platypterum*, sterile form, *robustum*, extra large fronds, *tinctum*, young fronds pinkish; *moorei* (syn. *Lomaria ciliata*), 1 to 1½ ft., New Caledonia, and vars. *grande* and *majus*, both larger; *occidentale*, 1 to 2 ft., Tropical America, Chile; *tabulare* (syn. *Lomaria boryana*), to 4 ft., W. Indies.

Recommended hardy kinds are *B. penna marina* (syn. *Lomaria alpina*), to 1 ft., South Temperate Zone, Antarctic; *spicant* (syn. *Lomaria spicant*), Hard Fern, Deer Fern, 9 to 18 in., Europe (Britain), Morocco, Azores, Madeira, N. America, Japan.

BLETILLA *Orchidaceae*. A small terrestrial genus of orchid with showy flowers in loose spikes.

Compost, equal parts fibrous loam and peat with an addition of leafmould and sand. *B. striata*, better known as *Bletia hyacinthina*, will withstand a few degrees of frost and can be grown outdoors in many places, or it can be grown in a frost-proof house. It should not be dried out in winter. Position, sunny or semi-shaded.

Increase by division after flowering.

The best kind is *B. striata* (syn. *Bletia hyacinthina*), very variable, rose, purple, or white, summer, China.

BOLTONIA – *Compositae*. Hardy herbaceous perennials with daisy flowers.

Soil, ordinary. Position, sunny or shady borders. Plant in spring or autumn.

Increase by division of roots in spring or autumn.

Recommended kinds are *B. asteroides*, False Chamomile, white, summer, 4 to 5 ft., N. America; *latisquama*, pink to purple, 3 to 5 ft., N. America.

BOMAREA – *Alstroemeriaceae*. Slightly tender climbing perennials with clusters of tubular or funnel-shaped flowers.

Compost, John Innes potting compost No. 1 or equivalent. Pot or plant in spring. Position, well-drained large pots, tubs or beds in a cool greenhouse, minimum winter temp. 7°C., or outdoors in sheltered nearly frost-free places. Water fairly freely in spring and summer, very little in autumn and winter. No shading required.

Increase by seeds sown in light sandy soil in temp. 18°C. in spring. Seedlings should be potted singly at an early stage. Also by division of roots in spring.

Recommended kinds are *B. acutifolia*, red, yellow and green, late summer, autumn, 5 to 6 ft., Mexico, Guatemala, and var. *ehrenbergiana*, orange and yellow; *caldasii*, orange, green and red, winter and spring, to 8 ft., Ecuador, Colombia; *carderi*, rose, autumn, 6 to 8 ft., Colombia; *edulis*, rose or yellow and green, summer, 5 to 6 ft., Tropical America; *multiflora*, red and orange, autumn, 6 to 8 ft., Colombia and Venezuela; *patacocensis* (syn. *conferta*), carmine, rose, summer, 6 to 8 ft., Colombia, Ecuador.

BORAGO (Borage) – *Boraginaceae*. Hardy annual and perennial plants. The common species, *B. officinalis*, is used for flavouring claret cup and as a bee food.

Soil, ordinary. Position, sunny, well drained, suitable for hot, dry places. Sow seeds of common borage annually in spring where required to grow, afterwards thinning seedlings to 8 in. apart.

Increase annuals by seeds sown as above; perennials by division of roots in spring.

Recommended kinds are *B. laxiflora*, per-

ennial, blue, summer, 1 ft., sprawling, Corsica; *officinalis*, Common Borage, annual, blue, summer, 1 to 2 ft., Europe (Britain).

BORONIA – *Rutaceae*. Tender evergreen shrubs with small, often fragrant, flowers. All are natives of Australia.

Compost, John Innes potting compost No. 1 without chalk and plus ¼ its bulk of peat. Position, cool, unshaded greenhouse, minimum winter temp. 7°C. Plants can be stood outdoors if desired in summer. In mild, nearly frost-free places boronias can be grown outdoors in lime-free soil. Pot directly after flowering. Drain the pots well and make the compost quite firm. Water moderately in spring and summer, rather sparingly in autumn and winter as roots may rot in wet soil. Prune fairly severely after flowering to prevent plants becoming straggly.

Increase by cuttings of firm young shoots in summer inserted in sand and peat in a propagator; by seeds sown in peat and sand in a cool greenhouse in spring.

Recommended kinds are *B. elatior*, rosy carmine, spring, 3 to 5 ft.; *heterophylla*, rosy crimson, spring, 4 to 6 ft.; *megastigma*, maroon and yellow, scented, spring, 2 to 4 ft.; *serrulata*, Australian Native Rose, rosy mauve, spring, 3 to 5 ft.

BOUGAINVILLEA – *Nyctaginaceae*. Tender climbing deciduous plants with coloured bracts which are their chief floral attraction.

Compost, John Innes potting compost No. 2 or equivalent. Pot or plant in spring. Position, pots, tubs or borders in a sunny cool greenhouse, minimum winter temp. 7°C. Water freely in spring and summer, rather sparingly in autumn and winter. No shading required at any time. Ventilate freely in summer. Feed once a week in late spring and summer with weak liquid fertilizer. Train stems to wire or trellis. In early spring cut back side shoots and remove weak or overcrowded stems, but do not prune *B. buttiana* too severely.

Increase by cuttings of young shoots in a propagator in summer.

Recommended kinds are *B. buttiana* (syn. Mrs Butt and Crimson Lake), crimson, summer, 5 to 15 ft., hybrid between *glabra* and *peruviana*, and orange vars. Orange King, Mrs McLean, and Louis Wathen; *glabra*, rose, summer, 5 to 8 ft., Brazil and vars. Snow White, white and green, *cypheri*, rosy purple, extra large, *sanderiana*, rich rose, very floriferous, *magnifica*, large, deep rosy purple; *spectabilis*, lilac-rose, summer, 15 ft., Brazil, var. *speciosa*, deep rose.

BOUVARDIA – *Rubiaceae*. Tender evergreen shrubs with clusters of tubular fragrant flowers.

Compost, John Innes potting compost No. 2 or equivalent. Position, pots in an intermediate greenhouse, minimum winter temp. 13°C. Shade lightly in summer or plants can be stood outdoors for a few months while the weather is warm. Water fairly freely in late spring and summer, moderately in autumn, sparingly for a few weeks after the flowers fade when the stems can be cut back considerably. Pinch out tips of young stems occasionally in spring and early summer to ensure a bushy habit.

Increase in spring by cuttings of young shoots inserted in sandy compost in a propagator; or by cuttings of roots inserted in similar soil.

Bouvardia longiflora

Recommended kinds are *B. angustifolia*, red, autumn, 2 ft., Mexico; *humboldtii corymbiflora*, white, autumn, winter, 2 to 3 ft., origin uncertain; *jasminiflora*, white, winter, 2 ft., S. America; *longiflora*, white, autumn, winter, 2 to 3 ft., Mexico, and var. *flammea*, pink; *triphylla*, scarlet, winter, 2 ft., Mexico; and numerous hybrids and garden varieties, some with double flowers.

BRACHYCOME – *Compositae*. Slightly tender annual with daisy-type flowers.

Soil, ordinary. Position, sunny border. Sow in spring in temp. 15 to 18°C. and harden off seedlings for planting out in late spring or early summer; alternatively sow outdoors in late spring where plants are to flower and thin seedlings to 6 in.

The best kind is *B. iberidifolia*, Swan River Daisy, blue, mauve, pink, purple or white, summer, 1 ft., Western Australia.

BRASSAVOLA – *Orchidaceae*. Tender epiphytic orchids, the majority with stem-like pseudobulbs, bearing a single leaf. Flowers with narrow sepals and petals and a heart-shaped lip.

Compost, equal parts fibre and sphagnum moss. Position, pans or baskets suspended in an intermediate house. Water freely while the plants are growing. In winter a long rest is beneficial with little water and the plants may be hung near the glass. Shade in spring and summer.

Increase by division in spring when the plants are large enough.

Recommended kinds are *B. digbyana*,

greenish white, spring, 12 in., Honduras; *fragrans*, white tinged green and pink, early autumn, 12 in., Brazil; *glauca*, light green, spring, 9 in., Mexico, Guatemala; *nodosa*, white, green tinged, autumn, 6 in., Central America; *perrinii*, white, shaded green, spring, early summer, 12 in., Brazil.

BRASSIA – *Orchidaceae*. Tender epiphytic orchids, usually fragrant, with narrow sepals and petals which give the flowers a somewhat spidery appearance.

Compost, two parts fibre and three parts sphagnum moss. A complete rest cannot be given as growths are often present in the winter. Position, pots in a cool or intermediate house. Water freely from early spring to autumn and maintain a very moist atmosphere. Water moderately and keep air drier in winter. Shade in spring and summer but only from direct sunshine.

Increase by division of plants in spring.

Recommended kinds are *B. elegantula*, light green, white, brown flushed, summer, 6 in., Mexico; *lawrenceana*, fragrant, yellow with dark purple spots, summer, 18 in., Brazil, var. *longissima*, larger sepals, Costa Rica; *maculata*, greenish yellow spotted brown, lip white, early summer, 2 ft., Jamaica; *verrucosa*, greenish with purple spots, spring, summer, 2 ft., Mexico, Guatemala.

x BRASSOCATTLAELIA – *Orchidaceae*. Trigeneric hybrids between the genera *Brassavola*, *Laelia* and *Cattleya*.

Cultivation and propagation as for cattleya. The numerous varieties mostly bear garden (cultivar) names.

x BRASSOCATTLEYA – *Orchidaceae*. Tender epiphytic orchids; bigeneric hybrids between the genera *Brassavola* and *Cattleya*, requiring similar treatment to the cattleyas.

Cultivation and propagation as for cattleya.

The many varieties have garden (cultivar) names and are constantly being added to or further improved.

x BRASSOLAELIA – *Orchidaceae*. Bigeneric hybrids between *Brassavola* and *Laelia*.

Cultivation and propagation as for cattleya. The numerous varieties mostly bear garden (cultivar) names.

BRIZA – *Gramineae*. Hardy annual and perennial grasses, the flowers of which are valuable for mixing with cut flowers, or drying for winter decoration.

Soil, ordinary. Position, sunny.

Sow in spring where plants are required to flower. Flowers should be cut and dried for winter decoration when fully developed.

Recommended kinds are *B. maxima*, Pearl Grass, annual, summer, 1 to 1½ ft., Medi-

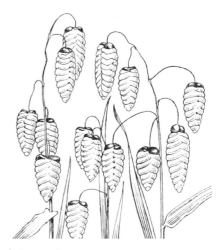

Briza maxima

terranean region; *media*, Quaking Grass, perennial, summer, 9 to 18 in., Europe (Britain), Temperate Asia; *minor*, summer, 6 to 18 in., Europe (Britain), Mediterranean region, annual.

BRODIAEA – *Alliaceae*. Hardy or slightly tender cormous plants with clusters of starry flowers on bare stems. See also Dichelostemma, Ipheion and Triteleia.

Soil, ordinary. Position, warm, sunny, well drained. Plant corms in autumn 4 in. deep.

Increase by seeds sown in sandy soil in a frame in spring; by offsets removed at planting time.

Recommended kinds are *B. californica*, lilac or violet, early summer, 9 to 12 in., California; *coronaria*, lilac or violet, early summer, 3 to 9 in., N. W. America; *elegans* (syn. *grandiflora*), violet, early summer, 6 to 12 in., Oregon, California.

BROMUS (Brome Grass) – *Gramineae*. Hardy ornamental annual grasses. Flower stems of the recommended kind are useful for drying for winter decoration.

Soil, ordinary. Position, open sunny. Sow in spring where plants are to flower and thin seedlings to 6 in. Cut flowers when fully developed.

The best kind is *B. briziformis*, 1 to 2 ft., summer, S. W. and Central Asia.

BROWALLIA – *Solanaceae*. Tender flowering annuals with trumpet-shaped flowers in loose spikes.

Sow in late winter for summer and autumn flowering and in early summer for winter and spring flowering in temp. 15 to 18°C. Pot seedlings singly in John Innes potting compost No. 1 or equivalent and grow in a cool or intermediate greenhouse, minimum temp. 7°C. Water fairly freely. No shading is required. Discard after flowering.

Recommended kinds are *B. demissa* (syn. *elata*), blue or white, summer, 1 to 1½ ft.,

Browallia speciosa

Peru; *speciosa*, purple, blue or white, late summer to spring, 1½ to 2 ft., Peru; *viscosa*, violet-blue, summer, 1 to 2 ft., S. America.

BRUCKENTHALIA – *Ericaceae*. Hardy evergreen, heath-like flowering shrub.

Soil, equal parts of loam, peat and leafmould. Will grow in soil containing a moderate amount of lime. Position, sunny; suitable as ground cover. Plant in spring.

Increase by division in spring; by seeds sown in sand and peat in spring; by cuttings in a propagator in summer.

The only species is *B. spiculifolia*, Spike Heath, pink, summer, 6 in., E. Europe, Asia Minor.

BRUNFELSIA – *Solanaceae*. Tender evergreen shrubs with clusters of large, periwinkle-like, sweetly scented flowers.

Brunfelsia calycina

Soil, John Innes potting compost No. 2 or equivalent. Position, pots or borders in a cool or intermediate greenhouse, minimum winter temp. 7°C. Water freely from spring to autumn but rather sparingly in winter. Maintain a moist atmosphere and shade in summer. Feed in late spring and summer with weak liquid fertilizer. Prune lightly in spring to keep the plants tidy.

Increase by cuttings of firm young shoots inserted in sand in a warm propagator in summer.

Recommended kinds are *B. americana*,

Lady of the Night, pale yellow or white, summer, scented at night, 4 to 8 ft., W. Indies; *calycina*, Brazil Raintree, violet-purple, lavender or white, fragrant, throughout the year in a warm temperature, 2 ft., Brazil, and var. *floribunda*, flowers with less warmth; *latifolia*, white, lavender or purple, autumn and spring, 3 to 6 ft., Tropical America.

BRUNNERA – *Boraginaceae*. Hardy herbaceous perennial with large leaves and flowers like forget-me-not. Formerly included in *Anchusa*.

Soil, ordinary. Position, sunny or shady. Useful as ground cover beneath trees. Plant in spring or autumn.

Increase by division in spring or autumn.

The best kind is *B. macrophylla* (syn. *Anchusa myosotidiflora*), blue, spring and early summer, 1½ ft., Siberia, Caucasus.

BRUNSVIGIA – *Amaryllidaceae*. Tender bulbs with clusters of funnel-shaped flowers on bare stems.

Compost, equal parts peat, loam and sand. Pot in autumn. Water only when new growth begins, then give a moderate quantity, cease to give any after the leaves turn yellow. Temperatures when grown under glass, winter 8 to 12°C., summer 15 to 18°C. Plants must have full exposure to sun.

Increase by offsets inserted in small pots and grown similarly to large bulbs; or by seeds sown as soon as harvested.

Recommended kinds *B. josephinae*, scarlet, summer, 1½ ft., S. Africa; *kirkii*, 1½ ft., Tropical E. Africa; *orientalis* (syn. *gigantea*), crimson, summer, 1½ ft., S. Africa; *radulosa*, pink, summer, winter hardy, S. African mountains.

BUDDLEIA (Butterfly Bush) – *Buddlejaceae*. Hardy and slightly tender evergreen and deciduous shrubs; many are fragrant and are singularly attractive to butterflies. Also spelled buddleja.

Buddleias will grow in any light garden soil, including chalky loam. Full sun is preferred. The more tender kinds need specially warm and sheltered places or a cool greenhouse. Plant in autumn or late winter.

Prune *B. davidii*, *fallowiana*, and other kinds which flower in late summer on the current season's growth, by cutting hard back each spring; *B. alternifolia*, which flowers on the previous year's growth, by cutting out much of the old flowering wood in summer immediately flowers fade; *B. globosa*, *colvilei* and other species which flower in early summer on short side growths or from terminal buds, by removing weak or dead stems in early spring.

Increase by summer cuttings in sandy soil. Seeds may also be sown under glass in spring, but *B. davidii* and varieties will produce many inferior forms.

Buddleia weyeriana

Recommended deciduous kinds are *B. alternifolia*, hardy, lilac-purple, early summer, to 12 ft., China; *auriculata*, tender, cream and yellow, winter, 10 ft., S. Africa; *colvilei*, rather tender, reddish purple, early summer, 10 to 20 ft., Himalaya; *davidii*, hardy, lavender and lilac-pink to purple, white, late summer, 6 to 12 ft., China; *fallowiana*, slightly tender, powder blue, white, late summer, grey foliage; *globosa*, slightly tender, evergreen in warm places, orange, early summer, 12 to 15 ft., Chile, Peru; *weyeriana*, hardy, orange flushed purple, summer, 12 to 15 ft., hybrid.

Recommended evergreen kinds, both rather tender, are *B. asiatica*, white, winter, 12 to 15 ft., East Indies; *madagascariensis*, yellow, winter, to 20 ft., Madagascar.

BULBOCODIUM – *Liliaceae*. Hardy bulbous plant flowering in spring before the leaves. Sometimes classified under *Colchicum*.

Soil, reasonably fertile. Position, sunny or partially shady. Plant bulbs 3 in. deep and 3 in. apart in late summer or early autumn. Lift and replant bulbs every second year.

Increase by offsets obtained when lifting the bulbs.

The only species is *B. vernum*, Spring Meadow Saffron, purple and white, early spring, 6 in., Alps, Spain.

BULBOPHYLLUM – *Orchidaceae*. Tender epiphytic orchids. The genus varies greatly, including deciduous and evergreen, minute and large-growing forms. The flowers are characterized by a lip which is delicately hinged at its base, so that it readily moves up and down.

Grow in osmunda fibre and sphagnum moss in equal quantities, mixed with good drainage material, in small pans, which can be suspended for the smaller-growing kinds, and in baskets for the larger. Most kinds succeed best in a warm house, minimum winter temp. 18°C., but a few will grow in an intermediate house. Water freely from spring to autumn, very sparingly in winter. Shade lightly in summer. Maintain a very moist atmosphere while in growth. Repot as growth restarts.

Increase by division of the pseudobulbs at potting time.

Recommended kinds are *B. barbigerum*, purple, dusky mahogany, with dark-haired lip, many flowers, summer, W. Central Africa; *dearei*, like *lobbii*, but the white lip marked with purple, summer, Borneo, Philippines; *ericssonii*, yellow-green and brown, summer, New Guinea; *grandiflorum*, large, olive green with whitish spots, summer, autumn, New Guinea; *lobbii*, large, buff yellow spotted with purple, summer, Burma to Java, var. *colossus*, flowers 4 in. across; *odoratissimum*, creamy white, scented, Burma.

BUPHTHALMUM (Yellow Oxeye) – *Compositae*. Hardy, herbaceous perennials with daisy flowers.

Soil, ordinary. Position, sunny or partially shaded. Suitable for borders and woodlands. Plant in spring or autumn.

Buphthalmum

Increase by division in spring and autumn; by seeds sown outdoors in spring.

The best kinds are *B. salicifolium*, yellow, summer, 2 ft., S. Europe; *speciosissimum* (syn. *Telekia speciosissima*), yellow, summer, 2 ft., Europe; *speciosum* (syns. *B. cordifolium* and *Telekia speciosa*), yellow, summer, 5 ft., Europe, Asia.

BUPLEURUM – *Umbelliferae*. The best kind, *B. fruticosum*, is a slightly tender evergreen shrub, loose spreading to 5 ft., and useful for wind-swept seaside localities, especially in chalky districts. It is a native of S. Europe. Plant in spring or autumn in ordinary or chalky soil and an open position.

Increase by cuttings in summer or early autumn. No regular pruning required but overgrown bushes can be cut hard back in spring.

BUTOMUS (Flowering Rush) – *Butomaceae*. Hardy perennial for shallow water, with rush-like leaves and umbels of flowers on long bare stems.

Soil, ordinary. Position, in shallow water on the margins of ponds, lakes, etc. Plant in spring.

Increase by division of roots in spring.

The only species is *B. umbellatus*, Flowering Rush, rose, summer, 2 to 3 ft., Europe (Britain).

BUXUS (Box) – *Buxaceae*. Hardy evergreen shrubs with small stiff leaves.

Soil, ordinary or chalky. Position, open or shady. Plant in spring or autumn. Dwarf box, *B. sempervirens suffruticosa*, can be used for edgings. Plant divisions with roots attached in a shallow trench 6 in. deep, allowing plants to nearly touch each other and with their tips about 2 in. above the soil. Firm soil well. Trim plants in spring and late summer. A nursery yard of box will make 3 yd. of edging.

For box hedges, dig the soil deeply, add decayed manure and plant ordinary green box 12 in. high about 12 in. apart. Trim in spring and summer.

Increase by cuttings or young shoots 3 in. long in a shady border in late summer or autumn; by division of old plants in spring or autumn; by layering in autumn.

Recommended kinds are *B. balearica*, 10 to 20 ft., Balearic Islands; *microphylla*, 3 ft., often prostrate, Japan, there are also various forms differing in habit and leaf character; *sempervirens*, to 20 ft., Europe, N. Africa, W. Asia, and numerous varieties including *argentea*, variegated grey and cream, *aureovariegata*, leaves variegated with yellow, *elegantissima*, leaves white edged, Gold Tip, yellow at shoot tips, *myrtifolia*, leaves very small, *rosmarinifolia*, dwarf, leaves various, *suffruticosa*, dwarf.

CAESALPINIA – *Leguminosae*. More or less tender shrubs the most useful of which for the garden are deciduous and capable of surviving a few degrees of frost. Most have elegant acacia-like leaves and are very spiny.

Soil, ordinary, well drained. Position, warm, sheltered, sunny or in a greenhouse with winter temp. 8 to 12°C. *C. japonica* suitable for training on a wall. Plant in autumn or late winter. Prune in spring cutting back some of previous year's growth

to prevent overcrowding of the branches.

Increase by seeds well soaked and sown in light sandy soil in temp. 15 to 18°C. in spring, seeds germinate more readily if hot water (87 to 88°C.) is poured over them and left to cool before sowing; by cuttings of short young shoots in a propagator in summer.

Recommended kinds are *C. gilliesii*, Paradise Poinciana, yellow with red stamens, summer, to 20 ft., Argentina; *japonica*, yellow with red anthers, 8 to 15 ft., Japan, the most reliable of the hardier species; *pulcherrima*, Barbados Flower Fence, red and yellow, summer, to 15 ft., Tropics, much used as a hedge in frost-free countries, but very tender.

CALADIUM – *Araceae*. Tender, tuberous-rooted deciduous perennials with arrow-shaped leaves, marked in many colours and patterns.

Compost, John Innes potting compost No. 1 plus one-quarter its bulk of peat. Position, pots in a warm greenhouse, spring to autumn temp. 18 to 24°C., but reduce the temperature to 13°C. in winter when plants are resting. Pot in early spring. Water sparingly at first, freely later but reduce water supply in autumn and keep only just moist in winter. Shade from strong sunshine but not too heavily as light helps to develop the leaf colours. Maintain a moist atmosphere while plants are growing.

Increase by division of tubers in early spring.

Recommended kinds are *C. bicolor*, leaves blue-green beneath, mottled and veined with red above and very variable, 1 ft., S. America, and many varieties; *humboldtii*, leaves light green and white, 9 in., Brazil; *marmoratum*, leaves grey-green beneath, dark green spotted grey or light green above, 12 to 15 in., Ecuador; *picturatum*, leaves green veined and spotted with white, pink and red, 1 ft., Peru, and many varieties. Varieties are more generally grown than the species and will be found in trade lists.

CALAMINTHA (Calamint) – *Labiatae*. Hardy herbaceous perennials and rock plants often included in the genus *Satureja*. Leaves aromatic.

Soil, ordinary, well drained. Position, full sun or light shade. Plant in spring or autumn.

Increase by seeds sown outdoors or under glass in spring; by cuttings of firm young growth in a propagator in summer; by division in spring.

Recommended kinds are *C. alpina*, purple, summer, 6 in., Mediterranean region; *grandiflora*, rosy red, summer 9 in., Europe; *nepeta*, lilac, summer, 1 to 2 ft., Europe (Britain).

CALANDRINIA (Rock Purslane) – *Portulacaceae*. Slightly tender, rather fleshy annuals and perennials with showy flowers.

Soil, light, moderately rich, well drained. Position, warm, sunny even rather dry. Plant perennials in spring; annuals when there is no longer any danger of frost.

Increase annuals and perennials by seeds sown in light soil in temp. 15 to 18°C. in spring, and perennials also by division of roots in spring.

Recommended kinds are *C. ciliata*, to 1 ft., purple or white, summer, annual, Peru, Ecuador, var. *menziesii* (syn. *C. speciosa*), crimson; *grandiflora*, light purple, summer, 1 ft., perennial, Chile; *umbellata*, magenta, all summer, 6 in., trailing, perennial, Peru. All can be grown as annuals.

CALANTHE – *Orchidaceae*. Tender terrestrial deciduous and evergreen orchids. The deciduous section is the more important as many garden varieties and hybrids have been produced. Their tall spikes and numerous brightly-coloured flowers are of great decorative value.

Compost, two parts peat and one part sand or polystyrene granules with a little old cow manure. Position, pots in a sunny intermediate house without shading. Pot annually in early spring. Water moderately at first, then freely but reduce water supply in autumn and keep dry in winter, except evergreen kinds which should be just moist. Feed in summer with weak liquid manure.

Calanthe vestita

A single bulb potted in spring will develop a new flowering bulb, the old bulb remaining behind it. It usually remains sound and may be separated and potted singly, or several placed in a shallow box, in the foregoing compost the following spring. Some will flower but, in any case, they will produce a basal growth.

Recommended kinds are *C. masuca*, violet and purple, summer, 2 ft., evergreen, India; *veratrifolia*, white and yellow, spring, 3 ft., evergreen, India to Australia; *vestita*, white and rose or red, winter, 2 ft., deciduous, India, and numerous varieties including one with pure white flowers.

CALATHEA – *Marantaceae*. Tender plants with tufted basal leaves splashed or striped in colours. Closely allied to *Maranta* with which they are sometimes confused.

Compost, equal parts loam, peat, leaf-mould, and sand. Position, well-drained pots in an intermediate or warm greenhouse or well heated room. Excellent for bottle gardens and Wardian cases. Water fairly freely in summer, moderately at other times. Shade from direct sunshine. Maintain a moist atmosphere at all times. Pot in spring, but little repotting is usually required.

Increase by division in spring.

Recommended kinds are *C. bachemiana*, leaves silvery grey and green, 9 in., Brazil; *insignis*, leaves various shades of green above, purple beneath, 4 to 6 ft., Brazil; *lietzei*, leaves dark green and silvery green above, purple beneath, 1 to 2 ft., Brazil; *lindeniana*, leaves various shades of green above, deep purple beneath, 1 ft., Peru; *louisae*, leaves various shades of green above, green and purple beneath, 7 in., origin uncertain; *makoyana* (syn. *Maranta makoyana*), Peacock Plant, leaves various shades of green and purple, 3 to 4 ft., Brazil; *ornata*, leaves green and pink or cream above, deep purple beneath, 1 ft., Brazil; *roseo-picta*, leaves green and red or pink above, purple beneath, 8 in., Brazil; *undulata*, leaves green and white above, purple beneath, 8 in., Peru; *veitchiana*, leaves various shades of green above, green and deep purple beneath, 2 ft., S. America; *vittata*, green and white leaves, to 3 ft., Brazil, Colombia; *zebrina*, Zebra Plant, leaves in shades of green above and of purple below, 1½ ft., Brazil.

CALCEOLARIA (Slipper Flower, Slipperwort) – *Scrophulariaceae*. Slightly tender and hardy shrubby and herbaceous plants with pouched flowers.

Culture of tender herbaceous kinds: Sow seed in John Innes seed compost or equivalent in temp. 13 to 15°C. in late spring or early summer. Prick out seedlings in similar compost and later pot singly in John Innes potting compost No. 1 or equivalent. Shade from direct sunshine, water fairly freely and ventilate freely. No artificial heat is necessary in summer and plants can stand in a frame but should be returned to a cool greenhouse, minimum temp. 7°C., before there is danger of frost. Pot on into 4- or 5-in. pots and John Innes potting compost No. 2 in early autumn. Give as much light as possible in winter and spring. Water rather sparingly in winter, keeping crowns dry, but water more freely in spring. Discard after flowering.

Culture of shrubby kinds: Grow in pots in John Innes potting compost No. 2 or in beds of good loamy soil in a cool greenhouse, minimum winter temp. 7°C., or

Calceolaria herbeohybrida

plant outdoors in fairly frost-free places. Water normally. No shade required. Shade from direct sunshine in summer. *C. integrifolia* and its varieties are often used for summer bedding, planted outdoors in summer but overwintered in a greenhouse or annually renewed from seed or cuttings.

Culture of hardy kinds: Soil, porous, rather moist, well enriched with leafmould. Position, partially shaded. Plant in spring. Water freely during hot, dry weather.

Increase shrubby kinds by cuttings inserted in sandy soil in a cool shady frame or greenhouse in late summer or early autumn; by seeds sown in temp. 15 to 18°C. in spring. Hardy kinds by division of roots in spring or by seeds sown in a cold greenhouse or frame in spring.

The best tender herbaceous kinds are *C. herbeohybrida*, yellow, orange, apricot, pink, red, usually heavily spotted with one colour on another, spring and early summer, 9 to 18 in., hybrids between *corymbosa*, *crenatiflora*, and possibly other species.

Recommended shrubby kinds are *C. burbidgei*, yellow, autumn, winter, 2 to 4 ft., hybrid between *deflexa* and *pavonii*; *deflexa* (syn. *fuchsiaefolia*), yellow, winter, spring, 2 ft., Peru; *integrifolia* (syn. *rugosa*), yellow to red-brown, summer, 1 to 3 ft., Chile, parent of the bedding calceolaria; *profusa* (syn. *clibranii*), yellow, winter, spring, 2 to 3 ft., hybrid of similar parentage to *burbidgei*.

Recommended hardy kinds are *C. biflora* (syn. *plantaginea*), yellow, summer, 4 to 12 in., Chile, Argentina; *darwinii*, bronze, yellow and white, summer, 4 in., Magellan Straits; *polyrrhiza* (syn. *acutifolia*), yellow, summer, 6 in., Chile.

CALENDULA – *Compositae*. Hardy annuals with showy daisy-type flowers.

Soil, ordinary. Position, sunny or partially shady.

Sow in spring or early autumn where plants are to flower and thin seedlings to 9 in. Once established they will usually reproduce themselves freely by self-sown seedlings but successive generations are likely to decline in quality.

The best kind is *C. officinalis*, Pot Marigold, Scotch Marigold, orange-yellow, summer, 12 in., S. Europe. There are many varieties with double flowers varying in form and in colour from yellow to deep orange.

CALLA – *Araceae*. Hardy aquatic perennial with arum-like flowers.

Soil, rich loam. Position, bog or shallow water at edge of pool. Plant in spring.

Increase by inserting portions of creeping rootstock in wet soil in spring.

The only species is *C. palustris*, Bog Arum, Marsh Calla, white, summer, scarlet berries, 6 to 12 in., Northern Hemisphere.

CALLICARPA – *Verbenaceae*. Hardy or slightly tender deciduous shrubs with ornamental berries most freely produced when several bushes are grown close together for cross fertilization of the flowers. Foliage often colours well in the autumn.

Soil, ordinary loam. Position, sheltered and sunny or in a sunny cool greenhouse. Plant in autumn. Cut out frost-damaged, weak or old worn-out stems in spring.

Increase by cuttings in summer or autumn or by seeds sown in temp. 15 to 18°C. as soon as ripe or in spring.

Recommended kinds are *C. bodinieri*, to 10 ft., flowers and fruits lilac, China, and var. *giraldii* (syn. *giraldiana*), similar; *dichotoma* (syn. *purpurea*), to 4 ft., flowers pink, summer, berries deep lilac, China, Japan; *japonica*, pale pink, summer, berries violet, 3 to 5 ft., Japan.

CALLIRHOE (Poppy Mallow) – *Malvaceae*. Hardy annuals and perennials with mallow-like flowers.

Soil, ordinary, well drained. Position, warm, sunny. Plant perennials in spring.

Increase annual species by seeds sown in light soil in 15 to 18°C. in spring, transplanting seedlings outdoors when danger of frost is over, or in warm places seeds may be sown outdoors in spring where plants are to flower; perennials by seeds sown in a similar way, or cuttings of young shoots inserted in sandy soil in a cold frame in spring.

Recommended annual species are *C. digitata*, rosy purple or violet, summer, 1½ ft., Southern U.S.A., Mexico; *pedata*, red-purple to lilac, summer, 2 ft., Texas.

The best perennial kind is *C. involucrata*, crimson, summer, 6 in., Southern U.S.A., Mexico.

CALLISTEMON (Bottle Brush Tree) – *Myrtaceae*. Rather tender evergreen flowering shrubs. Flowers produced in feathery spikes, hence the popular name Bottle Brush. All are Australian.

Grow in ordinary, well-drained, not chalky soils and in warm, sunny sheltered places, or in a cool greenhouse in equal parts of loam, peat and silver sand and minimum winter temp. 8°C. Plant in spring or autumn. Pruning is undesirable.

Callistemon citrinus

Increase by cuttings of firm shoots inserted in sandy peat in temp. 15 to 18°C. during summer, or by seeds, which is a slow method of obtaining large flowering plants.

Recommended kinds are *C. citrinus* (syn. *lanceolatus*), crimson, early summer, 15 ft. or more, and var. *splendens*, scarlet, 6 ft.; *linearis*, scarlet, summer, 3 to 5 ft.; *rigidus*, deep red, summer, 10 to 12 ft.; *salignus*, yellow, early summer, 6 ft.; *speciosus*, crimson, summer, 10 ft., sometimes much more.

CALLISTEPHUS (China Aster) – *Compositae*. Slightly tender annuals with daisy-type flowers.

Soil, ordinary, fertile. Position, open, sunny or partially shady.

Increase by seeds sown in temp. 13 to 15°C. in spring, transplant seedlings 2 in. apart in shallow boxes and harden off for planting out in late spring; or sow outdoors in late spring where plants are to flower and thin seedlings to 9 in.

The best kind is *C. chinensis*, pink, salmon, red, crimson, purple, blue, lavender, primrose, white, etc., summer, 6 in. to 2 ft., China. Numerous types are available differing in size, height and type of flower including singles, semi-doubles and full doubles, some with narrow quilled or long waved petals.

CALLITRICHE (Water Starwort) – *Callitrichaceae*. Good oxygenating aquatic perennials.

Soil, loam or aquarium compost. Position, ponds or tanks of any depth. Plant any time in spring or summer.

Increase by cuttings or divisions weighted with stones and dropped into a pool or aquarium.

Recommended kinds are *C. autumnalis*, entirely submerged, active during winter months, Europe (Britain), N. America; *verna*, upper leaves floating, pale green, Cosmopolitan.

CALLUNA (Heather, Ling) – *Ericaceae*. Hardy evergreen flowering shrubs.

Soil, dry to moderately moist, lime free, preferably with peat. Position, sunny and open or in light shade. Plant in spring or autumn. Prune in spring shortening previous year's growth but not cutting back into older wood.

Increase by division in spring or autumn; by cuttings in summer in sand and peat in a frame.

The only species is *C. vulgaris*, purple, late summer, to 2 ft., Europe (Britain), but it has many horticultural varieties varying in colour from white to crimson, some with double flowers and some with golden or bronze foliage.

CALOCEPHALUS – *Compositae*. Tender sub-shrub with white cottony stems. Used mainly for bedding.

Soil, ordinary. Position, sunny beds in summer only. Plant in late spring or early summer when danger of frost is past and lift in early autumn to overwinter in a light frost-proof greenhouse. Water very sparingly in winter.

Increase by cuttings inserted in a frame in summer.

The best kind is *C. brownii* (syn. *Leucophyta brownii*), 1 ft., Australia.

CALOCHORTUS (Butterfly Tulip, Star Tulip, Mariposa Lily) – *Liliaceae*. Hardy bulbs with tulip-like flowers from W. American mountains which require protection from winter wet rather than frost.

Frame culture: Prepare bed 12 in. deep with compost of equal parts loam, peat, leafmould, and sand. Plant bulbs 3 in. deep and 4 in. apart in early autumn, with sand immediately around the bulbs. Keep lights on in frosty weather, but off night and day in fair weather. Water only in dry weather and do not overwater in summer. Lift and replant every three years.

Pot culture: Use same compost as advised for frame culture. Place a dozen bulbs 2 in. deep in a 5-in. pot in early autumn. Cover pots with ashes in a cold frame, and give no water. Remove pots from ashes in late winter and place in a cool greenhouse near the glass. Water moderately till flowering is over, then gradually withhold it. Repot annually in early autumn.

Outdoor culture: Plant bulbs in similar soil and manner to that advised for frames. Beds must be dry in winter, as at the foot of a sunny wall.

Increase by seeds sown in pans of sandy soil in temp. 7 to 13°C. in spring, transplanting seedlings the following year into small pots and treating similarly to old bulbs; by offsets planted like bulbs in autumn.

Recommended kinds are *C. albus*, white, blotched chestnut, summer, 1 ft.; *amabilis*, yellow, fragrant, late spring, 1 ft.; *caeruleus*, lilac-blue, summer, 6 in.; *clavatus*, yellow, striped brown, summer, 2½ ft.; *gunnisonii*, white, summer, 2 ft.; *howellii*, white, summer, 18 in.; *kennedyi*, orange-red, summer, 2½ ft.; *luteus*, yellow, summer, 1 ft.; *macrocarpus*, pale lavender and green, summer, 1½ ft.; *monophyllus* (syn. *benthamii*), yellow, summer, 8 in.; *nuttallii*, white, summer, 6 in.; *plummerae*, soft lavender, summer, 2 ft.; *splendens*, lilac, summer, 1 ft.; *tolmiei*, white, lilac, 1 ft.; *uniflorus*, lilac, summer, 9 in.; *venustus*, summer, 18 in. A number of garden varieties will be found in specialists' lists.

CALTHA (Kingcup, Water Cowslip) – *Ranunculaceae*. Hardy perennials with large buttercup-like flowers in spring.

Soil, good, moist, loamy. Position, damp borders, or banks of ponds, streams or lakes. Plant in spring.

Increase by division of roots in spring after flowering.

Recommended kinds are *C. palustris*, Marsh Marigold, Water Cowslip, Kingcup, yellow, spring, 1 to 2 ft., Europe (Britain), Caucasus, N. America, and var. *plena*, double; *polypetala*, yellow, 2 to 3 ft., Asia Minor, Caucasus.

CALYCANTHUS – *Calycanthaceae*. Hardy deciduous flowering shrubs.

Soil, ordinary, with some peat added. Position, full sun. Plant in autumn or late winter. If overcrowded, cut out the older branches in spring.

Increase by seeds sown in light soil in spring; by layers in spring or summer or by cuttings in summer in a propagating frame.

Recommended kinds are *C. fertilis*, brownish purple, summer, 6 to 9 ft., South-eastern U.S.A.; *floridus*, Carolina Allspice, brownish purple, fragrant, summer, 6 to 9 ft., South-eastern U.S.A.; *occidentalis* (syn. *macrophyllus*), brownish purple, fragrant, summer, 8 to 10 ft., California.

CAMASSIA (Quamash) – *Liliaceae*. Hardy bulbs with flowers in spikes.

Soil, any ordinary loam. Position, beds or borders. Plant bulbs 4 in. deep and 4 in. apart in autumn. Topdress annually with leafmould or decayed manure. Lift and replant only when bulbs are overcrowded.

Increase by seeds sown in a sunny position outdoors in spring or in boxes of light soil in temp. 13°C. in late autumn; by offset bulbs in autumn or late winter.

Recommended kinds are *C. cusickii*, pale blue, summer, 3 ft., Oregon; *leichtlinii*, white, summer, 3 ft., Western N. America, var. *suksdorfii*, blue-violet; *quamash* (syn. *esculenta* Lindley), blue-violet to white, summer, 3 ft., Western N. America; *scilloides* (syns. *fraseri*, *hyacinthina*), blue-violet to white, summer, 2 ft., Eastern N. America, and mid U.S.A.

CAMELLIA – *Theaceae*. Hardy and slightly tender evergreen flowering shrubs for lime-free soil with some shelter from wind. Excellent for shady places but most kinds will succeed in full sun. Camellias can also be trained against walls or can be grown in pots or tubs of lime-free loam, peat and sand in unheated or cool greenhouses. Regular pruning is undesirable but growth of trained or pot-grown plants can be thinned after flowering and overgrown bushes can also be cut back in spring with loss of bloom the following year.

Increase by seeds sown in early spring, but seedlings of garden varieties usually vary considerably; or by summer cuttings in sandy peat in a propagating frame.

Single-flowered camellia

Recommended kinds are *C. cuspidata*, white, early spring, 6 ft., S. China; *japonica*, Common Camellia, large bush but eventually makes a small tree to 30 ft., late winter and spring, China, Japan, numerous named varieties in white, pink to scarlet and crimson, single, semi-double and double; *maliflora*, small-flowered, semi-double pink, late winter and spring, to 8 ft., China; *reticulata*, very large single or semi-double flowers, various shades of pink and red, late winter and spring, to 20 ft., China; *saluenensis*, pink, spring, 10 to 15 ft., China; *sasanqua*, white, pink to crimson, single, semi-double and double, autumn and winter, China; *williamsii*, free-flowering hybrid between *japonica* and *saluenensis*, white, pink to rose, single, semi-double and double, autumn to spring, 10 ft., or more.

Double-flowered camellia

CAMPANULA (Bellflower) – *Campanulaceae*. Hardy annuals, biennials and perennials with bell-shaped or saucer-shaped flowers.

Soil, ordinary, loamy for border kinds and easy rock garden kinds, gritty and well-drained scree for more difficult alpine kinds. Position, trailing species on sunny rock gardens and banks, mortarless terrace walls, etc., tall species in beds and borders, sunny or shady. Plant in spring or autumn.

Pot culture: Compost, equal parts of leafmould, loam, and sand. Grow trailing kinds in small pots or hanging baskets. Repot them in spring. Water moderately in winter, freely at other times. Tall kinds grow singly in 7-in. pots or three in a 10-in. pot. Sow seeds of these in a cold frame in summer, transplanting seedlings singly into 3-in. pots in autumn, into 5-in. pots in spring, and into 7-in. pots in late spring. Water moderately in winter, freely in summer.

Culture of annual species: Sow seeds in gentle heat in early spring, transplant seedlings into boxes, harden off in a cold frame in late spring and plant out in sunny borders early in summer.

Culture of biennial kinds: Sow seeds outdoors or in a frame in late spring or early summer. Transplant seedlings when 1 in. high, 6 in. apart in a nursery bed, and plant out in borders in autumn to flower the

Campanula isophylla

following year. *C. pyramidalis* is slightly tender and is often grown as a pot plant in a frost-proof greenhouse but pots can stand outdoors in summer.

Increase annuals by seed. Perennials by seeds sown in sandy soil in a frame or outdoors in spring; by division of roots in spring or autumn.

Recommended annual kinds are *C. macrostyla* (syn. *Sicyocodon macrostylus*), purple or mauve, summer, 1½ to 2 ft., Asia Minor; *ramosissima* (syns. *drabifolia* and *loreyi*), purple-blue, summer, 1 to 1½ ft., Italy.

Biennial species are *C. longestyla*, blue-purple, summer, 1½ to 2½ ft., Caucasus; *medium*, Canterbury Bell, blue, summer, 3 ft., S. Europe, and several white, rose and purple single and double varieties; *pyramidalis*, Chimney Bellflower, pale blue with darker centre, summer, 4 to 6 ft., S. Europe, and var. *alba*, white; *rapunculus*, Rampion, blue or white, summer, 2 to 3 ft., Europe (Britain); *speciosa*, violet, summer, 1 to 1½ ft., S. Europe.

Recommended perennial kinds are *C. alliariifolia*, cream, summer, 2 to 3 ft., Caucasus, Asia Minor; *allionii* (syn. *alpestris*), blue, early summer, 3 in., scree, Europe; *alpina*, blue, early summer, 4 in., Europe; *arvatica*, deep blue, summer, 2 in., scree, Spain, and var. *alba*; *aucheri*, violet-purple, early summer, 4 in., Caucasus; *barbata*, blue, early summer, 9 to 18 in., Europe; *burghaltii*, violet, summer, 2 ft., origin uncertain; *caespitosa*, blue, summer, 3 in., Europe, and var. *alba*; *carpatica*, blue, summer, 12 in., E. Europe, and innumerable garden varieties and hybrids such as *alba*, white, and *turbinata*, compact, 4 to 6 in.; *cenisia*, blue, prostrate, early summer, Italian Alps; *cochlearifolia* (syn. *pusilla*), blue, summer, 4 in., Alps, and numerous varieties with white or paler blue flowers; *collina*, blue, summer, 1 ft., Caucasus; *elatines*, purple, summer, 4 in., Piedmont, and var. *fenestrellata*, violet-blue; *formanekiana*, blue or white, 9 to 18 in., late spring, monocarpic, Greece; *garganica* (syn. *elatines garganica*), blue and white, late spring to early autumn, prostrate, Italy, and var. *hirsuta*, grey downy leaves; *glomerata*, blue, summer, 12 to 18 in., Europe (Britain) and several varieties including *acaulis*, 4 in., *alba*, white and *dahurica* (syn. *speciosa*), violet-purple; *isophylla*, lilac-blue, summer, trailing, slightly tender, Italy, and vars. *alba*, white, *mayi*, mauve, leaves variegated, downy; *lactiflora*, blue or white, 4 to 6 ft., summer, Caucasus, and vars. Loddon Anna, lilac-pink and Pouffe, 6 to 9 in.; *latifolia*, blue, summer, 4 to 5 ft., Britain, and var. *alba*, white, *persicifolia*, blue, summer, 3 ft., Europe, and many garden varieties with white, pale blue, deep blue and double flowers; *portenschlagiana* (syn. *muralis*), deep blue, summer, 6 in., S. Europe, and vars. *alba*, white, *major*, large flowers; *poscharskyana*, grey-blue, summer

and autumn, sprawling, Dalmatia, and var. *alba*, white; *pulla*, deep blue, summer, 4 in., E. Europe; *pulloides*, deep blue, summer, 6 in., hybrid between *carpatica turbinata* and *pulla*; *punctata* (syn. *nobilis*), cream spotted red, summer, 1½ ft., Siberia, Japan; *raddeana*, violet, summer, 9 in., Caucasus; *raineri*, blue, summer, 3 in., Alps, and var. *alba*; *rapunculoides*, deep blue, summer, 2 to 4 ft., Europe (Britain); *rhomboidalis*, blue or white, summer, 1 to 2 ft., Europe; *rotundifolia*, Harebell, blue, summer, 6 to 9 in., Northern Hemisphere (Britain), and many varieties; *sarmatica*, pale blue, summer, 1 ft., Caucasus; *saxatilis*, blue, 6 in., late spring, Crete; *stansfieldii*, purple, summer, creeping, hybrid between *tommasiniana* and *waldsteiniana*; *tommasiniana*, blue, summer, 6 in., Italy; *trachelium*, blue, summer, 3 ft., Europe (Britain), N. Africa, Siberia, and vars. *alba*, white, *alba plena*, double white, and *coerulea plena*, double blue; *waldsteiniana*, violet-blue, summer, 6 in., Croatia; *zoysii*, pale blue, summer, 2 to 3 in., scree, Italian Alps.

CAMPSIS (Trumpet Creeper, Trumpet Vine) – *Bignoniaceae*. Slightly tender vigorous deciduous climbing plants with orange or scarlet trumpet-shaped flowers. Plants climb by aerial roots like an ivy but may require some additional tying to suitable supports. All flower in late summer and autumn.

Soil, good rich loam with compost or well-decayed manure added. Position, warm and sunny against a wall, over old tree stumps or in a cool greenhouse. Plant in spring or autumn. Shorten previous year's growth fairly severely each spring to framework of main stems well spaced out.

Increase by cuttings of firm young shoots in temp. 15 to 18°C. in summer; by cuttings of riper growth in autumn or by layering outdoors in spring or summer. Root cuttings may also be taken in winter or seeds sown in 15 to 18°C. in spring.

Recommended kinds are *C. grandiflora*, scarlet, China; *radicans*, orange-red, N. America, and var. *flava*, yellow; *tagliabuana*, a variable hybrid between *grandiflora* and *radicans*, best planted in the form Madame Galen, deep salmon red.

CANNA – *Cannaceae*. Tender herbaceous plants with fleshy roots and very showy flowers in spikes.

Greenhouse culture: Soil, John Innes potting compost No. 2 or equivalent. Pot in late winter or early spring. Start into growth in temp. 15 to 18°C. and grow on in a sunny, frost-proof place. Water freely while in growth and feed frequently in summer with weak liquid manure or fertilizer. Gradually reduce water supply in autumn and keep dry in winter with protection from frost.

Outdoor culture: Start dormant roots into growth in spring as advised for green-

house culture. Harden off and plant outdoors in late spring or early summer in rich well-manured soil and a warm, sunny position. Water freely in dry weather. Feed with weak liquid manure or fertilizer. Lift roots in autumn, place them in boxes filled with ordinary soil, keep dry and in a frost-proof place till potting time.

Increase by seeds steeped for 24 hours in tepid water, then sown in temp. 25 to 30°C. in late winter or spring; by division of roots at potting time. It will facilitate germination if a slight notch is filed in the seed before soaking.

Recommended kinds are *C. indica*, Indian Shot, yellow and red, summer, 4 ft., W. Indies; *iridiflora*, deep cherry red, summer, 8 to 10 ft., Peru; *lutea*, yellow, purple spotted, summer, 2 to 3 ft., Tropical and Sub-tropical America. There are many garden varieties mostly of complex hybrid origin with *indica* and *lutea* among their parents. The names *generalis* and *orchioides* are sometimes used for groups of these hybrids which have very large flowers in a variety of shades of yellow, orange, red and crimson, often handsomely spotted or splashed with one colour or another.

CANTUA – *Polemoniaceae*. More or less tender evergreen flowering shrubs native to S. America.

Compost, two parts turfy loam, one part leafmould and sand. Position, in a cool greenhouse with minimum winter temperature 5°C., or outdoors in a warm, sunny position. *C. buxifolia* is the hardiest species and may survive a few degrees of frost. Plant or pot in spring.

Increase by cuttings of firm young growth in summer in a propagating frame, temp. 15 to 18°C.

Recommended kinds are *C. bicolor*, yellow and red, late spring, 4 ft., Bolivia; *buxifolia*, cherry red and yellow, late spring, 5 ft., Peru, Bolivia, Chile.

CAPSICUM (Red Peppers) – *Solanaceae*. Tender shrubby plants usually grown as annuals. Variable many seeded fleshy fruits differing in size, shape, colour and pungency under cultivation.

Soil, light rich. Position, pots in a sunny greenhouse or in a warm sunny position outdoors in summer.

Increase by seeds sown in temp. 15 to 18°C. in late winter or early spring. Transplant seedlings singly into 3-in. pots when large enough to handle and later into 5-, 6-, 7- or 9-in. pots according to the variety. Water freely. Gather fruit when full colour is attained.

Recommended kinds are *C. annuum*, red fruits, Tropics, and vars. *acuminatum*, slender fruits, *cerasiforme*, Cherry Pepper, *conoides*, Cone Pepper, *fasciculatum*, Red Cluster Pepper, *grossum*, Bell or Sweet Pepper, *longum*, Long Pepper, many types

including Chilli, Cayenne, Paprika, etc;
frutescens, very hot fruits mostly grown for
decoration, Tropics.

CARAGANA – *Leguminosae*. Hardy,
flowering, deciduous, easily grown shrubs
and small trees with compound leaves.

Soil, ordinary, succeeding in poor dry
soils and exposed places. Position, full sun.
Plant in autumn or late winter.

Increase by seeds well soaked in hot
water and sown as soon as ripe or in spring;
by cuttings in summer or early autumn; by
grafting choice species on *C. arborescens* in
spring.

Recommended kinds are *C. arborescens*,
yellow, late spring, 15 ft., Siberia, and vars.
lorbergii, *nana*, *pendula*; *frutex*, yellow, late
spring, 9 ft., Russia; *franchetiana*, buff-
yellow shaded maroon, early summer, 9 ft.,
China; *maximowicziana*, yellow, late spring,
weeping habit, to 4 ft., China, Tibet;
microphylla, yellow, late spring, early summer, 6 to 10 ft., N. Central Asia; *pygmaea*,
yellow, late spring, early summer, 3 ft.,
Caucasus to Tibet; *sinica* (syn. *chamlagu*),
reddish yellow, late spring, early summer, 3
to 4 ft., N. China; *tragacanthoides*, yellow,
early summer, 1 to 2 ft., Tibet to Siberia.

CARDAMINE (Bitter Cress) – *Cruciferae*.
Hardy herbaceous and tender aquatic plants.
C. lyrata is a very pretty submerged aquatic
not unlike Creeping Jenny.

Soil, ordinary. Position, moist, shady
border or in the bog garden. Plant in spring
or autumn. *C. lyrata* in a heated or unheated
aquarium or pool in frost-free places.

Increase by seeds sown outdoors in
spring; by division of roots in spring.

Recommended kinds are *C. bulbosa*, white.
spring and early summer, 6 in., Eastern
U.S.A.; *lyrata*, aquatic, white, summer,
submerged leaves, China, Japan; *pratensis*,
Lady Smock, Cuckoo Flower, white to
rose, spring, 1 to 2 ft., Northern Hemisphere (Britain), and var. *flore pleno*, double;
trifolia, white, spring, 3 to 4 in., S. Europe.

CARDIOCRINUM (Giant Lily) – *Liliaceae*. Hardy bulbous-rooted perennials
formerly included in the genus *Lilium*.

Soil, moist, well-drained rather rich
loam with leafmould, peat and sand. Position, open woodlands or other partially
shaded places. Plant in autumn only just
covering the bulbs. Bulbs die after flowering
but may leave offsets behind to flower again.

Increase by seeds sown in sandy peat and
loam in autumn, seedlings take about seven
years to flower; also by removal of offsets in
autumn.

The best kind is *C. giganteum* (syn. *Lilium
giganteum*), white, late summer, 6 to 12 ft.,
Himalaya.

CAREX (Blue Grass, Sedge) – *Cyperaceae*.
Hardy or slightly tender herbaceous peren-

nials, allied to grasses. Flowers in spikes.

Soil, ordinary, moist. Position, open or
partially shaded margins of pools. The
variegated kinds may be grown in pots in
ordinary good soil in cool greenhouses or
in rooms.

Increase by seeds sown in spring where
plants are to grow; by division of roots in
spring.

Recommended kinds are *C. morrowii
variegata*, leaves edged with white, 1 to 1½
ft., Japan; *pendula*, brown inflorescence,
summer, 3 to 6 ft., Europe (Britain), N.
Africa; *pseudocyperus*, Bastard Cyperus,
dark green spikelets, early summer, 3 ft.,
Temperate Zone; *riparia variegata*, leaves
striped white, Northern Hemisphere (Britain), S. America, and var. Bowles' Golden,
leaves golden yellow.

CARLINA (Carline Thistle) – *Compositae*.
Hardy perennials with handsome leaves and
thistle-like flowers.

Soil, ordinary. Position, open dryish
border. Plant in spring.

Increase by seeds sown in spring where
plants are required to grow.

Recommended kinds are *C. acanthifolia*,
white, summer, 18 in., S. Europe; *acaulis*,
white, early summer, 9 in., Europe.

Carpenteria californica

CARPENTERIA – *Philadelphaceae*.
Slightly tender evergreen flowering shrub.

Soil, light loamy. Position, warm sheltered shrub borders but requiring wall or
greenhouse protection in cold districts. In
spring remove some of the older stems to the
base to make room for young growth.

Increase by cuttings of young shoots in
summer, or from seeds sown in a temp. 15
to 18°C. in spring.

The only species is *C. californica*, Californian Mock Orange, white, fragrant,
summer, 8 ft., California.

CARPINUS (Hornbeam) – *Carpinaceae*.
Hardy deciduous trees frequently confused

with beech, but having in the European
species a rugged fluted trunk, that of the
European beech being smooth. Good for
hedging, retaining old leaves until spring,
as does beech used for this purpose.

Any ordinary soil including chalk and
clay, fairly dry or moist. Plant in autumn or
late winter. Trim hedges in autumn. Use *C.
betulus* for hedging and plant 18 in. apart.

Increase by seeds sown in autumn in fine
soil out of doors or stratified for four
months at 4°C. and then sown.

Recommended kinds are *C. betulus*, Common Hornbeam, 50 to 80 ft., Europe (Britain), with vars. *columnaris* and *fastigiata*,
excellent fastigiate trees, *incisa*, cut leaves,
pendula, branch tips weeping, and *purpurea*,
young leaves purplish; *caroliniana*, American Hornbeam, grey, smooth bark, spreading habit, 35 ft., America; *japonica*, spreading rather flat-topped habit, 40 ft., Japan;
laxiflora, drooping branch ends, 45 ft.,
Japan; *orientalis*, upright habit, 25 ft., S. E.
Europe; *tschonoskii*, freely branched, 35 ft.,
China, Japan; *turczaninowii*, young leaves
red, 25 ft., W. China.

CARPOBROTUS – *Aizoaceae*. Slightly
tender succulent plants. Formerly included
in *Mesembryanthemum*.

Soil, ordinary, well drained. Position,
sunny borders or banks, in sheltered districts. Will only survive a few degrees of
frost.

Increase by seeds sown in temp. 15 to
18°C. in spring; by cuttings in a similar
temperature and sandy soil any time from
spring to autumn.

Recommended kinds are *C. acinaciformis*
(syn. *Mesembryanthemum acinaciforme*),
purple, summer, trailing, S. Africa; *chilensis* (syn. *Mesembryanthemum chilense*), rose-
purple, summer, trailing, Chile, California;
edulis (syn. *M. edule*), Hottentot Fig, yellow
to purple, summer, trailing. S. Africa.

CARYA (Hickory) – *Juglandaceae*. Hardy
deciduous trees. Full-grown trees bear
edible nuts similar to walnuts.

Soil, ordinary. Position, open shrub
borders, woods or as single specimens on
lawns and in parks. Plant in autumn or late
winter. Prune in autumn but thin out misplaced or diseased branches only.

Increase by seeds stratified for four
months at 4°C. and then sown in temp. 15 to
18°C.

Recommended kinds are *C. cordiformis*,
Bitter Nut, to 90 ft., N. E. America; *glabra*
(syn. *porcina*), Pignut, 80 to 90 ft., N. E.
America; *laciniosa*, Shellbark Hickory, to
100 ft., Eastern U.S.A.; *pecan* (syn. *illino-
ensis*), Pecan, 100 to 150 ft., Southern
U.S.A.; *tomentosa*, Mockernut, 50 to 60 ft.,
E. America.

CARYOPTERIS (Blue Spiraea) – *Verbenaceae*. Hardy or slightly tender shrubs

with fluffy blue flowers carried in clusters.

Soil, well drained, including chalk. Position, warm, sunny. Prune previous season's shoots annually in spring to two buds.

Increase by cuttings in late summer in a frame.

Recommended kinds are *C. clandonensis*, blue, late summer, 2 ft., hybrid between *incana* and *mongolica*, and numerous varieties; *incana* (syn. *mastacanthus*), Bluebeard, blue, late summer, 4 ft., China; *mongolica*, blue, late summer, 1½ to 3 ft., Mongolia, China.

CASSIA (Senna) – *Leguminosae*. Evergreen shrubs and perennials a few of which are hardy though most are tender to varying degree according to species. The leaves and seed pods of some species provide the medicinal senna.

Grow in two parts loam, one part each of peat and sand in pots in a cool or intermediate greenhouse or in warm, sunny sheltered places out of doors. *C. corymbosa* can be trained against a wall and when so grown it may be necessary to prune each spring, shortening the previous year's stems to a few inches each. Plant all kinds in spring. In cold places protect the base of outdoor plants in winter with a covering of leaves or ashes.

Increase by seeds sown in light soil in temp. 18 to 20°C. in spring; by cuttings of previous year's shoots inserted in sandy soil in a similar temperature in spring.

Recommended kinds are *C. alata*, Candle Bush, yellow, winter, to 15 ft., Tropical America; *corymbosa*, yellow, summer, 6 to 10 ft., Argentina; *glauca*, yellow, all year, to 15 ft., S. E. Asia; *marylandica*, yellow, summer, 3 ft., Eastern U.S.A., the hardiest species, strictly a sub-shrub but often treated as a herbaceous perennial and cut to ground level each spring.

CASSIOPE – *Ericaceae*. Hardy evergreen flowering shrubs. Formerly known as andromeda.

Soil, sandy peat. Position, moist, cool, open.

Increase by seeds sown on the surface of sandy peat in spring; by layering in spring; by cuttings of firm young shoots in summer in a propagating frame.

Recommended kinds are *C. fastigiata*, white, spring, 9 to 12 in., Himalaya; *lycopodioides*, white, prostrate, spring, N. E. Asia and N. W. America; *mertensiana*, white, 6 to 10 in., spring, N. W. America; *selaginoides*, white, spring, 4 to 6 in., Asia; *stelleriana* (syn. *Harrimanella stelleriana*), white, prostrate, spring, N. W. America; *tetragona*, white, spring, 9 in., Arctic Europe, America; *wardii*, white, spring, 9 to 12 in., Asia.

CASTANEA (Chestnut) – *Fagaceae*. Hardy deciduous trees. Bears edible nuts, which

Castanea sativa

should be separated from the husks when the latter fall in autumn, then thoroughly dried in the sun or warm oven and stored in air-tight jars or boxes in a cool, dry place.

Soil, deep, rich, dry and sandy. Position, open, sunny. Plant in autumn or late winter.

Increase by seeds sown as soon as ripe in the open ground; choice varieties by grafting in spring on *C. sativa*.

Recommended kinds are *C. crenata*, Japanese Chestnut, 20 to 30 ft., Japan; *dentata* (syn. *americana*), American Chestnut, 50 to 90 ft., Eastern N. America; *mollissima*, Chinese Chestnut, 50 ft., China, Korea; *pumila*, Chinquapin, 10 to 20 ft., Eastern N. America; *sativa*, Spanish Chestnut, Sweet Chestnut, 50 to 80 ft., S. Europe, N. Africa, Asia Minor; *seguinii*, to 20 ft., sweet nuts, China.

CASUARINA (She-oak) – *Casuarinaceae*. Rather tender evergreen shrubs or trees with whip-like stems. All included are Australasian.

Soil, ordinary, well drained. Position, open, sunny, warm, particularly good near the sea, but will only survive a few degrees of frost. Plant in spring or autumn.

Increase by seeds sown in spring in a temperature of 15 to 18°C.; by cuttings of firm young growth in a warm propagator in summer.

Recommended kinds are *C. equisetifolia*, Horsetail Tree, 30 to 60 ft.; *nana*, 6 to 8 ft.; *stricta*, 20 to 30 ft.

CATALPA – *Bignoniaceae*. Hardy deciduous flowering and ornamental-leaved trees. Flowers borne in erect clusters like those of Horse Chestnut. Catalpas come into leaf very late.

Soil, ordinary, good, well drained. Position, sunny, they do well in town gardens. Plant in autumn or late winter. Remove dead or dying branch ends in spring. If

overgrown, branches can be cut back severely in late winter.

Increase by seeds sown as soon as ripe or in spring; by root cuttings in winter; by cuttings of firm young growth in summer in a propagating frame.

Recommended kinds are *C. bignonioides*, Indian Bean Tree, white, spotted purple and yellow, summer, 25 to 50 ft., U.S.A., and var. *aurea*, golden leaved; *bungei*, white, spotted purple, 30 ft., China; *fargesii*, lilac-pink, spotted purple, summer, 30 to 50 ft., W. China, and var. *duclouxii*; *ovata* (syn. *kaempferi*), white, spotted red, summer, 20 to 40 ft., China; *speciosa*, white, purple spotted, summer, 30 to 100 ft., Central U.S.A.

CATANANCHE (Cupid's Dart) – *Compositae*. Hardy perennials with cornflower-like flowers. Blooms may be cut and dried for winter decoration; gather when fully developed.

Soil, ordinary, well drained. Position, sunny warm borders. Plant in spring.

Increase by seeds sown in light soil in temp. 15 to 18°C. in spring; by division in spring.

The best kind is *C. caerulea*, Blue Cupidone, blue, summer, 2 ft., S. Europe, and vars. *alba*, white, *bicolor*, blue and white, *major*, blue, extra large.

CATHARANTHUS – *Apocynaceae*. Tender perennials or sub-shrubs closely allied to *Vinca* and sometimes included with them. Showy periwinkle-like flowers.

Catharanthus roseus, the most popular kind, though a perennial is generally grown as an annual. Sow in spring in temp. 18 to 21°C. Pot seedlings singly in John Innes potting compost No. 1 or equivalent and later move on into 5- or 6-in. pots and John Innes potting compost No. 2. Grow throughout in an intermediate or warm greenhouse, minimum winter temp. 13°C. Water normally. Shade from strong sunshine in summer. If grown on for several years repot as necessary in spring.

The best kind is *C. roseus* (syn. *Vinca rosea*), Madagascar Periwinkle, rose, all year, 1 to 2 ft., Tropics.

CATTLEYA – *Orchidaceae*. Tender evergreen epiphytic orchids. Not only are the species appreciated but orchid collections are enriched by great numbers of hybrids within the genus as well as intergeneric hybrids with *Laelia*, *Brassavola*, *Sophronitis*, etc. Many have showy flowers 6 to 8 in. across.

Compost, two parts fibre and three parts sphagnum moss or equivalent. Position, pots in an intermediate house. Water fairly freely from spring to autumn, moderately in winter. Shade from direct sunshine in late spring and summer only. Repot in spring but only when really necessary, per-

Cattleya (hybrid)

haps every two or three years, or even less frequently.

Increase by division of plants when potting. The rhizome may be cut through leaving four bulbs at least in front of the severance and an incipient 'eye' may then grow.

Recommended kinds are *C. aclandiae*, purple, yellow and rose, summer, 9 in., Brazil; *amethystoglossa*, rose, purple spotted, spring, 2½ ft., Brazil, var. *sanderae*, pure white; *bicolor*, bronze-green and rose-purple, autumn, 1 ft., Brazil; *bowringiana*, rose-purple, autumn, 1½ ft., Honduras; *citrina*, yellow, pendent, spring, Mexico; *dowiana*, yellow, purple and rose, summer, early autumn, 1 ft., Costa Rica; *guttata*, greenish yellow, purple and white, autumn, 1½ ft., Brazil; *intermedia*, pale rose and purple, summer, 15 in., Brazil, and numerous varieties including one with white flowers; *labiata*, rose, purple and yellow, late autumn, winter, 1 ft., Brazil, and many varieties including white; *lawrenceana*, purple and white, spring, early summer, 1 ft., British Guiana; *lueddemanniana*, purple, white and yellow, autumn, 1 ft., Venezuela, and many varieties including white; *mossiae*, pale rose and purple, frilled, late spring, early summer, 1 ft., Venezuela, and numerous varieties; *percivaliana*, pink and magenta, winter, spring, 1 ft., Colombia, Venezuela; *skinneri*, rose-purple, spring, 1 ft., Guatemala, var. *alba*, white; *trianae*, mauve and purple, winter, 1 ft., Brazil, and numerous varieties including white; *warneri*, rose and purple-red, summer, 1 ft., Brazil.

CAUTLEYA – *Zingiberaceae*. Herbaceous semi-tuberous-rooted plants with handsome leaves and stiff spikes of flowers. Sometimes wrongly spelled cautlea.

Soil, sandy, peaty, cool. Position, half-shade. Plant in spring or autumn.

Increase by seeds sown in temp. 15 to 18°C. in spring; by division of the roots in spring when growth starts.

Recommended kinds are *C. lutea*, yellow, 12 in., summer, Himalaya; *robusta*, yellow, summer and early autumn, 3 ft., Himalaya.

CEANOTHUS – *Rhamnaceae*. Hardy and slightly tender evergreen and deciduous flowering shrubs. The deciduous characteristic is much influenced by winter temperature and in warm places species commonly regarded as deciduous may retain their leaves. In warm localities most species make fine specimens in the open but in colder places are better for wall protection. Most are very adaptable for training.

Soil, light, ordinary, well drained. Position, warm and sunny, trained against walls or fences in cold districts or in pots in a cool greenhouse. Plant in spring, preferably from pots or other containers with as little root disturbance as possible. Prune deciduous kinds fairly severely in spring, the evergreen kinds should have flowering shoots shortened as blossoms fade but do not cut into old wood which will not produce new growth.

Increase by cuttings in summer; by seeds sown in spring in temp. 15 to 18°C.

Recommended deciduous kinds are *C. americanus*, New Jersey Tea, white, summer, 3 ft., E. America; *caeruleus* (syn. *azureus*), blue, all summer, 8 to 10 ft., Mexico; *delilianus* (syn. *arnouldii*), blue, all summer, 4 to 6 ft., hybrid between *americanus* and *caeruleus*, the well-known var. Gloire de Versailles belongs here; *integerrimus*, pale blue, early summer, 9 to 12 ft., California; *ovatus*, white, summer, 2 to 3 ft., U.S.A.

Recommended evergreen kinds are *C. arboreus*, blue, spring, to 20 ft., California; *burkwoodii*, blue, summer and early autumn, 8 ft., hybrid between *delilianus* and *dentatus*; *dentatus*, blue, late spring, 4 ft., California; *gloriosus*, lavender-blue, spring, prostrate, California; *impressus*, deep blue, late spring, 5 to 6 ft., California; *lobbianus*, blue, late spring and early summer, 10 to 15 ft., hybrid between *dentatus* and *thyrsiflorus*; *papillosus*, blue, late spring, 10 to 12 ft., California; *prostratus*, Squaw Carpet, blue, spring, prostrate, Western U.S.A.; *rigidus*, violet, spring, 6 to 12 ft., California; *thyrsi-*

florus, Californian Lilac, blue, occasionally white, early summer, 15 to 30 ft., one of the hardiest, California; *veitchianus* bright blue, spring, 10 ft., hybrid probably between *rigidus* and *thyrsiflorus*.

CEDRUS – *Pinaceae*. Hardy evergreen coniferous trees.

Soil, rich, deep, reasonably well drained. Position, open; warm and sheltered for *C. deodara*. *C. atlantica* does well in seaside gardens, and all are suitable for chalky soils. Plant in spring or autumn.

Increase by seeds sown outdoors as soon as ripe or immediately stratified for two months at 4°C. and then sown; garden forms by grafting on seedlings of the type plant in early spring.

Recommended kinds are *C. atlantica*, Mount Atlas Cedar, 80 to 100 ft., N. Africa, vars. *aurea*, golden, *glauca*, Blue Cedar, grey-blue, *pendula*, weeping; *brevifolia*, Cyprian Cedar, to 40 ft., Cyprus; *deodara*, Deodar, to 150 ft., Himalaya, and vars. *albospica*, needles white tipped, *aurea*, golden, *pendula*, broadly weeping; *libani*, Cedar of Lebanon, 80 ft., Asia Minor.

CELASTRUS – *Celastraceae*. Vigorous, hardy deciduous shrubby twiners. Grown for their attractive fruits. Plants often produce flowers of one sex only. Both male and female flowers are essential for fruit production, so either plants known to be hermaphrodite (i.e. with organs of both sexes) should be planted or several plants should be placed near one another.

Soil, ordinary. Position, walls, arbours or clambering over trees. Plant in autumn or late winter. Little pruning is necessary but dead vines should be cut out when seen.

Increase by layers of young shoots in autumn or spring; by cuttings in summer or autumn; by seeds sown outdoors as soon as ripe.

Recommended kinds are *C. orbiculatus* (syn. *articulatus*), the most reliable fruiting kind, capsules orange with scarlet seeds, N. E. Asia; *scandens*, American Bittersweet, 30 ft., fruits similar to *orbiculatus*, N. E. America.

Cedrus atlantica glauca

CELMISIA (New Zealand Daisy) – *Compositae*. Evergreen herbaceous perennials with white daisy flowers. Natives of Australasia.

Soil, well-drained sandy loam, deep and friable. Position, full sun, warm sheltered places.

Increase by seeds in a frame in spring or cuttings of side rosettes in summer.

Recommended New Zealand kinds are *C. coriacea*, early summer, 9 to 15 in.; *hieracifolia*, early summer, 6 to 10 in.; *spectabilis*, summer, 12 to 15 in.

CELOSIA – *Amaranthaceae*. Rather tender annuals with small brightly coloured flowers in plume-like sprays or cockscomb clusters.

Sow seeds in late winter or spring in open-textured soil such as John Innes seed compost in temp. 18 to 21°C. Pot seedlings singly in small pots in John Innes potting compost No. 1 or equivalent, and move on to larger pots as necessary using a richer compost such as John Innes potting compost No. 2. Keep in a sunny greenhouse throughout or plant out in a warm, sunny place when there is no longer any danger of frost. Discard plants after flowering.

Celosia argentea pyramidalis

Grow the Cockscomb in the same way but place pots on a shelf near the glass until the 'combs' show themselves. Select plants with the finest combs and place them in 4-in. pots; plunge these to the rims on a gentle hotbed (temp. 18 to 21°C.) and keep moderately moist at the roots. Syringe freely. Transfer plants when the pots are full of roots into 6-in. pots and treat as before. Give liquid manure when the combs are well advanced. A good specimen of a comb should measure 9 to 12 in. long, 3 to 6 in. wide.

The best kinds are *C. argentea cristata*, Cockscomb, red, crimson, orange or yellow, summer, to 1 ft.; *argentea pyramidalis* (syn. *plumosa*), scarlet, crimson, yellow, summer, 1 to 2 ft. The species from which these garden varieties have been developed has white flowers and is a native of the Tropics but is rarely cultivated.

CELSIA – *Scrophulariaceae*. Hardy or slight tender biennials and perennials with flowers in spikes similar to those of verbascum.

Soil, ordinary, well drained; John Innes potting compost No. 1 or equivalent if grown in pots. Position, warm and sunny outdoors, or in pots in a sunny greenhouse. Plant or pot in spring. Water moderately from spring to autumn, sparingly in winter.

Increase by seeds sown in a temp. 15 to 18°C. in spring, or for *C. cretica* also in early autumn for late winter and spring flowering.

Recommended kinds are *C. arcturus*, yellow with purple anthers, summer, 1 to 2 ft., Asia Minor, Crete; *cretica*, Cretan Mullein, yellow with brown spots, spring or summer, scented, 3 to 5 ft., Mediterranean region.

CELTIS (Hackberry) – *Ulmaceae*. Hardy deciduous ornamental-leaved trees.

Soil, ordinary. Position, sunny. Plant in autumn or winter. Prune, if necessary, in winter.

Increase by seeds stratified for three months at 4°C. and then sown outdoors or in a frame.

Recommended kinds are *C. australis*, Nettle Tree, 50 to 70 ft., S. Europe, N. Africa, Asia Minor; *laevigata* (syn. *mississippiensis*), long narrow leaves, 60 ft., Southeastern U.S.A.; *occidentalis*, spring, 40 to 130 ft., N. America.

CENTAUREA – *Compositae*. Hardy and slightly tender perennials and annuals.

Culture of annual species: Sow seeds outdoors in spring where plants are required to flower. Thin seedlings when an inch or so high to 4 or 6 in. apart. Ordinary, well-drained soil and a sunny position.

Culture of perennial species: Soil, ordinary, well drained. Position, sunny border; suitable for warm, rather dry places. Plant in spring or autumn.

Culture of tender species: Plants can be raised from seeds sown in temp. 15 to 18°C. in spring or from cuttings inserted in an unheated frame in late summer, lifting them when rooted and placing in pots in winter in a frost-proof greenhouse. Plant out in beds in summer when danger of frost is over. Can be grown outdoors all the year in well-drained soils in mild places and will withstand some frost particularly if growth is well ripened. The silvery foliage of these is valued for bedding.

Increase perennial kinds by seeds sown outdoors in spring; by division of roots in spring or autumn.

Recommended annual kinds are *C. cyanus*, Cornflower, blue, rose, white, etc., summer, 6 in. to 3 ft., Europe (Britain), *moschata*, Sweet Sultan, purple, mauve, pink, yellow, white, summer, 2 ft., Orient.

Recommended perennial kinds are *C. babylonica*, yellow, summer, 5 to 7 ft., Levant; *dealbata*, rose, summer, 2 to 3 ft., Caucasus, var. *steenbergii*, rose-magenta;

Centaurea cyanus

glastifolia, yellow, summer, 3 to 4 ft., Europe; *macrocephala*, yellow, summer, 4 to 5 ft., Caucasus; *montana*, blue, late spring, early summer, 2 ft., Caucasus, Pyrenees, and vars. *alba*, white, *rosea*, rose; *ruthenica*, pale yellow, summer, 3 to 4 ft., Caucasus and Siberia.

Recommended tender species, all with silver-grey leaves, are *C. gymnocarpa*, 2 ft., Caprera Island (near Sardinia); *ragusina*, 2 ft., Crete and Dalmatia; *rutifolia* (syns. *cineraria* and *candidissima*), to 3 ft., Italy.

CENTRANTHUS (Valerian) – *Valerianaceae*. Hardy herbaceous perennials. Sometimes spelled kentranthus.

Soil, ordinary, well drained. Position, sunny; excellent for hot, dry banks, terrace walls, etc. Plant in spring or autumn.

Increase by seeds sown in light soil in spring; by division in spring or autumn.

The best kind is *C. ruber*, Red Valerian, rose-red, summer, 18 in., Europe (Britain), and vars. *albus*, white, *coccineus*, crimson.

CEPHALARIA (Giant Scabious) – *Dipsacaceae*. Hardy herbaceous perennials with scabious-like flowers.

Soil, ordinary. Position, open, sunny. Plant in spring or autumn.

Increase by seeds sown in a sunny position outdoors in spring; by division in spring.

Recommended kinds are *C. alpina* (syn. *Scabiosa alpina*), yellow, summer, 5 ft., Europe; *tartarica*, yellow, summer, 6 ft., Siberia.

CEPHALOCEREUS – *Cactaceae*. Tender succulent perennial with columnar growth dotted with hairs, especially near the top, in some species.

Treatment is as for cereus but since it is young plants that usually give the best effect it is desirable to propagate fairly frequently by cutting off the tops of older plants and rooting them in a sandy compost.

Cephalocereus senilis

The best kind is *C. senilis*, Old Man Cactus, white, summer, to 40 ft., young plants clotted with long grey hairs, Mexico.

CEPHALOTAXUS (Plum Yew) – *Cephalotaxaceae*. Hardy evergreen coniferous trees. Leaves similar to those of yew.

Soil, ordinary, they succeed well on chalk. Position, open, or shady, even under large trees. Plant in spring or autumn.

Increase by seeds stratified as soon as ripe at 4°C. for three months and then sown outdoors or under glass; by cuttings of firm young shoots in a frame in late summer or autumn.

Recommended kinds are *C. fortunei*, to 30 ft., China; *harringtonia*, to 30 ft., said to be Japanese but origin uncertain, and vars. *drupacea*, Cow's Tail Pine, Japanese Plum Yew, *fastigiata*, erect habit, *prostrata*, dwarf and spreading.

CERASTIUM – *Caryophyllaceae*. Hardy perennials cultivated for their grey leaves and white flowers.

Soil, ordinary. Position, sunny, dryish borders, rock gardens, and banks. Plant in spring or autumn.

Increase by division of plants in spring.

Recommended kinds are *C. alpinum*, white, early summer, prostrate, Europe (Britain), var. *lanatum*, silvery woolly foliage; *biebersteinii*, white, late spring, early summer, 6 in., leaves silvery, mat forming, Asia Minor; *tomentosum*, Snow in Summer, white, early summer, 6 in., mat forming, spreads rapidly, leaves silvery, Europe.

CERATOSTIGMA – *Plumbaginaceae*. Hardy or slightly tender deciduous shrubs and herbaceous perennials often known as plumbago.

Soil, light, well drained loam, sunny position at the foot of a wall or on a rock garden. Cut older or dying shoots hard back in spring.

Increase by division in spring; by cuttings in summer.

Recommended shrubby kinds are *C. griffithii*, blue, late summer and autumn, 3 ft., Himalaya; *willmottianum*, sky blue, midsummer to early winter, 4 ft., W. China.

The best herbaceous kind is *C. plumbaginoides* (syn. *larpentae*), blue, late summer and autumn, 4 to 12 in., China.

CERCIDIPHYLLUM – *Cercidiphyllaceae*. Hardy deciduous tree with elegant foliage turning yellow or red in the autumn.

Soil, good loam, not liable to dry out severely. Position, sheltered from early frosts and cold winds.

Increase by seeds sown as soon as ripe; by cuttings in summer; by layering in spring.

The only species is *C. japonicum*, 50 to 100 ft., Japan, China.

CERCIS – *Leguminosae*. Hardy deciduous flowering trees.

Soil, rich, deep, sandy. Position, warm and sheltered. In cold places they may be trained against a sunny wall. Plant in autumn or late winter.

Increase by seeds sown in light sandy soil in temp. 15 to 18°C. in spring; by cuttings in summer; selected forms by grafting on to seedlings.

Recommended kinds are *C. canadensis*, Red-bud, rose, spring, 15 to 30 ft., N. America; *chinensis*, rosy purple, spring, 20 to 30 ft., rather tender, China; *racemosa*, rose, late spring, 20 to 30 ft., China; *siliquastrum*, Judas Tree, purple or rose, late spring, 20 to 30 ft., S. Europe.

CEREUS – *Cactaceae*. Tender succulent plants. Many species formerly included in this genus have been transferred to *Aporocactus*, *Echinocereus*, *Selenicereus*, etc. All are tall, stiffly erect plants. The flowers are not as a rule very attractive.

Compost, two parts fibrous loam, one part coarse sand and broken brick. Position, well-drained pots in a sunny greenhouse or window. Pot every two or three years as required. Water sparingly. Minimum winter temp. 7°C.

Increase by seeds sown in well-drained pots or boxes; by cuttings of stems inserted in pots of sand and kept just moist.

Recommended kinds are *C. alacriportanus*, to 6 ft., Brazil, Paraguay; *peruvianus*, the hardiest kind, to 40 ft. in nature, but usually much smaller, Brazil and Argentina, and var. *monstrosus*, with cristate stems.

CESTRUM (Bastard Jasmine) – *Solanaceae*. Tender evergreen or deciduous shrubs with tubular flowers.

Compost, two parts loam, one part leafmould and sand. Position, pots or beds with shoots trained on wall, pillars, or the roof of a cool or intermediate greenhouse or outdoors in warm, sheltered sunny places. Winter minimum temperature under glass

Cestrum fasciculatum

5°C. Plant or pot in spring. Prune into shape removing winter-damaged or old worn out growths in spring.

Increase by cuttings of firm young growth in summer in temp. 18 to 20°C.

Recommended kinds are *C. aurantiacum*, orange-yellow, summer, semi-climbing to 8 to 10 ft., Guatemala; *fasciculatum*, purplish red, 6 to 10 ft., Mexico, var. *newellii*, crimson; *parqui*, greenish yellow, summer, 7 ft., deciduous, one of the hardiest which will survive a few degrees of frost, Western S. America; *purpureum* (syn. *elegans*), carmine, summer and autumn, semi-climbing to 10 ft., Mexico, and var. *smithii*.

CHAENOMELES (Flowering Quince) – *Rosaceae*. Hardy deciduous and easily grown shrubs of great beauty, flowering in early spring before the leaves. The quince-like fruits are useful for preserves. Formerly included in the genus *Cydonia*. *Chaenomeles speciosa* is the Japonica of gardens.

All will grow in any garden soil. Position, open or trained against walls of any aspect, makes an attractive hedge. Plant in autumn or late winter. When trained, side growths that cannot be tied in can be shortened to five leaves in summer. Hedges should be trimmed after flowering and, if necessary, again in early autumn.

Increase by layering in winter or spring; by division in autumn or late winter; by cuttings in summer or autumn. Increase species or produce new varieties by seeds sown as soon as ripe or stratified for two months at 4°C. and then sown.

Recommended kinds are *C. cathayensis*, to 10 ft., white flushed pink, spring, China; *japonica* (syn. *Cydonia maulei*), 3 ft., orange or red, Japan; *speciosa* (syn. *Chaenomeles lagenaria*), to 6 ft., or if trained considerably higher, crimson, red, pink or white, late winter and spring, China, many named varieties including some with double flowers.

CHAMAECYPARIS (False Cypress) – *Cupressaceae*. Hardy evergreen coniferous trees with small scale-like leaves. Suitable for most soils, but less satisfactory on very dry or chalky soils. *C. thyoides* does well in boggy places. Position, open or partially shaded. Plant in autumn or spring. In general, chamaecyparis species are easier to transplant than cupressus species.

For hedges, trench soil, 3 ft. wide and 2 ft. deep, adding a little well-rotted manure. Plant 2 ft. apart. Trim twice annually in late spring and midsummer. *C. lawsoniana* is the best species for hedging. The various coloured forms with varying degrees of vigour are useful for formal planting and stand trimming well.

Increase by cuttings in summer or early autumn; by grafting garden varieties in spring on to seedlings; by seeds stratified as soon as ripe at 4°C. for three months and then sown outdoors or under glass, but seedlings of garden varieties may show considerable variation.

Recommended kinds are *C. lawsoniana*, Lawson's Cypress, pyramidal habit, 100 to 150 ft., California, and vars. *allumii*, glaucous, columnar, *argenteovariegata*, leaves flecked with white, *columnaris*, narrowly columnar, dark green, *elegantissima*, drooping habit, greyish green, *ellwoodii*, compact, columnar, grey-green, *erecta*, columnar, bright green, *filifera*, shrubby, thin drooping branchlets, *fletcheri*, slow growing, broadly columnar, grey-green, *forsteckiana*, dwarf, branchlets twisted, *glauca*, broadly columnar, steel blue, *intertexta*, weeping branchlets, greyish green, *lanei* and *lutea* both conical and yellow, *minima*, dwarf, rounded, green, *minima aurea*, similar to last but golden, *nana*, to 6 ft., rounded, green, *nidiformis*, horizontal branches from dense centre, drooping at tips, *pottenii*, columnar, green, *stewartii*, conical, yellow, *wisselii*, columnar, dark green, and many more differing in size, habit and foliage characteristics; *nootkatensis*, Nootka Cypress, pyramidal habit, weeping branch ends, 100 to 120 ft., Western N. America; *obtusa* (syn. *Retinospora obtusa*), Hinoki Cypress, spreading habit, 50 to 120 ft., Japan, and many varieties such as *albospica*, young leaves white, *filicoides*, ferny green foliage, slow growing, *lycopodioides*, bluegreen, moss-like foliage, *nana*, very dwarf dark green, *nana aurea*, similar to the last but golden, *nana gracilis*, broadly conical, dark green, compact, *pygmaea*, low, wide spreading, bronze-grey, *tetragona aurea*, golden moss-like foliage, and many more; *pisifera*, Sawara Cypress, (syn. *Retinospora pisifera*), broadly conical habit, 70 to 150 ft., Japan, and vars. *filifera*, drooping, whip-like branchlets, green, *filifera aurea*, similar to the last but golden, *plumosa*, compact feathery green, *plumosa aurea*, similar to the last but golden, *squarrosa*, soft blue-grey, and many more; *thyoides*, White Cedar, 20 to 50 ft., Eastern U.S.A. and vars. *ericoides*, bronze-purple in winter, *glauca*, blue-grey.

CHAMAEROPS – *Palmae*. Slightly tender palm with green fan-shaped leaves.

Compost, two parts rich loam, one part each decayed leafmould and sand. Position, well-drained pots in a cool greenhouse or sheltered well-drained beds outdoors in mild places. It can survive temperatures around – 5°C. Pot or plant in spring.

Increase by seeds sown in light soil in temp. of 25°C. in spring; suckers removed from parent plant in spring or late summer.

The recommended kind is *C. humilis*, Fan Palm, European Palm, 3 to 20 ft., S. Europe, N. Africa.

CHASMANTHE – *Iridaceae*. Hardy or slightly tender S. African corms formerly included in the genus *Antholyza*.

Soil, light sandy. Position, sunny welldrained border or pots in a cool greenhouse. Plant 6 in. deep and 6 in. apart in a border, or place six corms in a 6-in. pot in autumn. Lift after flowering, dry and store in a cool place till autumn.

Increase by offsets at planting time; by seeds sown in slight heat in spring.

Recommended kinds are *C. aethiopica* (syn. *Antholyza aethiopica*), red and yellow, summer, 3 to 4 ft.; *caffra* (syn. *intermedia*, hort.), bright red, late spring, 1 ft., slightly tender; *floribunda* (syn. *praealta*), orange and red, late spring, summer, 3 to 4 ft.; *vittigera*, yellow and red, summer, 3 ft.

CHEILANTHES (Lip Fern) – *Sinopteridaceae*. Tender or nearly hardy ferns mostly with very finely divided fronds.

Compost, equal parts peat, loam and coarse sand. Position, frost-free greenhouse for the hardier kinds or even very sheltered places outdoors but an intermediate greenhouse, minimum winter temp. 18°C., for *C. myriophylla*. Shade from direct sunshine. Water moderately in spring and summer, sparingly in autumn and winter. These ferns require less moisture than most. Pot or plant in spring.

Increase by spores similar to adiantum; or by division in spring.

Recommended kinds are *C. californica*, 9 in., California; *clevelandii*, 1 ft., N. W. America; *gracillima*, Lace Lip Fern, 9 in., W. America; *lanosa*, 9 in., South-eastern U.S.A.; *microphylla*, 1 ft., Tropical America; *myriophylla* (syn. *elegans*), 9 in., Central America; *pteridioides* (syns. *odora*, *suaveolens*), 6 in., S. Europe.

CHEIRANTHUS (Wallflower) – *Cruciferae*. Hardy perennials or sub-shrubs with evergreen leaves, often grown as biennials.

Soil, ordinary, well drained, not too heavy, preferably with lime or chalk. Position, sunny borders, beds or old walls.

Increase by seeds sown outdoors in spring. Seedlings of common wallflowers and *C. allionii* may be planted in a nursery bed in early summer, moved to flowering

quarters in late summer or early autumn and discarded after flowering. Seedlings of other species may be planted permanently and these kinds can also be increased by cuttings of firm young shoots in a frame in summer. To grow on old walls, sow a pinch of seed in crevices, adding a little soil and cow manure to supply food to young plants, or plant young seedlings in similar compost in spring.

Recommended kinds are *C. allionii*, orange, spring and early summer, 12 to 15 in., hybrid probably between *Erysimum dubium* and *E. perowskianum* but origin uncertain; *cheiri*, Wallflower, Gilliflower, yellow, chestnut, red, crimson, purple, lilac, white, scented, spring, 1 to 2 ft., Europe, and var. Harpur Crewe, double yellow; *kewensis*, sulphur, orange, purple, winter, 1 ft., hybrid between *cheiri* and *mutabilis*; *mutabilis*, pale yellow becoming lilac or purple, spring, early summer, 1 to 2 ft., slightly tender, Madeira, Canary Islands.

CHELIDONIUM (Greater Celandine) – *Papaveraceae*. Hardy perennial with furry foliage and orange sap.

Soil, ordinary. Position, open or semishady banks, unmortared terrace walls. Plant in spring.

Increase by seeds sown in shade outdoors in spring; by division in spring.

The only species is *C. majus*, yellow, late spring and summer, 1 to 3 ft., Europe (Britain), W. Asia, and vars. *flore pleno*, double, *laciniatum*, more finely divided leaves.

CHELONE (Turtle-head) – *Scrophulariaceae*. Hardy herbaceous perennials with spikes of penstemon-like flowers. Some species formerly known as chelone are now included under *Penstemon*.

Soil, moist, acid or neutral. Position, sunny, open. Plant in spring.

Increase by seeds sown in light soil in temp. 15 to 18°C. in spring; by cuttings in-

Chelone obliqua

serted in sandy soil in a cold frame in summer; by division of plants in spring.

Recommended kinds are *C. glabra*, white or pink, late summer, 3 ft., N. America; *lyonii*, purple, late summer, 2 to 3 ft., South-eastern U.S.A.; *obliqua*, Shell Flower, purple, late summer, 2 to 3 ft., Southern U.S.A.

CHIASTOPHYLLUM – *Crassulaceae.* Hardy succulent perennial, often included in *Cotyledon*. Flowers in short drooping spikes.

Position, light soil, in sun or half shade, rock garden or unmortared terrace wall.

Increase by cuttings in summer in a frame; by division in spring or autumn.

The only species is *C. oppositifolium* (syns. *Cotyledon oppositifolia, simplicifolia*), yellow, spring and early summer, 6 in., Caucasus.

CHIMONANTHUS (Winter Sweet) – *Calycanthaceae.* Hardy deciduous flowering shrub with very sweetly scented but not very showy flowers.

Soil, deep, rich, well drained, will succeed on chalk. Position, sunny and sheltered; may be trained against walls. Plant in autumn or late winter. Prune immediately after flowering when some of the older branches can be cut out if overcrowded and young stems trained in their place.

Chimonanthus praecox

Increase by layering shoots in winter or spring, or from seeds sown in spring.

The only species commonly cultivated is *C. praecox* (syns. *fragrans* or *Calycanthus praecox*), pale yellow and purple, winter, 6 to 9 ft., China, vars. *grandiflorus*, larger flowering, and *luteus*, without purple centre.

CHIONANTHUS (Fringe Tree) – *Oleaceae.* Hardy deciduous flowering trees or large shrubs.

Soil, reasonably good loam. Position, open, sunny. Plant in autumn or late winter.

Increase by seeds stratified for three

Chlorophytum comosum variegatum

months at 20 to 25°C., for a further three months at 4°C. and then sown outdoors or under glass; by cuttings of firm young growth in a frame in summer or autumn; by grafting on to ash in spring; by budding on to ash in summer.

Recommended kinds are *C. retusus*, white, summer, 8 to 15 ft., China; *virginicus*, Virginia Snowflower, white, early summer, 15 to 30 ft., Eastern N. America.

CHIONODOXA (Glory of the Snow) – *Liliaceae.* Hardy, spring-flowering bulbs.

Soil, ordinary, well-drained loam. Position, sunny rock garden or border, sunny edge of deciduous shrubs or woodland, well drained. Plant bulbs 1 in. apart and 3 in. deep in autumn. Lift and replant every three years.

Pot culture: Compost, equal parts peat, loam, leafmould and sand. Pot in autumn, planting twelve bulbs 1 in. deep in a well-drained 6-in. half-pot. Cover the pot with ashes outdoors or in a frame until well rooted, then remove to a window or greenhouse.

Increase by seeds sown in boxes of light soil in a cold frame in summer; by offsets treated as mature bulbs.

Recommended kinds are *C. cretica*, blue and white, 6 to 10 in., Asia Minor, and numerous varieties including white and pink; *gigantea*, blue, spring, 8 in., Asia Minor; *luciliae*, blue and white, spring, 6 in., Asia Minor; *sardensis*, intense blue, 6 in., Asia Minor.

CHLIDANTHUS – *Amaryllidaceae.* Slightly tender bulb with tubular flowers.

Grow in a warm, well-drained border outdoors in sandy loam with extra peat or leafmould or in pots in John Innes potting compost No. 1 or equivalent in a sunny frost-proof greenhouse. Plant bulbs 3 in. deep in spring. Lift outdoor bulbs before frost and store them in sand in a frost-proof place during winter. Water pot-grown plants moderately at first, freely when in active growth but keep dry from autumn until repotting time.

Increase by offsets in spring.

The only kind is *C. fragrans*, yellow, fragrant, summer, 10 in., Andes.

CHLOROPHYTUM – *Liliaceae.* Tender herbaceous perennials, one kind frequently grown as a foliage plant.

Grow in John Innes potting compost No. 1 or equivalent in pots or baskets in a frost-proof room or greenhouse. Water normally. Will succeed in sun or shade and may be planted outdoors in summer when there is no danger of frost. Repot when necessary in spring.

Increase by division of roots when repotting; *C. comosum* also by pegging down into soil the plantlets which form on long runners, and severing these when well rooted.

Recommended kinds are *C. capense mediopictum*, leaves centrally striped yellow; *capense variegatum*, leaves edged white; *comosum variegatum*, leaves striped with white. The native species of which these plants are variants are from S. Africa. *C. capense* is often known as *C. elatum*.

CHOISYA (Mexican Orange Blossom) – *Rutaceae.* Slightly tender evergreen flowering shrub with fragrant flowers.

Soil, ordinary loam, will succeed on chalk. Position, sheltered, sun or light shade; can be trained against walls. Good maritime shrubs. Plant in spring or autumn. Winter-damaged growth should be removed each spring. If overgrown, old branches can be cut hard back after flowering.

Increase by cuttings of firm shoots in temp. 15 to 18°C. in summer.

The species cultivated is *C. ternata*, white, spring, and usually again in autumn, 6 ft., Mexico.

CHORIZEMA (Flame Pea) – *Leguminosae.* Slightly tender evergreen shrubs with slender stems and pea-type flower. All are native to Australia.

Compost, equal parts fibrous peat and lime-free loam, one-fourth part sand. Position, pots, or in well-drained beds in a cool greenhouse, minimum winter temp. 7°C. Firm potting essential. Prune straggling shoots slightly after flowering. Water normally. No shade required at any time. In warm sunny places where wood gets well ripened, chorizemas will survive several degrees of frost and can be grown outdoors.

Increase by seeds sown in sandy compost in temp. 13 to 15°C. in spring; by cuttings in sandy peat in a propagator in summer or autumn. Grow young plants in pots as chorizemas resent root disturbance.

Recommended kinds are *C. cordatum*, purple, scarlet, and yellow, summer, 3 ft.; *ilicifolium*, crimson, red and yellow, summer, 2 to 3 ft.; *varium* (syn. *chandleri*), yellow, red and purple, summer, 4 ft.

CHRYSANTHEMUM – *Compositae*. A large genus of more or less tender and hardy perennials (some sub-shrubby) and hardy annuals.

Culture of annuals: Soil, ordinary. Position, open sunny. Sow seeds outdoors in spring where plants are to flower or sow under glass and plant out later.

Culture of Marguerites: Insert cuttings singly, or three in a 4-in. pot, in spring or summer in a propagator. Pot rooted cuttings in 3-in. pots in John Innes potting compost No. 1 or equivalent, moving into 5-in. pots and John Innes potting compost No. 2 when the smaller pots are filled with roots. Stand plants outdoors in full sun in summer but keep in a light frost-proof greenhouse in winter. Marguerites will survive a few degrees of frost and can be grown outdoors all year in mild climates but in colder places are either used as cool greenhouse plants or summer bedding plants. If grown as greenhouse plants water normally. Feed with weak liquid manure or fertilizer in summer. Marguerites can also be grown from seeds sown in a temp. 15 to 18°C. in spring, subsequent treatment being as for plants raised from cuttings.

Culture of Florists' Chrysanthemum: Best grown afresh from cuttings each year. Prepare cuttings in late winter and spring from young shoots growing directly from the roots of old plants. Insert cuttings in a mixture of equal parts of loam, peat and sand in a frame or propagator, air temp. 10°C., soil temp. 15°C. When rooted pot young plants singly in 3-in. pots in John Innes potting compost No. 1 or equivalent, and move on as necessary to 5-, 7- or 8-in. pots in John Innes potting compost No. 2. Early flowering (border) varieties need not be potted on but instead can be hardened off and planted outdoors in mid- to late spring in good, rather rich, loamy soil and a sunny open place. Space plants at least 15 in. apart and tie stems as they grow to canes or provide other suitable support. Late-flowering kinds, grown in pots throughout, may be stood outdoors in summer in a sunny, reasonably sheltered place. Water freely and feed every 7 to 10 days with weak liquid manure or fertilizer but discontinue feeding when flower buds start to open. If large flowers are required restrict the number of stems per plant to not more than seven, also restrict flower buds to one per stem, removing all others while still very small. Return late-flowering varieties to a cool greenhouse, minimum temp. 10°C., in early autumn before there is danger of frost but ventilate as freely as possible consistent with maintaining the required minimum temperature. Water carefully to avoid wetting leaves or flowers and maintain a dry atmosphere. After flowering cut down all stems to within 4 in. of the base but only keep enough plants to provide cuttings for the following year.

Alternatively, chrysanthemums can be grown from seeds sown in late winter or early spring in John Innes seed compost or equivalent in temp. 15 to 18°C., seedlings being pricked out in John Innes potting compost No. 1 and subsequently treated in the same way as plants from cuttings. This is a good way to grow the Charm and Cascade varieties with numerous relatively small single flowers.

Anemone-centred chrysanthemum

Incurved chrysanthemum

Pompon chrysanthemum

Reflexed chrysanthemum

Quill-petalled chrysanthemum

Single chrysanthemum

Culture of hardy perennial species:
Soil, ordinary, well drained for *C. còccineum* and varieties. Position, open, sunny. Plant in spring or autumn, *C. rubellum* in spring.

Increase hardy perennial species by division in spring; by seeds sown in a frame or outdoors in spring or early summer.

Recommended annual kinds are *C. carinatum*, Tricolor Chrysanthemum, white, red, purple, yellow, disk purple, summer, 2 ft., N. Africa, single- and double-flowered varieties; *coronarium*, yellow and white, summer, 3 ft., S. Europe, single- and double-flowered varieties; *multicaule*, yellow, summer, 6 to 12 in., Algeria; *segetum*, Corn Marigold, yellow, summer, 1½ ft., Europe (Britain), and vars. Eastern Star, primrose and brown, and Evening Star, large yellow flowers; *spectabilis*, yellow and white, summer, 3 to 4 ft., hybrid between *carinatum* and *coronarium*.

Recommended hardy species are *C. coccineum* (syn. *Pyrethrum roseum*), Pyrethrum, white to crimson, late spring, early summer, 1½ to 3 ft., Caucasus, Iran, and many varieties white, pink, red and crimson, single and double flowered; *leucanthemum*, Oxeye Daisy, white, summer, 2 ft., Europe (Britain), N. America; *maximum*, Shasta Daisy, white, summer, 2 to 3 ft., Pyrenees, and many varieties, some semi-double or double, some with fringed ray flowers; *nipponicum*, white, summer, 1½ to 2 ft., Japan; *parthenium* (syn. *Matricaria eximia*), Feverfew, white, summer, 2 ft., Europe, var. *aureum*, Golden Feather, yellow leaves; *uliginosum*, Giant Daisy, white, autumn, 5 ft., E. Europe.

Recommended other kinds are *C. frutescens*, Marguerite or Paris Daisy, white or yellow, summer, 3 ft., Canary Islands; Florists' Chrysanthemum, white, pink, salmon, crimson, purple, bronze, orange, yellow, etc., summer, autumn and winter, 1 to 6 ft., hybrids between *indicum*, yellow, China, Japan, *morifolium*, white, China, and possibly other species, available in a vast number of varieties, single, semi-double and fully double flowered in all manner of forms and types: Incurving, making ball-shaped flowers, Recurved, making mop-headed flowers, Quilled petalled, Spoon petalled, etc; *rubellum*, pink, summer and autumn, 2 to 3 ft., origin uncertain.

CHRYSOSPLENIUM (Golden Saxifrage, Water Carpet) – *Saxifragaceae*. Hardy perennial semi-aquatic herbs with clusters of small flowers.

Soil, boggy peat or wet loam. Position, damp and shady watercourses or ditches. Plant in spring or autumn.

Increase by division of plants in spring.

Recommended kinds are *C. alternifolium*, yellow, spring and summer, 3 in., Northern Hemisphere (Britain); *oppositifolium*, yellow, 3 in., Europe (Britain).

CIMICIFUGA (Bugbane) – *Ranunculaceae*. Hardy herbaceous perennials with slender spikes of small flowers.

Soil, ordinary, rather moist, preferably not alkaline. Position, shady. Plant in spring or autumn.

Increase by seeds sown in light soil in a frame in spring; by division of roots in spring or autumn.

Recommended kinds are *C. americana* (syn. *cordifolia*), late summer, 3 to 4 ft., N. America; *dahurica*, white, late summer, 6 to 7 ft., Asia; *foetida*, white, late summer, 4 to 5 ft., Russia, Japan, and var. *intermedia* (syn. *simplex*), usually unbranched flower spikes; *racemosa*, Snake-root, white, late summer, 4 to 6 ft., N. America.

CINNAMOMUM – *Lauraceae*. Rather tender evergreen trees grown both for ornament and for economic purposes, the bark of *C. zelanicum* yielding cinnamon and the wood of *C. camphora* oil of camphor.

Soil, ordinary, well drained. Position, open, warm, sunny, frost free or in a large frost-free greenhouse or conservatory. Plant in autumn or early spring. Prune in spring if necessary to restrict size.

Increase by seeds sown in spring in temp. 15 to 18°C., and transfer seedlings singly to small pots while still small so that they can be grown on without root breakage; by cuttings of young shoots in a warm propagator in spring or early summer.

The best kind is *C. camphora*, Camphor Tree, yellow, late spring, early summer, 20 to 40 ft., Japan, China, Malaysia.

CIRRHOPETALUM – *Orchidaceae*. Tender epiphytic orchids, closely allied to *Bulbophyllum*. In many species the flowers form a circle or part of a circle, the lower sepals elongated, and turned completely over. Lip mobile.

Culture and propagation are as for bulbophyllum.

Recommended kinds are *C. collettii*, maroon and yellow, summer, 9 in., Burma; *guttulatum*, pale yellow with maroon dots, variable flowering season, Himalaya; *mastersianum*, yellow, suffused red-brown, variable flowering season, 6 in., Java; *ornatissimum*, yellowish suffused purplish brown with darker stripes, autumn, winter, 6 in., Himalaya; *rothschildianum*, purple and yellow, various seasons, 6 in., India.

CISSUS – *Vitidaceae*. Tender evergreen climbers with ornamental leaves. Flowers inconspicuous.

Compost, John Innes potting compost No. 1 or equivalent. Position, pots or borders in a cool greenhouse, minimum winter temp. 7°C., for most kinds but an intermediate greenhouse, minimum temp. 13°C., for *C. discolor*. Water moderately at all times. Shade from strong sunshine. Provide wires, trellis or other supports for their

Cissus discolor

clinging tendrils. All except *C. discolor* make good house plants.

Increase by cuttings of firm growth in summer taken with a heel of old wood and inserted in a propagator; by seeds sown in spring in temp. 15 to 18°C.

Recommended kinds are *C. antarctica* (syn. *Vitis antarctica*), Kangaroo Vine, green leaves, Australia; *capensis*, green vine-like leaves, S. Africa; *discolor*, leaves velvety green mottled with white, purple and pink, Java; *sicyoides*, leaves green, leaf stalks crimson, Tropical America; *striata*, young leaves pink becoming green, Chile. See also Rhoicissus, Vitis.

CISTUS (Rock Rose) – *Cistaceae*. Hardy and slightly tender evergreen shrubs, mostly natives of S. Europe, but many are of garden origin. All flower in summer.

Although most will grow in any soil, for preference all should have light well-drained soil and sunny, reasonably sheltered positions. Plant from pots or other containers in spring or autumn. They are good rock garden shrubs and excellent for hot, dry places. No pruning except removal of dead portions following a severe winter.

Increase by seeds in sandy soil in a frame or unheated greenhouse in spring, transplanting seedlings singly into small pots;

by cuttings in sandy soil in summer.

Recommended kinds are *C. albidus*, rosy lilac, grey leaves, 5 ft.; *corbariensis*, white, 2 ft. hybrid between *populifolius* and *salvifolius*, one of the hardiest; *creticus* (syn. *villosus*), magenta, 2 to 4 ft., Mediterranean region; *crispus* (syn. *pulverulentus*), magenta, 2 ft., S. W. Europe; *cyprius*, white with chocolate blotches, 6 ft., hybrid between *ladanifer* and *laurifolius*; *florentinus*, white, 3 ft., hybrid between *monspeliensis* and *salvifolius*; *hirsutus*, white and yellow, 2 to 3 ft., Spain and Portugal; *ladanifer*, Gum Cistus, white, crimson blotches, 4 ft., S. Europe, N. Africa; *laurifolius*, hardiest white, 6 ft., S. W. Europe; *libanotis*, white, 1½ ft., Portugal; *loretii* white, crimson blotch, 3 to 4 ft., hybrid between *ladanifer* and *monspeliensis*; *lusitanicus*, white, carmine blotches, 3 ft., hybrid between *ladanifer* and *hirsutus*; *monspeliensis*, white, 2 to 4 ft., S. Europe, N. Africa; *palhinhae*, white, 1½ ft., hardy, Portugal; *populifolius*, white, to 6 ft., var. *lasiocalyx*, pure white, 3 ft., two of the hardiest, S. W. Europe; *purpureus*, reddish purple, chocolate blotches, 3 ft., rather tender, hybrid between *creticus* and *ladanifer*; *salivifolius*, white, 2 ft.; Silver Pink, pale pink, 2 ft., hybrid.

CITRUS – *Rutaceae*. Tender evergreen shrubs with fragrant flowers and thick-skinned, juicy, edible fruits. See also Aegle, Poncirus.

Soil, John Innes potting compost No. 2 or equivalent. Position, pots, tubs or borders in a cool greenhouse, minimum winter temp. 7°C. No shade required at any time. Plants may stand outdoors in summer when there is no danger of frost. Water freely in spring and summer, moderately in autumn, sparingly in winter. Feed in summer with weak liquid manure or fertilizer. Prune plants to shape after flowering, cutting out badly placed or overcrowded stems and shortening those that have grown too long but taking care not to remove young fruits in the process. *C. mitis* makes an excellent house plant for a light room, especially if it can be stood outside in summer.

Increase by seeds sown in John Innes seed compost in temp. 15 to 18°C. in spring or as soon as ripe; by cuttings inserted in small pots of sandy soil in a warm propagator in summer; by layering in autumn; by grafting choice varieties on to seedlings in a propagator in spring.

Recommended kinds are *C. aurantifolia*, Lime, to 15 ft., fruit thin skinned, yellow-green, very acid, Tropical Asia; *aurantium*, Bitter or Seville Orange, 20 ft., fruit loose skinned, orange, sour, Tropical Asia, var. *myrtifolia*, short-jointed, narrow-leaved form useful as a pot plant; *limonia*, Lemon, to 10 ft., fruit thin skinned, pale yellow, very sour, Asia; *maxima*, Shaddock, Pummelo, to 20 ft., rind bitter, fruit greenish yellow, large, round, Polynesia; *medica*, Citron, 10

Citrus mitis

ft., large, oval, warty fruit with scant acid pulp, used for candied peel, Asia; *mitis*, Calamondin Orange, fruit small, globular, skin orange, flesh acid, Philippines; *nobilis* var. *deliciosa*, Mandarin and Tangerine, to 15 ft., fruit yellow or orange with loose peel and easily divided flesh, China; *paradisi*, Grapefruit to 20 ft., fruit large, yellow, slightly bitter, origin uncertain probably E. Asia; *sinensis*, Common or Sweet Orange, to 30 ft., fruit orange, with solid core and sweet pulp, Asia; *tatsiensis*, Otaheite Orange, 2 to 3 ft., flowers pink outside, fruit small, yellow, lemon shaped, sometimes grown as a pot plant, origin unknown.

CLARKIA – *Onagraceae*. Hardy annuals with showy flowers in clusters or spikes. This genus is sometimes taken to include *Godetia*.

Soil, ordinary. Position, sunny or partially shady.

Clarkia elegans

Increase by sowing seeds in spring or early autumn where plants are required to flower. Thin seedlings to 8 in. apart when 3 in. high.

Recommended kinds are *C. elegans*, rosy purple, summer, 2 ft., California, and numerous varieties white, pink, rose, single and double; *pulchella*, lavender or white, summer, 1½ ft., California. Numerous superior varieties and hybrids are available, ranging in colour from white, through rose, pink, coral to brilliant scarlet and crimson, single and double.

CLAYTONIA (Spring Beauty) – *Portulacaceae*. Little spring-blooming perennials, suitable for use as ground cover in cool, shady places.

Soil, ordinary with leafmould or peat. Position, shady borders, woodlands, etc. Plant in spring or autumn.

Increase by seeds sown outdoors in spring; by division in spring or autumn.

Recommended kinds are *C. caroliniana*, white fading to pink, spring, 6 in., N. America; *sibirica*, pink, early spring, 3 to 6 in., Siberia; *virginica*, pink, spring, 4 to 6 in., N. America.

CLEMATIS (Virgin's Bower) – *Ranunculaceae*. Hardy and slightly tender climbers and herbaceous perennials, deciduous and evergreen. Many of the most decorative varieties are garden hybrids of fairly complex origin.

Soil, rich, deep, well-drained loam. Most kinds do well on chalk so long as they are not starved. Position for climbing kinds, sunny trellises, arches, old tree stumps, arbours, etc., also in beds with shoots trained over the surface. Plant in autumn or spring. Place so that roots are shaded but train shoots out into the sun. Mulch liberally every spring with rich compost or old manure.

Regular pruning is not essential but species and hybrids which flower in summer and autumn on growth made the same year can be cut back in late winter, either to within a few feet of ground level or fairly close to a larger framework of main vines. Species and hybrids that flower in spring or early summer may be thinned or shortened as soon as the flowers fade.

Herbaceous kinds should be grown in good loamy soil with or without lime or chalk. Position, sunny borders. Plant in autumn or spring. Topdress in autumn with decayed manure. Prune shoots close to soil level in autumn.

Increase by seeds sown in spring in light sandy soil in a cool greenhouse or frame (but seedlings of garden varieties may vary considerably); also by cuttings in sandy soil in spring or summer, or by grafting on roots of *C. viticella* or *C. vitalba* in spring; by layering shoots in summer; herbaceous kinds by division in spring.

Recommended climbing kinds are *C.*

alpina, blue, spring, 7 ft., Europe; *armandii*, evergreen, slightly tender, white, spring, 15 ft., China; *campaniflora*, bluish white, late summer and autumn, 15 ft., Portugal, Spain; *chrysocoma*, white, late spring, 20 ft., W. China; *fargesii*, white, summer, 15 ft., China, and var. *souliei*; *flammula*, white, sweetly scented, late summer and autumn, 12 to 15 ft., S. Europe; *florida*, white and purple, early summer, to 10 ft., China, and var. *sieboldii*, with ring of purple staminodes; *indivisa*, white, spring, 12 ft., distinctly tender will survive little frost, good cool greenhouse climber, New Zealand, and var. *lobata*; *jackmanii*, violet-purple, midsummer to autumn, 12 ft., hybrid; *jouiniana*, white and lilac, late summer and autumn, 10 ft., hybrid; *lanuginosa*, lavender or white, summer, 6 ft., China; *macropetala*, violet-blue, spring, 8 ft., N. China, and var. Markham's Pink, lilac-pink; *montana*, white, late spring, 30 ft., Himalaya, and var. *rubens*, soft pink; *orientalis*, yellow, late summer and autumn, 15 ft., N. Asia; *paniculata*, white, scented, autumn, 30 ft., N. China, Korea, Japan; *rehderiana*, buff yellow, scented, late summer and autumn, 20 ft., W. China; *tangutica*, yellow, autumn, 12 to 15 ft., Mongolia, N. W. China, and var. *obtusiuscula*; *texensis*, red, summer and autumn, 6 ft., slightly tender, Texas; *vedrariensis*, pink, late spring and early summer, 15 ft., hybrid; *vitalba*, Travellers' Joy, Old Man's Beard, greenish white, late summer and autumn, 30 ft., Europe (Britain); *viticella*, purple, crimson or white, summer and early autumn, 10 ft., S. Europe. There are also innumerable garden varieties.

Recommended herbaceous kinds are *C. fremontii*, purple, summer, 12 to 18 in., N. W. America; *heracleifolia*, blue, late summer, 2 to 3 ft., China, and var. *davidiana*; *integrifolia*, blue or white, summer, 3 ft., S. Europe; *recta*, white, summer, 3 to 4 ft., S. and E. Europe; *stans*, white or pale blue, autumn, 4 to 6 ft., Japan.

CLEOME (Spider Flower) – *Cleomaceae*. Slightly tender annuals with spider-like flowers.

Sow seeds in temp. 15 to 18°C. and harden

Cleome spinosa

off seedlings for planting outdoors in reasonably good soil and a sunny position when danger of frost is over, or sow outdoors rather late in spring where plants are to bloom.

The best kind is *C. spinosa* (syn. *pungens*), rose-purple or white, summer, 3 to 4 ft., Tropical America.

CLERODENDRUM – *Verbenaceae*. Tender and moderately hardy flowering shrubs and climbers. The hardier kinds can be grown outdoors in many temperate regions but may be killed to ground level by severe frost. They like good loamy soil and warm, sunny places. Plant in autumn or early spring. *C. bungei* can be pruned almost to ground level each spring; *C. trichotomum* can also be pruned in early spring, previous year's stems being shortened to a couple of growth buds each.

More tender kinds make excellent plants for an intermediate greenhouse in pots, tubs or borders of prepared soil. Grow in equal parts of loam, peat, leafmould, decayed manure and coarse sand. Pot in early spring. Prune shoots after flowering to within 2 or 3 in. of their base. Water freely in spring and summer, moderately in autumn and keep almost dry in winter. Maintain a winter temperature of 12 to 18°C. Little or no shading is required at any time.

Increase by seeds sown in sandy soil in temp. 25°C. in spring; by cuttings of young shoots in a similar temperature in spring.

Recommended tender kinds are *C. fragrans*, Glory Tree, white or blush, autumn, 6 ft., China, Japan, and var. *pleniflorum* with double flowers; *myrmecophilum*, orange, spring, 4 ft., Singapore; *speciosissimum* (syn. *fallax*), scarlet, summer, 2 to 4 ft., Java; *splendens*, scarlet, summer, 10 ft., Tropical Africa; *thomsonae* (syn. *balfouri*), crimson, summer, twining climber to 12 ft., Tropical Africa, and vars. *variegatum* and *magnificum*.

Recommended hardy kinds are *C. bungei* (syn. *foetidum*), rose, late summer and autumn, 5 ft., China; *trichotomum*, white and red, late summer and early autumn, followed by turquoise berries, 10 to 12 ft., Japan, and var. *fargesii*, white.

CLETHRA – *Clethraceae*. Hardy or slightly tender evergreen and deciduous shrubs all flowering in summer and scented. Grow in lime-free loam in open, sunny places. *C. alnifolia* succeeds well near the sea. Plant in autumn or late winter. Cut out some of the oldest stems each winter.

Increase by seeds sown as soon as ripe; by cuttings of firm shoots in summer; or by layering in spring or autumn.

Recommended kinds are *C. acuminata*, White Alder, cream, to 18 ft., South-eastern U.S.A.; *alnifolia*, Sweet Pepper Bush, Summersweet, white, 6 to 9 ft., Eastern N. America; *arborea*, evergreen, white, to 25 ft., Madeira, one of the more tender

species which will survive little or no frost; *barbinervis* (syn. *canescens*), white, 30 ft., Japan, China; *delavayi*, white, 10 to 12 ft., W. China; *fargesii*, white, 7 ft., China; *monostachya*, white, 10 to 12 ft., rather tender, W. China; *tomentosa*, white, 6 to 8 ft., South-eastern U.S.A.

CLIANTHUS – *Leguminosae*. More or less tender evergreen climbing shrubs with showy flowers.

Compost, two parts fibrous loam, one part peat or leafmould, one part sharp sand. Position, warm and sheltered, trained against walls or in a sunny greenhouse. Grow in well-drained borders, pots or *C. formosus* in hanging baskets. Pot or plant in spring. Water sparingly in autumn and winter, moderately in spring and summer. Good drainage is essential.

Increase by seeds sown in sandy soil in temp. 18 to 20°C. Cuttings of side shoots in sand with bottom heat. *C. formosus* does not thrive readily on its own roots, and is best grafted in the seedling state on to seedling stocks of *Colutea arborescens*, the latter being raised about ten days in advance of the seedling clianthus, and established singly in small pots before grafting. Grafted plants are placed in a propagating frame in temp. 18 to 20°C. until union is complete and growth starts, after which the temperature should be lowered gradually.

Recommended kinds are *C. formosus* (syn. *dampieri*), Glory Pea, red with black blotch, summer, sprawling, Australia; *puniceus*, Parrot's Bill, Lobster Claw, scarlet, lobster-claw flowers and fern-like foliage, handsome, 3 to 6 ft., summer, New Zealand, and vars. *albus*, white, *roseus*, and *magnificus*, a large form of the type species.

Clivia miniata

CLIVIA (Kafir Lily) – *Amaryllidaceae*. Tender evergreen plants with fleshy roots and lily-like flowers produced in clusters on stout stems.

Grow in John Innes potting compost No. 2 or equivalent compost in a cool greenhouse, minimum temp. 7°C. Water freely in spring and summer, sparingly in autumn and winter. Shade in summer. Repot when necessary in spring.

Increase by seeds sown in light soil in temp. 15 to 18°C. in spring; by division of roots at potting time.

Recommended kinds are *C. cyrtanthiflora*, orange-red, winter and early spring, hybrid between *miniata* and *nobilis*; *miniata*, scarlet and yellow, spring, 1 to 1½ ft., Natal and var. *aurea*, yellow; *nobilis*, orange and green, 1 to 1½ ft., S. Africa.

CNICUS – *Compositae*. Hardy annual with large leaves like those of a sow thistle but with silvery white veins.

Soil, ordinary. Position, sunny.

Increase by seeds sown in spring where plants are to grow.

The only recommended kind is *C. benedictus*, Blessed Thistle, yellow, 1½ to 2 ft., Mediterranean region.

COBAEA – *Cobaeaceae*. Slightly tender climbing perennials. *C. scandens* is usually grown as an annual.

Soil, mainly loam, with small additions of leafmould and coarse sand. Position, pots or beds in a sunny, frost-proof greenhouse, or against sunny walls, arches or trellises outdoors. In cold places it can be raised from seed under glass and hardened off for planting outdoors as soon as danger of frost is over. It grows so fast that it will cover a considerable area in one summer.

Increase by seeds sown in temp. 15 to 18°C. in spring; variegated variety by cuttings of firm young side shoots in a propagator in summer.

The best kind is *C. scandens*, Cups and Saucers, purple or white, summer and early autumn, 10 to 30 ft., Central and S. America.

COCHLIODA – *Orchidaceae*. A small genus of epiphytic orchids, allied to *Odontoglossum* and *Odontonia* with which it has been hybridized. Habit of odontoglossum but mostly small plants with lightly coloured flowers.

Culture as for odontoglossums.

Recommended kinds are *C. densiflora* (syn. *noezliana*), brilliant orange-scarlet, summer, 12 to 15 in., Peru; *rosea*, rose-carmine, spring, 15 to 18 in., Peru; *sanguinea* (syn. *Mesospinidium sanguineum*), rose-pink, scape often branched, autumn, Ecuador.

COCOS – *Palmae*. Tender palm producing the coconut of commerce. The only species

remaining in the genus, others having been transferred to *Arecastrum*.

Compost, two parts loam, equal parts peat and sand. Position, pots in a shady intermediate or warm greenhouse, minimum winter temp. 13°C. Pot in spring. Water normally.

Increase by seeds sown in light soil in temp. 25 to 30°C. at any time.

The only species is *C. nucifera*, Coconut Palm, 40 to 50 ft., Tropics.

CODIAEUM (Croton) – *Euphorbiaceae*. Tender evergreen shrubs grown extensively in hot houses for their coloured ornamental foliage.

Compost, John Innes potting compost No. 2 or equivalent. Position, pots in a warm or intermediate greenhouse, minimum winter temp. 13°C. Shade only from the strongest direct sunshine in summer and grow in as light a place as possible. Pot in spring. Water normally. Feed with weak liquid manure or fertilizer in summer. Pinch out tips of shoots occasionally to promote branching.

Codiaeum variegatum pictum

Increase by cuttings of the ends of shoots inserted singly in 2-in. pots filled with sandy soil in a warm propagator in spring or summer; air layering in spring.

The best kind is *C. variegatum pictum*, leaves green, yellow, red, etc., 3 to 10 ft., Malaysia, Pacific Islands, and many varieties differing in leaf colour and shape.

CODONOPSIS – *Campanulaceae*. Hardy perennial herbs, trailing or sprawling in habit and with bell-shaped flowers mostly unpleasantly scented.

Soil, good, well-drained loam. Position, sunny. Plant in spring or autumn.

Increase by seeds sown in a cold frame in spring, planting out seedlings in early summer; by cuttings in autumn.

Recommended kinds are *C. clematidea*, white and blue, summer, 3 ft., Asia; *convolvulacea*, light lavender, summer, 3 ft., twiner, slightly tender, Himalaya, China,

var. *forrestii* (syn. *C. tibetica*), larger flowers; *meleagris*, greenish white outside, dull purple inside, early summer, 10 in., China; *ovata*, blue-green veined purple, summer, 6 to 9 in., Himalaya; *vinciflora*, blue, summer, climber, Tibet.

COELOGYNE – *Orchidaceae*. Tender, mainly epiphytic orchids of which only a few species are commonly cultivated. By far the most popular is *C. cristata*, a small free-flowering attractive plant.

Compost, equal parts fibre and sphagnum moss or equivalent. Position, well-drained pans in a cool or intermediate greenhouse. Water freely from spring to autumn, sparingly in winter. Shade from direct sunshine. Maintain a moist atmosphere while in growth. Repot in early spring.

Increase by division in spring.

Recommended kinds are *C. asperata*, creamy white, summer, 2 ft., Borneo; *barbata*, white, autumn, winter, 1 ft., Assam; *cristata*, white and yellow, late winter, spring, 9 in., Himalaya, and var. *alba*, white; *dayana*, white, brown spotted, spring,

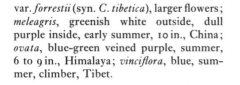

Coelogyne cristata

early summer, pendent, Borneo; *elata*, white and yellow, spring, 1 ft., N. India; *flaccida*, buff, white and yellow, spring, pendent, Nepal; *massangeana*, ochre and reddish brown, summer, pendent, Assam; *mooreana*, white and yellow, winter, spring, 9 in., Annam; *ochracea*, white and orange, spring, 9 in., N. E. India; *pandurata*, green and black, spring, 18 in., Borneo.

COIX – *Gramineae*. Slightly tender, ornamental, flowering annual grasses.

Soil, light, rich. Position, sunny.

Increase by sowing in John Innes seed compost or equivalent in spring in temp. 13 to 15°C. and harden off seedlings for planting outdoors in late spring or early summer, 6 in. apart; or sow outdoors in mid- to late spring where plants are to flower and thin seedlings to 6 in.

The best kind is *C. lacryma-jobi*, Job's Tears, 2 to 3 ft., pearly grey seeds are the chief attraction, Tropical Asia, var. *aurea zebrina*, leaves striped with yellow.

COLCHICUM (Autumn Crocus) – *Liliaceae*. Hardy corms with crocus-like flowers.

Soil, good, moist loam, enriched with decayed manure or leafmould. Position, sun or semi-shade; can be naturalized in grass. Plant corms 3 in. deep and 3 in. apart in summer. Foliage dies down in early summer and does not reappear until spring. It is usually 2 to 4 times the given flower heights.

Increase by seeds sown in fine soil outdoors or in a frame or cool greenhouse in summer as soon as ripe, transplanting seedlings 3 in., apart when two years old; by division of corms in summer. Seedling corms do not flower until four or five years old.

Recommended kinds are *C. agrippinum*, rose-purple and white, autumn, 3 to 4 in., S. Europe; *atropurpureum*, purplish red, autumn, 3 to 4 in., Europe; *autumnale*, Meadow Saffron, purple or white, 4 in., Europe (Britain), and numerous varieties; *byzantinum*, rose and purple, early autumn, 6 in., Greece; *decaisnei*, pale rose, late autumn, Mt. Lebanon; *giganteum*, soft rose and white, autumn; *speciosum*, lilac-purple, early autumn, 9 to 12 in., Caucasus, and var. *album*, white, E. Mediterranean to Iran; *variegatum*, rose and purple, autumn, 6 in., E. Europe and Asia Minor. Also many hybrids.

COLEUS – *Labiatae*. Tender perennials, some with richly coloured nettle-shaped leaves and some grown for their flowers. Often grown as annuals.

Coleus blumei

Compost, John Innes potting compost No. 1 or equivalent. Position, pots in a cool or intermediate greenhouse, minimum temp. 7°C., but overwintering is easier in a minimum of 13°C. Water freely from spring to early autumn, sparingly in late autumn and winter. Shade from strong sunshine in summer but leaf colours are developed best in good light. Pinch out tips of shoots of foliage varieties occasionally in spring and summer to improve branching.

Increase by seeds sown in John Innes

seed compost or equivalent in late winter or spring in temp. 18°C., transferring seedlings singly to small pots as soon as they can be handled; by cuttings of firm young shoots in a warm propagator in spring or summer. Cuttings rooted in late summer overwinter better than mature plants.

Recommended kinds are *C. blumei*, leaves green and bronze-red, 1 to 3 ft., Java, and many varieties with leaves in various shades of green, yellow, red, purple, copper, etc., often elaborately marked or mottled with several colours; *frederici*, purplish blue, winter flowering, 1½ to 2 ft., Angola; *thyrsoideus*, Winter-flowering Coleus, blue, winter, 3 ft., Tropical Africa.

COLLETIA – *Rhamnaceae*. Hardy or slightly tender evergreen shrubs. Branches armed with formidable spines. Flowers scented.

Soil, loamy, well-drained. Position, sheltered, warm and sunny. Plant in spring or autumn.

Increase by cuttings of firm shoots 6 in. long inserted in sandy soil in summer or early autumn.

Recommended kinds are *C. armata*, white, early autumn, bodkin-like spines, 6 to 8 ft., Chile, and var. *rosea*, buds pink opening white; *cruciata*, Anchor Plant, white, late summer and autumn, flattish triangular spines, occasionally bodkin like, 4 to 10 ft., Uruguay; *infausta* (syn. *horrida*), white, spring, bodkin-like spines, 10 ft., rather tender, Peru.

COLLINIA – *Palmae*. Tender palms.

Compost, John Innes potting compost No. 1 or equivalent. Position, pots in a greenhouse, minimum winter temp. 10°C., or in a room or bottle garden. Pot or plant in spring. Water normally. Maintain a moist atmosphere. Shade from direct sunshine.

Increase by seeds sown in temp. 18 to 21°C. in spring.

The best kind is *C. elegans* (syns. *Chamaedorea elegans*, *C. pulchella*, *Neanthe bella* and *N. elegans*), 1 to 4 ft., Mexico.

COLLINSIA – *Scrophulariaceae*. Hardy annuals with small two-lipped flowers in spikes or clusters.

Soil, ordinary. Position, open, sunny.

Increase by seeds sown outdoors in spring or early autumn where plants are required to flower. Thin seedlings to 6 in. apart.

Recommended kinds are *C. grandiflora*, Blue Lips, purple and blue, summer, 1 ft., W. America; *heterophylla* (syn. *bicolor*), purple and white, summer, 1 ft., California, var. *alba*, white; *verna*, Blue-eyed Mary, white and blue, late spring, 6 to 18 in., Eastern U.S.A.

COLUMNEA – *Gesneriaceae*. Tender evergreen trailing shrubs with showy flowers.

Compost, equal parts fibrous peat, sphagnum moss and loam. Position, hanging baskets. Plant in early spring. Water freely in summer, moderately in autumn, sparingly in winter. Minimum winter temp. 13°C. rising to 18 to 20°C. in summer. Shade in summer and maintain a moist atmosphere.

Columnea gloriosa

Increase by cuttings of firm shoots 3 in. long, in pots of the compost just described mixed with sand, in a warm propagator, temp. 25°C.

Recommended kinds are *C. banksii*, scarlet, spring, hybrid; *gloriosa*, scarlet and yellow, winter and spring, Costa Rica, var. *purpurascens*, scarlet and yellow, purple foliage; *magnifica*, scarlet, spring, Costa Rica; *microphylla*, scarlet and yellow, spring, Costa Rica; *schiedeana*, scarlet, summer, Mexico.

COLUTEA (Bladder Senna) – *Leguminosae*. Hardy deciduous flowering shrubs with pea flowers followed by distinctive inflated seed pods. Specially suitable for hot, dry places.

Soil, ordinary. Prune in late winter by simply cutting away weak shoots and shortening straggling ones, or may be restricted in size by hard pruning to a framework of more or less permanent stems.

Increase by seeds sown in spring; by cuttings of firm shoots inserted in sandy soil in summer and early autumn.

Recommended kinds are *C. arborescens*, yellow, summer, 10 ft., S. Europe; *media*, brownish red, summer, 8 to 10 ft., hybrid between *arborescens* and *orientalis*; *orientalis*, coppery red, summer, 4 to 6 ft., Orient.

COMMELINA – *Commelinaceae*. Hardy or slightly tender herbaceous perennials with flowers lasting only a day but renewed over a considerable period.

Soil, light, rich, well drained. Position, warm, sheltered or in a frost-proof greenhouse. Plant fleshy roots in spring. Outdoors protect roots during winter with thick layer of ashes or peat. In cold districts, lift roots of tuberous-rooted kinds such as *C. tuberosa* in autumn and store away as for dahlias in a frost-proof place, replanting in spring.

Increase by seeds sown in light soil in temp. 18 to 21°C. in spring; by division in spring.

Recommended kinds are *C. coelestis*, Day Flower, Blue Spiderwort, blue, summer, 1½ ft., Mexico, var. *alba*, white; *erecta*, blue, summer, 2 to 4 ft., South-eastern U.S.A.; *tuberosa*, blue, summer, 1 to 1½ ft., Mexico.

CONOPHYTUM (Cone Plant) – *Aizoaceae*. Tender succulent plants, all very small, with rounded or button-like leaves. All are natives of Namaqualand. All flower in summer or early autumn.

Grow in a mixture of two parts good loam, two parts coarse sand or grit and one part peat in well-drained pots in a sunny, frost-proof greenhouse or window, or in a bed on the greenhouse staging. Plant or pot in spring. Water fairly freely from late spring until mid-autumn, very little the rest of the year but at all times keep leaves dry and do not water plants overhead.

Increase by seeds or cuttings as for Lithops.

Recommended kinds are *C. albescens*, yellow; *bilobum*, yellow; *frutescens*, orange; *gratum*, magenta; *minutum*, mauve; *obcordellum*, yellow; *pearsonii*, magenta; *truncatellum*, yellow.

Conophytum

CONVALLARIA (Lily of the Valley, May Lily) – *Liliaceae*. Hardy herbaceous perennial, fragrant bell-shaped flowers.

Soil, good loam with some peat or leafmould. Position, beds or borders under shade of trees, high walls or fences for general culture; warm, sunny border for early flowering. Plant single crowns 2 or 3 in. apart, with points just below surface, in autumn. Lift and replant every four years, always planting largest crowns by themselves. Mulch bed annually in late winter with decayed manure. Apply liquid manure once a week from late spring to early autumn to beds more than a year old.

Strong roots can be forced. Place single crowns close together in shallow boxes with peat between the roots, and put boxes in temp. 25 to 26°C. Cover points of crowns with an inverted box or thick layer of moss until flowers appear, then remove. After forcing, crowns are of no value for flowering again, therefore discard them. Specially retarded roots flower quickly without much forcing.

Increase by seeds sown in light soil outdoors in spring; by division of roots in early autumn.

The only species is *C. majalis*, white, spring, 6 to 8 in., North Temperate Zone (Britain), var. *rosea*, pale pink.

CONVOLVULUS (Bindweed) – *Convolvulaceae*. Hardy annual and perennial plants mostly climbing or trailing, some sub-shrubby. Flowers broadly funnel shaped.

Soil, ordinary, well drained. Position, dwarf kinds in open sunny beds and borders; tall kinds at base of arbours, walls or trunks of trees, etc., *C. cneorum* and *mauritanicus* in sunny rock gardens. Plant perennials in spring. Sow annuals in spring where required and thin seedlings to 5 in. apart when 2 in. high.

Increase by seeds sown outdoors in spring; by division of roots in spring; sub-shrubby kinds by cuttings of firm young growths in a propagator in summer.

Recommended perennial kinds are *C. althaeoides*, rose-pink, summer, trailing, Mediterranean region; *cneorum*, white, tinged pink, summer, 1 to 2 ft., silvery leaves, S. Europe; *mauritanicus*, blue, summer, trailing, N. Africa.

The best annual kind is *C. tricolor*, blue, rose pink, summer, 1 ft., Spain, Portugal, Sicily.

See also Ipomoea.

CORDYLINE – *Agavaceae*. Tender or nearly hardy evergreen trees and shrubs grown primarily for their sword-shaped leaves. Allied to and often called *Dracaena*.

Grow in John Innes potting compost No. 2 or equivalent compost in large pots or tubs in a sunny greenhouse or plant *C. australis* outdoors in moderately rich well-drained soil and a warm, sunny, sheltered place; *C. indivisa* in moister soil and a semi-shady place. Both these species will survive several degrees of frost, but *C. terminalis* requires a minimum temperature of 10°C. and is most suitable for an intermediate or warm greenhouse.

Increase by seeds sown in pots of light soil in temp. 15 to 18°C. in spring (21 to 25°C. for *C. terminalis*); by cuttings of main stems cut into lengths of 1 in. and partially inserted horizontally in pots of sandy soil in a warm propagator in spring; by cuttings of fleshy roots inserted 1 in. deep in pots of sandy soil in spring in temp.

Cordyline terminalis

18 to 21°C.; by offsets inserted in sandy soil at any time; by air layering in spring or early summer.

Recommended kinds are *C. australis*, creamy white, scented, summer, leaves sword like and green, 15 to 40 ft., New Zealand; *banksii*, white, summer, ribbon-like leaves, 8 to 15 ft., New Zealand; *indivisa*, white, green and lilac, summer, leaves, green, broadly sword shaped, New Zealand; *terminalis*, white or pink, winter, leaves broad and green, 3 to 10 ft., Eastern Tropical Asia. There are many varieties with coloured or variegated leaves.

See also Dracaena.

COREOPSIS (Calliopsis, Tickseed) – *Compositae*. Hardy annual and perennial herbaceous plants.

Soil, ordinary. Position, sunny, well-drained beds or borders. Plant in spring.

Increase annuals by seeds sown outdoors in spring where plants are to flower; perennials by seeds sown outdoors in spring or early summer, transplanting seedlings to permanent position when large enough to handle; by division of roots in spring.

Recommended annual kinds are *C. drummondii*, yellow and crimson, summer, 1½ to 2 ft., Texas; *tinctoria* (syn. *bicolor*), yellow and purple, summer, 2 to 3 ft., N. America, and vars. *atropurpurea*, chestnut red, *flore pleno*, double, *nana*, dwarf, 8 in.

Recommended perennial kinds are *C. auriculata*, yellow and chestnut red, summer, 2 to 3 ft., Southern U.S.A.; *grandiflora*, yellow, summer, 2 to 3 ft., Southern U.S.A., and var. *flore pleno*, double-flowered form; *lanceolata*, yellow, summer, 2 to 3 ft., Eastern U.S.A.; *major*, deep yellow, summer, 2 to 3 ft., South-eastern U.S.A.; *palmata*, orange-yellow, summer, 1½ to 3 ft., Central U.S.A.; *pubescens*, yellow and purple, summer, 2 to 4 ft., Southern U.S.A., and var. *superba*, large flowered; *rosea*, rose-pink, summer, 9 to 24 in., U.S.A.; *verticillata*, yellow, summer, 2 ft. The plant grown in gardens as *C. auriculata* is usually *C. pubescens*.

CORNUS (Dogwood) – *Cornaceae*. Hardy or slightly tender, deciduous, flowering trees and shrubs. Some kinds are grown primarily for their variegated foliage, some for their coloured bark (specially brilliant on young stems), and some for the large white, cream or pink bracts which surround otherwise insignificant flowers.

Most will grow in a wide range of soils but *C. florida* and *C. nuttallii* do not as a rule succeed well on chalk and *C. canadensis* likes a deep mixture of peat or leafmould and sand. *C. alba* and *C. stolonifera* succeed well in damp places.

Position, open or shady. Plant in autumn or late winter. The flowering species require no pruning but those grown for beauty of stem, such as *C. alba* and varieties, *C. sanguinea* and *C. stolonifera*, may be cut hard back annually in spring.

Increase shrubby kinds by cuttings of firm shoots in summer or autumn; by layering shoots in spring; by suckers removed from plants in autumn and replanted at once; by grafting in spring on to related seedling stock; by seeds which may need stratification as soon as ripe to ensure good germination, most kinds for four months at 20 to 25°C. then for a further four months at 4°C. but seeds of *C. florida*, *kousa* and *stolonifera* require cold stratification only.

Recommended kinds are *C. alba*, white, summer, 8 to 10 ft., N. Asia, and vars. *elegantissima*, leaves variegated with white, *sibirica*, stems bright red, *spaethii*, leaves variegated with yellow; *alternifolia*, white, spring, 15 to 20 ft., Eastern U.S.A.; *canadensis*, white, early summer, creeping, N. America; *capitata* (syn. *Benthamia fragifera*), sulphur yellow, summer, followed by strawberry-like fruits, 20 to 30 ft., rather tender, Himalaya; *controversa*, white, late spring, 30 to 50 ft., Japan, China; *florida*, white, spring, 15 to 20 ft., Eastern U.S.A., and var. *rubra*, pink; *kousa*, white, early summer, 15 to 20 ft., Japan, Korea, and var. *chinensis*, a superior form; *macrophylla*, white, summer, 15 to 20 ft., Himalaya, China, Japan;

mas, Cornelian Cherry, yellow, late winter, 15 to 20 ft., Europe, and var. *variegata*, leaves edged with white; *nuttallii*, white, spring, 40 to 60 ft., slightly tender, Western U.S.A.; *sanguinea*, greenish white, early summer, 8 to 12 ft., purplish red stems, Europe (Britain); *stolonifera*, white, late spring, 6 to 7 ft., red stems, N. America, and var. *flaviramea*, yellow stems.

COROKIA – *Escalloniaceae*. Slightly tender evergreen shrubs.

Soil, light, well drained. Position, warm, sunny, sheltered. Plant in autumn or late winter.

Increase by cuttings of firm young growth in summer or early autumn or by layering in autumn.

The best kind is *C. cotoneaster*, 6 to 8 ft., a curious shrub with twisted and contorted growth, and minute starry, yellow flowers in profusion in early summer followed by orange berries, New Zealand.

CORONILLA – *Leguminosae*. Slightly tender and hardy shrubs and hardy perennials.

Soil, ordinary. Position for perennial kinds, sunny rock gardens or borders. Plant in spring or autumn.

Position for shrubby kinds, sheltered, warm shrub borders, or trained against sunny walls. *C. glauca* makes a good pot plant for a cool greenhouse. Cut out old, worn-out, frost-damaged or badly placed stems of all shrubby kinds in early spring.

Increase by cuttings inserted in sandy soil in summer or early autumn; seeds sown outdoors or under glass in spring but germination will be improved if hot water (87 to 88°C.) is poured over the seeds first and left to cool before sowing; perennial species by division of roots in spring or autumn.

Recommended shrubby kinds are *C. emeroides*, yellow, summer, 4 to 5 ft., Europe; *emerus*, Scorpion Senna, yellow, summer, 7 to 9 ft., Europe; *glauca*, yellow, most of the year, 6 to 10 ft., slightly tender, evergreen, S. Europe; *valentina*, yellow, summer, 4 ft., slightly tender, evergreen, S. Europe.

Coronilla glauca

Recommended herbaceous kinds are *C. cappadocica* (syn. *iberica*), yellow, summer, prostrate, Asia Minor; *varia*, Crown Vetch, pink and white, summer and autumn, 1 to 2 ft., trailer, Europe.

CORREA (Australian Fuchsia) – *Rutaceae*. Rather tender evergreen shrubs native to Australia and suitable for warm, sheltered places out of doors or may be grown as pot plants in a cool greenhouse. Shorten stems after flowering, which occurs in late winter or spring.

Compost, two parts peat, one part each of fibrous loam and sand. Increase by cuttings inserted in sandy peat in temp. 18 to 21°C. in spring or summer.

Recommended kinds are *C. alba*, creamy white, 3 to 4 ft.; *harrisii*, rose-scarlet, 3 ft., hybrid; *speciosa*, pink or red, 3 ft.

CORTADERIA (Pampas Grass) – *Gramineae*. Large, hardy or slightly tender perennial grasses with decorative plumes. Formerly known and still occasionally listed as gynerium.

Soil, rich, light, sandy. Position, warm, sheltered, sunny. Plant in spring. Gather plumes for winter decoration directly they are fully developed, female plumes are the most durable.

Increase by seeds sown in sandy soil in temp. 15 to 18°C. in spring; by division in spring.

Recommended kinds are *C. fulvida*, pale yellowish buff, late summer, 6 ft., slightly tender, New Zealand; *jubata*, yellowish white tinged purple, autumn, 8 to 10 ft., slightly tender, Western Tropical America; *richardii* (syn. *conspicua*), yellowish or silvery white, late summer, 4 to 10 ft., slightly tender, New Zealand; *selloana* (syn. *argentea*), silvery white, autumn, 4 to 10 ft., Temperate S. America, and vars. *carnea*, tinged pink, *pumila*, dwarf, 4 to 5 ft., *rosea*, tinged pink and violet.

CORYDALIS – *Fumariaceae*. Hardy perennial herbs with finely divided leaves and

Cornus kousa

spurred flowers borne in loose spikes.

Soil, ordinary, rather moist yet porous with leafmould or peat added. Position, sunny or partially shaded rock gardens, unmortared walls and borders.

Increase by seeds sown outdoors or in a frame in spring; by division after flowering; bulbous species by offsets in spring.

Recommended kinds are *C. cashmeriana*, blue, late spring, summer, 6 in., Himalaya; *cheilanthifolia*, yellow, spring and summer, 10 in., China; *lutea*, yellow, spring and summer, 1 ft., Europe (Britain); *thalictrifolia*, yellow, summer, 1 ft., China; *wilsonii*, yellow, spring, 9 in., China.

CORYLOPSIS – *Hamamelidaceae*. Hardy deciduous flowering shrubs and small trees. The scented cowslip-yellow flowers are produced in early spring in pendent racemes.

Soil, loamy, preferably slightly acid but will grow on deep, moderately rich chalk soils. Position, sheltered, sunny or semi-shade.

Increase by cuttings of firm, young shoots in spring or summer; by seed kept at 20 to 25°C. for five months, then at 4°C. for three months before sowing at 15 to 18°C.

Recommended kinds are *C. glabrescens*, 10 to 15 ft., Japan; *griffithii*, 10 ft., rather tender, Himalaya; *pauciflora*, 6 ft., flowers in short clusters, Japan; *sinensis*, 15 ft., China; *spicata*, 3 ft., Japan; *willmottiae*, 10 to 15 ft., China.

CORYLUS (Cobnut, Filbert) – *Corylaceae*. Hardy deciduous nut-bearing shrubs. The grey male flowers and crimson female flowers are borne in spring. Nuts ripen in autumn. For culture of cobnuts see page 234.

Soil, rich loam, well manured and deeply dug. Position, open, sunny.

Increase by seeds (nuts) sown 2 in. deep in autumn in the open garden, transplanting seedlings two years afterwards; by suckers removed from the base of old plants and replanted in autumn; by layering strong young shoots in late autumn; by grafting on to seedlings of *C. avellana* or *C. colurna* in spring, the latter is used to form standards, half standards and dwarf standards.

Recommended kinds are *C. americana*, 9 ft., Eastern N. America; *avellana*, Common Hazel, 10 to 15 ft., Europe (Britain), var. *aurea*, golden leaved, *contorta*, Corkscrew Hazel, twisted branches, *grandis*, Cobnut; *colurna*, Constantinople Nut, Turkish Hazel, tree to 70 ft., S. E. Europe; *maxima*, Filbert, 15 to 20 ft., S. Europe, var. *atropurpurea*, purple leaved.

COSMOS – *Compositae*. Slightly tender annuals with daisy-type flowers.

Soil, ordinary. Position, warm, sunny. Sow in John Innes seed compost or equivalent in temp. 13 to 18°C. in spring, transplanting seedlings out of doors 1 ft. apart in late spring.

Cotinus coggygria

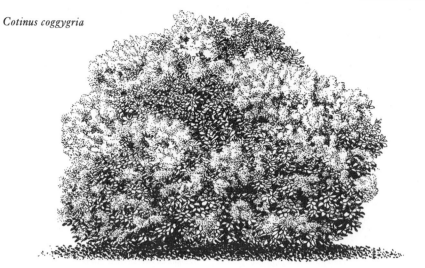

Recommended kinds are *C. bipinnatus*, white, pink to crimson, summer, 3 to 4 ft., Mexico, and numerous garden varieties, some with double flowers; *sulphureus*, pale yellow, summer, 2 ft., Mexico, and many varieties or hybrids from yellow to orange, some with double flowers.

COTINUS – *Anacardiaceae*. Deciduous shrubs grown for their foliage, which colours well in the autumn, and *C. coggygria* also for its curious inflorescences and fruiting bodies composed of numerous filaments which change colour from pink or pale purple to grey. Formerly included in the genus *Rhus*.

Soil, ordinary, well drained. Position, sunny. Keep young plants well watered until established. Plant in autumn or late winter. Regular pruning is unnecessary but if space is limited the previous year's stems can be shortened to two buds each in early spring.

Increase by layers in spring; by cuttings of firm young growth in summer; by seeds stratified for three months at 20 to 25°C., then for a further three months at 4°C. and then sown in temp. 15 to 18°C.

Recommended kinds are *C. americanus* (syn. *Rhus cotinoides*), to 20 ft., brilliant autumn colouring, South-eastern U.S.A.; *coggygria* (syn. *Rhus cotinus*), Smoke Tree, Wig Tree, Venetian Sumach, to 15 ft., S. Europe, var. *foliis purpureis*, leaves purple, *purpureus*, panicles with purple hairs.

COTONEASTER – *Rosaceae*. Hardy evergreen and deciduous shrubs and a few small trees bearing scarlet or black fruits in winter. All have white or pinkish flowers in summer. All are hardy and the wide variety of types makes them useful for many purposes in the garden.

Soil, ordinary. Position, shrub borders open or in shade, trailing species against walls or growing over tree roots and rocks or bare ground under trees. Plant in autumn or late winter.

Increase by seeds sown outdoors in spring. Germination of some kinds may be improved by stratification for three to five months at 20 to 25°C. followed by three months at 4°C. Cuttings of firm young growths of some kinds will root in summer in a propagator or hard-wood cuttings may root outdoors in autumn.

Recommended evergreen kinds, all with white flowers and red berries, are *C. buxifolius*, 1 to 2 ft., S. W. India; *congestus*, 1½ to 2 ft., Himalaya; *conspicuus*, 3 to 8 ft., Tibet, and var. *decorus*, 3 ft., compact habit; *dammeri*, prostrate, China; *franchetii*, 8 to 10 ft., W. China, and var. *sternianus* (often wrongly listed as *C. wardii*), more globose berries; *glabratus*, 8 to 10 ft., China; *glaucophyllus serotinus*, 20 to 30 ft., W. China; *harrovianus*, 6 ft., China; *lacteus*, 8 to 10 ft., China; *microphyllus*, 2 to 3 ft., spreading, will follow the surface of a wall, Himalaya, and var. *thymaefolius*, smaller and more prostrate; *pannosus*, 10 ft., S. W. China; *rotundifolius* (syn. *prostratus*), 3 to 5 ft., spreading, Himalaya; *salicifolius*, 10 to 15 ft., W. China and vars. *floccosus*, narrower leaves, *rugosus*, larger leaves; *turbinatus*, 10 ft., China; *watereri*, 15 ft., hybrids between *frigidus*, *henryanus* and *salicifolius*.

Recommended deciduous kinds, all with white flowers and red berries except where otherwise stated, are *C. acutifolius*, 10 ft., berries black, China, and var. *villosulus*, extra vigorous; *adpressus*, prostrate, China; *bullatus*, 10 ft., pink flowers, W. China; *dielsianus*, 6 ft., flowers pink, Central China; *divaricatus*, 6 ft., flowers rose, China; *frigidus*, 15 to 20 ft., Himalaya, and var. *fructuluteo*, yellow berries; *hebephyllus*, 8 ft., purplish crimson berries, China; *horizontalis*, spreading fishbone habit climbing against walls or to 3 ft. in the open, China; *lucidus*, 8 ft., pink flowers, black berries, N. Asia; *melanocarpus laxiflorus*, 6 ft., flowers pink, berries black, Siberia; *moupinensis*, 8 to 10 ft., flowers pink, berries black, China; *multiflorus*, 10 to 12 ft., China; *racemiflorus*, 6 ft., N. Africa, Asia; *simonsii*, 8 to 10 ft., evergreen in mild places, Assam; *zabelii*, 6 to 9 ft., flowers pink, China.

COTULA – *Compositae*. Hardy, evergreen, creeping rock plants. Any soil, even the poorest. Position, full sun; useful for carpeting in rock gardens and planting in crevices between paving slabs.

Increase by division in spring or autumn; by seeds sown outdoors or in a frame in spring.

The best kind is *C. squalida*, bronze carpets, New Zealand.

COTYLEDON – *Crassulaceae*. Tender evergreen succulent plants. Some species formerly included here have been reclassified and will be found in the genera *Chiastophyllum* and *Echeveria*.

Soil, John Innes potting compost No. 1 or equivalent. Position, pots in a sunny cool greenhouse, minimum temp. 7°C. Water fairly freely from spring to autumn, sparingly in winter. Repot when necessary in spring.

Increase by seeds sown in temp. 15 to 18°C. in spring; by cuttings in spring or summer.

Recommended kinds are *C. macrantha*, red, winter and spring, 1 to 2½ ft., S. Africa; *orbiculata*, red, drooping, summer, to 4 ft., S. Africa; *undulata*, cream and red, summer, 3 ft., S. Africa.

CRAMBE (Seakale) – *Cruciferae*. Hardy herbaceous perennials with large leaves and huge loose panicles of small flowers.

Soil, ordinary, rich. Position, open, sunny.

Plant in spring. Increase by seeds sown outdoors in spring; by cuttings of shoots or division of roots in spring.

The best kind is *C. cordifolia*, Flowering Seakale, white, summer, 5 to 6 ft., Caucasus.

CRASSULA – *Crassulaceae*. Tender succulent perennials, some with very showy flowers. Some are shrubby.

Grow in a light, moderately rich compost, such as John Innes potting compost No. 2 plus one-sixth of the total bulk of coarse sand, in well-drained pots in a sunny, frost-proof greenhouse, close to the glass. Pot in spring. Water freely in spring and early summer, moderately in late summer and autumn, very little in winter.

Increase by seeds sown in sandy soil and just covered with fine soil, in temp. 18 to 21°C. in spring, seedlings to be kept close to the glass and have little water; by cuttings of shoots 2 to 3 in. long in summer in sandy soil, placed on a greenhouse shelf and given very little water.

Recommended kinds, all from S. Africa, are *C. arborescens*, white becoming red, late spring, 2 to 10 ft.; *cooperi* (syn. *bolusii*), pink, spring, 3 in.; *falcata* (syn. *Rochea falcata*), red, summer, 6 to 24 in.; *lycopodioides*, greenish, grown for foliage only, 2

ft.; *perforata*, yellowish, summer, 2 ft.; *pyramidalis*, white, summer, 1 to 2 ft.; *radicans*, white, summer, sprawling; *rupestris*, yellow, spring, sprawling; *schmidtii*, carmine, autumn, 3 in.; *tetragona*, white, summer, 2 ft.

See also Rochea.

CRATAEGUS (Thorn) – *Rosaceae*. Hardy, spiny, deciduous shrubs and small trees with ornamental flowers and fruits.

Soil, ordinary, alkaline or acid. Position open, Common Quick (Hawthorn) in hedges. Plant in autumn or late winter. Pruning is not normally desirable but overgrown trees can be thinned or cut back in autumn. For hedges, plant Quickthorn 9 to 12 in. apart and trim in summer or autumn.

Increase by seeds sown outdoors in spring but germination is improved by stratification for three months at 20 to 25°C., and then for a further three months at 4°C.; by budding choice varieties on to Common Hawthorn in summer; by grafting in spring; by root cuttings in spring.

Recommended kinds are *C. arnoldiana*, white, spring, 20 ft., red fruits, North-eastern U.S.A.; *azarolus*, Azarole, white, early summer, 15 to 20 ft., N. Africa, W. Asia; *coccinioides*, white, late spring, 20 ft., red fruits, Eastern U.S.A.; *crus-galli*, Cockspur Thorn, white, early summer, 20 ft., red fruits, N. America; *douglasii*, white, late spring, 20 to 30 ft., black fruits, N. America; *intricata*, white, late spring, 8 to 10 ft., reddish brown fruits, Eastern U.S.A.; *lavallei* (syn. *carrierei*), white, late spring, 15 to 20 ft., orange-red fruits, hybrid; *macrantha*, white, spring, summer, 12 to 15 ft., crimson fruits, N. E. America; *mollis*, white and red, late spring, 20 to 30 ft., Eastern U.S.A.; *monogyna*, Hawthorn, May, Quick, white, 20 to 30 ft., red fruits, Britain, and vars. *biflora*, Glastonbury Thorn, sometimes flowers in winter as well as in spring, *stricta*, columnar habit; *nitida*, white, late

Crataegus orientalis

spring, 20 to 30 ft., red fruits, Eastern U.S.A.; *orientalis*, white, early summer, 15 to 20 ft., orange-red fruits, Orient; *oxyacantha*, Hawthorn, white, pink or red, late spring, 15 to 20 ft., red fruits, Britain, and vars. *coccinea plena*, Paul's Scarlet Thorn, double red flowers, *rosea flore pleno*, double pink flowers; *phaenopyrum*, white, early summer, 20 to 30 ft., scarlet fruits, South-eastern U.S.A.; *pinnatifida major*, white, late spring, 15 to 20 ft., deep red fruits, China; *prunifolia*, white, early summer, 15 to 20 ft., crimson fruits, hybrid; *punctata*, white, early summer, 20 to 30 ft., crimson fruits, N. E. America; *tanacetifolia*, white, early summer, 15 to 25 ft., yellow fruits, Asia Minor; *wattiana*, white, late spring, 15 to 20 ft., yellow fruits, China.

CREPIS (Hawk's Beard) – *Compositae*. Hardy herbaceous perennials with dandelion-like flowers.

Soil, ordinary, sandy. Position, sunny borders, banks or rock gardens. Plant in spring.

Increase by seeds sown in spring, or by division of roots in spring.

The best kind is *C. incana*, pink, 5 to 9 in., summer, Greece.

CRINODENDRON – *Elaeocarpaceae*. Rather tender evergreen flowering shrubs sometimes known as tricuspidaria. Native to Chile. Pendent flowers, urn or lantern shaped.

Soil, lime-free loam, with peat and leaf-mould. Position, in the open in mild places with some shade. In colder places may be grown against a partially shaded wall or in tubs or large well-drained pots in a frost-proof greenhouse. Plant or pot in spring or autumn.

Increase by cuttings of half-ripened shoots in sandy soil in a propagator in summer.

Recommended kinds are *C. hookerianum*, (syn. *Tricuspidaria lanceolata*), crimson hanging lantern-like flowers, late spring, 10 to 20 ft.; *patagua* (syn. *Tricuspidaria dependens*), white, late summer, 20 to 30 ft.

CRINUM – *Amaryllidaceae*. Tender or nearly hardy bulbs with handsome lily-like flowers.

Culture of tender species: Compost, two parts turfy loam, one part each of peat and coarse sand. Position, pots or deep beds in a cool or intermediate greenhouse. Water freely from spring to autumn, very little afterwards except for *C. americanum* which is a swamp plant. Repot every three or four years. Apply liquid manure to established bulbs in summer.

Culture of hardy species: Soil, rich, deep. Position, warm, sunny, well-drained border. Plant bulbs in spring with tops just level with soil surface. The hardiest kinds will withstand temperatures of about

− 10°C. if well ripened but may be protected with dry litter in winter.

Increase by seeds sown in sandy soil in a temp. of 18 to 21°C. in spring; also by bulbs at potting or planting time. Seedling plants take several years to flower.

Recommended tender species are *C. amabile*, red, fragrant, autumn, 3 to 4 ft., Sumatra; *americanum*, white, spring and summer, 1½ to 2 ft., South-eastern U.S.A.; *asiaticum*, white, summer, 3 to 4 ft., Tropical Asia; *macowanii*, pink and white, summer, 2 to 4 ft., Natal; *erubescens*, white, purplish red and pink, summer, 2 to 3 ft., Tropical America; *kirkii*, white and red, autumn, 3 to 4 ft., Zanzibar; *sanderianum*, white and red, late summer, 2 ft., Tropical Africa; *scabrum*, white and crimson, late spring, 2 to 3 ft., Tropical Africa; *zeylanicum*, white and red, spring, 2 to 3 ft., Tropical Asia and Africa.

Recommended hardy kinds are *C. bulbispermum* (syns. *longifolium* and *capense*), Cape Lily, white or pink, summer, 3 ft., S. Africa; *moorei*, pink and white, summer, 3 to 4 ft., S. Africa; *powellii*, rose, summer, 3 ft., hybrid between *bulbispermum* and *moorei*, and var. *album*, white.

CROCOSMIA – *Iridaceae*. Hardy or slightly tender S. African corms. The common montbretia of gardens is *C. crocosmiiflora*, a hybrid between *C. aurea* and *C. pottsii*.

Common montbretia grows in poor well-drained soil, other named varieties and species in ordinary or sandy loam. Position, sunny well-drained borders. Named varieties of montbretia can be treated like gladioli or, if left in the ground permanently, should be lifted, divided and replanted every three years. Plants left in the ground may need a covering of leaves or ashes during winter.

Pot culture: Compost, equal parts turfy loam, peat, leafmould and coarse sand. Position, cold frame or greenhouse. Pot in autumn, placing six bulbs in a 5-in. pot. Water when growth starts, keep moderately moist until foliage dies down, then keep dry.

Increase is from offsets which spread out around the old corm. Species can be grown from seeds sown as soon as harvested.

Recommended kinds are *C. aurea*, Coppertip, bright orange-yellow, to 4 ft.; *crocosmiiflora*, Montbretia, orange-crimson, 2 to 3 ft., late summer, hybrid, and many named varieties of it; *masonorum*, reddish orange, 2½ to 3 ft., arching stems, pleated leaves, summer, S. Africa; *pottsii*, orange-yellow, summer, 3 ft.

CROCUS – *Iridaceae*. Hardy corms which do best in light rich soil. Position for common kinds, margins of beds or borders or in grass plots and lawns, open or in shade; for choice kinds, sunny, well-drained beds, or on rock gardens.

Plant spring-flowering species and varieties in autumn; autumn-flowering species in late summer, as available. Depth and distance – common kinds, 3 in., choice and rare kinds, 2 in. Leave corms undisturbed for four or five years, unless their place is wanted for other plants. Lift when necessary in summer, drying corms and storing in a cool place till planting time. Foliage should not be removed until it turns yellow.

Strong-growing crocus can be grown in short grass: bore holes 3 in. deep and 2 in. apart, insert a corm in the bottom of each, then fill up with ordinary soil; or lift turf, fork up soil below, add a little bonemeal, set the corms in place and replace turf. Grass should not be cut till crocus foliage turns yellow.

All species and varieties do well in pots with light, rich, sandy soil. Position, 10 in a 5-in. pot, or four in a 3-in. size. Pot in autumn for spring flowering. After potting, place in a cold frame and cover with cinder ashes or peat till growth begins, then remove to a cool or cold greenhouse. Water freely when growth begins, give less as foliage fades. Corms forced in slight heat must not be so used a second time, but may be planted out in the garden. To force, plunge the pots outdoors and then place in temp. 13 to 18°C. in winter.

Increase is by fresh seeds sown in light sandy soil in a cold frame in autumn, transplanting seedlings in the summer of the second year; by offsets removed from old corms in summer and replanted at the same time 2 in. deep and 2 in. apart. Seedling corms flower when three or four years old.

Large Dutch Crocus

Recommended kinds are *C. asturicus*, violet, autumn, Spain; *ancyrensis*, orange, early spring, Asia Minor; *balansae*, orange-yellow, spring, Asia Minor; *banaticus* (syns. *byzantinus*, *iridiflorus*), purple and lilac, autumn, E. Europe; *biflorus*, Scotch Crocus, lavender, early spring, Tuscany; *cancellatus*, yellow, white and purple, autumn, Asia Minor; *chrysanthus*, orange-yellow, but very variable (many named kinds), late winter, S. E. Europe; *clusii*, white and purple, autumn, Spain; *dalmaticus*, yellow and purple, early spring, Dalmatia; *etruscus*, lilac and yellow, spring, Italy; *fleischeri*, yellow and purple, early spring, Asia Minor; *imperati*, lilac, winter, Italy; *korolkowii*, yellow, early spring, Central Asia; *kotschyanus* (syn. *zonatus*), rosy lilac and yellow, autumn, Asia Minor; *longiflorus*, lilac, yellow and

purple, fragrant, autumn, Italy; *medius*, white and purple, autumn, Italy; *minimus*, purple, late spring, Corsica; *nudiflorus*, purple, autumn, Pyrenees; *ochroleucus*, white and orange, autumn, Asia Minor; *pulchellus*, lavender, blue and yellow, autumn, Turkey; *reticulatus*, white, lilac and purple, early spring, E. Europe; *sativus*, Saffron Crocus, white, lilac and purple, early autumn, W. Asia; *sieberi*, lilac and yellow, early spring, Greece; *speciosus*, lilac and purple, autumn, Central Europe; *suaveolens*, orange, lilac and purple, spring, Italy; *susianus*, orange and brown, early spring, Crimea; *tomasinianus*, pale sapphire lavender, spring, S. E. Europe; *vernus*, lilac, violet and white, spring, Europe; *versicolor*, white to purple, spring, France and Italy. The numerous large flowered Dutch forms in cultivation were originally derived from *C. vernus*.

CROSSANDRA – *Acanthaceae*. Tender evergreen shrubs with showy flowers in short spikes.

Compost, John Innes potting compost No. 2 or equivalent. Position, pots in a warm greenhouse, minimum temp. 18°C. Water freely in spring and summer, sparingly in autumn and winter. Maintain a moist atmosphere at all times. Shade in summer from direct sunshine. Feed fortnightly while plants are in growth with weak liquid manure or fertilizer.

Increase by seeds sown in temp. 21 to 25°C. in spring; by cuttings of firm young shoots in a warm propagator in spring or summer.

Recommended kinds are *C. guineensis*, lilac, autumn, 6 in., Tropical W. Africa; *infundibuliformis* (syn. *undulaefolia*), orange-red, spring, 1 to 3 ft., India, Malaysia; *mucronata*, scarlet, summer, 2 ft., Tropical W. Africa; *nilotica*, terracotta, spring, 1 to 2 ft., Tropical E. Africa, Mozambique; *subacaulis*, orange, 6 in., spring, Tropical E. Africa.

CRYOPHYTUM – *Aizoaceae*. Annual succulent plant, formerly included in *Mesembryanthemum* and grown for its leaves and stems which are covered in translucent spots.

Compost, John Innes potting compost No. 1 with some extra sand. Position, cool greenhouse, sunny window or outdoors in a warm, sunny place. Sow seeds in spring in temp. 15 to 18°C. and either harden off seedlings for planting outdoors when danger of frost is over or pot singly and grow on in protection. Water fairly freely. No shading required, discard after flowering.

The only kind is *C. crystallinum* (syn. *Mesembryanthemum crystallinum*), Ice Plant, white or pink, summer, S. Africa.

CRYPTANTHUS (Earth Stars) – *Bromeliaceae*. Tender epiphytic plants with flat,

starfish-like rosettes of stiff, coloured leaves.

Compost, equal parts peat, osmunda fibre and coarse sand. Pot in spring. Position, well-drained pots or pans in an intermediate or warm greenhouse, minimum winter temp. 13°C., or in well-warmed reasonably light rooms. Shade in summer from direct sunshine. Water moderately from spring to autumn, sparingly in winter.

Increase by large offsets inserted singly in small pots in temp. 25°C. in spring; by seeds sown as soon as ripe on the surface of a thin layer of coarse sand over a much thicker layer of leafmould or peat in a temp. 25 to 30°C.

Recommended kinds are C. acaulis, leaves green above, whitish beneath, Brazil, and vars. roseus pink tinted, ruber, brownish red and zebrinus, striped; beuckeri, green and cream, Brazil; bivittatus, leaves green or pinkish striped with buff or reddish brown, Brazil; fosterianus, leaves reddish brown and grey, S. America; tricolor, leaves cream, green and pinkish, S. America; zonatus, leaves green and coppery brown, Brazil.

See also Tillandsia.

CRYPTOGRAMMA – *Cryptogrammataceae*. Hardy ferns with parsley-like fronds.

Soil, equal parts lime-free loam and peat with a liberal supply of broken bricks or stone, quite free from lime. Position, cool, moist shady rock garden, or C. acrostichoides in a hanging basket in a shady unheated greenhouse. Plant in spring.

Increase by division in spring; by sowing the spores as soon as they are ripe.

Recommended kinds are C. acrostichoides, 6 to 8 in., N.W. America; crispa (syn. Allosorus crispus), Parsley Fern, 3 to 6 in., Europe (Britain), Iceland, Corsica, Macedonia, Caucasus, Siberia.

CRYPTOMERIA – *Taxodiaceae*. Hardy evergreen coniferous tree native to Japan.

Soil, deep, rich, moist loam. Position, sheltered, sunny. Plant in spring or autumn.

Increase the type by seeds sown in temp. 15 to 18°C. as soon as ripe; selected garden varieties by cuttings of firm young growth in summer or early autumn in a frame or propagator.

The only species is C. japonica, Japanese Cedar, 70 to 100 ft., Japan, but it has numerous varieties such as compressa, dwarf and slow growing, elegans, delicate feathery, glaucous-green foliage changing to bronzy red in autumn, 20 to 30 ft., araucarioides, branchlets long and thin, globosa, dwarf, globose, branchlets stiffer and tufted, spiralis, dense habit, leaves twisted around the stems, usually dwarf but can make a large tree.

CUCURBITA – *Cucurbitaceae*. Tender annual edible or ornamental-fruited trailing plants. It is to this genus that marrows and cucumbers belong but here only the ornamental gourds are described.

Soil, rather rich, with plenty of well-rotted manure or compost. Position, beds at the base of a warm sunny fence or wall, or on the summits of banks, shoots growing at will up and over the former or down the latter. Sow seeds in temp. 15 to 18°C. in spring and harden off for planting outdoors when there is no danger of frost; or sow later in the spring, protecting seeds with cloches or frames and leaving seedlings to grow where they germinate. Water freely in dry weather. Apply liquid manure occasionally when plants are laden with fruit. Tie stems to suitable supports if they are to be trained upwards, otherwise allow them to grow unrestricted and sprawl on the ground. No pinching of shoots is required. Gather fruit when ripe and hang it up in a dry room till wanted for use.

Recommended kinds are C. ficifolia, Malabar Gourd, fruits large, green with white stripes, E. Asia; foetidissima, Calabazilla, fruits small, green and yellow, U.S.A., Mexico; maxima turbaniformis, Turban Squash, Turk's Cap Gourd, fruits large, curiously shaped, yellow, orange or red, origin unknown; pepo ovifera, fruits small, or various shapes, green, yellow or grey; pepo verrucosa, fruits warted, various colours. The two last are varieties of C. pepo, Pumpkin, Vegetable Marrow, origin unknown.

CUNNINGHAMIA – *Taxodiaceae*. More or less tender evergreen ornamental trees, not unlike araucaria in growth but softer in appearance.

Soil, deep, well-drained loam. Position, sheltered from cold winds. Plant in spring or autumn.

Increase by seeds sown in sandy soil in temp. 18 to 21°C. in spring.

Recommended kinds are C. konishii, 20 to 30 ft., distinctly tender, Formosa; lanceolata (syn. sinensis), Chinese Fir, 70 to 150 ft., will stand temperatures around −10°C., China.

CUPHEA – *Lythraceae*. Tender evergreen plants with small tubular flowers.

Grow in John Innes potting compost No. 1 or equivalent compost in 4-in. pots in a cool greenhouse, minimum winter temp. 7°C., or in sunny beds outdoors in summer when there is no danger of frost. Pot in spring. Water normally.

Increase by seeds sown in light soil in temp. 15 to 18°C. in spring; by cuttings of young shoots inserted in sandy soil in a warm propagator in spring or summer.

Recommended kinds are C. ignea (syn. platycentra), Cigar Flower, red and black, spring to autumn, 1 ft., Mexico; micropetala, scarlet and yellow, summer, 1 ft., Mexico; miniata, red, summer and early autumn, 1 to 2 ft., Mexico.

x CUPRESSOCYPARIS – *Cupressaceae*. Bigeneric hybrids between *Cupressus* and *Chamaecyparis*, all fast-growing hardy evergreen trees.

Soil, ordinary. Position, open or partly shaded. Plant in spring or autumn. If used as hedges or windbreaks may be pruned in late spring or early summer.

Increase by cuttings of firm young growth in a propagator in summer.

Recommended kinds are C. leylandii, dark green, columnar, to 100 ft., hybrid between *Cupressus macrocarpa* and *Chamaecyparis nootkatensis*; notabilis, dark grey-green, hybrid between *Chamaecyparis nootkatensis* and *Cupressus glabra*; ovensii, dark, glaucous green, hybrid between *Chamaecyparis nootkatensis* and *Cupressus lusitanica*.

CUPRESSUS (Cypress) – *Cupressaceae*. Hardy or slightly tender evergreen coniferous trees with small scale-like leaves. Some species formerly included in this genus have been transferred to *Chamaecyparis*.

Soil, ordinary, well drained. Position, sunny, open, as single specimens or to form windbreaks. Tender kinds in a frost-proof greenhouse. Plant in spring or autumn from containers since these plants resent root breakage.

Increase by seeds sown in light soil in spring, transplanting singly into small pots the following spring and planting out of

Cuphea micropetala

doors a year afterwards; by cuttings in sandy soil in a propagator in summer or in a cold frame in autumn.

Recommended kinds are *C. arizonica*, 30 to 40 ft., Arizona; *cashmeriana*, grey-green, pendulous branchlets, to 60 ft., rather tender, origin unknown; *funebris*, Mourning Cypress, weeping habit, 40 to 50 ft., China; *glabra*, grey-green, narrowly conical habit, to 35 ft., Arizona (often listed as *arizonica bonita*); *lusitanica*, grey-green, pendulous branchlets, to 50 ft., Mexico; *macrocarpa*, Monterey Cypress, spreading habit, 60 to 75 ft., California, and numerous varieties such as Goldcrest, yellow, columnar, *lutea*, yellowish green, spreading; *sempervirens*, dark green, 50 to 60 ft., S. Europe and vars. *horizontalis*, widely conical, *stricta*, Italian Cypress, narrowly columnar.

CURTONUS – *Iridaceae*. Hardy corm, formerly included in *Antholyza*. Noteworthy for its arched, branched inflorescence of montbretia-like flowers.

Soil, light, sandy. Position, sunny, well-drained borders, or pots in a cool greenhouse. Plant 4 in. deep and 6 in. apart in the border, or 6 in a 6-in. pot in autumn.

Increase by offsets or seeds in slight heat in spring.

The only species is *C. paniculatus* (syn. *Antholyza paniculata*), orange-red, late summer, 4 ft., Transvaal, Natal.

CYANANTHUS – *Campanulaceae*. Prostrate (trailing) alpine hardy herbaceous perennials with periwinkle-like flowers.

Soil, equal parts of loam, peat, leafmould and sand. Position, cool, semi-shady rock garden or peat beds. Plant in spring.

Increase by cuttings of shoots inserted in sandy peat in late summer in a propagator; by seeds sown in a frame in spring.

Recommended kinds are *C. incanus*, bright blue, late summer, Himalaya; *lobatus*, violet-blue, late summer, Himalaya, and vars. *alba*, white, *insignis*, larger flowers; *microphyllus* (syn. *integer*), violet-blue, late summer, N. India, Nepal; *sherriffii*, light blue, late summer, Bhutan, Tibet.

CYATHEA (Tree Fern) – *Cyatheaceae*. Tender evergreen tree ferns.

Compost, three parts peat, one part loam, one part coarse sand. Position, pots or tubs, well drained, in a shady greenhouse. Repot, only when essential, in spring; these plants do not mind having their roots restricted. Water very freely in summer, moderately in winter. The kinds recommended here can all be grown in a cool greenhouse, minimum winter temp. 7°C. Syringe frequently in summer and keep stems moist.

Increase by spores sown at any time on the surface of finely-sifted peat and sand in shallow, well-drained pans; cover with a sheet of glass and keep moist in a shady position in temp. 18 to 21°C.

Recommended kinds are *C. dealbata*, 10 ft. and more, New Zealand, Lord Howe Island; *dregei*, to 12 ft., South Africa; *medullaris*, Sago Fern, to 20 ft., New Zealand.

CYCAS (Sago Palm) – *Cycadaceae*. Tender evergreen plants with ornamental, feather-shaped dark green leaves.

Compost, John Innes potting compost No. 2 or equivalent. Position, large pots, tubs or beds in an intermediate or warm greenhouse, minimum winter temp. 13°C. Water normally. Shade from late spring to autumn and maintain a very humid atmosphere. Pot or plant in spring.

Increase by seeds sown in temp. 26 to 30°C. in spring; by suckers obtained from the base of the plant inserted in small pots in temp. 26 to 30°C. at any time.

Recommended kinds are *C. circinalis*, leaves to 10 ft. long, E. Indies; *revoluta*, leaves to 3 ft. long, China.

CYCLAMEN – *Primulaceae*. Hardy and tender tuberous-rooted perennial flowering plants.

Cyclamen persicum (variety)

The greenhouse hybrids, obtained from *C. persicum*, need a compost of two parts loam, one part each of leafmould (or peat) and sand. Position, pots in a greenhouse from autumn to the end of frosts, a cold frame other times. Repot in summer placing the tuber above the surface of the compost. Water moderately until new growth begins, then increase supply, decreasing it when plants have ceased to flower, keeping roots nearly dry and cool during summer. Apply liquid manure when in flower. Greenhouse temp. 10 to 13°C. Tubers should not be grown for more than two years. Best results are obtained from seedling plants one year old. Shade from sun essential.

Hardy species need rich, friable loam containing plenty of leafmould or peat. Position, sheltered, partially shady nooks of rock garden or in short turf under trees. Plant in early autumn, 2 or 3 in. apart and 1½ in. deep. Topdress with decayed manure and rich soil annually after the leaves die down, taking care not to cover the tubers.

May also be grown in pots or pans in a cold greenhouse or frame.

Increase by seeds sown in well-drained pans of light soil, greenhouse hybrids in a temperature of 13°C. in late summer or late winter; species by seeds sown similarly in a cold frame in the autumn, transplanting the seedlings the following spring. Cover surface of soil in seed pans with a layer of moss to keep soil uniformly moist. Seeds take several weeks to germinate.

The best greenhouse kind is *C. persicum* (syn. *indicum*), white or pink, fragrant, mottled leaves, winter, spring, scented, 6 to 12 in., Eastern Mediterranean, and many varieties with larger flowers, white, pink, red and purple, some double, rarely fragrant.

Recommended hardy kinds are *C. africanum*, red and white, autumn, 6 in., N. Africa; *atkinsii*, purple and white, hybrid; *coum*, a variable group including former species *hiemale*, *ibericum*, *orbiculatum*, etc., carmine, pink or white with crimson spots at the base of petals, late winter and early spring, 4 in., S. Europe to Iran; *europaeum* (syn. *purpurascens*), carmine, summer, early autumn, scented, 6 in., S. Europe to N. Carpathians; *graecum*, rose-red, autumn, 3 in., S. E. Europe; *neapolitanum* (syn. *hederaefolium*), red or white, summer or autumn, 6 in., Europe (Britain); *repandum*, rosy red, spring, 4 in., Mediterranean region.

CYCNOCHES (Swan Orchid) – *Orchidaceae*. Tender epiphytic orchids with long pseudobulbs and very distinctive flowers with a curved column, hence the popular name Swan Orchid.

Compost, equal parts fibre, sphagnum moss and peat. Position, pots in a warm greenhouse, but intermediate house temperatures suffice in winter. Water fairly freely from spring to autumn but keep almost dry in winter. Maintain a moist atmosphere while in growth and give plenty of light but shade from direct sunshine.

Cycnoches chlorochilon

Increase by division of plants when potting in spring.

Recommended kinds are *C. chlorochilon*, yellow or yellowish green, lip creamy white with a black-green blotch, summer, 2 ft., Brazil, Demarara; *loddigesii*, greenish, suffused purple-brown, lip whitish, red spotted, summer, Brazil.

CYDONIA (Common Quince) – *Rosaceae*. A small deciduous, much-branching tree grown primarily for its edible fruit, and as a rootstock for pears. It is quite decorative in flower. For Japanese Quince, see Chaenomeles.

Soil, ordinary. Position, sunny. Plant in autumn. Prune in winter as necessary to preserve the shape of the tree and prevent overcrowding of branches.

Increase by seeds kept for three months at 4°C. and then sown outdoors or in a frame; by cuttings in summer or autumn; by layering in autumn.

The only species is *C. oblonga* (syns. *vulgaris, Pyrus cydonia*), white or pale pink, late spring, to 18 ft., fruits yellow, scented, apple or pear shaped, Central Asia.

CYMBALARIA – *Scrophulariaceae*. Creeping herbaceous perennials, hardy or slightly tender, often included in the genus *Linaria*.

Soil, ordinary, well drained. Position, moist and partly shady; sunny or shady walls for *C. muralis* and *C. pallida*. Plant in spring or autumn.

Increase by division in spring or autumn; by seeds sown outdoors or in a frame in spring.

Recommended kinds are *C. aequitriloba*, pale violet, summer, mat forming, S. Europe; *hepaticifolia*, lilac, summer, trailing, slightly tender, Corsica; *muralis* (syn. *Linaria cymbalaria*), Kenilworth Ivy, Ivy-leaved Toadflax, Mother of Millions, lilac, summer, trailing, Europe (Britain); *pallida*, blue, summer, trailing, S. Europe, Italy; *pilosa*, lavender and yellow, summer, mat forming, Italy.

CYMBIDIUM – *Orchidaceae*. Epiphytic, semi-epiphytic and terrestrial orchids. The spikes are produced from the base of the pseudobulbs and in many carry large long-lasting flowers. An immense number of hybrids have been produced and have superseded the species as a much greater variety of colour is present.

Compost, two parts peat, one part sand or polystyrene granules. Position, pots in a cool or intermediate greenhouse. Repot, if necessary, in early spring as growth appears, earlier if extra heat can be maintained. Water fairly freely from spring to autumn. Usually growths or flower spikes are present through the winter and so some water must be given. Admit night air whenever conditions are favourable. Syringe freely in summer, and shade from direct sunshine.

Increase by division of plants, or healthy back bulbs may be removed and placed on compost in a damp position. Pot when growth is seen.

Recommended kinds are *C. canaliculatum*, olive green or purplish brown, spring, 1 ft., N. E. Australia; *devonianum*, olive green and purple, spring, pendent, Assam, Sikkim; *eburneum*, white and yellow, fragrant, early spring, 2 ft., N. India, Burma; *ensifolium*, greenish yellow and brown, fragrant, autumn, Assam, China, Japan; *erythrostylum*, white and red, autumn, 1 ft., Vietnam; *finlaysonianum*, tawny red to yellow, summer, pendent, S. W. Asia; *giganteum*, yellowish green striped brown, autumn, 2 ft., Himalaya; *insigne*, pink to white marked with red, spring, 3 to 4 ft., Vietnam; *lowianum*, yellowish green suffused with reddish brown, lip cream blotched red, spring, Burma, var. *concolor*, yellow, tinted green; *pumilum*, reddish brown, yellow and red, spring, 1 ft., Formosa; *tigrinum*, yellowish, marked crimson, summer, 1 ft., Burma; *tracyanum*, yellowish with red-brown lines, lip cream colour spotted red, scented, autumn, 3 ft., Burma.

CYNARA – *Compositae*. Hardy herbaceous perennials with handsome, divided grey leaves and large thistle-like flower heads. Grown as vegetables but also of great ornamental value.

Soil, light, deep, rich. Position, open and sunny. Plant in spring.

Increase by suckers removed in spring; by seeds sown outdoors or in a frame in spring.

Recommended kinds are *C. cardunculus*, Cardoon, purple, summer and early autumn, 4 to 6 ft., S. Europe; *scolymus*, Globe Artichoke, late summer and early autumn, 3 to 6 ft., origin uncertain, and var. *glauca*, blue-grey foliage.

CYNOGLOSSUM – *Boraginaceae*. Hardy perennials and biennials with forget-me-not-like flowers.

Soil, ordinary, well drained. Position, sunny beds and rock gardens. Plant in spring or early autumn.

Increase by seeds sown outdoors in spring; perennials also by division in spring or autumn. If seed of *C. amabile* is sown early under glass in temp. 15 to 18°C. and planted out in late spring, it will flower the same year.

Recommended kinds are *C. amabile*, blue, summer, 2 ft., best treated as a biennial, S. W. China; *officinale*, Hounds-tongue, purple, early summer, 1 to 3 ft., biennial, North Temperate Zone (Britain); *nervosum*, blue, summer, 2 ft., perennial, Himalaya; *wallichii*, sky blue, summer, 8 in., Himalaya.

See also Omphalodes.

CYPERUS – *Cyperaceae*. Greenhouse and hardy grass-like perennials with greenish yellow or brown flowers in umbrella-like heads.

Culture of greenhouse species: Compost, two parts loam, one part each of leaf-mould and sand. Position, pots in a shady greenhouse. Water moderately in winter, freely at other times. Repot in spring. Temperature, spring and summer, 13 to 18°C., autumn and winter, 7 to 13°C.

Culture of hardy species: Soil, ordinary, loamy, preferably rather moist. Position, sun or semi-shade, especially good near water.

Increase by seeds sown in spring, tender kinds in temp. 15 to 18°C., hardy kinds out of doors; by division of roots in spring.

Recommended greenhouse kinds are *C. alternifolius*, Umbrella Plant, 2½ ft., leaves green, Africa, vars. *variegatus*, leaves striped with white, *gracilis*, a dwarfer, more elegant form; *haspan*, 1 to 3 ft., Tropical America, S. Asia, Australia, var. *adenophorus*, 1½ ft.; *papyrus* (syn. *Papyrus antiquorum*), Papyrus, 8 to 10 ft., leaves green, Tropical Africa.

Recommended hardy kinds are *C. esculentus*, Chufa, producing underground edible tubers, 2 to 3 ft., N. America, Europe and Asia; *longus*, Galingale, 4 ft., Britain, S. Europe; *vegetus*, crowded heads of mahogany-coloured flowers, autumn and winter, 2 to 4 ft., South-eastern U.S.A., Chile.

CYPRIPEDIUM (Lady's Slipper Orchid, Moccasin Flower) – *Orchidaceae*. Hardy or slightly tender terrestrial orchids with distinctively pouched flowers. At one time the name embraced species which are now separately classified as *Paphiopedilum* and *Selenipedium* though still in gardens often collectively referred to as 'cypripediums'.

Compost, two parts peat, one part leaf-mould, one part fibrous loam and a little sharp sand and chopped sphagnum moss. Position, open to the sky but shaded from direct sunshine in beds, or in well-drained pots or pans in an unheated greenhouse or frame. Water freely in spring and summer if in containers, but keep compost only just

Cypripedium calceolus

moist in winter. A mulching of leafmould may be given in winter.

Increase by division of the plants in spring.

Recommended kinds are *C. acaule*, rose, green and purple, late spring, early summer, 6 to 12 in., Eastern N. America; *arietinum*, greenish brown, purplish red and white, late spring, early summer, 12 in., Northern U.S.A., Canada; *calceolus*, reddish brown and yellow, late spring, early summer, Europe (Britain), N. Asia; *candidum*, greenish brown and white, late spring, early summer, 12 in., North-eastern U.S.A.; *pubescens*, greenish yellow and brown, late spring, early summer, 18 in., Eastern N. America; *reginae* (syn. *spectabilis*), white and pink, early summer, 2 ft., Eastern N. America.

CYRTANTHUS – *Amaryllidaceae*. Slightly tender and tender bulbs from Eastern S. Africa.

Grow in a compost of two parts loam, one part sand and peat. Position, well-drained pots on a shelf in a light greenhouse. Pot bulbs when dormant, 2 in. deep.

Water little when dormant, especially summer-dormant kinds, but freely when in growth. Winter temperature, if dormant, 7 to 10°C., if growing, 10 to 13°C., summer 15 to 18°C.

Increase by offsets when transplanting, or seeds sown as soon as ripe in a temp. of 13 to 15°C.

Recommended kinds are *C. angustifolius*, orange, summer, 1 ft., winter foliage; *contractus*, Fire Lily, red, spring, winter dormant, 10 in.; *epiphyticus*, red, 1½ ft., grow on moss; *flanaganii*, yellow, early summer, 9 in., winter dormant; *mackenii*, white, winter, winter foliage, 1 ft., var. *cooperi*, yellow; *obliquus*, yellow and red, 9 to 12 in., late spring; *o'brienii*, pale scarlet, 1 ft., winter foliage; *ochroleucus*, pale yellow, fragrant, spring, winter dormant; *parviflorus*, bright red, 1 ft., winter foliage; *rhododactylus*, rose, 6 in., winter foliage; *sanguineus*, red, summer, 1 ft., winter dormant.

CYRTOMIUM – *Aspidiaceae*. Slightly tender ferns with large, thick, shining green segments (pinnae) to the fronds.

Compost, two parts peat or leafmould, one part medium loam and one part coarse sand. Position, pots in a cool greenhouse, minimum winter temp. 7°C., or in a room. Can be grown outdoors in mild places and will survive a few degrees of frost but may then lose its leaves. Shade in spring and summer. Water freely from spring to autumn, sparingly in winter. Pot in spring.

Increase by division of roots in spring, also by spores sown on fine sandy peat in temp. 15°C. at any time.

The best kind is *C. falcatum*, Holly Fern, 2 to 3 ft., fronds spreading or erect, Asia.

CYSTOPTERIS (Bladder Fern) – *Athyriaceae*. Hardy deciduous ferns with small, finely divided fronds.

Soil, rich, deep, sandy loam, freely mixed with pieces of limestone or dried mortar. Position, well-drained, shady, sheltered rock garden. Plant in spring. Water moderately in dry weather.

Pot culture: Compost, two parts good loam, one part leafmould and one part crushed chalk or limestone. Position, shady, moist but not waterlogged or in pots in a shady unheated greenhouse or frame. Water freely in spring and summer, moderately in autumn, very sparingly in winter.

Increase by spores sown on surface of fine sandy soil in pans, covered with sheet of glass and placed in a cold frame at any time; division of plants in spring; *C. bulbifera* by bulblets which form in the fronds and fall to the ground when ready.

Recommended kinds are *C. alpina*, 6 to 8 in., Europe, Asia Minor; *bulbifera*, 6 to 12 in., N. America; *fragilis*, 6 to 8 in., fronds deeply cut, Cosmopolitan (Britain); *montana*, 6 to 12 in., Europe (Britain), N. Russia, N. America.

CYTISUS (Broom) – *Leguminosae*. Slightly tender and hardy deciduous and evergreen flowering shrubs with small pea-type flowers. The genista of florists is *C. canariensis*.

Culture of tender kinds: Compost, John Innes potting compost No. 2 or equivalent. Position, pots in a sunny frost-proof greenhouse, minimum winter temp. 4°C. Pot in autumn. Water freely in spring and summer, sparingly in autumn and winter. No shading required at any time. Plants can stand outdoors in a sunny, sheltered place in summer. Shorten flowering stems when flowers fade but do not cut into old wood. Earlier flowers can be obtained by bringing plants in late winter into a temp. of 13 to 15°C.

Culture of hardy kinds: Soil, ordinary. Brooms will thrive in hungry, light and stony soils and enjoy dry root conditions and full sun. Plant in autumn or late winter from containers as brooms dislike root disturbance. Prune directly after flowering, shortening old shoots to the base of promising young ones but avoid cutting into old wood.

Increase by heel cuttings of young shoots 3 in. long in sandy soil in well-drained pots in a propagator in spring or summer; by seeds sown as soon as ripe or in spring in light soil in temp. 15 to 18°C. for tender kinds, outdoors or in a frame for hardy kinds; selected varieties by grafting in spring on to seedlings of a nearly related species. Seeds of common broom may be scattered on banks or in woodlands.

The best tender kind is *C. canariensis* (syn. *Genista canariensis*, the Genista of florists), yellow, fragrant, late spring, early

summer, to 6 ft., Canary Islands, and var. *ramosissimus*, small leaved.

Recommended hardy kinds are *C. albus* (syn. *multiflorus*), White Spanish Broom, white, late spring, 6 to 10 ft., Spain; *ardoinii*, yellow, spring, 4 to 6 in., Maritime Alps; *battandieri*, yellow, scented, summer 10 to 12 ft., Morocco; *beanii*, deep yellow, late spring, 6 to 18 in., hybrid; *burkwoodii*, cerise, crimson and yellow, late spring, early summer, 4 to 5 ft., hybrid; *dallimorei*, pink and red, late spring, early summer, 5 ft., hybrid between *albus* and *scoparius andreanus*; *kewensis*, creamy white, late spring, prostrate, hybrid between *ardoinii* and *albus*; *monspessulanus*, yellow, spring, 5 to 7 ft., S. Europe; *nigricans*, yellow, late summer, 4 to 6 ft., Europe, Russia; *praecox*, creamy yellow, spring, 4 to 6 ft., hybrid between *albus* and *purgans*; *prostratus* (syns. *maritimus* and *Sarothamnus scoparius prostratus*), yellow, late spring, early summer, prostrate, Britain, Channel Islands; *purgans*, deep yellow, late spring, early summer, 3 to 4 ft., France, Spain, N. Africa; *purpureus*, purple, spring, 1 to 1½ ft., Europe; *scoparius* (syn. *Sarothamnus scoparius*), Common Broom, yellow, spring, summer, 5 to 10 ft., Europe (Britain), var. *andreanus*, yellow and red.

Daboecia cantabrica

DABOECIA – *Ericaceae*. Two species of hardy or slightly tender evergreen flowering shrub of heath-like appearance.

Soil, sandy peat and loam free from lime. Position, sunny banks or rock gardens. Plant in spring or autumn.

Increase by cuttings inserted in sandy soil in summer in a frame; by layering shoots in autumn.

Recommended kinds are *D. azorica*, 6 in., bright rose, early summer, slightly tender, Azores; *cantabrica*, (syns. *D. polifolia*, *Menziesia polifolia*), Irish Heath, St Dabeoc's Heath, 18 in., purple, summer, Connemara, S. W. Europe, and vars. *alba*, white, *atro purpurea*, rich reddish purple, and *bicolor*, some flowers white, others purple, and some striped white and purple on the same plant.

DACRYDIUM – *Podocarpaceae*. Rather tender, ornamental evergreen trees with

75

small leaves and slender branches, related to the yew.

Soil, slightly moist but porous loam and peat in a sheltered position outdoors or in a cool greenhouse. Only *D. laxifolium* will survive more than a few degrees of frost. Water freely in spring and summer, moderately at other times. Plant or pot in spring or autumn.

Increase by cuttings of firm young growth in a propagator in summer; by seeds sown in sandy peat in a cool greenhouse as soon as ripe or in spring.

Recommended kinds are *D. cupressinum*, New Zealand Rimu, Red Pine, 20 to 50 ft., New Zealand; *franklinii*, Huon Pine, 15 to 40 ft., Tasmania; *laxifolium*, prostrate, New Zealand.

DAHLIA – *Compositae*. Tender herbaceous tuberous-rooted perennials with showy, daisy-type flowers.

Outdoor culture: Soil, ordinary, well enriched with manure. Position, open, sunny. Plant dormant tubers 3 in. deep in mid- to late spring, or start them in pots in temp. 13°C. in spring and harden them off for planting out in late spring or early summer when danger of frost is over. Alternatively, start afresh each year from seed or cuttings (see later). Stake all except Dwarf Bedding varieties securely as flowers are heavy and stems brittle. For very large flowers thin shoots to three on each plant; flower buds to one on each shoot. Apply liquid manure occasionally in summer or feed with a chemical fertilizer. Water freely in dry weather. When frost damages plants in autumn cut down stems to within 6 in. of the tubers. Then lift and store tubers in a frost-proof place.

Increase by seeds sown in John Innes seed compost or equivalent in temp. 15 to 18°C. in early spring, potting seedlings singly in John Innes potting compost No. 1 and hardening them off for planting out in late spring or early summer; by cuttings of shoots 3 in. long issuing from tubers, inserted in sandy soil in temp. 15 to 18°C. in spring, treating rooted cuttings as advised for seedlings; by division of tubers in spring. To secure a supply of suitable shoots to be used as cuttings, tubers should be started into growth in late winter or early spring by being potted singly, or packed close together in boxes with potting soil or peat around them, and brought into a light greenhouse temp. 13 to 18°C. Water moderately. Take cuttings just above the tubers.

The best kinds cultivated are all of hybrid origin derived from such species as *D. coccinea*, scarlet, orange or yellow, 4 ft., Mexico; *imperialis*, white and purplish red, 10 to 15 ft., Mexico; *juarezii*, scarlet, 3 ft., Mexico; *rosea* (syn. *pinnata* and *variabilis*), various colours, 3 to 5 ft., Mexico, and others.

Anemone-flowered dahlia

Paeony-flowered dahlia

Collerette dahlia

Cactus dahlia

Decorative dahlia

Pompon dahlia

The varieties produced from this hybridization are extremely varied in form, habit and colour and for garden purposes are classified in a number of types. Principal among these are Decorative, with strap-shaped petals; Cactus, with quilled petals; Ball, with more or less globular blooms composed of short, rolled petals; Pompon, similar to the last but under 2 in. in diameter; Single, with only one row of broad petals; Collarette, like singles but with a ring of short, coloured florets around the central disk; Anemone-flowered, like singles but with a pad of short, coloured petals in the centre; Paeony-flowered, two or more rows of petals; Dwarf Bedding, flowers of various types but plants under 4 ft. high. For exhibition purposes further sub-divisions are made to some of these groups according to the size of the flowers. Colours include all shades of yellow, orange, pink, red, crimson, purple, mauve, lavender, plus white.

DANAE – *Ruscaceae*. Hardy evergreen berry-bearing shrub with bamboo-like growth, useful for planting in shady places and for cutting as foliage.

Soil, ordinary moist. Position, shade including dense shade under trees; good carpeting shrub. Plant in spring or autumn.

Increase by seeds sown outdoors in autumn; by division in spring.

The only species is *D. racemosa* (syn. *Ruscus racemosus*), Alexandrian Laurel, greenish white flowers, succeeded by red berries, 2 to 3 ft., sprays used for indoor winter decoration, S. Europe.

DAPHNE – *Thymelaeaceae*. Hardy or slightly tender deciduous and evergreen shrubs with fragrant flowers.

Soil, loamy, moist in summer but well drained in winter, preferably with some chalk or lime for *D. mezereum*. Position, open, sunny, or shade for *D. laureola*.

Increase by cuttings of firm young side shoots in pots or pans of sandy peat in summer in a propagator, or in autumn in a frame; by layers in spring; by grafting on to *D. laureola* and *D. pontica* in spring; by seeds stratified for three months at 4°C. and then sown, or in cold places sown outdoors as soon as ripe.

Recommended evergreen kinds are *D. arbuscula*, pink, early summer, 6 in., Hungary; *bholua*, purple, winter, 4 to 6 ft., Himalaya; *blagayana*, white, spring, prostrate, S. E. Europe; *burkwoodii*, pale pink, spring, 3 ft., hybrid; *cneorum*, Garland Flower, rose-pink, spring, to 1 ft., Europe, and vars. *alba*, white and *eximia*, dwarf, deep rose; *collina*, purplish rose, late spring, 1 to 2 ft., slightly tender, S. Italy and var. *neapolitana*, rose pink, 2 to 3 ft.; *laureola*, Spurge Laurel, yellowish green, late winter, 3 to 4 ft., S. W. Europe (Britain); *odora*, purple, late winter and early spring, 2 to 3 ft., rather tender, China and Japan, and var.

Daphne burkwoodii

aureomarginata, leaves yellow edged, hardier than the type; *oleoides*, cream or pink, 2 to 3 ft., slightly tender, S. Europe; *petraea* (syn. *rupestris*), rose-pink, early summer, 2 to 3 in., Italy, and var. *grandiflora*, larger flowers; *pontica*, yellowish green, spring, 2 to 3 ft., Asia Minor; *retusa*, rose-purple, late spring, 1 to 2 ft., W. China; *tangutica*, rose-purple, spring, 2 to 3 ft., China.

Recommended deciduous kinds are *D. alpina*, white, spring, summer, 6 in., Europe; *caucasica*, white, spring, summer, 3 to 4 ft., Caucasus; *genkwa*, blue-lilac, spring, 3 ft., China, Japan; *mezereum*, Mezereon, reddish purple, winter, spring, 3 to 4 ft., Europe, Asia, and vars. *alba*, white, *grandiflora*, large and early flowered, *rosea*, pink.

DAPHNIPHYLLUM – *Daphniphyllaceae*. Hardy evergreen shrubs grown for their large rhododendron-like leaves. Flowers inconspicuous.

Soil, ordinary, rich. Position, moist, shady. Plant in spring or autumn.

Increase by cuttings of nearly ripe wood in a propagator in summer; by seeds sown in spring.

Recommended kinds are *D. humile*, 1½ to 2 ft., Japan; *macropodum*, 12 ft. (more under favourable conditions), China, Japan.

DARLINGTONIA – *Sarraceniaceae*. Slightly tender herbaceous insectivorous plant. Pitchers borne on summit of leaves, hood like, bright green mottled with white and pink.

Compost, equal parts peat, chopped sphagnum, sharp sand and loam. Position, cool, shady greenhouse, minimum winter temp. 4°C., either planted directly in recommended compost or in pots plunged in live sphagnum, or outdoors in sheltered, sunny but moist places where there is no danger of severe or prolonged frost. Pot or plant in spring. Water freely during growing season. Syringe greenhouse plants daily in spring and summer. Protect outdoor plants in winter with a frame or handlight.

Increase by seeds sown on the surface of a mixture of fibrous peat, charcoal, sphagnum and sand in a pan standing partly in water in a cool propagator in spring; by removal of rooted side shoots inserted in small pots at any time.

The only species is *D. californica*, Californian Pitcher Plant, yellow and green, spring, 6 to 36 in., California.

DATURA (Trumpet Flower) – *Solanaceae*. Tender annuals and shrubs with pendulous trumpet-shaped flowers.

Culture of annual species: Sow in spring in temp. 15 to 18°C. and harden off for planting outdoors in good soil and a warm sunny position in late spring or early summer. Alternatively, pot singly in John Innes potting compost No. 2 or equivalent and grow in a sunny, frost-proof greenhouse. Discard after flowering.

Culture of shrubby species: Compost, John Innes potting compost No. 2 or equivalent. Position, well-drained pots, tubs or borders in a cool or intermediate greenhouse, minimum winter temp. 7°C. Plants can stand outdoors or be planted outdoors as bedding plants in summer. *D. sanguinea* is sufficiently hardy to survive a few degrees of frost and so can be grown outdoors in mild places. Water freely in spring and summer, sparingly in autumn and winter. Feed fortnightly in summer with weak liquid manure or fertilizer. Prune in spring, cutting back previous year's stems quite hard to prevent branches becoming too long and breaking off. If desired restrict young plants to a single stem until they are about 4 ft. high and then pinch out the growing point, so making the plant produce a head of branches on a bare stem or trunk.

Increase by seeds sown as described for annual kinds; shrubby species by cuttings of firm young shoots in sandy soil in a propagator in spring or summer.

The best annual kind is *D. metel*, white, summer, 2 to 3 ft., India, and vars. *chlorantha*, greenish yellow, *fastuosa* (syn. *cornucopia*), double violet or red, *muricata*, double white, *rubra*, single violet.

Recommended shrubby kinds are *D. arborea* (syn. *Brugmansia arborea*), Angel's Trumpet, white, summer, 7 to 10 ft., Peru,

Chile; *cornigera*, Horn of Plenty, creamy white, summer, 10 ft., Mexico, and double-flowered form often erroneously named *knightii* (syn. *Brugmansia knightii*); *sanguinea* (syn. *Brugmansia sanguinea*), orange, yellow, summer, autumn, 4 to 6 ft., Peru; *suaveolens*, Angel's Trumpet, white, fragrant, summer, 8 to 10 ft., Mexico, and double-flowered variety.

DAVALLIA – *Davalliaceae*. Tender ferns with finely divided usually evergreen fronds and furry rhizomes.

Soil, two parts sphagnum peat or leaf-mould, one part medium loam and one part coarse sand or well-broken charcoal. Position, pots or hanging baskets in a cool or intermediate greenhouse, minimum winter temp. 7°C. (but 13°C. for *D. divaricata*, *solida* and *trichomanoides*). Shade at all times. Water freely from spring to autumn, rather sparingly in winter. Pot in spring.

Increase by spores sown on the surface of sandy peat in pans in a propagator at any time; by division of rhizomes in spring.

Recommended kinds are *D. bullata*, Squirrel's Foot Fern, dwarf, creeping, Japan, China, Tropical Asia; *canariensis*, Hare's Foot Fern, fronds to 1½ ft. long, Canary Islands to Spain and N. Africa; *divaricata* (syn. *polyantha*), fronds to 3 ft., young fronds pink or reddish, Tropical Asia; *solida*, fronds to 2 ft., Malaysia, Polynesia, Queensland, and vars. *fijiensis*, creeping, and *plumosa*, fronds drooping; *trichomanoides* (syn. *dissecta*), fronds to 9 in., Malaysia.

DAVIDIA – *Davidiaceae*. Hardy deciduous tree, unusual subject with the bearing of a lime tree. Each globular cluster of flowers is backed by two large white bracts hanging like handkerchiefs.

Soil, good, loamy. Position, open, preferably sunny, not subject to late spring frosts. Plant in autumn or late winter.

Increase by seeds stratified for five months at 20 to 25°C. and for a further three months at 4°C. and then sown outdoors; by cuttings of firm young growth in summer; by layering in spring or autumn.

The only species is *D. involucrata*, large white bracts, late spring, 40 to 65 ft., Central and W. China, and var. *vilmoriniana*, glabrous leaves.

DECAISNEA – *Lardizabalaceae*. Hardy deciduous ornamental shrub grown for its curious sausage-like grey-blue fruits. Flowers, greenish, pendulous.

Soil, rich loam, moist but well drained. Position, sunny, sheltered from winds. Plant in autumn or late winter.

Increase by seeds sown in temp. 15 to 18°C. in spring.

The only species is *D. fargesii*, yellowish green, early summer, grey-blue fruits, 2 to 3 pinnate leaves, 3 to 10 ft., W. China.

DELONIX – *Leguminosae*. Tender evergreen flowering trees with graceful, fern-like green leaves, and showy scarlet and yellow flowers.

Soil, ordinary. Position, in beds in large, sunny greenhouses or conservatories, minimum winter temp. 13°C.

Increase by seeds sown in light soil in temp. 24 to 27°C. in spring; by cuttings of short young shoots inserted singly in small pots filled with pure sand in a warm propagator in summer.

The best kind is *D. regia* (syn. *Poinciana regia*), Peacock Flower, Flamboyant, scarlet, summer, 20 to 30 ft., Madagascar, and var. *flavida*, yellow.

DELOSPERMA – *Aizoaceae*. S. African greenhouse succulent plants formerly included in *Mesembryanthemum*.

Soil, John Innes potting compost No. 2 or equivalent plus one-sixth its bulk coarse sand. Position, pots in a sunny, cool greenhouse, minimum winter temp. 7°C. Water fairly freely in spring and summer, sparingly in autumn and winter. Pot in spring. Cut back straggly stems in spring. No shade required.

Increase by seeds sown in porous compost in temp. 15 to 18°C. in spring; by cuttings in sandy soil in summer.

The best kinds are *D. echinatum* (syn. *Mesembryanthemum echinatum*), white or yellow, summer, 1 ft.; *robustum*, much branched shrub to 10 in., flowers reddish gold above, red below.

DELPHINIUM (Larkspur) – *Ranunculaceae*. Hardy annuals and herbaceous perennials with flowers in spikes.

Soil, ordinary, well drained but not dry; rather rich for garden varieties of *D. elatum*, Plant perennial kinds in spring or early summer.

Increase annuals by seeds sown in spring or early autumn where plants are to flower; perennial kinds by seeds sown outdoors or under glass as soon as ripe or in spring after being stored overwinter in temp. 4°C.; by cuttings of firm young shoots in a propagator in spring; by division in spring.

The best annual kind is *D. ajacis*, blue, white, pink or red, 1 to 3 ft., summer, S. Europe. There are many beautiful garden varieties differing in height, branching, colour and some with double flowers.

Recommended perennial kinds are *D. brunonianum*, blue and purple, early summer, 1 ft., Afghanistan, China; *cardinale*, scarlet, summer, 3 to 6 ft., California; *elatum*, blue, summer, 2 to 3 ft., Europe, Asia; *exaltatum*, blue, summer, 2 to 4 ft., Eastern N. America; *formosum*, blue-purple, summer, 2 to 3 ft., Caucasus, Asia Minor, and var. *coelestinum*, light blue; *grandiflorum* (syn. *chinense*), blue or white, summer, 1 to 3 ft., Siberia, N.W. America; *nudicaule*, orange-scarlet, 1 to 1½ ft., Cali-

Delphinium ajacis

fornia; *ruysii*, reddish or pink, summer, 2 to 4 ft., hybrid between *elatum* and *nudicaule*; *tatsienense*, sky blue, summer, 2 ft., China; *zalil*, yellow, summer, 2 ft., Iran. The popular garden delphiniums are hybrids between several species such as *elatum*, *exaltatum*, *formosum* and *grandiflorum*.

DENDROBIUM – *Orchidaceae*. Tender, usually epiphytic orchids. Something like 1000 species are included in this widely-spread Eastern genus and naturally considerable variation is present in both the flowers and plants. Some are very small, tufted in habit with stems rather than pseudobulbs, others have stem-like pseudobulbs several feet in height, usually with hard persistent leaves. Many beautiful and free-flowering hybrids have been obtained, chiefly by crossing *D. nobile*, and some of its varieties with *D. aureum*, *wardianum*, *pendulum* and *findlayanum*, but also from crosses between the hybrids themselves.

Dendrobium nobile (variety)

General compost, two parts of fibre or equivalent to one part of sphagnum moss, rather more moss for any kinds of soft texture. Position, pots or pans, well drained and as small as the plant size allows, should be used. The shorter-growing species may be suspended, the pendent-growing kinds suspended in baskets. So varied is the genus, and so widely distributed that only general directions can be given. Much will be gained by studying the character of the individual species. Shading is required in summer for the majority, but this should not be heavy, and very light for the hard-bulbed, hard-leaved kinds. Expose to full light in autumn, especially the deciduous kinds. Water freely in summer, when the temperature for the majority can rise to 30°C. by sun heat, with a humid atmosphere in the day. With exceptions, the Far Eastern species (Borneo, Java, etc.) require a winter night temperature of 18 to 21°C. with moderate humidity, deciduous kinds, especially those from Burma, a more decided rest in winter and minimum temp. 10°C. In none allow the pseudobulbs to shrivel or the leaves to approach flaccidity.

Increase by division of plants when re-potting. By young plants produced on the pseudobulbs in some species, taken off when roots are seen. Some of the noded stems may be cut in pieces with not less than two nodes, laid on sand or peat in shallow pans or boxes and placed in a propagating case with bottom heat.

Recommended kinds are D. aggregatum, yellow, spring, early summer, pendent, Burma, N. India, and var. majus, larger flowers; aureum (syn. heterocarpum), amber yellow and velvet brown, fragrant, spring, 1½ ft., Ceylon, Burma, India; brymerianum, yellow, early spring, 2 ft., Burma; chrysanthum, orange-yellow, crimson blotched, late summer, autumn, 4 to 5 ft., pendulous, N. India, Burma; chrysotoxum, yellow and orange, late autumn to spring, pendent, Burma, var. suavissimum (syn. D. suavissimum), fragrant, maroon blotch on lip; densiflorum, orange-yellow, spring, 1 ft., Assam, Burma; devonianum, creamy white, magenta, orange and yellow, spring, early summer, pendent, India, Burma; falconeri, white, purple and orange, pendent, spring, summer, Assam, Burma; fimbriatum, orange and yellow, spring, 2 to 4 ft., Nepal, Burma, var. oculatum, lip with maroon blotch; findlayanum, whitish, flushed mauve, lip with orange centre, winter, spring, 1½ ft., Burma; formosum, white, orange-yellow in lip, fragrant, autumn, 1½ ft., India; infundibulum, white and orange-yellow, late spring, early summer, 1½ ft., Burma; kingianum, white or purplish, spring, 1½ ft., Australia; moschatum, amber and rose, spring, summer, 3 to 5 ft., Burma; nobile, whitish flushed rose or purple, winter to spring, 2 to 3 ft., N. India, China, Burma, vars. album, white, cooksonianum, purple, sanderi-

anum, deep purple and white, and many other named vars.; phalaenopsis, rose-red to magenta-purple, late summer, autumn, 1 to 1½ ft., N. Australia, New Guinea; pierardii, blush white, rose to primrose yellow on lip, spring, N. India, Burma; speciosum, whitish, spotted purple, various seasons, 1 ft., Australia; spectabile, yellow, gold and crimson red, segments twisted, winter, New Guinea; superbiens, rose and white, purple, spring, 1 to 3 ft., N. Australia; superbum, variable, magenta, spring, 2 ft., Philippines, Malaysia; thyrsiflorum, white or purplish, lip yellow, spring, 12 to 15 in., Burma; victoriae reginae, whitish to purplish blue, various flowering times, pendent, Philippines; wardianum, white, amethyst purple, lip yellow, maroon blotched, winter, spring, Assam, Burma, var. album, white and yellow; williamsonii, fawn yellow, whitish, lip reddish, spring, 1 ft., Assam, Burma.

DENDROCHILUM – Orchidaceae. About 150 epiphytic species. Pseudobulbs small, usually clustered, and single leaved. Flowers small, numerous, the rachis often pendulous from an erect, laterally inclined, slender peduncle. Sometimes included in the genus Platyclinis.

Compost, equal parts fibre and sphagnum moss with just a little peat or leafmould. Position, well-drained pans which can be suspended near the glass in an intermediate house. Water freely when growing, fairly frequently in winter. Shade from direct sunshine at all times.

Increase by division of the plants in spring.

Recommended kinds are D. cobbianum, creamy white, autumn, Philippines; cucumerinum, greenish yellow, autumn, winter, Philippines; filiforme, Golden Chain Orchid, yellow, fragrant, early summer, Philippines; glumaceum, cream or whitish, fragrant, spring, Philippines; latifolium, creamy white tinted green, spring, Philippines; uncatum, green to brown, winter, Philippines.

DENDROMECON (Tree Poppy) – Papaveraceae. Rather tender, semi-woody, deciduous shrub. Flowers poppy like.

Soil, light, well drained. Position, warm, sunny and sheltered or in a sunny frost-proof greenhouse. Plant in autumn or early spring.

Increase by cuttings of well-ripened growth placed singly in sandy soil in small pots during summer; they should be put in a propagator with a little bottom heat till rooted. Also by seeds sown in temp. 15 to 18°C., but germination may be slow.

The recommended kind is D. rigida, yellow, summer, fragrant, to 10 ft., California.

DENTARIA (Toothwort) – Cruciferae. Hardy herbaceous perennials with flowers in short spikes.

Soil, peaty loam with leafmould and sand. Position, moist shady banks and margins of woodland. Plant in spring or autumn.

Increase by division in spring.

Recommended kinds are D. laciniata, white or purplish, spring, 8 to 12 in., N. America; pinnata, white or purplish, spring, 8 to 12 in., Switzerland.

DESFONTAINIA – Potaliaceae. Rather tender evergreen flowering shrubs. Leaves of D. spinosa oval, dark shiny green, with spiny margins resembling those of holly. Flowers tubular, scarlet and yellow.

Desfontainia spinosa

Soil, good, loamy, preferably slightly acid. Position, sheltered and partially shaded, or in cold places in a cool greenhouse shaded in summer.

Increase by cuttings inserted in sandy peat and loam in a propagator in summer; by seeds sown in temp. 15 to 18°C. in spring.

The recommended kind is D. spinosa, scarlet and yellow, late summer, 6 ft., Chile, Peru.

DESMODIUM – Leguminosae. Hardy and tender flowering perennials and semi-woody shrubs dying to ground level each winter. Leaves of D. gyrans animated, especially in sunshine.

Grow D. gyrans in a compost of equal parts peat, loam and coarse sand. Position, pots in an intermediate or warm greenhouse, minimum winter temp. 12°C. Water normally. Pot in spring.

Grow hardy kinds in light well-drained soil. Position, sunny and warm, even dry. Plant in autumn or late winter.

Increase by seeds sown in spring, those of D. gyrans in temp. 20 to 25°C., hardy kinds in 15 to 18°C.; hardy kinds also by division in spring.

The best tender kind is D. gyrans (syn. motorium), Telegraph Plant, violet, summer, 2 to 3 ft., herbaceous perennial sometimes grown as a tender annual, India.

Recommended hardy kinds are *D. canadense*, Tick Trefoil, purple, summer, 3 ft., herbaceous perennial, N. America; *tiliaefolium*, pale lilac to deep pink, late summer and autumn, 2 to 4 ft., sub-shrub, Himalaya.

DEUTZIA – *Philadelphaceae*. Hardy, deciduous shrubs with flowers in clusters or short spikes.

Soil, ordinary. Position, sunny. Plant in autumn or winter. Prune after flowering, cutting out stems that have borne flowers.

Increase by cuttings of young shoots in sandy soil in a propagator in summer, or firm young shoots 10 to 12 in. long in a frame or outdoors in autumn; by seeds sown in a frame or outdoors in spring or as soon as ripe.

Recommended kinds are *D. discolor*, white, early summer, China, and var. *major*, larger flowers; *elegantissima*, rose-pink, early summer, 4 ft., hybrid between *purpurascens* and *sieboldiana*; *gracilis*, white, spring, 3 to 4 ft., Japan, and var. *aurea*, leaves yellow; *hybrida*, rose to white, early summer, 5 to 6 ft., hybrid between *discolor* and *longifolia* and vars. Magician, purple, pink and white, Mont Rose, rose-pink and purple; *kalmiiflora*, pink and white, early summer, 6 ft., hybrid between *parviflora* and *purpurascens*; *lemoinei*, white, late spring, early summer, 7 ft., hybrid between *gracilis* and *parviflora*; *longifolia*, soft purple, early summer, 4 to 6 ft., China, and var. *veitchii*, lilac-pink; *magnifica*, double white, early summer, 7 to 8 ft., hybrid between *scabra* and *vilmoriniae*, and var. *longipetala*, larger flowers; *parviflora*, white, early summer, 5 to 6 ft., China; *purpurascens*, white flushed purple, early summer, 6 to 7 ft., China; *rosea*, soft rose, early summer, 4 ft., hybrid between *gracilis* and *purpurascens*, and vars. *carminea*, rose-carmine, and *multiflora*, white; *scabra* (syn. *crenata*), white, early summer, 7 to 10 ft., Japan, China, and vars. *plena* and Pride of Rochester, purplish pink and white, double; *setchuenensis*, white, summer, 3 to 6 ft., China; *vilmoriniae*, white, early summer, 7 to 10 ft., China.

DIANTHUS – *Caryophyllaceae*. Annual, biennial and perennial plants, some hardy and some slightly tender. Here belong the plants popularly known as Pinks, Carnations and Sweet Williams which are themselves subdivided into groups according to the colour and form of their flowers. Thus carnations may be Cloves, richly scented; Selfs, flowers all of one colour; Fancies, one colour striped or flaked on another; Picotees, a narrow edge of a different colour around each petal, etc. Laced Pinks have flowers of two colours, one clearly marked on another. Auricula-eyed Sweet Williams have the centre of each flower a different colour from the rest. Border Carnations are hardy and can be grown outdoors. Perpetual-flowering Carnations are less hardy and in colder countries are grown under glass. Malmaison Carnations have very large, richly scented flowers. There are many other types.

Culture of Border Carnations and Picotees: Soil, three parts decayed turfy loam, one part of a mixture of equal parts well-decayed cow manure and sand for the exhibition kinds; good, well-drained, ordinary or rich soil for the border kinds. Position, sunny beds or borders. Plant 12 in. apart in early autumn or spring. Topdress with manure or compost in spring. Thin flower buds to one on each shoot. Stake flower stems. Apply liquid manure once a week when buds form. Shade exhibition blooms from hot sun.

Pot culture: Compost, as advised for border carnations. Position, a cold frame in autumn and winter, cold greenhouse afterwards. Plant singly in 3-in. pots in early autumn and then in 6-in. pots in late winter. Give plenty of air.

Culture of Perpetual Carnations: Make 3-in. long cuttings of side shoots from midway up the flowering stems with a few of the lower leaves removed, and insert them in well-drained pots of pure sand from late autumn until spring. Place in a box or propagator, keep moist and shaded from sun till rooted. Temp. 10°C. and slight bottom heat. When rooted, transfer to small pots in a compost of two parts sandy loam and one

Perpetual carnation

part each of leafmould and sand. Stand in temp. 8 to 12°C. till pots are filled with roots, then transfer to larger pots in a compost of four parts fibrous loam, one part each sand and leafmould. Add carnation fertilizer at the rate suggested by the makers. Bonemeal, 4 oz. to each bushel of soil, is sometimes used instead of the fertilizer. Stop or pinch shoots at third or fourth joint after the first potting; again at intervals from the time when shoots are a few inches long till about midsummer. Feed with liquid manure when well rooted. Place outdoors in summer. Winter temp. 8 to 12°C. Ventilate freely in fine weather and give all the light possible. Water normally.

Culture of Malmaison Carnations: Layer shoots in summer. Plant rooted layers in small pots and place in a cold frame or greenhouse and transfer to 5- or 6-in. pots in autumn. Temp. 12 to 16°C. Feed with liquid manure when buds form. Shade in spring from strong sunshine. Admit air freely on fine days.

Culture of Pinks: Soil, ordinary, well drained, fairly rich. Position, sunny borders. Plant 9 in. apart in autumn or spring. Increase by cuttings (pipings) in a frame in summer; by careful division in spring.

Culture of annual species: Sow seeds in temp. 15 to 18°C. in spring, harden off seedlings in a cold frame and plant out in beds and borders when danger of frost is past.

Culture of Sweet Williams and other biennial kinds: Sow outdoors or in a frame in late spring or early summer. Transplant seedlings a few inches apart in a nursery bed as soon as they are large enough to handle and remove to flowering positions in the autumn.

Culture of rock garden and other hardy perennial kinds: Soil, ordinary, well-drained; excellent on chalk and limestone. Position, open, sunny, rock gardens, banks, unmortared terrace walls and borders. Plant in spring or autumn. Increase by seeds sown outdoors or in a frame in spring; by cuttings of firm young growth in a frame in summer; by careful division in spring.

Recommended kinds are *D. allwoodii*, white, pink, salmon, scarlet, crimson, summer, 6 to 15 in., hybrid between *plumarius* and *caryophyllus*; *alpinus*, rose to crimson, summer, 3 to 4 in., Alps; *arenarius*, white, summer, 6 to 15 in., N. Europe; *barbatus*, Sweet William, pink, red, crimson, white, 1 to 2 ft., Europe; *carthusianorum*, crimson, 1 to 2 ft., Europe; *caryophyllus*, Clove Pink, Carnation, various, 1½ to 3 ft., Europe; *chinensis*, Chinese or Indian Pink, various, 6 to 12 in., annual, E. Asia, var. *heddewigii*, a Japanese variety from which most garden annual pinks have been developed; *deltoides*, Maiden Pink, rose, summer, 6 to 9 in., Europe (Britain) to Japan, and vars. *albus*, white, Brilliant, crimson; *glacialis*, Glacier Pink, pink and white, summer, 4

Dicentra spectabilis

in., Europe; *gratianopolitanus* (syn. *caesius*), Cheddar Pink, rose, fragrant, late spring, early summer, 6 in., Europe (Britain); *knappii*, yellow, summer, 9 to 18 in., Europe; *neglectus*, rose, summer, 2 in., Pyrenees; *plumarius*, Cottage Pink, white, pink, red, late spring, early summer, 12 to 18 in., Europe; *superbus*, Fringed Pink, lilac, summer, 9 to 18 in., Europe, Asia. There are many hybrid forms of dianthus in cultivation.

DIASCIA – *Scrophulariaceae*. Slightly tender annuals and perennials with sprays of small, butterfly-like flowers.

Sow seeds in temp. of 15 to 18°C. in spring. Transplant into pots or boxes when large enough to handle. Gradually harden off, and plant out in good soil, in a sunny position when there is no danger of frost.

The best kind is *D. barberae*, rosy pink, summer, 1 ft., S. Africa, perennial but often grown as an annual.

DICENTRA – *Fumariaceae*. Hardy herbaceous, tuberous- and fibrous-rooted perennials. Formerly known as dielytra. Leaves finely divided, flowers two spurred in branched or arching racemes.

Soil, deep, light, rich, porous but not dry. Position, sunny or partially shaded. Plant in spring or autumn.

Increase by dividing the crowns in spring; by cuttings of fleshy roots 2 in. long inserted in sandy soil in spring or early summer; by seeds sown outdoors or under glass as soon as ripe or in spring.

Recommended kinds are *D. canadensis*, white, spring, 1 ft., N. America; *cucullaria*, Dutchman's Breeches, white or pinkish, spring, 1 ft., U.S.A.; *eximia*, reddish purple, late spring, summer, 1 ft., South-eastern U.S.A., and var. *alba* white; *formosa*, pink, spring, 1 to 1½ ft., Western N. America; *spectabilis*, Chinaman's Breeches, Bleeding Heart, Lyre Flower, rosy red and white, late

spring, early summer, 2 ft., Siberia, Japan, var. *alba*, white.

DICHELOSTEMMA – *Alliaceae*. Slightly tender perennials making corms and with clusters of tubular flowers. Many authorities include them in *Brodiaea*.

Soil, John Innes potting compost No. 1 or equivalent. Position, pots or pans in a cool or cold greenhouse, minimum winter temp. 0°C., or outdoors in warm, sunny, sheltered positions in reasonably frost-free areas. Pot or plant in autumn. Water moderately in autumn, fairly freely in spring and early summer until leaves die down when keep quite dry until planting time. No shade required at any time.

Increase by division of corm clusters at planting time; by seeds sown in a cool greenhouse in spring or as soon as ripe.

Recommended kinds are *D. congesta* (syn. *Brodiaea congesta*), blue, early summer, 9 to 12 in., Western U.S.A.; *ida-maya*, (syns. *Brodiaea ida-maya*, *Breevoortia ida-maya*), Californian or Floral Firecracker, red and yellow, early summer, 1½ to 2 ft., California; *multiflora* (syn. *Brodiaea multiflora*), lilac-blue, early summer, 3 ft., Western U.S.A.; *pulchellum*, (syn. *Brodiaea pulchella*), Blue Dicks, Wild Hyacinth, violet-blue, late spring, early summer, 1 to 2 ft., California; *volubilis* (syn. *Brodiaea volubilis*), mauve-pink, summer, 3 to 8 ft., twining, California.

DICKSONIA – *Dicksoniaceae*. Tender or nearly hardy tree ferns.

Grow in a mixture of two parts loam, two parts peat and one part coarse sand in well-drained pots or tubs or in a bed in a cool greenhouse, or plant *D. antarctica* outdoors in reasonably frost-free areas. Pot or plant in early spring. Water very freely in summer, moderately in winter. Syringe frequently in summer and keep trunks moist. Shade from all direct sunshine. Minimum temperature for greenhouse plants 7°C.

Increase by spores sown at any time on the surface of finely sifted peat and sand in well-drained pots, cover with a sheet of glass and keep moist.

Recommended kinds are *D. antarctica*, Australian Tree Fern, 10 to 30 ft., Australia; *fibrosa*, 10 to 20 ft., New Zealand; *squarrosa*, New Zealand Tree Fern, 15 to 20 ft., length of frond nearly equalling height of plant, New Zealand.

DICTAMNUS – *Rutaceae*. Hardy herbaceous perennials with fragrant foliage.

Soil, ordinary, well-drained. Position, sunny or partially shady. Plant in spring or autumn.

Increase by seeds sown in light soil outdoors when ripe in late summer or early autumn; by cuttings of fleshy roots inserted 2 in. deep in a frame in spring; by division of roots in spring or autumn.

Recommended kinds are *D. albus* (syn. *fraxinella*), Burning Bush, Dittany, Fraxinella, Gas Plant, white, early summer, 3 ft., Europe, and vars. *caucasicus*, giant form, *purpureus*, rosy red.

DIEFFENBACHIA (Dumb Cane) – *Araceae*. Tender evergreen perennials with oblong variegated leaves.

Compost, John Innes potting compost No. 1 or equivalent. Position, intermediate or warm greenhouse, minimum winter temp. 13°C., or in a warm room. Water freely in spring and summer, just sufficiently to keep soil moist in autumn and winter. Shade from direct sunshine and maintain a humid atmosphere. Feed in summer with weak liquid manure or fertilizer. Pot in spring.

Increase by cuttings each consisting of one node or joint and inserted in sandy soil in a warm propagator in spring; by offsets removed in spring and started in a warm propagator.

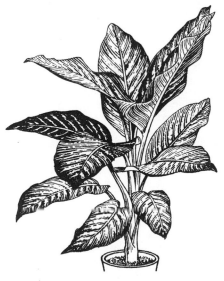

Dieffenbachia bowmannii

Recommended kinds are *D. bowmannii*, leaves blotched dark and light green, Colombia, Brazil; *chelsonii*, leaves green, grey and yellow, Colombia; *imperialis*, leaves green and cream, Peru; *oerstedii*, leaves dark green with ivory stripe, Central America; *picta*, leaves dark green and white or yellow, Brazil, and vars. *bausei*, light and dark green with silver spots, *jenmanii*, green blotched cream, *memoria*, silvery grey edged green, *roehrsii*, yellowish green marked with dark green and ivory; *regina*, leaves white and green, S. America; *seguine*, leaves green, white spotted, Brazil, and vars. *barraquiniana*, light green and white, *liturata*, green with white midrib and margin, *nobilis*, dark green blotched white.

DIERAMA (Wandflower) – *Iridaceae*. Hardy corms which do best treated as hardy perennials, with sword-shaped leaves and long graceful flower stems.

Soil, light or sandy. Position, well-drained border at the base of a sunny wall. Plant corms 3 in. deep and 3 in. apart in late autumn and do not transplant until very overcrowded.

Increase from seeds sown as soon as ripe or in spring; or by careful division of clumps in autumn.

Recommended kinds from S. Africa are *D. pendulum*, lilac, summer, 3 ft.; *pulcherrimum*, purple, carmine, rose, lilac, late summer, 4 to 6 ft., and var. *album*, white.

DIERVILLA (Bush Honeysuckle) – *Caprifoliaceae*. Deciduous suckering shrubs suitable for holding banks, colonizing, or as tall ground cover. For other species sometimes listed under this name, see Weigela.

Soil, ordinary, moist. Position, sun or partial shade. Plant in autumn or winter.

Increase by removal of suckers in autumn or winter.

Recommended kinds, all from Eastern N. America, are *D. lonicera*, yellow, summer, 3 ft.; *rivularis*, lemon yellow, summer, to 6 ft.; *sessilifolia*, sulphur yellow, summer, 2 to 4 ft.

DIGITALIS (Foxglove) – *Scrophulariaceae*. Hardy biennial and perennial herbs with tubular flowers in spikes.

Soil, ordinary. Position, sunny or shady. Excellent naturalized in woodlands and wild gardens. Plant in spring or autumn.

Increase by seeds sown in a shady border outdoors in spring or early summer. Transplant seedlings 3 in. apart in a shady bed when large enough to handle and remove to flowering quarters in autumn. Discard biennial kinds after flowering. When favourably placed foxgloves will often perpetuate themselves by self-sown seedlings but selected garden varieties may deteriorate in quality. Perennial kinds can also be increased by division in spring.

Recommended perennial kinds are *D.*

dubia, purple, early summer, 6 to 18 in., Balearic Isles; *grandiflora* (syns. *ambigua*, *ochroleuca*), yellow, summer, 3 ft., Europe; *lamarckii*, (syn. *orientalis*), buff veined rose, summer, 2 ft., Anatolia; *lanata*, grey, white and purple, summer, 2 to 3 ft., E. Europe; *mertoniensis*, crushed strawberry, summer, 2 ft., hybrid between *grandiflora* and *purpurea*.

Recommended biennial kinds are *D. ferruginea*, rusty red, summer, 4 to 6 ft., Europe; *purpurea*, Common Foxglove, purple, summer, 3 to 5 ft., Europe (Britain), and numerous varieties in white, pink and purple, some with larger flowers or flowers all round the spike instead of on one side only.

DIMORPHOTHECA (Cape Marigold) – *Compositae*. Slightly tender S. African annuals and perennials with daisy-type flowers, usually grown as annuals. See also Osteospermum.

Soil, ordinary, well drained. Position, sunny, warm. Sow in early spring in temp. 15 to 18°C. and harden off seedlings for planting outdoors in late spring or early summer, or sow in mid- to late spring where plants are to flower and thin to 8 in.

Recommended kinds are *D. chrysanthemifolia* (syn. *Calendula chrysanthemifolia*), yellow, summer, 2 to 3 ft.; *calendulacea*, orange-yellow, summer, to 12 in., Namaqualand; *pluvialis* (syn. *annua*), white and violet, summer, 1 ft., the opening and closing of the flowers (really dependent on temperature) was once thought to indicate rain; *sinuata* (often wrongly called *aurantiaca*), orange, summer, 1 ft. Most of the varieties grown in gardens are hybrids between these and possibly other species.

DIONAEA – *Droseraceae*. Slightly tender, herbaceous, insectivorous, perennial plant. The leaves are fringed with sensitive hairs and close together when touched.

Compost, equal parts peat and living sphagnum. Position, pots or pans well drained and partly immersed in pans of water, and placed under glass in a cool greenhouse, minimum winter temp. 5°C. Water freely always. Can be grown in full sun or partial shade.

Increase by seeds sown in a mixture of sphagnum moss and peat and kept moist in a propagator in spring; by division of plants in spring.

The only species is *D. muscipula*, Venus's Fly Trap, white, summer, 6 in., Carolina.

DIOSPYROS – *Ebenaceae*. Deciduous or evergreen trees and shrubs with juicy edible fruits.

Soil, ordinary. Position, warm, sunny and sheltered. Plant in autumn or late winter. Remove frost-damaged or dead growth each spring or early summer.

Increase by seeds sown outdoors in

autumn or stratified for three months at 4°C. and then sown.

Recommended kinds are *D. armata*, yellow fruits, 20 ft., half-evergreen, Central China; *kaki*, Chinese Persimmon, yellowish white, spring, yellow fruits, good autumn colour, deciduous, to 40 ft., China; *lotus*, Date Plum, reddish, white, summer, purple or yellow fruits, to 40 ft., W. Asia. China, Japan; *virginiana*, Persimmon, yellow, summer, pale yellow and red fruits, to 50 ft. or more, Eastern N. America.

DIPELTA – *Caprifoliaceae*. Hardy deciduous shrubs with flowers resembling those of weigela.

Soil, ordinary. Position, sunny, not too dry in summer. Plant in autumn. Cut out dead wood in winter and occasionally cut back old stems to new growth near the base of the bush.

Increase by cuttings inserted in a frame in autumn; by seeds sown as soon as ripe or in spring in a frame or cool greenhouse.

Recommended kinds are *D. floribunda*, pink and yellow, fragrant, late spring, 6 to 10 ft., China; *ventricosa*, deep rose and orange, late spring, 6 to 10 ft., W. China; *yunnanensis*, cream with orange markings, 10 ft., late spring, China.

DIPLADENIA – *Apocynaceae*. Slightly tender evergreen twiners with funnel-shaped flowers.

Compost, John Innes potting compost No. 2 or equivalent. Position, large pots or beds in an intermediate or warm greenhouse, minimum winter temp. 13°C. Water normally. Shade in summer and maintain a moist atmosphere. Cut back previous year's growth almost to the base in late winter, and in summer pinch out the tips of any shoots that are growing too long.

Increase by cuttings of young side shoots, 3 in. long, inserted in pots of sandy peat in a warm propagator in summer.

Recommended kinds are *D. boliviensis*, white and yellow, summer, 8 to 10 ft., Bolivia; *splendens*, pink and white, summer, 8 to 12 ft., Brazil, and vars. *amabilis*, rosy crimson, *profusa*, carmine, and *williamsii*, deep pink.

DISA – *Orchidaceae*. Slightly tender terrestrial tuberous-rooted orchids. The upper sepal is often hood like and developed into a short spur at its base.

Compost, three parts of finely shredded fibre or peat, two parts of sphagnum moss and a little loam fibre and sand. A cool moist atmosphere is necessary and the compost must never approach dryness. They may grow in a cold frame in summer with shading but require cool greenhouse temperatures in winter. Species from warmer parts of Africa need much more warmth and a winter rest with little water.

Increase the stronger crowns from offsets

which may be carefully removed and potted in early spring. Success is occasionally obtained from seeds sown on the compost given previously.

Recommended kinds from S. Africa are *D. cornuta*, white or mauve and purple, spring, 9 in.; *racemosa*, rose-purple or whitish to rose, summer, 1½ ft.; *tripetaloides*, whitish, suffused and dotted rose-pink, summer; *uniflora* (syn. *grandiflora*), crimson, shaded yellow, spring, summer, 2 to 3 ft.

DIZYGOTHECA (False Aralia) – *Araliaceae*. Tender evergreen shrubs with finger-like leaves.

Compost, John Innes potting compost No. 1 or equivalent. Position, pots in an intermediate or warm greenhouse, minimum winter temp. 13°C., or in a warm, light room. Water normally. Syringe or sponge leaves frequently to maintain a moist atmosphere. Shade in summer only from strong direct sunshine.

Dizygotheca elegantissima

Increase by stem cuttings in a warm propagator in summer; by root cuttings in similar conditions in spring.

The best kind is *D. elegantissima* (syn. *Aralia elegantissima*), narrow reddish bronze leaflets, 3 to 5 ft., New Hebrides, Pacific Islands.

DODECATHEON (American Cowslip) – *Primulaceae*. Hardy or slightly tender herbaceous perennials with flowers shaped like those of cyclamen.

Soil, light loam enriched with plenty of leafmould. Position, sheltered, lightly shaded, moist in summer but well drained in winter. Plant in spring. Can also be grown in 5- or 6-in. pots in a mixture of equal parts loam, leafmould and sand. Position, in a cold frame in winter, then in an unheated greenhouse till after flowering, when place

outdoors until late autumn. Then repot and return to a frame. Water moderately when new growth appears, freely when in full growth.

Increase by seeds sown in pots of light sandy soil in a cold frame as soon as ripe or in spring; by division of crowns in spring or autumn.

Recommended kinds are *D. alpinum*, magenta, yellow and white, late spring, 8 in., N. W. America; *clevelandii*, violet-blue and yellow or white, late spring, 1 ft., slightly tender, California; *cusickii*, purple, late spring, 8 in., N. W. America; *hendersonii*, violet and yellow, late spring, 1 ft., California; *integrifolium*, purple, late spring, 9 in., British Columbia; *jeffreyi*, purple-rose, spring, 6 in., California; *meadia*, rosy purple, white and lilac, late spring and early summer, 1 ft., N. E. America, vars. *album*, white, *lilacinum*, lilac; *pauciflorum*, lilac and yellow, late spring, early summer, 9 in., N. W. America.

DOLICHOS – *Leguminosae*. Tender evergreen twiners and sub-shrubs with pea-type flowers. *D. lablab* is a perennial but is usually grown as an annual.

Sow in early spring in John Innes seed compost or equivalent in temp. 15 to 18°C. and harden off seedlings for planting outdoors in a warm, sunny place in late spring or early summer when danger of frost is over. Provide wire, sticks or trellis for plants to twine around.

The best kind is *D. lablab*, Bonavist, Hyacinth Bean, rosy purple, summer, 1 to 2 ft., Tropics.

DOMBEYA – *Sterculiaceae*. Tender ornamental evergreen shrubs or trees with large leaves and flowers in clusters.

Compost, John Innes potting compost No. 1 or equivalent. Position, large pots, tubs or beds in an intermediate or warm greenhouse, minimum winter temp. 13°C. Water normally. Shade from direct sunshine in summer. Prune moderately after flowering. Plant or pot in spring.

Increase by cuttings of nearly ripe wood in sandy soil in a warm propagator in summer.

Recommended kinds are *D. dregeana*, white and pink, late winter, early spring, 6 to 10 ft., S. Africa; *mastersii*, white and pink, late winter, early spring, 6 ft., Tropical Africa; *natalensis*, white, winter, early spring, the hardiest kind, Natal; *spectabilis*, pink, winter, spring, 6 to 8 ft., Tropical Africa.

DORONICUM (Leopards-bane) – *Compositae*. Hardy herbaceous perennials with yellow daisy flowers in spring.

Soil, ordinary. Position, sunny or lightly shaded. Plant in spring or autumn. Plants can also be flowered early in a greenhouse for cut flowers in spring or early summer.

Increase by division of roots in spring or autumn; by seeds sown in spring or early summer.

Recommended kinds are *D. austriacum*, 1½ ft., Europe; *caucasicum*, 1 to 1½ ft., Europe, Asia, and var. Spring Beauty with double flowers; *cordatum*, 6 in., Europe, Asia Minor; *pardalianches*, 2 ft., Europe (Britain); *plantagineum*, 3 ft., Europe (Britain), var. Harpur Crewe (syn. *excelsum*), more robust with larger flower heads.

DOROTHEANTHUS – *Aizoaceae*. Tender succulent annuals and perennials formerly known as mesembryanthemum. Natives of S. Africa.

Soil, ordinary. Position, warm, sunny.

Increase by seeds sown in early spring in temp. 15 to 18°C.; the seedlings should be hardened off for planting out when there is no danger of frost.

The recommended kind is *D. bellidiformis* (syn. *Mesembryanthemum criniflorum*), Livingstone Daisy, pink carmine, crimson, apricot, buff, white, summer, prostrate, annual.

DOUGLASIA – *Primulaceae*. Hardy tufted evergreen plants related to androsace and similar in appearance.

Compost, equal parts peat, loam, coarse sand and limestone chippings. Position, sunny rock garden or moraine with plenty of water in summer but first-rate drainage in winter. Plant in spring.

Increase by seeds sown in sandy peat in a cold frame in spring; by division in spring.

Recommended kinds are *D. laevigata*, crimson, spring, 1 in., mountains of Oregon and Washington; *vitaliana* (syn. *Androsace vitaliana*), yellow, late spring, early summer, 2 in., mountains of Spain and the Alps.

DRABA (Whitlow Grass) – *Cruciferae*. Hardy perennial plants forming close cushions of growth studded with tiny yellow or white flowers.

Soil, ordinary, well drained. Position, sunny rock gardens, crevices in dry walls, raised beds, etc. Difficult kinds in well-drained pots or pans filled with a mixture of equal parts loam, leafmould (or peat) and coarse sand in a frame or unheated greenhouse. Water fairly freely while in growth, very sparingly in autumn and winter.

Increase by seeds sown in pans of sandy soil in spring; by division of roots in spring.

Recommended kinds are *D. aizoides*, yellow, spring, 3 in., Europe (Britain); *aizoon*, yellow, spring, 4 to 6 in., Alps, Carpathian Mountains; *alpina*, yellow, spring, 3 in., European Arctic Regions, *bruniifolia*, yellow, early spring, 3 in., Caucasus; *bryoides*, yellow, spring, 2 in., Caucasus, var. *imbricata*, even smaller; *dedeana*, white, spring, 2 to 3 in., Pyrenees; *mollissima*, yellow, 2 in., early spring, Caucasus; *polytricha*, yellow, 2 in., spring, Armenia; *rigida* (syn.

diacranoides), yellow, 3 in., spring, Asia Minor.

DRACAENA – *Agavaceae*. Tender evergreen plants grown for their handsome, often variegated, foliage.

Dracaena godseffiana

Compost, John Innes potting compost No. 3 or equivalent. Position, pots in an intermediate or warm greenhouse, minimum winter temp. 13°C., or in a warm room. Shade lightly in summer only. Water freely in spring and summer, very moderately in autumn and winter. Repot in spring. *D. draco* is nearly hardy and can be grown outdoors in frost-free localities.

Increase by stem cuttings in peat in a warm propagator in spring; by cuttings or 'toes' of fleshy roots in sandy peat in spring; by air layering in spring or summer; species by seeds sown in temp. 15 to 18°C. in spring.

Recommended kinds are *D. deremensis*, leaves long and pointed, 4 to 15 ft., Tropical Africa, and vars. *bausei*, centre of leaf silver, and *warneckii*, leaves white striped; *draco*, Dragon Tree, leaves glaucous, 40 to 50 ft., Canary Islands; *fragrans*, leaves green, 15 to 20 ft., Tropical Africa, and vars. *lindenii*, leaves edged gold, and *massangeana*, centre of leaf gold; *godseffiana*, leaves green, cream spotted, 3 ft., W. Tropical Africa; *goldieana*, leaves green and gold, 4 to 6 ft., W. Tropical Africa; *sanderiana*, leaves white and green, 5 ft., W. Tropical Africa.

DRACOCEPHALUM (Dragonhead) – *Labiatae*. Hardy perennial herbs with flowers in spikes.

Soil, light, ordinary. Position, cool, partially shady. *D. palustre* in shallow water at the edge of a pool. Plant in spring or autumn.

Increase by seeds sown in light sandy soil outdoors in spring; by cuttings of young shoots inserted in light sandy soil in a frame in spring; by division in spring or autumn.

Recommended kinds are *D. forrestii*, purple, summer, 1 to 1½ ft., China; *grandiflorum* (syn. *altaiense*), blue, summer, 1 ft., Siberia; *hemsleyanum*, light blue, summer, 1½ ft., Tibet; *palustre*, rose, 12 to 15 in., origin unknown; *ruyschiana*, purplish blue,

early summer, 12 to 18 in., Europe; *sibiricum* (syns. *Nepeta macrantha*, *N.* Souvenir d'Andre Chaudron), blue, summer, 4½ ft., Siberia.

See also Physostegia.

DRACUNCULUS (Dragon Arum) – *Araceae*. Hardy tuberous-rooted perennials. Unisexual flowers on spadices surrounded by deep reddish purple spathes, very offensive odour when in bloom.

Soil, ordinary, well drained. Position, sunny or partially shady. Plant tubers 3 in. deep in autumn.

Increase by division of tubers in spring or autumn.

The best kind is *D. vulgaris* (syn. *Arum dracunculus*), purple, summer, 3 ft., S. Europe.

DRIMYS – *Winteraceae*. Slightly tender ornamental evergreen shrubs and trees.

Soil, good loamy. Position, warm, sheltered, sunny or partially shaded. Severe damage is likely at temperatures below about −5°C. Plant in spring or autumn. Remove frost-damaged growth in spring when it can be seen where buds are bursting.

Increase by cuttings in summer or autumn, or by layering in spring.

Drimys winteri

Recommended kinds are *D. colorata* (syn. *Pseudowintera colorata*), greenish yellow, red-blotched leaves, 4 to 6 ft., New Zealand; *lanceolata* (syn. *aromatica*), white, spring, bronze-tinted leaves, 10 to 15 ft., Australia, Tasmania; *winteri*, ivory white, aromatic, spring, large shining leaves, 12 to 40 ft., S. America.

DROSERA – *Droseraceae*. Tender and hardy perennial insectivorous plants.

Compost, equal parts living sphagnum moss, peat, charcoal and sand. Position, well-drained pots in a moist position in a sunny greenhouse. Water freely except in winter. May also be grown in peat and sphagnum in a bog garden.

Increase by seeds sown on the surface of living sphagnum moss and peat in well-drained pots in a propagator in spring or

summer; by division of the crowns in spring; by root cuttings, ½ to 1 in. long, embedded in a pan of moss and peat in a warm propagator.

Recommended kinds are *D. binata*, white, summer, 4 to 6 in., Australia; *capensis*, purple, summer, 6 in., S. Africa; *filiformis*, purple, summer, 6 to 8 in., N. America; *intermedia*, white, summer, 6 in., N. America; *rotundifolia*, Sundew, white, summer, 4 to 6 in., Northern Hemisphere (Britain).

DRYAS – *Rosaceae*. Hardy evergreen creeping or trailing plants with flowers like small single roses.

Soil, moist peat with plenty of grit or coarse sand. Position, sunny. Plant in spring or early autumn.

Increase by seeds sown in sandy peat in shallow pans or boxes in a frame in spring; by cuttings inserted in sandy peat in a frame in autumn; by division of plants in spring.

Recommended kinds are *D. drummondii*, yellow, late spring, early summer, trailing, N. America; *octopetala*, Mountain Avens, white, late spring, early summer, trailing, N. Europe (Britain), N. America, and vars. *integrifolia*, leaves untoothed, *minor*, neat, compact habit; *suendermannii*, cream becoming white, late spring, early summer, trailing, hybrid between *drummondii* and *octopetala*.

DRYOPTERIS – *Aspidiaceae*. Hardy ferns, many with fronds arranged in shuttlecock form. Many ferns previously known as aspidium, lastrea, nephrodium and thelypteris are now included in this genus.

Soil, ordinary, freely mixed with leafmould or peat. Position, shady. Plant in spring. Water freely in dry weather from spring to autumn. Topdress annually with leafmould or well-decayed manure. Do not remove dead fronds until spring.

Increase by spores sown on the surface of sandy soil in a shady cold frame; by division in spring.

Recommended kinds are *D. abbreviata* (syn. *filix-mas pumila*), 1 to 2 ft., Britain; *aemula*, Hay-scented Buckler Fern, ½ to 2 ft., Britain, France, Madeira, Azores; *austriaca* (syn. *dilatata*), Broad Buckler Fern, 1 to 5 ft., Europe (Britain), Temperate Asia; *borreri* (syn. *Lastrea pseudomas*), 2 to 3 ft., W. Europe (Britain), S. W. Asia, and several crested varieties; *cristata*, Crested Buckler Fern, 1 to 3 ft., fronds crested, Europe (Britain), Russia, Siberia, Eastern N. America; *erythrosora*, 1½ to 2 ft., Japan; *filix-mas*, Male Fern, 2 to 4 ft., Europe (Britain), Temperate Asia, and numerous varieties; *linneana* (syn. *Thelypteris dryopteris*), Oak Fern, 4 to 16 in., N. Europe (Britain), Caucasus, Asia, N. America; *oreopteris* (syns. *Lastrea montana*, *Thelypteris oreopteris*), Mountain Fern, 1 to 3 ft., Europe (Britain), Asia, Madeira; *phegop-*

teris (syn. *Thelypteris phegopteris*), Beech Fern, 4 to 18 in., Europe (Britain), Asia, N. America; *villarsii*, Rigid Buckler Fern, 9 to 24 in., Europe (Britain).

ECCREMOCARPUS – *Bignoniaceae*. Rather tender climbing plant. Stems herbaceous in cold places but usually new growth breaks up from the fleshy roots in spring unless the soil is severely frozen.

Soil, light, rich. Position, warm, sheltered and sunny or in cool or intermediate greenhouses. Cut out dead or damaged growth each spring. Outdoors protect roots in autumn with a layer of cinder ashes on the surface of the soil.

Increase by seeds sown in light sandy soil in temp. 15 to 18°C. in spring. Seedlings grow so rapidly that, if seed is sown early, plants will flower the same summer and can be treated as half-hardy annuals.

The only kind grown is *E. scaber*, Chilean Glory Flower, scarlet or orange-yellow, summer, 10 to 12 ft., Chile.

ECHEVERIA – *Crassulaceae*. Tender succulent plants, sometimes included in the genus *Cotyledon*. Grown primarily for their ornamental rosettes of fleshy leaves but many also have attractive flowers.

Compost, John Innes potting compost No. 2 or equivalent. Position, pots in a cool greenhouse, minimum winter temp. 7°C., or in a sunny window. *E. secunda* is frequently planted outdoors in summer as a bedding plant. Water fairly freely in spring and summer but sparingly in autumn and winter when care should be taken not to wet the leaves unduly. No shade required at any time. Pot in spring.

Increase by seeds in temp. 15 to 18°C. in spring; by cuttings of leaves with the base inserted in well-drained pots of sandy soil in summer; by offsets removed in spring. Do not water leaves, cuttings or offsets until they begin to shrivel.

Recommended kinds from Mexico are *E. agavoides*, orange, autumn, 1 ft.; *coccinea*, red, autumn, 2 ft.; *derenbergii*, yellow or orange, summer, 2 to 3 in.; *elegans*, pink, summer, 3 in.; *gibbiflora*, red, autumn, 2 ft.; *glauca*, red and yellow, autumn, 1 ft.; *pulvinata*, scarlet, autumn; *secunda*, reddish, summer, 1 ft.

ECHINACEA (Purple Cone Flower) – *Compositae*. Hardy herbaceous perennials with large daisy flowers. Sometimes included with *Rudbeckia*.

Soil, deep, rich, light loam. Position, well drained, sunny. Plant in spring or autumn.

Increase by seeds sown in a cool greenhouse in spring, or outdoors in a sunny position in late spring or early summer; by division in spring or autumn.

The best kind is *E. purpurea* (syn. *Rudbeckia purpurea*), purplish red, summer, 3 to 4 ft., N. America.

ECHINOCACTUS – *Cactaceae*. Tender succulent plant producing thick, barrel-like growth.

Compost, John Innes potting compost No. 2 or equivalent plus one-sixth its bulk of coarse sand. Position, pots or beds in a sunny cool greenhouse, minimum winter temp. 7°C. Water freely in spring and summer, very sparingly in autumn and winter. No shade is required. Pot in spring, annually if it is desired to restrict size.

Increase by seeds sown in sandy soil in temp. 18 to 21°C. in spring, keeping soil moderately moist.

The best kind is *E. grusonii*, yellow, summer, to 4 ft., Mexico.

ECHINOCEREUS – *Cactaceae*. Tender plants with fleshy, spiny stems, without leaves. Formerly included in the genus *Cereus*. Many kinds with very attractive flowers.

Compost, John Innes potting compost No. 2 or equivalent plus one-sixth its bulk of coarse sand. Position, well-drained pots in a cool greenhouse or sunny window, minimum winter temp. 7°C. Water fairly freely in spring and summer, sparingly at other times. No shade required. Pot in spring.

Increase by seeds sown in well-drained pots or pans in temp. 18 to 21°C. in spring; by stem cuttings inserted in sand in summer and kept just moist; by grafting on other kinds in spring.

Recommended kinds are *E. coccineus*, scarlet, autumn, Southern U.S.A., Mexico; *engelmanii*, purple, South-western U.S.A.; *fendleri*, purple, Mexico; *knippelianus*, pink, spring, 2 to 3 in., Mexico; *pectinatus*, cerise, summer, 6 to 8 in., Mexico, and var. *rigidissimus*, Rainbow Cactus, various shades of pink; *pentalophus*, rose, summer, 6 in., Mexico, Texas; *reichenbachii* (syn. *Cereus caespitosus*), rose, summer, Texas, Mexico.

Echinops ritro

ECHINOPS (Globe Thistle) – *Compositae*. Hardy biennials and perennials with flowers in tight globular heads.

Soil, ordinary. Position, well drained, sunny. Plant in spring or autumn.

Increase by seeds sown in a sunny position outdoors in spring or early summer; by division of roots in spring; by root cuttings in winter in a frame or cool greenhouse.

Recommended kinds are *E. bannaticus*, violet-blue, summer, 2 to 3 ft., Hungary; *humilis*, blue, late summer, foliage silvery grey, 3 to 4 ft., Asia, and var. *nivalis*, white; *ritro*, blue, summer, 3 ft., S. Europe; *sphaerocephalus*, grey-blue, summer, 3 to 5 ft., Europe, Asia.

ECHINOPSIS – *Cactaceae*. Tender succulent plants with barrel-like growth and showy, often scented, flowers usually with a long tube.

Compost, John Innes potting compost No. 2 or equivalent plus one-sixth its bulk of coarse sand. Position, well-drained pots in a sunny, cool greenhouse or window, minimum winter temp. 7°C. Repot annually in spring. Water fairly freely in spring and summer, sparingly in autumn and winter.

Increase by seeds sown in sandy soil in temp. 18 to 21°C. in spring, keeping soil moderately moist; by cuttings of stems inserted in small pots of sandy soil, kept barely moist in summer; by grafting on common kinds in spring.

Recommended kinds are *E. eyriesii*, white, fragrant, summer, 4 to 6 in., Brazil, Uruguay, Argentina; *leucantha*, white, rose, summer, 1 ft., Argentina; *multiplex*, rose, summer, Brazil; *oxygona*, rose, summer, 6 in., Brazil; *tubiflora*, white, summer, 4 in., Argentina.

ECHIUM (Viper's Bugloss) – *Boraginaceae*. Hardy annuals and fairly tender biennials and monocarpic plants. Some kinds are dwarf but most of the tender kinds carry their flowers in stiff spikes which are sometimes of great size.

Soil, ordinary. Position, sunny, well drained; tender kinds only in warm, almost frost-free places. Plant monocarpic kinds in spring; biennials as soon as large enough to be planted out.

Increase all kinds by seed, that of annuals sown in spring or early autumn where plants are to flower; that of monocarpic and biennial kinds in spring or early summer outdoors or under glass.

The best hardy annual is *E. plantagineum*, blue, pink or white, summer, 9 to 24 in., Mediterranean region.

The best biennial or monocarpic kinds are *E. aubertianum*, blue, spring, summer, to 8 ft., Teneriffe; *candicans*, blue, spring, summer, to 6 ft., Madeira; *pininana*, lavender, to 10 ft., La Palma; *simplex*, white, to 12 ft., Teneriffe; *wildpretii* (syn. *bourgae-*

anum), rose, spring, summer, to 8 ft., Teneriffe.

EDGEWORTHIA – *Thymelaeaceae*.
Slightly tender, deciduous shrub bearing dense heads of fragrant little yellow flowers in early spring.

Soil, light loam, well drained but not dry. Position, sunny, sheltered. It will not stand temperatures lower than about −5°C.

Increase by cuttings in sandy soil in summer.

The only kind cultivated is *E. papyrifera* (syns. *chrysantha*), Paper Bush, Mitsumata, 4 to 6 ft., China, Japan.

EDRAIANTHUS – *Campanulaceae*.
Hardy, low tufted perennial plants closely allied to *Campanula* and very similar in appearance.

Grow in light loam with plenty of leaf-mould and sharp grit or coarse sand. Position, sunny or in well-drained pots in a frame or alpine house.

Increase by seeds sown in sandy soil in spring; by cuttings or tufts rooted in sand in a frame in spring.

Recommended kinds are *E. caudatus* (syn. *dalmaticus*), purple-blue, cluster headed, 6 in., summer, Dalmatia; *graminifolius*, blue, cluster headed, 9 in., summer, Dalmatia; *pumilio*, blue, 2 to 3 in., late spring, early summer, Dalmatia; *serpyllifolius*, deep purple-blue, prostrate, late spring, early summer, Balkans.

EICHHORNIA – *Pontederiaceae*.
Tender floating aquatic perennials with flowers usually in spikes.

Eichhornia crassipes

Grow in water up to 1 ft. deep with good loamy soil in the bottom into which plants can root. Plant *E. crassipes* by floating it on the surface, other kinds by planting in the bare soil or in soil-filled baskets and standing these in the pool. *E. crassipes* can be grown outdoors in summer when there is no danger of frost and can then be brought into a frost-proof greenhouse in early autumn and overwintered in wet soil. All kinds thrive in warmth, temp. 15 to 25°C.

Increase by division in early summer, or by severing the stolons from natural runners.

Recommended kinds are *E. azurea*, summer, spreading over water surface, lavender-blue and yellow, S. America; *crassipes* (syn. *speciosa*), Water Hyacinth, rounded habit, swollen petioles make it buoyant, violet, floating, Tropical America.

ELAEAGNUS – *Elaeagnaceae*.
Hardy deciduous and evergreen shrubs with insignificant but mostly fragrant flowers.

Soil, ordinary, well drained. Position, open, sheltered. Plant deciduous species in autumn or late winter, evergreen species in spring or autumn.

Increase by seeds stratified for three months at 4°C. (those of *E. multiflora* should have a prior five months at 18 to 21°C.), and then sown in temp. 15 to 18°C.; by cuttings in sandy soil in spring or autumn; by layering in spring; by root cuttings in spring.

Recommended evergreen kinds are *E. ebbingei*, silvery white, fragrant, autumn, leaves olive green above, silvery beneath, to 15 ft., hybrid; *glabra*, white, autumn, fragrant, autumn leaves green above brown beneath, semi-climbing to 20 ft., China, Japan; *macrophylla*, silvery white, fragrant, autumn, leaves silvery on both surfaces when young, 12 ft., Japan, Korea; *pungens*, silvery white, fragrant, autumn, leaves shining green above, white speckled brown below, 10 to 15 ft., China, Japan, and vars. *maculata*, gold in centre of leaf, *variegata*, gold edge to leaf.

Recommended deciduous kinds are *E. angustifolia*, Oleaster, yellow, fragrant, early summer, leaves narrow silvery grey, to 20 ft., Asia; *commutata*, Silverberry, yellow, fragrant, late spring, leaves silvery, 12 ft., N. America; *multiflora*, silvery, fragrant, spring, leaves silvery beneath, cherry-like edible fruits, 9 ft., Japan, China; *umbellata*, silvery, fragrant, spring, summer, leaves silvery, 12 ft., China, Korea, Japan.

ELODEA – *Hydrocharitaceae*.
Useful oxygenating plants for the aquarium or pond with completely submerged growth.

Plant any time during spring or summer, weight clumps with lead or stone and sink them in position in the pool or aquarium with some loam placed in the bottom into which the plants can root.

Increase by slips taken any time during the growing season.

Recommended kinds are *E. canadensis* (syn. *Anacharis canadensis*), E. Canada, for aquaria only; *densa* (syn. *Egeria densa*), small white flowers enclosed by broad loose spathe, S. America, for ponds.

EMBOTHRIUM – *Proteaceae*.
Rather tender evergreen shrubs or small trees. Soil, good loamy, lime free, well drained but not dry in summer. Position, sunny, but sheltered, or in light shade.

Increase by cuttings inserted in sandy peat in summer in a propagator; by seeds sown in sandy peat in temp. 18 to 21°C. in spring.

Recommended kinds are *E. coccineum*, Chilean Firebush, bright scarlet, honeysuckle shaped, late spring, 10 to 30 ft., Chile, vars. *lanceolatum*, Norquinco Valley form, narrow leaves, not fully evergreen, flowers all along branches, hardier than *E. coccineum*, *longifolium*, longer, more evergreen leaves.

EMILIA – *Compositae*.
Slightly tender annual with daisy-type flowers lacking ray florets.

Soil, ordinary. Position, sunny. Sow seeds in temp. 15 to 18°C. in early spring, pricking out seedlings into boxes as soon as they are large enough to handle, and hardening off for planting out in late spring; alternatively sow a little later outdoors where plants are to flower.

The best kind is *E. sagittata* (syn. *E. flammea*, *Cacalia coccinea*), Tassel Flower, scarlet, summer, 1 to 2 ft., Tropical America.

ENCEPHALARTOS (Kaffir Bread) – *Zamiaceae*.
Tender evergreen plants, some with quite long trunks; each carrying a shuttlecock head of feather-shaped leaves.

Compost, John Innes potting compost No. 2 or equivalent. Position, tubs or beds in an intermediate or warm greenhouse, minimum winter temp. 13°C. Water normally and maintain a humid atmosphere. Shade lightly in spring and summer. Pot in spring.

Increase by seeds sown in light soil in temp. 25 to 30°C. in spring.

Recommended kinds from S. Africa are *E. altensteinii*, 15 ft.; *caffer*, Kaffir Bread, 12 ft.; *horridus*, 3 ft.; *lehmannii*, 6 to 10 ft.

Endymion hispanicus

ENDYMION (Bluebell) – *Liliaceae*. Hardy bulbs with spikes of bell-shaped flowers. Formerly known as scilla.

Soil, ordinary, fertile, moist. Position, shady, woodlands, wild garden and borders. Plant in early autumn. Leave undisturbed for many years.

Increase by division of the bulb clusters in early autumn; by seeds sown in spring in moist soil with plenty of peat or leafmould.

Recommended kinds are *E. hispanicus* (syn. *Scilla hispanica*), Spanish Bluebell, blue, pink, white, late spring, 9 to 18 in., S. Europe, N. Africa; *non-scriptus* (syn. *Scilla non-scripta*), Bluebell, Wild Hyacinth, blue, pink, white, late spring, early summer, 9 to 18 in., Europe (Britain).

ENKIANTHUS – *Ericaceae*. Hardy deciduous shrubs with small bell-shaped flowers in spring and autumn-tinted foliage.

Soil, lime-free loam with peat or leafmould. Position, sheltered, sunny or partially shaded. Plant in spring or autumn. No pruning required.

Increase by cuttings of firm shoots in sandy soil in a propagator in summer, or by seeds sown in peaty soil in spring.

Recommended kinds are *E. campanulatus*, cream or buff, late spring, 10 ft., Japan; *cernuus*, white, late spring, 5 to 8 ft., Japan, var. *rubens*, flowers deep red; *chinensis* (syn. *sinohimalaicus*), salmon orange, late spring, early summer, 10 to 20 ft., W. China, Burma; *perulatus* (syn. *japonicus*), white, spring, 6 ft., Japan.

EOMECON – *Papaveraceae*. Hardy, rhizomatous, herbaceous, poppy-like perennial. It runs underground.

Soil, sandy peat and leafmould. Position, sunny, well drained in winter but not dry in summer. Plant in spring or autumn. Water freely in very dry weather.

Increase by division of the roots in spring.

The only species is *E. chionantha*, Snow Poppy, white, summer, 1 ft., China.

EPACRIS (Australian Heath) – *Epacridaceae*. Tender evergreen flowering shrubs with narrow heather-like leaves and spikes of tubular flowers.

Compost, three parts fibrous peat, one part coarse sand. Position, light, airy greenhouse, minimum temp. 7°C., but may be stood outdoors in a sunny place in summer. Repot in spring; good drainage is essential. Prune lightly after flowering. Water moderately at all times. Syringe plants daily while in active growth in spring and early summer.

Increase by seeds sown immediately they ripen on the surface of sandy peat in a propagator; by cuttings inserted in sandy peat in a propagator in spring or early summer.

Recommended kinds from Australia are *E. impressa*, red, pink, or white, winter, to

5 ft.; *longiflora*, crimson and white, winter, spring, 2 to 4 ft.; *purpurascens*, white and reddish purple, winter, 2 ft.

EPIDENDRUM – *Orchidaceae*. Tender epiphytic orchids, native in Tropical America and allied to *Cattleya*. There are a great many species, very variable, including some of dwarf habit. A number of hybrids have been raised.

Compost, two parts fibre and three parts sphagnum moss or equivalent. Position, well-drained pots in an intermediate house. Water fairly freely while in growth. The hard-bulbed, hard-leaved species must have a marked rest in winter, most of them at about 10°C. The stemmed section mostly needs a winter temp. of 13 to 15°C., shade from direct sunshine, and a more humid atmosphere throughout the year. Variation is so great that slight differences are necessary in treatment. The Nanodes section needs a moist atmosphere throughout the year, though high temperatures may not be needed. *E. radicans* can be trained like a climber.

Increase by division of plants. Stemmed kinds which produce stem roots by cuttings taken off below the roots.

Recommended kinds are *E. brassavolae*, yellow, lip whitish and purple, spring, Guatemala; *ciliare*, pale green and white, lip fringed, winter, Tropical America; *endresii*, white and violet, various seasons, 6 in., Costa Rica; *fragrans*, white or greenish, veined red, autumn, early winter, 9 in., Central America; *medusae* (syn. *Nanodes medusae*), yellowish green, lip purple-brown, fringed, pendent, Costa Rica; *parkinsonianum* (syn. *falcatum*), pale green and white, spring, pendent, Mexico; *prismatocarpum*, yellowish white, purplish spotted, summer, 12 to 15 in., Central America; *radicans*, red, all seasons, sprawling to 10 ft., Guatemala; *stamfordianum*, variable, white, yellow, red-spotted, fragrant, spring, Guatemala, Brazil; *vitellinum*, orange, red and yellow, autumn, winter, 1 ft., Mexico.

EPIGAEA – *Ericaceae*. Hardy evergreen perennials, with woody creeping stems and small flowers in clusters or short spikes. They are not easy to manage where the air is dry in summer.

Grow in a mixture of four parts leafmould (or peat) to one part each loam and coarse sand or grit in a cool, semi-shady place or in well-drained pots in a shady frame or alpine house. Plant or pot in spring after flowering.

Increase by seeds sown in spring in peat, leafmould and sand; by division in early autumn.

Recommended kinds are *E. asiatica*, pink, spring, prostrate, Japan; *intertexta* (syn. Aurora), pink, spring, hybrid between *asiatica* and *repens*; *repens*, American Ground Laurel, New England Mayflower,

Trailing Arbutus, white, fragrant, spring, trailing, N. America.

EPILOBIUM (Willow Herb) – *Onagraceae*. Hardy herbaceous perennials usually with showy flowers.

Soil, ordinary. Position, shady or sunny. *E. angustifolium* only suitable for wild gardens and woodland. Plant in spring or autumn.

Increase by seeds sown in shady position outdoors in spring or early summer; by division of roots in spring or autumn.

Recommended kinds are *E. angustifolium*, Rose Bay or French Willow, magenta, summer, 4 to 6 ft., Europe (Britain), var. *album*, white; *chloraefolium*, white or pink, summer, autumn, 6 to 12 in., New Zealand, and var. *kalkourense*, large white or cream flowers; *fleischeri* (syn. *dodonaei* and *rosmarinifolium*), rosy purple, summer, 9 to 12 in., Europe; *glabellum*, creamy white, summer, 9 to 12 in., New Zealand.

EPIMEDIUM (Barrenwort) – *Berberidaceae*. Hardy herbaceous perennials with attractive foliage and loose sprays of berberis-like flowers. They creep by rhizomes and make good ground cover.

Soil, ordinary. Position, cool, shady, will do well under trees. Plant in autumn or spring. Cut off old leaves and stems in autumn or winter after they have ceased to be decorative.

Increase by division of rhizomes in autumn.

Recommended kinds are *E. alpinum*, Bishop's Hat, garnet red and yellow, summer, 9 in., Europe; *grandiflorum* (syn. *macranthum*), pale violet and white, spring, summer, 9 in., Japan, and vars. *flavescens*, pale yellow, Rose Queen, carmine, *violaceum*, violet; *perralderianum*, bright yellow, early spring, 12 to 15 in., Algeria; *pinnatum*, bright yellow, spring, 9 in., Iran, and var. *colchicum*, to 15 in., Caucasus; *pubigerum*, white, pink and yellow, spring, 15 in., Bulgaria, Turkey, Caucasus; *rubrum* (syn. *alpinum rubrum*), crimson and yellow, spring, 9 in., hybrid, probably between *alpinum* and *grandiflorum*; *versicolor*, old rose and yellow, spring, 12 in., hybrid between *grandiflorum* and *pinnatum colchicum*, and vars. *neosulphureum* and *sulphureum* (syn. *E. sulphureum*), sulphur yellow; *warleyense*, coppery red and yellow, spring, 12 in., hybrid between *alpinum* and *pinnatum colchicum*; *youngianum*, greenish white, 9 in., spring, Japan, and vars. *niveum* (*E. niveum*), white, 6 in., *roseum* (syn. *E. concinnum*), rose, 6 in.

EPIPHYLLUM *Cactaceae*. Tender epiphytic succulent plants with showy flowers. Some species formerly included in this genus have been transferred to *Schlumbergera*, *Zygocactus*, etc.

Compost, three parts each of turfy loam and peat or leafmould, one part coarse sand.

Epiphyllum
(hybrid)

Position, pots or baskets in a cool or inter-mediate greenhouse, minimum winter temp. 7°C., or a well-lighted room. Water fairly freely in spring, summer and autumn, sparingly in winter. Shade from strong sun-shine in late spring and summer. In summer plants can be grown outdoors in a lath shelter or in baskets suspended from trees.

Increase by cuttings in sand in spring or summer; by seeds sown in well-drained pans in temp. 15 to 18°C. in spring.

The best species is *E. ackermannii*, crim-son, spring, early summer, 2 to 3 ft., Mexico, but most of the varieties grown are hybrids from this and other species. Most flower in spring and early summer, are from 2 to 3 ft. high and have a colour range from cream and soft pink to orange, carmine and purple.

ERAGROSTIS – *Gramineae*. Hardy annu-al and perennial flowering grasses with light, feathery and graceful inflorescences.

Soil, light, well drained. Position, open, sunny.

Increase by seeds sown in spring when danger of severe frost is over where plants are to grow. Gather inflorescences in sum-mer when fully developed and dry for winter use.

Recommended kinds are *E. capillaris*, Lace Grass, ½ to 2 ft., Eastern U.S.A.; *interrupta* (syn. *elegans*), Love Grass, 1 to 2 ft., Brazil; *japonica*, ½ to 2 ft., Tropical Asia, Australia; *maxima*, 2 to 3 ft., Madagascar; *mexicana*, Mexican Love Grass, to 3 ft., U.S.A., Mexico; *namaquensis*, to 4 ft., Tropi-cal and S. Africa; *obtusa*, ½ to 1½ ft., S. Africa; *pilosa*, Soft Love Grass, ½ to 1½ ft., warm regions; *spectabilis*, Purple Love Grass, to 2½ ft., U.S.A.; *tef* (syn. *abyssinica*, *abessinica*), 1 to 5 ft., Ethiopia, S.W. Arabia; *trichodes*, to 4 ft., perennial, Old World Tropics; *unioloides*, ½ to 1½ ft., Tropical Asia; *virescens*, 1 to 2½ ft., S. America.

ERANTHEMUM – *Acanthaceae*. Tender flowering plants with ornamental foliage. See Xantheranthemum for other species commonly called eranthemum.

Compost, John Innes potting compost No. 1 or equivalent. Position, pots in an intermediate or warm greenhouse, mini-mum winter temp. 13°C. Water normally. Shade lightly in summer only. Maintain a moist atmosphere in spring and summer. Pot in spring. Prune shoots to within 1 in. of the base after flowering.

Increase by cuttings of young shoots in-serted in sandy peat in a warm propagator in spring or summer.

The best kind is *E. pulchellum* (syns. *E. nervosum*, *Daedalacanthus nervosus*, *D. pul-chellus*), blue, winter, to 14 ft., India.

ERANTHIS (Winter Aconite) – *Ranuncu-laceae*. Hardy, winter and early spring flowering tubers with a single yellow flower above green bracts.

Soil, ordinary. Position, shady borders, lawns, under deciduous trees or shrubs or on rock gardens. Plant 2 in. deep and 2 in. apart in autumn. Tubers should not be lifted, but left permanently in the soil.

For pot plants use a compost of equal parts leafmould, loam and sand. Position, 3-in. pots or large pans in a cool greenhouse or window. Plant tubers ½ in. deep and close together in pots or pans in autumn. Water moderately. After flowering, plant tubers out of doors.

Increase by seeds sown as soon as ripe or, in the case of hybrid form, divide the tubers and replant pieces immediately in autumn.

Recommended kinds are *E. cilicica*, yel-low, 2 to 3 in., Greece, Asia Minor; *hyemalis*, yellow, 3 to 4 in., Europe (Britain); *sibirica*, yellow, 2 to 3 in., Siberia; *tubergenii*, large, shiny, golden yellow, hybrid between *cilicica* and *hyemalis*.

ERCILLA – *Phytolaccaceae*. Hardy ever-green climber, clinging by adhesive disks, with flowers in small spikes.

Soil, sandy loam. Position, walls or old tree trunks; sunny or semi-shady. Plant in spring or autumn. Prune after flowering, cutting away weak shoots and shortening strong shoots by a quarter.

Increase by cuttings in a propagator in summer; or by layers in autumn.

The best kind is *E. spicata* (syns. *E. volubilis*, *Bridgesia spicata*), purple, spring, 10 to 15 ft., Chile.

EREMURUS – *Liliaceae*. Hardy her-baceous perennials with thick fleshy or cord-like roots which resent disturbance. Flowers carried in long slender spikes.

Soil, light, deep, sandy, well-manured loam. Position, sunny, well-drained beds or borders. Plant in autumn. Mulch freely with well-decayed manure in autumn. Water copiously in hot weather. Protect in winter by a covering of bracken or dry litter.

Increase by division of roots in autumn or spring; by seeds sown in heat in spring, growing seedlings on in a cold frame for the first three years. Seeds are sometimes slow to germinate.

Recommended kinds are *E. himalaicus*,

Eremurus himalaicus

white, late spring, to 5 ft., Himalaya; *kaufmannii*, white and yellow, early sum-mer, to 3½ ft., Afghanistan; *olgae*, pink or white, summer, 2½ to 3 ft., Turkestan; *robustus*, Fox-tail Lily, pink, late spring, early summer, Turkestan; Shelford, white, yellow, orange-buff, pink, late spring, early summer, 2½ to 4 ft., hybrid between *olgae* and *stenophyllus*; *spectabilis*, sulphur and orange, early summer, to 5 ft., Asia Minor; *stenophyllus* (syn. *bungei*), yellow, early summer, to 4 ft., Iran, Russia.

ERICA (Heath) – *Ericaceae*. Hardy and tender flowering shrubs. The hardy kinds are of great garden value, suitable selections providing colour the whole year round. The majority of these are dwarf growing but a few species reach large shrub dimensions.

The hardy kinds like sandy peats but will grow in a wide variety of soils though only a few, including *E. carnea*, *mediterranea*, *ter-minalis*, *darleyensis* and their varieties, will tolerate lime. All grow best in open sunny places but will tolerate light shade. Plant in spring or autumn. The summer- and autumn-flowering kinds can be trimmed with shears or a hedge trimmer in early spring, winter- and spring-flowering kinds as soon as they have finished flowering. Most do not like being pruned into hard old wood but *E. arborea* can be cut right back and will sprout up again from the stumps.

The tender kinds can only be grown outdoors where there is no danger of frost. Elsewhere they can be grown in cool greenhouses in a compost of two-thirds fibrous peat, one-third coarse sand. Position, well-drained pots in light airy greenhouse in winter and early spring, sunny place outdoors in summer. Repot autumn- and winter-flowering kinds in spring, summer-flowering kinds in early autumn. Press the compost firmly in the pots. Water carefully always, giving sufficient to keep soil uniformly moist; rain, not spring water, essential. Prune flowering shoots to within 1 or 2 in. of the base immediately after flowering. Minimum winter temp. 7°C.

Increase tender kinds by cuttings of shoots 1 in. long inserted in a well-drained pot of sandy peat in a propagator in spring; hardy species by cuttings inserted in sandy peat in a frame in summer; by division of plants in autumn; layering shoots in spring.

Recommended hardy kinds are *E. arborea*, Tree Heath, white, fragrant, late spring, 10 to 15 ft., slightly tender, Mediterranean region, var. *alpina*, similar but hardier, 8 ft., Spain; *australis*, Spanish Heath, rather tender, rosy red, spring, 3 to 4 ft., Spain; *carnea*, dwarf to 1½ ft., winter flowering, Central Europe, in many varieties, white, pink to deep red; *ciliaris*, Dorset Heath, 1 ft., summer, rosy red, S. W. Europe (Britain), and var. *maweana*, rosy crimson; *cinerea*, Bell Heather, 1 ft., summer, early autumn, purple, W. Europe (Britain), and vars. *alba*, *atropurpurea*, *atrorubens* and *fulgida*, and many more in various shades of pink, red and white; *darleyensis*, very easily grown, rose-lilac, autumn till spring, 1½ ft., hybrid between *carnea* and *mediterranea*; *lusitanica* (syn. *codonodes*), rather tender, pretty foliage, pale rose, winter, spring, S. W. Europe; *mediterranea*, 3 to 6 ft., rosy lilac, honey scented, spring, W. Europe, vars. *alba*, *superba*, etc.; *terminalis* (syns. *corsica* and *stricta*), Corsican Heath, Hardy Tree Heath, 6 to 9 ft., erect, pale rose, late summer, autumn, Spain, Italy, Corsica; *tetralix*, Cross-leaved Heath, to 1½ ft., rose pink, summer, autumn, Europe (Britain), and vars. *mollis*, silver foliage, white flowers, *rubra*, dark red, etc.; *vagans*, Cornish Heath, 2 ft., spreading to 5 ft. wide, rosy lilac, summer, autumn, W. Europe (Britain), and numerous vars.; *veitchii*, a hybrid between *lusitanica* and *arborea*, a vigorous counterpart of the former, slightly tender.

Recommended tender kinds are *E. canaliculata* (often wrongly listed as *melanthera*), rose, winter, 4 to 6 ft., S. Africa; *cavendishiana*, yellow, spring, 1 to 2 ft., hybrid between *abietiana* and *depressa*; *glauca* (syn. *elegans*), mauve and green, summer, 1 to 2 ft., S. Africa; *gracilis*, pink, autumn, winter, 1 ft., S. Africa; *hyemalis*, pink and white, winter, 1 to 2 ft., probably a hybrid;

mammosa, white, mauve or purple, late summer, 3 to 5 ft., S. Africa; *pageana*, yellow, spring, S. Africa; *ventricosa*, pink, spring, 1 to 1½ ft., S. Africa.

ERIGERON (Fleabane) – *Compositae*. Hardy herbaceous perennials with daisy-type flowers.

Soil, well drained. Position, sunny. Plant in spring or autumn. Cut down stems after flowering.

Increase by seeds sown outdoors in late spring or early summer; by division of roots in spring or autumn.

Recommended kinds are *E. aurantiacus*, Orange Daisy, orange, summer, 1 ft., Turkestan; *aureus*, bright gold, summer, 4 in., Western N. America; *compositus*, lavender or white, early summer, 3 in., Western N. America; *glaucus*, Beach Aster, lavender or pink, summer, 9 in., Western N. America; *leiomerus*, lavender, early summer, 3 to 4 in., N. W. America; *macranthus*, violet-blue, summer, 1 ft., N. W. America; *mucronatus* (syn. *karvinskyanus*), white or pale pink, spring until autumn, 6 to 9 in., Mexico; *philadelphicus*, lilac-pink, summer, 1 to 2 ft., N. America; *speciosus*, violet-blue, summer, 1½ to 2 ft., N. America. There are also numerous hybrids and varieties with garden names.

ERINACEA – *Leguminosae*. Dwarf deciduous spring-flowering shrub with spiny growths and pea-type flowers.

Soil, equal parts loam, peat and coarse sand. Position, sunny, warm, well drained. Plant in spring.

Increase by seeds sown in sandy soil in spring in a frame. Pot seedlings singly and plant out without breaking the roots.

The only kind is *E. pungens* (syn. *anthyllis*), Hedgehog Broom, pale blue, spring, 1 ft., Spain.

ERINUS – *Scrophulariaceae*. Hardy tufted perennial with flowers in small spikes.

Soil, ordinary, well drained. Position, crevices of old sunny walls or dryish rock gardens. Plant in spring.

Increase by seeds sown where plants are to grow in spring; by division of plants in spring.

The only species is *E. alpinus*, violet-purple, spring, 6 in., Pyrenees, Alps, and vars. *albus*, white, and *carmineus*, carmine.

ERIOBOTRYA – *Rosaceae*. Rather tender evergreen flowering shrub. The edible fruits of the loquat are about the size of green walnuts, pale orange-red, but these only ripen in warm climates. The loquat is often grown for its large and handsome leaves.

Soil, light, deep loam. Position, sunny and sheltered or in large pots or tubs in a cool greenhouse in a mixture of two parts sandy loam, one part leafmould. Plant in

spring or autumn. Prune straggling shoots in spring.

Increase by seeds sown in pots of light soil in a cool greenhouse or frame in spring or autumn; by cuttings of firm shoots inserted in sandy soil in a frame or greenhouse in summer.

The only kind commonly grown is *E. japonica*, Loquat, white, fragrant, summer, 10 to 30 ft., China, Japan.

ERITRICHIUM – *Boraginaceae*. Hardy perennial alpine plants of tufted habit with flowers like myosotis (forget-me-not).

Grow *E. nanum* in a mixture of three parts coarse sand to one part of leafmould, other species in a mixture of equal parts loam, leafmould and coarse sand, in well-drained pots or pans in a cool, airy greenhouse or frame or outdoors in a well-drained sunny rock garden or scree. Protect foliage from excessive moisture in winter. Plant or pot in spring.

Increase by division of plants in spring; by seeds sown in sand and leafmould in a frame or greenhouse in spring.

Recommended kinds are *E. nanum*, Fairy Borage, Fairy Forget-me-not, sky blue and yellow, spring, 2 to 3 in., European Alps; *rupestre*, blue, late spring, 6 in., Himalaya, and var. *pectinatum*, leaves grey.

ERODIUM (Heron's Bill) – *Geraniaceae*. Hardy perennial herbs with small but attractive flowers. Grow in ordinary, reasonably well-drained soil and a sunny position, in rock gardens, dry walls, raised beds, etc. Plant in spring.

Increase by seeds sown in sandy soil in a frame in spring; by division in spring.

Recommended kinds are *E. absinthioides*, violet, rosy lilac or white, summer, 4 to 8 in., Asia Minor, and var. *amanum*, white, 2 in.; *chamaedryoides*, white and pink, summer, 2 to 3 in., Balearic Islands, and var. *roseum* (syn. *reichardii roseum*), rose; *chrysanthum*, pale yellow, summer, 9 in., Greece; *corsicum*, pink, summer, prostrate, Corsica, Sardinia; *guttatum*, pink, summer, 4 in., Mediterranean region; *macradenum*, rosy mauve and purple, summer, 6 in., Pyrenees; *manescavii*, purplish red, summer, 1 to 2 ft., Pyrenees.

ERYNGIUM – *Umbelliferae*. Hardy perennial herbs with spiny-toothed leaves; flower heads surrounded by spiny, coloured bracts.

Soil, light, well drained. Position, sunny. Plant in spring.

Increase by seeds sown in sandy soil in an unheated frame in spring; by division of plants in spring; by root cuttings in winter in a frame or cool greenhouse.

Recommended kinds are *E. agavifolium*, greenish, summer, 4 to 6 ft., a little tender, needs a specially warm place, Argentina; *alpinum*, metallic blue, summer, 2 to 3 ft., Europe; *amethystinum*, amethyst blue, summer, 1½ ft., Pyrenees; *giganteum*, ivory white, summer, 3 to 4 ft., seldom long lived and often grown as a biennial, Caucasus; *maritimum*, Sea Holly, blue, summer, 1 ft.,

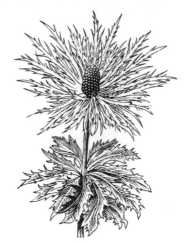

Eryngium alpinum

Europe (Britain); *oliverianum*, amethyst blue, summer, 3 ft., hybrid; *planum*, blue, summer, 2 to 3 ft., Europe; *tripartitum*, blue, summer, 3 to 3½ ft., S. Europe.

ERYSIMUM (Alpine Wallflower) – *Cruciferae*. Hardy annuals, biennials and perennials, closely allied to *Cheiranthus* (wallflower) and much confused with that genus.

Soil, ordinary. Position, dryish sunny beds or rock gardens. Plant in spring or early autumn.

Increase annual species by seeds sown in spring where plants are required to grow; biennials by seeds sown in a sunny place outdoors in late spring or early summer, transplanting seedlings to flowering positions in early autumn; perennials by seeds sown as advised for biennials, also by cuttings inserted in sandy soil or in a cold frame in summer.

The best annual species is *E. perofskianum*, reddish orange, spring to autumn, 1 ft., Afghanistan, but plants sold under this name often prove to be *asperum* or *murale*, both biennials.

Recommended biennial kinds are *E. asperum*, orange or yellow, spring and early summer, 1 to 3 ft., N. America; *murale*, yellow, spring and early summer, 1 to 1½ ft., Europe.

Recommended perennial kinds are *E. kotschyanum*, yellow, scented, spring, 3 to 4 in., Asia Minor; *linifolium*, rosy lilac, late spring and summer, 1 to 1½ ft., Spain, and var. *variegatum*, leaves variegated creamy white; *rupestre*, pale yellow, spring, 3 in., Asia Minor.

ERYTHRINA – *Leguminosae*. Rather tender semi-evergreen or deciduous shrubs and trees, usually thorny.

Plant in good, well-drained soil and a warm, sunny position or grow in large pots or tubs in a compost of equal parts loam, peat, well-decayed manure and sand, in a sunny greenhouse, minimum winter temp. 7°C. Pot or plant in spring. Prune shoots close to the old wood in autumn. Water freely from spring to early autumn, keep almost dry after that.

Store plants in pots on their sides in a greenhouse during winter. Place in a light part of the house in spring, then in a sunny position outdoors for the summer. Protect outdoor plants with a covering of ashes in winter in cold places.

Increase by cuttings of young shoots removed in spring with a portion of the old wood attached and inserted singly in well-drained pots of sandy peat in temp. 18 to 21°C.; by seeds sown in spring in a similar temperature.

Recommended kinds are *E. americanum* (syn. *corallodendrum*), scarlet, late spring, to 20 ft., deciduous, Tropical America; *caffra*, scarlet, late spring, to 50 ft., semi-evergreen, S. Africa; *crista-galli*, Coral Tree, scarlet, summer, 6 to 8 ft., deciduous, Brazil.

ERYTHRONIUM – *Liliaceae*. Hardy bulbs with pendulous flowers like small lilies.

Compost, equal parts loam, peat and leafmould. Position, sheltered, moist, rock gardens, beds, or under light shade of trees. Plant bulbs 3 in. deep and 2 in. apart in late summer. Transplant very seldom. Topdress annually with decayed manure.

Pot culture: Compost, same as above. Plant bulbs 1 in. deep and ½ in. apart in well-drained pots in late summer. Store pots in a cold frame during winter. Water very little until late winter then give a moderate supply. Place plants in a greenhouse or window in spring to flower.

Increase by offsets in summer; by seeds sown when ripe.

Erythronium dens-canis

Recommended kinds are *E. albidum*, white and yellow, spring, 6 in., Eastern N. America; *americanum*, Yellow Adder's-tongue, golden yellow and purple, spring, 6 in., N. America; *californicum*, creamy white, spring, 12 to 15 in., California; *citrinum*, cream with

yellow, spring, 6 in., Oregon; *dens-canis*, Dog's-tooth Violet, rose, spring, 6 in., Europe, Asia, and vars.; *grandiflorum*, yellow, spring, N. W. America; *hendersonii*, purple-rose, spring, 6 in., Oregon; *howellii*, yellow and orange, spring 6 in., Oregon; *multiscapoideum*, white to pale yellow, 6 in., California; *oregonum* (syn. *giganteum*), white, yellow base, 6 to 18 in., Oregon to British Columbia; *purpurascens*, yellow, purple, and orange, spring, California; *revolutum*, Trout Lily, rose-pink, spring, 8 to 12 in., California, and vars. *albiflorum*, white and maroon, and *johnsonii*, rosy pink; *tuolumnense*, deep golden yellow, spring, 9 to 12 in., California.

ESCALLONIA – *Saxifragaceae*. Hardy or slightly tender evergreen or deciduous shrubs.

Soil, ordinary, well drained, lime free for *E. virgata*. Position, sunny, warm, sheltered. Most kinds will withstand a few degrees of frost, the hardiest, such as *E. langleyensis* and *E. virgata*, temperatures of −10°C., perhaps even lower under favourable conditions.

Suitable for hedges in mild districts and excellent maritime shrubs. Plant in spring or autumn. Prune when necessary after flowering, shortening stems to side shoots or growth buds. There are numerous garden hybrids sold under 'fancy' names.

Increase by cuttings inserted in sand in summer; by layering shoots in spring; by suckers removed and replanted in spring; species by seeds sown in spring in temp. 15 to 18°C.

Recommended evergreen kinds are *E. edinensis*, carmine and pink, summer, 6 to 7 ft., hybrid; *exoniensis*, white or rose tinted, summer, 10 to 12 ft., hybrid between *pterocladon* and *rubra*; *illinita*, white, summer, 10 to 12 ft., Chile; *langleyensis*, rosy carmine, summer, 8 ft., hybrid between *punctata* and *virgata*; *macrantha*, crimson-red, summer, 6 to 10 ft., Chile; *montevidensis* (syn. *bifida*), white, summer, 10 ft., Montevideo; *organensis* (syn. *laevis*), rosy red, late summer, 5 to 6 ft., Brazil; *pterocladon* (syn. *rosea*), white, summer, 4 to 8 ft., Patagonia; *punctata*, red, summer, 6 to 10 ft., Chile; *revoluta*, pale pink or white, summer, 15 to 20 ft., Chile; *rubra*, red, summer, 6 ft., Chile; *viscosa*, white, summer, 10 ft., Chile.

The best deciduous kind is *E. virgata* (syn. *philippiana*), 6 to 8 ft., white, summer, hardy, Chile.

ESCHSCHOLZIA (Californian Poppy) – *Papaveraceae*. Hardy annuals with ferny leaves and showy, poppy-like flowers.

Soil, ordinary. Position, sunny well-drained beds or borders. Sow in spring or early autumn where plants are to flower. Thin seedlings out to 6 in. apart.

The best kind is *E. californica*, orange-yellow, summer, 1 to 2 ft., California, and numerous varieties, white, pink to carmine, some semi-double.

EUCALYPTUS (Gum) – *Myrtaceae*. More or less tender evergreen trees growing very rapidly. Fragrant leaves changing in shape as the tree ages. The juvenile type of foliage can be retained by pollarding trees each spring.

Soil, ordinary. Position, warm and sunny. Plant seedlings from pots in spring or early summer and stake securely for the first three or four years. Pruning is not essential but the previous year's stems can be cut hard back each spring if desired. Alternatively, grow in tubs in two parts fibrous loam, one part peat, one part sand in a cool sunny greenhouse, standing out of doors in summer. Water sparingly in winter, moderately at other times.

Increase by seeds sown in pots of sandy soil in temp. 15 to 18°C. in late winter or early spring.

Recommended kinds are *E. amygdalina*, Almond-leaved or Peppermint Gum, 15 to 30 ft., Australia, and vars. *angustifolia*, *numerosa*, *regnans*, Giant Gum; *citriodora*, Lemon-scented Gum, 50 ft., Australia; *coccifera*, 30 to 50 ft., Tasmania; *cordata*, 30 to 50 ft., Tasmania; *dalrympleana*, 50 to 100 ft., peeling bark, Australia; *ficifolia*, Scarlet-flowered Gum, 10 to 30 ft., Australia; *globulus*, Blue Gum, 50 to 150 ft., Tasmania; *gunnii*, 50 to 80 ft., Tasmania; *niphophila*, Snow Gum, 20 ft., Australia; *nitens*, Silver Top, 50 to 150 ft., Australia; *urnigera*, 50 to 100 ft., Tasmania, and var. *glauca*, blue-grey leaves; *viminalis*, Manna Gum, White Gum, 50 to 150 ft., Tasmania, Australia.

EUCHARIS – *Amaryllidaceae*. Tender evergreen bulbs which frequently produce two crops of fragrant white flowers in a year.

Compost, two parts fibrous loam, one part loam, one part peat, decomposed manure, sand and charcoal. Position, well-drained pots on a bed or stage heated beneath to a temp. of 30°C. in a warm house. Pot in spring or early summer, placing six bulbs in a 10-in. pot. Press compost down firmly. Repotting is not needed more often than once every three or four years. Water moderately in autumn, freely afterwards. Syringe freely in summer. Apply liquid manure twice a week when flower stems appear. Topdress established plants annually in the spring with rich compost. Temperature spring to end of summer 22 to 27°C., autumn 13 to 18°C., winter 18 to 26°C.

Increase by seeds sown in sandy soil in temp. 28 to 30°C. in late winter, by offsets removed from old bulbs and placed singly in 3-in. pots in summer.

Recommended kinds are *E. candida*, autumn, 1 ft., Colombia; *grandiflora* (syn. *amazonica*), Amazon Lily, tinged green, 1 to 2 ft., Colombia; *lowii*, spring, 1 to 2 ft.,

hybrid; *mastersii*, white, spring, 1 to 1½ ft., Colombia; *sanderi*, white, yellow within, spring, 1 to 1½ ft., Colombia; *stevensii*, white and yellow, spring, 1 ft., hybrid between *candida* and *sanderi*; *subedentata*, winter, 1½ ft., Colombia.

EUCOMIS – *Liliaceae*. Slightly tender bulbs, those included here are S. African.

Any rich, well-drained loam suits them. Position, well-drained pots in a light, cool greenhouse, or in warm sunny borders, protected in winter. Pot in autumn or spring, placing one bulb in a 5-in. pot. Winter temp. 7 to 10°C. Apply liquid manure occasionally when flower spike shows.

Increase by offsets removed and transplanted in autumn.

Eucomis bicolor

Recommended kinds include *E. bicolor*, greenish yellow, purple edged, summer, 1 to 2 ft.; *comosa* (syn. *punctata*), Pineapple Flower, green, fragrant, with purplish brown spots on foliage and stems, summer, 1½ to 2 ft.; *pallidiflora*, greenish white, 2 ft.; *pole-evansii*, pale green, 4 ft.; *regia*, King's Flower, green and purple, 2 ft.

EUCRYPHIA – *Eucryphiaceae*. Hardy and slightly tender evergreen and deciduous flowering trees of great beauty.

Soil, good loam, lime free, moist in summer but never waterlogged. Position, sheltered, sunny or lightly shaded. *E. cordifolia* will put up with lime in the soil but is better without it.

Increase by cuttings in summer or early autumn in peat and sand in a propagator; or by seeds sown in peaty soil in spring.

Recommended kinds are *E. cordifolia*, evergreen, white, summer, to 40 ft., Chile; *glutinosa* (syn. *pinnatifolia*), deciduous, white, summer, to 20 ft., Chile; *intermedia*, evergreen, white, summer, to 30 ft., hybrid between *glutinosa* and *lucida*; *lucida*, ever-

green, white, summer, 12 to 20 ft., Tasmania; *nymansensis*, evergreen, white, summer, to 30 ft., hybrid between *cordifolia* and *glutinosa*.

EUGENIA (Fruiting Myrtle) – *Myrtaceae*. Tender evergreen flowering shrubs and trees. The dried flower buds of *E. aromatica* provide the cloves of commerce.

Compost, two parts sandy loam, one part leafmould and sand. Position, pots in a cool or intermediate greenhouse or the least tender species, such as *E. myrtifolia*, out of doors in a warm, sheltered, sunny position. No kinds are likely to survive temperatures below about −5°C. Under glass it is desirable to maintain a winter temp. of 10°C. or more. Syringe with water in summer. Prune straggling shoots in spring.

Increase by cuttings of firm shoots inserted in sandy soil in a propagator in summer.

Recommended kinds are *E. aromatica*, Clove Tree, 20 ft., Moluccas; *jambos*, Rose Apple, white, summer, 20 ft., Tropical Asia; *malaccensis*, Malay Apple, scarlet, summer, 15 to 30 ft., Malaysia; *myrtifolia* (syn. *paniculata australis*), Australian Brush Cherry, white, late summer, 12 to 15 ft., Australia. For *E. apiculata* see *Myrtus apiculata*.

EUONYMUS (Spindle Tree) – *Celastraceae*. Hardy and slightly tender deciduous and evergreen shrubs or small trees. The evergreen kinds are grown primarily for their decorative foliage, variegated in some varieties; the deciduous kinds for the beauty of their autumn fruits.

Soil, ordinary. Position, deciduous species sunny, open; evergreen species, sunny or shady, *E. japonicus* as a hedge, especially in maritime districts. Plant deciduous species in autumn or late winter; evergreen in spring or autumn. Evergreen kinds may be trimmed as necessary in summer, any hard cutting back required being done in spring. Deciduous kinds do not as a rule require pruning.

Increase by cuttings of shoots of current year's growth, well ripened, inserted in sandy soil in a frame in autumn; *E. radicans* by division at planting time. Deciduous kinds from seeds sown in spring.

Recommended deciduous kinds *E. alatus*, 6 to 8 ft., grown for its rich autumn colour, China, Japan; *europaeus*, Common Spindle Tree, 10 to 15 ft., Europe (Britain), well known for its brilliant red and orange autumn fruits, with vars. *atropurpureus*, coloured foliage, *fructu-albo* and *fructu-coccineo*, white and scarlet fruits respectively; *latifolius*, 10 ft., a fine European species with large fruits similar to those of *europaeus*; *sachalinensis* (syn. *planipes*), 10 ft., very similar to *latifolius*, Japan; *yedoensis*, 15 ft., fruit pink, Japan.

Recommended evergreen kinds are *E.*

fortunei, green, creeping or climbing by aerial roots like an ivy, China, and numerous varieties such as *carrierei*, more bushy in habit to 6 ft., *coloratus*, leaves purple especially in winter, *radicans*, one of the best prostrate forms, *variegatus*, leaves grey-green edged white; *japonicus*, leaves green, 10 to 15 ft., China, Japan, and vars. *albomarginatus*, leaves margined with white, *aureus*, leaves yellow, *macrophyllus albus*, large leaves with broad white margin, *microphyllus*, small leaves, slow growth, *ovatus aureus*, leaves suffused creamy yellow.

EUPATORIUM – *Compositae*. Hardy and slightly tender herbaceous and shrubby plants.

Culture of tender species: Compost, John Innes potting compost No. 2 or equivalent. Position, pots in a light greenhouse, cool (min. temp. 7°C.) for *E. riparium* and *glandulosum*, but intermediate (min. 13°C.) for *E. atrorubens*. *E. ligustrinum* will survive some frost and can be grown outdoors in mild places. Prune immediately after flowering.

Culture of hardy species: Soil, ordinary. Position, open, sunny. Plant in spring or autumn.

Increase by cuttings of young shoots in sandy soil in temp. 15 to 18°C. in spring. Hardy species by division in spring or autumn.

Recommended tender kinds are *E. atrorubens*, red, winter, 1 to 1½ ft., Mexico; *glandulosum*, white, winter, spring, 3 to 6 ft., Mexico; *ligustrinum* (syn. *micranthum*, *weinmannianum*), white, autumn, 6 to 8 ft., Mexico; *riparium*, white, spring, 2 to 3 ft., Mexico.

Recommended hardy kinds are *E. ageratoides*, (syn. *rugosum*), white, late summer, 10 ft., N. America; *cannabinum plenum*, Double-flowered Hemp Agrimony, reddish purple, summer, 4 ft., Europe (Britain); *purpureum*, Joe-pye Weed, pink or purple, autumn, 3 to 6 ft., N. America.

EUPHORBIA (Spurge) – *Euphorbiaceae*. Tender and hardy flowering shrubs, herbaceous perennials, biennials and annuals. Some are succulent and adapted to live in desert places. In most the flowers are inconspicuous but in many are surrounded by showy bracts.

Culture of annuals: Sow seeds in spring in temp. 15 to 18°C. and harden off for planting out in late spring or early summer in good soil and a sunny place; or sow *E. marginata* in spring outdoors where it can remain.

Culture of biennials: Sow seeds outdoors in spring or early summer where plants are to flower. Once established plants will often renew themselves by self-sown seed.

Culture of tender non-succulent kinds: Compost, moderately rich, John

Euphorbia pulcherrima

Innes potting compost No. 2 or equivalent, in pots in a warm greenhouse, minimum winter temp. 18°C. Water freely in summer, moderately in autumn and winter and very sparingly for a few weeks in late winter or early spring after flowers fade. Little or no shading required. Flower stems can be cut for decoration or may be shortened when flowers fade.

Culture of Poinsettia: Compost as for other non-succulent kinds. Grow in pots in an intermediate or warm greenhouse, minimum winter temp. 13°C. Water as for other non-succulent kinds but feed fairly generously in summer while plants are making their growth and shade from strong sunshine at this season. After a resting period in late winter or early spring cut back all stems one-third and raise the temperature to at least 18°C.

Culture of tender succulent kinds: Compost, porous, not too rich, John Innes

Euphorbia splendens

potting compost No. 1 or equivalent, with extra sand for sharp drainage. Grow in pots in a cool or intermediate greenhouse, minimum winter temp. 7°C., or in a sunny window. Water freely in spring and summer, sparingly in autumn, hardly at all in winter. Pot when necessary in spring. No shade is required at any time. Prune *E. bojeri* and *splendens* in spring to improve their habit.

Culture of hardy kinds: Soil, ordinary. Position, sunny or in light shade. Some kinds make good ground cover beneath tall trees. Plant in spring or autumn.

Increase tender non-succulent kinds by cuttings of young shoots in a warm, moist propagator in spring. Poinsettias are usually grown anew from such cuttings every year. Succulent kinds by cuttings in a much drier, more airy atmosphere in summer; by seeds sown in spring in sandy soil in a temp. 18 to 21°C. Hardy kinds by seeds sown outdoors in spring or early summer, or by division in spring or autumn.

Recommended tender non-succulent kinds are *E. fulgens* (syn. *jacquinaeflora*), scarlet, autumn and winter, 2 to 3 ft., Mexico; *pulcherrima* (syn. *Poinsettia pulcherrima*), Poinsettia, scarlet, pink or white, autumn and winter, 3 to 6 ft., Mexico.

Recommended tender succulent kinds are *E. bojeri*, scarlet, most of the year, shrubby, 2 to 3 ft., Madagascar; *bubalina*, shrubby, to 3 ft., S. Africa; *bupleurifolia*, globose, 4 in., S. Africa; *caput-medusae*, snake-like stems, to 1 ft., S. Africa; *clandestina*, narrow leaves on erect stem, to 2 ft., S. Africa; *clava*, leaves at top of stem, to 3 ft., S. Africa; *echinus*, shrubby, to 3 ft., Morocco; *meloformis*, globose, ribbed, 6 in., S. Africa; *obesa*, globose or cylindrical, 6 in., S. Africa; *splendens* (syn. *milii*), Crown of Thorns, scarlet, most of the year, to 3 ft., Madagascar.

Recommended annual or biennial kinds are *E. heterophylla*, Painted Spurge, Annual Poinsettia, Mexican Fire Plant, Fire on the Mountain, scarlet, summer, 2 ft., annual, Central America; *lathyrus*, Caper Spurge, yellow-green, summer, 3 ft., biennial, Europe; *marginata*, Snow on the Mountain, green and white, summer, 2 ft., annual, N. America.

Recommended hardy perennial kinds are *E. amygdaloides*, yellowish green, spring, 1 to 1½ ft., Europe, S. W. Asia, and var. *variegata*, leaves cream edged; *capitulata*, yellow, spring and summer, mat forming, S. E. Europe; *characias*, green and maroon, spring and early summer, 4 ft., W. Mediterranean; *cyparissias*, Cypress Spurge, yellow, spring and summer, 9 to 12 in., Europe; *griffithii*, orange-red, late spring and early summer, 3 ft., Himalaya; *mellifera*, greenish yellow and brown, scented, late spring, 5 to 8 ft., rather tender shrub but will survive a few degrees of frost, Madeira; *myrsinites*, yellow, early summer, prostrate, S. Europe; *polychroma* (syn. *epithymoides*), lemon yellow, spring, 1½ ft., Europe; *rigida* (syn. *biglandulosa*), yellow, spring, Europe, S. W. Asia; *robbiae*, yellow, summer, 1½ ft., Asia Minor; *sikkimensis*, bracts yellow, young shoots red, summer, 4 ft., Himalaya; *veneta* (syn. *wulfenii*), greenish yellow, spring and summer, 4 ft., sub-shrub.

EURYOPS – *Compositae*. Slightly tender evergreen shrubs with yellow daisy flowers. All included here are natives of S. Africa.

Soil, light, well drained. Position, warm, sunny or in pots in a sunny greenhouse. Most kinds will survive a few degrees of frost.

Increase by seeds sown in sandy soil in temp. 15 to 18°C. in spring; by cuttings in a propagator or frame in summer.

Recommended kinds are *E. acreus*, late spring, early summer, 1 ft., grey leaves, often wrongly called *evansiana*, which is similar but distinct; *pectinatus*, late spring, early summer, 2 to 3 ft., grey leaves; *virgineus*, spring, 2 to 3 ft., green leaves.

EXACUM – *Gentianaceae*. Tender annuals, biennials or perennials. Only one kind, *E. affine*, is commonly grown and this must be renewed from seed annually.

Sow seed in porous soil such as John Innes seed compost in early spring for flowering in late summer and autumn, and in early summer for flowering in winter. Germinate in temp. 15 to 18°C. Pot seedlings singly in John Innes potting compost No. 1 or equivalent and grow in a cold or cool greenhouse with light shading in summer only, normal watering and a fairly damp atmosphere.

The recommended kind is *E. affine*, blue and yellow, scented, late summer to winter, 9 to 18 in., Socotra.

EXOCHORDA (Pearl Bush) – *Rosaceae*. Hardy deciduous flowering shrubs of great beauty, somewhat neglected in gardens.

Soil, ordinary. Position, sunny, but not too dry. Plant in autumn or late winter. Prune after flowering, shortening old flowering stems to young growths or side branches.

Increase by seeds sown in sandy soil in a frame in spring or autumn; by cuttings of young shoots inserted in sandy soil in a propagator in summer.

Recommended kinds are *E. giraldii*, white, late spring, 10 ft., N. and W. China, and var. *wilsonii* with larger flowers; *korolkowii* (syn. *albertii*), white, late spring, 12 ft., grows well in chalk, Turkestan; *macrantha*, hybrid between *racemosa* and *korolkowii*, white, spring, to 10 ft.; *racemosa* (syn. *grandiflora*), white, spring, 8 to 10 ft., very free flowering, China.

FABIANA (False Heath) – *Solanaceae*. Slightly tender flowering evergreen shrubs with heath-like foliage and tubular flowers.

Soil, good loamy, slightly moist but not waterlogged. Best on neutral or moderately acid soils but will survive on chalk if well fed. Position, sunny, warm, sheltered or in pots in a sunny frost-proof greenhouse. Plant or repot in spring.

Increase by cuttings of firm young shoots inserted in sandy soil in a propagator in summer.

Recommended kinds are *F. imbricata*, white, early summer, Peru, and vars. *prostrata*, mauve, 2 ft., hardier than type, *violacea*, lavender-mauve, to 8 ft.

FAGUS (Beech) – *Fagaceae*. Hardy deciduous trees.

Soil, sandy or chalky, and gravelly loam. Position, open dryish, lawns, copses, hedges; also good seaside trees. Plant in autumn or late winter. Common species (*F. sylvatica*) and its coloured-leaved forms are good hedge shrubs, plant 9 in. apart and keep sides closely trimmed in autumn or winter, but do not prune for the first two years so that plants become well established. Hard-pruned plants retain their dead leaves all winter and, since they can be grown to a considerable height, make excellent windbreaks.

Increase by seeds stratified for three months at 4°C. and then sown outdoors or in frames, transplanting seedlings when two years old; specially selected garden varieties by grafting in spring on common species.

Recommended kinds are *F. grandifolia*, American Beech, to 90 ft., but usually much less and tending to produce suckers, Eastern N. America; *sylvatica*, Common Beech, 70 to 90 ft., Europe (Britain), and vars. Dawyck, narrow columnar habit, *heterophylla* (syns. *asplenifolia*, *incisa* and *laciniata*), Cut-leaved Beech, Fern-leaved Beech, leaves narrow and deeply lobed, *pendula*, Weeping Beech, *purpurea*, Purple Beech, Copper Beech.

FATSHEDERA – *Araliaceae*. A hardy bigeneric hybrid between *Fatsia japonica* and *Hedera helix*, the common ivy. The evergreen leaves are lobed and leathery, like those of fatsia but smaller. The stems are long and flexible, easily trained to wires or trellis.

Soil, ordinary. Position, sun or shade or can be grown in pots as a room plant.

Increase by cuttings in a frame in summer or by layering in spring or autumn.

The only kind is *F. lizei*, and var. *variegata* with cream margin to leaves.

FATSIA – *Araliaceae*. Fairly hardy evergreen shrub. A popular room or greenhouse plant.

Compost, two parts sandy loam, one part each of leafmould, decayed manure and sand. Position, well-drained pots in a cool greenhouse or dwelling room. Pot or plant in spring.

Alternatively, plant outdoors in spring or autumn in a warm, sheltered sunny or partially shady place. Fatsia will survive temps. of about − 10°C.

Increase by cuttings of firm young growth in summer in a propagator; by root cuttings in early spring in a propagator with bottom heat.

The only species grown is *F. japonica* (syn. *Aralia sieboldii*), Japanese Aralia or Figleaf Palm, leaves green, palmate, 6 to 15 ft., Japan, and var. *variegata*, white variegated tips to leaf lobes.

FAUCARIA – *Aizoaceae*. Tender succulent plants with sharply toothed, jaw-like leaves. All are natives of S. Africa.

Grow in a fairly porous but not too rich compost, such as John Innes potting compost No. 1 with extra sand, in small, well-drained pots in a cool or intermediate greenhouse, minimum winter temp 7°C., or in a sunny window. Pot in spring. Water freely from late summer until midwinter, less freely in spring and summer. No shade is required at any time.

Faucaria tigrina

Increase by seeds sown in a close atmosphere, temp. 15 to 18°C., in spring or summer; by stem cuttings, which should first be dried, in late spring or early summer in temp. 15 to 18°C.; by division in spring.

Recommended kinds are *F. albidens*, yellow, autumn; *britteniae*, yellow, autumn; *felina* (syn. *Mesembryanthemum felinum*), Cat's Chaps, yellow, autumn; *lupina* (syn. *M. lupinum*), yellow, autumn; *tigrina* (syn. *M. tigrinum*), Tiger's Chaps, yellow, autumn; *tuberculosa* (syn. *M. tuberculosum*), yellow, autumn.

FEIJOA – *Myrtaceae*. Slightly tender, evergreen flowering shrubs.

Soil, ordinary. Position, sunny, sheltered, warm or in a frost proof greenhouse.

Increase by seeds sown in sandy soil during spring in temp. 15 to 18°C.; by cuttings of young growth taken during summer and rooted in a propagator.

The best kind is *F. sellowiana*, white and crimson, autumn, to 18 ft., Brazil.

FELICIA – *Compositae*. Slightly tender annuals or biennials and sub-shrubs mostly with blue daisy flowers.

Soil, ordinary, well drained. Position, beds or borders or a sunny frost-proof greenhouse. Sow seeds of annual kinds thinly in well-drained pans in early spring in temp. 15 to 18°C. Prick out seedlings when large enough to handle and harden off for planting out when there is no danger of frost.

Increase shrubby species by seeds sown in the same way or by cuttings of young shoots in spring or summer in a propagator. In cold places take some cuttings annually and overwinter in a frost-proof greenhouse or frame in case outdoor plants are killed.

Recommended kinds are *F. amelloides* (syn. *F. capensis*, *Agathaea coelestis*), Blue Marguerite, Blue Daisy, summer, blue, 12 to 18 in., sub-shrub, S. Africa; *bergeriana*, Kingfisher Daisy, blue, summer, 4 in., annual, S. Africa; *pappei* (syn. *Aster pappei*), blue, summer, 12 to 15 in., sub-shrub, S. Africa.

FEROCACTUS (Hedgehog Cactus, Barrel Cactus) – *Cactaceae*. Tender succulent plants usually large, globose or cylindrical, deeply ribbed and very spiny.

Compost, ordinary, porous and fairly rich, such as John Innes potting compost No. 2 with extra sand. Position, well-drained pots or pans in a sunny frost-proof greenhouse or window. Repot every two or three years in spring. Water fairly freely in spring and summer, very sparingly in autumn and winter. Minimum winter temp. 7°C.

Increase by seeds sown in sandy soil in temp. 18 to 21°C. in spring, keeping soil moderately moist; by stem cuttings inserted in small pots of sandy soil kept barely moist in summer; by grafting on common kinds in spring.

Recommended kinds are *F. acanthodes*, lemon yellow, summer, South-western U.S.A.; *latispinus* (syn. *cornigera*), purple, summer, Mexico; *lecontei*, yellow or red, summer, Arizona; *melocactiformis*, yellow, summer, Mexico; *rectispinus*, yellow, summer, S. California; *stainesii*, yellow, summer, Mexico.

FESTUCA (Fescue Grass) – *Gramineae*. Hardy perennial grass grown for its ornamental blue-grey foliage.

Soil, ordinary. Position, sunny. Plant in spring or early autumn.

Increase by division in spring.

The recommended kind is *F. ovina glauca*, Blue Fescue Grass, leaves very narrow, tufted, glaucous green, 9 in., a garden variety of a species found in all cool climates, including Britain.

FICUS (Fig) – *Moraceae*. Tender and hardy evergreen trees, shrubs and climbers, some grown as foliage plants in greenhouses,

Ficus elastica decora

rooms, etc., and one, *F. carica*, the fig cultivated both for ornament and for its edible fruits. Flowers unisexual, borne inside the young fruit.

Culture of tender species: Compost, moderately rich, John Innes potting compost No. 2 or equivalent. Position, erect species (*F. elastica*, etc.) in pots in an intermediate or warm greenhouse or dwelling room, minimum winter temp. 13°C. Creeping species (*pumila*, *radicans*) in beds with shoots clinging to walls, etc., in cool or intermediate greenhouses, minimum winter temp. 7°C. *F. pumila* will actually withstand a few degrees of frost and can be grown outdoors in mild places. Pot or plant in spring. Water normally. Maintain a moist atmosphere for erect species. Shade from direct sunshine. *F. elastica* will grow in quite poor light in a room.

Culture of the Fig: Soil, well drained, not too rich. Root spread restricted to a border about 3 ft. wide. Plant in the open in warm, sunny places or train against sunny walls outdoors or in a lean-to greenhouse. Plant from autumn until early spring. Water freely in spring and summer, sparingly in autumn and winter. Cut out thin or old stems and branches in autumn. Rub out unwanted shoots in spring and summer, and in early summer shorten good side shoots to five leaves where necessary to prevent overcrowding. Under glass and in warm climates two crops may be ripened each year, one in early summer from fruitlets already well formed on young stems the previous autumn; the second in late summer or early autumn from fruitlets that are still very small the previous autumn. In cool climates it is best to remove the more advanced fruits in autumn, retaining only the small ones which have the best chance to survive and ripen.

Increase tender species by cuttings of shoots inserted in sandy peat in a warm propagator in spring or summer; by stem cuttings 1 in. long, and with one leaf attached, slightly burying the stem portion in soil and supporting leaf with a stake, and placing in a warm propagator in summer; stem rooting in spring for tall plants of *F. benjamina*, *elastica* and *lyrata*. Fig by seeds sown in light soil in a temp. of 18 to 21°C. in winter or early spring; afterwards growing seedlings on in pots until they bear fruit and it can be seen if they are worth growing; by cuttings of previous year's shoots, 6 in. long and with a heel of older wood attached at the base, inserted in a frame or propagator in autumn; by cuttings of young shoots, 3 or 4 in. long, removed with a heel of older wood, and inserted in pots of light sandy soil in a warm propagator in summer; by layering shoots in summer; grafting by approach just after the tree comes into leaf; by budding in summer; or by suckers in autumn.

Recommended tender kinds are *F. benghalensis*, Banyan, Bengal Fig, large leathery dull green leaves, to 10 ft. (a tree in the tropics), India, Tropical Africa; *benjamina*, narrow leaves, weeping habit, 6 ft. (a tree in the tropics), Tropical Asia; *deltoidea* (syn. *diversifolia*), Mistletoe Fig, leaves sometimes khaki coloured beneath, 2 to 4 ft., India, Malaysia; *elastica*, India Rubber Plant, leaves large, leathery, shining dark green, to 10 ft. (much more in the tropics), Tropical Asia, and vars. *decora*, more compact habit, *doescheri*, leaves variegated pink and cream; *lyrata* (syn. *pandurata*), Banjo Fig, Fiddleback Fig, large leathery waisted leaves, 4 to 8 ft. (a tree in the tropics), Tropical Africa; *macrophylla*, Moreton Bay Fig, large leathery dark green leaves, to 10 ft. (tree outdoors in mild climates), Queensland, New South Wales; *nekbudu*, large leathery dark green leaves, to 10 ft. (tree in the tropics), Tropical Africa; *parcellii*, leaves green and ivory white, to 12 ft., Pacific Islands; *pumila* (syn. *repens*), Creeping Fig, climber, leaves small, dark green, stems self-clinging, China, Japan, and var.

Ficus benjamina

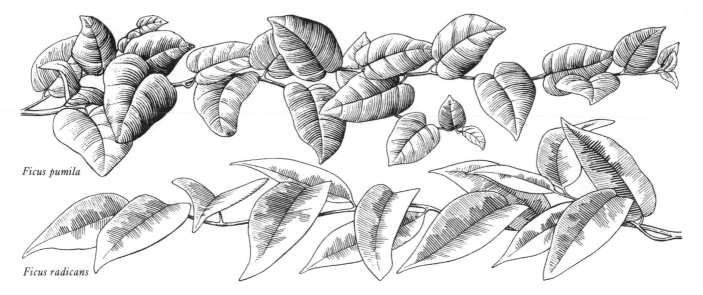

Ficus pumila

Ficus radicans

variegata, leaves variegated with white; radicans, climber, leaves small, stems self-clinging, habitat unknown, and var. variegata, leaves variegated with cream.

The hardy species cultivated is F. carica, Fig, leaves shining green, usually lobed, Western Asia.

FILIPENDULA (Meadowsweet) – Rosaceae. Hardy herbaceous perennials, formerly included in Spiraea. Small flowers carried in feathery heads or plumes.

Soil fairly rich and moist for most species but rather dry for F. hexapetala which succeeds well on chalk. Position, sunny, stream and pond sides; well-drained borders for F. hexapetala. Plant in spring or autumn.

Increase by division in spring or autumn; by seeds sown outdoors or in a frame in spring or early summer.

Recommended kinds are F. camtschatica, white, summer, 4 to 8 ft., Manchuria, Kamchatka, and var. rosea, pale pink; hexapetala (syn. Spiraea filipendula), Dropwort, white, early summer, 2 to 3 ft., Europe (Britain), Asia, and var. flore pleno, flowers double; palmata (syn. Spiraea digitata), pale pink, summer, 2 to 3 ft., Siberia, Kamchatka, and var. nana, 1 ft.; purpurea (syn. Spiraea palmata), pink or purple, 2 to 4 ft., summer, Japan, var. alba, white; rubra (syn. Spiraea lobata), Queen of the Prairie, pink, 2 to 8 ft., Eastern U.S.A., and vars. magnifica, larger flower clusters, and venusta (syn. Spiraea venusta), deep pink; ulmaria (syn. Spiraea ulmaria), Common Meadowsweet, white, summer, to 6 ft., Europe (Britain), W. Asia, and vars. aurea, leaves variegated with yellow, flore pleno, flowers double.

FITTONIA – Acanthaceae. Tender Peruvian perennial trailing plants with white or coloured veins on the leaves.

Grow in a moderately rich compost, such as John Innes potting compost No. 2, in an intermediate or warm greenhouse, minimum winter temp. 13°C. Repot in spring. Water normally. Maintain a moist atmosphere. Shade from direct sunlight. Can also be used as room plants, preferably in the moist air of a Wardian case, bottle garden or plant cabinet.

Increase by cuttings of firm shoots inserted in sandy soil in a warm propagator in spring or summer; by division of plants in early spring.

Recommended kinds are F. argyroneura, leaves green, veined white, creeping; gigantea, leaves dark green, veined carmine, 18 in.; verschaffeltii, leaves green, veined with red, creeping.

FITZ-ROYA (Patagonian Cypress) – Cupressaceae. One fairly hardy evergreen cone-bearing tree or large shrub, like a cypress with pendulous branchlets. Male and female organs on separate plants.

Soil, ordinary. Position, open but not very cold or exposed. Plant in autumn or early spring. Increase by seeds sown as soon as ripe in a cool greenhouse or frame.

The only species is F. patagonica, 15 to 50 ft., Patagonia, Chile.

FOENICULUM (Fennel) – Umbelliferae. Hardy perennial herbs, often rather short lived and grown as biennials or annuals. Ornamental, feathery foliage, strongly aromatic and used for flavouring, as are the seeds.

Two varieties are grown for their swollen stems which are blanched and cooked or used as salad.

Soil, well drained, moderately rich. Position, sunny. Plant F. vulgare in spring. Sow seeds of Florence Fennel and Carosella in drills 18 in. apart in spring where plants are to grow. Thin seedlings to 6 in. Remove flower stems. When plants are well grown draw up soil around the stems to blanch them.

Recommended kinds are F. vulgare, Common Fennel, yellow, summer, 4 to 5 ft., S. Europe, and vars. dulce, Florence Fennel, Finnochio, swollen stems, piperitum, Carosella, thickened stems, rubra, bronze foliage.

FORSYTHIA (Golden Bells) – Oleaceae. Hardy deciduous flowering shrubs. Popular for their early yellow blossom.

Soil, ordinary. Sunny or light shade, or F. suspensa may be trained against a wall or fence. Plant in autumn or late winter. Prune after flowering, cutting back old flowering stems to new shoots or side branches.

Increase by cuttings inserted in sandy soil in a propagator in summer, or in a cold frame in autumn; by layering in autumn.

Recommended kinds are F. intermedia, 10 ft., of upright growth, rich yellow, spring, hybrid between suspensa and viridissima, and vars. Lynwood, large flowers, spectabilis, extra free flowering, vitellina, deep yellow; ovata, amber yellow, early spring, 3 to 4 ft., Korea; suspensa, 10 ft. as a bush, rather sprawling and higher when trained to a wall, light yellow, spring, China, and var. atrocaulis, purplish black stems; viridissima, yellow, spring, 6 ft., China.

FOTHERGILLA (American Witch Hazel) – Hamamelidaceae. Hardy deciduous flowering shrubs grown primarily for their brilliant autumn colour. The white flowers are composed mainly of stamens.

Soil, lime free, loamy. Position, sunny, open. Plant in autumn or late winter.

Increase by seeds stratified for five months at 20 to 25°C. then for a further three months at 1°C. and then sown in sandy peat at 15 to 18°C.; by cuttings of firm young shoots in a propagator in summer; by layering shoots in autumn.

Recommended kinds are F. gardenii (syn. alnifolia), white, fragrant, spring, 3 ft., South-eastern U.S.A.; major, white, spring,

Fothergilla monticola

6 to 8 ft., Virginia and S. Carolina; *monticola*, white, spring, 6 ft., South-eastern U.S.A.

FRAGARIA (Strawberry) – *Rosaceae.* Hardy herbaceous perennials grown mainly as economic plants for their edible fruits, but a few kinds grown for ornament.

Soil, ordinary. Position, open or shady. Plant in spring or autumn.

Increase by rooting runners in summer, by division in spring.

The best kind is *F. vesca variegata*, white, summer, leaves variegated with white, prostrate, Europe (Britain).

FRANCOA (Maiden's Wreath; Bridal Wreath) – *Francoaceae.* Hardy and slightly tender perennial plants with flowers in slender spikes. All are natives of Chile.

Outdoor culture: Soil, light rich loam. Position, sunny and sheltered. Plant in spring.

Pot culture: Grow in a moderately rich compost, such as John Innes potting compost No. 2, in well-drained pots in a cool greenhouse, frame or window. Pot in spring. Water normally. Apply a little liquid manure to plants coming into flower.

Increase by seeds sown in temp. 15 to 18°C. in spring; by division of plants in spring.

Recommended kinds are *F. appendiculata*, rose, summer, 2 ft.; *ramosa*, white, summer, 2 to 3 ft.; *sonchifolia*, pink, summer, 2 ft.

FRANKENIA (Sea Heath) – *Frankeniaceae.* Hardy evergreen, flowering creeping plants.

Soil, light sandy. Position, sunny. Plant in spring.

Increase by division of plants in spring; by seeds sown in a frame in spring.

Recommended kinds are *F. laevis*, pink, summer, Europe (Britain); *thymifolia*, pink, 1 to 2 in., summer, bronze leaves, Spain.

FRAXINUS (Ash) – *Oleaceae.* Hardy deciduous trees grown mainly for their ornamental pinnate foliage but some species also have attractive white or greenish white flowers.

Soil, ordinary. Position, open, sunny or partially shady. Suitable for seaside gardens, towns, chalky or gravelly situations. Plant in autumn or late winter.

Increase by seeds stratified for five months at 20 to 25°C., then for three months at 4°C. (those of *F. americana* need only this cold stratification), then sown outdoors or in a frame, transplant seedlings when a year old; by grafting on common species in early spring.

Recommended kinds are *F. americana*, White Ash, to 120 ft., Eastern N. America; *angustifolia*, 60 to 70 ft., S. Europe, N. Africa; *excelsior*, Common Ash, 100 to 140 ft., Europe (Britain), and vars. *crispa*, Curl-leaved Ash, *aurea*, Golden Ash, *pendula*, Weeping Ash; *ornus*, Flowering or Manna Ash, greenish white flowers, late spring, 50 to 65 ft., S. Europe; *oxycarpa*, 50 ft., S. Europe, Iran, and var. Raywood, leaves purple in autumn; *pennsylvanica*, 40 to 60 ft., Eastern N. America; *spaethiana*, one of the most striking ashes on account of its yellow-tinged foliage, 30 to 50 ft., Japan; *velutina*, 30 to 40 ft., South-western U.S.A.; *xanthoxyloides*, Afghan Ash, unusual small tree with winged leaf stalks, Afghanistan.

FREESIA – *Iridaceae.* Slightly tender corms from S. Africa, often very fragrant. Those grown for cut flowers are complex hybrids.

Compost, John Innes potting compost

Freesia (hybrid)

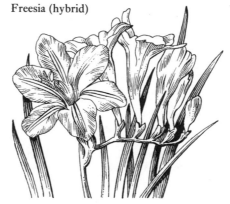

No. 2 or equivalent. Position, pots in a cool greenhouse, frame or window. Pot in summer to flower in midwinter, and at intervals till midwinter for late spring flowers. Plant corms 1 in. deep and 2 in. apart. Five-inch pots are a suitable size. Stand pots in a cool position and give very little water until growth starts, then water freely until the plants have flowered. After flowering gradually decrease water supply, keeping soil quite dry till foliage dies down. Temperature not lower than 5°C. Apply weak liquid or artificial manure to plants showing flower. Stake early, repot annually.

Freesia refracta is hardier than most of the hybrids and will survive a few degrees of frost. It may be grown outdoors in light, rich, sandy soil in sunny, warm, well-drained places only. Plant corms 2 in. deep and 2 in. apart in late summer and early autumn. Protect from frost in winter.

Increase by seeds sown in pots or pans of light sandy soil in a cool greenhouse or frame as soon as ripe or in spring; spacing the seeds or thinning the seedlings so that no transplanting is needed before flowering. Also by offsets at potting time.

Recommended kinds are *F. armstrongii*, rosy pink with yellow tube, 10 to 15 in.; *corymbosa* (syn. *odorata*), yellow and orange, 5 to 18 in., fragrant; *refracta*, white and orange, fragrant, summer, 1 to 1½ ft., and vars. *leichtlinii*, yellow and orange, *alba*, white. The many hybrids are white, yellow, pink, carmine, red, purple, mauve, 1½ to 2½ ft.

FREMONTIA – *Sterculiaceae.* Slightly tender evergreen flowering shrubs, also known as fremontodendron.

Soil, sandy loam. Position, against walls or fences, or in warm, sheltered, sunny places, or in a sunny cool greenhouse. Plant in spring or autumn.

Increase by seeds sown in sandy soil in temp. 15 to 18°C. in spring; by cuttings in a propagator in summer.

Recommended kinds are *F. californica*, golden mallow-like flowers, summer, to 10 ft. or more on a wall or in warm localities, California; *mexicana*, similar to last but narrower petals, California, Mexico.

FRITILLARIA (Fritillary) – *Liliaceae.* Hardy bulbs, many from mountainous regions and needing alpine house or frame protection from wet in winter, and thorough ripening in summer.

Those most commonly grown outdoors in ordinary, deep rich soil are the Crown Imperial, *F. imperialis*, and the Snake's Head Fritillary, *F. meleagris*, which can also be naturalized in turf; topdress Crown Imperials annually with decayed manure. Do not dig around the plants, keep the soil firm and do not transplant bulbs more often than once in four years. Plant the large bulbs of Crown Imperial 6 in. deep and 8 to 12 in.

apart, those of *F. meleagris* 4 in. deep and 4 to 6 in. apart in moist soil.

Pot culture in alpine house or frame: Compost, John Innes potting compost No. 1 or equivalent, with extra sand. Position, well-drained pots in a cold frame or cold greenhouse. Pot in autumn, placing one bulb in the centre of a 5-, 6- or 8-in. pot. The small bulbs are very fragile and liable to damage. Water very little till growth begins, then give a moderate supply. Apply liquid manure when plants show flower. After flowering gradually withhold water, keeping soil dry after foliage has died, but if in a frame raise the lights to give air.

Increase by seeds sown in pots or pans of sandy soil in a cold frame or greenhouse as soon as ripe, or in spring; by offsets at planting time. Do not transplant seedlings the first year. Seedlings do not flower until four to six years old.

Fritillaria pyrenaica

Recommended kinds are *F. acmopetala*, olive green and purple, spring, 20 to 30 in., Asia Minor; *assyriaca*, chestnut brown and yellow, spring, 12 to 15 in., Iraq, Iran; *aurea*, yellow and brown, 6 in., spring, Asia Minor; *citrina* (sometimes listed as *bithynica* var. *citrina*), green and yellow, 8 in., spring, Asia Minor; *elwesii*, green and brown, spring, 1 ft.; *imperialis*, Crown Imperial, yellow, reddish orange, spring, 2 to 3 ft., Orient; *meleagris*, Snake's Head, purple, white, usually chequered, spring, 1 to 1½ ft., Europe (Britain); *pallidiflora*, green flecked crimson, spring, 9 to 15 in., Siberia; *persica*, Persian Lily, violet-blue, early spring, 2 ft., Asia Minor; *pontica*, green, buff and brown, spring, 9 to 12 in., S. E. Europe; *pudica*, golden yellow, spring, 6 in., N. W. America; *pyrenaica*, plum, olive and maroon, late spring, 1½ ft., Pyrenees; *recurva*, orange-scarlet, spring, 2 ft., California; *ruthenica*, purplish black, spring, 1 ft., Caucasus.

FUCHSIA – *Onagraceae.* Variously tender flowering shrubs many with showy, pendent flowers produced over a long period.

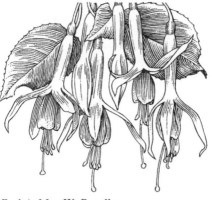

Fuchsia Mrs W. Rundle

Culture under glass: Grow in a moderately rich compost, such as John Innes potting compost No. 2, in pots, or pendulous kinds in hanging baskets, in a cool or intermediate greenhouse, minimum winter temp. 7°C. Water freely in spring and summer, very sparingly in winter if temperatures below 10°C. are likely, but normally in an intermediate house in which growth will continue most of the winter. Shade from strong sunshine in summer. Ventilate as freely as possible consistent with temperatures recommended. Pot in spring, or young plants as necessary to prevent them becoming pot bound.

Plants can be trained as standards or in other ways by removing unwanted shoots and pinching the tips of other shoots to obtain extra branches where required. Even the tender fuchsias can be planted outdoors in summer in most places, and potted and returned to the greenhouse in autumn before sharp frosts occur.

Culture outdoors: Soil, ordinary, deep, rich. Position, warm, sheltered, sunny or lightly shaded. Plant in spring. Cut back all dead or damaged growth in early spring, if necessary, to ground level. Protect roots in autumn by scattering dry litter, peat or coarse sand over them.

Increase by cuttings of young shoots inserted singly in small pots of sandy soil in a frame or cool propagator any time from spring to early autumn; species by seeds sown in temp. 15 to 18°C. in spring.

Recommended kinds are *F. arborescens*, rose, winter, 10 to 15 ft., Mexico; *boliviana*, red, summer, 2 to 4 ft., Bolivia; *corymbiflora*, deep red, summer, 10 to 15 ft., Ecuador, Peru; *excorticata*, green becoming red-purple, spring, 6 to 15 ft., New Zealand; *exoniensis*, scarlet, summer, 2 ft., spreading habit, garden hybrid; *fulgens*, scarlet, summer, 4 to 6 ft., Mexico; *magellanica*, scarlet and purple, summer, 6 to 10 ft., S. America, and vars. *alba* (syn. *molinae*), pale pink, *gracilis*, slender habit, *pumila*, dwarf, *riccartonii*, vigorous, stiffly branched, *variegata* (syn. *gracilis variegata*), leaves green, edged cream and pink, *versicolor*, leaves grey-green, cream and pink; *procumbens*, yellow

and blue, summer, magenta-crimson berries, habit trailing, New Zealand; *splendens*, scarlet, summer, 6 ft., Mexico; *thymifolia*, white to pink, summer, 2 to 3 ft., Mexico; *triphylla*, cinnabar red, summer, 1 to 2 ft., Santo Domingo.

There are hundreds of garden varieties mostly derived from hybrids between *magellanica*, *fulgens* and *coccinea*.

FURCRAEA – *Agavaceae.* Tender succulent plants with leaves in basal rosettes and whitish or greenish flowers in terminal panicles on tall scapes. Leaves, long, fleshy, spined.

Grow in porous compost, such as John Innes potting compost No. 1, in a light, sunny, cool greenhouse or plant outdoors in well-drained soil and a warm sunny position in frost-free areas. Pot or plant in spring. Water moderately in spring and summer, little in autumn and winter.

Increase by offsets inserted in small pots at any time.

Recommended kinds *F. bedinghausii*, green, summer, to 15 ft., Mexico; *elegans*, green, summer, 20 ft., Mexico; *foetida* (syn. *gigantea*), green and ivory white, summer, 20 ft., Tropical America.

GAGEA – *Liliaceae.* Small hardy bulbs.

Soil, sandy. Position, sunny borders or in turf. Plant 3 in. deep and 3 in. apart in autumn. Leave undisturbed.

Increase by offsets removed in autumn.

Recommended kinds are *G. fistulosa* (syn. *liottardii*), yellow, 4 in., late spring, Europe; *sylvatica* (syn. *lutea*), Yellow Star of Bethlehem, yellow, spring, 6 in., Europe (Britain).

GAILLARDIA – *Compositae.* Half-hardy annuals and hardy herbaceous perennials with showy daisy-type flowers.

Soil, ordinary. Position, sunny, well-drained beds or borders. Plant perennial kinds in spring. Plants are not usually long lived. Sow annual kinds in spring in temp. 15 to 18°C., prick off into boxes and harden off for planting outdoors in late spring or early summer.

Increase perennial species by seeds sown as for annual kinds; by division of plants in spring, or by root cuttings laid in sandy soil in early spring.

Recommended kinds are *G. aristata*, Blanket Flower, yellow, summer, 18 in., perennial, N. America, and many garden varieties with yellow and red or all red flowers; *pulchella*, crimson and yellow, summer, 2 to 3 ft., annual, N. America, and var. *picta*, orange, red and yellow, double, 1 ft.

GALANTHUS (Snowdrop, Fair Maids of February) – *Amaryllidaceae.* Hardy bulbs.

Soil, ordinary or rich. Position, margins of beds; groups in open or shady borders; banks, rock gardens or in turf, *G. nivalis* and

Galanthus nivalis

plicatus like shade, as in light woodland, or sun; most choice varieties need sun. Plant bulbs 2 in. deep and 1 in. apart in autumn or lift and divide clumps immediately after flowering.

Choice varieties should be grown permanently in pots, others can be forced in spring. Compost, John Innes potting compost No. 1 or equivalent. Position, alpine house, cool house, or frame. Pot in autumn, placing bulbs 1 in. deep and 1 in. apart in 4- or 5-in. pots or shallow pans. Place pots for forcing in a cold frame or outdoors and cover with cinder ashes or peat until growth begins. Water moderately till after flowering, then gradually cease. Plant forced bulbs outdoors the following autumn.

Increase by seeds sown as soon as ripe in light sandy soil, and place pans in a cool shady position; by offsets treated as bulbs, removed from clumps after flowering, and by division of clumps after flowering. Seedlings flower when three years old.

Recommended kinds are *G. byzantinus*, green and white, late winter, 9 to 12 in., S. E. Europe; *caucasicus*, white and green, late winter, spring, 6 in., Caucasus; *elwesii*, white, late winter, 9 to 12 in., Asia Minor, and varieties; *fosteri*, white, late winter, 6 in., Asia Minor; *ikariae*, white, spring, 8 in., Nikaria; *nivalis*, Common Snowdrop, white, late winter and spring, and var. *reginae-olgae*, autumn, 6 in., Europe, with many varieties; *latifolius*, white and green, early spring, 6 in., Caucasus, and *allenii*, a fine garden form, 6 to 9 in.; *plicatus*, Crimean Snowdrop, white, late winter, 10 to 12 in., Caucasus.

GALAX – *Diapensiaceae*. Hardy perennial with shining, evergreen leaves and white flowers in spikes.

Soil, lime-free loam and peat. Position, moderately shady, not liable to dry out in summer. Excellent as ground cover. Plant in spring or autumn.

Increase by division of plants in spring or autumn; by seeds sown in peaty soil in a frame in spring.

The only species is *G. aphylla*, Wand Plant, Carpenter's Leaf, white, summer, 1 ft., South-eastern U.S.A.

GALEGA – *Leguminosae*. Hardy perennial herbs with pea-type flowers in small spikes or clusters.

Soil, ordinary. Position, open. Plant in spring or autumn. Replant every two or three years.

Increase by seeds sown in spring or early summer in a sunny position; by division of roots in spring or autumn.

Recommended kinds are *G. officinalis*, Goat's Rue, blue, summer, 3 to 5 ft., S. Europe, and vars. *alba*, white, *carnea*, pink, *hartlandii*, blue and white; *orientalis*, blue, summer, 3 to 4 ft., Caucasus.

GALTONIA (Spire Lily) – *Liliaceae*. Hardy S. African bulbs, only one of which is commonly grown.

Any ordinary or rich well-drained soil. Position, open sunny borders. Plant in autumn or spring, placing bulbs 6 in. deep and 6 in. apart.

Galtonias can be forced in pots in any reasonably good compost such as John Innes potting compost No. 1. Grow in a cold or cool greenhouse. Pot in autumn to flower in spring; in spring to flower in autumn. Place one bulb with its apex just showing through the surface of the soil in a well-drained 6-in. pot. Cover with ashes in a cold frame until growth begins. Water moderately when leaves appear, freely when in full growth; keep nearly dry after flowering. Apply weak liquid manure occasionally to plants in flower. Plant outside after forcing.

Increase by seeds sown in sandy soil in a frame in autumn or spring; by offsets treated as bulbs in autumn. Seedlings flower when four or five years old. Small bulbs are liable to frost damage.

The best kind is *G. candicans* (syn. *Hyacinthus candicans*), white, fragrant, summer, 2 to 3 ft.

GARDENIA – *Rubiaceae*. Tender evergreen flowering shrubs or small trees usually with very sweetly scented flowers.

Grow in a moderately rich compost, such as John Innes potting compost No. 2, in pots in an intermediate or warm greenhouse, minimum winter temp. 13°C. Plants can be stood outdoors in summer in a sunny

Gardenia jasminoides

sheltered place. Pot in spring. Shade lightly in summer unless plants are out of doors. Prune into shape in spring. Apply liquid manure occasionally in late spring and summer to healthy plants. Plants one to two years old produce the best blooms.

Increase by cuttings of firm young side shoots 2 to 3 in. long inserted in well-drained pots of sandy peat in a warm propagator in spring.

The best kind is *G. jasminoides*, Cape Jasmine, white, fragrant, summer, China, Japan, and vars. *florida*, double white, *fortuniana*, large single flowers.

GARRYA – *Garryaceae*. Slightly tender evergreen shrubs. Flowers (pendulous catkins), male and female borne on separate plants.

Soil, ordinary, well drained. Position, against sheltered walls or in warm, sheltered places. They succeed well near the sea. Plant in spring or autumn.

Increase by cuttings of firm shoots in sandy soil in a propagator in summer; by layering shoots in autumn.

Recommended kinds are *G. elliptica*, Silk Tassel Bush, catkins greenish yellow, winter, female catkins followed by maroon-coloured fruits, 6 to 12 ft., California; *thuretii*, a vigorous hybrid with insignificant catkins but useful as a very fast growing windbreak in maritime and warm localities, 15 ft.; *wrightii*, short greenish yellow catkins in late summer, 6 ft., South-western U.S.A.

GASTERIA – *Liliaceae*. Tender succulent plants, stemless, or nearly so, with long thick leaves arranged fanwise, and flowers in loose pendent racemes. All are natives of S. Africa.

Grow in a moderately rich but very porous compost, such as John Innes potting compost No. 2 with extra sand or grit, in well-drained pots in a cool or intermediate greenhouse or window. Shade lightly in summer. Pot in spring. Water moderately from spring to early autumn, very little the rest of the year.

Increase by seeds sown in sandy soil, temp. 15 to 18°C. in spring; by offsets removed in spring or summer and rooted in sand or sandy soil.

Recommended kinds are *G. liliputana*, pink and green, summer, 6 in.; *lingua* (syn. *disticha*), red, leaves spotted with white, 6 to 9 in.; *maculata*, red, summer, leaves spotted white, 6 to 8 in.; *marmorata*, red, summer, 6 in.; *nigricans*, pink, summer, leaves spotted white, 6 to 8 in.; *trigona*, red, summer, leaves spotted white, 6 to 8 in.; *verrucosa*, red, summer, leaves with raised white spots, 6 to 9 in.

GAULTHERIA – *Ericaceae*. Mainly hardy evergreen shrubs with red, purple or blue berries, suitable for acid soils and shady places. They will thrive in a variety of places including quite moist situations. Plant in spring or autumn.

Increase by seeds sown in peaty soil outdoors in autumn; by removal of rooted offsets in spring; by cuttings in the summer or autumn.

Recommended kinds are *G. adenothrix*, white and pink, spring, summer, berries red, 1 ft., Japan; *cuneata*, white, summer, 9 in., berries white, W. China; *forrestii*, white, summer, berries blue, 3 ft., W. China; *miqueliana*, white or pinkish, early summer, berries white, 1 ft., Japan; *nummularioides*, white and pink, summer, trailing, berries blue-black, Himalaya; *procumbens*, Canada Tea, Partridge Berry, Creeping Wintergreen, white, summer, creeping, berries red, N. America; *shallon*, Shallon, white, early summer, 4 ft., N. W. America; *tetramera*, white, spring, summer, berries in varying shades of blue, W. China; *trichophylla*, pink, spring, 3 to 6 in., blue berries, Himalaya; *veitchiana*, white, early summer, 1 to 3 ft., berries blue, W. China.

GAURA – *Onagraceae*. Hardy herbaceous perennials and annuals, but only one kind commonly grown. Starry flowers in loose sprays.

Soil, light. Position, sunny well-drained beds or borders. Plant in spring.

Increase by seeds sown in light soil outdoors in spring.

The recommended kind is *G. lindheimeri*, white and rose, summer, autumn, 3 to 4 ft., Texas.

GAYLUSSACIA (Huckleberry) – *Ericaceae*. Evergreen or deciduous berry-bearing shrubs, to be grown in the same way as vaccinium.

Recommended kinds, both from the Eastern U.S.A., are *G. baccata*, Black Huckleberry, reddish, late spring, fruits black, 1 to 3 ft., deciduous; *brachycera*, white or pink, berries blue, 6 to 12 in.

GAZANIA (Treasure Flower) – *Compositae*. Slightly tender herbaceous perennials with showy daisy flowers. All those dealt with here are natives of S. Africa.

Grow in not too rich, well-drained soil in a warm sunny position. In areas in which frost is likely to occur bring plants into a frost-proof frame or greenhouse in early autumn and replant outdoors in spring when danger of frost is over. Alternatively, root cuttings in a frame or greenhouse in late summer and overwinter these in protection. *G. montana*, the hardiest species, will survive a few degrees of frost especially if soil is well drained.

Increase by cuttings in sandy soil or in a frame or unheated greenhouse in summer or early autumn; by seeds sown in sandy soil during spring in temp. 15 to 18°C.

Recommended kinds are *G. montana*, yellow and black, summer, mat forming;

pavonia, yellow, brown and white, summer, 1 ft.; *rigens*, yellow and black, summer, 1 ft.; *splendens*, orange, black and white, summer, 1 ft., hybrid. Also many hybrid varieties of varying colours including pink and purple.

GELSEMIUM – *Loganiaceae*. Rather tender evergreen twining shrubs with jasmine-like flowers.

Soil, ordinary. Position, warm sunny wall or pots in a sunny greenhouse or conservatory. Will survive a few degrees of frost. Pot or plant in spring. Prune as necessary after flowering.

Increase by seeds sown in temp. 15 to 18°C. in spring; by cuttings of firm young growth in a warm propagator in summer; by layering in spring.

The best kind is *G. sempervirens*, Carolina Jessamine, yellow, late spring, early summer, South-eastern U.S.A., Central America.

GENISTA (Broom) – *Leguminosae*. Hardy deciduous flowering shrubs; excellent for dry banks and stony ground.

Soil, ordinary, well drained. Position, open, sunny. Plant in autumn or late winter from containers as genistas resent root breakage. Prune after flowering, shortening flowering stems but do not cut into old, hard wood.

Increase by seeds sown outdoors or in a frame in spring.

Recommended kinds are *G. aethnensis*, Mt. Etna Broom, yellow, summer, 15 to 20 ft., Sardinia, Sicily; *anglica*, Needle Furze, yellow, late spring, summer, 1 to 1½ ft., Europe (Britain); *cinerea*, yellow, early summer, 6 to 10 ft., S. W. Europe; *hispanica*, Spanish Gorse, yellow, spring, summer, 1 to 2 ft., S. W. Europe; *lydia*, yellow, spring, summer, 1 to 2 ft., S. E. Europe; *pilosa*, yellow, late spring, 6 to 12 in., Europe (Britain); *sagittalis*, yellow, early summer, prostrate, Europe; *sylvestris*, yellow, summer, 6 to 9 in., S. E. Europe; *tinctoria*, Dyer's Greenweed, yellow, late summer, 1 to 2 ft., Europe, and var. *plena*, double flowers; *virgata* (syn. *tenera*), yellow, summer, 4 ft., Madeira.

GENTIANA (Gentian) – *Gentianaceae*. Hardy perennials frequently small and from mountainous places with tubular or funnel-shaped flowers.

Grow *G. acaulis* in fairly rich soil with chalk or lime; other mountain kinds in equal parts of lime-free loam, peat and coarse sand; *G. asclepiadea* in any ordinary soil with plenty of peat or leafmould. Most kinds need full sun but *G. asclepiadea* prefers light shade. Most need abundant moisture in summer and a few are bog plants. Plant in spring and topdress each spring with peat or well-decayed leafmould. *G. amoena*, *andrewsii*, *bavarica*, *cachemirica*, *calycosa*, *far-*

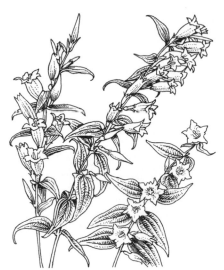

Gentiana asclepiadea

reri, *hexa-farreri*, *hexaphylla*, *kurroo*, *lawrencei*, *loderi*, *ornata*, *pneumonanthe*, *prolata*, *sikkimensis*, *sino-ornata*, *strangulata*, and *waltonii* dislike lime.

Increase by seeds sown deep in sandy peat in a cold frame in spring; by division of plants in spring. Seeds sometimes take one or two years to germinate and soil must be kept moderately moist.

Recommended kinds are *G. acaulis*, Gentianella (syn. *excisa*), deep blue, spring, 4 in., Europe, and vars. *alba*, white, *angustifolia*, narrow leaves, *clusii*, flowers with paler throat, *kochiana*, sky blue speckled green within; *alpina*, deep blue, spring, 3 in., Alps; *andrewsii*, blue, late summer, early autumn, 1 ft., Eastern N. America; *angulosa*, deep blue, spring, 3 in., Caucasus; *asclepiadea*, Willow Gentian, deep blue, summer, 2 ft., Europe, and var. *alba*, white; *bavarica*, blue, spring, 2 to 3 in., Central Europe; *bellidifolia*, white, summer, 6 in., New Zealand; *cachemerica*, blue and white, late summer, 4 to 6 in., Himalaya; *calycosa*, blue, spotted green, summer, trailing, Rocky Mountains; *dahurica*, dark blue, summer, prostrate, China, Asia Minor; *farreri*, blue and white, late summer and autumn, prostrate, China; *freyniana*, purplish blue, late summer, early autumn, 6 to 9 in., Asia Minor; *froelichii*, bright blue, summer, 2 in., Europe; *gracilipes* (syn. *purdomii*), purplish blue, late summer, prostrate, China; *hexa-farreri*, blue, autumn, 3 to 4 in., hybrid between *hexaphylla* and *farreri*; *hexaphylla*, blue, summer, 3 in., Tibet, China; *kurroo*, deep blue, autumn, 6 in., Himalaya; *lagodechiana*, deep blue, summer, 9 to 12 in., Caucasus; *lawrencei*, blue, summer, 4 in., Siberia, *loderi*, pale blue, summer, prostrate, Kashmir; *lutea*, yellow, summer, 4 to 5 ft., needs moist soil, Europe; *macaulayi*, deep blue, autumn, prostrate, hybrid between *farreri* and *sino-ornata*; *ornata*, pale blue, purple and white, late summer, prostrate, Nepal; *pneumonanthe*, Marsh Gentian, blue, late summer, 6 to 9 in., Europe (Britain), needs very wet soil; *prolata*, blue, summer, mat forming, China; *punctata*, yellow, spotted purple, summer, 1 to 2 ft., Europe; *pyrenaica*, violet-blue, late spring, early summer, Europe, Asia; *saxosa*, white, late summer, prostrate, New Zealand; *septemfida*, blue, summer, 9 to 12 in., Asia Minor; *sino-ornata*, deep blue, autumn, prostrate, China; *verna*, blue, spring, 2 to 3 in., Europe (Britain).

GERANIUM (Cranesbill) – *Geraniaceae*. Hardy and slightly tender herbaceous perennials with attractive foliage and flowers. For greenhouse geraniums see Pelargonium.

Soil, ordinary, well drained, many kinds thrive on chalk or limestone. Plant in spring or autumn. *G. palmatum* needs a frost-free place such as a cool greenhouse.

Increase by seeds sown in ordinary soil in a sunny position outdoors in spring or early summer, or in a cold frame or greenhouse in spring; by division in spring or autumn.

Recommended kinds are *G. aconitifolium*, white, dark veined, late spring, early summer, 1½ ft., S. Europe; *argenteum*, rose, summer, 1 ft., leaves silver grey, Alps, var. *purpureum*, intense crimson red; *cinereum*, pink, early summer, leaves grey, 6 in., Pyrenees, var. *album*, white; *dalmaticum* (syns. *macrorrhizum dalmaticum, microrrhizum*), light rose, early summer, 4 in., Dalmatia, and var. *album*, white; *endressii*, rose, summer, 1 ft., Pyrenees; *grandiflorum*, blue, summer, 1½ to 2 ft., Sikkim, and var. *alpinum*, 1 ft.; *ibericum*, blue, summer, 1½ to 2 ft., Caucasus, Turkey; *macrorrhizum*, pink, spring, summer, scented leaves, 12 to 15 in., S. Europe; *napuligerum* (syn. *farreri*), pink, late spring, early summer, grey leaves, 4 to 6 in., China; *nodosum*, lilac-pink, summer, 1 ft., Europe; *palmatum* (syn. *anemonifolium*), magenta, late spring, early summer, 2 ft., rather tender, Madeira, Teneriffe; *phaeum*, Mourning Widow, maroon, late spring, summer, 2 ft., Europe; *pratense*, blue, summer, 2 to 3 ft., N. Europe (Britain), and vars. *album*, white, *plenum*, double, *roseum*, pink, *striatum* (syn. *bicolor*), blue and white; *psilostemon* (syn. *armenum*), crimson magenta, late spring, early summer, 2 ft., Armenia; *pylzowianum*, pink, summer, 6 to 9 in., Tibet; *renardii*, lavender, summer, 9 in., Caucasus; *sanguineum*, crimson, summer, 1 ft., Europe (Britain), and vars. *album*, white, *prostratum*, dwarf form, *lancastriense*, prostrate, pale pink; *subcaulescens*, carmine, spring to autumn, 9 in., Balkans; *sylvaticum*, blue, summer, 2 to 3 ft., Europe (Britain), and var. *album*, white; *wallichianum*, purple, summer, sprawling, Himalaya, and var. Buxton's Blue, blue and white.

GERBERA (Transvaal Daisy) – *Compositae*. Slightly tender herbaceous perennials with elegant daisy-type flowers.

Compost, John Innes potting compost No. 1 or equivalent with one-quarter its bulk extra coarse sand. Position, well-drained pots or beds in a cool greenhouse, minimum winter temp. 7°C. Water fairly freely in spring and summer, sparingly in autumn and winter. Shade from strong sunshine in summer. Ventilate freely, consistent with maintaining necessary minimum temperature. Pot in spring. Best renewed frequently from seed.

Increase by seeds sown in sandy soil in spring in temp. of 15°C.

The best kind is *G. jamesonii*, Barberton Daisy, pink, red, terra-cotta, orange or yellow, late spring, summer, 18 in., S. Africa. There are single- and double-flowered varieties.

GESNERIA All the plants commonly grown under this name have been transferred to other genera and those still recognized by botanists as belonging to *Gesneria* are all rather difficult and not recommended. See Kohleria, Rechsteineria and Smithiantha for desirable kinds.

GEUM (Avens) – *Rosaceae*. Hardy perennial flowering herbs with showy flowers.

Soil, ordinary, well drained for most but moist for *G. rivale*. Position, sunny. Plant in spring or autumn. Cut down flower stems in autumn.

Increase by seeds sown in pots of light soil in a cold frame in spring, or in a sunny position outdoors in late spring or early summer; by division in spring.

Recommended kinds are *G. borisii*, orange, summer and autumn, 9 to 12 in., hybrid between *bulgaricum* and *reptans*; *bulgaricum*, yellow, summer, 12 to 18 in., Bulgaria; *chiloense* (often wrongly called *coccineum*, which is a different plant not much cultivated), scarlet, summer, 2 ft., Chile, and var. *plenum*, and numerous garden forms with yellow, orange or red flowers mostly double; *montanum*, yellow, early summer, 6 to 12 in., S. Europe; *reptans*, yellow, summer, trailing, Europe; *rivale*, Water Avens, old rose, summer, 9 to 12 in., Europe (Britain).

GILIA – *Polemoniaceae*. Annuals, biennials and perennials, those grown in gardens mostly being renewed annually from seed. The funnel-shaped flowers are often very showy and freely produced.

Soil, ordinary, well drained. Position, sunny. Sow seeds of annual kinds in spring where plants are to flower, thinning seedlings to 3 in. apart. Sow biennials in late summer or early autumn in a cool greenhouse unless the climate is very mild and winter drainage first class. Harden off seedlings for planting outdoors the following spring where they are to flower.

Recommended annual kinds are *G. achilleaefolia*, purplish blue, summer, 2 ft., Cali-

fornia; *capitata*, light blue, summer, 1½ to 2 ft., Western N. America; *hybrida* (syn. *Leptosiphon hybridus*), many colours, summer, 3 to 6 in., hybrid of uncertain origin; *lutea*, yellow, summer, 6 in., California, Mexico; *tricolor*, lavender, yellow and pink, summer, 1½ ft., Western N. America, and var. *nivalis*, white.

The best biennial kind is *G. rubra* (syn. *coronopifolia*), scarlet, summer, 3 to 6 ft., California.

GILLENIA – *Rosaceae*. Hardy perennials with small flowers in loose sprays.

Soil, peaty. Position, moist, shady. Plant in spring or autumn. Cut down flowering stems in autumn.

Increase by division of roots in spring; by seeds sown in spring.

The best kind is *G. trifoliata*, Indian Physic, red and white, summer, 2 ft., Eastern U.S.A.

GINKGO (Maidenhair Tree) – *Ginkgoaceae*. Hardy deciduous coniferous tree with ornamental foliage turning yellow in autumn. Male and female flowers borne on separate trees but males are most desirable for ornamental purposes as the fruits produced by the female trees fall and smell unpleasant when crushed.

Soil, ordinary, well drained. Position, open, sunny. Plant in autumn or late winter.

Increase by seeds sown in light sandy soil in a cold frame as soon as ripe; by cuttings in summer in a propagator; garden varieties by grafting in spring on to seedlings.

The only species is *G. biloba* (syn. *Salisburia adiantifolia*), fruit small, globular, 60 to 80 ft., China, vars. *fastigiata*, narrowly erect, *pendula*, weeping.

GLADIOLUS (Sword Lily) – *Iridaceae*. Slightly tender corms with showy flowers in spikes.

Outdoor culture: Soil, deep, rich, liberally manured. Position, sunny, well drained. Plant summer-flowering kinds in spring, spring-flowering kinds in autumn. Tie large-flowered kinds individually to canes or other supports. Lift plants six or seven weeks after flowers fade, cut off all top growth 1 in. above the corms, remove old shrivelled corms, which are useless, from the base of the new corms and store the latter in shallow trays in an airy place secure from frost.

Culture of early-flowering kinds under glass: Compost, John Innes potting compost No. 2 or equivalent. Plant or pot in autumn and grow in a sunny, frost-proof greenhouse. Water sparingly at first, moderately when growth starts, freely while flower stems are lengthening, at which period plants may be fed with weak liquid manure or fertilizer. Gradually reduce water supply after flowering and allow plants to die down, after which corms can be treated as for those outdoors.

Increase by seeds sown in light, rich soil in spring in temp. 15 to 18°C.; by cormels, which grow at the base of corms, planted 2 in. deep and 6 in. apart in sunny borders outdoors in spring; by the natural increase of the corms. Seedlings usually flower when three years old; cormels when two years old.

Most varieties grown are hybrids mainly from the following species: *G. blandus* (syn. *oppositiflorus*), white or pink, early summer, 1 to 1½ ft., S. Africa; *byzantinus*, magenta, early summer, 2 ft., Eastern Mediterranean; *cardinalis*, scarlet, summer, 2 to 3 ft., S. Africa; *cruentus*, scarlet and pale yellow, autumn, Natal; *cuspidatus*, white, rose or purple, late spring, early summer, S. Africa; *floribundus*, white and purple, late spring, 1½ ft., S. Africa; *primulinus* (syn. *natalensis primulinus*), yellow, summer, 1½ to 2 ft., Tropical Africa; *psittacinus* (syn. *natalensis*), red and yellow, autumn, 2 to 3 ft., S. Africa; *purpureo-auratus* (syn. *papilio*), yellow and purple, late summer, Natal; *recurvus*, yellow becoming blue, spring, 1 to 3 ft., S. Africa; *saundersii*, carmine, autumn, 2 to 3 ft., S. Africa; *tristis*, yellowish white and purple, scented, spring, 1½ ft., Natal. Not many of these species are commonly cultivated in gardens though all are attractive plants. Many of the early-flowering species produce their foliage during the winter. *G. byzantinus* is sufficiently hardy to remain undisturbed out of doors in sunny places even where quite severe winter frosts are experienced, and will naturalize itself.

For garden purposes the hybrids are split into various groups such as Giant and Large-flowered, with large, widely opened flowers closely packed on spikes 3 to 5 ft. high, flowering in late summer and early autumn; Miniature and Small-flowered, similar to the last but with smaller flowers; Primulinus, with small more or less hooded flowers in a loose spike, same flowering season, and Nanus, with small, open flowers in fairly loose spikes in spring or early summer.

GLAUCIUM (Horned Poppy, Sea Poppy) – *Papaveraceae*. Hardy biennials or perennials with poppy-like flowers.

Soil, light, sandy. Position, sunny.

Increase by seeds sown in spring or early summer in a frame or outdoors, seedlings transplanted into flowering position in late summer or early autumn.

The best kind is *G. flavum* (syn. *luteum*), yellow, summer, 1 to 2 ft., Europe (Britain), N. Africa, W. Asia.

GLEDITSIA – *Leguminosae*. Hardy ornamental deciduous trees with green, feathershaped leaves and shoots armed with exceptional spines, up to 6 in. long on *G. caspica*. The flowers are insignificant but

Large-flowered gladiolus

Gladiolus colvillei (early-flowering type)

Primulinus gladiolus

Butterfly gladiolus

Miniature gladiolus

the seed pods of some kinds are long and distinctive.

Soil, ordinary, well drained. Position, sunny, warm, excellent in hot dry places and in towns. Plant in autumn or late winter.

Increase by seeds carefully perforated or chipped and sown in light soil in a frame or cool greenhouse in spring.

Recommended kinds are *G. aquatica*, Water Locust, 20 to 30 ft., U.S.A.; *caspica*, Caspian Locust, 20 to 30 ft., N. Iran; *triacanthos*, Honey Locust, Three-thorned Acacia, to 60 ft. or occasionally more, attractive frond-like leaves, U.S.A., and vars. *elegantissima*, slow growing, ferny, to 15 ft., Sunburst, yellow leaves.

GLOBBA – *Zingiberaceae*. Tender herbaceous perennials with curiously formed flowers, often with coloured bracts, carried in terminal sprays at various times of the year according to conditions.

Soil, John Innes potting compost No. 1 or equivalent. Position, pots in a warm greenhouse, minimum winter temp. 18°C. Pot in spring. Water normally. Shade in summer from direct sunshine and maintain a humid atmosphere. Increase by division in spring.

Recommended kinds are *G. atrosanguinea*, red and yellow, 1 to 2 ft., Indonesia; *schomburgkii*, red and yellow, 1 to 2 ft., Indonesia; *winitii*, magenta and yellow, 1 to 2 ft., Thailand.

GLOBULARIA (Globe Daisy) – *Globulariaceae*. Hardy mat-forming perennials, herbaceous or sub-shrubby with small blue flowers packed into fluffy spherical heads.

Soil, ordinary, reasonably fertile and well drained. Position, sunny, suitable for rock gardens and crevices between paving. Plant in spring or autumn.

Increase by seeds sown on the surface of light sandy soil in a cold frame in spring; by division in spring.

Recommended kinds are *G. bellidifolia*, summer, 3 in., S. Europe; *cordifolia*, summer, 3 in., shrubby, Europe, W. Asia; *incanescens*, summer, 6 in., shrubby, Italy; *nudicaulis*, summer, 6 in., herbaceous, S. Europe; *trichosantha*, summer, 6 to 8 in., herbaceous, Asia Minor.

GLORIOSA – *Liliaceae*. Tender, deciduous, tuberous-rooted climbers with lily-type flowers.

Compost, John Innes potting compost No. 2 or equivalent. Position, one tuber in a 6-in. pot (or three tubers in an 8-in. pot) in an intermediate greenhouse, minimum winter temp. 13°C. Water rather sparingly at first but freely as growth appears. After flowering gradually reduce water supply and keep quite dry in winter until it is time to restart. If a temperature of 15°C. can be maintained tubers can be repotted and re-

Gloriosa simplex

started in midwinter, but with less artificial heat it is better to wait until spring.

Increase by seeds inserted singly in 3-in. pots filled with light soil in temp. 24°C. in early spring; by offsets removed from large tubers at potting time.

Recommended kinds are *G. rothschildiana*, ruby red and yellow, summer, to 6 ft., Uganda; *simplex* (syn. *virescens*), Mozambique Lily, yellow and red, summer, 5 ft., Tropical Africa, and vars. *grandiflora*, larger flowers, and *leopoldii*, petals curved inwards; *superba*, Glory Flower, orange and red, summer, 6 ft., Tropical Africa, India.

Godetia (hybrid)

GODETIA – *Onagraceae*. Hardy annuals, related to *Oenothera* and formerly included in that genus, and by others placed with *Clarkia*.

Soil, ordinary. Position, sunny or partly shady.

Sow seeds in spring or early autumn where plants are to bloom and thin seedlings to 6 in. apart.

Recommended kinds are *G. amoena*, Farewell to Spring, rose and crimson, summer, 1 to 2 ft., California, and var. *schaminii*, to 3 ft., white to carmine; *grandiflora* (syn. *Oenothera whitneyi*), red, crimson or white, summer, 6 to 12 in., California, and var. *azaleiflora plena*, double flowers; *viminea*, lavender and purple, summer, short branched, to 2 ft., California. See trade lists for numerous varieties, some of which are derived from hybrids between these species.

GOMPHRENA – *Amaranthaceae*. Rather tender annual with 'everlasting' flowers. Sow in spring in temp. 15 to 18°C. and harden off seedlings for planting outdoors in late spring or early summer in ordinary soil and a warm, sunny position. Alternatively, pot seedlings singly in John Innes potting compost No. 1 or equivalent and grow in a sunny frost-proof greenhouse. Water normally. No shade required. Cut flowers immediately they are fully developed for drying for winter decoration.

The best kind is *G. globosa*, Globe Amaranth, white, red or purple, summer, 12 in., India, and var. *nana* 4 to 6 in.

GORDONIA – *Theaceae*. Slightly tender evergreen shrubs or small trees with camellia-like flowers.

Soil, lime-free loam and peat. Position, warm, sheltered against a sunny wall or in the open in nearly frost-free places or in a frost-proof greenhouse or conservatory. Plant in spring.

Increase by seeds sown in a cool greenhouse in lime-free loam, peat and sand in spring or as soon as ripe; by cuttings of firm young growth in a propagator in summer.

Recommended kinds are *G. axillaris* (syn. *anomala*), creamy white, autumn until spring, 12 to 30 ft., China, Formosa; *chrysandra*, creamy white, scented, late winter, Yunnan; *lasianthus* (syn. *Hypericum lasianthum*), Loblolly Bay, white, summer, 20 to 70 ft., South-eastern U.S.A.

GREVILLEA – *Proteaceae*. Tender and nearly hardy evergreen flowering shrubs and trees.

Soil, lime free, well drained. Position, sunny, warm, sheltered, or tender kinds as pot or tub plants in a frost-proof greenhouse. *G. robusta* is often grown as a foliage plant only and discarded when it gets too big as it is easily raised from seed. Plant in spring or autumn. Remove weak or frost-damaged growth in spring.

Grevillea robusta

Increase by seeds sown in well-drained pots of light soil in temp. 18 to 21°C. in spring; by cuttings of young shoots in sandy soil in a propagator in summer; by layering in autumn.

Recommended kinds are *G. robusta*, Silk Bark Oak, orange, spring, to 150 ft., tender, Australia; *rosmarinifolia*, red, summer, 5 ft., Australia; *sulphurea*, pale yellow, summer, to 6 ft., Australia.

GRISELINIA – *Cornaceae*. Slightly tender evergreen shrubs. Male and female flowers produced on separate plants, berries are seldom seen. These shrubs are grown solely for their foliage. They are excellent near the sea and useful hedge shrubs.

Soil, ordinary, poor, well drained, including chalk. Position, open, sunny, will survive temperatures of about −10°C. Prune into shape in spring.

Increase by cuttings in sandy soil in a frame in summer or autumn.

The best kind is *G. littoralis*, 20 to 30 ft., New Zealand, and var. *variegata*, with white variegation.

GUNNERA (Prickly Rhubarb) – *Gunneraceae*. Hardy herbaceous perennials grown for their very large ornamental leaves but one kind is small and mat forming.

Soil, ordinary, rich. Position, damp, sunny sheltered margins of ponds or bogs. Plant in spring. Protect with leaves in winter.

Increase by seeds sown in peat and sand in temp. 15 to 18°C. in spring, transplanting seedlings outdoors in summer; by division of plants in spring.

Recommended kinds are *G. chilensis* (syn. *scabra*), Chile Rhubarb, leaves 4 to 6 ft. in diameter, 6 to 10 ft., Chile; *manicata*, leaves 5 to 10 ft. in diameter, 4 to 10 ft., Brazil; *magellanica*, very dwarf, leaves 2 to 3 in. across, mat forming, S. Chile.

GYMNOCLADUS – *Leguminosae*. Hardy deciduous tree with pinnate leaves and seeds in large pods.

Soil, ordinary, well drained. Position, sunny, open. Plant in autumn or late winter.

Increase by seeds perforated to admit moisture and sown in light soil in a cool greenhouse in spring; by root cuttings in spring.

The best kind is *G. dioica* (syn. *canadensis*), Kentucky Coffee Tree, greenish white, early summer, 60 ft., N. America, var. *variegata*, leaves variegated with creamy white.

GYNURA – *Compositae*. Tender perennials with ornamental purple-tinted leaves.

Grow in a not too rich compost, such as John Innes potting compost No. 1, in pots in partial shade in an intermediate or warm greenhouse or a light, fairly warm room. Pot in spring. Water normally.

Increase by cuttings in spring.

The best kinds are *G. aurantiaca*, leaves covered with violet down, 2 to 3 ft., Java; *sarmentosa*, leaves covered with violet down, trailing or twining, India.

GYPSOPHILA – *Caryophyllaceae*. Hardy perennial and annual herbs with abundant flowers produced in loose sprays and valuable for cutting as well as for garden decoration.

Soil, ordinary, well drained, preferably with lime or chalk. Position, sunny. Plant in spring or autumn. Cut down flower stems in autumn.

Grow annual species from seeds sown in spring where plants are to flower, thinning seedlings out to 3 to 6 in. apart when 1 in. high.

Increase perennial species by seeds sown in a sunny position outdoors in spring; by cuttings of secondary laterals, 2 in. long, in coarse sand in a propagator in summer; double-flowered kinds by grafting in spring on to seedlings of single-flowered species.

The annual species cultivated is *G. elegans*, white or pink, summer, 1 to 1½ ft., Caucasus.

Recommended perennial kinds are *G. acutifolia*, white or rosy, summer, 4 ft., Caucasus; *aretioides*, white, early summer, 1 in., Caucasus; *cerastioides*, white, veined red, summer, 3 in., Himalaya; *monstrosa* (syn. *repens monstrosa*), white, summer, to 3 ft., hybrid between *repens* and *stevenii*; *oldhamiana*, pink, summer, 2 to 2½ ft., Japan; *paniculata*, Chalk Plant, white, summer, 2 to 3 ft., Europe, and vars. Bristol Fairy, double white, superior to *flore pleno*, Flamingo, double pink, Rosy Veil (syn. Rosenschleier), double pink; *repens*, white, summer, 6 in., Alps and var. *rosea*, pink; *rokejeka*, 2 ft., pink or violet, Egypt, Asia Minor; *stevenii*, white, summer, 2 ft., Caucasus.

HABERLEA – *Gesneriaceae*. Hardy herbaceous perennial with rosettes of leathery leaves and widely funnel-shaped flowers in small clusters.

Grow in a mixture of equal parts loam, peat and coarse sand in vertical fissures of

Haberlea ferdinandi-coburgii

rock gardens, dry walls, etc., in shade. Plant in spring. Water freely in dry weather.

Increase by seeds sown in sandy peat in a frame in spring; by division of plants in spring; by leaf cuttings in a propagator in summer.

The only kinds are *H. ferdinandi-coburgii*, lilac and white, 4 in., late spring, early summer, Bulgaria; *rhodopensis*, blue-lilac, 6 in., late spring, early summer, Balkans, var. *virginalis*, white.

HABRANTHUS – *Amaryllidaceae*. Slightly tender, S. American bulbs, sometimes included in the genus *Zephyranthes*, which usually produce only one trumpet-shaped flower per bulb.

Grow in light, sandy loam. Position, well-drained sunny beds, borders or rock gardens. Plant in late summer and early autumn, placing bulbs 3 to 4 in. deep and 4 in. apart. Protect in winter by a layer of cinder ashes, peat or cloches. Lift and replant only when bulbs show signs of deterioration. Or grow in a cool greenhouse in pots or a border in John Innes potting compost No. 1 or equivalent.

Increase by offsets.

Recommended kinds are *H. andersonii* (syn. *Zephyranthes andersonii*), golden yellow, summer, 6 in., S. America; *brachyandrus* (syn. *Hippeastrum brachyandrum*), orchid pink above, reddish purple below, to 12 in., S. America; *cardinalis*, red and green, early summer, 6 in., S. America; *robustus*, rose-red, to 9 in., Argentina.

HAEMANTHUS (Blood Lily, Red Cape Tulip) – *Amaryllidaceae*. Tender bulbs with showy flowers in close rounded heads.

Grow in John Innes potting compost No. 1 or equivalent in well-drained pots exposed to full sun in a cool greenhouse whilst growing; on a sunny shelf or in a frame whilst at rest. Pot early-flowering species in late summer or autumn; late-flowering species in spring. Cover bulbs to only half their depth in compost. Water very little till growth begins, then moderately; gradually withhold water when flowers fade, and keep the soil quite dry from the time foliage turns yellow till repotting time. Apply weak liquid manure once or twice weekly to plants in full growth. Minimum winter temp. 7°C. Bulbs flower best when only repotted every three or four years.

Increase by offsets removed at potting time and placed in small pots.

Recommended kinds are *H. albiflos*, white, summer, 1 ft., S. Africa, and var. *pubescens*; *coccineus*, Blood Flower, scarlet, autumn, 10 to 12 in., S. Africa; *katharinae*, red, spring, 1 ft., S. Africa; *magnificus*, Royal Paint Brush, orange-scarlet or pink, summer, 12 to 15 in., S. Africa; *multiflorus* (syn. *kalbreyeri*), blood red, spring, 1 to 1½ ft., Tropical Africa; *puniceus*, orange-scarlet, summer, 1 ft., S. Africa.

HALESIA (Silver Bell) *Styracaceae.* Hardy flowering deciduous trees.

Soil, deep well-drained, lime-free loam. Position, sheltered, sunny or lightly shaded. Plant in autumn or late winter. Prune after flowering but only if necessary to maintain shape.

Increase by seeds stratified for five months at 20 to 25°C., then for three months at 4°C. and then sown in a frame or cool greenhouse.

Halesia carolina

Recommended kinds are *H. carolina* (syn. *tetraptera*), Snowdrop Tree, white, late spring, 15 to 30 ft., South-eastern U.S.A.; *diptera*, white, spring, to 20 ft., N. America; *monticola*, similar to *carolina* but stronger growing and with larger flowers, Central U.S.A.

x HALIMIOCISTUS – *Cistaceae.* Hardy or slightly tender dwarf evergreen shrubs. Bigeneric hybrids between *Halimium* and *Cistus.*

Soil, dry, light. Position, warm, full exposure to sun.

Increase by cuttings of half-ripened wood in a propagator in summer.

Recommended kinds are *H. ingwersenii*, white, all summer, 1½ ft., Portugal, believed to be a natural hybrid between *Halimium umbellatum* and *Cistus hirsutus*; *sahucii*, white, all summer, 1 ft., S. France, said to be a natural hybrid between *H. umbellatum* and *C. salviifolius.*

HALIMIUM – *Cistaceae.* Hardy or slightly tender evergreen shrubs similar to *Helianthemum* and formerly included in that genus.

Soil, dry. Position, warm, sunny. Subject to damage in severe winters but with good drainage and well ripened growth most will survive temperatures of about −7°C.

Increase by seeds sown in temp. 15 to 18°C. in spring; by cuttings in sandy soil in a frame in summer.

Recommended kinds are *H. alyssoides*, yellow, summer, 2 ft., Spain, Portugal; *halimifolium*, yellow, summer, 1 to 2 ft., rather tender, S. Europe, N. Africa; *lasian-*

thum (syn. *formosum*), yellow, summer, 2 to 3 ft., Portugal; *libanotis*, yellow, early summer, 1 to 1½ ft., Mediterranean region; *ocymoides* (syn. *Helianthemum algarvense*), flowers bright yellow with maroon blotch, summer, erect growing to 3 ft., young shoots downy, Spain, Portugal; *umbellatum*, white, early summer, to 2 ft., Mediterranean region.

HALIMODENDRON (Salt Tree) – *Leguminosae.* Hardy deciduous flowering shrub.

Soil, deep, sandy. Position, open; excellent near the sea. Plant in autumn or winter. Prune into shape in autumn.

Increase by seeds sown outdoors in spring; by grafting on to stocks of caragana, to which it is related, in spring.

The only species is *H. halodendron* (syn. *argenteum*), grey-spined leaves and pink pea-shaped flowers, summer, 4 to 6 ft., salt steppes, Siberia.

HAMAMELIS (Witch Hazel) – *Hamamelidaceae.* Hardy winter and early spring flowering deciduous shrubs or small trees.

Soil, deep, rich loam preferably moderately acid or neutral. Position, open and sunny or in light shade, with plenty of space as they have an open spreading habit. Plant in autumn or late winter.

Increase by layering in autumn; by grafting rare species on stocks of *H. virginiana*, raised from seed; species by seeds stratified for five months at 20 to 25°C., then for three months at 4°C. and then sown outdoors or in an unheated frame or greenhouse.

Recommended kinds are *H. intermedia*, yellow to red, winter, early spring, 10 to 20 ft., hybrid between *japonica* and *mollis* with numerous named garden forms; *japonica*, yellow to red, winter, 15 to 20 ft., Japan, and vars. *arborea*, red and yellow, and *zuccariniana*, sulphur yellow; *mollis*, yellow, winter, the best species with spicily fragrant flowers and autumn-tinted foliage, 10 ft., China, var. *pallida*, sulphur yellow; *virginiana*, Witch Hazel, yellow, autumn, winter, 10 to 15 ft., Eastern N. America.

HAWORTHIA – *Liliaceae.* Tender succulent plants with their leaves in rosettes or overlapping, arranged in several rows, short, blunt, pointed, fleshy, often covered with pearly tubercles or even more or less transparent. Flowers in long loose racemes, small and inconspicuous, whitish green. Flowering almost any time. Attractive easily grown little succulents suitable for room culture. All are natives of S. Africa.

Soil, well drained, rich, porous, such as John Innes potting compost No. 2 with extra sand. Position, room or cool house, minimum winter temp. 7°C. for most kinds, but 13°C. for *H. maughanii* and *truncata*. Rather liable to sunburn so some shade is desirable in spring and summer. Water freely in summer, less in winter but the plants should not be dried out for too long.

Increase by offshoots removed and rooted in sand. May easily be raised from seed but not recommended as they hybridize readily.

Recommended kinds are *H. arachnoides* (syn. *Aloe arachnoidea*), stemless rosettes, oblong leaves with bristly tips; *attenuata*, stemless rosette, white tubercles on leaves; *bolusii*, stemless rosette, leaf ends translucent; *cymbiformis*, rosettes stemless, offsets freely formed, leaves 1½ to 2 in.; *fasciata*, rosettes stemless, leaves white striped on back; *marginata* (syn. *albicans*), leaves 3 to 4 in.; *margaritifera*, stemless rosettes, leaves 3 in. long with large roundish pearly tubercles; *maughanii*, rosettes of truncated leaves with translucent ends; *reinwardtii*, rosettes with stems up to 6 in., leaves 1½ in., upper side with a few tubercles; *tortuosa*, rosette elongated to 5 in., stems branching from among the basal leaves, leaves in three spiral overlapping rows; *viscosa*, rosette to 8 in. long, leaves in three overlapping rows, erect.

HEBE – *Scrophulariaceae.* Slightly tender and hardy evergreen flowering shrubs, formerly included in *Veronica.* Most come from New Zealand, including those recommended here.

Soil, ordinary, well drained. Position, sunny, warm, specially suitable for maritime districts, or in large pots or tubs in a frost-proof greenhouse.

Increase by cuttings of young growths inserted in sandy soil in a propagator in summer; by cuttings of nearly ripened growth in a cold frame in early autumn; species by seeds sown in a temp. 15 to 18°C. in spring.

Recommended kinds are *H. andersonii variegata*, foliage margined with white, 2 to 3 ft., hybrid; *brachysiphon* (syn. *traversii*), white, summer, 4 to 6 ft.; *buchananii*, white, summer, 1 ft.; *buxifolia*, white, summer, 9 to 12 in.; *carnosula*, white, summer, 1 ft.; *catarractae*, white and pink, summer, 6 to 9 in.; *colensoi*, white, summer, 1 to 1½ ft.; *cupressoides*, pale blue, summer, 1 to 6 ft.; *elliptica*, white or blue tinted, summer, scented, 4 to 10 ft., New Zealand, Chile, Falkland Islands; *epacridea*, white, 4 to 6 in.; *franciscana*, violet, purple or white, summer, 2 to 4 ft., hybrid between *elliptica* and *speciosa*; *hectori*, white or pink, summer, 6 to 12 in.; *hookeriana*, white, summer, 8 to 12 in.; *hulkeana*, lilac, 3 to 5 ft.; *lewisii*, pale blue, summer, 4 to 6 ft.; *loganioides*, white, summer, 4 to 12 in.; *lycopodioides*, white, summer, 1 to 2 ft.; *macrantha*, large white flowers, late spring, 12 to 15 in.; *ochracea*, white, summer, 2 to 3 ft., tiny leaves old gold in colour (this species is usually sold as *H. armstrongii*, a different plant); *odora*, white, summer, 2 to 4 ft.; *pimeleoides*, purplish blue, summer, 1 to 1½ ft.; *pinguifolia pagei* (syn. *pageana*), white, late spring, 9 in.; *salicifolia*, white, summer, 6 to 10 ft.; *speciosa*, reddish purple, late summer, 4 to 5 ft., and numerous hybrids with flowers in various shades of blue, purple and crimson; *tetrasticha*, white, summer, 9 in.; *vernicosa*, white, summer, 1 to 2 ft. There are also a great many hybrids of uncertain parentage which are sold under garden names.

HEDERA (Ivy) – *Araliaceae*. Hardy evergreen climbing shrubs with insignificant green flowers followed by purplish black, orange or yellow berries. Tree ivies represent the adult stage of growth of many kinds; the climbing habit is lost and a large rounded, free-flowering bush is formed. The types usually grown are *H. helix arborescens*, common tree ivy, and *H. colchica arborescens*, the best large-leaved tree ivy.

Soil, ordinary. Position, sunny or shady, against walls of all aspects, railings, tree stumps, arbours, etc., on banks and under trees. Plant in spring or autumn. Peg shoots to the surface of the soil when first planted in any position. Prune in spring, cutting off old leaves and straggling shoots.

Ivies can also be grown in pots as room or cool greenhouse plants in a compost of two parts loam, one part each of leafmould, or decayed manure, and sand. Pot in spring or autumn. Prune into shape in spring. Apply liquid fertilizers to established plants in summer.

Increase by cuttings of firm shoots in ordinary soil in a shady sheltered place in autumn; by cuttings of younger growth in a propagator in spring or summer; by layering at any time.

Hedera helix sagittifolia

Recommended kinds are *H. canariensis*, large leathery leaves to 8 in. across, Canary Islands, N. Africa, and var. *variegata*, leaves grey-green and white; *colchica*, largest leaved of all ivies up to 10 in. across, Caucasus, Iran, and var. *dentata variegata*, leaves green, grey-green and cream; *helix*, Common Ivy, Europe (Britain), usually represented in gardens by varieties of which there are a great many, including *arborescens*, bushy habit, Buttercup, yellow leaves, *caenwoodiana*, small leaves with narrow lobes, *congesta*, stiff, slow growing, *con-*

Hedera canariensis variegata

glomerata, similar to the last but with wavy leaves, Glacier, leaves silvery grey and white, Gold Heart, leaves with central splash of yellow, *hibernica*, Irish Ivy, large leaves, *marginata*, leaves margined with white flushed pink, *poetica*, Italian Ivy, shallow-lobed leaves, yellow fruits, *sagittifolia*, narrow lobes to leaves, and *tricolor* (syn. *elegantissima*), leaves edged with white and pink.

HEDYCHIUM (Ginger Lily) – *Zingiberaceae*. Tender herbaceous perennials with fragrant flowers in broad spikes.

Grow in a fairly rich compost, such as John Innes potting compost No. 2, in well-drained pots, tubs or boxes, or plant in beds in an intermediate or warm greenhouse. Pot plants may be stood outdoors in summer. Pot or plant in spring. Water freely in spring and summer, moderately in autumn and winter if a temperature of 13°C. and above can be maintained, but very sparingly if temperature is likely to drop to 7°C. Apply liquid manure twice a week to plants in full growth. Cut down flower stems immediately after flowering. *H. gardnerianum* is suitable for outdoor culture in places where there is little frost.

Increase by division of rhizomes in spring.

Recommended kinds are *H. coccineum*, orange-red, summer, 4 to 6 ft., India, Burma; *coronarium*, Fragrant Garland Flower, white, summer, scented, 5 ft., India; *densiflorum*, coral red, late summer, early autumn, 4 to 6 ft., Himalaya; *flavum*, yellow and orange, summer, 5 ft., India; *gardnerianum*, lemon yellow, scented, summer, 4 ft., N. India.

HEDYSARUM – *Leguminosae*. Hardy herbaceous perennials or shrubs with pea flowers.

Soil, ordinary, well drained. Position, sunny and warm. Plant in spring or autumn.

Increase by seeds sown in a temp. 15 to 18°C. in spring; herbaceous kinds by division in spring; shrubby kinds by layering in spring or cuttings in summer.

Recommended kinds are *H. coronarium*, French Honeysuckle, red, summer, 3 to 4 ft., herbaceous, S. Europe, var. *album*, white; *multijugum*, magenta, all summer, 4 ft., shrubby, Mongolia.

HELENIUM (Sneezeweed) – *Compositae*. Hardy herbaceous perennials with showy daisy flowers.

Soil, ordinary. Position, sunny, well drained. Plant in spring or autumn. Cut down flower stems in autumn.

Increase by seeds sown outdoors in spring, transplanting seedlings in summer; by division in spring or autumn.

Recommended kinds are *H. autumnale*, yellow, late summer, autumn, 3 to 5 ft., N. America, and vars. *pumilum magnificum*, yellow, 2½ ft., summer, *rubrum*, chestnut red, *striatum*, yellow and brown, 4 ft., *superbum*, yellow, waved florets, 5 ft.; *bigelovii*, yellow and brown, summer and early autumn, 4 ft., California, and var. *aurantiacum*, yellow; *hoopesii*, yellow, summer, 2 ft., N. America. There are numerous garden varieties, hybrids between these species, with yellow to crimson flowers, 2 to 5 ft. high.

Helenium (hybrid)

HELIANTHEMUM (Sun Rose) – *Cistaceae*. Hardy flowering evergreen shrubs. A number of former species are now in the genus *Halimium*.

Soil, well drained, excellent on chalk or limestone. Position, sunny banks or rock gardens. Plant in spring or autumn. Prune into shape after flowering.

Increase by seeds sown in light soil in a cool frame or greenhouse in spring; by cuttings of firm young shoots 1 to 2 in. long inserted in sandy soil in a propagator in summer.

Recommended kinds are *H. apenninum*, white, summer, to 9 in., Europe, Asia Minor; *lunulatum*, yellow with orange spot at base, 6 in., Italy; *nummularium* (syn. *vulgare*), yellow, early summer, to 1 ft., Europe (Britain), and numerous double and single varieties in a range of colours including pink, red, crimson, orange, primrose and white.

HELIANTHUS (Sunflower) – *Compositae*. Hardy annual or perennial herbs with large showy daisy flowers.

Culture of annual species: Soil, ordinary. Position, sunny. Sow seeds in spring where plants are to flower, or in pots in temp. 15 to 18°C. in spring, transplanting seedlings outdoors after danger of sharp frost is over. Plant or thin to 2 ft.

Culture of perennial species: Soil, ordinary. Position, sunny, well drained. Plant in spring or autumn (*H. atrorubens* Monarch in spring only as this kind is slightly tender and may need winter protection in cold places). Cut down flower stems in autumn. Replant every second or third year.

Increase perennial species by seeds sown in a sunny place outdoors in spring or early summer; by division of the roots in spring or autumn.

Recommended annual kinds are *H. annuus*, Common Sunflower, yellow, summer, early autumn, 3 to 12 ft., Western U.S.A., and numerous varieties some with chestnut-red zones; *argophyllus*, yellow, 6 ft., Texas; *debilis* (syn. *cucumerifolius*), yellow, 3 to 4 ft., Southern U.S.A.

Recommended perennial kinds are *H. atrorubens* Monarch, yellow, disk black, autumn, 6 to 7 ft., South-eastern U.S.A.; *decapetalus*, sulphur yellow, late summer, early autumn, 4 to 6 ft., Canada, U.S.A., and vars. *flore-pleno*, double, *maximus*, large; *laetiflorus*, yellow, late summer, early autumn, 5 to 7 ft., N. America; *mollis*, yellow, late summer, early autumn, 3 to 4 ft., Central U.S.A.; *salicifolius* (syn. *orgyalis*), yellow, autumn, 6 to 7 ft., U.S.A.; *scaberrimus* (syn. *rigidus*), yellow, late summer, autumn, 3 to 6 ft., U.S.A. There are numerous varieties to be found in trade lists.

HELICHRYSUM (Everlasting Flower, Immortelle Flower) – *Compositae*. Slightly tender annuals, hardy perennials and slightly tender shrubs, often with chaffy 'everlasting' flowers.

Culture of annual species: Soil, ordinary. Position sunny. Sow seeds in temp. 15 to 18°C. in spring and harden off seedlings for planting outdoors when there is no danger of frost; or sow outdoors in late spring where plants are to flower. Plant or thin to 6 to 8 in. Gather flowers for winter decoration directly they are fully expanded.

Culture of perennial species: Grow in a mixture of equal parts loam, leafmould (or peat), and coarse sand or grit in well-drained pans in a sunny frame or greenhouse or outdoors in mild, fairly dry places. Water moderately from spring to early autumn, sparingly the rest of the year.

Culture of shrubby species: Soil, light, porous. Position, warm, sheltered. Most kinds will only survive a few degrees of frost.

Increase all kinds by seeds sown in temp. 15 to 18°C. in very porous soil in spring; perennial species by cuttings or divisions started in sand and leafmould or peat in a propagator in spring. Shrubby kinds by cuttings of firm young shoots in a propagator in summer.

The best annual kind is *H. bracteatum monstrosum*, white, pink, red, crimson, yellow, and orange, double, summer, 1½ to 2½ ft., garden variety of an Australian species.

Recommended perennial kinds, all with silvery or grey woolly leaves, are *H. bellidioides*, silvery white, summer, 3 to 4 in., New Zealand; *coralloides*, cream, early summer, 6 to 12 in., New Zealand; *frigidum*, white, late spring, early summer, 3 in., Corsica; *milfordiae* (syn. *marginatum*), white, early summer, 3 in., Basutoland; *orientale*, yellow to white, early summer, S. E. Europe; *scutellifolium*, cream, late spring, 1 to 2 ft., Tasmania; *selago*, white, summer, 6 to 12 in., New Zealand; *virgineum*, cream, late spring, 6 to 9 in., Greece.

The best shrubby kinds are *H. rosmarinifolium* (syn. *Ozothamnus rosmarinifolius*), red buds, white flowers, summer, 6 to 9 ft., Australia, Tasmania; *serotinum* (syn. *angustifolium*), Curry Plant, yellow, summer, narrow grey leaves, 1 ft., S. Europe; *splendidum* (syn. *trilineatum*), yellow, summer, autumn, 2 to 3 ft., grey leaves, S. Africa.

HELICODICEROS (Dragon's Mouth) – *Araceae*. Hardy tuberous-rooted perennial. Flowers arum like, with an unpleasant odour which is attractive to flies.

Soil, ordinary, well drained. Position, sunny. Plant in autumn or early spring.

Increase by offsets in autumn.

The only species is *H. muscivorus* (syn. *Arum crinitum*), spathe purplish brown, summer, 2 ft., Corsica, Balearic Islands.

HELICONIA (False Plantain) – *Heliconiaceae*. Tender herbaceous perennials. Flowers inconspicuous but enclosed by large, boat-shaped, often highly coloured bracts arranged zigzag up the stiff stems.

Compost, two parts fibrous loam, one part each of leafmould, peat and sand. Position, pots in a shady part of a warm greenhouse, minimum winter temp. 18°C. Pot in spring. Water freely in spring and summer, moderately in autumn, but do not give any in winter. Syringe daily in spring and summer.

Increase by division of roots in late winter, early spring.

Recommended kinds are *H. bihai*, bracts scarlet and yellow, summer, to 12 ft., West Indies; *magneriana* (sometimes wrongly called *humilis*), bracts red and green, 4 ft., Trinidad, Brazil.

HELIOPHILA – *Cruciferae*. Hardy annuals with flowers in slender spikes. All are native to S. Africa.

Soil, ordinary. Position, sunny, well drained.

Sow in spring where plants are to flower and thin seedlings to 4 to 6 in. Discard after flowering.

Recommended kinds are *H. leptophylla*, blue and yellow, summer, 9 to 18 in.; *linearifolia*, blue and yellow, 1½ to 3 ft.; *longifolia*, blue and white or yellow, 1½ ft.

HELIOPSIS – *Compositae*. Hardy herbaceous sunflower-like perennials from N. America.

Soil, ordinary rich. Position, sunny. Plant in spring or autumn. Cut down flower stems in autumn.

Increase by division in spring or autumn.

Recommended kinds are *H. helianthoides* (syn. *laevis*), North American Ox-eye, yellow, summer, 5 ft., and var. *pitcheriana*, larger, deep yellow flowers; *scabra*, yellow, summer, 4 ft., and vars. *incomparabilis*, orange, semi-double, *magnifica*, orange, semi-double, *patula*, orange-yellow, semi-double, *zinniaeflora* orange-yellow semi-double.

HELIOTROPIUM (Heliotrope) – *Boraginaceae*. Tender sub-shrubs with heads of small, fragrant flowers.

Compost, John Innes potting compost No. 2 or equivalent. Position, pots, tubs or beds in a cool or intermediate greenhouse or outdoors in summer. Pot in spring. Water fairly freely in spring and summer, moderately in autumn, sparingly in winter. Shading unnecessary. Prune in late winter cutting back previous year's growth as necessary to keep plants tidy. If used for summer bedding, plant outdoors in a sunny or lightly shaded place in late spring or early summer when danger of frost is past. Water freely in dry weather. Lift and return to the greenhouse in autumn before frost occurs, or discard plants and start anew the following year from seed. For bedding purposes heliotrope is commonly treated as a half-hardy annual.

Increase by seeds sown in John Innes seed compost or equivalent in late winter or early spring in temp. 15 to 18°C.; by cuttings of young shoots in a warm propagator in spring or late summer.

The best kind is *H. peruvianum* (syn. *arborescens*), Cherry Pie, blue, spring to winter, 1 to 6 ft., Peru, and numerous varieties differing in height, intensity of colour and scent.

HELIPTERUM (Australian Everlasting, Immortelle Flower) – *Compositae*. Hardy annuals with chaffy 'everlasting' daisy flowers.

Soil, light, well drained, reasonably fertile. Position, sunny.

Sow in early spring in temp. 15 to 18°C. and harden off seedlings for planting outdoors when danger of frost is past, or sow outdoors in late spring where plants are to flower. Plant or thin to 6 in. apart. Can also be grown as pot plants in a cool or unheated greenhouse in John Innes potting compost No. 1 or equivalent. Discard after flowering. Gather blooms when fully grown and dry thoroughly in summer for winter decorations.

Recommended kinds are *H. humboldtianum*, yellow, summer, 1½ ft., Australia; *manglesii* (syn. *Rhodanthe manglesii*), rosy pink or white, summer, 1 to 1½ ft., Australia; *roseum* (syn. *Acroclinium roseum*), rose, summer, 2 ft., Australia, and vars. *album*, white, and *plenum*, double.

Helleborus foetidus

HELLEBORUS (Hellebore) – *Ranunculaceae*. Hardy evergreen and deciduous perennials with saucer-shaped flowers in winter or spring.

Soil, rich, loamy. Position, shady, well drained. Plant in spring or autumn, 12 in. apart. Mulch with well-decayed manure in spring. Water freely in dry weather. Apply liquid manure occasionally in summer. Disturb roots as little as possible. Protect varieties of *H. niger* with handlights, cloches or frames, or cover the surface of the bed with moss to protect blooms from splashes.

Increase by seeds sown in John Innes seed compost or equivalent in a frame in spring or as soon as ripe, transplanting seedlings outdoors when a year old, seeds are often very slow in germinating; by division of roots in spring.

Recommended kinds are *H. abchasicus*, purplish green, winter, 1 ft., Caucasus, and var. *coccineus*, maroon; *antiquorum*, rose-pink, early spring, 1½ ft., Asia Minor; *atrorubens*, deep reddish purple, spring, 1 ft., S. E. Europe; *corsicus* (syn. *lividus corsicus*), apple green, late winter, spring, 2 ft., Corsica, Sardinia, Balearic Islands; *cyclophyllus*, purplish green, spring, scented, 1½

to 2 ft., Greece; *foetidus*, Stinking Hellebore, green and purple, late winter, early spring, 2 ft., Europe (Britain); *guttatus*, white and crimson, late winter, early spring, 1½ ft., Caucasus; *lividus*, green, late winter, early spring, Balearic Islands; *macranthus* (syn. *niger angustifolius*, *niger maximus*), white, winter, 1 ft., Italy to Greece; *niger*, Christmas Rose, white, winter, 6 to 15 in., Europe, and var. *altifolius*, white and purple, 1½ ft.; *odorus*, Fragrant Hellebore, yellowish green, late winter, early spring, scented, 1½ ft., Balkans; *olympicus*, white and green, spring, 1½ ft., Greece; *orientalis*, Lenten Rose, ivory white, greenish white or purple, spring, 1 to 2 ft., Greece, Asia Minor; *purpurascens*, greenish purple, early spring, 1 ft., Hungary; *viridis*, Green Hellebore, green, late winter, 1½ ft., Europe. Many varieties will be found in trade lists.

HEMEROCALLIS (Day Lily) – *Liliaceae*. Hardy herbaceous perennials with lily-like flowers which individually are short lived but are rapidly replaced by opening buds.

Soil, ordinary, deep, reasonably fertile. Position, open or slightly shaded. Plant in spring or autumn. Replant every three or four years. Mulch established clumps with decayed manure in spring. Remove faded flowers regularly.

Increase by division of roots in spring or autumn; by seeds sown in John Innes seed compost or equivalent in temp. 15 to 18°C. in spring or as soon as ripe; by offshoots removed from flower stems in summer and rooted in a frame or propagator.

Recommended kinds are *H. altissima*, yellow, scented, summer, 4 to 8 ft., Japan; *aurantiaca major*, Japanese Day Lily, purplish orange, summer, 3 ft., Japan; *citrina*, light yellow, summer, 4 ft., China; *dumortieri*, orange-yellow, late spring, early summer, 1½ ft., Japan; *flava*, lemon yellow, fragrant, late spring, early summer, 2 to 3 ft., S. Europe; *fulva*, orange-buff, summer, 3 to 4 ft., origin uncertain, and vars. *flore pleno*, double, *kwanso flore pleno*, semidouble, *rosea*, pink; *middendorffii*, orange, late spring, early summer, 2 ft., Siberia, Japan; *minor* (syn. *graminea*), lemon yellow, fragrant, 9 to 12 in., Siberia, Japan; *multiflora*, deep yellow and chestnut, late summer, 3 ft., China; *thunbergii*, lemon yellow, summer, fragrant, 3 ft., Japan. There are also many fine hybrids.

HEPATICA – *Ranunculaceae*. Hardy perennial herbs, sometimes included in the genus *Anemone*.

Soil, deep, porous, with leafmould or peat. Position, cool, partially shaded.

Increase by careful division in spring after flowering; by seeds sown in equal parts of loam, leafmould and sand in a frame or cool greenhouse in spring or as soon as ripe.

Recommended kinds are *H. acutiloba*,

pale blue, early spring, 6 to 9 in., Eastern N. America; *americana*, blue, early spring, 6 in., Eastern N. America; *transsilvanica* (syn. *Anemone transsilvanica*), rose, spring, 3 to 5 in., Hungary, Romania, and various colour forms.

HERACLEUM (Cow Parsley) – *Umbelliferae*. Hardy herbaceous perennials with large, flattish heads of small white flowers and large deeply divided leaves which can cause skin rash in some people.

Soil, ordinary, slightly moist. Position, open or semi-shady. Excellent plants to naturalize in thin woodland. Plant in spring or autumn.

Increase by seeds sown outdoors in spring or as soon as ripe; by division in spring or autumn.

Recommended kinds are *H. mantegazzianum*, white, summer, 8 to 12 ft., Caucasus; *villosum* (syn. *giganteum*), Cartwheel Flower, white, summer, 10 to 12 ft., Caucasus.

HERMODACTYLUS (Snakeshead Iris) – *Iridaceae*. A tuberous plant allied to *Iris*.

Treat as tuberous iris. Increase by seed; also by division.

The only species is *H. tuberosus* (syn. *Iris tuberosa*), violet, black and green, spring, 9 to 12 in., Mediterranean region.

HESPERANTHA (Evening-flower) – *Iridaceae*. Slightly tender corms with fragrant flowers opening in the afternoon or evening.

Compost, two parts fibrous loam, one part leafmould or peat, and a little sand. Position, well-drained pots in a cold frame, cool greenhouse or window until growth begins, then remove to temp. 7 to 13°C. Pot in late autumn placing five corms 3 in. deep in a 5-in. pot. Cover the pots with peat till growth begins. Water moderately from time growth starts until flowers fade, then gradually withhold, keeping corms quite dry from autumn to late winter.

Increase by seeds or offsets treated as advised for Ixia.

The species usually grown is *H. stanfordiae*, pale yellow, summer, 9 to 15 in.

HESPERIS – *Cruciferae*. Hardy perennial and biennial herbs with fragrant flowers.

Soil, moderately rich, moist but porous. Position, sunny. Plant perennial kinds in spring or treat as biennials, raising annually from seeds sown outdoors in spring or early summer, transferring plants to flowering quarters in late summer or early autumn and discarding them after flowering. Since the double-flowered varieties set no seed they must be grown as perennials. Mulch with decayed manure in spring. Apply liquid manure occasionally in summer to double varieties. Cut down flower stems in autumn. Lift and replant double kinds every second year.

Increase single kinds by seeds sown as described above; double kinds by cuttings of young shoots in sandy soil in a shady position outdoors in summer, also by division of roots in spring.

Recommended kinds are *H. matronalis*, Sweet Rocket, Dame's Violet, Dame's Rocket, white or lilac, late spring, early summer, 2 to 3 ft., perennial, S. Europe to Siberia, and vars. *alba plena*, double white, and *flore pleno*, double purple; *tristis*, white, cream or purplish, summer, to 2 ft., biennial, E. Europe.

HEUCHERA (Alum-root) – *Saxifragaceae*. Hardy perennial herbs with small flowers in spring. See x *Heucherella tiarelloides* for the bigeneric hybrid sometimes known as *Heuchera tiarelloides*.

Soil, ordinary. Position, open, sunny for *H. sanguinea* and varieties; partially shady for *H. americana*; sunny or shady for *H. brizoides*. Plant in spring or autumn.

Increase by division in spring; by seeds sown in light soil in a frame or outdoors in spring or early summer.

Recommended kinds are *H. brizoides*, pink, summer, 1 ft., hybrid; *sanguinea*, Coral Bells, red, summer, 1 to 1½ ft., Mexico, Arizona, and vars. *alba*, white, *atrosanguinea*, deep red, *rosea*, rose, *splendens*, crimson, and many more offered in trade lists.

x HEUCHERELLA – *Saxifragaceae*. Hardy herbaceous perennial with small flowers in elegant sprays. A bigeneric hybrid between *Heuchera* and *Tiarella cordifolia*. Sometimes included in *Heuchera* and similar to *H. brizoides*.

Soil, ordinary. Position, sun or half-shade. Plant in spring or autumn. Increase by division.

The various forms of this hybrid are grouped under the name *H. tiarelloides* (syn. *Heuchera tiarelloides*), pink or red, summer, 1 to 1½ ft.

HIBISCUS (Rose Mallow) – *Malvaceae*. Tender evergreen and hardy deciduous flowering shrubs, hardy annuals and perennials.

Culture of tender species: Grow in a moderately rich compost, such as John Innes potting compost No. 2, in well-drained pots or beds in a cool or inter-mediate greenhouse, minimum winter temp. 7°C. Pot or plant in spring. Prune into shape in spring. Water very freely in spring and summer, moderately in autumn and winter. Maintain a moist atmosphere while in growth. *H. manihot* makes a useful pot plant treated as a tender annual and grown in the greenhouse for summer flowering.

Culture of annual species: Soil, ordinary. Position, sunny beds or borders. Sow seeds of *H. trionum* in spring where plants are to flower; sow seeds of other annuals in

Hibiscus syriacus

well-drained pans in temp. 15 to 18°C. in spring and grow on in pots in a greenhouse or plant outdoors in early summer.

Culture of shrubby species: Soil, rich, light loam. Position, sheltered, sunny, well drained. Plant in autumn or late winter. Prune in spring, only thinning out weak and dead wood.

Increase tender species by seeds in well-drained pots of sandy peat in temp. 18 to 21°C. in spring; by cuttings of firm shoots in sandy peat in a warm propagator in spring or summer; by grafting in spring. Perennial species by seeds sown outdoors in spring, or division of roots in spring. Shrubby species by layering in spring or autumn or grafting in spring.

Recommended tender kinds are *H. archeri*, red, summer, 10 to 12 ft., hybrid between *schizopetalus* and *rosa-sinensis*; *arnottianus*, white, summer, scented, 10 to 15 ft., Hawaii; *coccineus*, scarlet, 6 to 8 ft., South-eastern U.S.A.; *grandiflorus*, pink and red, summer, 4 to 6 ft., South-eastern U.S.A.; *manihot*, yellow with large blotch of maroon, 9 ft., E. Asia; *mutabilis*, white or pink changing to red, summer, 10 to 15 ft., China; *rosa-sinensis*, Blacking Plant, crimson, summer, to 25 ft., Asia, and many garden vars., white, pink, yellow, red, single, semi-double and fully double; *schizopetalus*, orange-red, summer, 10 ft., E. Tropical Africa.

The best annual kind is *H. trionum* (syn. *africanus*), Flower of an Hour, pale yellow or white, with violet eye, summer, 2 ft., Africa.

The best hardy shrub is *H. syriacus*, Shrubby Althaea, white, blue, purple, pink, crimson, late summer and autumn, to 10 ft., E. Asia, and many varieties, some with double flowers.

HIERACIUM (Hawkweed) – *Compositae*. Hardy perennial herbs with dandelion-like flowers.

Soil, ordinary, well drained. Position, sunny. Plant in spring or autumn.

Increase by seeds sown outdoors in spring; by division in spring.

Recommended kinds are *H. aurantiacum*, orange-red, summer, 1 ft., Central Europe, naturalized in Britain; *bombycinum*, yellow, summer, silver hairy leaves, 9 in., Spain; *maculatum*, yellow, summer, 1½ ft., leaves marbled with black, Germany, Austria; *villosum*, yellow, summer, silver hairy leaves, 1 ft., Europe.

HIPPEASTRUM – *Amaryllidaceae*. Tender bulbs, popularly but incorrectly known as amaryllis.

The large-flowered hybrids require a moderately rich compost such as John Innes potting compost No. 2. Grow in well-drained pots in a light part of an inter-mediate or warm greenhouse or in a room. Pot from late summer to midwinter, burying the bulb about two-thirds of its depth. Water freely from the time growth begins until the leaves start to die back, when keep quite dry. Apply liquid manure when flower spike shows. Topdress large bulbs annually and repot every three or four years only, temperature during winter 10 to 13°C., spring to the end of growth 18 to 24°C.

Hippeastrum (hybrid)

Increase by seeds sown in sandy loam in temp. 18 to 21°C. in spring, placing seedlings singly in 2-in. pots and keeping them moderately moist all the year round for three years; by offsets removed at potting time and treated as old bulbs. Seedlings are three years or more before they flower.

Recommended kinds are *H. ackermannii*, crimson, summer, almost hardy, 1½ ft., hybrid; *aulicum*, crimson and orange, winter, 2 ft., Brazil; *bifidum*, orange-scarlet, spring 1 ft., Argentina; *equestre* (syn. *puniceum*) Barbados Lily, red, summer, 1½ ft., Tropical America; *pardinum*, green, yellow and scarlet, spring, 2 ft., Peru; *pratense*, scarlet, spring and early summer, 9 to 12 in., Chile; *procerum* (syn. *Worsleya rayneri*), bluish mauve, 3 ft., spring, Brazil; *psittacinum*, orange and scarlet, summer, 2 ft., Brazil; *rutilum*, bright crimson and green, spring, 1 ft., S. Brazil; *vittatum*, crimson

Hoheria lyallii

and white, spring, 2 ft., Peru. Numerous hybrids with very large flowers will be found in trade lists.

HIPPOPHAE (Sea Buckthorn) – *Elaeagnaceae*. Hardy, deciduous, berry-bearing shrubs or small trees. Male and female flowers, which are inconspicuous, are borne on separate plants. Both must be grown to ensure a crop of berries.

Soil, ordinary or sandy, well drained. Position, open, excellent in exposed places especially by the sea. Can be used as a windbreak. Plant in autumn or late winter.

Increase by seeds sown outdoors in autumn or stratified for three months at 4°C. and sown in spring; by root cuttings in winter; by layering shoots in autumn.

Recommended kinds are *H. rhamnoides*, silver leaves, 20 to 30 ft., orange-yellow berries, Europe (Britain); *salicifolia*, olive-green leaves, to 30 ft., yellow berries, Himalaya.

HOHERIA – *Malvaceae*. Slightly tender, flowering, evergreen and deciduous shrubs or small trees. All have small white mallow-like flowers produced freely in clusters in summer. All are native to New Zealand.

Soil, rich, deep loam. Position, sheltered, sunny; may be trained against sunny walls.

Increase by cuttings of half-ripened shoots in summer in sandy soil in a propagator; by seeds sown in spring in temp. 15 to 18°C.

Recommended kinds are *H. angustifolia*, to 25 ft., evergreen; *glabrata* (syns. *Gaya lyallii* and *Plagianthus lyallii*), to 30 ft., deciduous, probably the hardiest kind; *lyallii* (syn. *Gaya lyallii* and *Plagianthus lyallii*), to 30 ft., deciduous, this species has been much confused with *glabrata* but is distinct; *populnea*, 30 ft., evergreen; *sexstylosa* (syn. *populnea lanceolata*), similar to preceding but slightly less tender.

HOLBOELLIA – *Lardizabalaceae*. Hardy evergreen twiners with male and female flowers on separate plants. Fruits of some species are edible but are only produced if both sexes are grown.

Soil, ordinary, fertile. Position, sunny.

Plant in autumn or early spring to cover a pergola, screen or wall or climb into a tree. Fertilize by transferring pollen from male to female with a brush when flowers are fully open. This is only necessary if fruits are required.

Increase by seeds sown in a frame or cool greenhouse in spring; by cuttings of firm young stems in a propagator in summer; by layering in spring or summer.

Recommended kinds are *H. coriacea*, male flowers purplish, female greenish white tinged purple, spring, fruit purplish, China; *latifolia* (syn. *Stauntonia latifolia*), male flowers greenish white, female flowers purple, early spring, fruit purple, edible, Himalaya.

HOLCUS – *Gramineae*. Hardy ornamental perennial grass.

Soil, ordinary. Position, sunny or partially shady. Plant in spring or autumn.

Increase by division of plants in spring or autumn.

The best kind is *H. mollis albo-variegata*, leaves green striped white, 6 to 8 in., Europe (Britain), sometimes incorrectly called *H. lanatus albo-variegatus*.

HOLODISCUS – *Rosaceae*. Hardy deciduous flowering shrubs, formerly included in *Spiraea*.

Soil, good, ordinary, well drained. Position, sunny or partly shady.

Increase by seeds sown in a frame in spring; by layering in spring or autumn; by cuttings of firm young growth in summer.

The best kind is *H. discolor ariaefolius* (syn. *Spiraea ariaefolia*), Ocean Spray, creamy white, summer, 8 to 12 ft., Western N. America.

HOMERIA – *Iridaceae*. Handsome tender S. African corms.

In pots in a cool greenhouse use a compost of loam, leafmould (or peat) and sand in equal parts. Place corms 1 in. apart and 1 in. deep in 5-in. pots during the autumn. Stand in a cold frame and cover with a few inches of peat till growth begins, then remove to greenhouse. Plant in pots placed near to the glass. Water freely during active

growth. Keep nearly dry after flowers fade to ripen the corms. Repot annually in autumn.

In warm positions plant corms 3 to 4 in. deep in light, rich, well-drained soil in late autumn. Protect with bracken litter or cloches in winter.

Increase by seeds sown in spring or by offsets removed at planting time.

Recommended kinds are *H. collina* (syn. *Moraea collina*), red and yellow, spring, 1½ ft., vars. *aurantiaca*, orange, red and yellow, *miniata*, red, spring, 6 to 8 in.; *elegans*, yellow, brown and orange, summer, 1½ ft.; *lineata*, red and yellow, spring, 2 ft.

HOMOGLOSSUM – *Iridaceae*. Slightly tender S. African corms.

Grow in compost of loam, peat, sand and bonemeal. Plant in pots in autumn and keep watered throughout growth. Cool greenhouse temperature, not above 13°C.

Recommended kind is *H. salteri*, bright red, 2 ft., early spring.

HORDEUM – *Gramineae*. Hardy annual flowering grass. Inflorescence barley like, borne in spikes in summer, very useful for cutting.

Soil, ordinary. Position, open, dryish. Sow seeds in spring where plants are required to flower. Cut inflorescences when well developed.

The best kind is *H. jubatum*, Squirrel-tail Grass, 2 ft., N. America.

HOSTA (Plantain Lily) – *Liliaceae*. Hardy herbaceous flowering plants with ornamental foliage, formerly known as funkia.

Soil, ordinary, reasonably fertile, moist. Position, sunny or shady. Plant, spring or autumn. Topdress annually with decayed manure.

Increase by division in spring or autumn.

Recommended kinds are *H. albo-marginata*, mauve, late summer, 1½ ft., leaves edged white, Japan; *crispula*, lavender, summer, 2 ft., leaves wavy, edged white,

Hosta

Japan; *decorata* (syn. Thos. Hogg), violet, summer, 1½ to 2 ft., leaves broad, edged white, Japan; *elata* (syn. *fortunei gigantea*), violet, summer, 3 to 4 ft., leaves dark green, Japan; *fortunei*, reddish violet, summer, 2 to 3 ft., leaves large, green above, bluish white below, Japan, and vars. *albopicta*, leaves yellowish with green edge, and *aureomarginata*, leaves edged yellow; *lancifolia* (syn. *japonica*), violet, late summer, early autumn, 1 to 1½ ft., leaves glossy green, Japan; *plantaginea*, white, scented, late summer, early autumn, 2½ ft., China; *rectifolia*, violet-purple, late summer, early autumn, 2 ft., Japan, Kurile Islands; *sieboldiana* (syn. *glauca*), pale violet, summer, 2 ft., leaves large, heart shaped, blue-grey, Japan, and var. *elegans*, white tinged violet, leaves corrugated; *tardiflora*, pale purple, autumn, 1 ft., Japan; *undulata*, light violet, late summer, 9 to 12 in., leaves waved, light green, white in the middle, Japan, and vars. *erromena*, to 3 ft., and *univittata*, white stripe in centre of green leaf; *ventricosa*, dark violet, late summer, 3 ft., leaves shining green, E. Asia.

HOTTONIA (Water Violet) – *Primulaceae*. Hardy aquatic perennial herb grown as an oxygenating plant and for its whorls of lilac flowers.

Soil, loam. Position, shallow water in aquarium or pond. Plant in spring or early summer.

Increase by division, setting each plant separately in a pot or small basket and lowering in the water or weighing individually.

The best kind is *H. palustris*, lilac, 8 to 10 in. above water level, late spring, early summer, Europe (Britain), Siberia.

HOUSTONIA – *Rubiaceae*. Hardy herbaceous perennials with slender stems bearing numerous starry flowers.

Soil, loam with plenty of peat or leafmould and sand. Position, partially shaded crevices, nooks and crannies of moist rock gardens. Plant in spring.

Increase by seeds sown in peat and sand in a frame in spring; by division in spring.

Recommended kinds are *H. caerulea*, Bluets, blue, late spring, summer, 4 to 6 in., Eastern N. America, var. *alba*, white; *longifolia*, white, summer, 6 to 12 in., N. America; *purpurea*, pale purple, summer, 6 to 12 in., Central U.S.A.; *serpyllifolia*, white, summer, creeping, Eastern N. America.

HOUTTUYNIA – *Saururaceae*. Hardy aquatic perennial for the waterside.

Soil, heavy loam. Position, boggy or wet ground or in shallow water. Plant in spring.

Increase by division in spring.

The only species is *H. cordata*, white flowers, heart-shaped leaves, ½ to 2 ft., China, Japan.

HOWEIA – *Palmae*. Tender palms with feather-shaped, graceful leaves. Native to Lord Howe Island.

Compost, John Innes potting compost No. 2 or equivalent. Position, well-drained pots or beds in a cool or intermediate greenhouse, minimum winter temp. 7°C., or for short periods in rooms. Pot in spring. Water normally. Shade from strong direct sunshine in summer. Apply weak liquid manure to healthy plants once a week from late spring to early autumn and syringe plants daily. Sponge leaves of those grown in dwelling rooms once weekly.

Increase by seeds sown in light soil in temp. 24 to 26°C. in early spring.

The two species are *H. belmoreana* (syn. *Kentia belmoreana*), Sentry Palm, Curly Palm, 6 to 30 ft.; *forsteriana* (syn. *Kentia forsteriana*), Flat Palm, Thatch Leaf Palm, 6 to 30 ft.

HOYA – *Asclepiadaceae*. Climbing or trailing evergreen plants with scented wax-like flowers in flat clusters. Only two species are commonly cultivated.

Compost, John Innes potting compost No. 1 or equivalent. Position, *H. carnosa* in pots or beds in a cool or intermediate greenhouse, minimum winter temp. 7°C.; *H. bella* in pots or baskets in an intermediate or warm greenhouse, minimum temp. 15°C. Both kinds may also be grown in light warm rooms. Pot in spring. Water freely in spring and summer, rather sparingly in autumn and winter but never allow plants to become quite dry. Shade in summer from strong direct sunshine only. Provide wires, trellis or canes for stems of *H. carnosa* to twine around.

Increase by cuttings of firm young shoots in a warm propagator in summer; *H. carnosa* by layering in spring or summer; *H. bella* by grafting on to *H. carnosa* in a warm greenhouse in spring.

Recommended kinds are *H. bella*, white and crimson, summer, trailing, India; *carnosa*, Honey Plant, Wax Flower, pink and white, late summer, 10 to 12 ft., Queensland, and var. *variegata*, leaves splashed with yellow.

Hoya bella

HUMEA – *Compositae*. Tender biennial with arching sprays of small reddish-brown flowers. Leaves are incense scented.

Sow in late spring in John Innes seed compost or equivalent in temp. 15°C. Pot seedlings singly in John Innes potting compost No. 2 or equivalent and grow in a cool or intermediate greenhouse, minimum winter temp. 7°C. Repot in spring in 7- or 8-in. pots in similar compost. Stake flower stems individually. Water fairly freely in summer, moderately in spring and autumn, sparingly in winter. Discard plants after flowering. Plants can stand outdoors in summer and flowering plants are sometimes used in summer bedding schemes.

The best kind is *H. elegans*, Incense Plant, reddish brown, summer, early autumn, 5 to 7 ft., Australia.

HUMULUS – *Cannabidaceae*. Hardy perennial twining climbers. Male blooms borne in axillary panicles, and female blooms in cones in clusters on separate plants; the latter form is the hop of commerce and is the more ornamental.

Soil, deep rich and well-manured loam. Position, sunny. Plant in late winter or early spring. Topdress annually with decayed manure in early spring. Water freely in dry weather. Cut down plants in autumn. *H. japonicus* is often grown as an annual from seeds sown in temp. 15 to 18°C. in early spring, seedlings being hardened off for planting outdoors in late spring, or sown in late spring directly where plants are to grow.

Increase by seeds as described above or by division in spring.

Recommended kinds are *H. japonicus*, Japanese Hop, Japan, and var. *variegatus*, leaves blotched with white; *lupulus*, Hop, 10 to 15 ft., Europe (Britain), Asia, N. America, and var. *aureus*, leaves golden.

HUNNEMANNIA – *Papaveraceae*. Slightly tender Mexican perennial with poppy-like flowers, usually grown as an annual or biennial.

Soil, ordinary. Position, sunny, warm. well drained. Protect with dry litter in winter.

Increase by seeds sown in temp. 15 to 18°C. in spring and harden off seedlings for planting outdoors 9 in. apart when danger of frost is over; or sow in late summer in a frame or greenhouse and plant out in spring. Can also be grown in pots in John Innes potting compost No. 1 or equivalent in a sunny greenhouse.

The only species is *H. fumariifolia*, yellow, summer, 2 ft., Mexico.

HUTCHINSIA – *Cruciferae*. Hardy perennial herbs.

Soil, ordinary, well drained. Position, sunny or partially shaded. Plant in spring.

Increase by seeds sown in spring where

plants are required to grow; by division in spring.

The best kind is *H. alpina*, white, spring and summer, 3 in. Pyrenees.

HYACINTHUS (Hyacinth) – *Liliaceae*.
Hardy bulbs with bell-shaped flowers in spikes.

Culture of common or Dutch hyacinths in pots: Compost, fibrous loam, leafmould or peat and sharp sand, or in bowls with bulb fibre, i.e. peat with charcoal and crushed shell. Position, first plunge under cinder ashes or peat in a cold frame or outdoors, afterwards place in a window or greenhouse. Pot in autumn, placing one bulb half its depth in a 6-in. pot or three in an 8-in. pot. Keep moist until growth begins then water freely. Apply liquid manure occasionally when flower spikes form. After flowering plant bulbs outdoors.

Some hyacinth bulbs are specially prepared for forcing. Plant these immediately they are available. Less time is needed in the plunge bed than for untreated bulbs. Do not force a second time.

Hyacinthus orientalis

Culture in water: Hyacinths can be grown in water by placing the bulbs in autumn in special glasses so that the bases just touch the water. Use soft or rain water with a little charcoal, and add more water as required. Put in a dark position until roots form, then remove to the light. No feeding is needed.

Outdoor culture: Plant in ordinary or slightly sandy soil, enriched with manure the previous autumn. Position, open, sunny. Plant bulbs 3 to 4 in. deep and 8 in. apart in autumn. Protect the surface of the bed by a covering of peat. Apply liquid manure once or twice when flower spikes appear. Lift and dry bulbs when the leaves die down and store them in a cool place till planting time.

Culture of Roman hyacinths: These differ in size, density and number of spikes per bulb. Compost as advised above. Position, pots plunged under ashes or peat in a cold frame or outdoors till rooted then placed in a heated greenhouse or window. Pot in late summer and autumn, placing three in a 5-in. pot. Depth for planting 1 in. Keep moist until removed from the ashes and water regularly afterwards. Temperature when in the greenhouse or window 13 to 18°C.

Increase by seeds sown in a frame or outdoors in autumn; by offsets removed from old bulbs when lifted and planted 6 in. apart each way outdoors in autumn. Seedling bulbs flower when three years old, and attain full size when seven years old.

Recommended kinds are *H. amethystinus* (syn. *Brimeura amethystina*), Spanish Hyacinth, blue, spring, 1 ft., Pyrenees, var. *albus*, white; *azureus* (syns. *H. ciliatus*, *Hyacinthella azurea*), sky blue, 6 in., Asia Minor; *orientalis*, Common Hyacinth, various colours, spring, Mediterranean region, var. *albulus*, Roman Hyacinth, white.

For *Hyacinthus candicans* see Galtonia.

HYDRANGEA – *Hydrangeaceae*.
More or less tender and hardy deciduous flowering shrubs. Flowers are borne in clusters and are of two kinds, fertile, which are relatively small, and sterile, which are surrounded by large showy bracts. In certain varieties all the flowers are of this sterile type so that the inflorescence becomes globe or cone shaped; in other varieties only the outer ring of flowers are sterile resulting in a flat 'lace cap' inflorescence.

Hydrangeas, particularly garden varieties of *H. macrophylla*, make excellent pot or tub plants to grow on terraces or in cool greenhouses and other sheltered places. Grow in a compost of two parts rich loam, one part each of well-decayed manure and sharp sand. Pot in spring. Water abundantly in spring and summer, moderately afterwards. Prune after flowering, cutting back flowering stems to side growths or growth buds. The best blooms are obtained on plants propagated by cuttings taken annually during spring or early summer. Apply liquid manure frequently to plants showing flower. Temperature for early flowering 15 to 18°C. Blue flowers may be obtained in many kinds by planting in acid soil or by the use of one of the proprietary blueing powders used according to manufacturers' instructions. White varieties cannot be 'blued'.

Outdoors plants should be grown in ordinary, rich soil. Position, sunny or semi-shaded, preferably with protection from cold winds for all varieties of *H. macrophylla* which can be damaged by temperatures of −18°C. or thereabouts. *H. petiolaris* will climb against a sunny or partially shady wall or up a tree as it is self-clinging like an ivy. Young growth of *H. sargentiana* is liable to be injured by early spring frosts. Plant in autumn or spring. Topdress annually. Prune straggling or dead shoots in

Hydrangea macrophylla hortensia

spring. *H. arborescens* and *paniculata* can be pruned annually to within 1 in. of the base of the previous year's growth in spring. Water freely in dry weather.

Increase by cuttings of young shoots inserted singly in a propagator, temp. 15 to 18°C., in spring or early summer; by cuttings of points of firm shoots, 2 to 3 in. long, in sandy soil in a cold frame in late summer.

Recommended kinds are *H. arborescens grandiflora*, white, ball like, late summer, 4 ft., Eastern U.S.A.; *aspera* (syn. *villosa*), bluish purple, lilac, summer, 6 to 8 ft., thrives on chalk. E. Asia; *heteromalla*, white, summer, 10 ft., Himalaya, China, and var. *bretschneideri*, the best garden form; *macrophylla*, blue, purple, pink, red and white, summer, faded flower heads persisting all winter and often of a pleasing colour in autumn, 6 to 8 ft., China, Japan, and vars. *hortensia*, flowers all sterile forming a ball-like head, various colours, and *serrata*, flowers in flat clusters with only the outer flowers sterile, 2 to 3 ft.; *paniculata*, creamy white, late summer, 3 to 12 ft., China, Japan, and vars. *grandiflora*, larger flower heads, *praecox*, earlier than the type; *petiolaris* (syn. *anomala petiolaris*), self-clinging species, white, summer, to 50 ft., Japan; *quercifolia*, white, summer, scalloped leaves, 6 ft., South-eastern U.S.A.; *sargentiana* (syn. *aspera sargentiana*), pale violet, summer, 6 ft., large velvety leaves, rather tender, China.

HYDROCLEYS (Water Poppy) – *Limnocharitaceae*.
Slightly tender aquatic perennials with floating leaves and poppy-like flowers.

Grow in loamy soil in sunny shallow ponds, or in sunken tubs. Plant 6 in. below the surface of the water in spring. In cold districts plants are best wintered in a frost-proof greenhouse.

Increase by seeds sown in pots of rich soil just covered with water, or by division of the plants in spring.

The best kind is *H. commersonii* (syns. *H. nymphoides*, *Limnocharis humboldtii*), yellow, summer, Brazil.

HYMENOCALLIS *Amaryllidaceae.* Fragrant, tender bulbs, some of which are evergreen. Flowers carried in umbels. Formerly known as pancratium.

Compost, two parts sandy loam, one part decayed manure and half a part coarse sand. Position, well-drained pots in a sunny, warm or intermediate greenhouse. Margins of indoor pools for *H. crassifolia.* Pot in spring. Repotting is necessary every three or four years only. Water abundantly from spring to autumn then moderately, but keep deciduous kinds dry from midwinter to spring. Apply liquid manure once or twice a week during active growth. Temperature for warm house species 21 to 27°C. from spring to autumn, 13 to 18°C. in winter; intermediate greenhouse species, 13 to 18°C. from late spring to autumn, 7 to 10°C. from winter to late spring.

Increase by offsets removed from old bulbs in spring and treated as previously described.

Hymenocallis calathina

Recommended warm house kinds include *H. eucharidifolia,* white, spring, 2 ft., Tropical America; *macrostephana,* white, spring, 2 ft., hybrid between *calathina* and *speciosa,* evergreen; *ovata,* white, autumn, 1 ft., evergreen, W. Indies; *speciosa,* white, spring, 1 ft., evergreen, W. Indies.

Recommended for the intermediate greenhouse, *H. calathina* (syn. *narcissiflora*), white, spring, 1 ft., Peru.

HYPERICUM (St. John's Wort) – *Guttiferae.* Hardy or slightly tender evergreen and deciduous shrubs, sub-shrubs and perennials.

Soil, ordinary, well drained. Position, sunny for most kinds, but *H. calycinum* in sun or shade on banks or under trees, the tender kinds require wall protection. Small perennials and sub-shrubs on rock gardens, dry walls, etc. Plant shrubby kinds in autumn or late winter, perennial kinds in spring. Prune *H. calycinum* and *moserianum*

almost to ground level in spring, other kinds should have frost-damaged wood removed in spring.

Increase by seeds sown in a frame or cool greenhouse in spring; by cuttings in sandy soil in a frame in summer; by division in spring for many kinds including *H. calycinum* and tuft-forming perennials.

Recommended shrubby kinds are *H. androsaemum,* Tutsan, yellow, summer, followed by red (later black) capsules, 2 ft., Europe (Britain); *augustinii,* yellow, summer, 3 ft., China; *beanii* (syn. *patulum henryi*), yellow, summer, 3 to 4 ft., China; *calycinum,* Rose of Sharon, yellow, summer, trailing to 1 ft. high, evergreen, S. E. Europe; *forrestii* (syn. *patulum forrestii*), yellow, summer and early autumn, 3 ft., China, Assam, Burma; Hidcote, yellow, summer and autumn, 5 to 6 ft., semi-evergreen, origin unknown; *inodorum* (syn. *elatum*), pale yellow, summer, followed by red capsules, 3 to 4 ft., hybrid, and var. Elstead, salmon-red capsules; *leschenaultii,* deep yellow, summer, 4 to 5 ft., evergreen, distinctly tender, Sumatra; *moserianum,* yellow and red, late summer and autumn, 1½ ft., hybrid between *calycinum* and *patulum,* and var. *tricolor,* leaves variegated with pink and cream; *patulum,* yellow, summer, 3 ft., S. W. China, slightly tender; Rowallane (syn. *rogersii*), yellow, summer, 5 to 6 ft., semi-evergreen, slightly tender, origin unknown.

Recommended perennials, sub-shrubs and shrublets are *H. coris,* yellow, summer, 6 in., S. Europe; *empetrifolium,* orange-yellow, summer, 1 ft., Greece and var. *prostratum,* prostrate; *fragile,* pale gold, summer, 6 in., Greece; *olympicum,* golden yellow, summer, 1 ft., Asia Minor; *polyphyllum,* yellow, summer, 6 in., Cilicia; *repens,* yellow, summer, prostrate, S. E. Europe, Asia Minor; *reptans,* deep yellow, summer to autumn, prostrate, Himalaya.

HYPOCYRTA – *Gesneriaceae.* Tender evergreen perennials with small tubular flowers.

Soil, John Innes potting compost No. 1 or equivalent. Position, pots in a cool or intermediate greenhouse, minimum temp. 7°C., or in a light room. Pot in spring. Water normally. Trim shoots or pinch out their tips in spring and summer if the plants get too large.

Increase by cuttings of firm young growth in a propagator in summer.

The best kind is *H. glabra,* Clog Plant, Goldfish Plant, orange, summer, 1 to 2 ft., S. America.

HYPOESTES – *Acanthaceae.* Tender perennials and shrubs, but only one herbaceous kind commonly grown for its foliage.

Soil, John Innes potting compost No. 1 or equivalent. Position, pots in an intermediate greenhouse, minimum temp. 13°C.,

or in a room. Pot in spring. Water normally. Shade from strong sunshine, but leaf colour is best in good light.

Increase by seeds sown in temp. 15 to 18°C. in spring.

The recommended kind is *H. sanguinolenta,* Polka Dot Plant, leaves green spotted with pink, 1 ft., Madagascar.

HYPOXIS (Star Grass, Golden Star) – *Hypoxidaceae.* Slightly tender plants with corms or rhizomes and star-shaped yellow flowers.

Compost, two parts peat, one of leaf-mould and sand. Position, pots or beds in a frost-free frame or greenhouse or well-drained beds outdoors in nearly frost-free localities. Pot or plant in autumn. Water moderately from the time the bulbs begin to grow until the flowers fade, then gradually withhold it keeping bulbs dry until growth restarts.

Increase by offsets, removed in autumn and treated as old corms or rhizomes; by seeds sown in a cool greenhouse as soon as ripe.

Recommended kinds are *H. argentea,* yellow, winter, spring, 6 in., S. Africa; *hirsuta,* yellow, 6 in., North-eastern U.S.A.; *setosa,* yellow, spring, 6 in., S. Africa; *villosa,* yellow, winter, spring, 1 ft., S. Africa.

HYSSOPUS (Hyssop) – *Labiatae.* Small evergreen shrub with narrow aromatic leaves.

Soil, ordinary, well drained. Position, warm, sunny. Plant in spring. Prune in spring as necessary to keep it neat. Gather the shoots for distilling when the plants are in flower.

Increase by seeds sown in spring; by cuttings in spring or summer.

The only species is *H. officinalis,* blue, pink or white, summer, 1 ft., S. Europe.

IBERIS (Candytuft) – *Cruciferae.* Hardy annuals and evergreen perennials with flowers in spikes or close clusters.

Culture of annual species: Soil, ordinary. Position, sunny. Sow seeds where plants are to flower, in spring for flowering in summer, in early autumn for flowering in late spring. Thin out seedlings to 4 to 6 in. apart.

Culture of perennial species: Soil, light sandy loam. Position, sunny fissures or ledges of rock gardens or dry walls or on the margins of borders. Plant in spring or autumn.

Increase perennial kinds by seeds sown in sandy soil in a frame in spring; by cuttings of partially ripened shoots, from 1 to 2 in. long, inserted in sandy soil in a frame or propagator in summer; by division of roots in spring.

Recommended annual kinds are *I. amara,* Rocket Candytuft, white, summer, 6 to 12 in., W. Europe (Britain), and var. *coronaria,* to 1½ ft.; *umbellata*, Common Candytuft, purple, summer, 1 ft., S. Europe, and several varieties including *nana*, 6 in.

Recommended perennial kinds are *I. correaefolia*, white, late spring, early summer, 9 in., origin uncertain; *gibraltarica*, lilac, spring, summer, 1 ft., Spain, Morocco; *saxatilis*, white, late spring, 4 to 6 in., S. Europe; *sempervirens*, white, 9 to 12 in., S. Europe, and a number of garden varieties.

IDESIA – *Flacourtiaceae*. Hardy deciduous flowering tree with large leaves, small yellowish-green flowers in panicles followed by red berries. Male and female flowers are sometimes borne on separate trees, sometimes on the same tree.

Soil, good, loamy, preferably slightly acid. Position, well drained, sunny. Plant in autumn or late winter.

Increase by seeds sown in sandy soil in temp. 18 to 21°C. in spring; by cuttings of firm shoots, 3 to 4 in. long, inserted in sandy soil in a propagator in summer.

The only species is *I. polycarpa*, to 40 ft., Japan, and var. *vestita*, a hardy Chinese form.

ILEX (Holly) – *Aquifoliaceae*. Hardy and slightly tender evergreen and deciduous shrubs or trees. Greenish flowers sometimes bisexual and sometimes male and female borne on separate plants, which accounts for some specimens not berrying. Leaves, dark green or variegated with white or yellow, usually spiny but occasionally smooth edged.

Soil, ordinary. Position, sunny or shady, as specimen trees or bushes or as hedges or windbreaks. Plant in spring or autumn. Hollies are not always easy to move and must be well watered and constantly damped overhead if dry weather follows transplanting. Prune or clip in late spring and early summer.

For hedges, plant hollies which are about 18 in. high, 18 in. apart.

Increase by seeds stratified out of doors for twelve months from harvesting and then sown outdoors or in a frame or cool greenhouse; variegated kinds by budding in summer on common species; by grafting in spring; by cuttings of half-ripened side shoots in a propagator in summer.

Recommended kinds are *I. altaclarensis*, 20 to 40 ft., large red berries, hybrid between *aquifolium* and *perado*, and numerous varieties including *camelliifolia*, very large leaves and berries, Golden King, leaves edged yellow, and *hodginsii*, purple stems, variable leaves, *aquifolium*, Common Holly, 10 to 30 ft., red berries, Europe (Britain), and numerous horticultural forms including *bacciflava*, yellow fruit, *ferox*, Hedgehog Holly, leaves with short teeth and spines on surface, *heterophylla*, leaves entire, J. C. van Thol (syn. *polycarpa*), free fruiting, *pendula*, pendulous branches, *pyramidalis*, probably

the best berrying variety, and a great many silver or gold variegated varieties with garden names such as Golden Queen, Handsworth New Silver and Madame Briot; *cornuta*, to 9 ft., red berries, China; *crenata*, small leaves, black berries, 12 to 20 ft., Japan; *glabra*, Ink Berry, unarmed leaves, black berries, 10 to 20 ft., Eastern N. America; *latifolia*, large leaved, 20 ft., tender in exposed places, Japan; *opaca*, American Holly, 20 to 40 ft., U.S.A.; *perado* (syn. *maderensis*), Madeira Holly, 20 to 30 ft., red berries, Madeira, slightly tender; *pernyi*, red berries, 15 to 30 ft., Central and W. China; *serrata*, deciduous, 10 ft., heavy crops of very small scarlet berries, Japan; *verticillata*, deciduous, red berries, 6 to 10 ft., Eastern N. America; *vomitoria*, red berries, to 24 ft., Southeastern U.S.A.

ILLICIUM (Aniseed Tree) – *Illiciaceae*. Slightly tender evergreen shrubs with fragrant flowers and leaves with an odour of aniseed.

Soil, loamy, preferably lime free with some peat, well drained but not dry. Position, warm, sheltered, sunny or light shade or in pots or tubs in a cool, lightly shaded greenhouse. Plant in spring.

Increase by cuttings of firm young growth in a propagator in summer; by layering in spring.

Recommended kinds are *I. anisatum* (syn. *religiosum*), yellowish white, spring, 8 to 12 ft., Japan, Formosa; *floridanum*, purple-red, early summer, 8 ft., Florida.

IMPATIENS – *Balsaminaceae*. More or less tender and hardy annuals and perennials. Some with very showy flowers produced over a long season.

Even the perennials are commonly raised from seed though they can also be increased by cuttings of young growth in a warm propagator at any time in spring or summer. Cuttings must be used for varieties with variegated leaves. Sow seeds in spring in temp. 15 to 18°C. for tender kinds or outdoors for hardy kinds. Tender kinds may be hardened off for planting outdoors when there is no further danger of frost, or may be grown in pots in a fairly rich potting compost, such as John Innes potting compost No. 2, in a cool or intermediate greenhouse or *I. walleriana* in a light room. Water freely in spring and summer, moderately in autumn and winter. Shade from strong sunshine in summer.

Outdoors plants may be grown in sun or shade in any reasonably fertile soil that is not liable to dry out in summer. *I. noli-tangere* and *glandulifera* make good waterside plants but can spread so rapidly as to become a nuisance.

Recommended tender kinds are *I. balsamina*, Balsam, red, pink, purple, white, summer, 6 to 24 in., annual, India, Malay-

sia, China, and var. *camelliaeflora*, flowers large and double; *walleriana* (syns. *holstii* and *sultanii*), Busy Lizzie, Sultan Snapweed, Patience Plant, Chinaman's Pigtail, red, purple, pink, white, most of the year, 6 to 12 in., perennial, Tropical Africa, and numerous garden varieties.

Recommended hardy kinds are *I. glandulifera* (syns. *cornigera* and *roylei*), purple, pink, summer, 5 to 8 ft., annual, India; *noli-tangere* (syn. *noli-me-tangere*), yellow, 1½ ft., annual, Europe (Britain).

INCARVILLEA – *Bignoniaceae*. Hardy herbaceous perennials with trumpet-shaped flowers.

Soil, light, rich and well drained. Position, sunny and sheltered. Plant in spring. Protect crowns of the plants in winter by a covering of dry litter in cold places.

Increase by seeds sown in temp. 15 to 18°C. in spring, or in a frame or greenhouse in summer as soon as ripe; by division in spring. Seedlings grow slowly and may take several years to reach flowering size.

Recommended kinds are *I. delavayi*, rose, late spring, early summer, 2 to 3 ft., China, Tibet; *mairei* (syn. *grandiflora*), rose-red and yellow, late spring, early summer, 1½ to 2 ft., China, and var. *grandiflora*, leaves with fewer leaflets; *olgae*, pale pink, summer, 2 to 4 ft., Turkestan.

INDIGOFERA (Indigo) – *Leguminosae*. Hardy or slightly tender deciduous shrubs with pea-shaped flowers and elegant pinnate leaves.

Soil, ordinary, well drained. Position, warm and sunny; excellent for rather dry places. Plant in autumn or late winter. Prune to near ground level annually in spring.

Increase by seeds which germinate better if hot water (87 to 88°C.) is poured over them and left to cool, after which they should be sown immediately; by cuttings of firm young growth in a propagator in summer; by root cuttings in winter.

Recommended kinds are *I. amblyantha*, pink, summer, autumn, to 6 ft., China; *decora*, pink and white, summer, 1 to 2 ft., China, Japan; *gerardiana* (syn. *heterantha*), magenta, summer, early autumn, 2 to 4 ft., Himalaya; *potaninii*, pink, summer, autumn, 4 to 6 ft., China.

INULA – *Compositae*. Hardy herbaceous perennials with daisy flowers.

Soil, ordinary. Position, sunny or partially shaded; some are suitable for thin woodland. Plant in spring or autumn. Cut down flower stems in autumn.

Increase by division in spring or autumn; by seeds sown outdoors or in a frame in spring or early summer.

Recommended kinds are *I. acaulis*, yellow, summer, 2 in., Asia Minor; *ensifolia*, yellow, summer, 1½ ft., Caucasus; *glandu-*

losa (syn. *orientalis*), yellow, summer, 2 to 2½ ft., Caucasus; *helenium*, Elecampane, yellow, summer, 2 to 5 ft., Europe (Britain); *hookeri*, yellow, late summer, autumn, 2 ft., Himalaya; *oculus-christi*, yellow, summer, 2 to 3 ft., Europe; *royleana*, deep golden yellow, summer, autumn, 2 ft., Himalaya.

IONOPSIDIUM – *Cruciferae*. Hardy annual with numerous small four-petalled flowers.

Soil, ordinary. Position, shady. Suitable for rock gardens or crevices in paving.

Increase by seeds sown in spring or early summer where plants are to grow, just covering them with fine soil. Discard after flowering.

The only kind is *I. acaule*, Carpet Plant, Portugal Diamond Plant, Violet Cress, violet, summer, 3 in., Portugal.

IPHEION – *Alliaceae*. Hardy bulbous-rooted plants with clusters of starry flowers.

Soil, ordinary. Position, warm, sunny, well drained. Plant in autumn or spring.

Increase by division in autumn or spring.

The best kind is *I. uniflorum* (syns. *Brodiaea uniflora*, *Milla uniflora*, *Triteleia uniflora*), white or lilac, spring, 6 in., Peru, Argentina, and var. *coeruleum*, light blue.

IPOMOEA – *Convolvulaceae*. More or less tender annual and perennial twining plants with funnel-shaped flowers. Often known as convolvulus, and some species as pharbitis, quamoclit or mina.

Soil, any ordinary fertile. Position, warm, sunny.

Ipomoea tricolor

Sow annual kinds in spring in temp. 15 to 18°C., pot seedlings singly and either plant out in late spring or early summer when danger of frost is over or grow throughout in a sunny frost-proof greenhouse. Plant or pot perennial kinds in spring and grow in large pots, tubs or borders of good soil in a

cool or intermediate greenhouse or outdoors in frost-free places only.

Increase all kinds by seed as above.

Recommended annual kinds are *I. coccinea* (syn. *Quamoclit coccinea*, *Mina sanguinea*), Scarlet Starglory, Star Ipomoea, scarlet and yellow, scented, summer, Mexico, Arizona; *hederacea* (syn. *Pharbitis hederacea*), blue, summer, early autumn, Tropics; *imperialis* (syn. *Pharbitis imperialis*), Japanese Morning Glory, various colours, summer, hybrid between *hederacea* and *tricolor*; *lobata* (syn. *Mina lobata*), scarlet, orange and yellow, summer, Mexico; *quamoclit* (syn. *Quamoclit pennata*), Cypress Vine, Indian Pink, red, summer, Tropical America; *purpurea* (syns. *Convolvulus major*, *C. purpurea* and *Pharbitis purpurea*), blue, purple, red, pink and white, summer, Tropical America; *tricolor* (syns. *I. rubro-coerulea* and *Pharbitis tricolor*), white and red becoming purple or blue, summer, Tropical America.

The best perennial kind is *I. learii* (syn. *Pharbitis learii*), blue becoming purple, summer, Tropical and sub-tropical America.

IRESINE – *Amaranthaceae*. Tender herbaceous plants or sub-shrubs with brilliantly coloured leaves.

Compost, equal parts peat, loam, leafmould and sand. Position, sunny part of intermediate or warm greenhouse, minimum winter temp. 13°C. Pot in spring. Water normally.

Can be planted outdoors in sunny beds or borders in early summer when all danger of frost is over. Lift, repot and remove to a greenhouse in early autumn. Pinch off points of shoots frequently to induce bushy growth.

Increase by cuttings of young shoots inserted in light sandy soil in a warm propagator in spring or late summer.

Recommended kinds are *I. herbstii*, leaves maroon and crimson, 1 ft., S. America, and vars. *aureo-reticulata*, leaves green, gold and red, *brilliantissimum*, red and crimson; *lindenii*, leaves blood red, 1 ft., Ecuador, and var. *formosa*, yellow, veined crimson and green.

IRIS – *Iridaceae*. Hardy evergreen rhizomatous and bulbous-rooted perennials. This is a very large and varied genus which botanists split up into a number of sections according to the formation of the flowers and the character of the roots. Thus Bearded or Pogoniris have flowers in which the lower petals or 'falls' have a central band of hairs forming the 'beard'; Crested or Evansia Irises have a central crest to the falls; Apogon or Beardless Irises have neither beards nor crests on their falls; Regelia or Cushion Irises come mainly from mountainous regions in Asia and need perfect winter drainage; Juno and Xiphium Irises are bulbous rooted, and so on. From the

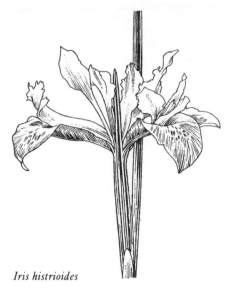

Iris histrioides

point of view of cultivation it is sufficient to divide irises into four groups: Border Irises, which can be grown in normal soils and conditions; Cushion Irises requiring special treatment; Moisture-loving Irises, some of which will actually grow in water, and Bulbous Irises which can be purchased as dry bulbs.

Culture of Border Irises: Soil, ordinary, well drained, and with plenty of lime for *I. germanica* and its numerous garden varieties and hybrids. Position, sunny. Plant in spring, autumn or summer immediately the flowers fade, keeping rhizomes near the surface. Topdress with superphosphate of lime in spring at the rate of 1 to 2 oz. per sq. yd. Lift and replant every third or fourth year.

Culture of Moisture-loving Irises: Soil, rather rich, lime free. Position, sunny, moist but not actually flooded except for *I. laevigata* and *pseudacorus*, which will thrive in a 2- to 3-in. depth of water. Plant in spring or autumn.

Culture of Cushion Irises: Soil, light, rich loam with liberal addition of crushed limestone or chalk. Position, raised bed against a south wall. Plant in autumn. Protect by a cold frame or handlight in winter. Lift rhizomes in midsummer and store in dry sand in a sunny shed or greenhouse until autumn.

Culture of Bulbous-rooted Irises: Plant choice kinds in early autumn in a compost of equal parts fibrous loam, leafmould and sharp sand. Place bulbs 3 in. deep and 3 in. apart; Spanish and English kinds in ordinary soil in sunny beds or borders in autumn, placing bulbs 3 in. deep and 6 in. apart. Lift and replant Spanish and English irises every third year but leave choice species undisturbed until overcrowded.

Pot Culture of bulbous species: Compost, equal parts loam, leafmould and coarse sand. Place in a cold frame till growth begins, when remove to a cold greenhouse or leave in a frame to flower. Pot in autumn, placing five bulbs of the Spanish or English kinds and *I. tingitana* in a 5-in. pot. Small species, such as *I. danfordiae, histrioides* and *reticulata*, should be spaced 2 in. apart in pots or pans. Water sparingly at first, fairly freely once growth appears. Withhold water after leaves begin to wither in late spring or summer. Spanish and English iris must not be placed in artificial heat. *I. tingitana* can be gently forced to flower from midwinter onwards.

Increase by seeds sown in sandy soil in a cold frame as soon as ripe; by division immediately after flowering or in spring or autumn; bulbous kinds by separation of bulb clusters in late summer when the leaves have died down.

Recommended border kinds are *I. aphylla*, purple, late spring, 9 to 15 in., Europe; *chamaeiris*, blue, purple, yellow or white, spring, 4 to 12 in., S. Europe, and numerous varieties; *chrysographes*, violet-purple and yellow, early summer, 1½ ft., China; *confusa*, lavender and orange, spring, 2½ ft., slightly tender, China; *cristata*, lilac and yellow, late spring, 3 to 4 in., Eastern U.S.A.; *douglasiana*, purple, buff or white, late spring, 9 to 12 in., California; *dykesii*, purple and yellow, early summer, 1½ ft., China; *ensata*, white to purple, spring, 1 to 1½ ft., Temperate Asia; *foetidissima*, Gladwyn, grey-blue, early summer, orange-scarlet seeds, 1½ ft., Europe (Britain); *forrestii*, yellow and purple, summer, 1½ ft., China; *germanica*, German Iris, purple, white and yellow, late spring, 2 to 3 ft., origin uncertain, and var. *florentina*, Fleur de Lys, Orris Root, white and pale lavender; *gracilipes*, lilac and orange, late spring, 9 in., Japan; *graminea*, reddish purple and violet, late spring, early summer, 9 to 12 in., Europe; *innominata*, buff-yellow and brown, spring, 6 in., North-western U.S.A.; *japonica* (syn. *fimbriata*), lilac or lavender, yellow and white, spring, Japan, China; *lacustris*, light blue, late spring, 3 in., Eastern U.S.A.; *mellita*, smoky purple, spring, 4 in., S. E. Europe, Asia Minor, and var. *rubromarginata*, red edged; *orientalis*, blue on white, late spring, early summer, 2 ft., E. Asia, Japan; *pallida*, lavender, late spring, early summer, 3 ft., Europe, and vars. *dalmatica*, larger flowers, *aurea variegata*, leaves striped yellow, *variegata*, leaves striped cream; *pumila*, blue, purple, yellow or white, spring, 4 to 6 in., Europe, Asia Minor; *ruthenica*, white or lilac and purple, spring, 1 to 8 in., E. Europe to Korea; *sibirica*, lavender to violet-purple, early summer, 3 to 4 ft., Europe, Asia, and var. *alba*, white, *tectorum*, blue, early summer, 1 ft., Japan, and var. *alba*, white; *tenax*, cream to reddish purple, late spring, 1 ft., North-western U.S.A.; *unguicularis* (syn. *stylosa*), Algerian Iris, lilac-blue, winter, 1 ft., Algeria, E. Mediterranean, and vars. *alba*, white, *speciosa*, violet-blue; *variegata*,

yellow and brown, late spring, early summer, 15 in., S. E. Europe. There are also a great many varieties derived from hybrids between *I. germanica, pallida, variegata* and other species, with a very wide range in colour and height and these are the most popular border irises.

Recommended cushion irises are *I. gatesii*, greyish white, purple veined, late spring, 1 to 1½ ft., Asia Minor; *hoogiana*, grey-blue, yellow beard, late spring, Turkestan; *korolkowii*, white and green, veined brown, late spring, 1 to 1½ ft., Turkestan; *lortetii*, creamy white veined maroon, late spring, 9 to 12 in., Lebanon; *susiana*, grey, veined blackish purple, late spring, 1 to 1½ ft., Asia Minor.

Recommended moisture-loving irises are *I. bulleyana*, lavender and yellow, early summer, 1½ ft., China; *crocea* (syn. *aurea*), yellow, early summer, 3 to 4 ft., Kashmir; *delavayi*, violet-purple and white, early summer, 3 to 5 ft., China; *fulva* (syn. *cuprea*), burnt orange to salmon, summer, 2 to 3 ft., Southern U.S.A.; *kaempferi*, Japanese Iris, blue, purple, rosy red, white, summer, 2 to 2½ ft., Japan; *laevigata*, blue-purple, early summer, 2 ft., Japan; *longipetala*, lilac and yellow, early summer, 2 ft., California; *missouriensis*, light blue and yellow, late spring, early summer, N. America; *monnieri*, yellow, summer, 3 to 4 ft., Crete; *ochroleuca*, creamy white, summer, to 5 ft., Asia Minor; *pseudacorus*, Yellow Flag, Water Flag, yellow, late spring, early summer, 2 to 3 ft., Europe (Britain), W. Asia; *setosa*, purple, late spring, early summer, 6 to 24 in., Siberia, Japan; *spuria*, lilac, purple and white, summer, 1 to 2 ft., Europe, Asia, Algeria; *versicolor*, purple, early summer, 2 to 3 ft., N. America.

Recommended bulbous irises are *I. aucheri* (syn. *sindjarensis*), azure blue and greenish yellow, late winter, early spring, 6 to 9 in., Mesopotamia; *bakeriana*, white, violet, and blue, fragrant, winter, 4 to 6 in., Iraq, Turkey, Iran; *bucharica*, white and yellow, spring, 1 to 1½ ft., Bukhara; *danfordiae*, yellow, winter, 4 in., Turkey; *graeberiana*, mauve and cobalt blue, spring, 6 to 12 in., Turkestan; *histrio*, bright blue and yellow, winter, 4 to 6 in., Asia Minor; *histrioides*, blue, white and yellow, winter, 3 to 4 in., Turkey, Iran, Asia Minor; *magnifica*, lavender-blue and orange, spring, 2 ft., Turkestan; *orchioides*, yellow, spring, 9 to 12 in., Turkestan; *persica*, white, greenish blue, purple, and orange, winter, 6 to 8 in., Asia Minor; *planifolia* (syn. *alata*), lilac and yellow, winter, 1 ft., N. Africa, Sardinia, S. Spain, and var. *alba*, white; *sindpers*, blue and greenish yellow, late winter, early spring, 4 in., hybrid between *aucheri* and *persica*; *reticulata*, violet, purple and yellow, violet scented, late winter, 6 to 8 in., Russia, Iran; *tingitana*, lilac-blue, deep blue and yellow, winter, 2 ft., slightly tender, N. W. Africa; *xiphioides*, English

Iris, various colours, summer, 1 to 2 ft., Pyrenees; *xiphium*, Spanish Iris, various colours, early summer, 1 to 2 ft., S. Europe, N. Africa. The plant known in gardens as *Iris pavonia* is actually *Moraea pavonia*.

ITEA – *Iteaceae*. Evergreen and deciduous, slightly tender, flowering shrubs.

Soil, moist, loamy, lime free for *I. virginica*. Position, sunny or partly shady, warm, sheltered. Can be trained against a wall. Plant in autumn or early spring. Prune after flowering, removing the oldest wood but retaining all strong young stems.

Increase by suckers removed in autumn; by cuttings in summer in sandy soil in a propagator with gentle bottom heat.

Recommended kinds are *I. ilicifolia*, 9-in. pendulous racemes of greenish-white flowers in summer, evergreen, 8 to 10 ft., China; *virginica*, Virginian Sweetspire, erect racemes of creamy-white fragrant flowers, summer, 3 to 5 ft., deciduous, Eastern U.S.A.

IXIA (African Corn Lily) – *Iridaceae*. Slightly tender cormous plants with showy flowers in spikes.

Outdoor culture: Soil, light, rich, sandy. Position, sunny, well-drained border. Plant in autumn 2 in. deep and 2 or 3 in. apart.

Pot culture: Compost, John Innes potting compost No. 1 or equivalent. Position, pots in a sunny cool greenhouse, minimum winter temp. 7°C. Pot in autumn, placing five to seven bulbs in each 4- or 5-in. pot. Water sparingly at first, freely while in growth but reduce the water supply after flowering and keep quite dry for a few weeks in summer before repotting.

Increase by offsets, treated as advised for bulbs; by seeds sown in a frame or cool greenhouse as soon as ripe or in early spring.

Recommended kinds are *I. maculata*, orange-yellow and purple or black, spring, 1 to 1½ ft., S. Africa; *polystachys*, white and green, spring, 1½ ft., S. Africa; *viridiflora*, blue-green, spring, 1 ft., S. Africa. Most of the ixias grown are hybrids flowering in spring, about 1½ ft. high, in a range of colours including cream, yellow, orange, scarlet, carmine, purple, and white with a red centre.

IXIOLIRION – *Amaryllidaceae*. Slightly tender bulbous plants with sprays of small trumpet-shaped flowers.

Soil, light, sandy loam. Position, warm, well-drained sunny borders. Plant bulbs 3 in. deep and 4 in. apart in spring. After flowering cover with a handlight to ensure thorough ripening of the bulbs. Lift the bulbs in autumn and store in dry sand in a cool, frost-proof place till planting time.

They may also be grown in a greenhouse in the same way as ixia.

Increase by offsets removed when the plants are lifted in autumn and treated as advised for normal bulbs; by seeds sown in a frame or cool greenhouse as soon as ripe or in spring.

The best species is *I. montanum*, blue, summer, 1 ft., W. Asia.

IXORA – *Rubiaceae*. Tender evergreen flowering shrubs with clusters of brilliantly coloured tubular flowers.

Compost, John Innes potting compost No. 1 or equivalent with one-quarter its bulk extra peat. Position, pots in a warm greenhouse, minimum winter temp. 18°C. Water normally. Shade in late spring and summer from direct sunshine and maintain a humid atmosphere. Prune into shape in late winter.

Ixora chinensis

Increase by cuttings of firm young shoots, 2 to 3 in. long, inserted singly in small pots in sandy peat in a warm propagator in spring or summer.

Recommended kinds are *I. chinensis*, orange, summer, 2 to 3 ft., China, and vars. *alba*, white, *rutilans*, crimson; *coccinea*, orange-scarlet, summer, 3 to 4 ft., East Indies, and numerous varieties; *rosea* (syn. *chinensis rosea*), pink, summer, 2 to 4 ft., India. There are also many hybrids grown under garden names.

JACARANDA – *Bignoniaceae*. Tender evergreen flowering trees with downy, fern-like leaves and clusters of funnel-shaped flowers.

Compost, John Innes potting compost No. 1 or equivalent. Position, pots or tubs in a cool or intermediate greenhouse, minimum winter temp. 7°C. Water normally. Give all the light possible. Cut back in spring to restrict size and obtain the best foliage development. In completely frost-free places jacaranda can be grown out of doors in ordinary soil and in a sunny position.

Increase by seeds sown in John Innes seed compost or equivalent in temp. 15 to 18°C. in spring. In greenhouses plants are usually grown for foliage only and are discarded when they become too large.

The best kind is *J. mimosifolia* (syn.

ovalifolia), blue, to 50 ft., Argentina. This tree is sometimes wrongly named *J. acutifolia*, a different, Brazilian species.

JACOBINIA – *Acanthaceae*. Tender herbaceous plants or sub-shrubs with tubular flowers sometimes in compact spikes, sometimes scattered singly.

Compost, John Innes potting compost No. 2 or equivalent. Position, pots (or *J. suberecta* in baskets) in an intermediate greenhouse, minimum winter temp. 13°C., but *J. pauciflora* can stand outdoors in a sheltered sunny place in summer. Water normally but keep *J. carnea, chrysostephana* a little dry for a few weeks after flowering, at which time they can be pruned fairly severely if desired. Rest *J. ghiesbreghtiana* in late summer, when plants can be pruned, stood outside for a few weeks and watered sparingly.

Increase by cuttings of young shoots inserted in sandy soil in a propagator in spring or summer.

Recommended kinds are *J. carnea* (syns. *magnifica carnea, Justicia carnea*), pink, late summer, early autumn, 3 to 6 ft., Brazil; *chrysostephana*, yellow, winter, 3 ft., Mexico; *ghiesbreghtiana* (syn. *Justicia ghiesbreghtiana*), scarlet, winter, 2 ft., Mexico; *pauciflora* (syn. *Libonia pauciflora*), scarlet and yellow, winter, 2 ft., Brazil; *pohliana*, pink, 4 to 6 ft., early autumn, Brazil, and var. *velutina*; *suberecta*, orange, 1 ft., summer, Uruguay.

For *J. coccinea* see *Pachystachys coccinea*.

JASIONE – *Campanulaceae*. Hardy herbaceous perennials with small, scabious-like flowers.

Soil, light, sandy loam. Position, sunny. Plant in spring.

Increase by seeds sown in light soil outdoors in spring; by division in spring.

Recommended kinds are *J. humilis*, blue, summer, 6 in., Pyrenees; *jankae*, blue, summer, 9 in., E. Europe; *perennis*, blue, summer, 9 in., W. Europe.

JASMINUM (Jasmine, Jessamine) – *Oleaceae*. Tender and hardy climbing, trailing or shrubby plants, evergreen and deciduous. The most tender kinds make good climbers for intermediate greenhouses with a minimum winter temperature of about 12°C. Grow less tender kinds in frost-proof greenhouses.

Compost, equal parts loam, peat and leaf-mould, with a little sand. Position, well-drained pots, beds or borders with shoots trained to walls, rafters or trellis. Pot or plant in early spring. Prune moderately in late winter.

Hardy and slightly tender kinds can be grown outdoors in reasonably good, loamy soil, twining kinds against a trellis or screen or ascending a tree, *J. nudiflorum* trained against a wall or fence, bushy kinds in

Jasminum polyanthum

sunny, sheltered places. Most prefer sun but *J. nudiflorum* will grow in shade. Plant in autumn or late winter. Prune *J. nudiflorum* moderately after flowering, only removing shoots that have flowered. Other kinds need little pruning but can be thinned in spring if overgrown.

Increase by cuttings of shoots, 3 to 6 in. long, inserted in sandy soil in a propagator in summer for tender kinds, a frame in late summer or autumn for hardy kinds; by layering in spring or summer.

Recommended evergreen tender kinds which will not stand any frost are *J. gracillimum*, white, winter, fragrant, climbing, Borneo; *grandiflorum*, white, summer, autumn, climbing, Himalaya; *sambac*, Arabian Jasmine, white, most of the year, fragrant, twiner, India.

Recommended slightly tender kinds that will survive some frost are *J. floridum*, yellow, late summer, autumn, sprawling, semi-evergreen, W. China; *mesnyi* (syn. *primulinum*), semi-double, yellow, spring, deciduous, 6 to 10 ft., China; *polyanthum*, white, late spring, summer, fragrant, evergreen, vigorous climber, China.

Recommended hardy kinds are *J. beesianum*, strong growing deciduous climber, fragrant rose-coloured flowers, late spring, early summer, shining black berries, W. China; *humile*, evergreen shrub, 3 to 6 ft., yellow, summer, S. E. Asia, and var. *revolutum*, larger flowers; *nudiflorum*, Winter Jasmine, deciduous, yellow, winter, best trained to a wall, any aspect, China; *officinale*, Common Jasmine, vigorous deciduous climber to 30 ft., better for wall protection in cold districts, white, very fragrant, all summer, Iran, Kashmir, China; *parkeri*, yellow, summer, prostrate, deciduous, N. W. India; *stephanense*, vigorous climber to 20 ft., pink, summer, hybrid between *beesianum* and *officinale*.

JEFFERSONIA – *Podophyllaceae*. Hardy perennial herbs with attractive, anemone-like flowers carried singly.

Soil, peaty loam, moderately acid or neutral. Position, shady, as in thin woodland. Plant in spring or autumn.

Increase by seeds sown in sand and peat in a cold frame in spring or early summer; by division in spring.

Recommended kinds are *J. diphylla*, Twin Leaf (syn. *binata*), white, spring, 6 in., South-eastern U.S.A.; *dubia* (syn. *Plagiorhegma dubium*), deep lilac, spring, 6 to 9 in., Manchuria.

JUGLANS (Walnut) – *Juglandaceae*. Hardy deciduous nut-bearing trees.

Soil, reasonably good, not waterlogged. Position, open, sunny. Plant in autumn or late winter. Plant deeply. Pruning is unnecessary. Gather nuts for pickling before the shells get too hard. Place ripe nuts in thin layers in a dry place until the husks fall off, then pack in alternate layers with sand in barrels or casks, or sprinkled with salt in jars. Grafted or budded trees bear earlier than seedlings. Walnuts planted for fruit production should be grafted specimens of named varieties of known cropping ability.

Increase by seed (nuts) sown 2 in. deep in light soil outdoors in autumn, or stratified as soon as ripe for four months at 4°C. and then sown outdoors or under glass; by budding in summer; by grafting in spring for selected varieties which do not come true from seed.

Recommended kinds are *J. cinerea*, Butternut, 50 to 60 ft., N. America; *nigra*, Black Walnut, 80 to 100 ft., N. America; *regia*, Walnut, 50 to 80 ft., Caucasus to Himalaya, and var. *laciniata*, Cut-leaved Walnut, leaflets deeply cut.

JUNCUS (Rush) – *Juncaceae*. Hardy bog plants.

Soil, ordinary. Position, wet ground or pond margin. Plant in spring or autumn.

Increase by division in spring or autumn.

The best kinds are *J. effusus spiralis*, 1½ ft., stems twisted in corkscrew fashion, N. America, Europe, Asia; *follicularis variegatus*, 2 ft., stems banded with white.

JUNIPERUS (Juniper) – *Cupressaceae*. Hardy evergreen coniferous trees. Leaves awl shaped when young, scale like on older trees.

Soil, ordinary, will grow well on lime-

stone or chalk. Position, open, sunny, as specimens, or the dwarf kinds in rock gardens. Plant in spring or autumn.

Increase by seeds stratified for about four months at 20 to 25°C., for a further three months at 4°C. and then sown outdoors or under glass; by cuttings of young shoots inserted in sandy soil in a cold frame in early autumn.

Recommended kinds are *J. chinensis*, to 60 ft., China, Japan, and vars. *aurea*, upright growth, young shoots gold, *columnaris glauca*, blue-grey, columnar, *pyramidalis*, dwarf, conical, *variegata*, compact growth, foliage tipped creamy white; *communis*, Common Juniper, to 40 ft., Europe, and vars. *hibernica*, Irish Juniper, slender column, *compressa*, slender column, very dwarf, *hornibrookii*, prostrate, *oblonga pendula*, to 15 ft., branch ends weeping; *horizontalis*, Creeping Juniper, grey-green or grey-blue, prostrate, N. America; *media*, a variable hybrid between *chinensis* and *sabina* grown in numerous selected varieties such as Blaauw, vase shaped, to 4 ft., *pfitzeriana*, wide shuttlecock, green, *pfitzeriana aurea*, similar to the last but young shoots golden, *plumosa*, wide spreading, plume-like growth; *procumbens*, Creeping Juniper, grey-green, spreading, to 2 ft. high, Japan; *sabina*, Savin, 5 to 10 ft., Europe and N. America, and var. *tamariscifolia*, grey-green, low spreading habit; *scopulorum*, Rocky Mountain Juniper, blue-green, conical, to 35 ft., Rocky Mountains, and numerous varieties; *squamata*, 3 ft., Himalaya, China, and var. *meyeri*, dense habit and metallic blue colouring; *virginiana*, Red Cedar, Pencil Cedar, 40 to 80 ft., N. America, and vars. *glauca*, blue foliage, columnar, *pendula*, branches drooping, *schottii*, columnar habit, bright green foliage, and Sky Rocket, blue-grey, very narrow column, 15 to 20 ft.

KALANCHOE – *Crassulaceae*. Tender succulent perennial plants with flowers in sprays or clusters.

Compost, John Innes potting compost No. 2 or equivalent plus one-sixth its bulk of coarse sand. Position, sunny intermediate greenhouse, minimum winter temp. 13°C. Water fairly freely in spring and summer, moderately in autumn and winter. No shade required at any time. Plants will survive in a cool house, minimum temp. 7°C., but winter-flowering kinds are unlikely to bloom freely.

Increase by seeds sown in sandy soil, just covered with fine soil, in temp. 15 to 18°C. in late winter or early spring; by cuttings of shoots 2 to 3 in. long in summer in well-drained pots of sandy soil, placed on a greenhouse shelf and given very little water; also by leaves laid on the surface of moist sand in summer.

Recommended kinds are *K. blossfeldiana*, scarlet, autumn, winter, 1 ft., Madagascar; *flammea*, orange-scarlet, summer, 1 ft., Som-

alia; *kewensis*, pink, winter, 1½ ft., hybrid between *flammea* and *teretifolia*; *marmorata*, white, summer, 2 ft., Abyssinia; *teretifolia*, white, winter, 3 ft., Arabia.

KALMIA – *Ericaceae*. Hardy evergreen shrubs with clusters of waxy, rose or pink blossoms in late spring.

Soil, lime-free loam, moist but not poorly drained; plants will also thrive in sandy peats provided these are not too dry. Position, cool, partially shaded. Plant in spring or autumn. Pruning is usually undesirable but straggly stems can be shortened in spring or immediately after flowering.

Increase by seeds sown in spring in sandy peat in a cold frame but germination is often better if the seed has been previously stratified for three months at 4°C.; by cuttings of young shoots inserted in sandy peat in a propagator in summer; by layering in spring.

Recommended kinds are *K. angustifolia*, Sheep Laurel, rosy red, early summer, 3 ft., N. America, and vars. *nana*, dwarf, *rosea*, pink, and *rubra*, red; *latifolia*, Calico Bush, American Laurel, Mountain Laurel, the best species for general cultivation, beautiful clear rose-pink, early summer, 6 to 10 ft., N. America, and var. *myrtifolia*, a good dwarf form for a confined space.

KALMIOPSIS – *Ericaceae*. Hardy evergreen dwarf shrub with flowers similar to those of kalmia.

Soil, lime-free loam and peat. Position, sunny, moist. Plant in spring.

Increase by cuttings in summer in acid, sandy soil in a propagator; by seeds sown in similar soil in a frame or cool greenhouse in spring or as soon as ripe.

The only kind is *K. leachiana*, to 15 in., bright pink, spring, N. W. America.

KERRIA (Jew's Mallow) – *Rosaceae*. Hardy deciduous flowering shrub.

Soil, ordinary. Position, sunny or shady; *K. japonica pleniflora* trained, if so desired,

Kerria japonica pleniflora

against a wall, fence or screen. Plant in autumn or late winter. Prune after flowering, cutting out old flowering stems to young growths or to near ground level.

Increase by cuttings of young shoots, 2 to 3 in. long, in sandy soil in a frame in summer; by layering shoots in spring; by removal of rooted suckers in autumn or late winter.

The only species is *K. japonica*, yellow, spring, 6 ft., China, and var. *pleniflora*, double flowered, to 10 ft. tall, and *variegata* (syn. *picta*), leaves variegated creamy white.

KIRENGESHOMA – *Hydrangeaceae*. Hardy, herbaceous perennial with sprays of nodding, bell-shaped flowers.

Soil, rich, leafy or peaty, moist. Position, cool, partially shaded. Plant in spring.

Increase by division in spring; by seeds sown in a shady frame or greenhouse in spring.

The only species is *K. palmata*, yellow, late summer, early autumn, 3 to 4 ft., Japan.

KLEINIA – *Compositae*. Tender perennials with fleshy cylindrical bluish-grey stems. Some authorities now classify these as *Senecio* to which they are closely allied.

Compost, John Innes potting compost No. 1 or equivalent. Position, sunny, cool greenhouse, minimum winter temp. 7°C., or in a sunny window. Water moderately in spring and summer, sparingly in autumn and winter.

Increase by cuttings of shoots dried for a few hours and then inserted in gritty compost in summer.

Recommended kinds are *K. articulata*, Candle Plant, yellow, winter, 1½ ft., S. Africa; *fulgens*, orange and red, late spring, 2 ft., S. Africa; *galpinii*, orange, autumn, 1 ft., S. Africa; *neriifolia* (syn. *Senecio kleinia*), yellow, autumn, 4 ft., Canary Islands; *pendula*, red and orange-yellow, autumn, sprawling, Abyssinia, Somalia, Arabia; *repens* (syn. *Senecio serpens*), white, summer, creeping, S. Africa.

KNIPHOFIA (Torch Lily, Club Lily) – *Liliaceae*. Hardy or slightly tender herbaceous perennials with tubular flowers in crowded spikes. Formerly known as tritoma.

Soil, good fertile loam, well drained in winter but not liable to dry out in summer. Position, sunny. Plant in spring. Topdress annually in spring with well-decayed manure. Water freely in dry weather during summer. Protect in severe weather by drawing the leaves together and tying them like a tent over the crown.

Increase by seeds sown in sandy soil in a frame or greenhouse in spring, transplanting seedlings outdoors when large enough to handle; by division of roots in spring.

Recommended kinds are *K. caulescens*, reddish salmon or nearly white, early summer, 4 ft., S. Africa; *erecta*, orange-scarlet, late summer, early autumn, 4 ft., hybrid;

foliosa, yellow and red, summer, 3 ft., Abyssinia; *galpinii*, orange, summer, 2½ ft., Transvaal; *macowanii*, orange-red, late summer, early autumn, 2 ft., S. Africa; *nelsonii*, orange-scarlet and yellow, summer, 1½ ft., S. Africa; *northiae*, yellow and red, summer, 3 ft., S. Africa; *praecox*, red and yellow, late spring, early summer, 2 ft., S. Africa; *rufa*, yellow and orange-red, summer, 1 to 1½ ft., Natal; *snowdenii*, orange-red and yellow, autumn, 3 ft., Uganda; *tuckii*, yellow and red becoming all yellow, early summer, 4 to 5 ft., S. Africa; *uvaria* (syn. *aloides*), red and yellow, late summer, early autumn, 3 to 4 ft., S. Africa, and vars. *grandis*, *maxima* and *nobilis*, all taller and with larger flower spikes. There are also many garden varieties and hybrids varying in colour from ivory white to deep scarlet and in height from 2 to 6 ft.

KOCHIA – *Chenopodiaceae*. Slightly tender annual with uninteresting flowers but making dense columns of narrow leaves which change from light green to a brilliant crimson-purple tint in early autumn.

Soil, ordinary. Position, sunny. Sow seeds

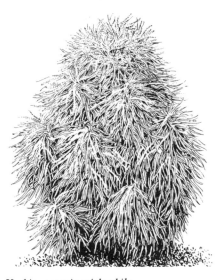

Kochia scoparia trichophila

in light soil in temp. 15 to 18°C. in spring. Transplant seedlings into pots or boxes, harden off in a frame, and plant out 2 ft. apart in late spring and early summer. In frost-free places seeds can be sown outdoors in spring where plants are to flower.

The best kind is *K. scoparia trichophila*, Summer Cypress, Fire Bush, 2 to 3 ft., S. Europe to Japan.

KOELREUTERIA – *Sapindaceae*. Hardy or tender deciduous trees. Attractive pinnate leaves, small flowers produced in large showy sprays.

Soil, ordinary. Position, warm, sunny, well drained, even rather dry. *K. formosana* will not survive frost and so is only suitable for very mild or sub-tropical climates.

Increase by seeds, perforated or chipped to admit moisture and sown as soon as ripe or in spring in temp. 15 to 18°C.; by root cuttings in winter.

Recommended species are *K. formosana*, Chinese Flame Tree, yellow, summer, 20 to 40 ft., red and orange bladder-like fruits, tender, Formosa; *paniculata*, Pride of India, China Tree, Golden-rain Tree, yellow, summer, followed by greenish bladder-like fruits, good autumn-tinted foliage, 30 ft., China, and vars. *apiculata*, doubly pinnate leaves, *fastigiata*, slow growing, erect columnar habit.

KOHLERIA – *Gesneriaceae*. Tender herbaceous perennials with rhizomatous roots and clusters of showy tubular or bell-shaped flowers. Formerly known as isoloma.

Compost, equal parts loam, leafmould and peat with two parts of coarse sand. Position, pots in an intermediate or warm greenhouse, minimum winter temp. 13°C. Pot in early spring, just covering the rhizomes. Water sparingly at first, freely as growth appears but after flowering gradually reduce water supply and keep quite dry

Kohleria eriantha

in winter. Shake out rhizomes in late winter, repot and treat as before. Shade from strong sunshine.

Increase by seeds sown in temp. 15 to 18°C. in spring; by division of rhizome clusters at potting time; by leaf or stem cuttings in a warm propagator in summer.

Recommended kinds are *K. amabile*, rose and purple, summer, 1 to 2 ft., Colombia, and a range of hybrids with white, red or deep purple flowers; *bogotensis*, yellow and red, summer, 1 to 2 ft., Colombia, and hybrids varying in flower colour; *eriantha*, red, yellow spotted, summer, 2 to 4 ft., Colombia (often wrongly grown as *Isoloma hirsutum*), and hybrids with larger flowers; *lindeniana*, white, yellow and violet, summer, Ecuador.

KOLKWITZIA – *Caprifoliaceae.* Deciduous hardy shrub with small flowers resembling weigela.

Soil, ordinary, well drained. Position, full sun. Cut out old and weak stems after flowering.

Increase by cuttings in sandy soil in a frame in summer; by layering in spring or autumn; by seeds sown in temp. 15 to 18°C. as soon as ripe or in spring, but seedlings may vary in colour and freedom of flowering.

The only species is *K. amabilis*, Beauty Bush, to 10 ft., pink with a yellow throat, spring, summer, China, varieties are available, such as Pink Cloud, with flowers of deep pink.

+ LABURNOCYTISUS – *Leguminosae.* Hardy deciduous flowering tree. A bigeneric graft-hybrid between *Laburnum anagyroides* and *Cytisus purpureus*, which produces typical yellow laburnum flowers, flowers of a similar type but yellowish purple, and purple flowers on broom-like growth. This strange tree is named *Laburnocytisus adamii*, grows to the same size as laburnum and should be treated in the same way.

LABURNUM – *Leguminosae.* Hardy deciduous flowering trees with trails of yellow pea flowers.

Soil, ordinary. Position, sunny, open. Plant in autumn or late winter. The seeds are poisonous.

Increase by seeds sown outdoors or under glass in spring. Germination is improved if warm water (87 to 88°C.) is poured over the seeds and left to cool before sowing; by cuttings of firm young growth in a propagator in summer; by layering in autumn; by grafting in spring or budding in summer on to seedlings of common species.

Recommended kinds are *L. alpinum*, Scotch Laburnum, yellow, scented, early summer, 15 to 20 ft., Europe; *anagyroides* (syn. *vulgare*), Golden Chain, yellow, late spring, 20 to 30 ft., Europe, and vars. *aureum*, golden leaved, *autumnale*, second flower crop in autumn, *quercifolium*, oak leaved, *carlieri*, long racemes, and *pendulum*, weeping; *watereri*, hybrid between *alpinum* and *anagyroides*, much like the former but variable and available in selected forms of which *vossii* is one of the best.

LACHENALIA (Cape Cowslip) – *Liliaceae.* Tender bulbous plants with tubular flowers in loose spikes. All are natives of S. Africa.

Compost, John Innes potting compost No. 1 or equivalent. Position, pots or baskets in a cool greenhouse, minimum winter temp. 7°C. Pot in late summer or early autumn, five or six bulbs in each 5-in. pot. Water sparingly at first, fairly freely when growth appears but gradually reduce the water supply in spring and keep quite

Lachenalia bulbifera

dry for a month or more in summer before repotting. No shade is required at any stage.

Increase by offsets removed and placed in separate pots at potting time; by seeds sown in John Innes seed compost or equivalent in a cool greenhouse in spring or as soon as ripe.

Recommended kinds are *L. aloides* (syn. *tricolor*), yellow, red and green, spring, 1 ft., and vars. *aurea*, bright orange-yellow, *lutea*, yellow, *nelsonii*, yellow and green, *quadricolor*, yellow, red, purple and green; *bulbifera* (syn. *pendula*), purple, red, yellow and green, winter, spring, 6 to 10 in.; *glaucina*, white or mauve, spring, 1 ft.; *mutabilis*, bluish mauve and orange, late winter, 6 to 8 in.; *orchioides*, white or yellowish, tinged red or blue, spring, 6 to 9 in. There are numerous hybrids mostly in shades of yellow and orange, more or less tinged with red and green.

LACTUCA – *Compositae.* Hardy perennials related to the lettuce and grown ornamentally for their handsome clusters of chicory-like flowers.

Soil, reasonably fertile loam. Position, sunny or semi-shady, not liable to dry out in summer, but well drained in winter. Plant in spring.

Increase by seeds sown in light sandy soil outdoors in spring or early summer; by division of roots in spring.

Recommended kinds are *L. alpina* (syns. *Cicerbita alpina*, *Mulgedium alpinum*), blue, summer, 3 ft., Arctic regions, Europe to Siberia; *plumieri* (syns. *Cicerbita plumieri*, *Mulgedium plumieri*), blue, summer, 8 ft., S. France.

LAELIA – *Orchidaceae.* Tender epiphytic orchids closely allied to *Cattleya*, with which genus many hybrids have been produced, also with *Brassavola*, *Epidendrum*, etc.

Compost, equal parts fibre and sphagnum moss. Broadly there are two sections, one much like the *Cattleya labiata* group requiring the same conditions in an intermediate house. The second has smaller, often ovoid, pseudobulbs and rather tall, slender scapes terminating in several flowers, usually smaller than those of the first section. These succeed in the cool house, but can be grown with the others suspended near the glass in pans during the summer, and given a rather severe rest in the cool house in winter. Otherwise treat as for Cattleya.

Increase by division of plants in spring.

Recommended kinds are *L. anceps*, pink, crimson and yellow, winter, 18 to 24 in., Mexico; *autumnalis*, rose, white and yellow, winter 2 ft., Mexico; *cinnabarina*, orange-red, spring, 9 to 12 in., Brazil; *crispa* (syn. *Cattleya crispa*), white, purple flushed, variable, summer, 12 in., Brazil; *gouldiana*, rose-pink and purple, winter, 18 in., Mexico; *harpophylla*, orange, spring, 12 in., Brazil; *perrinii*, rose, purple and crimson, autumn, winter, 12 in., Brazil, and var. *alba*, white; *pumila*, lilac-pink and yellow, autumn, 4 in., Brazil; *purpurata*, variable, light pink and rich crimson-purple, spring, summer, 12 in., Brazil, many varieties; *tenebrosa*, bronze and brown-purple, late spring, summer, 18 in., Brazil; *xanthina*, yellow, lip whitish suffused purple, spring, summer, 12 in., Brazil.

x LAELIOCATTLEYA – *Orchidaceae.* Bigeneric hybrids between *Cattleya* and *Laelia* combining some of the flower size of the former with the rich colouring of the latter.

Compost, conditions and temperatures as for cattleyas.

LAGENARIA (Bottle Gourd, Trumpet Gourd) – *Cucurbitaceae.* Rather tender, ornamental, fruiting annuals or perennials climbing by tendrils. Fruit not edible, oblong, bottle like, 1 to 6 ft. long. Grown for ornament and for making vessels.

Soil, fairly rich. Position, warm, sunny beds at the foot of walls, fences or trellis, or on the summits of sunny banks, shoots growing at will. Water freely and apply liquid manure when fruit has formed. No pinching of shoots is required. May also be grown in pots in a sunny greenhouse, the shoots being trained up the roof.

Increase by seeds sown in temp. 15 to 18°C. in spring; pot seedlings individually in John Innes potting compost No. 1 or equivalent and harden off for planting outdoors in late spring or early summer.

The recommended species is *L. vulgaris* (syn. *siceraria*), white, summer, 10 ft., Tropical Africa. *L. sphaerica* is similar but perennial.

LAGERSTROEMIA – *Lythraceae.* More or less tender deciduous flowering shrubs and trees.

Soil, ordinary, well drained. Position, warm, sunny, sheltered. *L. speciosa* will not survive any frost but, provided growth is well ripened in the autumn, *L. indica* will survive temperatures of about −12°C. If desired *L. indica* can be hard pruned each spring.

Increase by cuttings of firm young shoots inserted in sandy soil in a warm propagator in summer; by seeds sown in temp. 18 to 21°C. in spring.

Recommended kinds are *L. indica*, Crape Myrtle, pink, red, lavender or white, summer, 10 to 20 ft., polished grey bark, China, Korea, and vars. *nana*, dwarf, *prostrata*, prostrate; *speciosa*, lavender, pink, summer, to 60 ft., tender, India.

LAGURUS – *Gramineae*. Slightly tender ornamental annual grass. Inflorescence borne in downy egg-shaped heads. Very useful in the dried state for winter decorations.

Lagurus ovatus

Soil, ordinary, light. Position, open, sunny, warm. Gather inflorescences for drying when well developed.

Increase by seeds sown outdoors in spring where plants are required to grow.

The only species is *L. ovatus*, Hare's Tail Grass, 1 ft., S. Europe.

LAMIUM – *Labiatae*. Hardy herbaceous perennials grown primarily as ground cover for their ornamental leaves, though all flower.

Soil, ordinary. Position, sunny or shady. Plant in spring or autumn.

Increase by division in spring or autumn.

Recommended kinds are *L. galeobdolon* (syn. *Galeobdolon luteum*), Golden Dead Nettle, Yellow Archangel, yellow, late spring, early summer, sprawling, Europe (Britain), and var. *variegatum*, leaves silvery; *maculatum*, purple, spring to autumn, leaves green with white stripe, prostrate, Europe (Britain), and var. *aureum*, leaves greenish yellow; *orvala*, pink or purple, late spring, early summer, to 2 ft., Italy, France.

LAMPRANTHUS – *Aizoaceae*. Greenhouse succulent plants, formerly included

in *Mesembryanthemum*. Many have showy flowers produced in late spring and summer. All are natives of S. Africa.

Compost, John Innes potting compost No. 1 or equivalent plus one-sixth its bulk coarse sand. Position, pots in a sunny, cool greenhouse, minimum winter temp. 7°C. or many varieties outdoors in warm, sunny sheltered places where there is little or no frost. Water freely in spring and summer, sparingly in autumn, hardly at all in winter. No shade required at any time.

Increase by cuttings of firm young growth in a frame or propagator in summer; by seeds sown in John Innes seed compost or equivalent in spring in temp. 15 to 18°C.

Recommended kinds are *L. aurantiacus*, bright orange, 1 to 2 ft.; *aureus*, yellow, 1 ft.; *blandus*, pink, 1½ ft.; *brownii*, orange-red, 1 ft.; *coccineus*, scarlet, 1½ ft.; *emarginatus*, purple, 1 ft.; *roseus*, white to magenta, 1½ to 2 ft.; *spectabilis*, magenta, 1 ft.

LANTANA – *Verbenaceae*. Tender evergreen shrubs with close clusters of small flowers similar to those of verbena.

Compost, John Innes potting compost No. 1 or equivalent. Position, pots or beds in a cool or intermediate greenhouse, minimum winter temp. 7°C. No shading required. Water normally. Prune fairly severely in spring to prevent growth becoming straggly. Plants can be used out of doors as bedding in summer but should either be returned to the greenhouse before there is danger of frost in autumn or cuttings should be taken and overwintered in a greenhouse. Only in almost completely frost-free areas can lantanas be grown out of doors all the year.

Increase by seeds sown in John Innes seed compost or equivalent in temp. 15 to 18°C. in spring; by cuttings of firm young growth in a warm propagator in spring or summer.

The best kind is *L. camara*, orange-red and yellow, summer, autumn, 4 to 10 ft., Tropical America, and numerous varieties yellow, pink, white changing to mauve, yellow becoming red, etc.

LAPAGERIA – *Philesiaceae*. Rather tender evergreen flowering climber with hanging bell-shaped flowers of a waxy texture.

Soil, equal parts peat and lime-free loam. Position, warm, sheltered and shady. Can be allowed to twine up wires, trellis, etc., against a wall or grown in a shady greenhouse with minimum temp. 5°C. Water freely in spring and summer, syringe with water and maintain a rather moist atmosphere.

Increase by seeds sown in sandy peat and leafmould in temp. 15 to 18°C. in spring; by layering strong shoots in sandy peat in spring or autumn.

The only species is *L. rosea*, Chilean Bellflower, rose, summer, 12 to 15 ft.,

Lapageria rosea

Chile, and vars. *albiflora*, white, and Nash Court, pink and white.

LAPEIROUSIA – *Iridaceae*. Slightly tender cormous plants with starry, brightly coloured flowers. Previously known as anomatheca.

Soil, light, well drained. Position, warm, sunny, or in pots in a sunny frost-proof greenhouse. Pot in autumn. Plant in autumn or spring, preferably the latter except in warm, nearly frost-free places. Water sparingly at first, freely as growth appears but reduce water supply gradually after flowering and keep almost dry for a few weeks in summer. Outdoor plants can be covered with a cloche or handlight in winter.

Increase by offshoots removed at planting or potting time and treated as old corms; by seeds sown in sandy soil in a frame or greenhouse as soon as ripe or in spring.

The best kinds are *L. cruenta* (syn. *Anomatheca cruenta*), scarlet, summer, 1 ft., S. Africa, and var. *alba*, white.

LARIX (Larch) – *Pinaceae*. Hardy deciduous coniferous trees.

Soil, any except heavy poorly drained or very alkaline. Position, open, in groups or as single specimens. Plant in autumn. Pruning undesirable but dead branches should be removed in winter.

Increase by seeds stratified for three months at 4°C. and then sown in sand, peat and loam out of doors or in a frame.

Recommended kinds are *L. decidua* (syn. *europaea*), European Larch, 60 to 120 ft., Europe, and var. *pendula*, branchlets pendulous; *eurolepis*, Dunkeld Larch, Hybrid Larch, a vigorous hybrid between *decidua* and *kaempferi*; *kaempferi* (syn. *leptolepis*), Japanese Larch, 60 to 90 ft., Japan; *laricina* (syn. *americana*), American Larch, Tamarack, to 60 ft., America; *occidentalis*, 100 to 200 ft., N. America; *pendula*, Weeping Larch, pendulous branchlets, to 90 ft., believed to be a hybrid between *decidua* and *laricina*.

LATHRAEA – *Scrophulariaceae*. Herbaceous perennial, leafless, parasitic plants with attractive tubular flowers.

Sow seeds in spring or as soon as ripe in moist soil over the roots of those trees on which the species is parasitic; poplar and willow for *L. clandestina*, elm, hazel, etc., for *squamaria*.

Recommended kinds are *L. clandestina*, purple, spring, 3 in., Europe; *squamaria*, white, or pink, spring, 4 to 12 in., Europe (Britain), W. Asia.

LATHYRUS – *Leguminosae*. Hardy annuals and herbaceous perennials, mostly climbers, of which the sweet pea is the best known and most widely grown.

Culture of the Sweet Pea: Soil, rich, ordinary, well manured. Position, groups in sunny borders, shoots supported by brushy branches or bamboo canes; against sunny walls or fences; in rows in the open garden. Very dwarf kinds can be grown without support. Sow seeds, three or four in a 3-in. pot in light soil in temp. 10 to 15°C. in late winter, transplanting seedlings outdoors when sufficiently large; or sow in autumn in a similar temperature, grow throughout the winter in small pots in an unheated frame or greenhouse and plant out in spring; or sow seeds in spring where plants are to grow. Water liberally in dry weather. Apply liquid manure once or twice weekly to plants in flower. Remove seed pods as they form to ensure plenty of flowers.

For the finest quality flowers grow in rows 8 ft. apart. Dig trenches 18 in. wide and 2 ft. deep. Fork into subsoil 2 in. of rotted manure, then fill up the trench to within 2 in. of the top with ordinary soil and good loam. Sprinkle a little compound fertilizer in the trench and fork in. Sow five seeds in a 3-in. pot of good soil in a cold frame in autumn and plant out seedlings singly 6 in. apart in spring. Stake early, using bamboo canes at least 7 ft. high. Feed with liquid fertilizer from late spring until the plants finish flowering, following label instructions regarding strength. Remove all side growths, keeping each plant to a single stem. Nip off the points of shoots when the tops of the supporting sticks are reached, alternatively, untie each plant, loop the old growth round the bottom of its stake, and allow the growing point to climb to the top once more. Remove spent blooms daily.

Culture of perennial species: Soil, ordinary, deep, rich. Position, against sunny walls, fences, arbours, on tree stumps or banks. Plant in spring or autumn. Prune away stems close to the ground in autumn. Topdress with decayed manure or garden compost in spring.

Increase annuals by seed; perennials by seeds sown in spring or early summer, or by division of roots in spring.

Recommended annual kinds are *L. odoratus*, Sweet Pea, various colours, to 10 ft.,

Sicily; *tingitanus*, Tangier Pea, purple and red, summer, 4 to 6 ft., Tangier.

Recommended perennial kinds are *L. grandiflorus*, rosy crimson, summer, 5 ft., S. Europe; *latifolius*, Everlasting Pea, rose, pink or white, summer, 8 ft., Europe; *magellanicus*, Lord Anson's Pea, purple, summer, 6 to 8 ft., Straits of Magellan; *rotundifolius*, rosy pink, summer, 6 ft., Asia Minor; *splendens*, carmine, summer, rather tender, California; *vernus* (syn. *Orobus vernus*), purple and blue, spring 1 ft., bushy, Europe.

LAURUS (Bay Tree) – *Lauraceae*. Slightly tender evergreen shrubs or small trees. Small yellow flowers in clusters, male and female borne on separate plants; berries, dark purple. The dark green aromatic leaves are used for flavouring.

Soil, ordinary, well drained. Position, sunny, warm, sheltered but plants will stand exposure in mild maritime regions. *L. azorica* is unlikely to survive temperatures much below −5°C. but *L. nobilis* will survive −15°C. or even lower. Plant in spring or autumn. *L. nobilis* is a good shrub for clipping to a formal shape, may be purchased as pyramids or standards and is often grown in tubs to stand on terraces. Trim between late spring and midsummer.

If grown in tubs use a compost of two parts loam, one part each of leafmould and sand. Water sparingly in winter, freely afterwards. May stand in a sunny, sheltered position for the winter or in a cold greenhouse, since severe weather may cause browning of the leaves.

Increase by cuttings of shoots, 3 to 4 in. long, inserted in sandy soil in a frame in summer or early autumn; by layering in spring or autumn.

Recommended kinds are *L. azorica* (syn. *canariensis*), Canary Island Laurel, large leaves, to 60 ft., Canary Islands, Azores; *nobilis*, Sweet Bay, Victor's Laurel, Poet's Laurel, 20 to 40 ft., S. Europe.

LAVANDULA (Lavender) – *Labiatae*. Hardy or slightly tender evergreen flowering shrubs. The flowers are valued for their fragrance in a dried state and for distilling for perfumery, being grown commercially for the latter purpose.

Soil ordinary, well drained, good on chalk and limestone. Position, warm, sunny. Plant in spring or autumn. Prune straggly plants into shape in spring; this should be done regularly to lavender hedges to prevent them from getting bare at the base. Gather blossoms for drying just as they come into bloom and for distilling about a week later.

Increase by cuttings in ordinary soil in a frame in summer or out of doors in sheltered borders in early autumn.

Recommended kinds are *L. angustifolia* (syns. *officinalis*, *spica*), Old English Lavender, lavender, summer, 2 to 3 ft., S. W.

Europe, and numerous varieties or hybrids with *L. latifolia* such as *alba*, white, Hidcote, 1 to 1½ ft., blue-purple, *rosea*, pale pink, *vera*, Dutch Lavender, lavender-blue, 3 ft.; *dentata*, deep lavender-blue, summer, 1½ to 2 ft., slightly tender, S. Europe; *latifolia* (syn. *spica latifolia*), Spike Lavender, lavender, summer, 2 to 3 ft., S. W. Europe; *stoechas*, French Lavender, blue-purple, summer, 1 to 1½ ft., slightly tender, Mediterranean region.

LAVATERA (Tree Mallow) – *Malvaceae*. Hardy flowering sub-shrubs and annuals.

Soil, ordinary. Position, warm, sunny. Plant shrubby kinds in spring. Sow annual kinds in spring where they are to flower and thin (or transplant) seedlings 1 ft. apart.

Increase shrubby kinds by seeds sown in temp. 15 to 18°C. in spring; by cuttings of firm young shoots inserted in a propagator in summer.

The best shrubby kind is *L. olbia*, rosy pink, summer and autumn, 6 ft., S. Europe.

The best annual kind is *L. trimestris* (syn. *rosea*), rose, 3 ft., S. Europe, var. *alba*, white.

LAYIA – *Compositae*. Hardy annual with daisy flowers. Sow in spring outdoors in ordinary soil and a sunny position and thin seedlings to 6 to 8 in. Discard after flowering.

The best kind is *L. elegans*, Tidy Tips, yellow, and white, summer, 1 ft., California.

LEONOTIS – *Labiatae*. Rather tender sub-shrubs or perennials with showy whorls of orange-red flowers in autumn and early winter.

Soil, ordinary, well drained. Position, sunny, warm, sheltered or may be grown in pots in a frost-proof greenhouse. Plant in spring. Cut off all dead or damaged growth in spring.

Increase by seeds sown in temp. 15 to 18°C. in spring; by cuttings of firm young shoots in a frame or propagator in summer.

The best kind is *L. leonurus*, Lion's Ear, orange-scarlet, summer, 3 to 5 ft., shrubby, S. Africa.

LEONTOPODIUM – *Compositae*. Hardy perennial herbs with small flower heads surrounded by grey woolly bracts.

Soil, well drained, sandy. Position, sunny rock gardens. Plant in spring. Protect from heavy rain in autumn and winter by placing a square of glass, supported by sticks at each corner, a few inches above the plants. Gather flowers in summer and dry for preserving. Best results are obtained by raising fresh plants from seed annually, or by dividing old plants in spring.

Increase by seeds sown in spring in a well-drained pan filled with a mixture of two parts sharp sand, one part loam and one part either peat or leafmould in a frame in a cool shady spot; by division in spring.

The best kind is *L. alpinum*, Edelweiss,

Leontopodium alpinum

yellow, summer, surrounded by star-shaped cottony bracts, 6 in., Alps.

LEPTOSPERMUM – *Myrtaceae*. Hardy or slightly tender evergreen flowering shrubs.

Soil, loamy, lime free, well drained. Position, sunny, warm, sheltered for the more tender kinds. May be trained against sunny walls. Plant in spring. Little pruning is desirable but straggly shoots can be shortened in spring provided they are not cut back into hard old wood.

Increase by cuttings in sandy peat in pots in a propagator in summer; by seeds sown in sandy peat in temp. 15 to 18°C. in spring.

Recommended kinds are *L. humifusum* (syn. *scoparium prostratum*), white, early summer, prostrate, Tasmania; *lanigerum*, white, early summer, 4 to 6 ft., Australia, Tasmania; *scoparium*, South Sea Myrtle, Manuka, New Zealand Tea Tree, white, spring, summer, 6 ft. or more in warm localities, slightly tender, Australia, New Zealand, Tasmania, and vars. *chapmanii*, pink, *nicholl-sii*, crimson, and Red Damask, double, crimson.

LESCHENAULTIA – *Goodeniaceae*. Slightly tender evergreen shrubs with phlox-like flowers.

Compost, two parts fibrous peat and one part coarse sand. Position, well-drained pots in a sunny frost-proof greenhouse, minimum winter temp. 4°C., or outdoors in warm, sunny, nearly frost-free places. Water fairly freely in spring and summer, very sparingly in autumn and winter. Pot-grown plants can stand outdoors in a sunny place all summer. Pot or plant in spring.

Increase by cuttings of young growth inserted in sandy peat in a propagator in summer; by root cuttings in a cool greenhouse in winter. Grow on young plants in pots as they resent root disturbance.

The best kind is *L. biloba* (syns. *drummondii*, *grandiflora*), blue, summer, 2 to 3 ft., Australia.

LESPEDEZA (Bush Clover) – *Leguminosae*. Hardy shrubs with spikes of small pea-type flowers.

Soil, sandy loam. Position, warm, sunny. Plant in autumn or late winter. Prune slightly after flowering.

Increase by seeds sown in light soil in a frame or cool greenhouse in spring, the seeds germinate more readily if placed in water at 87°C. and left to cool before sowing; by cuttings of firm young shoots in a propagator in summer; by hard-wood cuttings in a frame or outdoors in autumn; by layering in spring.

Recommended kinds are *L. bicolor*, rosy purple, late summer, 9 ft., China, Japan; *cyrtobotrya*, rose-purple, late summer, 2 to 3 ft., Japan, Korea; *japonica* (syn. *bicolor alba*), white, autumn, 6 ft., Japan; *thunbergii* (syns. *L. sieboldii*, *Desmodium penduliflorum*), purple, autumn, 4 ft., China, Japan.

LEUCADENDRON – *Proteaceae*. Tender evergreen tree with silvery silky leaves.

Compost, two parts each of lime-free loam and peat, one part coarse sand. Position, pots or beds in a sunny, frost-proof greenhouse or outdoors in warm, sunny places where little or no frost occurs. Water moderately in spring and summer, very sparingly in autumn and winter. No shade is required at any time. Pot-grown plants can stand outdoors in a sunny place in summer.

Increase by seeds sown in sandy peat in temp. 13 to 15°C. as soon as ripe; by cuttings of firm shoots in sand in a propagator in summer.

The best kind is *L. argenteum*, Cape Silver Tree, 15 to 30 ft., S. Africa.

LEUCOCORYNE – *Alliaceae*. Slightly tender bulbous plants with clusters of ixia-like flowers.

Compost, John Innes potting compost No. 1 or equivalent. Position, pots in a sunny, frost-proof greenhouse or outdoors in a warm, sunny, well-drained position in places where there is little or no frost. Pot or plant in autumn, four or five bulbs in each 5-in. pot. Water sparingly at first, freely when growth appears but gradually

reduce water supply after flowering and keep quite dry for a month or more before repotting.

Increase by seeds sown in spring or as soon as ripe in sandy soil in temp. 13 to 15°C.; by offsets detached when bulbs are lifted and grown on in the same way.

The best kind is *L. ixioides* (syn. *odorata*), Glory of the Sun, blue and white, scented, late winter, early spring, 1 to 1½ ft., Chile.

LEUCOJUM (Snowflake) – *Amaryllidaceae*. Hardy bulbous plants with snowdrop-like flowers.

Soil, fertile, rather moist loam for *L. aestivum* and *vernum*. Position, sunny or shady in borders, rock gardens, woodlands, etc., or naturalized in grass. *L. autumnale* and *roseum* in porous, well-drained soil in a sunny, sheltered place or in pots of John Innes potting compost No. 1 or equivalent in an unheated greenhouse or frame. Plant bulbs 4 in. deep, *autumnale* and *roseum* in late summer, *aestivum* and *vernale* in early autumn. Bulbs do not usually flower the first year after planting, and only require to be lifted and replanted very occasionally.

Increase by offsets, removed and re-planted in autumn; by seeds sown in John Innes seed compost or equivalent in a frame or cool greenhouse in spring or as soon as ripe.

Recommended kinds are *L. aestivum*, Summer Snowflake, white and green, late spring, early summer, 1½ ft., Europe (Britain), Asia Minor, Caucasus; *autumnale*, white and pink, autumn, 4 in., Mediterranean region; *roseum*, pink, autumn, 4 in., Corsica; *vernum*, Spring Snowflake, white and green, early spring, 1 ft., Europe, and var. *carpathicum*, white and yellow.

LEUCOTHOE – *Ericaceae*. Hardy evergreen or deciduous shrubs with small bell-shaped or cylindrical flowers.

Soil, peaty loam, lime free. Position, open or shady. Plant in spring or autumn. Pruning is not necessary.

Increase by seeds sown in sandy peat in a frame in spring; by layering shoots in autumn; by division in autumn.

Recommended kinds are *L. catesbaei* (syn.

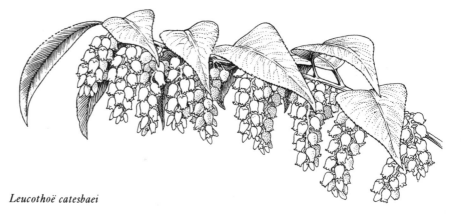

Leucothoë catesbaei

fontanesiana), white, late spring, 3 to 6 ft., an attractive shrub with arching growths and autumn foliage colour, South-eastern U.S.A., and vars. *nana*, shorter, Rainbow, leaves in various shades of green, copper, pink and red; *davisiae*, erect, sturdy habit, white, early summer, 3 ft., California; *keiskei*, prettily coloured young foliage, flowers cylindrical, white, summer, 3 to 4 ft., Japan; *racemosa*, deciduous, white or pink, late spring, 6 to 12 ft., good autumn colour, Eastern U.S.A.

LEWISIA (Bitterwort) – *Portulacaceae*. Hardy herbaceous perennials with attractive flowers carried singly or in clusters on bare stems.

Soil, equal parts sandy loam, peat and sand. Position, crevices of sunny rock gardens, moist in summer but well drained in autumn and winter. Plant in spring. Water in dry weather. Alternatively grow in well-drained pots or pans in an unheated frame or greenhouse, watering fairly freely while in growth, very sparingly in autumn and winter.

Increase by seeds sown in sandy loam and peat in a cool, shady frame in spring; by division in spring.

Recommended kinds are *L. brachycalyx*, white, late spring, 2 in., N. W. America; *columbiana*, pale pink, summer, 9 in., Northwestern U.S.A.; *cotyledon*, salmon pink, early summer, 9 in., California; *finchii*, rose, early summer, 6 in., California; *heckneri*, salmon pink, early summer, 6 ft., California; *howellii*, apricot pink, early summer, 9 in., Oregon; *leana*, white or soft pink, early summer, 6 in., California; *nevadensis*, pink, late spring, 2 in., Nevada; *oppositifolia*, white, late spring, 6 in., Oregon; *pygmaea*, pink, late spring, early summer, 1 in., Rocky Mountains; *rediviva*, Spatlum, soft pink, summer, 1 to 2 in., Western U.S.A.; *tweedyi*, salmon pink, early summer, 4 in., Washington.

LEYCESTERIA – *Caprifoliaceae*. Hardy or rather tender deciduous flowering shrubs with green, hollow, cane-like stems.

Soil, ordinary. Position, sunny or shaded or in a frost-proof greenhouse for *L. crocothyrsos*. Plant in autumn or late winter. Prune hard back to old wood annually in spring and feed well to ensure vigorous new growth, or simply cut out frost-damaged, old and weak stems each spring.

Increase by seeds sown in light soil outdoors or under glass in spring; by cuttings of firm shoots inserted in sandy soil in autumn; by division in autumn.

Recommended kinds are *L. crocothyrsos*, yellow, early summer, 6 to 8 ft., tender, Assam; *formosa*, Himalayan Honeysuckle, Flowering Nutmeg, wine-coloured bracts and white flowers, summer and early autumn, 6 to 8 ft., maroon berries, hardy, Himalaya.

LIATRIS (Blazing Star, Gayfeather) – *Compositae*. Hardy perennial herbs with flowers in closely packed stiff spikes.

Soil, light, fairly rich. Position, open, sunny, not liable to dry out severely in summer. Plant in spring. Mulch with decayed manure in spring. Water freely in dry weather.

Increase by seeds sown in light sandy soil outdoors in early autumn or in a cool greenhouse in spring; by division in spring.

Recommended kinds are *L. callilepis*, reddish purple, summer, 2 ft., U.S.A.; *elegans*, purple, summer, 3 to 4 ft., Southern U.S.A.; *pycnostachya*, Button Snake-root, purplish crimson, summer, 3 to 4 ft., Central U.S.A.; *scariosa*, purple, summer, 3 to 4 ft., Southeastern U.S.A.; *spicata*, purple, summer, 1 to 6 ft., Eastern N. America.

LIBERTIA – *Iridaceae*. Hardy or slightly tender evergreen perennials with sword-shaped or grass-like dark green leaves and white flowers in open spikes.

Soil, ordinary. Position, well drained, sunny. Plant in spring or autumn. In cold places protect by covering with dry fern, tree leaves or strawy manure in autumn.

Increase by seeds sown in sandy soil in a cold frame or greenhouse in spring; by division in spring.

Recommended kinds are *L. formosa*, white, late spring, 2 to 3 ft., Chile; *grandiflora*, white, summer, 2 to 3 ft., New Zealand; *ixioides*, white, summer, 2 ft., New Zealand; *pulchella*, (syn. *micrantha*), white, spring, 6 in., New Zealand.

LIBOCEDRUS – *Pinaceae*. Hardy or slightly tender, evergreen, coniferous trees also known as calocedrus.

Soil, good, loamy, well drained but not dry. Position, open, preferably with high atmospheric moisture. Excellent as specimens or planted in groups. Plant in autumn or late winter. Pruning undesirable.

Increase by seeds stratified for three months at 4°C. then sown in loam, peat and sand in a frame; by cuttings of firm young growth inserted in a frame or propagator in summer.

Recommended kinds are *L. chilensis* (syn. *Austrocedrus chilensis*), leaves dark green above whitish below, 40 to 80 ft., Chile, Argentina; *decurrens* (syn. *Calocedrus decurrens*), Incense Cedar, dark green, to 120 ft., South-western U.S.A., and var. *columnaris*, narrow, columnar habit; *formosana* (syn. *Calocedrus formosana*), bright green, 40 to 50 ft., rather tender, Formosa; *macrolepis* (syn. *Calocedrus macrolepis*), leaves green above, blue-grey beneath, 40 to 50 ft., slightly tender, S. W. China.

LIGULARIA – *Compositae*. Hardy herbaceous perennials with showy daisy-type flowers, sometimes included in the genus *Senecio*.

Soil, loamy. Position, partly shady, moist. *L. japonica* at the edges of ponds or lakes or in damp soil nearby. Plant in spring or autumn.

Increase by division in spring or autumn; by seeds sown outdoors in spring or early summer and kept well watered.

Recommended kinds are *L. dentata* (syn. *clivorum*), orange-yellow, late summer, 4 to 5 ft., China, Japan; *hessei*, orange, late summer, 5 ft., hybrid; *japonica*, orange-yellow, summer, 5 ft., Japan; *przewalskii*, yellow, summer, 3 to 4 ft., China; *stenocephala* (syn. *intermedia*), orange-yellow, late summer, 3 to 4 ft., China, Japan; *tussilaginea* (syn. *L. kaempferi*, *Senecio kaempferi*), late summer, yellow, 1 to 2 ft., Japan, and var. *aureo-maculata*, leaves blotched yellow, white or pink; *veitchiana*, yellow, summer, 3 to 6 ft., China; *wilsoniana*, golden yellow, summer, 3 to 5 ft., China.

LIGUSTRUM (Privet) – *Oleaceae*. Hardy deciduous and evergreen shrubs. *L. ovalifolium* and its golden-leaved variety are among the most popular hedge shrubs. Only a few varieties are worth growing for their clusters of small flowers or their black or deep purple berries.

Soil, ordinary. Position, sunny or shady. Plant in autumn or late winter. Trim hedges as necessary to keep them tidy in spring and summer; other kinds may be allowed to grow naturally with only a little thinning or shaping in spring.

For hedges, plant privet (1 to 3 ft. high), 1½ to 2 ft. apart.

Increase by cuttings of young shoots in summer; by cuttings of firm shoots 8 to 12 in. long in shady positions outdoors in autumn; by seeds stratified for three months at 4°C. and then sown outdoors or under glass.

Recommended kinds are *L. amurense*, Amur Privet, to 15 ft., deciduous, very hardy, N. China; *delavayanum* (syns. *ionandrum*, *prattii*), 6 ft., evergreen, small leaves, China; *henryi*, 8 to 12 ft., evergreen, China; *japonicum*, Japanese Privet, late summer, 10 to 12 ft., evergreen, Japan, and vars. *macrophyllum*, large dark green leaves, *rotundifolium*, slow growing to 6 ft.; *lucidum*, white, autumn, 15 to 30 ft., broad, lustrous evergreen foliage, China, and vars. *excelsum superbum*, leaves variegated cream and yellow, *latifolium*, larger, broader leaves, *tricolor*, variegated leaves, *compactum*, dense growth; *ovalifolium*, Oval-leaved Privet, semi-evergreen, 10 to 15 ft., Japan, and vars. *argenteum*, leaves with cream margin, *aureum*, Golden Privet, leaves yellow with green blotch; *quihoui*, white, late summer, 6 to 10 ft., deciduous, China; *sinense*, white, summer, purplish black berries, 10 to 20 ft., deciduous, the best flowering species, China; *vulgare*, Common Privet, deciduous, 6 to 10 ft., black berries, Britain, and var. *xanthocarpum*, yellow berried.

LILIUM (Lily) – *Liliaceae.* Hardy or slightly tender bulbous flowering plants. Some species formerly included in *Lilium* are now referred to other genera, see *Cardiocrinum* for *L. giganteum*, *Nomocharis* for *L. apertum*, *Notholirion* for *L. thomsonianum*.

Soil, ordinary, neutral or slightly acid, porous, well drained in winter but not dry in summer for most kinds. Markedly acid for *L. auratum, humboldtii, japonicum, parryi, sulphureum, superbum* and *wardii.* Preferably slightly alkaline with limestone or chalk for *L. candidum, carniolicum, chalcedonicum, henryi, martagon* and *testaceum.*

Plant *L. candidum* in late summer, others in autumn, see that basal roots are damaged as little as possible. Plant stem-rooting lilies, such as *L. amabile, auratum, aurelianense, brownii, bulbiferum, carniolicum, davidii, duchartrei, formosanum, hansonii, hollandicum, henryi, humboldtii, leucanthum, maculatum, nepalense, philippinense, primulinum, pumilum, regale, sargentiae, speciosum, sulphureum,* and *tigrinum,* 6 in. deep and mulch with peat or leafmould as growth progresses. Position, sunny or partially shady. Many lilies grow best when planted among low-growing perennials or shrubs which shade their roots but allow their stems to grow up into the sun.

Only just cover the bulbs of *L. candidum* and *testaceum* with soil. Other lilies plant 4 in. deep. Place a handful of sharp sand under each bulb and a little round it. Mulch with leafmould in spring. Do not cut down flower stems before the leaves have turned yellow. Water freely in dry weather. To prevent spread of virus diseases spray frequently in spring and summer against aphids. Any plants showing signs of virus infection (e.g. mottling or streaking and twisting of leaves or deformity of flowers due to adhering of petal tips) should be burned as soon as possible. Do not handle a healthy plant after touching a virus-infected one. Many lilies become virus-infected in the propagating frame when diseased stock and healthy stock are propagated side by side. *L. tigrinum* often carries virus disease.

Pot culture: Compost, John Innes potting compost No. 1 or equivalent. Pot in autumn, placing one bulb in a 5- or 6-in. pot or three in an 8- or 10-in. pot. For stem-rooting kinds put one-quarter drainage, then half-fill with compost, place bulbs on this and cover them with ½ in. of compost, topdress with similar compost as growth progresses. Other kinds may be potted about 3 in. deep in the ordinary way.

After potting, place pots in a cold frame, greenhouse or shed and cover with 2 in. of cinder ashes or peat. Allow them to remain thus till growth begins, remove them to a light airy part of the greenhouse until they flower, then stand them outdoors. Water sparingly at first, moderately when growth begins, freely when in full growth. Temperature for forcing *L. longiflorum* and *philip-*

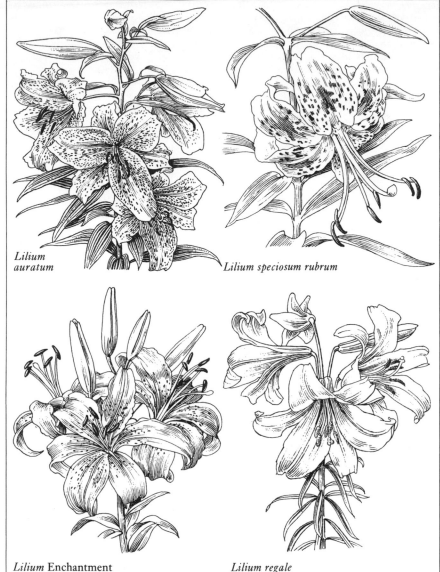

Lilium auratum

Lilium speciosum rubrum

Lilium Enchantment

Lilium regale

pinense, 13 to 18°C. Repot annually in autumn. After flowering, place plants in a sunny position outdoors, and gradually reduce water supply but never allow soil to become quite dry. Kinds most suitable for indoor culture are *L. auratum, formosanum, japonicum, nepalense, longiflorum, philippinense, primulinum, speciosum* and *sulphureum.*

Increase by seeds sown as soon as ripe or in spring in well-drained pans in a mixture of equal parts loam (lime-free for lime-hating kinds), peat and coarse sand; transplant the seedlings when large enough to handle into similar soil in deep trays or a bed in a frame or lath shelter. Seeds of some kinds germinate quickly; some may take 12 to 18 months to germinate, and some may grow below ground only for the first year, producing tiny bulbs but no leaves. Increase also by offsets or bulbils planted 1 in. deep and 2 or 3 in. apart in beds of peaty soil in a frame in autumn; by plump scales, broken

from bulbs just after flowering, planted in sand and moist peat in trays, pans or beds in a frame or cool greenhouse. Take care not to injure roots when transplanting young lilies however they have been raised.

Recommended kinds are *L. amabile,* red and black, summer, 2 to 3 ft., Korea, and var. *luteum,* yellow; *auratum,* Golden-rayed Lily of Japan, white, yellow and crimson, late summer, autumn, 4 to 8 ft., Japan, and numerous varieties and hybrids from almost all white to almost all red; *aurelianense,* yellowish orange, summer, 5 to 7 ft., hybrid between *henryi* and *sargentiae; brownii,* white inside, rose-purple outside, summer, 3 to 4 ft., China; *bulbiferum,* orange, purple spotted, summer, 2 to 3 ft., Europe, and vars. *chaixii,* yellow and orange, spotted purple, and *croceum* (syns. *L. aurantiacum, croceum*), Orange Lily, orange; *canadense,* yellow or orange, purple spotted, summer, 2 to 5 ft., Eastern N. America; *candidum,* Madonna Lily, white, summer, 3 to 5 ft.,

Balkans, Near East, and var. *salonikae*, producing seeds freely; *carniolicum*, red, summer, 1 to 3 ft., Balkans, and var. *jankae*, yellow; *cernuum*, purplish pink, summer, 1 to 3 ft., Korea, Manchuria; *chalcedonicum*, Scarlet Turk's Cap, Scarlet Martagon, scarlet, summer, 2 to 4 ft., Greece, and var. *maculatum*, scarlet, black spotted; *columbianum*, orange-yellow, summer, 2 to 6 ft., N. W. America; *concolor*, scarlet, summer, 1 to 2 ft., China; *dauricum* (syn. *dahuricum*), orange-red, summer, 1 to 2 ft., N. E. Asia; *davidii*, orange-red, black spotted, late summer, 3 to 5 ft., W. China, and vars. *macranthum*, 5 to 6 ft., *unicolor*, few or no spots, *willmottiae*, to 7 ft., arching flower stems; *duchartrei* (syn. *farreri*), white, purple spotted, summer, 2 to 4 ft., W. China; *formosanum*, Formosa Lily (syn. *philippinense formosanum*), white flushed purple outside, late summer, early autumn, 3 to 7 ft., slightly tender, Formosa, and var. *pricei*, 1 to 2 ft.; *hansonii*, orange-yellow, summer, 3 to 5 ft., Korea; *henryi*, light orange, late summer, early autumn, 5 to 8 ft., China; *humboldtii*, orange-red, maroon spotted, summer, 4 to 6 ft., California, and var. *ocellatum*, heavily spotted; *imperiale* (syn. *princeps*), white and yellow, purplish outside, summer, 4 to 6 ft., hybrids between *regale* and *sargentiae*; *japonicum* (syn. *krameri*), pink, summer, 2 to 3 ft., Japan; *lankongense*, pink, purple spotted, late summer, 2 to 4 ft., W. China; *leichtlinii*, lemon-yellow, brown spotted, late summer, 2 to 4 ft., Japan, and var. *maximowiczii*, orange, red; *leucanthum*, creamy white, summer, 3 to 4 ft., China, and var. *centifolium*, white, flushed green and purple outside; *longiflorum*, Easter Lily, white, summer, 2 to 3 ft., rather tender, Ryukyu Island, Formosa, and vars. *eximium*, flowers narrower, and *nobile*, flowers large; *mackliniae*, white flushed pink, early summer, 9 to 24 in., India, Burma; *maculatum*, (syns. *elegans*, *thunbergianum* and *fortunei*), yellow, orange, apricot or red, summer, 9 to 24 in., hybrids probably mainly between *dauricum* and *concolor*, and numerous varieties; *martagon*, Turk's Cap Lily, purple, summer, 2 to 5 ft., Europe, Asia, and vars. *album*, white, *cattaniae*, claret purple, *sanguineo-purpureum* (syn. *dalmaticum*), reddish purple; *monadelphum*, yellow, summer, 3 to 5 ft., Caucasus; *nepalense*, greenish yellow and maroon, late spring, early summer, 2 to 3 ft., slightly tender, Himalaya, and var. *concolor*, greenish yellow; *pardalinum*, Leopard Lily, Panther Lily, orange-red, spotted brown, summer, 3 to 7 ft., Western N. America, and var. *giganteum* (syn. Sunset), orange and yellow, spotted purple; *parkmannii*, red and white, late summer, early autumn, 4 to 6 ft., hybrid between *auratum* and *speciosum*; *parryi*, yellow, summer, 2 to 6 ft., California, Arizona; *philippinense*, white, late summer, early autumn, 2 to 3 ft., slightly tender, Philippine Islands; *pom-*

ponium, scarlet, early summer, 1½ to 2½ ft., S. Europe; *primulinum*, greenish yellow, late summer, autumn, 4 to 8 ft., rather tender, W. China, Burma, and vars. *burmanicum*, greenish yellow and maroon, *ochraceum*, 3 ft., fairly hardy; *pumilum* (syn. *tenuifolium*), scarlet, early summer, 15 to 18 in., N. E. Asia, and var. Golden Gleam, yellow; *pyrenaicum*, yellow, black spotted, late spring, early summer, 2 to 4 ft., Pyrenees, and var. *rubrum*, orange-red, maroon spotted; *regale*, white and yellow, flushed purple outside, summer, 3 to 6 ft., W. China; *rubellum*, rose-pink, late spring, early summer, 1½ to 2 ft., Japan; *sargentiae*, white and yellow, purplish brown outside, late summer, 4 to 6 ft., W. China; *speciosum*, white and pink or carmine, late summer, early autumn, 5 to 6 ft., Japan, and vars. *album-novum*, white, *magnificum*, carmine and white, Melpomene, crimson and white, *rubrum*, rose-purple spotted; *sulphureum* (syn. *myriophyllum*), yellow, late summer, early autumn, 6 to 8 ft., slightly tender, W. China, Burma; *superbum*, Swamp Lily, yellow or orange and green, spotted maroon, late summer, 4 to 8 ft., Eastern and Central N. America; *szovitsianum* (syn. *monadelphum szovitzianum*), yellow, early summer, 4 to 6 ft., Caucasus, Turkey; *testaceum*, Nankeen Lily, apricot, early summer, 4 to 6 ft., hybrid between *candidum* and *chalcedonicum*; *tigrinum*, Tiger Lily, orange-red, black spotted, late summer, early autumn, 4 to 6 ft., Japan, E. China, and var. *splendens*, deeper colour, later flowering; *wardii*, light purple, maroon spotted, late summer, 3 to 5 ft., Tibet. There are also a great many hybrids listed in trade catalogues.

LIMNANTHES – *Limnanthaceae*. Hardy annual making low mounds of feathery leaves covered in saucer-shaped yellow and white flowers. Much favoured by bees.

Soil, ordinary. Position, sunny. Sow for spring flowering in early autumn, for summer flowering in spring and thin seedlings to 6 in. Discard after flowering.

The best kind is *L. douglasii*, spring and summer, 6 in., California.

LIMONIUM (Sea Lavender) – *Plumbaginaceae*. Hardy and slightly tender evergreen perennials and annuals with small chaffy 'everlasting' flowers. Useful for cutting. Formerly known as statice.

Culture of greenhouse species: Grow in a porous but not over-rich compost such as John Innes potting compost No. 1. Pot in spring. Keep in a cool, sunny greenhouse, minimum winter temp. 7°C. Water freely in spring and summer, sparingly in autumn and winter. No shading required. Most can be grown outdoors in places where there is little frost.

Culture of hardy perennial species: Soil, ordinary, well drained. Position, sunny. Plant in spring. Gather flowers when well

developed and dry in a cool, airy place.

Culture of annual species: Soil, ordinary, well drained. Position, sunny. Sow seeds in sandy loam in spring in temp. 15 to 18°C. Prick off seedlings into John Innes potting compost No. 1 or equivalent and harden off for planting outdoors in late spring or early summer when there is no danger of frost. Treat flowers as for hardy perennial kinds.

Increase by seeds sown in pans of sandy soil in temp. 15 to 18°C. in spring; by root cuttings inserted in similar soil and in a cold frame in winter.

Recommended tender perennial kinds are *L. imbricatum*, blue, summer, 1½ ft., Teneriffe; *macrophyllum* (syn. *halfordii*), purplish blue and white, late spring, 1 to 2 ft., Canary Islands; *profusum*, blue and white, late summer, early autumn, 2 to 3 ft., hybrid between *macrophyllum* and *puberulum*, and var. *superbum*, larger flowers; *puberulum*, purple and white, summer, Canary Islands.

Recommended hardy perennial kinds are *L. bellidifolium* (syns. *L. reticulatum* and *Statice caspica*), lilac, summer, 6 to 9 in., Europe (Britain); *cosyrense*, violet, late summer, 3 to 4 in., S. Europe; *eximium*, rosy lilac, late summer, early autumn, 1 to 1½ ft., Central Asia; *globulariifolium*, pale lavender, summer, 9 to 18 in., Mediterranean region; *gmelinii*, blue and rose, summer, 1 to 2 ft., Europe; *gougetianum*, blue-mauve, summer, 6 in., Italy; *latifolium*, lavender-blue, late summer, Bulgaria, S. Russia, and var. *grandiflorum*, larger flowers; *tataricum*, red and white, summer, 1 ft., S. E. Europe to Siberia; *vulgare* (syn. *Statice limonium*), Common Sea Lavender, purplish blue, late summer, early autumn, 1 ft., Europe (Britain).

Recommended annual kinds are *L. bonduellii*, yellow, summer, 1 to 2 ft., Algeria; *sinuatum*, blue and white, summer, 1 to 2 ft., Mediterranean region, and several colour forms, really a perennial but always grown as an annual; *spicatum*, rose or white, summer, 6 in., W. Asia; *suworowii*, lilac-pink, summer, 1½ ft., Central Asia.

LINARIA (Toadflax) – *Scrophulariaceae*. Hardy annual and perennial herbs with spurred flowers like little 'snapdragons'. Some species formerly included in this genus have been transferred to *Cymbalaria*.

Culture of perennial species: Soil, ordinary, well drained, good on chalk and limestone. Position, sunny; most will grow well on walls. Plant in spring or autumn.

Culture of annual species: Soil, ordinary. Position, sunny. Sow seeds outdoors in spring for flowering in summer, in early autumn for flowering in spring. Thin seedlings to 6 in.

Increase perennial kinds by division in spring or autumn; by seeds sown outdoors or in a frame in spring or early summer.

The best annual kind is *L. maroccana*,

purple, crimson, mauve, yellow, white, summer, 9 to 15 in., Morocco.

Recommended perennial kinds are *L. alpina*, violet-blue and orange, summer, 3 in., Alps; *dalmatica*, yellow, summer, 3 to 4 ft., S. E. Europe; *purpurea*, purple, late summer, early autumn, 2 to 3 ft., S. Europe; *triornithophora*, purple and yellow, summer, 2 to 3 ft., slightly tender, Portugal, Spain; *vulgaris*, Common Toadflax, Butter and Eggs, yellow, summer, 2 ft., Europe (Britain).

LINDERA – *Lauraceae*. Hardy and slightly tender deciduous and evergreen flowering shrubs and trees. Leaves of the deciduous kinds turn yellow before they fall in autumn.

Soil, lime-free loam, moist but not badly drained. Position, open or light shade. Little pruning is required but weak, dead or frost-damaged stems can be removed in spring.

Increase by seeds stratified as soon as ripe for four months at 4°C. and then sown outdoors or in a frame; by cuttings of firm young shoots in a propagator in summer; by layering in spring.

Recommended species are *L. benzoin*, Benjamin Bush, Spice Bush, deciduous, greenish yellow, spring, 6 to 12 ft.; *megaphylla*, evergreen, black fruits, 15 to 20 ft., rather tender, Central China; *obtusiloba* (syn. *triloba*), deciduous, yellow, spring, black fruits, 20 to 25 ft., Japan, China, Korea.

LINNAEA – *Caprifoliaceae*. Dainty, creeping, hardy shrub, found wild in N. E. Britain.

Soil, peaty, lime free. Position, shady, moist.

Increase by division in spring; by cuttings in summer in a propagator.

The only species is *L. borealis*, Twinflower, creeping, pink or white, fragrant, summer, circumpolar, and var. *americana*, slightly larger and easier to grow.

LINUM (Flax) – *Linaceae*. Hardy annuals, perennials and small shrubs.

Culture of annual species: Soil, ordinary. Position, sunny. Sow seeds in spring

Linum grandiflorum

where plants are required to flower. Thin seedlings to 4 to 6 in. Discard after flowering.

Culture of perennial and shrubby species: Soil, good, ordinary, well drained. Position, warm, sunny. Plant in spring or autumn. Prune straggling shoots of *L. arboreum* into shape in spring.

Increase perennial species by seeds sown in well-drained soil outdoors or in a frame in spring or early summer, also by division in spring; shrubby species by cuttings of young shoots inserted in sandy soil in a propagator in summer; by seed as for perennial kinds.

The annual kinds grown are *L. grandiflorum*, rose, summer, 1 ft., Algeria, and vars. *album*, white and *rubrum*, Scarlet Flax, red.

Recommended perennial kinds are *L. alpinum*, blue, summer, 6 in., Europe; *campanulatum*, yellow, summer, 1 ft., Europe; *flavum*, yellow, summer, 1 to 1½ ft., E. Europe; *monogynum*, white, summer, 1 to 2 ft., New Zealand; *narbonnense*, blue, late spring, summer, 2 ft., S. Europe; *perenne*, blue, summer, 1½ ft., Europe (Britain), and var. *album*, white; *salsoloides*, white, tinged pink, early summer, 9 in., S. W. Europe.

The best shrubby kind is *L. arboreum*, yellow, summer, 1 ft., Crete.

LIPPIA – *Verbenaceae*. Slightly tender deciduous shrub with lemon-scented leaves.

Soil, ordinary, well drained. Position, warm, sunny, sheltered or trained against a sunny wall or grown in a frost-proof greenhouse. Prune away all weak, dead or frost-damaged growth each spring. New shoots will usually appear even from old wood.

Increase by cuttings of firm young shoots in sandy soil in a frame in summer or riper cuttings in autumn.

The best kind is *L. citriodora* (syn. *Aloysia citriodora*), Lemon-scented Verbena, lilac, late summer, 10 ft., Argentina, Chile.

LIQUIDAMBAR – *Altingiaceae*. Hardy or slightly tender deciduous trees. Flowers greenish yellow, inconspicuous, spring. Leaves palmate, colouring richly in autumn.

Soil, deep, moist, lime-free loam. Position, sunny. Little pruning is desirable.

Increase by seeds stratified as soon as ripe for three months at 4°C. and then sown outdoors or under glass; by layering shoots in spring.

Recommended kinds are *L. formosana*, 60 to 80 ft., slightly tender, China; *styraciflua*, Sweet Gum, 100 ft., Eastern U.S.A.

LIRIODENDRON – *Magnoliaceae*. Hardy deciduous trees with tulip-shaped flowers and curiously shaped bright green leaves turning gold in autumn.

Soil, deep rich loam. Position, sunny, open; makes an excellent specimen on a lawn. Plant in autumn or late winter. Prune straggling shoots into shape and remove wind-damaged branches in late winter.

Liriodendron tulipifera

Increase by seeds stratified as soon as ripe for three months at 4°C. and then sown out of doors or under glass; by layering in spring.

Recommended kinds are *L. chinense*, yellowish green, summer, 50 to 80 ft., China; *tulipifera*, Tulip Tree, yellow, summer, 100 to 200 ft., N. America, numerous forms in cultivation including *aureo-maculatum*, bright gold-mottled leaves, and *fastigiatum*, columnar in habit.

LIRIOPE – *Liliaceae*. Fairly hardy evergreen perennials. Grass-like foliage in tufts and flowers in stiff narrow spikes.

Soil, sandy loam. Position, sunny, sheltered, well drained or as small pot plants in a cool greenhouse or conservatory. Plant or pot in spring.

Increase by division at planting time.

Recommended kinds are *L. muscari*, lilac, autumn, 1 to 1½ ft., Japan, China and var. *variegata*, leaves yellow striped; *spicata*, pale lilac to white, autumn, 9 to 12 in., China, Japan.

LITHOPS (Stone-face, Living Stone) – *Aizoaceae*. Greenhouse succulent plants grown for the strange appearance of their pebble-like growth. All are natives of Namaqualand.

Lithops

Compost, John Innes potting compost No. 2 or equivalent plus one-third its bulk of coarse sand or stone chippings. Position, pots in a sunny greenhouse, minimum winter temp. 7°C. Water fairly freely from mid-spring to mid-autumn, very little for the rest of the year. Do not shade at any time. Plunge pots to their rims in gravel. Pot in spring.

Increase by seeds sown in sandy soil in a temp. 15 to 18°C. in spring; by careful division of plants in spring or insertion of pairs of leaves as cuttings in very sandy soil.

Recommended kinds are *L. bella*, plant body brownish yellow; *bromfeldii*, reddish brown; *fulleri*, grey and brown; *helmutii*, mottled shades of grey-green; *lesliei*, brown with greenish markings; *olivacea*, shades of olive green; *optica*, fawn with transparent area; *pseudotruncatella*, mottled brown.

LITHOSPERMUM (Gromwell) – *Boraginaceae*. Hardy, dwarf, trailing, evergreen flowering shrubs and perennials.

Soil, ordinary, well drained for most kinds but moderately acid, lime free for *L. diffusum*. Position, sunny, warm, excellent for terrace walls and ledges of sunny rock gardens. Plant in spring or autumn.

Increase by seeds in sandy soil in a frame in spring, transplanting seedlings when an inch high singly into 2-in. pots and growing in a frame till the following spring; by cuttings of firm shoots in sandy soil in a frame or propagator in summer or early autumn; by layering shoots in autumn or spring.

Recommended kinds are *L. diffusum* (syns. *L. prostrata* and *Lithodora diffusa*), blue, summer, prostrate, S. Europe, and vars. *album*, white, Heavenly Blue, extra fine flowers and colour; *oleifolium* (syn. *Lithodora oleifolia*), sapphire blue, summer, prostrate, Pyrenees; *purpureo-caeruleum*, red becoming blue, late spring, early summer, 9 to 12 in., Europe (Britain); *rosmarinifolium*, blue and white, winter, 1 to 2 ft., rather tender, Italy.

See also Moltkia.

LITTONIA – *Liliaceae*. Tender tuberous-rooted, climbing perennials with hanging bell-shaped flowers, allied to *Gloriosa*.

Soil, John Innes potting compost No. 1 or equivalent. Position, pots in a sunny cool or intermediate greenhouse, minimum temp. 7°C. Pot in spring. Water moderately at first, freely when in growth, but gradually reduce water supply after flowering and keep almost dry in autumn and winter. Provide canes or small branches or other support for the slender stems.

Increase by seeds sown in temp. 15 to 18°C. as soon as ripe or in spring; by careful division in spring.

The best kind is *L. modesta*, orange, summer, 3 to 6 ft., S. Africa, and var. *keitii*, vigorous and free flowering.

LOBELIA – *Campanulaceae*. Hardy and slightly tender herbaceous perennials some of which are commonly grown as annuals.

Soil, ordinary with sufficient humus to keep it moist in summer but well drained in winter. Position, sunny for most kinds but rather moist and slightly shady for *L. cardinalis*. Plant in spring. On cold, damp soils all the species (except *L. syphilitica*) are best lifted in autumn, placed in pots, stored in a cold frame till spring and then replanted.

Culture of tender kinds: Soil, ordinary. Position, pots in a cool greenhouse with minimum winter temp. 7°C.; dwarf kinds as edgings to beds outdoors in summer when danger of frost is over; trailing kinds in window boxes and hanging baskets.

Increase hardy perennial species by seeds sown in sandy loam and leafmould in temp. 15 to 18°C. in spring; by division in spring. Tender species by seeds sown in spring, the seedlings transplanted 2 in. apart in boxes, hardened off in a cold frame and planted out in late spring or early summer; by cuttings of young shoots inserted in sandy soil in a warm propagator in spring; by division in spring.

Recommended hardy kinds are *L. cardinalis*, Cardinal Flower, scarlet, late summer, autumn, 2 to 3 ft., N. America; *fulgens*, scarlet, late summer, autumn, 1 to 3 ft., Mexico; *syphilitica*, light blue, late summer, early autumn, 2 ft., Eastern U.S.A., and var. *alba*, white; *vedrariensis*, purplish blue, late summer, 2 to 3 ft., hybrid.

Recommended tender kinds are *L. erinus*, blue and white, summer, 6 in., S. Africa, and numerous varieties from white to carmine, some trailing; *tenuior*, bright blue, summer, 1 to 2 ft., W. Australia. There are several named varieties.

LOBULARIA (Sweet Alyssum) – *Cruciferae*. The correct name for the hardy annual which most gardeners call *Alyssum maritimum*.

Soil, ordinary. Position, sunny. Excellent for edging, ground cover and rock gardens.

Increase by seeds sown in spring under glass or directly outdoors where required to flower. Plant or thin to 4 to 6 in. Discard after flowering.

The only species is *L. maritima*, white, lilac, rose, violet, summer, 3 to 12 in., Europe, W. Asia.

LONICERA (Honeysuckle) – *Caprifoliaceae*. Hardy and slightly tender deciduous and evergreen shrubs and twiners. *L. nitida* is much used for hedges.

Soil, ordinary. Position for climbers, as far as possible choose a shaded and cool position for the roots, but where the top growth can reach full sun. For the more tender evergreen kinds choose a partially shaded wall or grow in a frost-proof greenhouse. Shrubby kinds in sun or shade, sheltered from wind and frost for those that flower in winter. Plant all deciduous kinds in autumn or late winter, evergreen kinds in spring or autumn.

Prune most twining kinds by removing some of the older stems after flowering; *L. japonica* by shortening the previous year's growth in spring; deciduous shrubs by cutting out old and weak stems in early spring or as soon as flowering is finished; evergreen kinds by cutting back as much as necessary in late spring and light clipping occasionally in summer.

Lonicera nitida is a bushy, small-leaved evergreen, suitable for hedges to 5 ft. high. Young specimens up to 18 in. high should be planted 18 in. apart.

Increase by cuttings of firm young growth in summer in a propagator or cuttings of riper growth in autumn out of doors or in a frame; by layering in spring or autumn; some kinds by division in autumn or spring; or by seeds stratified for three months at 4°C. and then sown out of doors or under glass.

Recommended twining kinds are *L. americana*, white becoming yellow, scented, summer, to 30 ft., deciduous, a natural hybrid between *caprifolium* and *etrusca*; *brownii*, Scarlet Trumpet Honeysuckle, orange-scarlet, spring and summer, to 15 ft., semi-evergreen, hybrid between *hirsuta* and *sempervirens*, and varieties; *caprifolium*, Perfoliate Honeysuckle, creamy white, summer, scented, to 20 ft., deciduous, Europe, Asia Minor; *etrusca*, creamy yellow, summer, scented, to 30 ft., deciduous, slightly tender, Mediterranean region; *heckrottii*, yellow and purple, scented, summer, autumn, semi-shrubby, to 10 or 12 ft., deciduous, hybrid probably between *americana* and *sempervirens*; *henryi*, yellow and purplish red, summer, to 20 ft., evergreen, W. China; *hildebrandtiana*, Giant Honeysuckle, cream changing to deep yellow, scented, summer, to 30 ft., or more, distinctly tender, Burma, Thailand, China; *hirsuta*, orange-yellow, summer, N. E. America; *japonica*, white changing to yellow, scented, summer, to 30 ft., evergreen, Japan, Korea, and vars. *aureoreticulata*, leaves netted with gold, *halliana*, green leaved, *repens*, less rampant; *periclymenum*, Woodbine, Common Honeysuckle, cream and purple, scented, summer, autumn, to 20 ft., deciduous, Europe, N. Africa, W. Asia, and var. *belgica* (syn. *serotina*), Dutch Honeysuckle, flowers red-purple outside; *sempervirens*, Trumpet Honeysuckle, orange-red and yellow, summer, to 30 ft. or more, evergreen, Eastern U.S.A.; *tellmanniana*, deep yellow, summer, to 20 ft., deciduous, hybrid between *tragophylla* and *sempervirens*; *tragophylla*, yellow, summer, to 30 ft. or more, deciduous, W. China.

Recommended shrubby kinds are *L. fragrantissima*, cream, late winter, spring, scented, 6 ft., deciduous, China; *korolkowii*, pink, early summer, 12 ft., deciduous, Turkestan; *nitida*, small evergreen leaves, to 6 ft., W. China, and var. *fertilis* (syn. *pileata yunnanensis*), stiffer growth; *pileata*, small semi-evergreen leaves, 4 ft., China; *standishii*, cream, scented, winter, 6 ft., deciduous, China; *syringantha*, pale lilac, late spring and early summer, scented, 4 to 6 ft., deciduous, China, Tibet; *tatarica*, pink, late spring early summer, 7 to 9 ft., deciduous, Central Asia, Russia; *thibetica*, lilac, scented, late spring and early summer, 4 to 6 ft., Tibet; *xylosteum*, Fly Honeysuckle, cream, late spring, followed by red berries, 9 ft., deciduous, Europe (Britain).

LOTUS – *Leguminosae.* Tender and hardy perennials. The water plants popularly known as 'lotus' are unrelated, see Nelumbo and *Nymphaea lotus*.

Culture of tender kinds: Grow in a not-over-rich compost such as John Innes potting compost No. 1 in pots or baskets in a cool greenhouse, minimum winter temp. 7°C., or outdoors as ground cover in warm, frost-free places. Water moderately in spring and summer, very sparingly in autumn and winter. No shade required at any time.

Culture of hardy species: Soil, ordinary, well drained. Excellent for chalk or limestone. Position, sunny. Plant in spring.

Increase greenhouse species by seeds sown in sandy soil in temp. 15 to 18°C. in spring. The hardy kind recommended by division in spring.

The best tender kind is *L. berthelotii* (syn. *peliorhynchus*), Coral Gem, scarlet, summer, 2 ft., Canary Islands.

The best hardy kind is *L. corniculatus flore plenus*, Bird's-foot Trefoil, yellow, double, summer, creeping, Northern Hemisphere (Britain).

LUCULIA – *Rubiaceae.* Rather tender evergreen or deciduous shrubs with very sweetly scented flowers.

Compost, equal parts fibrous loam, peat, charcoal and sand. Position, in large well-drained pots or, preferably, in beds in a cool or intermediate greenhouse with minimum winter temperature 7°C., or outdoors in very warm sheltered places. Pot-grown plants can be stood outdoors in summer. Pot or plant in spring. Cut back old flowering stems to a few inches as soon as the flowers

Luculia grandifolia

fade. Water freely from spring to autumn but keep nearly dry in winter.

Increase by seeds sown in light sandy soil in temp. 18 to 21°C. in spring; by cuttings of young shoots inserted in sandy soil in a propagator, temp. 20 to 25°C., in summer.

Recommended kinds are *L. grandifolia*, white, early summer, 6 ft., deciduous, Bhutan, probably the hardiest species; *gratissima*, rose, winter, 8 to 10 ft., evergreen, Himalaya; *pinceana*, rose, late spring to autumn, Assam.

LUNARIA – *Cruciferae.* Biennial and perennial flowering plants. Seed pods flat, oval, containing a parchment-like partition; useful for drying for winter decorations.

Soil, ordinary, well drained. Position, sunny or partially shaded.

Increase by seeds sown outdoors in spring or early summer, transplanting seedlings to a nursery bed or flowering quarters as soon as they can be handled. Established plants often renew themselves freely by self-sown seedlings and these can be thinned out or transplanted as convenient. Space 9 to 12 in. apart.

Recommended kinds are *L. annua* (syn. *biennis*), Honesty, Money Flower, Satin Flower, purple, late spring, early summer, 2 to 3 ft., biennial, Europe, and vars. *alba*, white, *variegata*, leaves blotched with white; *rediviva*, purple, fragrant, late spring, early summer, 2 to 3 ft., perennial, Europe.

LUPINUS (Lupin) – *Leguminosae.* Hardy sub-shrubby and herbaceous perennials and annuals with pea-type flowers in spikes.

Culture of sub-shrubby and perennial kinds: Soil, loamy, well drained, preferably lime free. *L. arboreus* will grow on sand. Position, sunny. Plant in spring or autumn. Remove flower spikes as soon as flowers fade to check the spread of self-sown seedlings. Renew fairly frequently from selected seed or cuttings.

Culture of annual kinds: Soil, ordinary, well drained, not too rich. Sow seeds outdoors in spring where plants are to flower and thin seedlings to 1 ft. Discard after flowering.

Increase sub-shrubby and perennial species by seeds sown outdoors in spring or as soon as ripe, transplanting seedlings into flowering positions when large enough to handle; herbaceous perennial kinds by cuttings of young growth taken in spring before they become hollow and rooted in sandy soil in an unheated frame; sub-shrubby kinds by cuttings in summer in a frame or propagator.

Recommended sub-shrubby kinds are *L. arboreus*, Tree Lupin, yellow, fragrant, summer, 6 ft., California, and var. *albus*, white; *chamissonis*, blue-purple, early summer, silvery-grey leaves, 1 to 2½ ft., California; *excubicus* (syn. *paynei*), violet-blue, late spring, 1 to 5 ft., California.

The best herbaceous species is *L. polyphyllus*, Perennial Lupin, blue, summer, 3 to 6 ft., California, and many varieties with a colour range from white to pink, carmine, purple, mauve, orange, apricot and yellow. 'Russell' lupins have the upper petals expanded to give a more solid flower spike.

Recommended annual kinds are *L. hartwegii*, blue, white and rose, summer, 2 to 3 ft., Mexico; *luteus*, yellow, summer, 1 to 2 ft., scented, S. Europe; *mutabilis*, white, blue and yellow, fragrant, summer, 4 to 5 ft., Colombia, and var. *cruckshanksii*, white, blue and yellow becoming violet; *pubescens*, violet-blue and white, summer, 1½ to 3 ft., Mexico, Guatemala; *subcarnosus*, blue and white on yellow, summer, 8 to 12 in., Texas; *tricolor*, white becoming pink or purple, summer, 1½ to 2 ft., hybrid.

LYCASTE – *Orchidaceae.* Tender terrestrial and epiphytic orchids (often on rocks). Flowers showy, borne singly on stems from the base.

Compost, equal parts fibre, sphagnum moss and peat. Position, well-drained pots in a cool or intermediate greenhouse. Water freely from spring to autumn and feed with liquid manure. Maintain a moist atmosphere and shade from direct sunshine. In winter water sparingly or not at all and give all the light possible. Repot when necessary in spring.

Lycaste skinneri

Increase by division of plants when repotting, or by sound back bulbs, removed singly, placed in a small pot filled with small pieces of broken pot and surfaced with sphagnum. Pot when roots are seen.

Recommended kinds are *L. aromatica* (syn. *Maxillaria aromatica*), orange-yellow, very fragrant, spring, 9 to 12 in., Mexico, and var. *majus*, larger, often with reddish stain at lip base; *cruenta* (syn. *Maxillaria cruenta*), yellow with dark red blotch, spring, 9 in., Guatemala; *deppei* (syn. *Maxillaria deppei*), green, red-spotted, white, lip yellow, winter, spring, 9 to 12 in., Mexico; *gigantea*, olive green, chocolate, orange-yellow, summer, 1½ to 2 ft., Ecuador;

skinneri, white, rose flushed, winter, spring, 1 to 2 ft., Guatemala, and numerous varieties from white to crimson.

LYCHNIS (Campion) – *Caryophyllaceae*. Hardy annuals and perennials with showy flowers.

Culture of perennial species: Soil, light rich loam for *L. alpina*, open dryish beds, banks or borders for other species. Plant in spring or autumn. Cut down flower stems in autumn or before seeds ripen if self-sown seedlings are not desired.

Culture of annual species: Soil, ordinary. Position, sunny. Sow where required to bloom, in spring for summer flowering, early autumn for spring flowering.

Increase by seeds sown in light soil in a sunny position outdoors in spring or early summer, transplanting seedlings into flowering positions in autumn; by division in spring.

Recommended kinds are *L. arkwrightii*, scarlet, late summer, 1½ ft., hybrid between *chalcedonica* and *haageana*; *chalcedonica*, Scarlet Lychnis or Jerusalem Cross, scarlet, summer, 3 ft., Russia, and vars. *alba*, white, *rosea*, pink and *flore-pleno*, double, scarlet; *coronaria* (syn. *Agrostemma coronaria*), Rose Campion, crimson, summer, grey leaves, 2 to 3 ft., S. Europe, and vars. *atrosanguinea*, crimson-red, *alba*, white; *coronata*, scarlet or salmon, summer, autumn, 15 to 30 in., China, Japan, and var. *sieboldii*, white; *flos-jovis* (syn. *Agrostemma flos-jovis*), Flower of Love, bright pink, summer, 1½ to 2 ft., European Alps; *fulgens*, scarlet, summer, 1 to 2 ft., Siberia; *haageana*, scarlet, summer, 9 to 12 in., hybrid between *fulgens* and *coronata sieboldii*; *viscaria*, magenta, late spring, summer, 1 to 1½ ft., Europe, and vars. *albiflora*, white and *splendens pleno*, double rose.

Recommended annual kinds are *L. coelirosa* (syn. *Agrostemma coeli-rosa*), Rose of Heaven, rose and purple, summer, 1 ft., Levant, and vars. *alba*, white, *kermesina*, red, and *oculata*, purple eyed.

LYCIUM (Boxthorn) – *Solanaceae*. Hardy erect and rambling deciduous shrubs with small flowers followed by berries, red in most species. Specially suitable for maritime areas.

Soil, light, sandy. Position, open, sunny suitable for dry poor soil, and especially seaside cliffs. Plant in autumn or late winter. Prune in late winter cutting out old and weak stems. Plants can, if desired, be cut hard back as new growth will come even from old wood.

Increase by cuttings of firm shoots, 6 to 8 in. long, inserted in sandy soil in a shady position in autumn; by layering in spring; by removing suckers with roots attached in autumn or winter.

Recommended kinds are *L. barbarum* (syn. *halimifolium*), pinkish, summer, 8 to 10 ft., S. E. Europe, W. Asia; *chinense*, Common Boxthorn, Duke of Argyll's Tea-tree, purple or pink, summer, 10 to 12 ft., succeeded by scarlet berries, China.

LYCORIS (Spider Lily) – *Amaryllidaceae*. Tender flowering bulbs with tubular flowers in clusters similar to those of nerine.

Compost, John Innes potting compost No. 1 or equivalent. Position, pots in a sunny, frost-proof greenhouse or in well-drained soil in a particularly warm, sunny position outdoors. Pot or plant in late summer. Water sparingly at first, moderately as growth appears, fairly freely in spring but gradually reduce water supply in late spring and keep quite dry for six or eight weeks from midsummer.

Increase by offsets removed in late summer and treated as bulbs; by seeds sown in John Innes seed compost or equivalent in a cool greenhouse as soon as ripe.

Recommended kinds are *L. aurea* (syn. *Amaryllis aurea*), Golden Spider Lily, yellow, late summer, early autumn, 12 to 15 in., China; *radiata* (syn. *Amaryllis radiata*), scarlet, late summer, early autumn, 1½ ft., China, the hardiest kind, and var. *alba*, white; *sanguinea*, crimson, late summer, 1 to 1½ ft., Japan; *squamigera*, rosy lilac, fragrant, late summer, 2 ft., Japan.

LYGODIUM (Climbing Fern) – *Schizaeaceae*. Tender climbing ferns with slender twining fronds.

Compost, two parts peat, one part each of loam and coarse sand. Position, pots or beds in a cool greenhouse, minimum winter temp. 7°C. Pot in spring. Water normally. Shade in spring and summer. Provide canes, wires or other supports for the climbing fronds.

Increase by spores sown on the surface of fine sandy peat in a warm propagator at any time; by division of plants at potting time.

Recommended kinds are *L. japonicum*, E. Asia; *palmatum*, Eastern U.S.A.; *scandens*, the most generally grown species, Africa, Asia, Polynesia, Tropical America.

LYSICHITUM – *Araceae*. Hardy herbaceous perennials with rhizomatous roots and showy, arum-like flowers.

Soil, loam. Position, open, sunny or lightly shaded, moist, bogs, margins of pools, streams, etc. Plant in spring.

Increase by division in spring; by seeds sown in a cool greenhouse or frame as soon as ripe or in spring and kept very wet.

Recommended kinds are *L. americanum*, Yellow Skunk Cabbage, yellow, spring, 1½ to 2½ ft., Eastern N. America; *camtschatcense*, white, spring, 1 to 2 ft., Kamchatka, Japan.

LYSIMACHIA (Loosestrife) – *Primulaceae*. Hardy herbaceous perennials with showy flowers.

Soil, ordinary, moist for most kinds but

Lysimachia punctata

sandy and well drained for *L. leschenaultii*. Position, sunny or shady. Plant in spring or autumn. Cut down flower stems of tall kinds in autumn.

Increase by division in spring or autumn; by seeds sown outdoors in spring or early summer.

Recommended kinds are *L. clethroides*, white, summer, early autumn, 3 ft., China, Japan; *ephemerum*, white, summer, 2 to 3 ft., S. W. Europe; *leschenaultii*, rose-purple, summer, 1 ft., Nilghiri Hills; *nummularia*, Creeping Jenny, Moneywort, yellow, summer, creeping, Europe (Britain), and var. *aurea*, yellow leaves; *punctata* (syn. *verticillata*), yellow, summer, 2 to 3 ft., Asia Minor; *thyrsiflora* (syn. *Naumburgia thyrsiflora*), yellow, summer, 1 to 2 ft., North Temperate Regions (Britain); *vulgaris*, Yellow Loosestrife, yellow, summer, 3 ft., Europe (Britain), Asia.

LYTHRUM (Purple Loosestrife) – *Lythraceae*. Hardy herbaceous perennials with showy flowers in narrow spikes.

Soil, ordinary. Position, sunny or partially shady; will succeed in moist spots beside streams or ponds. Plant in spring or autumn.

Increase by division in spring or autumn.

Recommended kinds are *L. salicaria*, reddish purple, summer, 3 to 4 ft., Britain, and varieties with pink or crimson flowers, *roseum superbum* and *tomentosum*; *virgatum*, magenta, summer, 3 ft., Europe.

MACLEAYA – *Papaveraceae*. Hardy herbaceous perennials with handsome foliage and sprays of small flowers. Sometimes included in the genus *Bocconia*.

Soil, rich, good loamy. Position, sunny. Plant in spring. Cut down flower stems after blooming.

Increase by division in spring; by seeds sown in spring.

The two species are *M. cordata* (syn. *Bocconia cordata*), Plume Poppy, Tree Celandine, cream or pink, summer, 6 to 8 ft., China, Japan; *microcarpa* (syn. *Bocconia microcarpa*), yellowish buff, summer, 6 to 7 ft., China.

MAGNOLIA – *Magnoliaceae*. Hardy and slightly tender, deciduous and evergreen flowering trees and shrubs.

Soil, deep, rich loam preferably lime free and moist yet well drained. Position, sunny or in light shade; some kinds, especially the evergreens, can be trained effectively against walls. Plant in spring or autumn. Mulch in spring with peat or leafmould. Little pruning is required but if necessary branches can be shortened or removed, in summer if deciduous, late spring if evergreen.

Increase by seeds stratified as soon as ripe for four months at 4°C. and then sown in sandy peat outdoors or under glass; by layering in spring or autumn; by cuttings of firm young growth in a propagator in summer or cuttings of riper wood outdoors in autumn.

Recommended deciduous kinds are *M. acuminata*, Cucumber Tree, greenish yellow, spring, summer, red fruits, 60 to 90 ft., Eastern N. America; *campbellii*, pink to rose, early spring, 40 to 60 ft., Himalaya, and vars. *alba*, white, *mollicomata*, pink to purple, hardier, quicker to flower; *dawsoniana*, pale pink, spring, 30 to 40 ft., China; *denudata* (syn. *conspicua*), Yulan, white, spring, scented, 20 to 40 ft., China; *kobus*, white, spring, 30 to 40 ft., Japan and vars. Leonard Messel, lilac-pink, *stellata* (syn. *M. stellata*), white, slow growing, *stellata rosea*, pale pink, slow growing; *liliiflora*, reddish purple and cream, spring and summer, 9 to 12 ft., China, and var. *nigra*, deeper purple; *obovata* (syn. *hypoleuca*), cream and red, early summer, scented, 60 to 100 ft., Japan; *salicifolia*, white, spring, scented, 20 to 30 ft., Japan; *sargentiana*, pink, spring, 30 to 40 ft., W. China, and var. *robusta*, larger deeper coloured flowers; *sieboldii* (syn. *parviflora*), white and crimson, spring, summer, scented, 15 to 20 ft., Japan, Korea; *sinensis*, white and red, scented, early summer, 12 to 15 ft., W. China; *soulangiana*, white flushed purple, spring, 15 to 20 ft., hybrid between *denudata* and *liliiflora*, and numerous varieties such as *alba superba*, white, *alexandrina*, white and purple, *brozzonii*, large white, *lennei*, reddish purple and cream, and *rustica rubra*, purple; *sprengeri*, deep rose, spring, scented, 30 to 40 ft., China; *tripetala*, Umbrella Tree, cream, spring, summer, scented, 25 to 35 ft., Eastern U.S.A.; *veitchii*, white and purple, spring, 30 to 50 ft., hybrid between *campbellii* and *denudata*; *virginiana*, Sweet Bay, Swamp Bay, creamy white, summer, scented, 30 to 60 ft., evergreen in very mild places, Eastern U.S.A.; *wilsonii*, white and crimson, spring, summer, scented, 20 to 30 ft., W. China.

Recommended evergreen kinds, all slightly tender, are *M. delavayi*, white, summer to autumn, 30 to 40 ft., China; *grandiflora*, white, summer, early autumn, scented, 40 to 80 ft., South-eastern U.S.A., and vars. Exmouth, large white flowers, leaves tawny beneath, *ferruginea*, leaves very tawny beneath, Goliath, flowers very large, *undulata*, leaves wavy; *nitida*, creamy white, spring, summer, scented, 20 to 30 ft., China, Tibet.

MAHONIA – *Berberidaceae*. Hardy or slightly tender evergreen flowering shrubs. Formerly included in the genus *Berberis*.

Soil, good loam. Position, sun or partial shade. Plant in spring or autumn.

Increase by seeds stratified as soon as ripe for three months at 4°C. and then sown outdoors or under glass; by cuttings of firm young shoots in a propagator in summer or riper cuttings in a frame in autumn; by layering in spring or autumn; some kinds by division in spring.

Recommended kinds are *M. acanthifolia*, pale yellow, autumn and winter, 15 to 20 ft., rather tender, Nepal, Assam, China; *aquifolium*, Oregon Grape, yellow, early spring, 3 to 4 ft., black berries, Western N. America; *bealei*, yellow, autumn to spring, to 12 ft., China; *fortunei*, yellow, autumn, 4 to 6 ft., China; *japonica*, pale yellow, autumn to spring, scented, to 10 ft., China; *lomariifolia*, deep yellow, winter, 12 to 15 ft., slightly tender, China, Formosa; *media*, deep yellow, autumn and winter, 10 to 15 ft., hybrid between *japonica* and *lomariifolia*, and var. Charity, a fine form; *napaulensis*, yellow, late winter and spring, 8 to 10 ft., slightly tender, Himalaya; *nervosa*, yellow, spring, 1½ ft., black berries, Western N. America; *pinnata* (syn. *fascicularis*), deep yellow, late winter, 10 to 12 ft., California; *repens*, yellow, spring, 1 ft., black berries, Western N. America; *undulata* (syn. *aquifolium undulata*), yellow, spring, 6 to 8 ft., origin unknown.

MAIANTHEMUM – *Liliaceae*. Hardy herbaceous perennial. Leaves and habit similar to the lily of the valley.

Soil, ordinary, moist. Position, shady, useful as ground cover. Plant in autumn. Water freely in dry weather.

Increase by division of creeping rootstocks in autumn.

Recommended kinds are *M. bifolium* (syn. *M. convallaria*, *Smilacina bifolia*), white, spring, 6 to 9 in., Europe, Asia; *canadense*, white, spring, 3 to 6 in., Northern U.S.A.

MALCOMIA – *Cruciferae*. Hardy annual with small confetti-like flowers.

Soil, ordinary. Position, sunny.

Sow seeds for summer flowering in spring where plants are required to grow, and in early autumn for flowering in spring.

The best kind is *M. maritima*, Virginian Stock, various colours, summer, 6 in., S. Europe.

MALOPE – *Malvaceae*. Hardy annuals with showy, mallow-like flowers.

Soil, ordinary. Position, sunny. Sow in spring or early autumn where plants are to flower and thin to 12 to 18 in. apart.

The best kinds are *M. trifida*, purple, summer, 2 to 3 ft., Spain, and vars. *alba*, white, *grandiflora*, crimson, large, *rosea*, pink.

Magnolia kobus (left) *Magnolia obovata* (right)

MALUS (Apple) – *Rosaceae*. Hardy deciduous, spring-flowering, fruit-bearing trees and shrubs. For apples grown for dessert and culinary use see page 232.

Soil, ordinary but a few kinds such as *M. ioensis plena* and *scheideckeri* prefer slightly acid or neutral soils of fairly high fertility. Position, sunny or open. Plant in autumn or late winter. Prune in autumn or winter as necessary to improve shape, prevent overcrowding of branches and restrict size to available place. Remove crossing branches and shorten branches where this is necessary either to the main trunk or limb from which they grow or to a side branch.

Increase by seeds stratified for three months at 4°C. and then sown outdoors; by grafting established varieties in spring; by budding in summer; some kinds by layering in autumn.

Recommended kinds are *M. aldenhamensis*, deep carmine, spring, small red-purple fruits, 15 to 20 ft., hybrid; *arnoldiana*, pink and white, spring, scented, small yellow and red fruits, hybrid probably between *floribunda* and *baccata*; *atrosanguinea*, deep carmine, late spring, small deep red fruits, 20 ft., hybrid; *baccata*, Siberian Crab Apple, white, spring, scented, yellow or red fruits, 15 to 25 ft., Asia; *coronaria*, double pink flowers, late spring, early summer, scented, 20 to 30 ft., Eastern N. America; *floribunda*, Japanese Crab Apple, carmine changing to white, spring, 15 to 25 ft., Japan; *halliana*, pink, spring, 12 to 15 ft., China, and var. *parkmanii*, weeping habit, double flowers; *hupehensis*, pink changing to white, late spring, early summer, scented, 20 to 25 ft., small yellow, red flushed fruits, China, Japan; *ioensis*, Prairie Crab Apple, white and pink, late spring, scented, U.S.A., and var. *plena*, double flowers; *lemoinei*, deep carmine, spring, 20 to 25 ft., hybrid probably between *niedzwetzkyana* and *atrosanguinea*; *niedzwetzkyana*, deep reddish purple, spring, 15 to 25 ft., small dark reddish purple fruits, Siberia, Turkestan; *prunifolia*, rosy red to white, spring, 20 to 30 ft., small red or yellow fruits, N. E. Asia; *purpurea*, deep carmine, spring, 20 to 25 ft., small purplish crimson fruits, hybrid between *niedzwetzkyana* and *atrosanguinea*; *robusta*, Cherry Crab Apple, white or pink, spring, 30 to 40 ft., cherry-like red or yellow fruits, hybrids between *baccata* and *prunifolia*, and vars. Red Siberian, red fruits, Yellow Siberian, yellow fruits; *sargentii*, white, spring, scented, 6 to 8 ft., red cherry-like fruits, Japan; *scheideckeri*, semi-double pink, spring, 12 to 15 ft., hybrid between *floribunda* and *prunifolia*; *sieboldii* (syn. *toringo*), pink changing to white, late spring, 8 to 10 ft., small red or yellow fruits, Japan; *spectabilis*, double pink flowers, spring, 20 to 25 ft., China, and var. *albi-plena*, double white; *toringoides*, white, late spring, scented, 15 to 20 ft., red and yellow fruits, W. China; *tschonoskii*, white and pink, spring, 25 to

35 ft., yellow and purple fruits, Japan; *yunnanensis*, white, spring, 20 to 25 ft., small deep red fruits, W. China, and var. *veitchii*, brighter red fruits. There are also many forms and hybrids with garden names such as Dartmouth, Golden Hornet, John Downie and Profusion, some grown primarily for their flowers, some also for ornamental fruit.

MALVA (Mallow) – *Malvaceae*. Hardy perennials with funnel-shaped flowers.

Soil ordinary. Position, sunny. Plant in spring or autumn. Increase by seeds sown in spring in a frame or out of doors; by division in spring; by cuttings in summer in a frame.

Recommended kinds are *M. alcea*, light rose, summer, 4 ft., Europe, and var. *fastigiata*, more erect in habit; *moschata*, Musk Mallow, rose, summer, 3 ft., Britain, and var. *alba*, white.

MALVASTRUM (False Mallow) – *Malvaceae*. Hardy perennials with flowers similar to malva.

Soil, ordinary. Position, sunny. Plant in spring. Protect in severe winters with a layer of cinder ashes or leafmould.

Increase by seeds sown in sandy soil in temp. 15 to 18°C. in spring; by cuttings inserted in a cold frame in summer.

The best kind is *M. coccineum*, brick red, summer, 6 to 9 in., Rocky Mountains.

MAMMILLARIA – *Cactaceae*. Tender succulent perennials. Growth leafless, cylindrical or globular, bearing small tubercles or teats crowned with rosettes or stars of spines evenly spaced over the surface. Flowers in a circle around the top of the plant.

Mammillaria elongata

Compost, John Innes potting compost No. 2 plus one-sixth its bulk of coarse sand. Position, well-drained pots in a sunny, cool greenhouse, minimum winter temp. 10°C. Water fairly freely in spring and summer, very sparingly in autumn and winter. Pot in

spring. Repot young plants annually, older plants only every third or fourth year. Plants may also be grown in sunny windows in reasonably heated rooms.

Increase by seeds sown in sandy soil in temp. 15 to 18°C. in spring; by cuttings of the tops of plants inserted in gritty compost in spring; by offsets removed in spring or summer and treated as cuttings; by tubercles removed and allowed to dry for 24 hours, then inserted as cuttings.

Recommended kinds are *M. bocasana*, cream or pink, late spring, 6 in., Mexico; *camptotricha*, whitish, spring to autumn, 4 in., Mexico; *candida*, white and pink, early summer, 3 in., Mexico; *celsiana*, carmine, late spring, 4 in., Mexico; *compressa* (syn. *angularis*), rosy purple, summer, 4 to 8 in.; *decipiens*, white or pink, 4 in., Mexico; *echinaria*, pink or cream, summer, 6 in., Mexico; *elegans*, purplish red, spring, 4 to 6 in., Mexico; *elongata* (syn. *stella-aurata*), yellow, summer, 3 in., Mexico; *geminispina* (syn. *bicolor*), purple, summer, 6 to 12 in., Mexico; *glochidata*, white, summer, 6 in., Mexico; *gracilis*, cream, spring, 4 in., Mexico; *haageana*, carmine-rose, summer, 4 in., Mexico; *karwinskiana*, cream, 3 in., Mexico; *microcarpa*, pink, summer, 3 in., Mexico; *microhelia*, greenish white or pink, summer, 6 in., Mexico; *parkinsonii*, pink, late summer, 6 in., Mexico; *perbella*, pink, early summer, 6 in., Mexico; *plumosa*, greenish white, winter, 3 in., Mexico; *prolifera* (syn. *pusilla*), yellow, 3 in., W. Indies; *schelhasei*, white and rose, summer, 4 in., Mexico; *schiedeana*, cream, summer, 3 in., Mexico; *spinosissima*, crimson, summer, 6 in., Mexico; *tetracantha*, rose, summer, 9 in., Mexico; *uncinata*, pink, early summer, 4 in., Mexico; *wildii*, white, summer, 3 to 4 in., Mexico.

MANDEVILLA – *Apocynaceae*. Tender flowering deciduous climbers with funnel-shaped flowers.

Compost, John Innes potting compost No. 2 or equivalent. Position, large pots, tubs or beds in a cool greenhouse, minimum winter temp. 7°C., or plant outside in warm, sunny places where there is little likelihood of frost. Water normally. Cut back previous year's growth nearly to the base in late winter. Provide trellis, wires or other supports for twining growth.

Increase by seeds sown in pans or beds of sandy peat in temp. 15 to 18°C. in spring; by cuttings of firm side shoots, 2 to 3 in. long, inserted in a warm propagator in summer.

The best kind is *M. suaveolens* (syn. *laxa*), Chilean Jasmine, white, fragrant, summer, 15 to 30 ft., Argentina.

MANETTIA – *Rubiaceae*. Tender evergreen climbers with small tubular flowers.

Compost, John Innes potting compost No. 1 or equivalent. Position, pots or beds in an intermediate or warm greenhouse, minimum winter temp. 13°C. Water normally. Shade from direct sunshine in spring and summer and maintain a moist atmosphere. Feed with weak liquid manure or fertilizer in summer. Cut back previous year's growth in late winter as necessary to fill available space.

Increase by seeds sown in sandy soil in temp. 15 to 18°C. in spring; by cuttings of young shoots in a warm propagator in late spring or early summer.

Recommended kinds are *M. bicolor*, scarlet and orange, all year in a warm atmosphere, 10 to 15 ft., Brazil; *glabra*, scarlet, winter to summer, 10 to 15 ft., S. America; *inflata*, scarlet and orange, all year in a warm atmosphere, 10 to 15 ft., Paraguay and Uruguay.

MARANTA – *Marantaceae*. Tender herbaceous perennials with ornamental foliage.

Compost, equal parts loam, leafmould and peat plus one-sixth its bulk of coarse sand. Position, pots in an intermediate or warm greenhouse, minimum winter temp. 13°C., or in a warm room. Water moderately at all times but a little more freely in summer. Shade from direct sunshine and maintain a humid atmosphere. Pot in spring.

Increase by division in spring.

Maranta leuconeura kerchoveana

Recommended kinds are *M. arundinacea*, Arrowroot, white, summer, to 6 ft., Tropical America, and var. *variegata*, leaves green and white; *bicolor*, leaves olive green, 1 ft., Brazil; *leuconeura*, leaves light and dark green, white and purple, 1 ft., Brazil, and vars. *kerchoveana*, leaves spotted with red, and *massangeana*, leaves white veined, purple beneath.

See also Calathea.

MASDEVALLIA – *Orchidaceae*. Tender epiphytic orchids with showy flowers some made more distinctive by the sepals being extended into long tails.

Compost, equal parts of fibre and sphagnum moss. Position, well-drained pans or baskets in a cool greenhouse. Water fairly freely from spring to autumn, moderately in winter. Maintain a moist atmosphere and shade. Repot when necessary in spring.

Increase by division of plants in early spring.

Masdevallia (hybrid)

Recommended kinds are *M. amabilis*, orange-red to orange-yellow with crimson veins, spring, summer, 8 in., Colombia; *bella*, yellowish thickly spotted chocolate red, autumn, winter, 6 in., Colombia; *caudata*, yellow, red, sepals mauve-purple, autumn to spring, 6 in., Colombia; *chimaera*, yellowish with brown spots, autumn to spring, 6 to 9 in., Colombia, and many varieties; *coccinea* (syn. *harryana*), magenta to crimson, spring, 1 to 2 ft., Colombia, many varieties including *alba*, creamy white, *armeniaca*, apricot, *atrosanguinea*, blood red, *gravesiae*, white tinged buff, *lindenii*, lilac-magenta and *sanderae*, white tinged yellow; *ignea*, cinnabar red, spring, 12 to 15 in., Colombia, and var. *militaris* (syn. *M. militaris*), red, scarlet and yellow; *muscosa*, yellow, lip projecting, on being touched by an insect it snaps up enclosing the insect for a short time, spring, autumn, 3 in., Colombia; *tovarensis*, white, winter, 6 in., Colombia.

MATRICARIA – *Compositae*. Hardy annual with feathery leaves and small ball-like flowers. For chamomile see *Anthemis nobilis* and for *Matricaria eximia* see *Chrysanthemum parthenium*.

Soil, ordinary. Position, open, sunny. Sow in spring where plants are to flower and thin seedlings to 6 in.

The recommended kind is *M. inodora plenissima*, Double Mayweed, white, double, summer, 1 ft., North Temperate Regions (Britain).

MATTHIOLA (Stock) – *Cruciferae*. Hardy or slightly tender annual, biennial or occasionally perennial herbs, notable for the fragrance of their flowers.

Culture of Ten-week Stock: Soil, deep, rich, well manured. Position, open, sunny. Sow seeds in light soil in temp. 15 to 18°C. in spring, transplanting seedlings outdoors in late spring or early summer. Plant dwarf kinds 9 in. and tall kinds 12 to 15 in. apart each way. Remove seed pods as they form. Discard after flowering. With 100% strains keep seedlings for a few days at 10°C. and then discard all those with dark green leaves

as these would produce single flowers. Those with light green leaves will produce double flowers and so are the ones to retain. The colour difference is less noticeable at higher temperatures.

Culture of Brompton Stocks: Soil as for ten-week stocks but well drained. Sow seeds in light soil in a cold frame in early or midsummer. Transplant seedlings when 1 in. high to a nursery bed of good soil in a sunny place spacing at least 4 in. apart in rows 1 ft. apart. Transfer to flowering quarters in late summer or early autumn spacing 9 to 12 in. apart. Alternatively in cold districts pot seedlings singly in John Innes potting compost No. 1 or equivalent and grow in a cold frame throughout the winter, planting out in spring when weather becomes mild. Remove seed pods as they form. Discard plants after flowering though occasionally in warm, well-drained places some plants may survive for several years.

Culture of Winter-flowering Stocks: Sow in early summer in John Innes seed compost or equivalent in an unheated frame or greenhouse. Pot seedlings singly in small pots in John Innes potting compost No. 1 or equivalent and grow on without heat. Repot as necessary, eventually into 5- or 6-in. pots and John Innes potting compost No. 2 or equivalent. Bring into a cool greenhouse, minimum temp. 7°C., in autumn. Water freely in summer, moderately in autumn and winter. Discard after flowering.

Matthiola incana

Culture of Night-scented Stock: Soil, ordinary. Position, sunny. Sow in spring outdoors where plants are to flower and thin to about 3 in. Discard after flowering.

Recommended kinds are *M. bicornis* (syn. *longipetala*), Night-scented Stock, lilac, purple, summer, fragrant at night, 1 ft., annual, Greece; *incana*, Brompton Stock, purple varying to red, violet, lavender, creamy yellow and white, fragrant, often double, spring to early summer, 1 to 2 ft., biennial or perennial, S. Europe, and var. *annua* (syn. *M. annua*), Ten-week Stock, Intermediate Stock, annual.

MAURANDYA – *Scrophulariaceae*. More or less tender climbing or trailing perennials with trumpet-shaped flowers.

Indoor culture: Compost, John Innes potting compost No. 2 or equivalent. Pot in spring. Position, well-drained pots with shoots draping over the front of the staging, or trained up trellises, walls, or rafters, or suspended in baskets in a sunny cool greenhouse, minimum winter temp. 7°C. Water freely from spring to early autumn, moderately in autumn, keep nearly dry afterwards. Apply liquid fertilizer to healthy plants in flower only.

Outdoor culture: Soil, ordinary, well drained. Position, against warm, sunny walls or in vases or window boxes in a sunny, sheltered place. Water freely in dry weather. Protect in winter with dry litter. Will survive a few degrees of frost in well-drained soil.

Increase by seeds sown in light soil in temp. 15 to 18°C. in spring, transplanting seedlings when 1 in. high singly into 2- or 3-in. pots; by cuttings of young shoots inserted in sandy soil in a warm propagator in spring or summer. *M. erubescens* is occasionally grown as an annual in warm climates, raised under glass as above and planted outdoors in late spring or early summer.

Recommended kinds are *M. barclaiana*, violet-purple or white, summer, Mexico; *erubescens* (commonly grown as *M. scandens*), rose, purple, summer, Mexico; *scandens*, lavender or violet, summer, Mexico.

MAXILLARIA – *Orchidaceae.* Tender epiphytic orchids, varying greatly, many of minor interest, others of considerable beauty. Flowers, sometimes fragrant, borne singly.

Compost, equal parts fibre and sphagnum moss. Position, well-drained pans or baskets suspended in a cool or intermediate greenhouse. Water fairly freely from spring to autumn and shade. The winter rest must be governed by the nature of the plant. For hard-bulbed, hard-leaved species rest is essential, so only occasional waterings may be required in winter. For species with strongly keeled leaves, e.g. *M. venusta*, *sanderiana*, water can seldom be withheld for more than a week or two, and their winter temperature should not fall below 13°C., nor should water be sprayed too freely on them or brown spots appear on their foliage. Other forms may be syringed as soon as the leaves are free. Repot when necessary in spring.

Increase by division of the pseudobulbs in spring.

Recommended kinds are *M. grandiflora*, white, lip yellow flushed crimson, spring, 8 in., Ecuador, Peru; *macrura* (syn. *longisepala*), greyish green, pink and yellow, summer, 6 in., Venezuela; *picta*, cream and purple, various seasons, 6 in., Brazil; *sanderiana*, white blotched blood red, spring, 18 in., Ecuador; *tenuifolia*, yellow and red, spring, 9 in., Mexico; *venusta*, creamy white, yellow and red, autumn, 12 in., Colombia.

MAZUS – *Scrophulariaceae.* Hardy dwarf perennial herbs, suitable for carpeting. Small 'snapdragon' flowers.

Soil, peaty or leafy, moist yet porous. Position, sunny. Plant in spring.

Increase by division of the tufts in spring.

Recommended kinds are *M. pumilio*, lilac and yellow, summer, prostrate, New Zealand; *radicans* (syn. *Mimulus radicans*), white, violet and yellow, summer, prostrate, New Zealand; *reptans*, rosy lavender, white and yellow, early summer, prostrate, Himalaya.

MECONOPSIS – *Papaveraceae.* Hardy monocarpic and perennial herbs with poppy-like flowers.

Sow seeds in a mixture of equal parts peat, leafmould and sharp sand in an unheated greenhouse or frame as soon as ripe or in the spring. Transplant seedlings when large enough to handle into a cold frame and plant out in permanent positions as soon as they have formed tufts of seven or eight leaves each. Soil, deep, lime-free loam with sand, leafmould and peat. Position, well drained but not dry, cool, partially shady. Water freely in summer; keep dry as possible in winter. Monocarpic species flower when two to four years old and afterwards die. Species most likely to prove perennial are

Meconopsis betonicifolia

M. betonicifolia, cambrica, grandis, quintuplinervia and *villosa*.

Recommended kinds are *M. betonicifolia* (syn. *baileyi*), Himalayan Poppy, Tibetan Poppy, Blue Poppy, azure blue, late spring, early summer, 3 to 4 ft., Tibet, Yunnan, Upper Burma; *cambrica*, Welsh Poppy, yellow, orange, late spring, summer, 1 ft., Europe (Britain), and var. *plena*, double flowered; *dhwojii*, primrose yellow, early summer, 2 to 2½ ft., Nepal; *grandis*, blue, late spring, early summer, 3 ft., Nepal, Tibet, Bhutan, Sikkim; *horridula*, light blue, reddish purple or white, early summer, 3 ft., Nepal, W. China; *integrifolia*, primrose yellow, summer, 1½ to 3 ft., Tibet, Upper Burma, W. China; *latifolia*, pale blue, early summer, 2½ ft., Kashmir; *napaulensis* (syn. *wallichii*), Satin Poppy, blue, pink, purple, red or white, summer, 4 to 6 ft., Nepal, S. W. China; *paniculata*, yellow, summer, 5 to 6 ft., Nepal to Assam; *quintuplinervia*, lavender-blue, late spring, 1 to 1½ ft., Tibet, W. China; *regia*, yellow, summer, ornamental foliage, 2 ft., Nepal; *sheldonii*, deep blue, late spring, early summer, 2 to 3 ft., hybrid between *betonicifolia* and *grandis*; *simplicifolia*, sky blue to purple, summer, 2 ft., Nepal to Tibet; *sherriffii*, pink, carmine, summer, 1 to 2 ft., Bhutan, Tibet; *superba*, white, late spring, early summer, 3 to 4 ft., Tibet, Bhutan; *villosa*, yellow, summer, 15 to 20 in., Nepal to Bhutan.

MEDICAGO – *Leguminosae.* Hardy annual. Flowers succeeded by curiously twisted pods. Leaves with red spots.

Increase by seeds sown in ordinary soil in a sunny position outdoors in spring. Thin seedlings to 6 in. apart.

The kind recommended is *M. echinus*, Calvary Clover, yellow, summer, 6 in., S. Europe.

MEDINILLA – *Melastomataceae.* Tender evergreen flowering shrub with showy pendent flower clusters.

Compost, John Innes potting compost

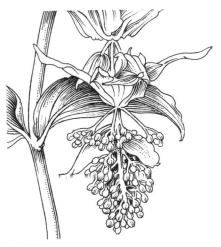

Medinilla magnifica

No. 2 or equivalent with one-quarter its bulk extra peat. Position, warm greenhouse, minimum winter temp. 15°C. Water freely in spring and summer, moderately in autumn, sparingly in winter. Shade in summer and maintain a moist atmosphere from spring to autumn. Feed fortnightly with weak liquid manure or fertilizer from late spring to late autumn.

Increase by cuttings of firm young side shoots inserted in sand, peat and leafmould in a warm propagator in spring.

The best kinds are *M. magnifica*, rosy pink, late spring, early summer, 3 ft., Philippines, and var. *superba*, flowers larger.

MELALEUCA – *Myrtaceae*. Slightly tender evergreen shrubs with bottle brush flowers.

Soil, lime-free loam and peat. Position, sheltered, warm and sunny in nearly frost-free places or in pots or beds in a sunny, frost-proof greenhouse. Water fairly freely in spring and summer, moderately in autumn, sparingly in winter. Pot or plant in spring. Shorten previous year's stems in late winter.

Increase by cuttings of nearly ripened shoots inserted in sandy peat in a frame or propagator; by seeds sown in peat and sand in a frame or cool greenhouse as soon as ripe. Grow on young plants in pots as they resent root disturbance.

Recommended kinds are *M. armillaris*, creamy white, summer, 10 to 30 ft., Australia; *elliptica*, carmine, summer, 6 to 8 ft., W. Australia; *gibbosa*, lilac-mauve, late spring, 3 ft., Tasmania, Australia; *hypericifolia*, red, summer, 6 to 8 ft., Australia; *leucadendra*, Cajeput Tree, creamy white, summer, autumn, 20 ft. or more, Australia; *squamea*, purple, late spring, 6 to 10 ft., Tasmania, Australia; *squarrosa*, pale yellow, summer, 3 to 9 ft., Australia; *wilsonii*, purplish pink, late spring, 3 to 6 ft.

MELANDRIUM – *Caryophyllaceae*. Perennial herbs closely allied to *Silene* and often listed as such.

Soil, equal parts loam, leafmould (or peat) and coarse sand. Position, sunny, well-drained rock gardens, raised beds, etc., or in pots or pans in an alpine house or frame. Plant or pot in spring. Water freely in spring and summer but very sparingly in autumn and winter.

Increase by seeds sown in spring in a frame or cool greenhouse.

Recommended kinds are *M. elisabethae* (syn. *Silene elizabethae*), magenta, summer, 4 in., Tyrol, Italy; *pennsylvanicum*, pink, early summer, 4 in., N. America; *wherryi*, pink, summer, 6 in., Western N. America.

MELIA – *Meliaceae*. Slightly tender deciduous flowering tree with graceful, feather-shaped green leaves.

Soil, sandy loam. Position, warm, sunny,

sheltered or large well-drained pots in a cool greenhouse or conservatory. Plant or pot in autumn or late winter. Water freely pot-grown plants from spring to autumn, but give little afterwards.

Increase by cuttings inserted in sand in a propagator in summer; by seeds sown in temp. 18 to 21°C. in spring.

The recommended kind is *M. azedarach*, Indian Lilac, Pride of India, Chinaberry, China Tree, Bead Tree, lilac, late spring, fragrant, orange globose fruits, to 40 ft., India, China and var. *umbraculiformis*, Texas Umbrella Tree, umbrella-shaped habit.

MELIANTHUS – *Melianthaceae*. Slightly tender evergreen sub-shrub with graceful, feather-shaped, grey-green leaves.

Soil, ordinary, well drained. Position, sunny beds or borders. Plant in spring. Cover roots and base of plant with dry litter in autumn in cold places as protection from frost, or lift, pot and winter in a cool greenhouse or conservatory. Plants can also be grown in large pots or tubs of loamy soil in a frost-proof greenhouse.

Increase by seeds sown in light, sandy soil in temp. 18 to 21°C. in spring; by cuttings inserted in sandy soil in a propagator in spring or summer.

The recommended kind is *M. major*, Cape Honey Flower, Large Honey Bush, reddish brown, summer, 4 to 6 ft., S. Africa.

MELIOSMA – *Meliosmaceae*. Hardy deciduous trees and shrubs with panicles of spiraea-like flowers.

Soil, good, loamy, neutral or acid. Position, sunny.

Increase by cuttings of half-ripened shoots inserted in sandy soil in a propagator in summer; by seeds sown in a cool greenhouse or frame as soon as ripe.

Recommended kinds are *M. beaniana*, creamy white, late spring, 40 to 80 ft., China; *cuneifolia*, yellowish white, fragrant, summer, 10 to 20 ft., W. China; *veitchiorum*, creamy white, late spring, purplish black berries, 30 to 50 ft., pinnate leaves turn yellow in autumn, W. China.

MELISSA (Balm) – *Labiatae*. Hardy herbaceous perennials with lemon-scented leaves; used in seasoning and liqueurs, and also as medicine.

Soil, ordinary, light. Position, warm, sunny. Plant in spring or autumn. For drying for winter use gather stems when the flowers are open. Cut stems off close to the ground after flowering.

Increase by seeds sown outdoors in spring; golden-leaved variety by division in spring or autumn.

Recommended kinds are *M. officinalis*, Balm, white or yellow, summer, autumn, 2 to 3 ft., Europe (Britain), and var. *aurea*, leaves golden.

MELITTIS – *Labiatae*. Hardy perennial with clusters of pink and white flowers in early summer.

Soil, fairly rich. Position, partially shaded. Plant in spring or autumn.

Increase by division of roots directly after flowering; by seeds sown in a frame or shady place outdoors in spring.

The only species is *M. melissophyllum*, Bastard Balm, 1 to 1½ ft., Europe (Britain).

MENISPERMUM (Moon Seed) – *Menispermaceae*. Hardy deciduous flowering climber with large leaves, inconspicuous flowers and black, poisonous fruits. Male and female flowers are produced on different plants and both are required for fruits to be produced.

Soil, ordinary. Position, moist, sunny or shady, against walls, arbours, pergolas or trellises. Plant in autumn or winter. Prune in early spring as necessary to keep in bounds.

Increase by cuttings of young shoots inserted in sandy soil in a frame in spring or summer; by layering in autumn; by seeds sown as soon as ripe or in spring in a frame or cool greenhouse.

The best kind is *M. canadense*, greenish yellow, summer, 10 to 15 ft., N. America.

MENTHA (Mint) – *Labiatae*. Hardy aromatic herbs grown for oil and as garden herbs and ornamental creeping plants.

Soil, light, rich. Position, open, sunny for most kinds but cool, moist and partially shaded for *M. requienii*, which is an excellent creeping plant for covering the surface of soil or paving. *M. aquatica* in shallow water at the margins of pools, etc.

Increase by summer cuttings in moist soil in a frame or propagator; by division in spring.

Recommended kinds are *M. aquatica*, Water Mint, mauve, summer, 6 to 36 in., Europe (Britain), W. Asia, N. and S. Africa, Madeira; *piperita*, Peppermint, purple, autumn, to 3 ft., hybrid between *aquatica* and *spicata*; *pulegium*, Pennyroyal, lilac, late summer, autumn, 4 to 12 in., Europe (Britain) and var. *gibraltarica*, Gibraltar Mint, leaves sometimes splashed with white; *requienii*, Corsican Mint, pale mauve, summer, creeping, Corsica, Sardinia; *rotundifolia*, Apple Mint, Round-leaved Mint, pinkish lilac, late summer, to 2 ft., Europe (Britain), Azores, and var. *variegata*, leaves blotched with white; *spicata* (*M. viridis* of trade lists), Green Pea Mint, Lamb Mint, Spearmint, purple, late summer, 1 to 3 ft., Europe.

MENTZELIA – *Loasaceae*. Hardy annuals, some with showy saucer-shaped flowers.

Soil, ordinary. Position, sunny. Sow in spring where plants are to flower and thin to about 9 in. Discard after flowering.

The best kind is *M. lindleyi* (syn. *Bartonia*

Mentzelia lindleyi

aurea), Blazing Star, yellow, summer, 1½ to 2 ft., California.

MENYANTHES – *Menyanthaceae*. Hardy perennial aquatics with floating leaves and attractive flowers.

Soil, ordinary. Position, shallow streams, pools, ponds, marshes and bogs. Plant in spring.

Increase by inserting pieces of creeping stems in the mud in spring.

The best kind is *M. trifoliata*, Buck Bean, Bog Bean, Marsh Trefoil, pinkish, fringed, fragrant, late spring, early summer, Europe (Britain).

MENZIESIA – *Ericaceae*. Hardy deciduous flowering shrubs with small bell-shaped flowers.

Soil, peaty lime-free loam. Position, sunny or partially shady. Plant in autumn or late winter.

Menziesia caliicalyx

Increase by seeds sown in sandy peat in well-drained pans during spring in temp. 15 to 18°C.; by cuttings of current year's growth during summer in sandy soil in a propagator; by layering in spring or autumn.

Recommended kinds are *M. ciliicalyx*,

cream or purple, late spring, 1½ to 2½ ft., Japan; *pilosa* (syn. *globularis*), yellowish white and pink, spring, summer, 2 to 6 ft., Eastern N. America.

See also Daboecia and Phyllodoce.

MERENDERA (Pyrenean Meadow Saffron) – *Liliaceae*. Hardy bulbous perennials with fragrant funnel-shaped flowers.

Soil, light, sandy loam with peat or leafmould. Position, sunny, sheltered, well drained, or in pots in an unheated frame or greenhouse. Plant bulbs 3 in. deep in late summer. Foliage dies down in early summer and does not reappear until after the plant has flowered.

Increase by seeds sown in a cold frame as soon as ripe or in spring, transplanting seedlings 3 in. apart when two years old; by division of bulb clusters in summer. Seedling bulbs do not flower until four or five years old.

Recommended kinds are *M. filifolia*, pink, late autumn, 3 in., W. Mediterranean; *montana* (syn. *bulbocodium*), rosy lilac, late summer, autumn, 3 in., Spain; *robusta*, purplish, spring, 3 in., Iran, India; *sobolifera* white, flushed pink, spring, 3 to 4 in., Bulgaria, Asia Minor; *trigyna* (syn. *caucasica*), mauve or white, spring, 3 in., Caucasus.

MERTENSIA – *Boraginaceae*. Hardy perennial herbs with curling spikes or clusters of funnel-shaped flowers.

Soil, sandy peat and loam, acid and lime free for *M. longiflora*. Position, partially shady borders, moist in summer. Plant in spring or autumn.

Increase by seeds sown in sandy peat as soon as ripe.

Recommended kinds are *M. ciliata*, blue, late spring, summer, 2 ft., N. W. America; *longiflora*, Small Bluebells, blue, summer, 9 in., N. America, Asia; *maritima*, Northern Shorewort, blue, spring, 6 in., Europe (Britain), Iceland; *sibirica*, purplish blue, late spring, summer, 6 in., Asia; *virginica*, Virginian Cowslip, light blue, late spring, early summer, 2 to 3 ft., Eastern U.S.A.

MESEMBRYANTHEMUM, see Carpobrotus, Conophytum, Cryophytum, Delosperma, Dorotheanthus, Faucaria, Lampranthus, and Lithops.

MESPILUS – *Rosaceae*. Hardy ornamental deciduous tree. Flowers white or tinted pink, solitary; cultivated for its fruits.

Soil, ordinary. Position, sunny shrub borders, or as specimens on lawns. Plant in autumn or late winter. Prune out weak and overcrowded wood in winter, but as a rule little pruning is required once the young trees have been formed. Pick fruit before the advent of frosts and store until very ripe or 'bletted'.

Increase by seeds stratified for five months at 20 to 30°C., then for a further

3 or 4 months at 4°C. after which they may be sown outdoors or under glass; by grafting in spring on seedling stock or on pear, quince or hawthorn; by budding on the same stocks in summer.

The only kind is *M. germanica*, Medlar, white, spring, summer, fruits brown, 15 to 20 ft., Europe, Asia Minor.

METASEQUOIA (Dawn Redwood) – *Taxodiaceae*. Hardy deciduous coniferous tree with feathery leaves similar to those of taxodium. Leaves turn russet brown before they fall.

Soil, good, rather moist loam. Position, open, sunny. Plant in autumn or late winter.

Increase by seeds sown outdoors or under glass as soon as ripe or in spring; by cuttings of firm young growth in a propagator in summer or riper cuttings in autumn.

The only species is *M. glyptostroboides*, to 100 ft., fast growing, China.

METROSIDEROS – *Myrtaceae*. Rather tender evergreen trees with small flowers with prominent stamens carried in short bottle brush-like spikes.

Soil, loamy, moderately acid or neutral. Position, warm, sheltered, sunny, as frost free as possible or in pots or tubs in a cool greenhouse.

Increase by cuttings of young growths during late spring and summer inserted in sandy soil in a propagator.

Recommended kinds are *M. lucida*, bright red, 15 to 50 ft., New Zealand; *robusta*, Rata, coppery red, late summer, 20 to 50 ft., New Zealand; *tomentosa* (syn. *excelsa*), dark red, 20 to 70 ft., New Zealand.

MICHAUXIA – *Campanulaceae*. Hardy biennials or monocarpic plants with bell-shaped flowers.

Sow in spring in a compost of equal parts loam, peat and coarse sand in a frame or greenhouse. Pot seedlings singly in similar compost and when large enough plant outdoors in moderately rich very porous soil and a sunny, sheltered position. Protect in winter from excessive rain. Discard after flowering and seed ripening. Plants may take two or three years to flower.

Recommended kinds are *M. campanuloides*, white, summer, 4 ft., Asia Minor; *tchihatcheffii*, white, summer, 5 to 7 ft., Asia Minor.

MICHELIA – *Magnoliaceae*. Slightly tender evergreen flowering trees and shrubs, closely allied to *Magnolia*.

Soil, rich, deep, lime-free loam. Position, sunny, warm, sheltered. Plant in spring.

Increase by seeds sown singly in small pots during spring in temp. 15 to 18°C.; by layering in spring; by cuttings of firm young growth in a propagator in summer.

Recommended kinds are *M. compressa*, pale yellow and purple, fragrant, late spring,

15 to 30 ft., Japan, Formosa; *doltsopa*, creamy white, fragrant, spring, 30 to 40 ft., China, Tibet, Himalaya; *fuscata* (syn. *figo*), yellowish green and purple, very fragrant, spring and summer, 15 ft., Japan.

MICROGLOSSA – *Compositae*. Hardy shrub with Michaelmas daisy-like flowers.

Soil, ordinary, well drained. Position, sunny. Plant in autumn or early spring.

Increase by seeds sown in sandy soil in a cold frame in spring; by cuttings in a propagator in summer.

The best kind is *M. albescens*, Shrubby Starwort, lilac-blue or bluish white, summer, 2 to 3 ft., Himalaya, China.

MILIUM – *Gramineae*. Hardy perennial grass cultivated for its yellow foliage.

Soil, ordinary, moist. Position, shady. Plant in spring. Increase by division in spring.

The recommended kind is *M. effusum aureum*, Golden Wood Millet, Bowles' Golden Grass, 1 to 3 ft., garden origin but the species is native to Europe (Britain), Siberia, Himalaya and N. America.

MILTONIA – *Orchidaceae*. Tender epiphytic orchids, every species with attractive flowers. Allied to *Odontoglossum* with which many beautiful hybrids have been raised, also with *Cochlioda* and *Oncidium*.

Compost, equal parts of fibre and sphagnum moss with a little dried cow manure. Position, the smallest pots that will contain the plants in an intermediate house, minimum temp. 13°C., but temperatures rather lower than normal in summer with shade, plenty of ventilation and moderate humidity. *M. vexillaria* may be potted in early spring or early autumn, the other species in early spring, the hybrids in spring or into summer. Avoid winter potting. Water most kinds moderately throughout but a few species with rather hard pseudobulbs are better for rather infrequent waterings in winter.

Increase by division of the plants when they are repotted.

Recommended kinds are *M. candida*, yellow, spotted brown, lip white spotted mauve, late summer, autumn, 18 in., Brazil; *clowesii*, yellow and brown, lip violet-purple and white, autumn, Brazil; *endresii* (syn. *Odontoglossum warscewiczii*), white, rose-purple in blotches, spring, summer, Costa Rica; *flavescens*, pale green, cream and purple, autumn, 12 in., Brazil; *phalaenopsis*, white, lip with two crimson-purple blotches, variable, summer, autumn, 9 in., Colombia; *roezlii*, white, purple and yellow, autumn, spring, 9 in., Colombia; *spectabilis*, white, rose flushed, lip rose-purple to whitish, variable, summer, 9 in., Brazil; *vexillaria*, variable, rose, lip often darker, streaked yellow and red, spring, summer, 1 to 2 ft., Ecuador, Colombia; *warscewiczii*, brownish red, tipped white, spring, summer, Peru, Brazil. There are many garden varieties and hybrids.

MIMOSA – *Leguminosae*. Tender shrubs, climbers and perennials with feather-shaped leaves, which in *M. pudica* and *sensitiva* fold on being touched. The spring flower sold as Mimosa is *Acacia dealbata*.

Compost, John Innes potting compost No. 1 or equivalent. Position, beds or pots in a cool or intermediate greenhouse, minimum winter temp. 7°C. Pot or plant in spring. Water normally. *M. pudica* and *sensitiva* are commonly grown as annuals, renewed from seed annually.

Increase by seeds sown in light soil in temp. 15 to 18°C. in spring; by cuttings of young shoots inserted in sandy soil in a warm propagator in spring or summer.

Recommended kinds are *M. pudica*, Humble Plant, rose, summer, 1 to 1½ ft., Tropical America; *sensitiva*, Sensitive Plant, purple, summer, 3 to 6 ft., Tropical America.

MIMULUS (Monkey Flower, Musk) – *Scrophulariaceae*. Hardy herbaceous perennials but some varieties are commonly grown as annuals. All have trumpet-shaped flowers.

Soil, ordinary. Position, moist, semi-shady. Plant in spring. May be grown in pots in a cool, shaded greenhouse in a fairly porous compost such as John Innes potting compost No. 1, watered very freely in summer, moderately at other times.

Mimosa pudica

Increase by seeds sown in spring on the surface of light soil and covered with a little sand or fine soil, in temp. 15 to 18°C.; by cuttings of young shoots inserted in light sandy soil in a propagator at any time; by division in spring.

Recommended kinds are *M. bartonianus*, rose-pink, summer, 2 ft., hybrid between *cardinalis* and *lewisii*; *cardinalis*, Cardinal Monkey Flower, scarlet, or scarlet and yellow, summer, 1 to 3 ft., N. America; *cupreus*, yellow becoming copper coloured, spotted brown, summer, 8 to 12 in., Chile, and numerous varieties such as Leopard, yellow and reddish brown, Whitecroft Scarlet, scarlet, 6 in.; *glutinosus* (syn. *Diplacus glutinosus*), orange, salmon or buff, summer, 3 to 5 ft., California, and var. *aurantiacus*, coppery red; *lewisii*, rose, summer, 1 ft., N. W. America; *luteus*, Monkey Musk, yellow, red spotted, summer, 8 to 24 in., Chile, and vars. *duplex*, hose-in-hose flowers, *guttatus*, spotted maroon; *moschatus*, pale yellow, summer, autumn, prostrate, Western N. America; *ringens*, violet, summer, 2 to 4 ft., N. America; *tigrinus* (syn. *hybridus*), yellow, pink to crimson, much blotched, summer, 12 to 15 in., hybrids between *cupreus*, *luteus* and *variabilis*, usually grown as annuals; *variegatus*, (syn. *luteus variegatus*), yellow, white, crimson and violet, summer, 1 to 2 ft., Chile.

MIRABILIS – *Nyctaginaceae*. Slightly tender tuberous-rooted perennials with heads of showy flowers.

Soil, good, ordinary. Position, sunny, warm. Plant tuberous roots in spring, seedlings in early summer. In cold places lift tubers in early summer and store in sand, peat or cinder ashes in a frost-proof place until spring.

Increase by seeds sown in light soil in temp. 15 to 18°C. in spring, transferring seedlings to a cold frame and planting out in early summer; by division of tubers at planting time. Marvel of Peru may be treated as an annual.

Recommended kinds are *M. hybrida*, various colours, summer, 2 ft., hybrid between *longiflora* and *jalapa*; *jalapa*, Marvel of Peru, white, yellow, red or striped, summer, fragrant, 2 to 3 ft., Tropical America; *longiflora*, white, pink, violet, summer, fragrant, 2 to 3 ft., Mexico; *multiflora*, purple, rose, summer, 2 to 3 ft., N. W. America.

MISCANTHUS – *Gramineae*. Hardy perennial grasses grown for their foliage.

Miscanthus sinensis variegatus

Soil, ordinary, well drained. Position, sunny. Plant in spring.

Increase by division in spring.

Recommended kinds are *M. sacchariflorus* (syn. *saccharifer*), grey-green leaves, 6 to 8 ft., E. Asia, and var. *variegatus*, leaves striped yellow; *sinensis* (syn. *Eulalia japonica*), Eulalia, green with white midrib, 3 to 9 ft., China, Japan, and vars. *gracillimus*, narrow leaved, *variegatus*, leaves striped yellow, and *zebrinus*, Zebra-striped Rush, leaves cross-banded yellow.

MITELLA (Bishop's Cap) – *Saxifragaceae*. Hardy perennial herb with slender spikes of small flowers and attractive heart-shaped foliage.

Soil, ordinary. Position, moist, shady. Plant in spring.

Increase by division in spring.

The best kind is *M. diphylla*, Mitre-wort, white, spring, 1 to 1½ ft., N. America.

MOLINIA – *Gramineae*. Hardy perennial grass grown for its narrow yellow-edged leaves and purplish flower plumes.

Soil, ordinary, well drained but not dry in summer. Position, open, sunny. Plant in spring or autumn.

Increase by division in autumn or spring.

The recommended kind is *M. caerulea variegata*, 1½ to 2 ft., garden form of the Purple Moor Grass, a species found wild in Europe (Britain), Asia Minor, Caucasus, Siberia and N. America.

MOLTKIA – *Boraginaceae*. Hardy subshrubs or perennials closely related to *Lithospermum* and often referred to that genus.

Soil, ordinary, well drained, will do well on chalk or limestone. Position, sunny. Plant in spring.

Increase by summer cuttings in a propagator; by layering in spring or autumn; *M. petraea* by seeds sown in sandy soil in a frame or greenhouse in spring.

Recommended kinds are *M. intermedia*, deep blue, summer, 9 in., hybrid between *petraea* and *suffruticosa*; *petraea*, pink becoming violet-blue, summer, 6 to 12 in., Greece; *suffruticosa*, pale blue, summer, 12 to 18 in., Italy.

MOLUCCELLA – *Labiatae*. A slightly tender annual grown for its cup-shaped, apple-green calyces which are much used in flower arrangements.

Soil, sandy loam. Position, warm, sunny beds or a cool greenhouse. Sow seeds in spring in sandy soil in temp. 15 to 18°C. Prick out seedlings when large enough to handle and gradually harden off for planting outdoors in late spring or early summer, or grow in pots in John Innes potting compost No. 1 or equivalent. Gather flower spikes when well developed and dry in a cool airy place.

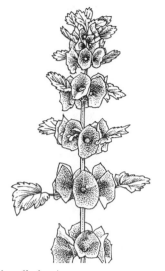

Moluccella laevis

The recommended kind is *M. laevis*, Shell Flower, white, summer, 2 to 3 ft., W. Asia.

MONARDA (Horsemint) – *Labiatae*. Hardy aromatic herbaceous perennials with flowers in whorls.

Soil, ordinary. Position, in sun or partial shade, not liable to dry out badly for *M. didyma* and varieties.

Increase by seeds sown in light soil in a partially shaded position outdoors in spring or early summer; by division of roots in spring.

Recommended kinds are *M. didyma*, Bee Balm, Oswego Tea, Sweet Bergamot, scarlet, summer, 2 to 3 ft., N. America, and var. *alba*, white; *fistulosa*, Wild Bergamot, purple, summer, 2 to 3 ft., N. America, and vars. *mollis*, pink or lilac, *purpurea*, purplish crimson, *rubra*, crimson, and *violacea superba*, violet-purple; *media*, reddish purple, summer, 2 to 3 ft., U.S.A. There are numerous garden varieties in red, pink and purple, probably hybrids between these species.

MONSTERA (Shingle Plant) – *Araceae*. Tender evergreen ornamental climbers. Leaves, large, handsome, perforated, dark green. Stems, creeping, furnished with aerial roots.

Compost, John Innes potting compost No. 1 or equivalent. Position, large pots, tubs or beds in an intermediate or warm greenhouse, minimum winter temp. 13°C., or in warm rooms. Water normally. Shade from direct sunshine in spring and summer. Pot or plant in spring. Feed in spring and summer with weak liquid manure or fertilizer.

Increase by cuttings in summer in a warm propagator (temp. 30 to 32°C.); by seeds sown in spring in temp. 25 to 27°C.

Recommended kinds are *M. deliciosa*, yellow, summer, to 20 ft., leaves to 2 ft.

Monstera deliciosa

across and 4 ft. long, Mexico; *pertusa* (syn. *adansonia*), yellow and white, summer, to 15 ft., leaves about 1 ft. wide and broad (often incorrectly known as *M. deliciosa borsigiana*), Tropical America.

MORAEA (Butterfly Iris) – *Iridaceae*. Slightly tender bulbous plants with iris-like flowers.

Soil, light, rich, sandy. Position, sunny, well drained. Plant in autumn, placing bulbs 4 in. deep and 2 in. apart. Mulch the surface of the bed in spring with well-rotted manure. Alternatively, grow in pots in a sunny, frost-proof greenhouse. Place five bulbs 3 in. deep in each 5-in. pot in autumn using a porous, moderately rich compost such as John Innes potting compost No. 1. Water moderately from the time the bulbs begin to grow until the flowers fade, then gradually cease, keeping bulbs dry from midsummer until autumn.

Increase by offsets, treated as advised for bulbs; by seeds sown in a cool greenhouse in spring or as soon as ripe.

Recommended kinds are *M. bicolor*, yellow and brown, summer, 2 ft., S. Africa; *gigandra*, cream, lilac, orange, green and dark blue, spring, 2 ft.; *glaucopsis*, white and blue-black, spring, 1 ft., S. Africa; *iridioides*, white, yellow and blue, spring, 1 to 2 ft., S. Africa; *papilionacea*, orange-red, salmon and yellow, spring, 4 to 6 in.; *pavonia* (syn. *Iris pavonia*), Peacock Iris, orange-red or yellow and blue-black, 1 to 2 ft., S. Africa; *robinsoniana* (syn. *Iris robinsoniana*), Wedding Flower, white, summer, 4 to 6 ft., Australia; *spathacea* (syn. *spathulata*), yellow and purple, 1 to 2 ft., S. Africa; *villosa*, purple, mauve, cream, yellow or orange, spring, 1 to 1½ ft., S. Africa.

MORINA (Whorl Flower) – *Morinaceae*. Hardy perennial herbs with thistle-like leaves and flowers in whorls on stiff stems.

Soil, deep, well-drained loam. Position, sunny. Plant in spring or autumn.

Morina longifolia

Increase by seeds sown in sandy soil in a cold frame in spring or autumn; by division of roots in spring.

The best kind is *M. longifolia*, rose and white, summer, 2 to 2½ ft., Nepal.

MORISIA – *Cruciferae*. Hardy dwarf alpine perennial with neat rosettes and stemless yellow flowers.

Soil, gritty, well-drained loam in a moraine or in a moist bed of stone chippings, loam and sand. Requires full exposure to the sun. Plant in spring.

Increase by seeds sown in sandy soil in a cold frame in spring or by root cuttings laid in sand in late winter or spring.

The only species is *M. monantha* (syn. *hypogaea*), golden yellow, early spring, Corsica and Sardinia.

MORUS (Mulberry) – *Moraceae*. Hardy deciduous trees grown for edible fruits, for foliage to feed silkworms and for ornament.

Soil, warm, deep and well-drained yet moist loam. Position, sunny, sheltered from cold winds. Plant in autumn or late winter, placing roots 6 in. below surface; avoid exposure and drying out and do not cut back fleshy roots as bleeding results. Prune thin overcrowded branches and remove

badly placed ones in early winter. Topdress area of soil equal to spread of branches with well-decayed manure in late autumn, winter or early spring. Allow fruit to ripen and drop on to a layer of straw or other soft material.

Increase selected varieties by cuttings 12 in. or more long, inserted to half their depth in light soil in a sheltered position outdoors in autumn; by shorter cuttings of firm young growth in a propagator in summer; by layering shoots in autumn; species by seeds stratified for three months at 4°C. and then sown in temp. 15 to 18°C.

Recommended kinds are *M. alba*, White Mulberry, to 40 ft., leaves used for silkworms, fruit white becoming pink, China, Europe, N. America, and vars. *pendula*, Weeping Mulberry, *pyramidalis*, erect branches, *tatarica*, Russian Mulberry, small, bushy, very hardy; *nigra*, Black Mulberry, to 30 ft., fruits deep crimson, the best for eating and preserve making, W. Asia; *rubra*, Red or American Mulberry, to 60 ft., fruits red, central U.S.A.

MUEHLENBECKIA – *Polygonaceae*. Slightly tender deciduous shrubs with wiry, tangled stems and climbing or clambering habit, flowers insignificant.

Soil, ordinary, well drained. Position, warm, sunny, may be allowed to stray over large rocks or tree stumps. Both species liable to damage by severe frost.

Increase by summer cuttings in a frame; by division of rootstock or rooted layers in spring.

Recommended kinds are *M. axillaris*, Creeping Wire Vine, creeping and dwarf habit, suitable for rock garden or ground cover, New Zealand; *complexa*, Wire Vine, 15 ft., New Zealand.

MUSA (Banana) – *Musaceae*. Tender herbaceous perennials. Some species grown for fruit, *M. basjoo* and *ensete* for garden decoration in summer.

Compost, John Innes potting compost No. 2 or equivalent. Position, large pots, tubs or beds in a cool or intermediate greenhouse, minimum winter temp. 7°C., or *M. basjoo* outdoors in warm, sheltered places, sunny or half-shady, in nearly frost-free districts. Water freely in spring and summer, moderately in autumn, sparingly in winter. Maintain a moist atmosphere in spring and summer, and feed with weak liquid manure or fertilizer. No shade is required. Pot or plant in spring. Plants may also be stood or plunged outdoors in summer for tropical bedding effects.

Increase by suckers removed from the parent plant and placed in pots in temp. 25°C. at any time of the year; seeds of ornamental kinds sown in spring in temp. 21 to 25°C.

Recommended kinds are *M. basjoo*, to 10 ft., Japan, the hardiest species; *caven-*

dishii, (syns. *acuminata* and *nana*), 5 ft., China, and numerous varieties all grown for their fruit; *ensete*, 15 to 25 ft., Abyssinia; *paradisiaca*, Plantain, to 25 ft., Tropical Asia, and many varieties of which *sapientum*, the seedless banana, has itself produced many sub-varieties widely cultivated in the tropics for fruit with one, *vittata*, having leaves green, white and pink; *textilis*, Manila Hemp, to 20 ft., Philippine Islands.

MUSCARI (Grape Hyacinth) – *Liliaceae*. Hardy bulbous plants with small flowers in close spikes.

Soil, ordinary. Position, sunny. Plant in autumn. Lift, divide and replant when overcrowded.

Increase by seeds sown in light soil in a frame or outdoors as soon as ripe or in spring; by division of bulb clusters in late summer or early autumn; by offsets from old bulbs removed when lifting. Seedlings flower when three to four years old.

Muscari macrocarpum

Recommended kinds are *M. armeniacum*, blue edged white, spring, 6 to 8 in., Asia Minor; *botryoides*, light blue, spring, 6 in., Europe, var. *album*, white; *comosum*, Tassel Hyacinth, green and violet-purple, 12 to to 18 in., S. Europe, Asia Minor, and var. *monstrosum*, Feather Hyacinth, blue, filamentous petals; *latifolium*, deep violet-purple and lilac-blue, spring, 12 to 15 in., Turkey, Asia Minor; *macrocarpum* (syn. *moschatum flavum*), yellow and purple, spring, 8 in., Aegean Islands; *moschatum* (syn. *muscerinii*), Musk Hyacinth, dull violet, becoming yellowish green, spring, 8 in., Asia Minor; *racemosum*, Starch Hyacinth, blue, spring, 6 in., Europe (Britain), Asia; *tubergenianum*, deep and light blue, spring, 8 in., Iran.

MUTISIA (Climbing Gazania) – *Compositae*. Hardy or rather tender flowering climbers with daisy-type flowers, climbing by tendrils.

Soil, rich, well drained. Position, warm, sunny, sheltered, supported on wires or trellis on a wall or climbing into a sparsely branched shrub, or in a sunny greenhouse. Plant in spring. Usually little pruning is required but if overgrown growth can be thinned in summer. Water freely in dry weather. Protect from slugs.

Increase by cuttings of firm young shoots inserted in sand in a propagator in summer; by seeds sown in sandy soil in a temp. 15 to 18°C. in spring.

Recommended kinds are *M. clematis*, orange, summer and early autumn, to 20 ft., rather tender, unlikely to survive frost, Andes of Colombia and Ecuador; *decurrens*, orange or orange-red, summer, 6 to 10 ft., Chile; *ilicifolia*, lilac-pink, summer and early autumn, 8 to 12 ft., Chile; *oligodon*, pink, summer, and early autumn, 4 to 5 ft., Chile.

MYOSOTIDIUM – *Boraginaceae*. Slightly tender herbaceous perennial with large shining green leaves and blue flowers in clusters in spring. Difficult to establish in hot, dry areas.

Soil, fertile, porous loam. Position, cool, damp, sheltered. Plant in spring. Water freely in dry weather.

Increase in spring by seeds sown singly in small pots filled with a mixture of equal parts of loam, peat and sand. This plant should be disturbed as little as possible and so seedlings should be planted in permanent quarters as soon as the pots are filled with roots.

The only species is *M. hortensia* (syn. *nobile*), Chatham Island Forget-me-not, 1 to 1½ ft., Chatham Islands.

MYOSOTIS (Forget-me-not) – *Boraginaceae*. Hardy perennials and biennials with small flowers freely produced.

Soil, ordinary, rather moist for most kinds but a mixture of equal parts of loam, peat, leafmould and sharp sand for mountain and New Zealand species. Position, open and sunny for most but *M. sylvatica* will grow in semi-shade, *M. palustris* likes wet places beside streams, ponds, etc.

Increase all kinds by seeds sown outdoors in spring or early summer, choice kinds in a frame or cool greenhouse. Perennial kinds also by division in spring.

Recommended kinds are *M. alpestris*, blue, summer, 2 to 8 in., European Alps (Britain), Asia, N. America; *azorica*, blue, early summer, 6 to 8 in., Azores; *caespitosa*, blue and yellow, early summer, 3 to 6 in., Europe (Britain), Asia, N. Africa; *dissitiflora*, sky blue, spring, 8 to 10 in., Switzerland, and var. *alba*, white; *palustris* (syn. *scorpioides*), sky blue, late spring, early summer, 6 to 18 in., Europe (Britain), Asia, N. Africa, N. America; *rupicola*, blue and yellow, early summer, 2 in., European Alps; *sylvatica*, blue and yellow, late spring, early summer, 6 to 18 in., Europe (Britain), Asia, and vars. *alba*, white, *rosea*, pink. There are numerous garden varieties.

MYRICA – *Myricaceae*. Hardy deciduous and evergreen shrubs with small catkin flowers followed in some species by glaucous or purple fruits. Leaves, lance shaped, green, highly fragrant.

Soil, light, lime free, peaty, moist for most species but *M. pensylvanica* will grow in dry places. Position, open. Plant in autumn or late winter. Cut out straggly shoots and generally tidy plants in summer.

Increase by seeds soaked in warm water as soon as ripe to remove waxy covering, then stratified for three months at 4°C., after which they should be sown in peat and sand outdoors or under glass; by layering in autumn; by division of plants in autumn.

Recommended kinds are *M. californica*, Californian Bayberry, evergreen, to 15 ft., rather tender, waxy, dark purple berries, California; *cerifera*, Candle-berry or Wax Myrtle, evergreen, 15 to 30 ft., America; *gale*, Sweet Gale, Bog Myrtle, deciduous, brown, late spring, 4 ft., N. Europe (Britain); *pensylvanica*, Bayberry, deciduous, grey-white berries, 9 ft., Eastern N. America.

MYRIOPHYLLUM (Water Milfoil) – *Haloragidaceae*. Pretty feathery submerged and shallow-water aquatics used as oxygenating plants in ponds and aquariums.

Soil, loam. Position, pools, aquaria, etc. Plant in spring and summer by dropping gently into the water or planting individual specimens in the aquarium.

Increase by slips broken from parent plants and inserted in pans containing a little loam and several inches of water.

Recommended kinds are *M. heterophyllum*, bronze-green, N. America; *proserpinacoides*, Parrot's Feather, grow at pond margin, feathery stems trail over sides of pool or fountain, slightly tender, S. Africa; *pinnatum*, reddish bronze, tender, Tropical and N. America; *spicatum*, green, Northern Hemisphere (Britain); *verticillatum*, green, Europe (Britain), Asia, N. America.

MYRRHIS (Myrrh) – *Umbelliferae*. Hardy perennial aromatic herb. Leaves finely divided, fern like, fragrant.

Soil, ordinary. Position, open, sunny. Plant in spring or autumn.

Increase by seeds sown in ordinary soil outdoors in spring or as soon as ripe; by division of roots in spring or autumn.

The only species is *M. odorata*, Sweet Cicely, white, late spring, early summer, 3 ft., Europe (Britain).

MYRTUS (Myrtle) – *Myrtaceae*. Slightly tender evergreen shrubs. Leaves fragrant when crushed; flowers also fragrant, small with prominent stamens, borne in clusters.

Soil, ordinary, well drained. Position, very sheltered, warm, sunny or against a sunny wall in cold places or in large pots or tubs in a sunny, frost-proof greenhouse or conservatory. May be trained as pyra-

Myrtus nummularia

mids or standards. Prune or trim in spring and early summer.

Increase by cuttings in sandy soil in summer in a propagator; by seeds sown in spring in temp. 18 to 21°C.

Recommended kinds are *M. apiculata* (syn. *luma*), white, late summer, early autumn, 15 to 25 ft., peeling cinnamon-coloured bark, Chile; *bullata*, Ramarama, white, spring, 15 to 25 ft., New Zealand; *communis*, Common Myrtle, to 10 ft., white, summer, W. Asia, with vars. *microphylla*, smaller leaved, *tarentina*, a smaller-growing dainty form, and *variegata*, leaves edged white; *lechleriana*, white, late spring, 15 to 25 ft., Chile; *nummularia*, white, late spring, early summer, prostrate, Argentina, Chile, Falkland Isles, the hardiest kind; *ugni* (syn. *Eugenia ugni*), Chilean Guava, pink, summer, 8 to 10 ft., berries which are pleasant to eat, freely borne, Chile.

NANDINA – *Nandinaceae*. Slightly tender evergreen flowering shrub, grown primarily for its bamboo-like foliage and clusters of red berries, but these are only freely produced in mild climates.

Soil, good loam. Position, sheltered, moderately moist yet well drained. Will survive a temperature around −8°C. but prefers warmer conditions. Plant in spring or autumn.

Increase by cuttings inserted in sandy peat in a propagator in summer, rooting is slow; by seeds sown as soon as ripe in a temp. 18 to 21°C.

The only kind is *N. domestica*, Sacred Bamboo, white, summer, 6 to 8 ft., leaves assume reddish tint in spring and autumn, China.

NARCISSUS – *Amaryllidaceae*. Hardy spring-flowering bulbs. Flowers typically composed of a tubular perianth opening out into almost flat, sometimes recurved segments, known as 'perianth segments' or sometimes simply as 'perianth', and a central cup or trumpet, sometimes called the 'corona'.

R.H.S. CLASSIFICATION: DIVISION I – Trumpet. One flower to a stem; trumpet or corona as long as or longer than the perianth segments: (a) Perianth coloured; corona coloured, not paler than the perianth. (b) Perianth white; corona coloured. (c) Perianth white; corona white, not paler than the perianth. (d) Any colour combination not falling into (a), (b) or (c).

Narcissus cyclamineus (hybrid)

DIVISION II – Large-cupped. One flower to a stem, cup or corona more than one-third but less than equal to the length of the perianth segments; sub-divisions (a), (b), (c) and (d) as in Division I.

DIVISION III – Small-cupped. One flower to a stem; corona not more than one-third the length of the perianth segments: sub-divisions (a), (b), (c) and (d) as in Division I.

DIVISION IV – Double. Flowers double.

DIVISION V – Triandrus. Characteristics of *Narcissus triandrus* clearly evident, 1 to 6 flowers per stem: (a) Corona not less than two-thirds the length of the perianth segments. (b) Corona less than two-thirds the length of the perianth segments.

DIVISION VI – Cyclamineus. Characteristics of *Narcissus cyclamineus* clearly evident, flowers inclined, perianth segments recurved. Sub-divisions (a) and (b) as in Division V.

DIVISION VII – Jonquilla. Characteristics of any of the *Narcissus jonquilla* group clearly evident, flowers several to a stem, scented. Sub-divisions (a) and (b) as in Division V.

DIVISION VIII – Tazetta. Characteristics of any of the *Narcissus tazetta* group clearly evident, several flowers per stem, corona much shorter than perianth segments.

DIVISION IX – Poeticus. Characteristics of the *Narcissus poeticus* group clearly evident without admixture of any other.

DIVISION X – Species, etc. All species and wild, or reputedly wild, forms and hybrids.

DIVISION XI – Miscellaneous. All narcissi not falling into any of the foregoing divisions.

Outdoor culture: Soil, ordinary, fertile, reasonably moist in spring when plants are in growth. Position, sunny or in partial shade in cultivated ground or naturalized in grass. If naturalized, grass must not be cut until daffodil leaves begin to turn yellow and die down in summer. Plant in late summer or early autumn, covering bulbs with their own depth of soil. Prior to planting dust the soil with bonemeal at 3 oz. per sq. yd. and repeat dressing annually each autumn. Bulbs can be lifted in summer when leaves have died down but this need not be done annually, only when bulbs are overcrowded and flower quality is beginning to suffer.

Indoor culture: Compost, John Innes potting compost No. 2 or equivalent. Position, pots in a light, unheated or cool greenhouse. Pot in late summer or early autumn, three to five bulbs in each 6-in. pot. Stand outdoors in a cool, shady place or in a frame or plunge in a bed of peat or sand for at least eight weeks to allow roots to fill the soil before pots are brought into the greenhouse. Water sparingly at first, freely from the time growth appears but gradually reduce supply after flowering and when all foliage has died down remove bulbs from pots and store dry in a cool, airy place until planting time. Do not grow the same bulbs in pots two years running.

Increase by seeds sown in sandy loam in a frame as soon as ripe, transplanting seedlings the following year 1 in. apart in a bed of good soil in a sunny but not dry place; by offsets, removed from old bulbs in summer when the leaves have died down and replanted at once as advised for parent bulbs. Seedling bulbs flower when three to eight years old.

Narcissus – Tazetta hybrid

Recommended kinds are *N. asturiensis* (syn. *minimus*), deep yellow, late winter, early spring, 3 to 4 in., Spain; *bulbocodium*, Hoop-petticoat Daffodil, early spring, 4 to 6 in., S. E. Europe, N. Africa, and vars. *citrinus*, lemon yellow, *conspicuus*, deep yellow and *romieuxii*, cream; *cantabricus monophyllus*, white, early spring, 4 in., S. E. Europe; *cyclamineus*, yellow, late winter, early spring, 4 to 8 in. Spain, Portugal; *jonquilla*, Jonquil, deep yellow, richly scented, spring, 1 ft., S. Europe, Algeria, and var. *flore pleno*, Queen Anne's Double

Narcissus – Trumpet

Jonquil, double; *juncifolius*, yellow, spring, 6 to 8 in., S. Europe; *minor*, pale and deep yellow, early spring, 6 to 8 in. Portugal; *obvallaris*, Tenby Daffodil, deep yellow, spring, 8 to 12 in., Britain; *odorus*, Campernelle, yellow, strongly scented, spring, 1 ft., origin uncertain, may be a hybrid; *poeticus* (syn. *majalis*), Poet's Narcissus, white, yellow, red and green, strongly scented, late spring, 1 to 1½ ft., S. Europe, and var. *recurvus*, Pheasant's Eye, perianth segments recurved; *pseudo-narcissus*, Lent Lily, yellow, early spring, 8 to 12 in., Europe (Britain); *rupicola*, deep yellow, richly scented, spring, 1 ft., Spain, Portugal; *tazetta*, Polyanthus Narcissus, white, yellow or yellow and white, winter, early spring, 1 to 2 ft., Mediterranean region, Asia to Japan, and var. *canaliculatus* (syn. *N. canaliculatus*), white and yellow, early spring, 6 to 8 in.; *triandrus*, Angel's Tears, white, spring, 8 to 10 in., Spain, and vars. *concolor*, yellow and *loiseleurii*, white or cream; *watieri*, white, spring, 4 to 6 in., Atlas mountains. There are a great many garden varieties.

NEILLIA (Nine Bark) – *Rosaceae.* Hardy deciduous flowering shrubs with small flowers in slender racemes.

Soil, ordinary. Position, open, sunny but not dry. Plant in autumn or late winter. Prune after flowering, cutting out the oldest stems to the base and shortening others to good side shoots or growth buds.

Increase by cuttings of half-ripened shoots in sand in a propagator in summer; by rooted offsets removed in autumn or late winter.

Recommended kinds are *N. longiracemosa*, rose-pink, summer, 6 to 8 ft., W. China; *sinensis*, pale pink, late summer, 6 ft., Central China; *thibetica*, pink, late spring, early summer, 6 ft., W. China; *thyrsiflora*, white, summer, 3 ft., Sikkim.

NELUMBO (Lotus) – *Nelumbonaceae.* Tender aquatic rhizomatous-rooted perennials with fragrant flowers and bluish-green, shield-shaped leaves 1 to 2 ft. in diameter. *N. nucifera* is one of the two plants known as the Lotus of the Nile, the other being *Nymphaea caerulea*.

Compost, six parts loam, one part well-decayed manure. Position, tanks or tubs of water heated to a temperature of 15 to 18°C. Plant rhizomes 1 to 2 in. below surface of water in spring. Temperature of air, spring to autumn 13 to 18°C., winter 7 to 13°C. Draw off water from tank in mid-autumn and keep rhizomes dry till late winter.

Increase by seeds sown in sandy soil, 2 to 3 in. below the surface of water heated to temp. 18 to 21°C. any time of the year, file seeds to facilitate germination; by division of rhizomes in early spring.

Recommended kinds are *N. lutea* (syn. *pentapetala*), American Lotus, Chinkapin, Duck Acorn, pale yellow, summer, Southern U.S.A.; *nucifera* (syns. *Nelumbium nelumbo*), rose paling with age, summer, Tropical Asia, and many varieties including double white, white edged red or green, rose, double rose and pygmy forms.

NEMESIA – *Scrophulariaceae*. Slightly tender S. African annuals with a wide colour range.

Soil, fertile, porous with plenty of humus, not liable to dry out. Position, open but not hot. Sow in spring in John Innes seed compost or equivalent and germinate in temp. 15 to 18°C. Prick off seedlings early into John Innes potting compost No. 1 or equivalent and harden off for planting out in late spring or early summer 6 to 8 in. apart. Alternatively, pot singly in John Innes potting compost No. 1 or equivalent and grow on in an unheated greenhouse. Water freely. Shade from strong direct sunshine. Discard after flowering. For pot culture in a cool greenhouse, minimum temp. 7°C., seeds can also be sown in late summer and treated as above to give plants which will flower in winter.

Recommended kinds are *N. strumosa*, all colours except blue, summer, 1 to 2 ft.; *versicolor*, blue, lilac, yellow, white, summer, 6 to 12 in. Races of hybrids between these two species are listed as *compacta grandiflora*, *suttonii*, etc., and include all colours, plus larger flowers and more compact habit, 8 to 12 in.

NEMOPHILA – *Hydrophyllaceae*. Hardy prostrate annuals with small flowers very freely produced. Sow seeds where plants are to flower in ordinary well-drained but not dry soil in a cool semi-shady or sunny place, in spring to flower in summer and, in mild places, in late summer or early autumn to flower in spring. Thin seedlings to 3 in. Water freely in dry weather. Discard after flowering.

The best kind is *N. menziesii* (syn. *insignis*), Baby Blue-eyes, white or blue, summer, spreading, California.

NEOREGELIA – *Bromeliaceae*. Tender evergreen plants making rosettes of stiff leaves often brilliantly coloured around the central 'vase'. Formerly known as aregelia.

Compost, equal parts peat, osmunda fibre and coarse sand. Position, well-drained pots in an intermediate or warm greenhouse, minimum winter temp. 13°C., or in a warm room. Pot in spring. Water normally and keep the 'vase' in the centre of each rosette constantly filled with water. Shade from direct sunshine and maintain a humid atmosphere.

Increase by removing offsets in spring and rooting them in a warm propagator.

Recommended kinds are *N. carolinae*, blue, summer, central leaves bright red, Brazil, and var. *tricolor*, leaves striped cream and pink; *cyanea*, violet, summer, leaves grey-green, Brazil; *marechati*, violet, summer, central leaves crimson, Brazil; *spectabilis*, blue, summer, leaves green above, red tipped and banded in shades of grey beneath, Brazil.

NEPENTHES (Pitcher Plant) – *Nepenthaceae*. Tender evergreen sub-shrubby perennials grown for their foliage, which is variously mottled with red, brown and crimson, terminating in a pitcher-like appendage in which insects are trapped.

Compost, two parts peat, and one part chopped live sphagnum moss. Position, hanging baskets in a warm greenhouse, minimum winter temp. 18°C. Plant in early spring. Water freely from spring to mid-autumn, moderately the rest of the year. Shade from direct sunshine throughout the year and maintain a very humid atmosphere.

Increase by seeds sown on the surface of a mixture of fibrous peat and sphagnum moss in well-drained pans in a warm propagator, temp. 26 to 30°C., in spring; by cuttings of one-year-old shoots in spring or summer inserted singly in small pots filled with peat and sphagnum moss and placed in a warm propagator as for seeds.

Recommended kinds with colours of pitchers are *N. albomarginata*, green, dull red and white, Singapore; *distillatoria*, green and red fringed, Ceylon; *gracilis*, green, purple spotted, Malaysia; *hookeriana*, pale green and red, Borneo; *khasiana*, green or purplish, India; *maxima* (syn. *curtisii*), green, crimson, and purple, Borneo; *mirabilis*, green, S.E. Asia; *rafflesiana*, greenish yellow and brown, India; *sanguinea*, blood red, Malaysia; *veitchii*, green, Borneo; *ventricosa*, green, brown, and crimson, Philippines. There are numerous hybrids between these species.

NEPETA – *Labiatae*. Hardy herbaceous perennials with lavender-like flowers and grey leaves. The plant most commonly cultivated in gardens as *N. mussinii* is in reality a hybrid, *N. faassenii*. The flowers are on longer spikes than in the true species.

Soil, ordinary, well drained, not too rich; good on chalk and limestone. Position, sunny. Plant in spring.

Increase by division in spring; by cuttings in a frame in spring or summer; by seed sown outdoors or in a frame in spring or early summer.

Recommended kinds are *N. cataria*, Catmint, white, purple spotted, summer, to 3 ft., Europe (Britain); *faassenii*, lavender-blue, summer, 1 ft., hybrid between *mussinii* and *nepetella*; *grandiflora*, lavender-blue, summer, 1½ to 2 ft., Caucasus, and var. Souvenir d'Andre Chaudron (syn. Blue Beauty), larger flowers; *mussinii*, lavender-blue, summer, 2 to 3 ft., Caucasus, Iran; *nepetella*, white or pink to violet, very variable, summer, 1 to 2½ ft., S.W. Europe; *nervosa*, violet-blue, summer, 1 to 2 ft., Kashmir.

NEPHROLEPIS (Sword Fern, Ladder Fern) – *Oleandraceae*. Evergreen ferns. Fronds long, narrow, pinnate, but the pinnae sometimes cut into fine, almost moss-like segments.

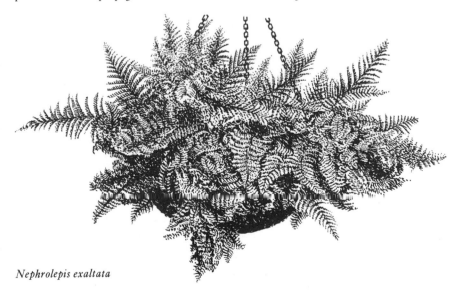

Nephrolepis exaltata

Compost, equal parts of loam and coarse sand, two parts of peat or leafmould. Position, in baskets suspended from the roof, or in well-drained pots or beds in an intermediate or warm greenhouse, minimum winter temp. 13°C., or in warm rooms. Pot or plant in spring. Water normally. Shade from direct sunshine at all times and maintain a fairly moist atmosphere.

Increase by spores sown on the surface of pans of sandy peat in a warm propagator at any time; by division in spring; or by pegging down creeping stems bearing young plants and removing these when rooted.

Recommended kinds are *N. acuminata* (syn. *davallioides*), 2 to 3 ft., Malaysia; *biserrata* (syn. *acuta*), 2 to 4 ft., Tropics; *cordifolia* (syn. *tuberosa*), 1 to 2 ft., Tropics and sub-tropics, and numerous varieties; *exaltata*, Ladder Fern, 2 to 3 ft., Tropics, and many fine crested and plumose varieties.

NERINE

NERINE – *Amaryllidaceae*. Variously tender bulbous plants, natives of S. Africa, with flowers borne in clusters on bare stems in late summer or autumn. Sometimes known as Diamond Lilies.

Pot culture: Pot bulbs in early autumn, one in each 4- or 5-in. pot in a porous compost such as John Innes potting compost No. 1, and covering the bulbs to only two-thirds of their depth. Grow in a sunny, frost-proof greenhouse. Water moderately at first, fairly freely while plants are in growth during winter and spring but keep quite dry when leaves die down in early summer, and stand pots in the warmest, sunniest part of the house to ripen the bulbs. Do not repot until bulbs are very crowded. Start to water again when flower spikes appear in late summer or autumn.

Nerine bowdenii

Outdoor culture: Soil, light, sandy. Position, warm, sunny, well drained. Plant in late summer or early autumn only just covering the bulbs. In cold places protect in winter with dry litter or handlights. Only replant when really overcrowded.

Increase by offsets, removed when repotting and treated as old bulbs; by seeds sown in sandy soil in a frame or cool greenhouse in spring or as soon as ripe.

Recommended kinds are *N. angustifolia*, deep pink, 1½ to 2 ft.; *appendiculata*, pale pink, 1 to 2 ft.; *bowdenii*, rose-pink, 1½ to 2 ft., the hardiest kind, and vars. *alba*, white, Fenwick's Variety, 2 to 2½ ft., deep rose; *filifolia*, rose, 9 to 18 in.; *flexuosa*, pale pink, 2 ft., and var. *alba*, white; *humilis*, rose-pink, 6 to 15 in.; *masonorum*, pale pink, 9 in.; *sarniensis*, Guernsey Lily, pink, rose, scarlet or crimson, 9 to 15 in., and vars. *corusca major*, *curvifolia* and *fothergillii*, all scarlet; *undulata*, rose, 9 to 18 in. There are also numerous hybrids between *bowdenii*, *flexuosa*, *humilis*, *sarniensis* and *undulata*, with a colour range from white and palest pink to red, crimson and purple.

NERIUM – *Apocynaceae*. Rather tender evergreen flowering shrubs. All parts of the plants are poisonous.

Nerium oleander

Soil, ordinary loamy, well drained. Position, sunny, warm, sheltered or in pots or tubs in a sunny frost-proof greenhouse or conservatory. Water freely from spring to autumn, very sparingly in winter. Prune after flowering, shortening the flowering stems as much as necessary to keep plants within bounds.

Increase by cuttings of firm young shoots in a propagator in spring or summer.

The best kind is *N. oleander*, Oleander or Rose Bay, white, cream, pink, red or purple, summer, to 20 ft., Orient, and numerous varieties, many with double flowers.

NERTERA – *Rubiaceae*. Rather tender creeping perennial herb with orange berries.

Compost, John Innes potting compost No. 1 or equivalent. Position, pots in a frost-proof greenhouse or outdoors in moist soil and shady places in nearly frost-free districts. Can be used for carpet bedding in summer and returned to the greenhouse in autumn. Pot in spring. Water normally. Shade from direct sunshine in spring and summer.

Increase by seeds sown in light soil in temp. 15 to 18°C. in spring; by division in spring.

The best kind is *N. granadensis* (syn. *depressa*), Bead Plant, Fruiting Duckweed, 1 in., flowers green, S. America, Australasia.

NICANDRA – *Solanaceae*. Hardy annual with bell-shaped lavender-blue flowers believed by some to keep off flies and some other insects.

Soil, ordinary. Position, sunny. Sow in spring where plants are to flower and either thin or transplant seedlings to 1 ft. apart. Discard after flowering.

The only species is *N. physalodes*, Apple of Peru, Shoo Fly Plant, blue, summer, 2 to 4 ft., Peru.

NICOTIANA (Tobacco Plant) – *Solanaceae*. Slightly tender annuals or perennials with funnel-shaped flowers. *N. tabacum* is the tobacco of commerce.

Soil, ordinary. Position, sunny or semi-shady. Sow in spring in temp. 15 to 18°C. and harden off seedlings for planting outdoors in late spring or early summer. In fairly frost-free places *N. alata* may live for several years but normally these plants are best treated as annuals and discarded after flowering. The leaves of *N. tabacum* should be gathered for drying as they become full grown.

Recommended kinds are *N. alata* (syn. *affinis*), Sweet-scented Tobacco, white, fragrant, summer, 3 to 5 ft., Brazil, and var. *grandiflora*, larger flowers; *forgetiana*, rose, summer, 2 to 3 ft., Brazil; *langsdorffii*, green or lime green, summer, opening by day even in poor light, to 5 ft., Brazil; *sanderae*, red, pink, carmine, etc., summer, 2 to 3 ft., hybrid between *alata* and *forgetiana*; *sylvestris*, white, summer, opening by day even in poor light, 3 to 4 ft., Argentina; *tabacum*, Tobacco Plant, rose, summer, 4 ft., S. America, var. *macrophylla* (syn. *N. macrophylla*), red, rose, or purple, summer; *tomentosa* (syn. *colossea*), pale green and yellow, tinged red, 10 to 20 ft., Brazil. Hybrid races have also been produced

Nicotiana alata

between *alata* and *langsdorffii* to produce varieties that will open their flowers in dull weather.

NIDULARIUM – *Bromeliaceae*. Tender evergreen plants with green, red or crimson bracts, and leaves in dense basal rosettes.

Compost, equal parts of peat, osmunda fibre and sand. Position, the smallest pots that will contain the plants placed in an intermediate or warm greenhouse, minimum winter temp. 13°C., or in a warm room. Pot in spring. Water normally and keep the hollow in the centre of the leaf rosette (the vase) constantly filled with water. Shade from direct sunshine and maintain a humid atmosphere.

Increase by largish offshoots inserted singly in small pots of sandy peat in temp. 26 to 28°C. in spring.

Recommended kinds are *N. fulgens*, white and violet, central leaves scarlet, 9 to 12 in., Brazil; *innocentii*, white, leaves tinted brown or red, central leaves crimson, Brazil; *purpureum*, red leaves flushed purple-brown, Brazil; *rutilans*, vermilion, leaves spotted dark green, Brazil; *striatum*, white, leaves white striped, central leaves red, to 1 ft., Brazil.

NIEREMBERGIA (Cup Flower) – *Solanaceae*. Hardy or slightly tender herbaceous perennials with open bell-shaped flowers.

Soil, equal parts loam, leafmould, peat and sharp sand. Position, warm, sunny, moist in summer but not too wet in winter. Plant in spring. Water freely in dry weather. Protect in very severe weather with a covering of litter. May also be grown in well-drained pots or pans in a frame or unheated greenhouse, watered freely in spring and summer, sparingly at other times. *N. coerulea* is often grown as a half-hardy annual, sown in temp. 13 to 15°C. in early spring, planted out when there is no further risk of frost and discarded after flowering.

Increase by seeds sown in sandy soil in temp. 13 to 15°C. in spring; by cuttings inserted in sandy soil in a shaded propagator in summer.

Recommended kinds are *N. coerulea* (syn. *hippomanica*), violet-blue, summer, early autumn, 9 in., Patagonia; *repens* (syn. *rivularis*), white and cream or pink, summer, prostrate, Argentina, Chile, Uruguay.

NIGELLA (Fennel Flower) – *Ranunculaceae*. Hardy annuals with cornflower-like flowers surrounded by a green lacy involucre. Foliage feathery.

Soil, ordinary. Position, sunny. Sow in spring or early autumn where plants are to flower and thin seedlings to 6 in. Discard after flowering.

Recommended kinds are *N. damascena*, Love-in-a-mist, Devil-in-a-bush, blue, summer, 1 to 2 ft., S. Europe, and vars. *alba*, white, *flore pleno*, double, Persian

Rose, old rose; *hispanica*, Fennel Flower, blue, summer, 1 to 2 ft., Spain, and var. *alba*, white.

NOLANA (Chilean Bell Flower) – *Nolanaceae*. Hardy annuals or perennials with bell-shaped flowers.

Soil, ordinary, reasonably fertile. Position, open, sunny. Sow in spring in temp. 15 to 18°C. and harden off seedlings for planting outdoors in late spring or early summer. Alternatively they may be grown in pots or hanging baskets in John Innes potting compost No. 2 or equivalent.

Nolana acuminata

Recommended kinds are *N. acuminata* (syn. *lanceolata*), sky blue, cream spotted, summer, 4 to 12 in., Peru; *paradoxa* (syn. *atriplicifolia*), Chilean Bell Flower, blue and yellow, 4 to 12 in., Chile.

NOMOCHARIS – *Liliaceae*. Hardy bulbous plants, sometimes included in *Lilium*. Flowers usually saucer shaped.

Soil, well-drained, lime-free loam with leafmould or peat added. Position, sun or half-shade, moist in spring and summer yet porous and well drained in winter.

Increase by seeds sown in peat and sand as soon as ripe or in spring in a frame or cool greenhouse and the seedlings transplanted

Nomocharis mairei

individually to small pots in a compost of lime-free loam, peat and sand soon after germination, or grown in deep seed pans and planted outdoors, without breaking up the soil block, the next spring or the spring following.

Recommended kinds are *N. aperta*, rose blotched with crimson, summer, 1 to 3 ft., W. China, Tibet; *farreri*, white with crimson spots, summer, 2 to 3 ft., Burma; *mairei*, white, usually spotted with red-purple, summer, 2 to 2½ ft., W. China, and var. *candida*, white; *pardanthina*, pink with crimson spots, summer, 2 to 3 ft., W. China; *saluenensis*, white or pale rose, purple spotted, 2 to 3 ft., W. China, Tibet, Burma.

NOTHOFAGUS (Southern Beech) – *Fagaceae*. Hardy or slightly tender evergreen or deciduous trees.

Soil, lime-free, rather moist but not poorly drained loam. Position, sunny or lightly shaded but sheltered from strong wind. Plant deciduous species in autumn or late winter, evergreen species in spring or autumn. Increase by layering in spring; by cuttings of firm young growth in a propagator in summer; by seeds sown in sand, peat and loam as soon as ripe or in spring.

Recommended deciduous kinds are *N. antarctica*, Antarctic Beech, 40 to 60 ft., Chile; *obliqua*, Robel Beech, 50 to 100 ft., Chile; *procera*, 60 to 100 ft., Chile.

Recommended evergreen kinds are *N. betuloides*, 40 to 60 ft., Chile; *cliffortioides*, Mountain Beech, 30 to 50 ft., New Zealand; *cunninghamii*, 20 to 40 ft., tender, Tasmania; *fusca*, Red Beech, 30 to 50 ft., New Zealand; *menziesii*, 30 to 50 ft., tender, New Zealand; *moorei*, Australian Beech, tinted young foliage, 30 to 50 ft., tender, Australia; *solandri*, Black Beech, 40 to 60 ft., New Zealand.

NOTHOLIRION – *Liliaceae*. Hardy bulbous plants with lily-like flowers and sometimes included in *Lilium*.

Soil, well-drained lime-free loam with peat or leafmould. Position, sheltered, cool, in half-shade, or in an almost unheated greenhouse with frost protection while the plants are making their growth in winter. Plant in autumn. In some species bulbs die after flowering but should first produce bulbils to continue in later years.

Increase by seeds sown in loam, peat and sand in a frame or cool greenhouse as soon as ripe or in spring; by bulbils formed round the base of the flower stems, these being separated and planted apart after flowering.

Recommended kinds are *N. bulbiferum* (syn. *hyacinthinum*), lilac and green, late summer, 3 to 5 ft., W. China, Tibet; *campanulatum*, crimson, early summer, 3 to 4 ft., N. Burma, Tibet, W. China; *macrophyllum*, pale mauve or lavender, late spring, early summer, 7 to 12 in., Himalaya; *thomsonianum*, pale mauve, spring, 2 to 4 ft., Himalaya, Afghanistan.

NOTHOPANAX – *Araliaceae*. Slightly tender, fast-growing evergreen shrubs with large palmate leaves. Sometimes included in *Pseudopanax*.

Soil, ordinary, well drained. Position, sheltered borders in nearly frost-free localities, or in pots, tubs or beds in a frost-proof greenhouse.

Increase by seeds sown in sandy soil in a frame as soon as ripe.

The recommended kind is *N. arboreum*, 15 ft., New Zealand.

NOTOSPARTIUM – *Leguminosae*. Slightly tender evergreen flowering shrubs closely resembling the brooms, to which they are related.

Soil, light well-drained loam. Position, sunny, sheltered, will survive temperatures around −10°C. Plant in spring, preferably from containers to avoid root breakage. Prune after flowering, thinning out weak wood only.

Increase by seeds sown in sandy soil in a frame in spring; by cuttings of firm young growth in a propagator in summer.

The best kind is *N. carmichaeliae*, New Zealand Broom, pink, summer, 4 to 10 ft., New Zealand.

NUPHAR (Yellow Water Lily) – *Nymphaeaceae*. Hardy aquatic perennials with floating and submerged leaves and cup-shaped or globular flowers.

Soil, strong rich loam. Position, sunny, or semi-shady but flowers are most freely produced in light places. Depth of water, 6 to 12 in.; plants will live in 4 to 6 ft. of water, but rarely bloom in such depths. Plant firmly in a basket in spring and drop into position.

Increase by division in spring.

Recommended kinds are *N. advena*, Spatterdock, Cow Lily, yellow, late spring till early autumn, Eastern U.S.A., var. *variegata*, variegated leaves, purplish yellow flowers; *intermedia*, yellow, summer, Europe, believed to be a natural hybrid between *lutea* and *pumila*; *japonica*, yellow, arrow-shaped leaves above and crimped ones below water, still water, summer, Japan, var. *rubrotincta*, orange-scarlet, reddish stamens; *lutea*, Brandy Bottle, yellow, summer, early autumn, Europe (Britain); *pumila* (syn. *minima*), yellow, summer, for shallow water, Europe (Britain); *polysepala*, yellow, summer, North-western U.S.A.

NYMPHAEA (Water Lily) – *Nymphaeaceae*. Tender and hardy aquatic tuberous-rooted perennials with floating leaves and large showy flowers.

Culture of tender species: Soil, rich turfy loam plus 4 oz. bonemeal per bushel. Position, large pots or baskets immersed 8 to 12 in. below the surface of the water in tanks fully exposed to light. Plant in spring. Temperature of the atmosphere, 18 to 24°C. spring to early autumn, 10 to 16°C. late autumn and winter. Temperature of the water 18 to 24°C. spring to autumn. Repot annually in early spring. Reduce the depth of water as soon as the foliage dies off and leave tubers in the mud all the winter. Alternatively, lift tubers in late autumn and store in moist sand in temp. 13 to 18°C. until spring; beware of rats during this period.

Culture of hardy species: Soil as for tender species. Depth of water 1½ to 2 ft. for strong-growing kinds, 1 to 1½ ft. for medium kinds, and 4 to 8 in. for the pygmies. Position, open sunny ponds or lakes. Plant in late spring. Methods of planting: (1) Place the plant in a plastic basket containing above compost and lower to the bottom of the pool. (2) Spread compost 4 in. deep over the floor of the emptied pool with ½ in. of gravel above it and plant direct into this. Run water in very gradually and at intervals as the plants grow.

Increase all kinds by division in spring; by seeds sown in loam and crushed charcoal in pans kept constantly wet, in a cool greenhouse or frame for hardy kinds, temp. 18 to 24°C. for tender kinds.

Recommended hardy kinds are *N. alba*, Common Water Lily, white, summer, Europe (Britain), and var. *rubra*, pink becoming red; *candida*, white, N. Europe; *caroliniana*, pink, scented, summer, hybrid between *odorata rosea* and *tuberosa*; *gladstoniana*, white, hybrid between *alba* and *odorata rosea*; *laydekeri*, rose, purplish, hybrid between *alba rubra* and (probably) *tetragona*, many named forms, series of hybrids of different parentage raised in France; *marliacea*, hybrids of mixed parentage, many named forms, *albida*, white, *carnea*, pink, *chromatella*, yellow, *ignea*, carmine, etc., all summer flowering and raised in France; *odorata*, white, scented, summer, N. America, and vars. *rosea*, pink, *sulphurea*, yellow; *pygmaea alba*, white, summer, origin uncertain, may be var. of *candida*; *pygmaea helvola*, primrose, summer, hybrid between *flava* and *tetragona*; *tetragona*, white, summer, America, Asia, Australia; *tuberosa*, white, summer, N. America, and var. *rosea*, pink. There are also many garden varieties raised by interbreeding these and other species.

Recommended tender kinds are *N. ampla*, white, summer, Central America; *burtii*, primrose, summer, Tanzania; *caerulea*, Blue Lotus of the Nile, sky blue, summer, N. and Central Africa; *capensis*, sky blue, scented, S. and E. Africa, Madagascar, and var. *zanzibariensis*, Royal Purple Water Lily, dark blue; *dentata*, white, summer, Sierra Leone; *flavo-virens*, greenish white, scented, Mexico; *gigantea*, sky blue, summer, Australia; *lotus*, White Lotus of the Nile, white, night blooming, scented, summer, Tropics of the Old World; *micrantha*, viviparous, bluish white, summer, W. Africa; *polychroma*, blue, early summer, Tanzania; *rubra*, foliage bronze, flowers bright red, nocturnal, summer, India.

NYMPHOIDES (Floating Heart, Bean Lily) – *Menyanthaceae*. Hardy and tender floating perennial aquatics. Formerly known as limnanthemum.

Soil, good rich loam. Position, ponds, pools or tanks, hardy kinds out of doors, tender kinds in a cool greenhouse, minimum temp. 7°C. Plant in spring in large pots or baskets sunk in position.

Nymphoides indica

Increase by seeds sown in pots of light soil immersed in water in spring in an unheated frame or greenhouse for hardy kinds, temp. 15 to 18°C. for tender kinds; or by division of the plants in spring; hardy species by seeds sown in mud in spring or by division of roots in spring.

Recommended kinds are *N. aquatica* (syns. *Villarsia aquatica*, *Limnanthemum lacunosum*, *L. trachyspermum*), Fairy Water Lily, white, summer, Eastern N. America; *cordata* (syn. *Villarsia cordata*), Floating Heart, white, late summer, Eastern N. America; *indica*, Water Snowflake, white and yellow, summer, tender, Tropics, N. Australia; *peltata* (syns. *Limnanthemum nymphoides*, *L. peltatum*, *Villarsia peltata*), Water Fringe, yellow, late summer, early autumn, Europe (Britain). Asia.

NYSSA – *Nyssaceae*. Hardy deciduous trees. Grown for the beauty of their richly coloured autumn foliage.

Soil, good, rather moist, lime-free loam. Position, open, sunny. Plant in autumn or late winter, preferably from containers or as very young plants to avoid root breakage.

Increase by layering in autumn; by seeds stratified as soon as ripe for three months at 4°C. and then sown in peat, sand and loam outdoors or under glass.

Recommended kinds are *N. sinensis*, Chinese Sour Gum, 20 to 60 ft., China; *sylvatica*, Tupelo, 30 to 90 ft., N. America.

x ODONTIODA – *Orchidaceae*. Tender epiphytic orchids, bigeneric hybrids between *Cochlioda* and *Odontoglossum*.

Culture as for the odontoglossums of the *O. crispum* type.

ODONTOGLOSSUM – *Orchidaceae*. Tender epiphytic orchids so popular that often a house is devoted to them. Many hybrids, now outnumbering the species, have been produced. Spikes from the base of the leading pseudobulbs may be few or many flowered, usually simple, sometimes branched. All have beautiful flowers.

Compost, two parts fibre and three parts sphagnum moss. Position, well-drained pots in a greenhouse with an equable temp. 11 to 18°C., with shade from direct sunlight at all times and a moist atmosphere.

Watering is required throughout the year but in reduced amounts in cold weather. This treatment suits *O. crispum* and most hybrids but the harder-bulbed kinds e.g. *O. grande*, *citrosmum*, need different treatment though they may be grown in the same house. They should be placed near the glass and, if they are matured by late autumn, should be watered only once or twice, if at all, from mid-autumn until late winter.

Repot the majority of species in spring as growth is seen. Hybrids may be at slight variance with this season, but never pot in winter.

Odontoglossum crispum

Increase by division of plants when potting. Each division should have four bulbs and a growth evident or incipient. Sound back bulbs may be removed singly or in twos, laid on a rather shady part of a shingle-covered stage, or placed in pans or shallow boxes filled with small pieces of broken pot and kept damp till growth is seen, then pot using a very small pot.

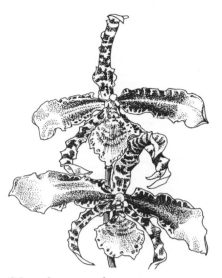

Odontoglossum grande

Recommended kinds are *O. bictoniense*, yellowish green blotched chestnut brown, lip rose, autumn, winter, 2 to 3 ft., Guatemala, Mexico, and numerous varieties; *cervantesii*, white or rosy, basal halves with concentric chocolate-red bars, autumn, semi-pendent, Mexico, Guatemala; *cirrhosum*, white spotted purplish crimson, spring, pendent, Ecuador, var. *hrubyanum*, white faintly spotted; *citrosmum*, white and rose, spring to summer, pendulous, Mexico; *cordatum*, yellow and chestnut brown, lip white brown spotted, spring, 12 to 15 in., Mexico, Guatemala; *crispum*, white or rose tinged or blotched red, variable flowering season, 1½ to 2 ft., Colombia, and many varieties; *grande*, yellow and chestnut brown, lip whitish with reddish spots, autumn, winter, 9 in., Guatemala, var. *aureum*, light and dark yellow; *hallii*, yellow, brown spotted, spring, 2 to 4 ft., Ecuador; *insleayi*, yellow and brown, autumn, winter, 1 ft., Mexico; *laeve*, yellowish green, brown white and purple, scented, spring, 2 to 3 ft., Mexico, Guatemala; *nobile* (syn. *pescatorei*), white or rose flushed, often purple spotted, spring, 1 to 2 ft., Colombia, many varieties; *pulchellum*, white and yellow, spring, fragrant, 1 ft., Mexico, Guatemala; *rossii*, white or rose flushed, spotted brown, very variable, autumn, 1 ft., Mexico; *schlieperianum*, yellow, barred brown, summer to autumn, 9 in., Costa Rica; *uroskinneri*, greenish, chestnut brown, lip rose marbled white, autumn, 2 to 3 ft., Guatemala.

x ODONTONIA – *Orchidaceae*. Tender epiphytic orchids, bigeneric hybrids between *Odontoglossum* and *Miltonia*. Culture as for odontoglossum.

OENOTHERA – *Onagraceae*. Hardy biennials and herbaceous perennials grown for their showy flowers.

Culture of biennial species: Soil, ordinary, well drained. Position, sunny for most kinds but *O. biennis* will succeed in semi-shade. Sow seeds outdoors in late spring or early summer, transplanting seedlings 4 in. apart into a nursery bed, transplanting again into flowering positions in early autumn or spring. *O. acaulis* and *trichocalyx* can be grown as annuals by sowing in early spring in temp. 15 to 18°C. and planting out in early summer.

Culture of perennial species: Soil, light sandy loam. Position, sunny, well drained. Plant in spring or autumn. Lift and replant *O. fruticosa* and *tetragona* every two or three years. Leave others undisturbed. Most are naturally short lived and may have to be renewed by seed every few years.

Increase perennial species by seeds sown as for biennial species; by cuttings of young shoots inserted in a shady propagator or frame in spring or summer; by division in spring.

Recommended biennial kinds are *O. biennis*, Evening Primrose, pale yellow, fragrant, summer, early autumn, 2 to 4 ft., Eastern N. America; *erythrosepala* (syn. *lamarckiana*), yellow, summer, autumn, 2 to 4 ft., habitat uncertain probably N. America; *grandiflora* (syn. *biennis grandiflora*), yellow, summer, 2 to 4 ft., N. America; *stricta* (syn. *odorata*), yellow becoming red, summer, early autumn, 2 to 4 ft., Chile.

Oenothera glaber

Recommended perennial kinds are *O. acaulis* (syn. *taraxacifolia*), white becoming blush, summer, 1 in., Chile; *caespitosa*, white becoming pink, fragrant, late spring, summer, 1 to 2 in., Central U.S.A.; *fruticosa*, Sun-drops, golden yellow, summer, 2 to 3 ft., U.S.A.; *glaber*, yellow, summer, bronze leaves, 15 to 18 in., origin uncertain; *missouriensis* (syn. *macrocarpa*), yellow, summer, trailing, S. Central U.S.A.; *perennis* (syn. *pumila*), yellow, summer, 9 to 18 in., Eastern N. America; *speciosa*, white becoming pink, summer, 1 to 2 ft., S. Central U.S.A., Mexico; *tetragona* (syns. *riparia*, *youngii*), lemon yellow, summer, 1 to 3 ft., Eastern N. America, and vars. *fraseri*, larger flowers, *fyrverkeri* (syn. Fireworks), red buds, yellow flowers, 1½ ft.

OLEA – *Oleaceae*. Slightly tender evergreen flowering trees and shrubs. Fruiting in warm climates.

Soil, ordinary, well drained. Position, sheltered, sunny, warm or trained against a sunny wall. Plant in spring or autumn. Prune as necessary in spring, cutting back badly placed growths, especially on trained trees. Olives will usually grow again even if cut back to within a foot or so of ground level in spring. Protect in very severe weather with litter or mats.

Increase by seeds sown in sandy peat in spring in temp. 18 to 21°C.; by cuttings of firm young growth inserted in sandy soil in a propagator in summer.

The best species is *O. europaea*, Olive, white, fragrant, late summer, 15 to 25 ft., Asia Minor, Syria.

See Osmanthus for *Olea fragrans*.

OLEARIA (Daisy Bush, Tree Daisy) – *Compositae*. Hardy and slightly tender evergreen flowering shrubs from Australia and New Zealand with small daisy flowers usually very freely produced.

Increase by cuttings of firm young shoots inserted in sandy soil in a propagator in summer.

Recommended kinds are *O. avicennifolia*, white, late summer, early autumn, scented, 10 to 15 ft., New Zealand; *forsteri* (syn. *paniculata*), white, autumn, scented, 10 to 20 ft., New Zealand; *gunniana*, (syn. *phlogopappa*), white, late spring, 4 to 5 ft., Tasmania, Australia; *haastii*, white, late summer, 6 to 8 ft., one of the hardiest, New Zealand; *ilicifolia*, Mountain Holly, white, summer, 6 to 10 ft., fairly hardy, New Zealand; *lyrata*, white, late spring, 8 to 10 ft., Tasmania; *macrodonta*, New Zealand Holly, white, summer, good maritime screen, 15 ft., New Zealand; *nummularifolia*, curious round yellowish leaves, white, summer, scented, 5 ft., New Zealand; *scilloniensis*, white, late spring, 5 to 7 ft., hybrid between *lyrata* and *gunniana*; *semidentata*, mauve, early summer, 5 to 8 ft., New Zealand; *stellulata*, white, late spring, 6 ft., Tasmania, var. *splendens*, mauve to rose-pink; *traversii*, white but insignificant, summer, 15 to 20 ft., Chatham Isles, rather tender but an excellent windbreak in mild maritime districts.

OMPHALODES (Navelwort) – *Boraginaceae*. Hardy annual and perennial herbs with forget-me-not-type flowers.

Culture of annual species: Soil, ordinary. Position, sunny. Sow seeds where required to grow in spring to flower in summer, or in early autumn to flower in spring.

Culture of perennial species: Soil, ordinary, rich, moist. Position, partially shaded, well-drained. Plant in spring or autumn. Water freely in dry weather.

Increase by seeds sown in a semi-shaded position in spring, transplanting seedlings when 1 in. high; by division of roots in spring.

The best annual kind is *O. linifolia*, Venus's Navelwort, white, spring, summer, 9 to 12 in., S. W. Europe.

Recommended perennial kinds are *O. cappadocica*, blue, spring, early summer, 9 in., S. Europe; *lojkae*, blue, spring, 6 in., Caucasus; *luciliae*, Rock Forget-me-not, blue, summer, 6 in., Asia Minor; *verna*, Creeping Forget-me-not, Blue-eyed Mary, blue, spring, 6 in., Europe, and var. *alba*, white.

ONCIDIUM – *Orchidaceae*. Tender epiphytal orchids, many kinds with rather small flowers borne in large sprays or clusters, though a few have much larger flowers, 4 to 5 in. in diameter. Yellow mottled with brown is the most usual colour scheme.

Oncidium varicosum

With such a varied group the needs of individual kinds must be studied. Compost for all as for odontoglossum, the dwarf-growing kinds placed in pans, the larger in pots. Drainage must be ample, from one-eighth to one-quarter of the pot in depth. Species with hard leaves and/or pseudobulbs must have a decided rest, *O. splendidum* at least two months, but pseudobulbs must not be allowed to shrivel; the cool house species may require a few soakings during the winter. Kinds suited to the warm or intermediate house treated as for odontoglossum but with fewer winter waterings. All when in vigorous growth need frequent watering and the cool house species in particular should be exposed to full light in autumn. Repot in late winter or early spring.

Increase by division of plants in spring. Pseudobulbs can be separated as suggested for odontoglossums, cymbidiums, etc., but do not respond as readily. A few species produce young plants on the flower spikes.

Recommended cool house kinds are *O. cheirophorum*, yellow, scented, autumn, winter, 2 ft., Colombia; *crispum*, red-brown and yellow, autumn, winter, 2 to 4 ft., Brazil; *forbesii*, red-brown and yellow, autumn, 1½ to 3 ft., Brazil; *incurvum*, white and purple, scented, autumn, 3 to 7 ft., Mexico; *macranthum*, yellow, brown and red, spring, early summer, 7 to 14 ft., Central America to Peru; *ornithorhynchum*, purplish pink, scented, autumn, winter, 1 to 1½ ft., Mexico.

Recommended warm or intermediate house kinds are *O. altissimum*, yellow and brown, late summer, autumn, 3 to 6 ft., Tropical America; *cavendishianum*, yellow, red spotted, scented, winter, spring, 2 to 3 ft., Guatemala; *cebolleta*, light yellow and brown, late summer, 1½ to 3 ft., Tropical America; *kramerianum*, red-brown and yellow, large flowers, all seasons, 2 to 3 ft., Central America; *marshallianum*, yellow and brown, large flowers, early summer, 3 to 5 ft.; *papilio*, Butterfly Orchid, red-brown and yellow, large flowers, all seasons, 2 to 4 ft.; *splendidum*, yellow and brown, winter, 2 to 3 ft., Guatemala; *tigrinum*, yellow and brown, winter, 2 to 3 ft., Peru, Brazil; *varicosum*, yellow and brown, autumn and winter, 4 to 5 ft., Brazil.

ONOCLEA – *Aspidiaceae*. Hardy deciduous fern. The barren fronds are broad, once divided and green; the fertile ones are narrow, contracted, once divided and brown.

Grow in two parts of good loam, one part leafmould or peat in a cool, semi-shaded, moist border or margin of a pond. Plant in spring.

Increase by spores sown on the surface of well-drained pans of sandy peat or leafmould, covered with glass and kept moderately moist in a shady position in a cold frame or greenhouse; by division of plants in spring.

The only kind is *O. sensibilis*, Sensitive Fern, 2 to 3 ft., N. America, N. Asia.

ONONIS (Rest-harrow) – *Leguminosae*. Hardy and deciduous shrubs and sub-shrubs.

Soil, ordinary. Position, warm, even dry borders and banks. Plant in autumn or late winter. Clip *O. fruticosa* with shears after flowering; cut back *O. rotundifolia* almost to ground level in late winter or early spring.

Increase by seeds sown in ordinary soil outdoors or under glass in spring.

Recommended kinds are *O. fruticosa*, rose-pink, summer, 2 to 3 ft., Europe;

rotundifolia, rose-pink, summer, 1½ ft., sub-shrub, Europe.

ONOPORDUM – *Compositae*. Hardy biennial or monocarpic plants with tall angularly branched grey stems, silver-grey leaves and purple thistle-like flowers in summer.

Increase by seeds sown in ordinary, well-drained soil in a sunny position outdoors in spring or early summer. Transplant seedlings in autumn where required to flower or thin to 2 to 3 ft. In porous soil plants will usually renew themselves by self-sown seedlings.

Recommended kinds are *O. acanthium*, Cotton Thistle, Scotch Thistle, 5 ft., Europe (Britain); *nervosum* (syn. *arabicum*), 8 to 10 ft., Spain, Portugal; *tauricum*, 6 ft., S. Europe.

ONOSMA (Golden Drop) – *Boraginaceae*. Hardy perennial herbs with tubular, pendent flowers.

Soil, two parts sandy loam, one part grit or small stones. Position, warm, sunny, crevices in rock gardens, dry walls, etc. Plant in spring.

Increase by cuttings in gritty soil in summer in a frame or propagator; by seeds sown in similar soil in spring or as soon as ripe in an unheated frame or greenhouse.

Recommended kinds are *O. albo-pilosum*, white and rose, summer, 9 in., Asia Minor; *cassium*, yellow, summer, 18 in., N. Syria; *echioides*, yellow, late spring, 6 to 12 in., S. Europe; *stellulatum*, yellow, early summer, 6 in., S. E. Europe; *tauricum* (syn. *stellulatum tauricum*), yellow, summer, 9 in., S. E. Europe.

OPHIOPOGON (Snake's Beard) – *Liliaceae*. Hardy or slightly tender evergreen perennial herbs with narrow leaves used as ground cover and for edging.

Soil, ordinary. Position, warm, sunny, sheltered. Plant in spring or autumn. Lift, divide and replant every four or five years.

Increase by division in spring.

Recommended kinds are *O. jaburan*, white, or mauve, summer, 1 ft., Japan, and vars. *aureus*, leaves striped yellow, and *variegatus*, leaves striped cream; *japonicus*, white flowers hidden among the 6- to 15-in. long, dense, grassy leaves, summer, Japan, and var. *variegatus*, leaves striped cream.

OPLISMENUS – *Gramineae*. Tender perennial trailing grass. Flowers insignificant. Leaves, variegated.

Compost, John Innes potting compost No. 1 or equivalent. Position, pots, hanging baskets or beds in an intermediate or warm greenhouse, or in a warm room. Pot or plant in spring. Water normally.

Increase by cuttings of young shoots inserted in a propagator in spring or summer; by division in spring.

The best kind is *O. hirtellus* (syn. *com-*

positus), Basket Grass, in its variegated vars. *albidus*, white and green, and *variegatus*, green, white and pink, trailing, West Indies.

OPUNTIA (Prickly Pear) – *Cactaceae*. Tender or hardy succulent plants, sometimes of tree-like size, some with flattened stems or 'pads' known collectively as 'tuna', some with cylindrical stems known as 'cholla', some with globular growth.

Compost, John Innes potting compost No. 2 or equivalent plus one-sixth its bulk of coarse sand. Position, pots or beds in a sunny, frost-proof greenhouse. Some can stand low temperatures provided growth is well ripened and the soil is dry. No shading required at any time. Water moderately in spring and summer, sparingly in autumn and winter. Pot or plant in spring. The hardier kinds can be grown outdoors in ordinary soil with plenty of sand and stone chippings to improve drainage and in a warm dry, sunny position.

Increase by seeds sown in sandy soil in temp. 15 to 18°C. in spring; by cuttings of portions of stems exposed for a few days, then inserted in small, well-drained pots of sandy soil in summer.

Recommended tender kinds are *O. bigelovii*, white and green, summer, 10 ft., California, Nevada, Arizona; *brasiliensis*, yellow, summer, 10 to 30 ft., Brazil; *cylindrica*, scarlet, summer, 4 to 6 ft., Peru, and var. *cristata*, crested; *diademata* (syn. *glomerata*), yellow, summer, Argentina; *imbricata*, purple, summer, 5 to 10 ft., South U.S.A., Mexico; *leucotricha*, yellow, summer, 12 to 15 ft., Mexico; *microdasys*, pale yellow, summer, 2 ft., Mexico, and *albispina*, white bristles, *pallida*, yellow bristles, *rufida*, red bristles; *salmiana*, pale yellow, summer, 1 to 3 ft., S. America.

Recommended hardy kinds are *O. cantabrigiensis*, yellow and red, summer, 3 ft., Mexico; *compressa*, yellow, summer, 1 ft., South-eastern U.S.A.; *macrorhiza*, yellow and red, summer, 1 ft., Southern U.S.A.; *polycantha*, (syn. *missouriensis*), yellow and red, summer, 6 in., N. America; *rhodantha*, carmine, summer, 1 ft., U.S.A.; *vulgaris*, Barbary Fig, yellow or reddish, summer, 1 to 20 ft., S. America.

ORCHIS – *Orchidaceae*. Hardy and tender terrestrial orchids with numerous small flowers in spikes.

Soil, loam with sufficient sand and peat or leafmould to ensure that it does not dry out rapidly in summer or become waterlogged in winter. Position, sunny or partially shady, moist in spring and summer. Plant in spring. Leave undisturbed as much as possible. Increase by careful division in spring.

Recommended kinds are *O. elata*, purple, late spring, early summer, 1½ to 2 ft., Algeria; *maderensis* (syn. *foliosa*), purple, 1 to 1½ ft., late spring, Madeira.

Orchis elata

ORIGANUM – *Labiatae*. Hardy or slightly tender perennial herbs or sub-shrubs cultivated for their aromatic foliage and attractive small purplish pink flowers borne in spikelets.

Soil, ordinary, well drained. Position, warm, sunny. Plant in spring.

Increase by seeds sown in a frame or greenhouse in spring; by cuttings in gritty soil in a frame or propagator in summer.

Recommended kinds are *O. dictamnus*, Cretan Dittany, pink, summer, 1 ft., slightly tender, Crete; *hybridum*, rosy purple, late summer, early autumn, 1 ft., Eastern Mediterranean; *laevigatum*, purple, late summer, 9 to 18 in., Turkey, Syria; *libanoticum*, pink, summer, 1 to 2 ft., Lebanon; *majorana*, Garden, Knotted or Sweet Marjoram, purple or white, early summer, 1 to 2 ft., N. Africa; *onites*, Sweet Marjoram, mauve-pink, summer, 1 ft., Mediterranean region; *vulgare aureum*, purple, summer, yellow leaves, 1 ft., garden form of European (British) wild plant.

ORNITHOGALUM – *Liliaceae*. Hardy and slightly tender bulbous plants with flowers in clusters or dense spikes on bare stems.

Outdoor culture: Soil, sandy. Position, sunny, warm and sheltered for slightly

Ornithogalum thyrsoides

tender kinds. Plant hardy kinds in autumn, and leave undisturbed until overcrowded. Plant slightly tender kinds in spring, lift in autumn and store dry in a cool but frost-proof place until the spring.

Indoor culture: Compost, John Innes potting compost No. 1 or equivalent. Position, pots in a sunny frost-proof greenhouse. Pot in autumn placing four or five bulbs in each 5-in. pot. Water sparingly at first, fairly freely when growth appears but reduce water supply after flowering and keep dry in a sunny place for a few weeks before repotting in autumn.

Increase by offsets removed from old bulbs; by seeds sown in John Innes seed compost or equivalent in a cool greenhouse as soon as ripe or in spring.

Recommended kinds are *O. arabicum*, white, fragrant, summer, 1 to 1½ ft., S. Europe; *lacteum*, white, summer, 1½ ft., slightly tender, S. Africa; *montanum*, white and green, spring, early summer, 1 to 1½ ft., S. Europe, Asia Minor; *nutans*, white and pale green, spring, 1 ft., Europe; *thyrsoides*, Chincherinchee, white, summer, 1½ ft., S. Africa, and vars. *aureum*, orange-yellow, *flavescens*, light yellow, and *flavissimum*, deep yellow; *umbellatum*, Star of Bethlehem, white, spring, 1 ft., Europe, Asia Minor.

ORONTIUM – *Araceae*. Hardy aquatic perennial with bluish-green leaves, floating in deep water, erect in shallow water. Small yellow flowers crowded in a narrow spadix.

Soil, good, loamy, deep. Position, ponds or slow-moving streams up to 1½ ft. deep. Plant in spring.

Increase by division of rootstock in spring; by seeds sown in spring in shallow pans kept constantly wet.

The only species is *O. aquaticum*, Golden Club, yellow, early summer, 1 to 1½ ft., N. America.

OSMANTHUS – *Oleaceae*. Hardy and slightly tender evergreen flowering shrubs.

Soil, ordinary, fertile. Position, sheltered, sunny borders or against sunny walls. *O. fragrans* in a sunny frost-proof green-

house. Plant in spring or autumn. Prune, when necessary, in spring, *O. delavayi* immediately after flowering but only for shortening or removal of overgrown branches. *O. heterophyllus* may be planted as a hedge and clipped closely each spring.

Increase by seeds sown in sandy peat in spring in temp. 15 to 18°C.; by cuttings of firm young shoots in sandy soil in a propagator in summer.

Recommended kinds are *O. americanus*, white, spring, scented, 15 to 30 ft., South-eastern U.S.A.; *armatus*, creamy white, autumn, scented, 8 to 15 ft., W. China; *delavayi* (syn. *Siphonosmanthus delavayi*), white, spring, very sweetly scented, 6 ft., China; *fortunei*, white, fragrant, autumn, 6 ft., hybrid; *forrestii*, large leaves, white, summer, scented, 15 ft., Japan; *fragrans* (syn. *Olea fragrans*), Fragrant Olive, white, summer, powerfully fragrant, 6 to 10 ft., China, Japan, will survive only a few degrees of frost; *heterophyllus* (syns. *aquifolium, ilicifolius*), white, autumn, scented, 10 to 20 ft., Japan and vars. *aureomarginatus*, leaves edged with yellow, *myrtifolius*, small leaves, compact habit, *variegatus*, leaves edged with cream.

x OSMAREA – *Oleaceae*. Hardy evergreen shrub. Bigeneric hybrid between *Osmanthus delavayi* and *Phillyrea decora*.

Soil, ordinary. Position, open or partially shaded borders, excellent for hot, dry soils. Makes a good screen or useful clipped hedge. Plant in spring or autumn. Clip when required in spring or early summer.

Increase by cuttings of firm young shoots in sandy soil in a frame in summer.

The only kind is *O. burkwoodii*, white, spring, fragrant, hardy, 6 to 10 ft.

OSMARONIA – *Rosaceae*. Hardy flowering shrub with fragrant flowers succeeded by purplish plum-like fruits. Previously known as nuttallia.

Soil, ordinary. Position, shady or sunny. Plant in autumn or late winter. Prune, when necessary, immediately after flowering.

Increase by seeds sown in ordinary soil in a shady position, outdoors in spring or autumn; by suckers removed from the parent plant in autumn or late winter; by cuttings of ripened shoots in a cold frame in autumn; by layering in autumn.

The only species is *O. cerasiformis*, Oso-berry, white, strongly almond scented, late winter, early spring, 6 to 10 ft., Western America.

OSMUNDA – *Osmundaceae*. Hardy deciduous ferns. Fronds, feather shaped, plain or crested; fertile portions contracted.

Soil, equal parts of lime-free loam, leafmould, and peat. Position, moist, sunny or shady margins of ponds, streams, bogs, etc. Plant in spring. Remove dead fronds in spring. Water plants growing elsewhere than

on the margins of ponds copiously in dry weather.

Increase by spores sown at any time on the surface of sandy peat and leafmould in well-drained pans. Cover with a sheet of glass or a handlight and keep in a shady part of a cool greenhouse. Also by offsets from established plants in spring.

Recommended kinds are *O. cinnamomea*, 2 to 4 ft., Eastern N. America, West Indies, Mexico, Brazil, E. Asia; *claytoniana*, 2 to 4 ft., N. America, Himalaya, China; *regalis*, Royal Fern, 3 to 6 ft., widespread in northern and southern hemispheres (Britain) and vars. *cristata*, crested, *gracilis*, more slender in growth.

OSTEOSPERMUM – *Compositae*. Slightly tender sub-shrubs and perennials with daisy-type flowers. All are natives of S. Africa and are closely allied to *Dimorphotheca*.

Soil, ordinary, well drained. Position, warm, sunny.

Increase by seeds sown in temp. 15 to 18°C. in early spring; seedlings being hardened off for planting outdoors in late spring or early summer; or sown outdoors in mid- to late spring where plants are to flower, seedlings being thinned to 8 in.; also by cuttings in sandy soil in a frame or propagator in summer.

Recommended kinds are *O. barberiae* (syns. *Dimorphotheca barberiae, D. lilacina*), lilac, summer, autumn, to 2 ft.; *ecklonis* (syn. *Dimorphotheca ecklonis*), white and violet, summer, 1 to 2 ft.

OSTROWSKIA (Giant Bell Flower) – *Campanulaceae*. Hardy herbaceous perennial with large bell-shaped flowers.

Soil, deep, sandy loam, with peat or leafmould to hold moisture in summer and improve drainage in winter. Position, warm, sheltered. Cover with a handlight after foliage has died down. Carrot-like roots penetrate the soil to a depth of 2 ft. Plant in spring. Do not disturb at any time. Plants are unlikely to be long lived and should be replaced as necessary by seedlings.

Increase by seeds sown in light soil in a frame or cool greenhouse in spring or as soon as ripe. Pot seedlings singly in John Innes seed compost or equivalent compost and grow on in pots without root disturbance until sufficiently large to be planted outdoors. Seedlings take several years to flower.

The only species is *O. magnifica*, mauve-lilac and white, summer, 4 to 5 ft., Turkestan.

OSTRYA – *Carpinaceae*. Hardy deciduous trees closely resembling hornbeam and with hop-like fruits in autumn.

Soil, ordinary, moist. Position, open. Plant in autumn.

Increase by seeds stored for four months at 4°C. and then sown outdoors in sandy soil; by grafting on the Hornbeam, *Carpinus betulus*, in spring.

Recommended kinds are *O. carpinifolia*, Hop Hornbeam, 50 to 60 ft., S. Europe, Asia Minor; *japonica*, 20 to 30 ft., Japan, China; *virginiana*, Iron-wood, 20 to 40 ft., Eastern N. America, Mexico.

OTHONNA (African Ragwort) – *Compositae*. Slightly tender trailing herb with grey-green, fleshy leaves and yellow, daisy-type flowers.

Compost, John Innes potting compost No. 1 or equivalent. Position, small well-drained pots or baskets suspended from the roof in a sunny greenhouse, minimum temp. 7°C., or in a warm, sunny place outdoors in summer. Pot in spring. Water freely spring to autumn, sparingly in winter. Full exposure to sun is essential.

Increase by cuttings of shoots inserted in sandy soil in a cool greenhouse or propagator in summer.

The best kind is *O. crassifolia*, yellow, summer, trailing, S. Africa.

OTHONNOPSIS – *Compositae*. Nearly hardy trailing perennial with fleshy grey leaves and yellow daisy flowers. Sometimes known as hertia.

Soil, sandy loam. Position, warm, sunny rock gardens, banks, etc. Protect in severe weather.

Increase by cuttings in summer in sandy soil in a frame or propagator.

The best kind is *O. cheirifolia*, yellow, late spring and summer, sprawling, N. Africa.

OURISIA – *Scrophulariaceae*. Hardy herbaceous perennials with tubular flowers.

Soil, equal parts loam, peat, leafmould and sharp sand. Position, semi-shady in a well-drained rock garden or raised bed or in pots or pans in a shady, freely ventilated frame or greenhouse. Pot or plant in spring. Water freely in summer but very little in winter.

Increase by division in spring; by seeds sown as soon as ripe in sand and peat in a frame or greenhouse.

Recommended kinds are *O. alpina*, pink, red and white, early summer, 6 in., Andes; *coccinea*, scarlet, late spring to early autumn, 9 in., Andes of Chile; *elegans*, commonly cultivated as *O. coccinea*, much more robust grower than the true *coccinea*, red, summer, 12 to 18 in., Chile; *macrophylla*, white, early summer, 9 in., New Zealand.

OXALIS (Wood Sorrel) – *Oxalidaceae*. Tender and hardy herbaceous perennials and fleshy rooted plants. Several species can be troublesome weeds.

Culture of tender species: Compost, porous, John Innes potting compost No. 1 or equivalent. Position, cool greenhouse or sunny window, minimum winter temp.

Oxalis enneaphylla

3 to 4°C. Pot in autumn, four or five 'bulbs' in a 4- or 5-in. pot. Water moderately till leaves appear, then freely. Apply liquid fertilizer occasionally when flowers form.

Gradually withhold water when flowers fade, and keep quite dry and cool till growth begins again. Repot annually.

Culture of hardy species: Soil, sandy loam. Position, sunny and warm for most kinds but cool, deep soil for *O. enneaphylla*, shady for *O. acetosella*. Plant *O. adenophylla* and *enneaphylla* in autumn, other species in spring.

Increase by seeds sown in light sandy soil in temp. 15 to 18°C. in spring; by division of roots or offsets at potting or planting time.

Recommended tender kinds are *O. cernua*, Bermuda Buttercup, yellow, spring, 6 in., S. Africa, nearly hardy, can be a troublesome weed outdoors in nearly frost-free places; *deppei*, rose-red, summer, 9 to 12 in., Mexico; *purpurata*, purple, summer, 9 to 12 in., Africa and var. *bowiei*, larger flowers.

Recommended hardy kinds are *O. acetosella*, Wood Sorrel, white, spring, 2 to 4 in., Europe (Britain), Asia, Japan, Eastern N. America, and var. *rosea*, pink veined; *adenophylla*, lilac-pink, late spring, summer, 3 in., Chile; *chrysantha*, yellow, summer, creeping, Brazil; *enneaphylla*, blush white, summer, 2 to 3 in., Falkland Isles, and var. *rosea*, pink; *floribunda* (syn. *rubra*), rose-red, spring and summer, 9 in., Brazil, and var. *alba*, white; *lobata*, yellow, autumn, 3 in., S. America; *magellanica*, white, summer, 1 in., S. America.

OXYDENDRUM – *Ericaceae*. Hardy deciduous tree with clusters of small white flowers in late summer, and good autumn colour in warm places.

Soil, lime-free loam. Position, open, well drained. Plant in autumn or late winter.

Increase by seeds sown as soon as ripe or in spring in sandy peat. Cover very lightly and place in a greenhouse or frame.

The only species is *O. arboreum* (syn. *Andromeda arborea*), Sorrel Tree, 20 to 60 ft., Eastern N. America.

PACHYSANDRA – *Buxaceae*. Hardy evergreen or deciduous procumbent sub-shrubs.

Soil, moist loam, preferably lime free. Position, shady, *P. terminalis* is excellent as evergreen ground cover. Plant in spring or autumn.

Increase by cuttings of nearly ripened growths in sandy soil in a propagator in summer; by division in spring or autumn.

Recommended kinds are *P. procumbens*, greenish white or purplish, spring, 6 in., nearly deciduous, South-eastern U.S.A.; *terminalis*, greenish white, late winter, early spring, to 12 in., Japan, and var. *variegata*, leaves variegated with white.

PACHYSTACHYS – *Acanthaceae*. Tender perennials or shrubs with flowers in close spikes.

Compost, John Innes potting compost No. 2 or equivalent. Position, pots in an intermediate or warm greenhouse, minimum winter temp. 13°C. Water freely in spring and summer, sparingly in autumn and winter. Shade lightly in spring and summer. Pot in spring.

Increase by cuttings of firm young growth in a warm propagator in summer.

Recommended kinds are *P. coccinea* (syns. *Jacobinia coccinea*, *Justicia coccinea*), scarlet, summer, 3 to 6 ft., Trinidad, S. America; *lutea*, yellow bracts, winter, spring, 2 to 3 ft., Tropical America.

PAEONIA (Peony, Paeony) – *Paeoniaceae*. Hardy herbaceous and shrubby perennials mostly with large and showy flowers.

Culture of herbaceous kinds: Soil, fertile loam. Position, sunny or semi-shady. Plant in spring or autumn. Topdress annually in spring with decayed manure. Water freely in dry weather.

Culture of Tree Peonies: Good, loamy, well-drained soil. Position, sheltered and sunny, not subject to late spring frosts. Plant in autumn or early spring. If grafted, bury the point of union between stock and

Paeonia suffruticosa

scion 3 in. below the surface. Mulch in spring with rotted manure or peat. Leave undisturbed as long as possible.

Increase herbaceous species by division in spring or autumn. Tree species by grafting in summer or by layering in spring or autumn. All species by seeds sown in a frame as soon as ripe or in the spring.

Recommended kinds are *P. anomala*, crimson, late spring, 1 to 1½ ft., Europe, Central Asia; *arietina*, dark purplish red, late spring, to 2½ ft., S. E. Europe, Asia Minor; *clusii* (syn. *cretica*), white, late spring, 9 to 12 in., Crete; *daurica* (syn. *triternata*), purplish rose, late spring, 1 to 2 ft., Crimea; *delavayi*, dark crimson, late spring, 5 ft., shrubby, W. China; *emodi*, white, spring, 1 to 2 ft., Kashmir; *humilis* (syn. *paradoxa*), red, late spring, 1 ft., S. W. Europe; *lactiflora* (syns. *albiflora*, *edulis*), Chinese Peony, white, scented, early summer, 2 ft., Siberia, Manchuria, N. China, Mongolia, and numerous varieties white, pink and red, single, semi-double and double; *lemoinei*, yellow, orange and red, late spring, early summer, 4 to 6 ft., hybrid between *lutea* and *suffruticosa*, shrubby; *lutea*, yellow, late spring, early summer, 6 ft., shrubby, W. China, Tibet, and var. *ludlowii*, larger flowers, 8 ft.; *mascula* (syn. *corallina*), crimson, late spring, 3 ft., S. Europe, W. Asia; *mlokosewitschii*, yellow, spring, 3 ft., Caucasus; *obovata*, white or magenta, late spring, 1½ ft., Siberia, China, and var. *willmottiae*, white, larger flowers; *officinalis*, crimson, late spring, 2 to 3 ft., S. Europe, and numerous varieties white, pink and red, fully double; *peregrina* (syns. *decora*, *lobata*), red, to 3 ft., S. E. Europe, Asia Minor; *potanini* (syn. *delavayi* var. *angustiloba*), deep maroon, late spring, shrubby, 5 ft., W. China, and vars. *alba*, white, *trollioides*, yellow; *suffruticosa* (syns. *arborea*, *moutan*), Tree Peony, rose to white and magenta, late spring, early summer, 3 to 6 ft., shrubby, China, and numerous varieties white, pink, red, single, semi-double, and double; *tenuifolia*, crimson, late spring, 1 to 1½ ft., Europe, Caucasus; *veitchii*, purplish red, to 2 ft., early summer, China, var. *plena*, purplish rose, *woodwardii*, rose; *wittmanniana*, yellow, spring, 3 ft., Caucasus.

PANCRATIUM – *Amaryllidaceae*. Hardy or slightly tender evergreen bulbous plants. Flowers cup shaped with spidery petals. For tender species sometimes known as pancratium see Hymenocallis.

Soil, ordinary, light. Position, warm, sunny, well drained, or in pots in John Innes potting compost No. 1 or equivalent in a sunny, well drained, or in pots in John Innes in early autumn. Plant near the surface so that bulbs can get properly ripened but protect in winter with a 3- or 4-in. layer of peat or leafmould. Water pot-grown plants sparingly in autumn and winter, freely in spring and summer. Do not allow soil to become quite dry at any time.

Increase by offsets removed from old bulbs in autumn; by seeds sown in John Innes seed compost or equivalent in a temp. of 15 to 18°C. in spring or as soon as ripe.

Recommended kinds are *P. illyricum*, white, late spring, early summer, 1 to 2 ft., Mediterranean region; *maritimum*, Mediterranean Lily, or Sea Daffodil, white, summer, early autumn, 2 to 2½ ft., Mediterranean region.

PANDANUS (Screw Pine) – *Pandanaceae*. Tender evergreen shrubs with strap-like serrated leaves.

Compost, John Innes potting compost No. 2 or equivalent. Position, intermediate or warm greenhouse, minimum winter temp. 13°C., or in a warm, light room. Water fairly freely in spring and summer, moderately in autumn, sparingly in winter. Maintain a moist atmosphere. Shade in summer only. Pot in spring.

Increase by suckers removed in spring and rooted in a warm propagator.

Recommended kinds are *P. baptistii*, leaves blue-green striped cream, 4 ft., New Britain Island; *candelabrum*, leaves green, 15 to 30 ft., Tropical Africa, and var. *variegatum*, green and white; *pygmaeus*, leaves green, 2 ft., Madagascar; *sanderi*, leaves green striped yellow, 3 ft., Timor; *veitchii*, leaves green edged with white, 3 ft., Polynesia.

PANICUM – *Gramineae*. Hardy annual grasses grown for their plume-like sprays of small flowers.

Soil, ordinary. Position, sunny. Sow in spring where required to flower. Thin seedlings when 1 in. high to 2 in. apart. Gather inflorescences in summer when well developed.

Recommended kinds are *P. capillare*, Witch Grass, purple or green, late summer, 1 to 3 ft., N. America; *violaceum*, green and violet, 3 ft., origin uncertain.

PAPAVER (Poppy) – *Papaveraceae*. Hardy annual and perennial herbs with showy flowers.

Culture of annual species: Soil, ordinary, well drained. Position, sunny. Sow in spring or early autumn where required to grow. Thin seedlings to 6 to 9 in. apart.

Culture of perennial species: Soil, deep, sandy loam. Position, sunny borders for tall species, rock garden or scree for *P. alpinum*. Plant in spring or autumn. *P. alpinum* and *nudicaule* are best grown as biennials, sown each year in late spring or early summer, planted in their flowering place in late summer or early autumn in very well-drained soil, and discarded after flowering and seeding.

Increase perennial species by seeds sown in a sunny place outdoors in spring or early summer; by division of roots in spring or root cuttings in sandy soil in a frame or cool greenhouse in winter.

Recommended annual kinds are *P. glaucum*, Tulip Poppy, scarlet, summer, 1½ ft., Asia Minor; *pavoninum*, Peacock Poppy, scarlet and black, 1½ ft., summer, Afghanistan; *rhoeas*, Corn or Shirley Poppy, red and black in wild type but white and pink, single and double in Shirley strain, summer, 1 to 2½ ft., Temperate Europe (Britain), Asia; *somniferum*, Opium Poppy, pink, red, lilac, mauve, purple, single and double, summer, 3 ft., Europe, Asia.

Recommended perennial kinds are *P. alpinum*, Alpine Poppy, yellow, orange, salmon, pink and white, summer, 6 in., Europe; *atlanticum*, orange, summer, 1½ ft., Morocco; *bracteatum*, crimson, sometimes with black blotch, late spring, early summer, 2 to 3 ft., Caucasus, Asia Minor; *nudicaule*, Iceland Poppy, yellow, orange and white, summer, 1 to 3 ft., Sub-arctic Regions; *orientale*, Oriental Poppy, orange-scarlet, late spring, early summer, 2 to 3 ft., Asia Minor, and several varieties white, pink, salmon, cherry red, scarlet and black, single and double; *pilosum*, scarlet or orange, summer, 2 to 3 ft., Asia Minor; *pyrenaicum*, yellow, orange or white, summer, 6 in., Pyrenees, Carpathians; *rupifragum*, Spanish Poppy, terra-cotta, summer, 2 ft., Spain.

PAPHIOPEDILUM – *Orchidaceae*. Tender terrestrial or epiphytic orchids. They have no pseudobulbs, are evergreen and the lip of the flower is pouch like as in cypripedium, with which they were once botanically united and with which they are still often confused. There are a great many hybrids which, from the gardening standpoint, are now of greater importance than the species because of the great size and substance of the flowers.

Compost, equal parts fibre and sphagnum moss. A little loam may help some kinds. Position, well-drained pots in a cool or intermediate greenhouse, the higher temperatures (minimum 13°C.) being advisable

Paphiopedilum insigne

for most species with mottled foliage. Water fairly freely from spring to autumn, moderately in winter. Shade at all times, rather heavily in summer. Repot annually after flowering.

Increase by division of plants with not less than four growths, six are preferable.

Recommended kinds are *P. argus*, green-purple, veined brownish purple, late spring, early summer, 12 to 18 in., Philippines; *barbatum*, greenish white, striped and flushed brown-purple, spring, summer, 10 in., Malacca, many varieties; *bellatulum*, white, spotted purple-maroon, late winter, early spring, 6 in., Burma; *callosum*, white, green, brown-purple, spring, summer, 12 in., Thailand; *concolor*, yellow dotted red, summer, autumn, 6 in., Thailand, Burma; *curtisii*, white, green and purplish brown, spring, 12 in., Sumatra; *fairieanum*, white, striped green and purple, summer, autumn, 6 to 8 in., Assam; *godefroyae*, whitish, marked brown-purple, spring, 6 in., Vietnam; *hirsutissimum*, green, pink and brown-purple, autumn, 10 in., Assam, N. India; *insigne*, variable, green, white and brown purple, winter, 6 to 9 in., N. India, Assam, Burma, and many varieties including *sanderae*, greenish yellow and white; *niveum*, white, spotted pink, winter, spring, 5 in., Malaysia; *philippinense* (syn. *robelinii*), white, yellow, green and purple, spring, 10 in., Philippines; *spicerianum*, white, green and brownish purple, autumn, 9 in., Assam; *venustum*, whitish, green veined, pouch brownish orange, autumn, winter, 8 in., Nepal; *villosum*, green, white and brownish yellow, winter, spring, 10 in., India.

PARADISEA – *Liliaceae*. Hardy herbaceous perennials with funnel-shaped flowers in slender spikes.

Soil, fertile loam. Position, partially shady. Plant in spring or autumn.

Increase by division of roots in spring or autumn; by seeds sown in a cold frame or greenhouse in spring.

The species grown is *P. liliastrum* (syn. *Anthericum liliastrum*), St Bruno Lily, white, fragrant, late spring, early summer, 1 to 2 ft., S. Europe, var. *major*, 3 to 4 ft., larger flowers.

PARNASSIA – *Saxifragaceae*. Hardy perennial herbs with saucer-shaped flowers.

Soil, peaty, moist, acid for *P. palustris*, but alkaline for *P. caroliniana*. Position, open, bogs, or margins of streams or ponds. Plant in spring.

Increase by seeds sown in moist peat in a shady frame in autumn or spring; by division in spring.

Recommended kinds are *P. caroliniana* (syn. *glauca*), white, summer, 6 in., N. America; *palustris*, Grass of Parnassus, white and green, summer, 6 in., Northern Hemisphere (Britain).

PAROCHETUS (Shamrock Pea) – *Leguminosae*. Slightly tender trailing herbaceous perennial with pea-type flowers.

Soil, ordinary. Position, sheltered, moist, partially shady banks or rock gardens. Plant in spring. Protect with a handlight or cloche in cold places in winter. Will survive a few degrees of frost.

Increase by seeds sown in sandy soil in a cool greenhouse in spring; by division of plants in spring.

The only species is *P. communis*, blue, late summer and autumn, trailing, Himalaya, East Africa.

PARROTIA – *Hamamelidaceae*. Hardy deciduous tree, leaves brilliantly coloured in autumn.

Soil, good, loamy. Position, open, sunny. Plant in autumn or late winter. Little pruning is required.

Increase by seeds stratified for five months at 20 to 25°C. then for a further three months at 4°C. after which they may be sown outdoors or under glass; by cuttings of firm young growth in a propagator in summer; by layering in spring or autumn.

The only species is *P. persica*, crimson, early spring, 15 to 50 ft., Iran, Caucasus.

PARTHENOCISSUS – *Vitidaceae*. Hardy or slightly tender shrubs, mainly deciduous, climbing by tendrils or adhesive pads and used to cover walls, fences and trees, etc. Formerly included in genera *Ampelopsis* and *Vitis*.

Soil, ordinary. Position, against walls, etc. in sun or light shade. Plant in autumn or late winter. Prune as necessary in autumn.

Increase by layering in spring or autumn; by cuttings of firm young growth in a propagator in summer; by cuttings of riper growth in a frame or outdoors in autumn.

Recommended kinds are *P. henryana* (syn. *Vitis henryana*), tall, leaflets bright green with silver and pink variegation colouring to red, slightly tender, China; *quinquefolia* (syns. *Vitis quinquefolia*, *V. hederacea*), Virginia Creeper, Eastern U.S.A.; *tricuspidata* (syn. *Vitis inconstans*), Japanese or Boston Ivy, furnished with short-branched tendrils that can hold fast to any surface, Japan, China, Korea, and var. *lowii*, leaves small; *veitchii* (syn. *Ampelopsis veitchii*), leaves purple when young.

PASSIFLORA (Passion Flower) – *Passifloraceae*. Variously tender climbing plants. *P. edulis* and *P. quadrangularis* produce edible fruit.

Compost, equal parts loam and peat, one-fourth part coarse sand, or good well-drained soil out of doors. Pot or plant in spring.

Prune in spring, thinning out weak shoots and shortening strong ones to a good growth bud near the base of each. In mild localities

Passiflora allardii

or under glass the plants may be allowed to form a substantial framework of more or less permanent main vines to which side growths are cut back annually. Young growth should be allowed to hang down.

Position, well-drained tubs, pots or beds, shoots trained up rafters or walls, sunny. Water copiously from spring to autumn, moderately afterwards. Minimum temperatures for very tender kinds, such as *P. alata*, *edulis*, *quadrangularis* and *racemosa*, 12°C.; for most kinds 5°C. *P. caerulea* and its varieties will survive temperatures as low as −10°C., especially if protected around the base in winter with straw, dry bracken or in some other way.

Increase by seeds sown in sandy soil in temp. 18 to 21°C. at any time; by cuttings of young shoots in sandy soil in a propagator in summer.

Recommended kinds are *P. alata*, crimson, white and purple, summer, 15 to 20 ft., Peru; *allardii*, white, pink and deep blue, summer and early autumn, 20 ft., hybrid between *caerulea* and *quadrangularis* and will survive a few degrees of frost; *antioquiensis* (syn. *Tacsonia van-volxemii*), crimson, autumn, 30 ft., Colombia; *caerulea*, pale pink or white and purple, summer, 20 to 25 ft., Brazil, the hardiest kind, and var. Constance Elliott, white; *edulis*, Purple Granadilla, white and purple, summer, 20 ft., Brazil; *exoniensis*, rose-pink and white, summer, 20 to 30 ft., hybrid between *antioquiensis* and *mollissima*; *mixta* (syn. *Tacsonia mixta*), pink, summer, 20 ft., Tropical America; *mollissima* (syn. *Tacsonia mollissima*), rose, summer, 20 to 30 ft., Andes; *quadrangularis* Giant Granadilla, red, violet and white, fragrant, summer, 20 ft., Tropical America; *racemosa* (syn. *princeps*), red, white and purple, summer, 20 ft., Brazil.

PAULOWNIA – *Scrophulariaceae*. Hardy deciduous trees with ornamental foliage and funnel-shaped flowers in erect clusters.

Soil, rich, well-drained loam. Position,

sunny, sheltered, warm or as specimens in lawns. Plant in autumn or late winter. Prune shoots annually in late winter to within 2 or 3 in. of the base if only foliage is desired; leave unpruned for flowering.

Increase by seeds sown in sandy loam in a frame or greenhouse as soon as ripe or in spring; by cuttings of roots inserted in sandy soil in a frame in winter.

Recommended kinds are *P. fargesii*, heliotrope, late spring, scented, 40 to 50 ft., W. China; *lilacina*, pale violet striped with pale yellow, late spring, 30 to 40 ft., W. China; *tomentosa* (syn. *imperialis*), violet, late spring, 30 to 40 ft., China.

PAVONIA – *Malvaceae*. Tender evergreen plants with showy, petal-like bracts in some species.

Compost, two parts loam, one part each of peat and sand. Pot in spring. Grow in warm house conditions with minimum winter temperature of 18°C. Shade in summer. Water normally and maintain a moist atmosphere in summer.

Increase by cuttings in fine sand in a warm propagator.

The best kind is *P. multiflora* (syn. *wioti*), purple flowers, narrow red bracts, autumn, 1 to 2 ft., Brazil.

PELARGONIUM – *Geraniaceae*. Tender and hardy herbaceous, evergreen, shrubby and tuberous-rooted perennials, some grown primarily for their flowers which are usually produced freely over a very long season, some for their ornamental foliage and some for their scented foliage. Popularly but erroneously known as geraniums.

Zonal pelargonium

Classification of types: (1) Zonal: leaves roundish, lobed, with or without zone or horseshoe mark near margin of upper surface. Flowers usually showy. (2) Variegated-leaved: Similar to Zonal but leaves variegated with cream, yellow or red. (3) Ivy-leaved: leaves ivy shaped, rather fleshy, five angled, green or variegated; stems trailing or climbing. Flowers usually showy. (4) Scented-leaved: Leaves variously

Regal pelargonium

shaped, scented. Flowers usually rather small. (5) Regal, Show and Lady Washington: Leaves rounded but without dark zone. Flowers large often conspicuously blotched with one colour on another. (6) Succulent: Stems fleshy, often contorted, leaves variously shaped, often with glandular teeth. (7) Other kinds: mainly species of less general garden value than the foregoing.

Culture of hardy herbaceous species: Soil, sandy loam. Position, sunny, well drained scree or raised bed. Plant in spring. Protect in winter with handlights.

Culture of Zonal Pelargoniums: Compost, John Innes potting compost No. 2 or equivalent. Position, pots in a sunny greenhouse, minimum winter temp. 10°C. Water moderately in spring and autumn, freely in summer, sparingly in winter unless temperatures of 15°C. or more are maintained when moderate watering should be continued. Pot in spring. Do not shade at any time. Maintain a rather dry, airy atmosphere. Plants may be used outdoors in summer when there is no danger of frost, either planted out as summer bedding, or in ornamental pots, tubs, window boxes, plant containers, etc. Feed in summer with weak liquid manure or fertilizer but avoid excessive feeding which may produce luxuriant leaf growth at the expense of flowers.

Culture of Variegated-leaved Pelargoniums: As for zonal varieties except that as the flowers are not usually very good it is best to pick them off in bud and concentrate the strength of the plants on producing leaves.

Culture of Ivy-leaved Pelargoniums: As for zonals except that stems should be tied to trellis work, wires, canes or other suitable supports. Alternatively, plants can be grown in hanging baskets or window boxes or be placed at the edge of the greenhouse staging and allowed to trail downwards. If planted out in summer stems can either be trained upwards as described or be pegged out to cover the whole surface of the ground, the natural habit of these plants in the wild.

Culture of Show, Regal and Lady Washington Pelargoniums: Compost, John Innes potting compost No. 2 or equivalent. Position, pots in a sunny greenhouse, minimum winter temp. 10°C. Do not shade at any time. Water freely in spring and early summer but after flowering cut plants back quite severely and stand outdoors or in a frame in a sunny place for a few weeks keeping soil just moist. When growth restarts repot and resume normal watering. Return plants to the greenhouse in early autumn before there is danger of frost and water moderately at first, sparingly in winter. Regal pelargoniums can be used outdoors in summer like zonal varieties but are not so useful because of their shorter flowering season.

Culture of Scented-leaved Pelargoniums: As for variegated-leaved varieties except that they are never used for summer bedding outdoors because of the lack of colour in flowers and foliage. Can be used as house plants in well-lighted rooms.

Culture of Succulent Pelargoniums: Compost, John Innes potting compost No. 2 or equivalent plus one-sixth its bulk of coarse sand. Position, sunny, cool or intermediate greenhouse, minimum winter temp. 7°C. Water moderately from spring to autumn, sparingly in winter. Pot in spring.

Increase by seeds sown in John Innes seed compost or equivalent in temp. 15 to 18°C. in spring; by cuttings in spring or summer in sandy soil in a frame or even outdoors in late summer for zonal varieties. Late summer cuttings of show, regal and Lady Washington varieties usually give the best results. All cuttings when rooted should be potted singly in John Innes potting compost No. 1 or equivalent and only be moved on to a richer compost when they require larger pots. Seedling pelargoniums are best grown throughout their first year in John Innes potting compost No. 1 since in richer compost they may make a great deal of growth but produce few flowers.

The best hardy herbaceous kind is *P. endlicherianum*, rose, summer, 9 to 12 in., Asia Minor, Armenia.

Recommended scented-leaved species are *P. capitatum*, rose scented, rose and purple, summer, 2 to 3 ft., S. Africa; *citriodorum*, citron scented, white, summer, 2 to 3 ft., hybrid; *crispum*, lemon scented, rose, summer, 2 to 3 ft., S. Africa, and var. *variegatum*, leaves cream variegated; *cucullatum*, rose scented, late summer, 3 ft., S. Africa; *denticulatum*, balsam scented, purple, summer, 1 ft., S. Africa, and var. *filicifolium*, fern leaved; *fragrans*, nutmeg scented, white and pink, summer, 2 to 3 ft., S. Africa; *graveolens*, lemon scented, rose and purple, 2 to 3 ft., S. Africa; *odoratissimum*, apple scented, white, summer, 1½ ft., S. Africa; *quercifolium*, oak leaved, musk

Ivy-leaved pelargonium

scented, pink and purple, late spring, 3 ft., S. Africa; *radula*, balsam scented, rose and purple, summer, 2 to 3 ft., S. Africa; *tomentosum*, peppermint scented, white, summer, 3 ft., S. Africa.

Other recommended kinds are *P. fulgidum*, scarlet, summer, $1\frac{1}{2}$ to $2\frac{1}{2}$ ft., S. Africa; *grandiflorum*, white and red, summer, $1\frac{1}{2}$ ft., S. Africa; *inquinans*, scarlet, rose or white, summer, 1 ft., S. Africa; *peltatum* (syn. *hederaefolium*), parent of the ivy-leaved pelargoniums, white, mauve or pink, summer, sprawling, S. Africa; *zonale*, Horseshoe or Zonal Geranium, white, pink or red, summer, 2 ft., S. Africa. The bedding and zonal pelargoniums of gardens are hybrids between *inquinans fulgidum* and *zonale*; the show, regal and Lady Washington pelargoniums, sometimes known as *P. domesticum*, are hybrids between *cucullatum, fulgidum* and *grandiflorum*.

PENNISETUM – *Gramineae*. Hardy and slightly tender perennial grasses with very graceful inflorescences useful for cutting and drying for winter decoration.

Soil, ordinary, well drained. Position, warm, sunny or in a cool greenhouse, minimum winter temp. 7°C. *P. villosum* best treated as a half-hardy annual, grown from seeds sown in spring in temp. 15 to 18°C., seedlings hardened off for planting out when danger of frost is past.

Increase most kinds by seeds; also by division in spring.

Recommended kinds are *P. alopecuroides*, green, yellow or purple, summer, 1 to 5 ft., Eastern Asia, Eastern Australia; *latifolium*, green, summer, 4 to 9 ft., S. America; *macrourum*, brown or purple, summer, to 6 ft., S. Africa; *orientale*, purple tinted, summer, 6 to 36 in., Asia; *setaceum*, Fountain Grass, purple tinted, summer, 9 to 36 in., tender, Africa, Asia, and var. *purpureum*, purple leaves and flowers; *villosum*, Feathertop, brown or purple, summer, 6 to 24 in., Africa.

PENSTEMON (Beard Tongue) – *Scrophulariaceae*. Hardy or slightly tender perennials, or sub-shrubs with tubular flowers.

Soil, ordinary, fertile, well drained. Position, sunny, well drained. Plant in spring. Protect tender kinds in winter in cold places (most will survive a few degrees of frost), or overwinter rooted cuttings in a frostproof frame or greenhouse.

Increase by seeds sown in light soil in temp. 15 to 18°C. in spring, transplanting seedlings outdoors in late spring or early summer; by cuttings of young shoots inserted in sandy soil in a cold frame in late summer; by division in spring.

Recommended kinds are *P. angustifolius* (syn. *coeruleus*), blue or white, summer, $1\frac{1}{2}$ ft., Central U.S.A.; *barbatus* (syn. *Chelone barbata*), scarlet, summer, 3 to 6 ft., Western U.S.A.; *barrettiae*, purple, late spring, early summer, 1 ft., Western U.S.A.; *cobaea*, purple or white, summer, 2 ft., Central U.S.A.; *davidsonii*, crimson, summer, 2 in., Western U.S.A.; *diffusus*, blue or purple, summer, 1 to 2 ft., Western N. America; *fruticosus* (syn. *lewisii*), purple, summer, 9 to 12 in., N. W. America; *glaber*, blue or purple, summer, 1 to 2 ft., Southwestern U.S.A.; *gloxinioides*, pink, red, lilac, purple, summer, autumn, 2 to 3 ft.,

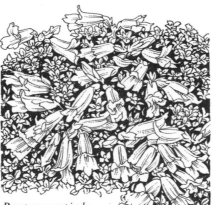

Penstemon rupicola

hybrids between *cobaea, hartwegii* and possibly other species; *hartwegii*, scarlet, summer, 2 ft., Mexico; *heterophyllus*, mauve to sky blue, summer, 1 to 3 ft., California; *hirsutus* (syn. *pubescens*), purple or violet, summer, 1 to 3 ft., U.S.A.; *isophyllus*, scarlet and crimson, summer, 4 to 6 ft., Mexico; *laevigatus*, white, summer, 2 to 3 ft., U.S.A.; *menziesii*, blue or purple, early summer, 6 to 12 in., N. W. America; *newberryi*, red, early summer, 9 to 12 in., Western U.S.A.; *ovatus*, blue to purple, summer, 2 to 3 ft., U.S.A.; *roezlii*, ruby red, summer, 9 in., Western U.S.A.; *rupicola*, ruby red, late spring, 2 to 3 in., N. W. America; *scouleri*, lilac, late spring, early summer, to 6 ft., N. W. America; *spectabilis*, rose-purple or lilac, summer, 2 to 4 ft., Mexico, S. California.

PEPEROMIA – *Peperomiaceae*. Tender herbaceous perennials with ornamental foliage.

Compost, John Innes seed compost or equivalent plus a little leafmould. Position, small pots in a cool or intermediate greenhouse, minimum winter temp. 7°C., or in rooms or bottle gardens. Pot in spring, but annual repotting is seldom necessary as peperomias make little root growth and get much of their food from the air. Water moderately at all times but maintain a moist atmosphere and shade from direct sunshine.

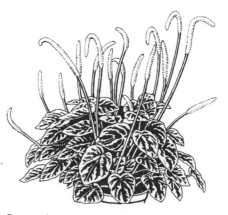

Peperomia caperata

Increase by cuttings of shoots, or single joints with leaf attached, inserted in sandy peat in a warm propagator in spring or summer; seeds in a temp. 15 to 18°C. in spring.

Recommended kinds are *P. argyreia* (syn. *sandersii*), leaves silvery veined green, 9 in., Brazil; *brevipes*, leaves brown and light green, Tropical America; *caperata*, leaves velvet green marked purple and grey, flowers white in slender spikes, 4 to 9 in., Brazil; *hederaefolia*, leaves grey, streaked dark green, 6 in., Brazil; *magnoliaefolia*, green, 6 in., West Indies, and var. *variegata*, leaves grey-green and cream; *metallica*, leaves coppery, 1 ft., Peru; *obtusifolia*, leaves green with dark red margins, 1 ft., flowers white, summer, Tropical S. America; *scandens*, leaves pale green and cream, trailing, S. America.

PERESKIA – *Cactaceae*. Tender semi-succulent shrubs and climbers, some with scented flowers. One, *P. aculeata*, is often used as a stock on which to graft other cacti.

Compost, John Innes potting compost No. 2 or equivalent plus one-sixth its bulk of coarse sand. Position, pots or beds in a sunny, cool or intermediate greenhouse, minimum winter temp. 7°C. Water freely in spring and summer, rather sparingly in autumn and winter but never allow soil to become quite dry. Tie stems of climbing species to canes, wires or trellis.

Increase by cuttings of stems inserted in sandy soil in temp. 18 to 21°C. in spring.

Recommended kinds are *P. aculeata*, Barbados Gooseberry, whitish or pale pink, scented, autumn, climbing to 30 ft., W. Indies, Mexico, Argentina; *bleo*, pink, 10 to 15 ft., Colombia, Panama; *grandifolia*, pink or white, 6 ft., Brazil.

PERILLA – *Labiatae*. Slightly tender annual, cultivated for its attractive coloured foliage, something like coleus.

Sow seeds in John Innes seed compost or equivalent in early spring in temp. 15 to 18°C. Transplant seedlings, when three leaves have formed, singly into 2-in. pots, or 2 in. apart in shallow boxes and gradually harden off for planting outdoors in late spring or early summer. Suitable for masses in borders or for lines in, or edgings to, beds.

The best kinds are *P. frutescens*, leaves green, purple spotted, 1 to 3 ft., China, Japan and Himalaya, and var. *nankinensis*, leaves bronze-purple, curled.

PERNETTYA (Prickly Heath) – *Ericaceae*. Hardy evergreen shrubs with brightly coloured berries persisting until spring. Cross pollination between different plants is necessary to ensure good fruiting with most varieties.

Soil, lime-free loam or peat. Position, moist, sunny or moderately shady. Plant in spring or autumn. Prune in spring as necessary to restrict sideways spread.

Increase by seeds sown in peaty soil outdoors in autumn; by layering shoots in spring; by division in spring.

Recommended kinds are *P. ciliata*, white, spring, summer, 1 ft., berries white, pink or lavender, S. America; *leucocarpa*, white, late spring, 9 to 12 in., berries white or pink, Chile; *mucronata*, white, spring, summer, 1½ to 3 ft., berries white to purple, Chile, Magellan Islands, and vars. *alba*, white berries, *atrococcinea*, ruby red, *lilacina*, lilac, and many more; *prostrata*, white, spring, summer, 9 to 12 in., berries black, Venezuela, Chile; *pumila*, white, spring, prostrate, berries white or pink, Magellan Straits, Falkland Isles; *tasmanica*, white, late spring, prostrate, berries red, Tasmania.

PEROVSKIA – *Labiatae*. Hardy, deciduous, semi-woody shrub with striking, greyish white shoots and leaves.

Soil, well-drained loam, also good on chalk or limestone. Position, sunny, excellent for maritime localities. Plant in spring from containers without root breakage. Prune previous year's stems to near the base each spring.

Increase by root cuttings in winter; by seeds sown in sandy soil under glass in spring.

Recommended kinds are *P. abrotanoides*, pink, late summer, autumn, 2 to 3 ft., Afghanistan, Himalaya; *atriplicifolia*, violet-blue, late summer, 3 to 5 ft., Himalaya,

Afghanistan, Tibet; *hybrida*, lavender, 3 to 4 ft., late summer, hybrid between *abrotanoides* and *atriplicifolia*.

PERSEA – *Lauraceae*. Tender evergreen trees, one species grown in warm countries for its edible fruits and occasionally grown as an ornamental foliage plant.

Soil, John Innes potting compost No. 2 or equivalent. Position, pots in a cool or intermediate greenhouse, minimum temp. 7°C. Water normally. Repot in spring; discard when too large.

Increase by seeds sown in spring in temp. 15 to 18°C. Pot seedlings singly as soon as they can be handled.

The recommended kind is *P. americana*, Avocado Pear, Alligator Pear, large leaves and dark green pear-shaped fruits, to 60 ft., Tropical America.

PETASITES – *Compositae*. Hardy herbaceous perennials, some of which can spread so rapidly as to become a nuisance.

Soil, ordinary. Position, sunny or partially shady; moist for *P. japonicus* which grows well beside a pool or stream. Plant in autumn.

Increase by division in autumn.

Recommended kinds are *P. fragrans*, Winter Heliotrope, pale lilac, fragrant, late winter, 6 in., Mediterranean region; *japonicus*, whitish, late winter, to 6 ft., very large broadly heart-shaped leaves, Sakhalin, and var. *giganteus*, even larger leaves.

PETREA – *Verbenaceae*. Tender deciduous small trees, shrubs and twiners with abundant flowers in terminal clusters.

Compost, John Innes potting compost No. 1 or equivalent. Position, large pots, tubs or beds in a sunny, cool or intermediate greenhouse, minimum winter temp. 7°C. Pot or plant in spring. Water normally. Do not shade at any time. Provide suitable supports for twining kinds.

Increase by cuttings of firm young shoots inserted in sandy soil in a warm propagator in spring or summer; by seeds sown in a temp. 18 to 21°C. in spring.

Recommended kinds are *P. arborea*, violet-blue, summer, 12 ft., shrub, Trinidad, Tropical S. America; *volubilis*, Purple Wreath, purple, summer, climber, to 15 ft., Tropical America, and var. *albiflora*, white.

PETUNIA – *Solanaceae*. Slightly tender annuals with trumpet-shaped flowers.

Soil, ordinary, fertile, well drained. Position, sunny, warm. Sow in spring in temp. 15 to 18°C. and harden off for planting out in late spring or early summer when there is no danger of frost. Petunias may also be grown in pots in a sunny greenhouse in John Innes potting compost No. 2 or equivalent. The double-flowered varieties make excellent pot, window box and balcony plants.

The garden varieties, of which there are hundreds, are all hybrids between two species, *integrifolia*, purple, summer, 18 in., Argentina, and *nyctaginiflora* (syn. *axillaris*), white, summer, 2 ft., S. America. There are single- and double-flowered forms, large-flowered (*grandiflora*), and medium-flowered (*multiflora*), in a wide range of colours including white, pale yellow, lavender, blue, purple, magenta, crimson, red and pink.

PHACELIA – *Hydrophyllaceae*. Hardy annuals with bell-shaped flowers in clusters. Good bee-attracting flowers.

Soil, ordinary, well drained. Position, sunny. Sow seeds where required to grow in spring or early autumn. Thin seedlings to 6 in. apart.

Phacelia campanularia

Recommended kinds are *P. campanularia*, blue, summer, 8 in., California; *tanacetifolia*, blue or lilac, summer, 1½ to 2½ ft., California; *viscida* (syn. *Eutoca viscida*), blue and pink or white, summer, 1 to 2 ft., S. California.

PHAIUS – *Orchidaceae*. Tender evergreen terrestrial orchids with spikes of flowers often on rather tall stems.

Compost, two parts peat, one part sand or polystyrene granules and a little dried cow manure. Position, pots or pans in an intermediate or warm greenhouse. Water rather freely from spring to autumn, moderately in winter. Shade from direct sunshine. Repot in spring.

Increase by division in spring. Healthy back bulbs removed and placed in a propagator will often produce growths.

Recommended kinds are *P. blumei*, buff yellow, lip whitish, red, spring, 3 to 4 ft., Java; *tankervilliae* (syn. *grandifolius*), yellow-brown or reddish brown, silvery behind, lip rose-purple bordered white, variable, winter, spring, 4 ft., China to Australia; *wallichii*, near *tankervilliae*, but stronger, tawny brown, yellow margined, lip whitish red lined, winter, 4 to 5 ft., N. India.

PHALAENOPSIS (Moth Orchid) – *Orchidaceae*. Tender epiphytic orchids with flowers produced on slender, arching, often branched stems. In addition to the species there are many very beautiful garden hybrids.

Compost, two parts fibre, one part sphagnum moss. The roots are extensive and clinging. Position, well-drained pans or baskets in a warm house shaded at all times, rather heavily in summer. The roots resent disturbance and the plants should not be disturbed until absolutely necessary. In the spring the old compost may be carefully picked out and new inserted. Later in the summer the operation may again be needed to a lesser degree. Water freely from spring to early autumn, moderately at other times. At no period should the compost be allowed to become really dry. Air must be carefully admitted, frequently by the bottom vents only as draughts and loss of atmospheric moisture are detrimental.

Young plants are sometimes produced on the flower spikes and occasionally on the roots. These, when rooted, can be potted.

Recommended kinds are *P. amabilis*, white, lip yellow and red spotted, autumn, winter, 1 ft., Java; *aphrodite*, white, lip with yellow stain and marked purple, various seasons, 9 to 12 in., Philippines; *equestris* (syn. *rosea*), pink, summer, 1 ft., Manila; *lueddemanniana*, white or yellow, barred or spotted pink to maroon, various seasons, to 2 ft., Philippines; *parishii*, white, lip brown spotted, spring, 8 in., Burma; *schilleriana*, pink, spotted purple, various flowering seasons, 2 to 3 ft., Philippines; *stuartiana*, white, spotted with purple, winter, spring, 2 ft., Philippines.

PHALARIS – *Gramineae*. Hardy annual and perennial ornamental grasses with flowers in dense spike-like sprays.

Culture of annual species: Soil, ordinary. Position, sunny. Sow seeds in spring where required to grow and thin seedlings to 6 in.

Culture of perennial species: Soil, ordinary. Position, sunny or semi-shady. Plant in spring or autumn. Lift, divide and replant every two or three years.

The best annual kind is *P. canariensis*, Canary Grass, whitish and green or purple, summer, 1 to 4 ft., W. Mediterranean region.

Recommended perennial kinds are *P. arundinacea*, greenish or purplish, summer, 2 to 6 ft., Europe, Asia, S. Africa, N. America, and vars. *picta* (syn. *variegata*), Gardener's Garters, Lady's Garters, Ribbon Grass, Silver Grass, leaves striped with silvery white, and *luteopicta*, leaves striped yellow.

PHILADELPHUS (Mock Orange) – *Philadelphaceae*. Hardy or slightly tender deciduous flowering shrubs often incorrectly known as syringa.

Philadelphus grandiflorus

Soil, ordinary, well drained. Position, sun or partial shade. Plant in autumn or late winter. Prune immediately after flowering, cutting back shoots that have bloomed to good side shoots or growth buds.

Increase by cuttings of young shoots inserted in sandy soil in a propagator in summer; by hard-wood cuttings of stronger growing kinds outdoors in autumn; species by seeds sown as soon as ripe or in spring outdoors or under glass.

Recommended kinds are *P. coronarius*, Sweet Mock Orange, creamy white, early summer, scented, 9 ft., S. E. Europe, and vars. *aureus* young leaves yellow, *variegatus*, leaves with cream margin; *delavayi*, white and violet, early summer, 8 to 10 ft., scented, China, Tibet, Burma; *grandiflorus*, white, early summer, scentless, 9 ft., South-eastern U.S.A.; *incanus*, white, summer, scented, 8 to 10 ft., China; *lemoinei*, white, early summer, scented, 4 ft., hybrid between *coronarius* and *microphyllus*, and numerous named varieties some up to 8 ft. tall; *maculatus* (syn. *coulteri*), white and purple, early summer, 6 ft., slightly tender, Mexico, Arizona; *microphyllus*, white, early summer, scented, 3 to 4 ft., South-western U.S.A.; *nivalis*, white, early summer, 6 ft., hybrid between *pubescens* and *coronarius*, and var. *plenus*, double flowers; *pubescens intectus* (syn. *P. intectus*), white, early summer, slightly scented, 12 to 15 ft., South-eastern U.S.A., often wrongly listed as *grandiflorus*; *purpurascens*, white and purple, scented, 8 to 10 ft., China; *purpureo-maculatus*, white and purple, early summer, scented, 4 to 6 ft., variable hybrid between *lemoinei* and *maculatus*, available in numerous named varieties; *schrenkii*, white, late spring, scented, 8 ft., Siberia, Manchuria, Korea; *splendens*, white, early summer, scented, 8 ft., hybrid, parentage uncertain; *virginalis*, white, double, early summer, scented, 5 to 8 ft., hybrid between *lemoinei* and *nivalis plenus*, and numerous named varieties.

PHILESIA – *Philesiaceae*. Slightly tender evergreen flowering shrub.

Soil, moist but not poorly drained, lime free, peaty. Position, partly shaded, shel-tered, not subject to temperatures below about −8°C., or in a cool, shady frost-proof greenhouse.

Increase by cuttings inserted in sandy peat in a propagator in summer; by suckers in spring.

The only species is *P. magellanica* (syn. *buxifolia*), rosy crimson, summer and early autumn, 6 in. to 2 ft., Chile and var. *rosea*, pink.

PHILLYREA – *Oleaceae*. Hardy evergreen flowering shrubs and small trees. *P. latifolia* is useful as a windbreak.

Soil, ordinary. Easily cultivated in any situation. Plant in spring or autumn. Prune straggly shoots only after flowering.

Increase by cuttings of firm shoots in sandy soil in a propagator in summer or cuttings of riper growth in a frame in early autumn.

Recommended kinds are *P. angustifolia*, Jasmine Box, cream, spring to summer, 8 to 10 ft., Mediterranean region, var. *rosmarinifolia*, rosemary leaved; *decora* (syn. *vilmoriniana*), white, scented, late spring, 8 to 12 ft., W. Asia; *latifolia*, white, late spring, 20 ft., Mediterranean region, and varieties.

See also Osmarea.

PHILODENDRON – *Araceae*. Tender evergreen dwarf or climbing plants, grown as foliage plants.

Compost, John Innes potting compost No. 2 or peat potting compost. Pot or plant in early spring. Grow in intermediate or warm temperatures or in a room with minimum temp. 13°C. Water normally. Shade in summer and maintain a moist atmosphere. Position, dwarf kinds in pots; tall ones in beds or borders, with shoots trained up walls or pillars.

Increase by cuttings of stems inserted in light soil in a warm propagator at any time; dwarf kinds by division in spring.

Recommended kinds are *P. andreanum*, climber, large arrow-shaped leaves, Colombia, and var. *melanochryson*, a juvenile form with dark green and coppery purple leaves; *bipinnatifidum*, dwarf, leaves divided, Brazil; *cordatum*, climbing, leaves heart shaped,

Brazil; *erubescens*, climbing, heart-shaped leaves, pink when young, Colombia; *gloriosum*, leaves green, white, and pink, climbing, Colombia; *giganteum*, broadly heart-shaped leaves, climbing, W. Indies; *hastatum*, climber, leaves heart shaped, Brazil; *imbe*, climber, leaves arrow shaped, Brazil; *micans*, climbing or trailing, leaves dark green and purple, Central America; *scandens*, climbing, leaves heart shaped, Central America, and var. *variegata*, leaves with cream blotch; *verrucosum* (syn. *lindenii*), dwarf, Colombia.

PHLOMIS – *Labiatae*. Hardy herbaceous or slightly tender perennials and evergreen shrubs

Soil, ordinary, well drained. Position, sunny, warm, even rather dry. Plant in spring or autumn. *P. fruticosa* is a good maritime plant, not hardy in cold districts.

Increase by seeds sown in light soil in temp. 18 to 21°C. in spring; herbaceous kinds also by division in spring; shrubs by cuttings inserted in a frame in summer.

Recommended herbaceous kinds are *P. samia*, yellow, summer, 4 ft., N. Africa; *tuberosa*, mauve, early summer, S. Europe and Asia Minor; *viscosa*, yellow, summer, 2 to 3 ft., Syria.

Recommended shrubby kinds are *P. chrysophylla*, yellow, early summer, 3 to 4 ft., yellowish grey leaves, Lebanon; *fruticosa*, Jerusalem Sage, yellow, early summer, 3 to 4 ft., grey leaves, S. Europe.

PHLOX – *Polemoniaceae*. Hardy perennial and slightly tender annual plants with showy flowers. Some kinds are tufted or mat forming and native to mountains.

Phlox nana

Culture of rock garden species: Soil, deep, rich, sandy loam containing a little leafmould or peat. Position, edgings to sunny borders or on ledges of rock gardens. Cool shady place for *P. adsurgens*. Plant in spring. Lift and divide in spring but only when they have grown too large for their position.

Culture of herbaceous perennials: Soil, deep, rich, not liable to dry out severely. Position, sunny or partly shaded.

Plant in spring or autumn. Water freely in dry weather. Cut down stems in autumn. Lift, divide and replant in fresh soil every two or three years.

Culture of annual species: Sow seeds in temp. 15 to 18°C. in spring. Transplant seedlings 2 in. apart in boxes or pots, gradually harden off and plant outdoors 6 in. apart in rich soil in a sunny position when there is no danger of frost. Nip off point of main shoot after planting to induce bushy growth. Water freely in dry weather.

Increase perennials by seeds sown in sandy soil in temp. 12 to 15°C. in autumn or spring; by cuttings of shoots from the base of old plants in sandy soil in a frame in spring; by division of plants in spring or autumn. *P. paniculata* varieties by cuttings of roots in winter in a cool greenhouse or frame as a precaution against eelworm infestation. Rock garden species by cuttings of shoots in sandy soil in a cold frame in summer; or by division in spring.

Recommended rock garden species are *P. adsurgens*, pink, spring, 4 in., California, Oregon; *amoena*, purplish pink, spring, 6 to 9 in., South-eastern U.S.A.; *divaricata* (syn. *canadensis*), bluish lilac or white, 12 in., Eastern N. America, and var. *laphamii*, larger, bluer flowers; *douglasii*, lavender, pink to white, spring, 2 to 3 in., Western N. America, numerous varieties and hybrids; *nana*, purple, pink or yellow, Texas, Mexico; *ovata*, purple, late spring and early summer, 12 to 15 in., N. America, and var. *pulchra*, pink; *procumbens*, pink, spring, 6 in., hybrid; *stolonifera*, violet or purple, spring, 6 in., Eastern N. America; *subulata*, Moss Pink, pink, purple, blue, lilac and white, early summer, Eastern U.S.A., many varieties and hybrids.

Recommended herbaceous perennial kinds are *P. arendsii*, lavender to mauve, summer, to 2 ft., hybrid between *divaricata* and *paniculata*; *carolina*, purple, rose and white, late spring, early summer, to 4 ft., Eastern U.S.A., early blooming varieties are widely cultivated as *P. suffruticosa*; *maculata*, Wild Sweet William, pink, purple or white, summer, fragrant, 2 ft., N. America; *paniculata*, purple and white, summer, fragrant, 3 to 4 ft., U.S.A. There are a great many garden varieties in shades of pink, red, purple, blue, lavender and white, often collectively known as *P. decussata*.

The annual species cultivated is *P. drummondii*, various, summer, 1 ft., Texas, and many varieties.

PHOENIX – *Palmae*. Tender feather palms. Dates are the fruits of *P. dactylifera*.

Grow in a fairly rich compost such as John Innes potting compost No. 2 in well-drained pots or tubs in a sunny part of a greenhouse with a minimum temp. 7°C., or plant outdoors in frost-free areas. Pot or plant in early spring. Water freely in

spring and summer, sparingly in autumn and winter. Shade greenhouse plants lightly in summer. Feed with weak liquid manure in late spring and early summer.

Increase by seeds sown 1 in. deep in light sandy soil or in a propagator in temp. 18 to 21°C. in spring.

Recommended kinds are *P. canariensis*, 30 to 40 ft., Canary Isles; *dactylifera*, Date Palm, 80 to 100 ft., N. Africa; *humilis*, 3 to 6 ft., India; *reclinata*, 25 to 35 ft., S. Africa; *roebelenii*, 2 to 6 ft., S. E. Asia; *rupicola*, 15 to 20 ft., N. India.

PHORMIUM – *Agavaceae*. Slightly tender evergreen perennial herbs with handsome, sword-shaped leaves.

Soil, light, deep loam. Position, warm, sunny, sheltered. In cold places protect crowns with dry litter in winter but plants will usually survive temperatures around −5°C. Plant in spring.

Increase by seeds sown in sandy soil in temp. 15 to 18°C. in spring; by division in spring.

Recommended kinds are *P. colensoi* (syn. *cookianum*), yellow and green, summer, 4 to 6 ft., New Zealand; *tenax*, New Zealand Flax, deep bronze, summer, 5 to 12 ft., New Zealand, and vars. *atropurpureum*, leaves purple, *variegatum*, leaves striped with cream, and *veitchii*, leaves striped soft yellow.

PHOTINIA – *Rosaceae*. Hardy and slightly tender deciduous and evergreen shrubs or small trees. Handsome foliage and hawthorn-like white flowers in spring or early summer followed in favourably warm places by red berries in autumn.

Soil, light, rich, well drained, preferably lime free though some kinds, including *P. serrulata*, will tolerate some lime. Situation warm, sunny and sheltered.

Increase by seeds stratified for three months at 4°C. then sown in peat, loam and sand outdoors or under glass; by layering in spring; by cuttings of firm young growth in a propagator in summer.

Recommended kinds are *P. beauverdiana*, deciduous, 15 to 18 ft., W. China; *davidsoniae*, evergreen, handsome young foliage, tinted bronze, 20 to 30 ft., slightly tender, Central China; *fraseri*, evergreen, 12 to 15 ft., hybrid between *glabra* and *serrulata*, and several named varieties with young foliage of a brighter red colour; *glabra* (syn. *prunifolia*), evergreen, 8 to 10 ft., Japan, and var. *rubens*, young leaves bright red; *serrulata*, Chinese Hawthorn, evergreen, young foliage copper, 15 to 30 ft., China; *villosa*, deciduous, handsome autumn foliage and fruits, 12 to 15 ft., Japan, Korea and China.

PHUOPSIS (Caucasian Cross-wort) – *Rubiaceae*. A small hardy herbaceous perennial similar to asperula (woodruff) in appearance and formerly known as cruci-anella.

Soil, ordinary, well drained, will succeed on chalk. Position, warm, sunny, rock gardens, raised beds, etc. Plant in spring.

Increase by seeds sown outdoors or in a frame in spring; by division in spring.

The only species is *P. stylosa* (syn. *Crucianella stylosa*) pink, summer, 9 to 12 in., Caucasus.

PHYGELIUS – *Scrophulariaceae*. Slightly tender evergreen sub-shrub with handsome narrowly tubular flowers carried in loose sprays.

Soil, ordinary, well drained. Position, warm, sheltered, sunny, in the open, or *P. capensis* trained as a climber against walls. Plant in spring. Prune in spring, shortening back any growth damaged by frost.

Increase by cuttings of half-ripened shoots in a propagator in summer; seeds sown in temp. 15 to 18°C. in spring; division in early spring.

The two species are *P. aequalis*, salmon and orange-red, late summer and early autumn, 2 to 3 ft., S. Africa; *capensis*, Cape Fuchsia, scarlet, summer and autumn, 2 to 6 ft., S. Africa, var. *coccineus*, crimson-scarlet.

PHYLLITIS – *Aspleniaceae*. Hardy ever-green ferns. Fronds, strap shaped, crested or contorted.

Soil, one part each fibrous peat and loam and one part of a mixture of sand, broken oyster shells and limestone. Position, shady. Plant in spring.

Increase by spores sown on the surface of fine peat in well-drained pans in a frame or cool greenhouse in spring or summer; by division in spring.

The best kind is *P. scolopendrium* (syn. *Scolopendrium vulgare*), Hart's-tongue Fern, 6 to 18 in., Europe (Britain), etc., and num-erous varieties with wavy edged, crested or divided fronds.

PHYLLODOCE – *Ericaceae*. Dwarf hardy evergreen shrubs with narrow leaves and heather-like flowers.

Soil, moist but porous lime-free peat. Position, cool, open. Plant in spring or autumn.

Increase by seeds sown in sand and peat in a cool shady frame in spring; by cuttings of nearly ripened shoots in a frame in summer; by layers in spring.

Recommended kinds are *P. breweri*, pur-plish rose, spring, summer, 6 to 12 in., California, *caerulea*, bluish purple, early summer, 6 in., Europe, Asia and N. America; *empetriformis*, reddish purple, spring, 6 to 9 in., Western N. America; *intermedia*, reddish purple, spring, 9 to 12 in., Western N. America; *nipponica*, white or pink, late spring, 4 to 8 in., Japan.

PHYLLOSTACHYS – *Gramineae*. Hardy or slightly tender bamboos with ornamental foliage.

Soil, rich, deep porous loam. Position, moist, sheltered, sunny or shady. Plant in spring.

Increase by division of plants in spring.

Recommended kinds are *P. aurea* (syn. *Sinoarundinaria aurea*), stems yellow, leaves green, 10 to 15 ft., China; *bambusoides* (syn. *quilioi*), leaves bright green, 10 to 15 ft., China; *flexuosa*, leaves dark green, 6 to 9 ft., China, and var. *sulphurea* (syn. Allgold), canes yellow; *niger* (syn. *puberula*), leaves dark green, stems yellowish green, 12 to 14 ft., China; *nigra*, Black Bamboo, leaves dark green, 8 to 10 ft., canes becoming black, China, Japan, and vars. *boryana*, canes yellow and purple, *henonis*, graceful arching habit; *sulphurea*, leaves green, 12 to 20 ft., China, Japan; *viridi-glaucescens*, leaves green above, glaucous beneath, 15 to 20 ft., canes yellowish green, China.

PHYSALIS – *Solanaceae*. Slightly tender and hardy perennial herbs and annuals. Fruit of Cape Gooseberry and Jamberberry edible – a berry enclosed in an inflated calyx.

Physalis alkekengi

Culture outdoors: Soil, rich. Position, sunny, well drained. Plant in spring. Lift, divide and replant in fresh soil every third year. Gather stems bearing fruits in early autumn and dry for winter decorations.

Culture of Cape Gooseberry: Soil, fairly rich such as John Innes potting com-post No. 2. Plant singly in 5- or 6-in. pots with shoots trained to sticks and placed close to the glass of a sunny frost-proof greenhouse, or planted in small beds with the shoots trained up the back wall. Pot or plant in spring. Water normally. Apply weak liquid fertilizer once or twice a week in summer. Gather fruit when ripe and fully coloured.

Culture of Jamberberry: Sow seeds in early spring in temp. 15 to 18°C. Grow seedlings in good compost, such as John Innes potting compost No. 1, in a frost-proof greenhouse and plant outdoors in a warm, sunny place when there is no danger of frost. In warm places it can be grown outdoors throughout. Gather fruits as they ripen. Discard plants when they have finished cropping.

Increase hardy species by seeds sown in a sunny spot outdoors in spring or early summer; or by division of roots in spring. Greenhouse species by seeds sown in pans of light soil in temp 18 to 21°C. in late winter or early spring; by cuttings inserted singly in pots of light, sandy soil and placed in a warm propagator in spring.

The best hardy kind is *P. alkekengi* (syns. *bunyardii*, *franchetii*), Bladder Herb or Winter Cherry, white, summer, fruit scarlet, 1 to 2 ft., S. E. Europe to Japan.

The best slightly tender kind is *P. peru-viana* (syn. *edulis*), Cape Gooseberry, white, summer, fruit edible, 3 ft., Tropics.

The best annual kind is *P. ixocarpa*, Jamberberry, Tomatillo, yellow and brown, summer, fruits purple, edible, 2 to 4 ft., Mexico.

PHYSOSTEGIA (False Dragonhead) – *Labiatae*. Hardy herbaceous perennials with tubular flowers in short spikes.

Soil, ordinary, not liable to dry out badly. Position, cool, partially shaded. Plant in spring or autumn.

Increase by seeds sown in light soil out-doors in spring; by cuttings of young shoots inserted in sandy soil in a frame in spring; by division in spring; by root cuttings in winter.

The best kind is *P. virginiana* (syn. *Dracocephalum virginianum*), rosy pink, summer, 1 to 4 ft., Eastern U.S.A., and vars. *alba*, white, Vivid, rose, 2 ft.

PHYTEUMA (Horned Rampion) – *Cam-panulaceae*. Hardy perennial herbs with curiously shaped sometimes flask-like flowers in close heads or spikes.

Soil, deep rich loam mixed with limestone

Phyteuma comosum

Phytolacca americana

grit and leafmould or peat. Position, sunny. Plant in spring. Lift, divide and replant only when overgrown. Topdress dwarf species with a mixture of peat, leafmould and ground chalk or limestone in spring.

Increase by seeds sown in sandy soil in a cold frame in autumn; by division in spring.

Recommended kinds are *P. charmelii*, blue, late spring, summer, 6 to 12 in., Apennines; *comosum*, amethyst blue, summer, 3 to 4 in., S. Europe; *hemisphaericum*, blue, early summer, 3 to 4 in., Alps; *orbiculare*, blue, summer, 6 to 12 in., Central Europe; *scheuchzeri*, purple, summer, 1 ft., Alps; *spicatum*, white, cream or blue, summer, 3 to 4 ft., Europe (Britain); *tenerum*, blue, summer, 6 to 12 in., W. Europe (Britain).

PHYTOLACCA (Pokeberry) – *Phytolaccaceae*. Hardy herbaceous perennials and rather tender shrubs. Flowers in dense spikes succeeded by deep purple berries in autumn.

Soil, good, ordinary. Position, sunny or semi-shady. Plant in spring or autumn. Shrubby kinds in a cool sunny greenhouse or nearly frost-free place outdoors.

Increase by seeds sown outdoors in spring or as soon as ripe; by division of plants in spring.

Recommended herbaceous kinds are *P. acinosa*, Indian Poke, white, summer, 5 ft., Himalaya; *americana* (syn. *decandra*), Virginian Poke, Red-ink Plant, Pigeon Berry, white, summer, 3 to 10 ft., N. America, berries poisonous; *clavigera*, pink, summer, 5 to 6 ft., red stems, China.

The best shrubby kind is *P. dioica*, (syn. *arborea*), greenish, summer, to 30 ft. in nature but usually much less in gardens, evergreen, S. America.

PICEA (Spruce) – *Pinaceae*. Hardy evergreen coniferous trees. Leaves needle shaped, spirally arranged. Branches always produced in tiers to form a pyramidal shape. Cones almost always pendulous. *P. abies*, the Common or Norway Spruce, is the Christmas Tree and also produces timber known as white deal.

Soil, deep, rich, moist. Situation open or in coppices and woodlands, preferring areas of heavy rainfall. Mostly timber trees but some species make handsome specimens up to 100 ft. or more and others are dwarf, suitable for rock gardens. Plant in autumn or late winter.

Increase by seeds in sandy loam outdoors or in a frame as soon as ripe or in spring; special forms grafted in spring on to seedlings of *P. abies*; some kinds by cuttings in a frame in summer or autumn.

Picea polita

Recommended kinds are *P. abies* (syn. *excelsa*), Common Spruce, Norway Spruce, 100 to 120 ft., Europe, and vars. *clanbrassiliana*, dense, slow growing, *echiniformis*, very dwarf, flat topped, *gregoryana*, dwarf, conical to 2 ft., *pendula* (syn. *inversa*), weeping, *nidiformis*, dwarf, flat topped, *procumbens*, prostrate, *pumila*, dwarf, dense growth, *pygmaea*, very dwarf, dome shaped, *reflexa*, semi-prostrate, *virgata*, Snake Fir, medium height, sinuous branches, and numerous others; *asperata*, vigorous, grey leaved, 50 to 70 ft., China; *bicolor* (syn. *alcockiana*), 80 ft., Japan; *brachytyla*, drooping branchlets, 40 to 80 ft., China; *breweriana*, branchlets pendulous, 80 to 100 ft., California; *engelmannii*, fine hardy tree, blue-green, 100 to 150 ft., dislikes lime,

Western N. America; *glauca* (syn. *alba*), White Spruce, 60 to 100 ft., N. E. America, and vars. *albertiana*, pyramidal to 150 ft., *aurea*, leaves tinged yellow, *caerulea*, leaves glaucous, and many dwarf forms including *conica*, *nana* and *echiniformis*; *jezoensis*, Yeddo Spruce, young shoots pale brown, not so hardy as var. *hondoensis*, 80 to 100 ft., Japan; *koyamai*, narrowly pyramidal, 50 ft., Japan; *likiangensis*, 60 to 80 ft., W. China, var. *balfouriana*, violet-coloured cones; *mariana* (syn. *nigra*), Black Spruce, 25 to 50 ft., young cones purple, N. America, var. *doumetii*, denser, rounded habit; *omorika*, Serbian Spruce, easily grown, narrowly conical, leaves white beneath, to 100 ft., Yugoslavia, var. *pendula*, narrowly erect with weeping branches; *orientalis*, Oriental Spruce, broadly conical habit, short dark green leaves, 100 ft., Caucasus, Asia Minor, with vars. *aurea*, young growth yellow, *nana*, dwarf; *polita*, Tigertail Spruce, stout prickly leaves, 50 to 90 ft., Japan; *pungens*, Colorado Spruce, rather slow growing, not so common as its beautiful forms *glauca*, Koster's Blue Spruce, *moerheimii*, even more blue-grey than the last, *pendula*, blue-grey, pendulous branches, *speckii*, bluish, etc., 50 to 100 ft., Colorado to N. Mexico; *rubens* (syn. *rubra*), Red Spruce, 70 to 80 ft., N. America, dislikes lime; *sitchensis*, Sitka Spruce, useful timber tree for moist places, to 140 ft., Alaska to California; *smithiana* (syn. *morinda*), West Himalayan Spruce, pendulous branchlets, 100 to 150 ft., Himalaya; *spinulosa*, East Himalayan Spruce, pendulous branches, 60 to 150 ft., Himalaya; *wilsonii* (syn. *watsoniana*), dense habit, young shoots white, to 70 ft., Central China.

PIERIS – *Ericaceae*. Hardy evergreen shrubs of great beauty with lily of the valley-like flowers. Some of the species were previously included in *Andromeda*.

Soil, lime-free loam such as suits rhododendrons. Position, sun or partial shade with some shelter from cold winds. Plant in spring or autumn. Little pruning is normally necessary but branches can be cut hard back after flowering.

Increase by seeds sown in sandy peat in a frame as soon as ripe or in spring; by cuttings of firm young growth in a propagator in summer; by layering shoots in autumn.

Recommended kinds are *P. floribunda*, white, late spring, 4 to 6 ft., South-eastern U.S.A.; *formosa*, white, spring, 8 to 12 ft., young shoots and leaves coppery red, Himalaya, and var. *forrestii*, young growths even brighter red, China, Burma; *japonica*, white, early spring, 9 to 10 ft., Japan, and var. *variegata*; *taiwanensis*, white, early spring, 4 to 6 ft., Formosa.

PILEA – *Urticaceae*. Tender perennial herbs grown for their ornamental foliage.

Compost, John Innes potting compost

No. 1 or equivalent. Position, pots in a cool or intermediate greenhouse, minimum winter temp. 7°C., or in a room. Water normally. Will grow in sun or shade. Pinch shoot tips of *P. cadierei* occasionally in spring and summer to encourage branching. Pot in spring.

Increase by cuttings of firm young shoots in a propagator in spring or summer.

Recommended kinds are *P. cadierei*, Aluminium Plant, leaves dark green, streaked silvery grey, 9 in., Annam; *involucrata* (syns. *pubescens* and *spruceana*), leaves bronze-green, flowers greenish, small, abundant, 6 in., Tropical America; *microphylla* (syn. *muscosa*), Artillery Plant, leaves very small, ferny, flowers insignificant, emitting puffs of pollen when disturbed, 6 in., Tropical America; *nummularifolia*, prostrate, W. Indies.

PILEOSTEGIA – *Hydrangeaceae*. Hardy evergreen shrubs climbing by means of aerial roots. Clusters of small flowers composed mainly of stamens.

Soil, good, loamy. Position, cool, shady, not dry, against a wall or to cover an old tree stump, etc. Plant in spring or autumn. Prune in spring, removing only such growth as cannot be accommodated.

Increase by layering in spring or autumn; by cuttings in a frame in summer or early autumn.

The best species is *P. viburnoides*, creamy white, late summer and autumn, India, China.

PIMELEA (Rice Flower) – *Thymelaeaceae*. Slightly tender evergreen flowering shrubs with small flowers borne in terminal heads.

Soil, light lime-free loam and peat with sufficient sand to ensure good drainage at all times. Position, pots or beds in a sunny frost-proof greenhouse or outdoors in a sunny position in nearly frost-free districts. Pot or plant in spring. Water fairly freely in spring and summer, sparingly in autumn and winter. *P. prostrata* can be grown in scree. All kinds can be pruned after flowering.

Increase by seeds sown in peat and sand in a temp. 15 to 18°C. in spring or as soon as ripe. Pot seedlings singly and grow on in pots without root disturbance which they resent.

Recommended kinds are *P. ferruginea* (syn. *decussata*), rose, spring, 2 ft., Australia; *hypericina* (syn. *ligustrina*), white, spring, 5 to 8 ft., Australia, Tasmania; *prostrata* (syn. *laevigata*), white, scented, summer, prostrate, New Zealand; *rosea*, pink, spring, 1 to 2 ft., Australia; *spectabilis*, pink, spring, 4 ft., Australia.

PINGUICULA (Butterwort) – *Lentibulariaceae*. Tender and hardy perennial insectivorous herbs.

Grow greenhouse kinds in a compost of equal parts fibrous peat, sphagnum moss, and powdered brick or earthenware crocks in well-drained pots or shallow pans in a very humid atmosphere such as that inside a Wardian case. Pot when necessary in spring. Water freely from spring to early autumn. Minimum winter temp. 7°C.; summer range 12 to 20°C.

Grow hardy kinds in peat and loam in a bog or where there is an almost constant trickle of water. Plant in spring. Mulch with peat or well-rotted leafmould each spring, but be careful not to cover the rosettes of leaves.

Increase by seeds sown on the surface of shallow pans filled with equal parts of sphagnum moss, peat and sand, placed in a propagator, temp. 12 to 15°C., and kept moist in spring; by division of plants at potting or planting time.

Pinguicula bakeriana

Recommended tender kinds are *P. bakeriana* (syn. *caudata*), carmine, autumn 6 in., Mexico; *gypsicola*, purple, summer, 6 in., Mexico.

Recommended hardy kinds are *P. alpina*, white and yellow, late spring, 4 in., Europe (Britain); *grandiflora*, blue and violet, summer, 4 in., Europe (Ireland); *vulgaris*, Bog Violet, Butterwort, violet, summer, 4 to 6 in., Europe (Britain).

PINUS (Pine) – *Pinaceae*. Hardy or slightly tender evergreen coniferous trees or occasionally shrubs. Leaves needle like, two to five in a whorl. Cones conical and erect.

Soil, preferably open and well drained; five-needled species usually rather intolerant of lime. Position, *P. nigra*, *mugo*, *radiata*, and *pinaster* suitable for seaside gardens and ordinary soils. *P. nigra* is a good town tree. *P. nigra*, *cembra*, *griffithii*, *leucodermis*, *pinaster*, *strobus* and *sylvestris* are suitable for gravelly or sandy soils. *P. nigra* is a good shelter tree and *P. sylvestris* will grow in the poorest soil and on rocky slopes.

Pines should be planted in their permanent quarters as early in life as possible. Plant in autumn or late winter.

Increase by seeds sown in sandy loam, as soon as ripe or in spring but seed will often germinate more freely if first stratified for three months at 4°C.; special varieties grafted in spring on common species.

Recommended kinds are *P. armandii*, blue-green, 50 to 60 ft., China, Korea, Formosa; *ayacahuite*, slender drooping needles, 60 to 100 ft., slightly tender, Mexico; *banksiana*, Jack Pine, 25 to 35 ft., Eastern N. America; *bungeana*, Lace Bark Pine, flaking grey-green and cream bark, 70 ft., N. China; *cembra*, Stone Pine, 60 to 100 ft., Central Europe; *cembroides*, Nut Pine, slow-growing round tree with edible seeds, 20 ft., Mexico; *contorta*, Beach Pine or Shore Pine, twisted leaves and branches, 30 ft., dislikes limes, West N. America, and var. *latifolia*, Lodge-pole Pine, to 75 ft.; *coulteri*, Big Cone Pine, 50 to 70 ft., California; *densiflora*, Japanese Red Pine, reddish bark, flat-topped habit, 60 to 100 ft., dislikes lime, Japan; *flexilis*, Limber Pine, 40 to 70 ft., N. W. America; *holfordiana*, slender blue-grey drooping needles, 60 to 100 ft., hybrid between *ayacahuite* and *wallichiana*; *jeffreyi*, long blue-green needles, 80 to 120 ft., South-western U.S.A.; *koraiensis*, Korean Pine, glaucous blue, slow growing, 50 to 80 ft., Korea, Japan; *lambertiana*, Sugar Pine, very large cones, 70 to 200 ft., N. W. America; *leucodermis*, dark green needles, 50 to 80 ft., Italy, Balkan Peninsula; *montezumae*, long slender blue-grey needles, 50 to 70 ft., slightly tender, Mexico; *monticola*, Mountain White Pine, 60 to 90 ft., Western N. America; *mugo* (syn. *montana*), Mountain Pine, varying in height from 5 to 15 ft., with var. *pumilio*, almost prostrate, Central Europe; *muricata*, Bishop Pine, 40 to 70 ft., dislikes limes, California; *nigra*, Austrian Pine, dark coloured bark, irregular branching, 70 to 100 ft., South-eastern Europe, and vars. *hornibrookiana*, dwarf, 2 ft., *maritima* (syn. *laricio*), Corsican Pine, straight stem and more regular branching; *parviflora*, Japanese White Pine, 30 to 40 ft., Japan; *patula*, slender drooping needles, 50 to 60 ft., slightly tender, Mexico; *peuce*, Macedonian Pine, conical habit, 40 to 60 ft., Macedonia; *pinaster*, Cluster Pine, 100 to 120 ft., Mediterranean region; *pinea*, Italian Stone Pine, dome-like head of branches, 40 to 60 ft., Mediterranean region; *ponderosa*, Western Yellow Pine, 100 to 150 ft., N. W. America; *radiata* (syn. *insignis*), Monterey Pine, deeply furrowed, dark-coloured bark, 100 to 120 ft., dislikes lime, slightly tender, California; *resinosa*, Red Pine, 50 to 70 ft., Eastern N. America; *rigida*, Northern Pitch Pine, 50 to 70 ft., dislikes lime, Eastern N. America; *sabiniana*, Digger Pine, 40 to 80 ft., California; *strobus*, Weymouth Pine, White Pine, 80 to 150 ft., dislikes lime, N. E. America; *sylvestris*, Scots Pine, reddish bark, picturesque habit, to 100 ft., Europe (Britain), and vars. *argentea*, Silver

Scots Pine, *beauvronensis*, dwarf, *fastigiata*, vertical branches, and *watereri*, slow growing, conical; *thunbergii*, Japanese Black Pine, twisted leaves and branches, 80 to 100 ft., Japan; *wallichiana* (syn. *griffithii* and *excelsa*), slender blue-grey drooping needles, 70 to 100 ft., Himalaya.

PIPTANTHUS – *Leguminosae*. Slightly tender evergreen or deciduous flowering shrubs.

Soil, ordinary, well drained. Position, warm, sheltered, sunny, in the open or trained against walls. Plant in spring or autumn. Prune in spring, cutting out old, weak or frost-damaged stems to ground level.

Increase by seeds sown in sandy soil out of doors or under glass in spring; cuttings of ripened shoots inserted in sandy soil in a frame in summer or early autumn.

The best species is *P. laburnifolius* (syn. *nepalensis*), Nepal Laburnum, Evergreen Laburnum (but in cold winters it will lose its leaves), yellow, late spring, 8 to 10 ft., Himalaya.

PISTACIA (Pistachio Nut) – *Pistaciaceae*. Hardy or rather tender evergreen and deciduous shrubs or small trees with handsome, compound leaves colouring in the autumn.

Soil, deep, ordinary. Position, sunny, warm, well drained but not dry, sheltered, with a temperature not below −5°C. even for *P. chinensis*, the hardiest kind. Plant in autumn or late winter.

Increase by seeds sown as soon as ripe but first soaked in water for several days to soften their coats. Sow in John Innes seed compost or equivalent in a temp. 18 to 21°C.; also by layering in autumn or spring.

The best kind is *P. chinensis*, Chinese Pistachio, deciduous, sumach-like leaves becoming orange to crimson in autumn, 10 to 50 ft., China.

PITTOSPORUM (Parchment-bark) – *Pittosporaceae*. Slightly tender evergreen flowering shrubs. Some species very fragrant.

Soil, ordinary, well drained, including chalk. Position, warm, sunny, even dry. Excellent as windbreaks in mild climates, particularly near the sea but require shelter in colder places. Many kinds will regenerate from the base even when top growth is killed. Popular kinds such as *P. tenuifolium* and *tobira* will usually survive temps. around −10°C. Plant in spring. Prune in spring as necessary to maintain shape or restrict size.

Increase by cuttings of moderately firm shoots, inserted in sandy soil in a propagator in summer.

Recommended kinds are *P. crassifolium*, Karo, purple, spring, 15 to 30 ft., New Zealand; *eugenioides*, Tarata, greenish yellow, spring, 20 to 40 ft., New Zealand; *ralphii*, dark purple, spring, 15 ft., New Zealand; *tenuifolium*, bright green leaves, wavy margins, black stems, chocolate-purple flowers, spring, summer, fragrant, 20 to 30 ft., New Zealand, and vars. Silver Queen, leaves silvery grey, Warnham Gold, leaves yellow; *tobira*, white, fragrant, spring to autumn, 10 ft., Japan and China; *undulatum*, Victorian Box, creamy white, spring, summer, 15 to 30 ft., Australia, and var. *variegatum*, leaves silver variegated.

PLAGIANTHUS – *Malvaceae*. Slightly tender deciduous shrubs and small trees with small, usually unisexual flowers of little beauty. Grown for their graceful habit. Native of New Zealand.

Soil, ordinary. Position, sunny, sheltered. Established plants will survive a few degrees of frost. Plant in autumn or late winter. Prune as necessary and remove frost-damaged growth in spring.

Increase by seeds sown in a temp. 15 to 18°C. in spring.

Recommended kinds are *P. betulinus*, New Zealand Lace Bark, white, late spring, 20 to 40 ft.; *divaricatus*, yellowish white, late spring, 8 ft. See also Hoheria.

PLATANUS (Plane Tree) – *Platanaceae*. Hardy deciduous trees with ornamental foliage, ball-like clusters of fruits hanging throughout winter, and characteristic peeling bark of trunks and branches.

Soil, deep, rich, moist loam, not very satisfactory on chalk. Position, open, sunny, as specimens or avenues. Plant in autumn or late winter. Prune into shape when desirable in winter.

Increase by seeds sown outdoors in autumn as soon as ripe; by cuttings of shoots, 6 to 8 in. long, inserted in moist soil in a sheltered position in autumn; by cuttings of younger growth in a propagator in summer.

Recommended kinds are *P. acerifolia* (syn. *hispanica*), London Plane, 70 to 100 ft., probably a hybrid between *occidentalis* and *orientalis*, also vars. *pyramidalis*, pyramidal habit, and *suttneri*, leaves blotched creamy white; *occidentalis*, Button-wood or American Plane, not very satisfactory in Britain, to 120 ft., Eastern N. America; *orientalis*, Oriental Plane, 60 to 80 ft., wide spreading habit, S. E. Europe.

PLATYCERIUM – *Polypodiaceae*. Tender evergreen ferns. Fertile fronds, erect, forked like antlers; sterile fronds broad, rounded, folded over the roots.

Position, intermediate or warm greenhouse or *P. bifurcatum* in a room. Best grown on a wad of live sphagnum moss bound to a block of wood or cork and suspended on its side. Alternatively, plants may be grown in well-drained pots in a mixture of equal parts chopped sphagnum

Platycerium bifurcatum

moss and peat. Water freely in spring and summer, preferably by immersing roots for a few minutes in water; much less frequently in autumn and winter. Shade from strong sunshine. Maintain a moist atmosphere. Pot or plant in spring.

Increase by offsets in spring; also by spores sown in sandy peat in temp. 24 to 26°C.

Recommended kinds are *P. bifurcatum* (syn. *alcicorne*), Stag's Horn Fern, fertile fronds grey downy, Australia, and var. *majus*, larger, greener, more leathery; *grande*, Elk's Horn Fern, fertile fronds to 6 ft., Malaysia, N. Australia, needs more warmth than *bifurcatum*.

PLATYCODON (Balloon Flower, Chinese Bell Flower) – *Campanulaceae*. Hardy herbaceous perennial with balloon-like flower buds and bell-shaped flowers.

Soil, fairly rich. Position, sunny, well drained. Plant in spring or autumn.

Increase by seeds sown in sandy soil in a frame or cool greenhouse in spring; by division in spring.

The only species is *P. grandiflorum*, blue, summer, 1 ft., China, Japan, and vars. *album*, white, Apoyama, violet-blue, 6 in., *mariesii*, deep blue; *roseum*, lilac-pink.

PLATYSTEMON – *Papaveraceae*. Hardy annual with small poppy-like flowers.

Soil, good, ordinary. Position, sunny. Sow seeds where required to grow in spring or early autumn. Thin seedlings to 4 in. apart when ½ in. high.

The best kind is *P. californicus*, Cream Cups, yellow, summer, 9 to 12 in., California.

PLECTRANTHUS – *Labiatae*. Tender perennial herbs and sub-shrubs allied to *Coleus*, and grown for their ornamental foliage and small spikes of 'dead nettle' flowers.

Compost, John Innes potting compost No. 1 or equivalent. Position, pots or hanging baskets in a cool or intermediate greenhouse. Pot in spring. Water normally. Shade in late spring and summer only. Pinch out tips of shoots that grow too long.

Increase by division in spring; by cuttings of firm young shoots in a propagator in spring or summer; by seeds in temp. 15 to 18°C. in spring.

The best kind is *P. oertendahlii*, whitish lavender, summer, leaves green veined bronze and white, trailing, S. Africa.

PLEIONE (Indian Crocus) – *Orchidaceae*. Tender or nearly hardy, partially epiphytic orchids. Allied to *Coelogyne*. Leaves deciduous, flowers fairly large, in many kinds produced on very short stems before the leaves gain size.

Compost, equal parts fibre, peat or loam, and sphagnum moss with a little leafmould, sand and small charcoal. Position, well-drained pans in a cool greenhouse or outdoors in frost-free places. Repotting is necessary every year before flowering, or shortly afterwards. Several bulbs may be placed in the pan at intervals. Bases of the bulbs must not be buried. They may have to be supported in position for a time. Winter night temp. about 7°C. Water may not be required throughout the winter. After repotting water sparingly till growths advance, then more often; less frequently as leaves mature. Suspend pans near the glass, shade lightly, summer temp. may reach 25°C. by sun heat.

Increase by division when repotting.

Pleione bulbocodioides

Recommended kinds are *P. bulbocodioides* (syn. *formosana*), pale rose and cream, spring, 4 in., Formosa, China, and numerous varieties sometimes listed as separate species under such names as *pricei*, *pogonoides* and *reichenbachiana*; *forrestii*, primrose, spring, 4 in., China; *hookeriana*, whitish or rose flushed blotched brown-purple and yellow, spring, early summer, 3 in., India, Nepal, Bhutan, Laos; *humilis*, white, sometimes rose tinted with deeper spots, autumn, winter, 3 in., India; *maculata*, white, lip streaked and blotched, late autumn, winter, 3 in., N. India, Burma, Bhutan, Thailand; *praecox* (syn. *lagenaria*), rose-purple, lip paler, summer to winter, 6 in., China, India, Nepal.

PLUMBAGO (Leadwort) – *Plumbaginaceae*. More or less tender evergreen flowering shrubs or climbers with clusters of phlox-like flowers.

Plumbago capensis

Compost, John Innes potting compost No. 2 or equivalent. Position, large pots, tubs or beds in a cool or intermediate greenhouse, minimum winter temp. 7°C. (but min. 13°C. for *P. rosea*), or *P. capensis* may be planted outdoors in summer in a sunny place or grown outdoors altogether in nearly frost-free districts, especially if it can be protected in winter. Pot or plant in late winter or spring. Water freely in spring and summer, rather sparingly in autumn and winter. Tie stems of *P. capensis* to wires, trellis or other suitable supports. Shorten previous year's growth to a few inches in late winter or early spring. Do not shade at any time. Feed with weak liquid manure or fertilizer in summer.

Increase by seeds sown in temp. 18 to 21°C. in spring; *P. capensis* by cuttings of firm young growth in a propagator in summer; *P. rosea* by cuttings of basal shoots in a warm propagator in spring.

Recommended kinds are *P. capensis*, Cape Leadwort, blue, summer, climbing or sprawling, to 15 ft., S. Africa, var. *alba*, white; *rosea*, scarlet, summer, 2 to 3 ft., East Indies.

PLUMERIA (Frangipani Plant) – *Apocynaceae*. Tender deciduous shrubs with clusters of showy, strongly scented flowers.

Compost, John Innes potting compost No. 1 or equivalent. Position, large pots, tubs or beds in a warm greenhouse, minimum winter temp. 18°C. Pot in spring. Water normally. Maintain a moist atmosphere but only shade lightly in summer. Cut back straggly shoots after flowering.

Increase by cuttings of firm shoots in sand and peat in a warm propagator in spring or summer.

The best kind is *P. rubra*, Frangipani Plant, white, yellow, pink or carmine, summer, early autumn, 10 to 15 ft., Tropical America, and vars. *acutifolia*, white and yellow, *lutea*, yellow, *tricolor*, white, pink and yellow.

PODOCARPUS – *Podocarpaceae*. Hardy and slightly tender evergreen trees related to yew.

Soil, good deep loam, well drained. Position, sunny, sheltered; tall kinds as specimens, dwarf kinds as ground cover. Tender species only suitable for mild climates where temps. are unlikely to fall below – 5°C. Plant in spring or autumn.

Increase by cuttings of firm young shoots in sandy loam in a propagator in summer.

Recommended kinds are *P. alpinus*, hardy, 3 to 4 ft., Tasmania; *andinus* (syn. *Prumnopitys elegans*), Plum-fruited Yew, Chilean Yew, 15 to 40 ft., Chile; *dacrydioides*, Kahika, 30 to 150 ft., New Zealand; *macrophyllus*, hardy, large yew-like leaves, 15 to 25 ft., dislikes lime, China, Japan; *nivalis*, Alpine Totara, hardy, 3 ft., New Zealand; *nubigenus*, 15 to 30 ft., Chile; *salignus* (syn. *chilinus*), slightly tender, elegant drooping branches, 15 to 30 ft., Chile; *spicatus*, bronze foliage, drooping branches, 60 to 75 ft., New Zealand; *totara*, 20 to 100 ft., yellowish green leaves, New Zealand.

PODOPHYLLUM – *Podophyllaceae*. Hardy herbaceous perennials with large, shield-shaped, divided, ornamental leaves, small flowers and conspicuous fruits.

Soil, rich, moist loam or peat. Position, partially shaded. Plant in spring.

Increase by division of roots in spring.

Recommended kinds are *P. emodi*, Himalayan May Apple, white, late spring, 1 ft., coral-red fruits, Himalaya; *peltatum*, Duck's Foot, May Apple, white, late spring, 12 to 15 in., yellow fruits, Eastern N. America.

PODRANEA – *Bignoniaceae*. Rather tender shrubby twiner with trumpet-shaped flowers in clusters.

Compost, John Innes potting compost No. 2 or equivalent. Position, large pots, tubs or beds in a sunny, cool or intermediate greenhouse, minimum winter temp. 7°C., or outdoors in sunny places in virtually frost-free districts. Pot or plant in spring. Water freely in spring and summer, moderately in autumn, sparingly in winter. Feed in summer with a high potash fertilizer. Cut back previous year's growth quite hard in late winter.

Increase by cuttings of firm growth in a propagator in summer; by layering in spring or autumn.

The only kind is *P. ricasoliana*, pink, climbing to 10 ft., S. Africa.

POLEMONIUM – *Polemoniaceae*. Hardy herbaceous perennials with feathery leaves and attractive flowers.

Soil, ordinary, porous but not dry. Position, open, sunny or semi-shady. Plant in spring or autumn. Cut off flower stems immediately after flowering unless self-sown seedlings are welcome.

Increase by seeds sown outdoors as soon

Polemonium caeruleum

as ripe or in spring; by division in spring.

Recommended kinds are *P. caeruleum*, Jacob's Ladder, Greek Valerian, blue, late spring, early summer, 2 ft., Northern Hemisphere (Britain), var. *album*, white; *carneum*, cream to rose, summer, 1 to 1½ ft., N. W. America; *confertum*, blue, summer, 6 to 8 in., N. W. America; *foliosissimum*, blue, summer, 1 to 2½ ft., Rocky Mountains, and var. *albiflorum*, white; *lanatum*, blue, summer, 6 in., Arctic, and var. *humile*, 4 in.; *pulcherrimum* (syn. *pulchellum*), blue and white or yellow, summer, Western N. America; *reptans*, blue, spring, 6 in., N. America; *richardsonii*, blue or purple, summer, 9 in., Arctic; *viscosum*, blue, spring, 4 in., Rocky Mountains.

POLIANTHES – *Agavaceae*. Slightly tender, tuberous-rooted plant with spikes of intensely fragrant flowers.

Compost, John Innes potting compost No. 1 or equivalent. Pot successively from autumn to spring, one tuber in each 4-in. pot or four tubers in a 6-in. pot. Grow throughout in a minimum temp. 15°C. but pots can be kept in a dark place until growth is two or three inches high when they should be removed to a light greenhouse. Water sparingly at first, freely when growth starts. After flowering gradually reduce water supply until growth dies down when tubers can be stored at a temp. of 18 to 21°C. for a second forcing, though it is usually more satisfactory to discard the old tubers and start afresh. In warm, sunny places polianthes can also be planted outdoors in spring to flower in summer but they will not survive frost so must be lifted in the early autumn except in frost-free places.

Increase by offsets removed when tubers are potted or planted.

The only species is *P. tuberosa*, Tuberose, white, fragrant, almost all the year according to the time at which tubers are started into growth, 3 ft., Mexico, and var. *flore-pleno*, double.

POLYGALA (Milkwort) – *Polygalaceae*. Hardy or slightly tender evergreen flowering shrubs, herbaceous perennials and annuals.

Soil, moist, peaty, lime free for *P. chamaebuxus*, *myrtifolia* and *vayredae*; gritty, well drained with lime or chalk for *P. calcarea*. Position, cool, half shady for peat lovers, sunny and open for lime lovers. Plant in spring or autumn, *P. myrtifolia* is slightly tender and in cold places should be grown in pots in a cool, moist, partially shaded and frost-proof greenhouse.

Increase shrubby kinds by cuttings inserted in sandy peat in a frame in autumn, or by suckers removed in autumn; herbaceous kinds by division in spring; all kinds by seeds sown in a frame either as soon as ripe or in spring.

The best herbaceous kind is *P. calcarea*, blue, spring, summer, prostrate, Europe (Britain).

Recommended shrubby kinds are *P. chamaebuxus*, Bastard Box, yellow, spring, summer, 6 to 9 in., Europe, and var. *grandiflora* (syn. *purpurea*), yellow and purple; *myrtifolia grandiflora*, purple, most of the year, 2 to 3 ft., S. Africa; *vayredae*, purple and yellow, spring, 4 in., Pyrenees.

POLYGONATUM (Solomon's Seal) – *Liliaceae*. Hardy herbaceous perennials with ornamental foliage and pendent tubular flowers.

Soil, ordinary. Position, shaded, excellent under trees. Plant in spring or autumn.

Increase by division in spring or autumn; by seeds sown outdoors or in a shady frame in spring.

Recommended kinds are *P. biflorum*, yellowish white, late spring, 2 to 3 ft., Eastern U.S.A.; *hookeri*, purple, late spring, 6 in., China, Tibet; *hybridum*, white and green, late spring, early summer, 3 ft., hybrid between *multiflorum* and *odoratum*; *latifolium*, white and green, summer, 2 to 3 ft., Europe; *multiflorum*, David's Harp, Common Solomon's Seal, white and green, late spring, early summer, 2 to 3 ft., Europe (Britain), Asia; *odoratum* (syn. *officinale*), Common Solomon's Seal, white, late spring, 1 ft., Europe (Britain).

POLYGONUM (Knotweed) – *Polygonaceae*. Hardy or slightly tender annuals, herbaceous perennials and shrubby climbers.

Culture of annual species: Soil, ordinary. Position, sunny, well drained. Sow outdoors in spring where plants are to flower. *P. capitatum*, though perennial, is usually grown as an annual, sown in spring in a temp. 15 to 18°C. and hardened off for planting out in late spring or early summer. It makes good ground cover.

Culture of perennial species: Soil, ordinary. The strong growing *P. cuspidatum* spreads quickly and is difficult to eradicate but is useful for wild gardens. *P. affine*, *tenuicaule* and *vaccinifolium* are useful for rock gardens. Other species for borders. Plant in spring or autumn.

Culture of climbing species: Soil, ordinary. Position, sunny. Useful for their quick and vigorous twining growth, to cover trellises, arbours, etc., or climb high into trees.

Increase perennials by seeds sown outdoors in spring or early summer; by division in spring or autumn; climbing kinds by cuttings in a propagator in summer or in an unheated frame in autumn.

Recommended annual kinds are *P. capitatum*, pink, summer, prostrate, N. India, strictly a perennial but flowers the first summer from seed; *orientale*, Prince's Feather, pink, late summer, autumn, 4 to 6 ft., Tropics, var. *variegatum*, variegated form.

Recommended perennial kinds are *P. affine* (syn. *brunonis*), pink, late summer, early autumn, leaves bronze-red in autumn, 6 to 9 in., Nepal, and vars. Darjeeling Red and Donald Lowndes, deep rose; *amplexicaule*, rose-red, late summer, early autumn, 3 ft., Himalaya, and vars. *album*, white, *oxyphyllum*, white, scented, *speciosum* (syn. *atrosanguineum*), red; *bistorta*, Bistort, Snakeweed, white or pink, summer, 1½ to 2 ft., Europe (Britain), Asia, and var. *superbum*, rose; *campanulatum*, blush pink, late summer, autumn, 2 to 3 ft., Himalaya, China, and var. *lichiangense*, white; *carneum*, pink, summer, 2 ft., Caucasus, Turkey,

Polygonatum odoratum

Iran; *cuspidatum* (syns. *sieboldii*, *Reynoutria japonica*), white, late summer, autumn, 6 to 9 ft., Japan, and vars. *compactum*, 2 to 3 ft., *variegatum*, leaves splashed creamy white, *reynoutria*, pink; *equisetiforme*, white, summer, 1½ ft., slightly tender, Mediterranean region; *milletii* (syn. *sphaerostachyum*), deep pink or crimson, summer, autumn, 6 to 18 in., China, Himalaya; *molle* (syn. *paniculatum*), white, late summer, autumn, 4 to 5 ft., India, Burma, China, Indonesia; *sachalinense* (syn. *Reynoutria sachalinensis*), white, autumn, 8 to 12 ft., Sakhalin Islands; *tenuicaule*, white, early spring, 4 in., Japan; *vaccinifolium*, pink, autumn, 6 in., Himalaya.

Recommended climbing kinds are *P. aubertii* (syn. *Bilderdykia aubertii*), white or greenish white, late summer, autumn, to 40 ft., China; *baldschuanicum* (syn. *Bilderdykia baldschuanica*), Russian Vine, white tinged pink, late summer, autumn, to 40 ft., Turkestan.

POLYPODIUM (Polypody) – *Polypodiaceae*. Tender and hardy evergreen and deciduous ferns.

Culture of tender kinds: Compost, two parts sphagnum peat or leafmould, one part each medium loam and coarse sand. Position, pots or baskets in a cool or intermediate greenhouse. Pot in spring. Water freely from spring to early autumn, just sufficiently to keep compost moist the rest of the year. Shade from direct sunshine at all times and maintain a moist atmosphere.

Culture of hardy species: Soil, equal parts of peat, turf loam, leafmould and coarse sand. Position, shady. Water in dry weather in spring and summer. Topdress annually in spring with peat or leafmould.

Increase by spores sown on the surface of sandy peat in a propagator in spring or summer; by division in spring.

Recommended tender kinds are *P. aureum*, fronds large, blue-green, W. Indies; *billardieri*, fronds deeply divided, Australia; *subauriculatum* (syn. *Goniophlebium subauriculatum*), drooping fronds to 6 ft., good for large baskets, India, Malaysia, Tropical Australia.

The best hardy kind is *P. vulgare*, Adder's Fern, Common Polypody, fronds simply divided, Europe (Britain), Asia, N. America, S. Africa, and many varieties such as *cambricum*, fronds cut into overlapping segments, *cornubiense*, fronds, large, much cut, and *omnilacerum*, erect fronds, to 2½ ft.

POLYSTICHUM – *Aspidiaceae*. Tender and hardy ferns. This genus includes many species previously classed as *Aspidium* and *Lastrea*.

Culture of tender species: Compost, two parts peat or leafmould, one part loam, one part coarse sand or broken charcoal. Pot in early spring. Water freely in summer, moderately in winter. Shade from sun.

Grow in cool or intermediate house conditions, minimum temp. 7°C. (12°C. for *P. viviparum*).

Culture of hardy species: Grow in loam to which plenty of peat or leafmould and some sand have been added. Position, shady. Plant in spring. Water freely in dry weather.

Increase by spores sown in sandy peat in a still, damp atmosphere at any time; by division in spring.

Recommended tender kinds are *P. adiantiforme*, to 3 ft., Southern Hemisphere; *aristatum*, to 3 ft., Asia, Australia; *tsussimense*, 1 ft., Japan; *viviparum*, 18 in., W. Indies.

Recommended hardy kinds are *P. acrostichoides*, 3 ft., N. America; *aculeatum*, to 2 ft., Europe (Britain), and numerous varieties; *braunii*, to 2 ft., Europe, N. America; *lonchitis*, to 2 ft., Europe (Britain); *munitum*, to 3 ft., Western N. America.

PONCIRUS (Hardy Orange) – *Rutaceae*. Hardy, deciduous, flowering, spiny shrub, allied to the orange. Used as a rootstock for citrus fruits to improve their hardiness.

Soil, deep, ordinary, well drained. Position, sunny, as a specimen or hedge. Clip in early summer if used as a hedge, otherwise little pruning is necessary.

Increase by seeds stratified for three months at 4°C. and then sown in a frame or greenhouse in spring; cuttings of half-ripened wood in a propagator in summer.

The only species is *P. trifoliata* (syns. *Aegle sepiaria*, *Citrus trifoliata*), white, spring, scented, small bitter fruits similar in appearance to oranges, sharply spined, 8 to 15 ft., China.

PONTEDERIA – *Pontederiaceae*. Hardy aquatic perennials with handsome leaves and showy spikes of small flowers.

Pontederia cordata

Soil, rich loam. Position, shallow ponds with no more than 6 in. of water over the crowns. Plant in late spring or early summer.

Increase by division of roots at planting time.

The best kind is *P. cordata*, Pickerel Weed, blue, summer, 2 ft., N. America, and var. *lancifolia* (syns. *P. angustifolia* or *lanceolata*), brighter blue but not as hardy as the type, 4 to 5 ft.

POPULUS (Poplar) – *Salicaceae*. Hardy deciduous trees. Flowers – catkins, male and female produced on separate trees in spring.

Soil, ordinary, moist, with few exceptions not very satisfactory on thin chalk. Dry soils are not suitable. Position, open, sunny, as specimens, in avenues or small coppices. *P. deltoides* and *P. nigra italica* are good trees for forming quick-growing screens. Plant in autumn or late winter. For screens, plant 4 to 6 ft. apart. Prune in winter.

Increase by cuttings of firm shoots inserted in ordinary soil outdoors in autumn or in a frame in summer; by suckers removed in autumn or late winter; species by seeds sown as soon as ripe outdoors or under glass.

Recommended kinds are *P. alba*, White Poplar, Abele, leaves green above, white beneath, 50 to 90 ft., Europe, N. Asia, etc., and vars. *richardii*, leaves dull yellow above, white beneath, and *pyramidalis* (syn. *bolleana*), erect branches, narrow columnar habit; *balsamifera* (syn. *tacamahaca*), Balsam Poplar, 80 to 100 ft., young leaves balsam scented, N. America; *berolinensis*, Berlin Poplar, vigorous, columnar shape, to 70 ft., hybrid between *laurifolia* and *nigra italica*; *canadensis*, Hybrid Black Poplar, variable, 100 to 150 ft., hybrids between *deltoides* and various forms of *nigra* (see *eugenei*, *regenerata* and *serotina*); *candicans*, Balm of Gilead, very fragrant young foliage, 60 to 90 ft., hybrid between *balsamifera* and *deltoides missouriensis*; *canescens*, Grey Poplar, grey leaves, to 100 ft., W. Europe (Britain), will succeed on chalk; *deltoides*, Cottonwood, 70 to 90 ft., Eastern N. America, and var. *missouriensis*, South-eastern U.S.A.; *eugenei*, young leaves coppery, to 150 ft., hybrid between *nigra italica* and *regenerata*; *generosa*, very vigorous hybrid between *angulata* and *trichocarpa*; *koreana*, apple-green leaves balsam scented when young, 60 to 80 ft., Korea; *lasiocarpa*, immense leaves, red stalks, 40 to 60 ft., Central China; *laurifolia*, balsam scented, 40 to 60 ft., Siberia; *maximowiczii*, large leathery leaves, white beneath, 70 to 90 ft., N. E. Asia, Japan; *nigra*, Black Poplar, not so common as vars. *betulifolia*, Downy Black Poplar, Manchester Poplar, to 100 ft., *italica*, Lombardy Poplar, well-known columnar tree to 125 ft., *thevestina*, similar to Lombardy but with a white trunk and *plantierensis*, similar to Lombardy Poplar but with downy twigs; *regenerata*, early leafing, will withstand atmospheric pollution, 100 to 130 ft., hybrid between *deltoides* and *nigra*; *serotina*, Black Italian Poplar, to 130 ft., hybrid between *deltoides* and *nigra*, and vars. *aurea*, Golden Poplar, young leaves yellow, and *erecta*, columnar habit; *simonii*, to 50 ft., N. China, and var. *fastigiata*, columnar habit; *suaveolens*, balsam odour, 50 ft., Siberia; *tremula*, Aspen, perpetually quivering leaves, 40 to 50 ft., Europe (Britain), with var. *pendula*, Weeping Aspen; *tremuloides*, American Aspen, pale yellowish bark, 50 to 90 ft., N. America; *trichocarpa*, Western Balsam, Black Cottonwood, the best of the balsam poplars, with scented young leaves, very quick growing, 75 to 150 ft., Western N. America.

PORTULACA – *Portulacaceae*. Slightly tender annuals with fleshy leaves and very showy flowers.

Soil, good, ordinary, well drained. Position, warm, sunny. Sow seeds in spring in temp. 15 to 18°C. and harden off seedlings for planting outdoors 6 in. apart in late spring or early summer when danger of frost is over.

Pot culture: Compost, John Innes potting compost No. 1 or equivalent. Raise plants from seeds as advised above. Transplant four seedlings into each 5-in. well-drained pot. Grow near glass in a sunny greenhouse. Water fairly freely.

The best kind is *P. grandiflora*, Sun Plant, red, yellow, rose, or white, summer, 6 in., Brazil, and numerous varieties, some double flowered.

POTAMOGETON (Pondweed) – *Potamogetonaceae*. Large genus of hardy, underwater aquatics, used in pools and rivers for oxygenating water and as cover for fish.

Soil, loam. Position, lakes, ponds, slow-moving streams, etc. Plant in spring to autumn in boxes, or weight clumps of plant and sink in water.

Increase by division in spring or summer.

Recommended kinds are *P. crispus*, Curled Pondweed, Old World (Britain); *natans*, Broad-leaved Pondweed, Northern Hemisphere (Britain); *pectinatus*, Fennel-leaved Pondweed, Cosmopolitan (Britain); *perfoliatus*, Perfoliate Pondweed, Northern Hemisphere (Britain), Australia.

POTENTILLA (Cinquefoil) – *Rosaceae*. Hardy herbaceous perennials and shrubs with showy flowers normally five petalled but double in some garden varieties.

Culture of herbaceous species: Soil, ordinary, reasonably fertile, well drained for most kinds but stony scree mixture for *P. nitida*. Position, sunny rock garden for dwarf species, sunny borders for tall species. Plant in spring or autumn. Lift, divide and replant border kinds in fresh soil every three or four years.

Culture of shrubby kinds: Soil, any reasonably well drained. Position, sunny. Plant in autumn or late winter. Prune in spring, cutting out weak stems and shortening others by a half to two-thirds.

Increase herbaceous species by seeds sown in sandy soil in a frame or outdoors in spring; by division of roots in spring or autumn; shrubby species by seeds sown as soon as ripe or by cuttings of firm young growth in a propagator in summer or of riper growth in autumn in an unheated frame.

Recommended herbaceous kinds are *P. alba*, white, spring, 6 to 9 in., Europe; *alchemilloides*, white, summer, 9 to 12 in., Pyrenees, Italy; *argyrophylla*, yellow, summer, silvery leaves, 2 to 3 ft., Himalaya; *atrosanguinea*, crimson, 2 to 3 ft., summer, Himalaya; *aurea*, yellow, summer, 4 to 6 in., Alps, Pyrenees, and var. *plena*, double; *cuneata* (syn. *ambigua*), yellow, summer, 4 to 6 in., Himalaya; *fragiformis* (syn. *emarginata*), yellow, summer, 9 in., Asia, Alaska; *megalantha*, yellow, summer, prostrate, Japan; *nepalensis*, rose-red, summer, 18 in., Himalaya, and vars. Miss Willmott, carmine, *roxana*, salmon red; *nitida*, rose, summer, 2 in., Europe, and var. *alba*; *recta*, yellow, summer, 12 to 15 in., Europe to Siberia, and var. *warrenii*, larger flowers; *rupestris*, white, summer, 6 to 18 in., Europe (Britain), Asia Minor, Siberia, and var. *pygmaea* (syn. *corsica*), prostrate; *tonguei*, terra-cotta, summer, 3 in., hybrid; *verna* (syn. *tabernaemontani*), yellow, summer, 4 to 6 in., Himalaya, and var. *nana*, dwarf. There is also a considerable number of garden varieties such as Gibson's Scarlet, single scarlet, William Rollison, double yellow and red, etc., said to be derived from hybrids between *argyrophylla*, *atrosanguinea* and *nepalensis*.

Recommended shrubby kinds are *P. arbuscula*, yellow, summer and autumn, 1 to 4 ft., Himalaya, and var. *beesii*, 1 to 1½ ft., silver foliage; Elizabeth, yellow, late spring to early autumn, 3 ft., hybrid between *arbuscula* and *fruticosa*; *fruticosa*, white, cream, yellow, late spring to early autumn, 2 to 6 ft., green or silvery leaves, North Temperate Zone, and numerous garden varieties.

PRATIA – *Campanulaceae*. Hardy creeping herbaceous perennials with lobelia-like flowers.

Soil, well-drained loam with peat or leafmould. Position, open, sunny, moist in summer but not waterlogged in winter. Can be naturalized in short grass or may be grown in pans in an unheated greenhouse or frame. Water freely in spring and summer, only sufficient to keep soil just moist in autumn and winter.

Increase by seeds sown in John Innes seed compost or equivalent in a frame or cool greenhouse as soon as ripe or in spring; by cuttings of young shoots in a propagator in summer.

The best kind is *P. angulata* (syn. *treadwellii*), white, summer, reddish purple berries, prostrate, New Zealand.

PRIMULA (Primrose) – *Primulaceae*. Slightly tender and hardy perennial plants of which the primrose and cowslip are familiar examples.

Culture of tender species: Sow seeds of *P. sinensis* and *P. obconica* in spring and early summer, *P. kewensis* and *P. malacoides* in summer, all in John Innes seed compost or equivalent and germinate in a temp. of 14 to 16°C. Shade from sun and keep just moist. Transplant seedlings when large enough to handle 1 in. apart in well-drained boxes or seed trays filled with the same compost. When leaves of seedlings meet each other, place singly in 3-in. pots in John Innes potting compost No. 1 or equivalent. Transfer when well rooted to 5-in. pots. Shade from sun, water moderately and feed every 10 to 14 days with weak liquid manure or fertilizer. Plants can stand in a frame or sheltered place outdoors in summer but should be returned to a cool greenhouse, minimum temp. 7°C., before there is frost. Give plenty of light in winter and ventilate as freely as possible consistent with maintaining cool greenhouse temperatures. Water moderately, taking care not to wet leaves unnecessarily.

Primula marginata

Culture of hardy species: Soil, porous but not dry, loamy, with leafmould or peat for most kinds. Position, cool, partially shady or open for *P. capitata*, *clarkei*, *farinosa*, *frondosa*, *juliae*, *involucrata*, *mooreana*, *nutans*, *pruhoniciana*, *sieboldii* and *viali*. Open, sunny, well drained but abundant moisture in summer for *P. allionii*, *auricula*, *clusiana*, *glutinosa*, *integrifolia*, *marginata*, *minima*, *pubescens*, *rubra* and *viscosa*. Open but not hot and dry with plenty of atmospheric moisture in winter but protection from excessive wet in winter for *P. chionantha*, *edgeworthii* and *sonchifolia*. Moist, very leafy or peaty, by waterside or in moist places for *P. alpicola*, *aurantiaca*, *beesiana*, *bulleyana*, *burmanica*, *chungensis*, *cockburniana*, *denticulata*, *florindae*, *helodoxa*, *japonica*, *poissonii*, *prolifera*, *pulverulenta*, *rosea*, *secundiflora*, *sikkimensis*, *waltoni* and *wilsoni*. Alpine house or frame for any of the high mountain species in a mixture of equal parts loam, leafmould and sand, with good drainage. Water freely in summer, sparingly in winter, moderately at other times. Avoid wetting foliage in winter. Ventilate freely at all times.

Culture of Florist's Auricula: Stems and blooms covered with mealy powder, blooms with more than one colour, and white-, grey- or green-edged petals. Desirable qualities, stem erect, elastic, carrying truss well above foliage, stalk proportionately long to size of petals; pips (blooms), seven to each truss, round; anthers, bold; eye, white, smooth and round; colours, well defined, rich; edges, distinct. Position, choice kinds in pots in John Innes potting compost No. 2 or equivalent in an airy frame or cold greenhouse; others in rich soil in shady borders. Pot and plant in spring. Water those in pots moderately in winter, freely at other times. Topdress with rich soil in spring plants that were not repotted. Apply liquid manure or fertilizer in weak solution to plants in flower.

Culture of Primrose and Polyanthus: Soil, ordinary but fertile, moist. Position, partly or wholly shaded. Plant in autumn. Mulch surface of beds containing choice kinds with rotted manure or compost in late winter. Lift those used for bedding directly after flowering, divide and replant 6 in. apart each way in a shady border until early autumn, then replant in flowering beds.

Increase by seed, that of tender kinds sown as already described; that of hardy kinds sown outdoors or in a frame or cool greenhouse as soon as ripe or in spring; some will regenerate by self-sown seedlings which can be thinned or transplanted as desired; also all hardy kinds by division in spring, immediately after flowering, or in autumn.

Recommended tender kinds are *P. floribunda*, yellow, spring, 4 to 9 in., Himalaya; *forbesii*, rose or lilac, winter and spring, 12 in., China; *kewensis*, yellow, winter and spring, 9 to 12 in., hybrid between *floribunda* and *verticillata*; *malacoides*, lilac and rose, winter and spring, 1 to 1½ ft., China, and many varieties white to carmine, single and double flowered; *obconica*, lilac, winter and spring, 6 to 9 in., China, and varieties with white, pink, red, magenta, mauve, and blue flowers; *sinensis*, Chinese Primrose, rosy purple, winter and spring, 9 in., China, and numerous varieties pink, carmine, crimson, salmon, orange and white; *verticillata*, yellow, spring, 12 in., Arabia.

Recommended hardy kinds are *P. allionii*, pink, rose, spring, 2 to 4 in., and var. *alba*, white, Maritime Alps; *alpicola* (syn. *microdonta alpicola*), yellow, purple or white, late spring, early summer, scented, 1½ to 2 ft., Tibet, Bhutan; *amoena* (syn. *altaica*), white to purple, spring, 6 in., Caucasus; *aurantiaca*, orange-red, summer, 9 to 12 in., China; *auricula*, various, spring, 6 to 8 in., Alps; *beesiana*, carmine, early summer,

Primula obconica

1½ to 2 ft., China; *bulleyana*, orange, early summer, 1½ ft., Yunnan; *burmanica*, magenta and yellow, early summer, 2 ft., Burma, China; *capitata*, violet-purple, summer, 6 to 12 in., Sikkim, Tibet, Bhutan; *carniolica*, rose and white, late spring, scented, 4 to 6 in., Alps; *chionantha*, white, late spring, scented, 15 to 30 in., Yunnan; *chungensis*, orange, early summer, 2 ft., China, Burma, Assam; *clarkei*, pink, spring, 2 in., Kashmir; *clusiana*, carmine and white, late spring, 2 to 3 in., Austria; *cockburniana*, orange-red, early summer, 1 to 1½ ft., Szechwan; *cortusoides*, rose, spring, 6 to 12 in., Siberia; *denticulata*, Drumstick Primrose, lilac, spring, 12 in., Himalaya, and vars. *alba*, white, *cachemiriana*, purple, and *rubra*, carmine; *edgeworthii* (syn. *winteri*), mauve and white, late winter, early spring, 3 to 4 in., Himalaya, and var. *alba*, white; *elatior*, Oxlip, yellow, spring, 9 in., Europe (Britain), Caucasus, Iran; *farinosa*, Bird's-eye Primrose, pink, spring, 4 to 6 in., Europe (Britain), N. Asia; *florindae*, primrose yellow, early summer, 2 ft., Tibet; *frondosa*, pink, spring, 6 in., Balkans; *glutinosa*, violet-blue, early summer, 3 in., Alps; *helodoxa*, yellow, early summer, 2 to 2½ ft., Yunnan, Burma; *integrifolia*, reddish lilac, 1 to 2 in., Pyrenees, Alps; *involucrata*, white, late spring, early summer, scented, 6 to 9 in., Himalaya, Tibet, Szechwan; *japonica*, crimson, magenta, early summer, 1½ ft., Japan, and Postford White, white and pink; *juliae*, red-purple, spring, 2 to 3 in., Caucasus; *marginata*, lavender, spring, 3 to 6 in., Alps; *minima*, pink, spring, 1 in., Alps; *mooreana*, deep violet-purple, summer, 9 in., Himalaya; *nutans*, lavender-blue, early summer, 9 in., Yunnan, Szechwan; *poissonii*, purple-crimson, early summer, 1½ ft., Yunnan, Szechwan; *pruhoniciana* (syn. *juliana*), pink to crimson-magenta, spring, 2 to 6 in., hybrids between *juliae*, *vulgaris*, and other species; *polyneura* (syns. *lichiangensis*, *veitchii*), pink to crimson, yellow eye, late spring, 9 to 12 in., China, Tibet; *prolifera*, yellow, spring, 1½ to 2 ft., Assam; *pubescens*, white, pink, lilac or crimson, 3 to 6 in., hybrids of

auricula with *rubra*, *villosa* and *viscosa*; *pulverulenta*, crimson, early summer, 2 ft., Szechwan, and vars. *alba*, white, Bartley Strain, shades of pink; *rosea*, deep rose, spring, 2 to 5 in., Himalaya; *rotundifolia*, mauve, late spring, 4 to 12 in., Nepal, Sikkim; *rubra* (syn. *hirsuta*), pink, early spring, 2 to 3 in., Alps, Pyrenees, and var. *nivea*, white; *secundiflora*, crimson, early summer, 1 to 1½ ft., Yunnan, Szechwan; *sieboldii*, white, rose or purple, late spring, 6 to 8 in., Japan; *sikkimensis*, primrose yellow, late spring, early summer, 1½ to 2½ ft., Nepal, Tibet, China; *sinoplantaginea*, purple, late spring, early summer, scented, 6 to 12 in., Yunnan, Szechwan; *sinopurpurea*, violet, late spring, early summer, 1 to 1½ ft., Yunnan; *smithiana*, yellow, early summer, 2 ft., Tibet, Bhutan; *sonchifolia*, lavender and yellow, late winter, early spring, 3 in., China, Tibet, Burma; *veris* (syn. *officinalis*), Cowslip, yellow, spring, scented, 6 to 9 in., Europe (Britain), Asia; *viali* (syn. *littoniana*), violet and red, summer, 1 to 2 ft., Yunnan, Szechwan; *viscosa*, lilac, late spring, scented, 2 to 5 in., Alps, Pyrenees; *vulgaris* (syn. *acaulis*), Primrose, pale yellow, spring, 4 to 6 in., Europe (Britain), and numerous varieties, white, pink, red, crimson, purple, blue, some double flowered, some, believed to be hybrids with *veris*, with many flowers on a stem (Polyanthus); *waltoni* (syns. *prionotes*, *vinosa*), pink or purple, late spring, early summer, 2 ft., Tibet, Bhutan; *wilsoni*, purple, early summer, 2½ ft., Yunnan, Szechwan.

PROBOSCIDEA – *Martyniaceae*. Half-hardy annuals with curious long-horned fruits, edible and used for making pickles.

Soil, fairly rich. Position, sunny, warm, well-drained, sheltered beds or borders. Sow seeds in John Innes seed compost or equivalent in temp. 15 to 18°C. in spring and either pot seedlings singly in John Innes potting compost No. 2 or equivalent, growing on in a sunny frost-proof greenhouse, or plant outdoors in late spring or early summer when danger of frost is past. Water normally. Gather fruits when young for pickling. Discard after fruiting.

The best kinds are *P. fragrans* (syn. *Martynia fragrans*), crimson-purple, summer, 2 ft., Mexico, Texas; *louisianica* (syns. *jussieui*, *Martynia louisiana*), Unicorn Plant, yellowish dotted purple, summer, 2 to 3 ft., sprawling, South-eastern U.S.A.

PROSTANTHERA – *Labiatae*. Rather tender flowering evergreen shrubs.

Compost, peat, lime-free loam and sand. Position, large well-drained pots in an unheated greenhouse, or sheltered, warm, sunny almost completely frost-free places out of doors. Water freely during summer, moderately in spring and autumn, little in winter. Pot or plant in spring. Prune after flowering, cutting back flowering stems. Remove frost-damaged growth in spring.

Increase by cuttings of young growth in sandy soil in a propagator in summer; by seeds in temp. 15–18°C. in spring with gentle bottom heat.

Recommended kinds are *P. lasianthos*, white tinged purple, spring, 3 to 6 ft., Australia, Tasmania; *ovalifolia*, soft purple, spring, 3 to 6 ft., Australia; *rotundifolia*, purple, spring, summer, 3 ft., Australia; *sieberi*, lavender, spring, 8 to 15 ft.; *violacea*, violet, spring, 6 to 8 ft., Australia.

PROTEA – *Proteaceae.* Tender evergreen shrubs; flowers enclosed in coloured bracts. All recommended kinds native to S. Africa.

Grow in rather poor, moderately acid loam with plenty of peat and coarse sand or stone chippings and perfect drainage. Plant in well-drained pots or tubs and grow in a cool, airy greenhouse, minimum temp. 7°C., or plant out of doors in sunny frost-free places. Do not shade at any time. Water moderately in summer, scarcely at all in winter. Proteas thrive best in hot, dry conditions.

Protea cynaroides

Increase by seeds sown in acid loam, peat and sand in spring in a cool greenhouse. Soak seeds in hot water (87 to 88°C.) and allow to cool before sowing.

Recommended kinds are *P. barbigera*, pink, red or yellow, winter and spring, 4 to 6 ft.; *cordata*, purplish red, spring, 3 to 4 ft.; *cynaroides*, pink, winter to summer, 2 to 4 ft.; *grandiceps*, pink, spring, 4 to 5 ft.; *latifolia*, carmine, summer, 5 to 10 ft.; *longiflora*, pink, cream or white, autumn and early winter; *mellifera* (syn. *repens*), white, pink or red; *nana* (syn. *rosacea*), crimson or orange-red, spring, 3 ft.; *neriifolia*, salmon to rose, spring, 6 to 8 ft.; *pulchella* (syn. *pulchra*), red or rose, spring, 4 to 6 ft.; *speciosa*, pink, spring, 3 to 4 ft.; *suzannae*, pink, winter and spring, 4 to 6 ft.

PRUNELLA (Selfheal) – *Labiatae.* Hardy herbaceous perennials with flowers in short spikes.

Soil, ordinary, light. Position, sunny, border or rock garden. Plant in spring or autumn. Lift divide and replant every two or three years.

Increase by division of roots in spring.

Recommended kinds are *P. grandiflora*, purple, summer, 1 ft., Europe, and vars. *alba*, white, and *rubra*, red; *incisa*, purple, summer, 9 to 12 in., Europe and var. *rubra*, red; *vulgaris laciniata*, white, summer, leaves finely cut, 1 ft., Temperate Regions of Northern Hemisphere (Britain).

PRUNUS – *Rosaceae.* A large genus of hardy flowering shrubs and trees, mostly deciduous but some evergreen. Those kinds grown for the edible fruits are dealt with on pages 234, 238 to 240.

Soil, ordinary, reasonably good, well drained for most deciduous kinds which also enjoy lime or chalk, but evergreen kinds do best in more moist, neutral or slightly acid soils.

Position, open and sunny for deciduous kinds, specially warm and sheltered for ornamental almonds, apricots and peaches which do not like low temperatures, particularly in spring when making their first growth. Plant deciduous kinds in autumn or late winter, evergreens in spring or autumn. Prune cherries, almonds and peaches as little as possible and then after flowering in late spring or early summer. *P. cerasifera, cistena, incisa* and *spinosa* are often grown as hedges or windbreaks and can be clipped after flowering and in late summer or early autumn. Evergreen kinds can be trimmed any time in summer but any hard cutting back necessary is best done in late spring.

For hedge or screen making plant *P. laurocerasus* 2 ft., apart, *lusitanica* 2 to 3 ft., *cerasifera* 2 ft., *cistena* 1½ ft.

Increase species by seeds stratified for four months at 4°C. and then sown out of doors or under glass; evergreen kinds by cuttings of firm young growth in a propagator in summer or cuttings of riper growth in an unheated frame in autumn; deciduous kinds by grafting in spring or budding in summer on to appropriate stocks such as seedling peach or plum stocks for peaches and almonds, plum stocks for plums, cherry stocks for cherries.

The following recommended kinds are grouped in their sections.

ALMONDS AND PEACHES. *P. communis* (syns. *amygdalus* and *dulcis*), Almond, pale pink, early spring, 20 to 30 ft., S. E. Europe, N. Africa, W. Asia, and vars. *alba*, white, *praecox*, extra early, *roseoplena*, double; *davidiana*, white or pink, late winter, early spring, 20 to 30 ft., China; *persica* Peach, pink, spring, 15 to 25 ft., China, usually planted for ornament in one of its garden varieties such as *alboplena* and Iceberg, double white, Aurora, Helen Borchers and Klara Mayer, double pink, Cardinal, Prince

Charming and Russell's Red, double red; *pollardii*, pink, spring, 20 to 25 ft., hybrid between *communis* and *persica* sometimes listed as a variety of *amygdalo-persica*; *tenella* (syn. *nana*), Dwarf Russian Almond, rosy red, early spring, 3 to 4 ft., Russia, S. E. Europe, and vars. *alba*, white and *gesslerana*, larger red flowers; *triloba*, double pink, spring, 10 to 20 ft., China.

CHERRIES. *Prunus avium*, Gean, Mazzard, Wild Cherry, white, spring, 30 to 60 ft., Europe (Britain), and vars. *plena*, double flowered, and *pendula*, semi-weeping; *campanulata*, Formosan Cherry, rose-red, early spring, 20 to 25 ft., rather tender, Formosa, Japan; *cerasus*, Sour Cherry, spring, white, 15 to 25 ft., Europe and var. *rhexii*, double flowers; *conradinae*, white or pale pink, late winter, early spring, 25 to 30 ft., China, and var. *semiplena*, semi-double flowers; *glandulosa*, Chinese Bush Cherry, pink or white, spring, 4 ft., China, and vars. *albiplena*, double white, and *sinensis* (syn. *japonica flore roseoplena*), double pink; *incisa*, Fuji Cherry, white or pale pink, early spring, 6 to 20 ft., Japan, and var. *praecox*, winter flowering; *japonica*, white or pale pink, spring, 4 to 5 ft., China, Korea; *mahaleb*, St Lucie Cherry, white, spring, scented, 20 to 30 ft., Europe, and var. *pendula*, weeping; *nipponica*, Nippon Cherry, Japanese Alpine Cherry, white or pale pink, late spring, 12 to 15 ft., Japan; *pumila*, Sand Cherry, white, late spring, 4 to 6 ft., North-eastern U.S.A.; *sargentii*, pink, spring, 20 to 40 ft., good autumn foliage colour, Japan, Korea; *serrula*, 20 to 25 ft., polished mahogany-red bark, W. China; *serrulata*, Oriental Cherry, Japanese Cherry, white, pink or pale lemon yellow, spring, 20 to 25 ft., China, Japan, and innumerable varieties, some single flowered, some double flowered, in habit spreading, shuttlecock shaped, columnar and weeping listed under Japanese, English and occasionally Latin names; *speciosa* (syn. *lannesiana speciosa*), Oshima Cherry, white, spring, 20 to 25 ft., Japan, parent of some of the garden Japanese cherries (see *serrulata*); *subhirtella*, Spring Cherry, pale pink, early spring, 20 to 30 ft., Japan, and vars. *autumnalis*, autumn and winter flowering and *pendula*, Weeping Rosebud Cherry, weeping; *tomentosa*, Manchu Cherry, white or pale pink, spring, 9 ft., China, Korea, Himalaya, can be clipped as a hedge; *yedoensis*, Yoshino Cherry, pink to white, spring, scented, 20 to 30 ft., hybrid between *speciosa* and *subhirtella*.

PLUMS. *Prunus blireana*, pink, double, scented, spring, 15 to 25 ft., hybrid between *cerasifera atropurpurea* and *mume*; *cerasifera*, Cherry Plum, Myrobalan, white, spring, 15 to 25 ft., W. Asia, Caucasus, with vars. *atropurpurea* (syn. *pissardii*, Purple Flash), Purple-leaved Plum, pale pink, early spring, brownish claret foliage, *nigra* (syn. Blaze), best form, deeper coloured flowers and foliage; *cistena*, Purple-leaved Sand Cherry, Crimson Dwarf, white, spring, reddish purple leaves, 4 to 6 ft., hybrid between *cerasifera pissardii* and *pumila*; *spinosa*, Sloe, Blackthorn, white, early spring, 8 to 10 ft., Europe (Britain), and vars. *plena*, double flowers, *purpurea*, purple leaves.

APRICOTS. *P. armeniaca*, Apricot, white or pale pink, spring, 20 ft., N. China, with ornamental vars. *ansu*, deeper pink, *flore pleno*, semi-double; *dasycarpa*, Black Apricot, white to pale pink, 12 to 15 ft., probably a hybrid between *armeniaca* and *cerasifera*; *mume*, Japanese Apricot, pink, late winter and spring, scented, 20 to 25 ft., Japan, with vars. *alba*, white, *alboplena*, double white, and *pendula*, weeping.

BIRD CHERRIES. All of these have small white flowers in slender racemes, *P. cornuta*, Himalayan Bird Cherry, late spring, 40 to 50 ft., Himalaya; *padus*, Bird Cherry, fragrant, late spring, 30 to 50 ft., N. Europe (Britain), N. Asia to Japan, with vars. *commutata*, early flowering, *plena*, semi-double and *watereri*, single, extra long racemes; *serotina*, Black Cherry, Rum Cherry, black fruits, bright leaves turning yellow in autumn, 30 to 90 ft., North-eastern N. America, and var. *salicifolia*, narrow leaves.

CHERRY LAURELS. All evergreen, *P. laurocerasus*, Cherry Laurel, white, spring, to 20 ft., fruit red then black, E. Europe, Asia Minor, and vars. *caucasica*, upright growth, rather narrow leaves, *magnoliaefolia*, leaves up to 12 in. long, *mischeana*, densely branched habit, Otto Luyken, narrow leaves, wide spreading habit, *rotundifolia*, good for hedging, *schipkaensis*, pyramidal habit, narrow leaves, very hardy, and *zabeliana*, dwarf spreading, hardy; *lusitanica*, Portugal Laurel, white, early summer, 10 to 25 ft., Spain and Portugal, with vars. *azorica*, large leaved, *myrtifolia* (syn. *angustifolia*), smaller leaves, dense habit, and *variegata*, leaves margined silver.

Prunus laurocerasus schipkaensis

PSEUDERANTHEMUM – *Acanthaceae*. Tender shrubs or sub-shrubs with ornamental foliage.

Compost, John Innes potting compost No. 1. Position, pots in an intermediate or warm greenhouse, minimum winter temp. 13°C., or in a warm light room. Water normally. Shade in spring and summer from strong sunshine and maintain a moist atmosphere. Pot in spring. Increase by cuttings in a warm propagator in spring or summer.

Recommended kinds are *P. albo marginatum*, leaves greyish with white edge, 3 to 4 ft., Polynesia; *atropurpureum*, leaves purple, 3 to 4 ft., Pacific Islands; *reticulatum*, leaves green, netted yellow, 4 ft., New Hebrides; *tricolor*, leaves green, pink and purple, 3 to 4 ft., Polynesia.

PSEUDOLARIX (Golden Larch) – *Pinaceae*. Hardy deciduous coniferous tree resembling a larch but with longer leaves, spirally arranged in clusters.

Soil, well drained, lime free. Position, open. Plant in autumn or late winter.

Increase by seeds sown in the open or under glass as soon as ripe or in spring.

The only species is *P. amabilis* (syns. *fortunei* and *kaempferi*), 100 to 120 ft., light green foliage turns rich yellow in autumn, E. China.

PSEUDOPANAX – *Araliaceae*. Rather tender evergreen shrubs or small trees grown for their ornamental foliage. The small dull green flowers are not attractive.

Compost, equal parts loam and peat or leafmould, or ordinary well-drained soil if out of doors. Position, pots or tubs in a sunny greenhouse, minimum temp. 8°C., or in a warm sunny sheltered place. All those listed below will survive a few degrees of frost. Plant or pot in spring. Little pruning is desirable but overgrown stems of *P. lessonii* may be cut back to side growths in spring.

Increase by cuttings of young shoots in a propagator in summer; by root cuttings in a warm propagator in spring.

Recommended kinds are *P. crassifolius*, 15 to 25 ft., leaves varying in shape with the age of the tree, New Zealand; *davidii*, 6 to 10 ft., leaves variable, China; *ferox*, narrow, toothed leaves, 12 to 20 ft., New Zealand; *lessonii*, Houmspara, or Houpara, compound leaves, to 15 ft., New Zealand.

PSEUDOTSUGA (Douglas Fir) – *Pinaceae*. Hardy evergreen coniferous tree.

Soil, good, deep lime-free loam, moist but porous. Position open, as specimens or in groups. Thrives in places where there is abundant rainfall.

Increase by seeds stratified for two months at 4°C. and then sown in the open or under glass.

The best kind is *P. menziesii* (syn. *doug-lasii* and *taxifolia*), 100 to 200 ft., Western N. America, and vars. *glauca*, Blue Douglas Fir, leaves glaucous above, extra hardy, *pendula*, branches pendulous, and *fretsii*, leaves short and broad, slow growing.

PSIDIUM – *Myrtaceae*. Tender evergreen flowering shrubs and trees. Fruit, yellow or claret coloured, round or pear shaped, aromatic, edible.

Grow in fairly rich soil such as John Innes potting compost No. 2 in well-drained pots, tubs or beds in a sunny frost-proof greenhouse (or out of doors in completely frost-free places). Pot or plant in spring. Prune into shape annually in late winter. Water normally. Syringe freely in spring and summer until fruit begins to ripen, then keep foliage dry.

Increase by cuttings of firm young shoots in sand in a warm propagator in summer; by seeds sown in spring in temp. 15 to 18°C.

Recommended kinds are *P. cattleianum*, Strawberry Guava, white, early summer, 15 to 25 ft., fruits purplish red, Brazil; *guajava*, Common Guava, white, summer, 20 to 30 ft., fruits yellow, Tropical America.

PTELEA – *Rutaceae*. Hardy deciduous flowering trees with elm-like fruits.

Soil, ordinary, well drained. Position, open or partially shaded. Plant in autumn or late winter. Regular pruning undesirable but overgrown branches can be cut back in winter.

Increase by seeds stratified for three months at 4°C. and then sown outdoors or under glass in spring; by layering shoots in spring.

The best species is *P. trifoliata*, Hop Tree, Wafer Ash, green, early summer, scented, 15 to 20 ft., N. America, var. *aurea*, leaves golden.

PTERETIS (Ostrich Fern) – *Aspidiaceae*. Large hardy deciduous ferns with long fronds in erect, narrow shuttlecocks.

Soil, two parts good loam, one part leafmould. Position, semi-shaded, cool moist border or margin of pond. Plant in spring.

Increase by spores gathered just before the cases burst and sown on the surface of a well-drained pan of sandy peat and leafmould, cover with glass and keep moderately moist in a shady position in a cold frame or greenhouse; by division in spring.

The best kind is *P. struthiopteris* (syns. *Matteuccia struthiopteris, Struthiopteris germanica*), 3 to 5 ft., Europe.

PTERIS (Ribbon Fern) – *Pteridaceae*. Large genus of mostly tropical ferns.

Compost, equal parts loam, leafmould, peat and sand. Position, pots or beds in a shady part of a cool (intermediate or warm for *P. biaurita* and varieties and *P. ensiformis*) greenhouse or in a room. Pot in spring. Water normally.

Pteris cretica

Increase by spores sown on fine sandy peat in well-drained pans in temp. 15 to 18°C. in spring or summer; by division at potting time.

Recommended kinds are *P. biaurita*, fronds to 1 ft. long, Tropics, and vars. *argyraea*, central white line to fronds, *tricolor*, young fronds red becoming silver variegated; *cretica*, fronds to 1 ft. long, Tropics and sub-tropics, and numerous varieties including *albo-lineata*, central white stripe to each frond segment; *ensiformis*, slender fertile fronds to 20 in., sterile fronds shorter, E. Asia, Malaysia, Australia, var. *victoriae*, segments banded with white; *multifida* (syn. *serrulata*), Spider Fern, slender fronds to 1½ ft long, China, Japan, there are many crested and other varieties; *tremula*, Australian Brake, fronds bright green to 3 ft. long, New Zealand, Australia.

PTEROCARYA (Wing Nut) – *Juglandaceae*. Hardy deciduous fast-growing trees resembling walnuts. Handsome pinnate leaves. Catkin-like flowers with male and female on the same tree.

Soil, deep moist loam. Position, as specimens in open places or on lawns, especially near water. Plant in autumn or late winter. Young plants liable to damage by late spring frosts.

Increase by seeds stratified for three months at 4°C. and then sown in open light soil outdoors or under glass in spring; by layering in autumn; or by suckers in autumn.

Recommended kinds are *P. fraxinifolia* (syn. *caucasica*), 50 to 100 ft., Caucasus, N. Iran; *rehderiana*, 50 to 80 ft., hybrid between *fraxinifolia* and *stenoptera*; *rhoifolia*, Japanese Wing Nut, 50 to 100 ft., Japan; *stenoptera*, 50 to 80 ft., China, less hardy than *fraxinifolia*.

PULMONARIA (Lungwort) – *Boraginaceae*. Hardy herbaceous herbs valuable for their early bloom and often ornamental foliage, sometimes spotted with white.

Soil, ordinary. Position, partially shaded.

Plant in spring or autumn. Lift and replant in fresh soil every four or five years.

Increase by seeds sown in ordinary soil in a shady position outdoors in spring; by division in spring or autumn.

Recommended kinds are *P. angustifolia* (syn. *azurea*), Blue Cowslip, pink becoming blue, spring, 6 to 8 in., Europe; *longifolia*, blue, spring, 6 to 8 in., Europe; *officinalis*, Jerusalem Cowslip, Common Lungwort, Spotted Dog, purple to violet, 6 to 12 in., Europe, Caucasus; *rubra*, brick red, spring, 6 to 9 in., Europe; *saccharata*, Bethlehem Sage, pink becoming blue, spring, summer, 1 ft., Europe, and var. Mrs Moon, rose-pink.

PULSATILLA – *Ranunculaceae*. Hardy herbaceous perennials, covered in down or silky hairs and with anemone-like flowers. Sometimes included with *Anemone*.

Soil, porous, alkaline for most kinds but lime free for *P. alpina sulphurea*. *P. vulgaris* and varieties succeed well on chalk. Position, open, sunny. Plant in spring, preferably young plants from pots as they do not transplant well. Leave undisturbed when established.

Increase by seeds sown in John Innes seed compost or equivalent in a frame or cool greenhouse as soon as ripe. Either transfer seedlings to flowering positions while very young or pot singly to avoid further root disturbance.

Pulsatilla vulgaris

Recommended kinds are *P. alpina* (syn. *Anemone alpina*), white, spring, 1 to 1½ ft., European Alps, and var. *sulphurea*, sulphur yellow; *vernalis* (syn. *Anemone vernalis*), white within, mauve without, early spring, 3 to 6 in., Europe; *vulgaris* (syn. *Anemone pulsatilla*), Pasque Flower, lavender to purple, spring, 6 to 8 in., Europe (Britain), and var. *alba*, white.

PUNICA – *Punicaceae*. Slightly tender deciduous small tree, ornamental flowers, edible fruit only produced in warm climates.

Soil, ordinary, well drained. Position, full sun. In the warmest areas a sheltered position in the open, elsewhere wall pro-

tection is essential. If sheltered plants can survive temperature around – 10°C.

Increase by seeds sown in temp. 15 to 18°C. in spring; by cuttings of half-ripened wood in a propagator in summer, or cuttings of fully ripe growth in a frame in autumn.

The best kind is *P. granatum*, Pomegranate, reddish scarlet, late summer, early autumn, 10 to 15 ft., Iran, Afghanistan, and vars. *alboplena* (syn. *multiplex*), double white, *flore pleno* (syn. *rubroplena*), double red, *nana*, dwarf. Yellow and orange-red varieties are also available.

PUSCHKINIA (Striped Squill) – *Liliaceae*. Hardy bulbous flowering plants with scilla-like flowers.

Soil, ordinary, light. Position, sunny, well drained. Plant bulbs 3 in. deep in autumn. Lift and replant only when overcrowded.

Increase by seeds sown in sandy soil in a frame or cool greenhouse as soon as ripe or in spring; by offsets, removed and planted as advised for old bulbs in autumn.

The best kind is *P. scilloides* (syns. *libanotica*, *sicula*), white or pale blue, striped with blue, spring, 4 in., Asia Minor, vars. *compacta*, dwarf, and *alba*, white.

PUYA – *Bromeliaceae*. Tender or nearly hardy plants making large rosettes of stiff spiny leaves and spike-like clusters of metallic-coloured flowers.

Compost, John Innes potting compost No. 1 or equivalent. Position, pots, tubs or beds in a sunny, frost-proof greenhouse or outdoors in warm, sunny, well-drained places in nearly frost-free districts. Water fairly freely in spring and summer, moderately in autumn, very sparingly in winter. Do not shade at any time. Pot or plant in spring.

Increase by suckers removed in spring and started in a propagator; by seeds sown in temp. 18 to 21°C. in spring or as soon as ripe.

Recommended kinds are *P. alpestris*, peacock blue, late spring, 2 to 4 ft., Chile; *caerulea*, deep blue, spring, 3 to 4 ft., Chile; *chilensis*, green and yellowish, summer, 6 to 10 ft., Chile, and var. *gigantea*, to 15 ft.

PYRACANTHA (Firethorn) – *Rosaceae*. Hardy and slightly tender, evergreen, flowering and berried shrubs.

Soil, ordinary, well drained; they succeed well on chalk and limestone. Position, full sun or partial shade. May be trained as wall climbers or as hedges, or will make bushy specimens. Excellent for screening. Plant in spring or autumn, preferably from containers to avoid root breakage. Hedges can be clipped occasionally in spring or summer; wall-trained plants may have badly placed growths shortened after flowering.

Increase by seeds stratified for three months at 4°C. and then sown in sandy soil in a cool greenhouse or frame during spring; cuttings of nearly ripened young growth in sandy soil in a frame during summer or early autumn.

Recommended kinds are *P. angustifolia*, white, late spring, early summer, 10 to 12 ft., orange-yellow berries persisting all winter, W. China; *atalantioides* (syn. *gibbsii*), white, late spring, early summer, 10 to 20 ft., scarlet berries persisting, China; *coccinea*, white, early summer, 10 to 15 ft., bright red berries, S. Europe, Asia Minor, and var. *lalandei*, more vigorous, orange-red berries; *crenato-serrata*, white, early summer, red berries, persisting, 10 to 15 ft., Central and W. China; *rogersiana* (syn. *crenulata rogersiana*), white, early summer, 10 to 12 ft., reddish orange berries, S. W. China, and var. *flava*, yellow berries; *watereri*, white, early summer, 10 to 12 ft., bright red berries, hybrid between *atalantioides* and *rogersiana*.

PYROLA (Wintergreen) – *Ericaceae*. Hardy perennial herbs with flowers in small spikes.

Soil, equal parts peat, leafmould and lime-free loam. Position, moist, shady. Plant in spring. Water freely in dry weather. Lift, divide and replant only when overgrown.

Increase by seeds sown thinly in spring in fine sandy peat where the plants are to grow; by division in spring.

Recommended kinds are *P. elliptica*, greenish white, scented, summer, 6 in., N. America; *media*, white tinged pink, summer, 6 in., Europe (Britain), Caucasus, Asia Minor; *rotundifolia*, white, 6 to 12 in., Europe (Britain), N. Asia, Asia Minor.

PYROSTEGIA – *Bignoniaceae*. Tender evergreen climbers with clusters of trumpet-shaped flowers.

Soil, John Innes potting compost No. 2 or equivalent. Position, sunny greenhouse, minimum temp. 7°C. or outdoors in frost-free places. Cut out damaged or overgrown stems in spring.

Increase by layering in spring or autumn; by cuttings of firm growth in a warm propagator in summer.

The best kind is *P. venusta* (syn. *ignea*), orange-red, winter, Brazil.

PYRUS (Pear) – *Rosaceae*. Hardy, deciduous, fruit-bearing and flowering trees. For pears grown for their edible fruits see page 238.

Soil, ordinary. Position, as specimens in open, preferably sunny, places. Plant in autumn or late winter.

Increase species by seeds stratified for three months at 4°C. and then sown outdoors or under glass; grafting in spring or budding in summer on to seedlings or pear stocks; selected varieties by layering in autumn.

Recommended kinds are *P. calleryana*, white, spring, 20 to 30 ft., China, and var. Bradford, similar but thornless; *salicifolia*, Willow-leaved Pear, flowers white, spring, 15 to 20 ft., narrow grey leaves, S. E. Europe, W. Asia, and var. *pendula*, weeping.

QUERCUS (Oak) – *Fagaceae*. Hardy or slightly tender deciduous and evergreen trees and shrubs.

Soil, good deep loam, preferably rather moist. Position, open or in coppices and woodlands. *Q. ilex* and *cerris* are particularly suitable for planting near the sea, and the former is often used as a windbreak. Plant evergreen kinds in spring or autumn, deciduous ones in autumn or late winter. Prune deciduous oaks in winter, evergreen kinds in spring.

Increase by acorns sown outdoors as soon as ripe or stored in moist sand outdoors until spring and then sown. Oaks transplant badly and are all the better for being sown where they are to grow. Choice deciduous kinds are grafted on common oak in spring. Most evergreen oaks can be increased by cuttings of firm young growth in a propagator in summer, and some by riper cuttings in a frame in autumn.

Recommended evergreen kinds are *Q. acuta*, 15 to 40 ft., Japan; *chrysolepis*, Californian Live Oak, Canyon Live Oak, Maul Oak, 15 to 60 ft., South-western U.S.A.; *ilex*, Holm Oak, Holly Oak, 60 ft., Mediterranean region; *suber*, Cork Oak, 50 to 60 ft., S. Europe, N. Africa, the source of the cork of commerce, only satisfactory in warm places; *virginiana*, Live Oak, 20 to 60 ft., South-eastern U.S.A., Mexico, Cuba, only satisfactory in warm places.

Recommended deciduous kinds are *Q. acutissima*, Sawtooth Oak, 30 to 40 ft., Japan, Korea, China; *alba*, White Oak, Quebec Oak, 30 to 90 ft., dislikes lime, Eastern U.S.A.; *bicolor*, Swamp White Oak, 60 to 70 ft., dislikes lime, Eastern N. America; *canariensis* (syn. *mirbeckii*), Algerian Oak, to 90 ft., handsome foliage retained till midwinter, N. Africa and Portugal; *cerris*, Turkey Oak, fast growing, to 120 ft., S. Europe, Asia Minor; *coccinea*, Scarlet Oak, fine autumn colour, 60 to 80 ft., dislikes lime, Eastern N. America, var. *splendens*, good autumn colouring form; *frainetto* (syn. *conferta*), large leaves warm tinted in autumn, to 100 ft., S. E. Europe; *garryana*, Oregon Oak, 40 to 90 ft., Western N. America; *hispanica*, often semi-evergreen, 60 to 100 ft., hybrid between *cerris* and *suber*, and var. *lucombeana*, Lucombe Oak, a good form which only loses its leaves in severe cold, *imbricaria*, Shingle Oak, long narrow leaves, autumn tints, 50 to 70 ft., Eastern U.S.A.; *libani*, Lebanon Oak, narrow leaves, 30 ft., Asia Minor; *lyrata*, Overcup Oak, leaves to 8 in. long, 60 to 80 ft., N. America; *macranthera*, 60 ft., Caucasus, Iran; *macrocarpa*,

Burr Oak, Mossy Cup Oak, enormous leaves, 50 to 100 ft., dislikes lime, Eastern and Central N. America; *marilandica*, Black Jack Oak, slow growing, autumn tints, 30 to 40 ft., dislikes lime, Eastern U.S.A.; *palustris*, Pin Oak, quick growing, autumn tints, 75 to 100 ft., dislikes lime, Eastern U.S.A.; *petraea* (syn. *sessiliflora*), Durmast Oak, Sessile Oak, 60 to 120 ft., Europe (Britain), good for moist soils; *phellos*, Willow Oak, willow-like leaves, 50 to 70 ft., dislikes lime, Eastern U.S.A.; *pontica*, large-ribbed leaves colouring in autumn, to 20 ft., dislikes lime, Armenia, Caucasus; *robur* (syn. *pedunculata*), Common Oak, to 100 ft., sometimes more, Europe (Britain), Asia Minor, many varieties including *concordia*, Golden Oak, *fastigiata*, Cypress Oak, columnar habit, *heterophylla*, leaves variously shaped, *pendula*, weeping, *variegata*, leaves marked with white or yellow; *rubra*, Red Oak, large leaves colouring in autumn, to 75 ft., dislikes lime, Eastern N. America; *velutina*, Black Oak, Yellow Bark Oak, bark permeated yellow, used for tanning, 70 to 100 ft., Eastern and Central U.S.A., and var. *rubrifolia*, Champion's Oak, extra large leaves colouring in autumn.

RAMONDA – *Gesneriaceae*. Hardy perennial plants making rosettes of leathery leaves and producing attractive flowers on bare stems.

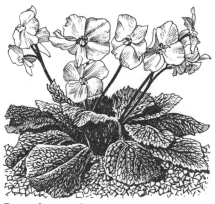

Ramonda myconi

Soil, light loam and peat. Position, semi-shaded aspect in vertical or horizontal crevices, not on the flat. Plant in spring. Water in dry weather. For pot culture use similar soil and grow in a cool position or in a shaded cold greenhouse or frame.

Increase by seeds sown in similar compost in spring in temp. 14 to 16°C.; by division of plants in spring or by leaf cuttings in summer.

Recommended kinds are *R. myconi* (syn *pyrenaica*), Rosette Mullein, lilac-blue and yellow, early summer, 6 in., Pyrenees, and vars. *alba*, white, *rosea*, pink; *nathaliae*, rich lavender, early summer, 4 to 6 in., Balkans; *serbica*, lavender, early summer, 4 in., Balkans, and var. *alba*.

RANUNCULUS (Buttercup, Crowfoot) – *Ranunculaceae*. Hardy and half-hardy, herbaceous, tuberous-rooted and aquatic perennials, some with very showy flowers.

Culture of tuberous-rooted species (Turban, Persian, French, Peony-flowered): Soil, good, ordinary, enriched with rotted manure and leafmould. Position, open, sunny, well drained in winter but not dry in summer. Plant in late winter or early spring in most places but in autumn in warm places or in sunny frames. Place tubers claw-side downwards 2 in. deep and 3 to 5 in. apart. Press tubers firmly into the soil and cover with fine soil. Water freely in dry weather. Feed with liquid manure or fertilizer in late spring and early summer. Lift tubers when flowers fade and leaves turn yellow in summer, dry them in the sun and store in sand in a cool place till planting time.

Culture of hardy species: Soil, ordinary for most kinds but scree for *R. alpestris, calandrinioides* and *glacialis*. Position, sunny, or partially shady for most kinds; sunny or alpine house for scree varieties. Plant in spring or autumn. Lift, divide and replant in fresh soil triennially. Ponds, and slow-moving streams for *R. aquatilis*, which is a useful oxygenator for water; shallow water or bog for *R. lingua*. Plant these aquatic or semi-aquatic kinds in spring or early summer.

Increase by seeds sown as soon as ripe in autumn in John Innes seed compost or equivalent in a frame or cool greenhouse; herbaceous and aquatic kinds by division in spring.

The best tuberous-rooted kind is *R. asiaticus*, Turban, Persian, French or Peony-flowered, various colours, late spring, summer, 6 to 12 in., Orient.

Recommended hardy kinds are *R. aconitifolius*, White Bachelor's Buttons, white, late spring, early summer, 1½ to 2 ft., Europe, var. *flore pleno*, Fair Maids of France, Fair Maids of Kent; *acris flore pleno*, Yellow Bachelor's Buttons, Double Buttercup, yellow, spring, 1½ ft., double-flowered form of the meadow buttercup native to Europe (Britain) and W. Asia; *alpestris*, white, spring, summer, 4 in., Europe; *amplexicaulis*, white, spring, 6 to 12 in., Pyrenees; *aquatilis*, Water Crowfoot, white, late spring, floating and submerged aquatic, Temperate Regions (Britain); *bulbosus pleniflorus*, Double Buttercup, yellow, spring, summer, 1 ft., double-flowered form of the bulbous buttercup, Europe (Britain), W. Asia; *calandrinioides*, large, white, winter, spring, 6 to 9 in., Morocco; *ficaria*, vars. *albus*, white, *aurantiacus*, orange, *flore pleno*, double yellow, *grandiflorus* (syn. *major*), large in leaf and flower, all forms of the Celandine, 6 to 9 in., late winter, early spring, Europe (Britain); *glacialis*, white and rose, summer, 6 in., Arctic Regions; *gramineus*, yellow, spring, early summer, 6 to 8 in., Europe; *lingua*, Greater Spearwort, yellow, summer, 3 to 4 ft., Europe (Britain); *montanus* (syn. *geraniifolius*), yellow, late spring, summer, 4 to 6 in., Europe; *parnassifolius*, white, summer, 6 in., Europe.

RAOULIA – *Compositae*. Small creeping perennial herbs grown for their foliage.

Soil, sandy loam. Position, sunny, well drained but not too dry in summer; suitable for carpeting the soil on rock gardens and screes. Plant in spring.

Increase by division in late summer.

Recommended kinds are *R. australis*, silvery foliage, yellow, New Zealand; *glabra*, emerald green foliage, white, New Zealand.

RECHSTEINERIA – *Gesneriaceae*. Tender herbaceous perennials forming tubers and with clusters of tubular flowers. Formerly known as gesneria, and also as corytholoma.

Compost, equal parts loam, leafmould and peat with two parts coarse sand. Position, pots in an intermediate or warm greenhouse, minimum winter temp. 13°C. Pot in early spring, one tuber only just covered in each 5-in. pot. Water sparingly at first, freely as growth appears but after flowering gradually reduce the water supply and in winter keep quite dry with pots on their sides. Shade from strong sunshine in spring and summer and maintain a fairly moist atmosphere.

Increase by seeds sown in late winter or early spring, in temp. 15 to 18°C.

Recommended kinds are *R. cardinalis*, scarlet, spring to autumn, 9 to 12 in., Brazil; *cyclophylla*, brick red and purple, summer, to 2 ft., Brazil; *leucotricha*, pink, white, and purple, summer, 6 to 10 in., Brazil; *splendens*, red, summer, 9 to 12 in., Brazil; *umbellata*, rose-pink, summer, 1 ft., Brazil. There are also hybrids between Rechsteineria and Sinningia.

REHMANNIA – *Scrophulariaceae*. Tender herbaceous perennials with loose spikes of trumpet-shaped flowers.

Compost, John Innes potting compost No. 2 or equivalent. Position, pots in a cool greenhouse, minimum winter temp. 7°C. Pot in spring. Water normally. Shade in summer from direct sunshine. *R. angulata* may be grown as a biennial.

Increase by seeds sown in early or mid-summer in an unheated greenhouse or frame, in John Innes seed compost or equivalent. Pot seedlings singly in John Innes potting compost No. 1 or equivalent, and later move on to John Innes potting compost No. 2 or equivalent. Pinch out the growing tip of each seedling when about 9 in. high.

The best kinds are *R. angulata*, purple, 2 to 3 ft., China, and var. Pink Perfection, pink.

REINWARDTIA – *Linaceae*. Tender evergreen flowering shrubs with clusters of showy yellow flowers.

Compost, John Innes potting compost No. 2 or equivalent. Position, large pots or a bed in a cool or intermediate greenhouse, minimum winter temp. 7°C. Pot or plant in early spring. Water normally. Do not shade at any time. Cut back previous year's stems in spring as soon as plants stop flowering.

Increase by cuttings of young growth in a propagator in spring.

The best kind is *R. trigyna* (syn. *Linum trigynum*), Winter Flax, yellow, autumn and winter, 2 to 3 ft., India.

RENANTHERA – *Orchidaceae*. Tender epiphytic orchids with slender stems bearing numerous rather spidery flowers.

Compost, equal parts fibre and sphagnum moss. Position, well-drained pots in an intermediate house. Shade from direct sunshine in spring and summer and maintain a moist atmosphere. Water freely while in growth, but rather sparingly in winter. Repot when necessary after flowering.

Increase by pieces of stem severed immediately below the aerial roots and started in a warm, close atmosphere.

Recommended kinds are *R. coccinea*, scarlet, crimson and yellow, summer, 4 to 20 ft., S. E. Asia; *imschootiana*, shades of red and yellow, spring, 3 ft., Assam.

RESEDA – *Resedaceae*. A hardy herbaceous perennial, but usually grown as an annual for its sweetly scented but not showy flowers.

Soil, ordinary, preferably containing lime or chalk. Position, sunny. Sow seeds outdoors in spring where plants are to grow and thin seedlings to 3 or 4 in. Water freely in summer. In warm, dry positions plants will survive the winter outdoors for several years. Plants can also be grown in pots in John Innes potting compost No. 1 or equivalent; sow directly in the pots and

Reseda odorata

thin to leave 3 or 4 plants in a 5-in. pot. Grow in a sunny greenhouse or window. No heat is required.

The best kind is *R. odorata*, Mignonette, yellow and white or green and red, summer, 1 to 2 ft., N. Africa.

RHAMNUS (Buckthorn) – *Rhamnaceae*. Hardy evergreen and deciduous trees and shrubs. Flowers small, followed by red or black berries.

Soil, ordinary. Position, sunny or semi-shady; good seaside shrubs. *R. alaterna, cathartica* and *frangula* occasionally used as hedges or windbreaks. Plant deciduous kinds in autumn or late winter, evergreen kinds in spring or autumn. Regular pruning is not essential but deciduous kinds can be pruned or clipped in autumn or late winter, evergreen kinds in spring or early summer.

Increase by seeds sown out of doors in autumn or stratified for three months at 4°C. and then sown out of doors or under glass; by cuttings of firm young growth in a frame in summer; by layering in spring or autumn.

Recommended kinds are *R. alaterna*, yellowish green, spring, fruits red, 10 to 20 ft., evergreen, S. W. Europe, and vars. *angustifolia*, and *argenteo-variegata*, leaves margined with creamy white; *californica*, 10 to 15 ft., evergreen, berries red becoming black, Western N. America; *cathartica*, Buckthorn, 10 to 20 ft., berries black, deciduous, Europe (Britain); *frangula*, 10 to 15 ft., fruits red becoming black, deciduous, Europe (Britain), and vars. *asplenifolia*, very narrow leaves, *columnaris*, columnar habit; *imeretina* (sometimes wrongly called *libanotica*), 10 ft., deciduous, fine autumn colour, Western Caucasus.

RHAPHIOLEPIS – *Rosaceae*. Slightly tender slow-growing evergreen flowering shrubs with leathery leaves.

Soil, good, loamy, well drained. Position, sunny, warm, sheltered. If wood is well ripened the hardiest kind, *R. umbellata*, will survive temperatures around − 10°C. All may be grown in a frost-proof greenhouse. Plant in spring or autumn. Prune straggling shoots in spring. Protect tender species in severe weather.

Increase by cuttings of firm shoots in a compost of equal parts sand, peat and loam in a frame in summer.

Recommended kinds are *R. delacouri*, pink, spring, 5 ft., hybrid between *indica* and *umbellata*; *indica*, Indian Hawthorn, white, tinged pink, spring and summer, 4 ft., China; *umbellata* (syn. *japonica*), hardy, withstands wind, white, fragrant, early summer, 4 to 6 ft., Japan.

RHAZYA – *Apocynaceae*. Hardy perennial with clusters of small flowers.

Soil, sandy loam. Position, sunny well drained. Plant in spring.

Increase by seeds sown in a greenhouse in spring; by division at planting time.

The best kind is *R. orientalis*, blue, summer, 12 to 18 in., Orient.

RHEUM (Rhubarb) – *Polygonaceae*. Hardy herbaceous perennials. Ornamental foliage plants, one species cultivated for its edible stalks.

Soil for the ornamental kinds, deep, rich, moist. Position, sunny or partially shaded. Plant in spring or autumn. Water copiously in dry weather.

Increase by seeds sown in spring out of doors or under glass; by division in spring.

Recommended kinds are *R. acuminatum*, reddish purple, summer, 3 ft., Himalaya; *alexandrae*, light buff bracts, summer, 3 to 4 ft., Tibet, China; *palmatum*, red, summer, 5 to 6 ft., N. E. Asia, and var. *tanguticum*; even larger leaves.

RHIPSALIDOPSIS – *Cactaceae*. Tender succulent perennials with showy flowers, both from Brazil.

Rhipsalidopsis rosea

Compost, John Innes potting compost No. 2 or equivalent plus one-sixth its bulk of coarse sand. Position, pots or baskets in a cool or intermediate greenhouse, minimum winter temp. 7°C., or in a warm light room. Water normally most of the year but rather sparingly for a few weeks after flowering. Shade from direct sunshine in summer when plants can be removed to a sheltered, semi-shady place outdoors.

Increase by cuttings in sandy soil in spring or summer; by grafting on *Pereskia aculeata* in spring.

Recommended kinds are *R. gaertneri* (syns. *Epiphyllum gaertneri* and *Schlumbergera gaertneri*), Easter Cactus, scarlet, spring, arching or pendulous; *rosea*, pink, early spring, arching. There are also hybrids between these two species.

RHIPSALIS – *Cactaceae*. Tender succulents, some kinds trailing, others erect.

Grow in a fairly rich, porous compost such as John Innes potting compost No. 2 with the addition of one-sixth its bulk of coarse sand or crushed brick, in well-drained pots in a light greenhouse. Pot in spring, pots to be drained to one-sixth of their depth for large plants, one-third for small plants. Water moderately in spring and summer, keep almost dry in autumn and winter. Shade from bright sunshine. Minimum winter temperature 7°C.

Increase by seeds sown in sandy soil in temp. 18 to 21°C. in spring; by stem cuttings inserted in sandy soil in summer.

Recommended kinds are *R. cassutha*, Mistletoe Cactus, yellow, late summer, trailing, Tropics; *cereuscula* (syn. *saglionis*), yellow, spring, to 2 ft., Brazil, Uruguay; *crispata*, white or cream, winter, 1 ft., Brazil; *houlletiana*, cream and red, winter, to 6 ft., Brazil; *mesembryanthoides*, white or pink, spring, 6 in., S. America.

RHODOCHITON – *Scrophulariaceae*. Greenhouse climbing perennial with pendent flowers.

Grow in a moderately rich compost such as John Innes potting compost No. 2 in well-drained pots or borders in a cool greenhouse, minimum winter temp. 7°C., with shoots trained up supports. Pot or plant in spring. Water normally. Shade from bright sun in summer. Thin out and shorten shoots moderately in late winter.

Increase by seeds sown in light soil in temp. 15 to 18°C. in spring, transplanting seedlings when 1 in. high singly in 2- or 3-in. pots; by cuttings of shoots inserted in sandy soil in a propagator in spring or summer.

The only species is *R. atrosanguineum* (syn. *volubile*), Purple Bellerine, Purple Bells, lilac-pink and maroon, summer, 10 to 15 ft., Mexico.

RHODODENDRON – *Ericaceae*. Hardy and more or less tender evergreen and deciduous shrubs. The shrubs commonly known in gardens as azaleas are classified by botanists as rhododendrons and so are included here.

In the main, the hybrid garden races of evergreen rhododendrons have sprung from such species as *R. catawbiense, ponticum, caucasicum, arboreum* and *griersonianum*. A lesser part has been played by *R. maximum, griffithianum, fortunei, thomsonii, williamsianum, dicroanthum, haematodes, eriogynum, repens, neriiflorum, elliottii, cinnabarinum, discolor* and *campylocarpum*. The deciduous hybrid azaleas have been obtained from *R. flavum, calendulaceum, nudiflorum, viscosum, occidentale, molle*, and others. The Ghent azaleas are, in the main, derived from *R. flavum, viscosum, nudiflorum, calendulaceum* and *luteum*. The dwarf Japanese azaleas, such as Hinodegiri, are closely allied to *R. obtusum*, those known as Kurume azaleas being forms raised over a period of many years by Japanese horticulturists round the city of Kurume, in the southern island of Kyushu, Japan.

It is impossible to cover fully, in a confined space, the immense variety of species and hybrids of rhododendron and their individual requirements. The species vary from low-creeping shrubs to large trees, and natural conditions in which they are found vary from shaded and sheltered woodland to elevated dry and exposed moorland. For full details refer to the Rhododendron Handbooks published by the Royal Horticultural Society. Only one species, *R. hirsutum*, will grow in soil containing free lime and most species prefer a rather acid soil but *R. ponticum* and its hybrids will grow in near neutral soils. The majority like cool, moist and humus-rich soil, and both heavy and light soils should receive heavy dressings of peat well dug in prior to planting. Hungry light soils should have some well-decayed manure mixed in also. All rhododendrons benefit from annual topdressing; useful material consists of compost, half-decayed leaves or bracken and peat. The best garden value for ordinary conditions is found amongst the numerous named garden hybrids, which are easily grown. Position, in open borders or semi-woodland glades with dappled shade from mixed plantations of evergreen and deciduous trees. Some species are equally easy but others require specialized positions. Always remove developing seed pods when the flowers have faded.

Though the varieties of Indian azalea can be grown out of doors in mild climates and will even survive some frost, particularly if planted under the shelter of trees, they make such excellent pot plants for winter and spring flowering that they are commonly grown in this way. The compost used is three parts peat, one part loam and one part equal proportions of leafmould and coarse sand. Position, well-drained pots in a sunny greenhouse from autumn to late spring, in partial shade out of doors in summer. Repot directly after flowering, firm potting essential. Prune only to shorten straggly growth. Syringe daily after flowering till plants are taken out of doors. Water moderately in autumn and winter, freely afterwards, never allowing roots to get dry. Apply weak liquid manure when flower buds form in summer. Minimum winter temperature 7°C. but this may be raised to 15 to 18°C. to bring plants into early bloom. Some varieties naturally flower earlier than others. Remove seed pods directly they form.

Increase species by seeds sown on the surface of sandy peat in late winter or early spring, slightly covered with fine sand and placed in a propagator, temp. 12 to 15°C., and kept moderately moist; species and garden varieties by cuttings of firm shoots in summer or early autumn inserted in three parts sand, one part granulated peat in a propagator temp. 7 to 12°C. at first, then 5°C. higher, steady bottom heat aids the rooting of large-leaved kinds; small-leaved kinds can be rooted without heat; take cuttings of the large-leaved kinds first and continue to the smallest-leaved varieties; by layering in spring or summer; by grafting on to common species in a propagator in spring.

The hardiness of the different species is indicated by a letter following the specific name, as follows:

A. Hardy

B. Slightly tender but usually able to survive temperatures of about −13°C.

C. Decidedly tender, some at risk at −3°C.

D. Tender, should not be exposed to frost.

For B and C inclusive, planting in open spaces in woodland usually gives the best results. The majority of species are most susceptible to frost when making their young growth in spring.

Rhododendron simsii (hybrid)

Recommended kinds are *R. aberconwayi*, A, white and pink, spring to summer, 4 to 6 ft., China; *ambiguum*, greenish yellow, spring, 8 to 10 ft., China; *arboreum*, B, C, red, pink or white, winter, early spring, 20 to 40 ft., Himalaya, Kashmir, Ceylon; *argyrophyllum*, A, white or pink, late spring, leaves silvery beneath, 15 to 20 ft., China; *augustinii*, A, B, blue, late spring, 10 to 15 ft., China, Tibet; *auriculatum*, A, white or pink, summer, 15 to 20 ft., China; *barbatum*, A, B, scarlet, early spring, 15 to 30 ft., Nepal, Sikkim, Bhutan; *bullatum*, C, white or tinged pink, late spring, very fragrant, 8 ft., China, Tibet, Burma; *calophytum*, A, white or pink, spring, 15 to 30 ft., China; *calostrotum*, A, purple, spring to summer, 4 ft., China, Burma, Assam, Tibet; *caloxanthum*, A, B, pale yellow and orange, spring, 4 to 6 ft., China, Burma, Tibet; *campanulatum*, A, rosy purple, spring, 12 to 18 ft., Himalaya; *campylocarpum*, A, B, yellow, spring, 4 to 12 ft., Kashmir to Bhutan; *campylogynum*, A, B, rose-purple to maroon, spring to summer, 2 to 18 in., China, Tibet, Burma; *catawbiense*, A, magenta, pink or white, early summer, 10 to 12 ft., South-eastern U.S.A.; *caucasicum*, A, pale yellow, late spring, 5 to 10 ft., Caucasus, Turkey; *cephalanthum*, A, white, late spring, 2 to 4 ft., China, Burma; *chaetomallum*, A, crimson or rose, spring, 8 to 10 ft., Tibet, China; *charitopes*, A, pink speckled crimson, spring, 2 to 3 ft., Burma, China; *ciliatum*, A, B, white or pink tinged, spring, 3 to 5 ft., Tibet, China; *ciliicalyx*, C, D, white or pale pink, spring, 6 to 10 ft., China, Tibet; *cinnabarinum*, A, cinnabar red, apricot or crimson, spring to summer, 8 to 12 ft., Himalaya; *concatenans*, A, apricot, spring, 6 to 8 ft., Tibet; *crassum*, B, C, white, cream or pink, summer, 8 to 12 ft., China, Burma, Tibet; *dalhousiae*, C, D, pale yellow or white, spring to summer, 8 to 10 ft., China, Tibet; *dauricum*, A, rose-purple, winter, early spring, 6 to 8 ft., semi-deciduous, N. Asia, and var. *sempervirens*, evergreen; *davidsonianum*, A, B, pink or purple, spring, 8 to 10 ft., China; *decorum*, A, white or pale pink, scented, spring, 12 to 20 ft., China; *desquamatum*, A, mauve, spring, leaves brown beneath, 15 to 25 ft., China, Burma, Tibet; *diaprepes*, B, white, or pale pink, early summer, 15 to 25 ft., China, Tibet; *dicroanthum*, A, orange or salmon, late spring, early summer, 6 ft., China; *discolor*, A, white or pink, scented, early summer, 15 to 20 ft., China; *edgeworthii*, C, white or pink flushed, scented, spring, 8 to 10 ft., Himalaya; *elliottii*, B, C, red, late spring, early summer, 10 to 12 ft., Manipur; *eriogynum*, B, C, red, early summer, China; *falconeri*, B, creamy white and maroon, spring, very large leaves, 20 to 50 ft., China, Nepal; *fargesii*, A, rose or white, spring, 12 to 20 ft., China; *ferrugineum*, A, rosy crimson, early summer, to 4 ft., Europe; *fictolacteum*, A, white, cream or pink and crimson, spring, leaves brownish beneath, 20 to 40 ft., China, Tibet; *formosum*, C, white and pink, scented, to 10 ft., Assam; *forrestii*, A, scarlet, spring, prostrate, Tibet, Burma, China; *fortunei*, A, lilac-pink, late spring, 15 to 30 ft., China; *fulgens*, A, scarlet, early spring, 6 to 12 ft., China, Assam, Tibet; *fulvum*, A, white to rose, early spring, 15 to 20 ft., China, Burma, Assam, Tibet; *giganteum*, C, D, rose-crimson, early spring, 30 to 80 ft., China; *grande*, C, white or cream and purple, early spring, 20 to 30 ft., very large leaves, silvery or tawny beneath, China, Bhutan; *griersonianum*, A, scarlet, early summer, 7 to 10 ft., China, Burma; *griffithianum*, C, white, late spring, 14 to 20 ft., China, Bhutan; *haematodes*, A, crimson, late spring to early summer, 3 to 10 ft., China; *hanceanum*, A, cream or yellow, spring, 2 to 4 ft., China and var. *nanum*, 6 in.; *hippophaeoides*, lavender to rose, early spring, 3 to 5 ft., China; *hodgsonii*, A, magenta-purple, spring, 12 to 20 ft., China, Nepal, Bhutan; *impeditum*, A, mauve or purplish blue, spring, to 18 in., China; *intricatum*, A, mauve, spring, 2 to 3 ft., China; *irroratum*, A, white or cream, sometimes pink flushed, spring, 15 to 25 ft. China; *javanicum*, D, orange-yellow and purple, various seasons, 4 to 6 ft., Java; *johnstoneanum*, B, pale yellow or white, scented, late spring, 10 to 15 ft. Assam, India; *keiskei*, A, lemon, spring, 3 to 8 ft., semi-evergreen, Japan; *keysii*, B, red tipped yellow or orange tipped red, early summer, 10 to 12 ft., Tibet, Burma, Assam; *lacteum*, A, yellow, spring, to 30 ft., China, Burma; *lepidostylum*, A, pale yellow, late spring, early summer, 2 to 3 ft., blue-green leaves, China; *leucaspis*, A, white, early spring, 1 to 2 ft., Burma, Tibet; *lindleyi*, C, white, scented, spring, 10 to 15 ft., China, Bhutan, Assam; *litiense*, A, yellow, late spring, to 12 ft., China; *loderi*, B, white or pink, scented, late spring, 12 to 15 ft., hybrid; *ludlowii*, A, yellow, spring, to 1 ft., Tibet; *lutescens*, A, primrose yellow and greenish yellow, early spring, 6 to 12 ft., China; *macabeanum*, B, yellow blotched purple, spring, 20 to 45 ft., large leaves greyish white beneath, India; *maddenii*, C, white, scented, early summer, 6 to 8 ft., China, Bhutan; *maximum*, A, pink spotted yellowish green, summer, 12 to 15 ft., Eastern U.S.A.; *moupinense*, A, white or pink, early spring, 2 to 4 ft., China; *mucronulatum*, A, magenta, late winter, 6 to 8 ft., Japan, Korea, China; *neriiflorum*, A, scarlet or crimson, spring, 6 to 9 ft., China, Tibet; *niveum*, A, blue-purple, spring, 12 to 15 ft., China, Bhutan; *nobleanum*, A, rose, late winter, early spring, 15 to 20 ft., hybrid and vars. *album*, white, *venustum*, pink; *nuttallii*, C, D, white or pale yellow, scented, spring, 15 to 30 ft., Bhutan; *orbiculare*, A, rose-pink, to 10 ft., China; *oreodoxa*, A, pink, spring, 12 to 20 ft., China; *oreotrephes*, A, mauve, spring, 12 to 20 ft., China, Tibet, Burma; *pachytrichum*, A, white or pale rose, early spring, 6 to 18 ft., China; *pemakoense*, A, mauve to purple, early spring, to 1 ft., Tibet; *ponticum*, A, mauve to purple, early summer, 12 to 15 ft., Asia Minor; *praecox*, A, rose-purple, early spring, 3 to 4 ft., hybrid; *racemosum*, A, pink and white, early spring, to 6 ft., China; *rex*, A, rose or white, crimson spotted, spring, 20 to 45 ft., large leaves, China; *roxieanum*, A, white and pink, spring, 5 to 9 ft., China, Tibet; *rubiginosum*, A, rosy lilac, spring, to 30 ft., China, Tibet; *russatum*, A, purplish blue, spring, 3 to 4 ft., China; *saluenense*, A, purple, spring, 3 to 4 ft., Tibet; *scintillans*, A, lavender or purplish rose, spring, 2 to 3 ft., China; *sinogrande*, B, cream or pale yellow, crimson blotched, spring, to 30 ft., very large leaves silvery when young, China, Burma, Tibet; *souliei*, A, white or pink, late spring, China, Tibet; *spinuliferum*, B, C, red, spring, 6 to 8 ft., China; *strigillosum*, A, crimson, early spring, 12 to 20 ft., China; *sutchuenense*, A, rosy lilac, or white flushed pink, early spring, 15 to 20 ft., China; *tagginium*, C, D, white, scented, spring, to 8 ft., China, Burma;

tephropeplum, A, magenta-rose, spring, 4 to 6 ft., Burma, China, Tibet, Assam; *thomsonii*, A, blood red, spring, 12 to 20 ft., China, Nepal, Bhutan, Tibet; *triflorum*, A, light yellow spotted green, late spring, early summer, to 10 ft., Assam, Tibet; *venator*, A, red, late spring, early summer, to 8 ft., Tibet; *wardii*, A, yellow, late spring, 10 to 20 ft., China, Tibet; *williamsianum*, B, pink, spring, to 5 ft., China; *xanthocodon*, A, yellow, late spring, 10 to 15 ft., Bhutan, Tibet; *yakusimanum*, A, pink fading to white, late spring, 4 ft., Japan; *yunnanense*, A, lavender, pink or white, late spring, 8 to 10 ft., China, Burma, Tibet.

Recommended kinds in the azalea section are *R. albrechtii*, A, rose or purple, spring, 3 to 5 ft., deciduous, Japan; *arborescens*, A, white or pinkish, summer, 8 to 15 ft., deciduous, Eastern N. America; *calendulaceum*, A, yellow, orange or red, late spring, early summer, 9 to 15 ft., deciduous, Eastern N. America; *indicum*, B, C, red, early summer, to 6 ft., evergreen, Japan, and vars. *balsaminiflorum*, double salmon, Gumpo, white, and several others; *japonicum*, A, red, late spring, 6 ft., deciduous, Japan; *kaempferi*, A, red, pink, white, late spring, early summer, to 10 ft., deciduous or semi-evergreen, Japan; *luteum* (syn. *Azalea pontica*), A, yellow, scented, late spring, to 12 ft., deciduous, E. Europe; *molle*, A, yellow or orange, late spring, to 4 ft., deciduous, China; *mucronatum* (syn. *Azalea ledifolia*), A, white, late spring, 3 to 6 ft., semi-evergreen, Japan, China; *nudiflorum*, A, white or pink, late spring, scented, to 9 ft., deciduous, Eastern N. America; *obtusum*, A, scarlet to crimson, late spring, to 3 ft., evergreen, Japan, and var. *amoenum* (syn. *Azalea amoena*), magenta, extra hardy; *occidentale*, A, white or pink with yellow blotch, early summer, scented, to 10 ft., deciduous, N. W. America; *quinquefolium*, A, white, green spotted, spring, 8 to 12 ft., deciduous, Japan; *schlippenbachii*, A, pale pink, spring, 8 to 12 ft., deciduous, Japan, Korea, Manchuria; *simsii* (syn. *Azalea indica*), C, D, red, late spring, to 6 ft., evergreen, China, Formosa and numerous varieties, white, pink and red, mostly with double flowers and mainly grown as pot plants; *vaseyi*, A, pink, spring, 8 to 12 ft., deciduous, Eastern N. America; *viscosum*, Swamp Honeysuckle, A, white, sometimes with pink blotch, scented, summer, 8 to 10 ft., deciduous, Eastern N. America; *yedoense*, A, rosy purple double flowers, late spring, 2 to 6 ft., Japan.

RHODOHYPOXIS – *Hypoxidaceae*. Dwarf, hardy bulbous plants with small, butterfly-like flowers.

Grow in a mixture of equal parts of lime-free loam, peat and coarse lime-free sand or grit, in a sunny place. Water freely in summer but keep rather dry in winter. Plant in spring and increase by division

then, or by seeds sown in sandy peat in a frame or cool greenhouse.

The only species is *R. baurii*, rose-red, pink or white, early summer, 2 in., S. Africa.

RHODOTYPOS – *Rosaceae*. Hardy deciduous flowering shrub with showy black berries in winter.

Soil, ordinary. Position, in sun or partial shade against walls or fences or in open borders. Plant in autumn. Prune after flowering, cutting off old or weak shoots.

Increase by cuttings of half-ripened shoots in sandy soil in a propagator in summer.

The only species is *R. scandens* (syn. *kerrioides*), white, late spring and early summer, 4 ft., China, Japan, Korea. This shrub is frequently erroneously called *Kerria japonica alba*.

RHOEO – *Commelinaceae*. Greenhouse herbaceous perennial with ornamental leaves.

Grow in a peat or loam compost, such as John Innes potting compost No. 1, in pots or hanging baskets in a cool or intermediate greenhouse or in a room. Shade in summer. Water normally.

Rhoeo discolor

Increase by cuttings of young shoots inserted in light soil in a warm propagator at almost any time.

The only species is *R. discolor* (syn. *Tradescantia discolor*), leaves dark green above, purple beneath, creeping, Mexico, West Indies, and var. *vittata* (syn. *Tradescantia variegata*), leaves striped with pale yellow.

RHOICISSUS – *Vitidaceae*. Tender climbers, one kind grown for its ornamental evergreen foliage.

Soil, John Innes potting compost No. 2 or equivalent. Position, pots in a cool or intermediate greenhouse or in rooms. Shade from direct sunshine. In rooms plants will grow in quite deep shade, but succeed better near windows. Water normally. Provide trellis, canes or other supports for the tendrils to cling to. Overgrown vines can

Rhoicissus rhomboidea

be shortened in spring and the tips of shoots can be pinched out at any time to encourage a more branching habit.

The best kind is *R. rhomboidea*, Natal Vine, young leaves bronze becoming green with age, Natal.

RHUS (Sumach) – *Anacardiaceae*. Hardy deciduous flowering trees, shrubs and climbers with brilliantly coloured foliage in autumn. Some species hardy in this country, *R. radicans*, *coriaria*, *toxicodendron* and *vernix* produce acrid and poisonous juices and should not be generally planted. A few species previously included in this genus have been transferred to *Cotinus*.

Soil, ordinary, well drained. Position, sunny borders or shrub border; walls or old tree trunks for *R. radicans*. Plant in autumn or late winter. Pruning is not essential but *R. glabra* and *typhina* can be cut back annually in late winter to within 3 or 4 in. of main branches. This, with good feeding, will produce extra large leaves.

Increase by cuttings of firm shoots in ordinary soil in a cold frame in autumn; by root cuttings, 2 or 3 in. long, planted 3 in. deep in sandy soil in autumn; by layering shoots in autumn; by rooted suckers removed in autumn or late winter.

Recommended kinds are *R. aromatica* (syn. *canadensis*), yellow, spring, 3 to 5 ft., N. America; *chinensis*, yellowish white, late summer, 15 to 25 ft., Japan, China, Korea; *copallina*, Shining Sumach, yellowish, summer, 5 to 30 ft., red fruits, Eastern N. America; *glabra*, Smooth Sumach, 4 to 15 ft., close erect panicles of small fruits densely covered with crimson hairs, U.S.A., and var. *laciniata*, leaves finely cut; *radicans*, Poison Ivy, red-tinted foliage in autumn, self-supporting climber to 20 ft., Eastern U.S.A.; *toxicodendron*, Poison Oak, 2 to 5 ft., South-eastern U.S.A.; *typhina*, Stag's Horn Sumach, 15 to 25 ft., crimson panicles of small fruits, var. *laciniata*, feathery

foliage; *vernix*, Poison Sumach, to 20 ft., leaves orange and scarlet in autumn but highly poisonous to the touch, U.S.A.

RIBES – *Grossulariaceae*. Hardy, deciduous and evergreen, flowering and fruit-bearing shrubs.

Soil ordinary. Position, sunny or shady. Plant in autumn or late winter. Pruning, remove some of the older wood after flowering.

Increase by cuttings of firm young growth inserted in ordinary soil out of doors in autumn.

Recommended kinds are *R. alpinum*, Alpine Currant, greenish yellow, fruit scarlet, spring, 3 to 6 ft., Europe, and var. *aureum*, leaves yellow; *americanum*, American Black Currant, yellowish, spring, black fruits, crimson and yellow foliage in autumn, 3 to 4 ft., N. America; *gordonianum*, yellow and red, spring, 6 to 8 ft., hybrid between *aureum* and *sanguineum*; *laurifolium*, greenish white, early spring, 2 to 3 ft., evergreen, China; *odoratum*, Buffalo Currant, Clove Currant, yellow, clove scented, spring, 4 to 6 ft., good autumn colour, Central U.S.A.; *sanguineum*, Flowering Currant, rose, spring, 6 to 10 ft., Western N. America, vars. *album*, white, *splendens*, fine deep red; *speciosum*, Fuchsia-flowered Gooseberry, rich red flowers, spring, 6 to 9 ft., semi-evergreen, California.

RICINUS – *Euphorbiaceae*. Tender tree usually grown in gardens as an annual for its large, handsome, deeply lobed leaves.

Steep seeds for a few hours in warm water and then sow in a temp. of 18 to 21°C. in spring. Pot seedlings individually and either grow on as pot plants in John Innes potting compost No. 2 or equivalent in a frost-proof greenhouse, or harden off and plant out of doors in good soil and a warm, sunny position as soon as danger of frost is over.

The only species is *R. communis*, Castor Oil Plant, 3 to 6 ft., Tropical Africa, but it has numerous garden varieties such as *borboniensis arboreus*, red stems and bronzy-green leaves, *cambodgensis*, deep purple leaves, *gibsonii*, maroon leaves, *zanzibarensis*, green leaves with white veins.

ROBINIA (False Acacia) – *Leguminosae*. Hardy deciduous flowering trees and shrubs.

Soil, ordinary, well drained. Position, sunny, excellent for hot dry places. Plant in autumn or late winter. Prune, if necessary, to restrict size in autumn or late winter. Rose Acacia, *R. hispida*, may be grown against warm, sunny walls but is not suitable for exposed places as shoots and branches are brittle.

Increase choice varieties by grafting on the common species, *R. pseudoacacia*, in spring; other kinds by seeds soaked for several hours in warm water (30 to 35°C.)

and then sown in sandy soil out of doors or under glass; by suckers removed with some roots from parent tree and planted in autumn.

Recommended kinds are *R. ambigua*, pink, early summer, 20 to 25 ft., hybrid between *pseudoacacia* and *viscosa*; *boyntonii*, rose-pink, late spring, early summer, 6 to 8 ft., South-eastern U.S.A.; *elliottii*, rosy lilac, late spring, early summer, 5 to 6 ft., South-eastern U.S.A.; *hispida*, Rose Acacia, rose, late spring to early summer, 6 to 8 ft., South-eastern U.S.A., var. *macrophylla*, with fewer prickles; *kelseyi*, rose, early summer, 8 to 12 ft., Eastern U.S.A.; *pseudoacacia*, Common Acacia, False Acacia, Black Locust, white, early summer, 70 to 80 ft., Eastern U.S.A., and vars. *aurea*, golden leaved, *bessoniana*, larger but fewer leaflets, *frisia*, leaves golden, *inermis*, mop headed, no spines, and *semperflorens*, flowering throughout the summer.

ROCHEA – *Crassulaceae*. Tender succulent plants with clusters of small flowers.

Grow in a fairly rich but well-drained soil, such as John Innes potting compost No. 2 with the addition of one-sixth its bulk of sharp sand, in well-drained pots in a light greenhouse, close to the glass. Pot in spring. Water freely in spring and summer, moderately in autumn, very little in winter. No shading required. Minimum winter temperature about 12°C.

Increase by cuttings of firm young shoots in very sandy soil in a propagator in late spring or summer.

The best kind is *R. coccinea* (syn. *Crassula coccinea*), scarlet, summer, 1 ft., S. Africa.

RODGERSIA – *Saxifragaceae*. Hardy herbaceous perennials with large, bronze-green leaves.

Grow in rather rich, moist soil in a partially shaded place. Very suitable plants for margins of pools or streams. Plant in spring. Water freely in dry weather.

Increase by division in spring.

Recommended kinds are *R. aesculifolia*, white, summer, 3 to 4 ft., bronze foliage, China; *pinnata*, pink, summer, 3 to 4 ft., China, and vars. *alba*, white, and *superba*, more bronzed leaves; *podophylla*, Rodger's Bronze Leaf, creamy white, summer, 3 to 4 ft., China; *sambucifolia*, white, summer, leaves divided, 2 to 3 ft., China; *tabularis*, creamy white, summer, 3 ft., bright green foliage, China.

ROMNEYA (Californian Tree Poppy) – *Papaveraceae*. Slightly tender perennials with large, poppy-like flowers, blue-grey leaves and semi-woody stems.

Soil, sandy loam. Position, well drained, sheltered and sunny. Plant in spring from containers taking care not to break the roots. Protect in severe weather with a covering of sand, boiler ashes or dry litter.

Romneya hybrida

Increase by seeds sown in sandy soil in spring in temp. 12 to 15°C.; by root cuttings in sandy compost in late winter in a frame or cool greenhouse, placing cuttings singly in small pots to avoid root disturbance later on.

The two species are *R. coulteri*, white and gold, fragrant, late summer and autumn, 6 to 7 ft., California; *trichocalyx*, white, fragrant, late summer and autumn, 6 to 7 ft., California. *R. hybrida* is a hybrid between them.

ROMULEA – *Iridaceae*. Hardy and slightly tender corms with crocus-like flowers.

Soil, light, rich, sandy. Position, sunny, well drained. Plant in autumn, placing tubers 4 in. deep and 2 in. apart. Protect in winter in cold localities with cloches or portable frames or grow throughout in a sunny, frost-proof greenhouse.

Increase by division of corms in autumn; by seeds sown in a frame or greenhouse in spring.

Recommended kinds are *R. bulbocodium*, yellow and violet, late winter and spring, 4 to 6 in., Europe; *clusiana*, lavender and orange, spring, 9 in., Spain; *requienii*, violet, spring, 4 in., Corsica and Sardinia; *rosea*, carmine, spring, 6 in., S. Africa.

ROSA (Rose) – *Rosaceae*. Hardy and slightly tender deciduous and evergreen flowering shrubs, mostly prickly.

For garden purposes roses are classified as shown in the chart on page 176.

Soil, good, rich, well drained but not dry. Dig thoroughly before planting and work in plenty of well-rotted manure or compost. Dust the surface with bonemeal or a compound fertilizer prior to planting. Position, open, preferably sunny; climbing roses trained against walls, screens, etc., or over arches, pergolas and the very vigorous kinds up trees. Plant in autumn or late winter, bush varieties 1½ to 2 ft. apart, shrub roses 3 to 4 ft. apart, climbers 6 to 10 ft. apart.

After planting prune all good stems to within 4 to 6 in. of soil level and remove thin, damaged or diseased stems altogether. Prune established roses in late winter or early spring (or summer non-recurrent climbers immediately after flowering). Remove all very old, worn out, diseased, weak or damaged stems. With bush roses shorten remaining healthy and vigorous stems, to 4 to 6 in. for naturally weak-growing varieties or if extra large blooms are required, to 9 to 12 in. for naturally vigorous varieties or if big bushes bearing a considerable number of flowers are required. With climbers simply shorten remaining stems as necessary to fit them to available space. Many shrub and species roses require little further pruning after removal of old and badly placed growth. With recurrent flowering roses remove faded flowers or flower trusses, cutting back to the first young growth or good growth bud. Remove all sucker growths from roses budded or grafted on to stocks.

Feed roses with a well-balanced compound fertilizer in spring and again in early summer. Spray occasionally from spring to autumn with a reliable insecticide and fungicide to keep down pests and diseases.

Increase roses by cuttings of firm young growth in summer in a propagator; by cuttings of riper growth in autumn in an unheated frame or outdoors; by budding in summer on to selected stocks or grafting in spring for kinds that are difficult to bud; by seeds sown outdoors as soon as ripe or stratified for three months at 4°C. and then sown outdoors or under glass. Seedlings from garden varieties show wide variation, those from species usually closely resemble the parent plants.

Most of the roses cultivated in gardens are complex hybrids. Since there are thousands of varieties which are added to yearly, and since these are fully described in trade catalogues and other publications and it is usually the more recently introduced varieties that are most popular, no useful purpose would be served by making recommendations about such varieties here. The following are all species or fairly simple (and therefore stable) hybrids which have garden merit particularly in shrub borders and in the wilder parts of gardens. *R. alba*, White Rose of York, white, early summer, grey leaves, red hips, 6 ft., hybrid between *canina* and *damascena*; *arvensis*, Field Rose, white, summer, dark red hips, trailing, Europe; *banksiae*, Banksian Rose, Lady Banks's Rose, double white rosette flowers, late spring, early summer, 20 to 25 ft., slightly tender, China, and var. *lutea*, Yellow Banksian Rose, identical but soft yellow; *bracteata*, Macartney Rose, white, summer, 6 to 12 ft., evergreen, a little tender, China; *canina*, Dog Rose, white or pink, summer, 6 to 10 ft., scarlet hips, Europe (Britain), W. Asia, used as a stock for garden hybrids; *cantabridgiensis*, soft yellow, late spring, early summer, 7 to 9 ft., hybrid between *hugonis* and *sericea*; *carolina*, rose, summer, 3 ft., red hips, Eastern N. America; *centifolia*, Cabbage Rose, Provence Rose, double rose, summer, 3 to 5 ft., Caucasus, and vars. *cristata*, Crested Cabbage Rose, Crested Moss Rose, large, crested calyx segments, *muscosa*, Moss Rose, moss-like glands on calyx and flower stems; *chinensis*, China Rose, crimson, pink or white, summer and early autumn, 3 to 6 ft., scarlet hips, China, and vars. *minima*, Fairy Rose (syns. *lawranceana* and *roulettii*), small flowers and leaves, *mutabilis*, flowers buff changing to carmine, *semperflorens* (syn. Old Blush), Monthly Rose, pink, *viridiflora*, Green Rose, green; *cinnamomea*, Cinnamon Rose, lilac-pink, late spring, early summer, 6 ft., red hips, Europe, Asia; *complicata*, pink and white, early summer, 6 ft., hybrid of *gallica*; *damascena*, Damask Rose, double, white, pink or red, summer, 4 to 6 ft., Asia Minor, and vars. *trigintipetala*, pink, *versicolor*, York and Lancaster Rose, white and rose; *davidii*, rose-pink, early summer, to 12 ft., large red hips, China; *dupontii*, pale pink, summer, 6 to 8 ft., hybrid; *ecae*, deep yellow, late spring, early summer, 3 to 4 ft., Afghanistan; *farreri persetosa*, Threepenny-bit Rose, red buds and pink flowers, early summer, 4 to 6 ft., coral-red fruits, China; *filipes*, white, summer, to 20 ft., red hips, China, and var. Kiftsgate, extra vigorous; *foetida*, Austrian Yellow, Austrian Briar, yellow, early summer, 3 to 5 ft., needs a warm sunny place, S. W. Asia, and vars. *bicolor*, Austrian Copper, coppery red and yellow, *persiana*, Persian Yellow Rose, double yellow; *gallica*, French Rose, rose, early summer, 2 to 3 ft., red hips, Europe and vars. *officinalis*, Apothecary's Rose, Red Rose of Lancaster, Provence Rose, semi-double, rosy crimson, *versicolor*, Rosa Mundi, rosy red and white; *gigantea*, white, late spring, early summer, 20 to 40 ft., semi-evergreen, China, Burma; *harrisonii*, Harrisons' Yellow, Hogg's Double Yellow, semi-double yellow, summer, 2 to 3 ft., hybrid between *foetida* and *spinosissima*; *heleniae*, white, early summer, 15 to 20 ft., orange-red hips, China; *highdownensis*, crimson, early summer, 6 to 10 ft., scarlet hips, hybrid; *hugonis*, yellow, late spring, 6 to 7 ft., dark red hips, China; *laevigata*, Cherokee Rose, white, late spring, early summer, 10 to 15 ft., China; *macrantha*, pink fading to white, early summer, 4 to 5 ft., red hips, hybrid between *canina* and *gallica*; *macrophylla*, cerise, early summer, 8 to 10 ft., red hips, Himalaya; Max Graf, pink, summer, trailing, hybrid between *rugosa* and *wichuraiana*; *moschata*, Musk Rose, creamy white, late summer and autumn, 10 to 15 ft., Asia; *moyesii*, crimson, summer, 6 to 12 ft., large bright red hips, China; *multibracteata*, rosy lilac, summer, 6 to 10 ft., small red hips, China; *multiflora* (syn. *polyantha*), white,

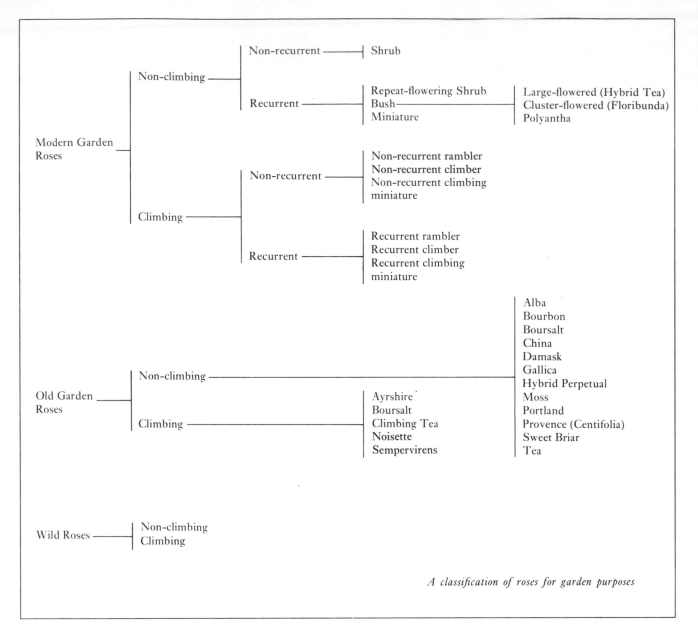

A classification of roses for garden purposes

early summer, 10 to 15 ft., red hips, Japan, Korea, and var. *platyphylla*, Seven Sisters Rose, double purple; *nitida*, rose-red, summer, 2 to 3 ft., red hips, good autumn foliage colour, Eastern N. America; *noisettiana*, white or pink, semi-double, summer, 7 to 10 ft., hybrid between *chinensis* and *moschata*; *omeiensis* (syn. *sericea omeiensis*), white, spring, early summer, 7 to 12 ft., red and yellow hips, China, and var. *pteracantha*, very broad, wing-like translucent crimson thorns; *pendulina* (syn. *alpina*), rose, early summer, thornless, 3 ft., red hips, Europe; *pimpinellifolia* (syn. *spinosissima*), Scotch Rose, Burnet Rose, white or pink, late spring, early summer, 3 to 4 ft., black hips, Europe (Britain), Asia, and numerous varieties, some with double flowers, white, pink and red and *altaica* (syn. *R. altaica*), creamy white; *primula*, primrose, late spring, 6 to 8 ft., red hips,

Turkestan; *roxburghii*, Burr Rose, Chestnut Rose, pink, early summer, 6 to 7 ft., orange hips, China; *rubrifolia*, pink, summer, 6 to 8 ft., grey purple-tinted leaves, red hips, Europe; *rugosa*, Ramanas Rose, magenta, summer, 5 to 6 ft., red hips, N. E. Asia, and numerous varieties some white, some double flowered and *scabrosa*, extra large flowers and hips; *sericea*, white, pink or pale yellow, late spring, 6 to 8 ft., Himalaya; *setigera*, Prairie Rose, pink, summer, 8 to 12 ft., trailing, Eastern and Central U.S.A.; *setipoda*, pink, summer, 6 to 8 ft., large bright red hips, China; *soulieana*, white, summer, 10 to 12 ft., orange-red hips, China; *sweginzowii*, pink, summer, 9 to 12 ft., large bright red hips, China; *villosa* (syn. *pomifera*), Apple Rose, pink, summer, 6 ft., large red hips, Europe, Asia, and var. *duplex*, Wolley-Dod's Rose, flowers semi-double; *virginiana*, pink, summer, 6 ft.,

red hips, Eastern N. America and var. *plena* (syn. Rose d'Amour), St Mark's Rose, flowers double; *wichuraiana*, white, summer, 8 to 12 ft., trailing, semi-evergreen, red hips, Japan; *xanthina*, yellow semi-double, late spring, 6 to 9 ft., China, Korea.

ROSCOEA – *Zingiberaceae*. Dwarf hardy perennials with fleshy roots and distinctive flowers.

Soil, sandy loam and leafmould. Position, woodland gardens or half-shady sheltered borders. Plant the fleshy tuberous roots 6 in. deep in spring.

Increase by division of the roots in spring, or by seeds sown in peaty soil in a cool greenhouse in spring.

Recommended kinds are *R. alpina*, purple, summer, 6 in., Himalaya; *cautleoides*, yellow, summer, 12 in., China; *purpurea*, purple, summer, 12 in., Himalaya.

Rubus Tridel

ROSMARINUS (Rosemary) – *Labiatae*. Hardy or slightly tender evergreen fragrant shrubs with narrow aromatic leaves.

Soil, ordinary well drained. Position, warm and sunny. Excellent for rather dry places. Plant in spring.

Increase by cuttings of half-ripened young shoots in a frame in summer or early autumn.

Recommended kinds are *R. lavandulaceus* (syn. *officinalis prostratus*), lavender-blue, spring, early summer, prostrate, rather tender, Mediterranean region; *officinalis*, violet-blue, spring, 3 to 6 ft., S. Europe, with vars. *albus*, white, *fastigiatus* (syn. *pyramidalis*), upright growth, useful for hedges, *roseus*, lilac-pink.

RUBUS (Blackberry) – *Rosaceae*. Hardy deciduous or evergreen shrubs and climbers grown for their flowers and some kinds for their stem colour or fruits.

Soil, ordinary. Position, sunny or shady. Plant in autumn or late winter. Prune varieties grown for their flowers as soon as the flowers fade, varieties grown for their fruits after these have fallen or been eaten, varieties grown for bark colour in late winter or early spring. In all cases cut out as much as possible of the old growth retaining strong young stems for further flowering or fruiting.

Increase by cuttings of firm young growth in summer or autumn; by layering in spring or summer; some kinds by division in autumn or late winter or by removal of rooted suckers or offshoots; species by seeds stratified for three months at 20 to 25°C., then for a further three months at 4°C. and then sown outdoors or under glass.

Recommended kinds are *R. cockburnianus* (syn. *giraldianus*), Whitewash Bramble, purple, early summer 8 to 10 ft., black fruits, white stems, China; *deliciosus*, white, late spring, early summer, 6 to 10 ft. Rocky Mountains; *henryi*, climbing evergreen, pink, early summer, to 20 ft., China, var. *bambusarum*, short-stalked leaflets; *illecebrosus*, Strawberry-Raspberry, white, summer, 6 to 15 in., insipid strawberry-like fruits, semi-herbaceous, Japan; *odoratus*, Flowering Raspberry, unarmed, rose-purple, summer, 6 to 7 ft., fruits red, edible, Eastern N. America; *phoenicolasius*, Wineberry, pink, summer, 7 to 9 ft., red bristly stems, orange-red edible fruits, Japan, China, Korea; *spectabilis*, Salmonberry, rosy red, spring, 4 to 6 ft., orange-yellow edible fruits, Western N. America; *tricolor*, white, summer, trailing evergreen, red edible fruits, China; Tridel, white, late spring, early summer, 7 to 9 ft., hybrid between *deliciosus* and *trilobus*; *trilobus*, white, late spring, summer, to 8 ft., Mexico; *ulmifolius bellidiflorus*, double pink, flowers, summer, 10 ft., sprawling, Europe (Britain).

RUDBECKIA (Coneflower) – *Compositae*. Hardy annuals, biennials and herbaceous perennials with showy daisy flowers.

Culture of annual species: Soil, ordinary. Sow in temp. 15 to 18°C. in early spring and harden off for planting out when there is no danger of hard frost, or sow in later spring outdoors where plants are to flower and thin seedlings to 1 ft. Sow or plant in well-drained soil and a sunny place. Plants will sometimes survive the winter and flower a second year especially in warm well-drained places.

Culture of perennial species: Soil, ordinary. Position, sunny well drained. Plant in spring or autumn. Lift, divide and replant in a fresh position triennially.

Increase by seeds sown in ordinary soil and a sunny position in spring or early summer, transplanting seedlings into flowering positions the following autumn; by division of plants in spring or autumn.

Recommended annual and biennial kinds are *R. bicolor*, yellow and maroon, late summer, 1 to 2 ft., annual, N. America; *hirta*, Black-eyed Susan, yellow and dull brown, summer, 2 to 3 ft., biennial or annual, N. America; *triloba*, deep yellow and brown, summer, 2 to 5 ft., biennial or annual, N. America.

Recommended perennial kinds are *R. fulgida*, yellow and black, late summer and autumn, to 2 ft., N. America, and vars. *deamii*, 3 ft., *speciosa* (syn. *newmanii*), 2 ft., *sullivantii*, large flowers; *laciniata*, yellow, summer, 6 to 10 ft., N. America, var. *hortensia*, Golden Glow, double; *maxima*, yellow and blackish brown, late summer, 7 to 9 ft., Southern U.S.A.; *nitida*, yellow, late summer, 4 ft., N. America, var. Herbstsonne, 6 ft., golden yellow, reflexed petals; *subtomentosa*, yellow and brown, late summer, 3 to 5 ft., N. America.

See also Echinacea.

RUELLIA – *Acanthaceae*. Tender perennial herbs or shrubs with funnel-shaped flowers.

Grow in a moderately rich compost, such as John Innes potting compost No. 2, in a cool or intermediate greenhouse or *R. ciliosa* outdoors in a warm, sheltered place. Pot or plant in spring. Water normally, shade lightly in summer. Prune shrubs hard back each spring. Rest winter-flowering kinds in summer.

Increase all kinds by seeds sown in temp. 15 to 18°C. in spring; shrubby kinds by cuttings in a propagator in summer; herbaceous kinds by division in spring.

Recommended kinds are *R. ciliosa*, blue, summer, 1 to 2½ ft., U.S.A.; *macrantha*, Christmas Pride, rosy purple, winter, 2 to 3 ft., shrubby, Brazil.

RUSCUS – *Ruscaceae*. Hardy evergreen shrubs with flattened stems in place of leaves and showy red fruits on the female plants provided there are male plants nearby for pollination.

Ruscus aculeatus

Soil, ordinary. Position, shady or sunny borders or woods; useful for dense shade. Plant in spring or autumn.

Increase by suckers; by division of plants in spring.

Recommended kinds are *R. aculeatus*, Butcher's Broom, green, spring, 3 ft., scarlet cherry-like berries, Europe (Britain); *hypoglossum*, yellow, inconspicuous, spring, to 1½ ft., red berries, S. Europe. The Alexandrian Laurel, frequently known as *Ruscus racemosus*, is correctly *Danaë racemosa*.

RUTA (Rue) – *Rutaceae*. Hardy aromatic evergreen shrub, with ferny, milky-green leaves.

Soil, ordinary, well drained, succeeds well on chalk. Position, sunny, makes an excellent dwarf edge to a formal bed. Prune the plants closely in spring. Plant in spring.

Increase by seeds sown out of doors in spring; by cuttings of firm young growth inserted in a frame in summer or early autumn.

The only kind grown is *R. graveolens*, Herb of Grace, yellowish green, summer, 3 ft., S. Europe, and var. Jackman's Blue, leaves blue-grey.

SAGINA (Pearlwort) – *Caryophyllaceae*. Hardy perennial evergreen tufted herbs with creeping stems.

Soil, ordinary. Position, sunny borders or rock gardens. Plant small tufts in spring, 2 in. apart, to make dense ground cover or form patterns in carpet bedding.

Increase by division in spring.

Recommended kinds are *S. glabra*, white, summer, prostrate, Alps, and var. *aurea*, yellow leaves; *subulata*, white, summer, prostrate, Europe (Britain).

SAGITTARIA (Arrowhead) – *Alismataceae*. Hardy and tender perennial aquatic herbs usually with arrow-shaped leaves and white flowers in spikes.

Soil, good rich loam. Position, open, sunny ponds or lakes for hardy species. Tender species in pots in a frost-proof greenhouse in autumn and winter, in borders of ponds outdoors in summer. Depth of water, 3 to 6 in. Plant in spring or early summer.

Increase by seeds sown in rich soil kept constantly wet in spring; by division in late spring.

Recommended kinds are *S. lancifolia*, white, summer, tender, 2 to 5 ft., West Indies; *latifolia* (syn. *variabilis*), Duck Potato, white, summer, 3 to 4 ft., N. America; *montevidensis*, white and purple, summer, 4 to 6 ft., tender, Argentina to Peru; *sagittifolia* (syn. *japonica*), white and purple, summer, 1 to 3 ft., Europe (Britain), Asia, N. America, and var. *flore pleno*, double.

SAINTPAULIA – *Gesneriaceae*. Tender rosette-forming herbaceous perennials with slightly violet-like flowers produced over a long season.

Compost, John Innes potting compost No. 1 or equivalent plus one-quarter its bulk of peat. Position, pots in an intermediate or warm greenhouse or in a warm room. Pot in spring. Water normally but be careful to apply water direct to the compost and not to wet the leaves unduly, particularly in winter. Shade from direct sunshine at all seasons. Maintain a moist atmosphere, particularly in spring and summer. Can also

Double-flowered saintpaulia

be grown in Wardian cases, plant cabinets and bottle gardens.

Increase by seed sown in John Innes seed compost or equivalent in spring or summer in temp. 18 to 21°C.; by cuttings of mature leaves, removed with their stalks and inserted, stalk first, in peat and sand in a warm propagator in summer.

The best kind is *S. ionantha*, African Violet, violet, all year, 3 to 4 in., Tropical Africa, and numerous varieties, white, pink, rose, lavender, mauve, single and double flowered.

SALIX (Willow) – *Salicaceae*. Hardy deciduous trees and shrubs grown for their foliage, catkins, distinctive habit of growth and in some cases bark colour. There are a great many species differing in character and in size from small, prostrate mountain plants to large moisture-loving trees.

Soil, ordinary, loamy, some preferring really moist conditions and none enjoying really dry soils. Position, open, sunny or lightly shaded, moisture-loving species beside lakes, pools and streams. Plant in autumn or late winter. Prune in autumn or late winter, but only as necessary to restrict spread or improve shape, except when grown for bark colour when all the previous year's stems can be cut back to within 2 or 3 in. of the main trunk or branches in late winter or early spring.

Increase by cuttings of young stems in summer in a frame, or of riper growth in autumn outdoors; by layering in autumn; species by seeds sown as soon as ripe outdoors or under glass.

Recommended kinds are *S. aegyptiaca* (syn. *medemii*), showy catkins, late winter, 12 to 18 ft., Asia, Russia; *alba*, White Willow, 50 to 80 ft., Europe (Britain), Asia, N. Africa, and vars. *aurea*, yellow leaves, *chermesina* (syn. *britzensis*), Scarlet Willow, orange-red stems, *sericea*, Silver Willow, silvery leaves, *vitellina*, Golden Willow, yellow stems; *babylonica*, Weeping Willow, 30 to 50 ft., wide head, pendulous branches, China; *bockii*, 3 to 4 ft. W. China; *caerulea*, Cricket-bat Willow, 70 to 100 ft., Britain; *caprea*, Goat Willow, Sallow, 15 to 25 ft., Europe (Britain), W. Asia, var. *pendula*, Kilmarnock Willow, stiff, pendulous;

crysocoma, Golden Weeping Willow, young pendulous stems yellow, 20 to 40 ft., hybrid; *daphnoides*, Violet Willow, 30 to 40 ft., shoots covered with plum-coloured bloom, Europe (Britain), Asia; *discolor*, Pussy Willow, to 20 ft., N. America; *elaeagnos* (syn. *incana*), Hoary Willow, young leaves grey, 10 to 15 ft., Europe, Asia Minor; *elegantissima*, 30 to 40 ft., pendulous branches, hybrid between *babylonica* and *fragilis*; *fargesii*, shining reddish brown stems, 6 to 10 ft., China; *fragilis*, Crack Willow, 60 to 70 ft., deeply furrowed bark, Europe (Britain), N. Asia; *gracilistyla*, showy yellow catkins, early spring, 6 to 10 ft., Japan, Korea, China; *herbacea*, Dwarf Willow, creeping, Europe (Britain), N. America; *irrorata*, attractive white stems, red catkins, 8 to 10 ft., Colorado to N. Mexico; *lanata*, Woolly Willow, 2 to 3 ft., N. Europe (Britain); *magnifica*, 6 to 20 ft., W. China; *matsudana*, Pekin Willow, pyramidal tree to 40 ft., China, vars. *pendula*, weeping and *tortuosa*, Corkscrew Willow, spirally twisted leaves and branches; *moupinensis*, polished red-brown stems, 8 to 12 ft., China; *nigra*, Black Willow, dark brown, rough scaly bark, to 35 ft., N. America; *pentandra*, Bay Willow, Laurel Willow, 20 to 50 ft., Europe (Britain), N. Asia; *purpurea*, Purple Osier, shoots reddish purple, 10 to 18 ft., Europe (Britain), Asia; *repens*, Creeping Willow, to 3 ft., Europe (Britain), Asia; *reticulata*, 6 to 12 in., Europe (Britain), N. America; *retusa*, 4 to 8 in., Europe; *sachalinensis*, shining red-brown stems, 15 to 25 ft., N. E. Asia, and var. Sekka, Japanese Fan-tail Willow, flattened, contorted branchlets; *viminalis*, Osier Willow, the species grown to yield osiers, 12 to 20 ft., Europe, N. Asia.

SALPIGLOSSIS – *Solanaceae*. Slightly tender annuals with showy trumpet-shaped flowers.

Salpiglossis sinuata

Soil, good, ordinary. Position, sunny. Sow seeds in John Innes seed compost or equivalent in temp. 15 to 18°C. in spring. Transplant seedlings into John Innes potting compost No. 1 or equivalent and harden off for planting outdoors in late spring or early summer. Alternatively, plants can be potted on in the same compost and grown throughout in a sunny greenhouse. Water freely. Feed in summer with weak liquid manure or fertilizer. Discard after flowering. Seeds can also be sown in late summer or early autumn, seedlings potted and over-wintered in a cool greenhouse, minimum temp. 7°C., for spring flowering.

The best kind is *S. sinuata*, Painted Tongue, various colours, summer, 2 ft., Chile, the parent of the beautiful strains grown in gardens.

SALVIA (Sage) – *Labiatae*. Hardy annuals and biennials, tender perennials best treated as annuals, hardy herbaceous perennials, and slightly tender shrubs or sub-shrubs mostly deciduous but some semi-evergreen.

Culture of annual kinds and those best treated as such: Soil, ordinary. Position, warm, sunny. Sow hardy kinds in spring or early autumn where required to flower and thin to 6 or 8 in. Sow tender perennials in late winter or early spring in temp. 15 to 18°C. Transplant (or pot singly) in John Innes potting compost No. 1 or equivalent and harden off for planting outdoors in late spring or early summer when there is no danger of frost. Discard after flowering.

Culture of biennial kinds: Soil, ordinary, well drained. Position, sunny. Sow in late spring or early summer where plants are to flower. Thin seedlings to 1 ft. or transplant some elsewhere when large enough to handle easily. Do not discard until seeds have ripened the following summer as, in congenial conditions, plants will often regenerate from self-sown seedlings.

Culture of hardy perennial kinds: Soil, ordinary. Position, sunny. Plant in spring or autumn. Lift and divide every second or third year. *S. patens* has tuberous roots and is rather tender. In fairly frost-free places it can be grown outdoors winter and summer. In colder places tubers can be lifted in autumn and stored in a frost-proof place to be replanted outdoors in spring or it can be grown as described for tender annuals.

Culture of shrubby kinds: Soil, ordinary, well drained. Position, sunny, warm, will survive a few degrees of frost particularly if growth is well ripened. Plant in spring or autumn. Cut down stems close to the ground or main stems in early spring.

For the culture of sage as a culinary herb, see page 247.

Increase shrubby kinds by cuttings of young shoots inserted in sandy soil in a frame or propagator in summer or early autumn. Hardy perennials by division in spring or autumn; by seeds sown outdoors in late spring or early summer. Sage by seeds sown in spring in temp. 14 to 16°C.; by cuttings as for shrubby kinds.

Recommended hardy perennial kinds are *S. azurea*, blue, late summer, early autumn, 4 to 6 ft., N. America, and var. *pitcheri* (syn. *grandiflora*), larger flowers; *haematodes*, blue, early summer, 2 to 3 ft., Europe; *jurisicii*, violet, pink or white, summer, 1 to 1½ ft., Serbia; *lavandulifolia*, lavender, early summer, 9 to 12 in., Spain; *nemorosa* (syn. *sylvestris*, *sylvestris superba*, *virgata nemorosa*), purple, late summer, 2 to 3 ft., Europe, S. W. Asia, and numerous varieties differing mainly in height and habit (the kind often listed as *S. superba* belongs here); *pratensis*, Meadow Clary, blue, summer, 2 to 3 ft., Europe (Britain), and vars. *alba*, white, *atroviolacea*, dark violet, *rosea*, rosy purple, *rubicunda*, rose-red and *variegata*, blue and white; *uliginosa*, sky blue, late summer, autumn, 3 to 8 ft., Eastern S. America.

Recommended biennial kinds are *S. argentea*, white, summer, densely white woolly leaves, to 3 ft., Eastern Mediterranean, and var. *alpina*, dwarf; *sclarea*, Clary, lilac, rose and white, summer, 3 to 4 ft., Europe, S. W. Asia, and var. *turkestanica*, paler colours. In warm, well-drained places these may live for several years.

Recommended tender perennials best grown as annuals, are *S. farinacea*, lavender blue, late summer, autumn, 2 to 4 ft., nearly hardy, will survive a few degrees of frost, Texas, New Mexico; *splendens*, Scarlet Sage, scarlet, summer, autumn, 1 to 3 ft., Brazil, and numerous varieties, white, pink, purple, crimson, some dwarf and compact, all decidedly tender.

Recommended shrubby kinds are *S. greggii*, carmine, summer and early autumn, 3 to 4 ft., slightly tender, Mexico; *microphylla* (syn. *grahamii*), scarlet, summer and early autumn, 3 to 4 ft., Mexico, and var. *neurepia*, magenta, late summer and autumn, 5 to 7 ft.; *officinalis*, Common Sage, blue-purple, summer, 2 to 3 ft., Europe and vars. *albiflora*, white, *purpurascens*, Purple-leaf Sage, *tricolor*, leaves green, purple, pink and white; *rutilans*, Pineapple Sage, scarlet, summer, 3 ft., origin unknown.

The best hardy annual kind is *S. horminum*, lilac, pink, purple and white, summer, 1½ ft., S. E. Europe.

SALVINIA – *Salviniaceae*. Tender, floating, annual aquatic ferns. Rounded leaves, arranged in pairs and covered with silky hairs.

Soil, not necessary. Position, a tank of water in an intermediate or warm greenhouse or in an indoor aquarium, minimum winter temp. 13°C. Place in the tank at any time.

Increase by division during the growing period.

The best kind is *S. natans*, small, bright green, Warm Temperate Regions.

SAMBUCUS (Elder) – *Sambucaceae*. Hardy deciduous shrubs, small trees or herbaceous perennials. Green, golden or white pinnate leaves, small white or cream flowers in large flat heads followed by black or scarlet berries.

Soil, ordinary, preferably rather moist. Position, sun or partial shade; excellent for wild gardens. Plant in autumn or late winter. Prune in winter, cutting out older stems or, for the best foliage effect, shortening previous year's basal growth by one-half and removing all other growth.

Increase by cuttings of firm young shoots in a frame in summer, cuttings of riper growth outdoors in autumn; by root cuttings in winter; species by seeds stratified for three months at 4°C. and then sown outdoors or under glass.

Recommended kinds are *S. canadensis*, white, summer, to 12 ft., black berries, Eastern N. America, and vars. *acutiloba*, leaves deeply dissected, *aurea*, yellow leaves, red berries, *maxima*, extra large leaves and flower clusters; *ebulus*, Dwarf Elder, herbaceous, white tinged pink, late summer, 3 ft., Europe, N. Africa; *nigra*, Common Elder, white, early summer, 20 ft., Europe (Britain), and vars. *aurea*, Golden Elder, *laciniata*, Cut-leaved Elder, *rosea flore-pleno*, flowers double, rosy tinted; *racemosa*, white, spring, scarlet berries in summer, 8 to 12 ft., Europe, Asia, and vars. *plumoso-aurea*, toothed, golden-yellow foliage, *tenui-folia*, leaflets finely dissected.

SANDERSONIA – *Liliaceae*. Tender tuberous-rooted perennial with nodding, lantern-shaped flowers.

Soil, John Innes potting compost No. 1 or equivalent. Position, pots in a sunny cool or intermediate greenhouse, minimum winter temp. 7°C. Pot in early spring. Water moderately at first, freely when growing

Sandersonia aurantiaca

and flowering, but gradually reduce water supply in late summer and keep almost dry in autumn and winter. Support stems with canes.

Increase by seeds sown in temp. 15 to 18°C. as soon as ripe or in spring; by careful division in spring.

The only kind is *S. aurantiaca*, orange, summer, 2 ft., Natal.

SANGUINARIA – *Papaveraceae*. Hardy perennial low-growing herb with white, cup-shaped flowers and orange-red sap.

Soil, deep sandy lime-free loam or peat. Position, cool, open or semi-shady. Plant in early autumn. Water freely in dry weather. Leave undisturbed as long as possible.

Increase by seeds sown in equal parts of leafmould, peat and sand in a frame or cool greenhouse in early autumn or spring, transplanting seedlings outdoors when large enough to handle; division of branched rhizome in early autumn.

The only species is *S. canadensis*, Bloodroot, white, spring, 6 in., Eastern N. America, and vars. *grandiflora*, larger flowers, *plena* (syn. *multiplex*), double flowers.

SANGUISORBA (Burnet) – *Rosaceae*. Hardy perennial herbs with flowers in bottle brush spikes. Sometimes known as poterium.

Soil, ordinary or slightly acid, moist. Position, sunny or shady. Plants appreciate abundant moisture during the growing season. Plant in spring or autumn.

Increase by seeds sown in moist loam, peat and sand in spring or summer; by division in spring.

Recommended kinds are *S. canadensis* (syn. *Poterium canadense*), American Burnet, White Burnet, white, late summer, early autumn, 4 ft., N. America; *obtusa* (syn. *Poterium obtusum*), pink, summer, 2 to 3 ft., Japan, var. *alba*, white; *tenuifolia*, red, summer, 3 to 4 ft., China, and var. *alba*, white.

SANSEVIERIA (Bowstring Hemp, Angola Hemp) – *Agavaceae*. Tender herbaceous perennials grown for their ornamental leaves.

Compost, John Innes potting compost No. 2 or equivalent. Position, pots in a cool or intermediate greenhouse, minimum winter temp. 7°C., or in a room. Water rather sparingly at all times. Will grow in sun or shade. Feed monthly in summer with weak liquid manure or fertilizer. Pot in spring.

Increase by division of the rhizomes in spring.

Recommended kinds are *S. cylindrica*, leaves cylindrical, 3 to 4 ft. long, banded dark green, Tropical Africa; *hahnii*, leaves short, mottled grey-green, forming a rosette, 6 in., Tropical Africa; *trifasciata*, leaves narrow, banded light and dark green, 2 to 4 ft., Tropical Africa and var. *laurentii*, leaves edged with yellow.

SANTOLINA (Lavender Cotton) – *Compositae*. Evergreen aromatic shrubby plants.

Soil, ordinary, well drained. Position, sunny, useful for rather dry places. Plant in spring or autumn. Clip over with shears annually after flowering or cut hard back in early spring.

Increase by cuttings of firm young growth in a frame in summer, or riper cuttings in autumn outdoors or in a frame.

Recommended kinds are *S. chamaecyparissus* (syn. *incana*), yellow, summer, to 2 ft., leaves covered with cottony grey down, S. Europe, and var. *nana* (syn. *corsica*), 1 ft.; *virens*, Holly Flax, yellow, summer, 2 ft., leaves green, S. Europe.

SANVITALIA – *Compositae*. Hardy annual with yellow, black-centred daisy-type flowers.

Soil, ordinary. Position, sunny. Sow in open ground in spring where plants are to flower and thin seedlings to 4 or 5 in. apart. Discard after flowering.

The best kind is *S. procumbens*, yellow and black, summer to late autumn, prostrate, Mexico, var. *flore pleno*, flowers double.

SAPONARIA (Soapwort) – *Caryophyllaceae*. Hardy annuals and perennials, mostly with small flowers freely produced.

Culture of annual species: Soil, ordinary. Position, sunny. Sow seeds where plants are required, in spring for summer flowering; early autumn for spring flowering. Thin seedlings to 3 or 4 in. apart.

Culture of perennial species: Soil, ordinary, well drained. Position, sunny rock gardens, walls, banks or borders for *S. ocymoides*; sunny or shady borders or wild garden for *S. officinalis*. Plant in spring or autumn.

Increase perennial species by seeds sown outdoors in spring or early summer; by cuttings inserted in sandy soil in a frame in autumn; by division in spring or autumn.

The best annual kind is *S. calabrica*, rose, summer, 6 to 12 in., Italy, and var. *alba*, white. For the plant sometimes known as *Saponaria vaccaria* see *Vaccaria pyramidata*.

Recommended perennial kinds are *S. caespitosa*, rose, late spring, early summer, 4 in., Pyrenees; *ocymoides*, Rock Soapwort, rosy purple, summer, trailing, Alps and Jura Mountains; *officinalis*, Bouncing Bet, Fuller's Herb, pink, late summer, early autumn, 1 to 2 ft., vars. *alba plena*, white, double, *rosea plena*, pink, double.

SARCOCOCCA (Sweet Box) – *Buxaceae*. Hardy evergreen shrubs, mostly with fragrant unisexual flowers produced in winter and early spring.

Soil, ordinary, rather moist, does well on chalk. Position, shady, thrives under trees. Plant in spring or autumn.

Increase by cuttings of firm young growth in a propagator in summer, or riper cuttings in an unheated frame in autumn.

Recommended kinds are *S. confusa*, white, winter, fruits black, up to 6 ft., origin unknown, probably China; *hookeriana*, white, autumn, fruits black, 2 to 3 ft., Himalaya, and var. *digyna*, narrower leaves, China; *humilis*, white, winter, fruits black 2 ft., China; *ruscifolia*, white, winter, fruits red, to 4 ft., China, and var. *chinensis*, longer and narrower leaves.

SARRACENIA (Pitcher Plant) – *Sarraceniaceae*. Slightly tender or hardy herbaceous perennials with tubular, pitcher-shaped leaves in which insects are trapped.

Indoor culture: Compost, two parts fibrous peat and one part chopped sphagnum moss. Position, well-drained pots in a cool, moist greenhouse, fernery or frame, or Wardian case in a living room, minimum winter temp. 4°C. Pot in spring. Water freely from mid-spring until mid-autumn, sparingly in winter. Maintain a moist atmosphere. Shade from direct sunshine.

Outdoor culture: Compost, as for pot plants with the addition of a little lime-free loam. Position, bog garden. Plant in spring. Keep surface of soil covered with a layer of living moss. Water freely in summer and cover with a handlight or cloche in winter.

Increase by division in spring; by seeds sown on constantly damp peat and sphagnum moss in a temp. 13 to 15°C. in spring.

Recommended kinds are *S. drummondii*, flowers purple, spring, leaves white, green and purple, 2 ft., South-eastern U.S.A.; *flava*, Huntsman's Horn, Trumpet Pitcher Plant, flowers greenish yellow, spring, 2 to 3 ft., South-eastern U.S.A.; *purpurea*, Common Pitcher Plant, Huntsman's Cup, Indian Cup, Sidesaddle Flower, flowers reddish purple, spring, 1 to 1½ ft., leaves veined purple, the hardiest species, Eastern N. America. There are numerous hybrids.

Sarracenia
(hybrid)

SASA – *Gramineae*. Hardy bamboos with ornamental foliage. Formerly included in *Arundinaria* and *Bambusa*.

Soil, good, loamy, preferably rather moist. Position, sheltered, sunny or in partial shade. Plant in spring or autumn.

Increase by division in spring.

Recommended kinds are *S. palmata*, 6 to 7 ft., Japan; *tessellata*, large leaves, 3 to 5 ft., Japan, China; *veitchii* (syns. *albo-marginata*, *Arundinaria* and *Bambusa veitchii*), withered leaf margins create a variegated impression, 2 to 3 ft., quick growing, Japan.

SASSAFRAS – *Lauraceae*. Hardy deciduous aromatic trees grown for their foliage.

Soil, deep loam. Position, sheltered. Plant in autumn or late winter.

Increase by seeds stratified as soon as ripe for three months at 4°C. and then sown in well-drained pots in a frame or greenhouse; by root cuttings in late winter or early spring.

The best species is *S. albidum* (syn. *officinale*), greenish yellow, late spring, round dark blue fruits, 50 to 60 ft., good autumn foliage colour, Eastern U.S.A.

SAUROMATUM (Monarch of the East) – *Araceae*. Nearly hardy tuberous-rooted perennials with arum-like flower spathes.

Sauromatum venosum can be grown without soil if the tubers are kept moist. It is sometimes grown in this way in a saucer on a window sill and is planted out when it comes into flower as its smell is overpowering. This is a curiosity, but better results are obtained by potting in autumn or late winter in John Innes potting compost No. 1 or equivalent, keeping the compost just moist at first but watering normally when growth appears. In summer, the water supply is gradually reduced until by the time growth is complete the soil is quite dry. Pot- or saucer-grown plants must be kept in a reasonably light, frost-free place, but in many areas plants can be grown outdoors if the tubers are planted 5 or 6 in. deep in porous soil in a warm, sunny sheltered place and protected with a cloche or a 2-in. layer of peat in winter.

Increase by removal of offsets when tubers are lifted; by seeds sown in spring in temp. 15 to 18°C.

The only kind cultivated is *S. venosum* (syn. *guttatum*), purple, yellow and green, winter or spring, 1½ to 2 ft., Sub-tropical Asia and Africa.

SAURURUS (Lizard's Tail) – *Saururaceae*. Hardy aquatic perennials with heart-shaped leaves and small flowers in slender spikes.

Soil, heavy loam. Position, margins of ponds in 3 to 6 in. of water. Plant in spring. Increase by division in spring.

The only two species are *S. cernuus*, American Swamp Lily, white, fragrant, summer, 1 to 2 ft., N. America; *chinensis*

(syn. *loureirii*), yellowish white, summer, 1 to 2 ft., China, Japan.

SAXIFRAGA (Saxifrage, Rockfoil) – *Saxifragaceae*. A very large genus of mainly hardy perennial plants suitable for the rock garden. Many have evergreen leaves though there are also herbaceous species which die down completely in winter and a few annuals, none of great garden merit.

The genus falls botanically into fifteen sections and one sub-section (Engleria of horticulture equals sub-section Media of Kabschia section). Cultivation differs to some extent from section to section and is described below. The sections are numbered 1 to 16 and in the list of recommended kinds the section number appears in brackets after each name.

1. BORAPHILA. Leaves form a soft, leathery rosette. Flowers in spikes or loose showers. Cool, moist places and peaty acid soil.

2. HIRCULUS. Mat-forming plants with deciduous leaves for very moist screes.

3. ROBERTSONIA. Rosettes of more or less spoon-shaped, leathery leaves. Flowers in loose, open showers. Easily grown in shady, rather moist places and ordinary soil.

4. MISCOPETALUM. Tufted habit, rather leathery leaves, leafy stems bearing sprays of small flowers. Ordinary soil. Shady position.

5. CYMBALARIA. Small, freely-branching annuals for cool, shady places.

6. TRIDACTYLITES. Not very decorative annuals or biennials with basal rosettes of leaves. Leafy stems carry small white flowers. Soil, sandy, well drained. Position, sun or shade.

7. NEPHROPHYLLUM. Deciduous, often with bulbils at the base or in the leaf axils of the flowering stems. Few are good garden plants but *S. granulata* is an exception and is suitable for ordinary, well-drained, neutral or alkaline soil and open places.

8. DACTYLOIDES. The Mossy Saxifrages belong here and make soft, dense mats of leaves in rosettes. Easily grown in ordinary, rather moist soil and cool, semi-shady places.

9. TRACHYPHYLLUM. Mostly small, mat-forming species of little garden merit. Soil, lime-free loam, peat and coarse sand. Position, sunny.

10. XANTHIZOON. There is only one species in this section, *S. aizoon*, a sprawling plant which likes very porous yet moist soil. It grows in Britain by mountain streams and on wet, stony mountain slopes.

11. EUAIZOONIA. The Silver Saxifrages, so called because of their attractive rosettes of firm, silvery leaves. The flowers are carried in loose sprays. Soil, porous, alkaline, with crushed limestone or chalk. Position, open but not too hot, some shade is desirable around mid-day.

12. KABSCHIA. Cushion-forming densely

tufted plants with small, narrow, pointed leaves. Flowers single or several on short stems. Soil and situation as for 11 but with extra good drainage to prevent rotting in winter. All make excellent pot or pan plants for an alpine frame or house in equal parts of loam, leafmould and limestone chippings, with a scattering of chippings only on top.

13. ENGLERIA. (Really sub-section Media of the Kabschia group.) Plants forming tight rosettes of broad, overlapping silvery leaves. Flowers often rather dowdy but carried on stems with coloured bracts. Culture as for 12 with even greater emphasis on pot or pan cultivation.

14. PORPHYRION. Mat-forming plants of which the best for garden purposes is *S. oppositifolia*. Soil very porous yet moist in summer but not waterlogged in winter. Position, sunny. Can be grown in pots or pans in a mixture of equal parts loam, leafmould and coarse sand.

15. TETRAMERIDIUM. The only species that has been introduced, *S. nana*, is tufted with four-petalled flowers but is of little decorative merit.

16. DIPTERA. Herbaceous plants mostly with quite large leaves and small flowers in large, loose sprays. Soil, loam and leafmould or peat. Position, cool, semi-shade. Some kinds are slightly tender and *S. stolonifera* is often grown in pots as a cool greenhouse or window plant.

Plant or pot all kinds in spring, or spring-flowering kinds as soon as flowers fade. Increase by offsets or division in spring but some, especially hybrids of Kabschia and Engleria sections, are best increased by tiny cuttings rooted in a frame in a mixture of five parts sand to three parts finely sieved moss peat; the cuttings should be taken as soon as the growths are long enough to handle after flowering in spring or summer. All species by seeds sown in sand and peat as soon as ripe or in spring. Hybrids do not breed true from seed.

Recommended kinds are *S. aizoides* (10), yellow or orange, 3 to 4 in., summer, Alpine and Arctic Europe (Britain), Asia, and vars. *atrorubens*, blood red, *aurantia*, orange, and *autumnalis*, orange, autumn; *aizoon* (11), white or purple spotted, 6 in., N. America,

Saxifraga burseriana

Europe, and innumerable varieties such as *lutea*, yellow, *minor*, smaller in all its parts, *rosea*, pink; *andrewsii* (3 x 11), white, purple spotted, summer, 9 in., hybrid; *apiculata* (12), yellow, spring, 4 in., hybrid; *arcovalleyi* (12), rose, spring, 1 in., hybrid; *aretioides* (12), yellow, spring, 2 in., Pyrenees; *aspera* (9), pale yellow, speckled orange, early summer, 3 in., Europe; *borisii* (12), yellow, spring, 3 in., hybrid; *boydii*, (12), citron yellow, spring, 3 in., hybrid; *brunoniana* (2), yellow, summer, 3 in., Himalaya; *bryoides* (9), pale yellow, spotted red, early summer, 3 in., Europe; *burseriana* (12), white, early summer, 3 in., limestone Alps, and many fine varieties; *caesia* (12), white, summer, 2 in., Pyrenees, E. Alps; *callosa* (11) (syn. *lingulata*), white, early summer, 9 to 12 in., Maritime Alps, and numerous varieties; *camposii* (8) (syn. *wallacei*), white, 9 in., summer, Spain; *canis-dalmatica* (11), white spotted red, summer, 6 in., hybrid; *cartilaginea* (11), white, early summer, 6 in., Caucasus; *cebennensis* (8), white, spring, 3 in., Central France; *clibranii* (8), deep red, spring, 6 in., hybrid; *cochlearis* (11), white, 6 in., early summer, Maritime Alps, and var. *minor*, smaller, more compact; *cortusaefolia* (16), white, early autumn, 12 in., Japan, and var. *rosea*, pink, dwarf; *corymbosa* (13), yellow, late spring, 4 in., Asia Minor, Bulgaria; *cotyledon* (11), white, summer, 1½ to 2 ft., Alps, Arctic, Pyrenees, and numerous varieties; *crustata* (11), white, summer, 3 to 6 in., limestone Alps; *cuneifolia* (3), white, late spring, 3 in., Apennines, Alps; *diapensioides* (12), white, 1 in., late spring, early summer, Alps; *elizabethae* (12), soft yellow, spring, 3 in., hybrid; *engleri* (11), white, early summer, 9 in., Carinthian and Venetian Alps, natural hybrid; *exarata* (8), cream, spring, 3 in., Pyrenees to Balkans, Iran; *ferdinandi-coburgii* (12), yellow, spring, 4 in., Bulgaria; *fortunei* (16), white, autumn, 12 to 15 in., China, Japan; *geum* (3), white, early summer, 4 to 6 in., Europe (Britain); *granulata* (7), Meadow Saxifrage, Fair Maids of France, white, summer, 12 in., Europe (Britain), and var. *flore pleno*, double; *grisebachii* (13), rose flowers, crimson bracts, summer, 9 in., S. E. European Mountains; *haagii* (12), yellow, spring, 3 in., hybrid; *hirculus* (2), yellow, summer, 6 in., Europe (Britain); *hostii* (11), cream, summer, 12 in., limestone Alps; *hypnoides* (8), Dovedale Moss, white, summer, 4 in., Europe (Britain), N. America, and many garden hybrids; *irvingii* (12), pink, spring, 2 in., hybrid; *juniperifolia* (12), yellow, late spring, 3 in., Caucasus, and var. *macedonica*, 4 in.; *kellereri* (12 x 13), soft pink, late winter, early spring, 4 in., hybrid; *lilacina* (12), lilac, spring, prostrate, Himalaya; *longifolia* (11), white, summer, 2 ft., monocarpic, Pyrenees; *macnabiana* (11), white, spotted red, summer, 12 in., hybrid; *marginata* (12), white, 4 in., early spring, Italy and vars. *coriophylla*, smaller, *karadzicensis*,

2 in., *rocheliana purpurea*, purple buds, white flowers, *rocheliana lutea*, yellow; *media* (13), pink, spring, 4 in., limestone Pyrenees; *moschata* (8), white, pink, pale yellow or purple, summer, 3 in., Pyrenees to Caucasus, (parent of many garden hybrids); *muscoides* (8), white, summer, 3 in., Europe; *oppositifolia* (14), purple, spring, prostrate, Europe (Britain), N. Asia, N. America, and many varieties such as *alba*, white, *splendens*, large flowers extra rich colour, Wetterhorn, small flowers, deep purple; *pedemontana* (8) (syn. *allionii*), white, summer, 4 in., Europe; *petraschii* (12), white, early spring, 3 to 4 in., hybrid; *porophylla* (13), pink, spring, 6 in., Italy; *retusa* (14), red, summer, 1 in., Pyrenees to Bulgaria; *rosacea* (8) (syn. *decipiens*), white, pink to crimson, spring, early summer, 3 to 6 in., Europe, and many varieties and hybrids varying in height, habit and colour; *rotundifolia* (4), white, speckled pink, early summer, 1 to 2 ft., Northern Hemisphere; *salomonii* (12), white, spring, 3 in., hybrid; *sancta* (12), yellow, spring, 4 in., Greece, Asia Minor; *scardica* (12), white, late spring, 4 in., limestone, Macedonia; *stolonifera* (16) (syn. *sarmentosa*), Mother of Thousands, Strawberry Saxifrage, white, red spotted, summer, 9 to 12 in., spreading by stolons, China, Japan; *stribrnyi* (13), pink flowers, crimson bracts, spring, 4 in., Bulgaria; *taygetea* (4) (syn. *rotundifolia taygetea*), white spotted pink, early summer, 4 to 6 in., Greece; *tenella* (8), white, summer, 2 to 3 in., E. Alps; *tombeanensis* (12), white, early summer, 2 in., Europe; *umbrosa* (3), London Pride, pink, summer, 12 to 18 in., Europe (Britain), and vars. *colvillei*, 6 to 9 in., *primuloides*, 4 to 6 in., *variegata*, leaves splashed with yellow; *valdensis* (11), white, early summer, 2 to 3 in., French Alps; *vandellii* (12), white, early summer, 3 to 4 in., limestone, Italian Alps; *veitchiana* (16), white, late summer, 6 to 9 in., China.

SCABIOSA (Scabious, Pincushion Flower) – *Dipsacaceae*. Hardy annual and perennial herbs. Flowers useful for cutting.

Culture of annual species: Soil, moderately rich, ordinary. Position, sunny. Sow seeds in light, sandy soil in temp. 14 to 16°C. in late winter or early spring and plant out in late spring; alternatively, sow a little later outdoors where plants are to flower and thin to 8 or 9 in.; or sow in early autumn outdoors or in a frame to flower the following spring and early summer.

Culture of perennial species: Soil, ordinary, moderately rich preferably with lime or chalk for *S. caucasica*. Position, sunny, well drained. Plant in spring. Lift, divide and replant every second or third year.

Increase by division in spring; by cuttings of firm young shoots in a frame in spring; by seeds sown in very porous soil in a frame or cool greenhouse in spring.

The best annual kind is *S. atropurpurea*, Sweet Scabious, Mournful Widow, Pincushion Flower, crimson, scented, 1 to 3 ft., S. W. Europe, and numerous varieties white, pink, red, maroon and blue.

Recommended perennial kinds are *S. caucasica*, Caucasian Scabious, light blue, summer, to 2 ft., Caucasus, and white and deep blue varieties; *columbaria*, blue, 2 ft., summer, Europe, Africa, Asia, and var. *graminifolia*, mauve, 1 ft., S. Europe; *ochroleuca*, yellow, summer, early autumn, 3 ft., Europe.

See also Cephalaria.

SCHISANDRA – *Schisandraceae*. Hardy deciduous aromatic twining shrubs with large leaves and scarlet berries. Male and female flowers are borne on different plants; only females can produce berries and then only if fertilized by a nearby male. Flowers small but pleasing, pendent. Sometimes spelled schizandra.

Soil, good, loamy. Position, partially shady on walls, screens or up trees. Plant in spring or autumn. Prune in late winter, cutting out old and weak stems.

Increase by cuttings of firm shoots inserted in sandy peat in a propagator in summer; by layering in spring.

Recommended kinds are *S. chinensis*, pale rose, fragrant, late spring, 20 to 30 ft., China, Japan; *grandiflora*, pink, late spring, early summer, Himalaya, var. *rubrifolia*, red; *propinqua*, orange, late summer and autumn; *sphenanthera*, orange-red, late spring, early summer, W. China.

SCHIZANTHUS (Butterfly or Fringe Flower, Poor Man's Orchid) – *Solanaceae*. Slightly tender annual herbs with large sprays of small, butterfly-like flowers in many colours.

Sow in spring for summer flowering or in late summer for spring flowering, in John Innes seed compost or equivalent and germinate in a temperature of about 15°C. Pot seedlings singly in John Innes potting compost No. 1 or equivalent and later move on into larger pots and John Innes potting compost No. 2 or equivalent. Grow in a sunny, cool greenhouse, minimum winter temp. 7°C., or in summer plants can stand outdoors in their pots or be planted in sunny beds to flower in the open. Water normally. Feed well-grown plants occasionally with weak liquid manure or fertilizer. Support growth early either with twiggy branches through which the stems can grow or with three or four thin canes and encircling ties. Discard after flowering.

The best kind is *S. wisetonensis*, white, pink, salmon, carmine, purple, mauve, yellow and apricot, 1 to 2 ft., spring and summer, a hybrid between *grahami*, lilac or rose and yellow, summer, 2 ft., Chile, and *pinnatus*, purple or violet and yellow, summer, 2 ft., Chile.

SCHIZOPETALON – *Cruciferae*. Half-hardy annual with divided leaves and fringed petals.

Soil, ordinary, reasonably fertile. Position, warm, sunny, well drained. Sow in spring in temp. 15 to 18°C. and pot seedlings singly in John Innes potting compost No. 1 or equivalent in small pots. Harden off for planting out in late spring or early summer. Alternatively, in warm places sow outdoors where plants are to flower and thin seedlings to 6 in., as seedlings transplant badly. Support plant with small bushy twigs.

The best kind is *S. walkeri*, white, almond scented, summer, 1½ to 2½ ft., Chile.

SCHIZOPHRAGMA – *Hydrangeaceae*. Hardy, deciduous, self-clinging, climbing flowering shrubs of very great vigour, closely related to hydrangea.

Soil, ordinary. Position, shady, requiring space, high walls, tree trunks, old tree stumps, etc. Plant in autumn or late winter. Little pruning required but excessive growth can be removed in winter.

Increase by cuttings of firm young growth in a propagator in summer; by layering in spring or autumn; by seeds sown as soon as ripe or in the spring.

Recommended kinds are *S. hydrangeoides*, creamy white, summer, 20 to 30 ft., Japan; *integrifolium*, creamy white, summer, to 40 ft., China.

SCHIZOSTYLIS (Kaffir Lily, Crimson Flag) – *Iridaceae*. Hardy or rhizomatous-rooted perennial with flowers in slender spikes.

Schizostylis coccinea

Soil, ordinary, well drained. Position, warm, sunny. Plant in spring. Lift and replant when plants become overcrowded. Protect in severe weather with a covering of dry litter.

Increase by division in spring.

The best kind is *S. coccinea*, crimson, autumn, 1 to 2 ft., S. Africa, and vars.

major, larger flowers, Viscountess Byng, pink.

SCHLUMBERGERA (Leaf-flowering Cactus) – *Cactaceae*. Greenhouse succulent plants with showy flowers. The genus, consisting of two species from Brazil, was formerly known as *Zygocactus*.

Compost, John Innes potting compost No. 2 or equivalent plus one-sixth its bulk of peat. Position, pots or baskets in a cool or intermediate greenhouse, minimum winter temp. 7°C. (but 13°C. for winter-flowering kinds), or in a warm, light room. Winter flowering can be inhibited by the use of artificial lighting to shorten night length. Water fairly freely most of the year but sparingly for a few weeks after flowering. Shade from direct sunshine in summer at which time plants can be removed to a sheltered semi-shady place outdoors.

Schlumbergera buckleyi

Increase by cuttings inserted singly in 3-in. pots filled with sandy soil in spring or summer; by grafting on to stock of *Pereskia aculeata* in temp. 18 to 21°C. in spring.

Recommended kinds are *S. buckleyi*, Christmas Cactus, Candlemas Cactus, rose or magenta, winter, arching or pendulous, hybrid between *russelliana* and *truncata ruckeri*; *russelliana*, magenta, late winter, spring, arching or pendulous; *truncata*, Crab Cactus, Lobster Cactus (syn. *Zygocactus truncatus*), rose, autumn, winter, spreading.

SCIADOPITYS (Umbrella Pine, Parasol Pine) – *Taxodiaceae*. Hardy evergreen conifer. Stiff, narrow glossy leaves borne in tufts at the end of shoots like parasols; the leaves are green with yellow grooves on their lower surfaces.

Soil, rich, moist, lime-free loam. Position, sunny or partially shady, sheltered from piercing winds. Plant in spring or autumn.

Increase by seeds sown in sandy loam and placed in a cold frame or greenhouse, or outdoors in spring in a moist bed of sandy loam, transplanting seedlings the next year.

The only species is *S. verticillata*, slow growing, pyramidal shape, 80 to 120 ft., Japan.

SCILLA (Squill) – *Liliaceae*. Hardy and slightly tender bulbs with flowers in racemes. For bulbs commonly known as Bluebells see Endymion.

Soil, deep, sandy loam. Position, sunny. Plant in autumn, covering the bulbs with from 2 to 4 in. of soil. Lift, divide and replant when overcrowded.

Scilla sibirica

Increase by seeds sown in sandy soil in a frame or outdoors as soon as ripe or in spring; by offsets from old bulbs removed when lifting and treated as advised for full-sized bulbs. Seedlings flower when three to four years old.

Recommended kinds are *S. bifolia*, blue, early spring, 6 in., Europe, and vars. *alba*, white, *rosea*, rose; *peruviana*, lilac, late spring, early summer, 6 to 12 in., slightly tender, Algeria, and var. *alba*, white; *sibirica*, Siberian Squill, blue, early spring, 3 to 6 in., East Russia, Siberia, and var. *alba*; *tubergeniana*, light blue, late winter, early spring, 6 in., Iran.

SCINDAPSUS – *Araceae*. Tender evergreen climbers, grown for their shining green foliage.

Compost, John Innes potting compost No. 2 or equivalent. Position, large pots or beds in an intermediate or warm greenhouse, minimum winter temp. 10°C., or in a warm room. Water freely in spring and summer, moderately in autumn, rather sparingly in winter. Shade in spring and summer from direct sunshine. Feed occasionally in late spring and summer with weak liquid manure or fertilizer. Pot or plant in spring. Provide canes or trellis for support or make moss- or bark-covered pillars into which the climbing stems can root.

Increase by cuttings of firm young growth in a warm propagator in summer.

Recommended kinds are *S. aureus*, leaves blotched with pale yellow, 20 ft., Solomon Islands; *pictus*, leaves dark green, spotted light green, 20 ft., E. Indies, and var. *argyraeus*, silver-spotted leaves.

SCIRPUS (Club Rush, Bulrush) – *Cyperaceae*. Tender and hardy perennial marsh or water plants. *S. cernuus* is hardy but almost invariably cultivated as a greenhouse pot plant.

Culture of hardy species: Soil, loamy. Position, margins of lakes, streams and ponds in boggy soil or shallow water. Plant in spring.

Culture of greenhouse species: Compost, John Innes potting compost No. 1 or equivalent. Position, small pots in a cool greenhouse, minimum winter temp. 7°C. Pot in spring. Water abundantly from spring to autumn, moderately in winter. Increase by division in spring.

Recommended kinds are *S. holoschoenus variegatus*, leaves banded green and white, 1 to 1½ ft., a variety of a plant native to Europe (Britain), Siberia and S. Africa; *lacustris*, Bulrush, reddish brown, summer, 3 to 8 ft., Europe (Britain), Asia, Africa, Australia, Polynesia, N. and Central America; *maritimus*, Sea Club Rush, inflorescence golden brown, summer, 3 to 5 ft., Cosmopolitan; *setaceus* (syn. *Isolepis setacea*), brownish purple, summer, 1 to 6 in., Europe (Britain), Africa, Asia, Australia; *tabernaemontani*, similar to *lacustris*, glaucous, S. Europe, Temperate Asia, the Arctic, and var. *zebrinus* (syn. *Juncus zebrinus*), Porcupine Quill Rush, Zebra Rush, stems banded in green and white, 4 to 5 ft.; *triquetrus*, triangular stems, 2 to 3 ft., Europe (Britain), W. Asia, N. and S. Africa, N. America.

The recommended greenhouse species is *S. cernuus* (syn. *Isolepis gracilis*), Club Rush, 6 to 12 in., stems slender and drooping, Cosmopolitan.

SCROPHULARIA (Figwort) – *Scrophulariaceae*. Hardy herbaceous perennials, mostly weeds but one kind grown for its variegated foliage.

Soil, ordinary, rather moist. Position, open. Plant in spring or autumn.

Increase by division at planting time.

The recommended kind is *S. aquatica variegata*, Variegated Water Betony, leaves variegated with cream, 3 ft., Europe (Britain), N. Africa, Azores.

SCUTELLARIA (Helmet Flower, Skull Cap) – *Labiatae*. Those dealt with here are hardy herbaceous perennials with small tubular hooded flowers.

Soil, ordinary. Position, open, sunny. Plant in spring.

Increase by seeds sown outdoors in spring; by division in spring.

Recommended hardy kinds are *S. alpina*, purple, late summer, 6 to 8 in., Europe, Asia, and vars. *alba*, white, *bicolor*, purple and white, *lupulina*, yellow, *rosea*, pink; *baicalensis* (syn. *macrantha*), purplish blue, late summer, 1 ft., E. Asia, and var. *coelestina*, bright blue; *indica japonica*, violet-purple, summer, 4 to 6 in., Japan; *orientalis*

(syn. *grandiflora* and *pulchella*), yellow, late summer, creeping, to 9 in., S. Europe, Central Asia; *scordifolia*, deep blue, late summer, 6 in., slightly tender, Siberia.

SEDUM (Stonecrop) – *Crassulaceae*. Succulent tender and hardy evergreen and deciduous perennials, biennials, annuals and monocarpic plants.

Culture of tender species: Compost, John Innes potting compost No. 1 or equivalent. Position, well-drained pots or pans in a sunny frost-proof greenhouse or room. Pot in spring. Water freely from mid-spring to mid-autumn, very little afterwards. No shade is necessary at any time.

Culture of hardy perennial species: Soil, ordinary, well drained for most but moist for *S. pulchellum*. Position, sunny, rather dry. Plant in spring or autumn.

Culture of annual and biennial species: Soil and position as for hardy perennial kinds. Sow *S. coeruleum* in spring in temp. 15 to 18°C. and plant out 4 in. apart in late spring or early summer. Sow *S. pilosum* in spring or early summer in a greenhouse or frame and plant out when large enough to handle conveniently.

Increase tender kinds by seeds sown in well-drained pots or pans filled with porous compost such as John Innes seed compost in spring in temp. 14 to 16°C.; also by cuttings of shoots inserted in sandy soil in a propagator in summer, and by division at potting time. Hardy species by seeds sown outdoors in spring; by division in spring; by cuttings in spring or summer in sandy soil in a frame.

Recommended hardy perennial kinds are *S. acre*, Wall Pepper, yellow, summer, 2 in., Europe (Britain), Asia, N. Africa, and vars. *aureum*, young leaves yellow, *majus*, larger; *aizoon*, yellow, summer, 12 in., Siberia to Japan; *album*, white, summer, 4 in., Europe, N. Africa and Asia, and vars. *micranthum*, a miniature form, *murale*, deep purple leaves, pink flowers, *pallens* (*chloroticum*), yellowish leaves, green-tinted flowers; *amplexicaule*, yellow, late spring, early summer, 3 in., Mediterranean region; *anacampseros*, purple, summer, sprawling, grey-green stems and leaves, Central Europe; *anglicum*,

white, tinged pink, summer, 2 in., Europe (Britain); *anopetalum*, rich cream, summer, 6 in., Spain, Asia Minor; *bithynicum*, pink, summer, creeping, Balkans, Asia Minor; *brevifolium*, blue-grey leaves, white flowers, summer, 2 in., Europe and N. Africa, and var. *quinquefolium*, twice as large; *cauticola*, rose-crimson, late summer, autumn, trailing, Japan; *crassipes* (syns. *asiaticum* and *wallichianum*), greenish, or purplish white, early summer, 6 to 12 in., Himalaya, Tibet, China; *dasyphyllum*, blush pink, summer, 2 in., S. Europe (Britain), and vars. *glanduliferum*, very hairy form, *macrophyllum*, twice as large as the type; *divergens*, golden, early summer, 2 to 3 in., Western N. America; *douglasii*, yellow, summer, 12 in., Western N. America; *ellacombianum*, yellow, late summer, 6 in., Japan; *ewersii*, pink, late summer, 9 in., Himalaya to Mongolia, and var. *homophyllum*, condensed form; *gracile*, white spotted red, summer, 2 in., Caucasus, Iran; *gypsicolum*, white, summer, 3 in., Spain, Portugal; *hispanicum* (syn. *glaucum*), white, early summer, 2 in. Caucasus, Asia Minor, Italy, and var. *aureum*, leaves yellow in summer; *hybridum*, yellow, spring and autumn, creeping, stems 4 in., Siberia; *kamtschaticum*, orange-yellow, late summer, 6 in., N. E. Asia, and var. *variegatum*, leaves variegated cream and pink, seed vessels red; *lydium*, white, early summer, leaves red in summer, prostrate, Asia Minor; *maximum*, greenish white, 2 ft., summer, Europe, and var. *atropurpureum*, mahogany leaves and reddish flowers; *middendorffianum*, yellow, late summer, 4 to 6 in., Siberia, Manchuria; *oreganum*, golden, late summer, green and red leaves, creeping, Western N. America; *populifolium*, white or pink, fragrant, late summer, 1 to 1½ ft., Siberia; *primuloides*, white, summer, 2 to 3 in., China; *pruinatum*, pale yellow, summer, 9 to 12 in., Portugal; *pulchellum*, pink, summer, prostrate, U.S.A.; *reflexum*, Stone Orpine, yellow, summer, prostrate, Europe; *roseum* (syn. *rhodiola*), Rose-root, greenish yellow, late spring, early summer, 12 to 15 in., Europe, Asia, America, and var. *atropurpureum*, purple; *rupestre*, yellow, late summer, 6 in., Europe (Britain); *sediforme* (syn. *altissimum*), yellow, summer,

Sedum bellum

6 to 24 in., Mediterranean region, and var. *latifolium* (syn. *nicaeense*), larger leaves, 2 ft.; *sempervivoides*, crimson, summer, monocarpic, 4 to 6 in., Caucasus, Asia Minor; *sexangulare*, yellow, summer, 2 in., Europe (Britain); *spathulifolium*, yellow, late spring, early summer, prostrate, Western N. America, and vars. Cappa Blanca, leaves covered with white meal, *purpureum*, leaves purple; *spectabile*, pink, late summer, early autumn, 12 to 15 in., Japan, and var. *atropurpureum*, rose-red; *spurium*, pink, late summer, prostrate, Caucasus, Iran, and var. *album*, white, Schorbusser Blut, deep magenta; *stribrnyi*, yellow, summer, 6 in., Bulgaria, Greece; *telephium*, Orpine, pink, late summer, autumn, 8 to 24 in., Europe (Britain), Temperate Asia, N. America, and vars. Autumn Joy, salmon pink becoming bronze red, Munstead Red, dusky red; *ternatum*, white, late spring, early summer, 3 to 6 in., Eastern U.S.A.; *winkleri*, white and green, summer, 1 to 2 in., Spain.

Recommended annual and biennial kinds are *S. coeruleum*, pale blue, summer, 3 to 4 in., slightly tender, annual, S. Europe, Algeria; *pilosum*, rose-red, late spring, early summer, 2 to 4 in., biennial, Iran, Caucasus, Asia Minor.

Recommended tender kinds are *S. adolphi*, white, spring, 1 ft., Mexico; *allantoides*, greenish white, summer, 1 ft., Mexico; *bellum*, white, spring, prostrate, Mexico; *humifusum*, yellow, spring, early summer, prostrate, Mexico; *lineare variegatum*, yellow, spring, summer, prostrate, leaves edged white, China, Japan; *moranense*, white, summer, 4 in., Mexico, and var. *arboreum*, like a miniature tree, 6 in.; *morganianum*, Burro's-tail Stonecrop, red, summer, grey-green leaves trailing, Mexico; *pachyphyllum*, yellow, spring, leaves red tipped, 4 in., Mexico; *palmeri*, orange, late spring, early summer, 9 in., Mexico; *praealtum*, yellow, late spring, early summer, 1 to 2 ft., Mexico; *rubrotinctum*, yellow, leaves green becoming red in hot sunshine, 6 in., Mexico; *sieboldii*, pink, summer, 9 in., Japan, and var. *mediovariegatum*, cream blotch in centre of leaf; *stahlii*, yellow, summer and autumn, leaves reddish, 4 to 8 in., Mexico; *treleasei*, yellow, spring, 1 ft., Mexico; *weinbergii*, white, late spring, early summer, 8 in., rosettes of glaucous leaves becoming purple, Mexico.

SELAGINELLA – *Selaginellaceae*. Tender evergreen moss-like plants, allied to ferns. Fronds creeping or erect, branched, green or variegated.

Compost, equal parts fibrous peat and chopped sphagnum moss. Position, pots or pans in a cool or intermediate greenhouse, minimum winter temp. 7°C. Pot or plant in spring. Water copiously and syringe daily from mid-spring to early autumn, moderately afterwards. Shade from direct sunshine at all times.

Increase in spring and summer by scattering pieces of growth on the above compost in a propagator or in a pan covered with a sheet of glass; by spores sown on the surface of similar compost in a propagator in spring or summer.

Recommended kinds are *S. braunii*, 1 to 1½ ft., China; *douglasii*, creeping, pale green, British Columbia to California; *grandis*, 1½ to 2 ft., Borneo; *involvens* (syn. *caulescens*), 1 to 2 ft., China, Japan; *kraussiana*, creeping or trailing, S. Africa; *martensii*, 6 to 12 in., Mexico; *pallescens* (syn. *cuspidata*), 6 in., Mexico; *pulcherrima* (syn. *caulescens amoena*), 1 ft., Mexico; *uncinata* (syn. *caesia*), trailing, China.

SELENICEREUS – *Cactaceae*. Tender succulent plants with slender stems bearing very large flowers usually opening at night. Formerly included in *Cereus*.

Compost, John Innes potting compost No. 2 or equivalent plus one-sixth its bulk of coarse sand. Position, well-drained pots in a sunny, cool greenhouse, minimum winter temp. 7°C.; can be trained up the greenhouse wall. Water fairly freely in spring and summer, sparingly in autumn and winter. Pot in spring.

Increase by seeds sown in sandy soil in spring in temp. 15 to 18°C.; by cuttings in sandy soil in a cool greenhouse in summer.

Recommended kinds are *S. grandiflorus*, Queen of the Night, white, scented, summer, trailing, Jamaica; *macdonaldiae*, white, summer, trailing, Argentina, Uruguay.

SEMPERVIVUM (Houseleek) – *Crassulaceae*. Hardy succulent-leaved perennials grown for their ornamental rosettes of leaves. The usually pink, purple or whitish flowers are borne in clusters on stout, leafy stems. Tender species native to Canary Islands and Madeira have been transferred to *Aeonium*, *Aichryson* and *Greenovia*.

Soil, ordinary, light, sandy, preferably alkaline or neutral with lime or chalk. Position, open and sunny, chinks, crevices or ledges of rock gardens, walls, etc., or in well-drained pans, trough gardens. Plant in spring. Topdress annually in spring with equal parts leafmould and limestone chippings. *S. tectorum*, suitable for growing on sunny roofs or crevices of old walls, plant in a mixture of cow dung and clay in spring.

Increase by seeds sown in spring in John Innes seed compost or equivalent in well-drained, shallow pans, lightly covered with fine soil, in a sunny frame or greenhouse, temp. 14 to 16°C.; by cuttings inserted in sandy soil in summer; by division in spring.

There are too many species with, in many instances, differences too slight for brief descriptions to justify a detailed list here. The figures given in the following list refer to the approximate diameter of rosettes.

Recommended kinds are *S. allionii* (syn.

Sempervivum arachnoideum

Jovibarba allionii), pale green, sometimes red tipped, 1 in., Alps; *S. andreanum*, blue-green, purple tipped, 1 in., Spain; *arachnoideum*, Cobweb Houseleek, green or reddish covered with 'cobweb' hairs, 2 in., Pyrenees to Carpathians, and var. *tomentosum* (syn. *laggeri*), extra dense cobweb; *arenarium* (syn. *Jovibarba arenaria*), pale green, ½ in. Alps; *armenum*, green, purple tipped, 2 in., Turkey; *atlanticum*, green or grey, 2½ in., Morocco; *ballsii*, green, 1½ in., Greece; *borisovae*, green and purplish red, 1 in., Caucasus; *calcaratum*, milky purple and crimson, to 6 in., hybrid; *cantabricum*, green, purple tipped, 2 in., Spain; *ciliosum*, grey-green, 1½ in., S. E. Europe; *erythraeum*, purple, 1½ in., Bulgaria; *funckii*, green and purple, 1½ in., hybrid; *giuseppi*, grey-green, 1½ in., Spain; *grandiflorum*, green, 3 in., Alps; *heuffelii* (syn. *Jovibarba heuffelii*), grey-green, sometimes dark tipped, to 6 in., S. E. Europe; *hirtum* (syn. *Jovibarba hirta*), green and brownish purple, 1½ in., Alps, Hungary, Dalmatia; *ingwersenii*, light green, 1 in., Caucasus; *kindingeri*, light green, 3 in., Macedonia; *kosaninii*, green, dark tipped, 2½ in., Yugoslavia; *macedonicum*, green, 1 in., Yugoslavia; *marmoreum*, green or dull purple, 3 in., Eastern Europe; *montanum*, green, 1 in., Alps, Carpathians; *nevadense*, pinkish bronze or purple, 1 in., Spain; *octopodes*, green, purple tipped, hairy, 1 in., Macedonia; *reginae-amaliae*, grey-green or purplish red, 1½ in., Greece, Albania; *ruthenicum*, green, purple tipped, 3 in., Eastern Europe; *soboliferum* (*Jovibarba sobolifera*), Hen and Chicken Houseleek, light green and red, numerous offsets, ¾ in., N. Europe, Asia; *tectorum* (syn. *triste*), Common Houseleek, green, purple tipped, 3 in., Europe, and vars. *alpinum*, leaves red at base, smaller rosettes, *calcareum*, milky green, purple tipped; *thompsonianum*, light green and reddish purple, 1 in., Macedonia; *thompsonii*, green, hairy, 1½ in., hybrid; *zelebori*, grey-green, downy, 2 in., Bulgaria, Rumania.

SENECIO (Groundsel, Ragwort) – *Compositae*. Tender and hardy annuals, evergreen herbs or climbers, herbaceous perennials and evergreen shrubs with daisy-type flowers. *S. smithii* is grown in the water garden. Florists' cinerarias are hybrids or varieties of *S. cruentus*. For other plants often listed as senecio see Ligularia.

Culture of annual species: Soil, ordinary. Position, sunny. Sow seeds in spring in temp. 14 to 16°C. and harden off seedlings for planting outdoors in late spring or early summer, or, for *S. elegans*, sow outdoors in spring where required to grow and thin seedlings 4 to 6 in. apart.

Culture of climbing species: Compost, John Innes potting compost No. 2 or equivalent. Position, well-drained pots or borders in a sunny greenhouse, minimum winter temp. 7°C. Allow to twine around pillars, trellis or wires. Pot or plant in spring. Water normally. No shade required at any time. Prune in spring to fill available space.

Culture of hybrid cinerarias (*S. cruentus*): Sow in spring and early summer in John Innes seed compost or equivalent in temp. 14 to 16°C. Prick out seedlings into similar compost and later pot singly in 3-in. pots in John Innes potting compost No. 1 or equivalent. Grow during the summer in a light, airy greenhouse or frame but in early autumn before there is danger of frost bring the plants into a light well-ventilated greenhouse, minimum temp. 7°C. Repot as necessary in John Innes potting compost No. 2 or equivalent. Water fairly freely in summer, sparingly in winter, at all times taking care not to wet leaves and crowns unnecessarily. Discard after flowering.

Culture of S. cineraria and S. leucostachys: Soil, ordinary, well drained. Position, warm, sunny places outdoors but in cold or wet places bring the plants into a sunny frost-proof greenhouse in autumn and do not plant outdoors again until late spring.

Culture of hardy herbaceous perennial species: Soil, deep, rich loam. Position, partially shady, moist. *S. smithii* in bog or shallow water. Plant in spring or autumn. Mulch with decayed manure annually in spring. Water freely in dry weather.

Culture of shrubby species: Soil, ordinary well drained. Position, warm, sunny, excellent in rather dry places. Plant in spring or autumn.

Increase climbing kinds by seeds sown in spring in temp. 14 to 16°C.; by cuttings in spring or summer in a propagator or frame; by layering in spring or summer. *S. cineraria* and *leucostachys* by seed as above, or by cuttings in spring or summer in a frame or propagator. Hardy perennial kinds by division in spring or autumn; by seeds sown in spring or early summer outdoors or in a frame. Shrubby species by cuttings of nearly ripe wood in sandy soil in a propagator in summer, and by seed as for hardy perennial kinds.

Recommended annual kinds are *S. arenarius*, lavender, purple, pale yellow and apricot, summer, 1 ft., S. Africa; *elegans* (syn. *Jacobaea erecta*), rose, purple, crimson, single and double, summer, 1½ to 2 ft., S. Africa.

The best greenhouse kind is *S. cruentus* (syn. *Cineraria cruenta*), parent of the well-known cinerarias, purple, summer, 1 to 2 ft., perennial but grown as an annual, Canaries, and many garden varieties in a wide range of colours including blue, purple, crimson and scarlet often with a white zone around the central disk. Double varieties are known. There are also large-flowered (*grandiflora*), medium-flowered (*multiflora*), and small-flowered (*stellata*) strains as well as dwarf varieties.

Senecio cruentus (large-flowered)

The best climbing kind is *S. mikanioides*, German Ivy, yellow, winter, vigorous twiner with light green, shining, ivy-like leaves, S. Africa.

Recommended hardy perennial kinds are *S. cineraria*, yellow, summer, white woolly leaves, 2 to 3 ft., sub-shrub, S. Europe; *leucostachys*, similar to last but leaves more finely divided, Patagonia; *macrophyllus* (syn. *Jacobaea macrophylla*), golden yellow, summer, 4 to 5 ft., Caucasus; *smithii*, white, early summer, 3 ft., Chile, Falkland Islands; *tanguticus*, golden yellow, autumn, 6 to 7 ft., W. China.

Recommended shrubby kinds are *S. greyi*, yellow, summer, 3 ft., slightly tender, New Zealand; *laxifolius*, yellow, summer, 2 to 4 ft., New Zealand; *monroi*, yellow, summer, 2 ft., New Zealand; *rotundifolius* (syn. *reinoldii*), yellow, summer, 6 to 8 ft., New Zealand.

SEQUOIA (Californian Redwood) – *Taxodiaceae*. Hardy evergreen coniferous tree, notable for its great size and regular conical shape.

Soil, deep loam. Position, sunny, sheltered, excellent as a specimen but needs plenty of room. Plant in autumn or late winter.

Increase by seeds in sandy soil in a cold frame in spring; variegated kinds by grafting on common species, or by cuttings of firm young growth in a propagator in summer.

The only species is *S. sempervirens*, 100 to 300 ft., California, and vars. *adpressa* (syn. *albo-spica*), leaves and ends of shoots white tipped, *prostrata*, dwarf, spreading.

SEQUOIADENDRON (Wellingtonia) – *Taxodiaceae*. Tall evergreen coniferous tree with deeply furrowed reddish brown spongy bark. It makes a broader cone than the related *Sequoia sempervirens* and has a thicker trunk but does not grow so tall.

Soil, deep loam. Position, open, sunny; makes a handsome specimen but requires plenty of space.

Increase by seeds stratified for two months at 4°C. and then sown under glass; selected garden varieties by grafting on to seedlings of the common kind; by cuttings of firm young growth in sandy peat in a propagator in summer.

The only species is *S. giganteum* (syn. *Wellingtonia gigantea*, *Sequoia wellingtonia*), Giant Sequoia, Californian Big Tree, Wellingtonia, to 100 ft. or more, trunk many feet in diameter and bark to 20 in. thick, California, and vars. *glaucum*, leaves bluish grey, *pendulum*, branches stiffly pendulous, usually on one side only making a very freakish looking tree.

SETCREASEA – *Commelinaceae*. Tender herbaceous perennials with ornamental foliage.

Compost, John Innes potting compost No. 1 or equivalent. Position, pots in an intermediate or warm greenhouse, minimum winter temp. 13°C., or in a warm, fairly light room. Pot in spring. Water normally. Shade from strong sunshine only – leaf colour is best developed in good light. Pinch the tips of shoots occasionally to improve branching habit.

Increase by cuttings of firm young growth in a warm propagator in spring or summer.

The best kind is *S. purpurea*, Purple Heart, magenta, summer, leaves and stems purple, sprawling, Mexico.

SHORTIA – *Diapensiaceae*. Hardy evergreen herbs with leathery leaves and attractive flowers on bare stems. Some species were formerly known as schizocodon.

Soil, equal parts sandy peat and leafmould. Position, partially shady border, rhododendron bed or frame. Plant in spring. Water freely in dry weather.

Increase by division in spring.

Recommended kinds are *S. galacifolia*, white flushed pink, spring, early summer, 3 to 6 in., N. Carolina, and var. *rosea*; *uniflora*, Nippon Bells, pink, spring, 6 in., Japan, and var. *grandiflora*, larger flowers.

SIDALCEA – *Malvaceae*. Hardy perennial herbs with flowers in slender spikes.

Soil, ordinary. Position, sunny. Plant in spring or autumn. Lift, divide and replant every three or four years.

Increase by seeds sown in light soil outdoors in spring or summer; by division in spring or autumn.

Recommended kinds are *S. candida*, white, summer, 3 ft., Rocky Mountains; *malvaeflora*, lilac, summer, 3 ft., California, and numerous varieties in shades of pink, rose and crimson.

SILENE (Catchfly) – *Caryophyllaceae*. Hardy annuals, biennials and herbaceous perennials with campion-like flowers.

Culture of annual and biennial species: Soil, ordinary, light, well drained. Position, sunny. Sow seeds in early autumn for spring flowering. In cold or wet places overwinter *S. armeria* and *pendula* in a frame and plant out in early spring. Sow also in spring where plants are to flower in summer and thin seedlings to 6 in.

Culture of perennial species: Equal parts loam, leafmould (or peat) and coarse sand for *S. acaulis* and *hookeri*; ordinary well-drained soil for other kinds. Position, sunny crevices or ledges of rock gardens for *S. acaulis*, *alpestris*, *hookeri*; open, sunny for other kinds. Plant in spring.

Increase perennials by seeds sown in pans or boxes of sandy loam and peat in spring; by cuttings of young shoots inserted in sandy loam in a frame in summer; by division in spring.

Recommended annual and biennial kinds are *S. armeria*, pink, summer, 1 to 1½ ft., Europe; *compacta*, rose-pink, summer, 9 to 12 in., Russia, Asia Minor; *oculata* (syn. *Viscaria oculata*), white, pink, red, carmine, blue, summer, 1 to 1½ ft., N. Africa; *pendula*, pink, spring, trailing, Mediterranean region, and many varieties, white to crimson.

Recommended perennial kinds are *S. acaulis*, Cushion Pink, Moss Campion, pink, late spring, early summer, 2 in., North Temperate Zone (Britain), and var. *alba*, white; *alpestris* (syn. *Heliosperma alpestre*), Alpine Catchfly, white, summer, 6 in., Alps; *caroliniana*, Wild Pink, white to pink, early summer, 6 to 8 in., U.S.A.; *hookeri*, pink and white, summer, 2 in., California; *maritima* var. *florepleno*, Witch's Thimble, white, double, summer, trailing, Europe (Britain), N. Africa; *saxifraga*, white, tinged green or pink, summer, 6 in., S. Europe, Asia Minor; *schafta*, rose-magenta, late summer and autumn, 4 to 6 in., Caucasus; *virginica*, Fire Pink, scarlet, spring, early summer, 2 ft., N. America.

See also Melandrium.

SILPHIUM – *Compositae*. Hardy perennials with large daisy-type flowers, from Eastern U.S.A.

Soil, ordinary. Position, sunny. Plant in spring or autumn. Lift, divide and replant every two or three years.

Increase by division in spring or autumn.

Recommended kinds are *S. laciniatum*, Compass Plant, Pilot Weed, Polar Plant, yellow, summer, 6 to 8 ft.; *perfoliatum*, Cup Plant, yellow, late summer, early autumn, 4 to 8 ft.

SILYBUM – *Compositae*. Hardy biennial herb. Leaves, large, variegated with broad white veins.

Soil, ordinary. Position, open. Sow seeds in spring or early summer where plants are to grow, thinning or transplanting seedlings to 1 ft. apart when large enough to handle.

The best kind is *S. marianum*, Blessed Thistle, Holy Thistle, Our Lady's Milk Thistle, rose-purple, summer, 1 to 4 ft., Mediterranean region.

SINNINGIA – *Gesneriaceae*. Tender tuberous-rooted deciduous flowering plants with rosettes of velvety leaves and showy trumpet-shaped flowers. The most commonly grown, *S. speciosa*, is known as gloxinia.

Start tubers into growth in late winter or early spring in damp peat in a temp. 15 to 18°C. When leaves appear pot singly in John Innes potting compost No. 2 or equivalent and grow in a similar temperature throughout. Water fairly freely and maintain a reasonably moist atmosphere. In late spring and summer shade from direct sunshine. In autumn gradually reduce water supply and when foliage has died down place pots on their sides and keep quite dry in a minimum temp. 10°C. Shake out tubers when it is time to start them into growth again.

Sinningia (hybrid)

Increase by seeds sown on surface of fine John Innes seed compost or equivalent in well-drained pots or pans in temp. 15 to 18°C. in early spring, covering the seed pans with glass and paper until germination occurs. Prick out seedlings in similar compost and later pot singly in 3-in. pots in John Innes potting compost No. 1 or equivalent. Use a richer compost such as John Innes potting compost No. 2 when the plants are ready for 4-in. pots. Growing conditions as for plants grown from tubers.

The best kind is *S. speciosa* (syn. *Gloxinia speciosa*), violet, summer, 6 to 12 in., Brazil, parent of the lovely strains of gloxinias grown in gardens in various colours including red, pink, violet, purple, often netted or with white throats.

SISYRINCHIUM (Satin Flower) – *Iridaceae*. Hardy and half-hardy perennials with small but attractive flowers.

Soil, two parts sandy loam, one part peat. Position, sunny, sheltered. *S. californicum* does best in moist soil. Plant in spring or autumn.

Sisyrinchium striatum

Increase by division in spring; by seeds sown in a frame or greenhouse in spring or as soon as ripe.

Recommended kinds are *S. angustifolium* (syn. *gramineum*), Blue-eyed Grass, blue, summer, 6 to 8 in., N. America; *bellum*, violet-blue and yellow, summer, 4 in., N. America; *bermudiana*, blue and yellow, late spring, early summer, 12 to 15 in., Bermuda; *douglasii* (syn. *grandiflorum*), Spring Bell, Rush Lily, purple, spring, 9 in., N. W. America, and var. *album*, white; *filifolium*, Pale Maidens, white, late spring, 6 in., Falkland Islands; *striatum*, yellow, veined purple, early summer, 2 ft., Chile, and var. *variegatum*, leaves striped white.

SKIMMIA – *Rutaceae*. Hardy, evergreen, flowering, berry-bearing shrubs with ornamental foliage. Flowers in spikes, fragrant. Some species, notably *S. japonica* and *laureola*, produce male and female flowers on separate plants. Only the females of these kinds can produce berries and then only if fertilized from a nearby male.

Soil, ordinary, but not shallow and dry; *S. reevesiana* on lime-free soil. Position, shade or sun, good for exposed positions. Plant in spring or autumn.

Increase by seeds sown when ripe in sandy loam and peat in a cold frame; by cuttings of firm shoots inserted in a propagator in summer; by layering in autumn.

Recommended kinds are *S. japonica*, white, spring, 3 to 4 ft., spreading, Japan, and vars. *foremanii*, female extra vigorous, *fragrans*, large panicles, fragrant male flowers, *rubella*, male, red buds; *laureola*, greenish yellow, scented, spring, 2 to 3 ft.; Himalaya; *reevesiana* (syn. *fortunei*), white, spring, 1½ to 2 ft., hermaphrodite, crimson pear-shaped fruits, China.

SMILACINA – *Liliaceae*. Hardy perennials with ornamental leaves and plumy clusters of small flowers.

Soil, ordinary, deep, rich. Position, partially shady, moist. Plant in spring or autumn.

Increase by division of roots in spring or autumn; by seeds sown in sand and peat in spring or as soon as ripe outdoors or in a frame.

Recommended kinds are *S. racemosa*, False Spikenard, white, late spring, 2 ft., N. America; *stellata*, Star-flowered Lily of the Valley, Starry Solomon's Seal, white, late spring, 1 ft., N. W. America.

SMILAX (Sarsaparilla Plant, Greenbriar) – *Smilacaceae*. Hardy or tender evergreen and deciduous climbers, often very spiny. The smilax of florists is *Asparagus medioloides*.

Soil, ordinary. Position, sunny, warm. Plants often spread underground and can become inpenetrable thickets. Plant in spring or autumn.

Increase by division of roots at planting or potting time.

Recommended kinds are *S. aspera*, Prickly Ivy, pale green, fragrant, late summer to early autumn, 10 to 15 ft., evergreen, slightly tender, Mediterranean region, Canary Islands, and var. *maculata*, leaves blotched white; *megalantha*, Coral Greenbriar, green, summer, male and female on separate plants with coral-red berries, evergreen, twining to 18 ft., China.

SMITHIANTHA (Temple Bells) – *Gesneriaceae*. Tender herbaceous perennials forming rhizomes. They have tubular flowers in spikes, and heart-shaped green or crimson velvety leaves. Native to S. Mexico. Formerly known as naegelia.

Compost, equal parts loam, leafmould and peat with two parts coarse sand or vermiculite. Position, pots in an intermediate or warm greenhouse, minimum winter temp. 13°C. Pot in early spring only just covering the rhizomes, which should be placed one in each 4- or 5-in. pot. Water sparingly at first, then freely as growth appears, but after flowering gradually reduce the water supply and keep dry, with only enough water to prevent the rhizomes from shrivelling in winter. Shake out rhizomes in early spring and repot as before. Shade from direct sunshine.

Increase by division of rhizomes; by

Smithiantha (hybrid)

seeds sown in late winter or early summer in temp. 15 to 18°C. Treat early seedlings like plants grown from rhizomes, but keep summer-sown seedlings growing throughout their first winter and only rest them after they have flowered the following year.

Recommended kinds are *S. cinnabarina*, rose or red with white or pale yellow, summer, 2 ft.; *fulgida*, red and orange, summer, to 2 ft.; *multiflora*, creamy white, summer, 2 to 2½ ft.; *zebrina*, yellow and scarlet, summer, 2 to 2½ ft. There are also many hybrids with a colour range including cream, yellow, orange, vermilion, deep red, carmine, rose and pink.

SOBRALIA – *Orchidaceae*. Tender, chiefly terrestrial orchids. In a number, though the individual flowers only last a few days, they are large and very handsome, not unlike a large cattleya flower in shape.

Compost, equal parts sphagnum moss, fibre, peat or leafmould and loam. Position, fairly large, well-drained pots in an intermediate house. Water liberally in summer, moderately in winter, but the compost should never get really dry. Shade from direct sunshine only in spring and summer but give full light in autumn and winter. Repot every second year in spring.

Increase by division of plants in early spring.

Recommended kinds are *S. leucoxantha*, creamy white, lip shaded yellow and orange, summer, 2 to 5 ft., Guatemala, Costa Rica; *macrantha*, shades of rose with whitish throat and yellowish blotch, summer, 4 to 6 ft., Mexico, Guatemala; *xantholeuca*, yellow and orange, summer, 3 to 6 ft., Guatemala.

SOLANDRA – *Solanaceae*. Tender evergreen shrubs or climbers with trumpet- or goblet-shaped flowers.

Compost, John Innes potting compost No. 1 or equivalent. Position, tubs or beds in an intermediate or warm greenhouse, minimum winter temp. 10°C., with shoots trained up rafters or round trellises. Pot or plant in spring. Water freely from early autumn to late spring, but keep rather dry

in summer when growth is ripening. Plant in early spring.

Increase by cuttings inserted in light soil in a warm propagator in spring.

Recommended kinds are *S. grandiflora*, Peach Trumpet Flower, cream and purple, scented, spring, climber to 30 ft., Tropical America, Jamaica; *guttata*, Gold Cup, Chalice Vine, yellow and purple, scented, winter, spring, climber to 20 ft., Mexico; *hartwegii* (syn. *nitida*), yellow, striped maroon, scented, winter, spring, climber to 20 ft., Mexico, much confused with *guttata*.

SOLANUM – *Solanaceae*. A large genus including tender and hardy, flowering, berry-bearing and ornamental-leaved plants, shrubs, climbers, vegetables and medicinal plants.

Culture of berry-bearing species: Compost, John Innes potting compost No. 1 or equivalent. Position, pots in a cool greenhouse, minimum winter temp. 7°C., or outdoors in a sunny place in summer. Useful for room decorations in winter. Water normally. Syringe daily in early summer when plants are in flower to improve setting of the fruits. Pinch out tips of young shoots occasionally to improve branching. Cut previous year's growth hard back in early spring when fruits have fallen and then repot. Do not shade at any time.

Solanum pseudocapsicum

Culture of climbing species: More or less tender climbing kinds in ordinary, well-drained soil and a warm, sunny, sheltered place. *S. crispum* does well on chalk soils. All can also be grown in a sunny frost-proof greenhouse. Plant in spring or autumn. Prune in early spring cutting out all weak or frost-damaged growth.

Culture of ornamental-leaved species: Compost, John Innes potting compost No. 3 or equivalent. Position, pots in an intermediate greenhouse, minimum temp. 13°C. from autumn to spring, outdoors in a warm, sunny place in summer. Often used as sub-tropical bedding. Water normally. Do not shade at any time. Discard biennial kinds at the end of the second summer. Perennial kinds can be lifted, repotted and returned to the greenhouse.

Increase berry-bearing species by seeds sown in temp. 18 to 21°C. in late winter or early spring, transplanting seedlings into small pots in John Innes potting compost No. 1 or equivalent, and removing points of shoots when 3 in. high and later transferring plants to 5-in. pots. Climbing species by cuttings of young shoots in sandy soil in a propagator in summer; by layering in spring or autumn. Ornamental-leaved species by seeds sown in a temp. 18 to 21°C., in spring for perennial kinds, in late summer or early autumn for biennials. Pot seedlings singly in John Innes potting compost No. 1 and move later to larger pots and John Innes potting compost No. 3.

Recommended berry-bearing kinds are *S. capsicastrum*, Star Capsicum, Winter Cherry, flowers white, summer, fruits scarlet, winter, 1 to 2 ft., Brazil; *pseudocapsicum*, Jerusalem Cherry, white, summer, fruits orange-red, 2 to 4 ft., Madeira. Wetherill's hybrids are the result of crosses between the two species.

Recommended climbing kinds are *S. crispum*, bluish purple, summer and early autumn, bush or climber, 12 to 15 ft., in cold winters stems may be killed to near ground level, China, var. *autumnalis*, deeper colour, extended flowering season; *jasminoides*, Jasmine Nightshade, blue, summer, 15 to 30 ft., Brazil, var. *album*, white, tender.

Recommended ornamental-leaved kinds are *S. giganteum*, blue, summer, leaves large, wedge shaped, 8 in. long, 10 ft., biennial, East Indies; *hispidum* (syn. *warszewiczii*), white, summer, stems hairy, red and prickly, leaves green with prickly midribs, 3 to 4 ft., perennial, S. America; *macranthum*, violet, summer, leaves very large, to 15 in. long, 6 to 14 ft., perennial, Brazil; *marginatum*, white and purple, summer, stems woolly and prickly, leaves prickly, white beneath, green above and margined with white, 3 to 4 ft., biennial, N. Africa; *robustum*, white, summer, stems woolly, leaves velvety above, reddish beneath and spiny, 2 to 4 ft., perennial, Brazil.

SOLDANELLA (Blue Moonwort) – *Primulaceae*. Hardy perennial herbs with bell-shaped fringed flowers.

Compost, equal parts peat, leafmould, loam and sharp sand. Position, sheltered, cool, semi-shady. Plant in spring. Mulch surface of the soil in spring with leafmould.

Increase by seeds sown as soon as ripe in well-drained pans filled with equal parts loam, peat and sand in a cold, shady frame; by division of the plants immediately after flowering.

Recommended kinds are *S. alpina*, blue, spring, 3 in., Alps, Pyrenees; *ganderi*, palest lilac, early spring, 2 in., hybrid between *alpina* and *minima*; *minima*, lilac or white

Soldanella alpina

lined purple, spring, 2 in., Alps; *montana*, lavender, spring, 6 to 9 in., Alps, Carpathians; *pindicola*, lilac, spring, 3 in., Balkans; *pusilla*, pale violet, early spring, 2 to 4 in., Alps; *villosa*, lavender, spring, 6 in., Pyrenees.

SOLEIROLIA (syn. Helxine) (Baby's Tears) – *Urticaceae*. Hardy perennial with creeping shoots. Useful for making a green carpet in shady places.

Soil, ordinary. Position, cool, shady, rather moist. Plant at any time from spring to autumn.

Increase by division when transplanting.

The only species is *S. soleirolii* (syn. *Helxine soleirolii*), 2 to 3 in., tiny neat green leaves, very invasive, Corsica, Sardinia, and var. Golden Mat, leaves yellow.

SOLIDAGO (Golden Rod) – *Compositae*. Hardy herbaceous perennials with branched sprays of small yellow daisy-type flowers.

Soil, ordinary. Position, sunny or shady. Plant in spring or autumn. Lift, divide and replant every two or three years.

Increase by division of roots in spring or autumn; by seeds sown outdoors in spring or summer.

Recommended kinds are *S. canadensis*, yellow, late summer, autumn, 1 to 6 ft., Eastern N. America; *graminifolia* (syn. *lanceolata*), yellow, early autumn, 2 to 4 ft., Eastern N. America; *virgaurea*, Common Golden Rod, yellow, late summer, autumn, ½ to 2½ ft., Europe (Britain), and many varieties differing mainly in size and including *brachystachys* (syn. *S. brachystachys*), 6 in.

x SOLIDASTER – *Compositae*. A bigeneric hybrid of horticultural origin between *Aster ptarmicoides* and an unknown species of *Solidago*.

Culture and propagation as for solidago.

The only kind is *S. luteus* (syns. *Aster hybridus luteus* and *Solidago missouriensis* hort.), yellow, summer, early autumn, 2½ ft.

SOLLYA – *Pittosporaceae*. Rather tender evergreen twining shrubs, natives of Australia.

Compost, two parts peat, one part turfy loam, and half a part coarse sand. Position, well-drained pots or beds, with shoots trained to a wire trellis or up rafters or pillars in a frost-proof greenhouse or in a warm sunny place outdoors in mild areas. Sollyas are unlikely to survive more than a few degrees of frost. Pot or plant in spring.

Increase by cuttings of shoots inserted in a propagator, temp. 15 to 18°C., spring or early summer; by seeds sown in a similar temperature in spring.

The only species are *S. fusiformis* (syn. *heterophylla*), Australian Bluebell Creeper, blue, summer and autumn, 4 to 6 ft.; *parviflora* (syn. *drummondii*), dark blue, summer and autumn, 4 to 6 ft.

SONERILA – *Melastomataceae*. Tender flowering perennials grown as foliage plants.

Grow in a fairly rich compost, such as John Innes potting compost No. 2, in an intermediate or, better still, a warm greenhouse, minimum winter temp. 15°C. Water freely most of the year provided good temperatures can be maintained. Shade from sun in spring and summer and maintain a moist atmosphere.

Increase by seeds sown in sand and peat in a warm propagator (temp. 20 to 24°C.) in spring; by cuttings in similar conditions at almost any time.

The best kind is *S. margaritacea*, rose, summer, leaves white and green above, purplish beneath, Java, Burma. There are numerous varieties.

SOPHORA – *Leguminosae*. Hardy and slightly tender evergreen and deciduous shrubs and trees, with attractive pinnate foliage and ornamental flowers.

Soil, well-drained loam. Position, warm, with full sun; some kinds can be trained against sunny walls. Plant evergreen kinds in spring or autumn, deciduous kinds in autumn or late winter. Pruning is generally undesirable but badly placed branches can be removed in late summer.

Sophora microphylla

Increase by seeds sown as soon as ripe but first soaked for several hours in warm water (85 to 88°C.), and then sown in sandy soil in a temp. 18 to 21°C.; also by cuttings of half-ripened young shoots in a propagator in summer, and by layering in autumn.

Recommended kinds are S. davidii (syn. viciifolia), deciduous, blue and white, early summer, 6 to 8 ft., China; japonica, Japanese Pagoda Tree, deciduous, creamy white, late summer and autumn, trees do not flower when young, 50 to 75 ft., China, with vars. pendula, stiffly pendulous branches, variegata, leaves margined creamy white, and violacea, flowers rosy violet; microphylla, evergreen, yellow, late spring, 8 to 12 ft., slightly tender, New Zealand and Chile; tetraptera, Kowhai, New Zealand Laburnum, golden yellow, late spring, 15 to 25 ft., New Zealand, Chile, with var. grandiflora, the best form, both are slightly tender but evergreen in sheltered places.

x SOPHROCATTLEYA – Orchidaceae.
Bigeneric hybrids between the genera Sophronitis and Cattleya. Cultivation as for cattleya.

x SOPHROLAELIA – Orchidaceae. Bi-
generic hybrids between the genera Sophronitis and Laelia. Cultivation as for cattleya.

x SOPHROLAELIOCATTLEYA –
Orchidaceae. Trigeneric hybrids between the genera Sophronitis and Laeliocattleya. Cultivation as for cattleya.

SOPHRONITIS – Orchidaceae. Tender
epiphytic orchids, dwarf and with small, brightly coloured flowers. All are natives of Brazil.

Compost, equal parts fibre and sphagnum moss. Position, pans or pieces of bark or cork in a cool or intermediate house. Shade in summer and maintain a moist atmosphere. Water moderately throughout the year. Repot when necessary in spring.

Increase by division in spring.

Recommended kinds are S. cernua, cinnabar red, winter, 3 in.; coccinea (syn. grandiflora), red and orange-yellow, winter, 3 in.; violacea, deep violet, winter, 3 in.

SORBARIA (False Spiraea) – Rosaceae.
Hardy deciduous shrubs, formerly included in Spiraea. Plumy panicles of white or cream flowers.

Soil, moist, rich. Position, open, sunny. Plant in autumn or late winter. Prune in late winter shortening previous year's growth to a few inches.

Increase by rooted suckers dug up in autumn or late winter; by cuttings of firm young growth in autumn; by root cuttings in winter; by seeds sown as soon as ripe or in spring.

Recommended kinds are S. aitchisonii, white, late summer, 8 to 10 ft., Afghanistan,

Kashmir; arborea, white, late summer, 18 ft., China; sorbifolia, white, late summer, 3 to 6 ft., N. Asia, Japan; tomentosa (syn. lindleyana), white, late summer, early autumn, 12 to 20 ft. Himalaya.

SORBUS – Rosaceae. Hardy deciduous
ornamental flowering and fruiting trees, formerly included in Pyrus.

Soil, ordinary well drained. The Whitebeams and Service Trees are excellent on chalk or limestone. Position, open and sunny. Plant in autumn or late winter. Little pruning is required but badly placed or overgrown branches can be removed in winter.

Sorbus scalaris

Increase species by seeds sown out of doors as soon as ripe or stratified for three months at 4°C. and then sown out of doors or under glass; hybrids and selected varieties by grafting in spring or budding in summer on seedlings of related species.

Recommended kinds are S. alnifolia, white, late spring, 20 to 40 ft., red berries, good autumn colour, Japan; americana, American Mountain Ash, white, late spring, early summer, 20 to 30 ft., red berries, good autumn colour, Eastern N. America; aria, Whitebeam, white, late spring, 30 to 50 ft., crimson berries, leaves white beneath, Europe (Britain), and vars. decaisneana (syn. majestica), larger leaves, lutescens, leaves creamy white above, white beneath; aucuparia, Mountain Ash, Rowan, white, late spring, 30 to 50 ft., scarlet berries, Europe (Britain), and vars. asplenifolia, deeply cut leaflets, beissneri, young shoots red, leaves yellow-green, fern like, edulis, large berries, fastigiata (syn. pyramidalis), branches erect, pendula, branches weeping, xanthocarpa (syn. fructuluteo), berries deep yellow; cashmiriana, pale pink, late spring, 20 to 30 ft., white berries, Kashmir; commixta, white, late spring, 20 to 30 ft., columnar, red berries, good autumn colour, Japan;

cuspidata, Himalayan Whitebeam, white, late spring, 30 to 40 ft., brownish fruits, leaves silvery beneath, Himalaya; decora, white, late spring, early summer, 20 to 30 ft., red berries, N. E. America; discolor, white, spring, 20 to 30 ft., berries cream and pink, good autumn colour, China; domestica, Service Tree, white, late spring, 30 to 60 ft., green and red fruits, Europe; esserteauana, white, late spring, 20 to 35 ft., red berries, good autumn colour, China; folgneri, white, late spring, 20 to 30 ft., purplish red berries, China; hupehensis, white, early summer, 20 to 30 ft., white or pale pink berries, good autumn colour, China; hybrida (syn. fennica), white, late spring, 20 to 35 ft., red berries, N. Europe; insignis, white, late spring, 20 to 30 ft., pink berries, Assam; intermedia, Swedish Whitebeam, white, late spring, 20 to 40 ft., red berries, leaves grey beneath, N. W. Europe; Joseph Rock, white, late spring, early summer, 20 to 30 ft., yellow berries, good autumn colour, origin uncertain, may be a hybrid; pohuashanensis, white, late spring, 25 to 35 ft., orange-red berries, China; sargentiana, white, late spring, 15 to 30 ft., scarlet berries, good autumn colour, China; scalaris, white, late spring, early summer, 15 to 20 ft., red berries, good autumn colour, China; scopulina, white, late spring, 15 to 18 ft., stiffly erect stems, scarlet berries, Western N. America; torminalis, Wild Service Tree, white, early summer, 30 to 40 ft., brown fruits, Europe (Britain), Asia Minor, N. Africa; vilmorinii, white, early summer, 15 to 20 ft., pink and white berries, China.

SPARAXIS (Harlequin Flower) – Iridaceae.
Slightly tender perennials grown from corms. All are native to S. Africa.

Soil, light, rich, sandy. Position, sunny well-drained border or in pots or pans in a light, frost-proof greenhouse. Plant or pot in autumn. Cover outdoor plants with dry bracken or straw in winter as a protection against frost.

Water pot plants moderately from the time the corms begin to grow until the flowers fade, then gradually cease, keeping the corms dry until potting time in autumn. Temperature in winter 5 to 10°C., at other times 10 to 16°C.

Increase by division of corm clusters; by seeds sown in temp. 15 to 18°C. in spring.

Recommended kinds are S. grandiflora, violet-purple or white with maroon blotch, spring, 1 to 1½ ft.; tricolor, orange-yellow, red, pink, or purple, and black, spring, 12 to 15 ft., S. Africa, and var. flore-pleno, double in a wide range of colours.

SPARMANNIA – Tiliaceae. Tender ever-
green shrub with large leaves and clusters of flowers.

Compost, John Innes potting compost No. 2 or equivalent. Position, pots, tubs or beds in a sunny, cool greenhouse, minimum winter temp. 7°C. Can be stood outdoors in summer or may be grown outdoors in nearly frost-free areas. Water normally. Do not shade at any time. Pot or plant in spring. Cut back straggly stems in late winter.

Increase by cuttings inserted in sandy soil in a propagator in spring; by seeds sown in a temp. 15 to 18°C. in spring. Grow young plants individually in pots with as little root disturbance as possible.

The best kind is *S. africana*, African Hemp, white and yellow, all year, 10 to 15 ft., S. Africa, and var. *florepleno*, double flowered.

SPARTIUM – *Leguminosae*. Hardy deciduous flowering shrub.

Soil, ordinary, well drained. Position, sunny open borders or dry banks, excellent maritime shrub. Plant in autumn or late winter. The previous year's growth may be pruned or clipped in spring but not into older branches which will not produce new growth.

Increase by seeds sown in fine soil in a sunny position outdoors in autumn or spring. Young plants should be pot grown until planted out.

The only species is *S. junceum*, Spanish Broom, yellow, sweetly scented, summer, 6 to 10 ft., S. Europe.

Spartium junceum

SPATHIPHYLLUM – *Araceae*. Tender evergreen perennials with small, arum-like flowers.

Compost, John Innes potting compost No. 2 or equivalent. Position, pots in an intermediate or warm greenhouse or in a warm room. Water normally. Shade at all times. Feed regularly in late spring and summer with weak liquid manure or fertilizer. Repot annually in spring.

Increase by seeds sown in temp. 24 to 26°C. in spring, or by division in spring.

Recommended kinds are *S. floribundum*,

white and yellowish, foliage rich green, 1 ft., Colombia; *wallisii*, White Sails, green becoming white, spring and autumn, 9 to 12 in., Colombia.

SPECULARIA – *Campanulaceae*. Hardy annuals with bell-shaped flowers freely produced. Some botanists call this genus *Legousia*.

Soil, ordinary. Position, sunny. Sow in spring where required to grow. Thin seedlings to 3 to 6 in. apart. Support plants with small twigs when 3 to 6 in., high.

The best kind is *S. speculum* (syn. *Campanula speculum, Speculum veneris*), Venus's Looking Glass, purple, summer, 1 ft., Europe, and vars. *alba*, white, and *grandiflora*, large flowered.

SPIRAEA – *Rosaceae*. Hardy deciduous flowering shrubs. Some species formerly included in this genus are now classified in *Astilbe, Aruncus, Filipendula, Holodiscus* and *Sorbaria*.

Soil, ordinary loam, a few kinds dislike very alkaline soils. Position, open sunny borders or shrub borders. Plant in autumn or late winter. Prune those which flower on young wood, such as *S. japonica*, *bumalda*, Anthony Waterer, *margaritae*, *menziesii*, etc., to within a few inches of ground level in early spring or retain some of the most vigorous stems and shorten them by about one-third. Those which flower early on one-year-old wood, such as *S. arguta, prunifolia plena* and *thunbergii*, and also the later flowering species with a similar flowering habit, such as *S. canescens*, *nipponica*, *vanhouttei*, *trichocarpa*, and *veitchii*, should have much of the older and weaker growth removed after flowering.

Increase by cuttings of young shoots in a frame during summer; by cuttings of riper growths out of doors in autumn; by offsets removed and planted in autumn.

Recommended kinds are *S. albiflora*, white, late summer, 1½ ft., Japan; *arguta*, Bridal Wreath, Foam of May, white, spring, 5 to 6 ft., hybrid between *multiflora* and *thunbergii*; *billiardii*, rose, summer, 6 ft., dislikes chalk, hybrid between *douglasii* and *salicifolia*, and var. *triumphans* (syn. *menziesii triumphans*), bright rose colour; *bullata* (syn. *japonica bullata*), deep rose, summer, 12 to 15 in., Japan; *bumalda*, carmine, summer, 2 ft., hybrid between *albiflora* and *japonica*, and var. Anthony Waterer, brighter colour, some leaves cream variegated; *canescens*, white, summer, 6 to 8 ft., Himalaya; *cantoniensis*, white, early summer, 4 to 6 ft., China; *chamaedryfolia*, white, late spring, 4 to 6 ft., Europe, Siberia, and var. *ulmifolia*, larger flowers; *decumbens*, white, late spring, to 1 ft., S. Europe; *douglasii*, purplish rose, summer, 5 to 6 ft., dislikes chalk, Western N. America; *henryi*, white, early summer, 6 to 8 ft., China; *japonica* (syn. *callosa*), rosy

red, summer, 3 to 5 ft., Japan, Korea, China, and vars. *alpina*, 1½ to 2 ft., *atrosanguinea*, crimson; *latifolia*, white or pale pink, summer, 5 to 6 ft., dislikes chalk, N. America; *margaritae*, bright pink, late summer, 4 ft., hybrid between *japonica* and *superba*; *menziesii*, purplish rose, late summer, 3 to 5 ft., Western N. America; *mollifolia*, creamy white, early summer, 4 to 6 ft., China; *nipponica* (syn. *bracteata*), white, early summer, 5 to 8 ft., Japan, and var. *rotundifolia*, larger foliage and flowers; *prunifolia plena*, white double, spring, 6 ft., autumn colour, China; *salicifolia*, pink, summer, 5 to 6 ft., dislikes chalk, Europe, Asia, Japan; *thunbergii*, white, early spring, 3 to 5 ft., autumn colour, China; *trilobata*, white, early summer, 3 to 4 ft., Asia; *vanhouttei*, white, early summer, 5 to 6 ft., hybrid between *cantoniensis* and *trilobata*; *veitchii*, white, summer, 8 to 10 ft., China; *wilsonii*, white, early summer, 6 to 7 ft., China; *yunnanensis*, white, late spring to early summer, 5 to 6 ft., China.

SPREKELIA – *Amaryllidaceae*. Slightly tender bulbous plant with widely flared and lipped flowers.

Compost, John Innes potting compost No. 1 or equivalent, or fertile, porous loam. Position, pots in a cool greenhouse or warm, sunny sheltered position outdoors. Pot or plant in spring. Water freely from the time growth begins (late winter) until autumn and then keep quite dry. Topdress large bulbs annually and repot every three or four years only. Minimum winter temp. 4°C. Outdoors protect in winter with a covering of dry litter.

Increase by seeds sown in sandy loam in temp. 15 to 18°C. in spring, placing seedlings singly in 2-in. pots, and keeping them moderately moist all the year round for three years; by offsets, treated as old bulbs. Seedlings are six to seven years before they flower.

The only species is *S. formosissima* (syn. *Amaryllis formosissima*), Jacobean Lily, crimson, summer, 1 to 1½ ft., Mexico and Guatemala.

STACHYS (Woundwort, Betony) – *Labiatae*. Hardy herbaceous perennials, some with ornamental foliage.

Soil, ordinary. Position, sunny, well drained. Plant in spring or autumn.

Increase by division in spring or autumn.

Recommended kinds are *S. corsica*, cream and pink, summer, mat forming, 1 in., Mediterranean region; *lanata*, Lamb's Ear, magenta, summer, leaves white and woolly, 1 ft., Caucasus, and var. Silver Carpet, non flowering; *lavandulifolia*, purplish rose, summer, grey leaves, sub-shrub, Caucasus, Asia Minor; *macrantha* (syns. *S. grandiflora*, *Betonica grandiflora*), violet, late spring, early summer, 1½ to 2 ft., Caucasus, and vars. *rosea*, pink, and *superba*, purple;

Stachys macrantha

officinalis (syns. *S. betonica*, *Betonica officinalis*), Bishop's-wort, purple, summer, to 3 ft., Europe, Asia Minor, and vars. *alba*, white, *grandiflora*, rose, large.

STACHYURUS – *Stachyuraceae*. Hardy deciduous flowering shrubs. Flowers produced early in the year in stiffly pendulous trails.

Soil, good, loamy. Position, sun or semi-shade. Plant in autumn or late winter.

Increase by cuttings of firm young growth in a propagator in summer.

Recommended kinds are *S. chinensis*, pale yellow, late winter, early spring, 6 to 12 ft., China; *praecox*, pale yellow, late winter, early spring, 6 to 12 ft., Japan.

STANHOPEA – *Orchidaceae*. Tender epiphytic orchids with extraordinary flowers growing from the base and often appearing through the compost below the plant.

Compost, equal parts fibre and sphagnum moss. Position, teakwood baskets which can be suspended are preferable, without drainage crocks so that the flower spikes can grow out of the bottom of the basket. Grow in an intermediate house, water freely while in growth from spring to autumn but sparingly while in flower and little in winter. Shade in spring and summer only. Maintain a moist atmosphere at all times. Repot every three or four years in spring.

Increase by division of large plants is best but two or three healthy back bulbs may be removed in spring, placed on small crocks in a pot, surfaced with sphagnum and put into a propagating case; gentle bottom heat is an aid to growth. Pot when roots are seen but return to the case for a week or two.

Recommended kinds are *S. devoniensis*, fragrant, creamy or fawn yellow, marked purplish red, summer, Mexico; *grandiflora* (syn. *eburnea*), fragrant, white, speckled purple, summer, Venezuela, Guiana, Brazil, Trinidad; *hernandezii* (syn. *tigrina*), large, scented, yellow, orange and maroon, summer, Mexico; *insignis*, large, fragrant, yellow, purple spotted, late summer, autumn, Brazil, Peru; *oculata*, large, fragrant, yellow, with ocellated red spots, summer, Brazil, Guatemala, Mexico; *platyceras*, green and yellow, spotted red-purple, summer, autumn, Mexico; *wardii*, large, fragrant, yellow or orange, spotted and blotched maroon, summer, Guatemala, Venezuela.

STAPELIA (Carrion Flower) – *Asclepiadaceae*. Tender evergreen succulent-stemmed plants. Flowers shaped like a starfish, sometimes disagreeably scented. Those listed are all S. African.

Compost, John Innes potting compost No. 2 or equivalent plus one-quarter its bulk of coarse sand. Position, pots in a sunny greenhouse, minimum winter temp. 10°C. Water freely in spring and summer, sparingly in autumn and winter. Shade lightly in summer only. Repot annually in spring.

Increase by cuttings in spring and summer of stems exposed to air on a shelf in the greenhouse for two or three days, then inserted in sandy soil in a temp. 15 to 18°C.; by seeds sown as soon as ripe in sandy soil in temp. 18 to 21°C.

Recommended kinds are *S. asterias*, Starfish Flower, violet, yellow and purple, summer, 9 in.; *flavirostris*, purple and white, summer; *geminiflora*, dark brown, spotted yellow, autumn, 6 in.; *gettleffii*, purple and yellow, summer, prostrate; *gigantea*, yellow, red, brown and purple, summer, 6 in.; *grandiflora*, dark brown, autumn, 1 ft.; *hirsuta*, cream and purple, summer, 8 in.; *mutabilis*, greenish yellow, purple and red, summer, 9 in., hybrid; *nobilis*, buff and purple, summer, 6 to 8 in.; *pillansii*, maroon, summer; *rufa*, violet-purple with red, summer, 6 in.; *variegata*, greenish yellow and purplish brown, summer, 4 to 6 in.

STAPHYLEA (Bladder Nut) – *Staphyleaceae*. Hardy deciduous shrubs with ornamental flowers and foliage and curious inflated fruits.

Soil, moist, loamy. Position, sunny or partially shaded. Plant in autumn or late winter. Prune straggling shoots immediately after flowering or cut back whole plant to within a few inches of ground level.

Increase by seeds stratified as soon as ripe for three months at 20 to 30°C., and then for a further three months at 4°C. before sowing outdoors or under glass; by cuttings of firm shoots inserted in sandy soil in a propagator in summer or outdoors in autumn; by layering shoots in autumn; by suckers removed and planted in autumn or late winter.

Recommended kinds are *S. bumalda*, greenish white, late spring, early summer, 4 to 6 ft., good autumn foliage colour, Japan, Korea, China; *colchica*, white, late spring, 7 to 10 ft., Caucasus; *holocarpa*, white, spring, 8 to 12 ft., Central China, with its more attractive var. *rosea*, pale pink, slightly larger flowers; *pinnata*, white, late spring, early summer, 10 to 15 ft., Europe, Asia Minor.

STAUNTONIA – *Lardizabalaceae*. Slightly tender evergreen twining shrub with flowers in racemes and edible fruits.

Soil, ordinary, reasonably fertile. Position, warm, sheltered, sunny or partially shady. Plant in spring or autumn and provide wires, trellis or other support for the twining stems.

Increase by cuttings of firm young growth in a propagator in summer.

The best kind is *S. hexaphylla*, white and violet, scented, spring, to 30 ft., fruits purplish but only produced in warm places, Japan, Korea.

STENANDRIUM – *Acanthaceae*. Tender herbaceous perennial with ornamental leaves.

Compost, John Innes potting compost No. 1 or equivalent. Position, pots in an intermediate greenhouse, minimum winter temp. 13°C., or in a warm, light room. Water moderately in spring and summer, rather sparingly in autumn and winter. Shade lightly in summer. Pot in spring.

Increase by cuttings of young shoots in a propagator in late spring or early summer.

The best kind is *S. lindenii*, yellow, summer, leaves dark green and grey-green with yellow veins, 6 to 12 in., Peru.

STENANTHIUM – *Liliaceae*. Hardy herbaceous perennial, somewhat bulbous. Flowers small, bell shaped, in plumes or close sprays.

Soil, fertile, porous loam and peat. Position, moist, yet warm and shaded. Plant in spring.

Increase by seeds sown in pans of moist peat and sand in a cool greenhouse or frame in spring; by offsets detached at planting time.

The only species is *S. robustum*, white or greenish, summer, 5 ft., Eastern U.S.A.

STEPHANANDRA – *Rosaceae*. Hardy deciduous ornamental-leaved shrubs with attractive stems, sepia tinted in winter.

Soil, moist loam. Position, sun or semi-shade, suitable for the waterside. Can be hard pruned in early spring. Plant in autumn or late winter.

Increase by suckers or divisions at planting time; also by cuttings in summer in a propagator.

Recommended kinds are *S. incisa* (syn. *flexuosa*), greenish white, early summer, fern-like foliage, 4 to 7 ft., Japan and Korea, and var. *crispa*, dwarf, 1½ to 3 ft., suitable for ground cover; *tanakae*, yellowish white, summer, foliage turns orange in autumn, 4 to 6 ft., Japan.

STEPHANOTIS – *Asclepiadaceae*. Tender evergreen twining shrubs with clusters of tubular scented flowers.

Compost, John Innes potting compost No. 1 or equivalent. Position, pots in an intermediate or warm greenhouse, minimum winter temp. 13°C. or in a warm, light room. Water freely in spring and summer, rather sparingly in autumn and winter. Feed in late spring and summer with weak liquid manure or fertilizer and shade from direct sunshine. Pot in spring. Provide canes, trellis or other support for the twining stems.

Stephanotis floribunda

Increase by cuttings of firm young shoots in sand and peat in a warm propagator in spring or early summer.

The best kind is *S. floribunda*, Clustered Wax Flower, Madagascar Jasmine, white, fragrant, spring and summer, 10 to 15 ft., Madagascar, and var. *elvastonii*, a dwarfer and more free-flowering form.

STERNBERGIA – *Amaryllidaceae*. Hardy bulbous plants with crocus-like flowers which appear before the foliage.

Soil, deep, reasonably fertile loam. Position, sunny, sheltered. Plant bulbs in late summer, 3 in. deep and 4 to 6 in. apart. Lift and replant only when bulbs show signs of deterioration. May also be grown in pots in a cold greenhouse in John Innes potting compost No. 1 or equivalent, watered moderately in autumn and winter, more freely in spring and not at all in summer after the leaves die down.

Increase by offsets, removed when replanting in late summer.

Recommended kinds are *S. clusiana*, yellow, autumn, 4 in., Asia Minor; *colchiciflora*, yellow, autumn, 2 in., on limestone, Hungary; *fischeriana*, yellow, spring, 4 to 6 in., Caucasus, Mediterranean region; *lutea*, Winter Daffodil, Yellow Star Flower,

yellow, autumn, Greece, Asia Minor, and var. *major*, flowers larger than the type.

STEWARTIA – *Theaceae*. Hardy deciduous flowering shrubs, allied to *Camellia*, with considerable beauty of flower in summer, and attractive autumn foliage. Flaking bark on trunks and main branches is a further attraction. The name is sometimes incorrectly spelled Stuartia.

Soil, lime-free loam, well drained but moist, and containing a generous addition of peat, leafmould or compost. Dry situations not suitable. Position, sheltered, semi-shady, suitable for planting in open woodland or among well-spaced trees. Plant in autumn or late winter. Little pruning is required but main trunks may be cleared of shoots or side branches.

Increase by cuttings of firm shoots inserted in sandy soil in a propagator in summer or outdoors in autumn; by layering shoots in autumn; by seeds stratified as soon as ripe for five months at 20 to 30°C. and then for a further three months at 4°C., after which they should be sown in sandy peat and lime-free loam outdoors or under glass.

Recommended kinds are *S. malacodendron*, white, purple stamens, summer, 12 to 20 ft., South-eastern U.S.A.; *monadelpha*, ivory white, purple anthers, summer, 15 to 30 ft., Japan, Korea; *ovata* (syn. *pentagyna*), white, orange anthers, summer, 10 to 15 ft., South-eastern U.S.A.; *pseudocamellia*, white, cup shaped, summer, 20 to 30 ft., Japan, and var. *koreana*, 15 to 20 ft., Korea; *serrata*, white, flushed red on outside, early summer, 20 to 30 ft., Japan; *sinensis*, white, fragrant, decorative peeling bark, summer, 15 to 30 ft., China.

STIPA (Feather Grass) – *Gramineae*. Hardy perennial flowering grasses. Inflorescences borne in feathery panicles.

Soil, ordinary. Position, dryish, sunny. Plant in spring. Gather inflorescences for drying for winter decoration when well developed in summer.

Increase by seeds sown in light soil in a cool greenhouse or frame in early spring or outdoors in mid- to late spring; also by division in spring.

Recommended kinds are *S. gigantea*, purplish, summer, 3 to 4 ft., Spain; *pennata*, summer, pinkish brown, 2 ft., Europe, Siberia.

STOKESIA (Stoke's Aster) – *Compositae*. Hardy herbaceous perennial herb with aster-like flowers.

Soil, ordinary. Position, sunny, well drained. Plant in spring. In cold districts protect in winter with a cloche or handlight, or pot in John Innes potting compost No. 1 or equivalent and bring into a cool greenhouse for autumn flowering.

Increase by division in spring; by seeds

sown in spring in a cool greenhouse or frame.

The only species is *S. laevis* (syn. *cyanea*), blue, late summer and autumn, 1½ to 2 ft., South-eastern U.S.A.

STRANVAESIA – *Rosaceae*. Hardy evergreen trees and shrubs with handsome foliage often turning red in the autumn, white flowers, and hawthorn-like berries.

Soil, ordinary, loamy or peaty, well drained. Position, partial shade or full exposure. Plant in spring or autumn. Little pruning is desirable.

Increase by cuttings of half-ripened shoots in sandy soil in a propagator in summer; by cuttings of riper wood in autumn; by seeds stratified for three months at 4°C. and then sown outdoors or under glass.

Recommended kinds are *S. davidiana*, white, early summer, 20 to 30 ft., scarlet berries, W. China, with vars. *fructuluteo*, berries yellow, *undulata*, 8 to 12 ft., spreading, coral berries; *salicifolia* (syn. *davidiana salicifolia*), white, early summer, red fruits, 20 to 30 ft., upright habit, China.

STRELITZIA – *Strelitziaceae*. Tender rhizomatous perennials from S. Africa with showy flowers somewhat resembling a crested bird.

Compost, John Innes potting compost No. 2 or equivalent. Position, large pots, tubs or beds in a cool or intermediate greenhouse, minimum winter temp. 7°C. Water freely in spring and summer, sparingly in autumn and winter. Do not shade at any time. Pot or plant in early spring.

Increase by seeds sown in a compost of leafmould, peat and loam in temp. 18 to 21°C. in spring; by offsets or division of old plants in spring.

Recommended kinds are *S. parvifolia*, orange and blue, spring, 3 to 4 ft., and var. *juncea*, rush-like leaves; *reginae*, Bird of Paradise Flower, orange and blue, spring, 3 to 4 ft.

STREPTANTHERA – *Iridaceae*. Slightly tender corms with showy flowers. Native to S. Africa.

Soil, ordinary, well drained. Position, warm, sunny, raised bed, rock garden, etc., or in pots of John Innes potting compost No. 1 or equivalent in a sunny, frost-proof greenhouse. Plant or pot in early autumn. Water pot plants moderately in autumn and winter, freely in spring, but keep almost dry in summer. In cold places protect outdoor plants with cloches in winter.

Increase by seeds sown in temp. 15 to 18°C. as soon as ripe or in spring; by division of corm clusters in early autumn.

Recommended kinds are *S. cuprea*, orange and purple, early summer, 6 to 8 in., and var. *coccinea*, orange-red; *elegans*, white and purple, early summer, 6 to 8 in.

STREPTOCARPUS (Cape Primrose) – *Gesneriaceae.* Tender herbaceous perennials with clusters of trumpet-shaped flowers.

Compost, John Innes potting compost No. 1 or equivalent. Position, pots in a cool greenhouse, minimum winter temp. 7°C., but in autumn a minimum of 13°C. should be maintained for plants still in flower. Water fairly freely throughout the year. Shade from direct sunshine in spring and summer.

Streptocarpus Constant Nymph

Increase by seeds sown in John Innes seed compost or equivalent in late winter or early spring in a temp. 15 to 18°C.; mature leaves in summer treated as cuttings with their stalks inserted in peat and sand in a propagator, or excise midrib and lay each half leaf flat on the surface of similar compost so that plantlets form along cut edges.

The best kinds are *S. hybridus*, blue, mauve, pink, red or white, late spring to autumn, 9 to 12 in., hybrid between numerous species including *cyaneus*, mauve, *dunnii*, terra-cotta, *parvifolius*, white and mauve, *polyanthus*, light blue, *rexii*, white or purplish, *saundersii*, lilac, *wendlandii*, purple, and *woodii*, mauve, all natives of S. Africa; Constant Nymph, Paula, Louise, etc., blue, pink, red, white, smaller but more numerous flowers, some winter flowering, hybrids between *hybridus* and *johannis*; *johannis*, purple, spring to autumn, 6 in., Natal.

STREPTOSOLEN – *Solanaceae.* Tender evergreen flowering shrub with clusters of orange flowers.

Compost, John Innes potting compost No. 2 or equivalent. Position, pots or beds in a sunny frost-proof greenhouse, minimum winter temp. 4°C. Pot or plant in spring. Water normally. Do not shade at any time. Either train sprawling stems to

Styrax japonica

trellis, wires or other supports or pinch out the tips of shoots occasionally to make the plants more bushy. Cut back previous year's growth fairly severely in late winter.

Streptosolen jamesonii

Increase by cuttings inserted in light, sandy soil in a propagator in spring or summer.

The only species is *S. jamesonii* (syn. *Browallia jamesonii*), orange, summer, 6 to 8 ft., Colombia.

STROBILANTHES (Cone Head) – *Acanthaceae.* Tender shrubby or herbaceous plants, some with ornamental foliage.

Compost, John Innes potting compost No. 1 or equivalent. Position, large pots or beds in an intermediate or warm greenhouse, minimum winter temp. 13°C. Water freely in spring and summer, moderately in autumn, rather sparingly in winter. Shade in spring and summer and maintain a humid atmosphere. Pot or plant in early spring. Cut back previous year's growth in late winter.

Increase by cuttings in a warm propagator in summer.

Recommended kinds are *S. dyerianus* (syn. *Perilepta dyeriana*), violet and blue, autumn, leaves violet above, purple below, 3 ft., Burma; *isophyllus* (syn. *Goldfussia isophylla*), blue and white, winter, 2 to 3 ft., India.

STYRAX (Snowbell) – *Styracaceae.* Hardy and slightly tender deciduous flowering shrubs, flowers white, bell shaped, pendent, produced in early summer.

Soil, rather moist, lime-free loam. Position, sheltered, sunny or in semi-shade. Plant in autumn or late winter.

Increase by seeds stratified as soon as ripe for five months at 20 to 30°C., then for a further three months at 4°C. and then sown in peaty soil under glass; by cuttings of half-ripened wood in a propagator in summer; by layering in spring or autumn.

Recommended kinds are *S. hemsleyana*, 15 to 25 ft., China; *japonica*, 15 to 25 ft., Japan, Korea; *obassia*, fragrant flowers in clusters, slightly tender, Japan; *officinalis*, fragrant, for warmer localities only, 10 to 12 ft., Greece, Asia Minor; *wilsonii*, dense growth, flowering when very small, 4 to 8 ft., W. China.

SWAINSONA (Darling River Pea) – *Leguminosae.* Tender evergreen flowering shrubs with pea-type flowers.

Compost, John Innes potting compost No. 1 or equivalent. Position, pots or beds in a sunny cool greenhouse, minimum winter temp. 7°C. Pot or plant in spring. Water normally. Do not shade at any time. Prune to within about 12 in. of the base in late winter or early spring after flowering.

Increase by seeds sown in temp. 15 to 18°C. as soon as ripe.

The best kind is *S. galegifolia*, mauve, pink, red, crimson or white, summer, 3 to 4 ft., Australia.

SYCOPSIS – *Hamamelidaceae.* Hardy evergreen winter-flowering trees related to witch hazel.

Soil, good loamy. Position, sun or semi-shade. Plant in spring or autumn. Little pruning is required but, if overgrown, branches can be shortened in spring.

Increase by cuttings of half-ripened wood in a propagator in summer.

The best species is *S. sinensis*, reddish brown bracts, yellow stamens, late winter, 12 to 20 ft., China.

SYMPHORICARPOS – *Caprifoliaceae.* Hardy deciduous flowering and berry-bearing shrubs. Flowers small but much sought after by bees.

Soil, ordinary. Position, sunny or shady. Plant in autumn or late winter. Prune in late winter, simply thinning out old or decayed wood, or cutting back hard if severely overgrown.

Increase by cuttings of firm wood inserted in ordinary soil in a shady position out of doors in autumn; by suckers removed with roots in autumn or late winter.

Recommended kinds are *S. albus* (syn. *racemosus*), Snowberry, pink or rose, summer, berries white, 2 to 3 ft., Eastern N. America; *chenaultii*, pink, summer, 2 to 3 ft., berries purplish red, hybrid between *microphyllus* and *orbiculatus*; *doorenbosii*, pink, summer, 5 to 6 ft., berries pink or white, hybrid between *chenaultii* and *rivularis*; *occidentalis*, Wolfberry, pink, summer, berries white, 4 to 6 ft., N. America; *orbiculatus*, Indian Currant, Coral Berry, white, late summer, berries purplish red, 3 to 6 ft., Eastern U.S.A.; *rivularis* (syn. *albus laevigatus*), pink, summer, 5 to 6 ft., white berries, Western N. America.

SYMPHYANDRA (Pendulous Bellflower) – *Campanulaceae.* Hardy perennials resembling campanulas.

Soil, ordinary, well drained. Position, sunny or partially shaded. Plant in spring or autumn.

Increase by seeds sown in sandy soil out of doors, in spring or early summer; by cuttings of young shoots inserted in sandy soil in a cold frame in spring; by division of roots in spring.

Recommended kinds are *S. hofmannii*, white, summer, 1 to 2 ft., Yugoslavia, may prove difficult to keep after flowering in which case it is best treated as a biennial; *wanneri*, blue, summer, 6 in., Alps.

SYMPHYTUM (Comfrey) – *Boraginaceae.* Hardy herbaceous perennials with short curling spikes of tubular flowers.

Soil, ordinary. Position, sunny or shady, moist borders or margins of streams. Plant in spring or autumn. Lift, divide and replant every three or four years.

Increase by division of roots in spring.

Recommended kinds are *S. asperum* (syn. *asperrimum*), Prickly Comfrey, rose changing to blue, summer, 3 to 6 ft., Caucasus, and var. *aureovariegatum*, yellow-edged leaves; *caucasicum*, blue, summer, 1 to 2 ft., Caucasus; *grandiflorum*, yellowish

white and brick red, spring and early summer, 9 to 18 in., Caucasus; *orientale*, creamy white, 2 ft., Turkey; *peregrinum*, rose changing to blue, 3 to 6 ft., Caucasus, Iran; *tauricum*, yellowish white, 1 to 1½ ft., S. Russia; *tuberosum*, yellowish white, summer, 1 to 1½ ft., Europe (Britain).

SYNTHYRIS – *Scrophulariaceae.* Hardy herbaceous perennial with shining green leaves and short spikes of blue flowers, from the mountains of Western N. America.

Soil, loamy. Position, partially shady bed or rock garden. Plant in spring or autumn. Water freely in summer.

Increase by division in spring; by seeds sown in sandy soil in pans in a cold greenhouse or frame in spring.

The best kinds are *S. reniformis*, blue, early summer, 6 to 9 in.; *rotundifolia*, blue, summer, 6 in., and vars. *alba*, white and *cordata*, leaves heart shaped.

SYRINGA (Lilac) – *Oleaceae.* Hardy deciduous flowering shrubs. The name syringa is frequently erroneously applied to the mock orange, correctly named philadelphus.

Soil, reasonably good, loamy; excellent on chalk. Position, sunny. Plant in autumn or late winter. Prune moderately after flowering, removing all shoots with spent flowers, and thinning out the weaker shoots. Remove all suckers from grafted plants. For the finest flowers feed annually in early spring with a compound fertilizer or well-rotted manure or compost.

Increase named varieties by layering in spring or autumn; by grafting, either on to common lilac or on privet, and from such plants suckers will be either common lilac or privet but suckers from layered plants will resemble the parent; by cuttings of half-ripened wood in frames in summer; by removal of rooted suckers of species and from garden varieties on their own roots (not grafted); species from seeds stratified for two months at 4°C. and then sown out of doors or under glass.

Recommended kinds are *S. amurensis*, Amur Lilac, white, early summer, 12 to 15 ft., Manchuria, China, Korea; *chinensis*, Rouen Lilac, lavender, late spring, fragrant, 10 to 12 ft., hybrid between *persica* and *vulgaris*, and vars. *metensis*, lilac-pink and *saugeana* (syn. *rubra*), lilac-red; *correlata* (syn. *chinensis alba*), white, late spring, 10 to 12 ft., hybrid; *emodi*, Himalayan Lilac, white or purple tinted, early summer, 10 to 15 ft., Himalaya; *henryi*, white to violet, early summer, 10 to 15 ft., hybrid between *josikaea* and *villosa*; *josiflexa*, rose-pink, late spring, early summer, 10 to 15 ft., hybrid between *josikaea* and *reflexa*, and var. Bellicent, the best form; *josikaea*, Hungarian Lilac, deep lilac, early summer, 10 to 12 ft., Europe; *julianae*, pale lilac, late spring, early summer, fragrant, 5 to 7 ft., China; *microphylla*, rose-lilac, early summer

and early autumn, fragrant, 4 to 6 ft., China; *oblata*, lilac-blue, spring, 15 to 20 ft., China, and vars. *alba*, white, *dilatata*, lilac-pink and *giraldii*, purplish violet; *pekinensis*, creamy white, early summer, scented like privet, 15 to 20 ft., China, and var. *pendula*, weeping branches; *persica*, Persian Lilac, mauve, late spring, fragrant, 4 to 6 ft., hybrid, and vars. *alba*, white and *laciniata*, lilac, lobed leaves; *prestoniae*, Canadian Hybrid Lilacs, lilac-pink to deep purplish red, late spring and early summer, 10 to 15 ft., hybrid between *reflexa* and *villosa*, and numerous varieties; *reflexa*, purplish pink, late spring, early summer, 10 to 12 ft., China; *sweginzowii*, pink, late spring, early summer, fragrant, 6 to 9 ft., China; *velutina* (syn. *palibiniana*), Korean Lilac, lilac-pink, late spring, early summer, 4 to 6 ft., Korea; *vulgaris*, Common Lilac, lilac, late spring, fragrant, 12 to 20 ft., E. Europe and numerous varieties, some with single flowers, some double, white, lilac, pink, mauve to deep reddish purple; *yunnanensis*, lilac-pink, early summer, fragrant, 10 to 15 ft., China.

TAGETES (Marigold) – *Compositae.* Half-hardy annuals with showy daisy-type flowers.

Soil, ordinary, reasonably fertile. Position, sunny. Sow seeds in John Innes seed compost or equivalent in spring in temp. 15 to 18°C. Transplant seedlings when three leaves form 3 in. apart in John Innes potting compost No. 1 or equivalent and gradually harden off for planting outdoors in late spring or early summer when there is no danger of frost. If grown to provide flowers for exhibition, thin shoots to about four on each plant, each carrying one bloom. Water freely in dry weather. Apply liquid fertilizer when well established.

Recommended kinds are *T. erecta*, African Marigold, yellow, summer, 2 to 3 ft., Mexico; *patula*, French Marigold, orange, red and brown, summer, 1 to 1½ ft., Mexico; *tenuifolia* (syn. *signata*), yellow, summer, 1 to 1½ ft., Mexico, and var. *pumila*, 9 in. There are many garden varieties of each species varying in colour, size and flower form, and also hybrids between the African and French marigolds which are intermediate in character.

TAMARIX (Tamarisk) – *Tamaricaceae.* Hardy deciduous shrubs with small, heather-like leaves and slender racemes of small flowers.

Soil, ordinary, well drained. Position, open, sunny, particularly suitable for maritime areas and excellent wind resisters. Plant in autumn or late winter. Prune early-flowering kinds, such as *T. parviflora* and *tetrandra*, after flowering, shortening the younger stems as much as necessary to keep the shrubs tidy and removing very old and worn out branches. Prune later flowering kinds, such as *T. gallica, hispida, pentandra* and *ramosissima*, in early spring cutting back previous year's growth to within a few inches of the main branches. This considerably reduces maximum height and improves flower quality.

Increase by cuttings of firm young shoots in a propagator in summer or cuttings of riper growth out of doors in autumn.

Recommended kinds are *T. gallica* (syn. *anglica*), Common Tamarisk, pink, late summer and autumn, 10 to 30 ft., S. Europe; *hispida*, pink, glaucous foliage, late summer, early autumn, 3 to 4 ft., Caspian; *juniperina* (syn. *chinensis*), bright pink, late spring, 10 to 15 ft., China; *parviflora*, pink, late spring, 10 to 15 ft., Europe; *pentandra* (syn. *hispida aestivalis*), rosy pink, late summer, early autumn, 12 to 15 ft., Asia; *ramosissima* (syn. *odessana*), pink, summer, 10 to 15 ft., Caspian; *tetrandra*, pink, late spring, early summer, 10 to 15 ft., Mediterranean region.

TANACETUM (Tansy) – *Compositae*. Hardy herbaceous perennials closely allied to *Chrysanthemum*.

Soil, ordinary for *T. vulgare*; gritty and well drained, for the silver-leaved kinds. Position, sunny. Plant *T. vulgare* 12 in. apart in rows 18 in. apart in spring or autumn; remove flower stems as they form; replant every three or four years; leaves aromatic, used for flavouring puddings, etc., and for garnishing. Plant silver-leaved kinds in spring or grow in pots in an alpine house or frame.

Increase by seeds sown out of doors in spring; by division of the roots in spring.

Recommended kinds *T. argenteum* (syn. *Chrysanthemum argenteum*), white, summer, silvery foliage, 9 in., Asia Minor; *densum*, yellow, summer, grey-green leaves, 9 in., Syria, Anatolia; *haradjanii* (syn. *Chrysanthemum haradjanii*), yellow, summer, 9 to 15 in., grey downy leaves, Anatolia; *herderi*, yellow, summer, silvery white foliage, 9 in., Turkestan; *praeteritum*, white, summer, grey or silvery green leaves, 9 in., Anatolia; *vulgare*, yellow, summer, 3 ft., Europe (Britain), var. *crispum*, finer, more crisped leaves.

TANAKAEA (Japanese Foam Flower) – *Saxifragaceae*. Dwarf evergreen perennial with leathery, fringed, rich green leaves.

Soil, light lime-free loam, containing plenty of humus. Position, woodland or partially shaded cool border. Plant in groups in spring.

Increase by division of tufts in spring.

The only species is *T. radicans*, white, spring, early summer, 6 to 9 in., Japan.

TAXODIUM (Deciduous Cypress, Swamp Cypress) – *Taxodiaceae*. Hardy deciduous coniferous trees. Leaves, feather shaped, bright green, changing to rusty red in autumn.

Soil, moist loam. Position, margins of ponds and rivers in damp places or even in shallow water, growth less satisfactory in dry places. Plant in autumn or late winter.

Increase by seeds stratified for two months at 4°C. and then sown in pans of light soil in a cold frame; by cuttings of ripened shoots in a shady frame and sandy soil in autumn and kept moist.

Recommended kinds are *T. ascendens*, narrowly columnar habit, 20 to 40 ft., South-eastern U.S.A., and var. *nutans*, older branchlets nodding; *distichum*, 70 to 100 ft., Southern U.S.A., and var. *pendens*, branches drooping.

TAXUS (Yew) – *Taxaceae*. Hardy evergreen tree. Leaves poisonous to cattle.

Soil, good deep loam is the most suitable, although the yew will grow in any soil, including chalk, but cultivation should be thorough prior to planting. Position, sunny or shady. Plant, spring to autumn. For hedges space plants 18 in. apart for trees 2 ft. high; 2 ft. apart for trees 3 ft. high; and 3 ft. apart for trees 3 to 5 ft. high. Clipping is best done twice yearly in late spring and in midsummer. The Common Yew, or its golden form, is the best shrub for training and clipping for topiary work.

Increase species by seeds stratified for five months at 20 to 30°C., for a further three months at 4°C. and then sown in light soil out of doors or under glass; all kinds, including selected garden varieties, by cuttings of shoots inserted in sandy soil in a propagator in summer or in an unheated frame or out of doors in autumn; by grafting variegated kinds on common yew in spring; by layering in spring or autumn.

Recommended kinds are *T. baccata*, Common Yew, 15 to 50 ft., Europe (Britain), Iran, N. Africa, and numerous varieties such as *adpressa*, dense spreading habit, *aurea*, Golden Yew, leaves yellow the first year, *cavendishii*, 2 to 3 ft., *dovastoniana*, Westfelton Yew, horizontal branches, pendulous branchlets, *elegantissima*, leaves yellow first year, yellow edged thereafter, *erecta*, Fulham Yew, broadly columnar, *fastigiata*, Irish Yew, narrowly columnar, *fastigiata aurea*, Golden Irish Yew, narrowly columnar, leaves yellow edged, *lutea* (syn. *fructuluteo* and *xanthocarpa*), fruits yellow, *repandans*, semi-prostrate, *semperaurea*, leaves yellow dulling with age, *standishii*, narrowly columnar, leaves golden yellow, *variegata*, wide shuttlecock habit, young leaves bright yellow, old leaves white edged, *washingtonii*, wide shuttlecock habit, leaves bright yellow becoming yellowish green; *canadensis*, Canadian Yew, 3 to 6 ft., erect, Canada, North-eastern U.S.A.; *celebica* (syn. *chinensis*), Chinese Yew, 12 to 20 ft., S. E. Asia; *cuspidata*, Japanese Yew, 15 to 50 ft., Japan, and vars. *aurea*, leaves yellow first year, *densa*, compact habit, *nana*, 2 to 4 ft.; *media*, 10 to 20 ft., hybrid

between *baccata* and *cuspidata* and numerous varieties such as *brownii*, dense, rounded, *hicksii*, broadly columnar, *sargentii*, dense, erect, and *thayerae*, wide shuttlecock habit.

TECOPHILAEA – *Tecophilaeaceae*. Slightly tender plant with rich gentian-blue flowers, grown from corms.

Soil equal parts loam, leafmould, peat and coarse sand. Position, well-drained bed in a cold frame or at the foot of a south wall, or pots in a sunny unheated greenhouse.

Plant the corms 2 in. deep and 6 in. apart in late summer or early autumn. Pot singly in 3½-in. pots or three in a 5-in. pot. Water moderately while plants are in growth but keep dry after foliage turns yellow until growth restarts. No artificial heat required except to exclude frost. Admit air freely to plants in pots.

Increase by offsets removed at potting time, but only disturb plants where really necessary.

The best kind is *T. cyanocrocus*, Chilean Crocus, blue and white, fragrant, spring, 6 in., Chile, and var. *leichtlinii*, white and two shades of blue.

TELLIMA – *Saxifragaceae*. Hardy herbaceous perennial allied to *Mitella*. Useful as ground cover.

Soil, ordinary. Position, open or partially shady borders or wild gardens. Plant in autumn or spring.

Increase by division in spring.

The only species is *T. grandiflora*, greenish becoming reddish, spring and early summer, 2 ft., Western N. America.

TELOPEA – *Proteaceae*. Rather tender evergreen shrub with dense heads of flowers.

Soil, sandy, well drained yet moist, lime-free loam. Position, sunny and sheltered or in a sunny frost-proof greenhouse with a rather dry atmosphere but plenty of ventilation in summer. Water sparingly in winter, freely in summer.

Increase by cuttings of young shoots inserted in sandy soil in a propagator in summer.

The best kind is *T. truncata*, Tasmanian Waratah, crimson, early summer, 8 to 15 ft., Tasmania.

TEUCRIUM (Germander) – *Labiatae*. Hardy perennial plants, sub-shrubs and a slightly tender evergreen shrub grown for flower and foliage.

Culture of perennial species and sub-shrubs: Soil, ordinary, well drained for most kinds, but rather moist and limy for *T. scordium*. Position, sunny. Plant in spring.

Culture of shrubby species: Soil, light, well drained. Position, sunny, warm, sheltered. Can be trained against a sunny wall. Plant in spring or autumn. Prune in spring, cutting out all frost-damaged growth and shortening straggly stems.

Increase shrubby species by cuttings of half-ripened shoots inserted in sandy soil in a frame in summer; perennial species by division in spring or seeds sown in sandy soil outdoors or in a frame in spring or early summer.

Recommended perennial kinds are *T. chamaedrys*, Wall Germander, rosy purple, summer, early autumn, 1 ft., Europe; *marum*, Cat Thyme, purple, summer, 1 ft., S. Europe; *polium* (syn. *aureum*), yellow, white or purple, summer, 4 to 6 in., grey leaves, Europe, W. Asia; *pyrenaicum*, cream and lilac, summer, prostrate, S. Europe; *scordium*, Water Germander, purple, summer, early autumn, 6 to 24 in., Europe (Britain), and var. *crispum*, leaves wavy edged.

The best shrubby species is *T. fruticans*, lavender, blue, summer and autumn, 3 to 5 ft., stems and leaves covered with white down, S. Europe, N. Africa.

THALIA – *Marantaceae*. Slightly tender aquatic perennials with handsome canna-like leaves and flowers in large loose sprays.

Soil, peaty loam. Position, pool up to 2 ft. deep. Plant in spring, requires a warm, sheltered spot. In cold places plant in tubs or baskets and remove to a frost-proof greenhouse in winter.

Increase by division in spring.

The best kind is *T. dealbata*, purple, summer, 6 ft., S. California.

THALICTRUM (Meadow Rue) – *Ranunculaceae*. Hardy herbaceous perennials with foliage reminiscent of maidenhair fern and small flowers in clusters or loose sprays.

Soil, ordinary for most kinds; deep, porous yet slightly moist with abundant humus for *T. chelidonii, delavayi, diffusiflorum* and *dipterocarpum*. Position, sunny or partially shady; *T. diffusiflorum* prefers some shade. Plant in spring or autumn, but spring only for *T. chelidonii, delavayi, diffusiflorum* and *dipterocarpum*. Topdress annually in spring with peat, leafmould or decayed manure. Lift, divide and replant only when absolutely necessary.

Increase by division in spring; by seeds sown in John Innes seed compost or equivalent in spring or early summer in a frame or outdoors.

Recommended kinds are *T. alpinum*, purplish yellow, summer, 4 to 6 in., Northern and Arctic Regions (Britain); *aquilegifolium*, lilac, summer, 3 ft., Europe (Britain); *chelidonii*, rosy lilac, summer, 1½ to 3 ft., Himalaya; *delavayi*, lilac, summer, 2 to 4 ft., W. China, much confused with *dipterocarpum*, and var. Hewitt's Double (syn. *dipterocarpum plenum*), flowers double; *diffusiflorum*, lilac and yellow, summer, 3 to 10 ft., Tibet; *dipterocarpum*, mauve, summer, 5 to 7 ft., W. China, and

Thalictrum aquilegifolium

var. *album*, white; *flavum*, yellow, summer, 2 to 3 ft., Europe (Britain); *kiusianum*, rose-purple, spring, 6 in., Japan; *minus*, greenish, summer, 1 ft., Europe (Britain), and vars. *adiantifolium*, very fine foliage, and *majus*, larger; *speciosissimum* (syn. *glaucum*), pale yellow, summer, 5 ft., S. W. Europe, N. W. Africa.

THERMOPSIS – *Leguminosae*. Hardy herbaceous perennials with lupin-like flower spikes.

Soil, ordinary. Position, open, sunny. Plant in spring.

Increase by seeds sown in light soil in sunny position outdoors in spring or late summer as soon as ripe, transplanting seedlings when large enough to handle; by division in spring.

Recommended kinds are *T. caroliniana*, golden yellow, summer, 4 to 5 ft., Southeastern U.S.A.; *montana* (syn. *fabacea*), golden yellow, summer, 2 to 3 ft., Rocky Mountains; *rhombifolia*, yellow, summer, 1 ft., N. America.

THLASPI – *Cruciferae*. Hardy perennial herbs forming mats or low cushions of growth and with small, cress-like flowers.

Soil, equal parts loam, leafmould and coarse sand. Position, sunny rock gardens or well-drained pots or pans in an airy unheated greenhouse or frame. Plant or pot in spring.

Increase by seeds sown in peat and sand in a cold frame or greenhouse during spring; by division at planting time.

The best kind is *T. rotundifolium*, rosy lavender, scented, late spring, 2 in., Alps.

THUJA (Arbor-Vitae) – *Cupressaceae*. Hardy evergreen coniferous trees and shrubs, leaves small and scale-like in flattened, fan-like sprays. Often spelled thuya. *T. occidentalis* and *plicata* make excellent hedges and windbreaks.

Soil, ordinary, well drained. Position, sun or shade. Plant in autumn or late winter.

Specimen plants are best left unpruned but badly placed branches can be removed in spring.

Distance apart for hedge planting: 2 ft. for trees up to 3 ft. high; 2½ ft. for trees to 4 ft.; and 3 ft. for taller specimens. Clipping is best done twice in late spring and mid-summer.

Increase by cuttings of firm young growth in a propagator in summer or cuttings of riper growth in a frame in autumn; species can also be increased by seeds stratified for two months at 4°C. and then sown outdoors or under glass.

Recommended kinds are *T. koraiensis*, leaves white beneath, spreading habit, to 20 ft., Korea; *occidentalis*, American Arbor-Vitae, 50 to 60 ft., N. E. America, and vars. *aurea nana*, dwarf, globular, yellowish green, *ellwangeriana*, low broad pyramid, *ericoides*, dwarf, *lutea*, bright yellow pyramidal form, *ohlendorfii*, dwarf, 'whipcord' and normal foliage, *pendula*, branches drooping, Rheingold, bronzy gold, slow growing, *spiralis*, narrowly columnar, *vervaeneana*, small and dense, etc.; *orientalis*, Chinese Arbor-Vitae, 30 to 40 ft., China, and vars. *elegantissima*, compact, bright yellow in spring, *juniperoides* (syn. *decussata*), dwarf bushy form, *meldensis*, dwarf, globular, *semperaurea*, rounded, leaves yellow when young, bronze later, etc.; *plicata* (syn. *lobbii*), Western Red Cedar, over 100 ft., N. W. America, and vars. *cuprea*, dwarf, golden, *fastigiata*, columnar form, *pendula*, drooping, branches, *zebrina*, leaves banded with gold; *standishii* (syn. *japonica*), Japanese Arbor-Vitae, 20 to 30 ft., Japan.

THUJOPSIS – *Cupressaceae*. Hardy evergreen coniferous tree with small leaves arranged in flat fan-like sprays. Allied to *Thuja* and requiring similar cultivation.

The only species is *T. dolabrata* (syn. *Thuja dolabrata*), 15 to 45 ft., leaves dark green above, white banded below, Japan, and vars. *aurea*, golden yellow, *hondai*, taller growth, *nana*, dwarf, lighter green, *variegata*, tips creamy white.

THUNBERGIA – *Thunbergiaceae*. Tender annual and perennial twining or bushy plants with widely flared trumpet-shaped flowers.

Culture of annual kinds: Sow in early spring in John Innes seed compost or equivalent in temp. 15 to 18°C. Pot seedlings singly in John Innes potting compost No. 1 or equivalent and grow in a sunny frost-proof greenhouse or plant outdoors in warm, sunny places when there is no danger of frost. Water fairly freely. Provide canes, trellis, wires or twiggy branches as support for twining growths. Do not shade at any time. Discard after flowering.

Culture of perennial kinds: Compost, John Innes potting compost No. 1 or equivalent. Position, pots in an intermediate or

Thunbergia alata

warm greenhouse, minimum winter temp. 13°C. Pot in early spring. Water freely in spring and summer, moderately in autumn, sparingly in winter. Shade from direct sunshine in summer. Maintain a moist atmosphere in spring and summer.

Increase by seeds sown as described for annual kinds; by cuttings of firm young shoots, inserted in a mixture of equal parts of leafmould, peat and sand in a warm propagator in spring or summer.

Recommended kinds are *T. alata*, Black-eyed Susan, Black-eyed Clockvine, orange and black, summer, twining, perennial but usually grown as an annual, S. Africa, and vars. *alba*, white and black, *aurantiaca*, yellow and black, and *lutea*, all yellow; *capensis*, pale yellow, summer, twiner, annual, S. Africa; *coccinea*, red, summer, twiner, India, Burma; *erecta*, blue and yellow, summer, 6 ft., shrub, West Africa; *fragrans*, creamy white, summer, twiner, perennial, India; *grandiflora*, pale blue or white, summer, twiner, perennial, N. India; *laurifolia*, light blue, summer, twiner, perennial, Malaysia; *mysorensis*, yellow and purple, summer, twiner, perennial, India.

THUNIA – *Orchidaceae*. Tender terrestrial orchids with fairly tall stems bearing clusters of large flowers.

Compost, equal parts fibre, sphagnum moss and peat or loam. Position, well-drained pots in a warm greenhouse. Water freely while in growth in spring and summer, but in autumn when leaves turn yellow, stop watering and store dry in a light place with minimum temp. 10°C. Shade lightly in summer and maintain a moist atmosphere. Repot annually in spring and renew watering but sparingly until growth appears.

Increase by division in spring.

Recommended kinds are *T. alba*, white, yellow and mauve, early summer, 2 to 3 ft., Nepal, Assam, Burma; *bensoniae*, magenta, white and yellow, early summer, 2 ft., Burma; *marshalliana*, white and orange or yellow, summer, 2 to 3 ft., Burma.

THYMUS (Thyme) – *Labiatae*. Hardy aromatic evergreen or semi-evergreen shrubs, sub-shrubs and mat-forming perennials.

Soil, light, preferably calcareous, with sand or gravel, well drained. Position, sunny, prostrate kinds useful for paving and for carpeting over spring bulbs. Plant in spring or autumn.

Increase by seeds sown outdoors in spring; division in spring; gold and silver kinds by cuttings in a frame in summer.

For culture of thyme as a culinary herb see page 248.

Recommended kinds are *T. caespititius* (syns. *azoricus*, *micans*), lilac-pink, summer, 2 in., Spain, Portugal, Madeira, Azores; *carnosus*, white, pale lilac, summer, 9 in., Portugal, often wrongly named *nitidus*; *citriodorus*, Lemon Thyme, lilac, summer, 4 to 12 in., hybrid between *pulegioides* and *vulgaris*, and var. Silver Queen, silver variegated; *comosus*, lilac-pink, summer, 3 to 6 in., Rumania, turpentine scented; *doerfleri* (syn. *hirsutus doerfleri*), purple, summer, mat forming, grey hairy, Albania, Yugoslavia; *drucei*, Mother of Thyme, rose-purple, summer, prostrate, W. Europe (Britain), much confused with *serpyllum* which it closely resembles, and vars. *albus*, white and *coccineus*, crimson; *herba-barona*, light purple, summer, foliage scented like carraway seed, 6 in., Corsica, Sardinia; *hirsutus*, lilac, summer, mat forming, Crimea, Balkan Peninsular; *lanuginosus* (syn. *serpyllum lanuginosus*), purple, summer, mat forming, grey woolly leaves, Europe (Britain), Siberia; *membranaceous*, greenish or pinkish white, summer, 4 to 6 in., Spain; *nitidus* (syn. *richardii nitidus*), rosy lilac, early summer, 9 in., Sicily; *nummularius*, mauve, summer, 4 to 12 in., Caucasus, Asia Minor; *pallasinianus* (syn. *odoratissimus*), purple, summer, 2 to 4 in., S. Russia; *pseudo-lanuginosus*, pink, early summer, mat forming, grey hairy, origin uncertain; *pulegioides*, (syn. *chamaedrys*), Larger Wild Thyme, rose-purple, summer, 4 to 10 in., Europe (Britain); *serpyllum*, Wild Thyme, rose-purple, summer, prostrate, N. Europe (Britain); *vulgaris*, Garden Thyme, purple, summer, 6 in., S. Europe, and vars. *aureus*, leaves yellow, and Silver Queen, leaves silver variegated.

TIARELLA – *Saxifragaceae*. Hardy perennial herbs with sprays of small flowers, allied to *Heuchera*.

Soil, ordinary. Position, cool, shady. Plant in spring or autumn.

Increase by division in spring; by seeds sown outdoors or in a frame in spring.

Recommended kinds are *T. cordifolia*, Foam Flower, False Mitrewort, white, spring, early summer, 6 to 12 in., Eastern N. America; *wherryi*, white or pinkish, spring, early summer, 6 to 12 in. Eastern N. America.

TIBOUCHINA – *Melastomataceae*. Tender shrubs with velvety evergreen leaves and clusters of showy flowers.

Compost, John Innes potting compost No. 2 or equivalent. Position, large pots, tubs or beds in a cool or intermediate greenhouse, minimum winter temp. 7°C. Pot or plant in early spring. Water normally. Shade lightly in summer only. Train long stems to trellis, wires or other supports, or pinch tips of growth occasionally to produce a more branching habit. Cut out or shorten unwanted growth in late winter.

Increase by cuttings of firm young growth in spring or summer in a warm propagator.

The best kind is *T. semidecandra* (syns. *T. urvilleana*, *Lasiandra macrantha*), Brazilian Spider Flower, Brazilian Glory Bush, violet-purple, summer, autumn, to 10 ft., Brazil.

Tibouchina semidecandra

TIGRIDIA (Tiger Flower, Tiger Iris) – *Iridaceae*. Slightly tender bulbs with showy blooms which individually last only a day but are produced in succession for many weeks.

Soil, reasonably fertile, porous and well drained in winter but fairly moist in summer. Position, warm, sunny, sheltered. Plant in spring. Water freely in summer if weather is dry. Cover bulbs with dry litter or cloches in winter or lift and store in a frost-proof place until spring.

Pot culture: Compost, John Innes potting compost No. 1 or equivalent. Pot the bulbs in spring, 5 to 7 bulbs in each 4- or 5-in. pot. Position, sunny greenhouse or frame, minimum temp. 7°C. Water sparingly at first, moderately after growth begins; freely when well advanced. Apply weak liquid fertilizer occasionally when flower stems show. After flowering gradually withhold water until foliage turns yellow, then keep quite dry. During winter either store the bulbs in pots laid on their sides in a frost-proof place or remove them and store them dry like gladiolus corms.

Increase by seeds sown in John Innes seed compost or equivalent in temp. 15 to 18°C. in spring; by offsets removed and treated as advised for old bulbs in spring.

The best kind is *T. pavonia*, red, yellow and purple, summer, 1 to 2 ft., Mexico, and vars. *alba*, white, red spotted, *albu immaculata*, white, *aurea*, yellow, and *conchiflora*, rich yellow, etc.

TILIA (Lime Tree, Linden, Basswood) – *Tiliaceae*. Hardy deciduous trees. The small whitish yellow flowers in summer are sweetly scented and yield abundant nectar which is eagerly sought by bees.

Soil, good, ordinary. Position, open, sunny, as specimen trees or as screens. Also suitable for training over arches to form a shady path in summer; will stand severe pruning and may be pleached to form formal avenues or walks. Plant in autumn or late winter. Prune in autumn or winter as necessary to maintain required shape.

Increase by seeds stratified for five months at 20 to 30°C., then for a further four months at 4°C., after which they should be sown outdoors or under glass; grafting on common species in spring for choice kinds.

Recommended kinds are *T. americana*, American Lime, large leaves, 60 to 120 ft., E. and Central N. America; *cordata*, Small-leaved Lime, neat habit, slow growing, 50 to 90 ft., Europe (Britain); *dasystyla* (syn. *caucasica*), 40 to 60 ft., Europe, S. W. Asia; *euchlora*, good foliage and habit, 40 to 60 ft., hybrid between *cordata* and *dasystyla*; *europaea* (syn. *vulgaris*), Common Lime, suckers badly, to 130 ft., hybrid between *cordata* and *platyphyllos*; *moltkei*, very vigorous, pyramidal, 40 to 60 ft., hybrid between *americana* and *petiolaris*; *mongolica*, Mongolian Lime, very hardy and graceful small tree, 20 to 30 ft., N. China, Mongolia; *petiolaris*, Weeping Silver Lime, graceful and very sweet scented, often overpowering bees, leaves white beneath, 60 to 90 ft., origin doubtful; *platyphyllos*, Large-leaved Lime, superior to Common Lime, to 120 ft., Europe, with numerous vars. *aurea*, golden twigged, *fastigiata* (syn. *pyramidalis*), upright branches, *laciniata*, cut leaved, *rubra*, red-twigged lime; *tomentosa* (syn. *argentea*), Silver Lime, leaves silvery beneath, broadly pyramidal, 60 to 100 ft., Europe.

TILLANDSIA – *Bromeliaceae*. Tender epiphytic perennials, some with showy flowers and bracts.

Grow in equal parts fern or peat fibre and chopped sphagnum moss in baskets or wired to a piece of wood or bark and suspended in a warm greenhouse, minimum winter temp. 13°C., or in a warm room. Keep moist throughout the year and maintain a humid atmosphere if possible. Shade from strong direct sunshine only. Pot in spring but annual repotting is unnecessary.

Increase by offsets inserted in small pots

of sandy peat in temp. 20 to 25°C. in spring.

Recommended kinds are *T. cyanea*, blue and pink, spring, 1½ to 2 ft., Guatemala; *erubescens* (syn. *ionantha*), violet and red, spring, 3 to 4 in., Tropical America; *lindenii* (syn. *lindeniana*), violet and pink, spring, Peru.

TITHONIA – *Compositae*. Slightly tender annuals with daisy-type flowers.

Soil, ordinary. Position, sunny. Sow in John Innes seed compost or equivalent in temp. 13 to 18°C. in spring. Harden off for planting out in late spring or early summer when there is little danger of frost. Discard after flowering.

Tithonia rotundifolia

The best kind is *T. rotundifolia* (syn. *speciosa*), Mexican Sunflower, orange-yellow, summer, 3 to 6 ft., Mexico, Central America.

TOLMIEA – *Saxifragaceae*. Hardy herbaceous perennial with small green flowers and heart-shaped leaves which often produce plantlets by which it can be propagated.

Soil, ordinary. Position, shady outdoors or in pots of John Innes potting compost No. 1 or equivalent in a shady greenhouse or as a room plant. Plant or pot in spring.

Increase by division in spring or by pegging leaves to the soil and detaching when plantlets are well rooted.

The only species is *T. menziesii*, Pick-a-back Plant, Thousand Mothers, Youth-on-age, green, spring, 1 to 2 ft., N. W. America.

TORENIA – *Scrophulariaceae*. Tender annuals with small, trumpet-shaped flowers.

Sow in spring in John Innes seed compost or equivalent in temp. 13 to 18°C. Pot seedlings singly in John Innes potting compost No. 1 or equivalent and grow in a sunny, frost-proof greenhouse. Water normally. Support the slender stems with branching twigs or split canes and encircling ties. Discard after flowering.

The best kinds are *T. baillonii*, yellow and purple, summer, autumn, 1 ft., Vietnam, often wrongly called *flava*, an inferior species; *fournieri*, blue, purple, yellow and black, summer, autumn, 1 ft., Vietnam.

TORREYA – *Taxaceae*. Slightly tender evergreen coniferous tree with yew-like foliage and small plum-like fruits.

Soil, ordinary, excellent on chalk. Position, sheltered, sunny or shady. Plant in autumn or late winter. Can be pruned if necessary in late spring.

Increase by seeds stratified for three months at 4°C. and then sown outdoors or under glass; by cuttings of firm young growth in a propagator in summer.

Recommended kinds are *T. californica*, Californian Nutmeg, 40 to 60 ft., California; *nucifera*, 15 to 75 ft., Japan.

TRACHELIUM (Blue Throatwort) – *Campanulaceae*. Slightly tender herbaceous perennials with clusters of small flowers. Usually grown as an annual or biennial.

Sow, in spring for late summer flowering, or about midsummer for spring and early summer flowering, in John Innes seed compost or equivalent in temp. 15 to 18°C. Pot seedlings singly in John Innes potting compost No. 1 or equivalent and move on to 5- or 6-in. pots for flowering. Grow throughout in a light, frost-proof greenhouse. Water normally.

The best kind is *T. caeruleum*, blue, spring or summer, 2 ft., S. Europe, and var. *album*, white.

TRACHELOSPERMUM – *Apocynaceae*. Slightly tender evergreen twining shrubs with fragrant, jasmine-like flowers.

Soil, light loam, well drained, with some leafmould or peat. Position, warm, sunny, sheltered walls or in a sunny frost-proof greenhouse. In cold places, protect outdoors in winter with nets, sacking or polythene.

Increase by cuttings of half-ripened shoots in a warm propagator in summer.

Recommended kinds are *T. asiaticum* (syns. *crocostemon*, *divaricatum*), white becoming cream, summer, 12 to 15 ft., the hardiest species, Japan, Korea; *jasminoides* (syn. *Rhyncospermum jasminoides*), Chinese Jasmine, white, very fragrant, summer, 10 to 12 ft., China, with vars. *variegatum*, foliage green, silver, and pink, and *wilsonii*, narrow, veined leaves.

TRACHYCARPUS – *Palmae*. Hardy or slightly tender palms with fan-shaped dark green leaves.

Soil, ordinary, well drained. Position, sunny but sheltered from cold winds which damage the leaves. Plant in spring or autumn. Remove dead leaves and leaf stalks in spring.

Increase by seeds sown in temp. 18 to 21°C. in spring. In favourable places self-

Tradescantia fluminensis Quicksilver

sown seedlings often appear freely around mature specimens.

The best species is *T. fortunei* (syn. *Chamaerops excelsa*), Chusan Palm, Windmill Palm, 25 to 30 ft., China.

TRACHYMENE (Blue Lace Flower) – *Umbelliferae*. Slightly tender annuals and perennials with small flowers in flat clusters. The kind commonly cultivated is an annual, often known as *Didiscus coeruleus*.

Soil, ordinary. Position, sunny. Sow in temp. 15 to 18°C. in spring, transplant seedlings 2 in. apart in pots or boxes and harden off for planting out in late spring or early summer. Alternatively, pot seedlings singly in John Innes potting compost No. 1 or equivalent in 4-in. pots and grow throughout in a sunny, frost-proof greenhouse. Water fairly freely. Discard after flowering.

The best kind is *T. coerulea*, blue, summer, 8 in., Australia.

TRADESCANTIA (Spiderwort) – *Commelinaceae*. Hardy herbaceous and tender perennials grown for flowers and foliage.

Culture of hardy species: Soil, ordinary. Position, partially shady or sunny. Plant in spring or autumn. Lift, divide and replant every two or three years. Excellent for town gardens.

Culture of tender species: Compost, John Innes potting compost No. 1 or equivalent. Position, well-drained pots in a cool or intermediate greenhouse, minimum winter temp. 7°C., or in a room. Pot in spring. Water normally. Can be grown in sun or shade but this may affect the colour of the leaves, which is usually best in fairly strong light. *T. fluminensis* will often grow well under the greenhouse staging.

Increase hardy species by division in spring; by seeds sown outdoors or in a frame in spring or as soon as ripe; tender species by cuttings inserted in sandy soil in a warm propagator in spring or summer; by division in spring.

Recommended hardy kinds are *T. andersoniana*, blue, purple, rose, pink or white,

summer, autumn, 1½ to 3 ft., hybrids between *subaspera*, *virginiana* and other species, usually listed in gardens as varieties of *virginiana*; *canaliculata*, purple, blue, rose or white, summer, autumn, 2 ft., Eastern U.S.A.; *subaspera*, purple, blue, white, summer, autumn, 2 ft., Central U.S.A.; *virginiana*, Flower of a Day, Spiderwort, blue, purple or white, summer, autumn, 1 to 3 ft., Eastern U.S.A.

Recommended tender kinds are *T. blossfeldiana*, trailing, leaves green above, purple beneath, Argentina; *fluminensis* (syn. *tricolor, viridis vittata*), Wandering Jew, prostrate, leaves green or purple sometimes striped with white or yellow.

TRAPA (Water Chestnut) – *Trapaceae*. Tender or hardy annual aquatic floating herbs with spiny edible fruit.

Soil, rich loamy. Position, sunny, water basins, tubs or pools in a cool greenhouse, or *T. verbanensis* outdoors. Sow seeds in water in spring where plants are to grow. Germinate in temp. 18 to 21°C. When growing the temperature can be lowered and in summer no artificial heat should be necessary.

Recommended kinds are *T. bicornuta*, fruits two horned, China; *bispinosa*, fruits with two to four spines, India, Ceylon; *natans*, Water Calthrops, Water Chestnut, Jesuit's Nut, fruits edible, 2 in. in diameter, Europe; *verbanensis*, two-horned fruits, hardy, Italy.

TRICHOMANES – *Hymenophyllaceae*. Tender filmy ferns. Fronds of some kinds semi-transparent.

Compost, equal parts loam, peat or leafmould, sphagnum moss, sandstone chippings and coarse sand. Position, moist, shady recesses of rock gardens, in a cool, shady greenhouse or in a Wardian case. Plant or pot in spring. Water freely from spring to autumn, moderately afterwards. Damp atmosphere and shade essential. Protect from frost. Constant moisture essential.

Increase by spores sown on the surface of sandy peat in a shallow pan covered with

glass in temp. 15 to 18°C. at any time; by division at potting time.

The best kind is *T. speciosum* (syn. *radicans*), Killarney Fern, Bristle Fern, fronds finely divided, 3 to 12 in., Ireland, Britain, Pyrenees, Spain, Portugal, and vars. *andrewsii*, pinnae somewhat widely separated, *densum*, compact, *dilatatum*, larger, *dissectum*, very finely cut fronds.

TRICYRTIS (Toad Lily) – *Liliaceae*. Slightly tender perennials with lily-like, often spotted flowers.

Soil, equal parts loam, peat and sand. Position, partially shady, sheltered, moist in summer but not waterlogged in winter. In cold places plants may need protection from frost. Plant rhizomes 2 in. below the surface in autumn or early spring. Plants grown outdoors do not flower until autumn but if grown in an unheated greenhouse or frame will bloom in summer.

Increase by offsets, removed at planting or potting time; by seeds sown in peat and sand in a cool greenhouse as soon as ripe or in spring.

Recommended kinds are *T. hirta*, white or pale lilac and purple, autumn, 1 to 3 ft., Japan; *macrantha*, pale yellow and brown, autumn, 2 ft., Japan; *macropoda*, greenish yellow, spotted purple, autumn, 2 to 3 ft., China, Japan, and var. *striata*, leaves striped white.

TRILLIUM (Wood Lily) – *Trilliaceae*. Hardy herbaceous perennials with rhizomatous roots and three-petalled flowers.

Soil, fertile, porous acid loam with peat or leafmould. Position, shady, moist yet well drained. Plant in autumn. Topdress annually in spring with peat or leafmould; lift and replant only when absolutely necessary.

Trillium grandiflorum

Increase by seeds sown in sandy peat, in a shady unheated frame in spring or as soon as ripe; by division of roots in autumn.

Recommended kinds are *T. cernuum*, white or pinkish, spring, 6 to 18 in., N. America; *erectum*, purplish maroon, spring, 1 ft., N. America; *grandiflorum*, Wake Robin, American Wood Lily, white, spring, early summer, 1 ft., N. America; *nivale*, Snow Wood Lily, white, early spring, 6 in., Southeastern U.S.A.; *ovatum*, white to pink, early spring, 1½ ft., N.W. America; *recurvatum*, maroon, spring, 1 ft., U.S.A.; *rivale*, white and purple, spring, 6 to 8 in., Western U.S.A.; *sessile*, purple, early spring, 9 to 12 in., U.S.A.; *undulatum*, white and purple, spring and early summer, 1½ ft., N. America.

TRITELEIA – *Alliaceae*. Slightly tender cormous perennials with tubular or funnel-shaped flowers. Many authorities include them in *Brodiaea*.

Soil, John Innes potting compost No. 1 or equivalent. Position, pots or pans in a cool or cold greenhouse, minimum winter temp. 0°C., or outdoors in sunny, sheltered places in reasonably frost-free areas. Plant or pot in autumn. Water moderately until spring then freely until foliage dies down in summer when keep dry until planting time.

Increase by seeds sown in a cool greenhouse in spring or as soon as ripe; by division of corm clusters at planting time.

Recommended kinds are *T. bridgesii* (syn. *Brodiaea bridgesii*), blue or mauve, early summer, 9 to 12 in., Western U.S.A.; *crocea* (syn. *Brodiaea crocea*), Old Maids, yellow, late spring, early summer, 6 in., California; *grandiflora* (syns. *Brodiaea elegans*, *B. grandiflora*, *B. douglasii*), violet-blue, early summer, 6 to 9 in., N.W. America; *hyacinthina* (syn. *Brodiaea hyacinthina*), white or pinkish, early summer, 1½ ft., Western U.S.A.; *ixioides* (syn. *Brodiaea ixioides*), Golden Star, Pretty Face, yellow and purple, summer, 1½ ft., Western U.S.A.; *laxa* (syn. *Brodiaea laxa*), violet-blue or purple, summer, 1½ to 3 ft., California; *peduncularis* (syn. *Brodiaea peduncularis*), white or pink, summer, 1½ ft., California; *tubergenii* (syn. *Brodiaea tubergenii*), blue, summer, 1½ ft., hybrid between *laxa* and *peduncularis*.

For *Triteleia uniflora* see Ipheion.

TRITONIA – *Iridaceae*. Slightly tender cormous perennials with showy flowers. All are native to S. Africa. The common montbretia of gardens is *Crocosmia crocosmiiflora*, although often known as tritonia.

Soil, sandy loam. Position, warm, sunny, well drained. Plant 3 in. deep in spring. Water in very dry weather. Lift plants in autumn and place in shallow boxes filled with dry soil and keep in an unheated frame or greenhouse until planting time. Practically no water is required until growth starts in early spring. In sheltered gardens corms may be left in the ground with a covering of dry litter during winter. Alternatively, grow in pots in John Innes potting compost No. 1 or equivalent. Pot in autumn or late winter, four or five corms in each 4- or 5-in. pot. Keep in a cool greenhouse, minimum temp. 7°C. Water moderately from the time plants begin to grow until flowers fade, then occasionally till the plants die down, and keep dry till late winter.

Increase by offsets removed at planting or potting time; by seeds sown in John Innes seed compost or equivalent in spring in temp. 13 to 18°C.

Recommended kinds are *T. crocata*, tawny red, late spring, early summer, 2 ft., and vars. *aurantiaca*, orange-red, *coccinea*, scarlet, *purpurea*, purple, *sanguinea*, blood red, etc.; *fluvida*, yellow, late spring, 2 ft.; *rosea*, bright red spotted yellow at base, early summer, 1½ ft.

TROLLIUS (Globe Flower) – *Ranunculaceae*. Hardy herbaceous perennials with flowers like large, usually globular, buttercups.

Soil, deep, moist loam. Position, partially shady borders or margins of ponds or streams. Plant in spring or autumn. Water freely in dry weather. Lift, divide and replant every three or four years.

Increase by seeds sown in moist, loamy soil in a shady position outdoors in spring or as soon as ripe; by division in spring or autumn.

Recommended kinds are *T. asiaticus*, orange, late spring, early summer, 1½ to 2 ft., Siberia, Turkestan; *europaeus*, lemon yellow, late spring, early summer, 1½ to 2 ft., Europe (Britain), and vars. *albidus*, cream, *giganteus*, 2½ ft., *nanus* (syn. *humilis*), 3 to 8 in., *superbus*, large soft yellow flowers; *ledebouri*, orange, late spring, early summer, 2 to 3 ft., Siberia; *pumilus*, yellow, summer, 6 to 8 in., Himalaya, China; *yunnanensis*, yellow, late spring, 1½ to 2 ft., China.

TROPAEOLUM – *Tropaeolaceae*. Tender or hardy perennial and annual dwarf or climbing herbs with showy spurred flowers.

Culture of Canary Creeper: Soil, good, ordinary. Position, against a sunny or shady wall, fence, arbour or trellis. Sow seeds in light soil in temp. 13 to 15°C. in spring, harden off seedlings in a cold frame and plant outdoors in late spring or early summer, or sow in mid- to late spring outdoors where required to grow. Water freely in dry weather. Discard after flowering.

Culture of Nasturtium: Soil, ordinary. Position, sunny. Sow seed 1 in. deep in spring where plants are required to grow. Remove seed pods as they form to ensure free flowering. Discard after flowering.

Culture of T. peltophorum: Soil, John Innes potting compost No. 1 or equivalent. Position, well-drained pots or border in a sunny, frost-proof greenhouse, shoots trained up canes, wires, trellis, etc. Alternatively, can be planted outdoors in late spring or early summer in warm sunny places in the autumn before frost occurs.

Culture of tender tuberous-rooted species: Compost, John Innes potting compost No. 1 or equivalent. Position, well-drained pots in a light airy greenhouse, minimum winter temp. 7°C. Pot in late summer or autumn. Place one tuber only in a 4- or 5-in. pot and bury this about one inch. Water very little till plants grow freely, then give an abundant supply. Withhold water entirely when foliage turns yellow and until growth restarts. Apply weak liquid feeds occasionally when plants are in flower. Train shoots to wire trellis fixed in pots or up rafters. After growth ceases store pots in a cool but frost-proof place till potting time.

Culture of hardy or slightly tender species: Soil, light, sandy loam for *T. pentaphyllum*; ordinary soil for *polyphyllum*; equal parts loam, peat, leafmould and sand for *speciosum*; poorish soil for *tuberosum*. Position, warm, sunny wall or fence for *pentaphyllum*; sunny bank or dry wall for *polyphyllum*; shaded wall or hedge for *speciosum*; sunny border for *tuberosum*. Plant *tuberosum* in spring; *polyphyllum* in late summer or autumn, 5 or 6 in. deep; *speciosum* and *pentaphyllum* in spring or autumn. Water freely in dry weather. Lift tubers of *tuberosum* in autumn (except in almost frost-free areas) and store in sand in a frost-proof place till spring; leave the others undisturbed.

Increase *T. peltophorum* by cuttings of shoots, 2 to 3 in. long, inserted in sandy soil in a warm propagator in spring; by seed as for Canary Creeper. Greenhouse tuberous-rooted species by seeds sown in light, sandy soil in temp. 13 to 15°C. in spring; by cuttings of shoots inserted in sandy soil and similar temperature in spring or summer. Hardy species by seeds sown in loam, leafmould and sand in a frame in spring; by cuttings in a propagator in summer; by division of roots at planting time. *T. majus* by seeds sown outdoors in spring.

Recommended annual kinds are *T. majus*, Tall Nasturtium, yellow, orange, salmon, red, summer, 5 to 10 ft., Peru, and vars. *nanum*, Tom Thumb Nasturtium, 6 to 9 in., *flore pleno*, double flowered, Gleam, semi-double; *peregrinum* (syn. *canariense*), Canary Creeper, yellow, summer, 3 to 10 ft., Peru.

Recommended tender perennial kinds are *T. peltophorum* (syn. *lobbianum*), orange-scarlet, summer, autumn, 6 to 10 ft., Colombia, Ecuador, and double-flowered varieties; *pentaphyllum*, vermilion and purple, summer, climbing, tuberous rooted, Argentina; *tricolorum* (syn. *tricolor*), scarlet and black, summer, climbing, Chile, Bolivia.

Recommended hardy or slightly tender perennial kinds are *T. polyphyllum*, yellow, early summer, trailing, Chile, Argentina; *speciosum*, Flame Flower, crimson, summer, 10 ft., Chile; *tuberosum*, yellow and red, autumn, climbing, tuberous rooted, Peru, Bolivia.

TSUGA (Hemlock) – *Pinaceae*. Hardy evergreen coniferous trees with an elegant habit of growth.

Soil, rich, rather moist loam; most dislike chalk but a few, including *T. canadensis*, will grow on chalk provided there is plenty of good soil on top. Position, sun or shade;

should be given plenty of room to develop their natural wide conical habit. Plant in autumn or late winter. Pruning is normally undesirable but branches can be cut back in late spring.

Increase by seeds stratified for three months at 4°C. and then sown in sandy soil outdoors or under glass; by cuttings of firm young growth in a propagator in summer or cuttings of riper growth in a frame in autumn.

Recommended kinds are *T. canadensis*, Canadian Hemlock, Eastern Hemlock, 70 to 90 ft., Eastern N. America, with vars. *albo-spica*, young shoots tipped white, and *pendula*, beautiful weeping form, wider than high, seldom over 6 ft.; *caroliniana*, Carolina Hemlock, compact habit, 40 to 70 ft., South-eastern U.S.A.; *chinensis*, slow growing, elegant, 40 to 150 ft., W. China; *diversifolia*, Japanese Hemlock, slow growing, pyramidal, 30 to 70 ft., Japan; *heterophylla*, Western Hemlock, 100 to 200 ft., Western N. America; *mertensiana*, Mountain Hemlock, bluish-green leaves, purple cones, 70 to 100 ft., S. Alaska to California; *sieboldii*, slow-growing graceful tree, 40 to 100 ft., Japan.

TULIPA (Tulip) – *Liliaceae*. Hardy bulbous-rooted plants flowering in spring.

Soil, ordinary light, fertile, well enriched with manure or compost. Position, open, sunny. Plant 3 to 4 in. deep, 6 to 8 in. apart in autumn and mulch the surface of the soil with compost or well-rotted manure. Bulbs grown in beds can be lifted directly after flowering and replanted at once into a reserve border to finish growth, or left till their foliage has died down and then lifted and stored in a cool, dry place till planting time. Bulbs may be left in the ground if desired, lifted, divided and replanted every two to four years.

Pot culture: Compost, John Innes potting compost No. 1 or equivalent, or special bulb fibre containing peat, crushed charcoal and oyster shell if grown in bowls without drainage holes. Pot in autumn, placing three bulbs in a 4-in. pot or five in a 6-in. pot, or leaving at least ½ in. between bulbs in bowls and burying the bulbs just below the surface. Place pots or bowls in a cold frame and cover with cinders or peat for at least eight weeks. Remove to a window, frame or greenhouse when growth begins and water freely. Temperature for forcing 13 to 18°C.

Increase by seeds sown in early spring in light sandy soil in a frame or cool greenhouse, transplanting in the autumn of the following year to a bed of rich soil outdoors; by offsets removed from the parent bulb in summer when foliage has died down. Seedling bulbs flower when four to six years old, offsets more rapidly according to size.

Recommended kinds are *T. acuminata*, Turkish Tulip, Horned Tulip, red or yellow, narrow petals, late spring, 1½ ft.,

Early single tulip

garden origin; *batalinii*, pale yellow, late spring, 6 to 9 in., Turkestan; *biflora*, cream and purple, spring, 4 to 12 in., S. Russia; *celsiana* (syn. *persica*), yellowish bronze, late spring, 6 in., Spain, N. Africa; *clusiana*, The Lady Tulip, white and rose, spring, 8 to 12 in., Iran, Afghanistan, Kashmir; *eichleri*, scarlet, spring, 12 to 15 in., S.W. Asia; *fosteriana*, scarlet and black, spring, 1 to 1½ ft., Central Asia; *gesneriana*, orange to crimson, spring, 1 to 1½ ft., origin uncertain; *greigii*, scarlet, yellow and black, spring, 1 to 2 ft., Central Asia; *hageri*, coppery red, spring, 6 in., Greece, Asia Minor; *hoogiana*, scarlet, yellow and black or green, late spring, 12 to 15 in., Central Asia; *humilis*, rose or purple and yellow, late winter, early spring, 4 in., Iran, Turkey; *kaufmanniana*, Water-lily Tulip, white or yellow and red, early spring, 6 to 12 in., Turkestan; *kolpakowskiana*, yellow and rose, early spring, 6 to 12 in., Turkestan; *linifolia*, scarlet and deep purple, spring, 6 to 9 in., Central Asia; *montana*, red, late spring, 9 to 12 in., Iran; *orphanidea*, coppery orange, spring, 8 to 12 in., Greece, Turkey; *praestans*, scarlet, spring, 9 to 12 in., Central Asia; *primulina*, creamy yellow, spring, 8 to 12 in., Algeria; *pulchella*, carmine and purple, late winter, early spring, 6 in., Asia Minor; *saxatilis*, lilac and yellow, early spring, 9 to 12 in., Crete; *sprengeri*, dull crimson, late spring, 1 to 1½ ft., Asia Minor; *sylvestris*, yellow, red and green, spring, 1 ft., Europe, Iran, N. Africa; *stellata*, white and pink, spring, 6 to 9 in., Kashmir, Afghanistan, and var. *chrysantha*, carmine and yellow; *tarda*, yellow and white, spring, 3 to 6 in., Turkestan, often wrongly known as *dasystemon*; *tubergeniana*, scarlet, spring, 1½ to 2 ft., Central Asia; *turkestanica*, white, cream and green, late winter, early spring, 9 to 12 in., Turkestan; *urumiensis*, yellow and bronze, purple, spring, 9 in., Iran; *violacea*, violet-purple, late winter, early spring, 6 in.,

Iran, Kurdestan; *viridiflora*, flowers marked with green, 15 to 24 in., spring, garden origin; *whittallii*, orange-buff and green, spring, 12 to 15 in., Turkey.

There are also large numbers of garden varieties obtained by hybridizing various species. These are classified in numerous groups determined by the time of flowering (Early Single, Early Double, May Flowering), by flower form (Parrot, Peony Flowered, Lily Flowered), relationship (Greigii Hybrids, Fosteriana Hybrids, Kaufmanniana Hybrids), and other characteristics.

TUNICA – *Caryophyllaceae*. Hardy herbaceous perennials with small flowers in loose, airy sprays.

Soil, ordinary, light. Position, sunny, well-drained rock gardens or dry walls. Plant in spring or autumn.

Increase by seeds sown in sandy soil in a frame in spring; by cuttings of non-flowering growths in a frame in summer, or by division at the same time.

The best kind is *T. saxifraga* (syn. *Petrorhagia saxifraga*), pink, summer, 6 in., Europe, Iran, and vars. *alba*, white and *flore pleno*, double.

TYPHA (Cat-tail, Reed Mace) – *Typhaceae*. Hardy aquatic perennials with brown cigar-like inflorescences.

Soil, ordinary, moist. Position, margins of shallow rivers or ponds. They may be grown in 1 to 6 in. of water. Plant in spring.

Increase by division in spring; by seeds sown in wet peat and sand in spring.

Recommended kinds are *T. angustifolia*, summer, 5 to 10 ft., Europe, Asia, N. America; *latifolia*, summer, 4 to 8 ft., North Temperate Region (Britain); *minima*, summer, 1 to 1½ ft., Europe, Asia.

ULEX (Furze, Gorse, Whin) – *Leguminosae*. Very spiny hardy evergreen shrubs with golden-yellow flowers.

Soil, poor and dry but seldom satisfactory on chalk. Position, full sun, excellent for hot banks and seaside gardens. Overgrown or leggy plants may be hard pruned in spring. Common gorse makes a good boundary hedge especially in maritime localities.

Increase species by seeds sown in light soil out of doors in spring, preferably where the plants are to grow or in pots, as all forms transplant badly; by cuttings of firm young growth inserted in sandy soil in a propagator in summer for the double form, which does not set seed.

Recommended kinds are *U. europaeus*, Common Gorse, gold flower principally in spring but a few appear all the year round, 3 to 6 ft., Europe (Britain), and var. *plenus*, double flowered, slow growing, compact; *gallii*, late summer and autumn, 2 ft., W. Europe (Britain); *minor* (syn. *nanus*), Dwarf Gorse, 1 to 2 ft., W. Europe (Britain).

ULMUS (Elm) – *Ulmaceae*. Hardy deciduous trees. Flowers small, reddish, appearing before the leaves.

Soil, ordinary for most species, but deep rich well-drained loam for Wych Elm, moist loam for American Elm. Position, open and sunny for all kinds. Not very suitable as garden trees owing to their extensive root systems which impoverish the soil. The Wych Elm is excellent near the sea. Large specimens of Common Elm are liable to shed branches without warning. Plant in autumn or late winter.

Increase by suckers removed and planted in autumn or late winter; by layering shoots in autumn; by budding choice kinds on common species in summer, or by grafting similarly in spring; by seeds gathered as soon as ripe and sown outdoors.

Recommended kinds are *U. americana*, American or White Elm, graceful habit, 100 to 120 ft., Central N. America; *angustifolia cornubiensis* (syns. *carpinifolia cornubiensis* and *stricta*), Cornish Elm, 80 to 100 ft., Britain, France; *carpinifolia* (syn. *nitens*), Smooth-leaved Elm, deeply fissured bark, to 90 ft., Europe, N. Africa, and vars. *pendula*, weeping, *variegata*, leaves mottled with white; *glabra* (syn. *montana*), Wych Elm, Scotch Elm, does not sucker, large rough leaves, 100 to 120 ft., Europe, Asia, and vars. *camperdownii*, Camperdown Elm, weeping, *exoniensis* (syn. *fastigiata*), Exeter Elm, upright growth, *lutescens*, young leaves yellow, *pendula*, low growing, weeping, good lawn specimen; *hollandica*, quick growing, variable to 120 ft., hybrids between *carpinifolia*, *glabra* and *plottii*, and numerous varieties such as *belgica*, Belgian Elm, to 100 ft., *hillieri*, dwarf, 4 ft., *major* (syn. *U. major*), Dutch Elm, 80 to 120 ft., *smithii* (syn. *pendula*), Downton Elm, 20 to 30 ft., pendulous branches, *vegeta*, Huntingdon Elm, Chichester Elm, 80 to 100 ft.; *plottii*, 60 to 90 ft., pendulous branchlets, England; *procera* (syn. *campestris*), English Elm, common in S. England, rarely sets seeds, 100 to 150 ft., England, and vars. *argenteo-variegata*, leaves spotted white, Louis van Houtte (syn. Van Houttei), yellow leaves; *pumila*, dwarf, 10 to 30 ft., E. Siberia, N. China; *rubra* (syn. *fulva*), Slippery Elm, Red Elm, 40 to 60 ft., N. America; *sarniensis* (syn. *stricta sarniensis*), Jersey Elm, Wheatley Elm, narrowly conical, 80 to 100 ft., Jersey, N. France; *viminalis*, slow growing, arching branches, 40 to 60 ft., hybrid, and vars. *aurea*, young leaves yellow, and *marginata*, leaves mottled grey.

UMBELLULARIA – *Lauraceae*. Slightly tender evergreen shrub or small tree; purple pear-shaped fruits in favoured localities. Leaves pungent when bruised. Small, greenish yellow flowers in clusters.

Soil, loamy, well drained. Position, sunny, warm, sheltered; will survive a temperature of about −10°C. for short periods. Plant in spring or autumn. Prune if necessary in late spring after flowering.

Increase by seeds sown in sandy soil in a cool greenhouse during spring; by layering in spring.

The only species is *U. californica* (syn. *Oreodaphne californica*), yellowish green, spring, 20 to 80 ft., California, Oregon.

UMBILICUS – *Crassulaceae*. Succulent perennial plants, sometimes included in the genus *Cotyledon*.

Soil, ordinary, preferably acid. Position, sunny walls or rock gardens. Plant in spring or autumn.

Increase by seeds sown outdoors in spring or as soon as ripe; by division in spring or autumn.

The best kind is *U. rupestris* (syns. *U. pendulinus*, *Cotyledon umbilicus*), Navelwort, Pennywort, greenish white, summer, 8 to 12 in., Europe (Britain), Madeira, Azores.

URSINIA – *Compositae*. Slightly tender annuals with showy daisy-type flowers.

Soil, ordinary, well drained. Position, warm, sunny. Sow in spring in temp. 15 to 18°C. in John Innes seed compost or equivalent and harden off seedlings for planting outdoors in late spring or early summer; or sow in late spring outdoors where plants are to flower and thin seedlings to 6 to 8 in.

Ursinia anethoides

Recommended kinds are *U. anethoides*, orange and purple, summer, 1 to 2 ft., S. Africa; *anthemoides*, yellow and purple, summer, 1 ft., S. Africa; *cakilifolia*, yellow or orange, summer, 9 to 12 in., S. Africa; *versicolor* (syn. *pulchra*), orange, summer, 9 in., Namaqualand. There are also hybrids between some of these species.

UTRICULARIA (Bladderwort) – *Lentibulariaceae*. Hardy aquatic submerged carnivorous herb.

Soil, unnecessary. Position, ponds or tubs in up to 2 ft. of water. Plant in spring by dropping plants into the water.

Increase by division at planting time.

The best kind is *U. vulgaris*, yellow, floating, summer, Europe (Britain), N. Africa, Siberia, N. America.

UVULARIA (Bellwort) – *Liliaceae*. Hardy herbaceous perennials with hanging, bell-shaped flowers.

Soil, peaty loam. Position, cool, partially shaded, moderately moist. Plant in spring or autumn.

Increase by division in spring or autumn; seeds sown in peat or leafmould and sand outdoors or in a frame as soon as ripe.

The best kind is *U. grandiflora*, yellow, spring, early summer, 1 ft., N. America.

VACCARIA – *Caryophyllaceae*. Hardy annuals with loose sprays of flowers.

Soil, ordinary. Position, sunny. Sow in spring or early autumn where plants are to flower and thin seedlings to 9 in. Discard after flowering.

The best kind is *V. pyramidata* (syns. *V. vulgaris*, *Saponaria vaccaria*), pink, summer, 2 ft., S. Europe, Mesopotamia, and var. *alba*, white.

VACCINIUM – *Ericaceae*. Hardy deciduous and evergreen flowering and berry-bearing shrubs. Edible red or bluish-black berries in autumn.

Soil, rather moist lime-free loam or peat. Position, shady. Plant in spring or autumn.

Increase by seeds in moist sandy peat in spring; cuttings of semi-matured shoots in sandy moist peat in a propagator in shade in summer; by layering in autumn; by division in spring or autumn.

Recommended deciduous kinds, all with bloomy black berries unless otherwise stated, are *V. angustifolium*, Lowbush Blueberry, white, tinted red, spring, 8 in., North-eastern N. America; *arctostaphylos*, Caucasian Whortleberry, white, tinted crimson, summer, autumn, 6 to 8 ft., Caucasus; *corymbosum*, Swamp Blueberry, High-bush Blueberry, pinkish, late spring, 6 to 12 ft., good autumn foliage, Eastern N. America; *cylindraceum*, yellowish green and red, late summer, autumn, 6 to 10 ft., semi-evergreen, Azores; *hirsutum*, Hairy Huckleberry, white tinged pink, late spring, 3 to 5 ft., South-eastern U.S.A.; *myrtillus*, Bilberry, Blaeberry, Whinberry, Whortleberry, pale pink, late spring, 6 to 18 in., Europe (Britain), Asia; *parvifolium*, Red Bilberry, pinkish, late spring, early summer, 2 to 10 ft., red berries, Western N. America.

Recommended evergreen kinds are *V. bracteatum*, white, scented, late summer, autumn, 4 to 6 ft., red berries, Japan, Korea, China; *delavayi*, white and pink, late spring, early summer, 2 to 5 ft., purple berries, China; *floribundum*, pink, early summer, 3 ft., red berries, Ecuador; *macrocarpum* (syn. *Oxycoccus macrocarpus*), American Cranberry, pink, summer, prostrate, red berries,

Vaccinium corymbosum

Eastern N. America; *nummularia*, rose-red, late spring, early summer, 1 ft., black berries, slightly tender, Himalaya; *ovatum*, white or pink, late spring, early summer, 6 to 10 ft., red berries turning black, Western N. America; *oxycoccus* (syn. *Oxycoccus palustris*), Cranberry, pink, late spring, early summer, prostrate, red berries, Northern Hemisphere (Britain); *vitis-idaea*, Cowberry, white and pink, summer, creeping, red berries, Europe (Britain), Asia.

VALERIANA – *Valerianaceae*. Hardy perennial herbs with ornamental flowers or foliage.

Soil, ordinary for *V. phu*, equal parts loam, leafmould (or peat) and coarse sand for the mountain kinds. Position, open, sunny. Cut down flowering stems of *V. phu* in autumn and pick off flower buds as they form.

Increase by seeds sown in light soil in a sunny position outdoors in spring; by division of roots in spring.

Recommended kinds are *V. arizonica*, pink, early summer, 2 to 3 in., Arizona; *montana*, rose-pink, summer, 6 in., Europe; *phu*, Cretan Spikenard, white, summer, 2 ft., Caucasus, var. *aurea*, young shoots golden yellow; *supina*, rose-pink, spring and early summer, 3 to 4 in., Europe.

VALLISNERIA – *Hydrocharitaceae*. Half-hardy submerged aquatic herbs with long, grass-like leaves. Useful as oxygenating plants in pools, aquaria, etc.

Soil, rich loam. Position, pools, deep tubs or aquaria. Plant in small baskets or in a bed of soil in the bottom of the tank, etc., in spring. Best in a minimum temp. of 4°C. but will grow in outdoor pools in mild places.

Increase by division in spring.

Recommended kinds are *V. gigantea*, leaves to 3 ft. long, S. America; *spiralis*, Eel Grass, Tape Grass, white, long narrow leaves, S. Europe, and var. *torta*, with twisted foliage.

VALLOTA – *Amaryllidaceae*. Tender bulbous plant with clusters of lily-like flowers on bare stems.

Compost, John Innes potting compost No. 1 or equivalent. Position, pots in a sunny, cool greenhouse, minimum winter temp. 7°C. Water fairly freely in summer from the time the flower spikes appear until mid-autumn, then moderately until early summer, after which the soil should be kept just moist for a few weeks while the bulbs are resting and ripening. No shade required at any time. Pot in autumn after flowering but do not repot annually as plants flower most freely when rather crowded.

Vallota speciosa

Increase by offsets removed at potting time; by seeds sown in John Innes seed compost or equivalent in a temp. 15 to 18°C. as soon as ripe.

The only kind is *V. speciosa* (syns. *V. purpurea*, *Amaryllis purpurea*), Scarborough Lily, scarlet, late summer, early autumn, 2 ft., S. Africa, var. *alba*, white.

VANCOUVERIA – *Berberidaceae*. Hardy perennials with creeping rootstocks, attractive divided leaves and small flowers.

Soil, rich loam with leafmould or peat. Position, cool, shady. Plant in spring or autumn.

Increase by division in spring or autumn.

Recommended kinds are *V. hexandra*, white, late spring, 12 to 18 in., N. W. America; *planipetala* (syn. *parviflora*), white, late spring, 9 to 12 in., California, Oregon.

VANDA – *Orchidaceae*. Tender epiphytic orchids with beautiful flowers often scented and carried in sprays or clusters.

Compost, equal parts fibre and sphagnum moss. Position, pots filled to at least one-third with drainage. The wide distribution of species in the wild demands difference in their treatment; *V. amesiana*, *caerulea*, *caerulescens*, *cristata* and *teres* will grow well in the intermediate house, minimum temp. 13°C., but *sanderiana* and *tricolor* prefer the warm house, minimum temp. 18°C. All require liberal watering when growing and the syringe should be used freely. In winter, water should be given more sparingly but plants must never be dry. Shade lightly in summer but give plenty of light at other times. Avoid draughts.

The taller stemmed kinds lose their bottom leaves after a while and the stems can then be severed below some healthy stem roots in spring and potted carefully. The decapitated base may remain in the old pot and usually develops new growths. Basal growths are sometimes produced without severance of the stem.

Recommended kinds are *V. amesiana*, fragrant, white flushed rose, winter, spring, 2 to 3 ft., Burma, N. India; *caerulea*, soft bluish grey to deep blue, autumn, 2 to 3 ft., Assam, Burma, Thailand, many named varieties; *caerulescens*, violet-blue, spring, summer, 1½ to 2 ft., Burma; *cristata*, greenish yellow and white, striped maroon, spring, summer, 9 in., N. India; *insignis*, yellow with chocolate spots, lip white and rose, late spring, early summer, 1½ ft., Moluccas; *sanderiana* (syn. *Euanthe sanderiana*), pinkish white tawny spotted and flushed red, lip small, tawny and very variable, mainly late summer, 2 to 3 ft., Philippines; *teres*, white, rose, veined purple, late summer, 2 to 3 ft., Burma, Thailand, many varieties; *tricolor*, pale yellow spotted maroon, lip violet-purple but very variable, spring and autumn, 3 to 5 ft., Java, and numerous varieties.

VELTHEIMIA – *Liliaceae*. Tender bulbous plants with tubular flowers in poker-like spikes. Native to S. Africa.

Compost, John Innes potting compost No. 1 or equivalent. Position, pots in a sunny, cool greenhouse, minimum winter temp. 7°C. Pot bulbs in late summer or early autumn. Water rather sparingly at first but freely as growth appears. In late spring gradually reduce the water supply and keep quite dry for a few weeks before repotting. Plants can stand out of doors in a warm sunny place in summer. The leaves of *V. bracteata* do not die down until after the new rosette appears so this species must not be dried off at any stage.

Increase by offsets removed from parent bulbs at potting time; by seeds sown as soon as ripe in sandy soil in temp. 15 to 18°C. Seedlings take two to three years to flower.

Recommended kinds are *V. bracteata* (syn. *viridifolia*), pink and green, late winter, spring, 1 to 1½ ft., much confused with *capensis*; *capensis* (syn. *glauca*), yellow to red, often spotted, spring, 1 to 1½ ft., and var. *deasii*, 1 ft., leaves wavy edged.

x VENIDIO-ARCTOTIS – *Compositae.* Slightly tender perennials with daisy-type flowers.

Soil, ordinary, well drained. Position, warm, sunny. Plant in late spring or early summer. Protect in winter with cloches or remove plants in autumn to a frame or cool greenhouse.

Increase by cuttings in spring or summer in sandy soil in a propagator. Pot rooted cuttings singly and overwinter in a frost-proof greenhouse.

The best kind is Sutton's Triumph, yellow, orange, salmon, bronze, red, crimson and claret purple, summer, autumn, 1½ to 2 ft., hybrids between *Arctotis grandis*, *A. breviscapa* and *Venidium fastuosum*.

VENIDIUM – *Compositae.* Slightly tender annuals with showy daisy-type flowers. Native to S. Africa.

Soil, ordinary, well drained. Position, sunny borders. Sow seeds in John Innes seed compost or equivalent in spring in temp. 15 to 18°C., transplanting seedlings outdoors in late spring or early summer.

Recommended kinds are *V. decurrens*, yellow and purplish brown, early summer, 2 ft., and var. *calendulaceum*, differing in minor leaf characteristics; *fastuosum*, orange and purplish black, summer, 2 to 3 ft. There are also hybrids between the species.

VERATRUM (False Hellebore) – *Liliaceae.* Hardy herbaceous perennials with large, prominently ribbed, green leaves, poisonous roots and small flowers packed in dense, branched spikes.

Soil, fertile, porous loam with peat or leafmould. Position, sunny or partially shady, moist. Plant in spring.

Increase by seeds sown in peaty soil in a cool greenhouse in spring or as soon as ripe; division in spring. Seed frequently takes many months to germinate.

Recommended kinds are *V. album*, greenish white, summer, 3 to 4 ft., Europe, N. Africa, Siberia; *californicum*, greenish cream, summer, to 6 ft., Western U.S.A.; *nigrum*, maroon, summer, 4 to 5 ft., S. Europe, Siberia; *viride*, yellowish green, summer, 5 to 8 ft., N. America.

VERBASCUM (Mullein) – *Scrophulariaceae.* Hardy biennial and perennial herbs with flowers in spikes.

Culture of biennial species: Soil, ordinary, well drained. Position, sunny. Sow seeds in light soil in a sunny position outdoors in late spring or early summer, transplanting seedlings when three or four leaves form 6 in. apart in a sunny position until the following spring, then plant where required to flower.

Culture of perennial species: Soil, ordinary, deep, light. Position, sunny, warm, even rather dry. Plant in spring or autumn. Increase by seeds as advised for biennial species; also by root cuttings taken early in the year and rooted in a frame or greenhouse.

Recommended biennial kinds are *V. blattaria*, Moth Mullein, yellow or whitish, summer, early autumn, 3 ft., Europe (Britain), Asia, N. Africa, and var. *grandiflorum*, larger white flowers; *bombyciferum* (syn. *broussa*), pale yellow, summer, whole plant densely white hairy, 4 to 6 ft., Asia Minor; *nigrum*, Dark Mullein, yellow and purple, summer, early autumn, 2 to 4 ft., Europe (Britain), Macedonia, Caucasus; *thapsus*, Aaron's Rod, yellow, summer, densely white woolly leaves and stems, 2 to 7 ft., Europe (Britain), Asia.

Recommended perennial kinds are *V. chaixii*, Nettle-leaved Mullein, yellow, summer, 3 ft., S. W. Europe; *dumulosum*, lemon yellow and crimson, spring, 1 ft., white felted leaves, sub-shrubby, Turkey, needs protection from wet in winter; *longifolium*, yellow, summer, 4 to 6 ft., Europe; *olympicum*, yellow, summer, early autumn, grey felted leaves, 5 to 6 ft., Bithynia; *pestalozzae*, yellow, spring, white woolly leaves, 8 to 12 in., Asia Minor; *phoeniceum*, Purple Mullein, violet, purple, lilac-pink or white, late spring to early autumn, 2 to 3 ft., S. Europe, N. Asia; *spinosum*, yellow, summer, 1 ft., shrubby, Crete; *thapsiforme* (syn. *densiflorum*), yellow, summer, to 5 ft., covered in yellow hairs, Europe; *wiedemannianum*, blue and purple, summer, to 3 ft., Asia Minor. There are numerous hybrids.

VERBENA (Vervain) – *Verbenaceae.* Hardy and slightly tender perennials with flowers in clusters.

Culture of hardy kinds: Soil, ordinary, well drained (but rather moist for *V. corymbosa*). Position, sunny. Plant in spring. Protect *V. peruviana* with cloches in winter or remove to a frame or cool greenhouse in autumn in cold places.

Culture of tender kinds: Soil, ordinary, reasonably fertile. Position, sunny. Sow seeds in temp. 15 to 18°C. in spring and harden off seedlings for planting out in late spring or early summer when there is no danger of frost; or grow from cuttings of firm young shoots in spring or summer rooted in sandy soil in a propagator, overwintering late struck cuttings in a frost-

Verbena (hybrid)

proof frame or greenhouse and planting outdoors when danger of frost is past. Verbenas also make good pot plants for a sunny, frost-proof greenhouse grown in John Innes potting compost No. 1 or equivalent with normal watering, but are usually renewed from seed or cuttings annually.

Increase tender kinds by seed or cuttings as described; hardy kinds by seeds sown outdoors or in a frame in spring or as soon as ripe; by cuttings in sandy soil in a frame in spring or summer; by division in spring.

The best tender kind is *V. hybrida*, red, pink, blue, purple, white, summer, autumn, 9 to 18 in., garden origin.

Recommended hardy kinds are *V. bipinnatifida*, lavender or purple, summer, 3 ft., Central U.S.A., Mexico, can be grown as an annual; *bonariensis*, purplish lilac, summer, 4 to 5 ft., Brazil, Paraguay, Argentina; *canadensis* (syn. *aubletia*), purple or lilac, summer, 1 to 2 ft., Central and Southern U.S.A. and numerous varieties including *drummondii*, leaves doubly cut; *corymbosa*, purple and lavender, summer, 2 to 3 ft., Southern S. America; *hastata*, purple, pink or white, summer, N. America; *peruviana* (syn. *chamaedrifolia*), scarlet, summer and autumn, trailing, Southern S. America; *rigida* (syn. *venosa*), violet-purple, summer, 1 to 2 ft., Argentina, Brazil, and var. *alba*, white; *tenera*, blue or lilac, summer, trailing, Southern S. America, can be grown as an annual.

VERNONIA (Ironweed) – *Compositae.* Hardy herbaceous plants with daisy-type flowers.

Soil, sandy loam. Position, sunny. Plant in spring or autumn.

Increase by seeds sown in sandy soil in a frame in spring or outdoors in a sunny border in spring; also by division of the roots in spring.

Recommended kinds are *V. altissima*, purple and violet, autumn, 7 ft., U.S.A.; *crinita* (syn. *arkansana*), purple, autumn, 5 to 7 ft., N. America; *novehoracensis*, purple, summer, 3 to 6 ft., U.S.A.

VERONICA (Speedwell) – *Scrophulariaceae*. Hardy herbaceous perennials with small flowers in clusters or spikes. See Hebe for many shrubs formerly known as veronica.

Soil, ordinary. Position, sunny. Plant in spring or autumn. Lift, divide and replant every third year.

Increase by division of roots in autumn or spring; by seeds sown in light soil outdoors in spring.

Recommended kinds are *V. allionii*, violet-blue, summer, prostrate, Alps; *chamaedrys*, Germander Speedwell, blue, late spring, 1 to 1½ ft., Europe (Britain); *cinerea*, blue, early summer, grey leaves, 3 to 6 in., Asia Minor; *filiformis*, china blue, late spring, prostrate, very invasive, Asia Minor; *fruticans* (syn. *saxatilis*), Rock Speedwell, blue and red, summer, shrubby, 4 in., Europe (Britain); *gentianoides*, light blue, spring, early summer, 1½ ft., Caucasus, and vars. *nana*, 9 in., *variegata*, leaves variegated with white; *incana*, blue, summer, grey leaves, 1 to 1½ ft., Russia; *longifolia* (syn. *maritima*), lilac-blue, summer, early autumn, 1½ to 2 ft., Europe, N. Asia, and var. *subsessilis*, deep blue; *orientalis*, pink, summer, 6 to 8 in., Asia Minor; *pectinata*, blue and white, late spring, early summer, mat forming, Asia Minor; *prostrata* (syn. *teucrium prostrata*), blue, summer, prostrate, Europe, N. Asia, and vars. *alba*, white, *rosea*, pink; *repens*, pale blue, autumn, creeping, Corsica, Spain; *spicata*, blue, summer, 6 to 18 in., Europe (Britain), and vars. *alba*, white, *corymbosa*, pale blue, and *rosea*, pink; *teucrium*, blue, summer, 6 to 36 in., S. Europe, N. Asia, and var. Trehane, yellow leaves; *virginica*, white or pale blue, autumn, 3 to 5 ft., Eastern N. America.

VIBURNUM – *Caprifoliaceae*. Hardy deciduous and evergreen flowering shrubs. Some have beauty of blossom, others of fruit and autumn-tinted foliage.

Soil, ordinary, reasonably fertile. Position, sunny or in light shade. *V. macrocephalum* trained against a wall in cold places. Plant deciduous kinds in autumn or late winter, evergreens in spring or autumn. Prune, when necessary, after flowering removing some of the older stems to prevent overcrowding.

Increase by cuttings of half-ripened shoots inserted in sandy soil in a propagator in summer, riper cuttings in a frame in autumn; by layering in spring or autumn; by removal of rooted suckers or offsets at normal planting times.

Recommended deciduous kinds are *V. betulifolium*, white, early summer, 10 to 15 ft., red berries, China; *bitchiuense*, white and pink, scented, spring, 6 to 10 ft., Japan; *bodnantense*, pink, scented, winter and early spring, 8 to 12 ft., hybrid between *fragrans*

Viburnum plicatum grandiflorum

and *grandiflorum*; *carlcephalum*, white, scented, late spring, 6 to 8 ft., hybrid between *carlesii* and *macrocephalum*; *carlesii*, white, scented, spring, 4 to 5 ft., Korea; *dilatatum*, white, late spring, early summer, 6 to 9 ft., red berries, Japan, and var. *xanthocarpum*, yellow berries; *foetens*, white, scented, winter and early spring, 6 to 8 ft., Himalaya, Korea; *fragrans* (syn. *farreri*), pink and white, scented, late autumn and winter, 7 to 9 ft., China and vars. *candidissimum* (syn. *album*), white, and *nanum*, dwarf; *grandiflorum*, rose-pink, late winter, early spring, 8 to 10 ft., Himalaya; *hupehense*, white, late spring, early summer, 6 to 8 ft., red berries, China; *juddii*, white and pink, scented, spring, 5 to 8 ft., hybrid between *bitchiuense* and *carlesii*; *lantana*, Wayfaring Tree, creamy white, late spring, early summer, 10 to 15 ft., red berries becoming black, Europe (Britain), Asia Minor, N. Africa; *lentago*, Sheepberry, creamy white, late spring, early summer, 15 to 30 ft., blue-black fruits, Eastern N. America; *lobophyllum*, white, early summer, 10 to 15 ft., red berries, China; *macrocephalum*, Chinese Snowball, white, late spring, 8 to 10 ft., slightly tender, China; *opulus*, Guelder Rose, Water Elder, white, summer, 10 to 15 ft., red berries, Europe (Britain), Asia, Africa, and vars. *aureum*, leaves yellow, *compactum*, 5 to 6 ft., *fructuluteo*, berries lemon yellow, *sterile* (syn. *roseum*), European Snowball, flowers in globular heads, *xanthocarpum*, berries golden yellow; *plicatum* (syn. *tomentosum plicatum* and *tomentosum sterile*), Japanese Snowball, white in globular heads, late spring, early summer, 9 ft., Japan, China, and vars. *grandiflorum*, larger flower heads, *tomentosum*, flat heads of flowers of the lace-cap type, fruits red becoming black; *prunifolium*, white, spring, 10 to 15 ft., blue-black berries, good autumn foliage colour, Eastern N. America; *sargentii*, white, summer, 12 ft., red berries, Asia; *setigerum*, white, early summer, 8 to 10 ft., orange-yellow berries becoming red, China; *sieboldii*, creamy white, late spring,

early summer, 10 to 15 ft., berries pink becoming blue-black, Japan; *trilobum* (syn. *americanum*, *oxycoccus*), white, summer, 12 ft., red berries, Northern N. America and var. *compactum*, shorter; *wrightii*, white, late spring, 9 ft., red berries, Japan, Korea, China.

Recommended evergreen kinds are *V. burkwoodii*, white, fragrant, late winter and spring, 6 to 8 ft., hybrid between *carlesii* and *utile*; *davidii*, dull white, early summer, attractive turquoise-blue berries, leathery leaves, 2 to 3 ft., China; *harryanum*, white, late spring, 5 to 8 ft., black berries, W. China; *henryi*, white, early summer, fruits red changing to black, 10 ft., China; *japonicum*, white, scented, early summer, 6 ft., berries red, Japan; *odoratissimum*, white, scented, late summer, 10 to 15 ft., berries red becoming black, rather tender, Malaysia; *rhytidophyllum*, dull white, late spring, fruits red then black, large wrinkled leaves, vigorous, 10 to 15 ft., China, with var. *roseum*, flowers pink; *tinus*, Laurustinus, white, autumn until spring, 10 to 15 ft., berries blue becoming black, S. E. Europe, and vars. *hirtulum* (syn. *hirtum*), larger leaves and taller, rather tender, *lucidum*, larger, glossier leaves, rather tender, and *variegatum*, leaves yellow variegated; *utile*, white, scented, late spring, dark blue fruits, leaves white beneath, 4 to 6 ft., China.

VICTORIA (Queen Victoria Water Lily) – *Euryalaceae*. Tender aquatic perennials usually cultivated as annuals. Leaves roundish, flat, with turned-up edges, bronze green, 4 to 6 ft. diameter, floating. The scented flowers open in the evening and last until the following day, changing from creamy white to purple or rose.

Compost, two parts good rich turfy loam, one part decayed cow manure. Position, large tanks 4 to 6 ft. deep, with water temp. 25 to 30°C. No shade required.

Increase by seeds sown in a pot of loam submerged 2 in. deep in water heated to a temperature of 30°C. and placed in a light position in winter. When the seedlings appear above the surface, transplant singly in small pots and put in water, again moving on as necessary to larger pots and deeper water until by late spring they can reach their final flowering position. Plants are discarded in autumn after flowering as it is difficult to keep them through the winter.

The best kinds are *V. amazonica* (syn. *regia*), Royal Water Lily, white, rose and purple, summer, Tropical S. America; *cruziana*, Santa Cruz Water Lily, white becoming pink, summer, Paraguay.

VINCA (Periwinkle) – *Apocynaceae*. Hardy or slightly tender evergreen and deciduous trailing sub-shrubs or herbs with attractive flowers. For the tender plant often known as *Vinca rosea* see Catharanthus.

Soil, ordinary. Position, flowers best in

Vinca major

sunny places beneath hedges or on banks but is also useful as ground cover in shady places beneath trees. *V. major* can be cut back in early spring if it becomes straggly or overgrown. Plant in spring or autumn.

Increase by division at planting time or by layering in spring or autumn.

Recommended kinds are *V. difformis* (syns. *acutifolia* and *media*), pale lilac-blue, autumn and early winter, 1 ft., rather tender, S. W. Europe; *major*, Greater Periwinkle, bright blue, spring, early summer, trailing, 1 to 2 ft., Europe (Britain), and var. *variegata* (syn. *elegantissima*), leaves blotched and margined yellow-white; *minor*, Lesser Periwinkle, blue, spring, summer, trailing, Europe (Britain), and numerous varieties with single or double flowers, white to deep purple, also *aureovariegata*, leaves blotched with yellow, and *variegata*, leaves variegated creamy white.

VIOLA (Violet, Pansy) – *Violaceae*. Hardy or slightly tender herbaceous perennials grown for their attractive flowers.

Culture of Pansies, Violas and Violettas: Soil, deep, rich loam. Position, open, light, preferably shaded from mid-day sun. Plant pansies in spring or autumn. Water freely in dry weather. If exhibition blooms are desired allow only one bloom to grow on each shoot. Feed once a week during the growing season with weak liquid fertilizer. Though perennials, these plants are often treated as annuals or biennials, renewed from seed each year and discarded after flowering.

Culture of Sweet Violet: Soil, ordinary, fertile, with peat or leafmould. Position, partially shady, cool. Plant 6 to 12 in. apart in spring. Water freely in dry weather. Feed in summer with weak liquid fertilizer. Remove runners, i.e. shoots that issue from the crowns, as they form during summer. For winter flowering lift plants in early autumn and replant 6 to 8 in. apart in equal parts of good soil and leafmould in an unheated sunny frame. Protect from frost. Replant annually.

Culture of other kinds: Soil, ordinary, fertile. Position, slightly moist, partially shaded. Plant in spring. *V. hederacea* in a sheltered reasonably frost-free place or in a shady frost-proof greenhouse.

Increase pansies, violas and violettas by seeds sown in a temp. of 13 to 15°C. in early spring, or outdoors or in an unheated frame in late spring or early summer. Harden off early seedlings for planting out in late spring or early summer to flower that same year. Transplant late seedlings to a sunny bed and from that to the flowering place in early autumn or the following spring. Plants can also be grown from cuttings inserted in shady frames in late summer or early autumn; divisions in spring or autumn. Violets by runners in spring and summer, division in spring or autumn, or by seed as for violas. Other kinds by seeds sown in spring or as soon as ripe; by division in spring.

Recommended kinds are *V. altaica*, yellow or violet, spring, early summer, creeping, Crimea, Turkestan; *cornuta*, Horned Violet, blue, summer, 6 to 12 in., Pyrenees, one of the parents of the garden viola or Tufted Pansy, and var. *alba*, white; *cucullata*, violet, spring, 3 to 4 in., Eastern N. America, and vars. *albiflora*, white, and *thurstonii* (syn. *striata*), white and purple; *elegantula* (syn. *bosniaca*), rosy mauve, late spring, early summer, 4 in., S. W. Europe; *gracilis*, Olympian Violet, violet-purple, summer, 4 to 6 in., Macedonia and Asia Minor; *hederacea* (syn. *Erpetion hederaceum*), Australian Violet, purple and white, summer, 2 to 3 in., slightly tender, Australia; *labradorica purpurea*, violet, spring, purple leaves, creeping, N. America, Greenland; *odorata*, Sweet Violet, blue, spring, 6 in., Europe (Britain), and numerous varieties, some with double or semi-double flowers, also white, pink, creamy yellow, mauve, lavender and deep purple-blue; *pedata*, Bird's-foot Violet, violet and lilac, spring, 6 in., Eastern N. America; *saxatilis* (syn. *alpestris*), yellow, summer, 4 to 8 in., E. Europe, Asia Minor, and var. *macedonica*, violet-purple; *visseriana*, blue, purple, yellow or white, summer, 4 to 6 in., hybrids between *cornuta* and *gracilis*; *tricolor*, Heartsease, yellow, purple and white, summer, 6 in., Europe (Britain), one of the parents of the pansy; *williamsii*, Viola, Violetta, various colours, spring, summer, 4 to 9 in., hybrids between *wittrockiana* and *cornuta*; *wittrockiana*, Pansy, various colours, spring, summer, 4 to 9 in., hybrids between *tricolor*, *altaica* and other species.

VISCUM (Mistletoe) – *Viscaceae*. Hardy evergreen parasitic berry-bearing plants. Male and female flowers are borne on separate plants of *V. album*, the only species commonly cultivated.

Cut a notch in the bark on the underside of a branch and press a ripe berry into it in spring; young plants grow slowly for two or three years. Trees suitable for mistletoe culture are apple, hawthorn, poplar, lime, maple, mountain ash, cedar, larch and oak.

The best kind is *V. album*, green, spring, white translucent berries, Europe (Britain), N. Africa, Asia.

VITEX – *Verbenaceae*. Slightly tender, deciduous, aromatic, flowering shrubs.

Soil, ordinary, well drained. Position, sheltered, warm borders or against a sunny wall. Plant in autumn or late winter. Prune in early spring, thinning out previous year's growth or shortening stems to within a few inches of the main branches.

Increase by cuttings of firm young growth in a propagator in summer; by cuttings of riper growth in a frame in autumn; by seeds stratified for three months at 4°C. and then sown in temp. 18 to 21°C.

The best kinds are *V. agnus-castus*, Chaste Tree, Tree of Chastity, violet-blue, autumn, to 10 ft., S. Europe, and var. *alba*, flowers white; *negundo*, Chinese Chaste Tree, lavender-blue, autumn, 10 ft., China, and var. *incisa*, deeply toothed leaves.

VITIS (Vine) – *Vitidaceae*. Hardy and slightly tender climbers, some species grown for fruit and others for screen or wall cover. Some species formerly included in this genus are now reclassified under *Parthenocissus* and *Cissus*. For Grape Vine, see page 237.

Soil, ordinary, fertile; suitable for chalk and limestone. Position, sunny walls or fences, arbours, trellises, poles, pergolas, etc. Plant in autumn. Prune in winter, shortening the current year's growth as necessary to furnish available space.

Increase by seeds stratified for three months at 4°C. and then sown in temp. 15 to 18°C.; by cuttings of firm young shoots in a propagator in summer or riper cuttings in a frame in autumn; by layering shoots in spring or summer.

Recommended kinds are *V. amurensis*, large leaves colouring to scarlet, Manchuria; *coignetiae*, enormous leaves colouring to yellow, orange and crimson, very vigorous, Japan; *davidii*, shoots spiny, leaves dark green colouring scarlet, edible fruits, China; *flexuosa*, slender climber, small glossy green leaves, Japan, China, and var. *parvifolia*, leaves a metallic bronze-green; *labrusca*, Fox Grape, vigorous, leaves variable, dark green above, white or rust coloured beneath, edible musk-flavoured grapes, Eastern U.S.A.; *riparia* (syns. *odoratissima*, *vulpina*), vigorous, scented flowers, Eastern N. America, *vinifera*, Grape Vine, vigorous, many varieties such as Brandt, leaves becoming purple in autumn, purplish black grapes, *incana*, Dusty Milk Grape, leaves grey-green, cobwebby, black grapes, *purpurea*, Teinturier Grape, leaves red-purple, bluish-purple grapes.

VRIESEA – *Bromeliaceae*. Tender epiphytic perennials with rosettes of rather stiff leaves around a central 'vase' and spikes of flowers in sheaths of coloured bracts.

Compost, equal parts peat, osmunda fibre, and sand. Position, pots in an intermediate or warm greenhouse, minimum winter temp. 13°C. or in a warm room. Pot in spring. Water normally and keep the 'vase' in the centre of each rosette constantly full of water. Maintain a moist atmosphere and shade in spring and summer.

Increase by offsets inserted in small pots of sandy peat in temp. 24 to 26°C.

Recommended kinds are *V. carinata*, Painted Feather, yellow and red, autumn, 6 to 8 in., Brazil; *fenestralis*, greenish yellow, summer, leaves marked brown, to 1½ ft., Brazil; *hieroglyphica*, yellowish, spring, leaves banded dark green and brown, 1 ft., Brazil; *saundersii* (syn. *Encholirium saundersii*), yellow, summer, leaves green, grey and red, 1½ ft., Brazil; *splendens* (syns. *speciosa*, *Tillandsia zebrina*), yellow and red, late summer, leaves dark green banded purple, 1½ to 2 ft., Guyana.

See also Tillandsia.

WAHLENBERGIA (Bellflower) – *Campanulaceae*. Hardy perennial herbs with slender growth and bell-shaped flowers.

Soil, well-drained gritty loam, containing plenty of well-rotted leafmould. Position, sunny, reasonably moist during the summer months but well drained in winter. Protect Australasian species with handlights during the winter. Plant in spring. Some kinds such as *W. albo-marginata* and *hederacea* may be treated as annuals or biennials.

Increase by seeds sown in loam, leafmould and sand in a frame or greenhouse as soon as ripe or in spring; by cuttings in a propagator in summer; by division in spring.

Recommended kinds are *W. albo-marginata*, white or blue, early summer, 3 to 6 in., New Zealand, frequently wrongly named *saxicola*; *hederacea* (syn. *Campanula hederacea*), Creeping Harebell, blue, summer, trailing, Europe (Britain); *matthewsii*, lilac and white, summer, 4 in., New Zealand; *saxicola*, white or pale blue, late spring, 3 to 4 in., Tasmania.

See also Edraianthus.

WALDSTEINIA – *Rosaceae*. Hardy perennial herbs with attractive foliage and flowers in loose sprays.

Soil, ordinary. Position, sunny or partially shady. Plant in spring or autumn. Cut away flower stems in late summer.

Increase by seeds sown in a frame or outdoors in spring or as soon as ripe; by division in spring or autumn.

Recommended kinds are *W. fragarioides*, Barren Strawberry, yellow, late spring, early summer, 6 in., N. America; *ternata* (syns. *trifolia*, *sibirica*), yellow, summer, 3 to 4 in., foliage colours in autumn, Europe.

WATSONIA (Bugle Lily) – *Iridaceae*. Slightly tender cormous perennials with flowers in spikes rather like gladioli. All those listed are natives of S. Africa.

Soil, deep, moderately rich loam with some peat or leafmould. Position, warm, sunny, sheltered, well drained. Plant in spring. Place corms 4 in. deep and 6 in. apart with a little sharp sand under each. Protect in winter with cloches or dry litter. Lift and split up clusters of corms every three or four years.

Increase by seeds sown in John Innes seed compost or equivalent in temp. 13 to 15°C. in spring or as soon as ripe; division of corm clusters in spring.

Recommended kinds are *W. ardernei*, white, summer, 3 ft.; *beatricis*, red, summer, 3 ft.; *coccinea*, scarlet, summer, 1 ft.; *comptonii*, scarlet, summer, 2½ ft.; *densiflora*, rose, summer, 2 ft.; *humilis*, pink, summer, 9 to 18 in.; *longifolia*, white, pink or red, summer, 4 ft.; *marginata*, pink, summer, 4 to 5 ft.; *meriana*, pink or rose, late spring, early summer, 3 ft.; *pyramidata*, rose, early summer, 4 ft.; *stanfordiae*, rose-purple, summer, 3 to 4 ft.

WEIGELA – *Caprifoliaceae*. Hardy deciduous flowering shrubs, formerly included in *Diervilla*.

Soil, ordinary, fairly rich. Position, sun or slight shade. Prune directly after flowering by shortening shoots that have borne flowers.

Increase by cuttings of firm young shoots in sandy soil in a propagator in summer; by cuttings of firm shoots in a frame in autumn; by layering in autumn.

Recommended kinds are *W. coraeensis* (syn. *Diervilla grandiflora*), pale rose to carmine, early summer, to 15 ft., Japan; *florida* (syn. *rosea*), rose, late spring, early summer, 4 to 6 ft., China, Korea, Japan, and vars. *foliis purpureis*, purplish leaves, pink flowers, *variegata*, leaves edged cream, pale pink flowers, *venusta*, free flowering, hardy; *hortensis*, carmine, late spring, early summer, 6 to 8 ft., Japan, var. *nivea*, white; *japonica*, pale rose, late spring, 6 to 7 ft., Japan; *middendorffiana*, sulphur yellow, spring, 4 ft., Japan, China; *praecox*, rose, late spring, to 6 ft., Korea, Japan. There are also numerous garden varieties of mixed parentage all growing about 5 ft. high, flowering in late spring and early summer, and with a colour range from white and pale pink to crimson.

WISTERIA – *Leguminosae*. Hardy deciduous climbing flowering shrubs. Flowers pea-like in pendent racemes. Often, but not originally, spelt wistaria.

Soil, good, loamy. Position, full sun on walls, pergolas, arbours, trellis or scrambling over a tree. Easily trained as a bush or standard. Plant in spring. Prune in midsummer, shortening side growths to five leaves and, if necessary, again in winter when side growths can be further shortened to two growth buds and unwanted extension growths removed. Large plants growing over trees, etc., need not be pruned.

Increase by layering young shoots in spring or summer; by cuttings of firm young growth in a propagator in summer or riper cuttings in a frame in autumn; species by seeds soaked in warm water for several hours and then sown in a temp. 15 to 18°C.

Recommended kinds are *W. floribunda*, Japanese Wisteria, violet-blue, scented, late spring, early summer, to 15 ft., Japan, and vars. *alba* (syn. *multijuga alba*), white, extra long racemes, *macrobotrys* (syn. *W. macrobotrys*), racemes up to 3 ft. long, *rosea* (syn. *multijuga rosea*), pale pink, extra long racemes; *sinensis*, Chinese Wisteria, deep lilac, scented, late spring, early summer, 40 to 60 ft., China, and vars. *alba*, white, Black Dragon, purple, double, *plena*, lilac, double; *venusta*, white, late spring, early summer, 20 to 30 ft., Japan, and var. *violacea*, violet.

WOODWARDIA (Chain Fern) – *Blechnaceae*. Hardy or slightly tender evergreen ferns, some with very large fronds.

Soil, rather acid peat or leafmould and loam. Position, moist, shady beds outdoors or tender kinds in a shady frost-proof greenhouse. Plant in spring. Keep fairly moist throughout the year. *W. areolata* and *virginica* are bog species but *radicans* will thrive in drier conditions.

Increase by spores sown on the surface of fine peat in well-drained pans in a cool greenhouse in spring or summer; by division of plants in spring.

Recommended kinds are *W. areolata*, 1½ to 2 ft., Eastern U.S.A.; *radicans*, 3 to 8 ft., Canary Islands, S. Europe, Asia; *virginica*, 3 to 4 ft., Eastern N. America.

WULFENIA – *Scrophulariaceae*. Hardy herbaceous perennials with tubular flowers in short spikes.

Soil, reasonably fertile sandy loam. Position, partially shady, moist in summer but well drained in winter.

Increase by seeds sown in a frame in spring; by division in spring.

Recommended kinds are *W. baldaccii*, blue, summer, 3 to 6 in., Balkans; *carinthiaca*, violet, summer, 1 ft., Carinthia; *orientalis*, heliotrope, late spring, 9 to 15 in., Asia Minor.

XANTHERANTHEMUM – *Acanthaceae*. Tender sub-shrub with ornamental foliage.

Compost, John Innes potting compost No. 1 or equivalent. Position, pots in an intermediate or warm greenhouse, minimum winter temp. 13°C., or in a warm room. Water moderately in spring and summer, rather sparingly in autumn and winter. Shade from strong sunshine in spring and summer and maintain a moist atmosphere.

Increase by cuttings in a warm propagator in spring or summer.

The only species is *X. igneum* (syns. *Chameranthemum igneum, Eranthemum igneum*), leaves green, yellow veined, sprawling, Peru.

XANTHOCERAS – *Sapindaceae*. Hardy deciduous flowering tree with flowers in erect panicles.

Soil, ordinary, fertile, moist, not very satisfactory on chalk. Position, shady. Plant in autumn or late winter.

Increase by seeds sown in light soil outdoors in autumn or spring or by root cuttings inserted in pans of sandy soil in a cool greenhouse in winter.

The only species is *X. sorbifolium*, white, stained carmine, late spring, 10 to 20 ft., China.

XERANTHEMUM (Immortelle) – *Compositae*. Hardy annuals with chaffy, daisy-type flowers which last for a long time. Flowers, single and double, suitable for winter decoration.

Soil, ordinary, well drained. Position, sunny. Sow seeds in spring outdoors where plants are to flower and thin to 6 in., or sow in John Innes seed compost or equivalent in early spring in temp. 15 to 18°C., harden off seedlings and plant out in late spring or early summer. Gather flowers for winter decoration directly they are fully expanded. Discard after flowering.

The best kind is *X. annuum*, purple, summer, 2 ft., S. Europe, and vars. *album*, white, *roseum*, pink, *ligulosum*, double, and *perligulosum* (syn. *superbissimum*), very double.

YUCCA – *Agavaceae*. Hardy and rather tender evergreen shrubs or small trees with rosettes of sword-shaped leaves and flowers in stiffly erect racemes.

Yucca gloriosa

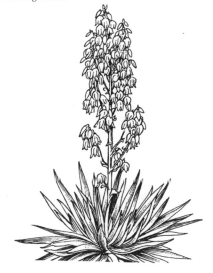

Soil, ordinary, light, well drained. Position, warm, sunny. Plant in spring or autumn. Protect the tender kinds in severe weather with mats or grow in a sunny, frost-proof greenhouse.

Increase by offsets or suckers in spring; by root cuttings inserted in sand in temp. 15 to 18°C. in spring.

Recommended kinds are *Y. aloifolia*, Spanish Bayonet, creamy white, summer, 10 to 24 ft., rather tender, Southern U.S.A. and Mexico, and vars. *draconis*, leaves drooping, *tricolor*, leaves variegated with white, green and yellow, and *variegata*, leaves striped with white; *filamentosa*, Adam's Needle, creamy, summer, 3 to 6 ft., South-eastern U.S.A., and var. *variegata*, leaves variegated yellow or white; *flaccida*, creamy, summer, 3 to 4 ft., hardy, South-eastern U.S.A.; *glauca* (syn. *angustifolia*), greenish white, summer, Southern U.S.A.; *gloriosa*, Spanish Dagger, creamy, summer, early autumn, 6 to 9 ft., Southern U.S.A., and var. *variegata*, leaves striped light yellow; *recurvifolia*, leaves recurving, creamy, summer, to 6 ft., hardy and of easy culture, South-eastern U.S.A., and var. *variegata*, two shades of green; *whipplei*, greenish white, scented, late spring, early summer, 6 to 10 ft., rather tender, California.

ZANTEDESCHIA (Arum or Calla Lily) – *Araceae*. Tender rhizomatous perennials with small flowers crowded in a spike-like spadix and enclosed in a large spathe. Formerly known as richardia.

Compost, John Innes potting compost No. 1 or equivalent. Position, pots in a cool or intermediate greenhouse, minimum winter temp. 7°C., or *Z. aethiopica* outdoors in mild localities, where frosts are neither severe nor prolonged. It will thrive in open or shady places in ordinary or boggy soil and is often grown at the margins of pools in water 3 or 4 in. deep. Pot or plant in late summer. Water pot plants sparingly at first, moderately as growth appears, freely in spring but reduce the supply after flowering and keep plants nearly dry for a few weeks before repotting. *Z. elliottiana* does best in the warmer atmosphere of the intermediate house, minimum temp. 13°C.

Increase by seeds sown in John Innes seed compost or equivalent in temp. 18 to 21°C. in spring; by division of plants when planting or repotting.

Recommended kinds are *Z. aethiopica* (syn. *Richardia africana*), white, spring, 3 to 4 ft., S. Africa, and vars. Crowborough, hardier than the type, Little Gem (syn. *compacta*), 1 to 1½ ft., *viridiflora*, spathes splashed with green; *albo-maculata* yellow, sometimes purple at the base, summer, 2 ft., leaves spotted white, S. Africa; *elliottiana*, yellow, late spring, early summer, 3 ft., S. Africa; *pentlandii*, yellow, early summer, 2 ft., S. Africa; *rehmannii*, pink to rosy purple, spring, early summer, 2 ft., Natal.

ZANTHOXYLUM – *Rutaceae*. Hardy deciduous, usually prickly shrubs or trees with aromatic young branches, flowers insignificant.

Soil, ordinary. Position, sunny or partially shady. Plant in autumn or late winter.

Increase by seeds stratified for three months at 20 to 30°C. and then for a further four months at 4°C. before sowing in a frame or cool greenhouse; by root cuttings in winter.

Recommended kinds are *Z. ailanthoides*, greenish yellow, early autumn, large compound leaves, 15 to 20 ft., Japan, Korea, China, Formosa; *americanum*, Prickly Ash, yellowish green, spring, 15 to 20 ft., Eastern N. America; *piperitum*, greenish yellow, late spring, early summer, 10 to 15 ft., Japan, Korea, China; *planispinum*, yellow, spring, 8 to 12 ft., Japan, Korea, China, Formosa; *schinifolium*, green, late summer, 10 to 15 ft., Japan, Korea, China; *simulans* (syn. *bungei*), greenish yellow, early summer, 6 to 10 ft., China.

ZAUSCHNERIA – *Onagraceae*. Slightly tender sub-shrubs with showy tubular flowers.

Soil, sandy loam. Position, warm, sunny, well-drained rock garden, raised bed or unmortared terrace wall. Plant in spring. Remove dead or damaged growth in spring.

Increase by seeds sown in light, sandy soil in spring in a temp. of 15 to 18°C.; by cuttings of young side shoots inserted in sandy soil in a propagator in summer, protect the rooted cuttings in a greenhouse until the following spring, then plant out; also by division of old plants in spring.

Recommended kinds are *Z. californica*, Californian Fuchsia, scarlet, late summer, autumn, 1 to 2 ft., California; *cana* (syn. *microphylla*), scarlet, to 2½ ft., California.

ZEA – *Gramineae*. Tender annual with broad, grass-like leaves, green or variegated with white and seeds in 'cobs'.

Sow seeds individually in small pots in spring in John Innes seed compost or equivalent and temp. 15 to 18°C., or sow outdoors in late spring where plants are to grow. Plant out pot-grown seedlings in late spring or early summer, when there is little danger of frost, in good soil and a warm, sunny position. Water freely in dry weather. Gather cobs of ornamental-seeded varieties when ripe. It is best to plant ornamental-seeded varieties in blocks or groups of several plants for cross pollination and to assist this further by shaking the plants when the flower tassels are well developed to distribute the pollen.

The only kind is *Z. mays*, Maize, Indian Corn, 3 to 12 ft., habitat uncertain, available in ornamental varieties with white- or yellow-striped leaves and with white, yellow, red or black seeds, often several colours in the same cob.

ZEBRINA – *Commelinaceae*. Tender herbaceous trailing perennials with ornamental leaves.

Compost, John Innes potting compost No. 1 or equivalent. Position, pots or baskets in a cool or intermediate greenhouse, minimum winter temp. 7°C., or in a light room. Water normally. Shade from strong sunshine but leaf colours are best in good light. Pot in spring.

Increase by cuttings of young shoots inserted in light soil in a warm propagator in spring or summer.

Recommended kinds are *Z. pendula* (syn. *Tradescantia zebrina*), Wandering Jew, foliage striped dark green, grey-green and purple, purple beneath, trailing, Mexico, and var. *quadricolor*, foliage striped with red, white and shades of green; *purpusii* (syn. *Tradescantia purpurea*), leaves in shades of purple, trailing, Mexico.

ZELKOVA – *Ulmaceae*. Hardy deciduous trees, closely allied to and resembling the elms.

Soil, deep, moist loam. Position, open, sunny, beside lakes, streams and in similar damp places. Plant in autumn or late winter.

Increase by seeds sown outdoors or under glass as soon as ripe; by cuttings of firm young growth in a propagator in summer.

Recommended kinds are *Z. carpinifolia* (syn. *crenata*), to 80 ft., Caucasus; *serrata* (syn. *acuminata*), to 100 ft., leaves turn bronze-red in autumn, Japan, Korea, China.

ZENOBIA – *Ericaceae*. Hardy deciduous or semi-evergreen flowering shrub with attractive lily of the valley-like flowers.

Soil, peat or sandy loam, lime free. Position, semi-shade. Plant in spring or autumn. Prune to prevent seed formation by cutting away portions of shoots which have flowered as soon as the flowers fade.

Increase by cuttings of half-ripe shoots inserted in sandy soil in a propagator in summer; by layering in spring or autumn.

The only species is *Z. pulverulenta* (syn. *speciosa*), white, waxy, summer, fragrant, 4 to 6 ft., Eastern U.S.A., and var. *nuda*, leaves green, flowers smaller.

ZEPHYRANTHES (Zephyr Lily, Flower of the West Wind) – *Amaryllidaceae*. Hardy and tender bulbous-rooted perennials with funnel-shaped flowers.

Soil, light, sandy loam. Position, well drained, sunny. Plant in autumn or spring, placing bulbs 3 in. deep. Protect in winter by a layer of sand, peat or dry litter. Lift and replant only when bulbs show signs of deterioration. Alternatively, grow in John Innes potting compost No. 1 or equivalent in well-drained pots in a sunny frame or

Zenobia pulverulenta

greenhouse with minimum winter temp. 7°C. Pot in autumn, placing four or five bulbs in each 5-in. pot. Water very little till growth begins, then freely. Withhold water when leaves wither and keep soil quite dry till potting time.

Increase by offsets removed in autumn and treated as advised for large bulbs.

Recommended kinds are *Z. atamasco*, white and pink, spring, 6 to 10 in., tender, South-eastern U.S.A.; *candida*, white, autumn, 4 to 8 in., Argentina, Uruguay; *citrina*, yellow, autumn, 6 in., tender, British Guiana; *grandiflora*, pink, summer, 5 to 9 in., Guatemala, slightly tender, West Indies; *rosea*, pink, late summer, autumn, 4 to 6 in., tender, West Indies.

ZIGADENUS – *Liliaceae*. Hardy herbaceous plants, some with bulbs and with flowers in loose spikes.

Soil, equal parts loam, peat, leafmould and sand. Position, partially shady, moist. Plant in autumn.

Increase by division in autumn; by seeds sown in sandy soil in a frame in spring.

Recommended kinds are *Z. elegans*, green and white, summer, 1 ft., N. America; *glaucus*, creamy white, late summer, early autumn, 1 ft., N. America; *nuttallii*, greenish white, early summer, 6 to 18 in., Southern U.S.A.

ZINGIBER – *Zingiberaceae*. Tender perennials with fleshy roots, handsome leaves and flowers in spikes.

Compost, John Innes potting compost No. 1 or equivalent. Position, pots or beds in a warm greenhouse, minimum winter temp. 18°C. Pot in spring. Water freely from spring to autumn, little in winter. No shade required at any time.

Increase by division of the rhizomes in late winter.

Recommended kinds are *Z. officinale*, Ginger, yellowish green and purple, summer, to 3 ft., Tropical Asia; *spectabile*, red and yellow, summer, 5 to 6 ft., Malaysia.

ZINNIA (Youth-and-old-age) – *Compositae*. Slightly tender annuals with showy daisy-type flowers.

Soil, reasonably fertile, porous loam. Position, warm, sunny. Sow seeds in John Innes seed compost or equivalent in temp. 13 to 15°C. in spring. Transplant seedlings when third leaf forms 2 in. apart in shallow boxes filled with John Innes potting compost No. 1 or equivalent and harden off for planting outdoors in late spring or early summer. Alternatively, sow in late spring outdoors where plants are to flower and thin seedlings to about 9 in. Water liberally in dry weather. Apply weak liquid fertilizer when the plants start to flower. Discard after flowering.

Recommended kinds are *Z. angustifolia* (syn. *haageana*), orange-scarlet, summer, 1 ft., Tropical America; *elegans*, yellow, orange, pink, scarlet, crimson, purple, summer, 2 to 3 ft., Mexico, and many garden varieties from ½ to 2 ft., with single, semi-double and fully double flowers.

ZYGOPETALUM – *Orchidaceae*. Tender terrestrial or epiphytic orchids with flowers in erect spikes.

Compost, equal parts fibre, sphagnum moss and leafmould or peat. Position, well-drained pots. Grow in an equable temperature of 11 to 18°C., as for odontoglossums. Shade in spring and summer from direct sunshine. Repot when necessary in spring. Water liberally in summer, infrequently in winter.

Increase by division of the plants in spring.

Recommended kinds are *Z. crinitum*, greenish yellow and brown, lip white veined purple, autumn, winter, scented, 1 to 1½ ft., Brazil; *intermedium*, yellowish green, flushed or blotched red-brown, lip whitish lined and spotted violet-purple, autumn, winter, scented, 1 to 2½ ft., Brazil; *mackaii*, greenish yellow blotched brown, lip white lined purple, autumn, winter, scented, 15 to 30 in., Brazil, much confused with *intermedium* which it closely resembles.

INDEX OF COMMON NAMES
& SYNONYMS

A

Aaron's Beard see Hypericum
Aaron's Rod see Verbascum
Abele see Populus
Absinthium see Artemisia
Acacia, False, see Robinia
Acacia, Rose, see Robinia
Aconite see Aconitum
Aconite, Winter, see Eranthis
Acroclinium see Helipterum
Adam's Needle see Yucca
Adder's Fern see Polypodium
Adder's Tongue see
  Polypodium
Adder's Tongue, Yellow, see
  Erythronium
Aegle see Poncirus
African Corn Lily see Ixia
African Daisy see Arctotis
African Hemp see Sparmannia
African Lily see Agapanthus
African Marigold see Tagetes
African Ragwort see Othonna
African Violet see Saintpaulia
Agathaea see Felicia
Agrostemma see Lychnis
Alder see Alnus
Alder, White, see Clethra
Alexandrian Laurel see Danaë
Alkanet see Anchusa
Alligator Pear see Persea
Allspice see Calycanthus
Almond see Prunus
Aloe, American, see Agave
Aloysia see Lippia
Alpine Totara see Podocarpus
Aluminium Plant see Pilea
Alum Root see Heuchera
Alyssum, Sweet, see Lobularia
Amaranth see Amaranthus and
  Gomphrena
Amaryllis see Hippeastrum
Amazon Lily see Eucharis
American Aloe see Agave
American Cowslip see
  Dodecatheon
American Currant see Ribes
American Ground Laurel see
  Epigaea
American Laurel see Kalmia
American Spikenard see Aralia
American Swamp Lily see
  Saururus
Ampelopsis see Parthenocissus
Amygdalus see Prunus
Anchor Plant see Colletia
Andromeda see also Pieris and
  Cassiope
Angelica Tree see Aralia
Angel's Tears see Narcissus
Angel's Trumpet see Datura
Angola Hemp see Sansevieria
Aniseed Tree see Illicium
Apple see Malus
Apple Berry see Billardiera
Apple, Malay, see Eugenia
Apple, Rose, see Eugenia
Apple of Peru see Nicandra

Apricot see Prunus
Aralia, Japanese, see Fatsia
Arbor-vitae see Thuja
Arbutus, Trailing, see Epigaea
Archangel, Yellow, see Lamium
Aregelia see Neoregelia
Arrowhead see Sagittaria
Arrowroot see Maranta
Artichoke, Globe, see Cynara
Artillery Plant see Pilea
Arum see also Helicodiceros
Arum, Bog, see Calla
Arum, Devil, see Dracunculus
Arum Lily see Zantedeschia
Asarina see Antirrhinum
Ash see Fraxinus
Ash, Mountain, see Sorbus
Ash, Prickly, see Zanthoxylum
Ash, Wafer, see Ptelea
Aspen see Populus
Asphodel see Asphodeline,
  Asphodelus
Aspidium see Dryopteris
Aster, Beach, see Erigeron
Aster, China, see Callistephus
Aster, Stoke's, see Stokesia
Auricula see Primula
Autumn Crocus see Colchicum
Avens see Geum
Avocado Pear see Persea
Australian Bluebell Creeper
  see Sollya
Australian Brake see Pteris
Australian Brush Cherry see
  Eugenia
Australian Everlasting Flower
  see Helipterum
Australian Fuchsia see Correa
Australian Heath see Epacris
Australian Honeysuckle see
  Banksia
Australian Native Rose see
  Boronia
Austrocedrus see Libocedrus
Azalea see Rhododendron
Azarole see Crataegus

B

Baboon Root see Babiana
Baby Blue-eyes see Nemophila
Baby's Tears see Soleirolia
Badger's Bane see Aconitum
Balloon Flower see Platycodon
Balm see Melissa
Balm, Bastard, see Melittis
Balm, Bee, see Monarda
Balm of Gilead see Populus
Balsam, Western, see Populus
Bamboo see Arundinaria,
  Bambusa and Sasa
Bamboo, Black, see
  Phyllostachys
Bamboo, Sacred, see Nandina
Banana see Musa
Baneberry see Actaea
Banyan see Ficus
Barbados Flower Fence see
  Caesalpinia

Barbados Gooseberry see Pereskia
Barbados Lily see
  Hippeastrum
Barbary Fig see Opuntia
Barberry see Berberis
Barberton Daisy see Gerbera
Barrel Cactus see Ferocactus
Barren Strawberry see Waldsteinia
Barrenwort see Epimedium
Bartonia see Mentzelia
Basket Grass see Oplismenus
Basswood see Tilia
Bastard Balm see Melittis
Bastard Box see Polygala
Bastard Cyperus see Carex
Bastard Jasmine see Cestrum
Batchelor's Buttons see
  Ranunculus
Bayberry, Californian, see Myrica
Bay, Loblolly, see Gordonia
Bay, Swamp, see Magnolia
Bay, Sweet, see Magnolia
Bay Tree see Laurus
Beach Aster see Erigeron
Bead Plant see Nertera
Bead Tree see Melia
Bean Lily see Nymphoides
Bearberry see Arctostaphylos
Beard Tongue see Penstemon
Bear's Breech see Acanthus
Beauty Bush see Kolkwitzia
Bee Balm see Monarda
Beech see Fagus and Nothofagus
Beech Fern see Dryopteris
Beech Wormwood see Artemisia
Belladonna Lily see Amaryllis
Bellflower see Campanula and
  Wahlenbergia
Bellflower, Chilean, see
  Lapageria and Nolana
Bell Flower, Chinese, see
  Platycodon
Bell Flower, Giant, see Ostrowskia
Bellflower, Pendulous, see
  Symphyandra
Bell Heather see Erica
Bellwort see Uvularia
Benjamin Bush see Lindera
Bergamot, Sweet, see Monarda
Bermuda Buttercup see Oxalis
Bethlehem Sage see Pulmonaria
Betonica see Stachys
Betony see Stachys
Big Tree see Sequoiadendron
Bilberry see Vaccinium
Bindweed see Convolvulus
Birch see Betula
Bird Cherry see Prunus
Bird of Paradise Flower see
  Strelitzia
Bird's-foot Trefoil see Lotus
Birthwort see Aristolochia
Bishop's Cap see Mitella
Bishop's Hat see Epimedium
Bishop's-wort see Stachys
Bistort see Polygonum
Bitter Cress see Cardamine
Bitter Nut see Carya
Bitterwort see Lewisia

Black Bamboo see Phyllostachys
Blackberry see Rubus
Blackcurrant, American, see Ribes
Black-eyed Clockvine see
  Thunbergia
Black-eyed Susan see
  Rudbeckia and Thunbergia
Blacking Plant see Hibiscus
Black Locust see Robinia
Bladder Fern see Cystopteris
Bladder Herb see Physalis
Bladder Nut see Staphylea
Bladder Senna see Colutea
Bladderwort see Utricularia
Blaeberry see Vaccinium
Blanket Flower see Gaillardia
Blazing Star see Liatris, Mentzelia
Bleeding Heart see Dicentra
Blessed Thistle see Cnicus and
  Silybum
Bletia see Bletilla
Blood Flower see Asclepias
  and Haemanthus
Blood Lily see Haemanthus
Bloodroot see Sanguinaria
Bluebeard see Caryopteris
Bluebell see Endymion
Bluebell Creeper, Australian,
  see Sollya
Bluebells, Small, see Mertensia
Blueberry see Vaccinium
Blue Cowslip see Pulmonaria
Blue Cupidone see Catananche
Blue Daisy see Felicia
Blue Dicks see Dichelostemma
Blue-eyed Grass see Sisyrinchium
Blue-eyed Mary see Collinsia
  and Omphalodes
Blue Grass see Carex
Blue Gum see Eucalyptus
Blue Marguerite see Felicia
Blue Lace Flower see Trachymene
Blue Moonwort see Soldanella
Blue Poppy see Meconopsis
Blue Spiraea see Caryopteris
Bluets see Houstonia
Bocconia see Macleaya
Bog Arum see Calla
Bog Bean see Menyanthes
Bog Myrtle see Myrica
Bog Rosemary see Andromeda
Bog Violet see Pinguicula
Bonavist see Dolichos
Borage see Borago
Borage, Fairy, see Eritrichium
Bottle Brush Tree see
  Callistemon, Melaleuca and
  Metrosideros
Bottle Gourd see Lagenaria
Bouncing Bet see Saponaria
Bowles' Golden Grass see Milium
Bowstring Hemp see Sansevieria
Box see Buxus
Box, Bastard, see Polygala
Box Elder see *Acer negundo*
Box, Jasmine, see Phillyrea
Box, Sweet, see Sarcococca
Boxthorn see Lycium
Box, Victorian, see Pittosporum

Bramble, Whitewash, see Rubus
Brandy Bottle see Nuphar
Brazilian Glory Bush see
  Tibouchina
Briar see Rosa
Bridal Wreath see Francoa
  and Spiraea
Bristle Fern see Trichomanes
Brittonastrum see Agastache
Brome Grass see Bromus
Broom see Cytisus, Genista
  and Spartium
Broom, Hedgehog, see Erinacea
Broom, New Zealand, see
  Notospartium
Broom, Spanish, see Spartium
Buck Bean see Menyanthes
Buckeye see Aesculus
Buckler Fern see Dryopteris
Buckthorn see Rhamnus
Buckthorn, Sea, see Hippophaë
Bugbane see Cimicifuga
Bugle see Ajuga
Bugle Lily see Watsonia
Bugloss see Anchusa
Bullock's Heart see Annona
Bulrush see Scirpus
Bunya-bunya Tree see Araucaria
Burnet see Sanguisorba
Burning Bush see Dictamnus
  or Kochia
Burro's-tail Stonecrop see Sedum
Bush Clover see Lespedeza
Bush Honeysuckle see Diervilla
Busy Lizzie see Impatiens
Butcher's Broom see Ruscus
Butter and Eggs see Linaria
Buttercup see Ranunculus
Buttercup, Bermuda, see Oxalis
Butterfly Bush see Buddleia
Butterfly Flower see
  Schizanthus, Bauhinia
Butterfly Iris see Moraea
Butterfly Milkweed see
  Asclepias
Butterfly Orchid see Oncidium
Butterfly Tree see Bauhinia
Butterfly Tulip see Calochortus
Butternut see Juglans
Butterwort see Pinguicula
Button-wood see Platanus
Button Snake-root see Liatris

C

Cactus, Barrel, see Ferocactus
Cactus, Candlemas, see
  Schlumbergera
Cactus, Christmas, see
  Schlumbergera
Cactus, Crab, see
  Schlumbergera
Cactus, Easter, see Rhipsalidopsis
Cactus, Hedgehog, see Ferocactus
Cactus, Leaf-flowering, see
  Schlumbergera
Cactus, Lobster, see
  Schlumbergera
Cactus, Mistletoe, see Rhipsalis

Cactus, Old Man, see
  Cephalocereus
Cactus, Rainbow, see Echinocereus
Cajeput Tree see Melaleuca
Calabazilla see Cucurbita
Calamint see Calamintha
Calamondin Orange see Citrus
Calico Bush see Kalmia
Calico Flower see Aristolochia
Californian Bayberry see Myrica
Californian Big Tree see
  Sequoiadendron
Californian Firecrackers see
  Dichelostemma
Californian Fuchsia see
  Zauschneria
Californian Mock Orange see
  Carpenteria, Philadelphus
Californian Nutmeg see Torreya
Californian Pitcher Plant see
  Darlingtonia
Californian Poppy see Eschscholzia
Californian Redwood see Sequoia
Californian Tree Poppy see
  Romneya
Calla Lily see Zantedeschia
Callicore see Amaryllis
Calliopsis see Coreopsis
Calocedrus see Libocedrus
Calvary Clover see Medicago
Campernelle see Narcissus
Campion see Lychnis and Silene
Campion, Moss, see Silene
Canada Tea see Gaultheria
Canary Creeper see Tropaeolum
Canary Grass see Phalaris
Candle-berry see Myrica
Candle Bush see Cassia
Candlemas Cactus see
  Schlumbergera
Candle Plant see Kleinia
Candytuft see Iberis
Candytuft, Lebanon, see
  Aethionema
Cane Reed see Arundinaria
Canterbury Bell see Campanula
Cape Cowslip see Lachenalia
Cape Figwort see Phygelius
Cape Fuchsia see Phygelius
Cape Gooseberry see Physalis
Cape Honey Flower see
  Melianthus
Cape Jasmine see Gardenia
Cape Leadwort see Plumbago
Cape Lily see Crinum
Cape Marigold see Dimorphotheca
Cape Pondweed see Aponogeton
Cape Primrose see Streptocarpus
Caper Spurge see *Euphorbia
  lathyrus*
Cape Silver Tree see
  Leucadendron
Capsicum, Star, see Solanum
Cardinal Flower see Lobelia
Cardoon see Cynara
Carline Thistle see Carlina
Carnation see Dianthus
Carolina Allspice see Calycanthus
Carosella see Foeniculum
Carpenter's Leaf see Galax
Carpet Plant see Ionopsidium
Carrion Flower see Stapelia
Cartwheel Flower see Heracleum
Castor Oil Plant see Ricinus
Catchfly see Silene
Catmint see Nepeta
Cat's Chaps see Faucaria
Cat-tail see Typha
Cat Thyme see Teucrium
Cedar see Cedrus
Cedar, Incense, see Libocedrus
Cedar, Japanese, see Cryptomeria
Cedar, Pencil, see Juniperus
Cedar, Red, se Juniperus
Cedar, Western Red, see Thuja

Cedar, White, see Chamaecyparis
Celandine see Ranunculus
Celandine, Greater, see
  Chelidonium
Celandine, Tree, see Macleaya
Century Plant see Agave
Cerasus see Prunus
Chain Fern see Woodwardia
Chalice Vine see Solandra
Chalk Plant see Gypsophila
Chamaedorea elegans see Collinia
Chamomile see Anthemis
Chamomile, False, see Boltonia
Chamomile, Red, see Adonis
Chaste Tree see Vitex
Chatham Island Forget-me-not
  see Myosotidium
Checker-berry see Gaultheria
Chenille Plant see Acalypha
Cherimoyer see Annona
Cherry see Prunus
Cherry, Australian Brush, see
  Eugenia
Cherry Laurel see Prunus
Cherry Pie see Heliotrope
Cherry Plum see Prunus
Cherry, Winter, see Physalis and
  Solanum
Chestnut see Castanea, Aesculus
Chestnut, Water, see Trapa
Chilean Bellflower see
  Lapageria and Nolana
Chilean Crocus see Tecophilaea
Chilean Fire Bush see
  Embothrium
Chilean Glory Flower see
  Eccremocarpus
Chilean Guava see Myrtus
Chilean Jasmine see Mandevilla
Chile Pine see Araucaria
Chile Rhubarb see Gunnera
China Aster see Callistephus
Chinaberry see Melia
Chinaman's Breeches see Dicentra
Chinaman's Pigtail see Impatiens
China Tree see Koelreuteria,
  Melia
Chincherinchee see Ornithogalum
Chinese Bell Flower see Platycodon
Chinese Fir see Cunninghamia
Chinese Flame Tree see
  Koelreuteria
Chinese Gooseberry see Actinidia
Chinese Hawthorn see Photinia
Chinese Jasmine see
  Trachelospermum
Chinese Pistachio see Pistacia
Chinese Sour Gum see Nyssa
Chinkapin see Nelumbo
Chinquapin see Castanea
Chokeberry see Aronia
Christmas Cactus see
  Schlumbergera
Christmas Pride see Ruellia
Christmas Tree see Picea
Chufa see Cyperus
Chusan Palm see Trachycarpus
Cicely, Sweet, see Myrrhis
Cicerbita see Lactuca
Cigar Flower see Cuphea
Cineraria see Senecio
Cinquefoil see Potentilla
Citron see Citrus
Clary see Salvia
Climbing Fern see Lygodium
Clog Plant see Hypocyrta
Clover, Bush, see Lespedeza
Clover, Calvary, see Medicago
Clove Tree see Eugenia
Club Lily see Kniphofia
Club Rush see Scirpus
Cobnut see Corylus
Cockscomb see Celosia
Cockspur Thorn see *Crataegus
  crus-galli*

Coconut Palm see Cocos
Coffee Tree, Kentucky, see
  Gymnocladus
Columbine see Aquilegia
Comfrey see Symphytum
Compass Plant see Silphium
Coneflower see Rudbeckia and
  Echinacea
Cone Head see Strobilanthes
Cone Plant see Conophytum
Constantinople Nut see Corylus
Convolvulus see also Ipomoea
Copper-leaf see Acalypha
Coppertip see Crocosmia
Coral Bells see Heuchera
Coral Berry see Symphoricarpos
Coral Gem see Lotus
Coral Plant see Berberidopsis
Coral Tree see Erythrina
Cornelian Cherry see Cornus
Cornflower see Centaurea
Corn Marigold see
  Chrysanthemum
Corytholoma see Rechsteineria
Cotton, Lavender, see Santolina
Cotton Thistle see Onopordum
Cottonwood see Populus
Cowberry see Vaccinium
Cow Lily see Nuphar
Cow Parsley see Heracleum
Cowslip see Primula
Cowslip, American, see
  Dodecatheon
Cowslip, Blue, see Pulmonaria
Cowslip, Cape, see Lachenalia
Cowslip, Jerusalem, see
  Pulmonaria
Cowslip, Virginian, see Mertensia
Cowslip, Water, see Caltha
Cow's Tail Pine see Cephalotaxus
Crab see Malus
Crab Cactus see Schlumbergera
Cradle Orchid see Angulosa
Cranberry see Vaccinium
Cranesbill see Geranium
Crape Myrtle see Lagerstroemia
Cream Cups see Platystemon
Creeping Forget-me-not see
  Omphalodes
Creeping Harebell see
  Wahlenbergia
Creeping Jenny see Lysimachia
Creeping Wintergreen see
  Gaultheria
Cress, Bitter, see Cardamine
Cress, Purple Rock, see Aubrieta
Cress, Rock, see Arabis
Cress, Violet, see Ionopsidium
Cress, Wall, see Arabis
Cretan Dittany see Origanum
Cretan Mullein see Celsia
Cretan Spikenard see Valeriana
Crimson Flag see Schizostylis
Crocus, Autumn, see Colchicum
Crocus, Chilean, see
  Tecophilaea
Crocus, Indian, see Pleione
Cross-wort, Caucasian, see
  Phuopsis
Croton see Codiaeum
Crowfoot see Ranunculus
Crown Imperial see Fritillaria
Crown of Thorns see Euphorbia
Crown Vetch see Coronilla
Crucianella see Phuopsis
Cuckoo Flower see Cardamine
Cuckoo Pint see Arum
Cucumber see Cucumis
Cucumber Tree see Magnolia
Cup Flower see Nierembergia
Cupid's Dart see Catananche
Cup, Indian, see Sarracenia
Cup Plant see Silphium
Cups and Saucers see Cobaea
Curly Palm see Howeia

Currant see Ribes
Currant, Indian, see
  Symphoricarpos
Curry Plant see Helichrysum
Cushion Pink see Silene
Custard Apple see Annona
Cyperus, Bastard, see Carex
Cypress see Cupressus,
  Chamaecyparis and
  Cupressocyparis
Cypress, Bald or Deciduous,
  see Taxodium
Cypress, False, see Chamaecyparis
Cypress, Lawson's, see
  Chamaecyparis
Cypress, Patagonian, see Fitz-Roya
Cypress, Summer, see Kochia
Cypress, Swamp, see Taxodium
Cypress Vine see Ipomoea

D

Daffodil see Narcissus
Daffodil, Sea, see Pancratium
Daffodil, Winter, see Sternbergia
Daisy see Bellis
Daisy, African, see Arctotis,
  Dimorphotheca and
  Osteospermum
Daisy, Barberton, see Gerbera
Daisy, Blue, see Felicia
Daisy Bush see Olearia
Daisy, False, see Bellium
Daisy, Globe, see Globularia
Daisy, Kingfisher, see Felicia
Daisy, Michaelmas, see Aster
Daisy, New Zealand, see Celmisia
Daisy, Orange, see Erigeron
Daisy, Shasta, see Chrysanthemum
Daisy, Swan River, see
  Brachycome
Daisy, Transvaal, see Gerbera
Dame's Rocket see Hesperis
Dame's Violet see Hesperis
Darling River Pea see Swainsona
Date Palm see Phoenix
Date Plum see Diospyros
David's Harp see Polygonatum
Dawn Redwood see Metasequoia
Day Flower see Commelina
Day Lily see Hemerocallis
Dead Nettle see Lamium
Deer Fern see Blechnum
Deodar see Cedrus
Devil-in-a-bush see Nigella
Devil's Walking Stick see Aralia
Diamond Lily see Nerine
Diamond Plant see Ionopsidium
Didiscus see Trachymene
Dielytra see Dicentra
Diervilla see Weigela
Dittany see Dictamnus
Dittany, Cretan, see Origanum
Dog's-tooth Violet see
  Erythronium
Dogwood see Cornus
Douglas Fir see Pseudotsuga
Dove Tree see Davidia
Dragon Arum see Dracunculus
Dragonhead see Dracocephalum
Dragonhead, False, see
  Physostegia
Dragon's Mouth see Helicodiceros
Dragon Tree see Dracaena
Dropwort see Filipendula
Duck Acorn see Nelumbo
Duck Potato see Sagittaria
Duck's Foot see Podophyllum
Duckweed, Fruiting, see Nertera
Duke of Argyll's Tea Tree see
  Lycium
Dumb Cane see Dieffenbachia
Dusty Miller see Anthemis,
  Centaurea gymnocarpa and
  Primula auricula

Dutchman's Breeches see
  Dicentra
Dutchman's Pipe see Aristolochia
Dyer's Greenweed see Genista

E

Earth Stars see Cryptanthus
Easter Cactus see Rhipsalidopsis
Edelweiss see Leontopodium
Eel grass see Vallisneria
Elder see Sambucus
Elder, Box, see *Acer negundo*
Elder, Water, see Viburnum
Elecampane see Inula
Elk's Horn Fern see Platycerium
Elm see Ulmus
Eulalia see Miscanthus
European Palm see Chamaerops
Evening Flower see Hesperantha
Evening Primrose see Oenothera
Everlasting Flowers see
  Anaphalis, Antennaria,
  Helichrysum, Helipterum,
  Limonium and Xeranthemum
Everlasting Pea see Lathyrus

F

Fair Maids of February see
  Galanthus
Fair Maids of France see
  Ranunculus
Fair Maids of Kent see
  Ranunculus
Fairy Borage see Eritrichium
Fairy Forget-me-not see
  Eritrichium
Fairy Moss see Azolla
False Acacia see Robinia
False Daisy see Bellium
False Goat's Beard see Astilbe
False Heath see Fabiana
False Hellebore see Veratrum
False Mitrewort see Tiarella
False Spikenard see Smilacina
False Spiraea see Sorbaria
Fan Palm see Chamaerops
Farewell to Spring see Godetia
Feather Grass see Stipa
Feather Hyacinth see Muscari
Feathertop see Pennisetum
Fennel see Foeniculum
Fennel Flower see Nigella
Fern, Asparagus, see Asparagus
Fern, Beech, see Dryopteris
Fern, Bladder, see Cystopteris
Fern, Bristle, see Trichomanes
Fern, Buckler, see Dryopteris
Fern, Climbing, see Lygodium
Fern, Elk's Horn, see Platycerium
Fern, Hard, see Blechnum
Fern, Hare's Foot, see Davallia
Fern, Hart's-tongue, see Phyllitis
Fern, Hay-scented, see Dryopteris
Fern, Holly, see Cyrtomium
Fern, Killarney, see Trichomanes
Fern, Ladder, see Nephrolepis
Fern, Lady, see Athyrium
Fern, Maidenhair, see Adiantum
Fern, Male, see Dryopteris
Fern, Mountain, see Dryopteris
Fern, Oak, see Dryopteris
Fern, Ostrich, see Pteretis
Fern, Parsley, see Cryptogramma
Fern, Ribbon, see Pteris
Fern, Royal, see Osmunda
Fern, Sago, see Cyathea
Fern, Sensitive, see Onoclea
Fern, Shield, see Dryopteris
  and Polystichum
Fern, Spider, see Pteris
Fern, Squirrel's Foot, see Davallia
Fern, Stag's Horn, see Platycerium
Fern, Sword, see Nephrolepis

Fern, Tree, see Cyathea and
   Dicksonia
Fescue Grass see Festuca
Feverfew see Chrysanthemum
Fig see Ficus
Fig, Barbary, see Opuntia
Figleaf Palm see Fatsia
Fig Marigold see Carpobrotus
Figwort see Scrophularia
Filbert see Corylus
Finnochio see Foeniculum
Fir see Abies
Fir, Chinese, see Cunninghamia
Fir, Douglas, see Pseudotsuga
Fir, Snake, see Picea
Fire Bush see Kochia
Fire Bush, Chilean, see
   Embothrium
Firecrackers, Californian or
   Floral, see Dichelostemma
Fire Lily see Cyrtanthus
Fire on the Mountain see
   Euphorbia
Fire Pink see Silene
Fire Plant, Mexican, see
   Euphorbia
Firethorn see Pyracantha
Fireweed see Epilobium
Flag see Iris
Flag, Crimson, see Schizostylis
Flag, Sweet, see Acorus
Flamboyant see Delonix
Flame Flower see Tropaeolum
Flame Pea see Chorizema
Flamingo Plant see Anthurium
Flat Palm see Howeia
Flax see Linum
Flax, Holly, see Santolina
Flax, New Zealand, see Phormium
Flax, Winter, see Reinwardtia
Fleabane see Erigeron
Fleur de Lys see Iris
Floating Hear see Nymphoides
Floral Firecrackers see
   Dichelostemma
Floss Flower see Ageratum
Flowering Nutmeg see Leycesteria
Flowering Quince see
   Chaenomeles
Flowering Rush see Butomus
Flower of a Day see Tradescantia
Flower of an Hour see Hibiscus
Flower of Love see Lychnis
Flower of the West Wind see
   Zephyranthes
Foam Flower see Tiarella
Foam Flower, Japanese, see
   Tanakaea
Foam of May see Spiraea
Forget-me-not see Myosotis
Forget-me-not, Chatham
   Island, see Myosotidium
Forget-me-not, Creeping, see
   Omphalodes
Forget-me-not, Fairy, see
   Eritrichium
Forget-me-not, Rock, see
   Omphalodes
Fountain Grass see Pennisetum
Four o'clock Flower see Mirabilis
Foxglove see Digitalis
Fox Grape see Vitis
Fox-tail Lily see Eremurus
Fragrant Garland Flower see
   Hedychium
Frangipani Plant see Plumeria
Fraxinella see Dictamnus
Fremontodendron see Fremontia
French Honeysuckle see
   Hedysarum
French Marigold see Tagetes
French Willow see Epilobium
Fringe Flower see Schizanthus
Fringe Tree see Chionanthus
Fritillary see Fritillaria

Fruiting Myrtle see Eugenia
Fuchsia, Australian, see Correa
Fuchsia, Californian, see
   Zauschneria
Fuchsia, Cape, see Phygelius
Fuchsia-flowered Gooseberry
   see Ribes
Fuller's Herb see Saponaria
Funkia see Hosta
Furze see Genista and Ulex

G

Galeobdolon see Lamium
Galingale see Cyperus
Gardener's Garters see Phalaris
Garland Flower see Daphne
   and Hedychium
Gas Plant see Dictamnus
Gaya see Hoheria
Gay Feather see Liatris
Gazania, Climbing, see Mutisia
Gean see Prunus
Gentian see Gentiana
Gentianella see Gentiana
Germander see Teucrium
German Ivy see Senecio
Gesneria see Kohleria,
   Rechsteineria and Smithiantha
Giant Bell Flower see Ostrowskia
Giant Lily see Cardiocrinum
Ginger see Zingiber
Ginger Lily see Hedychium
Gladwyn see Iris
Globe Amaranth see Gomphrena
Globe Artichoke see Cynara
Globe Daisy see Globularia
Globe Flower see Trollius
Globe Thistle see Echinops
Glory Bush, Brazilian, see
   Tibouchina
Glory Flower see Gloriosa and
   Eccremocarpus
Glory of the Snow see Chionodoxa
Glory of the Sun see Leucocoryne
Glory Pea see Clianthus
Glory Tree see Clerodendron
Gloxinia see Sinningia
Goat's Beard see Aruncus
Goat's Beard, False, see Astilbe
Goat's Rue see Galega
Gold Cup see Solandra
Gold Dust see Alyssum
Golden Bells see Forsythia
Golden Chain see Laburnum
Golden Chain Orchid see
   Dendrochilum
Golden Club see Orontium
Golden Dead Nettle see Lamium
Golden Drop see Onosma
Golden Larch see Pseudolarix
Golden-rain Tree see
   Koelreuteria
Golden Rod see Solidago
Golden Saxifrage see
   Chrysosplenium
Golden Star see Chrysogonum,
   Hypoxis and Triteleia
Goldfish Plant see Hypocyrta
Goldilocks see *Aster linosyris*
Goniophlebium see Polypodium
Gooseberry, Barbados, see
   Pereskia
Gooseberry, Cape, see Physalis
Gooseberry, Chinese, see Actinidia
Gooseberry, Fuchsia-flowered,
   see Ribes
Gorse see Genista and Ulex
Gourd see Cucurbita and
   Lagenaria
Granadilla see Passiflora
Grape, Dusty Milk, see Vitis
Grapefruit see Citrus
Grape Hyacinth see Muscari
Grape, Oregon, see Mahonia

Grape, Teinturier, see Vitis
Grape Vine see Vitis
Grass, Basket, see Oplismenus
Grass, Blue, see Carex
Grass, Blue-eyed, see
   Sisyrinchium
Grass, Bowles' Golden, see
   Milium
Grass, Brome, see Bromus
Grass, Canary, see Phalaris
Grass, Eel, see Vallisneria
Grass, Feather, see Stipa
Grass, Fescue, see Festuca
Grass, Fountain, see Pennisetum
Grass, Hair, see Aira
Grass, Hare's Tail, see Lagurus
Grass, Lace, see Eragrostis
Grass, Love, see Eragrostis
Grass, Pampas, see Cortaderia
Grass, Pearl, see Briza
Grass, Purple Moor, see Molinia
Grass, Quaking, see Briza
Grass, Ribbon, see Phalaris
Grass, Silver, see Phalaris
Grass, Squirrel-tail, see Hordeum
Grass, Star, see Hypoxis
Grass, Tape, see Vallisneria
Grass, Whitlow, see Draba
Grass, Witch, see Panicum
Grass of Parnassus see Parnassia
Greenbriar see Smilax
Grey Sage Bush see Atriplex
Gromwell see Lithospermum
Ground Laurel see Epigaea
Groundsel see Senecio
Guava see Psidium
Guava, Chilean, see Myrtus
Guelder Rose see Viburnum
Guernsey Lily see Nerine
Gum see Eucalyptus
Gum, Chinese Sour, see Nyssa
Gum Cistus see Cistus
Gum, Sweet, see Liquidambar
Gynerium see Cortaderia

H

Hackberry see Celtis
Hair Grass see Aira
Handkerchief Tree see Davidia
Hard Fern see Blechnum
Harebell see Campanula
Harebell, Creeping, see
   Wahlenbergia
Hare's Foot Fern see Davallia
Hare's Tail Grass see Lagurus
Harlequin Flower see Sparaxis
Hart's-tongue Fern see Phyllitis
Hawk's Beard see Crepis
Hawkweed see Hieracium
Hawthorn see Crataegus
Hawthorn, Chinese, see Photinia
Hawthorn, Indian, see
   Rhaphiolepis
Hawthorn, Water, see
   Aponogeton
Hazel see Corylus
Heartsease see Viola
Heath see Daboecia, Erica
Heath, Australian, see Epacris
Heath, False, see Fabiana
Heath, Prickly, see Pernettya
Heath, Sea, see Frankenia
Heath, Spike, see Bruckenthalia
Heather see Calluna and Erica
Hedgehog Broom see Erinacea
Hedgehog Cactus see Ferocactus
Heliosperma see Silene
Heliotrope see Heliotropium
Heliotrope, Winter, see Petasites
Hellebore see Helleborus
Hellebore, False, see Veratrum
Helmet Flower see Scutellaria
Helxine see Soleirolia
Hemlock see Tsuga

Hemp, African, see Sparmannia
Hemp Agrimony see Eupatorium
Hemp, Angola, see Sansevieria
Hemp, Bowstring, see Sansevieria
Herb Christopher see Actaea
Herb of Grace see Ruta
Hercules' Club see Aralia
Heron's Bill see Erodium
Hickory see Carya
Himalayan Honeysuckle see
   Leycesteria
Himalayan May Apple see
   Podophyllum
Himalayan Poppy see Meconopsis
Hinoki Cypress see
   Chamaecyparis
Hogweed, Giant, see Heracleum
Holly see Ilex
Holly Fern see Cyrtomium
Holly Flax see Santolina
Hollyhock see Althaea
Holly, Mountain, see Olearia
Holly, New Zealand, see Olearia
Holm Oak see Quercus
Holy Thistle see Silybum
Honesty see Lunaria
Honey Bush see Melianthus
Honey Flower, Cape, see
   Melianthus
Honey Locust see Gleditsia
Honey Plant see Hoya
Honeysuckle see Lonicera
Honeysuckle, Australian, see
   Banksia
Honeysuckle, Bush, see Diervilla
Honeysuckle, French, see
   Hedysarum
Honeysuckle, Himalayan, see
   Leycesteria
Hop see Humulus
Hop Hornbeam see Ostrya
Hop Tree see Ptelea
Hornbeam see Carpinus
Hornbeam, Hop, see Ostrya
Horned Poppy see Glaucium
Horned Rampion see Phyteuma
Horse Chestnut see Aesculus
Horsemint see Monarda
Horsetail Tree see Casuarina
Hottentot Fig see Carpobrotus
Houmspara see Pseudopanax
Hound's-tongue see Cynoglossum
Houpara see Pseudopanax
Houseleek see Sempervivum
Huckleberry see Gaylussacia
Huckleberry, Hairy, see Vaccinium
Humble Plant see Mimosa
Huntsman's Cup see Sarracenia
Huntsman's Horn see Sarracenia
Hyacinth see Hyacinthus
Hyacinth Bean see Dolichos
Hyacinth, Feather, see Muscari
Hyacinth, Grape, see Muscari
Hyacinth, Musk, see Muscari
Hyacinth, Starch, see Muscari
Hyacinth, Tassel, see Muscari
Hyacinth, Water, see Eichhornia
Hyacinth, Wild, see
   Dichelostemma and Endymion
Hyacinthella see Hyacinthus

I

Ice Plant see Cryophytum and
   Sedum spectabile
Immortelle see Helichrysum,
   Helipterum and Xeranthemum
Incense Cedar see Libocedrus
Incense Plant see Humea
Indian Bean Tree see Catalpa
Indian Corn see Zea
Indian Crocus see Pleione
Indian Cup see Sarracenia
Indian Currant see
   Symphoricarpos

Indian Hawthorn see
   Rhaphiolepis
Indian Lilac see Melia
Indian Physic see Gillenia
Indian Pink see Ipomoea and
   Dianthus
Indian Shot see Canna
India Rubber Plant see Ficus
Indigo see Indigofera
Indigo, False, see Baptisia
Inkberry see Phytolacca
Iris, Butterfly, see Moraea
Iris, Peacock, see Moraea
Iris, Snakeshead or Widow,
   see Hermodactylus
Iris, Tiger, see Tigridia
Iron Cross see Begonia
Ironweed see Vernonia
Iron-wood see Ostrya
Isoloma see Kohleria
Ivy see Hedera
Ivy, Boston, see Parthenocissus
Ivy, German, see Senecio
Ivy, Japanese, see
   Parthenocissus
Ivy, Kenilworth, see Cymbalaria
Ivy, Poison, see Rhus
Ivy, Prickly, see Smilax
Ivy-leaved Toadflax see
   Cymbalaria

J

Jack-in-the-Pulpit see Arisaema
Jacobaea see Senecio
Jacobean Lily see Sprekelia
Jacob's Ladder see Polemonium
Jamberberry see Physalis
Japanese Aralia see Fatsia
Japanese Cedar see Cryptomeria
Japanese Ivy see Parthenocissus
Japanese Pagoda Tree see
   Sophora
Japanese Plum Yew see
   Cephalotaxus
Japanese Quince see Chaenomeles
Japonica see Chaenomeles
Jasmine see Jasminum
Jasmine, Bastard, see Cestrum
Jasmine Box see Phillyrea
Jasmine, Cape, see Gardenia
Jasmine, Chilean, see Mandevilla
Jasmine, Chinese, see
   Trachelospermum
Jasmine, Madagascar, see
   Stephanotis
Jasmine, Nightshade, see Solanum
Jasmine, Rock, see Androsace
Jerusalem Cherry see Solanum
Jerusalem Cowslip see Pulmonaria
Jerusalem Cross see Lychnis
Jerusalem Sage see Phlomis
Jessamine see Jasminum and
   Gelsemium
Jessamine, Carolina, see
   Gelsemium
Jesuit's Nut see Trapa
Jewel Orchid see Anoectochilus
Jew's Mallow see Kerria
Job's Tears see Coix
Joe-pye Weed see Eupatorium
Jonquil see Narcissus
Joy Weed see Alternanthera
Judas Tree see Cercis
June Berry see Amelanchier
Juniper see Juniperus
Justicia see Jacobinia

K

Kaffir Bread see Encephalartos
Kaffir Lily see Clivia and
   Schizostylis
Kaki see Diospyros
Kale, Sea, see Crambe

Kangaroo Paw see Anigozanthos
Kangaroo Vine see Cissus
Karo see Pittosporum
Kenilworth Ivy see Cymbalaria
Kentranthus see Centranthus
Kentucky Coffee Tree see Gymnocladus
Killarney Fern see Trichomanes
Kingcup see Caltha
Kingfisher Daisy see Felicia
King's Flower see Eucomis
King's Spear see Asphodeline
Knapweed see Centaurea
Knotweed see Polygonum
Kowhai see Sophora

L

Laburnum, Evergreen, see Piptanthus
Laburnum, Nepal, see Piptanthus
Laburnum, New Zealand, see Sophora
Lace Grass see Eragrostis
Ladder Fern see Nephrolepis
Lad's Love see Artemisia
Lady Fern see Athyrium
Lady of the Night see Brunfelsia
Lady's Garters see Phalaris
Lady's Mantle see Alchemilla
Lady Smock see Cardamine
Lady's Pincushion see Armeria
Lady's Slipper Orchid see Cypripedium
Lamb's Ear see Stachys
Larch see Larix
Larch, Golden, see Pseudolarix
Larkspur see Delphinium
Lasiandra see Tibouchina
Lastrea see Dryopteris
Laurel see Aucuba, Laurus and Prunus
Laurel, Alexandrian, see Danaë
Laurel, American, see Kalmia
Laurel, American Ground, see Epigaea
Laurel, Bay, see Laurus
Laurel, Cherry, see Prunus
Laurel, Mountain, see Kalmia
Laurel, Portugal, see Prunus
Laurel, Sheep or Swamp, see Kalmia
Laurel, Spurge, see Daphne
Laurustinus see Viburnum
Lavender see Lavandula
Lavender Cotton see Santolina
Lavender, Sea, see Limonium
Lawson's Cypress see Chamaecyparis
Leadwort see Plumbago
Leaf-flowering Cactus see Schlumbergera
Lebanon Candytuft see Aethionema
Legousia see Specularia
Lemon see Citrus
Lemon Balm see Melissa
Lemon-scented Verbena see Lippia
Lent Lily see Narcissus
Leopards-bane see Doronicum
Leptosiphon see Gilia
Lettuce see Lactuca
Libonia see Jacobinia
Lilac see Syringa
Lilac, Indian, see Melia
Lily see Lilium, Cardiocrinum, Nomocharis and Notholirion
Lily, African, see Agapanthus
Lily, African Corn, see Ixia
Lily, Amazon, see Eucharis
Lily, American Swamp, see Saururus
Lily, Arum, see Zantedeschia
Lily, Barbados, see Hippeastrum

Lily, Bean, see Nymphoides
Lily, Blood, see Haemanthus
Lily, Bugle, see Watsonia
Lily, Calla, see Zantedeschia
Lily, Cape, see Crinum
Lily, Club, see Kniphofia
Lily, Cow, see Nuphar
Lily, Day, see Hemerocallis
Lily, Fire, see Cyrtanthus
Lily, Fox-tail, see Eremurus
Lily, Giant, see Cardiocrinum
Lily, Ginger, see Hedychium
Lily, Guernsey, see Nerine
Lily, Jacobean, see Sprekelia
Lily, Kaffir, see Clivia and Schizostylis
Lily, Lent, see Narcissus
Lily, Mariposa, see Calochortus
Lily, May, see Convallaria
Lily, Mediterranean, see Pancratium
Lily, Mozambique, see Gloriosa
Lily, Perisan, see Fritillaria
Lily, Peruvian, see Alstroemeria
Lily, Plantain, see Hosta
Lily, Rush, see Sisyrinchium
Lily, St Bernard, see Anthericum
Lily, St Bruno, see Paradisea
Lily, Scarborough, see Vallota
Lily, Spider, see Lycoris
Lily, Spire, see Galtonia
Lily, Sword, see Gladiolus
Lily, Toad, see Tricyrtis
Lily, Torch, see Kniphofia
Lily, Trout, see Erythronium
Lily, Wood, see Trillium
Lily, Zephyr, see Zephyranthes
Lily of the Incas see Alstroemeria
Lily of the Valley see Convallaria
Lily of the Valley, Star-flowered, see Smilacina
Lime see Citrus
Lime Tree see Tilia
Limnanthemum see Nymphoides
Limnocharis see Hydrocleys
Linden see Tilia
Ling see Calluna
Lion's Ear see Leonotis
Lion's Foot see Leontopodium
Living Stone see Lithops
Lizard's Tail see Saururus
Loblolly Bay see Gordonia
Lobster Cactus see Schlumbergera
Lobster Claw see Clianthus
Locust see Robinia
Locust, Honey, see Gleditsia
Lomaria see Blechnum
London Pride see Saxifraga
Loosestrife see Lysimachia
Loosestrife, Purple, see Lythrum
Loquat see Eriobotrya
Lords and Ladies see Arum
Lotus of the Nile see Nelumbo and Nymphaea
Love Grass see Eragrostis
Love-in-a-mist see Nigella
Love-lies-bleeding see Amaranthus
Love's Lad see Artemisia
Lungwort see Pulmonaria
Lupin see Lupinus
Lyre Flower see Dicentra

M

Madagascar Jasmine see Stephanotis
Madagascar Lace Plant see Aponogeton
Madagascar Periwinkle see Catharanthus
Madrona see Arbutus
Madwort see Alyssum
Maidenhair Fern see Adiantum
Maidenhair Tree see Ginkgo

Maiden's Wreath see Francoa
Maize see Zea
Malay Apple see Eugenia
Male Fern see Dryopteris
Mallow see Malva
Mallow, False, see Malvastrum
Mallow, Jew's, see Kerria
Mallow, Poppy, see Callirhoë
Mallow, Rose, see Hibiscus
Mallow, Tree, see Lavatera and Hibiscus
Maltese Cross see *Lychnis chalcedonica*
Mandarin see Citrus
Manila Hemp see Musa
Manuka see Leptospermum
Maple see Acer
Marguerite see Chrysanthemum
Marguerite, Blue, see Felicia
Marigold, African, see Tagetes
Marigold, Cape, see Dimorphotheca
Marigold, Corn, see Chrysanthemum
Marigold, French, see Tagetes
Marigold, Marsh, see Caltha
Marigold, Pot, see Calendula
Marigold, Scotch, see Calendula
Mariposa Lily see Calochortus
Marjoram see Origanum
Marrow see Cucurbita
Marsh Mallow see Althaea
Marsh Marigold see Caltha
Marsh Rosemary see Andromeda
Marsh Trefoil see Menyanthes
Marvel of Peru see Mirabilis
Mask Flower see Alonsoa
Masterwort see Astrantia
Matteuccia see Pteretis
May see Crataegus
May Apple see Podophyllum
Mayflower, New England, see Epigaea
May Lily see Convallaria
Mayweed see Matricaria
Meadow Clary see Salvia
Meadow Foam see Limnanthes
Meadow Foxtail see Alopecurus
Meadow Rue see Thalictrum
Meadow Saffron see Colchicum and Merendera
Meadowsweet see Filipendula
Mediterranean Lily see Pancratium
Medlar see Mespilus
Megasea see Bergenia
Mexican Orange Blossom see Choisya
Mexican Poppy see Argemone
Mexican Sunflower see Tithonia
Mezereon see Daphne
Michaelmas Daisy see Aster
Mignonette see Reseda
Milfoil see Achillea
Milfoil, Water, see Myriophyllum
Milk Thistle see Silybum
Milkweed see Asclepias
Milkwort see Polygala
Milla see Ipheion
Millet, Golden Wood, see Milium
Mina see Ipomoea
Mind-your-own-Business see Soleirolia
Mint see Mentha
Mistletoe see Viscum
Mistletoe Cactus see Rhipsalis
Mitre-wort see Mitella
Mitrewort, False, see Tiarella
Mitsumata see Edgeworthia
Moccasin Flower see Cypripedium
Mockernut see Carya

Mock Orange see Carpenteria and Philadelphus
Monarch of the East see Sauromatum
Money Flower see Lunaria
Moneywort see Lysimachia
Monkey Flower see Mimulus
Monkey Puzzle see Araucaria
Monkshood see Aconitum
Montbretia see Crocosmia
Moon Daisy see *Chrysanthemum leucanthemum*
Moon Seed see Menispermum
Moor Grass, Purple, see Molinia
Moreton Bay Pine see Araucaria
Morning Glory see Ipomoea
Moss Campion see Silene
Moss Pink see Phlox
Mother of Millions see Cymbalaria
Mother of Thousands see *Saxifraga stolonifera*
Mother of Thyme see Thymus
Moth Orchid see Phalaenopsis
Mountain Ash see Sorbus
Mountain Avens see Dryas
Mountain Fern see Dryopteris
Mountain Holly see Olearia
Mountain Laurel see Kalmia
Mountain Tobacco see Arnica
Mount Atlas Daisy see Anacyclus
Mournful Widow see Scabiosa
Mourning Widow see Geranium
Mouse-tail Plant see Arisarum
Mozambique Lily see Gloriosa
Mulberry see Morus
Mulgedium see Lactuca
Mullein see Verbascum
Mullein, Cretan, see Celsia
Mullein, Rosette, see Ramonda
Musk see Mimulus
Musk Hyacinth see Muscari
Musk Mallow see Malva
Myrobalan see Prunus
Myrrh see Myrrhis
Myrtle see Myrtus
Myrtle, Bog, see Myrica
Myrtle, Crape, see Lagerstroemia
Myrtle, Fruiting, see Eugenia
Myrtle, South Sea, see Leptospermum

N

Naegelia see Smithiantha
Nasturtium see Tropaeolum
Natal Vine see Rhoicissus
Navelwort see Omphalodes and Umbilicus
Neanthe bella see Collinia
Nemu Tree see Albizia
Nepal Laburnum see Piptanthus
Nephrodium see Dryopteris
Nettle Tree see Celtis
New Jersey Tea see Ceanothus
New Zealand Broom see Notospartium
New Zealand Burr see Acaena
New Zealand Daisy see Celmisia
New Zealand Flax see Phormium
New Zealand Holly see Olearia
New Zealand Laburnum see Sophora
New Zealand Rimu see Dacrydium
New Zealand Tea Tree see Leptospermum
Nightshade, Jasmine, see Solanum
Nine Bark see Neillia
Nippon Bells see Shortia
Nootka Cypress see Chamaecyparis
Norfolk Island Pine see Araucaria
Nut, Bitter, see Carya

Nut, Cob or Filbert, see Corylus
Nutmeg, Californian, see Torreya
Nutmeg, Flowering, see Leycesteria

O

Oak see Quercus
Oak Fern see Dryopteris
Oak, Poison, see Rhus
Oak, She-, see Casuarina
Oak, Silk Bark, see Grevillea
Oat see Avena
Obedient Plant see Physostegia
Ocean Spray see Holodiscus
Old Maids see Triteleia
Old Man see Artemisia
Old Man Cactus see *Cephalocereus senilis*
Old Man's Beard see Clematis
Oleander see Nerium
Oleaster see Elaeagnus
Olive see Olea
Olive, Fragrant, see Osmanthus
Orach see Atriplex
Orange see Citrus
Orange Blossom, Mexican, see Choisya
Orange, Hardy, see Poncirus
Orchid, Butterfly, see Oncidium
Orchid, Golden Chain, see Dendrochilum
Orchid, Lady's Slipper, see Cypripedium
Orchid, Moth, see Phalaenopsis
Orchid, Poor Man's, see Schizanthus
Orchid, Swan, see Cycnoches
Orchid Tree see Bauhinia
Oregon Grape see Mahonia
Oreodaphne see Umbellularia
Orobus see Lathyrus
Orpine see Sedum
Orris Root see Iris
Osier see Salix
Osoberry see Osmaronia
Ostrich Fern see Pteretis
Oswego Tea see Monarda
Otaheite Orange see Citrus
Our Lady's Milk Thistle see Silybum
Oxeye Daisy see *Chrysanthemum leucanthemum*
Oxeye, North American, see Heliopsis
Oxeye, Yellow, see Buphthalmum
Oxlip see Primula
Oxycoccus see Vaccinium
Ozothamnus see Helichrysum

P

Pagoda Tree see Sophora
Painted Feather see Vriesea
Painted Tongue see Salpiglossis
Pale Maidens see Sisyrinchium
Palm, Chusan, see Trachycarpus
Palm, Coconut, see Cocos
Palm, Curly, see Howeia
Palm, Date, see Phoenix
Palm, Fan, see Chamaerops
Palm, Figleaf, see Fatsia
Palm, Flat, see Howeia
Palm, Hardy, see Trachycarpus
Palm, Parlour, see Aspidistra
Palm, Sago, see Cycas
Palm, Sentry, see Howeia
Palm, Thatch Leaf, see Howeia
Palm, Windmill, see Trachycarpus
Pampas Grass see Cortaderia

Pansy see Viola
Paper Bush see Edgeworthia
Papyrus see Cyperus
Paradise Poinciana see
  Caesalpinia
Parasol Pine see Sciadopitys
Parchment-bark see Pittosporum
Parlour Palm see Asparagus
Parrot's Bill see Clianthus
Parrot's Feather see
  Myriophyllum
Parsley Fern see Cryptogramma
Partridge Berry see Gaultheria
Pasque Flower see Pulsatilla
Passion Flower see Passiflora
Patience Plant see Impatiens
Pea see Lathyrus
Pea, Darling River, see
  Swainsona
Pea, Shamrock, see Parochetus
Peacock Flower see Delonix
Peacock Iris see Moraea
Peacock Plant see Calathea
Peach see Prunus
Pear see Pyrus
Pear, Alligator, see Persea
Pear, Avocado, see Persea
Pear, Prickly, see Opuntia
Pearl Bush see Exochorda
Pearl Grass see Briza
Pearlwort see Sagina
Pearly Everlasting see Anaphalis
Pebble Plant see Lithops
Pecan see Carya
Pelican Flower see Aristolochia
Pencil Cedar see Juniperus
Pennyroyal see Mentha
Pennywort see Umbilicus
Peony see Paeonia
Pepper Bush, Sweet, see Clethra
Peppermint see Mentha
Peppers see Solanum
Periwinkle see Vinca
Periwinkle, Madagascar, see
  Catharanthus
Persian Lily see Fritillaria
Persimmon see Diospyros
Peruvian Lily see Alstroemeria
Petrorhagia see Tunica
Pharbitis see Ipomoea
Pheasant's Eye see Adonis
  and Narcissus
Pick-a-back Plant see Tolmiea
Pickerel Weed see Pontederia
Picotee see Dianthus
Pigeon Berry see Phytolacca
Pignut see Carya
Pilot Weed see Silphium
Pimpernel see Anagallis
Pincushion Flower see Scabiosa
Pine see Pinus
Pine, Huon, see Dacrydium
Pine, Moreton Bay, see Araucaria
Pine, Norfolk Island, see
  Araucaria
Pine, Parasol, see Sciadopitys
Pine, Red, see Dacrydium
Pine, Screw, see Pandanus
Pine, Umbrella, see Sciadopitys
Pineapple see Ananas
Pineapple Flower see Eucomis
Pink see Dianthus
Pink, Cushion, see Silene
Pink, Fire, see Silene
Pink, Indian, see Ipomoea
Pink, Moss, see Phlox
Pink, Sea, see Armeria
Pink Siris Tree see Albizia
Pistachio see Pistacia
Pitcher Plant see Nepenthes
  and Sarracenia
Pitcher Plant, Californian, see
  Darlingtonia
Plagianthus see also Hoheria
Plane Tree see Platanus

Plantain see Musa
Plantain Lily see Hosta
Plantain, Water, see Alisma
Pleurisy Root see Asclepias
Plum see Prunus
Plum, Cherry, see Prunus
Plumbago see also Ceratostigma
Plume Poppy see Macleaya
Plum Fir see Podocarpus
Plum Yew see Cephalotaxus
Poet's Laurel see Laurus
Poinciana see Delonix and
  Caesalpinia
Poinsettia see Euphorbia
Poison Ivy see Rhus
Poison Oak see Rhus
Pokeberry, Pokeweed see
  Phytolacca
Polar Plant see Silphium
Polka Dot Plant see Hypoëstes
Polyanthus see Primula
Polypody see Polypodium
Pomegranate see Punica
Pondweed see Potamogeton
Poor Man's Orchid see
  Schizanthus
Poplar see Populus
Poppy see Papaver and
  Meconopsis
Poppy, Californian, see
  Eschscholzia
Poppy, Californian Tree, see
  Romneya
Poppy, Horned, see Glaucium
Poppy Mallow see Callirhoë
Poppy, Mexican, see Argemone
Poppy, Plume, see Macleaya
Poppy, Prickly, see Argemone
Poppy, Sea, see Glaucium
Poppy, Snow, see Eomecon
Poppy, Tree, see Dendromecon
Poppy, Water, see Hydrocleys
Porcupine Quill Rush see
  Scirpus
Portugal Diamond Plant see
  Ionopsidium
Portugal Laurel see Prunus
Poterium see Sanguisorba
Pot Marigold see Calendula
Pretty Face see Triteleia
Prickly Ash see Zanthoxylum
Prickly Heath see Pernettya
Prickly Ivy see Smilax
Prickly Pear see Opuntia
Prickly Poppy see Argemone
Prickly Rhubarb see Gunnera
Prickly Thrift see Acantholimon
Pride of India see
  Koelreuteria and Melia
Primrose see Primula
Primrose, Cape, see Streptocarpus
Primrose, Evening, see
  Oenothera
Prince of Wales' Feather see
  Celosia argentea plumosa
Prince's Feather see
  Amaranthus and Polygonum
Privet see Ligustrum
Prophet Flower see Arnebia
Pseudosasa see Arundinaria
Pummelo see Citrus
Pumpkin see Cucurbita
Purple Bellerine see
  Rhodochiton
Purple Bells see Rhodochiton
Purple Heart see Setcreasea
Purple Loosestrife see Lythrum
Purple Moor Grass see Molinia
Purple Rock Cress see Aubrieta
Purple Wreath see Petrea
Purslane, Rock, see Calandrinia
Purslane, Tree, see Atriplex
Pyrenean Meadow Saffron see
  Merendera
Pyrethrum see Chrysanthemum

Q

Quaking Grass see Briza
Quamash see Camassia
Quamoclit see Ipomoea
Queen of the Night see
  Selenicereus
Queen of the Prairie see
  Filipendula
Queen Victoria Water Lily see
  Victoria
Quince, Common, see Cydonia
Quince, Japanese, see
  Chaenomeles

R

Ragwort see Senecio
Ragwort, African, see Othonna
Rainbow Cactus see Echinocereus
Ramarama see Myrtus
Rampion see Campanula
Rampion, Horned, see Phyteuma
Raspberry, Flowering, see Rubus
Rata see Metrosideros
Rat's Tail Cactus see Aporocactus
Red-bud see Cercis
Red Cape Tulip see Haemanthus
Red Cedar see Juniperus
Red Chamomile see Adonis
Red-hot Cat-tail see Acalypha
Red-hot Poker see Kniphofia
Red-ink Plant see Phytolacca
Red Valerian see Centranthus
Redwood, Californian, see
  Sequoia
Redwood, Dawn, see Metasequoia
Reed, Giant, see Arundo
Reed Mace see Typha
Rest-harrow see Ononis
Rhodanthe see Helipterum
Rhubarb see Rheum
Rhubarb, Chile, see Gunnera
Rhubarb, Prickly, see Gunnera
Rhynchospermum see
  Trachelospermum
Ribbon Fern see Pteris
Ribbon Grass see Phalaris
Rice Flower see Pimelea
Rock Cress see Arabis
Rock Cress, Purple, see Aubrieta
Rocket, Dame's, see Hesperis
Rocket, Sweet, see Hesperis
Rockfoil see Saxifraga
Rock Forget-me-not see
  Omphalodes
Rock Jasmine see Androsace
Rock Purslane see Calandrinia
Rock Rose see Cistus
Rodger's Bronze Leaf see
  Rodgersia
Rose see Rosa
Rose Acacia see Robinia
Rose Apple see Eugenia
Rose, Australian Native, see
  Boronia
Rose Bay see Nerium
Rosebay Willow Herb see
  Epilobium
Rose Campion see Lychnis
Rose, Guelder, see Viburnum
Rose Mallow see Hibiscus
Rosemary see Rosmarinus
Rose of Heaven see Lychnis
Rose of Sharon see Hypericum
Rose, Rock, see Cistus
Rose-root see Sedum
Rose, Sun, see Helianthemum
Rosette Mullein see Ramonda
Rowan see Sorbus
Royal Fern see Osmunda
Royal Paintbrush see
  Haemanthus
Royal Water Lily see Victoria
Rubber Plant see Ficus

Rue see Ruta
Rue Anemone see Anemonella
Rue, Meadow, see Thalictrum
Rush see Juncus
Rush, Club, see Scirpus
Rush, Flowering, see Butomus
Rush Lily see Sisyrinchium
Rush, Porcupine Quill, see
  Scirpus
Rush, Sea Club, see Scirpus
Rush, Zebra, see Scirpus
Rush, Zebra-striped, see
  Miscanthus
Russian Sage see Perovskia
Russian Vine see Polygonum

S

St Bernard's Lily see
  Anthericum
St Bruno Lily see Paradisea
St Dabeoc's Heath see
  Daboecia
St John's Wort see Hypericum
Sacred Bamboo see Nandina
Saffron see Crocus
Saffron, Meadow, see Colchicum
Saffron, Pyrenean Meadow,
  see Merendera
Saffron, Spring Meadow, see
  Bulbocodium
Sage see Salvia
Sage, Bethlehem, see Pulmonaria
Sage Bush, Grey, see Atriplex
Sage, Jerusalem, see Phlomis
Sago Fern see Cyathea
Sago Palm see Cycas
Sallow see Salix
Salmonberry see Rubus
Salt Bush see Atriplex
Salt Tree see Halimodendron
Sandwort see Arenaria
Santa Cruz Water Lily see
  Victoria
Sarsaparilla Plant see Smilax
Satin Flower see Lunaria and
  Sisyrinchium
Satureja see Calamintha
Savin see Juniperus
Sawara Cypress see
  Chamaecyparis
Saxifrage see Saxifraga and
  Bergenia
Saxifrage, Golden, see
  Chrysosplenium
Scabious see Scabiosa
Scabious, Giant, see Cephalaria
Scarborough Lily see Vallota
Scilla see Endymion
Scolopendrium see Phyllitis
Scorpion Senna see Coronilla
Scotch Bluebell see *Campanula
  rotundifolia*
Scotch Marigold see Calendula
Scotch Thistle see Onopordum
Screw Pine see Pandanus
Sea Buckthorn see Hippophaë
Sea Club Rush see Scirpus
Sea Daffodil see Pancratium
Sea Heath see Frankenia
Sea Holly see Eryngium
Seakale see Crambe
Sea Lavender see Limonium
Sea Pink see Armeria
Sea Poppy see Glaucium
Sedge see Carex
Selfheal see Prunella
Senna see Cassia
Senna, Bladder, see Colutea
Senna, Scorpion, see Coronilla
Sensitive Fern see Onoclea
Sensitive Plant see Mimosa
Sentry Palm see Howeia
Sequoia, Giant, see
  Sequoiadendron

Service Berry see Amelanchier
Service Tree see Sorbus
Shadbush see Amelanchier
Shaddock see Citrus
Shallon see Gaultheria
Shamrock Pea see Parochetus
Shasta Daisy see
  Chrysanthemum
Sheepberry see Viburnum
Sheep Laurel see Kalmia
Shell Flower see Chelone and
  Moluccella
She-oak see Casuarina
Shield Fern see Dryopteris
  and Polystichum
Shingle Plant see Monstera
Shoo Fly Plant see Nicandra
Shooting Star see Dodecatheon
Shorewort, Northern, see
  Mertensia
Shrimp Plant see Beloperone
Shrubby Althaea see Hibiscus
Sidesaddle Flower see
  Sarracenia
Silk Bark Oak see Grevillea
Silk Tassel Bush see Garrya
Silk Tree see Albizia
Silver Bell see Halesia
Silverberry see Elaeagnus
Silver Grass see Phalaris
Silver Rod see Asphodelus
Silver Tree see Leucodendron
Siphonosmanthus see Osmanthus
Skull Cap see Scutellaria
Skunk Cabbage see Lysichitum
Slipper Flower see Calceolaria
Slipper Orchid see
  Paphiopedilum
Slipperwort see Calceolaria
Sloe see Prunus
Smilax see Asparagus
Smoke Tree see Cotinus
Snake Fir see Picea
Snake-root see Cimicifuga
Snake-root, Button, see Liatris
Snake's Beard see Ophiopogon
Snake's Head see Fritillaria
Snakeshead Iris see
  Hermodactylus
Snakeweed see Polygonum
Snapdragon see Antirrhinum
Sneezeweed see Helenium
Sneezewort see Achillea
Snowball see Viburnum
Snowbell see Styrax
Snowberry see Symphoricarpos
Snowdrop see Galanthus
Snowdrop Tree see Halesia
Snowflake see Leucojum
Snowflake, Water, see
  Nymphoides
Snow in Summer see Cerastium
Snow on the Mountain see
  Euphorbia
Snow Poppy see Eomecon
Snowy Mespilus see Amelanchier
Soapwort see Saponaria
Solomon's Seal see Polygonatum
Solomon's Seal, Starry, see
  Smilacina
Sorrel Tree see Oxydendrum
Sorrel, Wood, see Oxalis
Sour Gum, Chinese, see Nyssa
Sour Sop see Annona
South African Thistle see
  Berkheya
Southern Beech see Nothofagus
Southern Cane see Arundinaria
Southernwood see Artemisia
South Sea Myrtle see
  Leptospermum
Sowbread see Cyclamen
Spanish Bayonet see Yucca
Spanish Bluebell see Endymion
Spanish Broom see Spartium

Spanish Dagger see Yucca
Spanish Moss see Tillandsia
Spatlum see Lewisia
Spatterdock see Nuphar
Spearmint see Mentha
Spearwort, Greater, see
  Ranunculus
Speedwell see Veronica
Spice Bush see Lindera
Spider Fern see Pteris
Spider Flower see Cleome
Spider Flower, Brazilian, see
  Tibouchina
Spider Lily see Lycoris
Spiderwort see Tradescantia
Spiderwort, Blue, see Commelina
Spike Heath see Bruckenthalia
Spikenard, American, see Aralia
Spikenard, Cretan, see Valeriana
Spikenard, False, see Sorbaria
Spindle Tree see Euonymus
Spiraea, Blue, see Caryopteris
Spiraea, False, see Sorbaria
Spire Lily see Galtonia
Spleenwort see Asplenium
Spotted Dog see Pulmonaria
Spring Beauty see Claytonia
Spring Bell see Sisyrinchium
Spring Meadow Saffron see
  Bulbocodium
Spruce see Picea
Spurge see Euphorbia
Spurge Laurel see Daphne
Squash see Cucurbita
Squill see Scilla
Squill, Striped, see Puschkinia
Squirrel's Foot Fern see Davallia
Squirrel-tail Grass see Hordeum
Stag's Horn Fern see
  Platycerium
Stag's Horn Sumach see Rhus
Star Capsicum see Solanum
Starch Hyacinth see Muscari
Starfish Flower see Stapelia
Star Flower, Yellow, see
  Sternbergia
Star Glory, Scarlet, see Ipomoea
Star Grass see Hypoxis
Star of Bethlehem see
  Ornithogalum
Star of Bethlehem, Yellow,
  see Gagea
Star Tulip see Calochortus
Starwort, Shrubby, see
  Microglossa
Statice see Limonium
Stock see Matthiola
Stock, Virginian, see Malcomia
Stoke's Aster see Stokesia
Stone Cress see Aethionema
Stonecrop see Sedum
Stonecrop, Burro's-tail, see
  Sedum
Stone-face see Lithops
Stone Orpine see Sedum
Strawberry see Fragaria
Strawberry, Barren, see
  Waldsteinia
Strawberry-Raspberry see Rubus
Strawberry Tree see Arbutus
Strawflower see Helichrysum
Stuartia see Stewartia
Sultan Snapweed see Impatiens
Sumach see Cotinus, Rhus
Summer Cypress see Kochia
Summersweet see Clethra

Sundew see Drosera
Sun-drops see Oenothera
Sunflower see Helianthus
Sunflower, Mexican, see Tithonia
Sun Plant see Portulaca
Sun Rose see Helianthemum
Swallow-wort see Asclepias
Swamp Bay see Magnolia
Swamp Cypress see Taxodium
Swamp Lily see Saururus
Swan Orchid see Cycnoches
Swan River Daisy see
  Brachycome
Sweet Alyssum see Lobularia
Sweet Bay see Magnolia, Laurus
Sweet Bergamot see Monarda
Sweet Box see Sarcococca
Sweet Briar see Rosa
Sweet Cicely see Myrrhis
Sweet Corn see Zea
Sweet Flag see Acorus
Sweet Gale see Myrica
Sweet Gum see Liquidambar
Sweet Maudlin see Achillea
Sweet Nancy see Achillea
Sweet Olive see Osmanthus
Sweet Pea see Lathyrus
Sweet Pepper Bush see Clethra
Sweet Rocket see Hesperis
Sweet Sop see Annona
Sweetspire, Virginian, see Itea
Sweet Sultan see Centaurea
Sweet William see Dianthus
Sweet William, Wild, see Phlox
Sweet Woodruff see Asperula
Sword Fern see Nephrolepis
Sword Lily see Gladiolus
Swan Orchid see Cycnoches
Sycamore see Acer

T

Tacsonia see Passiflora
Tail Flower see Anthurium
Tamarack see Larix
Tamarisk see Tamarix
Tangerine see Citrus
Tansy see Tanacetum
Tape Grass see Vallisneria
Tarata see Pittosporum
Tassel Flower see Emilia
Tassel Hyacinth see Muscari
Tea, Oswego, see Monarda
Tea Tree, Duke of Argyll's,
  see Lycium
Tea Tree, New Zealand, see
  Leptospermum
Tecoma see Campsis
Teinturier Grape see Vitis
Telegraph Plant see Desmodium
Temple Bells see Smithiantha
Thatch Leaf Palm see Howeia
Thea see Camellia
Thistle, Blessed, see Cnicus
  and Silybum
Thistle, Cotton, see Onopordum
Thistle, Globe, see Echinops
Thistle, Holy, see Silybum
Thistle, Our Lady's Milk, see
  Silybum
Thistle, Scotch, see Onopordum
Thistle, South African, see
  Berkheya
Thorn see Crataegus
Thorn Apple see Datura
Thousand Mothers see Tolmiea

Thrift see Armeria
Thrift, Prickly, see
  Acantholimon
Throatwort, Blue, see
  Trachelium
Thuya see Thuja
Thyme, Cat, see Teucrium
Tickseed see Coreopsis
Tick Trefoil see Desmodium
Tidy Tips see Layia
Tiger Flower see Tigridia
Tiger Iris see Tigridia
Tiger's Chaps see Faucaria
Toadflax see Linaria
Toadflax, Ivy-leaved, see
  Cymbalaria
Toad Lily see Tricyrtis
Tobacco Plant see Nicotiana
Tomatillo see Physalis
Toothwort see Dentaria
Torch Lily see Kniphofia
Totara see Podocarpus
Transvaal Daisy see Gerbera
Traveller's Joy see Clematis
Treasure Flower see Gazania
Tree Fern see Cyathea and
  Dicksonia
Tree-groundsel see Baccharis
Tree Mallow see Lavatera and
  Hibiscus
Tree of Chastity see Vitex
Tree of Heaven see Ailanthus
Tree Poppy see Dendromecon
Tree Purslane see Atriplex
Trefoil, Bird's-foot, see Lotus
Trefoil, Marsh, see Menyanthes
Trichosporum see Aeschynanthus
Tricuspidaria see Crinodendron
Tritoma see Kniphofia
Trout Lily see Erythronium
Trumpet Creeper see Campsis
Trumpet Flower see Datura
Trumpet Flower, Peach, see
  Solandra
Trumpet Gourd see Lagenaria
Trumpet Vine see Campsis
Tuberose see Polianthes
Tulip see Tulipa
Tulip, Butterfly, see Calochortus
Tulip, Red Cape, see
  Haemanthus
Tulip, Star, see Calochortus
Tulip Tree see Liriodendron
Tupelo see Nyssa
Turk's Cap see Lilium
Turtle-head see Chelone
Tutsan see Hypericum
Twin Flower see Linnaea
Twin Leaf see Jeffersonia

U

Umbrella Pine see Sciadopitys
Umbrella Plant see Cyperus
Umbrella Tree see Magnolia
Umbrella Tree, Texas, see
  Melia
Unicorn Plant see Proboscidea

V

Valerian see Valeriana
Valerian, Greek, see Polemonium
Valerian, Red, see Centranthus
Velvet Flower see Amaranthus
Venetian Sumach see Cotinus

Venus's Fly Trap see Dionaea
Venus's Looking Glass see
  Specularia
Venus's Navelwort see
  Omphalodes
Verbena, Lemon-scented, see
  Lippia
Vervain see Verbena
Victorian Box see Pittosporum
Victor's Laurel see Laurus
Villarsia see Nymphoides
Vine see Vitis
Vine, Cypress, see Ipomoea
Vine, Kangaroo, see Cissus
Vine, Russian, see Polygonum
Vine, Wire, see Muehlenbeckia
Violet see Viola
Violet, African, see Saintpaulia
Violet Cress see Ionopsidium
Violet, Dame's, see Hesperis
Violet, Dog's-tooth, see
  Erythronium
Violet, Water, see Hottonia
Violetta see Viola
Viper's Bugloss see Echium
Virginia Creeper see
  Parthenocissus
Virginian Cowslip see
  Mertensia
Virginian Stock see Malcomia
Virginian Sweetspire see Itea
Virginia Snowflower see
  Chionanthus
Virgin's Bower see Clematis
Viscaria see Lychnis and Silene

W

Wafer Ash see Ptelea
Wake Robin see Trillium
Wall Cress see Arabis
Wallflower see Cheiranthus
  and Erysimum
Wall Pepper see Sedum
Walnut see Juglans
Wandering Jew see
  Tradescantia and Zebrina
Wandflower see Dierama
Wand Plant see Galax
Waratah, Tasmanian, see Telopea
Water Calthrops see Trapa
Water Carpet see Chrysosplenium
Water Chestnut see Trapa
Water Cowslip see Caltha
Water Elder see Viburnum
Water Fringe see Nymphoides
Water Hawthorn see
  Aponogeton
Water Hyacinth see Eichhornia
Water Lily see Nymphaea,
  Nuphar
Water Lily, Fairy, see
  Nymphoides
Water Lily, Queen Victoria,
  see Victoria
Water Lily, Royal, see Victoria
Water Lily, Santa Cruz, see
  Victoria
Water Lily, Yellow, see Nuphar
Water Milfoil see Myriophyllum
Water Plantain see Alisma
Water Poppy see Hydrocleys
Water Starwort see Callitriche
Water Violet see Hottonia
Wattle see Acacia
Wax Flower see Hoya

Wax Flower, Cluster, see
  Stephanotis
Wayfaring Tree see Viburnum
Wedding Flower see Moraea
Wellingtonia see Sequoiadendron
Welsh Poppy see Meconopsis
Western Balsam see Populus
Western Red Cedar see Thuja
West Wind, Flower of the, see
  Zephyranthes
Whin see Ulex and Genista
Whinberry see Vaccinium
White Alder see Clethra
Whitebeam see Sorbus
White Cedar see Chamaecyparis
White Sails see Spathiphyllum
Whitlow Grass see Draba
Whorl Flower see Morina
Whortleberry see Vaccinium
Wig Tree see Cotinus
Wild Hyacinth see
  Dichelostemma and
  Endymion
Willow see Salix
Willow Herb see Epilobium
Windflower see Anemone
Windmill Palm see Trachycarpus
Wineberry see Rubus
Wing Nut see Pterocarya
Winter Aconite see Eranthis
Winter Cherry see Physalis
  and Solanum
Winter Daffodil see Sternbergia
Winter Flax see Reinwardtia
Wintergreen see Pyrola
Wintergreen, Creeping, see
  Gaultheria
Winter Heliotrope see Petasites
Winter Sweet see Chimonanthus
Wire Vine see Muehlenbeckia
Witch Grass see Panicum
Witch Hazel see Hamamelis
Witch Hazel, American, see
  Fothergilla
Witch's Thimble see Silene
Wolfberry see Symphoricarpos
Wolf's Bane see Aconitum
Woodbine see Lonicera
Wood Lily see Trillium
Woodruff see Asperula
Wood Sorrel see Oxalis
Wormwood see Artemisia
Woundwort see Stachys
Wreath, Purple, see Petrea

Y

Yarrow see Achillea
Yellow Archangel see Lamium
Yellow Water Lily see Nuphar
Yew see Taxus
Yew, Plum, see Cephalotaxus
Yew, Plum-fruited, see
  Podocarpus
Youth-and-old-age see Zinnia
Youth-on-age see Tolmiea
Yulan see Magnolia

Z

Zebra Plant see Calathea
Zebra Rush see Scirpus
Zephyr-striped Rush see
  Miscanthus
Zephyr Lily see Zephyranthes
Zygocactus see Schlumbergera

GARDEN DESIGN

Kenneth Midgley

Planning and Design

The making of a garden can be a relaxing and rewarding activity. Even those who profess a dislike of the subject have been known to find an awakening of interest, when circumstances, such as the acquisition of an undeveloped plot of land, force them into doing something about it.

It is a task which should be approached with an open and enquiring mind, and frustration lies in the path of anyone starting with vague ideas about 'style', 'surprises', 'vistas' and so on, which they believe are essentials, or the feeling that there is some mysterious mumbo-jumbo, known only to the experts, and without which they must fail.

The seasoned craftsman can, and often does, design as he goes along, but for the less experienced in garden design this is not a practice to be recommended, since a mistake or change of mind during progress of work can be expensive. It is wiser to make an overall scheme before starting work, even if minor but essential details have to be left over for further thought later on.

The designer of no matter what, must have at the outset a mental appreciation of the end product – in this case a garden – and must be clear as to its purpose; any scheme used should take into account the reasons for wanting a garden. These may be summarized as: a play space for children and pets; relaxation for older members of the family; the growing of vegetables and, for the colour hungry, a place for flowers, but of primary importance is the provision of a suitable setting for the house. These reasons all call for an adjustment of one's approach to the problem.

I suggest that the strongest reason for wanting a garden is that we all like to have our own bit of nature at home on our doorsteps. Man belongs to Nature, and even though he has been forced by overcrowding and lack of living space to draw away, as at present, he has always battled to impose his will on nature. For example, in the 17th century and earlier, forests, where they existed, were thick and extensive and held a certain terror for man. However, within the safety of the homestead, or the castle wall, he could assert his superiority and he laid out gardens in orderly rows and patterns, even cutting plants and trees into decorative and sometimes extravagant shapes. Because the properties belonged to the wealthy the houses were large and tall and the gardens were designed to look well from upper windows as almost two-dimensional ground pattern. As upkeep was no problem, they were also extensive with long straight walks connecting rectangular compartments, each devoted to elaborately shaped beds and pools.

Like most good ideas these formal gardens were overdone, and in the 18th century reaction, inspired by painters and writers, set in. It was realized that a tree left to itself was beautiful, and trees, if grouped, could be arranged to create pictures – provided one was prepared to wait for results. Incidentally, there was an economic reason for tree planting: to replace the forests as they were cleared for their valuable ship and building timber. The landscape designers of the period did this without hope of ever seeing the eventual results of their efforts, it is we who are in a position to appreciate the beauty of the parkland which makes such a wonderful contribution to what we call the English landscape. Instead of long fingers of formality reaching into the surrounding countryside, the latter was encouraged to come rolling right up to the house. Of course, just as there were critics of formality in the previous century, there were now critics of the 'natural' style, particularly as this involved the deliberate introduction of mock ruins and so on. There were few flowers and no intimate gardens in which people might live, and by the end of the century geometry again played a part and soon Italian terraces made their appearance; these were used in conjunction with the building to form a transition between the house and the informal setting in which it stood.

This is all over-simplified and these observations are not offered as a condensed story of gardening but rather as a reminder that gardening has a history, and one that is spread over a long period of development.

It might be said that what was done to the great gardens of the past has nothing to do with the little plots of today, and this would be true as far as size goes, but it is also correct to say that the making of a garden in today's restricted space presents just as much of a problem as any expansive acreage, and that one can find the same principles of design at work in both. It is, therefore, helpful for the would-be garden maker to do some thoughtful observation in older gardens which are open to the public, as so many of them demonstrate the use of these principles. In the following pages, I have tried to determine the reasons for their success and to apply the findings to contemporary work.

It is of the greatest help to look for a moment at a basic factor – what is meant by 'design'? The word is one with a wide application, for example, if an engineer can produce a tool for use in making something else, provided it is functional its appearance is not important and it can be said to be well designed. On the other hand, the seat of a car, or a chair, must not only do all that is expected of it from the point of view of comfort and convenience, but to be well designed it must also be pleasing in appearance – beauty and usefulness must be combined. It is as well to remember that there are some things which, to be well designed, have merely to be beautiful with no practical value, such as a painting or a piece of sculpture. So in thinking about design there is the useful, the useful and beautiful, and the exclusively beautiful.

One dictionary says that 'design' is 'to formulate a plan, an outline or sketch' and another 'the arrangement of lines or forms which make up the plan of a work of art, with special regard to the *proportions, structure, movement and beauty of line of the whole*'. If this had been written with gardens in mind it could not be a more appropriate definition.

Garden design is an art in many ways comparable with drawing, painting, sculpture, architecture, and even music, poetry and literature, but the medium is different. This need be no cause for dismay in those who say 'I can't draw a line', or 'I only know what I like', because there is something of the artist in most people – it merely needs developing. It shows in the way they dress themselves and their children, the way they furnish their houses, and so on, and a great many people find an outlet for this latent ability in needlecraft, hobbies, and flower arranging.

The arts, and this in the broad sense includes garden design, stem not from rules and laws, but from inspiration and the controlled play of the imagination. An artist will paint, a sculptor will model in a certain way because he *feels* that that is how it should be done, and he might even have difficulty in explaining why; it is left to others to dissect and to analyse in order to find some lesson.

The painter produces three-dimensional effects on a flat canvas by the use of perspective, tone and lighting; the sculptor works in three dimensions, and evolves shapes which are beautiful from whatever angle, while the architect creates sculpture which the viewer can enter and become a part. This is what the gardener must do, and just as in a church one can discover new shapes unfolding as one moves, so in the garden, with the sky for a ceiling, one is compelled to move slowly to enjoy the change evoked by the placing of a single tree in an open space.

Have you ever noticed how difficult it is to hurry in a garden? Watch the people next time you visit one of the gardens which are open to the public, apart from the small boy who thinks he is a jet aircraft with a great lawn on which to manoeuvre, everyone moves as though they are about to slide into the nearest pew.

The gardener has another dimension to consider, that of time. His materials are not static like those of the painter and sculptor; he must think several years ahead, for a little tree will become a big one, perhaps too big for the design, and while a group of three trees will serve a purpose for, say, ten years, he must arrange them so that when two are later removed the remaining one will still be satisfying. He does, however, have some advantage over the painter with a blank canvas, in that he can look to the site for assistance in making a start, and to the climate and the dictates of function which will also prod him into a particular line of action. There are three main elements to be considered: 1. The site, its location, character, soil, climate, and so on. 2. The medium, i.e. the materials available for use. 3. The designer's own wishes (or if working for someone else, those of his client).

The main aim will be – in a word – *composition*, a composition of form, tone, texture and colour, and to achieve this the gardener will be guided by the principles which lead to good composition in the other arts. The dictionary definition gives a lead here 'with special regard to the proportions, structure, movement and beauty of line'.

The first of these requisites, proportion, is allied to scale and balance, which in turn lead to structure, involving in the process movement and beauty of line, so that it is almost impossible to separate the principles into water-tight compartments and say that any one is more important than another.

Proportion will call for a pleasing relationship, not only between length, breadth and height of a feature, such as a grouping of shrubs, but with the scale of that feature relative to its immediate surroundings. Proportion is something often best judged on site whenever possible, since perspective plays a part; for instance what is said to be perfect proportion – 10 by 6 – when seen drawn as a rectangle on paper, will, when marked out on the ground and seen from normal eye level, appear shorter when viewed down its length, and much narrower when seen across its width. See below.

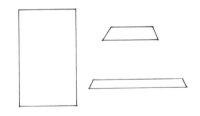

One must remember that with most gardens the house – a dominating feature – sets the scale, and while a classical colonnade springing from the corner of a large period house may well be fitting, the same thing of similar dimensions from the end of a little bungalow, would be out of scale.

It is not difficult to find examples of what, for want of a better term, I would call the disproportionate lawn. This can occur on any but the smallest of sites, caused probably by timid planting, or the need for play space. Too great an area is open grass, making the thin band of surrounding

planting insignificant, in fact, out of proportion. It is easily corrected by re-shaping and enlarging the planting areas, and if practicable breaking the lawn with a group of trees, or by a single specimen shrub in the case of the small plot. Open space and planting then complement each other on equal terms. This is illustrated below.

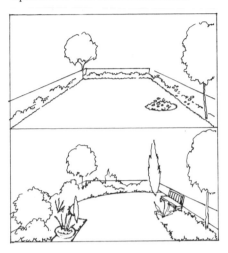

Proportion and scale are affected by the movement of the viewer within the composition. Planting along the edge of a drive traversed by cars at 30 or 40 miles an hour would need to be large trees at ten paces apart, rather than clipped box at 6-ft. intervals which is more suited to border a footpath where one walks at a mere two miles an hour.

A principle which is felt in painting or sculpture more by its absence than presence is balance. Good composition, whether in a picture, a piece of sculpture or a garden, is so satisfying that it is accepted without remark, but let there be too much weight on one side, let the sculpture appear as though about to topple, and the lack of balance is immediately felt.

Balance does not necessarily mean the even distribution of weight equally about a centre line, producing two matching halves. This type of balance we call symmetry. It is easily achieved, effective and restful and many of the early formal gardens one can still see today are based on an axial line, with further axial lines at right angles. Anyone making such a garden, particularly in a small space near the house, should remember that the building is the dominant note, and that the axis of the development will spring from the centre of an important window, door or other strong feature.

When walking in a symmetrically planned garden, there is little danger of feeling a loss of balance because one is steered along the axis at all times, but in a less formal layout, though it may be modelled to look balanced from the house, movement will be less restricted, and care must be taken to see that as walking opens up new views, these are also balanced. This is not easy, since what is

used to create balance in the main view may well upset the balance of some secondary view. It is a good practice, when in doubt, to stand on the site and place easily visible canes or poles (hang a sack or newspaper on them to make them more telling). Then move among them to judge whether or not these markers, representing substantial planting accents, are in the best places. The choice of position for these 'canes' may be the result of a groping for composition, or of a need to mask something unsightly outside the site; they may frame a view, or even fulfil a practical need such as a desire to grow fruit. They are, however, the first steps in creating a basic framework on which to build up a scheme. Collectively, they become the 'structure' mentioned in the dictionary definition of the word 'design'.

The principles of proportion, balance and now structure can, of course, apply to two-dimensional pattern where height is absent or negligible. A moment's reflection and you will find them at work in such familiar things as the design of wallpaper or tiles, or the design of this page. They will be essential to the ground pattern of the garden which, if well constructed, is halfway to a satisfying three-dimensional whole. An example of this can be seen in an arrangement of beds where the aim is to achieve a display of blocks of colour, as in a rose garden.

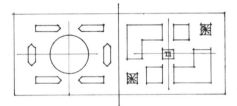

In the left-hand diagram, there is evidence of structure but proportion is bad, whereas in the right-hand one with similar structure, the faults in proportion have been corrected.

Nevertheless, in thinking of structure we think of something rising from the ground like the framework of a building – we are visualizing form not pattern and it is this grasp of three dimensions which is vital to composition in the garden, and which makes it important that the designer should know his medium if he is to use it properly. The most significant of the materials at his disposal are trees and shrubs, valuable chiefly for their form but with the added bonus of texture and the colour of blossom and leaf. Similar qualities will be found in herbaceous plants, roses and annuals, and, of course, any of these are quite useless without suitable soil in which they can grow. Plants and soil will be aided and abetted by inert materials such as timber, brick, stone, glass, and such products as perspex.

With the few basic principles of scale, proportion, balance and structure as a guide, it will help to go through the stages of planning a garden and look for other principles in the process. Using a hypothetical plot of rectangular shape, 56 ft. wide by 112 ft. long, and with typical problems, it is possible, step by step, to build up a scheme which satisfies the needs of the site, possible personal wishes, and at the same time forms a pleasing composition.

As a simple outline sketch the site seen from the house might look like this.

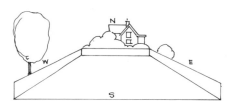

And looking in the opposite direction from the end of the plot back to the house, like this.

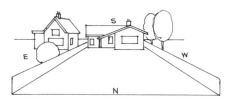

In many cases gardens are overlooked on both flanks, but for the purpose of this exercise a plot is chosen which has a neighbour on one side only, as would be the case at the corner of a road. The points to note first are the practical ones of aspect, screening and privacy, and it will be seen that the garden is overlooked at the far end, but that near the house only one side is affected in this way – the east, which is in view from the neighbour's upper windows. The west side is already screened by trees outside the plot.

So some screening is needed at 'A' and near 'B', the latter to take care of the oblique view from the neighbouring house on the east side. The natural action is to place one or more trees in each position. As young nursery trees look so inadequate, the tendency is often to use too many. For the moment I suggest placing only two trees at 'A' and two at 'B', as shown below.

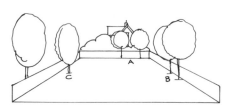

There is now too much weight on the east side and by placing the trees against the fence (a common practice) the lines of the boundaries are emphasized. Except in cases

where the aim is to build a garden based on geometric shapes, i.e. a formal garden, as opposed to one where shapes flow freely, or informally, the marking of the boundaries is, in my view, a mistake. Trees can, with advantage, be brought into a site whenever there is sufficient space to allow for this, and in this case balance must be maintained by adding a tree at 'C' whether there is a practical reason for this or not. In the last diagram the tree at 'C' has been added and by blocking it out with a finger it is easy to see the lop-sided effect that is created by having all the planting where it is needed most. There is, in any case, plenty of room along the west boundary and more planting can be sited there. There are a great many shrubs, such as syringa (lilac) and philadelphus (the mock orange), which grow to sizeable plants and these will have a marked effect in keeping weight on the west side.

Looking at these suggestions in the form of a three-dimensional diagram, a new factor emerges, namely perspective. This is a word used by the artist to mean a drawing which, though on a flat surface, successfully shows the three dimensions (especially, in this case, a sense of distance), as distinct from a plan or an elevation, each of which shows only two dimensions.

Perspective is what makes objects of the same size appear smaller in direct ratio to the increase in distance from the eye of the viewer. It makes the space between the two edges of a straight road, or a railway track, decrease until the edges meet at a point known as the 'Vanishing Point'. Any other parallel lines such as those of a parallel building and its roof standing at the roadside will also go to the same point.

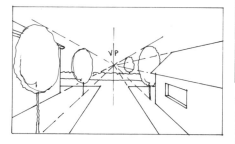

It follows that in order to block out an undesirable view, the same tree which appears small at the far end of the garden will be larger and more effective as a screen the nearer it is to the viewer's eye.

This must be an argument in favour of bringing the trees at 'A' in the diagram closer to the house where they might serve as the nucleus of a block of planting forming a division between two compartments of the garden. If the far end of the garden is to be used for something like a vegetable plot, privacy in this area would not be of major concern, but if it is necessary to ensure privacy here then the trees in the middle distance would be in addition to those at 'A'.

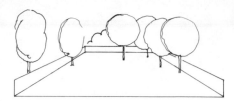

The drumstick symbols in these sketches are sufficient to indicate trees but, when making a composition in form, it is as well to remember that while many trees do make rounded heads, there are variations on this shape. The possibilities can be examined in greater detail later but, for the moment, a glance over the landscape or mature garden will show some trees which are up-reaching or conical, some downsweeping, popularly styled 'weeping', and others which branch out sideways, and so on. There are innumerable combinations of these shapes to use in juxtaposition, so that each enhances the character of the other. There are no rules, you simply bring together shapes which you feel add to the beauty of the space sculpture you are modelling.

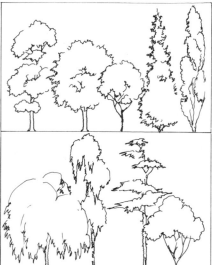

Whatever their silhouettes, however, the trees are being placed to serve a purpose and the designer's preference for formal or informal treatment will govern not only the position but also the character of the tree. If, for any reason, formality is desirable, the screening trees can follow the fence and turn across the plot to form the background to a geometric arrangement. To add to the effect the trees used can be uniform and of formal outline such as certain cherries or conifers, as shown here.

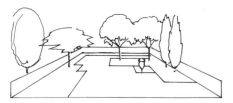

Informality, on the other hand, demands that the trees break away from straight rows and become a group – though satisfying as such, this group can be supported by shrubs and contained in a shape, which as the dictionary suggests has 'grace and movement'.

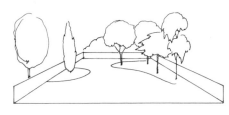

However, the lines here tend to lead the eye out of the picture and this can be corrected simply by the compensation of a line swinging in again. It is often enough to create such a line by the division between mown and unmown grass. See below.

In passing, I would like to point out here that if a plot has a view which is there for the borrowing, the lines mentioned above would, in fact, be shaped to take the eye to that view, and trees arranged to frame it. Such a variation is shown below.

Whatever we may require of a garden, we can, I hope, expect it to be peaceful. Where there is conflict and confusion there can be no calm, and so it is important that the shapes and lines created should be related in some way. Those so far drawn can be said to associate well – they move easily and harmoniously across the plot and, incidentally, in so doing help to preserve a sense of width. They are, so to speak, conscious of each other's presence, and if one can only imagine lines and shapes within a design as having this regard for each other, we realise that the mutual awareness leads to a wholeness of effect. This simple scheme is beginning to assume the essential quality of unity. This is a quality which will be in evidence not only in the whole of a small garden, but in the larger plot broken into sub-divisions, each of which, while being a separate entity, is so keyed to its surroundings that if removed it would be missed.

A call for harmony does not mean that there cannot be contrast, one of the designer's most useful aids. Contrast is stimulating and forceful and I have already mentioned its use in the bringing together of trees of differing shapes. Many a gardener who admits to having no extensive knowledge of the subject will agree that the most pleasing effects in his garden, often created by contrast, are accidental. Nevertheless one cannot rely on happy accidents and contrast must be organized, though in a way which does not appear contrived. Two shapes can be in complete contrast, and yet combined will produce a hybrid which is satisfying because it has character. Take, for example, a square and a circle, about as different as any two shapes can be. Bring them together. Each will now emphasize the basic quality of the other – the curve looks strong against the angularity of the square and vice versa, and the new shape which results is pleasing.

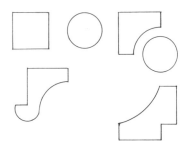

Contrast is used right through garden design, not only in ground shapes but in the juxtaposition of foliage and other textures, tones and colours.

It can even play a part in achieving unity. Imagine, for example, a border of shrubs in conjunction with a low building of marked horizontal character. There are low scrambling plants as a ground work, a horizontally branched larger shrub picking up the lines of the building, plus a single strong vertical provided by a cypress. Such an arrangement is shown in the next drawing.

Now take the cypress away – it is missed because, even though in contrast to most of the lines and shapes (admittedly not with the verticals in the building), it firmly 'pegs' the whole group to the surface of the ground.

The build up of the garden scheme has so far been a three-dimensional exercise because I think it essential to work this way, placing trees for screening in a balanced arrangement. These have been linked with planting areas so shaped that the whole looks right from the house. This at least makes sure that unity between the building and that part of the garden which is visible from the building is not lost.

When designing a garden it is helpful to see everything marked out on the ground even if, wisely, there has been some preliminary sketching on paper. Canes, poles, and little pegs mean much more than marks on paper. Incidentally, a practical point, never try to mark out curves on the ground with sticks or canes only, it is very difficult to produce good curves that way, and you finish up with a forest of markers so confusing as to be meaningless. The best way is to lay a hose (a plastic one should be warmed on a cold day to make it pliable) along the desired curve. It is often possible to anchor one end, and 'fling' the hose into a pleasing line. Rope, chain, heavy twine or a long measuring tape are good alternatives.

Such a marker is seen at a glance and, once satisfied with the effect, small pegs can be placed or it can be 'nicked' out or, if left for a few days on short grass, the hose will bleach a line itself. It is, however, not always practicable to go straight on with the preparation of the land and then a record must be made, so that everything can be re-staked at a later date. This record is made in the form of a plan and I will give suggestions for convenient ways of transferring 'ground to paper' later. The plan of the example plot is shown at the top of the column overleaf. Continuing the quest for unity it is necessary to consider how the informal arrangement is going to link up with the geometric lines of the house. The wisdom of having a formal area around the building designed to form a link with the informality beyond, was an idea which took centuries to develop and cannot be disregarded.

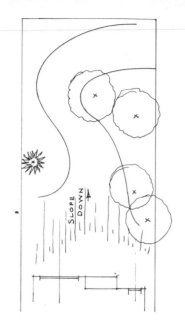

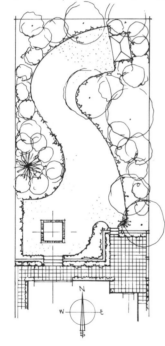

SCALE | 1̥o   2̥o   3̥o   4̥o   5̥o   6̥o |
                                    FT.

It may be said that there can be no parallel between a mansion in unlimited acres of open country, and the contemporary plot, measured in feet and standing among a hundred others. In terms of size this is true, in terms of principles it is false.

It would be unwise to underestimate the difficulties involved in trying to bring Nature into the homes of countless people who have to live in a tightly packed space. Until it becomes the practice to give everyone a share in a common garden maintained by local authority, all that can be attempted is to produce for each householder his own small slice of Nature's cake. As plots be-

come smaller it is necessary to scale down a little by making everything a fraction smaller; using, for example, 1-ft. square or 18-in. square paving tiles instead of 2-ft. square slabs, or a laburnum or a mountain ash where in a bigger garden an oak would be used, and so on.

To look at the problem for a moment in the form of a plan: there are two lines coming towards the house; they have been designed to look 'right' from the house but do not yet connect. As the shapes pull the eye to the left some way of counteracting this with a strong accent to the right must be established. It can be seen in earlier diagrams that the house is facing north, which means that any sitting out area must be sited away from the shadow of the building. Assuming some drop from the level of the building to that of the yet unmade garden, a terrace can be created which has an extension carried out into the sun. This extension makes for unity if it is opposite one of the main windows, and the steps to the lower garden can be sited opposite the other. Thus the basic shape is a reversed letter L. This is shown in the bottom plan on the left.

The sitting space will become a feature, especially when it carries its garden furniture, and will, in fact, provide the accent where it is needed. This L shape is particularly useful when the land falls diagonally from near right to far left, and in extreme cases a development can be a terrace on two levels.

Where there is a tendency to be overlooked from the right the projecting arm of terrace can be sheltered with a line of sawn timber posts or brick columns bearing either a single overhead beam, panels of trellis or both.

Without altering the shape the projection could hold a pool with fountain jet and the sitting-out area made on the lower level in the angle of the reversed L.

Looking back at the house now, the general lines of the scheme look like this.

The previously unconnected shapes can now be united with the terrace, which forms a close-up centre of interest using the further part of the garden as a backcloth. The completed scheme is shown on the right.

The eye goes first to the right foreground, it may well move to the left foreground, where there is another point demanding attention, but it is then drawn on down the curving glade of lawn and one feels compelled to move into the plot. At the end one turns and out of sight of the house is a new arresting feature in the form of a seat, an ornament or a summer house, which would be very suitable on this plot as it would face west.

Giving the eye something on which it can fix, or the establishment of a focal point, is an elementary principle offered to beginners in photography. Since the camera may well be of fixed focus, the advice is concerned less with technicalities, than with composition.

The novice soon learns that however beautiful the subject may be, to point the camera and shoot without careful consideration can produce a picture which is restless, falling apart and with, perhaps, an interesting feature disappearing off the edge of the print. This is understood and the lesson learned when it is Auntie who appears to have been suspended in midair and scalped, but the subsequent care which goes into the composing of a portrait is often missing when the subject is landscape.

Study of a good painting will show how the artist, by positioning for balance, by lighting, the use of perspective, and so on, will immediately hold the attention on the main subject. Then, if the composition contains other interests, the eye moves easily from one to the other guided by the basic shaping of the whole, but it does not run off the edge of the canvas.

This focus of attention is a principle to be observed in garden composition. The most important question to be decided is where the viewer is standing – at a window, a door, or at some point outside – and it is for the designer to choose. If the garden is regarded as an extension of the house then some accent is desirable opposite the window of a much-used room. At least one person sits for half an hour at a time with a view through the dining room window, and in many cases the kitchen window is particularly important. There are instances, however, when something of interest viewed

*An impression of the scheme discussed in the
accompanying text. The projection opposite
the study window is paved to take chairs.
This sitting-out area is sheltered by posts and
trellis but the far end is left open to allow the
border to be viewed from the window.*

*Opposite the living room on the lower level
is a pool with a figure or fountain jet.*

A scheme for an area which takes in (as sometimes happens) the lower end of the neighbour's plot. This allows room for a vegetable garden, which is approached by a path following the right-hand hedge and not seen in full.

Opposite the main window of the house is a square of paving in old York stone with a brick or tile pattern.

There is a drop to the lawn linked by three or four shallow steps radiating from the centre point of a circular pool – note that the pool is centred on the window. At the bottom of the steps to the right is a sheltered sitting-out alcove backed by a clipped hedge.

The lawn is open and uncluttered except for a single specimen tree, and the right-hand border curls round to screen the kitchen garden without making a hard line of fence or hedge.

WINDOW

from a favourite sitting area outside is to be preferred.

The way the focus of attention is created is less important than that it should exist. It might be an inert object like a bowl or ornament, a pool, a striking group of plants or a view down a path, but if it can be something which invites a closer look it will be instrumental in creating movement within the garden.

The ever present temptation in garden design is over elaboration. It is all too easy to go on adding frills and ornamentation, and to create intricate unworkable shapes. Our Victorian forebears found the temptation difficult to resist and would strew beds shaped like stars and crescents on an unoffending lawn, as though dropped from the sky. Examples of such enthusiasm are still to be found, especially in town and suburban gardens made about the turn of the century, but it is also easy to find the same fervour at work today. There are highly ornamental and castellated walls where a simple one would suffice, wriggling curves where a graceful sweep would be more effective, too many accessories such as urns, pots and vases, and the indiscriminate cutting of small beds which are in no way related to their surroundings. It is all rather like pinning ribbons, bows, and brooches to a well-tailored suit.

In garden planning it is wise to bear in mind at all stages the value of simplicity, and to err on the side of omission than on the addition of extra detail.

A garden cannot be produced by the application of a set of rules or instructions; any scheme resulting from such procedure would be mechanical and uninspired. Rather it will arise from the controlled play of the imagination, and the observance of the principles outlined here will ensure that your aspirations and ideas are brought to the site in the most effective yet restrained way.

Translating ground work to paper

If you design the main ground shapes of your garden in the way already discussed, i.e. by placing out marker pegs for trees and hose or line for the planting areas, you may well find it necessary to make a record of your work. This may depend on the time of year, whether or not you are in a position to go ahead with digging at once, and so on. On the other hand you may prefer to work out a scheme in the form of a plan on paper. Whichever you do there must be a procedure for committing work on the ground to paper and vice versa.

Assuming the first situation and you have a hose lying on the ground, or a rope or whatever was the most convenient way of describing a curve. First, lay down a long measuring tape (or even a straight tight string marked off at 10 ft. intervals) in a position which can be related accurately to a fence or the face of the house. This line should be as close as possible to the newly laid curve. Then from zero on the tape move along and at convenient intervals (say 10 ft.) take measurements square off the tape to the hose line and note them. Where the curve is moving sharply measurements taken a little closer than 10 ft. apart would be an advantage. If a line is now drawn on a piece of squared paper, the offset measurements can be set off at the appropriate intervals and these will give a series of points which can be joined up to describe the correct curve. The hose can be removed or if the curve has been marked by rope and/or pegs the lot can be taken up. At some later date the tape can be relaid in exactly the same position, the offsets recorded can be set off and marked with canes, which can be connected to reproduce the curve originally laid and removed. This is also the way to transfer a curve designed on paper to the ground. Draw the line on your plan, mark off to scale 10 ft. intervals, measure the offsets to the curve, write in on the plan, then translate outside.

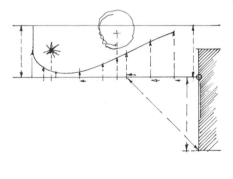

Colour

Little mention has so far been made of colour. This is deliberate because I want to stress the need to think first in terms of form, even though plants with coloured foliage or flower mass may be used to build up that form. One cannot rely upon colour to save a bad composition and I suggest that it should not be regarded as an end in itself. Its use, however, in what might otherwise be a restful, though perhaps sad study in greens and browns, will bring life and uplift, particularly on a dull day.

A careful grouping can become a focal point, a desirable feature which has already been discussed. For example, the use of blending and contrasting foliage, variegated, golden, and red with a range of greens; yellow roses in front of deep shadow, or red ones emphasized by a mass of white and so on.

Many people instinctively employ colour without even thinking of the theory behind it; however, it may be helpful if I give a brief appraisal of surface colour, even if this means the risk of stripping a complicated subject to the bare bones. It must be remembered that we are not dealing with dyed fabrics, paint, or rainbows but pigments contained in the surface of plant leaves, bark and flowers, and arranged by Nature in a complex and subtle way. For example, what we might call a green leaf, on examination, proves to be not merely green as paint or dye of that name would be, but a green veined and broken by other colours, shaded and marked so that it is vibrant and alive.

I feel I cannot do better than take what I hope will be a thought-provoking look at what is usually called the colour circle. Imagine three unadulterated primary pigments – yellow, red and blue – set out at equal spacing around the white disc of a clock face (a convenient way of referring to positions), the yellow at 12 o'clock the blue at 4 and the red at 8. Then allow them to blend gradually with the neighbour on each side, and in imperceptible gradations the yellow changes to orange at 10 o'clock and continues to change through red-orange to red at 8. The red gradually becomes purple at 6 o'clock and continues to blue at 4. Blue goes through blue-green to green at 2 o'clock and on to yellow-green and finally to yellow. See colour circle overleaf.

The colour at any point is a *hue* denoting a character of its own (an orange-yellow or green-blue for instance). This is clear colour which can be brought to maximum saturation or purity, when it can be said to be at its brightest or of high *tone*. The hue can also be thinned gradually by the addition of white to a *tint*. Having been strengthened or weakened it can take in grey in varying quantity producing a range of greyed tints and shades of the particular hue. The grey is produced by adding the right quantity of the hue radially opposite on the circle and when the red–yellow and blue are in balance they make a rich neutral grey or near black.

The most difficult hues to bring together are those which are unadulterated and in their most brilliant form, but one can safely group any within the same third of the circle, for example, yellow, with its immediate neighbours as far as red. However, those hues lying on each side of the red, i.e. the orange side and the blue side are, for the cautious, happier apart. This is worth considering when grouping roses, or placing, for example, a patch of strong orange near to a rose which is of a red which contains even a little blue.

The less 'fierce' hues are easier, in fact the more grey and white one adds the nearer to a monochrome, which is no problem at all.

A garden about the length of a tennis court where the primary wish is for a swimming pool. The pool measures approximately 15 by 24 ft., and there is an area for chairs at its shallow end, which is the one further from the house. Three steps lead down to the lawn on the right-hand side of the pool, and beside the right-hand hedge is a narrow service path to a small vegetable patch at the far end of the plot.

This is an arrangement suitable for many plots which are overlong and where surplus space is given to vegetables or orchard, while still leaving room for a well-proportioned lawn and borders.

The scheme is orientated to allow maximum sun to reach the pool.

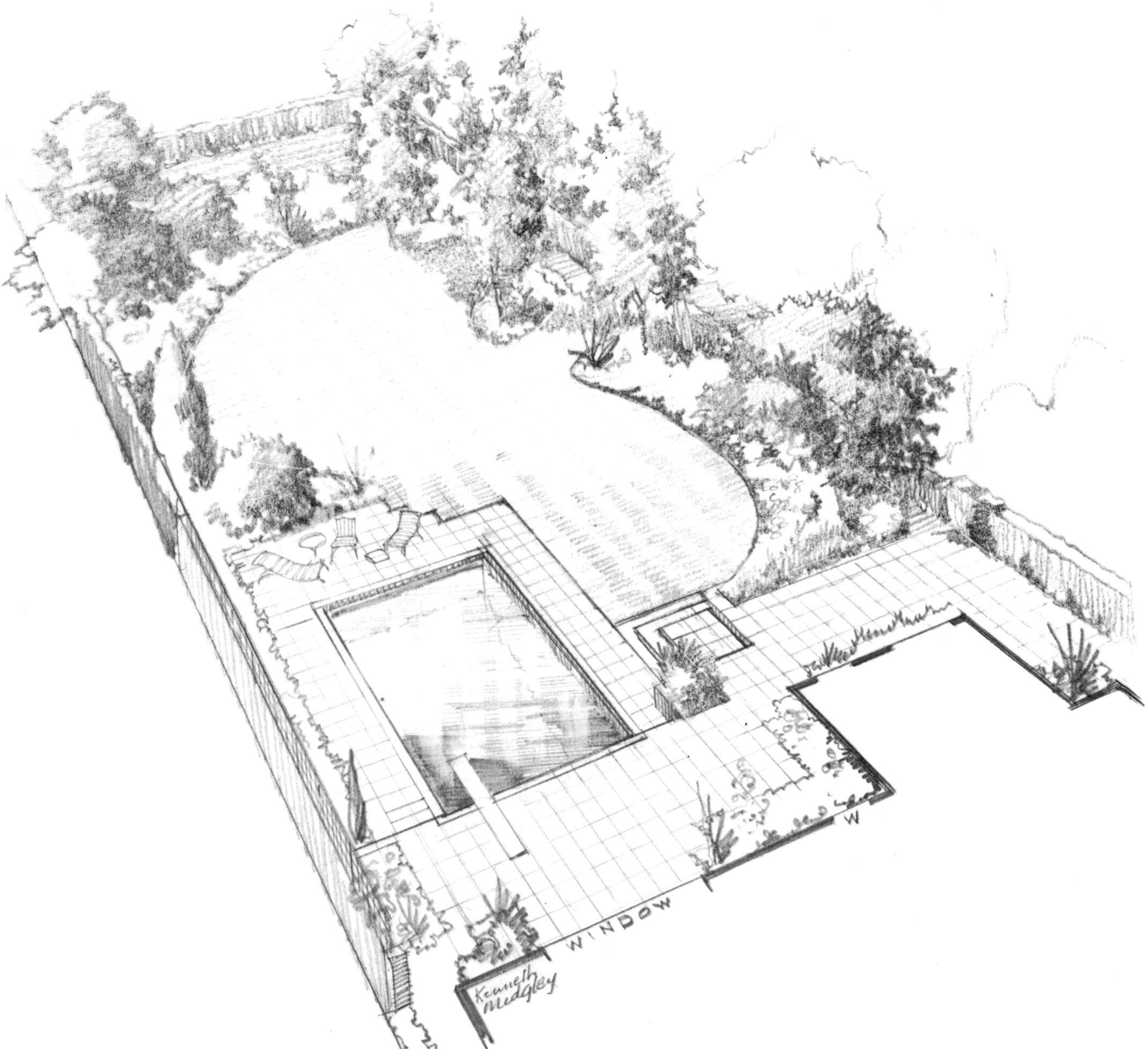

Kenneth Medgley

WINDOW

W

There is pleasure and interest in grouping plants with hues that blend, particularly the range of delicate pale tints and greyed shades, but for punch one needs contrast.

Contrasts can be chosen if necessary by reference to the colour circle. Hues which are radially opposite each other with a little latitude either side are good contrasts, for instance yellow with purple, red-purple and blue-purple. An old trick to find the right contrasting colour is to let your eye do it. Stare hard for a few moments at any hue against a white background. Then look at a plain white sheet and the shape on which you have been concentrating will appear for a moment in a pale tint of the complementary hue. A little rough and ready but it helps.

Sometimes a combination of colours does not work out as well as expected although in theory it should. In such a case the first thing to suspect is tone. The hues in the circle fall into a tonal order. Yellow is the brightest, then working both ways round the circle the brightness diminishes until 6 on the clock face is reached where there is deep purple. When using yellow and purple together, a light yellow is better with a deep purple than a strong yellow with a watered-down purple – mauve in other words. An orange which is lighter than red is better than a strong orange with a pink (a pale red), and a pale orange with its contrasting blue as a deep shade is more pleasing than a strong orange with a delicate pale blue, and so on.

The warm colours, which are those in the orange sector, tend to assert themselves, while the cool hues, in the blue sector, are recessive. This is important when trying to create an impression of length in a small garden. The assertive colours, the yellows, oranges and whites, can be planted in the foreground while the recessive hues from the blue-red range, particularly those containing grey, can be placed further away where their tendency to recede creates an illusion of greater depth. Of course when you look back to the house the effect is lost.

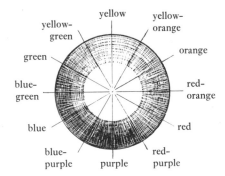

A diagram of a colour circle

Fortunately for us Nature takes care of a good deal. Pluck a pink rose and examine it, it is not easy to give the colour a name which describes it, the outer petals may be white at the base shaded with yellow, the white is overlaid with red veining and a touch of blue but note the way in which the red is carried down the stalk and into the leaf. Nature ensures that the green foliage which becomes the background to the rose has the right amount of tone to set off the flower and, in fact, the greens and the brown of the soil will help to such an extent that you are not likely to go wrong, and, if you do, next year you can alter it.

The Shape of Trees

Any attempt to classify and catalogue plants according to shape and size might be said to be treating them as merchandise produced to order and specification, and only the nurseryman need of necessity do this.

Perhaps to our advantage, they refuse to fall into sharply defined compartments and can only be grouped broadly according to their overall characteristics. For example, we might think of them under the headings: Rounded, Vertical, Horizontal, Weeping and Specially Decorative. It may be difficult sometimes to decide under which heading a tree will fall or if, in fact, it should be placed under two headings. However, the object here is not to produce written tables but to initiate a way of thinking.

Within each shape group there will be a range of sizes. This is important since there are some which, though admirable in woodland or park, are unsuitable for most small gardens, while there are others which are ideal. Any group must also contain large, small and dwarf shrubs and under the various headings below are given examples ranging from forest trees to miniatures.

ROUNDED

This is the most common outline and in it I would include such variations as up-ended pear and egg shapes, and trees which have a 'V' formation. *Examples* of trees falling into this group are as follows (where possible common well-known names are given in brackets).

Forest, Park or Large *Acer platanoides* (Norway Maple), *Acer pseudoplatanus* (Sycamore), *Aesculus hippocastanum* (Horse Chestnut), *Betula* (Birch), *Carpinus* (Hornbeam), *Castanea sativa* (Sweet Chestnut), *Fagus* (Beech), *Fraxinus* (Ash), *Quercus* (Oak), *Tilia* (Lime) and *Ulmus* (Elm).

Medium of garden size *Crataegus* (Thorn), *Laburnum*, *Malus* (Crab Apple), *Prunus* (Cherry), *Prunus pissardii* (Purple Plum), *Sorbus aria* (Whitebeam), and *Sorbus aucuparia* (Mountain Ash).

Shrub size This covers many of the bigger growing shrubs up to 10 ft. or so.

Some *Berberis*, *Camellia*, *Cotoneaster*, *Laurus* (Laurel), *Philadelphus* (Mock Orange), *Rhododendron*, *Rhus* (Sumach), *Syringa* (Lilac), *Viburnum tinus* (Laurustinus).

Small and dwarf A range from the smallest to about 4 ft. *Cytisus* (Broom), *Genista hispanica* (Spanish Gorse), *Hebe* (Veronica), *Ruta* (Rue), *Santolina* (Lavender Cotton), *Senecio*.

VERTICAL

These are the up-reaching fastigiate plants and those making a spire-like outline, though many such plants also have a marked horizontal structure. Shrubs include those with generally vertical shoots.

Large *Carpinus betulus fastigiata* (upright Hornbeam), *Cupressus* and *Chamaecyparis*, *Fagus sylvatica* Dawyck· (Dawyck Beech), *Larix* (Larch), *Libocedrus decurrens* (Incense Cedar), *Picea abies* (Spruce), *Populus nigra italica* (Lombardy Poplar).

Medium *Arundinaria* (Bamboo), *Crataegus stricta* (upright Thorn), some Cypress, *Eucryphia*, *Prunus* Amanogawa (upright cherry), *Taxus baccata fastigiata* (Irish Yew).

Shrub size *Chaemaecyparis fletcheri*, *Juniperus* Skyrocket, *Philadelphus erectus*, *Viburnum fragrans*.

Small and dwarf *Berberis thunbergii erecta*, *Juniperus communis compressa* (dwarf Juniper), *Picea albertiana conica*, *Thuja* Rheingold.

HORIZONTAL

These are trees which have pronounced horizontal branching or with horizontal shadows in the foliage. Some, such as *Pinus sylvestris* in the juvenile form, might be classified as vertical but when mature have horizontal form too.

Large *Cedrus libani* (Cedar of Lebanon), certain *Picea* (Spruce) of spire shape but with laminated shadow effects, *Pinus nigra austriaca* (Austrian Pine), *Pinus sylvestris* (Scots Pine).

Medium *Crataegus crus-galli* (Cockspur Thorn), *Prunus* Shiro Fugen, *P.* Shimidsu Sakura, *Taxus dovastoniana*.

Shrub size *Acer palmatum dissectum*, *Pyracantha angustifolia*, *Viburnum tomentosum mariesii*.

Small and dwarf *Chaenomeles simonii* (Quince), *Cotoneaster horizontalis*, *C. microphyllus*, *Cytisus kewensis*, several prostrate junipers including *Juniperus horizontalis*, *J. procumbens*.

WEEPING

This group would include not only trees with downward sweeping branches, but those which go up but with 'dripping' branchlets. It would include among the shrubs those which form a dome shape.

Large *Betula pendula dalecarlica* (Swedish Birch), *Fagus sylvatica pendula* (Weeping Beech), *Fraxinus excelsior pendula* (Weeping Ash), *Picea breweriana* (Brewers Weeping Spruce).

Medium *Betula pendula youngii* (Young's Weeping Birch), *Prunus subhirtella pendula* (Weeping Rosebud Cherry), *P.* Kiku-shidare Sakura (Oriental Weeping Cherry), *Pyrus salicifolia pendula* (Weeping Pear).

Shrub size *Acer palmatum dissectum, Buddleia alternifolia, Cotoneaster hybridus pendulus, Escallonia langleyensis.*

Small and dwarf *Cedrus deodara pendula* (Dwarf Weeping Cedar), *Cotoneaster conspicuus decorus, Juniperus depressa aurea, Viburnum davidii.*

DECORATIVE

A loose grouping for plants of special character or particular favourites.

Large *Araucaria araucana* (Monkey Puzzle), *Ginkgo biloba* (Maidenhair Tree), *Liquidambar* (Sweet Gum), *Liriodendron tulipifera* (Tulip Tree), *Pinus strobus* (Weymouth Pine), *Pinus sylvestris* (Scots Pine), *Robinia pseudoacacia frisia* (Mock Acacia, golden form).

Medium *Acer palmatum* (Japanese Maple), *Arbutus unedo* (Strawberry Tree), *Genista aetnensis* (Mount Etna Broom), *Magnolia, Parottia persica, Prunus serrula tibetica.*

Small and dwarf Japanese azaleas, miniature conifers, *Pernettya.*

Plant Arrangement

The main shrub planting is as much a part of the design of the garden as the trees and the ground plan so far discussed. Having gone to so much trouble over the latter it is wise to give thought to the selection and arrangement of the shrubs. The importance of this is not always fully appreciated and too often a border is furnished with an odd lot ordered at random.

The choice is wide and the number of ways in which they can be arranged seems limitless, but since we are concerned with design in general rather than anyone's particular problems, it is best to look at a few useful general principles.

First, a practical note, the enclosed spaces within the lines marked on the ground for planting should be deeply dug (two spits) and cleared of perennial weeds, so that new shrubs can root freely and receive the maximum benefit from rain. This, for a time at least, exposes a lot of bare soil which has to be kept clean, but it is a better method than having spot beds in grass which make mowing difficult.

The planting scheme can be worked out in the form of a scale plan on squared paper,

or on site using labelled canes. Obviously the latter is something which is done only after the ground is ready, though it does have the advantage of allowing the designer to visualize the shrubs in position and judge the amount of space needed for each.

To supplement the basic information given elsewhere in this book about any favoured plant, a catalogue from a good nursery will be helpful. Many provide information on height and eventual spread, time of flowering, colour, the aspect needed and, of course, the cost.

Aspect is important and from observation you will be able to judge how sunny or shaded is the position of the proposed group or border. It is necessary too, at this stage, to decide whether or not tall shrubs are needed for providing privacy and, if so, how tall? Is privacy in the winter important, demanding the use of evergreens? Perhaps the whole group has to be low-growing to avoid blocking a view.

You are working very much in three dimensions and in time the profile of the border as a whole can be a pleasantly varied line.

Except in the case of a hedge, a solid even wall of shrubs of similar height, with medium and small growers ranged evenly in front, is to be avoided. The border can be made interesting and attractive by varying the height of the back, and here and there bringing forward a taller shrub to stand as a specimen in a drift of low plants, as in the diagram above.

Small trees, those under the heading 'garden size', will help the border but remember that in time a tree will form a canopy of shade and possibly keep off rain, so suitably tolerant shrubs must be planted around it.

An early decision is the vexed question of allowing time for development. Is the border to be effective during the next five years or so, demanding close planting and subsequent wastage? Or can you wait for well spaced, slow growers to achieve their height and put up with bare earth in the meantime, alternatively, infilling with cheaper plants, herbaceous plants, roses or annuals until such time as the shrubs take over. There is a compromise which will be found as work proceeds.

The slower growers – the plants for the future which often include the expensive ones like magnolia, *Acer palmatum* (Japanese Maple, *Arbutus unedo* (Strawberry Tree) camellia, ilex (holly), syringa (lilac) and so on – are placed so that they will have room

to develop without cramping each other. Between and around them can be planted equally attractive but faster growing shrubs which can be thinned out later. A great many of these lend themselves to grouping so that they appear as one plant, or a mass of foliage and flower. At a later date the odd one here and there can go, without spoiling the effect. Even some of the larger growers can be grouped, but in this one must be guided by the character of the plant. For instance, three lilacs can be planted 4 or 5 ft. apart, too close to allow any one making a fine single specimen, but the habit is such that they interlock as one, whereas three arbutus planting in the same way may always appear to be struggling for possession.

Where necessary trees can also be grouped closely, provided all are of the same kind. While three thorn, *or* three laburnum, *or* three crab stems making one head are striking and acceptable, a mixed group comprising one of each striving for existence is unhappy to say the least. 'Garden size' trees should be kept about 18 ft. apart, except for fastigiate subjects which have little spread and can be closer. Once these have been approximately positioned, select and place out any big evergreens needed for screening or as background. These will be plants such as *Cotoneaster lacteus, Berberis stenophylla, Elaeagnus ebbingei*, laurel, and the odd cypress and, on acid soil, rhododendron. Most of such tall-growing plants are capable of reaching out 4 or 5 ft. from the stem and therefore need to be planted approximately 8 ft. apart. For a quicker effect they can be closer, but it is better to plant a temporary shrub such as buddleia between and slightly in front of them.

Where evergreen foliage is important, other evergreen shrubs of slightly smaller stature such as osmarea, *Berberis darwinii, Cotoneaster franchetii* and *Choisya ternata* can be used to fill in the gaps, but these should be placed a little forward in the border.

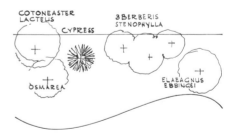

Once the choice of background plants has been made place out the special plants mentioned earlier. The bare earth between can then be occupied by a host of other decorative and beautiful shrubs which can be used to build up the group. Try using contrasts in foliage, the finely cut leaves and the small leaves with the big ones, plants with near

The overall layout, with no attempt to show detail, for a bigger, country plot.

The house has a shallow terrace with a hedge-enclosed rose garden to one side, while at the kitchen end of the building is an area for drying laundry. There is a kitchen garden beyond the garages.

The drop to the main lawn is accomplished by a main flight of steps, and there is another approach by way of the rose garden and an iris garden, complete with ornamental pool. From the pool area a pergola leads between borders to a summerhouse which looks out over the informal pond in the foreground.

Sports facilities are kept together in the left foreground. The swimming pool is well protected by a curving hedge and the one which forms a background for the tennis court.

In an area of this size it is possible to arrange for grass walks between the shrubs.

This scheme is best suited to a house facing south.

Kenneth Midgley.

Formality and informality blended in a small plot (40 by 20 yd.) with space allowed for vegetables.

The scheme is balanced about an axial line from the centre of the garden door in the centre foreground, and is adaptable to varying aspects provided the main sitting-out area near the projecting window is exposed to sunshine at the most useful time of day, and that the small summerhouse and pool are not in permanent shade.

There is a drop of about 15 in. from terrace to lawn, these two features being linked by three steps of equal depth. It is possible to walk dry shod from the stone-paved terrace down to the summerhouse, and, behind it (though not visible in the sketch),

to the vegetable garden. As an alternative a narrow path could be taken right down the plot under the left-hand hedge.

The two projecting side hedges help to give shelter to the sitting-out area and provide a sense of enclosure without masking from view what lies beyond.

Where children playing in the garden must be watched from the house, the big beds and urn in the left foreground could be omitted and the area used as an open play lawn.

WINDOW

DOOR

vertical stems or 'V' formation like bamboo, leycesteria, *Viburnum fragrans* and rubus, behind or beside those which reach out like *Viburnum tomentosum* Lanarth, or rounded shapes such as hebe (veronica).

Consider the effect of the light-coloured foliage of such plants as *Cornus alba variegata*, or *Weigela florida variegata* associated with the leaves of *Cotinus coggygria* in its red form or *Berberis thunbergii atropurpurea*. These latter and other red-leaved plants might themselves be neighbours of *Senecio*

laxifolius, which is silver grey, or *Philadelphus coronarius aureus*, which is gold. The opportunities are intriguing and endless, especially as you work forward to the 'knee high' plants such as some potentillas, caryopteris, ceratostigma, and so on, all of which have not only soft muted foliage, but delicate harmony in the flower association. Such small subjects can be planted as close as 2 ft. for immediate effect and will make a billowing mass, out of which may rise a small cypress or a taller growing shrub. At

some later date, a few can be taken out if any thinning is necessary.

It is important to guard against the tendency to make an even covering for the bed, as plants soon grow and if groups, as well as single plants, are too close, the effect is confusing and irritating to anyone with a tidy mind. Bare earth, kept hoed, makes a pleasant background and there are plenty of creeping and prostrate plants with which to make a carpet for anyone who has no time or inclination to use a hoe.

FRUITS & VEGETABLES

Fruit Growing

Strawberries fit well into the vegetable garden regime since they need to be renewed fairly frequently, but most other kinds of fruit require permanent positions where they can be left undisturbed for many years. Blackberries and loganberries can be trained on fences and screens or used to cover outbuildings. Raspberries require a plot to themselves where they can be trained to wires. Apples, pears, plums, cherries and peaches can all be grown naturally as standard or bush trees. Alternatively, they can be trained in various ways either against walls, fences etc., or on posts and wires, in which case they may be useful as divisions, both ornamental and useful, between one part of the garden and another. Gooseberries and red and white currants can also be used semi-ornamentally but black currants are best grown as bushes in a plot of their own.

All fruit trees make many feeding roots close to the surface so they should not be planted where frequent soil cultivation has to be carried out as this would destroy these roots. Some fruit trees, and most notably apples and pears, need fairly frequent spraying to keep them free from pests and diseases and this may limit the ornamental plants or vegetables which can be grown underneath them.

APPLE (*Malus sylvestris*)

Apples grow in most soils which are reasonably fertile and well cultivated and which are neither so porous that they dry out rapidly in summer nor so close that they readily become waterlogged in winter.

Nursery-grown apple trees are always grafted on to an apple stock. This stock should be chosen to suit the variety of apple and the purpose for which it is required. For standard trees a vigorous stock such as Malling 16 or 25 will be used, whereas if a small single-stemmed cordon tree is required a much less vigorous stock such as Malling 9, 7, 26 or Malling-Merton 106 may be the one selected. For bush trees, that is those with a short main trunk bearing numerous branches, a moderately vigorous stock such as Malling 2 or Malling-Merton 3 will be used.

Prepare the ground for apples by digging or forking it well and working in rotted manure or garden refuse at 1 cwt. to 15 sq. yd. Before planting give a topdressing of a good compound fertilizer at 3 to 4 oz. per sq. yd., and in each successive year give a top-dressing of manure or compost in late winter followed by a topdressing of compound fertilizer at the same rates.

Plant from autumn to early spring if the trees are lifted from the open ground or at any time of the year if they are purchased in containers. Plant them 1 in. deeper than in the nursery bed or container – the planting level will be indicated by the soil mark on the main stem. Standard apple trees should be spaced 20 to 25 ft. apart, bush trees 12 to 15 ft. apart, horizontal-trained trees 12 to 15 ft. apart and single-stem cordons 2 ft. apart. The last two types of tree should be placed against walls or fences or trained to strained wires in rows set at least 6 ft. apart. Stake or tie all trees immediately after planting to prevent windrocking.

Prune young apple trees immediately after planting. Shorten all young stems by about one third and make each cut just above a growth bud which points away from the centre of standard or bush trees, or in the direction the new growth of horizontal-trained or cordon trees is required to take.

For the first few years continue to prune the trees much as in the first year, but shorten some of the thinner side growths that are not required to make main branches

APPLES	USE	SEASON	COLOUR	FLOWERING	FERTILITY	COMMENTS
American Mother	D	mid-season	yellow and red	late	PSF	irregular cropping, distinctive flavour
Arthur Turner	C	early	yellow and brown	mid-season	PSF	good cropping, handsome blossom
Beauty of Bath	D	early	yellow and red	early	PSF	ripens and drops suddenly
Bramley's Seedling	C	late	green	mid-season	SS	makes a lot of growth, fine blossom
Charles Ross	D	mid-season	green and red	mid-season	PSF	very handsome but indifferent quality
Court Pendu Plat	D	late	yellow and russet	late	PSF	good cropping, small fruits
Cox's Orange Pippin	D	mid-season	yellow and russet red	mid-season	PSF	susceptible to scab and canker, fine flavour
Crawley Beauty	C	late	green and red	late	SF	good cropping, wide-spreading habit
Early Victoria	C	early	yellowish green	mid-season	PSF	also known as Emneth Early
Edward VII	C	late	green	late	PSF	heavy fruits which cook pink
Egremont Russet	D	mid-season	russet	early	PSF	resistant to scab
Ellison's Orange Pippin	D	early	yellow and red	mid-season	PSF	irregular cropping distinctive flavour
Golden Delicious	D	late	yellow	mid-season	PSF	heavy and regular cropping
Grenadier	C	early	green	mid-season	SF	good cropping

APPLES	USE	SEASON	COLOUR	FLOWERING	FERTILITY	COMMENTS
Heusgen's Golden Reinette	D	late	yellow and red	late	PSF	good cropping
Howgate Wonder	C	late	yellow and red	mid-season	PSF	very large fruits
James Grieve	D	early	yellow and red	mid-season	PSF	susceptible to scab and canker
Lane's Prince Albert	C	late	green and red	mid-season	PSF	good cropping, compact habit
Laxton's Epicure	D	early	yellow and red	mid-season	PSF	good flavour but soon spoils
Laxton's Fortune	D	early	yellow and red	early	PSF	a very handsome apple
Laxton's Superb	D	late	yellow and brown	mid-season	PSF	inclined to bear biennially
Lord Lambourne	D	mid-season	yellow and red	early	PSF	good cropping, compact habit
Merton Charm	D	mid-season	yellow	mid-season	PSF	fruits juicy but rather small
Rev. William Wilks	C	mid-season	pale yellow	early	PSF	very large fruits, compact habit
Ribston Pippin	D	mid-season	yellow and russet red	early	SS	fine flavour, good cropping
Scarlet Pimpernel	D	early	yellow and red	early	PSF	handsome, rather sharp flavoured fruits
Sturmer Pippin	D	late	yellow and russet	early	PSF	ripens slowly and may take months to develop full flavour
Sunset	D	mid-season	yellow and red	mid-season	PSF	good flavour and easy to grow
Tydeman's Early	D	early	yellow and red	mid-season	PSF	earlier and better flavoured than Worcester Pearmain
Tydeman's Late Orange	D	late	yellow and russet	mid-season	PSF	rather like Cox but keeps later
Wagener	CD	late	green and brown	mid-season	PSF	good cropper, resistant to scab and canker
Worcester Pearmain	D	early	yellow and red	mid-season	PSF	handsome fruit but must be picked and used ripe

D = dessert C = cooking
CD = cooking or dessert SF = self-fertile
SS = self-sterile PSF = partially self-fertile

Fully self-fertile varieties can be planted alone. Fully self-sterile varieties must have another variety of apple nearby for pollination. Partially self-fertile varieties will crop on their own but will usually give better crops with another variety nearby for cross pollination. Pollinators should be chosen from varieties that bloom at the same time.

or stems to 1 or 2 in. This will help them to form fruit buds and eventually spurs.

As standard and bush trees mature they require progressively less pruning, eventually only needing the old or overcrowded branches, stems and spurs to be thinned out in autumn or winter.

Horizontal-trained trees and cordons require special pruning to maintain their shapes and to restrict their growth. Much of this can be done in summer.

Start when the young stems of the year are about the thickness of a pencil at the base and beginning to get woody. Shorten each side shoot growing direct from a main stem or branch to four leaves, not counting the rosette of partly developed leaves which cluster around the base of most young shoots. Continue to do this as the shoots reach this stage, but do no pruning of this kind after late summer.

In autumn or winter shorten main stems (those continuing the line of the main branches) by about one-third or, if the trees have filled the available space, cut these extension stems right out. With horizontal-trained trees cut the central stem off at a point 15 to 18 in. above the uppermost pair of horizontal arms. Then the following spring train the shoot from the topmost bud straight up to continue the central stem of the tree and the shoots from the two buds below it to right and left to form two new horizontal arms. Remove all other shoots from the central stem.

If apple trees set very heavy crops it may be necessary to thin the young fruits to relieve the strain on the trees, improve the size of the fruits and increase the likelihood of the trees cropping again the next year.

Start to thin fruits in early summer when they are no larger than marbles but do not complete the thinning until after mid-summer as there is often a heavy natural fall of fruits just prior to this. Apples are borne in clusters and usually the central fruit is thick stalked and should be removed first. Retain the best two in each cluster for dessert varieties, but only one per cluster for cooking varieties.

Pick apples as soon as the fruits part readily from the trees. This will be in late summer for early varieties, in early autumn for mid-season varieties and in mid-autumn for late varieties.

Late apples may be stored in boxes in a cool, slightly damp place, such as a shed with an earthen floor, but early apples should be used as soon as possible.

Before any apple tree can produce fruit the female organs in the flowers must be fertilized with pollen from the male organs. This may not occur if there is a shortage of insects, particularly bees, which carry ripe pollen from flower to flower; if the weather is bad at blossom time so that the blossom is damaged or insects are prevented from visiting it; or if the tree lacks food reserves at this critical stage of development.

Fertilization can also be prevented by lack of suitable pollen. Some varieties of apple are almost totally self-sterile: they are incapable of being fertilized by their own pollen and must be pollinated by another variety of apple. If no other apple tree grows nearby or the only ones that do flower at a different time (a few days may make all the difference), they will never crop.

Most varieties of apple tree are partially self-sterile: they will set some fruit with their own pollen, but will produce far better crops if they receive pollen from another variety of apple.

It is wise, therefore, to plant several different varieties chosen to pollinate each other. An alternative method is to graft several varieties of apple on one tree.

APRICOT (Prunus armeniaca)

Apricots require rather rich, well-cultivated and well-drained soil and a warm, sunny, sheltered position. Like peaches and nectarines they are usually fan trained against sunny walls or are grown in greenhouses with little or no artificial heat. Apricots are always budded on to plum stocks.

Soil preparation, planting and general care are the same as for peaches and nectarines, except for pruning. Apricots bear their best fruit on the older stems and branches, and are mainly pruned in summer. Start in early summer by rubbing out badly placed or unwanted shoots which cannot readily be tied in. In midsummer shorten other young side shoots to six leaves. In autumn shorten the young shoots extending the main branches by about one-third or cut them out altogether if the wall space is already filled.

BLACKBERRY, LOGANBERRY
(Rubus ursinus, R.u. loganobaccus)

There are numerous varieties of blackberry differing from each other in several features including that of being thornless.

There are both armed and thornless varieties of loganberry, which bear identical, rather acid, but pleasantly flavoured fruits.

Place blackberries and loganberries against fences or sheds on which they can be trained, or provide heavy wires strained between strong posts to support their considerable weight.

Plant one-year-old canes of blackberries and loganberries in autumn or winter and cover their roots with 2 to 3 in. of soil. Shorten the canes by a foot or so and attach them to the supports provided.

Sprinkle a little compound fertilizer around the thornless varieties each spring but do not feed the vigorous varieties. Blackberries and loganberries may be permitted to carry some fruit the first year, if growing well.

When the fruit has been gathered, cut out as much as possible of the growth that has fruited, but retain the best young canes. With blackberries a few of these may grow from near the base of old canes so it may not be possible to cut the whole of each old cane out. If there are more young canes than can be trained in conveniently some of these may be removed as well.

CHERRY (Prunus avium, P. cerasus)

Cherries like well-drained, well-cultivated soils and do especially well where the subsoil is chalk or limestone. They flower early and so in many places the blossom is subject to frost damage, which may be severe in valleys where cold air collects.

Cherries are budded on stocks, the best for general purposes being the Common Gean or Mazzard. Sweet or dessert cherries are usually grown as standard trees. They become very large in time and are highly decorative when in flower and fruit but in country districts the fruit is often taken by birds. They can also be grown as bushes or as single-stem cordons. Acid or cooking cherries are grown as small standards, bushes or as fan-trained trees against walls or fences, where they will thrive without direct sunshine.

Preparation of the ground for cherries is the same as for apples except that manure or decayed garden refuse may be worked in at 1 cwt. to 10 sq. yd. Planting times are also the same as for apples.

Standard cherries should be spaced 30 ft. apart, bushes 15 ft. apart, and fan-trained trees 12 to 15 ft. apart.

The pruning of standard or bush sweet cherries is similar to that for plums and may be done in winter, spring, or immediately the crop has been gathered.

The pruning of cordon sweet cherries is similar to that of cordon apples except that the side shoots are pruned earlier while still soft enough for the tips to be pinched out. They should be pinched back to four or five leaves and any secondary shoots developing after that should be pinched again at one or two leaves.

Acid cherries bear on the previous year's growth, not on old growth, and need different treatment. Leave the main stems of standard or bush trees unpruned. Shorten those of fan-trained trees as described for fan-trained plums. Cut out side shoots that have borne fruits if there are enough young shoots to take their place, but, if not, keep some of the older side shoots unpruned and shorten others to about 2 in. to encourage new side shoots to develop the following year.

No thinning of cherries is required. The fruit is picked and used as it ripens. Cherries cannot be stored but they may be bottled, canned or frozen.

Some acid cherries, such as Morello and Flemish Red, are self-fertile, that is, they can be fertilized with their own pollen, so that a Morello cherry planted alone can still produce good crops.

Sweet cherries are self-sterile; they will not crop unless fertilized with pollen from another variety of cherry. Morello will effectively pollinate all varieties of sweet cherry. Sweet cherries themselves fall into groups, the members of which will not fertilize each other but will fertilize varieties of other groups. It is important, therefore, when selecting a cherry from any of these groups to select also a variety from another group or an acid cherry, flowering at the same time, as pollinator.

COBNUT (Corylus avellana)

Cobnuts and filberts can be grown in a variety of soils either in sun or shade. Preparation of the soil is as for apples. Nuts are nearly always planted as bushes spaced about 10 ft. apart but are sometimes planted closer as screens. Autumn and winter are the best planting seasons.

Prune in late winter when the nuts are carrying catkins. Cut out ingrowing stems and suckers – stems growing straight from the roots – and shorten each side growth to the catkin nearest its tip, or, if there are no catkins, to the first female flowers (these are small and red and set close to the stems). Shoots that have catkins only should be left unpruned until spring and then shortened to about 1 in.

BLACK CURRANT (Ribes nigrum)

There are numerous varieties of black currant which differ in time of ripening, flavour, size of berry, vitamin C content, cropping capacity, etc.

CHERRIES	USE	SEASON	COLOUR	FERTILITY	RECOMMENDED POLLINATORS
Bigarreau de Schrecken	D	early	reddish black	SS	Governor Wood, Elton Heart
Bigarreau Napoleon	D	late	yellow and red	SS	Governor Wood, Bradbourne Black, Elton Heart
Black Eagle	D	mid-season	black	SS	Bigarreau Napoleon, Emperor Francis, Elton Heart
Bradbourne Black	D	late	dark red	SS	Frogmore Early, Governor Wood, Bigarreau Napoleon
Early Rivers	D	early	black	SS	Bigarreau de Schrecken, Elton Heart, Merton Favourite, Merton Heart
Elton Heart	D	early	yellow and red	SS	Bigarreau Napoleon, Merton Bigarreau
Emperor Francis	D	late	red	SS	Governor Wood, Frogmore Early
Frogmore Early	D	early	yellow and red	SS	Bigarreau Napoleon, Elton Heart
Governor Wood	D	early	red and yellow	SS	Bigarreau Napoleon, Elton Heart
Kent Bigarreau	D	mid-season	yellow and red	SS	Bigarreau Napoleon, Elton Heart, Governor Wood
Kentish Red	C	early	red	SF	Needs no pollinator and will pollinate all other varieties
Merton Bigarreau	D	late	black	SS	Early Rivers, Governor Wood, Elton Heart, Merton Heart
Merton Favourite	D	early	black	SS	Early Rivers, Merton Heart
Merton Glory	D	early	cream and red	SS	Bigarreau de Schrecken, Bigarreau Napoleon, Early Rivers, Merton Bigarreau, Merton Favourite
Merton Heart	D	early	black	SS	Bigarreau de Schrecken, Early Rivers, Waterloo
Morello	C	very late	dark red to black	SF	Needs no pollinator and will pollinate all other varieties
Waterloo	D	early	reddish black	SS	Bigarreau Napoleon, Elton Heart

D = dessert   SS = self-sterile
C = cooking   SF = self-fertile

All sweet cherries are self-sterile and should not be planted singly. For cross pollination purposes they fall into groups the members of which are inter sterile but will pollinate varieties of other groups that are in flower at the same time. Sour cherries are self-fertile and require no pollinators. They will also pollinate sweet cherries that are in bloom at the same time.

Black currants are usually grown as bushes with numerous stems coming direct from the roots. They can also be trained fanwise against wires or a fence or wall, which can be convenient in small gardens.

They are purchased as one- or two-year-old bushes, and can be planted at any time from autumn to spring. Space the bushes at least 5 ft. apart each way, with fan-trained plants 5 ft. apart in the row.

Take particular care to remove all perennial weeds and weed roots before planting as black currants fill the soil with a mass of fine roots, making cultivation difficult once they have become established. Plant rather deeply so that the stems come through the soil rather than from above the soil. Immediately after planting cut all stems down to within about 6 in. of soil level. No fruit will be produced during the first season and no further pruning will be needed that year.

Spread manure or well-rotted garden refuse around black currants each year in late winter or early spring, and a month later sprinkle a well-balanced compound fertilizer around the plants at the rate recommended by the manufacturer. Give a further application of fertilizer at half this rate in early summer.

A crop should be produced during the second year and each succeeding year and treatment becomes routine. When all the fruit has been gathered, cut out the stems that have just borne fruit but retain all the strong young stems to flower and fruit the following year. Alternatively, the stems may be cut complete with fruit and brought indoors for picking.

RED AND WHITE CURRANTS
(Ribes sativum)

Red and white currants only differ from each other in the colour of their berries. They are related to black currants but they grow in a different way and so do not require the same treatment.

They may be grown as bushes on a short main stem or 'leg' so that all branches are above soil level, or can be trained as 'cordons' with one, two or three stems tied to wires on a fence or wall. Red and white currants will succeed in sun or light shade and are usually sold as two- or three-year-old plants.

Space bushes at least 4 ft. apart each way; single-stem cordons 1 ft. apart in the row, double-stem cordons 2 ft. apart and

BLACK CURRENTS	SEASON	COMMENTS
Amos Black	late	one of the last to ripen
Baldwin	late	high vitamin C content
Blacksmith	mid-season	should be picked directly it is ripe
Boskoop Giant	early	one of the first to ripen
Laxton's Giant	early	very large berries
Malvern Cross	late	rather tough skins to berries
Mendip Cross	early	can beat Boskoop Giant for earliness
Seabrook's Black	mid-season	long bunches but sometimes all fruits do not form
Tor Cross	early	heavy cropping and holds fruits well
Wellington XXX	mid-season	heavy cropping, should be picked directly it is ripe

any grown as triple-stem cordons 3 ft. apart.

Plant so that all roots are covered with at least 2 in. of soil, but the stems are not buried as for black currants. Remove 4 or 5 in. from the tip of each main stem and shorten side shoots to about 1 in.

Spread some rotted manure or garden refuse on the surface around the plants each year in late winter or early spring.

A light crop can be taken during the first year provided the plants are growing well. If they are not, remove all the fruit at an early stage, give the soil a light dusting of a compound fertilizer and keep well watered.

Red and white currants bear their fruits on the older stems. The fruit buds are produced in little clusters which are quite prominent by the autumn. Be careful not to cut any of these off when pruning unless they are damaged, diseased or have become exhausted with age, when they should be removed complete.

In the autumn when most leaves have fallen, shorten by about 6 in. the new growth that has extended the main branches and shorten side growths to about 1 in. from the main stem. With bushes a few strong, well-placed side growths may be retained to form further main branches, but do not overcrowd the bush with these. From 8 to 12 branches for each bush is quite enough.

No extra branches should be retained on cordons unless there is room to train them in at the proper spacing (approximately 1 ft.). With cordons be especially careful to shorten all side growths so that the neat habit of the plants is always preserved.

FIG (*Ficus carica*)

Figs like a warm, sunny, sheltered place and well-drained but not very rich soil. They are trained as fans against sunny walls out of doors or against the back wall of a lean-to greenhouse. They may also be grown as large bushes in the open or as pot plants in the greenhouse.

Prepare the ground by thorough digging or forking and work in manure or decayed garden refuse at 1 cwt. to 20 sq. yd., dusting the soil with bonemeal at 4 oz. per sq. yd.

Plant in autumn if the plants are lifted from the open ground, or at any time if they are planted from containers and can be kept watered in dry weather.

Give a light topdressing of manure or decayed garden refuse each spring, plus bonemeal at 4 oz. and sulphate of potash at 1½ oz. per sq. yd.

During the spring and early summer remove badly placed shoots that could not easily be tied in on fan-trained trees, and during summer shorten all good side shoots to about five leaves. In winter cut out weak or overcrowded shoots. Two crops may be obtained if there is sufficient warmth to start growth in late winter. Elsewhere only one late summer crop can be expected. After the first crop has ripened in summer thin out the year-old stems to expose the second crop, already forming, to the light. Brown Turkey and Negro Largo are the hardiest varieties.

GOOSEBERRY (*Ribes grossularia*)

There are a great many different varieties of gooseberries, differing in the colour, size and flavour of their fruits and in their habit of growth.

Gooseberries are purchased as two- or three-year-old bushes on a short main stem or 'leg' with all branches above soil level. They can also be grown as single-, double- or triple-stemmed cordons like red and white currants.

Space bushes at least 4 ft. apart, cordons 1, 2 or 3 ft. apart in the rows, according to the number of stems.

Plant gooseberries so that all their roots are covered with at least 2 in. of soil, but so that all their branches are clear of the soil. Shorten the main stems by 3 or 4 in. after planting and the side stems to about 2 in.

If the plants grow well a crop can be taken during the first year, but if they grow poorly treat as advised for red and white currants.

Prune in autumn or early winter when most of the leaves have fallen. Shorten the main stems by 4 or 5 in. or, in the case of varieties with a weeping habit, cut each branch to the top of its arch and to a bud which is facing upwards. This will induce a more erect habit.

Shorten all side shoots to about 2 in. or retain a few a good deal longer if there is room for them to make new stems. Cut out stems that are growing inwards through the middle of the bush as these make picking difficult. Prune cordons in a similar manner to red and white currant cordons.

Annually in late winter or early spring topdress with manure or well-rotted garden refuse. About a month later give a compound fertilizer with a fairly high level of phosphoric acid and potash and repeat at half strength in early summer.

RED and WHITE CURRANTS	SEASON	COMMENTS
Jonkheer Van Tets	early	one of the first to ripen
Laxton's No. 1	early	heavy cropper with upright habit
Red Lake	mid-season	very large berries
White Dutch	mid-season	rather spreading habit
White Leviathan	mid-season	large berries
White Versailles	early	erect habit, heavy cropping

GOOSEBERRIES	USE	SEASON	COLOUR	HABIT
Careless	C	mid-season	green	spreading
Crown Bob	DC	mid-season	red	arching
Early Sulphur*	D	early	yellow	bushy
Golden Drop	D	mid-season	yellow	upright
Keepsake	DC	early	green	rather spreading
Lancashire Lad	C	mid-season	red	bushy
Lancer	DC	late	yellow-green	spreading
Langley Gage	D	mid-season	greenish white	upright
Leveller*	DC	mid-season	greenish yellow	spreading
Whinham's Industry	DC	mid-season	red	arching
Whitesmith	DC	early	yellowish white	bushy

* These varieties are damaged by lime sulphur sprays

GRAPES *(Vitis vinifera)*

Vines can be grown out of doors trained against sunny walls or over screens, pergolas etc., or on wire or other supports. It is also possible to prune them hard each year and so restrict them sufficiently to be grown without support or to be tied down and covered with cloches while the fruit is ripening.

The choicest varieties of dessert grapes are usually grown in greenhouses. They can be grown in large pots or tubs but then require a great deal of watering and feeding. The better method is to plant in specially prepared borders either inside or outside the greenhouse. Inside borders give greater control over growth and enable vines to be started earlier in the year but outside borders need less watering. If planted outside, the main stem of the vine is led into the house through a hole in the wall.

Borders should be the full length and width of the house and 3 ft. deep, with some hard rubble in the bottom for drainage. Fill with good loamy soil with each cubic yard of which 14 lb. each of ground chalk, wood ashes and coarse bonemeal have been well mixed.

Plant two-year-old canes in autumn, winter or early spring. If the multiple-stem system of training is to be adopted one vine will in time fill a house of considerable size but more usually, nowadays, the single-stem system is used, in which case plants should be spaced 5 or 6 ft. apart. Either way, wires running lengthwise 9 in. below the rafters and 15 in. apart must be provided for support.

After planting cut all vines to within about 2 ft. of ground level. The following spring, if the single-stem system is to be used, train the topmost shoot towards the ridge of the house or, if the multiple-stem system is to be adopted, horizontally just below the eaves of the house. Pinch out the tip of this main stem when it is 6 ft. long.

Water fairly freely in spring and summer but sparingly at other times. Feed with weak liquid manure or a vine fertilizer occasionally from late spring until late summer. Ventilate fairly freely in summer, very freely in winter until it is desired to re-start growth, when the ventilators should be closed and temperatures raised to a night minimum of 10°C.

Under the single-stem system allow side shoots to form along the length of each main stem approximately 15 in. apart, and train these to right and left along the training wires provided. Under the multiple-stem system allow a side shoot to develop about every 4 ft. along the horizontal stem and train these side shoots towards the ridge, treating each like the main stem of a single-stem vine. The horizontal stem can be continued to produce more side growths until the whole house is filled.

Fruit is borne on the young laterals and these are renewed annually. Pinch out the tip of each lateral two leaves beyond the first flower cluster it produces or, if there is no flower cluster, when it is 3 ft. long. Pinch out the tips of any secondary laterals at the first leaf.

In autumn cut all laterals back to two growth buds. As vines become older they will build up woody spurs on the main rods from which all new laterals will be borne. Allow only one new shoot to grow from each pruned lateral, choosing the sturdiest and rubbing out any others.

When growth starts syringe vines daily with clear water but do not continue this after they come into flower. When in flower allow the temperature to rise to a night minimum of 13°C. and dust pollen from flower to flower with a camel-hair brush. When berries are well formed thin them with pointed scissors taking out rather more fruits near the bottom of the bunch than around the shoulders. In summer maintain as equable a temperature as possible, 15 to 21°C. by day and 13 to 15°C. by night being ideal. After cutting ripe bunches open ventilators widely and use no artificial heat, so that the vines rest and lose their leaves.

When grown out of doors similar pruning and training systems are used though vines may be given greater freedom if there is space. If to be ripened under cloches plant the canes 3 ft. apart and in winter cut each vine to two dormant growth buds. Allow two stems to grow the following summer and in autumn shorten one of these to two buds to provide two further shoots the following spring, the other to six dormant buds for fruiting. Tie this shortened fruiting cane horizontally to a wire or cane so that when necessary it can be easily covered with a cloche. Repeat this process of restriction and renewal annually.

MEDLAR *(Mespilus germanica)*

Medlars like rich, well-cultivated soil and a warm, sunny place. Prepare the ground as for plums. Nurserymen graft medlars on to pear stocks and usually offer standard trees. If more than one tree is planted space them 20 ft. apart.

Planting and subsequent care are the same as for apples except that once the trees start to drop they usually require little pruning. Gather the fruit in autumn and store in single layers, eyed ends downwards, in a dry store or room as for pears. Medlars are ready for use when they turn brown and become soft, which may take several weeks. Dutch, Nottingham and Royal are the best varieties.

MULBERRIES *(Morus nigra, M. alba)*

These also like rich soil, but not one that is too light and liable to dry out rapidly. They are nearly always grown as standards and need staking as they are easily blown over.

In the early stages of growth prune mulberries like apples, thinning out over-crowded or badly placed stems and forming a good, evenly spaced head of branches. Later, little pruning is required.

The Black Mulberry *(Morus nigra)* is the kind grown for fruit; the White Mulberry *(M. alba)* for the foliage which is used as a food for silkworms.

PEACH, NECTARINE (*Prunus persica*)

Though they look so different nectarines are simply smooth-skinned varieties of peach and the cultivation of peaches and nectarines is identical. They like good, well-cultivated and well-drained soil and warm, sunny, rather sheltered positions. They are often grown against sunny walls, or against the back wall of a lean-to greenhouse.

Prepare the ground by thorough digging or forking and work in rotted manure or vegetable refuse at 1 cwt. to 10 sq. yd. Unless the ground is on chalk or limestone give a topdressing of ground chalk at 4 oz. per sq. yd. before planting.

Nursery trees are always budded on plum or seedling almond, but peaches and nectarines can also be grown from stones and this is often done by home gardeners. Such trees need no grafting, but may take a few years before they start cropping. Seedling trees are likely to differ from their parents in such features as the size and quality of their fruits and the time of ripening.

Peaches and nectarines are grown as bushes or as fan-trained trees. Planting times and methods are the same as for apples. Occasionally they are grown in large pots or tubs, in which case John Innes potting compost No. 3 or equivalent compost should be used and the potting done in autumn. Use pots at least 10 in. in diameter and only fill them to within 3 in. of the rim, leaving a space for topdressing later with a mixture of equal parts of good soil and rotted manure.

Flowers are produced in early spring and out of doors they may need protection against frost with muslin or fine mesh netting. When the blossom is fully open, distribute the pollen from flower to flower with a camel-hair brush.

Keep wall-trained trees well watered in dry weather, especially when the fruits are swelling rapidly. Start to thin fruits when they are as large as marbles but do not complete the thinning until the stones are formed inside the fruits as there may be a considerable natural fall of fruit at this stage. At first reduce the fruits to one per cluster, but later thin to a distance of from 9 to 12 in.

Feed with a compound fertilizer early each spring at 3 to 4 oz. per sq. yd. and spread a 1-in. thick layer of manure or decayed garden refuse round each tree.

Young trees are pruned like plums but when they start to crop a different system of pruning is necessary. Fruit is borne on side stems which grew the previous year and pruning is designed to maintain enough of this young growth. With bush trees it is usually sufficient to feed them well and then, as soon as the fruit has been picked, to cut out as many as possible of the stems that have just borne fruit, but to keep all the best of the new growth for fruiting the following year.

With fan-trained trees a process of disbudding is usually adopted to encourage growth where it is required. Start in late spring and gradually rub out all young growths except two for every old stem, one as near the bottom of this stem as possible and one at the tip. Pinch out the tip of the top shoot when it has made about five leaves. When the fruit has been gathered, cut out each of these old stems just above the young growth retained near the bottom, leaving this to take its place. The aim should be to have enough young shoots to fill the whole available space when they are tied in at 3 to 4 in. apart.

In greenhouses give free ventilation in winter when the trees are resting, and also in summer. Close the ventilators in late winter or early spring to start the trees growing and protect the blossom, but do not allow the temperature to rise above 10°C. at night or 15°C. by day. Syringe the trees frequently with clear water in summer and water the paths and walls to maintain moisture in the air. In a hot, dry atmosphere leaves become scorched and red spider mite is encouraged.

All peaches and nectarines are self-fertile so it is not necessary to plant several different varieties to ensure fertilization.

PEAR (*Pyrus communis*)

Pears require similar soil conditions to apples but appreciate a warmer situation. They resent heavy, poorly drained soils even more than apples and are more tolerant of light sandy or gravelly soils.

Pears are grafted by nurserymen on stocks, seedling pear sometimes being used for large trees, though most are grafted on some form of quince, that known as Malling A for vigorous bushes, Malling B for small bushes and horizontal-trained trees, and Malling C for single-stem cordons.

Preparation of the ground, planting times and the method of planting and spacing are the same as for apples.

Pruning also follows much the same general lines, but pears form fruit buds more readily and freely than apples and, provided they have been worked on suitable stocks, often require less pruning to keep them in shape. Trained trees should be summer pruned like apples, but pear growth starts to ripen a little earlier and so pruning can usually start about midsummer.

NECTARINES	SEASON	COMMENTS
Dryden	mid-season	white fleshed, good flavour
Early Rivers	early	excellent flavour, can be ripened outdoors
Elruge	mid-season	hardy and reliable
Humboldt	mid-season	flowers open rather late
Lord Napier	early	good under glass
Newton Pineapple	late	fine flavour, good under glass

PEACHES	SEASON	COMMENTS
Amsden June	early	should be well thinned
Barrington	late	good outdoors or in an unheated greenhouse
Bellegarde	late	hardy and reliable
Duke of York	early	very large fruits produced extra early
Hale's Early	mid-season	good but not as early ripening as its name suggests
Peregrine	mid-season	one of the most popular round peaches
Rochester	mid-season	even hardier and more prolific than Peregrine
Royal George	late	can be grown outdoors or under glass
Sea Eagle	very late	should be grown under glass

The stems are often slightly thinner than comparable apple wood.

Old bush and standard pear trees usually require a minimum of pruning, little more than the removal of diseased or damaged branches.

Fruits may need to be thinned, especially if very large individual fruits are required, and the same methods should be used as for apples. After thinning the fruits may be spaced from 5 to 6 in. apart.

As pears ripen they are sometimes badly infested by wasps and it may be necessary to protect the individual fruits in muslin bags. Picking should be done progressively as the fruits ripen.

Use early pears as soon as possible after picking. They do not keep well and quickly go soft and rotten in the centre. Store late pears in shallow trays in a cool but dry storage place, such as a room or a cupboard. They must be used as soon as ripe, which is indicated by softening of the flesh near the stem. Examine pears in store every few days, since they will ripen suddenly and then rapidly go rotten.

Varieties are numerous and may be wholly or partly self-sterile. It is, therefore, wise to avoid planting pears singly and to plant the trees so that each is near at least one other variety which is in flower at the same time.

PLUM (Prunus domestica)

Plums like rather rich, loamy, well-cultivated soil. They grow rapidly, make large trees and do not take kindly to hard pruning, for which reasons they are not very suitable

PEARS	USE	SEASON	FLOWERING	FERTILITY	COMMENTS
Beurré d'Amanlis	D	early	early	SS	should be used as soon as ripe
Beurré Hardy	D	mid-season	late	PSF	a hardy, free-cropping pear
Beurré Superfin	D	mid-season	mid-season	PSF	excellent flavour and good cropping
Bristol Cross	D	mid-season	mid-season	PSF	should not be grafted on quince
Catillac	C	late	late	SS	a very hard, long-lasting pear
Clapp's Favourite	D	early	late	PSF	should not be grafted on quince
Conference	D	mid-season	mid-season	PSF	a very heavy cropping variety
Doyenné du Comice	D	mid-season	late	PSF	one of the best flavoured pears
Dr Jules Guyot	D	early	late	PSF	should not be grafted on quince
Durondeau	D	mid-season	mid-season	PSF	large fruits freely produced
Emile d'Heyst	D	mid-season	early	PSF	compact growth, good cropping
Fondante d'Automne	D	early	mid-season	PSF	compact growth, good cropping
Glou Morceau	D	late	late	PSF	best in a warm, sunny place
Hessle	D	mid-season	mid-season	PSF	small fruits freely produced. Also known as Hasel
Improved Fertility	CD	early	late	SF	one of the heaviest croppers but inferior quality
Jargonelle	D	early	early	SS	should not be grafted on quince
Joséphine de Malines	D	late	mid-season	PSF	needs fairly rich soil to do well
Louise Bonne of Jersey	D	mid-season	early	PSF	fine quality and good cropping
Packham's Triumph	D	mid-season	late	SF	should not be grafted on quince
Pitmaston Duchess	CD	mid-season	late	SS	huge fruits but not of top quality
Thompson's	D	mid-season	mid-season	PSF	should not be grafted on quince
Williams' Bon Chrétien	D	early	mid-season	PSF	should not be grafted on quince

D = dessert C = cooking
CD = cooking or dessert
SF = self-fertile SS = self-sterile
PSF = partially self-fertile

Fully self-fertile varieties can be planted alone. Fully self-sterile varieties must have another variety of pear nearby for pollination. Partially self-fertile varieties will crop on their own but will usually give better crops with another variety for cross pollination. Pollinators should be chosen from varieties that bloom at the same time.

for small gardens where space is limited.

Plums are grown by nurserymen on stocks, but no really dwarfing stocks are available. Myrobalan B is commonly used for large trees, and Pershore for small trees, including those that are to be trained. Common Mussel and Common Plum are of intermediate vigour.

Preparation of the ground is similar to that for apples but manure or decayed vegetable refuse may be used at 1 cwt. to 10 sq. yd. Space standard plum trees 25 to 30 ft. apart and bush plums 15 ft. apart.

Plums are not satisfactory as cordons or horizontally trained but some varieties give good results fan trained against walls or fences, when they should be spaced 15 ft. apart.

In the early years pruning of bush and standard trees is similar to that of apples and pears, but, when trees start to fruit, pruning is reduced to a minimum because of the risk of disease entering through pruning wounds. For the same reason pruning is then done in late summer or early autumn after the crop has been gathered, when the danger of infection is lower than in autumn

PLUMS	USE	SEASON	COLOUR	FLOWERING	FERTILITY	COMMENTS
Bryanston Gage	D	late	yellow	mid-season	SS	fine flavour, good cropping
Cambridge Gage	D	mid-season	green	late	PSF	one of the best cropping greengages
Coe's Golden Drop	D	late	yellow	early	SS	requires a warm sunny place
Czar	C	early	purple	mid-season	SF	heavy cropping but susceptible to silver leaf
Denniston's Superb	D	early	yellow	early	SF	fine flavour, good cropping
Early Transparent Gage	D	early	yellow and red	late	SF	one of the best for early eating
Giant Prune	C	mid-season	purple	late	SF	heavy cropping but susceptible to bacterial canker
Green Gage	D	early	green	late	SS	needs a warm sunny place
Jefferson	D	mid-season	yellow	early	SS	fine flavour, good cropping
Kirke's Blue	D	mid-season	purple	mid-season	SS	requires a warm sunny place
Marjorie's Seedling	CD	late	blue-black	late	SF	when fully ripe it is of fair dessert quality
Merryweather Damson	C	mid-season	black	mid-season	SF	heavy cropping and makes a fine tree
Monarch	C	late	purple	early	SF	said to be resistant to silver leaf
Oullin's Golden Gage	CD	early	yellow	late	SF	a useful dual purpose plum
Pershore	C	early	yellow	mid-season	SF	heavy cropping but indifferent quality
Rivers' Early Prolific	C	early	purple	mid-season	PSF	small fruits very profusely produced
Severn Cross	D	mid-season	yellow and pink	mid-season	SF	grows and crops well
Victoria	CD	early	red	mid-season	SF	a favourite but susceptible to silver leaf
Warwickshire Drooper	CD	mid-season	yellow	early	SF	weeping habit, immense crops

D = dessert
C = cooking
CD = cooking or dessert
SS = self-sterile
SF = self-fertile
PSF = partially self-fertile

Self-fertile varieties can be planted alone. Self-sterile varieties must have another variety of plum nearby for pollination. Partially self-fertile varieties will crop on their own but will usually produce heavier crops if another variety is growing nearby.

Pollinators should be chosen from varieties that bloom at the same time.

or winter. Large wounds made when pruning should be covered with Stockholm tar or a proprietary tree-wound dressing.

Fan-trained trees require different treatment. Cut out the central stem and train the side stems like the ribs of a fan. Each winter shorten the new growth at the end of each branch to a point where it is 7 to 9 in. from its neighbours, so forcing it to branch the following year and produce more 'ribs' to keep the space on the wall or fence fully occupied. Tie in any side shoots at full length between these main branches where there is room for them, but to prevent overcrowding pinch out the tips of some of the side shoots during the summer. This should be done a little at a time as soon as it can be seen where there will be room to tie the growth in.

Plums are not usually thinned, but if large fruits are required they may be reduced to one every 2 in. when the stones have formed.

Fruits should be picked and used as soon as ripe. They will not keep in store.

Many plums are self-fertile and all set better crops when pollinated by a different variety.

RASPBERRY (Rubus idaeus)

Raspberries like rather rich soil that remains fairly moist in summer but does not become waterlogged in winter. Prepare by thorough digging and work in manure at 1 cwt. to 8 to 10 sq. yd. plus sulphate of potash at 2 oz. per sq. yd.

Raspberries are purchased as young canes, each of which is simply one stem with roots. It is important to buy canes certified virus free. The best planting season is from mid-autumn to early spring.

Space the canes 15 in. apart in rows at least 5 ft. apart. Spread the roots out widely in a planting hole of just sufficient depth to permit the topmost roots to be covered with 2 in. of soil. Cut the canes down to within 6 in. of the ground in late winter.

Do not allow raspberries to fruit the first year. Summer-ripening varieties are unlikely to attempt to do so, but autumn-ripening kinds may produce a few flowers, which should be picked off.

Do not prune at all the first year. More stems or 'canes' will appear around the parent cane during the summer and should be tied to wires strained between posts firmly driven into the ground.

Feed with manure or rotted garden refuse annually in late winter or early spring and about a month later give a sprinkling of a compound fertilizer. Repeat the application of manure or well-rotted garden refuse in early summer.

Prune autumn-fruiting varieties in later winter by cutting all canes to ground level. They will then produce new canes direct from the roots and these will bear fruit. Prune summer-fruiting varieties immedi-

ately the crop has been gathered. Cut out at ground level all the old canes that have just borne fruit, and thin out the young canes to about 6 in. apart, retaining the strongest. Tie these canes to training wires and in late winter shorten them all to a level of 6 ft. or thereabouts.

RASPBERRIES	SEASON	COMMENTS
Glen Cova	early to late	crops over a long period
Lloyd George	mid-season and autumn	susceptible to virus infection, fine flavour
Malling Enterprise	mid-season	susceptible to cane blight
Malling Exploit	early	excellent quality
Malling Jewel	mid-season	slow to increase
Malling Orion	mid-season	heavy cropping
Malling Promise	early	heavy cropping, spreads rapidly
Norfolk Giant	late	tall canes, large fruits
September	autumn	the best for late summer and autumn

STRAWBERRY (Fragaria chiloensis)

There are three quite distinct types of strawberry, namely Summer Fruiting, with large fruits; Perpetual or Remontant, mostly with medium-sized fruits, and Bush or Alpine with small fruits.

Strawberries are sold as young plants in autumn and spring. It is important to obtain only virus-free stock. Plants may be

STRAWBERRIES	TYPE	FRUIT SIZE	COMMENTS
Alexandria	Alpine	small	grow from seed
Baron Solemacher	Alpine	small	grow from seed
Cambridge Favourite	Summer	large	crops for several weeks
Cambridge Rival	Summer	large	resistant to red core disease
Cambridge Vigour	Summer	medium	resistant to red core disease
Gento	Perpetual	medium	one of the best perpetuals
Grandee	Summer	very large	distinctive flavour
Hampshire Maid	Perpetual	medium	needs a porous soil with plenty of moisture in summer
Red Gauntlet	Summer	very large	heavy cropping
Royal Sovereign	Summer	large	fine flavour, subject to virus
Sans Rivale	Perpetual	below medium	heavy cropping
Senga Sengana	Summer	large	heavy cropping
Sonjano	Perpetual	medium	can be trained as a climber
Talisman	Summer	large	plant early to establish before winter
Triplex	Perpetual	large	one of the largest fruited 'perpetuals'

sold as lifted from the open ground (known as open-ground runners) or be in small pots or other containers. The latter transplant most easily.

Space summer-fruiting and remontant strawberries 1½ ft. apart. Alpine varieties do not make such large plants and may be spaced 1 ft. apart. They make attractive edgings to beds.

Provided they grow well, autumn-planted strawberries may be allowed to fruit the following year. Spring-planted summer-fruiting strawberries should not be allowed to fruit the first year and all the flowers should be picked off. Remontant and alpine strawberries may be allowed to fruit from late summer onwards.

Early each spring sprinkle a well-balanced compound fertilizer around the plants at the recommended rate. In late spring, spread clean straw under summer-fruiting straw-berries, and do this in early summer for remontant strawberries. Remove the first flowers from remontant strawberries so that they start to crop after the summer-fruiting kinds. Cover the plants with nets while the fruits are ripening to protect them against bird damage.

Remove all runners as they appear on summer-fruiting strawberries. Alpine varieties do not make runners, and some runners may be retained on remontant strawberries to continue the supply of fruit into the autumn.

Re-make beds at least every third year. Many gardeners only keep strawberries for two years and replant half the bed every year, so that there is a constant succession of healthy young plants.

Alpine strawberries can be raised from seed sown in a greenhouse or frame in spring. Other strawberries are increased by pegging down selected runners in summer.

WALNUT (*Juglans regia*)

Walnuts thrive in moist, well-cultivated soils but do not succeed in cold, damp or frosty places. Nurserymen sometimes offer seedling trees, but these are often unreliable in cropping and selected varieties propagated by grafting or budding are to be preferred. Franquette is a popular and satisfactory variety but Chaberte, Glady, Stutton Seedling and Northdown Clawnut crop more heavily.

Walnuts are almost always planted as standard trees which eventually grow to considerable size. The only pruning necessary is to remove overcrowded or badly placed branches, which is best done in autumn.

Vegetable Growing

Some vegetables can be grown in any garden, however tiny. It is even possible to grow mustard and cress in containers on the kitchen window-sill and herbs of several kinds in boxes or tubs in a yard. Vegetables can also be associated with flowers in the manner of cottage gardens. However, if more than a few rows of vegetables are to be grown, it is wise to set aside a plot for the purpose, if possible in an open situation since, though some vegetables will grow in shade, most prefer plenty of light.

It is wise to arrange the plot so that some kind of rotation can be carried out.

The simplest system is a three-part one in which the plot is divided into three roughly equal parts; one devoted to green crops such as cabbage, brussels sprouts, broccoli and kale; a second to peas, beans and salads; and a third to root crops, including potatoes, carrots, beetroots, parsnips and turnips.

Then each year there is a kind of 'musical chairs', the greens going to the previous year's peas, beans and salad plot, these moving on to the root crop plot and the root crops going to the former greens plot.

There is no need to stick too rigidly to any such scheme but this general principle of movement should be borne in mind. Each crop has its particular food requirements and pests, and a change of site does it good.

ARTICHOKES

There are three types of artichoke: the Jerusalem Artichoke (*Helianthus tuberosus*), the Chinese Artichoke (*Stachys sieboldii*) and the Globe Artichoke (*Cynara scolymus*). All have a very distinctive appearance.

The Jerusalem artichoke is grown for its tubers, which are not unlike those of the potato. It will grow in any reasonably well-cultivated soil. Plant the tubers in late winter or early spring, 6 in. deep and 15 in. apart in rows 2½ ft. apart. Keep weed free and draw soil towards the rows when hoeing. Dig the tubers up as required for use in autumn or winter or lift and store them like potatoes.

The Chinese artichoke is grown in a similar manner, except that tubers are planted 4 in. deep and 1 ft. apart in rows 18 in. apart. It is best to leave the tubers in the ground and lift them as required for use, as they deteriorate rapidly in store.

The globe artichoke is a handsome plant with large, divided grey leaves and very large, purple, thistle-like flowers. It is cultivated for its unopened flower heads. Rooted offsets are planted 3 ft. apart each way in spring in well-cultivated and manured soil. All flower stems are removed in the first year, so that strong plants can be built up. Dead leaves should be removed in autumn and the plants protected with dry straw or bracken in winter. In subsequent years, cut flower heads regularly as soon as they are plump with fleshy scales.

Remake beds every third or fourth year from rooted offsets removed in spring. Plants can also be grown from seed sown in spring ½ in. deep (or in a greenhouse). Transplant seedlings 6 in. apart in rows 1 ft. apart and remove to cropping bed the following spring.

ASPARAGUS (*Asparagus officinalis*)

Asparagus is a crop which needs to be grown in the same place for many years. Prepare the ground by thorough digging or forking and work in manure or well-rotted garden refuse at 1 cwt. to 15 sq. yd. Unless the soil is already alkaline, apply hydrated lime as a topdressing at 6 to 8 oz. per sq. yd.

Two-year-old roots should be planted in spring in trenches 6 in. deep. Space the roots 1 ft. apart and return the soil over them. Keep free from weeds and cut off the top growth of the asparagus in late autumn. Topdress with well-rotted manure or garden refuse in late winter and apply a compound fertilizer in early spring. The second year after planting, draw soil from between the rows towards the plants to form low ridges. Start to cut asparagus for use the third year after planting. Cut 4 in. below soil level when young shoots (spears) are showing 3 in. above the soil. Cropping should continue from mid-spring to midsummer only. Continue cultural treatment and feeding as before.

Plants can also be raised from seed sown thinly in drills, 1 in. deep and 15 in. apart, in spring. Leave for two years, discard any seedlings which produce berries (female plants) and plant the remainder as already described.

Pedigree varieties and selected male plants are to be preferred and these can be bought at reputable nurseries.

AUBERGINE
(*Solanum melongena ovigerum*)

This is also known as the Egg Plant, though the edible parts are of various shapes from nearly round to sausage-like. They may be white, purple or striped but dark purple varieties are most popular. All are grown as annuals. Sow in a temperature of 15 to 18°C. in late winter or early spring, pot seedlings singly in John Innes potting compost No. 1 or equivalent and later move on to 6- or

7-in. pots and John Innes compost No. 2.

In warm districts aubergines can be planted outdoors like tomatoes in early summer in a sunny place but are more usually grown under glass throughout.

Water fairly freely. Pinch out the growing tip of each plant when 6 to 8 in. high to encourage branching. Tie stems to stakes or wires. Restrict each plant to a maximum of six fruits. Gather these when ripe.

VEGETABLE	YIELD PER ACRE	YIELD PER SQUARE YARD	YIELD PER FOOT OF ROW
Beans, broad	4 tons	2 lb	8 oz
Beans, french	3 tons	1½ lb	4 oz
Beans, runner	10 tons	5 lb	4 lb
Beans, haricot*	15 cwt	5–6 oz	1 oz
Beetroot	12 tons	5½ lb	14 oz
Broccoli	8 tons	3¾ lb	19 oz
Brussels sprouts	4 tons	2 lb	9 oz
Cabbage (spring)	9 tons	4 lb	11 oz
Cabbage (autumn and winter)	15 tons	7 lb	1½ lb
Cauliflower	6 tons	3 lb	1 lb
Carrots (main crop)	14 tons	6½ lb	12 oz
Carrots (early)	8 tons	3¾ lb	5 oz
Endive	—	10 heads	¾ head
Kale	10 tons	5 lb	1½ lb
Leek	10 tons	5 lb	13 oz
Lettuce	—	10–13 heads	1½–2 heads
Mushrooms	—	10 lb	—
Onions	12 tons	5½ lb	10 oz
Parsnips	10 tons	5 lb	13 oz
Peas	3 tons	1½ lb	6 oz
Potatoes (main crop)	10 tons	5 lb	1½ lb
Savoys	15 tons	7 lb	1½ lb
Shallots	—	8 lb	10 oz
Spinach (summer)	8 tons	3¾ lb	5 oz
Swedes	13 tons	6 lb	14 oz
Turnips (main crop)	13 tons	6 lb	14 oz
Tomatoes (under glass)	30 tons	15 lb	6 lb per plant
Tomatoes (outdoors)	20 tons	10 lb	4 lb per plant

* Seeds only

BROAD BEANS (Vicia faba)

Broad beans are grown for their seeds which may be white or green. Both are excellent in quality, but the green beans look more appetizing when canned or frozen.

Prepare ground well and apply manure or rotted garden refuse at 1 cwt. per 15 sq. yd. Rake a compound vegetable fertilizer into the seed bed when preparing it.

Sow in spring in drills 2 in. deep and 2 ft. apart, spacing the seeds 6 in. apart in the drills. In sheltered places where the soil is well drained, seed can be sown in autumn for an early crop. Seed can also be sown 2 in. apart in boxes in late winter and germinated in a warm greenhouse to give seedlings for planting out in spring after proper hardening off.

Pinch out the growing tip of each plant when the first clusters of pods start to swell. This hastens cropping and discourages attacks of blackfly.

Gather pods as soon as the seeds are large enough for use, but while they are still young and tender.

FRENCH AND HARICOT BEANS (Phaseolus vulgaris)

These may be dwarf or climbing. French beans are grown for their pods, haricot beans for their seeds.

Prepare ground as for broad beans. Sow in mid- to late spring, in drills 2 in. deep and 18 in. apart, spacing seed 3 to 4 in. apart and thinning the seedlings to 6 to 8 in. Earlier crops can be produced by sowing seeds 2 in. apart in boxes in early spring, germinating in a greenhouse or frame and hardening off for planting out in late spring. The plants are not fully hardy.

Climbing varieties, also known as Pole Beans, are grown in rows 3 to 4 ft. apart and are provided with tall pea sticks or poles after the manner of runner beans.

Start to gather pods of french beans as soon as they reach usable size and pick regularly to keep plants cropping.

Leave haricot beans to complete their growth, then pull up the plants, tie them in bundles and suspend in a dry, airy shed or greenhouse before shelling out the seeds and storing for winter use.

RUNNER BEANS (Phaseolus multiflorus)

Prepare ground as for broad beans. Sow seeds in late spring 8 in. apart in drills 2 in. deep, either in single rows 6 ft. apart or in double rows 18 in. apart with 6 ft. between each pair of rows. Place double lines of poles or canes 1 ft. apart along the rows, crossing them near the top and lashing them to horizontal poles to make a rigid framework. Poles should extend at least to 7 ft. above soil level.

Alternatively, sow in circles about 5 ft. in diameter and support on poles or canes arranged in the form of a cone or wigwam, lashed together at the top. Runner beans can also be grown on netting stretched between posts or they can be used to clothe walls or fences provided they have wires or netting to twine around. There are also naturally bushy varieties which require no support and can be grown like dwarf french beans.

Seed may also be sown 2 in. apart in boxes as for french beans and seedlings planted out 8 in. apart in late spring or early summer. Keep watered in dry weather and spread manure or decayed vegetable refuse beside the rows in early summer.

Start to gather beans as soon as they attain usable size and continue to pick regularly to keep plants cropping.

BEETROOT *(Beta vulgaris)*

Dig or fork ground thoroughly and work in manure or well-rotted garden refuse at 1 cwt. to 20 sq. yd. Rake or fork in a compound fertilizer before sowing seed.

Sow from mid-spring until early summer in drills 1 in. deep and 12 in. apart. Space seeds about 1 in. apart and thin seedlings to 6 in. Beetroot seed usually takes several weeks to germinate, so it is particularly important to sow on ground which is free from weeds.

Beetroots are lifted by grasping the leaves firmly and pulling them, at the same time levering up the soil with a fork if they refuse to pull out easily. Be very careful not to damage the roots when lifting or they will bleed and lose colour. Start to pull roots as soon as they are large enough to use, but leave some until early autumn to be lifted for storing in a clamp or in boxes of peat, sand or dry soil in a shed. Twist off the tops before storing, but do not cut or injure the roots.

Varieties are divided into three main groups: Globe, with ball-like roots; Long, with long, tapering roots; Intermediate, with cylindrical roots. The globe-rooted type is the most useful for gardens. Though red is the usual colour there are white-fleshed varieties.

BROCCOLI *(Brassica oleracea italica)*

At one time this name was applied both to heading varieties forming one large curd per plant which differed little from cauliflowers except that they were hardier, and also to sprouting varieties. Nowadays all heading kinds are known as cauliflowers and only the sprouting kinds as broccoli, though there are two distinct types of these. One type, Calabrese, crops in summer and early autumn producing a small to medium size green or white central head, followed by smaller side heads or spears. The other type,

which crops in winter or spring, produces a succession of small white, green or purple spears.

Sow in spring, the summer and autumn varieties fairly early, the winter and spring varieties fairly late. Sow thinly ¼ in. deep in rows 6 in. apart and transplant seedlings when 6 to 8 in. high to well dug, rather rich soil in an open, sunny position, spacing plants 2 ft. apart each way. Cut heads or spears with several inches of stem while the buds are still tightly packed.

BRUSSELS SPROUTS
(Brassica oleracea gemmifera)

These are grown both for the cabbage-like head at the top of each plant and for the button-like sprouts that form beneath it down the whole length of the stem. Varieties are available to mature successively from late summer until about midwinter.

Prepare ground as for cabbages. Sow seed in early spring as for cabbages or in boxes in a greenhouse or frame in late winter, pricking out seedlings 2 in. apart into other boxes and hardening off for planting out in spring.

Plant as for cabbages, but space plants 2 ft. apart in rows 2½ ft. apart. Keep plants well watered in dry weather and feed with one or two light dustings of a compound fertilizer in summer. Stake tall plants in early autumn. Cut and use tops when the lower sprouts are nearly ready for picking. Pick sprouts as they become usable.

CABBAGES *(Brassica oleracea capitata)*

There are three types of cabbage: Pointed, with a conical heart; Drumhead or Ball-head, with a globular or slightly flattened heart, and Savoy, similar to the drumhead in form but with prominent veins which give the leaves a wrinkled appearance. Some varieties are quick growing and suitable for summer or early autumn cutting, some are slow growing (savoys are of this type) and suitable for autumn and winter cutting, and some can be sown in summer to be cut late the following spring or in early summer.

Prepare ground for summer, autumn and winter cabbages by thorough digging or forking. Work in manure or well-rotted garden refuse at 1 cwt. to 10 sq. yd. and rake in a compound fertilizer prior to planting out. Cabbages for spring cutting may be planted on ground cleared of early crops after the soil has been given a dressing of compound fertilizer only.

Sow summer and autumn varieties in early or mid-spring, winter varieties, including savoy cabbages, in late spring. Sow for spring cutting between mid- and late summer. Sow in drills ½ in. deep and 6 in. apart. Rake 4 per cent. calomel dust into the seedbed before sowing.

Transplant seedlings when 4 to 6 in. high, spacing plants 18 in. apart in rows 2 ft.

apart, (1 ft. and 18 in. for spring cutting). Sprinkle 4 per cent. calomel dust in each hole as a preventive to cabbage root fly maggots and club root disease.

CARDOON *(Cynara cardunculus)*

This plant is closely related to the globe artichoke. It has similarly handsome, grey, divided leaves but is grown for its stems not its flower heads.

Sow seed in spring in a greenhouse, frame or sheltered place outdoors. Plant seedlings outdoors in late spring or early summer as advised for globe artichoke. In autumn draw the leaves together and tie them at the top. Wrap brown paper round them from soil level to near the top and then draw soil towards the plants, making ridges as when celery is earthed up. Leave to blanch for at least two months, after which plants can be lifted as required. Since cardoons are not very hardy it is wise to protect them with straw in winter in cold places.

CARROTS *(Daucus carota)*

Carrots may be stump-rooted, i.e. more or less cylindrical and blunt-ended, or tapering. Stump-rooted varieties are most popular for kitchen use, tapering varieties for exhibition. Both types have numerous varieties differing in length and earliness.

If possible, choose a place for carrots that has been manured for a previous crop, since too rich a soil may cause roots to 'fork'. Dig thoroughly and before sowing rake or fork in a compound fertilizer. Sow an early variety every 3 or 4 weeks from early spring to midsummer for use as young carrots, and a larger, slow-maturing variety in mid-spring for lifting and storing.

Sow thinly in drills ¼ in. deep and 9 in. apart for early varieties; 1 ft. apart for carrots to be grown to maturity. Thin storing carrots to 4 in. and sprinkle flake naphthalene along the rows after thinning to keep the carrot fly from laying eggs. Early carrots should need no thinning until the most forward roots can be pulled for use.

In early autumn lift carrots with a fork for storing. Cut off the tops and store the carrots in clamps or in boxes filled with peat, sand or dry soil placed in a shed.

Very early carrots can be produced by sowing an early variety in a frame or under cloches in late winter.

CAULIFLOWER
(Brassica oleracea botrytis cauliflora)

Cauliflowers are grown for their large white curds.

Prepare ground as for cabbages. Sow in spring as for cabbage and plant out in the same way, spacing plants 2 ft. apart each way. For summer cutting, sow in early autumn in a frame or in late winter in a greenhouse, temp. 13 to 15°C., hardening off seedlings for planting out in mid-spring.

Keep plants well watered in dry weather. Bend the inner leaves over the curds to keep them white, and to protect winter and spring kinds from frost.

Cut curds when well formed.

CELERIAC (*Apium graveolens*)

This belongs to the same species as celery but has a swollen root. It is sometimes known as Turnip-rooted Celery. Sow seed during spring in pans of John Innes seed compost or a peat-based seed compost and germinate in a greenhouse or frame, at a temperature of 15°C. Prick out seedlings 1½ in. apart and harden off for planting out in late spring, 1 ft. apart in rows 18 in. apart, in well-cultivated soil. Keep clear of weeds, but do not draw soil around plants as with celery. Large, swollen roots will develop, and these can be used as required, either raw in salads, or cooked in soups and stews. The crop should be completely lifted in autumn and stored in sand, peat or dry soil in a shed.

CELERY (*Apium graveolens*)

There are two main types of celery: the Autumn and Winter Celery which must be blanched, and the Summer or Self-blanching Celery which is not blanched and is less hardy than the pink- and white-stemmed varieties of autumn and winter celery.

For autumn and winter celery prepare trenches 15 in. wide and 3 ft. apart by digging out the soil to a depth of 18 in., forking over the bottom and returning half the soil with a generous quantity of manure or compost.

Sow seed in boxes from late winter to mid-spring in a greenhouse or frame at a temperature of 12 to 15°C. Prick out seedlings 2 in. apart in boxes filled with John Innes potting compost No. 1 or equivalent and harden off for planting out in early summer. Plant 1 ft. apart down the centre of each trench. Water in freely and keep well watered.

In early autumn, remove shoots round the base of the plants, draw stems together with string and return the rest of the soil from the trenches. Throw more soil from between the rows around the plants to form ridges with only the leaves showing. This will blanch the stems and plants can be lifted about six weeks later.

Seed of self-blanching celery is sown in the same way but the seedlings are planted 1 ft. apart each way in blocks. The ground should be well manured. No earthing up is required but the celery should be used before hard autumn frosts occur.

There are both pink- and white-stemmed varieties of autumn and winter celery and the pink varieties are hardier.

CHICORY (*Cichorium intybus*)

This is a useful winter salad. Prepare the ground as for endive, and sow the seed in late spring in drills ½ in. deep and 15 in. apart. Thin seedlings to 9 in. apart.

From late autumn onwards, lift roots as required for forcing. Pack them quite close together in large pots or boxes of moist soil or peat and bring into a warm greenhouse or shed. Cover with an inverted pot or box to exclude all light (even the drainage holes of pots must be filled). Cut the blanched heads when about 5 to 6 in. long.

Chicory can also be blanched out of doors by covering the roots in late winter.

CHINESE CABBAGE (*Brassica cernua*)

This looks more like a cos lettuce than a cabbage and can either be cooked like cabbage or used raw as a salad. Sow in late spring and early summer in good rich soil in drills ½ in. deep and 1 ft. apart. Thin seedlings to 9 in. Cut as plants grow sufficiently large to be usable.

CHIVES (*Allium schoenoprasum*)

This relative of the onion is a perennial grown for its leaves, which are chopped and used as flavouring. Plant small tufts or divisions in early spring in reasonably good soil and an open position. Space 6 in. apart. Plants make attractive edges to beds. Cut a few leaves at a time as required but never strip any plant completely.

COUVE TRONCHUDA
(*Brassica oleracea costata*)

A relation of the cabbage but with very large white midribs to the leaves. These can be cut out and used like seakale, the green parts being cooked like cabbage.

Sow in spring as for cabbage and plant out seedlings when large enough 2 ft. apart each way in rich soil. Water freely in dry weather. Cut leaves as they attain usable size. This vegetable is sometimes known as Portuguese Cabbage.

CRESS (*Lepidium sativum*)

Sow under glass at any time in a temperature of 15°C. or out of doors in spring and summer. Scatter seed broadcast and cover lightly with soil outdoors but only with glass and paper when grown in a greenhouse. Water freely. Cut with scissors when seedlings are 2 to 3 in. high. Provided the temperature is right cress takes 12 to 18 days from sowing to cutting.

CUCUMBERS (*Cucumis sativus*)

Frame Cucumbers are grown in greenhouses or frames, and Ridge Cucumbers out of doors like marrows but on mounds of rich soil in a sunny place.

Sow seed of frame cucumbers in pairs in 3-in. pots from late winter to late spring in John Innes seed compost or a peat-based seed compost, and germinate in a temperature of 15 to 18°C. Reduce seedlings to one in each pot and water well.

Prepare a 6-in. deep bed of loam and well-rotted manure, in the proportion of 3 to 1. At intervals of 3 ft. make low mounds, each consisting of 2 bucketfuls of the same mixture.

When seedlings have two rough leaves each, plant one seedling on the summit of each mound. In a greenhouse, train the main stem upwards under the roof towards the apex of the house and spread side shoots out horizontally. In frames, plant one cucumber in the centre of each frame in late spring, pinch out the tip of the plant when 6 in. high and train side shoots towards each corner. Male and female flowers are produced, and the male flowers must be removed. Some varieties produce female flowers only.

Water and syringe the plants freely so that the air is constantly moist, shade from direct sunshine and topdress with rich soil or well-rotted manure when white roots appear on the surface of the soil.

Sow seed of ridge cucumbers in the same way but not before mid-spring. Harden off seedlings and plant outdoors when there is no danger of frost. Space at least 2 ft. apart in heavily manured soil and a sunny position. Water freely in dry weather. Do not remove male flowers as it is desirable that the female flowers should be fertilized.

ENDIVE (*Cichorium endivia*)

This is a salad plant which is particularly useful in autumn and winter as it is hardier than lettuce and can, therefore, be used as a substitute. Prepare the ground by thorough digging or forking and work in manure at 1 cwt. to 10 sq. yd. Rake in a compound fertilizer before sowing at the rate of 2 to 4 oz. per sq. yd.

Sow every three or four weeks from mid-spring until late summer in drills ½ in. deep and 1 ft. apart. Thin seedlings to 9 in. apart and transplant the thinnings elsewhere if desired. When plants are well grown, place a slate, tile, piece of board or an inverted saucer over each one to exclude light and blanch the leaves. Cut for use about six weeks later. There are both cut-leaved and plain-leaved varieties, the latter being hardier.

GARLIC (*Allium sativum*)

The cultivation of garlic is very similar to that of shallots except that each bulb is composed of several separate pieces, or 'cloves', the whole enveloped in a paper-like membrane. To propagate garlic these bulbs are broken up and each clove is planted separately. Soil, spacing and treatment are as for shallots.

HORSERADISH (Cochlearia armoracia)

This is grown for its roots which have a hot flavour and are used in sauces. It is grown from pieces of root, each 3 or 4 in. long, planted in early spring right way up in dibber holes 1 ft. apart in rows 18 in. apart. The top of each root should be just below soil level. Plant in well dug soil and keep clear of weeds.

Lift the roots in autumn, keeping the thickest for kitchen use and others for re-planting the following year. Store all in sand or peat in a sheltered place outdoors.

KALE or BORECOLE
(Brassica oleracea acephala)

There are several different types of kale or borecole, all related to the cabbage but grown for their leaves or shoots picked separately and not forming close heads or hearts. Green Curled is one of the most popular, others being Asparagus (grown for its shoots), Hungry Gap (it comes in spring when there is a shortage of green vegetables) and Russian.

Grow all from seed sown in spring or summer as advised for cabbage, transplanting seedlings when a few inches high to good soil and spacing them 18 in. apart in rows $2\frac{1}{2}$ ft. apart. Gather leaves or shoots as required.

KOHL RABI
(Brassica oleracea caulorapa)

This is grown for its swollen stems which are used in the same way as turnips. Prepare the ground by thorough digging or forking and work in manure or well-rotted garden refuse at 1 cwt. to 20 sq. yd. Rake in a compound fertilizer prior to sowing, at the rate of 2 to 4 oz. per sq. yd. Sow seed every three weeks from mid-spring to midsummer in drills $\frac{1}{2}$ in. deep and 15 in. apart. Thin seedlings to about 8 in. and pull plants for use when stems attain a diameter of about 3 in.

LEEKS (Allium porrum)

Prepare the ground for leeks by thorough digging or forking and work in manure or well-rotted garden refuse at 1 cwt. to 10 sq. yd. Rake or fork in a compound fertilizer before planting at the rate of 2 to 4 oz. per sq. yd.

Sow seed during early spring in a separate seed bed of well-broken soil in drills $\frac{1}{4}$ in. deep and 9 in. apart. For an early crop, sow in a greenhouse, temp. 13 to 15°C., in late winter, prick out seedlings $1\frac{1}{2}$ in. apart and harden off for planting out in late spring.

Plant the seedlings with a dibber in holes 9 in. deep and 1 ft. apart in rows 18 in. apart. Let each plant drop to the bottom of its hole and water in with a watering-can without a rose. This deep planting is necessary to blanch the stems.

For longer stems, plant in trenches 1 ft. wide, 6 in. deep and at least 2 ft. apart. Space the plants 1 ft. apart and as they grow gradually fill in the trench.

With either method, more soil can be drawn around the stems from between the rows in late summer. Lift the plants as they are required for use. Leeks are quite hardy and can remain in the ground all winter.

LETTUCE (Lactuca sativa)

Varieties are divided into three main types: Cabbage Lettuces with ball-like hearts; Cos Lettuces with long hearts; and Loose-leaf Lettuces with no hearts at all. Cabbage lettuces are subdivided into two groups: Crisphead with brittle leaves and Butterhead with soft leaves.

Prepare soil with manure or decayed vegetable refuse worked in at 1 cwt. to 10 sq. yd. and a compound fertilizer raked or forked into the seedbed immediately prior to sowing.

Make small successional sowings at intervals of two to three weeks from early spring to late summer. Sow thinly in drills $\frac{1}{2}$ in. deep and 1 ft. apart, and thin seedlings to 8 to 12 in. apart. Surplus seedlings carefully lifted with a hand fork can be replanted elsewhere. For an early crop, sow seed in a frame or greenhouse in late winter, harden off seedlings and plant out in spring. For a still earlier crop, sow in a frame or under cloches in autumn and either thin out or transplant seedlings to other frames or cloches in late winter.

Keep lettuces well watered in summer. Cut as they form hearts and before they run to seed, which they may do rapidly in hot weather.

MINT
(Mentha spicata and M. rotundifolia)

Obtain roots in spring, spread them out thinly all over the bed in which they are to grow and cover with 1 in. of soil. Mint succeeds best in moderately rich soil and a sunny place. A bed can remain undisturbed for years but if the vigour of the plants shows signs of declining the roots should be dug up and replanted in another place in spring.

Early crops can be obtained by lifting roots, placing them in a box of soil and bringing this into a warm greenhouse any time between October and February.

The Spearmint or Common Green Mint, Mentha spicata, is the kind commonly grown but many people regard the Round-leaved Mint, M. rotundifolia, as superior in flavour.

This species has an attractive variety with white variegation on the light green leaves which is often grown for ornament and is sometimes known as Apple Mint. All these kinds can be grown in the manner described.

MUSHROOMS (Psalliota campestris)

The most satisfactory way of growing mushrooms is in boxes of any size and 9 to 12 in. deep. These are filled with specially prepared horse manure or with straw rotted with one of the chemical preparations sold for the purpose. If straw is used the instructions on the composting accelerator must be followed. If manure is used it should be obtained fresh with a fair amount of straw and be immediately built into a stack 3 ft. high and wide and of any convenient length. The manure is turned every five days for three weeks, any dry places being wetted at each turning. By then it should have an even texture throughout, brown and easily broken and with no smell of ammonia.

Fill the boxes with the prepared manure or compost, take a temperature reading daily well down in the box and spawn when the temperature drops to between 21 and 24°C. Pure culture spawn is best. Break this into small pieces and plant in the boxes 1 in. deep and 9 in. apart. Place boxes in a dark shed or other convenient place in a temperature of 15 to 16°C. and cover with clean straw. After 10 days lift the straw and examine the compost. If it is becoming covered with a cobweb of white filaments cover with a 1-in. layer of a mixture of equal parts broken chalk and peat, and replace the straw. Four or five weeks later the first mushrooms should appear and cropping may continue for a further four to six weeks.

Mushrooms can also be grown in beds 2 to 3 ft. wide and about 9 in. deep. The method is the same as for boxes.

MUSTARD
(Brassica nigra and Sinapis alba)

This is grown in exactly the same way as cress. It grows more rapidly so should be sown three days after cress if both are required at the same time.

ONIONS (Allium cepa)

Dig or fork ground thoroughly and work in manure or rotted garden refuse at 1 cwt. to 10 sq. yd. Rake in bonfire ashes at 8 oz. per sq. yd. and also give a dressing of a compound fertilizer prior to sowing. Onions need a particularly crumbly seed bed.

Sow in spring in drills $\frac{1}{2}$ in. deep and 1 ft. apart. Thin seedlings to 6 in. when large enough for use as salad onions.

For an earlier crop, sow in boxes in a warm greenhouse in late winter, prick off seedlings 2 in. apart into other boxes and harden off for planting out in mid-spring. Alternatively, sow outdoors in late summer and transplant seedlings in spring, 6 in. apart in rows 1 ft. apart in ground prepared as described above.

Yet another way of growing onions is from 'sets' i.e. small bulbs specially grown for planting. Plant these in spring 6 in. apart in rows 1 ft. apart, barely covering with soil. As they grow they will work themselves on to the top of the soil.

When bulbs are well formed in summer, bend over the leaves, and 2 or 3 weeks later lift the bulbs with a fork and lay them in a dry sunny place for a few days to ripen before storing them in trays in a cool, dry place.

Salad onions are produced by sowing fortnightly from spring to late summer in rows 8 in. apart and pulling seedlings when large enough for use.

PARSLEY *(Petroselinum crispum)*

Sow in early spring and again in midsummer in drills $\frac{1}{4}$ in. deep in good soil and a sunny position. Thin seedlings to 6 in. Gather leaves a few at a time as soon as plants are well grown. In autumn transplant some plants from the last sowing to a frame for winter supplies.

PARSNIPS *(Peucedanum sativum)*

Dig or fork ground deeply so that roots can grow down easily without forking (dividing). Rake in a compound fertilizer before sowing. Sow in spring in drills 1 in. deep and 15 in. apart. Thin seedlings to 6 in. apart. Give a further light application of fertilizer in early summer and hoe in. When roots attain usable size lift them a few at a time as required. They are quite hardy and can be left in the ground all winter.

PEAS *(Pisum sativum)*

There are many varieties of pea, differing in height and the time taken to reach maturity. Dwarf varieties, $1\frac{1}{2}$ to 2 ft. high, need little or no support. Medium and tall varieties, 3 to 4 ft. high, must be supported on twiggy branches or netting. Early varieties take about twelve weeks from sowing to first picking, maincrop varieties about fourteen weeks.

Prepare ground as for broad beans. Sow every two or three weeks from early spring until midsummer using an early variety for the first sowings and a maincrop variety for the late sowings. Sow thinly in drills 2 in. deep and spaced at about the height of the variety, i.e. dwarf varieties 18 in. apart, tall varieties 3 ft. apart. Alternatively, sprinkle seeds thinly all over flat-bottomed drills, 1 in. deep, which have been scooped out with a spade.

Push pea sticks firmly into the soil on both sides of each row as soon as seedlings are 3 to 4 in. high. Keep well watered in dry weather.

Start to gather pods as soon as the peas are of usable size.

POTATOES *(Solanum tuberosum)*

There are early, second early, maincrop and late varieties differing in the time they take to reach maturity. In general, early varieties do not crop so heavily as those that grow more slowly.

For all varieties dig or fork ground thoroughly and work in manure or well-rotted garden refuse at 1 cwt. to 15 sq. yd. Fork or rake in a compound fertilizer prior to planting.

Obtain certified virus-free planting 'sets' (small tubers or 'seed' potatoes) in late winter and place them, 'eyed' ends uppermost, in single rows in boxes. Stand in a light but frost-proof place to sprout.

Plant in spring in V-shaped trenches 5 to 6 in. deep and $2\frac{1}{2}$ ft. apart for early varieties, 3 ft. for maincrop and late varieties. Place tubers, sprouts upwards, 1 ft. apart and carefully return the soil over them.

As soon as shoots appear, draw soil from between the rows over them (earthing up). Continue to do this every few days until ridges 4 to 6 in. high have been formed.

Lift early and second early varieties with a fork as soon as tubers are of usable size. Leave maincrop and late varieties until leaves and stems start to die down in late summer or autumn. Spray with Bordeaux mixture or other copper fungicide in midsummer and again in late summer if growth is not already dying down by then.

Store only sound tubers for winter use in a frost-proof shed or clamp. Keep quite dark or tubers will become green and unfit for consumption.

PUMPKIN *(Cucurbita maxima)*

This is related to the vegetable marrow and is grown in a similar manner. It enjoys good rich soil containing plenty of manure or decayed garden refuse, adequate supplies of water while growing and a warm, sunny position.

Pumpkins may be used young, like vegetable marrow, or may be allowed to grow to full size and ripen, then be cut and stored in a dry frost-proof place.

RADISH *(Raphanus sativus)*

These like rich soil and plenty of water while growing. Dig or fork ground thoroughly, working in manure or rotted garden refuse at 1 cwt. per 10 sq. yd. and raking in a compound fertilizer before sowing. Sow thinly every fortnight from early spring to late summer in drills $\frac{1}{4}$ in. deep and 8 in. apart. Keep well watered in dry weather

and pull roots as they attain usable size. The variety Chinese Rose makes large roots and can be lifted in autumn and stored for winter use if sown about midsummer.

RHUBARB *(Rheum rhaponticum)*

This is a perennial which may occupy the same site for many years. Prepare the soil by thorough digging or forking and work in manure or well-rotted compost at 1 cwt. to 15 sq. yd.

Plant strong roots in spring, spacing them 3 ft. apart each way, with the crowns just appearing on the surface. Feed with a top-dressing of manure or garden compost each spring.

Pull off the sticks of rhubarb (leaf stalks) for use as required, but do not crop in the first year after planting or in late summer and autumn.

To force rhubarb, cover established roots in winter with barrels, boxes, earthenware forcing pots, or anything else that will exclude light, and heap dead leaves, straw or other dry litter around them to exclude cold. Gather the sticks as required.

For even earlier supplies of forced rhubarb, lift strong roots in autumn and bring them into a warm greenhouse or heated shed. Surround them with soil in some place that can be kept dark. Keep well watered and pull as available. Roots can be replanted in the garden after forcing, but should not be forced again for two or three years.

Old plants can be lifted and divided in spring or rhubarb can be raised from seed sown in spring.

SAGE *(Salvia officinalis)*

A small shrub grown for its aromatic leaves which are used for flavouring. Plant in spring in well-drained soil and a sunny position. Do not crop the first year. In subsequent years gather leaves as required but never strip a plant completely. About midsummer young shoots can be cut, tied in small bundles and hung in a dry, airy place. When completely dry and brittle, leaves are crumbled and stored in jars for use at any time.

Sage can be raised from seed sown in spring or from cuttings in summer. There are ornamental-leaved varieties which are equally satisfactory for flavouring.

SALSIFY *(Tragopogon porrifolius)* and SCORZONERA *(Scorzonera hispanica)*

Both these vegetables are grown for their long, rather parsnip-like roots. Salsify is sometimes known as Vegetable Oyster because the roots, when cooked, are said to taste like oysters. Both salsify and scorzonera require similar treatment.

Prepare the ground by thorough digging or forking and rake in a compound fertilizer, at the rate of 2 to 4 oz., per sq. yd., prior to sowing. Sow in spring in drills ½ in. deep and 1 ft. apart and thin seedlings to 6 or 8 in. apart.

Lift roots carefully in autumn and store in sand or ashes in a sheltered place for use as required.

The skin of the scorzonera root is black, but the flesh is white. The young leaves of salsify can be used in salads.

SEAKALE (Crambe maritima)

Seakale is grown for forcing in winter and it is the blanched shoots that are eaten. It is grown from root cuttings or 'thongs' cut from mature plants before they are forced. Each thong should be about 6 in. long and of finger thickness. Plant in spring in well-cultivated soil. Use a dibber to make holes slightly more than the depth of the thongs, drop one thong into each hole, right way up, and just cover with soil. Space 1 ft. apart in rows 18 in. apart. Keep free of weeds and give a dusting of a compound fertilizer in early summer.

In autumn dig up all roots, trim off the side roots which will be kept for replanting the following spring and pack the main roots, crowns uppermost, in sand or ashes in a sheltered place. If a sloping cut is made at the bottom of each side root as it is removed it will be easy to tell the top from the bottom of the cutting. Tie these roots in bundles and lay in sand or ashes out of doors.

Pot the main roots a few at a time for forcing. Place fairly close together in pots or deep boxes and bring into a warm greenhouse or shed. Cover to exclude light or force in a dark place. Cut shoots at soil level when 6 to 9 in. long.

Alternatively, some roots can be left in the ground and soil thrown up over them in winter. New shoots grow up into this soil and are blanched.

SHALLOTS (Allium ascalonicum)

These are grown for their clusters of bulbs which have a mild onion flavour. They are produced from small bulbs planted in late winter or early spring.

Prepare the ground by thorough digging or forking and work in manure or rotted garden refuse at 1 cwt. to 15 sq. yd. Rake or fork in a compound fertilizer prior to planting at the rate of 2 to 4 oz. per sq. yd.

Plant only good sound bulbs. Space them 6 in. apart in rows 1 ft. apart, barely covering each bulb with soil. Later they will work out on top of the soil, which is their natural habit, but if they get dislodged by birds, wind, frost or any other cause they must be replanted.

Keep the ground clear of weeds and when the new bulbs are well formed draw soil away from them to expose them to the sun for ripening. Lift with a fork when leaves turn yellow and spread the bulbs out in a dry sunny place to complete ripening. Then store in a cool, dry shed.

SPINACH (Spinacia oleracea)

This is a fast-growing annual cultivated for its leaves which are cooked. There are two types, Summer or Round-seeded Spinach, and Winter or Prickly-seeded Spinach.

Dig or fork ground thoroughly and work in manure or well-rotted garden refuse at 1 cwt. to 10 sq. yd. Rake in a compound fertilizer before sowing.

Sow summer spinach every three weeks from early spring until midsummer and winter spinach in late summer or early autumn. Sow in drills 1 in. deep and 1 ft. apart and thin seedlings to 6 in. Water freely in dry weather. Start to pick outer leaves as soon as they reach usable size, or take the centre out of each plant as soon as large enough to use, when the buds below will make new growth. Pick regularly until plants run up to flower.

SPINACH BEET, SEAKALE BEET (Beta vulgaris cicla)

These both belong to the same species as the beetroot but seakale beet is grown for the fleshy mid-rib of the leaf which can be used as an alternative to seakale, the green of the leaf being cooked like spinach, and spinach beet is also grown for its leaves. It stands hot weather better than true spinach, and will continue to crop for months.

Prepare ground for both these crops as for spinach. Sow in spring and again in late summer in drills 1 in. deep and 18 in. apart and thin seedlings to 9 in. Gather leaves a few at a time from each plant as required.

SWEET CORN (Zea mays)

Prepare ground in a sunny, warm place by thorough digging or forking and work in manure or rotted garden refuse at 1 cwt. to 15 sq. yd. Before sowing or planting, rake in a compound fertilizer at the rate of 2 to 4 oz. per sq. yd.

Sow in late spring in drills 1 in. deep and 2 ft. apart, putting two or three seeds every foot along each drill. Reduce seedlings to one at each point after germination. Alternatively, sow seed in mid-spring, two in each 3-in. pot, in John Innes seed compost or equivalent compost, germinate in a frame or greenhouse, reduce seedlings to one in each pot and harden off for planting out in late spring or early summer. Space plants 1 ft. apart in rows 2 ft. apart. It is better to have several short rows in a block rather than one long row, because if grown in a block the flowers are fertilized more readily.

Water freely in hot weather. Examine cobs (seedheads) as they form by carefully drawing aside the sheathing husks and cut cobs when the seeds are well formed and golden. If punctured with the thumb nail, milky sap should seep out.

THYME (Thymus vulgaris)

A small shrubby plant grown for its aromatic leaves which are used as flavouring. Plant in spring or autumn 9 in. apart in reasonably good, well-drained soil and a sunny position. Allow young plants to become well established before picking shoots from them and even then only gather a few at a time from each plant except in early summer when plants can be clipped all over and the shoots tied in small bundles and hung up to dry in a sheltered, airy place. When thoroughly dry, leaves can be crumbled and stored in well-stoppered jars. Thyme can be raised from seed sown outdoors in spring or by cuttings in a frame in summer.

TOMATOES (Lycopersicon esculentum)

Sow seed of tomatoes in winter or early spring for cropping under glass, and in spring for outdoor planting. Sow in John Innes seed compost or equivalent, just covering the seeds, and germinate in a temperature of 15 to 18°C. Prick out seedlings 2 in. apart in John Innes potting compost No. 1, or equivalent, and, before they become overcrowded, pot singly in 3-in. pots in the same compost.

Grow throughout this period in a light greenhouse with an average temperature of 15°C. and a minimum temperature of 10°C. and water well.

In late spring harden off the plants for outdoor planting and plant out when there is no further danger of frost, 18 in. apart in rows 3 ft. apart in well-cultivated soil in a sheltered, sunny position. Remove all side shoots as they appear and tie each plant to a 4-ft. stake. Remove the top of each plant when it has produced four flower trusses. Support is not necessary for bush varieties nor need side shoots or tops be removed from them.

Spray all outdoor plants with a copper fungicide about midsummer and repeat every two or three weeks.

Pick fruits as they turn yellow and allow them to finish ripening in boxes indoors. Gather all remaining green fruits before there is danger of frost and ripen in boxes or use for chutney.

Under glass, tomatoes can be grown in 9-in. pots, boxes of about 1 cu. ft., beds of soil or bottomless rings. For pots or boxes use John Innes potting compost No. 4. Prepare soil beds by thorough forking, the addition of manure or well-rotted compost at 1 cwt. to 15 sq. yd. and a dusting of a well-balanced compound fertilizer.

Pot or plant in spring or according to the

degree of heat available. Tomatoes need a fairly steady temperature of 15°C. for growth, so it is no use planting very early in unheated or poorly-heated houses. In beds, space plants 18 in. apart in rows 2½ ft. apart.

Rub off all side shoots as they appear and keep each plant to a single stem. Tie this to a cane or attach soft string near the base of the plant and to the greenhouse rafters and gently twist the plant around this as it grows.

Keep well watered at all times and feed once a week with a liquid fertilizer directly tiny fruits start to form on the lowest flower trusses.

Ventilate freely when possible, but keep a temperature of 15°C. Syringe plants with water to assist flowers to set (form fruits). Remove the top of each plant when it reaches the roof of the greenhouse. Gather fruits as they ripen.

Ring culture is another satisfactory method of growing tomatoes under glass or outdoors. Plants are raised in the usual way but when 5 to 6 in. high they are planted in bottomless 'rings' about 10 in. in diameter and 9 in. deep, usually made of tough, rot-proof paper. These are filled with John Innes potting compost No. 4, or equivalent, and are placed 18 in. apart from centre to centre on a 6-in. deep bed of well-weathered boiler ashes or pea-sized gravel isolated from the soil below by a sheet of polythene.

The young plants are well watered in until excess water trickles out of the bottoms of the rings. Subsequently, all water is applied to the bed of ashes or gravel and some will soak up into the compost in the rings. Very soon the plants will root down into the bed of ashes or gravel and obtain their water directly from it.

Training is exactly as for plants grown in the ordinary way. When feeding is necessary it is given to the compost in the rings, not to the bed of ashes or gravel.

TURNIP, SWEDE (*Brassica rapa*)

Both these vegetables belong to the same species and are grown for their swollen roots. Both grow best in fairly rich soil and turnips in particular need to grow fast if they are to be tender fleshed and mild flavoured.

Sow turnips every 3 or 4 weeks from early spring to midsummer in drills ½ in. deep and 12 in. apart. Thin seedlings to 4 in. apart and pull roots for use as they attain sufficient size. Roots from the last summer sowing may be left to reach a greater size, lifted in autumn and stored in a clamp or in sand, peat or dry soil in a shed.

Sow swedes in late spring or early summer in drills ½ in. deep and 15 in. apart. Thin seedlings to 8 in. and lift as required for use. Swedes are hardy and can be left in the ground all the winter.

VEGETABLE MARROW, SQUASH (*Cucurbita pepo*)

Plants may be either trailing in habit or bushy according to variety.

Dig or fork ground thoroughly and work in manure or well-rotted garden refuse at 1 cwt. to 10 sq. yd. Alternatively, prepare a site 2 ft. sq. for each plant, forking in a large basketful of manure or compost.

Sow seeds in spring, two in each 3-in. pot in John Innes seed compost, or equivalent, and germinate in a temperature of 15 to 18°C. Reduce to one seedling in each pot

and harden off for planting out 3 ft. apart in late spring or early summer. Alternatively, sow when there is little further likelihood of frost outdoors, placing two or three seeds at each place where a plant is required. Cover with a cloche or a large jam jar. Remove this when seedlings appear and thin to one plant at each point.

Keep plants well watered in dry weather. Pinch out the growing tips of trailing varieties when stems are 3 ft. long. Side shoots will then grow and these usually fruit more freely than main stems.

Cut fruits as soon as they are large enough to use; courgettes when about 5 in. long. If left to grow large, cropping will be reduced.

WATERCRESS (*Nasturtium officinale*)

This is best grown in watertight beds (they can be lined with concrete or plastic sheeting) 8 to 10 in. deep. Good loamy soil is spread over the bottom to a depth of 3 in., a little gravel or sand is spread on top and watercress cuttings are dibbled into this, 6 in. apart, in spring, summer or early autumn. The bed is then flooded to a depth of 1½ in.; more water is admitted as the plants grow but the final depth should not be more than 4 in. Cutting can start as soon as the bed is well covered with growth.

Alternatively, crops can be grown in trenches prepared as for celery but about 2 ft. in width. Seed is sown in spring or summer, or cuttings planted as already described, and the trenches are kept well watered.

TABLE OF VEGETABLE TYPES AND VARIETIES

KIND	TYPES	CHARACTERISTICS	VARIETIES
Broad Bean	Longpod	very long seed pods	Aquadulce Claudia, Bunyard's Exhibition, Dreadnaught, Green Masterpiece
	Windsor	broad seed pods	Giant Four-seeded White Windsor, Giant Four-seeded Green Windsor, Fillbasket
	Dwarf	height about 1 ft., well branched plant	The Sutton
French Bean	Ordinary	flattish pods, dwarf habit	Canadian Wonder, Masterpiece, The Prince
	Stringless	almost tubular pods, dwarf habit	Processor, Tendergreen, Tenderlong
	Wax (golden podded)	yellow pods, dwarf habit	King Horn Wax
	Haricot	grown for ripened seeds, dwarf habit	Brown Dutch, Comtesse de Chambord, Masterpiece
	Climbing	similar to dwarf varieties but tall and twining	Blue Lake Stringless, Kentucky Wonder, Brown Seeded

KIND	TYPE	CHARACTERISTICS	VARIETIES
Runner Bean	Climbing	tall, twining growth	Achievement, Goliath, Prizewinner, Scarlet Emperor, Streamline
	Dwarf	dwarf, bushy, non-twining	Hammond's Dwarf Scarlet
Beet	Globe	ball-shaped roots	Avonearly, Boltardy, Detroit, Burpee's Golden, Snow White
	Intermediate	cylindrical roots	Cylindra
	Long	long tapering roots	Cheltenham Greentop, Long Blood Red
	Leaf	grown for leaves or leaf mid-ribs	Perpetual Spinach, Silver or Seakale, Ruby Chard
Broccoli	Calabrese	medium size heads and side sprouts (the clustered flower buds)	Calabrese Atlantic, Calabrese Emerald Corona, Calabrese Green Comet
	Sprouting	many small sprouts (the clustered flower buds)	Early Purple Sprouting, Early White Sprouting, Late Purple Sprouting, Late White Sprouting
Brussels Sprouts	Open pollinated	cabbage head and button-like sprouts packed around stem	Bedford (various selections), British Allrounder, Cambridge No. 1, Cambridge No. 5, Irish Elegance, Roodnerf (various selections)
	F_1 Hybrid	similar but more uniform in habit and cropping time	Jade Cross, King Arthur, Peer Gynt, Thor
Cabbage	Round or Ball headed	leaves fold over to form a tight ball	Autumn Monarch, Christmas Drumhead, Golden Acre, Primo, Summer Monarch, Winter Monarch
	Pointed (for spring sowing)	leaves folded round one another to form a tight conical centre	Greyhound, Winnigstadt
	Pointed (for summer and autumn sowing)	similar to above but suitable to stand the winter as young plants and be cut in spring	April, Avoncrest, Early Offenham (various selections), Harbinger, Wheeler's Imperial
	Savoy	ball headed but with wrinkled leaves	Best of All, January King, Ormskirk Late
	Pickling	ball headed, usually red	Mammoth Red Rock, Nigger Head, Stockley's Red
Carrot	Stump-rooted	roots cylindrical, rounded at base	Autumn King (various selections), Amsterdam Forcing, Chantenay Red Cored, Early Horn, Early Nantes
	Intermediate	roots tapering, medium length	James' Scarlet Intermediate
	Long	roots tapering, very long	Long Red Surrey, St Valery
Cauliflower	Summer	ready to use from mid- to late summer	All the Year Round, Alpha, Polar Ice, Snow King, Snowball, Early Super
	Autumn	ready to use in autumn	Autumn Giant (various selections), Early September, Flora Blanca (several selections), Snowcap, South Pacific
	Winter	ready for use in winter and spring	English Winter (various selections), Knight's Protecting, Roscoff (various selections), Leamington, Snow's Winter White, Walcheren Winter (various selections)
Celery	White blanching	white stems when blanched	Giant White (several selections), New Dwarf White
	Pink blanching	pink stems when blanched, slightly hardier than white type	Giant Red, Giant Prize Pink

KIND	TYPE	CHARACTERISTICS	VARIETIES
Celery *continued*	Self-blanching	greenish or yellowish stems without blanching, less hardy than blanching type	Avon Pearl, Green Fayre, Golden Self-blanching, Lathom Self-blanching
Cucumber	Ridge	suitable for growing outdoors	Bedfordshire Prize, Burpee Hybrid, Burpless Perfection, King of the Ridge, Victory
	Frame or Greenhouse	suitable for growing under glass	Butcher's Disease Resisting, Conqueror, Feminex, Fertila, Green Spot, Improved Telegraph
Leek	Ordinary	long stems	The Lyon, Musselburgh, Autumn Mammoth (various selections)
	Pot	short thick stems	No varieties, strains selected by growers, mostly for exhibition
Lettuce	Cos	long leaves, upstanding plant	Little Gem, Lobjoit's Green, Paris White, Winter Density, Valmaine
	Cabbage (Butterhead)	broad soft leaves, ball-like plant	All the Year Round, Avondefiance, Continuity, Tom Thumb, Trocadero, Suzan
	Cabbage (Crisphead)	broad crisp leaves, ball-like plant	Avoncrisp, Iceberg, Unrivalled, Webb's Wonderful
	Loose leaf	little or no heart but cabbage habit of growth	Buttercrunch, Salad Bowl
	Glasshouse	suitable for cultivation under glass	Amanda, Cheshunt Early Giant, Kloek, Kwiek
Onion	Flat	bulbs rather flattened	Giant Zittau, Reliance (several selections), White Spanish
	Globe	bulbs globular or taller than wide	Ailsa Craig, Bedfordshire Champion, James' Long Keeping, Rijnsburger (several selections)
	Salad	mild flavour to be pulled as seedlings	White Lisbon, White Portugal
	Pickling	small bulbs	Barletta, Nocera, Paris Silverskin, White Portugal, Stuttgart Brown Skin Pickling
Parsnip	Short to medium	thick roots, not very long	Avonresister, Offenham, Student
	Long	long tapering roots	Coopers Champion Hollow Crown, Tender and True
Pea	Round seeded	hardy, suitable for autumn	Feltham First, Foremost, Gradus, Meteor, Pilot Improved, Progress No. 9
	Wrinkle seeded, first early	sweet, ready in 10–11 weeks	Beagle, Kelvedon Wonder, Little Marvel
	Wrinkle seeded, second early	sweet, ready in 12–13 weeks	Canice, Green Shaft, Early Onward, Witham Wonder
	Wrinkle seeded, maincrop	sweet, ready in 13–14 weeks	Alderman, Kelvedon Monarch, Lord Chancellor, Onward, Senator, Stratagem
	Wrinkle seeded, late	sweet, ready in 15–16 weeks	Gladstone
Potato *continued overleaf*	Early	ready to dig about 3 months after planting	Arran Pilot, Duke of York, Epicure, Home Guard, Sharpe's Express, Ulster Chieftain, Ulster Sceptre
	Second early	ready to dig about 4 months after planting	Catriona, Craig's Royal, Maris Peer
	Maincrop	ready to dig about 5 months after planting	Arran Banner, Desiree, Dr McIntosh, King Edward, Majestic, Pentland Dell, Red King Edward

KIND	TYPE	CHARACTERISTICS	VARIETIES
Potato *continued*	Late	ready to dig about 6 months after planting	Golden Wonder, Kerr's Pink, Pentland Crown
Radish	Turnip or Oval	globular or egg-shaped roots	Cherry Belle, French Breakfast, Saxa, Scarlet Globe, Sparkler
	Long	long tapering roots	Long Scarlet, Long White, Icicle
	Winter	large roots, long or round	China Rose, Spanish Black Round
Sweet Corn	Open pollinated	cheaper seed	Golden Bantam
	F_1 Hybrid	more uniform habit and improved cropping	Earliking, John Innes Hybrid, Kelvedon Glory, Sugar King
Tomato	Ordinary, open pollinated	grown on a single stem	Ailsa Craig, E.S.1., Histon Ideal, Infinity Cross, Kondine Red, Market King, Outdoor Girl, Potentate, Sunrise
	Ordinary, F_1 hybrid	similar but more uniform	Big Boy, Eurocross (several selections), Maascross, Supercross
	Bush	short branching habit	Amateur, Easicrop, Histon Cropper
	Yellow fruited	yellow fruits, both ordinary and bush types available	Golden Amateur (bush), Golden Sunrise, Mid-day Sun, Yellow Perfection
Turnip	White	roots all white	Early Snowball, Milan White
	Golden	roots all yellow	Golden Ball
	Green top	roots white, green on upper half	Manchester Market
	Purple top	roots white, purple on upper half	Coopers Early Purple Top, White Globe, Purple Top Milan
Vegetable Marrow	Bush	bushy habit	Custard White, Long Green Bush, White Bush
	Trailing	trailing growth	Long Green Trailing, Long White Trailing
	Courgette	free fruiting can be cut very young	All Green Bush, Golden Courgette, Zucchini

GARDEN MANAGEMENT

ABSCISSION LAYER A layer of thin-walled cells formed between leaf stalks and stems and also between fruit stalks and stems before the leaves or fruits fall. It is at this layer that the break occurs. On the stem side of the abscission layer a corky layer is formed to seal the wound.

ACARICIDE Any chemical which will kill mites. The term is often used in describing sprays or dusts produced for the purpose of killing red spider mites.

ACAULESCENT A botanical term meaning stemless or practically stemless. The specific epithets *acaulis* and *acaule* are derived from the same root and are often applied to plants with flowers which are either stemless or carried on extremely short stems.

ACHENE A botanical term for a seed vessel or fruit that is dry, contains only one seed and does not split open along a clearly defined line or lines. The fruits of a buttercup are of this type.

ACICULAR A botanical term usually applied to leaves and meaning needle shaped.

ACID Chemically an acid is a substance, an aqueous solution of which will turn the blue litmus dye pink in contrast to a base or alkali which turns pink litmus dye blue. As far as the gardener is concerned he can think of acid substances most helpfully as those which are sharp and sour and have the property of combining with alkalis to form salts which are in the main neutral in reaction, i.e. neither acid nor alkaline.

The term is important to gardeners because soils are either acid, neutral or alkaline and this may have an important bearing on their fertility, the kinds of plants which they will grow and even the susceptibility which these plants may show to certain diseases. For example, most members of the heather family, *Ericaceae*, which includes heathers, rhododendrons, pieris and andromeda, will only thrive in soils which are to some extent acid. By contrast, most members of the brassica family, *Cruciferae*, which includes cabbages, brussels sprouts, kale and wallflowers, succeed best in soils which are neutral or slightly alkaline; if planted in markedly acid soils, they are often heavily infected with club root disease.

Acidity and alkalinity can be measured by various means, but are usually expressed in terms of a scale which is known as the pH of the substance tested. If the substance is described as being pH 7.0 it is neutral, that is to say, neither acid nor alkaline. If it is described as having a pH above 7.0, for example pH 7.5, it is alkaline, whereas if the figure is below 7.0, for example pH 6.5, the substance is acid. In general the most satis-

factory reaction for a garden soil, in which many different plants are to be grown, is between pH 6.5 and pH 7.0. Soils with readings below 6.0 become difficult for many plants except those that thrive in acid conditions. Similarly, above pH 8.0 trouble may be experienced with many plants and there may be signs of severe mineral deficiency (a form of starvation), owing to the locking-up of certain essential foods in the soil.

Any soil that is being cultivated extensively will tend to become more acid in time and this increasing acidity will be most rapid when heavy applications of dung or compost are made. It is part of the gardener's task to assess from time to time the acid–alkaline reaction of his soil and maintain it at the level most suitable for the particular plants he proposes to cultivate. The test can be carried out in several ways, most simply, and for most purposes sufficiently accurately, by the barium sulphate colour test, but still more accurately by an electrical apparatus. Reagents for the barium sulphate test, with a suitable colour chart, can be purchased in the form of proprietary kits from garden centres and garden sundriesmen.

In the British Isles, the degree of acidity of most soils is controlled by the amount of lime they contain. A soil containing free lime will always be to some degree alkaline and therefore unsuitable for the really acid-loving plants. It is, however, possible for lime to be present in the soil without being free. This so-called active lime (i.e. lime that has combined with humus and the finest soil particles or colloids) is a vital constituent of all fertile soils. The less active lime there is, the more acid the soil will usually be; harmful acidity can, in consequence, always be remedied by giving dressings of lime (see Lime). Acidity may be caused by an excess of organic matter in the soil and also by poor aeration (see Aeration). In consequence, besides treatment with lime, cultivation,

which improves both aeration and drainage, must be considered as a possible method of counteracting acidity.

One effect of an acid soil which gardeners often turn to account is that coloured hydrangeas produce blue flowers when grown in it, whereas in alkaline soils the flowers are pink. White hydrangeas remain white no matter what the pH of the soil. Therefore, if the gardener wishes to have blue flowers, he must take care to see that the soil is suitably acid. If it is naturally acid, he need do nothing, but if it is neutral or alkaline, he may give it fairly heavy dressings of either sulphate of aluminium, alum or sulphate of iron, or he may add heavy dressings of acid organic matter such as sphagnum peat, oak leafmould or the residue of an old cucumber bed.

ACORN The fruit of the oak.

ACRE An area of 4,840 sq. yds.

ACUMINATE A botanical term usually applied to leaves, indicating that they taper to a rather long and narrow point and that the sides of this point are themselves curved inwards.

ACUTE A botanical term often applied to leaves, indicating termination in a sharp point. The term differs from acuminate in that in this instance the sides of the point are either straight or curved slightly outwards.

ADPRESSED, see Appressed

ADVENTITIOUS A botanical term for a growth or organ produced by a plant at a place which would not normally have a growth or organ of that type. For example, if a willow stem is cut off and inserted in the soil in autumn or winter, it will almost certainly produce roots from the base; these are known as adventitious roots because

There are various proprietary kits for testing the acid–alkaline reaction of soils

they would not have been produced had the branch been left to grow on the tree. In the same way, if a tree is cut down, buds and, later, shoots may be produced near the top of the stump, despite the fact that there were no buds there previously. These are known as adventitious buds. It is sometimes possible to produce adventitious growth by chemical means. For example, if one of the root-forming hormones is smeared or painted on the shoot of a growing plant, it is possible that a few weeks later roots will appear at this point despite the fact that the shoots may be nowhere near the soil and the roots are quite useless to the plant.

AERATION Applied to gardening this means the presence of air spaces between the soil particles, an important factor in all fertile soils. Many cultural operations are concerned with the improvement or maintenance of satisfactory aeration. For example, a lawn which has been subject to heavy wear will become so consolidated that little or no air can penetrate the soil. To remedy this the gardener perforates it with a spiked roller, or even with the prongs of an ordinary garden fork, so letting in air and restoring the fertility of the soil.

Coarse sand is a usual ingredient of most loam-based seed and potting composts and some soilless ones because it prevents the more adhesive constituents of the mixture from binding too closely together and so excluding air. Digging, forking and hoeing, though necessary for other reasons, are also valuable because they increase aeration. In a soil which contains insufficient air, harmful bacteria and other micro-organisms thrive and acid conditions are rapidly produced.

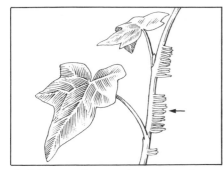

Aerial roots assist some plants, such as ivy, to climb

AERIAL ROOT Any root which appears above ground level is known by this name. Aerial roots are most important to certain orchids which in nature live on trees where there is little or no soil. These orchids obtain most of their nourishment from the moisture in the air which they absorb by means of these aerial roots, as well as by their leaves. Some climbing plants, such as ivy, cling by means of aerial roots.

AEROBIC A term used to describe bacteria which require air, in contrast to those that can live without it and are therefore described as anaerobic. In general, anaerobic bacteria are harmful from the garden standpoint whereas many aerobic bacteria perform useful functions such as releasing the plant food stored in organic matter. Part of the benefit gained by soil cultivation is due to the fact that it permits air to penetrate more freely and so stimulates aerobic and discourages anaerobic bacteria. See Bacteria.

AEROSOL A colloidal suspension of any substance in a gas. Aerosols of various chemicals are sometimes used in greenhouses to destroy pests but the method has been superseded to a considerable extent by smokes carrying the same or similar chemicals. A method commonly employed to produce an aerosol is to prepare a solution of the chemical in a volatile fluid, place this in a closed metal chamber and drive it out with great force through a fine jet by discharging a sparklet bulb of compressed carbon dioxide into the chamber. As a result, very fine particles of the chemical are left suspended in the air and eventually become deposited as a fine film on all exposed surfaces such as the leaves and stems of plants or the bodies of insects. Azobenzene is often used as an aerosol to destroy red spider mites.

AGGREGATE The hard material used to form the bulk of concrete or to act as the rooting medium in soilless cultivation (q.v.). Gravel and sand are the materials most commonly employed, but broken clinkers are sometimes used.

AIR LAYERING A method of rooting branches of shrubs by wounding them, encasing the wound in damp sphagnum moss, and covering this with a sleeve of thin polythene. See Layering.

ALBINO This term is more commonly applied to animals than to plants and signifies an individual in which the normal colouring matter is absent, but occasionally white forms of normally coloured flowers are known as albinos.

ALGAE Very simple plants which include those that form a green film on damp surfaces of stone and wood and the thread-like green growths found in ponds. Seaweeds are also algae. In the main, they are not harmful from the garden standpoint but excess of algal growth in ponds can be a nuisance. The pond growth popularly known as flannel weed is an alga. It can be killed with copper sulphate used at the rate of 23 grains to a thousand gallons of water but this remedy must be used with great caution as an excess will kill ornamental aquatics and fish. The correct quantity of

copper sulphate required to treat the pond should be placed in a muslin bag tied to a string, and should then be dragged through the water until dissolved. Copper wires stretched just below the surface of the water will help to control algae.

ALGINATE, see Soil Conditioner

ALKALINE The opposite of acid; a substance the aqueous solution of which turns pink litmus paper blue. See Acid.

ALLOTMENT, GARDEN Any plot of land not exceeding a quarter of an acre and rented for the purpose of growing crops for home consumption. Most allotments in England are about one quarter of that size. Usually the plot is rectangular, 30 ft. in width and 90 ft. in length. The Allotments Act of 1950 governs such matters as tenure and compensation.

ALLUVIAL Strictly speaking the term means 'that which has been washed'. It is important to gardeners because certain types of soils are geologically known as alluvial. These are all soils which have been deposited by rivers and are composed very largely of silt. Large areas in Lincolnshire and Norfolk are composed of soil of this character, and are important as market-gardening, potato-growing and bulb-growing districts, because of the extremely workable and fertile nature of the soil.

ALPINE Strictly speaking an alpine is a plant which grows naturally on mountains. In gardens the term has come to be applied to almost any plant suitable for cultivation in rock gardens, in fact it is to all intents and purposes synonymous with rock plant. Genuine mountain plants are for the most part dwarf and compact in habit and they thrive best where light is good and drainage quick. Many of them are adapted to finding their living in very stony places, and they have long roots capable of penetrating a great distance in search of food and moisture. Often they have to be dormant for many months under a deep protective covering of snow and then crowd the whole of their growth, including the production of flowers and the ripening of seeds, into three or four months during which they have the benefit of the clear mountain atmosphere and an abundant water supply from snow melting on the higher slopes. These plants are not always easy to grow under our lowland conditions with our ever-changing weather, lack of sunshine and the absence of protective winter snow. See Moraine.

ALTERNATE A term applied to leaves which are placed singly on the stem at different heights in contrast to leaves which are in pairs opposite one another or in whorls, several together. See overleaf.

An alternate arrangement of leaves

ALUM There are numerous alums but in garden terminology this is applied to sulphate of aluminium which is sometimes used as a slug killer or as a bird deterrent, and is also employed to increase the acidity of soil. For the first two purposes 4 oz. of powdered alum are dissolved in 1 gallon of water. This solution, if watered on vacant ground or on greenhouse staging and floors, will kill any slugs with which it comes in contact. The same solution sprayed on buds of fruit trees or ornamental plants will make them so bitter that as a rule birds will not touch them. Dry alum can also be sprinkled in a narrow ring round any plant likely to be attacked by slugs. To increase the acidity of soil, alum is raked or forked in at rates of up to 1 lb. per sq. yd. or may be mixed with potting soil at the rate of 2½ lb. per cwt. of soil.

It is the substance chiefly used to promote the production of blue flowers in hydrangeas. See Acid.

AMERICAN BLIGHT A name frequently given to a pest of apples, also known as woolly aphid. It is described under that name.

AMERICAN GOOSEBERRY MILDEW, see Gooseberry Mildew

AMMONIA Pure ammonia is a gas which very readily unites with water to form the familiar liquid ammonia (ammonium hydroxide) of the kitchen. This powerful and volatile alkali is seldom used directly in the garden, despite the fact that it is a potential source of nitrogen which itself is an important plant food. The difficulty is that ammonia is an inconvenient substance to use as a fertilizer because of its scorching effect on plants and its volatility. Ammonia can, however, be applied to the soil in the form of various ammonium salts the most popular of which is sulphate of ammonia (q.v.). Kitchen ammonia may also be added with advantage to water that is to be used to wash greenhouse glass as it has marked cleaning properties. Incidentally, ammonia is often given off by decomposing dung and can be smelt strongly. This indicates bad storage, as all ammonia lost in this way represents a loss of nitrogen.

ANNUAL A plant that completes its cycle of life within a year, germinating, flowering, setting seed and then dying. It should be understood that this cycle need not necessarily be within any one calendar year. It is quite possible to sow many annuals in September and over-winter them so that they flower the following spring or early summer and then set their seed and die. Nor need the annual take anything like a year in completing its life cycle. Many annual weeds, such as groundsel and chickweed, complete the cycle so quickly that they are quite capable of producing several generations in a year, and are termed ephemeral.

The annual may be contrasted with the perennial, which lives for an indefinite number of years and may flower and seed many times, and also with the monocarpic plant, which, like the perennial, lives for an indefinite number of years but only flowers once, then sets seed and dies.

No completely satisfactory scientific explanation of the annual's behaviour has yet been made, although it has been suggested that death after seed production may be due to an accumulation of poisonous substances within the plant, a suggestion which seems to imply that if some method could be discovered of dispersing these poisons, the annual would behave like a perennial.

From the gardener's point of view, annuals are subdivided into three groups – hardy, half-hardy and tender. Members of the first group can be grown out of doors at any time of the year without protection, e.g. clarkia, godetia, calendula and cornflower.

Members of the second group can only be grown out of doors in the warm weather and must usually be started under glass, though occasionally this aid can be dispensed with, e.g. ten-week stocks, annual asters, French and African marigolds and zinnias. Tender annuals require greenhouse cultivation most if not all of the time and are in general unsuitable for growing out of doors, e.g. celosia, browallia and *Torenia fournieri*.

Hardy annuals can usually be sown where they are to flower and after thinning out in the seedling stage can be left to grow on undisturbed. Alternatively, some varieties may be raised in a nursery bed and transplanted to their flowering quarters when large enough. The best sowing times are usually March to May and again in early September. Most varieties thrive in good ordinary soil and do not require any special care.

Half-hardy annuals are, in general, raised in a greenhouse or frame in a temperature of 16 to 18°C. They may then be pricked out into pans or boxes and hardened-off for planting out when the weather is sufficiently mild, usually towards the end of May or early in June. Sowing time may be anything from early January to late March. In favourable places some half-hardy annuals may be sown out of doors in late April or early May and left to mature where they germinate.

Tender annuals must always be germinated in the greenhouse in a temperature of 16°C. or more and sowing time will depend upon the season at which flowers are required.

ANTERIOR A botanical term meaning front or on the front. Thus the anterior lobe of a flower is the front lobe.

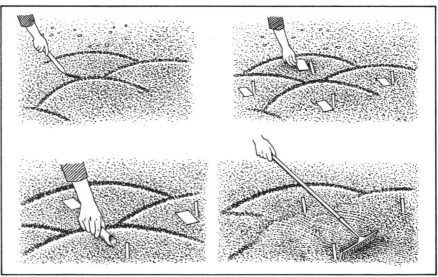

One of the most effective ways of growing annuals is in a border. First, mark out the design with a pointed stick and then allocate the seeds, checking for height and colour. The seeds should be sprinkled thinly over the soil and raked in

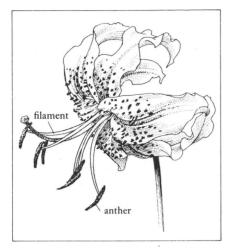

filament

anther

ANTHER That part of the flower which produces pollen, the male sex cells of the plant. The anther itself forms part of the stamen, the remainder of which usually consists of the filament, a thread-like stem which bears the anther. In some flowers anthers are of considerable size and add greatly to the decorative properties of the bloom, e.g. the central cluster of golden anthers in a single rose, the large yellow anthers in a white lily or the nearly black anthers in some tulips.

Plant breeders often remove the immature anthers from flowers which have been selected as seed parents. This is done in order to prevent fertilization with their own pollen and the process of removal is known as emasculation.

ANTHOCYANINS A class of pigments which are found dissolved in the cell sap of plants. They may be contrasted with flavones which are pigments occurring as minute particles, or plastids, in the cytoplasm, the living layer within the plant cells. The anthocyanin colours range from blue to red.

ANTHRACNOSE, BEAN A disease which is fairly common in french and haricot beans and is occasionally found in runner beans. It is caused by a fungus which attacks pods, leaves and stems, causing dark, wrinkled or cratered spots to appear on the first two and black, cankered areas on the stems. Seeds, too, may show dark patches caused by the fungus. Such seeds should not be sown. If the disease has been troublesome in former years, all plants should be sprayed with half-strength Bordeaux mixture once or twice before flowering. After flowering they may be sprayed with lime sulphur, 1 fl. oz. to 4 gallons of water, every fortnight or three weeks until the pods are half grown.

ANTS These are enemies to the gardener for two reasons; they loosen the soil and so disturb the roots of plants, and particularly

of seedlings, and they transport aphids from one plant to another. They do not themselves attack plants directly. Ants can be destroyed by dusting the soil around their nests with BHC or derris or by watering the nests with trichlorphon. Several proprietary ant-killing preparations are also offered and these should be used according to manufacturers' instructions.

APETALOUS A term applied to flowers which have no petals.

APICAL At the summit or tip of a branch or any other organ.

APICULATE Coming to a small but sharp point. A term often applied to leaves.

APHID The collective name for the many louse-like plant pests which are known in gardens by such popular names as greenfly, black fly or dolphin fly, American blight and blue fly. Aphis is the scientific name of one genus. Though aphids differ considerably in appearance and in the plants which they attack, all the numerous species have this in common, that they obtain their food by sucking the sap of plants. As a result of their attack plants are weakened and shoots or leaves frequently become curled or otherwise distorted. More serious still, aphids frequently act as carriers of virus diseases, picking up the virus from infected plants and inoculating previously healthy ones with it.

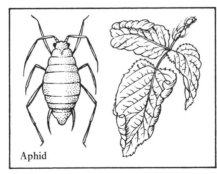

Aphid

Aphids are capable of breeding at a tremendous rate under favourable conditions. A change in the weather will often bring an attack to a sudden end but the gardener who relies upon this would be asking for trouble. Some of the flies are winged and can travel considerable distances but the majority are wingless and their powers of locomotion are small. A crop planted 100 yd. or so away from another of the same kind may remain quite clean though its neighbour is heavily infested with aphids. Most aphids prefer the young shoots and leaves and will be found clustered around the tips of the former and on the lower surfaces of the latter; but some species are confined to the roots. See Root Aphids.

The substances most effective in killing

aphids are BHC, demeton-s-methyl, derris, diazinon, dimethoate, formothion, malathion, menazon, nicotine, parathion, pyrethrum and schradan. In general insecticides should be used immediately aphids are seen and be applied directly to the insects in the form of a wetting spray. Nicotine and derris may also be applied as dusts but these are as a rule less effective. In any case it is desirable to repeat the application two or three times at intervals of about a week in order to catch the new generations before they start to breed. However, these methods can be modified when using systemic insecticides which are actually absorbed by the plant and enter its sap. As systemic insecticides are more persistent and do not need to come directly into contact with the insects that are to be killed, they may be applied in advance of an expected attack and applications need not be repeated so frequently. Systemic insecticides in the above list are demeton-s-methyl, dimethoate, formothion, menazon and schradan, see Systemic.

Before the beginning of winter, eggs are laid and these remain throughout the winter and so provide a means of reinfestation the following spring. On fruit trees the eggs can often be seen quite clearly and in great numbers on the ends of the shoots. They are very small and dark coloured. It is partly to destroy these aphid eggs that fruit trees are sprayed in winter with tar oil wash or DNC winter wash.

APPLE BLOSSOM WEEVIL, see Weevils

APPLE MILDEW, see Mildew

APPLE SAWFLY, see Sawfly

APPLE SCAB, see Scab

APPLE SUCKER, see Sucker, Apple

APPRESSED A botanical term meaning closely pressed together and often applied to leaves which are closely pressed to the stem. Adpressed has the same meaning.

AQUATIC Broadly speaking any plant which lives either wholly or partly in water, though it is more exact to say that the aquatic lives entirely in water and to reserve the term subaquatic for the marginal plants which are occasionally under water but more often above it. Aquatics are of many different and quite unrelated genera. Because of this there is very little that can be said in a general way about their cultivation, which will differ according to the particular variety under consideration. As a rule the best planting season for aquatics is from April to June and it is seldom wise to disturb them during the autumn or winter when they are at rest. Some of the large water

Water lilies and other large aquatics are best planted in baskets which can be sunk in the pool. See page 355

lilies thrive in water as much as 3 ft. deep and will cover considerable areas, whereas others such as the Flowering Rush, butomus, and the Arrow Head, sagittaria, would be killed by water more than a few inches deep. There are hardy aquatics which can be grown in the open air throughout the year, e.g. many of the popular water lilies such as *Nymphaea laydekeri* and *N. gladstoniana*; others which are half-hardy and require greenhouse protection in winter, *Calla palustris*, and yet others which are tender and require greenhouse protection throughout the year, e.g. the Water Hyacinth, *Eichhornia speciosa*.

One particular group of aquatics grows completely submerged in the water and has the valuable property of giving oxygen to the water and so keeping it fresh. Aquatics of this type include vallisneria, elodea and myriophyllum, and are known as oxygenating plants.

ARACHNOID A botanical term meaning like a cobweb. The specific epithet *arachnoideus* is derived from the same root. Thus *Sempervivum arachnoideum* is a houseleek in which the rosettes of leaves are densely covered with fine white filaments like cobwebs.

ARBORETUM A garden or park devoted exclusively or mainly to the cultivation of trees and shrubs, though in practice the term is usually confined to collections of botanical interest.

ARCURE A system of training fruit trees chiefly applied to apples and pears. Young branches are bent in the form of horizontal bows so that the upward flow of sap is checked. The topmost growth bud of each arch is permitted to grow and the resultant shoot is itself bent over to form yet another arch until all available space is filled. Other side growths are kept pruned to form fruiting spurs, see page 362.

ARMED In botany this term is applied to any plant having spines, thorns or prickles.

AROID Any plant belonging to the botanical family *Araceae*. This includes the arum lilies, anthurium, philodendron and monstera.

ARTICULATE Jointed; a term used botanically to describe any part of a plant which has nodes or joints at which separation from the parent plant may be expected to occur naturally.

ASCENDING A term applied to stems which are neither prostrate nor erect but curve upwards, or are produced obliquely.

ASEXUAL Literally sexless. In gardening chiefly used for methods of propagation not involving seed, e.g. division, cuttings, layers, runners, grafts and buds. See also Vegetative Propagation.

ASHES Wood ashes, if they have not been long exposed to rain, are useful as a fertilizer as they contain carbonate of potash. Soft coal ashes are of little value in the garden but ashes from hard coal or coke, if coarse and gritty, may be used to lighten heavy soil. They contain little, if any, plant food. Ashes make a useful medium in which to plunge flower pots to prevent excessive evaporation or rapid changes in temperature. See Potash and Plunge Bed.

ASPARAGUS BEETLE The adult beetle is small but rather handsome – jet black with several orange markings. The greenish grey grub or larva feeds on the foliage of asparagus often eating the stems quite bare. The remedy is to spray the foliage, at the first sign of trouble, with derris, BHC or malathion.

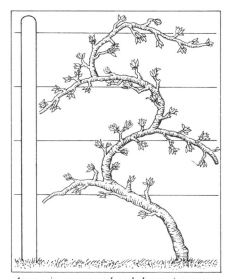

Arcure is an unusual and decorative system which can be used for training fruit trees against wires

ASTER WILT A common fungus disease of annual asters, callistephus, which attacks the main stem near soil level causing it to turn black and die. As a result the whole plant wilts and collapses. The disease is soil borne and for that reason difficult to control. Seed of annual asters should be sown in sterilized soil and this should also be used for the seedlings when they are pricked out. Plants should not be put out in ground on which wilt has occurred. Wilt resistant varieties of callistephus are available.

ATTENUATE Tapering narrowly or drawn upwards. Thus an attenuated shoot is one that has grown taller yet thinner than normal.

AURICULATE Provided with ear-like attachments. The term auricle is the noun from the same root. Auricles or ear-like portions are characteristic of the leaves or flowers of some plants.

AWL SHAPED Tapering to a fine or needle-like point. The term is often applied to leaves.

AWN Any thread-like attachment to a fruit or seed, though the term is most commonly applied to the beard of some grasses and cereals.

AXIL The angle between a leaf stalk or leaf and the stem on which it grows. At this point there is usually a bud, either a growth bud or a flower bud, and this may be referred to as the axillary bud. It is growth buds of this character that are used in the particular form of grafting known as budding.

AZOBENZENE A chemical which can be used in the form of aerosols or smokes for the destruction of red spider mites under glass. These preparations must be used according to manufacturers' instructions. They are most effective and least liable to cause foliage injury if the temperature of the greenhouse is at or above 24°C. They are liable to damage schizanthus, sweet peas and zinnias.

BACTERIA These are very simple forms of life, each individual consisting of no more than one cell. Ordinary fertile soil teems with bacteria of many different kinds and they are so minute and so prolific that they may number millions in a few grams of soil. Some bacteria may be harmful to plants, but many are indirectly beneficial because they assist in the decay of organic matter in the soil, in the release of chemical plant foods and, in some cases, in the actual fixing of nitrogen (itself one of the most important plant foods) from the atmosphere.

Broadly speaking bacteria may be grouped, from the point of view of horticulture, under two headings – those which require a fair amount of air if they are to survive and are known as aerobic, and those which thrive with little or no air and are known as anaerobic. The distinction is important, because most of the aerobic bacteria are beneficial, or at least not harmful, whereas the majority of the anaerobic kinds have a bad effect on soil or plants. Much soil cultivation is concerned with the improvement of aeration, partially, of course, for the direct benefit of plant roots which themselves need air but also to encourage the increase of beneficial bacteria and to discourage the harmful kinds.

What is sometimes erroneously known as soil sterilization (erroneously because it is only very partial sterilization) is also particularly concerned with the destruction of harmful bacteria and it is, perhaps, fortunate for the gardener that in general the more useful kinds of bacteria appear to be more resistant to heat than those which are less desirable; therefore, if soil is not oversterilized (a temperature of $93°$C. for 20 to 30 minutes is usually recommended as the optimum) most harmful bacteria are killed and sufficient of the beneficial kinds remain to restock the soil in a matter of a few weeks.

Of the bacteria which fix nitrogen direct from the atmosphere, the most important are azotobacter, which exists free in the soil, and the various bacteria which inhabit the nodules found on the roots of most leguminous plants, i.e. plants belonging to the pea family. These nodules, far from being harmful to the plants, are directly beneficial as they provide an additional source of valuable nitrogen. In some cases great benefit has resulted from the artificial stocking of land with a particular bacterium, as for example in the agricultural cultivation of alfalfa, which requires a nodule-forming bacterium often absent from British soils. This side of bacterial activity has not received much attention in gardens.

Some plant diseases are caused by bacteria. One of the most striking is that popularly known as crown gall. This attacks many different types of plant, always causing large, roughened and tumour-like swellings. The particular bacterium responsible is known as *Bacterium tumefaciens*. The soft rot or heart rot, which sometimes causes havoc in crops of celery and cabbages and also in stored carrots, is caused by either *Pectobacterium carotovorum* or *Erwinia caratovora*, both species of bacterium. No really satisfactory remedy has been discovered for these diseases.

BACTERIAL CANKER A common disease of cherries, plums and peaches, caused by the bacterium *Pseudomonas morsprunorum*. Small round holes appear in the leaves, a symptom which is sometimes known as shot-hole and was once believed to be a separate disease. The bark may be

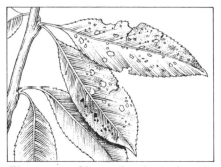

The presence of bacterial canker is shown by the appearance of small holes in the leaves

killed, particularly at or near to the crotch, and gum is likely to ooze from the damaged bark. Whole branches may wither and die quite rapidly and eventually the whole tree may be killed. Since the bacterium enters the tree through wounds principally in autumn and winter, no pruning should be carried out at these seasons but instead should be done between May and August.

Some rootstocks, such as Mazzard F 12/1 for cherries and Myrobalan B for plums and peaches, are fairly resistant to the disease and varieties worked on these stocks are less likely to be attacked. Trees can also be sprayed heavily with Bordeaux mixture applied three times, in late August, mid-September and early October.

BAGGING HOOK, see Sickle

BALL This term is used by the gardener for two quite different purposes – one to describe the ball of soil and roots with which a pot-grown plant can be removed from its container, or the ball of soil with which some plants, notably rhododendrons, azaleas and many conifers, can be lifted when young from a nursery bed; the other to describe a peculiar condition of roses, particularly very double forms, which in bad weather fail to open properly but instead decay in the half-open bud – a trouble known as balling. Some varieties are very subject to this fault particularly early in the summer or during wet seasons. The remedies are protection from rain and the avoidance of excessive feeding or thinning of the buds, as it is very big buds that are most subject to the fault.

It is important that the pot ball, or ball of soil and roots, should be obtained intact and it is for this reason that experienced gardeners make a point of cleaning old pots thoroughly. If this precaution is not taken, roots will cling to the dirty wall of the pot and when the plant comes to be removed for repotting or planting the pot ball will be broken and many roots damaged. With some nursery stock, particularly evergreen shrubs, it is important that the ball of soil and roots should be preserved intact, for which purpose it is closely wrapped in hessian, polythene or some other suitable material. This should not be removed until the plant is

actually standing in its new site, then the covering can be slipped away leaving the ball complete.

BARK BEETLES, see Shot-hole Borers

BARK-BOUND If trees or shrubs grow very slowly, through lack of moisture, lack of plant foods in the soil, injury to the roots or any other cause, the bark tends to become so hard that it is unable to expand in the normal way and actually strangles further development of the trunk or branches. Trees in this condition are described as barkbound and may continue to make very little growth long after the removal of the conditions which originally caused them to become bark-bound. Sometimes they will effect their own cure by splitting their bark longitudinally, an occurrence which may cause the gardener great alarm though in fact it is really a good thing. The best remedy for this bark-bound condition is to slit the bark right up the affected trunk or branch with a sharp knife or billhook and then to feed the soil round the tree or shrub generously and keep it well watered in dry weather. The most favourable time to carry out this artificial slitting is in the spring, just as growth is beginning. Some gardeners think it advisable to protect the slits against infection with warm grafting wax, Stockholm tar or one of the proprietary wound dressings.

BARK RINGING, see Ringing

BASAL ROT A name rather loosely applied to several quite distinct diseases which all attack bulbs, causing a decay of the base of the bulb. Roots are destroyed or are very weak and few in number. Narcissi (including daffodils) and tulips are most likely to be affected. In all these the decay is caused by fungal attack but the particular fungus responsible differs according to the precise nature of the basal rot. However, this is a point of academic rather than garden importance as treatment is the same in all cases. All bulbs should be examined carefully before being planted and any that show signs of decay at the base should be burnt. Great care should be taken to avoid bruising bulbs when they are lifted and stored. The store shed should be cool and dry. It is possible that treatment prior to planting with one of the advertised organomercurial fungicides prepared for seed treatment or with quintozene may be of some benefit in preventing the spread of basal rot. If narcissus bulbs have to be given warm–water treatment against eelworm, formalin (40 per cent. formaldehyde) may be added to the bath at the rate of 4 fl. oz. to 5 gallons to kill fungi and spores.

BASAL STEM ROT A disease of cucumber and melons, sometimes known as canker and caused by the same bacterium which produces soft rot in some other plants. The main stem is attacked, usually just above soil level but occasionally higher up, and as a result it rots and the plant collapses. The incidence of this disease can be curtailed by planting cucumbers and melons on low mounds of soil and putting metal collars around the stems to protect them from water splashings. Soil should be steam sterilized before use. In addition the base of each plant can be dusted with copper fungicidal dust or a mixture of 3 parts flowers of sulphur, 3 parts finely powdered copper sulphate and 10 parts hydrated lime. See Soft Rot.

BASIC SLAG A valuable fertilizer which is obtained as a waste material from the lining of blast furnaces. It contains lime and phosphoric acid and therefore has a dual value in the garden. The proportion of these chemicals varies considerably: poor samples may contain as little as 8 per cent. phosphoric acid, whereas good ones may be as high as 18.5 per cent. Moreover, the availability of the phosphoric acid also varies and the higher this is, the more valuable the sample is as a fertilizer. Availability is estimated on the basis of solubility in citric acid. Good samples may show a solubility of 80 per cent. or even more, whereas poor samples may be below 40 per cent. soluble.

Basic slag is a comparatively slow-acting fertilizer, though its rate of action will depend to some extent on the fineness to which it is ground. The finer the powder, the more rapidly will its chemical contents be released. Good samples should pass through a 100-mesh sieve. It is most suitable for autumn and winter application and particularly for the more acid types of soil. Rates may vary from 4 to 8 oz. to the sq. yd.

BASTARD TRENCHING An alternative name for double digging. See Digging.

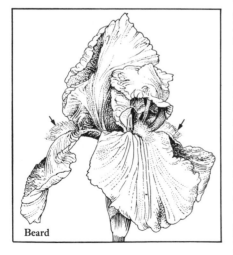

Beard

BEARDED With long hairs, as in the case of the dense growth of hairs which occurs on

Summer bedding plants should be planted in late spring. By working from a board placed on the bed the soil is prevented from becoming too compacted

the lower petals or falls of some irises. A beard of this character can often add considerably to the beauty of a flower. The long awns of barley and certain ornamental grasses are also known as the beard, e.g. bearded wheat.

BEDDING PLANT Any plant used for temporary display in the garden, a feature which is known as bedding out. Bedding plants may be annuals, biennials or perennials, and can be hardy or half-hardy. A typical example is the geranium (correctly called pelargonium), a half-hardy perennial which is grown in great numbers for planting out in late May or early June and provides a bright display in the garden during the summer months. Bedding plants are usually planted at two main seasons, in early autumn when plants such as wallflowers, forget-me-nots, double daisies, tulips and hyacinths are put in for a spring display, and in late spring, when plants such as geraniums, marguerites, heliotropes, French and African marigolds, stocks and asters are put in for a summer display.

BEES The common honey bee is usually a friend to the gardener for by carrying pollen from flower to flower it helps to ensure fertility in fruit trees and seed production in a great many other plants. Occasionally this activity may be a nuisance, for example if the gardener is attempting to make particular crosses between one plant and another and needs to be certain that they have not already been pollinated by means outside his control. Under such circumstances he will be well advised to protect, with muslin, Cellophane or paper bags, those flowers which have been selected to produce seed and to do this early before there is any chance that they are ready to receive pollen.

The humble bee is also a great distributor

of pollen and because of its long proboscis it is capable of pollinating some flowers which are beyond the powers of the honey bee. Because of its size it can make a mess of delicate flowers and is occasionally a nuisance, particularly to exhibitors.

Another kind of bee is a real pest in the garden because of its habit of cutting pieces out of the leaves of roses, lilacs, privet and rhododendrons. It uses the pieces to build its nest. The pieces are usually bitten out of the edge of the leaf, which has a deeply scalloped appearance as a result. The damage is sometimes attributed to slugs but the holes are cleaner and more regular in outline than those made by slugs. Unfortunately there is no very satisfactory remedy though some leaf-cutting bees may be caught with butterfly nets.

The term bee is also applied to the petaloid centre of a delphinium floret.

BEET AND MANGOLD FLY The small whitish maggots of this fly tunnel their way through the leaves of beetroot, mangolds and spinach. All affected leaves should be picked off and burned and, when the crop has been harvested, any waste refuse should also be burned. In severe attacks spraying with BHC, carbaryl, malathion or trichlorphon may be necessary.

BEETLE In general, beetles are friends rather than foes in the garden for many are carnivorous and do not attack plants. In this they differ markedly from weevils, which they closely resemble, though they lack the long snout so characteristic of the weevil. Almost all weevils are garden foes. A few beetles must also be classed as enemies. Principal among these are the asparagus beetle, the flea beetle, the pea and bean beetle, the raspberry beetle and the pollen beetle, which are described under their respective names. Beetles can as a rule be destroyed quite easily by spraying or dusting any plants attacked with an insecticide containing either BHC or carbaryl.

BELL GLASS The true bell glass was developed in France by market gardeners who used it for the intensive cultivation of early crops. It was a large glass jar of bell shape which could be placed over individual plants or groups of small plants. Nowadays it has been superseded by the cloche.

BENOMYL A systemic fungicide which is particularly effective against black spot and powdery mildew. It is available as a wettable powder to be stirred into water at the rate of ½ oz. to 3 gallons of water and applied as advised by the manufacturers.

BENZENE HEXACHLORIDE, see BHC

BERRY Botanically a berry is a fruit in which the seeds are protected only by a fleshy wall formed from the ovary. The term is very loosely applied in gardens to many fruits which are not strictly speaking berries at all. Gooseberries and currants are both true berries in the botanical sense, but raspberries and blackberries are not, as they are made up of a number of small drupes, i.e. fruits in which the seed is protected by a hard wall or stone as well as by the flesh. The fruits of cotoneaster and hawthorn are not really berries either as the seeds are not only contained within a hard wall formed from the ovary (the true fruit), but also within a fleshy covering or false fruit formed from the organ known as the receptacle. Curiously enough many true berries in the botanical sense are not recognized as such by the gardener, e.g. tomato, cucumber, melon and orange.

BESOM A broom made of twigs, usually those of a birch tree though occasionally heather is used. At one time the besom was

to be found in every gardener's tool shed and it is a pity that it has become less common, as it is still the best type of broom with which to remove dead leaves, debris and worm casts from lawns.

BHC powder is an effective insecticide. Here brassica seedlings are being treated

BHC A synthetic chemical, the full name of which is benzene hexachloride, used as an insecticide. There are several different forms of this chemical and the most effective as an insecticide is the gamma isomer usually known as gamma-BHC or lindane. This will kill aphids, weevils, beetles and their larvae, leaf miners, caterpillars, capsid bugs, scale insects, wireworms, cutworms, leather jackets and many other pests. It can be obtained in various forms including dusts mixed with a suitable carrier and ready for application; wettable powders to be dissolved in water and applied as sprays; in liquid form for spraying; in canisters combined with a suitable pyrotechnic for use as a smoke, or in powder form for raking or forking into the soil as a soil insecticide. All these are proprietary formulations and manufacturers' instructions should be followed.

In some instances BHC imparts a musty taint to the crops on which it is used. This is particularly liable to happen when samples containing other isomers of BHC in addition to the gamma isomer are used as soil insecticides on land on which root crops are to be grown immediately.

Gamma-BHC is not effective against red spider mite and, as it is likely to kill many of the insects which prey on red spider mites, its use at unsuitable times of the year, for example after mid-April on fruit trees, may result in an increase of red spider. It is poisonous to warm-blooded animals but it is unlikely to cause any injury at the concentration usually employed.

BICOLOR This botanical term means two coloured and is usually applied to flowers in which one colour is sharply contrasted with another.

BIENNIAL A plant which flowers and seeds in its second year from seed, after which it dies. It may be contrasted with the annual which also dies after seeding but completes its cycle in one year or less, and with the monocarpic plant which dies after seeding but takes an indefinite number of years to reach this stage. Some very popular garden flowers are biennials, e.g. Canterbury bells and foxgloves, but a great many plants, which are treated as biennials in gardens and are often referred to as such, are, in fact, perennials which would flower and seed many times if given suitable conditions. Hollyhocks, Sweet Williams, wallflowers and double daisies are examples of this latter class. They are usually sown in late spring, planted out and allowed to flower the following year after which they are destroyed, but this does not make them true biennials.

BIG BUD A most troublesome condition of currants, principally black currants, though red currants are sometimes affected and big bud has even been occasionally reported on gooseberries. The dormant

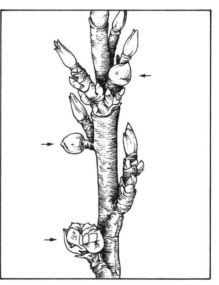

A black currant shoot showing the swollen globular buds which have been attacked by big bud mite

buds become swollen and globular, standing out prominently on the naked stems in winter. This swelling is caused by the presence within the buds of great numbers of minute white mites. These mites leave the buds in the spring and migrate to other buds. It is during this migration that they are most vulnerable and a strong application of lime sulphur (q.v.) applied in spring when the most forward leaves are an inch in diameter will usually destroy most of the mites. The lime sulphur is used at twice the normal winter strength and may cause some leaf scorching but the bushes usually recover quickly. However, this treatment cannot be used on sulphur-shy currants such as Davidson's Eight, Edina, Goliath, Victoria, Wellington XXX. Where only a few buds are affected they may be picked off in late winter and burned. In very severe cases it may be necessary to prune back all growth to within a few inches of the ground in winter and burn the prunings. The big bud mite also carries the virus which causes reversion and so the two conditions are usually associated. See Reversion.

BILLHOOK A hatchet-like hook with a fairly long curved blade used primarily for trimming hedges and rough undergrowth.

BIPINNATE Twice pinnate; a botanical term applied to leaves which are composed of several separate segments which are themselves divided into separate segments.

BIRDS From the gardener's standpoint birds may be roughly classified in three groups, one composed of kinds such as the owls, wagtails, flycatchers, tits, swallows, woodpeckers, swifts, cuckoos; robins and hedge sparrows, which are entirely, or almost entirely, beneficial; a second composed of such birds as the thrush, blackbird, starling, magpie, rook, jay and chaffinch, which do some harm but probably, on balance, more good and so are to be reckoned as friends rather than foes; and a third, of which the wood pigeon, stock dove, bullfinch and house sparrow are notorious members, which do more harm than good and are, in consequence, to be regarded as enemies.

Jays can do considerable damage to peas and fruit but they also eat great numbers of insects, slugs, mice and other garden pests. They can be kept away from the pea pods if pea rows are covered with netting. Small fruit bushes can be protected in the same way. Some birds pick up seeds but few are capable of scratching and so have no means of getting at seeds which have been properly covered; in any case vulnerable seeds can be efficiently protected with dark thread drawn tightly between sticks to form a network over the seed bed. Sparrows often do a great deal of damage to brightly coloured flowers, especially to early blooms such as those of crocus and polyanthus. Here again the most effective remedy is to cover the plants with tightly drawn and dark-coloured thread. Bullfinches attack the buds of fruit trees and bushes, often pecking them out quite wilfully and not for the sake of food. Protection with netting is often the only effective remedy though bird scarers fixed among the trees may have some effect. The damage, incidentally, is usually done in late winter as the buds start to swell.

Tits are also sometimes accused of destroying buds but on closer examination it will almost always be found that these buds are already attacked by insects and that it is the latter, not the buds themselves, that the tits have been after. Even if such buds had not been damaged by the tits, it is very unlikely that they would have developed into healthy shoots or flowers. Spraying with various proprietary bird repellents may do some good but usually it is necessary to repeat the application of these after heavy rain.

BITTER PIT A curious condition of apples, pears and, occasionally, quinces in which the flesh just beneath the skin decays in small spots or patches, causing the skin itself to sink in a series of small, irregular spots, often slightly darkened in colour. The disorder may be caused by an irregular flow of sap as it occurs severely in seasons during which periods of heavy rainfall alternate with periods of drought. Some varieties are much more susceptible than others and may have to be eliminated altogether in gardens in which the trouble is common.

BLACK FLY The name given to some of the many species of aphids characterized by their black colour. The black fly of broad beans, *Aphis fabae*, is also known as bean aphid, collier and dolphin fly. It is particularly common on broad beans but is also found on dwarf and runner beans, beetroot, spinach, turnips, rhubarb, docks and many other plants. Black flies usually congregate round the ends of tender young shoots. In the case of beans it is often possible to prevent an attack by pinching out the soft tip of each plant as soon as the first few trusses of pods are beginning to swell. The pest can be destroyed by spraying with BHC, demeton-s-methyl, derris, diazinon, dimethoate, formothion, malathion, menazon, nicotine, parathion, pyrethrum or schradan. See Aphid.

BLACKLEG A disease of potatoes which attacks the haulm just above ground level causing it to decay and turn black. Later tubers may be affected and will rot to a jelly at the end at which they are attached to the plant. Usually only an occasional plant is attacked and the disease seldom does extensive damage. No remedy is known. All affected plants should be lifted and burned as soon as noticed. No tubers showing a jelly-like rot at one end should be planted. See also Botrytis.

BLACK SPOT This name is sometimes applied loosely to almost any disease which causes black spots to appear on the plant attacked, but it properly belongs to one disease only, which is caused by a fungus and confines itself to roses. The fungus attacks the leaves causing these to develop circular black spots which increase in size until the whole leaf is destroyed or falls off. It is one of the most serious diseases of roses and one of the most difficult to control. In winter resting spores of the fungus remain in the surface soil and from these new infections spread the following summer. Two methods of checking the disease are to remove the surface inch of soil from the rose beds in winter and burn it, replacing with fresh soil from some place in which roses have not grown, and to cover the whole surface of the bed in early spring with an inch-thick mulch of grass clippings or clean peat so that spores cannot readily rise from the soil to the rose leaves. Such a mulch should be maintained throughout the summer and be disturbed as little as possible. Infected rose leaves should always be picked off and burned. If the disease has proved troublesome in other years it is wise to carry out preventive spraying with maneb, captan, thiram, or colloidal copper at about fortnightly intervals from April until August inclusive, or with one of the systemic fungicides, such as benomyl, chloraniformethan or thiophanate-methyl, at least once a month. If the disease makes its appearance,

Netting is one of the most effective remedies against bird attack

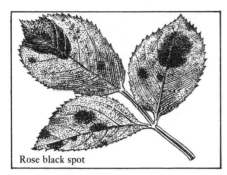

Rose black spot

one rather heavy spraying should be given in midwinter with copper sulphate, 1 oz. to a gallon of water. This must not be used while any leaves remain on the plant as it is very caustic. It may be allowed to fall fairly heavily on the soil to kill spores lying on it.

BLANCHING This is an important factor in the cultivation of certain vegetables, notably leeks, celery, endive and seakale. The purpose of blanching is to prevent the normal colouring matter of leaf or stem being produced, making vegetables more delicate in flavour and more attractive in appearance.

Blanching is always carried out by excluding light, but the methods employed vary considerably. With celery and leeks it is effected by drawing soil round the stems or by enclosing these in cardboard or paper collars. Endive is frequently blanched by inverting a saucer, or placing a slate or piece of wood over the heart of each plant, while seakale is usually blanched by bringing it into a darkened shed or cupboard. As a rule, blanching checks growth and therefore must not be carried out until the plant has reached a satisfactory stage of development, for instance celery blanching is usually delayed until September, by which time the plants are well grown. An exception can be made with leeks which can be blanched a little at a time by gradually drawing soil round the growing leaves from midsummer onwards. By this method blanched 'stems' of exceptional length can be produced.

Self-blanching varieties of celery are available and with these no earthing up is necessary, but it helps to plant in blocks so that the foliage cuts down the amount of light reaching the stalks.

BLEEDING The gardener describes as bleeding any overflow of sap from a plant. It is liable to occur in spring on almost any shrub or tree that has been pruned so late that the pruning wounds have not had an opportunity to heal over. Sometimes bleeding can be quite spectacular. In the case of grape vines which have been pruned late in the winter, quantities of sap may drip from the severed ends of the rods. It is widely held amongst gardeners that bleeding is harmful, but in fact scientific investigation does not seem to uphold this view. As a rule, the bleeding stops of its own accord after a few

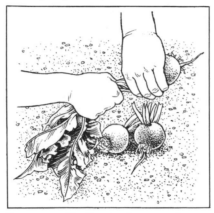

To prevent bleeding in beetroot, the tops should be twisted off

days and the wound heals over quite normally. Various remedies have been suggested, as for example the sealing of wounds with a red-hot iron, or their treatment with a caustic substance such as a styptic.

Bleeding is also likely to occur in beetroots if the skin or flesh is damaged, and can result in a serious loss of colour which may spoil the appearance of the roots. It is, therefore, usually recommended to twist off the

tops of beetroots when they are lifted and not to cut them off with any sharp implement which might damage the flesh.

BLIGHT This term is used very vaguely by most gardeners to describe almost any kind of pest or disease. Thus a bad infestation of greenflies may be referred to as blight and so will the black sooty mould (caused by fungus) which is likely to follow this infestation. Because of this vagueness it is an unsatisfactory term and one which would be best dropped. It is only justifiably used in connection with the common disease known as potato blight. This is caused by a fungus, *Phytophthora infestans*, which attacks the leaves causing black spots to appear. These quickly spread so that the whole haulm withers. Later the disease may pass to the tubers, causing soft, brown patches of decay in the flesh. This disease can be prevented by spraying the haulm thoroughly with Bordeaux mixture or other copper fungicides or with maneb or zineb. The first application should be made early in July followed by another, if necessary, three or four weeks later.

BLIND A plant is said to be blind when loss of the growing point causes cessation of growth. This condition is frequent in the case of seedlings of cabbage and other members of the brassica family, particularly if these have been attacked by maggots of the cabbage root fly. At first sight the plants can appear quite healthy, but a closer examination will show that they have no central growing shoots and that, in fact, growth is at a standstill. Such plants are quite useless and should be discarded, as no treatment will make them regain their growing points.

BLINDS The gardener may use blinds of one kind or another in the greenhouse and occasionally on frames, either to protect plants from excessive sunshine or in an attempt to prevent excessive loss of heat at night. Blinds used mainly for shading are made of translucent PVC, wooden slats,

To blanch celery: 1. *Remove small offsets*

2. *Wrap paper collars round the stems*

3. *Draw soil up around the plant*

hessian or split bamboo. They should be fitted in such a way that they can be quickly removed or rolled up when not required. Blinds of this type are not very useful for trapping heat and the most effective material yet discovered for this purpose is aluminium foil. This foil has remarkable heat insulating properties and is said to give an insulation equivalent to a 2-in. thickness of cork. Aluminium foil is extremely flexible and, if mounted on some tough paper core, is fairly durable. See also Shading.

BLOOD All blood contains nitrogen which is valuable as a plant food. Fresh blood is unpleasant to handle and is seldom used, though it may be applied freely on vacant ground and immediately dug in. However, it is dried blood that is commonly used and this is a fine dry powder easy to handle and suitable for use either on vacant ground or around plants in growth. An average sample contains about 12 per cent. nitrogen and can be applied at rates up to 1 oz. per sq. yd. or as a liquid manure well stirred into water at rates up to 1 oz. per gallon. As a rule it is not fully soluble, hence the instruction about stirring well to keep it in suspension.

BLOSSOM END ROT A disorder of tomatoes which causes a small dark spot to develop on the fruit at the end farthest from the stalk. This spot usually increases in size fairly rapidly and becomes black. The flesh beneath the spot shrinks and that part of the fruit becomes flattened. Despite its appearance to the contrary this trouble is not caused by a fungus but is the result of a collapse of some of the fruit cells due to lack of moisture.

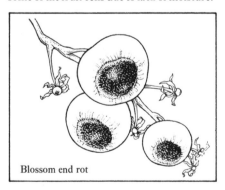
Blossom end rot

The disorder is usually an indication that at some previous time, probably several weeks earlier, the soil has been dry, though another possible cause, particularly on acid soils, is shortage of calcium. Affected fruits should be removed and every care taken to see that the plants have an adequate water supply at all times and that the soil, if acid, is well dressed with hydrated lime before tomatoes are planted.

BLOSSOM FALL, see Bud Stages

BLOSSOM WILT A disease of apples, apricots, damsons and plums caused by a

fungus which attacks the flowers causing them to wilt. It then passes on to the spurs and sometimes to the main stem, causing die-back. Infected flower clusters, spurs and shoots should be cut out and burned and the trees sprayed with tar oil at the late dormant stage and with lime sulphur at green bud and again at pink and white stages. See Bud Stages.

BLOTCHY RIPENING A term applied to a condition of tomato fruits in which, instead of ripening evenly all over, some parts remain green or at most only become yellowish. It is often associated with potash deficiency in the soil but may also be brought about by inadequate watering, possibly because when water is short it is difficult for the roots to take up sufficient potash. The condition is common in high temperatures and light intensities. The disease can be prevented by providing ample potash in the soil balanced by nitrogen and phosphates and plenty of water at all times. If it occurs, it is advisable to water plants every few days with 1 pint each of a solution made by dissolving 1 oz. of sulphate of potash in 5 gallons of water. Alternatively, make use of a high potash liquid fertilizer according to manufacturers' instructions. It is also advisable to leave sufficient foliage to protect ripening fruits from the strongest sunshine.

A rather similar blotchy appearance of the fruits can also be caused by virus disease but in this case the flesh does not remain hard and unripe as in true blotchy ripening. Virus disease cannot be cured by application of potash or, for that matter, by anything else.

BLUEING, see Acid

BLUESTONE, see Copper Sulphate

BOG GARDEN This is a construction intended to simulate the marshy conditions which are often found near rivers and on low-lying ground generally, and in which a specialized type of flora exists. Most bog plants will not tolerate long periods of complete inundation, nor will they withstand long periods of comparative drought. The problem, therefore, is to arrange the water supply so that the water level in the bog garden is more or less constant, winter and summer. If the water supply is entirely artificial, as for example from a well or water main, this is a fairly simple problem, as it consists mainly in regulating the flow of water by suitably placed cocks. If, however, the bog garden is made as an adjunct to a natural stream or pool, constructional problems are likely to arise. It is almost certain that sluice gates will be necessary to regulate the flow of water to the bog garden, maintaining the level in summer when the flow is at its lowest, but allowing surplus to escape freely at flood periods in the autumn and winter.

Most bog plants thrive best in a somewhat spongy soil mixture. It must never be so close in texture that free percolation of water is impeded. A suitable general mixture consists of rather heavy, fairly rich loam mixed with half its bulk of good quality horticultural peat. Avoid mud from pond bottoms and stream sides. Do not use dung and as far as artificial manures are concerned at most give a light sprinkling of bonemeal only.

Small bog gardens in which the water supply is to be entirely artificial must always be enclosed in cement or with beaten clay or plastic sheeting. The construction is very similar to that of a pool with the two important differences that there must be more frequent and larger outlets for surplus moisture and that the whole cemented area must be filled with soil. Concrete for this purpose should be prepared in exactly the same way as for pool construction (see page 354) and the walls of the bog garden should be similar in thickness to those of a pool.

In the case of natural bog gardens – that is to say those made alongside an existing stream, river or pond – it is usually quite unnecessary to use cement in any part of the construction, in fact if the soil is naturally of a heavy clay nature, it may even be necessary to break this up somewhat and open it with sand or broken clinkers to prevent too sluggish a movement on the part of the water. This is essential, for, though all bog plants must have abundant moisture, few thrive in stagnant conditions such as may occur where there is practically no movement of water through the soil.

There are a great many beautiful plants suitable for planting in bog gardens. Among the best are moisture-loving primulas such as *Primula japonica, P. pulverulenta, P. helodoxa* and *P. florindae*, dodecatheons, astilbes, trollius, calthas, lysichitums, *Iris kaempferi* and *I. sibirica*, and the Royal Fern, *Osmunda regalis*.

BOLTING A term used to describe plants that produce flowers and seeds prematurely. Thus lettuces will normally make a good and serviceable heart of leaves and hold it for several weeks before they start to run up to flower, but under some circumstances they may either form no hearts at all or start to run to flower very soon after forming hearts. This is particularly likely to happen in very hot dry weather. Bolting is often caused by a check to growth either through drought or starvation.

Sometimes bolting is an inherited tendency and breeders take pains to eliminate it from their stocks by careful selection and the rejection of all plants that show any inclination to bolt. Beetroot tends to bolt if sown too early when night temperatures are too low, though efforts are being made to breed varieties that will not bolt even if sown in March or early April.

BONE MANURES The bones of all animals contain certain elements that are valuable as plant foods and particularly phosphorus and calcium, together with smaller quantities of nitrogen. Unfortunately whole bones decompose so slowly in the soil that it takes many years for these plant foods to be liberated. Therefore such bones are of little value to the gardener. If, however, the bones are crushed into a fine powder, the rate of release of plant foods is greatly increased. As a result, finely ground bone flour is not only a valuable fertilizer, but is also, contrary to popular opinion, a fairly quick-acting one. Coarser grades of bonemeal will give up their supplies of phosphorus more slowly, and crushed bones, in which many of the pieces may be the size of peas, are sometimes used in the preparation of vine borders and other more or less permanent beds, because they will provide supplies of phosphorus over a number of years. It will be seen, therefore, that the rate of action of bone manures is proportionate to the fineness to which they are ground.

Frequently, bones are steamed to extract the gelatine from them before they are prepared as garden fertilizers. In the case of steamed bones there is very little nitrogen left and their value as a plant food can be determined solely on their content of phosphoric acid. Analysis, in any case, varies greatly from sample to sample. For raw bones it may be anything from 15 to 32 per cent. of phosphoric acid and up to 5 per cent. of nitrogen. With steamed bones, the phosphoric acid content will be a little smaller than that of raw bones with the nitrogen content as low as 1 per cent. The usual rate of application for bone manures is 3 to 4 oz. per sq. yd. with very finely ground samples such as those described as bone flour, and up to 8 oz. for the coarser grades of meal and crushed bone. Bonemeal can also be used with advantage in potting composts at the rate of about 4 oz. to each bushel and is preferred by some gardeners to the smaller quantities of superphosphate of lime recommended in the standard John Innes potting composts.

Bonemeal is a perfectly good fertilizer which can be used for all kinds of plants. Coarser grades should, as a rule, be used in the autumn or winter so that they may become partially decomposed before plants require the food which they contain. The finest samples can be used as spring dressings.

BONSAI This is the Japanese name for artificially dwarfed trees or shrubs. They can be grown in containers of any kind including ordinary flower pots but as a rule special ornamental containers are used. These are raised on little legs or feet to keep them off the soil or greenhouse bench as this discourages the plants rooting through the

A good bonsai formed from a group of the five-needled pine

drainage holes and so becoming overvigorous. Single specimens or groups of several trees or shrubs may be grown in a container but either way the aim is usually to create a rather romantic effect such as might be expected from a mature tree or trees that have grown in a very exposed place.

Bonsai can be formed from small seedlings dug up in the wild or from seedlings or cuttings specially raised for the purpose. They should be placed in a very light place as this helps to keep them dwarf. They can be grown in John Innes potting compost No. 1, or equivalent compost, and should be kept well watered. Growth is restricted by repotting every one, two or three years according to vigour (the most vigorous plants most frequently) and removing some of the coarser roots each time. Just before growth starts each spring rub out any growth buds that are not required to extend or shape the specimen. Throughout the spring and summer badly placed shoots can be shortened or cut out unless it is possible to train them where they are required. This can be done with canes and fillis, or by twisting copper wire around the stems and then gradually bending them to the required shape and position. All stakes, ties and wires should be removed as soon as they have served their purpose and the stems have become sufficiently stiff to remain in place without further assistance.

A good bonsai should be characteristic of its species when mature. The trunk should be substantial, the branches well spaced and some roots should appear on the surface of the soil, dipping naturally into it after a few inches. Ideally bonsai should look attractive from all sides, though as a rule one side is more beautiful than any of the others.

BORAX This natural salt is used in the garden as a fertilizer and also as an insecticide. As a fertilizer it provides the most convenient source of boron, one of the essential plant foods which is, however, required in such minute amounts that it is generally present in the soil in sufficient quantity for the plant's needs. Boron in excess acts as a plant poison and care must be exercised in its application. Boron deficiency occurs in a few places and is responsible for the disease known as brown heart in swedes, turnips, beetroot and mangolds. The central leaves turn brown and wither, the crown becomes brown and decay develops in the centre of the root. Where boron is discovered to be lacking in the soil, borax can be applied at the rate of 2 oz. over 30 sq. yd. in spring. It must be spread evenly. As an insecticide it is used principally as an ant killer, equal parts of borax and castor sugar being mixed together and placed where ants are seen.

BORDEAUX MIXTURE One of the most valuable of general-purpose fungicides, that is to say chemical mixtures which have the property of killing fungi. Bordeaux mixture is prepared from copper sulphate and lime and gets its name from the fact that it was developed in the Bordeaux area of France as a remedy for downy mildew on vines. It was subsequently discovered that Bordeaux mixture is effective against many other diseases caused by fungi and that it can be used with safety on a great variety of plants. It is now the standard remedy for potato blight (phytophthora) for which purpose at least two applications should be given, the first early in July and the second three or four weeks later. It can also be used to control scab disease of apples and pears and is particularly suitable for the latter, as it does not cause leaf scorching so readily as lime sulphur.

Three formulae are in general use in gardens and they are described respectively as strong solution, standard solution and reduced solution. The recipes are as follows:

STRONG SOLUTION For use against potato

blight and on other strong-leaved plants not liable to be scorched.

> 9 oz. copper sulphate
> 6 oz. quicklime
> 5 gallons water

STANDARD SOLUTION For use against apple and pear scab and as a general fungicide.

> 6 oz. copper sulphate
> 6 oz. quicklime
> 5 gallons water

REDUCED SOLUTION For use on tender-leaved plants liable to be scorched.

> 4½ oz. copper sulphate
> 9 oz. quicklime
> 5 gallons water

When Bordeaux mixture is prepared from the raw ingredients, fresh hydrated lime can be used in place of quicklime, but it is desirable to increase the quantities slightly, say to 7 oz. for the strong and standard solutions and 10 oz. for the reduced solution.

The copper sulphate should always be dissolved first of all in a portion of the water and the quicklime slaked in the remaining water in a separate vessel. Then add the slaked quicklime, a little at a time, to the copper sulphate solution, stirring all the while. The mixture should be used at once as there may be a tendency for it to precipitate after a time. It is advisable to test the strong solution before use. This can be done with blue litmus paper – if the paper turns pink, a little more lime should be added until the litmus paper remains blue. The fact that it turns pink is an indication that the mixture is still slightly acid, a condition in which it may cause damage to foliage.

Bordeaux mixture can also be purchased in various commercial brands as either a paste or a powder, ready for mixing with water. When using all these proprietary brands, manufacturers' instructions regarding strength must be followed.

BORDER A term with a rather wide and loose application in gardens, but in general it may be taken to refer to any bed which is prepared for some special purpose. An example is the vine border which is usually completely enclosed by concrete or brick walls to prevent the vine roots from penetrating beyond the specially prepared soil with which the border is filled. Then we have the herbaceous border devoted exclusively to the cultivation of hardy herbaceous perennials; the shrub border devoted exclusively to shrubs; the mixed border which may include shrubs, herbaceous plants and even annuals and semitender plants, such as pelargoniums, marguerites and antirrhinums, and the annual border devoted exclusively to plants raised from seed and flowering in their first season.

The term is sometimes used to distinguish certain kinds of plant which are hardy enough to be grown in the open from other similar kinds which need greenhouse protection. For example, one class of carnation is known as border carnation because it can be grown out of doors without any protection in contrast to the perpetual flowering carnations which require protection in winter. Similarly with chrysanthemums the term border chrysanthemum is sometimes used instead of early flowering chrysanthemum to denote any variety which is hardy enough and flowers early enough to be grown in the open. Border phlox is occasionally used to distinguish varieties of *Phlox paniculata* (*decussata*) from the alpine phloxes derived from *P. subulata* and other species.

BORECOLE An alternative name for kale.

BOTANY The scientific study of plants. While the practical gardener is under no compulsion to turn himself into a botanist, there is no doubt that some knowledge of the subject will make him a better gardener.

There are two main divisions, plant physiology, dealing with the manner in which plants function, and taxonomy, dealing with form and classification.

There are too many good elementary books on the subject to enumerate. The gardener should investigate his public library and be guided by his own personal preferences.

BOTRYTIS A fungus known as *Botrytis cinerea* attacks a great variety of plants causing rapid decay of their tissues followed by an outgrowth of fluffy grey mould on the diseased portions. For this latter reason the disease is often known as grey mould. The decayed tissue usually turns black and this feature has given rise to another popular name, blackleg, but this is also the name of a quite different disease of potatoes.

Botrytis rot may be found on vines, tomatoes, cucumbers, melons, marrows, lettuces, strawberries, pelargoniums, roses, sunflowers and many other plants. It thrives in damp, cold conditions, is most prevalent in autumn, can be a plague in badly ventilated or inadequately heated greenhouses and is always very difficult to control once it starts. Plants may be dusted with flowers of sulphur, quintozene or dicloran, may be sprayed with colloidal sulphur, captan or

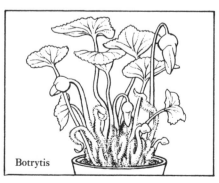

Botrytis

thiram or, under glass, may be fumigated with smoke generators containing tecnazene. Badly infected plants should be removed and burnt at once. See also Grey Mould.

BOTTLE GARDEN Some plants, particularly small specimens of those kinds frequently referred to as house plants (q.v.), can be grown very successfully in large bottles, jars or carboys. A little moist soil, peat or potting compost is placed in the bottle, the plants are planted in this using improvised tools, such as a teaspoon tied to a stick as a trowel, a cotton reel wedged on a cane to firm the compost, and long 'chop sticks' to move the plants about.

For planting up a bottle garden, improvised tools, such as a teaspoon tied to a stick, are used

Plants should be watered in, after which the bottle is stood in a room or any other sheltered place where there is a reasonable amount of light but, for preference, not in direct sunlight. Since the plants grow in an almost static atmosphere with little ventilation and consequent change of air, they require very little watering. The soil, peat or compost must be kept moist but often two or three waterings a year are sufficient for this. There is usually sufficient nourishment in the soil, peat or compost to keep them healthy for a considerable period and since vigorous growth is not desired, no feeding need, as a rule, be attempted. Eventually after a period of a few years some of the plants may begin to fail and then it is best to replant the bottle garden with new plants in a fresh rooting medium.

BOTTOM HEAT Heat applied from below, usually to warm beds of soil used in the propagation of tender or half-hardy plants or those which for one reason or another are somewhat difficult to strike from cuttings or raise from seed. One ancient method of producing bottom heat is by means of a bed of decomposing manure known to gardeners as a hotbed (q.v.). The most modern system relies on electrically warmed cables (see page 318) which are actually buried in the soil or in a layer of sand or ashes immediately below it. Sometimes the hot water pipes used for normal greenhouse heating are passed through a bed of soil which may itself be covered by a frame further to trap heat and maintain a close atmosphere in which seeds germinate most freely and cuttings root most readily.

An important point to note is that whatever system is used, the soil must only be warm and not raised to a high temperature which would do more harm than good. As a rule the temperature for hotbeds is between 18 and 24°C. Where electricity is used to warm the soil a thermostat may be fitted to control the temperature.

As the warmth tends to dry soil out rapidly, it is usually necessary to use a moisture-holding compost – that is to say one containing plenty of peat or leafmould which will soak up moisture like a sponge.

BOWLING GREEN A lawn developed specially for the purpose of the game of bowls. For this an absolutely true and level surface is required and very close mowing is necessary, so that the surface is almost as smooth as that of a billiard table. Only certain grasses will put up with this close mowing and give the required surface. Favourites are the finer fescues, such as Chewing's fescue and red fescue and the bent grasses, particularly brown bent and New Zealand bent or browntop, all of which can be raised from seed sown in the same way as for other lawn grasses. Another method is to turf the bowling green with the very fine, sea-washed turf usually sold as Cumberland turf. A drawback to this is that the turf frequently fails to thrive in inland districts and becomes patchy and moss or weed infested after a while.

The dimensions for a full-sized bowling green are 126 ft. square and there should be a surrounding ditch 1 ft. wide and about 6 in. deep. In addition there should be a surrounding path or grass border which can be of any convenient size. Crown greens are constructed with a rise of from 8 to 10 in. in the centre.

BRACT A modified leaf found at the base of a flower stalk, or on the stem of a flower cluster, or forming part of the flower head itself, as in the involucral bracts found in members of the daisy family, Compositae. Bracts are sometimes highly coloured and as decorative as the flowers with which they are associated or even more so. Examples of this kind are to be found in *Salvia horminum*, which has showy purple bracts, the Poinsettia, *Euphorbia pulcherrima*, which has scarlet bracts and *Saxifraga grisebachii*

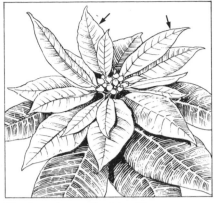

The showy bracts of a poinsettia

which has crimson bracts. In globe artichokes the fleshy bases of the involucral bracts are the edible portion.

BRAND The popular name applied to a fungal disease of Sweet Williams. Occasionally it is found on other species of dianthus. Brown spots, more or less circular in outline, appear on the undersides of the leaves and may spread very rapidly. Affected plants are so unsightly that they can scarcely be overlooked. There is no cure once the disease has started and affected plants should be pulled up and burned as soon as noted. If the disease has proved troublesome it is wise to spray plants occasionally with colloidal copper or thiram as a preventive measure.

BRASSICA The name of a botanical genus which includes such popular vegetables as cabbage, cauliflower, broccoli, brussels sprouts, kale, turnips and swedes.

BREAK A term much used by chrysanthemum growers and occasionally in connection with other plants. A break is a branch or fork and to make a plant break means to make it produce a branch or fork when otherwise it would not do so. Chrysanthemum growers often pinch out the growing tips of their plants quite early in the season to make them branch or fork early. If a rooted chrysanthemum cutting is left to its own devices, it will, after a time, produce an abortive flower bud at the top of the stem, which will prevent further lengthening of this particular stem and force it to produce side shoots or breaks. In consequence, this abortive flower bud is often known as the break bud.

BREAST-WOOD Shoots which grow forward from fruit trees or shrubs trained against walls or espalier fences and in consequence are inconvenient for training against the walls or fences. Breast-wood must usually be cut out and this is generally done during the summer so that light and air may penetrate to the fruits and also to more favourably placed shoots.

BROADCAST The practice of scattering seeds more or less evenly all over the surface of soil instead of confining them to straight lines or drills. In the garden broadcasting is used for grass seed to form a lawn and occasionally for seed of annuals which are to form irregular groups. Sometimes cabbages, broccoli, brussels sprouts and other plants which are to be transplanted as seedlings are raised from broadcast seed, as this saves space, but a drawback is that weeding is much more difficult than when the seeds are sown in straight lines with clear ground between them. A little skill is required to broadcast seed evenly by hand. It should be done with a quick flick of the wrist and care should be taken to pick up a similar quantity of seed each time.

Broadcast seed may be covered either by scattering fine soil over it or by raking the surface after sowing. See also Seed Sowing.

BROKEN A term applied by gardeners to certain varieties of tulip in which the normal petal colour has split up into an elaborate pattern of stripes or feathers on a groundwork of a different colour. This breaking of the normal colour is brought about by virus infection which does not seem to weaken the plants to any marked degree. In the past only the broken varieties were prized by tulip fanciers who kept the plain flowered plants solely as parents in the hope that they would break into some particularly delightful or unusual pattern. The plain flowered varieties were, therefore, referred to as breeders. There is still a class of breeder tulips and all the modern Rembrandt varieties have broken colours.

BROWN HEART A deficiency disease, that is to say one caused by a shortage of some essential food material, in this case boron. It affects turnips, swedes and beetroots causing internal brown decay of the roots. Good general cultivation will help to prevent the disease and so will an adequate water supply. Where these measures fail it will probably be necessary to add extra boron which may be done by topdressing the soil with powdered borax at the rate of 2 oz. to 30 sq. yd. prior to sowing the crop.

BROWN ROT A most distinctive fungal disease of fruits, including apples, pears, plums, cherries and, very occasionally, peaches and nectarines. The disease affects the fruits themselves and, to a lesser degree, the spurs from which they grow. The fruit develops a brown decay which spreads rapidly until the whole fruit may be affected. Whitish or buff coloured pustules appear on the decayed flesh and are arranged in a series of concentric rings. This striking feature makes the disease easy to recognize. Later the whole fruit shrivels and may become so mummified that it hangs on the tree throughout the winter. Such mummified fruits are centres of infection and should be removed and burned whenever seen. Fruit spurs may also be attacked and killed. When pruning a close watch should be kept for dead or dying spurs and all such should be removed and burned.

There is no complete remedy for the disease itself but as the fungus almost always finds entry through some bruise or insect injury (with apples it often follows in the wake of codling moth) anything done to prevent such damage will also reduce the frequency of brown rot. Reduction of the disease can also be effected by spraying with tar oil wash in January and with captan at three-week intervals from early July to late September.

BRUTTING The practice of fracturing young shoots about half way and leaving the broken ends hanging. It is used as a form of summer pruning and is principally applied to hazels.

BUCK-EYE ROT A disease of tomato plants caused by a species of fungus of the genus *Phytophthera*, which also causes the disease known as foot rot (q.v.). The resultant decay proceeds in concentric rings of dark and light brown, hence the name buck-eye. All diseased plants should be burned and care taken to tie up lower trusses and prevent water splashes from reaching the fruit. Soil around plants may be watered with Cheshunt compound, soluble copper or captan.

BUD An embryo shoot, flower or cluster of flowers. Buds vary greatly in shape and character and a study of them is often of great practical assistance to the gardener, enabling him to judge the progress of growth and to decide how and when a shoot should be pruned or whether any pruning is neces-

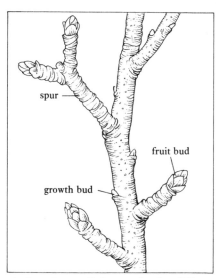

A shoot from a fruit tree showing different types of buds and a spur

sary. In particular, the fruit grower must learn to distinguish between growth buds and fruit buds. In general, growth buds of fruit trees are comparatively small and lie close against the shoots, whereas fruit buds are larger and more prominent and often stick out from the shoot or form extensive clusters known as spurs. A growth bud contains within itself the embryo of a shoot but it may in time change its character and develop into a fruit bud which, despite its name, contains not a fruit but a flower bud or buds capable of producing fruits.

Terminal bud describes a bud found at the extreme tip of a shoot. It may be either a growth bud or a fruit bud. Some varieties of fruit tree frequently produce fruit buds at the tips of shoots and are known as tip-bearers. The apple Worcester Pearmain is of this type. See also crown bud below.

Axillary bud is one which is found in the axil of a leaf, i.e. in the angle between the leaf and the stem on which it grows. Bud scales are the scale-like covering of the bud (usually brown) and as the bud develops, these scales loosen and eventually fall off – a condition known as bud burst and important to the gardener in the case of fruit trees, because it is the signal for the application of certain sprays such as BHC or carbaryl against apple blossom weevil, or for the cessation of the use of other sprays, such as tar oil or DNC winter wash. See Bud Stages.

Crown bud is the term used by chrysanthemum growers to denote flower buds (other than the first abortive flower bud or break bud) which are surrounded by shoots, in distinction to terminal buds which are flower buds surrounded by other flower buds and with no shoots to continue growth. See Stopping.

BUD BLAST A fungal disease of the flower buds of rhododendrons which kills them. They turn brown or grey and develop black spots but remain fixed firmly to the stems. All affected buds should be removed and burned. Bordeaux mixture may be applied fortnightly in spring until the buds start to open, and monthly in summer after the flowers have faded. It is wise to add BHC to the Bordeaux mixture as this will kill leaf hoppers which puncture the rhododendron buds and allow the disease to enter.

BUD BURST, see Bud Stages

BUDDING A method of grafting widely used for the propagation of certain plants, notably apples, pears, plums, cherries, peaches, nectarines, apricots and roses.

As in other forms of grafting, the essential operation is the joining of a portion of the plant to be increased (this portion is known as the scion) to the roots or stems of another

plant (known as the stock) which will provide it with nourishment. The essential difference between budding and other forms of grafting is that in budding the scion consists of one bud only, with a small piece of bark attached, whereas in other methods of grafting the scion is formed of a shoot or portion of shoot containing several buds.

The method varies in detail according to the kind of plant being budded but the general principles are the same. Budding is done while the plant is in full growth, usually some time between midsummer and the end of August. Buds are cut from firm young shoots of the current year's growth. The buds near the tips of these shoots are usually too young and immature while those at the base may be poorly developed or over-ripe. Therefore it is the buds in the middle portions of such shoots that are most useful. They should be plump and undamaged.

The shoots which are cut from the parent plants, to provide these buds, are known as budding sticks. They are prepared by cutting off the unripened tips and also the leaves, but the leaf stalks should be left. The budding sticks should then be tied up in small bundles according to variety, carefully labelled and placed, right way up, in a jar containing about half an inch of water.

Stocks are usually smaller than those used for grafting. In general, budding is only satisfactory on fairly young stocks or on young shoots produced from older stocks. It is seldom possible to insert buds satisfactorily where the bark is thick, hard and old and a good test to ascertain whether the stock is in suitable condition for budding is to make a small L-shaped incision in the bark and then try to lift the flap of bark formed in this way from the underlying wood. If the bark lifts freely and cleanly, the stock is ready, but if it adheres to the wood and can only be torn from it, the stock must be left a few weeks longer or a younger shoot chosen. Watering the roots freely may also help.

The commonest method of budding used is that known as shield budding. The stock is prepared to receive the bud by making a T-shaped incision in it and then carefully lifting the flaps of bark on each side of this incision. For this purpose a budding knife with a bone or plastic handle like a scalpel is the most convenient instrument. The blade is used to make the incision and the

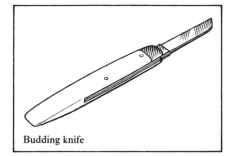

Budding knife

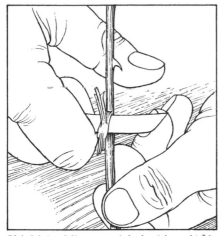

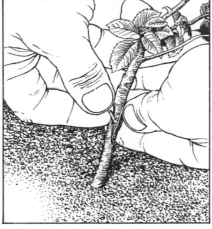

Shield budding. 1. *A bud with a shield-shaped portion of bark is prepared*

2. *The bud is slipped beneath flaps of bark in a T-shaped cut made on the rootstock*

3. *The bud is bound firmly in position with broad, soft raffia*

thin end of the handle to lift the bark without injury.

A bud for shield budding is then cut from the budding stick with a shield-shaped portion of bark attached as shown in the illustration. The knife should be inserted about ½ in. below the bud and drawn out about ½ in. above it and should not penetrate more than half way through the shoot. The bud is then held by the leaf stalk which has been left for this purpose. It will be seen that within the bark there is a tiny slip of wood which has been cut with it. Most experts like to remove this slip of wood by raising it with the point of the knife, gripping it with the thumbnail and flicking it out, but it is possible to make a good union without removing this wood. The next step is to cut the shield-shaped piece of bark squarely across about ¼ in. above the bud. The pointed end of the shield is then slipped beneath the raised flaps of bark on the stock and the whole shield is pushed downwards until it lies snugly against the bark of the stock. In this position it is bound with broad, soft raffia, soft twine, or one of the proprietary bud ties. Care should be taken to start the tie well below the T-shaped incision and to continue it well above this, so that the bark of the stock cannot gape. No further protection is necessary.

After a few weeks the bud should be examined. If it is still fresh and plump, it has almost certainly made a union with the stock; if it is dry and withered, it has died and another bud may be inserted on another part of the stock. If the tie is cutting into the bark, it should be removed and, should the bud appear at all loose, another tie should replace it.

Fruit tree stocks are usually budded between 6 in. and 1 ft. above ground level. Fairly young stocks are used for the purpose; they certainly should not be thicker than an ordinary walking stick and are usually rather less than this. The buds are placed directly in the bark of the main stems, usually one bud to a stock. Occasionally

when standard or half-standard trees are to be formed, the stock is allowed to grow to a height of 5 or 6 ft. and then a bud inserted high up at the level at which the first branches are to be formed. This form of top working is not very desirable, as there is always a danger that the head of branches will blow out at the point of budding.

Bush roses are usually budded on small seedling stocks and sometimes on young rooted cuttings. In both cases one bud is inserted direct on the main stem just below soil level. To enable this to be done a little soil is first scraped away with a trowel from around the stock. The soil is not returned immediately after budding, though it may be drawn back in the following autumn as protection for the bud in winter.

Standard roses may be budded on either wild English dog rose, *Rosa canina*, or on the Japanese brier, *R. rugosa*. With the former, strong and comparatively old stems are cut back in winter to a height of about 5 ft. (3½ ft. for half-standards) and then, the following spring, each stem is allowed to form three young shoots near the top, all other shoots being rubbed out. In the summer one bud is inserted near the base of each of these young shoots. When *Rosa rugosa* is used the buds are inserted direct in the bark of the main stem at a height of 5 ft. above ground level for standards and 3½ ft. for half-standards.

Another method of budding is known as patch budding. Here a square patch of bark with a bud in the centre is cut from the budding stick. A similar patch is removed from the stock and the bud fitted into position and tied in place. Great accuracy is called for and this is most easily attained if a special knife with parallel blades is used, the blades being the right distance apart to cut opposite sides of the square patch at once. Such a knife can be made with razor blades fastened to a piece of wood.

Patch budding is used for walnuts and for these the patch is about ½ in. square, and the buds are cut from well-ripened growth

made the previous season. This method of budding can be used for other plants with thick bark.

BUD DISEASE A name sometimes given to a withering of the flower stem just behind the bud or opening flower. It occurs in a good many different plants but is particularly common in roses and peonies. Various causes have been suggested but the trouble remains somewhat obscure. It may on occasion be due to attack by biting or sucking insects and sometimes to attack by fungus, but more often it appears to be a purely physiological condition, probably due to weakness. When big flowers such as those of roses and double peonies begin to open they require large supplies of moisture and food. If the plant is weak, and in particular if the flower stem is not very stout, it may be impossible for adequate supplies to reach the flower; as a result the stem starts to wither. Another possible cause is strong sunshine on the soft stem, and some experts believe this is particularly liable to cause damage if it occurs early in the morning while the stems are still wet with dew. Remedies take the form of spraying with an insecticide such as BHC, carbaryl or trichlorphon to kill any possible weevils; spraying with fungicide such as Bordeaux mixture or colloidal sulphur to kill fungi; feeding and watering the plant to counteract weakness; applying sulphate of potash to the soil at 1 oz. to a sq. yd. to make growth more resistant to this trouble, and shading the flower stems.

BUD DROPPING A trouble which often causes the loss of numerous flowers, particularly in tomatoes, runner beans, sweet peas, lupins and begonias. Bud dropping is not caused by insect or fungal attack but is a purely physiological disorder due to unsuitable atmospheric conditions. Cold draughts and low night temperatures are common causes. Over-watering and bad drainage may also account for some bud

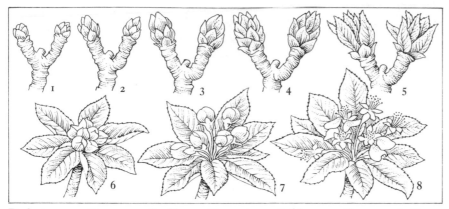

Bud stages. 1. *Dormant.* **2.** *Swelling.* **3.** *Green tip.* **4.** *Bud burst.* **5.** *Mouse ear.* **6.** *Green cluster.* **7.** *Pink bud.* **8.** *Blossom fall*

dropping. Plants should be given good cultivation, be kept out of draughts and, if under glass, low night temperatures should be avoided.

BUD STAGES Fruit growers use various terms to describe the different stages of fruit bud growth. These are important because spray applications in winter and spring are usually determined by the state of growth rather than by the precise calendar date. The terms commonly employed are dormant, swelling, breaking or green tip, bud burst, mouse ear, green bud or green cluster, pink bud or white bud, full blossom and blossom fall. With plums the term cot split is also used.

Dormant – the stage at which the blossom buds are, to all outward appearance, quite inactive, a period roughly extending from November to the end of January.

Swelling – a condition following the dormant stage when the buds are rapidly increasing in size and the scales enclosing the buds are starting to loosen.

Breaking or green tip – the tips of the green leaves within the bud begin to protrude through the loosened scales at the end of the bud.

Bud burst – the leaf tips are beginning to separate.

Mouse ear – the stage at which the individual leaves become apparent as they unfold themselves from the buds and the tips of the green blossom buds can be seen.

Green cluster or green bud – the scales have now completely dropped off and the cluster of tight green flower buds is revealed in the centre of a rosette of leaves.

Pink or white bud – at this stage the flower buds have expanded sufficiently to reveal a trace of petal colour, pink with apples, white with pears and plums.

Full blossom – the stage at which 80 to 90 per cent. of the blossom is fully open.

Blossom fall – the stage at which 80 to 90 per cent. of the blossom has fallen.

Cot split – the yellow calyx splits away from the tiny fruitlets of the plum about a week after petal fall.

BUG A member of the order *Hemiptera*, which consists of insects with biting and sucking mouthparts, and contains, apart from species of direct interest to the gardener, such well-known characters as the bed-bug, water-boatmen or pond-skaters. The frog hopper or cuckoo spit insect is a well-known garden pest. The majority of the 1,500 British species are sap suckers, which makes the order one of very great importance in horticulture. It includes, for example, the capsid bud (q.v.) and also many species of aphid, popularly known as greenfly, white fly, black fly and plant lice. Mealy bug on vines and greenhouse plants generally is also included and so are the various scale insects which attach themselves like limpets to the bark, stems or leaves of plants, sucking their juices. Lastly there is the rhododendron bug, a small black creature which attacks rhododendron leaves, giving them a rusty appearance beneath and a mottled look above. All these insects are detailed under their particular names.

BULB A bulb may be regarded as a much modified bud. It is a storage organ, usually formed underground, with fleshy scales or swollen leaf bases which serve to store food for a resting period. A typical example of a true bulb is an onion and if this is cut in half, the separate leaf bases of which it is formed can be seen very readily. In the centre of the bulb is an embryo shoot, as in the case of an ordinary bud, and often there is also a complete embryo flower.

However, the term bulb is often used loosely in the garden to cover all kinds of fleshy growths which store food and have the power of growing into new plants. Thus

a bulb catalogue is likely to contain descriptions of plants with tuberous roots or which form corms, besides plants which form true bulbs.

Many totally different kinds of plants form bulbs and it often happens that within one genus of plants some members are bulb forming whilst others are not, e.g. in the iris family there are various species, such as *Iris reticulata* and the Spanish, English and Dutch irises which form true bulbs, others such as the so-called German or flag iris which form rhizomes (fleshy stems formed on or near the surface of the soil) and yet others, such as *Iris unguicularis* and *I. sibirica*, which are fibrous rooted without bulbs, rhizomes or other methods of storing large quantities of food. Some bulbs are hardy, some are half-hardy and others are tender. Some have a long resting period and others practically no resting period at all.

During the resting period, the bulb is seldom completely dormant as important physiological changes may be going on within it, preparing it for its next season of growth. It is sometimes possible, by special treatment, to hasten or alter these changes, a fact that has been exploited by gardeners in the vernalization of hyacinths, tulips and daffodils. These vernalized bulbs are treated to periods of carefully regulated temperatures as a result of which they grow much more rapidly than untreated bulbs and can be used to produce very early supplies of flowers.

Most bulbs form offsets or small bulbs around themselves and sometimes the parent bulb itself will split into two or three separate and smaller bulbs. These offsets and divided bulbs can be detached and used to increase stock and the usual time for doing this is when growth dies down and the bulb becomes dormant. In a few instances new

Lilies can be propagated by rooting scales detached from the bulbs

bulbs can also be formed from separate bulb scales, a system of propagation often used for lilies. The scales of fully developed bulbs are carefully detached and laid in moist sand, peat or leafmould, sometimes in an unheated frame or greenhouse and sometimes in a steam-warmed room with a very humid atmosphere. After a few months, small bulbs are formed at the bases of the scales and these can then be treated like normal offsets.

BULB FIBRE Where bulbs are grown for indoor decoration in ornamental bowls, which are not provided with drainage holes, these containers cannot be filled with ordinary soil or soil compost as this would soon become sour due to the lack of drainage. In consequence a special compost is used which is often described as bulb fibre. It may either be purchased ready for use or it can be prepared at home from the following ingredients.

        6 parts of loose bulk of peat
        2 parts of oyster shell
        1 part of crushed charcoal
Mix well and moisten very thoroughly before use.

BULBIL The very small bulbs which form on some plants and which, if detached and planted in suitable soil and situation, will, in time, grow into full sized bulbs. The Tiger Lily, *Lilium tigrinum*, is a familiar example of a plant that forms bulbils on the flowering stems, in the axils of the leaves.

BULLATE A botanical term meaning puckered or blistered in appearance. It is sometimes applied to leaves which have a naturally irregular surface, e.g. *Rhododendron bullatum*.

BUNCH Any collection of flowers tied together or fruits in a natural cluster, as for example a bunch of grapes. The term is occasionally used in show schedules, for example there may be a class for a 'bunch of garden flowers'. If this is not qualified in any other way, it may be taken to be any number of flowers of any kind, tied together by their stems to form a bunch of any size. It is, therefore, a bad description without some qualification such as the number of stems which may be included, the total size of the bunch or something of that kind. Occasionally, small vegetables such as shorthorn carrots and spring onions are also asked for in show schedules, bunched. This means they should be held together by a tie around their stems or leaves.

BURGUNDY MIXTURE A preparation for the prevention of diseases caused by fungi. It is closely allied to Bordeaux mixture, which has almost superseded it. It gets its name from the fact that it was first developed in the Burgundy district of France for use on vines. Like Bordeaux mixture, it makes use of copper sulphate, but the acidity of this is neutralized by washing soda instead of lime. The formula is:

        8 oz. copper sulphate
        10 oz. washing soda
        5 gallons water
Dissolve the copper sulphate in 4 gallons of water and the washing soda in the other gallon. Pour the washing soda solution into the copper sulphate solution, stirring well. Prepare in a wooden or enamel container. Use at once.

BUSH The term is used in three ways by gardeners. A bush may be another way of saying shrub. A bush tree is one that branches from low down with no more than a short main trunk, in contrast to a standard tree which has a tall main trunk or a half-standard tree which has a trunk of intermediate height. Bush fruit may be used to distinguish fruits which naturally grow on small bushes, e.g. currants and gooseberries, from fruits which naturally grow on trees, e.g. apples, pears, plums and cherries, and which are known as top fruits.

BUSHEL This is a dry measure – an Imperial bushel consists of 8 gallons or 44 pecks and contains 1.28 cu. ft. Bushel measures can be purchased, or a measure which will hold approximately a bushel (certainly close enough for ordinary garden purposes) can be made from a box measuring 10 by 10 by 22 in. Bushel baskets were frequently used by market gardeners for conveying their produce to market. Another market container is known as the bushel flat, but this does not hold a bushel despite its name. It measures 21 by 16 by 10 in. It should be noted that a bushel is a measure of bulk and not of weight and that the weight contained in a bushel measure will depend on the substance being measured, e.g. a bushel of basic slag will weigh much more than a bushel of sand which will in turn weigh much more than a bushel of dry peat.

BUTTERFLIES Most butterflies are harmless as far as the gardener is concerned, and some are actually beneficial as they help to carry pollen from flower to flower and so effect pollination. There are, however, some exceptions to this general rule, notable among them the cabbage white butterflies, both large and small. The bright green caterpillars of these familiar creamy white butterflies attack not only cabbages but all

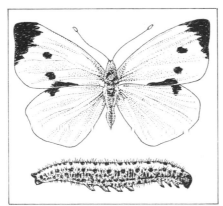

Cabbage white butterfly and larva

kinds of brassicas and many other plants as well. They eat holes in the leaves and are capable of defoliating plants completely. The best remedy is to spray or dust directly an attack is observed with a good insecticide such as derris, carbaryl or trichlorphon. On a small scale hand picking will be found useful.

CABBAGE APHID One of the many species of aphids. It attacks cabbages and allied brassicas. For treatment see Aphid.

CABBAGE BUTTERFLY, see Butterflies

CABBAGE DOWNY MILDEW A disease which sometimes attacks cabbages and other brassicas, particularly in the early stages of growth. The leaves turn yellow and develop a grey downy mould on their undersides. Considerable damage may be done, particularly in wet weather, in overcrowded beds. The best preventive is to give plants plenty of room at the outset and to spray with Bordeaux mixture or zineb if the disease is reported in the locality or has been troublesome in previous years.

CABBAGE GALL WEEVIL The adult weevil is a small beetle-like insect which does not itself damage plants, but it produces eggs which hatch out into small white grubs that attack cabbages and other brassicas, including turnips, at or near soil level, causing them to develop galls. Plants that are attacked can be recognized by these galls or lumps, each about the size of a pea, clustered around the base of the stem or the upper part of the main root. Sometimes these swellings are mistaken for those caused by club root disease, but they can be distinguished by the fact that the club root swellings are on the roots themselves including subsidiary roots, whereas the galls are only on the stem and that portion of the root which is a continuation of the stem. Moreover, if one of these galls is broken open, it will be found to be hollow within and most likely the small white grub which has caused the damage will be found in this hollow. The galls are unsightly but appear to inflict little damage on the plant. In serious outbreaks it may be desirable to dress the soil with a soil insecticide containing BHC, but in most instances it is sufficient to break open the galls and destroy the larvae when transplanting brassica seedings. This pest can also attack radishes making them inedible.

CABBAGE MOTH The caterpillars of this greyish moth attack cabbages and all kinds of brassica as well as some other plants. These caterpillars are sometimes confused with the caterpillars of cabbage white butterflies. They may be distinguished by the fact that though they are greenish when very young, they soon change to a dull olive green or brownish colour or at most a dirty

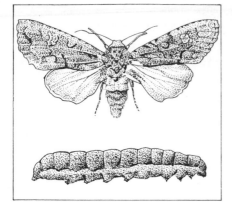

Cabbage moth with its larva

brownish green, and are not bright green throughout like the caterpillars of the cabbage butterfly. In any case accurate identification is not important from the gardener's standpoint as the remedy for both cabbage white butterfly and cabbage moth attack is the same, namely dusting or spraying with a good insecticide such as derris, carbaryl or trichlorphon. Cabbage moth caterpillars are less easy to hand pick as they burrow into the heart of the plant.

CABBAGE ROOT FLY This insect pest, which in appearance is rather like a small housefly, lays its eggs in the soil near the roots of cabbages and allied plants. These eggs soon hatch out into small white maggots which feed on the roots. In severe cases the plants are killed outright, and even when this does not occur they are severely checked and often become blind. Most of the damage occurs during May and June, though successive broods may be produced throughout the summer. One of the most effective preventives is to sprinkle 4 per cent. calomel dust on the surface of the soil close to the base of plants likely to be attacked. This may be done to brassica seedlings in the seed rows, and also to the same seedlings after they have been planted out. An inch-wide band of calomel dust round every plant or on each side of the seedling row will be sufficient to give protection. An alternative is to spray the seedlings and young plants with lindane. An old-fashioned preventive which is quite effective is to cut circular disks of tarred felt, each disk about 3 in. in diameter. A cut is then made to the centre of each disk so that it can be fitted around the stem of a brassica and pressed closely on the surface of the soil. This prevents the female flies from laying their eggs near the base of the plant. Such disks should be placed in position as the seedlings are planted out. In the case of brussels sprouts the eggs are also laid in the developing buttons, and early spraying with lindane is the best treatment.

CABBAGE WHITE FLY A form of the white fly so troublesome in greenhouses;

it attacks plants in the open and is particularly fond of cabbages and allied brassicas. See White Fly.

CACTUS A member of the natural order *Cactaceae*. The term is often misused by gardeners to cover almost any kind of plant with fleshy leaves. The correct word to use in this general sense is succulent. All cacti are succulents but not all succulents are cacti.

CALCAREOUS Containing chalk or lime. This term is applied in the garden principally to soils containing chalk or lime, which are sometimes referred to as calcareous soils. A calcareous rock is one composed mainly or entirely of chalk or limestone.

CALCICOLOUS, CALCIPHILOUS Both words have a similar import, the first meaning living on chalk, the latter chalk loving. They are applied in gardens to those plants that like lime or chalk in the soil and may be contrasted with calcifuge (q.v.).

CALCIFUGE Disliking lime or chalk in any form. The term is frequently used to describe plants which are lime-haters, such as most rhododendrons and heathers.

CALCIUM A chemical element which is an essential plant food. In soils calcium commonly occurs as calcium carbonate (chalk or limestone). See Lime.

CALLUS The growth which forms naturally over any wound made in a plant, e.g. if the limb of a tree is cut off, after a few weeks a thickening of the tissues underlying the bark will occur round the wound and this callus will gradually extend until the whole wound is covered and new bark is formed over it. In a similar manner a cutting forms a callus at the base and this callus in time covers and seals it. In this case roots may appear both from the callus and from the tissues immediately above it.

CALOMEL A popular name for mercurous chloride, a chemical used by the gardener to kill the maggots of the onion fly and cabbage root fly, the fungus which causes club root disease, and several of the fungi which may attack lawn grass. For fly maggots and club root control 4 per cent. calomel dust is employed and must be purchased as a proprietary article. To kill the fly maggots this powder is sprinkled in a narrow band around each cabbage or onion plant or in a narrow band along each side of every row of young plants. The most effective time to use it is in May and early June. For club root one teaspoonful of the powder is mixed with the soil in each hole prepared for a cabbage or other brassica seedling. If necessary the seed bed can also be sprinkled lightly with 4 per cent. calomel dust before

the seed is sown. This same preparation may be dusted on grass suffering from corticium disease, or dollar spot; or special formulations for lawns may be purchased and should be used according to manufacturers' instructions.

Calomel on its own or in combination with sulphate of iron is also used as a moss killer, either stirred into water and applied from a watering-can or as a dry powder top-dressing. Label instructions should be followed.

CALYX The outer whorl of a flower, formed of sepals, in contrast to the inner whorl formed of petals. These sepals are sometimes united in the form of a cup or tube and are sometimes separate. Frequently the calyx is green and not particularly conspicuous or decorative, but in some instances the calyx segments are highly developed and more brightly coloured than the petals. This is notably the case with the many varieties of clematis, in which the showy part of the flower is formed of the calyx, and the petals are either completely absent or inconspicuous. Many of the highly developed garden forms of hydrangea also depend on large, coloured calyces (plural of calyx) for their decorative value. In some flowers, e.g. magnolias and lilies, there is little or no differentiation between sepals and petals all of which play an equally conspicuous part in forming the flower. They may then be collectively known as tepals, (q.v.).

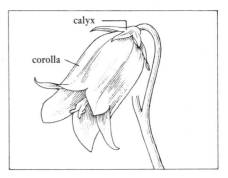

Carnation and pink growers have good cause to be familiar with the word, because the calyx of these flowers is tubular and often unable to contain the expanding petals which burst through it and so form a misshapen or irregular flower. This bursting is particularly troublesome with certain varieties. To overcome it carnation growers often place an elastic band round the calyx at an early stage.

CAMBIUM Botanically this name may be given to any plant tissue other than that at the growing points (shoot and root tips and buds) which retains the power of growth. However, when the term is used in horticulture, it is almost invariably confined to the very narrow layer of active tissue which exists between the bark and wood of dicotyledons. It is of vital importance to the grafter because it is at this point alone that active cell growth can take place to unite stock and scion. When the bark is peeled from a young stem that is in active growth, part of the cambium adheres to the wood and part to the bark. It is this fact which makes it possible to bud plants by placing a piece of bark carrying a bud in close contact with the 'wood' (it is actually the thin layer of cambium cells covering the wood) of a stock from which a small portion of bark has been peeled. When a cutting is inserted in the rooting medium it forms a callus from the exposed ring of active cambium at the base and it is from the cambium and this callus that new roots (or, in the case of root cuttings, shoots) are formed.

CAMPANULATE Bell shaped; a botanical term applied to flowers which are of this form. The genus *Campanula*, to which the harebell belongs, gets its name from the fact that so many of its members have campanulate flowers.

CANE BLIGHT A fungal disease of raspberries which attacks the canes causing dark patches, above which the whole cane may wither. Alternatively, the cane may snap off at ground level. This disease is usually associated with attacks of raspberry cane midge, the fungal spores entering the canes through the wounds caused by this insect. Affected canes should be cut off well below ground level and burned and healthy canes should be sprayed with BHC in early May and again a fortnight later to destroy raspberry cane midge.

CANE FRUITS Those fruits which produce long, cane-like stems, such as blackberries, loganberries and raspberries. Usually the canes are renewed annually, young canes growing to replace the old ones that have fruited and have either died or been removed by pruning.

CANE SPOT A familiar disease of raspberries, blackberries, loganberries and most other bramble fruits. It is caused by a fungus which attacks the canes. The first symptom of attack is the appearance of purplish spots or patches on the young canes. These increase in size until eventually the bark itself splits and canker-like wounds are formed. As a result of this, growth is weakened and the tops of the canes may even be killed. The most effective preventive is to spray with lime sulphur fungicide in March using it at twice the normal winter strength (22 fl. oz. of lime sulphur to 2 gallons of water). A further application of lime sulphur at double the normal summer strength (6 fl. oz. of lime sulphur to 2 gallons of water) may be given as soon as the first flowers open. Alternatively, thiram may be used before blossom

time but not after if the fruit is to be canned or frozen.

CANKER A general name given to various diseases which cause the bark or skin of plants to split and decay, the diseased area often being surrounded by enlarged tissue growth. When this happens on trees, e.g. apples and cherries, growth above the canker wound may at first merely be checked, but later, if the wound spreads so that it completely encircles the branch, all that area above the canker is killed. Some varieties of apple are particularly susceptible to canker, caused in this instance by the fungus *Nectria galligena*. There are proprietary remedies on the market which will often cure canker wounds and, if not, will usually prevent their spread. These should be used in accordance with manufacturers' directions. It is always wise to cut away the cankered bark and wood until clean healthy tissue is reached. This should be done with a sharp pruning knife and afterwards the clean wound should be painted with Stockholm tar or some other approved wound dressing.

The rose is also subject to attack by a fungus which causes canker, the scientific name in this instance being *Conothyrium fuckelii*. The symptoms are very similar to those of apple canker though the fungus is entirely distinct and infection cannot spread from rose to apple or vice versa. The only effective remedy is to cut off and burn all affected shoots, making each cut well below the canker and into clean healthy tissue.

A stem disease of tomatoes is also known as canker. This is caused by the fungus *Didymella lycopersici*. It attacks the main stem turning it brown and causing it to shrink and decay. As a rule the point of attack is near the base of the stem. All affected plants should be removed and burned and the soil around neighbouring plants may be watered with Cheshunt compound to prevent infection. As a precaution stems of

young plants and the soil around them may be sprayed with captan two days after planting. After the crop has been gathered the soil should either be changed or sterilized.

The name canker is also applied to a rusty decay of the upper part or shoulder of the parsnip. In this instance it does not appear that the trouble is caused by a fungus. The actual cause is somewhat obscure and may be physiological as the trouble is most apparent when parsnips are grown on heavily manured ground. A useful preventive appears to be to dress the soil with lime and sulphate of potash prior to sowing parsnip seed. Hydrated lime is used at the rate of 8 oz. per sq. yd. and sulphate of potash at 1 oz. per sq. yd. Soil may also be dusted with lindane prior to sowing parsnips to kill maggots of the carrot fly which may attack the roots and predispose them to canker.

CAPILLARY ATTRACTION The force which causes liquid to rise through any very fine tube or the tiny spaces between closely packed particles. It is capillary attraction which draws moisture through a sheet of blotting paper or oil up the wick of an oil lamp, and it is the same force which enables moisture to rise in the soil from the water reserves below. At one time it was supposed that hoeing was effective in preventing loss of moisture by evaporation from the surface because, by loosening the surface soil, the fine spaces through which water may rise by capillary attraction were broken up. Experiment has not supported this belief, for it has been shown that the loss of moisture by evaporation from unhoed soil is no greater than that from soil which has been hoed frequently. Apparently in this case the dried cap of soil which forms on unhoed soil is as effective in preventing loss of moisture as the layer of broken soil.

CAPILLARY WATERING A method of watering pot plants by standing them on a

One of the automatic watering systems, such as this capillary bench, can be an aid to the busy gardener

wet surface such as well-moistened sand or peat or by placing a wick in the bottom of each pot and allowing it to hang down into water. In each case the effectiveness of the method depends upon capillary attraction which causes the water to rise into the soil in the pot as this becomes dry. In practice capillary watering has proved very satisfactory for a wide range of plants. It is essential that the soil in the pots comes into direct contact with the wet sand or peat below. No drainage crocks should be used in the pots and, when earthenware pots are used, it may be necessary to pass a wick through the drainage hole. Plastic pots are sufficiently thin to permit the soil within to touch the sand or peat without. All manner of ingenious devices are available for keeping a bed of soil or peat constantly wet but quite simple methods can also be used, such as a large narrow-necked jar filled with water and inverted in a small water container, or trickle irrigation tubes laid on the capillary bed and left permanently on. Even when pot plants are watered in the ordinary way from above, if they are standing on some moisture absorbent material such as sand or peat, they will draw some moisture from it by capillary attraction.

CAPSID BUGS A group of insects some of which are plant pests though some are useful as they prey on other insects, notably red spider mites. The harmful capsids are small greenish or reddish insects. They obtain their food by sucking sap from the leaves, stems, fruits and flowers of plants. As a result the plants are weakened and there is usually considerable distortion and sometimes the formation of corky-looking scabs. This last symptom is common on apple fruits. Flower buds which are attacked by capsid bugs frequently fail to develop properly and may be one sided, a deformity often noted in chrysanthemums. Relatively few capsid bugs appear able to cause a great amount of damage, no doubt partly because they are fairly active insects which pass readily from one part of a plant to another or from one plant to another. Capsid bugs can be killed by spraying with BHC or nicotine and, on fruit trees, DNC or winter petroleum emulsions may be applied just before the buds burst fully. In greenhouses nicotine may be used as a spray or fumigant or diazinon as a spray or aerosol.

CAPSULE A dry fruit which splits to discharge its seeds and which has more than one carpel. Examples are the seed pods of the poppy, iris and cabbage.

CAPTAN A fungicide specially useful for controlling scab in apples and pears. It is also effective against black spot of roses. Unlike lime sulphur it has no ill effect on the leaves of any variety, but it needs to be renewed fairly frequently to be fully effective.

CARBARYL An insecticide used primarily to kill caterpillars, including those of the codling moth. It is available as a wettable powder for mixing with water according to manufacturers' instructions and application as a spray. The fluid should be kept agitated. It is harmful to bees so should not be used on open flowers; nor within a week of harvesting an edible crop.

CARBON DIOXIDE This gas, which forms a part of the atmosphere, provides plants with their sole source of carbon, an essential element in all organic compounds such as sugars, starches, proteins and cellulose. It is used in the process of photosynthesis which is carried on in the leaves of the plant during daylight or under sufficiently intense artificial illumination and there is usually enough of it to meet the plant's requirements. But in certain circumstances, as when plants are being grown very intensively in greenhouses, an extra supply of carbon dioxide may prove beneficial and many commercial growers of lettuces, tomatoes and cucumbers actually supplement the supply of it in the greenhouse atmosphere. Carbon dioxide may be produced by burning propane gas in the greenhouse; by placing frozen carbon dioxide (carbon dioxide snow) in the house; by using cylinders of compressed carbon dioxide or even from rotting beds of straw, since carbon dioxide is one of the natural products of decay. The additional carbon dioxide is only of value if there is sufficient illumination and warmth to enable the plants to make use of it.

CARBON DISULPHIDE This is also known as carbon bisulphide. It is an evil smelling, inflammable and volatile liquid which is used in the garden as a soil fumigant. See Fumigation.

CARPEL The female unit of a flower consisting of stigma, style and ovary. In many flowers there are several carpels, either joined as in the tomato, or separate as in delphinium or peony.

CARROT FLY A common pest of carrots. The adult fly is not unlike a small housefly and lays its eggs on the roots of carrots. It is particularly liable to choose plants growing in loose soil, as for example soil which has been disturbed by careless thinning of overcrowded seedlings. The eggs hatch out into white maggots which bore into the roots of the carrots. The attack usually starts in late April or early May, but successive broods may be produced throughout the summer. An old-fashioned remedy which is quite effective is to dust the surface soil every 10 days or so with finely powdered naphthalene, from about early May until the end of June. The smell of this keeps the flies away. Lindane dust can be worked into

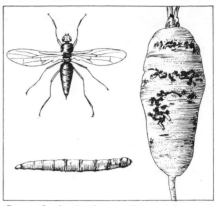

Carrot fly showing larva, adult and damage

the soil prior to sowing or diazinon may be applied to the seed drills. Careful thinning is an obvious precaution and the soil should be well firmed around any seedlings that are accidentally loosened.

CASTOR MEAL A by-product of the manufacture of castor oil used mainly as a fertilizer. An average analysis would be 5 to 6 per cent. nitrogen, 1 to 2 per cent. phosphoric acid and 1 per cent. potash. It can be used for any crops or ornamental plants and also for lawns on which it will quickly improve the growth and colour of the grass but may also increase the worm population.

CATCH CROP A crop grown rapidly on a piece of ground previously prepared for some other purpose, e.g. lettuces are sometimes grown in the trenches prepared for celery before the celery is ready to be planted.

CATERPILLAR The larval stage of a butterfly or moth, the complete cycle being (1) egg, (2) caterpillar or larva, (3) pupa, chrysalis or cocoon, and (4) adult insect or imago (butterfly or moth). There are, therefore, as many different kinds of caterpillars as there are butterflies and moths, but by no means are all garden pests. Nevertheless a considerable number of caterpillars, and particularly the caterpillars of moths, do feed on garden plants, and some inflict a great deal of loss on the gardener.

For the purpose of treatment caterpillars may be conveniently split into three groups – (1) those that feed on the outside aerial parts of the plant, mainly leaves, but occasionally shoots as well; (2) those that feed within the tissues of the plant either by tunnelling holes into the fruits as do the caterpillars of the codling moth, or by tunnelling into the shoots or branches, as do the caterpillars of the leopard moth and currant clear wing moth; and (3) those caterpillars that feed on the underground parts of the plant. Caterpillars of this third group are frequently referred to as cutworms. They spend their lives in the soil and gnaw the roots or those parts of the stem which are at or beneath the soil level.

Caterpillars which move by looping their bodies are known as loopers.

Leaf- and stem-eating caterpillars are usually dealt with by means of insecticides such as BHC, derris, trichlorphon or carbaryl. The object is to cover the leaves and stems with a fine film of poison either just before an attack is likely to start or as soon as one is observed. Then the caterpillars are poisoned directly they begin to feed.

Stem- and fruit-boring caterpillars are not so easy to deal with, in fact in the case of stem-borers it is usually necessary to extract them one by one from their tunnels with the aid of a length of flexible wire. Fruit-borers may be killed with the aid of stomach poisons provided these are applied to the fruits before the caterpillars have entered them. This method is adopted to counter the attacks of the codling moth (q.v.).

Cutworms or soil caterpillars may be dealt with by dusting the soil with a fumigant such as finely powdered naphthalene or paradichlorbenzene and hoeing this in, or by dusting or watering the soil with lindane, carbaryl or trichlorphon.

CATKIN A particular kind of flower spike, usually unisexual and pendulous, in which the flowers are stalkless and have small, scale-like bracts. The hazel, birch and willow are familiar examples of catkin-bearing trees.

CELERY BLIGHT or LEAF SPOT, see Leaf Spot

CELERY FLY Also known as the celery leaf miner. The small white maggot of this fly tunnels the leaves of celery and, occasionally, parsnips. Attacked leaves should be removed and burned and rags soaked in paraffin can be hung near the plants to deter flies from laying their eggs. Leaves can also be sprayed with BHC, carbaryl, trichlorphon or malathion.

CELL The unit of plant tissue, microscopic in size and consisting, as a rule, of a nucleus embedded in protoplasm and cell sap, and bounded by a thin wall. Cells at the tips of shoots and roots and in the cambium layer have the power of multiplication by division, by which means the plant grows.

CENTIPEDE Yellow or orange coloured creatures with long, narrow bodies and many legs which may often be seen moving about very actively in the soil. They are friends of the gardener as they are entirely carnivorous and destroy many of the soil insects that harm plants. Centipedes are sometimes mistaken for millepedes which are foes and not friends. They may at all

times be distinguished by the fact that they are yellow or orange, whereas millepedes are blackish, grey or a dirty pinkish white; that they are very active whereas millepedes are rather slow in their movements and that they have fewer and larger legs than millepedes.

CHAFERS A name given to various flying beetles of which the best known is the cockchafer. This usually flies at dusk, making a considerable droning noise and often colliding with obstacles. It is a large brown beetle with a black head and foreparts. These chafer beetles themselves eat leaves and flowers, but even greater damage is done by their large, whitish and somewhat prawn-like larvae which may be found curled up in the soil. They are very slow in their movements, but nevertheless are capable of doing a great deal of damage by feeding on the roots and other subterranean parts of plants. They attack a great variety of plants including trees and shrubs. The beetles themselves may be killed by spraying the stems and leaves with BHC. The larvae may be attacked with soil fumigants such as flaked naphthalene or paradichlorbenzene forked or raked into the soil, or carbon disulphide either injected into the soil with a special tool or poured into holes made with a dibber every 9 to 12 in.; such holes should be about 9 in. in depth and each should receive from one teaspoonful to a dessertspoonful of carbon disulphide. The holes should be refilled at once with soil to trap the fumes.

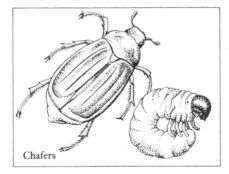
Chafers

CHALCID WASP, see Predators

CHALK Chalk, which is one of the common geological formations in the British Isles, is carbonate of lime, otherwise known as calcium carbonate, and is chemically identical with limestone, though it is much softer. Chalk is converted into quicklime by burning it in kilns, and quicklime in turn is converted into hydrated lime by slaking it with water or by exposing it to a damp atmosphere. Chalk itself is valuable in the garden for correcting acidity, but it should be ground finely as, if applied in lumps, it is extremely slow in action, in fact the lumps may remain practically unchanged for many years. Some gardeners prefer using finely ground chalk to hydrated lime because it is

less likely to scorch tender leaves and roots, it is more pleasant to handle and its effect is steadier and lasts longer. It is also said to be better for light, sandy soils because of its tendency to hold moisture and therefore to correct the natural dryness of these soils. It can be employed in potting composts in place of ground limestone and is in fact one of the recognized ingredients of the John Innes seed and potting composts. For this purpose it is usually applied at the rate of ¾ oz. chalk to each bushel of compost. In the open garden, it is used at rates varying from 6 oz. to 2 lb. to the sq. yd. according to requirements. It can be applied at any time of the year but should not be used at the same time as dung or sulphate of ammonia, with either of which it will combine to liberate ammonia gas with resultant loss of nitrogen.

Gardens on chalky soils present their own problems as the soil is likely to be alkaline and therefore unsuitable for the cultivation of acid-loving plants such as rhododendrons and heathers. Moreover, an excess of chalk may result in the locking up of certain other essential plant foods, notably iron, magnesium and potassium. It is because of this lack of available iron and magnesium on chalk soils that plants growing in such places often have yellow foliage – a condition known as chlorosis and due to lack of chlorophyll or green colouring matter. Iron and magnesium are both essential ingredients of chlorophyll. It is not possible to overcome these deficiencies simply by adding iron and magnesium as ordinary salts such as sulphate of iron or sulphate of magnesium, as these almost immediately become locked in the soil, but special chelated forms of these chemicals are available which remain available to plants for a considerable time. They are also referred to as sequestrols (q.v.).

It may be possible to lower the alkalinity of such soils by giving heavy dressings of acid substances such as dung, peat and oak leafmould. Chalky soils tend to be very wasteful of humus and consequently high rates of manuring with bulky manures such as dung and compost are likely to be required to maintain full fertility.

Plants which thrive in chalky soils include aubrieta, most members of the dianthus family, *Caryophyllaceae*, including the pink and border carnation, gypsophila, irises, centranthus, helianthemums, scabious, wallflowers, clematis and also all members of the cabbage family, *Cruciferae*. Some saxifrages grown on chalky soil secrete a solution from special glands on the edges of the leaves which evaporates leaving the chalk on the surface of the plant.

CHARCOAL This is produced by burning or smouldering wood in a heated cylinder or covered fire with a very limited air supply. Powdered or crushed charcoal is useful in the garden because of its power of absorbing poisonous substances. It may be used in potting composts to keep them sweet and is an important ingredient of the special bulb fibre (q.v.) used when bulbs are grown in undrained bowls or pans. It has little or no value as a plant food and is too expensive for use in the open ground.

CHELATED COMPOUNDS, see Sequestrols

CHESHUNT COMPOUND A mixture used to check the spread of damping-off disease and other soil-borne fungus diseases, particularly those that attack the stems of plants at or near soil level. Cheshunt compound is made by mixing 2 parts by weight of finely ground copper sulphate with 11 parts by weight of fresh ammonium carbonate. This mixture must be stored in a stoppered glass jar for at least 24 hours before use, after which it can be kept for any reasonable time. It is prepared for use by dissolving 1 oz. of the mixture in a little hot water and making up to two gallons with cold water. This solution is sprinkled on seedlings and soil from an ordinary watering-can fitted with a fine rose, and must be used as soon as prepared.

CHIMAERA In most plants the living tissues throughout are of the same genetical character, i.e. if any portion of a plant is separated and induced to form a new plant it will have exactly the same characteristics as the parent. However, there are exceptions to this general rule of uniformity and many plants are known in which tissues of two or more kinds exist side by side, each maintaining its separate identity. Such plants are known as chimaeras.

There are several different kinds of chimaeras differentiated according to the manner in which one kind of tissue is associated with the other. In some the outer covering or skin is of one character and the inner tissues of another. A familiar example of this kind of chimaera is the potato Golden Wonder which has a russet skin. This russet skin is of a different genetical character from the cells composing the flesh of the potato, a fact which can be demonstrated by raising plants from buds or eyes induced to form from the flesh. Such plants will produce smooth-skinned potatoes which are identical in every respect with the old variety Langworthy; in fact, Golden Wonder is merely Langworthy with a skin of a different character.

Variegation in some plants is caused by a similar phenomenon; for example, there are pelargoniums in which a colourless or nearly colourless epidermis (skin) overlies tissues of the normal green character. Where colourless skin overlies green tissue it is not observed; the leaf has a normal green colour, but the edge of the leaf is formed from the epidermis only and is, therefore, white. The

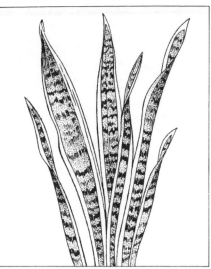

The yellow-edged form of Sansevieria trifasciata is a chimaera. The leaves are composed of two types of tissue, one overlying the other. It cannot be reproduced from cuttings

epidermis does not exist on the roots of a plant and so new plants of this kind of pelargonium, raised from root cuttings, are of the normal green-leaved type without a white margin. The opposite kind of variegation also occurs, namely a green skin overlying colourless cells. With this the reverse result will be obtained if plants are raised from root cuttings – the plants will be completely devoid of green colouring matter and will soon die.

In another type of chimaera one kind of tissue lies alongside the other and does not fit over it like a glove.

Chimaeras may occur naturally through a change in the genetical characteristics of one or more growing cells, or they may sometimes be produced by grafting. One of the best-known graft chimaeras is *Laburnocytisus adamii*. This was produced by grafting common laburnum on *Cytisus purpureus*. Instead of the tissue of stock and scion remaining entirely separate, one supplying the roots and the other the aerial parts of the tree, they became mixed though each retained its separate identity. As a result *Laburnocytisus adamii* produces normal laburnum growth and also broom-like growth. This latter produces the typical purplish flowers of *Cytisus purpureus* while the laburnum growth will bear not only normal yellow laburnum flowers but also other flowers similar to the laburnum in form, but of a purplish colour. All three characters may be observed at random throughout the aerial parts of the tree, which thus presents a very odd appearance.

CHINESE LAYERING, see Layering

CHLORANIFORMETHAN A systemic fungicide which is particularly good for controlling powdery mildew. It is an emulsi-

fiable concentrate and is used at the rate of 1 fl. oz. to 6 gallons of water.

CHLORBENSIDE A chemical used to control red spider mites by killing both the mites themselves and their eggs. It is sold as a wettable powder to be well stirred into water according to label instructions and applied immediately as a spray. For fruit trees an application in May or early June is advised. For other plants it should be used as soon as red spider mites are seen. Chlorbenside is rather slow in action but usually very effective. It should not be used on cucumbers, marrows, gourds and melons.

CHLORDANE A chemical used as a worm killer which has the advantage that the worms die in the soil and do not come to the surface as they do when mowrah meal is used. It is a liquid which is diluted with water according to manufacturers' instructions and watered on the turf or other areas to be treated. It should not be used on grass less than three months old from seed.

CHLOROPHYLL The green colouring matter of plants which is particularly developed in the leaves. Chlorophyll is a highly complex substance, which has the unique property of being able to utilize the energy of sunlight for the purpose of synthesizing the complex chemicals upon which plants live from simple chemicals supplied from the soil and air. This process is known as photosynthesis. Oxygen is formed during photosynthesis. Plants with white or yellow leaves lack chlorophyll, and are unable to carry out photosynthesis. Lack of chlorophyll may be brought about by many causes including the action of viruses or inherited genes and the lack of certain chemicals in the soil such as iron and magnesium. See Chlorosis.

CHLOROSIS Loss of chlorophyll or green colouring matter in a leaf or leaves as a result of which they become yellow or white. As it is the chlorophyll which enables the plant to manufacture its food from raw materials obtained from air and soil, it follows that without chlorophyll the plant will become starved and may in severe cases be killed. Chlorosis may be a symptom of disease, notably of certain virus diseases, but in such cases it is more usually referred to as mosaic, the term chlorosis being reserved for yellowing caused by purely physiological conditions. Two of the commonest causes are lack of iron and lack of magnesium. Lack of iron is itself usually due to excessive alkalinity and cannot be countered directly by applying iron salts to the soil, as this iron is rapidly rendered unavailable. See Chalk.

CHLORPROPAM A selective residual herbicide used mainly to prevent growth of weed seedlings in various bulb crops and around black currants, gooseberries and strawberries. It is liable to damage plants growing in soils that lack humus. It is available in various proprietary formulations, usually in combination with other herbicides, and should be used according to label instructions.

CHOCOLATE SPOT A familiar disease of broad beans, resulting in the production of chocolate coloured spots on the leaves. These spots may increase rapidly in size until the whole plant presents a withered appearance. The disease is caused by the same fungus as that which produces grey mould. It is most likely to be severe in spring following very cold or wet weather. The best preventive is to give early sowings of beans a rather sheltered position, or to protect them with cloches. Good cultivation, and in particular the provision of ample potassic and phosphatic food in the soil, will help to prevent this disease occurring and plants may also be sprayed with Bordeaux mixture.

CHROMOSOME The rod-like bodies found in all living cells and containing the numerous genes which control the development of the plant. As the cells divide the chromosomes also divide so that the number in each cell remains constant. When the sex cells are formed a special kind of division occurs which results in each such cell having half the usual number of chromosomes. When two sex cells meet and fuse, each contributes its half complement of chromosomes so that the original number is restored. It is by this means that each parent contributes its share to the heredity of the offspring. Every species of plant has its characteristic basic number of chromosomes. Sometimes this number is altered by natural accidents in cell division or by irregular cell division brought about by chemical or other means. Plants with abnormal numbers of chromosomes are known as polyploids and often look different from the normal or diploid plants. Sometimes the polyploids are bigger and more valuable for garden purposes.

CHRYSALIS A stage in the life of an insect between the larva (caterpillar or grub) and the perfect insect (or imago: butterfly, moth or fly). Another name for chrysalis is pupa. It is a stage of relative inactivity when outwardly there is little sign of life or movement though, within the chrysalis, important changes are taking place.

CILIATE Fringed with hairs, a botanical term applied mostly to leaves which have margins of this character, as in *Rhododendron ciliatum*.

CLADODE A stem which has taken on the function of a leaf. A well-known example is the apparent leaf of the common Butcher's Broom, *Ruscus aculeatus*, which is not really a leaf at all but a flattened stem. It can be observed that the small white flowers are borne in the centres of these 'leaves' which proclaims their true character as stems.

CLAMP A method of storing potatoes and some other tender roots in the open so that they are protected from frost and rain. A clamp consists of a conical or ridge-like heap of the roots to be stored, covered with a thick layer of clean straw which is itself covered with soil beaten smooth. As a rule, ventilating shafts are made at intervals along the ridge or at the apex of the cone by pulling wisps of straw through the soil covering. These chimneys allow damp, warm air to escape from the interior of the clamp.

There are several points to observe when making a clamp. First of all it should stand on well-drained ground or, if this is not possible, a trench should be dug right round the proposed site of the clamp and the excavated soil should be used to build up a platform on which the clamp can stand. Next a good thick layer of straw or twigs should be placed on the ground before any roots are put into position. The covering layer of straw over the roots should be at least 1 ft. thick and the outer covering of soil should be at least 9 in. thick, beaten down smoothly with the back of a spade. Clamps may be of any convenient size but the sides should be as steep as possible. Convenient dimensions for a ridge-shaped clamp are 4 to 5 ft. through at the base and 3 to 4 ft. high at the ridge.

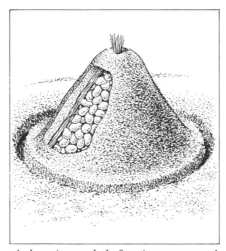

A clamp is a method of storing potatoes and other tender roots out of doors

Though clamps are principally used in gardens for potatoes, it is by no means their only use. Dahlia tubers can be stored successfully in clamps; beetroots are occasionally clamped and so are carrots, but the last named are hardy, and a somewhat different method is usually employed. The roots are stacked, top ends outwards and are only just covered with sand or sifted ashes, no covering of straw or soil being used.

When clamps containing tender roots such as potatoes are opened to get at the contents, care must be taken to seal them up again properly or frost may penetrate and do considerable damage. Care should be taken to clamp only healthy roots as disease can spread very rapidly within a clamp.

CLASPING Botanists apply this term to leaves which partly or wholly surround the stem from which they grow.

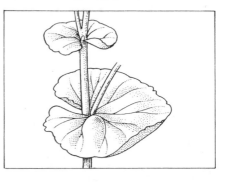

CLASSIFICATION Classification of plants is a matter for botanists, but it is of interest to gardeners because they frequently use the names which have been applied by botanists working to their classification rules. Popular names are used in some cases, as for example for roses, wallflowers, forget-me-nots, marigolds, lilac, but for many plants no popular names exist or there are so many different species bearing the same popular name that confusion occurs. A good example of this is the barberry, of which there are now close on 200 species in cultivation, any of which can be referred to as a barberry. In order to make it quite clear which species is being referred to, it is almost essential to make use of botanical nomenclature.

This nomenclature is based upon scientific examination of the plants in an effort to trace their relationship one to another – a kind of family tree. The system of nomenclature is governed by international rules which are respected in every country throughout the world. Because of this the gardener as well as the botanist has an international language at his disposal, by which he may communicate with gardeners in other lands and, if he desires, purchase plants from abroad with reasonable certainty that he will make his requirements quite plain.

The primary classification of plants is into those which flower and which are botanically called phanerogams, and those which do not flower and are called cryptogams. Ferns and fungi are familiar examples of non-flowering plants.

Flowering plants are obviously of greater importance to the gardener, and these are again subdivided into two great groups

277

according to the method of carrying their seeds. In one group, known as gymnosperms, the ovule or female cell, which, when fertilized, will develop into a seed, is exposed, whereas in the other class, known as angiosperms, the ovule is protected in an ovary. Pines, firs, cedars and other cone-bearing trees are familiar examples of gymnosperms, while apples, roses, tomatoes and peas are angiosperms.

The angiosperms are themselves sub-divided into two classes according to the number of seed leaves or cotyledons which they produce when the seed germinates. One class is known as monocotyledon because its members only have one seed leaf – the onion and the lily are examples known to everyone. The other class is known as dicotyledon because normally its members produce two seed leaves – tomatoes and marigold are of this type.

Within these major divisions of the vegetable kingdom the individuals are grouped according to their families, genera, species and varieties or cultivars. From the gardener's point of view, it is the last three which are of most importance, but it is desirable to have some understanding of the whole system in order to be able to understand the relationship between plants.

The species is the unit and all plants within the species will resemble each other closely, only differing in minor qualities such as colour, size of flower, earliness and so on. Species which resemble one another fairly closely and may be considered to have some common ancestry, are grouped together in genera, and genus and species between them provide the botanist with his mechanism for nomenclature, known as the binominal system. By this, each plant receives two names, the first designating the genus to which it belongs and the second the species. Thus *Ranunculus* is the generic name of the various species of buttercup, of which there are many. The common Creeping Buttercup is known as *Ranunculus repens*; the Meadow Buttercup, which is more erect in habit and does not creep about to the same extent, is *Ranunculus acris*; and the Marsh Buttercup, *Ranunculus lingua*. Exactly the same principle applies to garden plants – the barberries all belong to the genus *Berberis*, but each separate species has its own name so that the common barberry found in this country is *Berberis vulgaris*, while the beautiful deciduous barberry found in China by the collector Wilson, is known as *Berberis wilsonae*; the Holly-leaved Barberry which fills our gardens with orange blooms in April is *Berberis darwinii*; and so on.

Example of Classification

FAMILY : *Ranunculaceae*
GENUS : *Delphinium*
SPECIES : *elatum*
VARIETY : Bridesmaid

Any small variation within the species may be indicated by varietal names; thus, *Berberis thunbergii atropurpurea* is a form of Thunberg's barberry which has purple-coloured leaves. Sometimes varietal names are given as fancy or vernacular names. This is common with species or hybrids which are very variable and have been highly developed in gardens, as with roses and chrysanthemums. With these, such names as Etoile de Hollande, Crimson Glory, Shot Silk, The Favourite, Loveliness and so on, are really varietal names in English form, and this is permitted by the international rules of nomenclature. Such names are referred to as horticultural names as distinct from true botanical names. In botanical nomenclature varieties which have arisen in cultivation are known as cultivars to distinguish them from varieties that have occurred in nature but this distinction is rarely of much importance to gardeners. It should be noted that names of genera and species can only be given after a plant has been properly examined and identified by a trained botanist and a full description published in a magazine or other publication accepted by botanists for this purpose. Horticultural names of garden-raised varieties could, however, be given by gardeners who have no botanical qualifications, but rules are laid down, and among the most important of these is that no two plants of the same genus can bear the same varietal name, and all fancy names should be as simple as possible, and not include titles such as Mr, Mrs, Captain and so on, which might cause confusion. Horticultural names are only valid if published with a recognizable description in a recognized horticultural or botanical periodical or in a dated horticultural catalogue.

Genera are themselves grouped in families, according to their supposed relationship in the evolutionary scheme. Thus the buttercup already referred to belongs to the family *Ranunculaceae*, a family which also includes the obviously allied marsh marigold or caltha, together with other plants not, to the layman, so obviously related, as for example columbine (aquilegia), aconitum, delphinium and love-in-a-mist (nigella).

CLAY Pure clay is a mixture of very fine sand with an intensely sticky substance known as alumina. It is useful for making bricks and pottery and also for lining ponds or bog gardens, but is no use in the garden as a medium for the culture of plants. What is loosely referred to as a clay soil may be almost any mixture containing a proportion of clay together with coarser sand and humus. Clay soils themselves may be roughly classified as heavy and medium, the former containing a fairly high percentage of pure clay and the latter much larger proportions of coarse sand and/or humus.

Clay soils in general are retentive of moisture and may be difficult to work in wet weather but, if they can be improved in texture, they are usually very fertile. Moreover, they hold what is put into them and are often more economical to cultivate than sandy soils through which water percolates so quickly that many foods are washed out almost as quickly as they are put in.

Lime exercises an important function in improving the texture of clay soil, see page 333. Clay soils can be improved also by draining; by frequent digging, particularly when not too wet; by being left rough so that frosts and wind may break them up; by being left in ridges for the same purpose, and by being given heavy dressings of the lighter forms of dung such as stable manure or strawy farmyard manure, and of such substances as peat, leafmould, coarse sand and ashes. See also Soil Conditioners.

CLICK BEETLE The popular name of the beetle, the larva of which is the wireworm (q.v.).

CLOCHE Originally this term was applied to a small handlight or bell glass which could be quickly moved from one place to another and used for the protection of cuttings or

Rigid plastic cloches can be used to force an early crop of strawberries

seedlings or for the forcing of early vegetables. Nowadays, however, almost all cloches are of the continuous type, that is to say they are shelters which can be used to form a continuous line over a row, or rows, of plants. There are a great many different types, most with some peculiar advantages of their own. Some are made with glass, some with more or less rigid plastic and some with plastic film stretched over wires or other framework to form low tunnel-like structures. Clear plastic is used for crops requiring maximum light, white or clouded plastic for crops and cuttings requiring shade.

CLONE All plants produced vegetatively from one original parent.

CLOVE The individual bulbs clustered within the membranous coat of garlic (*Allium sativum*). The word is also used to describe a particular type of very fragrant border carnation known as a clove-scented carnation or sometimes just as a 'clove'.

Cloves used for flavouring in cooking are the dried and strongly aromatic flower buds of the clove tree, *Eugenia aromatica*.

CLUB ROOT A familiar disease of cabbages and other brassicas, caused by a fungus which exists in the soil and may attack the roots of these plants causing them to swell and eventually decay with a very unpleasant odour. Club root is most likely to be severe on acid soil and the fungus which causes it is unable to exist in soil that is markedly alkaline. Therefore, the best method of preventing club root disease from appearing is to maintain the soil used for brassicas in a slightly alkaline condition by giving adequate dressings of lime. When the disease has become established liming will not, as a rule, produce an immediate cure though, if continued, it will eventually clear the soil. For a quick result, the soil in each planting hole should be dusted with 4 per cent. calomel dust or the roots of the

Dipping brassica seedlings in a paste of calomel as a protection against club root

brassica seedlings should be dipped in a strong suspension (almost a thin paste) of calomel before being planted out. Seed beds may also be dusted with 4 per cent. calomel dust. All plants that are attacked by club root should be lifted and burned, roots and all.

The damage caused by club root is often confused with that caused by the cabbage gall weevil. Points of difference to observe are that the club root swellings are always on the roots whereas the roundish lumps caused by the gall weevil are on the base of the stem or that part of the root which is an extension of the stem, and that the club root swellings are solid throughout whereas the gall weevil lumps, if broken open, will be found to be hollow and quite likely to contain the small white maggot of the weevil.

CLUSTER CUPS A kind of rust disease which attacks gooseberries and occasionally red and black currants. A rather similar disease is also found on violas. The name refers to the orange or yellow blister-like swellings which appear on the leaves and, in gooseberries, also on fruits and occasionally young stems as well. Affected leaves or fruits should be picked off and burned and plants sprayed with Bordeaux mixture or zineb. As the fungus which causes gooseberry cluster cups can also be found on sedges, it is a good plan to drain bogs and other damp places in or near the garden.

COCKCHAFER, see Chafer

COCKROACH These flat deep brown or dark grey beetle-like insects once common in old houses may prove troublesome in the greenhouse for they eat seeds, seedlings and the young leaves and stems of plants. Proprietary cockroach traps may be purchased and should be used according to manufacturers' instructions. Cockroaches can also be trapped in jam jars sunk into the soil so that their rims are just level with the surface and then half filled with beer or treacle diluted with water. Cockroaches can also be poisoned with powdered borax mixed with an equal bulk of castor sugar.

CODLING MOTH This moth appears from June to August and lays its eggs on the young fruits of apple trees. From these eggs small white caterpillars hatch out and eat their way into the fruits, feeding on the flesh and producing a considerable cavity which may later become infected with the fungus causing brown rot disease. The damage caused by codling moth caterpillar is very similar to that caused by the larva of the apple sawfly, but the two may be distinguished by the fact that the sawfly attack usually starts in late May or early June and causes the fruits to fall while they are still immature, whereas the codling moth attack starts about a month later and fruits may

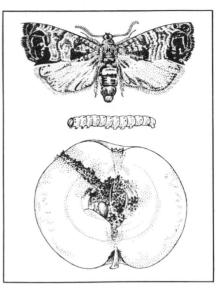

Codling moth, larva and damage

continue to develop to full size and ripeness despite the fact that there are caterpillars inside them. Moreover, an unpleasant smell is emitted from the holes produced by the sawfly larvae but not from the holes produced by the codling moth caterpillars. A codling moth caterpillar has eight legs whereas the sawfly larva has ten.

The best preventive is to spray with derris, carbaryl, malathion or arsenate of lead in mid-June and again in early July. Where attacks have been severe a precautionary spray may also be given in mid-May or, more exactly, as soon as the petals have fallen. Arsenate of lead is extremely poisonous and so is little used in private gardens today.

COLCHICINE A very poisonous drug obtained from the colchicum and sometimes used in plant breeding. In very minute doses it has the effect of producing abnormal growth, occasionally growths with more than the normal number of chromosomes. Some tetraploids (plants with double the normal number of chromosomes) have been artificially produced by colchicine treatment. The method usually employed is to soak seeds for a few hours in a dilute solution of colchicine. An alternative method is to treat buds that are just starting into growth, or the growing tips of seedlings soon after germination. An overdose will kill the seedling of the plant and even when a correct dose is given there is no guarantee that any useful mutation will result. The concentration and dosage at which colchicine should be used varies from one species of plant to another, and only by experiment can the correct rates be ascertained. As an indication, however, seedlings of flax have responded to a 48-hour treatment in a 0.1 per cent. solution of colchicine, while dwarf beans have responded to a 2-hour treatment in a 0.5 per cent. solution.

COLLAR That part of a plant where the stem or stems join the roots. With some plants it is important to keep the collar at soil level.

COLLAR ROT A general name given to various diseases which attack plants at the collar. The damping-off disease which attacks seedlings is really a form of collar rot and, in fact, when the fungus which causes damping-off attacks older plants it is referred to as collar rot and not as damping-off. These diseases are caused by soil-borne fungi and soil sterilization prior to planting or sowing provides a considerable measure of protection. Such sterilization may be carried out either with heat or with a chemical such as formaldehyde (see Sterilization). As a rule once collar rot fungi have attacked a plant no remedy is possible, but the fungus can sometimes be prevented from spreading to other nearby plants by watering the soil around these with Cheshunt compound, soluble copper, thiram or captan.

COLLOID A name given to a substance which is in a colloidal state, intermediate between a solution and a suspension. In a solution of common salt (sodium chloride) in water, the salt is dissociated into sodium ions and chloride ions, which are kept in solution by electrochemical forces. In a suspension of chalk (calcium carbonate), the particles are undissolved and eventually will settle, merely by force of gravity. In a colloid, the particles, although not dissociated, are so small that they remain in suspension. Colloids need not necessarily consist of a solid in a liquid. Glues and jellies are colloids (a liquid in a solid – colloid is derived from a Greek word meaning glue), so are smokes (a solid in a gas), aerosols (a liquid in a gas), emulsion (a liquid in a liquid) and most coloured glass (a solid in a solid).

Most of the humus in the soil is present in colloidal condition and it is in this state that it is most suitable as a medium for the growth of bacteria; in fact, the provision of an adequate supply of colloids in the soil is an important element in maintaining soil fertility. Usually this is achieved by working in dung, leafmould, peat and other humus-forming substances, but various substitutes have been recommended including alginates obtained from seaweed.

Some insecticides and fungicides are prepared in colloidal form and it is claimed that because of their extremely fine texture they can be dispersed more evenly and will form a thinner, more continuous film on the surfaces of stems and leaves than similar chemicals prepared in the form of powder or pastes.

COLLOIDAL COPPER A name given to certain proprietary preparations of copper used as fungicides. They have the merit of mixing very readily with water and pro-ducing a very thin and even film on the leaves or stems on which they are sprayed. Colloidal copper can be used to control most of the diseases for which Bordeaux mixture is also applicable.

COLLOIDAL SULPHUR A name given to certain proprietary preparations of sulphur used as fungicides. They mix readily with water and produce a very thin and even film of sulphur on leaves and stems. Colloidal sulphur may be used for most of the purposes for which lime sulphur is applicable. These include the control of apple and pear scab, mildews and red spider mite.

COLORADO BEETLE A serious pest of potatoes in many places but not established in the British Isles. The $\frac{1}{2}$-in. long beetle is yellow with black longitudinal stripes and the grub is reddish yellow. Both feed on the leaves of potatoes and are capable of stripping the plants. All cases of infestation must immediately be reported to the Ministry of Agriculture, Fisheries and Food.

COLUMN Botanically this term is used for the column-like outgrowth which, in the flowers of orchids, carries the anthers and stigmas. It is also sometimes applied to the tube-like structure caused by the union of the stamens surrounding the pistils in flowers of the mallow family, e.g. hollyhocks and sidalceas.

COMPOSITE A member of the daisy family in which many small individual flowers or florets are united in one head. See Compound Flower.

COMPOST This word is used by gardeners in two quite distinct ways. A compost heap is a heap composed of garden refuse of one kind and another, such as grass clippings, soft hedge trimmings, vegetable leaves and so on, possibly with the addition of dung and straw which will rot down and provide suitable material for digging into the soil. Compost is also the term employed by the gardener for all kinds of soil mixtures used for rearing seedlings or growing pot plants.

Compost heaps are of many different kinds and many theories exist as to the way they should be treated. On two points, however, most gardeners appear to be in agreement; one that the compost heap should be reasonably well aerated, the other that adequate, but not excessive, moisture must be present.

In order to ensure proper aeration, the heap should not be too wide or high, though it can be of any convenient length. The usual recommendation is that heaps should not be more than 3 ft. wide or 3 ft. high when first built – they are likely to sink considerably as they rot. Some experts also like to make holes in the heap with a pointed stick after a few weeks to let in further air.

Decay is brought about by the action of fungi and bacteria and as the bacteria require abundant supplies of nitrogen as food, the rate of decay can, as a rule, be increased by supplying some readily available nitrogen. This may be done by sprinkling the refuse as it is placed on the heap with a nitrogenous fertilizer such as sulphate of ammonia or Nitro-chalk or by placing layers of rich, fresh, animal manure between the layers of garden refuse. There are a number of proprietary preparations on the market which have the same effect of accelerating decay. Some compost users believe that herbal extracts are valuable in assisting decay and keeping the compost sweet.

Acids are produced as by-products of decay and too great an accumulation of acid will arrest decay. This danger can be avoided by including some lime in the heap, either powdered chalk or limestone or a fertilizer or dressing containing lime, such as Nitro-chalk. It should be noted that chalk or lime must not be brought into direct contact with sulphate of ammonia or fresh dung or animal manure of any kind or ammonia will be liberated and nitrogen lost as ammonia gas. If any of these are to be used with lime they should be kept to alternate layers, one layer being sprinkled with fertilizer or manure, the next with lime or chalk, then back to fertilizer or manure and so on until the heap is completed.

Ordinary green refuse, such as grass clippings and vegetable leaves, contain sufficient moisture, but dry refuse, such as bracken and straw, will need to be watered as it is built into the heap. Some gardeners like to turn their compost heaps after a period of three weeks or a month and, when doing so, usually water any parts which appear dry. They also advocate that the outer portions of the heap should be turned inwards and the inside brought out to achieve an even rate of rotting.

Refuse of all kinds decays most readily and satisfactorily in a fairly warm temperature and damp atmosphere. In consequence, decay will be more rapid in spring and autumn than in winter and will also be rapid in summer if the heap is placed out of the direct rays of the sun which otherwise may dry it too much.

Bins can be used to hold the decaying refuse; these are certainly convenient and clean, but care must be taken to see that there is ample provision for aeration, which can be done by making the sides of the bin of slats or boards spaced a little apart.

If compost is exposed for long to rain, much of its nutrient value may be lost by leaching. Therefore if the compost has to be stored it is desirable that it should be kept in an open-sided shed or some similar kind of shelter.

Sieving the loam which is to be used in potting or seed composts

Opinions differ as to precisely how long compost should be kept before it is in ideal condition for digging into the soil. Certainly it should be decayed to such an extent that the individual ingredients of which it is composed can no longer be distinguished. Some experts advise keeping it until it is a rich brown colour throughout, but others contend that by this stage there has usually been a considerable loss of plant food. It is probable that in warm weather soft refuse will take at least two months to decay, but in winter it may take five or six months. The harder the refuse, the slower the process of decay.

Soil composts for the cultivation of seedlings and pot plants were at one time of many diverse kinds as it was believed that quite different mixtures were required for plants of differing character of growth. Extensive research work carried out by the John Innes Horticultural Institution has shown that it is possible to accommodate practically all the plants commonly grown in gardens and greenhouses in a few standard mixtures.

The John Innes recommendations centre round three basic composts – one for seed, one for pot plants and one for cuttings. In all these mixtures, three ingredients figure prominently: loam, which should be of good quality without free lime, but not too acid (pH 6.5 is ideal) and neither too heavy nor too light; peat, which must be fibrous or granular and reasonably free from fine dust, and sand which must be very coarse and sharp, ranging in particle size up to $\frac{1}{8}$ in. It is recommended that the loam, prior to use, should always be sterilized, preferably by being steamed at a temperature of 93°C. for 20 minutes.

The seed mixture is prepared as follows:
2 parts by loose bulk of medium loam
1 part by loose bulk of peat
1 part by loose bulk of sand

To each bushel of this mixture is added:
$1\frac{1}{2}$ oz. superphosphate of lime
and
$\frac{3}{4}$ oz. either finely ground chalk or finely ground limestone
One of the unique features of the mixtures is the inclusion of fertilizers. Previous to the experimental work at the John Innes Horticultural Institution, it was generally believed that fertilizers could not be used in seed mixtures without danger of injury to the tender roots of seedlings.

The loam used in this seed compost will probably have to be sieved but it is undesirable to use a sieve with too fine a mesh. One with a $\frac{1}{2}$-in. mesh will serve for most seed composts except those which are to be used for very small seeds such as those of meconopsis and begonias.

The standard John Innes potting compost is prepared with:
7 parts by loose bulk loam
3 parts peat
2 parts sand
Here again chemicals are added. A special mixture is prepared as follows:
2 parts by weight hoof and horn meal
2 parts superphosphate of lime
1 part sulphate of potash
This is added to the compost at the rate of 4 oz. to each bushel and $\frac{3}{4}$ oz. of finely ground chalk or ground limestone to the bushel is also added.

This standard mixture will suit almost all greenhouse plants. With some plants, particularly vigorous growing types which have progressed beyond the 4-in. pot, it has been found necessary to double the dose of fertilizers and chalk or limestone, 8 oz. instead of 4 oz. of the first and $1\frac{1}{2}$ oz. of the second being used to the bushel. For very sturdy plants grown in pots above 8 in. in diameter, a treble dose of fertilizer and chalk or limestone is used, namely 12 oz. and $2\frac{1}{4}$ oz. to the bushel respectively. These three mixtures,

one with a single or 4 oz. dose of fertilizer, one with a double or 8 oz. dose and the third with a treble or 12 oz. dose, are often known respectively as John Innes potting composts No. 1, No. 2 and No. 3 or J.I.P. 1, J.I.P. 2 and J.I.P. 3.

These composts are not suitable for lime-hating plants such as azaleas and many heathers for which the John Innes seed compost should be used but with $\frac{3}{4}$ oz. flowers of sulphur in place of the $\frac{3}{4}$ oz. of ground chalk or limestone.

When preparing loam for potting composts it is even more important than when preparing seed composts not to sieve finely; in fact when dealing with big plants in pots of 6 in. size or over, the sieve may usually be discarded altogether and the loam prepared simply by breaking it up with the fingers. Even when dealing with much smaller plants, a sieve with a $\frac{1}{2}$-in. mesh will usually meet all requirements and the loam should be rubbed through the sieve so that as much as possible of the fibre passes into the potting compost. Finely sieved soils lacking in fibre will bind badly.

The compost recommended by the John Innes Horticultural Institution as a rooting medium for cuttings is composed of:
1 part by loose bulk of medium loam
2 parts of peat
1 part of coarse sand
No fertilizers are added to this mixture.

Soilless composts Since these John Innes composts were devised and proved successful many other seed and potting composts have been made up, some of which dispense with soil altogether as being the most difficult ingredient to standardize and the one most likely to introduce diseases, pests or weed seeds. Some of these are based on peat, sand and fertilizers, some on peat and vermiculite and some on peat and fertilizers only. Highly satisfactory results are obtained with all types but rather different techniques must be adopted in potting and aftercare, mainly little or no firming of the compost and less frequent watering. All the same, care must be taken not to allow peat composts to become really dry as it is then very difficult to get them moist again.

COMPOUND This term is used by botanists to describe leaves, flowers or fruits which are composed of two or more similar parts. Thus a rose has a compound leaf composed of several leaflets joined to a common stalk.

COMPOUND FLOWER A flower which consists of a number of separate florets, or small flowers, united in one head as in the daisy family, *Compositae*, and also in the teasel or scabious family, *Dipsaceae*.

CONE The clustered flowers or fruits of conifers. The flowers are unisexual and the female clusters develop into the typical scaly, and usually hard, cones which open to discharge the seeds they contain.

CONIFER Literally any tree which bears cones, familiar examples of which are the various pines, spruces, firs and cedars. However, in gardens the term is usually expanded to include the whole class of *Coniferae*, which includes many trees and shrubs that do not produce the typical cones, e.g. yew, ginkgo and podocarpus.

CONSERVATORY A greenhouse, usually attached to a dwelling house, and forming a part of it. Conservatories were popular features of the larger Victorian houses and were often very extensive structures which provided an annex to the drawing room or ballroom. They were used for the display of plants which had been brought to maturity elsewhere, usually in a greenhouse of more utilitarian design, and also for the cultivation of plants often grown in beds within the conservatory. The modern equivalent of the conservatory is often called a house extension.

CONTAINER-GROWN PLANTS Many plants, including small specimens of shrubs and trees, are grown by nurserymen for sale in containers from which they can be transplanted to the garden with a minimum of root disturbance. In consequence, provided the plants are subsequently watered in dry weather until they are properly established, they can be planted at any time of the year when soil conditions are suitable. The containers may be tins, pots of various kinds or quite thin polythene bags. Before being sold plants should be sufficiently established within the container to permit this to be removed without the soil falling off the roots. All containers, except those made of com-

pressed peat, sawdust or treated paper, must be removed before planting and care should be taken to do this without damaging the roots or disturbing the soil. The plants should then be planted in the ordinary way and well watered in if the soil is dry. Trees and shrubs may require staking until they become established.

COPPER Formulations of copper oxide, copper oxychloride and possibly other copper compounds are sold as fungicides for use against a variety of plant diseases. All should be used according to label instructions. They have much the same range of effectiveness as Bordeaux mixture.

COPPER–LIME DUST A fungicide which is obtained as a dry dust ready for application. It may be used as substitute for Bordeaux mixture.

COPPER NAPHTHENATE A chemical sold under trade names as a wood preservative. It is considerably more efficient than creosote and has the additional merit of being harmless to plants so that it can be used with safety on seed boxes, wooden frames, greenhouse stagings and so on. It is a liquid which can be applied to wood with a paintbrush or may be sprayed on. The normal colour is a bluish-green, but specially prepared colourless copper naphthenate can be obtained and it can also be obtained combined with a brown stain.

COPPER SULPHATE (Sulphate of copper) This is popularly known as bluestone or sometimes as blue vitriol. It is one of the most powerful fungicides in the gardener's possession, but it can seldom be used by itself because of the severe scorching effect it has on leaves and tender shoots. Occasionally a simple copper sulphate spray

is recommended for winter use on woody plants, notably roses which have suffered from black spot disease, but care must be taken to delay application until all leaves have fallen. The recommended strength for this is 1 oz. of copper sulphate to each gallon of water. It is more generally used in combination with some alkaline substance such as lime or washing soda, which will neutralize its acidity, and so make it safe for application to plants in leaf. Mixtures of this character are described under the headings Bordeaux mixture and Burgundy mixture. Copper sulphate is also sometimes used as a weedkiller. It is very effective against broad-leaved weeds and can be used either dry, as fine powder at the rate of 4 oz. per sq. yd. or, more economically, in solution at 4 oz. per gallon of water – a gallon to 4 or 5 sq. yd. Of course in this state it must not be allowed to fall on garden plants or crops as it will kill these as readily as it kills weeds.

Copper sulphate is sometimes used to clear ponds of green scum, blanket weed and other algae. It is not a very safe method as it is very easy to kill all water plants and fish by giving a slight overdose. The correct quantity to use is 23 grains to a thousand gallons of water. The copper sulphate may be placed in a small muslin bag tied to a fishing rod, and dragged through the water until it is dissolved.

CORDATE Heart shaped; a botanical term applied, as a rule, to leaves which have a pair of rounded lobes at the base.

CORDON Any plant which would normally branch but is restricted to a single stem (or, occasionally, two or three stems) by pruning, pinching or other cultural methods. The term is most commonly applied in gardens to fruit trees and sweet peas. For fruit trees cordon training provides a method of growing many varieties in a comparatively small space. It is necessary that the trees should be grown on dwarfing stocks, otherwise it will be extremely difficult to keep them to the cordon form without destroying fruitfulness. In view of the absence of true dwarfing stocks for plums and sweet cherries, cordon cultivation is not recommended for these fruits, nor is it advised for Morello cherries, peaches or nectarines, all of which fruit most freely on young growth which is largely removed under cordon cultivation. Cordon treatment has proved extremely successful for some varieties of apple and pear when worked on suitable stocks such as Malling 7 or Malling 9 for apples, or Quince C for pears. The usual method is to train the main stem obliquely, at first at a fairly steep angle, but gradually at a more acute angle, the trees being lowered a little annually as they increase in length. By this method a greater length of stem can be obtained while still keeping the whole tree within arm's reach from ground level.

A modern type of conservatory

Cordon training is a useful way of growing fruit trees in a small garden

Many methods of pruning have been recommended for cordon-trained fruit trees. One of the simplest and most successful consists in a combination of summer and winter pruning as follows. Each summer, towards the end of July or early in August, all side growths (laterals) from main stems are shortened to a length of five well-developed leaves. In November, these summer-pruned side shoots are further shortened to two or three buds. Young shoots from fruiting spurs are shortened to two leaves in summer and, if they grow again, are cut to one bud in autumn or winter. Only one leading growth is retained to each tree and this is left unpruned until the tree reaches the maximum desired length, which may be as much as 12 ft. in the case of very obliquely trained trees. After this the leader is cut right out in November and if further leaders form, these are cut out in succeeding autumns.

A modification of this system which has proved successful with some rather vigorous varieties, such as the apple Laxton's Superb, is to carry out all the pruning in summer, usually during the first fortnight in August. At this time, all side shoots are cut back to the basal rosette of leaves, roughly a length of ¾ in. from the base. No autumn pruning is carried out at all and the same treatment as in the former system is given to the leaders.

Cordon apple and pear trees can be planted as close as 2 ft. apart in the rows, but the rows themselves should be at least 7 ft. apart. It is desirable that the rows should run approximately north and south so that each side receives some direct sunlight. There is some difference of opinion as to whether oblique cordons should slope to north or south, but in fact it does not seem to make much difference which way they slope.

The cordon method of training is occa-sionally used for gooseberries, though instead of these being restricted to one stem, they are usually allowed to form two, in which case they are known as double cordons, and occasionally carry three stems, when they are known as triple cordons; moreover, gooseberries are usually grown vertically and not obliquely. The system of pruning is similar to that employed for apples. Red and white currants may be grown in the same way, usually as single-stemmed vertical cordons.

Another variation of the cordon system of training fruit trees is that known as horizontal cordons. In this the stem is bent over about one foot above the ground level and then trained horizontally and sometimes two stems are taken in opposite directions. Horizontal apple or pear cordons may be seen in some old gardens as edgings to paths, but are seldom planted nowadays.

With sweet peas, a cordon system of cultivation is almost invariably used when flowers of large size and on long stems are required for cutting and exhibition. The point is pinched out of the seedling sweet pea when it is 2 or 3 in. in height. As a result two or three side shoots will form. The best of these is retained and the others are rubbed out. After this the plant is not permitted to branch again. The stem retained is trained vertically up a bamboo or suitable support. All side shoots which form are rubbed or pinched out. Even the tendrils with which the sweet pea would normally cling to the support are removed so that the whole of the strength of the plant is concentrated upon the production of one stem. Because the tendrils are removed it is necessary to tie the stem to the support. Sweet peas grown in this very artificial manner are much more liable to suffer from nutritional and other physiological troubles than are those grown naturally, in fact it is difficult to grow certain varieties as cordons. Nevertheless, it is the only system of cultivation by which really fine flowers can be obtained. Because all the growth goes into one stem, cordon sweet peas often grow very tall. A common practice is to untie the plants when they reach the top of 7- or 8-ft. canes, lay them along the ground for 3 or 4 ft. and then train them up a cane further along the line, a process known as layering.

CORM A storage organ differing from a true bulb in being composed mainly of thickened stem and therefore in being solid throughout and not made up of separate layers or scales. Such scales as it possesses are thin and papery and serve only for protection. Familiar examples of corms are gladiolus and crocus, which may be compared with the sectioned bulb of onion and daffodil or the scaled bulb of lily. The tiny corms that form round the parent corms are known as cormels or cormlets, page 284.

Sweet peas being grown on a cordon system. When the plants reach the top of the stakes, untie them, lay them along the ground and then train them up a cane further along the row

As gladiolus plants begin to die down, the corms should be lifted and stored in a frost-proof place for the winter. The tiny cormlets can also be grown on in the spring

COROLLA The inner leafy whorl of a flower composed of the petals. It may be contrasted with the outer whorl or calyx which is composed of sepals. In most flowers it is the corolla which provides the display, the calyx being less showy and of a more protective character. However, there are occasions when the calyx is more showy than the corolla, as for example in clematis, and there are other flowers in which corolla and calyx contribute equally to the showiness of the bloom, as in the lily.

CORONA Botanically any appendage which separates the corolla of a flower from its anthers, but in gardens the term is almost exclusively reserved for the cup, crown or trumpet of a narcissus (daffodil).

CORROSIVE SUBLIMATE, see Mercuric Chloride

CORYMB A botanical term for a flat-topped or nearly flat-topped flower cluster, in which the stalks of the various flowers which compose it do not start from a common point as in an umbel. The youngest flowers are in the centre. A familiar example of a flower cluster of this type is to be found in the yarrow – *Achillea millefolium*.

COT SPLIT, see Bud Stages

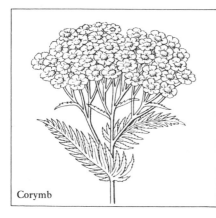

Corymb

COTYLEDON A seed leaf, of which there is only one in monocotyledons and two in dicotyledons. The seed leaves are usually the first to appear, though in some plants, e.g. pea, they remain below ground. As a rule they differ considerably in character from the leaves which appear later. Usually they are much simpler in structure and are generally completely undivided and regular in outline. Cotyledons are important to the gardener because their state of development is an indication of the best time at which seedlings should be pricked out. Also the gardener should learn to distinguish the cotyledons of cultivated plants from those of weeds, so that he may destroy the latter at an early stage before they have had time to rob the garden plant seedlings of food. It used to be considered that seedlings should not be pricked off until they had formed at least their first true leaves beyond the cotyledons, but more recent research has suggested that many seedlings pricked out in the cotyledon stage give the most satisfactory results.

CRANE FLIES The long-legged flies, often known as daddy-long-legs, which may be seen in great numbers in the summer and are the adult stage of the insect, the larvae of which are known as leather jackets (q.v.). Though crane flies themselves do not harm plants, leather jackets feed on the roots of grass and other plants and are most destructive.

CRENATE A botanical term applied to leaves the margins of which have shallow, more or less rounded teeth.

CREOSOTE A coal derivative which is much used as a wood preservative. Creosote is a brown, free-flowing liquid which can be applied with a paintbrush or can be sprayed on. Alternatively wood may be allowed to soak in a creosote bath. As a preservative it is not as effective as copper naphthenate and suffers from the further drawback that it

may scorch plants very severely and gives off fumes which have the same effect. Moreover, in warm weather wood that has been creosoted many months previously and has become quite dry may, nevertheless, still give off sufficient fumes to do damage to nearby plants.

CRESYLIC ACID A chemical used for sterilization of soil. It is not as effective against fungi as formalin, but it is more effective against some insects, including soil caterpillars and the larvae of chafer beetles and certain kinds of eelworms. See Sterilization.

CRICKETS These familiar insects, closely allied to grasshoppers and cockroaches, can cause damage in greenhouses in which they may attack seedlings of young plants in much the same manner as cockroaches. Remedies are the same as for cockroaches (q.v.). Crickets may also be trapped in inverted flower pots placed on sticks to raise them an inch or so above soil level.

CRISTATE A term meaning crested or cockscomb-like and applied horticulturally to certain abnormal, usually fasciated, forms of plants with flowers, leaves or stems of this kind. Some are highly prized by gardeners for their beauty or oddity. *Celosia argentea cristata* has a flower of this kind and is popularly known as Cockscomb. Many ferns have forms with crested leaves and there are numerous cacti in which the whole plant is cristate.

CROCKS Broken flower pots which are used by gardeners as drainage material in clay flower pots, pans and seed boxes. The term crocking is used to describe this process of placing drainage material in containers of one kind or another. The usual method of crocking a pot is to place one rather large crock, convex side upwards, over the drainage hole in the bottom of the pot. This is covered with a layer of smaller pieces of crock and this in turn is covered with some of the coarse material left in the sieve when preparing potting composts or with a wad of sphagnum moss. Crocking is only important when using fairly close-textured or heavily firmed composts through which moisture moves with some difficulty. It is not as a rule necessary with modern, open-textured composts, particularly those containing large quantities of sphagnum peat, coarse sand or vermiculite and is hardly ever used nowadays in commercial glass-house nurseries. It is unnecessary to crock plastic pots or other plastic containers.

CROSS-BRED, see Hybrid

CROSS-FERTILIZATION A flower is said to be fertilized when pollen reaches the ovules and unites with them to start the formation of seeds. It is said to be self-fertilized or self-pollinated when the pollen comes from the same plant as that producing the ovules and cross-fertilized (cross-pollinated) when the pollen comes from another plant. It should be noted that cross-fertilization does not mean merely the transference of pollen from one flower to another, but from the flower of one plant to that of another plant.

Cross-fertilization is useful to the gardener because it often enables him to combine the characteristics of two different varieties. It is also sometimes of supreme importance to the fruit grower because certain varieties of fruit do not crop, or only crop very sparsely, when fertilized with their own pollen, though they crop freely when fertilized with the pollen of another variety of the same kind of fruit. Varieties of this character are said to be self-sterile or partly self-sterile according to the degree of their inability to produce fruit from their own pollen. By contrast, trees which will produce full crops when fertilized with their own pollen are known as self-fertile varieties.

Cross-fertilization is sometimes favoured by nature and some flowers have elaborate methods of ensuring that they do not become fertilized with their own pollen but only with that from other flowers.

The hybridizer, who makes use of cross-fertilization for the purpose of breeding new plants, must take certain precautions if he is to be sure of his results. In the first place, the bloom which is to bear seed should be emasculated at an early stage to prevent any possibility of its being fertilized with its own pollen. Emasculation is achieved by removing the anthers, which can usually be done by carefully opening the flower before it is fully expanded and drawing out the anthers with a pair of small forceps. After this the bloom should be covered in some way to prevent chance pollination from other flowers by wind or insects. Grease-proof paper or muslin bags are often used for this purpose. The pollen from the flower selected as a male parent must be collected when fully ripe – a condition in which it becomes dry and powdery and is easily distributed. It may be collected with a camel-hair brush and transferred direct to the stigma of the flower selected as a female parent or, if there is much cross-pollination to be done, the pollen may be collected in a small box or glass phial from which it can be taken as required with a brush. If more than one variety of plant is being used as a pollen parent, care must be taken to clear the brush entirely of pollen grains between the applications of each variety of pollen. The most effective method of doing this is to dip the brush into a bottle containing alcohol or methylated spirits after which the brush must be allowed to dry. The bag used to cover the seed-producing flower must, of course, be removed for the purpose of pollination, but should be replaced immediately afterwards and left in position until the seed pod or fruit begins to form, after which it can be discarded with safety.

As a rule, cross-fertilization is only successful with plants that are closely related. Varieties of the same species can usually be cross-fertilized without difficulty though, as already remarked, this is not always so with fruit trees. Plants belonging to different species, but of the same genus, can sometimes be cross-fertilized, but it is seldom that plants belonging to different genera can be successfully cross-fertilized. Gardeners sometimes hear tales of dahlias being crossed with chrysanthemums, tulips with daffodils and so on. These can be dismissed as sheer nonsense.

CROSSING, see Cross-fertilization and Hybrid

CROSS-POLLINATION, see Cross-fertilization

CROTCH The point at which the main trunk of a tree divides into branches.

CROWN The upper part of the rootstock from which the shoots grow. The term is usually confined to plants with a fairly fleshy or woody crown as in peony, lupin, delphinium and rhubarb. The term is also occasionally used loosely to cover the whole of a root, particularly of a root lifted for forcing, for example, rhubarb and seakale.

CROWN BUD, see Bud and Stopping

CROWN GALL Curious tuber-like outgrowths which occur on the stems or roots of many different kinds of plant. They are particularly common on fruit trees and roses and on the former sometimes attain a great size. The name crown gall refers to the fact that these galls frequently occur at the crown of the plant (where stem joins roots) but they are by no means confined to this position. The swellings are caused by infection by a bacterium, but as a rule the disease does not appear to have any markedly harmful effect. It is disfiguring rather than dangerous. No satisfactory remedy has been discovered but when the galls occur on stems it is best to cut them off and burn them. If they occur on the crown it is very difficult to do this without injuring the plant and there the galls are best ignored.

CROWN ROT A disease which is peculiar to rhubarb and which attacks the plant at the crown causing this to turn brown and become decayed. The early symptoms are weak stems and dull coloured leaves. If the plants are examined more closely, it will usually be found that the crowns can be very easily knocked off owing to the decay which has already started. The disease is caused by a bacterium. No remedy is known; all affected plants should be burnt.

CRUCIFER Any plant belonging to the family *Cruciferae*. The name has reference to the four petals arranged in the form of a cross which is characteristic of the flowers of all plants in this family, e.g. wallflower, arabis and cabbage.

CUCKOO SPIT A popular name for a small insect pest which attacks many different kinds of plant. It is also known as frog hopper but must not be confused with the frog fly which is a totally different insect. The adult cuckoo spit insect is a bug (q.v.), not unlike a tiny grasshopper in appearance, pale yellow in colour, which jumps vigorously if disturbed. The larva, which does most of the damage, is also pale yellow or greenish, but it does not jump and is, in fact, comparatively slow in all its movements. It

Seakale crowns being boxed up for forcing. This is usually done in winter

lives by sucking sap from the plant and obtains protection by covering itself with a mass of froth. As the insect is most troublesome in late spring, the cuckoo season, it was erroneously associated by country people with the cuckoo, hence the name cuckoo spit. The insect can be killed with nicotine, malathion or BHC but any of these insecticides should be mixed with an efficient wetter and should be applied in the form of a very forceful spray to break through the frothy covering and come directly into contact with the insects. When it occurs on a small scale, hand picking is the most effective remedy.

CULTIVAR A botanical term for a variety that has either arisen or is maintained in cultivation as distinct from a variety that occurs naturally in the wild.

CUP, see Corona

CURD The 'head' of a cauliflower or broccoli.

CUTTING Any portion of stem, leaf or root separated from a plant and prepared and treated so that it will grow into a complete new plant. A cutting may be contrasted with a division which is also a piece separated from a parent plant and prepared and treated so that it grows into a complete new plant, but at the time of separation is not a single portion of stem, leaf or root, but a composite portion containing roots, shoots or buds. The cutting may also be contrasted with the layer which resembles it in many respects but is treated in such a way that it produces roots before and not after its separation from the parent plant.

Cuttings may be of many different kinds and can be prepared from different portions of a plant according to its nature and kind. Cuttings can be classified as stem cuttings, leaf cuttings and root cuttings. Leaf and root cuttings need not be further differentiated, but there are so many different kinds of stem cuttings that it is convenient to divide these into soft, half-ripe and hard-wood or naked cuttings, and to further sub-divide each of these into nodal, internodal and heel cuttings or slips.

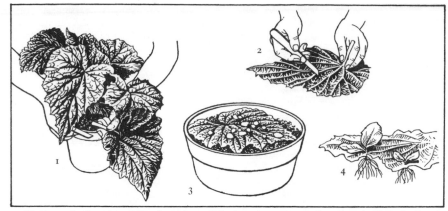

1. *Taking a leaf cutting of Rex begonia.* 2. *Slit the veins at intervals and,* 3, *hold the leaf to the soil with wire pins or pebbles.* 4. *Roots and plantlets form from each incision*

Leaf Cuttings are used chiefly for propagating a few greenhouse plants, notably begonias, gloxinias, streptocarpus and saintpaulias. They may also be used for a few hardy plants such as ramondas and haberleas. For many of these no preparation is necessary, all that is required is to remove a well-developed leaf complete with its leaf stalk and press the latter into a bed of very sandy soil, or a mixture of sand and peat, in such a way that the lower surface of the leaf lies flat on the bed. With some large leaves, such as those of Rex begonias, it is convenient to peg the leaf firmly to the surface of the sand or compost with pieces of wire bent like hairpins. These pegs should be placed over the main veins. Also with these large and heavily veined leaves, it sometimes pays to slit the veins crosswise every inch or so. When this is done, roots are formed from every incision and new crowns or shoots may also appear at each incision, so that one leaf will give rise to several new plants. These leaf cuttings are usually kept in a fairly damp, close atmosphere, and for leaf cuttings of greenhouse plants, in a warm atmosphere as well, usually with bottom heat.

Bud Cuttings closely resemble leaf cuttings but each leaf is removed with a small portion of stem including a growth bud in the axil of the leaf stalk. No further preparation is required and the cutting is inserted with the bud and leaf stalk in the rooting material but

A rooted bud cutting of Camellia japonica

with the leaf itself clear. The cuttings are usually rooted in a close frame or under mist (see Mist Propagation). This is an excellent method of propagating camellias.

Root Cuttings are generally, though not invariably, used as a means of increase for plants which have fairly thick roots, for instance hollyhocks, anchusas, perennial stattice, verbascums, oriental poppies, romneyas, horseradish and seakale. It must not be assumed, however, that all plants with thick roots can be increased in this way, nor does it follow that because a plant has thin roots it cannot be propagated by root cut-

1. *Streptocarpus can be propagated from leaf cuttings*

2. *The leaf stalk and lower part of the leaf are inserted in a pot of sandy compost*

3. *Eventually roots and a small plant will develop at the base*

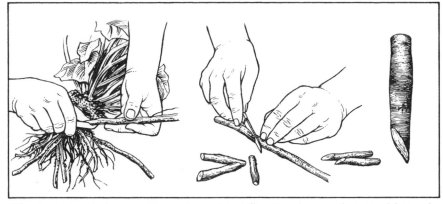

When preparing thick root cuttings it is usual to differentiate between the top and bottom by making a square cut at the top and a sloping one at the bottom.

tings, e.g. such cuttings can be used very effectively to increase phloxes and gaillardias, both of which have fibrous roots. As a rule root cuttings are taken while the plant is dormant, which means, generally, in winter. They are prepared by cutting the roots into sections, each from 1½ to 2 in. long. When taking cuttings of thick roots, it is desirable, though not essential, to keep them the right way up when they are inserted and, as it is difficult to tell one end of a root cutting from another, it is usual when preparing the cuttings to cut them squarely through at the top but to make a sloping cut at the base. Thinner cuttings are generally laid on their sides and so it is not necessary to distinguish one end from the other. The cuttings are placed in sandy soil or a mixture such as John Innes cutting compost (see page 281). The thick cuttings are simply pushed into the compost or into holes prepared with a dibber. The tops of the cuttings should be just beneath the surface of the compost. Thinner cuttings are strewn thinly on the compost and covered with a further half inch of compost. Root cuttings of most hardy plants can be kept in an unheated frame or greenhouse or even in a sheltered place out of doors. They will form buds and shoots in the spring and

will, in general, be ready for planting in a nursery bed by early summer. It may be noted that where phlox are suffering from eelworm attack, plants raised from root cuttings are usually free of the pest, which lives in the shoots and not in the roots.

Soft Stem Cuttings are those prepared early in the season of growth, while the shoots are still quite succulent. They provide a useful method of increasing a great many plants, including chrysanthemums, perpetual flowering carnations, pelargoniums, delphiniums and lupins. These cuttings are almost always of the nodal type, which means that they are severed at the base just below a node or joint. The method of preparation is to trim off the lower leaves with a sharp knife and cut the base of the cutting cleanly through immediately below a joint. The length of the completed cutting will depend on the character of the plant from which it is taken and may be anything from ¾ in. for plants with small shoots such as lobelia and ageratum, to 3 or 4 in. for plants with comparatively large shoots such as delphiniums, lupins and pelargoniums.

As cuttings of this type are very liable to lose moisture freely, it is essential to keep them in a fairly close, damp atmosphere and

to encourage them to form roots as quickly as possible. Under favourable conditions they may be rooted in three or four weeks. Treatment with rooting powder or liquid increases the rate and reliability of rooting (see Hormones). Soft cuttings are frequently inserted in a propagating case or box within the greenhouse, that is to say, a small frame or box with a closed lid, placed on the greenhouse staging. This can be half filled with peat or sand in which the pots or boxes containing the cuttings can be plunged. A very damp atmosphere can be maintained within such a propagating case and, if bottom heat can be applied, rooting will be effected very rapidly. Most soft stem cuttings may also be rooted very effectively under mist. See Mist Propagation.

Soft cuttings may be rooted in pure sand, vermiculite, peat, perlite or compost such as the John Innes cutting compost (see page 281). If pure sand, vermiculite or perlite are used, it is important to remove the cuttings to an ordinary compost containing soil directly they form roots, otherwise they will soon be starved. The cuttings must be inserted firmly to about a quarter their own depth and the rooting medium should be made firm round the base of each cutting. Usually a small wooden dibber or pointed stick is used, both to make the hole to receive the cutting and to firm the sand or compost round it. It is frequently recommended that when soft cuttings are inserted in earthenware pots or pans, they should be placed round the edge of these receptacles so that they are partly in contact with the earthenware, and it certainly seems that in this position they form roots more rapidly than when placed in the middle of the pot or pan.

At first, soft cuttings usually flag a little even when they are shaded from all strong sunshine, but in a suitably close atmosphere they will soon pick up. Directly roots are formed the cuttings will start to grow again, an indication that they are ready to be transferred to more normal growing conditions.

When propagating chrysanthemums, it is

1. Preparing a soft stem cutting of lupin. The base is cut just below a joint

2. Treatment with hormone rooting powder increases the rate of rooting

3. The cuttings are inserted in a propagating case

usually advised that soft cuttings should be prepared only from basal shoots growing direct from the roots and not from soft shoots coming from the old woody flower stems. For propagating perpetual flowering carnations, soft cuttings prepared from non-flowering side shoots appearing midway up the flowering stems are the most suitable. In this instance the shoots are pulled off where they join the main stem and no further preparation is needed beyond removal of basal leaves and the trimming of any strip of 'bark' which may have been removed with the cuttings. This is what is known as a heel cutting or slip.

Half-ripe Cuttings are those prepared from shoots or stems that have nearly completed their growth but have not yet become fully woody. They provide an important method of increasing many shrubby plants, including heathers. Half-ripe cuttings are usually taken in June, July and early August; they are often of the nodal type (i.e. severed at the base immediately below a joint) but some gardeners prefer to take heel cuttings (i.e. side shoots pulled away with a strip or heel of the main stem attached). In just a few instances internodal cuttings are taken. These are cuttings severed at the base midway between two joints and not just below a joint. Some gardeners believe that internodal cuttings of clematis root better than nodal cuttings, though there is not general agreement on this point.

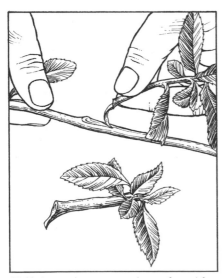

Half-ripe cuttings are sometimes taken with a heel of mature wood attached

Half-ripe cuttings are less succulent than soft cuttings and therefore less liable to lose moisture rapidly. Therefore they do not require quite as damp an atmosphere, though they are usually kept in a close frame or propagating case and usually respond well to mist (see Mist Propagation). Treatment with root-forming powders or liquids is helpful, see Hormones.

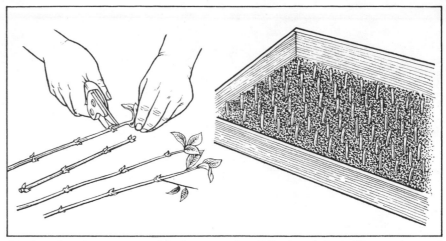

Hard-wood cuttings are prepared in the autumn from fully ripened shoots. They can be rooted in an unheated frame or out of doors

Rooting media are the same as for soft stem cuttings, and they are prepared in exactly the same way except that when cuttings are taken with a heel it is only necessary to trim off the ragged portions of this leaving the small lump of older wood to form the base of the cutting. As a rule half-ripe cuttings taken in midsummer will be rooted and ready for transference into pots or beds of freshly prepared soil by early autumn.

Hard-wood or naked cuttings are those which are prepared from fully ripened growth of the current year's production. They are taken at the end of the growing season usually, in the British Isles, in October or November. They provide an important method of increasing many shrubby plants including most soft fruits such as gooseberries and currants. As a rule they are nodal cuttings, though again some gardeners think that heel cuttings root more successfully.

Because of their ripe nature, hard-wood cuttings do not so readily lose moisture and therefore it is unnecessary and unwise to keep them in a close atmosphere or to try to force them to root very rapidly. Frequently they can be inserted out of doors without protection and this is the normal method employed with soft fruits and many hardy shrubs. With some cuttings, and particularly with those of evergreen trees and shrubs, it pays to give the cuttings the protection of an unheated frame, with the light used occasionally in severe weather or replaced by a screen of thin wood laths spaced a little apart so that air can circulate but some shelter is provided.

Hard-wood cuttings are as a rule considerably larger than either soft or half-ripe cuttings, and may be as much as one foot in length for many soft fruits and shrubs. With deciduous trees and shrubs, the leaves will already have fallen or be on the point of falling, and nothing further need be done about them, but when making hard-wood cuttings of evergreen plants, it is desirable to remove the lower leaves as for soft and half-ripe cuttings. If root-forming powders or liquids are used they should be of the special strength prepared for hard-wood cuttings (see Hormones). The cuttings should be inserted firmly 2 to 4 in. deep according to size. The usual method is to chop out a straight-backed trench 2 to 4 in. deep, in a sheltered place out of doors, scatter a little coarse sand in the bottom of this trench, place the cuttings upright in it, 2 or 3 in. apart, and replace the soil, pressing it firmly round the cutting with the foot. As a rule hard-wood cuttings, taken in the autumn, will not start to make roots until the following spring, and will not be ready for transplanting until the following autumn, that is approximately one year from the time they were taken.

Cuttings such as those of red and white currants and gooseberries, which are required on a leg, should have all buds removed from that part of the cutting which is in the soil and for a couple of inches above, to prevent sucker growth.

CUTWORMS An American term which has now been widely adopted in this country for those kinds of caterpillar which live in the soil. One of the most troublesome of these is the turnip moth caterpillar, while another is the caterpillar of the yellow underwing moth. Such caterpillars can be killed or driven away by dusting the surface soil with finely powdered naphthalene, with lindane or paradichlorbenzene and either hoeing or raking this in.

CYCLAMEN MITE, see Tarsonemid Mite

CYME A head of flowers in which the oldest flower ends the growth of the stem and younger ones come from one or more side shoots behind it, each in turn ending its growth. Where there are many branches the head is often in the shape of an inverted cone, with the oldest flower in the centre; where the stems are solitary the whole head may tend to curl up as in the borage family. In the pink family two branches usually occur at each forking. Compare with a raceme, a type of flower head in which the youngest flower ends the growth.

DADDY-LONG-LEGS A popular name for crane flies (q.v.).

DAISY GRUBBER, see Spud

DALAPON A selective weedkiller used mainly to kill grass, including couch grass. Provided reasonable care is taken in application it can be used around fruit trees and bushes, also around many ornamental trees and shrubs. It is purchased as a powder to be dissolved in water according to the manufacturers' instructions and applied as a spray or from a dribble bar. Care should be taken to prevent drift on to plants that are not to be killed.

DAMPING DOWN When plants are grown in greenhouses it is important to maintain the correct degree of moisture in the atmosphere. This will vary according to type of plant, e.g. cucumbers require very much more atmospheric moisture than do tomatoes. There are several ways in which moisture can be supplied to the atmosphere, but one of the most important is that known as damping down. This means that paths, stages and even the walls of the greenhouse are moistened. The degree and frequency of damping down will depend on the degree of moisture desired. For those plants which require a very humid atmosphere, it is usual to cover the stagings with gravel or coarse ashes as these hold moisture better than a solid staging of wood, brick or concrete. For the same reason, a soil or ash floor is better for moisture-loving plants than a floor made of concrete or bricks. In hot weather and for moisture-loving plants,

Damping down the path of a greenhouse

it may be necessary to damp down three or four times a day. The work is done either with a watering-can fitted with a fine rose, or with a syringe. It should be noted that the object of damping down is to wet the surroundings of plants and not the plants themselves. In the absence of adequate damping down, many plants will suffer from scorched foliage and serious attacks of red spider mite.

DAMPING-OFF A general name given to various diseases which affect seedlings at or near soil level causing the stems to decay and the whole seedling to topple over and die. All these diseases are caused by fungi but several quite distinct species are involved. However, the gardener need not attempt to distinguish between one kind and another as prevention and treatment are the same for all. The fungi are soil borne so soil sterization, either by heat or with a chemical

A box of seedlings affected by damping-off

such as formalin, will give reasonable protection. Damping-off tends to be prevalent where seedlings are overcrowded and with too little air and too much moisture, so thin sowing, early pricking out, careful watering and free ventilation are cultural points to be observed. If the disease does occur, its spread can usually be prevented by watering the soil and remaining seedlings with Cheshunt compound, captan or zineb and this treatment can also be used in advance as a preventive.

DAY LENGTH The ratio between the length of day and night has a controlling effect on the growth and flowering of many plants, a phenomenon known as photoperiodism. Some, such as the chrysanthemum, grow when days are long and nights short and flower when the days are short and the nights long. They are known as shortday plants and their growth (and hence height) and flowering time can be controlled by artificial manipulation of the day length. This is achieved by covering plants with a blackout for a period each day or by illuminating them fairly brilliantly (as, for example, with mercury vapour lamps) for a

period at night. By using these techniques and varieties of chrysanthemum specially bred to suit them it has proved possible to produce chrysanthemum flowers on a commercial scale throughout the year and also to produce flowers on dwarf plants.

Other plants, such as the fuchsia, flower when days are long and nights are short and are known as long-day plants. Sometimes they can be induced to flower by using artificial illumination at night and the most economical method of doing this seems to be to use the light to break the night into two more or less equal portions. In some instances quite short periods of comparatively low level illumination, for about $\frac{1}{2}$ to 1 hour with tungsten lamps, used in the middle of each night have proved sufficient, when combined with adequate temperatures, to promote winter or early spring flowering in plants that would not normally flower in temperate regions until summer.

DAZOMET A soil sterilizer used to kill eelworms and some soil-borne diseases. It is available as a dust to be sprinkled on the soil according to manufacturers' instructions (usually 1 lb. to 100 sq. ft.) and immediately worked in to a depth of about 1 ft. It can also be applied to potting soil (usual rate 7 oz. to each cu. yd.). The heap must be covered for three weeks after which it should be uncovered and turned occasionally for another four or five weeks. Nothing should be planted or sown in treated soil for eight weeks.

DD The abbreviation commonly used for the mixture dichloropropane-dichloropropene. This is a fluid used as a soil fumigant against the root-knot eelworm of tomatoes. The liquid is applied by injecting it into the soil with an instrument rather like a giant hypodermic syringe. It is used at rates varying from $2\frac{1}{4}$ to $3\frac{1}{2}$ lb. to 30 sq. yd. Injections are made to a depth of 8 in. and 12 in. apart and care should be taken in handling this chemical which has a highly irritating effect on the skin. Treatment is carried out on vacant ground at least six weeks before it is to be planted.

DEAD HEADING The removal of faded flower heads. It is an important operation in the cultivation of some very free-flowering rhododendrons as, if the flower heads are allowed to remain and carry seed, few flower buds are likely to be formed for the following year.

DECIDUOUS A name given to plants which lose their leaves in winter. It is particularly applied to trees and shrubs and may be contrasted with the term evergreen, which is applied to a plant which retains its leaves throughout the winter. Deciduous trees and shrubs are of many different kinds and may have little in common, but there is one important cultural point which applies to most of them, namely that they are best transplanted during the period when they are leafless or practically leafless, roughly from about the end of October to the end of March. For town planting deciduous plants have the advantage over evergreens, that they start afresh each year with a clean lot of leaves. The old leaves of evergreens are apt to get so coated with grime and soot that they are more of a liability than an asset to the plant.

DECUMBENT A botanical term used to describe stems which lie on the ground for part of their length and then turn upwards.

DEHISCENT A botanical term used to describe a seed pod or anther which splits open to discharge its contents.

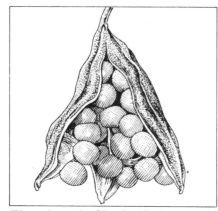

The seed capsule of Iris foetidissima is a good example of a dehiscent fruit

DEHORNING Shortening the main branch of a tree usually by cutting it back to a point at which another branch grows from it. This can be a useful method of restoring the vigour and at the same time reducing the size of old fruit trees. See Pruning.

DEMETON-S-METHYL A systemic insecticide used to kill aphids and red spider mites. It is poisonous to all warm-blooded animals, including man, and protective clothing must be worn when using it. It is a liquid for dilution with water according to manufacturers' instructions. No edible crop should be sprayed within three weeks of harvesting, it should not be applied to open blossom or be allowed to get into ponds and streams.

DENDROLOGY The study of trees.

DENITRIFICATION Loss of soil nitrogen usually due to bacterial activity. See Bacteria.

DENTATE A botanical term used to describe leaves which have rather coarsely toothed edges.

DERRIS An insecticide obtained from the roots of certain tropical plants. The active principle of derris is a chemical named rotenone and the effectiveness of any particular sample of derris will depend upon the percentage of rotenone it contains. Proprietary dust formulations may contain from 0.2 to 0.5 per cent. rotenone and wettable powders or liquid formulations from 1 to 6 per cent. rotenone. All should be used according to manufacturers' instructions. Derris is effective against most caterpillars, weevils, beetles and their larvae, slugworms, aphids, red spider mites and wasps.

Derris is very poisonous to fish but not to warm-blooded animals. It can be applied at any time of the year.

DIAZINON An insecticide used mainly to kill aphids, capsid bugs, thrips and red spider mites. It is poisonous to all warm-blooded animals including man. It should not be used on cucumbers or tomatoes in early spring. Diazinon is available as an aerosol, as a liquid and as a wettable powder for dilution with water when it must be kept agitated while being applied as a spray or it will settle out.

DIBBER (Dibble) A tool used for making holes in soil. Dibbers are of many sizes and types, from the small wooden dibbers about the thickness of an ordinary lead pencil, which are used for making holes into which cuttings are inserted, to the large steel or steel-shod dibbers as thick as a spade handle and a foot or more in length used for planting potatoes, bulbs, brassicas and so on.

There is no objection to the use of dibbers for inserting cuttings, but for planting large things, such as bulbs, potatoes and brassica seedlings many gardeners prefer to use a spade or trowel, because the dibber tends to consolidate the soil too much round the plant and may also make too pointed a hole, in which the potato or bulb will be suspended with an air space beneath. Nevertheless the planting of many seedlings can be done more rapidly with a dibber than with a trowel. All dibbers should have rounded rather than pointed tips. Small dibbers used for planting cuttings or pricking out seedlings are often made from hazel branches, whittled down and smoothed off.

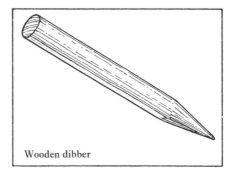

Wooden dibber

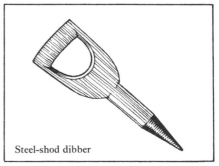

Steel-shod dibber

DICAMBA A selective weedkiller usually available only in a mixture with other weedkillers such as MCPA and mecoprop. It kills many broad-leaved weeds including clover and knotgrass and is used for weed control on lawns. Mixtures containing dicamba should be diluted with water according to manufacturers' instructions and applied as a spray or from a sprinkle bar, care being taken that the chemical does not drift on to plants that are not to be killed.

DICHLOBENIL A granular herbicide which acts through the soil and gives good long-term control of a large number of weeds. It is non-selective and at high rates of application it will kill all plant growth. At low rates it remains in the surface layer of soil where it kills small herbaceous plants and emerging seedlings without damaging deep-rooting fruit trees and bushes, shrubs, roses and hedges.

DICHLOFLUANID A fungicide used primarily for the control of botrytis in strawberries and other soft fruits and of black spot in roses. It should not be used on fruit within a fortnight of harvesting. It is available as a wettable powder to be stirred into water at the rate recommended by the manufacturers and applied as a spray.

DICLORAN A fungicide primarily used to control botrytis on lettuce and also tulip fire. It is available as a dust for direct application. Treated crops should not be harvested for at least three weeks.

DICOFOL A chemical used to kill red spider mites and their eggs. It is available as an aerosol and as a liquid for spraying. It should not be used when plants are exposed to strong sunshine and may injure young plants, particularly early in the year.

DICOTYLEDON A plant with two cotyledons or seed leaves in contrast to those which have only one cotyledon or seed leaf and are known as monocotyledons. The distinction is very important from the botanical viewpoint and provides one of the fundamental methods of grouping plants for classification.

DIDYMELLA A disease of tomatoes which causes a canker or decay of the stems. It is commonly known as tomato canker and is described under Canker.

DIE-BACK A general term applied to several quite different diseases which cause growths to die from the tips backwards. A familiar example occurs in roses. If a plant that is suffering from die-back is closely examined, it will be found to have a ring of dead bark either at the base of the particular stem that is dying or towards the base of the plant itself. It is this ring which is strangling the plant by preventing the proper flow of sap. In roses, gooseberries and certain other plants, the disease is caused by the same fungus, *Botrytis cinerea*, as that which also produces grey mould disease under different circumstances. In plums die-back is caused by a different fungus and there is an absence of the customary ring of decayed bark. Apricots, peaches and nectarines are also subject to die-back diseases.

Affected branches should always be cut back to completely healthy tissue and the wounds should be painted with white lead paint, Stockholm tar of some other approved wound dressing. When treating gooseberries some benefit can be obtained by spraying with copper sulphate at 1 oz. to each gallon of water plus 1 fl. oz. of cottonseed oil just before the buds burst in early spring. The same remedy can be tried in winter on roses, but must never be used on plants that have leaves or bursting buds. Bordeaux mixture may also be applied to gooseberries as soon as the flowers have set, and to roses at any time during spring and summer. Good cultivation and, in particular, an adequate supply of potash in the soil will help to keep die-back from occurring.

DIGGING There are many different methods of digging the soil, but all have two main objects – the destruction of weeds and the breaking up of the soil so that air may penetrate and the natural processes of decay, by which plant foods are liberated, may be speeded up. Sometimes digging also provides a convenient opportunity for mixing manures or fertilizers with the soil.

There are three principal systems of digging, which may be described as plain digging or single spit digging; double digging or digging to a depth of two spits, and trenching or digging to a depth of three spits. A spit is the depth of the blade of a spade, roughly 10 in.

Plain or single spit digging is accomplished by driving the spade or fork into the soil to the full depth of its blade or tines, lifting the soil and turning it right over. In order that this work may be done conveniently and neatly it is necessary to maintain a small trench between dug and undug soil. Before starting to dig any piece of ground, a trench 10 in. deep and approximately the same in width should be opened across one

end of the plot, and the soil transported to the other end. The digger then starts at one end of the opened trench and turns the soil, spadeful by spadeful, forward and over so that any weeds it may contain are completely reversed and buried. He progresses along the length of the trench until a complete narrow strip has been turned into it, so opening a second trench of approximately the same dimensions as the first. He then proceeds to turn another strip of soil, spadeful by spadeful, into this trench and continues in this manner, strip by strip, until he reaches the far end of the plot where the soil removed from the first trench is used to fill the last one.

In dealing with very long plots, it is sometimes more economical of labour to divide them in half lengthwise, opening a trench across one half of the plot only, and transporting the soil to the other half, but at the same end. The digger then works down one half of the strip and back up the other half, finishing alongside the point at which he started. This saves the labour of carrying soil from one end to the other.

Double digging can also only be done properly if an open trench is maintained throughout, but the trench must be considerably wider than that prepared for plain digging. It should be opened at one end of the plot as for plain digging and should be 10 in. deep and 2 ft. wide. The soil is transported to the other end of the plot or, where this is a long one, it can be divided in half and the soil removed to one side as already described for plain digging. Before starting to turn more soil into the opened trench, the digger should take a fork, step into the bottom of the trench and break up the soil in this to the full depth of the tines of the fork. This is done in the same way as for plain digging, working from one end of the trench to the other. In this way the soil is broken up to a depth of approximately 20 in.

Now a further strip of ground 2 ft. wide is marked out and the topsoil from this is turned forwards and over into the first trench. In this way a further 2-ft. wide strip of second spit soil is exposed which is in turn broken up with a fork. The work proceeds in the same way until the final trench is reached, which is filled with the soil removed from the first trench. It will be seen that by this method, though the soil is cultivated to a depth of about 20 in., the topsoil remains on top and the second spit soil remains beneath it. Double digging and trenching are both useful in breaking up the hard layer of soil, or pan, that occurs naturally on some soils and can almost always be induced in time by repeated shallow cultivation, particularly with plough or rotary hoe.

Trenching is the third method of cultivation. By this, soil can be cultivated to a depth of 30 in. or more. Again it is necessary to start with a trench, but this time it should be at least 3 ft. wide. The soil from this is removed to a depth of 10 in. and transported to the other end of the plot, or to one side as for long plots which are divided lengthwise. Next, the trench so opened is divided in half lengthwise and the soil from the forward half is removed to a further depth of 10 in. This is also transported to the other end of the plot or to one side, but is kept in a separate heap from the soil removed from the top spit. Now the digger gets into the bottom of the 18-in. wide and 20-in. deep trench and breaks up the subsoil with a fork, as for double digging, but in this case breaking it up to a depth of about 30 in.

The next step is to dig the 18-in. wide step of second spit soil on to the forked subsoil. When this is completed a further 18-in. strip of subsoil will be exposed and this, in turn, is broken up with a fork to a further depth of 10 in., making the total depth cultivated 30 in. or thereabouts.

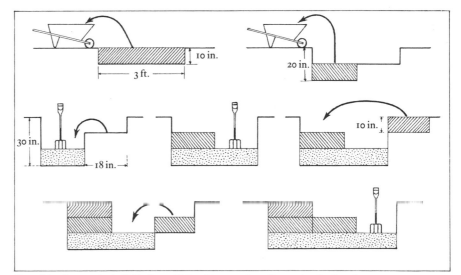

Trenching is a method of digging which cultivates the soil to a depth of 30 in.

Now a further 18-in. wide strip of topsoil is marked out. The soil from this is turned well forward on to the step of second spit soil in the first trench. By this means another 18-in. wide strip of second spit soil is exposed and this is turned forwards on to the forked subsoil in the first trench. The subsoil in the second trench is now broken up with a fork. Work proceeds in the same manner until the end of the plot is reached, when the smaller heap of second spit soil is used to fill the remaining second spit trench and the larger heap of top spit soil is used to fill the top spit trench. It will be seen that by this method, though the soil is broken up to a depth of about 30 in., the top spit remains on top, the second spit remains beneath it and the third spit is broken up but not raised.

A variation of this method of trenching is to bring some or all of the subsoil to the top and bury some or all of the topsoil. This is advocated by some gardeners as a method of rapidly increasing the depth of fertile soil, but if the subsoil is very infertile or of an unworkable character, as for example stony or clayey, it is a method which may land the gardener into serious difficulties. Really it is only in exceptional circumstances that it is justified.

DIGITATE Hand like; a botanical term used to describe leaves which are composed of several separate leaflets all joined at one point as in the Horse Chestnut.

DILUTOR A device by means of which regulated quantities of a liquid, usually a fertilizer though it may be an insecticide or fungicide, are mixed with the water flowing through a pipe line. Dilutors are much used in commercial glasshouses for feeding plants while watering them and are often made so that they can be attached to permanently installed irrigation systems. Small dilutors for attachment to ordinary garden hoses are also available for domestic use.

DIMETHOATE A systemic insecticide primarily used to kill aphids and red spider mites. It is purchased as a liquid for dilution with water according to manufacturers' instructions and applied as a spray. It is poisonous to warm-blooded animals, including man, and edible crops should not be harvested for at least a week after use.

DINOCAP A fungicide used to control powdery mildews of all kinds. It is not very poisonous but should not be inhaled and the concentrated chemical should be kept off the skin. It is available as a liquid for dilution or as a wettable powder to be stirred into water and kept agitated while being applied as a spray. Manufacturers' instructions regarding strength should be followed.

DIOECIOUS A botanical term applied to plants in which the flowers on any one plant are either entirely male, i.e. with stamens and no pistils, or entirely female, i.e. with pistils and no stamens. An example is *Skimmia japonica*, and if the female plants of this are to produce berries, a male plant must be placed near to them. The same thing applies to some varieties of holly and also to the Sea Buckthorn, hippophaë. See Monoecious.

DIPLOID A plant with the normal number of chromosomes for the species to which it belongs. See Polyploid.

DIQUAT A weedkiller of similar character to paraquat and sometimes sold in a mixture with it. It acts through the foliage or green stems and severely damages or kills most plants. It is inactivated by the soil and can therefore be used selectively if applied only to the leaves and young stems of the weeds that are to be destroyed. Diquat is a liquid to be further diluted with water according to manufacturers' instructions and applied as a spray or by means of a sprinkle bar. Care should be taken to prevent drift on to the plants that are not to be killed.

DISBUDDING The process of removing surplus buds or shoots. Disbudding is an important item in the cultivation of many flowers particularly when required for show. Roses are restricted to one flower to each stem, other flower buds being removed at an early stage. Carnations are frequently restricted in the same way to one flower to each stem, and the practice is common with chrysanthemums when large flowers are required. As a rule, it is the central or terminal bud that is retained and the side or axillary buds that are removed, but occasionally this rule is reversed. It may, for example, be reversed where roses with very full flowers are concerned, particularly early in the season or when the weather is unusually wet, the reason being that the central or terminal buds are liable to be too full of petals and to ball (q.v.) or fail to open properly as a result. The smaller side buds will give slightly smaller flowers which will open with less difficulty when conditions are adverse.

The disbudding of chrysanthemums is often referred to as taking the bud, a rather misleading term as, in fact, the bud is not taken in the sense of being taken away but precisely the opposite. See Take.

As a rule, when plants are disbudded the buds which are removed are alternative flower buds, but with chrysanthemums it is very often growth buds or small shoots which have to be removed and not flower buds. This is always the case when the bud that is to be retained is a crown bud (see Bud), for crown buds are surrounded by other shoots and not by flower buds.

By removing shoots or buds the gardener concentrates the whole strength of that particular stem on the remaining bud and forces it to develop to its fullest extent. As a rule disbudding is carried out as early as possible, which in practice means just as soon as the buds that are to be removed can be conveniently handled. If the work is delayed, the development of the bud that is to be retained will be checked and occasionally the gardener makes use of this fact as by delaying disbudding he can produce a slightly later and, if necessary, a slightly smaller flower.

Disbudding is usually done by pinching or rubbing out the unwanted buds between the first finger and thumb, but occasionally the point of a penknife is used.

DISEASE A term used by gardeners to cover any ailment of plants produced by physiological causes such as malnutrition, over-watering and so on, by attacks by other members of the vegetable kingdom such as fungi and bacteria and also by virus infection. It is often used in contrast to pest (q.v.).

DISK OR DISC FLORETS The small, often tubular florets or flowers which form the compact centre of the compound flowers

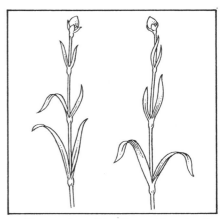

Disbudding carnations. 1. *Shoots before disbudding*

2. *Shoots after disbudding with only the central bud retained*

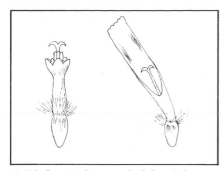

A disk floret is shown on the left and the more showy ray floret on the right

of daisies and other members of the *Compositae* or daisy family. Usually these florets are surrounded by ray florets which makes the whole head or flower more showy.

DIVISION Many plants, particularly herbaceous plants though also a few shrubs, can be increased simply by being divided into several pieces each provided with shoots and roots. Some can be divided simply by pulling them apart with the fingers but others are too tough for this and then a couple of hand forks or border forks may be thrust back to back through the plant and levered apart so exerting great pressure on it. This is better than using a knife or spade which might sever shoots from roots whereas by levering the plant breaks at the weakest place and most pieces come away well provided with shoots and roots. All the same, a knife may be required to cut through the hard, tough crowns of some plants such as delphiniums, peonies and rhubarb.

Plants that make large clumps, such as Michaelmas daisies and shasta daisies (*Chrysanthemum maximum*) tend to die out in the middle and when divided only the younger outside portions should be retained. With these very vigorous plants it may pay to divide drastically to single pieces with roots, but for most plants divisions should have several shoots or crowns. Plants should be divided at the normal planting or repotting period, which is very often in early spring.

DNC An abbreviation, also sometimes written as DNOC, for the chemical named dinitro-ortho-cresol, a bright yellow dye which is used in the garden both as an ingredient of petroleum winter washes for the destruction of hibernating insects and insect eggs, and also occasionally as a weed-killer. It is a poison, but when prepared with petroleum oil as a winter wash for fruit trees the amount of DNC present is not likely to cause injury to human beings or animals provided it is used with proper care and not allowed to come into contact with skin and eyes. The concentrated chemical should also be stored well away from foodstuffs. As a weedkiller DNC is used at much greater strength and fatal accidents have occurred.

DNC winter wash must be purchased as a proprietary article and should be prepared according to manufacturers' instructions, the usual strength being $2\frac{1}{2}$ to 3 pints of the purchased emulsion to 5 gallons of water. The spray will stain the skin and particularly the nails, and inflame the eyes, so protective clothing and gloves should be worn including goggles, and any exposed skin should be smeared with vaseline. DNC winter wash can be applied later than tar oil winter wash, the usual time being from the middle of February to the second week in March.

As a weedkiller DNC must also be purchased as a proprietary article for which manufacturers' instructions should be obtained. It is diluted with water and applied as a fine spray. It is particularly effective in killing cleavers, wild chamomile, corn marigold, spurrey, mayweed, veronica and fumitory.

DOLLAR SPOT A fungal disease of lawns which produces small, more or less circular brown or whitish patches. It is particularly likely to occur on weak, poorly fed lawns so good cultivation and feeding is the first line of defence. In addition, affected patches may be watered once a month with calomel.

DOLPHIN FLY A name sometimes used

for black fly (q.v.), particularly that species of black fly that attacks broad beans.

DORMANT A condition of temporary cessation of activity. Few plants are completely dormant in the sense that no changes are going on within them, but some plants and particularly those with storage organs such as bulbs, corms or tubers, may have a prolonged period of apparent dormancy. This is usually, though not invariably, in winter. Familiar examples of plants which are dormant in summer are nerine, the bulbs of which are almost completely at rest from about midsummer until August, and the greenhouse cyclamen which has a period of semi-dormancy at the same time of year. Deciduous trees and shrubs, that is those which lose their leaves in autumn, are described as being dormant from the time their leaves drop until the buds begin to swell in late winter or early spring.

Buds are said to be dormant when they are inactive. Buds of this type are to be found on most trees and shrubs at any time of the year.

Many seeds have a period of dormancy after they ripen and during this time will not germinate however favourable the conditions. There are, however, other seeds which have no such period and can be germinated as soon as they are ripe. See Vernalization.

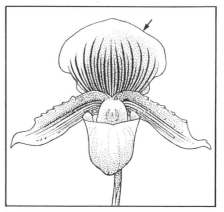

The dorsal sepal of a cypripedium

DORSAL Back; a term which in garden use is practically confined to the description of the flowers of some orchids. Thus the dorsal sepal of a cypripedium is the sepal which stands erect at the back of the flower and is often the most striking feature of it.

DOT PLANT A plant of taller growth used in a groundwork of lower plants to stand out as an individual specimen. In formal bedding schemes dot plants are often used to break up the monotonous line that would result from using nothing but plants of the same height. Any plant can be used as a dot plant if it is naturally taller than the plants with which it is to be associated or if it can

1. Dividing Michaelmas daisies by using two forks back to back

2. The pieces can be further split up with the hands

be trained to make it stand up above them. Sometimes the same kind of plant can be used both as groundwork and dot plants, e.g. ivy-leaved pelargoniums may be allowed to sprawl on the ground except for an occasional specimen which is trained up a stick.

DOUBLE FLOWERS, see Flore Pleno

DOWNY MILDEW, see Mildew

DRAINAGE The drainage of soil is most important, since if water cannot move fairly freely through it, air may be excluded and the more beneficial micro-organisms (see Bacteria) may be destroyed. Badly drained soils are often sour and even after drainage has been improved it may be necessary to correct this condition by suitable dressings of lime. Moreover, the roots of plants require air and will die if deprived of it. Another bad effect of waterlogging is that the soil is chilled and growth is retarded.

Natural drainage is ensured by a sufficiency of coarse, gritty material or sand in the soil, also small stones and spongy organic matter or humus. Clay soils tend to be the most unsatisfactory as regards drainage, but bad drainage may also occur in soils which have a hard pan, or layer of consolidated soil, beneath them. A pan can occur as a result of repeated ploughing or other forms of cultivation which tend to consolidate the lower layers of soil. The remedy in this case is to break up the pan by deeper ploughing or other deep cultivation and so let the surplus water find its way through into the subsoil.

Land drain pipes laid in a herringbone pattern are an effective form of drainage

The drainage of clay soils can often be improved sufficiently by treating them with lime, which makes the finer particles of clay cling together into larger granules (see Flocculate), and also by further cultivation

and the incorporation of bulky matter such as strawy manure, compost, leafmould and peat. Coarse sand and sharp boiler ashes are other useful materials for improving clay soils. Some clay may also be burnt to a red ash, which, when returned to the soil, helps to lighten and improve its texture.

Sometimes cultural methods and soil dressings are not sufficient and drains must be installed to remove the surplus moisture. The most effective drains are those made with earthenware land drain pipes laid end to end. The pipes should, for preference, be laid on a layer of gravel or coarse cinders and should be surrounded and covered with more of the same material. Trenches dug to receive land drains should have a slope in one direction, though it is not necessary for this slope to be more than 1 in 40. The drainage plan may be varied according to the site, but a convenient basic plan is that known as the herringbone pattern in which there is a central drain running the length of the plot with side drains leading into it on both sides. Whatever system is employed, the drain or drains should communicate at their lowermost point with some suitable outlet such as a stream, ditch, main drain or soakaway. The last-named is a large and deep hole filled with stones or clinkers. This soakaway will receive surplus water and allow it to percolate slowly into the subsoil. It is most effective if it can be dug sufficiently deep to penetrate through the impervious layer of subsoil that is holding up the moisture and so reach more porous soil beneath.

An alternative to laying pipe drains is to dig narrow trenches in the same way as for pipe drains and partly fill them with stones, brickbats or large clinkers between which water can flow. This layer of hard rubble should be covered with smaller stones, clinkers or gravel and then the trench should be filled with soil. A third system is to use bundles of brushwood laid in the bottom of the trenches and cover these with soil. Brushwood drains often last for a number of years, but may in time need to be replaced as the brushwood will decay and collapse.

DRAWN If plants are grown in the dark or crowded together they will become excessively tall, thin and weak, a condition described as drawn. Seedlings and young plants grown in greenhouses or frames are particularly susceptible and it is for this reason that they are often placed on shelves near the glass or raised on inverted pots placed on the staging so that they get as much light as possible. It is also partly to avoid this danger that it is recommended that seeds be sown thinly and seedlings pricked out early.

DRILL A narrow furrow or groove made in soil for the purpose of receiving seeds which are to be sown in straight lines, as

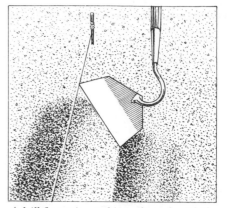

A drill for sowing seed is easily made with the corner of a hoe. Note how the line is used to guide the direction of the hoe

opposed to broadcast sowing. The act of preparing such drills is described as drawing drills or drilling. There are various ways in which this may be done. Frequently a draw hoe is used for the purpose, in which case it is held with one corner to the soil and pulled along in a series of smart but controlled jerks. Some gardeners prefer to use a dutch hoe held almost vertically, again with one corner only presented to the soil. The hoe is then drawn smartly towards the body. For making small drills in frames or small beds a pointed stick is often used, and another useful method is to press a rake handle into the soil. There are also mechanical implements which will not only prepare the furrow, but also drop the seeds into it at regular intervals. See Seed Drill.

The important thing in all drilling is that the drills shall be of the same depth throughout and that this shall be the correct depth at which the seeds should be sown. Beginners usually have a tendency to make drills which are too deep and vary in depth. The work is made much easier if the seed bed itself has been well prepared, and is even in texture and free from large stones. A garden line should be stretched tightly to mark the line of the drill and the tool which is to be used should be kept close to this line throughout. It will be found that if the tool, whether it be hoe, stick or mechanical implement, is operated firmly and rather rapidly it will be less liable to be deflected by small inequalities or obstacles in the soil.

For most seeds, drills should be no more than ½ in. deep. For just a few large seeds such as those of peas and beans, drills of 1 to 2 in. deep are required.

When seeds have been sown in drills, they are covered by drawing back the displaced soil into the drill and this is best done either with a rake drawn diagonally across the drill or with a small stick or a wooden tally used on edge.

DROUGHT Officially a drought is any period of fourteen consecutive days or more without measurable rainfall. The gardener uses the term loosely to describe any comparatively rainless period when plants show signs of suffering from lack of moisture. As plants absorb all nourishment from the soil in the form of solutions, it follows that water is of the utmost importance. It has been shown that in a normal southern English summer, the addition of 2 in. of artificial rain (by means of overhead irrigation) during the growing season, will double the crop of carrots and the same kind of thing is true of most other plants. It is therefore one of the gardener's first tasks to avoid drought. This he can do partly by digging soil deeply so that plants are encouraged to root deeply into layers of soil not so readily affected by sudden spells of dry weather; partly by working in plenty of bulky organic matter, such as dung, compost or peat, which will retain moisture like a sponge, and partly by making provision for artificial watering during dry periods. Despite statements to the contrary, artificial watering is extremely valuable provided it is adequate. Trouble only arises when water is supplied in inadequate quantity or spasmodically, whereby roots are encouraged to grow near the surface and are then scorched when the soil dries out. A fine spray of water applied for an extended period is more beneficial than a flood of water applied over a short period.

Mulching helps to prevent the effects of drought by checking evaporation from the surface of the soil and by killing weeds and so preventing unnecessary competition for available water supplies. Hoeing is also useful to destroy weeds.

Some plants are adapted by nature to survive long periods of drought. Notable examples are cacti and other succulents which are able to store moisture in their thickened leaves or stems and so survive even under prolonged desert conditions. Many plants with bulbous or tuberous roots are also able to survive drought at particular times of the year, usually when top growth has died down and they are more or less dormant.

DRUPE A fruit in which the seed is protected by a hard wall or stone as well as by flesh. Familiar examples are the plum and cherry. The individual sections of a blackberry, raspberry or loganberry fruit are drupels, i.e. little drupes.

DRY ROT A general name applied to various diseases which cause the dry decay of plants. One of the most familiar is the dry rot which attacks potatoes, particularly tubers in store. Dry, shrunken patches appear on the tubers with brown decay beneath and later whitish pustules form on these patches. All such tubers should be burned. Some varieties are particularly subject to it and should be avoided on that account. Dry rot of potatoes is most likely

to be troublesome in a damp, badly ventilated store. The disease can be controlled by dusting potatoes with tecnazene at ½ lb. to the cwt. before they are stored.

Another kind of dry rot attacks gladioli while they are in growth; the main stem decays just above the corm and as a result the leaves wither from the tips. Close examination will reveal the presence of many tiny black spots on the outer leaf sheaths near soil level. Small more or less circular black spots will also be found on the corms. Affected plants or corms should be burnt. Where the disease has occurred it is desirable to dip supposedly healthy corms in a suspension of calomel or captan or dust them with a mercurial seed dressing prior to planting.

DRY SET A physiological disorder of tomatoes which results in the fruits apparently setting but refusing to swell, each remaining no larger than a pin's head. Crop failures from this cause must not be confused with crop failures due to bud dropping, when the whole flower falls off at the knuckle. Dry set is only likely to occur under glass when the atmosphere is too hot and dry. It may be prevented by syringing the plants daily while they are producing flowers.

DWARF Some plant varieties are naturally smaller than the typical plants of the same species. The common juniper, *Juniperus communis*, grows to a height of about 30 or 40 ft. but it has a variety known as *compressa* which seldom exceeds one foot in height and will take many years to attain even this stature. The dwarf character of these plants is a hereditary quality. Other plants may be dwarfed by artificial treatment though they are not genetically dwarfs. This is so with many of the tiny shrubs and trees familiar in Japanese gardens. Such plants are dwarfed by constricting and pruning their roots, starving them and so on. See Bonsai.

With fruit trees, it is a notable and valuable fact that some of the stocks upon which garden varieties of fruit are grafted or budded have a dwarfing effect on the scions worked upon them. For example the apple Bramley's Seedling is normally a very vigorous variety and if grown on its own roots or on a seedling crab stock it will make a tree 20 or 30 ft. in height and at least as much through. But if this same variety of apple is grafted on the Paradise apple stock known as Jaune de Metz or Malling 9, it will only reach a height of 8 or 10 ft. with a similar spread, and this without any special treatment in the way of pruning or feeding. This dwarfing characteristic of certain stocks can be used to great advantage to produce small trees in limited space, such as cordons, espaliers and dwarf pillars. See Stock.

Some plants can be dwarfed by treatment with chemicals such as B9, CIPP and phos-

phon. The treatment has been applied to chrysanthemums, azaleas and a variety of bedding plants, and usually results in early flowering as well as shorter jointed and therefore dwarfer plants. As yet, however, these chemicals are not generally available to private gardeners, and are confined to commercial growers and experimental workers. The strength and timing of application are critical and considerable damage can be caused by their misuse.

Yet another way of dwarfing some plants is by controlling the day length in which they are grown. See Day Length.

EARTHING UP The process of drawing soil towards and round plants. It serves several purposes, including the blanching of stems, the covering of roots and tubers, and the provision of extra anchorage to secure plants during windy weather.

Earthing up with the aim of blanching is used for both celery and leeks and is an important item in the cultivation of these vegetables. With celery, earthing up must be delayed until the plants are fully developed for, after earthing up, they make little or no further growth. With leeks this is not so and earthing up is usually a progressive operation carried out at intervals during the summer and early autumn. Another point of difference is that with celery care must be taken to prevent soil working down between the stems into the hearts of the plants, whereas no such precaution is necessary with leeks. The usual method adopted with celery is to tie the stems together before starting to draw soil round them and possibly to wrap paper round them as an additional protection. See also Blanching.

Earthing up to cover tubers is usually adopted in the cultivation of the potato, though some experts believe that equally good crops and well-covered tubers are

Earthing up a crop of potatoes

obtained without earthing up. If started early when shoots first appear through the soil, it also serves the useful purpose of protecting them from frost.

Earthing up to ensure improved anchorage is sometimes carried out with broccoli, cauliflowers and the taller varieties of kale – soil being drawn round the stems when they are well developed.

Earthing up is often done with a draw hoe which is used to pull soil from between the rows towards the plants. This is the method almost invariably used when earthing up potatoes, broccoli, cauliflowers or kale. With celery a steeper and higher bank of soil is required and for this purpose a spade is commonly used, soil being dug from between the celery trenches and banked round the plants. The steep ridge formed in this way is usually smoothed off with the back of the spade. Occasionally when very large leeks are required for exhibition, earthing up is effected by placing a plank or planks on edge along each side of every row of plants and 4 or 5 in. away from them. The trough formed in this way is then gradually filled with fine soil.

EARTHWORMS In the main earthworms are of benefit to the gardener. By tunnelling through the soil they help to aerate it and by dragging leaves and other vegetable matter into the soil they help to provide it with humus. In a series of famous experiments Charles Darwin observed that layers of stones that had been spread over fields of uncultivated soil were after a few years covered to a depth of one or two inches purely as a result of the activities of earthworms burrowing through the soil and throwing their casts on to the surface. Worms thrive in soils that are rich in humus, and are few in number in soils that are dry and sandy.

Earthworms do no direct damage to plants, but they may do indirect damage if admitted to pots or boxes containing small plants, for in these the soil disturbance they cause can interfere with root development and worm casts may block the drainage holes. Worms can also be a nuisance on lawns, because the casts thrown on to the surface tend to be trodden down and, being rather sticky, they smother and kill the grass so causing small bare patches. Earthworms in lawns can be destroyed by spreading mowrah meal at the rate of 4 to 8 oz. to the sq. yd. and then watering very freely, or by watering the lawn with either chlordane or carbaryl, chemicals which should be used according to the manufacturers' instructions. The best time to carry out this treatment is between March and May and again in September and October, particularly in damp close weather. After treatment with mowrah meal the worms will come to the surface in a few hours and should be swept up at once, but chlordane and carbaryl kill

Trimming grass at the lawn edges is made easy with long-handled shears

worms in the soil and no further action need be taken.

With pot-grown plants care should be taken to exclude worms from the potting compost and to prevent them entering through the drainage holes. This latter may be done by setting the pots on a bed of ash or gravel or by placing a perforated zinc disk over each drainage hole.

EARWIGS Flowers and small seedlings are a favourite food of these creatures, and they can be very troublesome in the garden. Dahlias are particularly liable to be attacked, and the earwigs frequently hide themselves by day between the tightly packed petals of the flowers. Leaves that have been attacked often have a somewhat rusty, ragged appearance, while holes of a very similar type to those made by slugs and caterpillars may be eaten in petals.

Earwigs dislike daylight, and usually con-

A simple earwig trap can be made from an inverted hay-filled flower pot

ceal themselves by day in dark crevices. If inverted pots lightly stuffed with hay, or slightly opened empty match boxes are placed among the plants, many earwigs will go into them by day and can be collected and destroyed. Alternative remedies are to dust or spray the plants with BHC insecticide, and under glass BHC smoke generators are effective.

EDGING This term may be used in several ways; to describe the act of trimming the edges of lawns or the selection or use of plants to edge beds and borders.

Lawn edging may be done with a special tool (see Edging Iron) or with a sharp spade, and the grass that grows over the edges may be trimmed with long-handled shears or a variety of mechanical devices made specially for this purpose. When actually cutting the soil to straighten a lawn edge, a line should first be stretched to ensure that the cut really is straight, alternatively a long straight-edged plank can be used held in place with the feet.

A great many small plants are used for edging and one dwarf form of evergreen box, *Buxus sempervirens suffruticosa*, is known as edging box because of its popularity for this purpose. It can be kept to a height and width of a few inches by repeated clipping and is often used for edging formal beds.

Lawns are sometimes edged with rectangular paving slabs laid just below the level of the turf so that the mower can be run over them. This overcomes the difficulty of plants growing out over the turf and killing it but unless a clear channel is maintained between the turf and the paving it will be difficult to prevent the grass growing out over the paving and producing an irregular, untidy edge.

Special edging tiles were once very popular for making a clear tidy edge to borders but have tended to be replaced, where this kind of edging is required, by various metal or plastic strips.

EDGING IRON A tool with a straight handle and a half-moon blade used for cutting the edges of lawns.

EELWORMS A general name given to a number of different species of nematode worms. Many eelworms are microscopic in size and all are transparent and eel-like in shape. By no means are all species plant pests, in fact some of the larger nematode worms are mainly scavengers, but there are numerous eelworms which live within the tissues of plants, weakening them and usually producing withering or distortion of stems and leaves. One species attacks chrysanthemums by ascending the plants from the soil, swimming up the moisture on the outer skin to enter the leaves by way of the breathing pores. As a result the leaves develop purplish patches between the veins and these later turn brown, so that the whole plant may present the appearance of withering from the base upwards. Another species attacks phlox causing the stems to become puffy or gouty and the leaves to become curled, divided or extremely narrow. Badly attacked plants are completely stunted. Yet another common species of eelworm attacks potatoes, causing the plants to become weak and yellow and produce little or no crop.

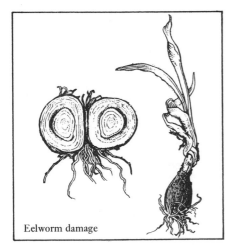
Eelworm damage

Close examination of the roots and tubers will reveal the presence of small whitish specks or cysts on them. Narcissi are also subject to attack by a particular species of eelworm and in these plants small thickened patches are formed on the leaves and can be felt if a leaf is drawn between forefinger and thumb. The leaves become distorted and develop pale green or yellowish streaks. Tomatoes are subject to attack by a species of eelworm which lives in the roots and forms galls or nodules on them for which reason it is called the root-knot eelworm. Plants are progressively weakened. Strawberries are attacked by eelworms which cause the leaves to become puckered,

brittle and blotched with grey. Plants may also become blind.

As all the eelworms spend at least a part of their time in the soil, soil sterilization is a possible means of controlling them, but is usually only practicable under glass. For this purpose steam may be used, or a chemical such as cresylic acid, DD, methamsodium or dazomet, the last primarily for potato root eelworm. Outdoors, rotation of crops is a possible means of keeping down the eelworm population. Clean phlox plants may be produced from affected plants if the roots only are employed as cuttings and the stems burnt. Clean plants raised in this way must not be replanted in the same eelworm-infested soil. Chrysanthemum plants that are to be used for propagation but are suspected of being infested with eelworm may be sterilized by placing them for 20 to 30 minutes in water at a temperature of 43°C. If potatoes develop eelworm, no further potato crop should be grown on the same site for three or four years. If seed potatoes are suspected of being infested they should be washed thoroughly before being planted. If a crop of mustard is grown on the ground and dug in just before coming into flower, some reduction in the number of eelworms may be expected.

Bulbs that are infested may be sterilized in a similar way to chrysanthemum stools, in water at 43°C. but the period of immersion is longer varying from one hour for irises to three hours for narcissi. Strawberry runners for propagation should only be taken from healthy plants. They can also be immersed in hot water, 46°C., for five minutes for leaf and bud eelworms and for seven minutes for stem eelworms. All these times and temperatures for hot water treatment are critical, which makes it difficult for amateur gardeners to carry them out efficiently without the expensive apparatus which commercial growers use.

Tomatoes can also be protected from rootknot eelworm by being grafted on an eelworm-resistant stock such as K.N.

EGG-KILLING CHEMICALS, see Ovicides

EMASCULATION The act of removing the anthers from a flower to prevent it from becoming pollinated with its own pollen. It is often a necessary preliminary to cross-fertilization (q.v.).

EMBRYO The earliest stage in the development of multicellular living organisms. In botany the term is applied to the rudimentary plant within the seed.

ENDOSULFAN An insecticide used to control big bud mite on currants but it is highly poisonous to all warm-blooded animals, including man, and so must be used with great care. Full protective clothing

should be worn while mixing and applying the spray and it must not be used within six weeks of picking currants.

ENTOMOLOGY The name given to the scientific study of insects. A person who practises this science is, therefore, known as an entomologist. Since many plant foes are insects the scientist who makes plant foes his special study is usually an entomologist, but it by no means follows that the name is confined to the study of harmful insects.

EPIDERMIS The outer skin or covering of the young parts of a plant including the upper surface of the leaves. In woody plants the epidermis of the stem is later replaced by the bark of branches and trunk.

EPIPHYTE A plant which grows upon another plant without actually being a parasite upon it. Many orchids are epiphytic, growing in the branches of trees but obtaining their nourishment from the air and from decaying matter collected in crevices of the bark.

ERICACEOUS Belonging to the heather family, *Ericaceae*, which includes, in addition to the heathers themselves, *Erica* and *Calluna*, such allied genera as *Daboecia*, *Rhododendron* (including azaleas), *Kalmia*, *Arbutus*, *Vaccinium*, *Gaultheria* and *Pernettya*. Many members of this family dislike lime and prefer acid soils.

ERMINE MOTH A number of species of small moths the caterpillars of which protect themselves in dense webs. The small ermine moth caterpillars do much damage to apple trees and hawthorn. The willow ermine attacks willows, the spindle ermine attacks euonymus and the sedum ermine attacks *Sedum telephium*. All can be controlled by spraying forcibly with carbaryl and on fruit trees winter spraying with tar oil wash will kill hibernating insects.

ESPALIER A system of posts with wires strained horizontally between them and used for the training of fruit trees. A good espalier will have a stout upright every 10 ft., the upright being embedded at least 2ft. in the soil and standing at least 5ft. out of it. Horizontal wires will be strained at intervals of about 15in. from bottom to top of these posts and the wires themselves should be no thinner than 10 gauge. The end posts of the espalier should be further supported by diagonal stays so that the wires can be strained really tight without displacing the posts.

The usual method of training fruit trees on such espaliers is that known as horizontal training in which the main stem or trunk is trained vertically and from this side branches are trained to right and left horizontally along each wire. Trees trained in

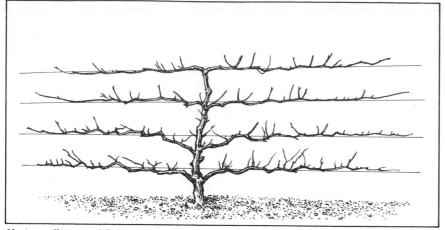

Horizontally-trained fruit trees grown on espaliers need careful pruning to maintain their shape. See page 360

this way are frequently erroneously referred to as espaliers; in fact this term applies to the training fence and not to the trees, though the trees may correctly be referred to as espalier-trained trees.

Espalier-trained trees are often used as a dividing line between one part of the garden and another in place of an ornamental hedge. In old gardens they may be seen as a dividing line between vegetable beds and paths.

When several rows of espaliers are placed in one plot they should be spaced at least 6 ft. apart and should, for preference, run north and south so that the trees trained upon them do not shade one another unduly.

ETIOLATED Blanched; a term used to describe the pale, thin and elongated growth produced by plants grown in the dark or in very poor light.

EUROPEAN GOOSEBERRY MIL-DEW, see Gooseberry Mildew

EVERGREEN Any plant which retains its leaves throughout the year, in contrast to a deciduous plant which loses its leaves and then, after a period of dormancy, produces new ones. However, even evergreens do shed their leaves and produce new ones, though the process is more or less continuous and there is no time at which the plant is bare. Some plants behave in an intermediate manner, shedding all or most of their leaves in very cold weather but retaining them throughout a mild winter. The common privet is an example and such plants may be termed semi-evergreen.

Evergreen trees and shrubs play an important part in the furnishing of the garden, particularly since they will provide foliage at all times of the year. Too great a reliance on evergreens can, however, give a heavy appearance to the garden and they should be suitably interspersed with deciduous types.

Evergreen trees and shrubs are of many different kinds and no general treatment can

be prescribed to suit all, but one feature which most of them have in common is that, unlike deciduous trees and shrubs, they have no marked period of dormancy and cannot be transplanted while dormant. Experience proves that, in general, evergreens, with the exception of evergreen conifers, transplant most satisfactorily either in early autumn (September, October) or in spring (April, May). Evergreen conifers can be transplanted successfully between November and March like deciduous trees and shrubs.

EVERLASTING A popular, though slightly misleading name for certain flowers, which, because of their dry and chaffy petals, can be kept for a long period. Familiar examples are statice and helichrysum. Everlasting flowers of this character should be cut just before they reach their maximum development. They should be dried by tying the stems in small bundles and hanging them head downwards in a cool airy shed or similar place where they are not directly exposed to sunshine. Frequently the dry stems have not sufficient strength to carry the rather heavy flowers and must be replaced by wires.

EXHIBITION The term is occasionally used by gardeners to distinguish certain varieties of flowers, fruits or vegetables particularly suitable for showing, from other varieties of the same kind of flower, fruit, or vegetable which are principally of value for garden decoration or table use. For example, violas are frequently classified as exhibition or bedding, according to whether they have the large, perfectly formed flowers required for show purposes or the tufted free-flowering habit so desirable for garden display. In the same way chrysanthemums, dahlias and roses are sometimes divided into exhibition and garden categories.

EXHIBITION BOARD At one time many flowers were displayed for show purposes on

boards, the dimensions of which were carefully specified by the rules. Present-day tendency is towards more informal methods of display, but boards or boxes are still used for roses, chrysanthemums, dahlias, violas, show pinks and begonias.

The sizes of boards for chrysanthemums are specified by the National Chrysanthemum Society as follows: for 12 large exhibition blooms, the board should be 28 in. long, 21 in. wide, 7 in. high at the back and 4 in. high at the front. Holes should be drilled in this board, 7 in. apart and $3\frac{1}{2}$ in. from the edge of the board – each hole to take 1 metal tube in which the flower stem can be placed. Alternatively, a bigger board may be used in which the holes are 10 in. apart.

The sizes of exhibition boards for roses are fixed by the National Rose Society as follows: for 24 blooms the board is to be 3 ft. 6 in. long and 18 in. wide and for 18 blooms it is to be 2 ft. 9 in. long and 18 in. wide; for 12 blooms it is to be 2 ft. long and 18 in. wide and for 9 blooms, 18 in. long, 18 in. wide; for 6 blooms it is 1 ft. long and 18 in. wide. These boards are usually made up into the form of a box with a lid which can be closed over the blooms to protect them on their way to the show.

EXOTIC Any plant which is not a native of the country. The term is often used, erroneously, as though it applied only to tender plants, but this is by no means so. Many exotics are actually hardier than natives because they come from countries with a colder climate.

EXSERTED Projecting; a botanical term sometimes applied to stamens or pistils which project beyond the other parts of a flower.

EYE A term used in several distinct ways by gardeners. It may be applied to the centre of a flower when differently coloured from the remainder of the bloom; to the growth bud of a tuber, e.g. the 'eyes' of a potato; or to a single growth bud removed from a stem, usually with a portion of the stem or surrounding bark, for the purpose of propagation. Eyes, or single bud cuttings, of this last-named type are sometimes used to increase grape vines and camellias. See Cuttings.

F₁ HYBRID Literally a first-filial, i.e. a first generation hybrid. Hybrids of this type can be valuable because of their vigour and uniformity. They are made from parents carefully selected for their desirable qualities and their proved suitability for producing reliable progeny in the first generation. As a rule pollen from the selected male parent must be conveyed by hand to the selected female parent, a slow and costly proceeding which partly accounts for the higher price of F_1 hybrid seed compared with open-

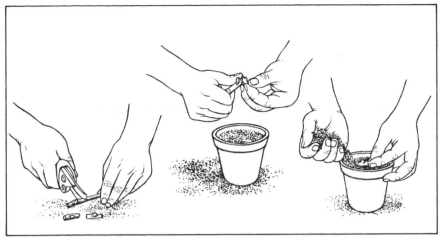

Eyes, or single bud cuttings, are used to increase vines. First, strong side shoots are cut into pieces, each carrying a single bud or eye. The cut edges are trimmed and the cuttings placed in pots of sandy compost

pollinated seed of similar plants. But sometimes it is possible to make use of male-sterility or other in-bred peculiarities to enable F_1 hybrid seed to be produced without hand pollination. The F_1 hybrid must be remade every time it is required. If a plant of the F_1 is fertilized with its own pollen an F_2 hybrid will be produced, i.e. a second generation hybrid, and if a plant of this generation is self-fertilized an F_3 hybrid will result, i.e. a third generation hybrid. Usually these second and third generation hybrids differ markedly from the F_1 but occasionally stable hybrids can be produced, at least at the F_2 stage, and as these can be produced much more cheaply by open pollination in the field, they have a commercial value.

FAIRY RINGS A popular name given to a fungus which attacks grass, weakening but not, as a rule, killing it. The fungus spreads slowly in the form of a ring and the grass immediately outside the ring is stimulated so that it grows more luxuriantly and assumes a darker green colour. It is this phenomenon which gave rise to the country name of fairy ring. Toadstools often appear round the outside of the ring. The remedy is to water with sulphate of iron at 4 oz. per gallon of water or with a mercurial lawn fungicide such as calomel according to manufacturers' instructions. The chemical should be applied principally to the outer part of the ring and the turf immediately outside it where the fungus is most active.

FALLOW The practice of allowing ground to lie idle for a period so that its fertility may be increased by natural processes such as the action of wind, rain and frost and the activity of soil micro-organisms, including bacteria. Fallowing is more common as an agricultural than as a horticultural practice and at one time formed a regular part of the farmer's cycle. It is of greatest importance

in gardens when soil has become infected with some disease-causing organism, or is heavily infested with a plant pest. Familiar examples are club root disease of brassicas and the cyst-forming eelworm of potatoes. With these it often pays to leave the ground vacant for a period, or at least not to grow any crop on which the pest or disease-causing organism can thrive.

FALLS The sepals of certain types of iris which hang downwards in contrast to the petals which stand up and form that part of the flower known as the standards (q.v.).

FAMILY A group of related genera. See Classification.

FANCY In a wide sense this term is used to denote the general body of breeders of any plant, or for that matter animal, specifically for show purposes; e.g. one may speak of the pigeon fancy with reference to the practice of breeding pigeons specifically for show purposes and of the rose fancy in a similar sense. It has, however, a more particular application in horticulture, to flowers, and particularly show flowers, with variegated markings. A familiar example is the fancy carnation which is always a variegated bloom in contrast to the self carnation in which the flower is of one colour throughout.

FAN TRAINED A system of training applied to fruit trees, particularly cherries, plums, peaches and nectarines, and also occasionally to ornamental shrubs. All the main branches are spread out in one plane like the ribs of a fan and other subsidiary branches are trained from them in the same general pattern. It is usually considered important not to have a central vertical stem which might monopolize the sap flow. See also page 360.

FARINA The powdery covering on the stems and leaves of some plants as, for example, those of the auricula and of *Primula pulverulenta*. This powdery covering is usually white, though occasionally bluish or yellowish in colour, and may add considerably to the attraction of the plant.

FARMYARD MANURE Nowadays this consists mainly of cattle manure with the possible addition of some pig manure and poultry droppings and varying quantities of straw. It is very variable in content and analysis but in all forms is a most valuable manure for garden use. An average analysis shows 0.6 to 0.7 per cent. nitrogen, 0.2 to 0.3 per cent. phosphoric acid and 0.3 to 0.35 per cent. potash. Farmyard manure has a marked effect on the texture of soil and many crops thrive better when fed with farmyard manure plus chemical fertilizers than they do with chemicals alone. Farmyard manure is described as long when relatively fresh with the straw undecomposed and as short when it is sufficiently rotted for the straw to have broken down into small fragments. Short manure is to be preferred provided decomposition has taken place under shelter or in a closed pit so that the nutrients have not been washed out of it. Farmyard manure is used at rates from 10 to 15 lb. to the sq. yd.

FASCIATION A condition in which several stems become fused together, the effect being of one stem of abnormal width and often carrying an exceptional number of flowers. This is a freak which is common in certain plants and in some seasons. It appears to be encouraged by conditions which favour very rapid growth, as for example an exceptionally rich soil or very

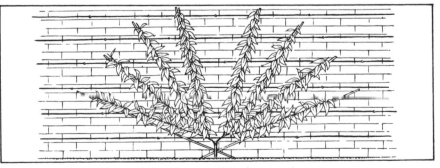

Peaches are one of the trees which can be successfully fan trained

mild and warm weather. Extraordinary examples of fasciation, in which many stems are fused together, are occasionally seen in delphiniums and some species of lily. Nothing can be done to prevent this freak, and it is possible that a plant which suffers from it in one year will be quite free from it the following year.

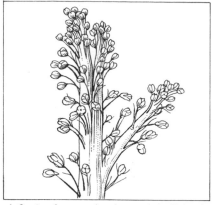

A fasciated stem. An abnormal condition in which several stems become fused

FASTIGIATE A botanical term meaning erect in habit. It is applied chiefly to trees and shrubs which in normal forms have spreading branches but in particular varieties have branches which are upright. Two familiar examples are the Lombardy Poplar, which is a fastigiate form of the Black Poplar, and the Irish Yew, which is a fastigiate form of the common yew.

FEATHERED A term sometimes applied to year-old (maiden) trees which, besides forming a main stem, have produced some side growths. These side growths are known as feathers.

FEMALE FLOWER A flower which bears pistils but no stamens, in contrast to a male flower which bears stamens and no pistils, and a hermaphrodite flower which has

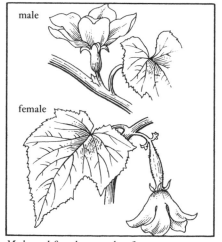

Male and female cucumber flowers

both pistils and stamens. Familiar examples are to be found in the vegetable marrow and the cucumber, both of which bear some flowers which are female only and some which are male only. In both these examples the female flower can be distinguished very readily because immediately behind it is an embryo fruit, recognizable as a rudimentary marrow or cucumber, whereas the male flower has no such embryo behind it but only a slender stem.

FENCING Fences can be utilitarian or purely ornamental. They may be used to increase privacy, to give protection from wind, to keep out intruders, including animals, or merely to serve as a line of demarcation. Solid wood or interwoven fences are excellent for all these purposes but are comparatively costly to erect and maintain. Simple post and chain or post and rail fences are among the cheapest but they serve little purpose except those of appearance and demarcation. Wrought iron fences, or fences erected with panels of wrought iron, are the most decorative of all but also amongst the most expensive.

Fences that are to keep out rabbits must either be solid or else must include wire netting well buried in the soil (see Rabbits). Fences to keep out wild deer need to be at least 6 ft. high and strongly constructed.

Wattle hurdles make useful temporary fences easily moved from one place to another and so, too, do split chestnut pales united by wire.

Fences can often be made more attractive if clothed with plants, either with climbing plants such as rambler roses, honeysuckle and clematis or with shrubs such as pyracantha, ceanothus, and chaenomeles (quince) trained against the fence.

FENURON A residual herbicide which in large doses will kill most plants but in carefully regulated quantities can be selective. It is available in various formulations, usually mixed with other herbicides, and for application as a spray or sprinkle after dilution according to label instructions.

FERN Non-flowering plants belonging to the group named *Filices*. The leaves of ferns are known as fronds and are often very beautiful. Ferns do not produce seeds but spores (q.v.).

FERTILE That which is able to produce abundantly. The term is used by gardeners both to describe varieties of plants which are able to produce good crops, in contrast to other varieties of the same kind of plant which do not produce so abundantly, and also to describe soils which are rich, in contrast to those which are poor. The term self-fertile, frequently applied to certain varieties of fruit, means that these varieties are capable of producing abundant crops

when fertilized with their own pollen, in contrast to self-sterile varieties which will not produce crops unless fertilized with pollen from another tree or bush of the same kind of plant, but of a different variety.

FERTILIZATION The union of two cells of opposite sex to produce a new individual. In flowering plants fertilization is effected by the growth of a pollen grain down the pistil of a flower until the male cell in it fuses with the ovule. As a result a seed is formed and this on germination produces a new plant. Fertilization is not only important as a means of producing new plants but also from the gardener's standpoint it is important as a means of producing fruits as many plants will not develop their fruits unless fertilized. The problem is further complicated by the fact that, though some plants are self-fertile i.e. they will produce seeds and fruits from a union between their own pollen and ovules, others are self-sterile, i.e. they will only produce seeds and fruits when cross-fertilized with pollen from another variety of the same kind of

Hand pollinating female flowers of a melon

plant. Many special precautions are taken to ensure good fertilization of some crops. Fruit growers import hives of bees to their orchards to ensure a thorough distribution of pollen from flower to flower and they also plant different varieties of the same kind of fruit near together to ensure cross-fertilization. Under glass, the flowers of peaches and nectarines are lightly dusted with a camel-hair brush or a rabbit's tail tied to a stick to scatter the pollen, and the atmosphere of such houses, and also of vineries, may be allowed to become a little warmer and drier than usual to allow the pollen to become thoroughly ripe.

Plant breeders carry out their controlled fertilization of particular flowers by emasculating the intended seed parents some time in advance and covering these prepared flowers with greaseproof paper or muslin bags to protect them from chance fertilization. The chosen pollen can then be brought to these flowers on a camel-hair brush when the stigmas are sticky and in a suitably receptive condition.

Melon growers take great care to fertilize a specified number of female flowers per plant all at one time, doing this by plucking well-developed male flowers and scattering the pollen from them over the stigmas of the female flowers. Ridge cucumbers and vegetable marrows are fertilized in a similar manner except that there is no restriction of the number of female flowers treated on each plant. Curiously enough greenhouse cucumbers are not fertilized as they will produce better, seedless fruits without this. Such fruits are said to be parthenocarpic. Similar results can be produced in certain instances by treating the flowers or tiny fruits with a suitable hormone and such hormones are used for getting a good set of fruit on the bottom trusses of tomatoes.

Frost and bad weather may seriously affect the fertilization of fruit blossom out of doors and it is for this reason that it is advised that fruit trees should not be planted in hollows and valleys in which cold air is apt to collect. Weakness and lack of available plant food in the soil, particularly lack of readily available nitrogen in May and June, may also adversely affect the fertilization of fruit trees.

FERTILIZER Any substance used in fairly concentrated form as a plant food in contrast to bulky manures such as dung, compost, sewage sludge and seaweed. Popular fertilizers are sulphate of ammonia, nitrate of soda, dried blood, hoof and horn meal, bonemeal, basic slag, superphosphate of lime, sulphate of potash and muriate of potash. See Organic and Inorganic.

FIBROUS This term is used by gardeners in two ways: to distinguish plants with masses of fine roots from those with much coarser or more fleshy roots, e.g. fibrous-rooted begonias from tuberous-rooted begonias; and to describe loam containing a lot of plant roots, particularly roots of grass, which give it a fibrous texture. Such loam is the best to use for potting and seed composts.

FILAMENT The slender stalk which bears an anther.

FILLIS Soft string used for tying.

FIMBRIATE Fringed; a botanical term usually applied by gardeners to petals with fringed margins.

FINGER AND TOE An alternative name for club root disease (q.v.).

FIRE (Tulip) A disease of tulips caused by a fungus which attacks both leaves and flowers, causing them to become brown and

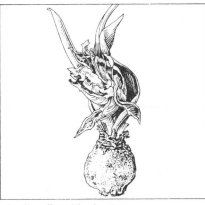
A tulip affected by fire disease

withered as if they had been burned. Sometimes the whole plant may be destroyed. The soil should be treated with quintozene dust at planting time and the plants sprayed frequently with maneb, zineb, captan or thiram from the time growth is one inch high until flower buds are about to open. Infected bulbs, which have a blistered appearance when the outer brown scale is removed, should not be planted.

FIRE BLIGHT A bacterial disease of pears which also attacks hawthorn, whitebeam, mountain ash, cotoneaster, pyracantha and stranvaesia. Infection is spread by insects, including bees, and also by rain. Blossom is first infected, especially late blossom, and as a result it withers; the decay passes back into the spurs, twigs and branches causing leaves to turn black, the bark to develop cankers and the wood immediately beneath the bark to be stained reddish brown. The pear Laxton's Superb is particularly susceptible.

There is no remedy, affected trees or bushes should be lifted and burned and it is compulsory under the Fire Blight Disease Orders 1958 and 1966 that the Ministry of Agriculture Fisheries and Food should be notified.

FISH REFUSE All animal matter is capable of decaying in the soil and producing humus in the process, in addition to liberating plant foods, and fish is no exception to this rule. Fish waste is, in consequence, a useful manure. Fresh fish waste can be used but is a rather unpleasant substance to handle unless it can be dug in directly it is received. Where fish scraps can be purchased cheaply it is good policy to keep a trench open on a vacant plot of ground, spread the scraps in this trench as received and cover at once with soil. Large quantities of fish waste are also dried and prepared in various forms, sometimes with the addition of other chemicals, and then sold as fish guano and fish manure. All such preparations are valuable garden manures which should be used strictly in accordance with manufacturers' instructions as they may

vary greatly in strength. No general analysis can be given though a plain sample of dried fish waste to which no chemicals have been added is likely to contain between 8 and 10 per cent. nitrogen, 4.5 to 9 per cent. phosphoric acid and 2 to 3 per cent. potash. Such plain dried fish manure may be used at the rate of 3 to 4 oz. to the sq. yd. in late winter and early spring. Undried fish waste should be used at rates varying between 1 cwt. to 6 sq. yd. and 1 cwt. to 24 sq. yd.

FLAKED A term used by exhibitors and plant fanciers for certain varieties of flowers in which two colours are combined in broad streaks or bands, e.g. flaked carnations are bicoloured varieties which can be compared with fancy carnations but differ from them in the bolder and broader markings of the flowers.

Petal markings of a flaked carnation

FLAMED Another term used by exhibitors and plant fanciers, particularly for certain broken varieties of tulip in which each petal is marked with a broad central band of a contrasting colour which runs out into narrow streaks or feathers (q.v.).

FLEA BEETLE Very small black or dark coloured beetles which live on the leaves of cabbages and other members of the cabbage family (*Cruciferae*) including turnips and radishes. The beetles make small round holes in the leaves and when disturbed they jump vigorously – hence the popular name. Seedlings are most liable to be attacked but damage can be done to plants of any age. Complete control can be effected by dusting the plants with BHC, carbaryl or derris. This pest is also known as turnip fly.

FLOCCULATE To join small particles together into larger granules. Horticulturally this term is used to describe the process of improving the texture of a clay soil by giving it a coarser and more porous structure. This effect may be produced by treating such soils with lime and also by dressing them with certain other materials such as alginates. See Lime and Soil Conditioners.

FLORA All the plants that grow in a particular country or locality or a book describing such plants.

FLORAL Anything pertaining to a flower. Thus petals, sepals, anthers and stigmas are all floral parts.

FLORE PLENO A botanical term used to describe flowers which are double, that is to say, which have more than the characteristic number of petals, e.g. the familiar double flowered form of *Gypsophila paniculata* is botanically known as *Gypsophila paniculata flore pleno*.

A double-flowered form of hollyhock

FLORET One of the individual flowers which make up the head of a composite flower, as in the daisy. The florets which form the cushion-like centre of a composite flower are known as disk florets, while the outside florets which carry ornamental petals are known as ray florets.

FLORIST In a wide sense anyone who deals in flowers or produces floral designs is known as a florist, but the gardener sometimes uses the term to designate those flowers which have been highly developed in gardens, in contrast to natural species and varieties, e.g. certain forms of roses, dahlias, chrysanthemums, gladioli, auriculas and tulips may appropriately be described as florist flowers.

FLOWER A flower is a short reproductive shoot, the stem or axis of which may be thickened or flattened (receptacle).

In a perfect flower the leaf or leaves at the end of this stem have been modified to form the carpel(s) or female organ(s). These are surrounded by stamens which are leaves altered to bear the male organs. These in turn are frequently surrounded by attractively coloured leaves or petals, protected by green leaves or sepals.

In semi-double or double flowers the stamens and/or the carpels develop in a

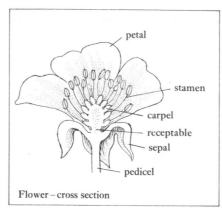

Flower – cross section

more leaf-like form as petaloids or extra petals and often halfway stages can be found with one half a stamen and the other a petal.

An opened pea pod can be seen as a leaf with seeds borne on the margins, supplied by veins from a midrib.

FLUE DUST The sweepings from factory chimneys in which the boiler has forced draught. Because of the intense heat much of the nitrogen, which is present as sulphate of ammonia in ordinary soot, is driven off and frequently the resultant dust has little or no garden value. A few samples, however, contain appreciable quantities of potash, as much as 8 per cent. occasionally. Flue dust should only be purchased where an analysis is available. A sample with 1 per cent. of potash would be worth one-fiftieth the price of sulphate of potash. Better samples can be calculated accordingly.

FLUSH A plentiful supply; often applied to mushrooms and roses which tend to crop intermittently.

FLY A general term used by gardeners not only for a number of genuine flies which are pests in the garden, but also for some insects which are not flies at all. Among the latter may be mentioned the black fly and the greenfly, both of which are aphids; the white fly which is closely related to the scale insects and superficially is more like a tiny moth than a fly, and the frog fly which resembles an aphid rather than a fly.

Among genuine flies which are troublesome in the garden the most important are the cabbage root fly, carrot fly, celery fly, mushroom fly, narcissus fly, marguerite fly (see Leaf Miner), onion fly and crane fly. Without exception it is the maggots (larvae) and not the flies themselves which cause the damage and, in many instances, they do this by boring into the roots or, with the narcissus and onion flies, into the bulbs of the plants attacked. Some, such as the celery fly and the marguerite fly, produce maggots which tunnel their way through the leaves, in consequence of which they are usually referred to as leaf miners. These various

pests are dealt with in greater detail under their particular names.

Sawfly is a name given to various small fly-like insects which are more closely related to wasps than to the familiar house fly. The maggots of all these sawflies feed on plants, usually on the leaves or stems. Among the most troublesome are the apple sawfly (a fruit eater), the currant sawfly, the gooseberry sawfly and the rose sawfly.

FOOT ROT A name given to a fungal disease of cucumbers, melons and tomatoes, caused by a species of *Phytophthora*. It attacks the main stem of the plant, usually just above soil level, though occasionally higher up and in tomatoes also attacks the fruits causing a rot known as buck-eye (q.v.). The damage closely resembles that caused by the diseases known as collar rot and damping-off, though these are caused by totally different organisms. As a result of the decay the upper part of the plant is deprived of sap and quickly collapses.

The most effective remedy is to keep the base of the plant rather dry, and to make it easier to do this it is a good plan to plant on small mounds of soil and place a metal collar around the base of each plant to prevent water splashing on to it. Some gardeners plant out their cucumbers and melons in the small pots in which they have been raised, merely knocking off the bottom of each pot so that the roots can grow out into the new soil. The pot is allowed to project an inch or so above the surface of the bed and so this acts as a collar or shield to keep the base of the plant dry.

Plants should be grown as far as possible in sterilized compost and the surface around tomatoes mulched with peat or clean straw to prevent fungus spores being splashed on to fruits. Soil around plants may be watered with Cheshunt compounds, soluble copper, thiram or captan.

FORCING The practice of hurrying plants into growth, flower or fruit by the application of heat or some other means. A forcing house is a greenhouse or shed specially designed for this class of work.

Some subjects force more rapidly and readily in the dark. This is notably so with rhubarb, which is often forced under the greenhouse staging, in warm sheds or even in cellars. Seakale, dandelion and chicory are forced in the same way and for these plants the darkness has the additional advantage that it blanches the stems, which is necessary to make them palatable.

Forcing bulbs It is most important that before bulbs are introduced to heat, they should be given a period during which they can develop an adequate root system. With narcissi, tulips and hyacinths, this is ensured by plunging the pots or other receptacles containing the bulbs, in a cool place out of

Rhubarb can be forced in boxes under the greenhouse staging. It is essential that all light is excluded

doors, for a period of at least eight weeks before they are introduced to a greenhouse. Sand, sifted ashes or peat are materials commonly used for plunging and the pots or boxes are completely covered to a depth of 2 or 3 in. Other bulbs are not plunged but are placed in an unheated frame or sheltered place out of doors for a similar period before being forced.

With some bulbs, it has been found that treatment prior to planting can have a marked effect on the speed of growth when they are forced, e.g. daffodils, if placed in cold storage for a period of several weeks in August and September, will force much more rapidly than untreated bulbs. With tulips and hyacinths slightly less cold temperatures have been found to produce the same result and some commercial growers have found it worth while to install large refrigeration plants for pre-treatment of bulbs in these ways. See Vernalization.

Another method is to retard growth for a period and then bring the plants into warmth. This produces remarkable results with some kinds of plants and is much used for lily of the valley. Selected crowns, lifted during their period of dormancy in winter, are placed in cold store and so prevented from growing at their normal time the following spring. They are kept in cold store throughout the spring and summer and are then potted and brought into warmth in the autumn. Growth is very rapid and flower spikes are produced within a few weeks.

Plants and bulbs that have been forced are usually so much weakened by the process that they are either of very little use afterwards or else must be allowed several years of normal culture before being forced again.

Forcing shrubs Many shrubs, including roses, are potted and brought into the greenhouse for forcing. Only strong, well-grown plants should be used for this purpose and it is an advantage if they are really well established in the pots before they are forced. The plants in their pots are grown in the open for most of the year, usually with the pots plunged to their rims in a bed of sand or ashes to reduce evaporation. They are brought into a cool greenhouse in the autumn or early winter and are only subjected to a really warm atmosphere for the last few weeks before flowers are required. Indian azaleas, *Deutzia gracilis*, lilacs, *Prunus triloba*, hydrangeas and *Cytisus fragrans* are popular subjects for forcing in this way. Provided great heat is not used and the plants are well looked after during the summer, being properly and regularly fed, watered and pruned, they will not suffer in constitution and can be gently forced several years in succession. After hard forcing, however, a prolonged period of recuperation may be required.

FORK Several different kinds of fork are useful to the gardener. The two most familiar are the digging fork, usually with four tines or prongs, which are square in cross section, and the hand fork, which is similar to a trowel but with three or four prongs instead of a solid blade.

A digging fork can be used for many tasks besides digging. It is, for example, one of the best tools for breaking down large clods of soil after winter weathering, for which purpose it is used with swinging, sideways blows. It is also quite a useful tool for lifting potatoes and other crops, though some gardeners prefer for this purpose a special lifting fork with tines which are slightly more curved than those of a digging fork and round instead of square in section. A similar fork, but with five instead of four round-sectioned prongs, is also useful for spreading manure and compost. Another type of fork is that with flat, rather broad tines, usually four in number. This is specially useful for digging the lighter types of soil which would pass too readily through an ordinary square-tined digging fork.

A border fork is really a small digging fork and is sometimes known as a lady's fork. It is most useful for light work and for loosening the soil round growing plants, as for example in the herbaceous border. A hand fork can also be used for this purpose, particularly in confined spaces such as between seedlings or in the rock garden. A hand fork is useful for lifting seedlings that are to be transplanted and for removing weeds.

All the larger types of fork may be manufactured with either T or D handles and there appears to be a strong regional preferences for these.

FORKING The practice of breaking up ground with a fork. It differs in no essential respect from digging and on many heavy soils a fork is a better tool to use than a spade for digging. A fork is not, however, a suitable tool with which to turn over the top spit of ground covered with turf or dense weeds, as for both these it is necessary to use the blade of a sharp spade to chop through the grass or woody roots so that the soil can be lifted cleanly and easily.

FORMAL GARDEN A term used to describe any garden or part of a garden designed on a more or less geometrical pattern, in contrast to an informal garden in which the lines are more flowing and irregular and the balance less obvious. It was rarely used in connection with gardens until the publication of *The Formal Garden in England* by Reginald Blomfield in 1892. No hard and fast rules can be given for formal gardens and every kind of intermediate type exists between the completely formal garden, as exemplified by the old English knot gardens in which beds contained elaborate patterns in clipped box or other plants and were arranged with absolute symmetry, to the completely informal wild or woodland gar-

Bulbs for forcing should be removed from the cold frame and brought indoors when shoots are showing above the rims of the pots

dens, which became so popular towards the close of the 19th century and in which it is sometimes difficult to have any organized plan.

FORMALIN The commercial name for the 40 per cent. solution of formaldehyde gas in water, usually sold for horticultural purposes. It is a useful chemical with which to sterilize partially soil which has become infected with disease-causing organisms, see Sterilization.

Formalin is also used as a disinfecting agent for certain seeds, particularly those of celery, which have suffered from leaf spot, a seed-borne disease. The seed is soaked for 3 hours before sowing, in a solution made by adding 1 teaspoonful of formalin to ½ gallon of water.

FORMOTHION A systemic insecticide specially useful for killing aphids and red spider mites. It is only moderately poisonous to warm-blooded animals, including man, but should not be used on edible crops within one week of harvesting. It is a liquid which should be diluted with water according to manufacturers' instructions and applied as a spray. Chrysanthemums, nasturtiums and African marigolds may be damaged by it.

FRAME A structure which can be covered by removable lights, glazed with either glass or glass substitute.

Frames are of many different types and sizes. The old-fashioned garden frame was usually made to accommodate lights measuring 6 ft. by 4 ft., each light being made with several sash bars and glazed with numerous panes of glass, generally about 10 in. broad and 12 in. deep. This type of frame is still much used, but has been replaced for many purposes, particularly in commercial gardens, by the dutch frame, which is designed to take lights measuring 62 in. by 25 in. and glazed with one pane of glass. Dutch lights are much lighter than the old-fashioned English lights and can be handled by one person. Moreover, as they have no sash bars, they transmit more light,

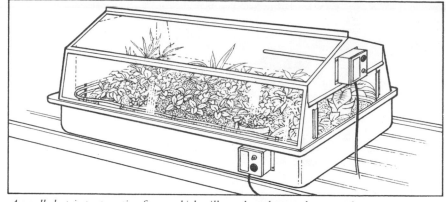

A small electric propagating frame which will stand on the greenhouse staging

which is better for the plants growing beneath them. Smaller frames for private gardens are often made to accommodate lights measuring 3 ft. by 4 ft. each with several sash bars and glazed with comparatively small panes of glass as in the 6 ft. by 4 ft. lights.

The lights may be made of wood or metal, but wood is still the more popular material as there is some difficulty in manufacturing a metal light which has no tendency to whip when lifted by one corner, as it may have to be when it is raised for inspection of the plants and watering.

Frames are as varied as the lights used to cover them. They may be portable or permanent, made of brick, wood, metal or plastic. The old-fashioned garden frames usually had brick walls about 1 ft. high in front and 18 in. to 2 ft. high at the back. They were provided with broadly-rabbeted cross members on which the lights could be slid easily backwards or forwards, for both ventilation and inspection of the plants. Small frames for private gardens are often made with a hinged light which can be thrown right open but cannot be removed from the frame. Dutch lights are often used on improvised frames which can very readily be taken to pieces and erected elsewhere. These may be made of 1-in. thick planks bolted or screwed to 2 in. by 2 in. uprights driven into the ground. As a rule no cross

members are provided. Frequently, the walls of these dutch frames are the same height front and back and the necessary tilt to run off rain is secured by banking up the soil on, which the frame is placed. This method has the advantages that all plants can be the same distance from the glass and that, if the tilt is towards the south, the frame receives maximum illumination with the minimum amount of shade thrown by the walls.

Various kinds of plastic may be used in place of glass for frames. Some manufacturers make frames in such materials, or corrugated plastic sheeting suitably stiffened with a light wooden framework, can take the place of glazed lights.

Cold frame is the name given to any type of frame which is not heated.

Propagating frame is the name given to any frame specially reserved for the propagation of plants and particularly for the germination of seed and the striking of cuttings. As a rule, propagating frames are comparatively small, often with only one light, and they must always be well made so that, when the light is in position, the frame is practically airtight. This is necessary to ensure the close atmosphere essential for the propagation of some plants. Such frames are often placed within the greenhouse for additional protection and may have hot water pipes or other heating apparatus placed beneath them or be provided with soil-warming electric cables to produce bottom heat (see page 318).

A sand frame is a particular type of propagating frame in which pure sand is used in place of soil or a mixture of soil, sand and peat. It is a device developed for the rooting of certain rather difficult cuttings, particularly those of some shrubs. The sand frame is often placed in full sunshine and is not shaded at any time. In order to prevent the cuttings flagging under such conditions frequent watering is necessary even to the extent of three or four times each day. It is obvious that such a device is of more service

This wooden frame is covered with dutch lights. The lack of sash bars allows more light to be transmitted

to the professional gardener who can give his whole time to the work, than to the amateur who may have to be away from his garden for fairly long periods.

A more practical development of this idea is the mist propagator. See Mist Propagation.

Frames fulfil three distinct functions in the garden. They provide a means of hastening the germination of seeds or the rooting of cuttings and are thus valuable to the propagator. They enable the gardener to obtain certain crops at times when they could not be obtained out of doors, and this is particularly true of early supplies of such things as lettuces, radishes, cucumbers, french beans, vegetable marrows, beetroots and carrots. Lastly, they provide a convenient method of hardening-off plants which have been raised in a greenhouse and are to be grown on in the open air.

In general, the best aspect for a frame is one that is open to the south but has some shelter from the north and east. If a greenhouse is included in addition to frames in the garden equipment, it often pays to have at least some of the frames against the south or west wall of the greenhouse as in this position the frame will get a certain amount of protection as well as some warmth if the greenhouse is heated.

Frames for some classes of alpine plants are sited to face north in order to provide cool, moist conditions.

Frames which are mainly used for accommodating plants grown in pots, pans or boxes are best provided with a floor of sifted boiler ashes, shingle, or peat as these materials will retain an adequate amount of moisture without encouraging insects or worms. Frames in which plants, cuttings or seeds are to be grown in a bed of soil should be filled with a suitable compost (see page 281). Concrete is seldom a satisfactory material as a floor for frames because it will not hold moisture and reflects sun heat too strongly. If it is used, adequate outlets for water must be provided.

The warming of frames can be carried out in a variety of ways. Hot water pipes may be passed through them as in the case of greenhouse heating. They may be equipped with electrical air heaters or electric soil-warming cables may be buried in the soil. An old-fashioned system which still has much to commend it is the hotbed (q.v.).

FRIABLE Easily broken up; a term used to describe soil that is in the right condition to be broken down to a fine, crumbly state.

FROG FLY, see Leaf Hopper

FROG HOPPER Another name for the insect commonly referred to as cuckoo spit (q.v.).

FROND The leaf of a fern or a palm.

Protecting the crowns of herbaceous plants that are likely to suffer frost damage. Dry bracken is held in place with wire netting or split canes

FROST A great many plants are damaged to a greater or lesser degree by temperatures below freezing point. In consequence, frost is one of the big problems with which the gardener has to contend. There are three principal ways in which this problem can be tackled (1) by protecting plants, either all the time or when frost threatens; (2) by preventing frost, at any rate at those periods when it is likely to do most damage; (3) by producing varieties which are resistant to frost.

Protection against frost Familiar methods of protection against frost are the greenhouse and the frame (q.v.). There are, however, other methods which the gardener may employ, particularly with plants which for one reason or another cannot be readily removed to a greenhouse or frame during cold spells of weather. A covering of ashes, peat, chopped bracken, straw or some other materials with good heat insulating properties will often serve to protect the crowns of herbaceous plants that are subject to frost damage, e.g. eremurus and gunnera. Such a protective covering should be placed in position as soon as the leaves die down in autumn and need not be removed until shoots begin to appear the following spring. It is often desirable to keep the protective covering out of direct contact with the dormant crown of the plant. This is particularly so with gunneras and the method employed is to place some bushy hazel twigs over the plant, or make a low, tent-like structure with fine-meshed, galvanized wire netting and then place the protective material over the twigs or netting. If chopped bracken or straw is used, it is also convenient to have a further outer covering of wire netting pegged down over this material to prevent it being blown away.

Hessian or old sacking is sometimes used as a protective screen for plants, particularly for shrubs such as hydrangeas, which are liable to suffer during frosty weather. No attempt should be made to cover the plants completely with such material, as this would exclude too much light and encourage premature or weak growth. The method is to place a screen closely around the specimen to be protected but to leave the top open for ventilation. Such a screen will give a large measure of protection, though it will not save plants from damage if frost is severe or protracted.

A third method is to use wattle hurdles as a screen. This is serviceable for large specimens or groups of plants which could not easily be protected by sacking or hessian as just described, but is more effective as a protection from wind than against frost.

Although most fruit trees grown in the British Isles are perfectly hardy, their blossom is often very susceptible to frost damage and, if this occurs, the crop may be much reduced or completely destroyed. Small bushes can be protected from moderate spring frosts by covering them with muslin. Old net curtains or any loose-meshed materials can be used for this purpose. Such protective coverings should only be used just before and during the blossom period when frost threatens and in general will only be required at night, being removed each day. Wall-grown fruit trees, such as peaches and nectarines, are often protected while in blossom by hanging hessian in front of them. Some measure of protection is provided by a screen of fish netting as used for protecting raspberries and other soft fruits against birds.

Portable cloches can be used to give frost protection to small plants and seedlings and the use of these is described elsewhere (see page 278).

Protection against short duration frosts,

such as those that often occur towards dawn during the late spring, can be given by allowing a water sprinkler to play over the plants continuously during the period of the frost and until any ice that has formed on the leaves and stems as a result of this treatment has melted. The finer and more mist-like the spray the better.

Prevention of frost It is only practicable to consider the prevention of frost out of doors for short periods during the spring months, but as these are often the most damaging frosts in the garden, especially where fruit is concerned, this is a measure which deserves attention. Spring frosts and particularly those frosts which occur during the last half of April and throughout May, are generally of the type known to meteorologists as radiation frosts, which may be contrasted with wind or convection frosts. The latter are due to cold streams of air which may be coming from many hundreds of miles away. Very little can be done to check wind frosts, except, possibly, the erection of walls or the planting of screening hedges. By contrast, radiation frosts are most liable to occur when the air is still. They are caused by loss of heat from the earth's surface by radiation into outer space and this loss occurs most rapidly when the sky is cloudless. If on an April or May evening the wind gradually dies away and the sky becomes completely clear, the gardener may suspect that a frost will occur by dawn the following morning. His suspicion may become a near certainty if at the same time a wet thermometer (page 324) placed out of doors gives a higher reading on the wet than on the dry bulb. Usually such frosts are foretold by the meteorological experts and announcements are made beforehand on radio or television. The fruit grower should pay particular attention to such warnings just before and during the blossom period.

There are four methods of preventing radiation frost. As the air is undisturbed it will tend to move very slowly, but none the less surely, according to its own weight, which will be governed by its temperature, cold air weighing more than warm air. As a result the cold air will flow downhill like a stream of water, filling hollows and valleys and leaving the high ground. This accounts for the fact, which so often puzzles gardeners, that exposed gardens on the tops of hills often suffer far less from spring frost than those situated in sheltered valleys. This slow flow of cold air may be impeded by any fairly solid obstacle such as a wall or dense hedge. In consequence, on sloping land walls and hedges erected as a protection against wind frosts may actually serve as a trap for the cold air caused by radiation frosts. This air will pile up on the higher ground above the wall or hedge and may cause severe damage to plants growing on it. By cutting large holes in walls or by trim-ming the bottoms of hedges for a height of a foot or so to allow the cold air to flow through frost may often be prevented. It is prudent also to plant tender subjects or fruit trees and bushes, the blossom of which is liable to be damaged by frost, on high rather than on low ground. It is the relative rather than the absolute height of the ground that matters. A hollow situated on a high plateau may be a frost pocket, whereas a knoll in lowland country may stand clear of the surrounding frost.

A second method of preventing spring frost is to warm the air. In some large fruit orchards kerosene burners are placed at frequent intervals and lit when frost threatens, but the cost of running is high and the method is only reasonably efficient where a fairly considerable area is covered by burners. In small orchards cold air flows in too quickly from outside. The smoke from these burners checks loss of heat by radiation.

A third method is to stir up the air and to draw down the comparatively warm air which will be found above the cold layer near soil level. Experiments have been made in the use of propellers mounted on towers, to draw a column of air from above into the garden or orchard. A certain degree of success has been obtained, but once again the method is of more interest to the commercial grower than to the private gardener as it is not economical on small areas.

The fourth method is by slowing down the radiation from the earth's surface to the sky. This may be done by covering the whole area with a dense fog or smoke such as that produced from damp bonfires. Such methods are much used on the Continent for protecting vines and may have some value, though experts differ on this matter.

Frost-resistant varieties There are two main lines on which the breeder may work in producing frost-resistant varieties. One is to breed varieties the tissues of which are actually more resistant to frost than older varieties of the same kind of plant. There are limits to which such increase in hardiness can be pushed and too much must not be expected from it. Examples of this kind of variability in resistance may be seen in apples. The blossom of Bramley's Seedling is very susceptible to frost damage, whereas that of Lord Lambourne is comparatively resistant.

An alternative line of approach, and one which holds out much hope for the fruit grower, is based on the fact that it is the young growth and blossom of woody plants which is most likely to be damaged. If varieties can be produced which start into growth and produce their blossom late, they may escape the period in which frost is likely to occur. A notable example of this is to be seen in the apple Crawley Beauty which seldom blossoms until the end of May, by which time it is unlikely that any severe frost will occur except in the coldest parts of the British Isles. Other late flower-ing apples which are useful for planting in frosty districts are Edward VII and Court Pendu Plat.

FRUIT Literally the seed-bearing organ of a plant. A dry pea pod is as much a fruit in this sense as is a peach. In gardens, how-ever, the term is usually confined to edible fruits.

FRUIT BUD Any dormant bud which will produce a flower or cluster of flowers with the possibility of fruit following. On fruit trees fruit buds can usually be distinguished from growth buds (page 268) by their greater size and prominence. Some fruit trees, and notably in apples and pears, fruit buds on the older branches tend to pro-liferate into branched clusters known as spurs (q.v.). It is necessary to be able to dis-tinguish between fruit buds and growth buds when pruning. In late winter and early spring fruit buds pass through clearly defined stages of development which are important for determining the correct timing of certain spray applications, see Bud Stages.

FRUIT CAGE A structure designed to protect fruit bushes and canes from the attacks of birds. Such cages usually consist of a framework of wood or metal, which may be permanent or portable, over which is stretched string, nylon, galvanized wire or plastic-covered wire netting. To be effective the mesh of this netting should not exceed ¾ in. Cages are most likely to be required when buds are expanding in late winter and early spring and again as the fruit ripens.

FULL BLOSSOM, see Bud Stages

FUMIGATION A method of destroying pests or disease-causing organisms by ex-posing them to insecticidal or fungicidal gases or smokes. For obvious reasons fumi-gation is of more use in greenhouses or other closed structures than out of doors, though it can be practised out of doors with special

For fumigating a greenhouse there are various types of smoke generator including nicotine shreds

apparatus. For example, a method has been devised for fumigating strawberries against aphids. A large drag sheet is pulled slowly across the crop and the insecticidal gas is blown underneath this sheet. This method has not yet been applied to small areas though there seems to be no theoretical objection to it. Fumigation of individual plants can also be accomplished by placing them in a box or other container and introducing the necessary gas or smoke.

Before fumigating a greenhouse it is necessary to make certain that ventilators and doors can be shut tightly and that there are no broken or missing panes through which fumes might escape. If there are gaps round the edges of doors and ventilators, provision should be made to cover these with wet sacks or some other suitable material. As a rule the house must be kept closed for several hours in order that the fumigation may be effective but modern smoke generators work quite rapidly and usually will have deposited their chemically effective film on plants and insects within one hour.

The chemicals most frequently used for greenhouse fumigation are azobenzene, BHC, nicotine and tecnazene. Tetrachlorethane is still occasionally used against white fly, sulphur against red spider mite and fungal diseases and naphthalene against thrips, but they have been largely superseded by more modern treatments.

Another purpose for which fumigation can sometimes be used very effectively is to clear soil of pests. In this instance some substance which gives off fumes, such as naphthalene, paradichlorbenzene, DD, metham-sodium or carbon disulphide, is either injected into the soil by means of a special gun or placed in holes bored in the soil at frequent intervals, the holes then being sealed with soil to prevent the escape of fumes.

Methods of fumigation At one time many different methods had to be used for various kinds of fumigation. Calcium cyanide and tetrachlorethane were simply sprinkled on the floor of the greenhouse, nicotine, sulphur and naphthalene were vaporized over special lamps, and so on. Nowadays, the almost universal adoption of smoke generators has standardized practice. These generators, usually in the form of pellets or small canisters, are supplied with full instructions regarding the space in which they are effective. Having calculated the cubic capacity of the greenhouse by multiplying length, breadth and height to a point midway between eaves and ridge, all measured in feet or fractions of feet, the correct number of pellets or canisters are spaced out down the centre of the house and ignited, starting at the far end from the door and working as quickly as possible back to the door. After which the house is im-

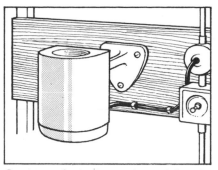

Continuous fumigation can be carried out by an electrically operated fumigator

mediately vacated and the door and ventilators kept closed until all trace of smoke has disappeared.

An alternative method of continuous fumigation can be carried out either by special electrically heated containers holding chemicals which are slowly vaporized, or by suspending bars, usually of a resinous nature, impregnated with a volatile chemical. The electrically heated containers are usually supplied and serviced by a firm which undertakes complete control, leaving nothing to the gardener. With both these types of fumigation it is safe to work in the house despite the presence of the insecticidal and fungicidal fumes.

FUNGICIDE Any substance which will kill fungi. As many plant diseases are caused by fungi, fungicides are of great importance to the gardener. The ideal substance is one which, while very poisonous to fungi, is completely harmless to garden plants. This may never be fully attained but several chemicals or combinations of chemicals come sufficiently close to it to have a wide application in the garden. One of the most useful general fungicides is Bordeaux mixture, which is composed of copper sulphate and quicklime. Copper sulphate itself is very poisonous to fungi, but unfortunately it is also damaging to foliage and soft shoots and can only be used on deciduous plants in the winter months, and then only with great care. Sulphur is another excellent fungicide and is often used by itself in finely powdered form, either as flowers of sulphur or as green horticultural sulphur which is really the flowers of sulphur with colouring matter added to make it less conspicuous on plants. Lime and sulphur are combined in the fungicide known as lime sulphur. This must be purchased as a concentrated solution which is then diluted with water according to manufacturers' instructions. Other popular fungicides are benomyl, calomel, chloraniformethan, dinocap, maneb, quintozene, tecnazene (TCNB), thiophanate-methyl, thiram and zineb. All these substances are described more fully under their respective names.

FUNGUS One of the important divisions of the vegetable kingdom. Fungi are of many different kinds and differ greatly in appearance, habit and method of growth. All are alike, however, in lacking green colouring matter and therefore in being unable to manufacture their food from simple chemicals, using for the process energy derived from the sun. In consequence they must obtain food supplies ready made and this many of them do by attaching themselves to living plants which possess the green colouring matter necessary for photosynthesis. They are, in fact, parasites and like most parasites they can live only by weakening or, in some cases, actually killing their hosts. It is for this reason that many fungi are correctly regarded by the gardener as enemies, for they are the cause of many plant diseases.

Not all fungi are similarly harmful. Many are not parasites but saprophytes, living on plant tissue or other organic matter which is already dead. Frequently these saprophytic fungi perform a very useful function in promoting the decay of dead material and hastening the liberation of the chemical plant foods which it contains and also the production of the humus which is so valuable in the maintenance of soil texture. There are even some fungi which are valuable as human food. The most familiar is the mushroom which has become an important commercial crop.

The most spectacular part of many fungi is the reproductive or spore-producing organ and it is frequently mistaken by the uninstructed for the fungus itself. In fact, it is no more the fungus than the flower of a flowering plant is the plant. The main body of the fungus is composed of a multitude of thread-like growths collectively known as mycelium. If a mushroom bed in full crop is opened, it will be found that the bed is filled with this mycelium so that most of the compost has a whitish appearance. When a parasitic fungus, such as that which causes black spot in roses, attacks a plant, this thread-like mycelium penetrates the living tissues drawing nourishment from the growing cells and destroying them in the process. It is for this reason that the area destroyed gradually increases in extent as the mycelium penetrates further and further into the plant in search of more living tissue from which to draw its nourishment.

Another feature which all fungi have in common is that they reproduce themselves by spores. These are often compared to the seeds of flowering plants, though in fact they differ in many vital features. However, they have this in common with seeds, that they are produced in great numbers, are widely distributed and, that when they find suitable conditions, they germinate and give rise to new specimens of their own kind. Spores are so extremely small as to be dust like. In consequence they can be carried considerable distances by wind or may be spread in water or on the feet of animals and birds. Many fungi produce a special type of spore in the autumn which is capable of resisting cold and other adverse conditions, remaining dormant for a long period and so ensuring the survival of the species during the winter months.

FUSARIUM PATCH One of the most troublesome diseases of lawns which causes the grass to die in more or less circular yellowish brown patches, becoming shiny and often developing a pinkish white outgrowth. It is most likely to occur in autumn or winter on lawns that have had too much nitrogenous feeding late in the summer. One form of the disease commonly appears after grass has been covered by snow and is known as snow mould. Nitrogenous fertilizers should not be used after about mid-August. Diseased patches should be watered with calomel. Any treatment which might raise the pH of the soil above 6 should be avoided.

GALL An abnormal outgrowth which may be due to a variety of causes. Many galls are produced by insects, one of the most familiar being the gall often found on the base of the stems of cabbage and other brassica seedlings which is caused by the maggots of the cabbage gall weevil. Oak trees seem to be particularly susceptible to galls of one kind and another, all of which are caused by the irritation set up by minute insects feeding in the tissues. The curious marble-like structures known as oak apples are galls. Roses suffer from a curious and rather beautiful gall often known as a bedeguar or Robin's pincushion. This may be the size of a Spanish chestnut complete with its outer husk. It is covered all over with hair-like growths, some of which may be green and others red.

However, not all galls are caused by insects. One of the most spectacular is the crown gall caused by a bacterium. It grows on a great many different kinds of plants and particularly on fruit trees where it is usually found at or near soil level. Crown galls often attain considerable size – maybe as big as a football. They seem to have little or no effect on the vigour and health of the plant which they attack.

In general, galls are extremely difficult to control as the pests or other organisms which cause them are more or less completely protected by the gall itself. Fortunately, galls seldom do much damage and are to be considered more as curiosities than as actual pests or diseases.

GALL WEEVIL This small white grub which attacks the base of the stems of cabbages and other brassicas causing them to develop lumps or galls, is described more fully under the name cabbage gall weevil.

GAMMA-BHC, see BHC

GARDEN CENTRE A place in which plants and seeds as well as horticultural chemicals, accessories, tools and machinery can be purchased on a self-service basis. Many plants are likely to be container grown though some may be pre-packed. Some garden centres grow all or most of the plants they sell, but many act as distributors for specialist wholesale growers. Advantages of the garden centre are that much of the cost of packing and carriage is avoided, that the customer can inspect and select the plants, and take them away for immediate planting at practically any time of the year.

GAZEBO A small two-storey pavilion from which fine views of the garden or landscape can be enjoyed.

GENE The physical unit of inheritance. The development of every characteristic feature in a plant or animal is controlled by a gene or genes. It will be realized, therefore, that even a fairly simple organism will have a great many genes, yet each is so small that the complete set characteristic of that organism is reproduced in every living cell. Individual genes are collected together into rod-like bodies known as chromosomes which themselves form a part of the nucleus of each living cell.

In the ordinary cells genes commonly occur in pairs which separate when sex cells are formed so that these special cells only contain one of each pair of genes. The pairs may be identical or dissimilar. In a very simple example, such as the pair of genes which control flower colour in the Four O'Clock Flower, *Mirabilis jalapa*, the petals may be red, white or pink depending on whether both genes are of the type which produces colour, both of the type which inhibits colour or one of each type.

It is not usually as simple as that. Commonly one variant of each pair is dominant over the other so that when both are present the effect of one is completely masked. A familiar example of this is the round-seeded or wrinkled-seeded feature in peas. These characters are controlled by a pair of genes. If both are for the round-seeded character all seeds will be of this kind. If both are for the wrinkled-seeded character all seeds will be wrinkled. But if a plant carries opposite genes the seeds are not intermediate, but are all of the round-seeded type. The importance of this will appear when such hybrid peas are used as parents, for the genes never lose their identity even when masked in this way. Each sex cell will have either a gene for the wrinkled type of seed or one for the round type and they will be produced in equal numbers. In consequence, if a hybrid pea of this type is fertilized with its own pollen it will produce some offspring of the pure round-seeded type and they will be produced in approximately the proportion of one each of the pure types to two of the hybrid type.

Since the hybrids look outwardly like the pure round peas the proportion will appear to be 3 pure round to 1 wrinkled until tested by breeding. With each generation, genes for the wrinkled character again come together and that character will re-appear.

Plants which carry many genes of opposite characters, such as the round- or wrinkled-seeded factor in peas, are described as heterozygous and are said to be hybrid-breeding, whereas those in which all or nearly all the genes are of identical pairing kind are said to be homozygous or pure-breeding. One of the problems confronting the seedsman who wishes to place a seed on the market is to ensure that all, or nearly all, heterozygous plants are eliminated, and that, in consequence, this novelty will breed true from seed. Many plants, including most fruit trees, cannot be raised true to type from seeds because of the number of contrasting genes which they contain.

GENETICS The science of heredity which includes that of breeding.

GENUS A group of closely related species, see Classification.

GERMINATION The first stage in the growth of a seed. In order to ensure germination, the seed must not only be living, but also must be provided with certain physical conditions, including a reasonable quantity of moisture, a sufficiently high temperature and some air. The precise degree of temperature required for germination varies from one species to another and almost invariably plants from tropical regions require a higher temperature than those from temperate regions. These temperatures may vary from as little as 7°C. for plants from cold regions to as much as 27°C. for tropical plants.

Many seeds lose their power of germination fairly quickly, and with all seeds the power of germination tends to be lowered with the passage of time. Stories concerning the germination of seeds after many thousands of years can be dismissed as false, but it is quite possible for some seeds to germinate after periods of 10, 20, 50, or possibly even 100 years. It has been estimated that delphinium seeds lose at least 50 per cent. of their germinating power within the first 6 or 8 months.

The majority of seeds appear to germinate most readily and satisfactorily when the soil in which they have been sown is exposed to a fair amount of light, but some seeds will only germinate in the dark. Air is essential to germination, and it is often through lack of air that seeds buried too deeply fail to germinate or germinate badly.

Many seeds go through a period of dormancy after ripening during which they cannot germinate no matter what the conditions. Others will germinate the moment they are ripe or even before they are fully ripe.

The provision of a good tilth for seed beds or of a suitable compost for seed pans and boxes is very important because this kind of tilth or compost provides the physical conditions of moisture and air which are essential to germination. If the tilth is faulty or the compost too fine, the soil will pack down so closely over the seeds that air will be excluded and germination prevented or retarded. If the soil is too loose it will dry out so quickly that there may not be sufficient moisture to complete germination. See Seed Sowing.

GISHURST COMPOUND A proprietary preparation containing soap and sulphur and used in the greenhouse to kill mealy bugs. It is applied to the dormant rods of vines and similar hard-wooded plants with a rather stiff, wet paintbrush. Gishurst compound should only be used in winter when growth is dormant.

GLABROUS Strictly speaking this term means no more than not hairy though it is frequently wrongly used in the more positive sense of smooth.

GLASS In the garden glass is used principally in the construction of greenhouses, frames and cloches. For all these purposes it is important that it should be reasonably free of bubbles which may act as lenses and so focus beams of sunlight on to plants in the manner of a burning glass, possibly causing serious damage. It is also important that glass should be reasonably thick, partly because thin glass is very liable to be broken, but even more because the heat insulation properties of glass depend a good deal on its thickness. Contrary to popular belief, glass is a fairly good insulator when compared, thickness for thickness, with other materials such as plastic, wood or brick. The thickness of glass is always indicated by the weight of a sheet measuring one square foot. Thus 21-oz. glass, which is the usual weight for horticultural work, weighs 21 oz. per sq. ft. Sometimes 24-oz. glass is employed and this gives superior protection.

It is not essential that glass for horticultural use should be completely clear, though it must not be very opaque. However, the type of glass usually referred to as rolled glass can be used and is cheaper than clear glass.

Ordinary glass, though transparent to all visible light, does not allow the ultra-violet rays to pass through. Special glass can be manufactured which is translucent to these rays and it has sometimes been claimed that this has special value for horticultural purposes, but experiments have not substantiated this.

GLASSHOUSE, see Greenhouse

GLAUCOUS Bluish grey, covered with a bloom. A term often used in the description of leaves or stems.

GOOSEBERRY MILDEW Two quite distinct fungi cause mildew diseases on gooseberries. One is known as American gooseberry mildew, and the other as European gooseberry mildew, and the former is by far the more serious. They can be distinguished by the fact that the American gooseberry mildew produces a greyish or brownish, felt-like outgrowth on the fruits and leaves, particularly on the tips of the young shoots. As a result growth is crippled. Though the fruits can be washed clean and are then quite palatable, much time is wasted and the crop is seriously damaged from a commercial point of view. European gooseberry mildew produces a powdery white outgrowth on the leaves and does not affect the fruits.

Both these mildews can be kept in check by spraying with lime sulphur or washing soda and soft soap. One application of lime sulphur at summer strength (page 334) applied as soon as the fruits have set, is usually sufficient to control European gooseberry mildew, but two applications are likely to be required for American gooseberry mildew, the first when the fruits are set and the second three weeks later. If washing soda and soft soap (page 409) are used, 5 to 6 applications should be given at intervals of two or three weeks, from the time the fruits are set until they are nearly ripe. The washing soda treatment has the merit that the fruits are not marked in any way and that it can be used with safety on all varieties whereas some, such as Cousen's Seedling and Leveller, may be damaged by sulphur in any form.

GRAFT HYBRID A hybrid which has resulted from the intermingling of the cells of stock and scion after grafting. See Chimaera.

GRAFTING Graft is the name applied to any union made between one plant and another or even between two branches of the same tree or shrub and it may occur naturally, as when two branches in a hawthorn hedge rub together and eventually wound each other sufficiently to produce calluses which then fuse into one. This is really the essential feature upon which grafting relies – the ability of a wounded surface of living plant tissue to produce a callus of new growth to cover the wound. If two artificially wounded surfaces are bound together and the right conditions are provided, they will unite through their respective calluses, provided that the plants themselves are sufficiently closely related. The gardener makes use of this characteristic to propagate many plants which would otherwise be difficult because they do not root readily from

cuttings or cannot be raised true from seed. Budding, which is really a form of grafting, has already been described (see page 268).

There are a good many different ways of grafting, all of which rely on the same principle but which differ in the details of their application. Some have been found in practice to be more suitable for certain kinds of plant than others and also some, by their nature, are more suitable for joining parts of plants which differ greatly in their diameter, e.g. the thin shoot of an apple to the thick trunk of an old apple tree. By contrast, other methods are more valuable where the parts to be joined are roughly of the same diameter, e.g. where a young apple shoot is to be joined to a young apple stock.

Before describing the most important of these methods, it is necessary to explain two terms which are used in connection with every kind of grafting. They are stock, which is the name given to that part of a plant destined to provide the roots, and scion, which is applied to that part which supplies the branches or top growth.

Grafting is usually done just as the plants are starting into growth; for example, the grafting of apple and pear trees is done at the end of March or early in April. It is desirable that the stock should be a little more advanced in growth than the scion, and to ensure this suitable young shoots of apple or pear from which scions may be prepared are usually cut in December or January and planted, right way up, in soil, in the coolest and shadiest place possible, such as the north side of a wall. Here they will keep plump and in good condition but perfectly dormant for several weeks after shoots on the tree have broken into leaf. However, though this use of retarded scions helps grafting, it is not essential to it.

If the grafting is successful, the scions will usually start to make leaves and new shoots within a few weeks. A month or so after this, the wax and tie should be very carefully removed to prevent the latter from cutting into the swollen bark. When this has been done, make quite certain that the scion has made a firm union with the stock by the formation of new callus growth. If there is any doubt on this point, do not disturb the scion but retie at once. It should not be necessary to rewax.

Bridge grafting This, unlike other methods of grafting, is not used as a method of propagation but as a means of repairing. It is particularly serviceable where trees have been badly barked by rabbits or other animals or cankered. If the bark has been removed right round the trunk of the tree destroying a complete ring of cambium, the plant is almost certain to die in time as there will be no passage for the return of food from leaves to roots. To overcome this the gardener can bridge the gap with a series of grafts prepared from young shoots of the same or a similar tree. The method of preparing the grafts in this case is very much the same as for rind grafting, except that the scions must be long enough to bridge the gap with a little to spare and must be cut to a tapering wedge at each end. Similarly two vertical incisions are made in the bark of the damaged tree, one above and one below the area of damaged bark. One prepared wedge of the bridge is then inserted in the lower incision and the other in the upper incision and both are bound in place and waxed. As a rule it is necessary to insert several of these bridges round the trunk where it has been barked. The bridges, as their name implies, carry sap over the wounded area. In time they will increase in girth and serve to support the tree and maintain it in healthy growth for many years.

Cleft grafting This is used mainly for the reworking of old fruit trees. It is not a particularly good method as it necessitates splitting the top of the stock and water is apt to collect in this split and cause decay. It has, however, the merit of simplicity. The stock is beheaded as for whip and tongue or rind grafting (see later) and is then split down the middle with a chopper or billhook which can be driven in with a hammer. The scions, which are made from year-old shoots, are cut at the base in the form of a long tapering wedge, two cuts being made on each scion, one on each side. There are thus two exposed surfaces instead of one as with whip and tongue and rind grafting. The taper wedge is then inserted in the cleft in such a manner that the cambium layer on one side coincides with the cambium layer of the stock. As a rule a wooden or metal wedge is used to keep the cleft open while the scion is being inserted and then the wedge is removed so that the cleft closes together and grips the scion in position. It is common practice to insert two scions in each cleft, one at each side. After this the scions are bound in position and the wound covered with grafting wax.

This form of grafting is sometimes used in the propagation of double-flowered forms of the perennial gypsophila (*Gypsophila paniculata flore pleno*). In this instance roots of the ordinary single flowered strain are used as stocks. Pieces of roots about $\frac{1}{4}$ in. in thickness are cut up into lengths of from 2 to 3 in. The top end of each piece of root is then split downwards for a length of about one inch. The scion is prepared from a firm young shoot of the double gypsophila and the bottom of this shoot is cut on both sides to form a narrow wedge. It is then inserted in the split rootstock as already described and bound up but no wax is applied. The grafted plant is then potted in a sandy compost, the whole of the wounded area being covered by this. The pots containing the grafts are finally plunged in a warm propagating frame. This kind of gypsophila

propagation is usually done in late spring or early summer.

Framework grafting This name is applied to a system of reworking old fruit trees in which, instead of the main branches being cut back to short stumps, practically the whole of the original branch system of the tree is retained and a great many grafts are inserted on this extensive framework. The method is laborious and requires a lot of grafting material, but has the advantage that a full-sized cropping tree can be obtained in a year or so, whereas, if the main branches are cut away, several years must elapse before a new branch system is elaborated. Frameworking is sometimes known as porcupine grafting, because of the quill-like appearance of the grafts studded all over the tree.

Four methods of grafting are commonly used when renewing trees by the framework method, whip and tongue grafting, stub grafting, oblique side grafting, and bark or inverted grafting.

Stub grafts are inserted in the bases of side growths, usually growths not above $\frac{1}{2}$ in. in thickness. The side growth is prepared to receive the graft by making a short downward cut on its upper surface just above the point at which it joins the main branch. The scion is prepared from part of a well-grown, year-old shoot cut at the bottom to form a rather short, double-sided wedge. The side growth is bent downwards so that the incision in it opens. The wedge of the scion is thrust into this and the shoot is then released so that it springs back and grips the scion in position. No tying is necessary. The shoot is severed at once just above the graft and the whole wound is then covered with wax.

Oblique side grafting is done directly on to main branches and stems too thick for stub grafting. An incision is made in the bark of the branch or stem. The scion is made from similar material as that used for stub grafting and is cut in the form of a tapering wedge, the two faces of which are inclined towards one another so that where

they meet they form a knife-like edge. This wedge is then thrust obliquely into the incision in the bark in such a way that one face lies snugly against the exposed wood of the branch and the other against the interior face of the flap produced by the incision. The springiness of the flap of bark is usually sufficient to grip the scion in position, but if it does appear to be at all insecure, it can be further fixed with a gimp pin. The wounded area should then be covered with grafting wax.

Bark or inverted-L grafting is also a method by which scions may be inserted directly on the main branches or stems. First of all an incision is made in the bark of the stem in the form of a rather obtuse-angled L. The flap of bark formed by this incision is then gently raised from the wood beneath with the thin, scalpel-like end of a budding knife. The scion is made from similar material to that used for the other grafts, and is prepared by cutting it in the form of a wedge at the base, one side of the wedge being considerably longer than the other. It is inserted beneath the flap of bark in such a manner that the longer surface of the wedge lies against the exposed wood of the tree, while the shorter surface is in contact with the interior layer of the flap of bark, and it is fixed in this position with a gimp pin driven right through the bark and scion, into the wood beneath. Once again the whole wounded surface must be protected with grafting wax.

Whip and tongue grafting This is probably the most widely used method of grafting where young stocks are concerned. It is the method employed by most nurserymen for propagating apples and pears and it is also used for many ornamental trees. It is not a good method to use where there is a great difference in diameter between stock and scion, though it can be used when the stock is as much as twice the diameter of the scion.

The essential wounding in this method is done by removing, with a sharp knife, a long slip of wood from both stock and scion.

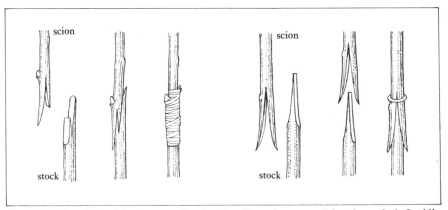

Two kinds of grafting: left, the stages involved in whip and tongue; right, the method of saddle grafting

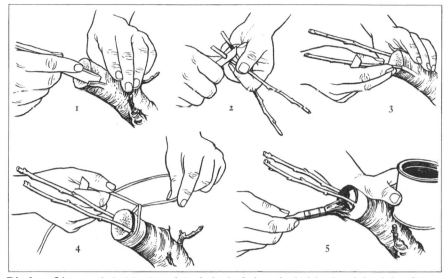

Rind grafting. 1. *An incision is made in the bark of a branch which has been beheaded.* **2.** *Scions are prepared and,* **3,** *inserted under the bark.* **4.** *Raffia is used to secure them and,* **5,** *the wounded area is covered with grafting wax*

The stock is usually a young seedling or well-rooted cutting and it should be well established in the soil. First of all this stock is prepared by being beheaded. When using young fruit stocks, this is generally done at a height of 9 to 10 in. above ground level. Any side shoots which may remain on the stock are then removed. The main cut is made by inserting the blade of the knife about 2 in. below the point of beheading and drawing it upwards so as to remove a slip of bark and wood 2 in. long and $\frac{1}{4}$ to $\frac{1}{3}$ in. wide. The scion generally consists of part of a well-grown one-year-old shoot. As a rule a piece 4 to 5 in. long is adequate. The knife is inserted 2 in. from the bottom of this shoot and drawn downwards so as to remove another slip of bark and wood 2 in. long and if possible also $\frac{1}{4}$ to $\frac{1}{3}$ in. wide, so that the cut surfaces of both stock and scion may be fitted exactly together. If the shoot is too thin to permit of a cut of this width being made, the two cut surfaces must be ranged together on one side only. It is essential that the cambium layer of the stock must actually touch the cambium of the scion on one side if not on both sides.

To complete the whip and tongue graft, two further incisions are made on the cuts already formed, but in an opposite direction, to give two tongues of wood which can be fitted together. The sole purpose of these tongues is to hold the scion in position on the stock while the gardener binds them together with soft twine or raffia after which the wound must be covered with grafting wax to prevent the rapid loss of sap by evaporation. This completes the operation.

Rind grafting This is the method most commonly employed in regrafting old trees. It can also be applied to younger material if there is a fair difference in diameter between stock and scion. The stock is beheaded as

for whip and tongue grafting. In the case of old trees that are being reworked, this beheading is usually carried out a foot or so above the crotch, each branch stump receiving one or more scions. Sometimes one branch is left unpruned to keep the stock growing until the scions have united and grown sufficiently to take over.

The stock is prepared by making a 2-in. incision vertically in the bark, starting from the point of beheading. The knife should penetrate right through the bark to the hard wood beneath. If the stock is in correct condition, it should then be possible to lift the bark away from the wood on each side of this cut. The scion, which is prepared from a well-grown, year-old shoot as for whip and tongue grafting, is prepared by making a 2-in. long, wedge-like cut on its lower part. The point of this thin wedge is inserted beneath the flaps of bark and pressed down until the whole cut surface of the scion lies against the wood of the stock. It is then bound in position with raffia or soft string and covered with grafting wax. If the stock is very thick it is quite possible to insert several scions round it, but they should be placed at least 3 in. apart. Further treatment is exactly the same as for whip grafting.

Saddle grafting This is a system of grafting often employed in the propagation of rhododendrons and some other choice shrubs. Stock and scion should be as nearly as possible of the same diameter. As a rule this kind of grafting is done in a propagating frame within the greenhouse, for which purpose young stocks are potted some months in advance. However, there is nothing in the method itself which makes this treatment essential, but simply that it is usually applied to subjects which require more nursing than fruit trees.

The stock is prepared by being beheaded

a few inches above ground level and then cut on both sides to form an upward-pointing wedge. The scion is split upwards from the base so that it can be fitted like a saddle over this wedge. It is essential that the cambium layer of the scion shall touch that of the stock on at least one side. If stock and scion are of equal diameter, it will be possible for them to touch on both sides, which is ideal. In either case, when in position the scion is bound to the stock with raffia or soft twine.

Splice grafting This is the simplest method of grafting as far as the actual preparation of the cuts is concerned. A simple oblique cut is made on both the base of the scion and the top of the stock, the two cuts to be as nearly as possible of the same length and width. The two cut surfaces are then placed in contact and bound together, after which the wounded surface is covered with grafting wax. It will be seen that the method very closely resembles whip and tongue grafting without the tongue which so conveniently holds the scion in position while it is being bound to the stock.

Inarching This method of grafting is sometimes known as grafting by approach – a term which describes it very well. It is used to graft plants without actually severing the scion from its own roots until the union has been made with the stock. It is usual, though not always essential, to have both the plant that is to provide the stock and that which is to provide the scion, growing in pots. The two pots are then placed side by side, a slip of bark and wood about 2 in. long is removed from one side of the stock and a similar slip of bark and wood is removed from one of the more pliable stems of the scion-bearing plant. The two cut surfaces are then fitted together as neatly as possible and bound in this position with raffia or twine after which the whole wounded surface is covered with grafting wax. After a few months the two cut surfaces should have made a proper union and then the grafted shoot can be severed from the scion-bearing plant just below the point of union.

GRAFTING WAX Preparations, based on beeswax, tallow, resin, bitumen, paraffin wax and other ingredients, used to seal the wounds caused when grafting and sometimes also to protect wounds caused when pruning. Some waxes can be used cold but more generally satisfactory are those that must be warmed to make them sufficiently fluid to be applied to the injured surface with a paintbrush or stick. Home made preparations are seldom used nowadays since they are difficult and messy to prepare and excellent proprietary grafting waxes are readily available.

GRASS HOOK, see Sickle

GRASSING DOWN The practice of covering the ground around fruit trees with grass instead of leaving it bare and cultivated. Grassing down reduces the amount of water in the surface soil and also alters the balance of available plant food. The immediate effect is to slow down the rate of growth of the trees and increase the formation of fruit buds but if the grass is permitted to grow too vigorously the trees may become starved and stunted and fruits may be few or small after a time. As a rule, grassing down of orchards is not carried out until several years after the trees have been planted and when they have made their initial growth and been properly shaped. It is at this stage that it is desired to bring the trees into bearing.

An agricultural long ley grass seed mixture may be used for grassing down, consisting of perennial rye grass, meadow grass and clover. The grass should be kept mown to about 2 in. and even more closely in spring when radiation frosts are likely.

GREASE BANDING This is a device closely allied to the domestic fly paper as its purpose is to trap insects which ascend or descend the trunks of trees. It is mainly used by fruit growers to protect apple trees from the winter moth, the reason being that the female winter moths are wingless and, after emerging from pupae in the soil, must crawl up the trunks of apple trees in order to lay their eggs on the shoots.

Usually the band is formed by tying a strip of greaseproof paper about 4 in. wide right round the tree about 3 ft. above ground level, and then smearing this with a very tacky substance specially manufactured for the purpose. The paper band is to keep the grease out of contact with the bark of the tree which it might otherwise damage. In point of fact most modern brands of grease contain no substance harmful to the bark of trees and can be applied direct to the bark with safety. Nevertheless there is still something to be said in favour of using the paper

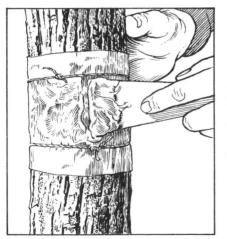

Smearing grease on a paper band which is to act as a trap for the winter moth

bands which can be readily removed and burnt when no longer required.

It is essential to have the bands in position before the female winter moths begin to emerge from their summer period of pupation and ascend the trees to start their egg laying, and there is not much point in retaining the bands once the egg-laying period is ended. This means that it is desirable to fix the bands by the middle of September and to retain them until about the middle of March. It may be necessary to add to the covering of grease from time to time as it loses its stickness with prolonged exposure to air and rain.

In the case of bush trees which have no main trunk 3 ft. or more in height, efficient protection may be given by placing one band round each main branch at least 3 ft. from ground level. The reason for this insistence on a minimum distance of 3 ft. from the ground is that the female moths can be carried for short distances by the winged males and may thus get over bands which are too close to the soil.

GREENBACK A common disorder of greenhouse grown tomatoes which prevents the fruits from ripening evenly and causes them to remain green around the stem or, at most, turn yellowish. Greenback is not caused by any foreign organism such as a fungus or bacterium, but appears to be due to inadequate or unbalanced feeding. It is most likely to occur on soils that are deficient in potash and magnesium and so one precaution is to provide an adequate supply of these plant foods. This may be given in the form of sulphate of potash and sulphate of magnesium both in the preparation of the bed and in topdressings while plants are in growth. Some varieties are highly susceptible to greenback and others comparatively resistant to it.

GREEN BUD/GREEN CLUSTER, see Bud Stages

GREENFLY, see Aphid

GREENHOUSE Any structure mainly of glass or glass substitute large enough to be entered by the gardener and intended for the cultivation of plants. The purpose of the greenhouse is to make it possible to grow plants which are too tender to be cultivated in the open air; to encourage plants to make their growth at an earlier date than they would otherwise do, and to provide congenial conditions for the raising of seeds and the striking of cuttings. With regard to the first of these objects, it is important to realize that in prolonged cold spells the temperature within an unheated greenhouse will tend to fall very nearly as much as that outside. In consequence an unheated greenhouse does not provide adequate protection for really tender plants except in the mildest

parts of the country or in exceptionally mild winters. In other places and in normal weather some form of artificial heating is essential if frost-tender plants are to be grown in winter.

There are a number of temperature regimes which can be adopted in greenhouses and these can be defined under four main headings: warm house, intermediate house, cool house and cold house.

Warm house This term is synonymous with stovehouse and is used for any house in which the temperature range in spring and summer is between 21 and 27°C. and does not fall below 18°C. in winter. Such temperatures are expensive to maintain in Britain and are only necessary for some tropical plants.

Intermediate house Here the spring and summer temperature ranges between 16 and 21°C. and does not fall below 13°C. in winter. This is a house in which a fairly wide range of plants can be cultivated.

Cool house This is a greenhouse in which the spring and summer temperature ranges between 12 and 18°C. and the minimum winter temperature is 7°C. This is the most useful class of house from the amateur's point of view as it enables him to grow a wide range of plants without too much expense. In most parts of Britain it is possible to maintain the correct temperatures for two thirds of the year without artificial heat, and only during the coldest periods is continuous heating likely to be required.

Cold house This simply means one that is not provided with any permanent heating apparatus. An oil lamp or electric radiator may be used occasionally to keep out really severe frost. Inevitably this class of house is of somewhat limited use as it will be impossible to exclude frost entirely throughout the winter, thus precluding the growing of frost-tender plants.

Greenhouses are of many different types. They may be classified according to the method of construction of the roof, which is termed a span roof when both sides slope either to ground level or to approximately the same height above ground level; three-quarter or hip-span when the roof on one side comes much nearer to ground level than that on the other, and lean-to when the roof slopes in one direction only, the reverse side of the house being formed by a wall.

Greenhouses may also be classified according to their function. Thus there are forcing houses, usually comparatively narrow and low and designed to permit a fairly high temperature to be maintained with the utmost economy in fuel consumption; plant houses, which are usually more lofty and airy and designed to admit the maximum

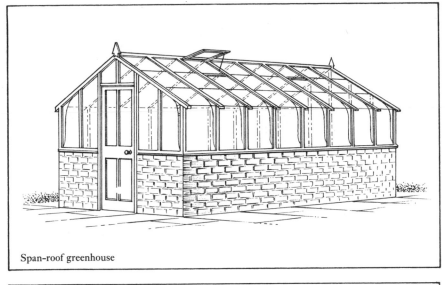

Span-roof greenhouse

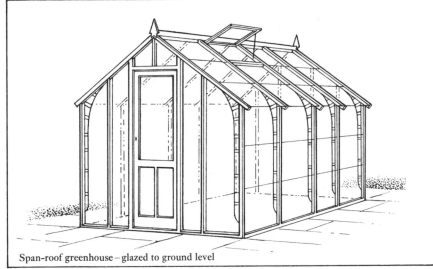

Span-roof greenhouse – glazed to ground level

Lean-to greenhouse

more utilitarian structures in other parts of the garden.

The so-called aeroplane house is used mainly for commercial purposes and consists of a number of successive spans carried on light steel or wood uprights, thus allowing a large area of ground to be covered with glass with minimum interference to cultivation and maximum transmission of light.

The dutch light house is constructed of the single pane frame lights known as dutch lights, which measure approximately 4 ft. by 2 ft. each. These lights are screwed, bolted or clipped to a light framework which is usually portable. Houses of this type can be taken down very quickly and re-erected in any place and are used mainly by commercial growers. Readily portable houses are also made of polythene sheeting stretched over a tubular metal (usually aluminium alloy) framework. As a rule, the polythene covering has to be renewed every second year. Some portable houses are also made by blowing air constantly into a kind of large 'bag' of polythene. The blown air can be cooled in hot weather and heated in cold weather.

Greenhouses may be glazed right to soil level, or they may have vertical walls partly made of brick, concrete, metal or wood and partly glazed. The merit of a house which has vertical walls partly of glass and partly of some solid material is that this method of construction gives good head room inside, even in the smaller widths, and retains the heat better than a house which is glazed right to the ground. If plants are to be grown on stages there is not much point in having glass below the stage level but if plants are to be cultivated directly in beds of soil on the floor of the house, much is gained by glazing to ground level as plants will get more light and be less liable to become drawn.

Rafters and sash bars of greenhouses may be of wood, steel, aluminium alloy or reinforced concrete. Supporting walls may also be made from any of these materials or of breeze block or asbestos-cement sheeting. There is something to be said in favour of each of these materials and no doubt something to be said against. Wood is the traditional material for the construction of rafters and sash bars and has the merit of being comparatively cheap, fairly readily replaceable and a good insulator. It suffers from the drawback that in time it will rot, and to prevent this must be fairly frequently painted. Some woods, however, are much more resistant to decay than others and both teak and western red cedar may be expected to last for fifty to sixty years without special treatment. One other slight drawback to wood is that, in comparison with metal, rafters and sash bars must be made of fairly substantial section and this means that more shade will be cast inside the house.

Aluminium alloys are now generally preferred to steel because they are practically

amount of light; propagating houses, often with propagating frames built inside them and intended mainly for the increase of plants by cuttings, grafts and seeds; vineries, usually tall and airy structures, often built against a south-facing wall and intended primarily for the cultivation of vines, and conservatories, usually attached to a dwelling house and intended primarily for the display of plants which have been reared in unaffected by the atmosphere once they have acquired their initial corrosion. Maintenance costs are consequently reduced to a minimum and no painting is required.

GREENHOUSE HEATING, see Heating

GREEN MANURING The practice of growing certain crops specifically for the purpose of turning them into the soil at a later date to rot and act as manure. Green manuring is of value for several reasons. It is a good method of maintaining the humus content of the soil. It is also useful to lock up temporarily plant foods which might otherwise be washed out of the soil. For example, if a readily soluble nitrogenous fertilizer, such as sulphate of ammonia or nitrate of soda, has been used rather freely and it is believed that a considerable quantity remains in the soil and may be washed out in winter, a green manure crop may be sown at once to absorb the surplus plant food. Then when the crop has been dug in and, after a period of some months, has decayed, the nitrogen will again become available for a following crop. In most instances green manuring does not actually enrich the soil in chemicals but only in humus. However, if clover, vetches, annual lupins or some other leguminous crop is used which is capable of making a symbiotic association with nitrifying bacteria, the result will be the addition of nitrogen to the soil. This may amount to the equivalent of an application of 1 cwt. or more of sulphate of ammonia per acre.

The principal crops used for green manuring are mustard, rape, rye grass, annual lupins and vetches. Mustard grows very rapidly and may be sown at the rate of $\frac{1}{8}$ oz. per sq. yd. any time from March until mid-August. Rape can be sown at the rate of $\frac{1}{12}$ oz. per sq. yd. at any time from March to July. Rye grass should be sown at about 2 oz. per sq. yd. at any time from March till July. The season is also the same for annual lupins which are sown at the rate of $\frac{1}{2}$ oz. per sq. yd. Vetches are comparatively slow in growth and are best sown between March and May at the rate of $\frac{3}{4}$ oz. per sq. yd. With all these the best time for digging in is just before the plants flower.

GREEN TIP, see Bud Stages

GREY MOULD A popular name given to some of the diseases caused by the fungus *Botrytis cinerea*. This fungus attacks a great many kinds of plant and produces different symptoms which often result in distinctive names being given to the disease, e.g. chocolate spot when found on broad beans, dieback when present on roses and gooseberries. Grey mould refers to a particular kind of symptom produced when *Botrytis cinerea* attacks lettuces, strawberries and pelargoniums. The leaves, or in straw-

berries the fruits, become soft and may turn black; shortly afterwards a dense greyish, fluffy mould appears all over the diseased area. This disease can be particularly troublesome with the large annual sunflowers grown for their seed, and in a damp season it is difficult to harvest the seeds undamaged by grey mould.

Botrytis cinerea thrives in stuffy, damp atmospheres during wet, dull weather. Under glass it can be avoided to some extent by good ventilation, maintenance of temperatures above 12°C., adequate spacing of plants and careful watering. See Botrytis.

GROWTH SUBSTANCES, see Hormones

GUANO Originally guano was a term used exclusively for the deposits left by sea birds in certain rainless or nearly rainless areas of South America, mainly in Peru. Through the centuries the droppings of these birds collected in great quantities, and as there had been little or no rain to wash the soluble chemicals out of them, they represented rich stores of plant food. The demand was so great, however, that most of the supplies have long since been exhausted and little genuine bird guano is now available. The term is now often used for almost any concentrated fertilizer, and is particularly applied to fish manures which are frequently termed fish guano.

Genuine bird guano, often referred to as Peruvian guano, is a general fertilizer particularly rich in nitrogen and phosphoric acid. An average sample may contain 10 to 14 per cent. of nitrogen, 9 to 11 per cent. phosphoric acid and 2 to 4 per cent. potash. Out of doors it can be used in the final preparation of seed beds or as a topdressing to plants in growth at the rate of 2 to 3 oz. per sq. yd. It is also very valuable as a topdressing for pot plants or for plants growing in beds of soil in the greenhouse, for which purpose it may be used at the rate of 1 oz. per sq. yd. or a heaped teaspoonful per pot, repeated about once a fortnight while plants are in full growth.

GUMMING All stone fruit trees such as plums, cherries, peaches, nectarines and apricots are liable to exude resin which is gum-like in appearance. This is most likely to occur if the bark is accidentally injured and often no harm results. There are occasions, however, when considerable quantities of gum oozing from a tree are an indication that it is in poor health or has been attacked by capsid bugs, sawfly larvae or bacterial canker. This last is a common disease of cherry trees and the gum produced often has a cloudy appearance. Close examination will usually reveal a cankered area of bark close to the gum. Sometimes branches that gum badly will be observed to be slowly dying back from the tip and in

such cases bacterial canker can frequently be diagnosed by close examination. Gumming also occurs on trees that are in poor condition or that have been too heavily pruned. The gum itself is not harmful and no steps need to be taken about it, but trees that are gumming should always be carefully examined in case of more serious trouble. See Bacterial Canker.

Gumming, Cucumber Gum may also appear on cucumber fruits, and here it is a symptom of the disease known as gummosis which is caused by a fungus. Dark sunken spots first appear on the fruits and it is from these that an amber coloured gum exudes. Later, a velvety olive-grey mould may grow on each spot and the fruits start to split. The remedy for this is to increase ventilation and to dust the plants with flowers of sulphur. The disease is not likely to occur if a cucumber bed is sufficiently porous and well drained.

GUMMOSIS, see Gumming, Cucumber

GYPSUM The popular name of sulphate of lime. It has a mild flocculating effect on clay soils, thereby improving their texture, and has been recommended for this purpose in place of calcium carbonate (chalk or limestone) or calcium hydroxide (hydrated lime) where it is not desirable to raise the pH of the soil. It has been recommended also for the treatment of soil that has been spoiled by inundation with sea water. A third use is to sprinkle it on manure heaps to fix free ammonia and so prevent wastage of nitrogen and possible scorching of plant leaves by ammonia gas.

Nearly half the weight of superphosphate of lime is composed of gypsum and it may, therefore, be used for some of the purposes for which gypsum is recommended, e.g. $\frac{1}{2}$ cwt. of superphosphate of lime may be mixed with one ton of stable manure to fix ammonia as just described.

HALF-HARDY, see Hardy

HALF-STANDARD, see Standard

HALO BLIGHT A disease of beans also sometimes known as halo spot. It is caused by a bacterium and the outward symptom is the appearance of small angular spots on the leaves. These spots are at first water soaked and later become dry and brown. In severe attacks the whole plant may collapse. Seeds from affected plants are usually slightly blistered. Such seeds should not be sown. No remedy is known for the disease and all plants that are affected should be burned as soon as the crop has been gathered. Certain varieties show a great degree of resistance.

HANDLIGHT A special type of cloche, usually made in the form of a rectangle with

Preparing a hanging basket. 1. *The basket is lined with moss*

2. *The plants are placed in position, the sides being planted first*

3. *The basket is gradually filled with compost and the final plants positioned*

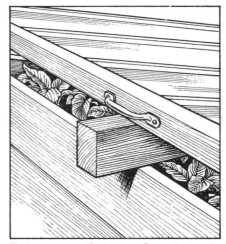

To increase ventilation in a frame during the hardening-off process the light can be propped open with a block of wood

a removable cover in the form of a four-sided pyramid, the whole structure being glazed. Such handlights are useful for the protection of individual plants or as portable miniature frames for the protection of small batches of cuttings or seedlings.

HANGING BASKET A device which enables plants to be grown suspended from the rafters of a greenhouse or over balconies, porchways and similar places. Hanging baskets can be constructed of wood, but nowadays are usually made of wire either galvanized or covered with plastic to prevent rusting, except for special purposes such as orchid culture. They can be purchased in a variety of sizes from most dealers in horticultural sundries. Occasionally square baskets are offered but usually they are shaped like a shallow pudding basin.

Before being filled with plants the baskets should be lined with a thick layer of moss, preferably sphagnum moss. The plants are then placed in position and the roots surrounded with an ordinary potting compost (see Compost). A great many plants can be grown successfully in this manner, notably ivy-leaved pelargoniums, pendent begonias, lantanas, *Lobelia tenuior*, *Campanula isophylla*, *Asparagus sprengeri*, smilax, achi-

menes, *Rhoeo discolor*, fuchsias, marguerites, heliotropes and *Saxifraga sarmentosa*.

Plants in hanging baskets will, as a rule, require watering rather more frequently than those in pots and most certainly should never be allowed to become really dry. Care should be taken not to hang the baskets in very draughty places.

A few orchids can also be grown in hanging baskets, notably those, such as stanhopea, that have a trailing habit or produce their flowers below their leaves. For these, special baskets made of teak strips or slats are usually employed.

HAPLOID The basic number of chromosomes normal to the sex cells of any particular species of plant.

HARDENING-OFF The process of gradually accustoming plants to a cooler atmosphere than that in which they have previously been grown. If the change from one temperature to another is made too rapidly, plants will suffer a severe check to growth which may retard them by many weeks or even kill them outright. Hardening-off is particularly important when plants are raised in a warm greenhouse for the purpose of being transplanted out of doors later on.

The plants should first be moved to the coolest part of the house and then, after a week or so, taken to a frame. The lights of the frame must be kept closed at first but after a few days may be opened an increasing amount on all fine days until eventually they can be removed altogether. If a cold wind is blowing it may be possible to raise the frame lights on the leeward side and so continue to harden-off the plants within, without exposing them to chilling draughts. At all times the appearance of the plants must be the gardener's guide as to how quickly he can proceed. If they continue to grow and they remain a normal colour, all is well, but if growth suddenly stops and leaves begin to turn blue or develop brown streaks or blotches, it is highly probable that the change to a lower temperature is being made too rapidly.

HARDY A rather ambiguous term which means no more than that the plant to which it is applied will survive frost. Without some qualification it says nothing about the degree of frost the plant will stand and this varies

Trailing orchids may be grown in special wooden-slatted baskets

greatly not only from one species to another but also between individuals within a species and according to the locality from which they have been obtained. Other factors, such as soil and air moisture, feeding, the degree of ripening the plant has received and its stage of growth, affect its hardiness. In general, young growth is more susceptible to cold than old growth, young plants more susceptible than old ones and all plants more susceptible when the soil is wet, the air humid or growth is soft because of an excess of nitrogen in the soil.

Zoning as practised in the U.S.A. and some other countries with very varied climates is an attempt to group plants according to the degree of cold they will survive, but for the reasons just stated it can at best only provide a rough and ready guide which needs to be checked by local experiments.

Plants may become temporarily tender if grown for some time in a greenhouse, but will recover their hardiness if they are gradually accustomed to cooler temperatures. It is for this reason that plants reared in the greenhouse in late winter or early spring must be gradually hardened-off before they are planted out in the late spring or early summer.

Half-hardy The term half-hardy is used for plants which will stand little or no frost and can be grown out of doors during the summer months but require protection in winter. A half-hardy annual is one which is too tender to be sown out of doors until quite late in the spring, but can be raised in a greenhouse or frame from a late winter or early spring sowing and can then be planted out in late spring or early summer.

HASTATE In the form of an arrow-head or halberd. A botanical term usually applied to leaves which are of this shape.

HAULM The stems of certain plants are given this name, notably those of potatoes and peas.

HAY BAND An old-fashioned method of reducing the numbers of codling moths – the moths which are responsible for one kind of grub which eats into apples and feeds in the flesh and core. When the codling moth caterpillar is fully grown, it leaves the fruit and seeks a sheltered place in which to turn into a pupa. If bands of hay or old sacking are tied round the branches or main trunks of apple trees in early summer and left until the autumn, it will be found that many of the caterpillars have formed pupae beneath them. The bands can then be removed in autumn and the pupae collected and burned.

HEAD Botanically this term is used to describe a dense cluster or a short dense spike

of flowers. Gardeners often use it in a much looser sense to cover such unrelated objects as a head of lettuce, a head of cauliflower, a head of cabbage, a head of celery – meaning one well developed specimen of the vegetable named.

HEADING, HEARTING The inward folding of leaves in some brassicas, e.g. cabbage, savoy, also in most varieties of lettuce. Sometimes used of the curd formations in broccoli and cauliflowers.

HEADING BACK The process of cutting back trees or shrubs very severely by shortening some or all of the main branches. When young fruit stocks are cut back to receive grafts in spring, the operation is referred to as heading back, in fact the term may be used for any drastic pruning or pollarding. Dehorning (see Pruning) is a mild form of heading back.

HEART ROT A name given to various internal decays of root crops and celery of which the two commonest are soft rot (q.v.) and brown heart (q.v.).

HEART SHAPED A term synonymous with cordate and used, as a rule, to describe leaves which have pairs of basal lobes giving them roughly the form of the heart on a playing card.

HEART-WOOD The innermost and hardest wood of the branch or trunk of a tree.

HEATH OR HEATHER GARDENS Gardens devoted largely, but not necessarily exclusively, to heaths or heathers, e.g. to species and varieties of *Calluna* and *Erica*. By careful selection of varieties such gardens can be colourful and attractive throughout the year. They require a minimum of attention since the dense, spreading growth of many kinds of heather effectively smothers most weeds. Coniferous trees and birches can often be associated very satisfactorily with heathers. An admirable example of a garden of this type is to be found in the Royal Horticultural Society's gardens at Wisley, Surrey.

HEATING Heating is of importance to the gardener for four reasons (1) to enable him to cultivate plants which are not sufficiently hardy to be grown without some extra heat at certain times of the year; (2) to enable him to grow plants out of season; (3) to enable him to dry the atmosphere and so accommodate certain plants which resent damp conditions, and (4) to stimulate the production of roots, a matter which is particularly important when cuttings are being struck. For these four purposes a great quantity of equipment of different types exists, and it is important to choose the kind most suitable for the particular end in view.

Heating apparatus may be classified in two ways – first according to whether it is required to heat the air or the soil and secondly according to the type of fuel to be consumed.

Air heating is most important for the purposes (1), (2) and (3) above, that is for the protection of plants against cold, for the cultivation of plants out of season and for the drying of the atmosphere. Soil heating is valuable for purpose (2) either on its own or in conjunction with air heating, and is also most important for purpose (4), namely to stimulate root growth of cuttings. Combined with air heating, it is of great value in raising early seedlings of many kinds of plants, particularly those that are tender or half-hardy.

The principal fuels available are coal, coke, gas, electricity, paraffin and fuel oil. Coal and coke have the merit of comparative cheapness and the drawback that much of the apparatus designed for their combustion demands more attention than that required for other types of fuel. For stoking large coal and coke boilers, it is usually possible to install a mechanical stoker of some kind which may even be automatically controlled to stoke the boiler in accordance with the varying demands made upon it by fluctuating temperatures.

Gas-fired boilers have not been much developed for greenhouse use, yet they are clean and they have the merit of being labour saving – in fact if the burner is fitted with a thermostatic control and a pilot jet, they can be left to run without attention for weeks on end.

Though the combustion products of coal gas are harmful to plants those of natural gas are not, so this can be burned inside a greenhouse without flues of any kind. This is a convenient and economical method of heating greenhouses particularly small ones where there are no great problems of heat distribution. Suitable stoves are manufactured specially for greenhouse heating with natural gas.

Electricity is, as a rule, a comparatively costly means of heating but it is extremely convenient, clean and labour saving; in fact, suitably installed electric heating apparatus with thermostatic control will require hardly any attention at all. Moreover, all danger of damage from fumes is eliminated.

Paraffin oil stoves, adequate to keep frost out of small greenhouses, can usually be run for quite a modest cost. The stoves themselves usually compare very favourably in cost with apparatus designed for any other fuel and are readily portable from one greenhouse to another. The principal drawback is that, even with the best designed apparatus, there is always some danger that damaging fumes may be liberated in the house. Some plants are very sensitive to such fumes and easily scorched by them. The danger is greatly increased if the stoves are not kept scrupulously clean, if they are subjected to draughts, or if poor-grade paraffin oil is used.

For soil warming, electricity is the fuel most commonly used, though hot water pipes from a boiler heated by coal, coke, gas or fuel oil, may be used. Yet another method of warming soil is by a heap of decaying horse manure, see Hotbed.

Solid fuel boilers Many patterns and sizes are manufactured, from small boilers with a horseshoe-shaped water jacket surrounding the fire grate, to large tubular boilers similar to those used in factories. With almost all the smaller installations the heat is used to warm water which is then conducted round the house in pipes by the thermosyphon system. This depends on the fact that warmer water rises and the cooler water sinks; in consequence, if a pipe is connected to the top of the water jacket surrounding the boiler and is led from this point steadily, though not necessarily steeply, uphill to the furthest point which is to be heated, after which it is allowed to run downhill to the lower part of the water jacket, the water when heated in the boiler will, of its own accord, circulate round the pipes without any mechanical assistance.

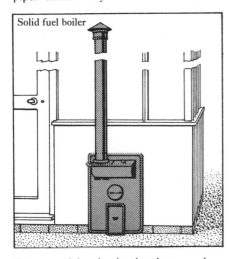
Solid fuel boiler

The essential point in the thermosyphon system is that the rise and fall of the pipes must be continuous, though not necessarily always at the same inclination. If the pipes switchback, air pockets may be formed in them and the flow of water will be impeded or stopped. Another important feature of any hot water system is that at some point there should be an expansion box or pipe to allow for the expansion of the water as it is heated. This is usually placed at the highest point or positioned to rise above the highest level of the water. Without this the pipes will be subjected to considerable pressure and will either burst or leak at the joints.

Generally, pipes 4 in. in diameter are used for hot water installations in small greenhouses but occasionally 2-in. pipes

are employed. These, however, are far less efficient than the larger diameter pipes. It is always wise to install a boiler which is a little larger than is absolutely necessary according to makers' specifications. This will give some reserve of heat so that the boiler is never pushed to its capacity. For a small house not exceeding 12 ft. in width, it is usually sufficient to have one 4-in. diameter flow pipe and one 4-ft. diameter return pipe running the length of the house. If, however, it is intended to grow hot-house plants requiring temperatures of over 18°C. even in winter, the pipes should be carried round three sides of the house. This is also the best form of installation for houses much over 12 ft. in width.

If the house is required mainly for the protection of tender or partly tender plants, the heating pipes should be kept fairly close to soil level, but if the purpose is mainly to dry the atmosphere, as, for example, when growing perpetual flowering carnations, the pipes may with advantage be slung from the roof rafters only a few inches below the glass itself. This will secure the necessary circulation of air without warming the atmosphere too much.

It is always desirable to have the fire and draught doors of a boiler protected to some extent. In large installations the whole boiler is often accommodated in a pit dug some feet below soil level or in a special boiler house. For small boilers this is seldom possible, but it may be practicable to place a potting shed at the end of the greenhouse and have the boiler in this shed. If this cannot be done, a small shelter may be built round the boiler. If wind can blow directly on the boiler, the draught may vary considerably from hour to hour and the rate of fuel consumption (and therefore the amount of heat generated) will also vary accordingly.

Gas-fired boilers Gas-fired boilers are also, as a rule, connected with pipes circulating water on the thermosyphon system. The only difference in installation is that, as the gas heating is less sensitive to draughts

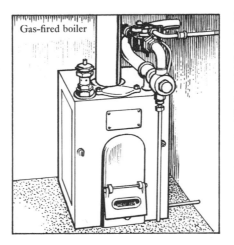
Gas-fired boiler

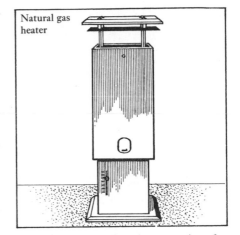
Natural gas heater

than a coal or coke fire, the precautions for protecting the boiler need not be quite so stringent. Great care should be taken, however, to see that an escape pipe for fumes from the gas boiler is carried well above the house since coal gas fumes can be very harmful to plants. This is unnecessary if natural gas is used.

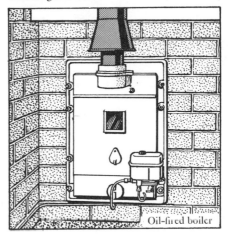
Oil-fired boiler

Fuel-oil boilers These are hot water boilers of similar types to those used for domestic heating. They have all the advantages of solid fuel boilers without the labour of stoking or so great a risk of variation in temperature. Such boilers usually have thermostatic control.

Electrical heating This may be applied in a number of ways. One that is much used is the low temperature tubular radiator, which outside looks rather like a small-diameter hot water pipe, but in fact consists of electrically heated elements without liquid of any kind. The heat is not too concentrated and so no fans are required to distribute it. The electric loading of these tubular heaters is usually 60 watts per ft. and 10 ft. will give sufficient heat to exclude frost from a greenhouse 250 cu. ft. in capacity. Twice this length of pipe will heat a greenhouse of twice the capacity and so on. If a minimum temperature of 7°C. is required it is desirable to double the amount of pipe.

Another type of electric air heater is the

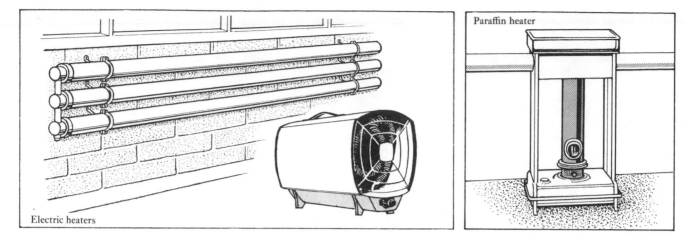

Electric heaters

Paraffin heater

convection heater designed so that a current of warm air is delivered from the stove into the greenhouse. Several patterns exist and manufacturers' instructions should be followed with regard to both installation and selection of a suitable size.

A third type of electric heater is the turbo-heater or fan heater in which the hot air from a comparatively small but intensely hot element is blown out by a fan. Such heaters are very compact and portable and usually quite efficient though it is necessary to be a little careful where they are placed in the greenhouse so that even circulation of heat is obtained without too great a concentration on any one plant or group of plants.

It is always advisable to connect electric air heaters with a thermostatic control, which will switch them off as soon as the desired temperature is reached and switch them on again immediately the temperature falls below this predetermined level. This thermostat not only ensures much more efficient heating, but also effects great economy in fuel consumption.

SOIL WARMING may be carried out with either low voltage current or mains current. If low voltage is used the warming wires need not be insulated. The mains supply is brought to a transformer which delivers the reduced voltage current to a length of naked galvanized wire, which is laid in a zigzag 6

Soil-warming cables

to 8 in. below the surface of the soil. Current is usually supplied at 6 volts, but occasionally 12 volts are used and sometimes up to 25. In all methods great care should be taken to see that the transformer is of a suitable type and properly protected from damp. It is very desirable to use specially manufactured apparatus and not to attempt home-made installations. Soil warming of this kind is usually applied on the dosage system, i.e. no thermostat is employed, but the current is switched on for a specified number of hours per day according to the requirements of the crop. It has been found that it makes no difference to the crop whether a certain degree of heat is applied throughout the 24 hours, or twice that degree for 12 hours or even three times that degree for 8 hours with no heat at all during the remaining hours. The sole essential feature is that the right total amount of heat should be transmitted to the soil.

For mains-voltage soil warming, insulated cable specially manufactured for this purpose must be used either with or without a thermostat. Manufacturers' instructions must be followed regarding installation and the amount of cable required for a given area. Since there is danger of receiving an electric shock if the cable is accidentally damaged, e.g. by striking it with a spade or trowel, it is desirable to protect it in some way, such as by laying fine mesh galvanized wire over it and then placing the soil on top of this.

Paraffin oil Two principal forms of paraffin heater are available, the blue flame and the white flame. The former has a much greater degree of efficiency and is, in general, to be preferred, though it is perhaps a little more temperamental and a little more likely to be put out of steady burning by draughts than the less efficient white flame heater. No general data concerning the size of heater required for any given size of house can be given and manufacturers' instructions should be obtained on this matter. As with solid fuel boilers, it is always wise to install a larger heater (or more heaters) than

appears necessary to warm the house to the degree required. Scrupulous cleanliness must always be maintained, and particular care should be taken to see that the air vents round or below the wick are quite clear. There should be no smell in the house when the heater is operating.

Fuel-oil heaters Special space heaters running on fuel oil and heating the air without water as an intermediary are available for use in greenhouses. As a rule they are used in conjunction with a fan, the hot air being blown through perforated tubes made of fairly thin polythene which can be laid on the ground or suspended from the rafters. Such heaters have the merit of great simplicity and are highly efficient if properly installed but are intended mainly for use in quite large greenhouses.

HEDGE A term applied to any continuous line of shrubs planted with the intention of forming a boundary or a division in the garden. Many hedges also serve the purpose of windbreaks and in very exposed gardens it may well be that the establishment of such a windbreak must precede most other planting.

Although the popular hedging plants are comparatively few in number, hedges can be formed of a great many shrubs and, indeed, it is difficult to exclude any kind as long as it is properly handled. However, the ideal hedging shrub should fulfil the following conditions. It must be capable of growing well, even when planted with neighbours jostling it closely on either side. It should be freely branched and not sparse in habit. It should start to branch close to ground level and maintain its foliage at the base even when it has grown to a considerable height. Further, it must be amenable to fairly severe pruning and even frequent clipping. It is an advantage, though not essential, that it should be evergreen. Beech and hornbeam are popular because, although they are deciduous, they have the peculiarity of holding their dead leaves throughout the winter when they are grown as hedges.

The most favoured hedging shrubs are privet, particularly the broad-leaved form, *Ligustrum ovalifolium*, the variegated privet, *Ligustrum ovalifolium variegatum* and golden privet, *Ligustrum ovalifolium aureo-marginatum*; *Lonicera nitida*; box, *Buxus sempervirens*; holly, *Ilex aquifolium*; cherry laurel, *Prunus lusitanica*; *Aucuba japonica* and its variegated form; *Euonymus japonicus* and its variegated form; yew, *Taxus baccata*, with the fastigiate form known as Irish Yew, *Taxus baccata fastigiata*, and the variegated form, *Taxus baccata variegata*; *Cupressus lawsoniana* and its several forms, notably *allumii* and *erecta viridis*; *C. macrocarpa*; *Thuja plicata*, frequently known as *Thuja lobbii*; *Thuja occidentalis*; beech, *Fagus sylvatica*; hornbeam, *Carpinus betulus*; hawthorn, *Crataegus monogyna*; and Myrobalan plum, *Prunus cerasifera*. In addition *Tamarix gallica* is often used in seaside areas and so is *Atriplex halimus* which, though rather untidy in growth, has the merit of thriving in very poor sandy soils and withstanding the most salt-laden gales. The common gorse, *Ulex europaeus*, is also a good hedge subject on sandy soil and in seaside areas. Flowering hedges are often formed of various species of berberis, notably *Berberis darwinii* and *Berberis stenophylla*, and sometimes of roses, particularly sweet briers, hybrid musk roses, the more vigorous floribunda varieties, and also rambler roses trained along wires to form a kind of hedge or screen. *Rosa rugosa* and its hybrids are also used to form large hedges which do not need to be cut to too formal a shape.

Before planting it is important to prepare the soil really well as, once the shrubs are planted, further cultivation of the soil will become practically impossible. Nevertheless, hedges should be fed, even when they have been established for many years, and this can be done by giving an annual top-dressing of rotted dung, or of a good compound fertilizer used according to manufacturers' instructions.

The frequency of clipping or pruning and the time at which this work should be done will depend very much on the purpose for which the hedge is required and the material of which it is composed. In general evergreen hedges should be clipped occasionally from May to September and any hard cutting required should be done in May, whereas deciduous hedges should be pruned mainly in autumn or winter.

Large-leaved hedges, such as those of cherry laurel and aucuba, should never be clipped with shears but always pruned with secateurs, the reason being that the shoots themselves should be cut and not the leaves, for if the latter are damaged with shears they look very unsightly.

It is possible to reduce the labour of hedge clipping very considerably by making use of one or other of the mechanical devices available for the purpose. These include hedge trimmers incorporating an electric motor to obtain current from a mains supply or a portable generator, or trimmers directly powered by flexible drive from a small petrol-engined power unit or garden cultivator. Battery operated trimmers are also available.

HEEL When a cutting of a plant is prepared by pulling a side shoot away from the main shoot from which it grows, the small strip of bark and wood which will be dragged away from the main shoot and remain attached to the bottom of the cutting is referred to as a heel. In consequence this type of cutting is sometimes called a heel cutting. As a rule it is the practice to trim off the thin end of the heel leaving only a small piece, like a little knot, at the base of the cutting. Some cuttings seem to strike more readily or with greater certainty if taken with a heel, whereas others do better if prepared entirely from young growth with no older wood attached at the base. Unfortunately there is not sufficient information available to say which plants respond best to either method. See also Cuttings.

HEELING-IN The process of planting temporarily until permanent planting can be undertaken. If the plants arrive from the nursery or elsewhere during bad weather or when for any other reason it is inconvenient to plant them in their final positions a trench may be dug out in any convenient place and the plants laid close together with their roots in this. The soil is then returned and made firm over the roots with the foot. Plants heeled-in in this manner will usually remain in good condition for several weeks if necessary.

HERB This term has two distinct meanings being applied both to those savoury vegetables which are grown principally for the seasoning of foods, e.g. sage, thyme, parsley, and also to any plant which has soft growth in contradistinction to woody growth. In this latter sense it is synonymous with herbaceous. A herbaceous perennial is a plant of this character which also continues to grow from year to year.

HERBACEOUS, see Herb

HERBACEOUS BORDER A border set apart mainly or wholly for the cultivation of herbaceous perennials. As a rule the plants are arranged in irregular groups of a kind, carefully placed for colour harmony or contrast and chosen either to flower all at one time or else to flower successively in such a manner that the later flowering groups tend to grow up and screen those plants that have flowered earlier. Plants of different heights will also be used in such a manner as to give the border a pleasing contour.

A great deal of ingenuity can be shown in the arrangement of plants in a herbaceous border, and there is scope for almost infinite variation according to the fancy of the gardener. As a rule an irregular and outwardly informal herbaceous border is really as much an artifice as the most elaborately designed piece of geometric bedding out (and much more difficult to carry out successfully) and its purpose is much the same – to associate plants in an effective, and even spectacular manner so that each kind is displayed to the best possible effect.

While no hard-and-fast rules can be given regarding the planning and planting of herbaceous borders, the following general suggestions can be made. Narrow borders are difficult to plan effectively. Five feet may be regarded as the minimum width for a border which is to be viewed from one side only, and nine feet for a border which is to be viewed from both sides. The plants should be arranged in irregular groups, not in straight lines. While the taller plants will, in general, be kept towards the back in borders which are to be viewed from one side only, and in the middle in borders that are to be viewed from both sides, there should be no rigid division. Some groups of the taller kinds should be brought forward to give an irregular contour and split the border up into a series of bays of varying height.

When planning colour associations care should be taken to see that the plants under consideration will flower at the same time. It is easy to spoil a scheme if flowers which were meant to set one another off flower successively instead of together.

As a rule it is easier to adopt a pleasingly irregular arrangement of the various groups if they are themselves composed of irregular numbers of plants of each kind. The groups themselves should in general be longer than they are broad, as narrow drifts are more easily concealed when they pass out of flower than are broad ones.

HERBAL Originally this term was used for almost any book describing plants or their medicinal uses. Nowadays its application is confined almost exclusively to books of the latter type.

HERBARIUM A collection of dried plants. Such collections are of great use to botanists in studying the structure of plants, establishing their relationship and providing them with proper names according to the international rules of nomenclature.

HERBICIDE Any chemical that will kill plants. All weedkillers are herbicides and since weeds are simply plants in the wrong place, a subtle distinction which no chemical can make, herbicide is the more scientific term. However, gardeners usually refer to such chemicals as weedkillers and they are more fully described under that heading in this book.

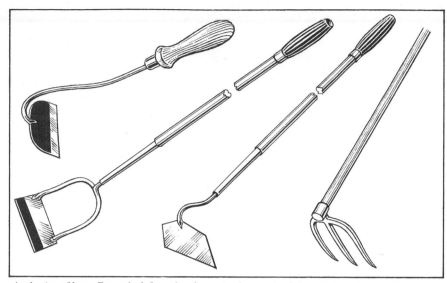

A selection of hoes. From the left – a hand or onion hoe, a dutch hoe, a draw hoe, and a canterbury hoe

HERMAPHRODITE Of both sexes. In botany applied to flowers which have both anthers (male organs) and pistils (female organs).

HIP (or Hep) The fruit of a rose.

HIRSUTE Hairy; a botanical term used to describe the coarse or rough hairs which are to be found on the leaves or stems of some plants.

HISPID Bristly; a botanical term used to describe the stiff hairs or bristles which are to be found on the leaves or stems of some plants.

HOARY A botanical term used to describe leaves or stems which are covered with dense, short, white or whitish hairs giving them the appearance of being frosted.

HOE A tool designed to cut through the surface soil, so breaking it up and destroying any weeds which may be growing in it. Many different patterns are made but they may be broadly divided into two main types, the dutch hoe and the draw hoe.

The dutch hoe This has the blade set nearly in the same plane as the handle and it is used by pushing the handle forwards, with the whole blade almost flat on the soil. The blade is then drawn back ready for a second stroke and, at the same time, the operator moves slowly back. In this way the surface soil is cut up and is not walked on after it has been hoed.

The draw hoe This has a blade set almost at right angles to the handle and it is used with chopping motions, the blade at the same time being drawn towards the body. In other words the cutting stroke is made in the reverse direction to that used with the dutch hoe. At the same time the operator moves slowly forward across the ground and so walks on the soil that has just been hoed. This is a minor drawback to this type of hoe, but advantages which may be claimed for it are greater control and more power. In consequence the draw hoe is often the better type to use when working very closely around plants, particularly those that are planted irregularly, and also when working on hard ground or amongst a dense growth of weeds.

The dutch hoe can be obtained in a great many sizes varying in width from very small hoes, usually known as spuds, not more than an inch in breadth, to wide hoes which may measure as much as 10 in. across. For practical purposes the 4-in., 6-in. and 8-in. hoes will be found serviceable. One type of dutch hoe is attached to the handle on one side of the blade only and in consequence can be worked very much more closely round plants.

Draw hoes are also manufactured in many different forms, one of the most popular being the swan-necked hoe, which has a blade shaped like a half moon and a steel shaft shaped in a curve like a swan's neck, which attaches it to the wooden handle. Another type has a rectangular blade attached to the handle by a steel stirrup, and in a variation of this pattern, the blade fits into slits in the stirrup and is easily removed with a tap from a hammer for replacement when worn out.

What is virtually a modification of the draw hoe, is a type known as the canterbury hoe in which the blade consists of several fork-like prongs attached to the handle at right angles. It is very useful for breaking up rough ground and can also be used for dragging out surface rooting weeds such as grass.

Yet another variation of the draw hoe is the onion hoe which resembles a very small swan-necked hoe and is only about 15 in. long. It is intended to be used with one hand, close around plants and gets its name from the fact that it is frequently used for thinning and weeding onions.

Hoeing is an important part of soil cultivation. Its main purposes are to break up the surface soil, so admitting air, and to destroy weeds. It also checks evaporation by leaving a mulch of loose soil on the surface. Whether this is of much practical account is open to doubt since unhoed soil usually forms a hard dry cap in hot weather which seals it equally effectively. However, weeds, if left to grow, will waste a great deal of soil moisture and hoeing is usually the quickest and most effective method of getting rid of them in the garden. Also, soil that has become capped through drought tends to throw off water whereas broken soil readily accepts it.

To be effective in destroying weeds, it is desirable that they should be cut off just below soil level and not merely dragged out of the soil, in which case they might easily take root again. In order that this cutting may take place, it is essential that the whole blade should be kept sharp.

HOLLOW HEART A trouble sometimes experienced with potatoes. The tubers, instead of being solid throughout, are hollow in the centre. This condition is not caused by an infection or by the attack of any insect, but appears to be due to soil and climatic conditions. It is most likely to occur when extremes of dry and wet weather follow one another quickly during the growing season. Varieties of potato which normally make very large tubers are most likely to suffer. Good preparation of the soil will help to prevent this disease occurring. Where it has proved troublesome, varieties known to make very large tubers should be avoided.

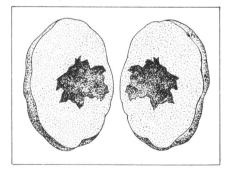

HOLLOW-TINE FORK A special fork with hollow tines which remove a thin core of soil when pushed into the ground. They are used to aerate lawns that have become too consolidated.

HOOF AND HORN A valuable nitrogenous manure made by grinding hooves and horns to a fairly fine powder. Because of its organic origin this fertilizer has a more beneficial effect on the texture of the soil than some inorganic nitrogenous fertilizers. The more finely the hooves and horns are ground up, the more rapidly will the nitrogen they contain be liberated in the soil. An average rate of use is 2 oz. per sq. yd. or it may be used in potting soils at the rate of 1 to 4 oz. per bushel. This fertilizer can be applied at any time of the year and may be used for any plants which require nitrogenous feeding.

HOOK, see Sickle

HONEY FUNGUS, see Root Rot

HOPS Spent hops can sometimes be purchased at a reasonable price from breweries and, if allowed to stand for a few months, become a valuable source of humus, which can be dug into the ground at the rate of 10 lb. per sq. yd. As the hops decay in the soil, small quantities of nitrogen and other plant foods will be liberated, but the manurial value of hops in this respect is comparatively small. Their principal use is in improving the texture of the soil by enriching it with humus.

Hop manure is the name given to spent hops which have been treated with various chemicals to increase their value as plant food. Because of this chemical treatment, hop manure is richer than spent hops and for the same reason it must be applied much more sparingly. The actual rate of application will vary according to the proprietary brand being used, and may be as little as 4 oz. or as much as 12 oz. per sq. yd.

Spent hops can be applied at practically any time of the year but as hop manure is usually treated with soluble fertilizers such as sulphate of ammonia and superphosphate of lime, it is more economical to apply it in spring as a topdressing or pricked into the surface soil.

HORMONES A name given to certain organic chemicals, some of which are formed naturally in the tissues of plants and some produced artificially, which exercise a controlling influence on some aspects of growth or development though they are not themselves plant foods. Hormones may initiate some vital change in the plant without actually taking part in it. For example, if a very dilute solution of alpha-naphthalene-acetic acid is smeared on the stem of a tomato plant, roots will develop on that part of the stem, though the chemical is not itself used in the formation of roots. Similarly, the production of minute quantities of hormone in the fertilized fruits of an apple or pear causes the fruit to develop and become fleshy, though the hormone is not one of the essential chemicals used in the development of the fruit.

Root formation in some plants is assisted if the bases of cuttings are dipped into hormone rooting powder

Hormones artificially applied enable the gardener to promote changes in the development of plants at times of the year, or under conditions, when they would not normally occur. Root-forming hormones such as alpha-naphthalene-acetic acid can be exceedingly useful in hastening the formation of roots by cuttings or layers. They are prepared commercially both in liquid form for dilution with water and as powders in which the base of a cutting can be dipped or which can be sprinkled on the wounded portion of a layer.

The powders are sometimes prepared in two or three different strengths, the weakest for soft cuttings, the strongest for hardwood cuttings. Manufacturers' instructions should be consulted regarding this. Liquid formulations are diluted according to the type of cutting (soft, half-ripe or hardwood) and the cuttings are either dipped into this individually or prepared in a bundle to be dipped together. In either case it is only the bottom $\frac{1}{4}$ in. of each cutting which need be moistened.

It has been found possible, by spraying suitable hormones on the open flowers of fruit trees, to induce the formation of fruits even when fertilization has not occurred or has been rendered impossible by the destruction of stamens and stigmas by frost.

It is also possible to delay the natural falling of apples and other fruits by spraying them in August or September with a suitable hormone solution. This has proved particularly useful for varieties of apples, such as Beauty of Bath, that are subject to a very heavy drop of fruit before the fruits are fully ripe.

Hormones can be used to retard growth and have been applied to potatoes before these have been placed in store to prevent premature sprouting. Other hormones produce longer internodes between the leaves or buds and so induce larger plants.

If hormones are applied in excess they will check or kill plants and as some plants are much more sensitive to this effect than others, it is possible to use hormones as selective weedkillers. Grasses have proved more resistant than broad-leaved weeds to excess application of certain hormones and,

if the dose is carefully controlled, these hormones can be used to kill the weeds on lawns with little or no check to the grass.

These useful plant hormones can all be purchased in proprietary formulations which should be used strictly in accordance with manufacturers' instructions.

Among the chemicals most commonly used as plant hormones are the following:

For root formation Alpha-naphthalene-acetic acid, indolyl-butyric acid, beta-indolyl-acetic acid and naphthoxyacetic acid. The first three are generally used at strengths of from 10 to 25 parts per million for herbaceous plants, 30 to 60 parts per million for half-ripened shoots of shrubs and trees, and 60 to 200 parts per million for hard-wood shoots. Naphthoxyacetic acid is used at still lower concentrations ranging from 2 parts per million for herbaceous plants to 25 parts per million for hard-wood cuttings.

For fruit formation Indolyl-butyric acid at 50 to 100 parts per million, beta-naphthoxy-acetic acid at 40 parts per million.

To prevent fruit drop Alpha-naphthalene-acetic acid at 10 parts per million.

To retard growth Methyl alpha-naphthalene acetate at one part to ten thousand parts (by weight) of potatoes.

To kill weeds 2,4-dichlorophenoxyacetic acid (2,4-D) and 4-chloro-2-methylphenoxyacetic acid (MCPA) at the rate of $\frac{1}{10}$ to $\frac{1}{5}$ oz. to 30 sq. yd. 2-(4-Chloro-2-methylphenoxy)propionic acid (Mecoprop) at $\frac{1}{5}$ to $\frac{1}{3}$ oz. to 30 sq. yd. and 2,4,5-trichlorophenoxyacetic acid (2,4,5-T) at $\frac{1}{5}$ to $\frac{2}{3}$ oz. active ingredient to 30 sq. yd. All these chemicals should be purchased as proprietary formulations and must be used strictly in accordance with manufacturers' instructions.

HORSE MANURE This is one of the most valuable of all the animal manures, both because it is comparatively rich and well balanced in nitrogen, phosphate and potash and also because it is light in texture and therefore excellent for improving the porosity of heavy soils. Moreover, fresh horse manure is one of the best substances from which to form a hotbed (q.v.), and is also the only animal manure that is reliably satisfactory for mushroom beds.

Horse manure can be used safely for all plants and crops for which animal manure is desirable. It can be applied at practically any time of the year, but it is usually rather wasteful to use rotted horse manure in the autumn on light sandy soils, as much of the goodness may be washed out before crops are ready to use it the following spring and summer. On such soils it is usually best to use horse manure in late winter or early spring unless it is fresh, when it should be given more time to decay in the soil before crops need to make use of it. Rates of application on all types of soils may vary from 10 to 15 lb. per sq. yd.

HOSE Garden hose for conveying water is made in various diameters from $\frac{1}{2}$ in. upwards and of either rubber or plastic. Measurement of hose is always of the aperture and does not take into account the thickness of the material of which it is constructed. Plastic hose has the merit of being extremely durable but is not quite so flexible as rubber hose. When hose is intended to take high pressure, as, for example, when it is used for high pressure spraying, it is reinforced with canvas. Neither rubber nor plastic hose should be subjected to frequent and sudden changes of temperature nor should either be left out of doors during frosty weather. When not in use it is best rolled on a special reel and placed in a cool, dark place.

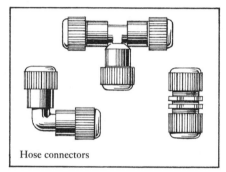
Hose connectors

HOSE-IN-HOSE A term used for a type of abnormality which sometimes affects flowers, particularly those of primroses, cowslips and mimulus. In these abnormal forms the bloom appears to be duplex, one perfect flower being carried inside another. Sometimes these hose-in-hose varieties have considerable beauty and have been selected and cultivated as garden plants.

HOST PLANT Any plant which provides the food for another plant, fungus, bacterium or virus which is parasitic upon it. Thus a rose bush attacked by black spot disease is a host plant for the fungus *Diplocarpon rosae*, which causes this disease, and an apple tree carrying mistletoe is acting as host plant to it. Often diseases troublesome in the garden also attack wild plants or spend some part of their life cycle on them and then control or elimination of these wild plants which act as hosts may become an important item in the control of the disease itself.

HOTBED An old-fashioned but excellent method of warming soil in order to encourage the early production of crops. Hotbeds are usually made from fresh horse manure, but they can also be prepared from horse

Hotbed

manure mixed with dead leaves and also from straw or chaff treated with one of the numerous rotting agents which usually contain nitrogen and lime.

The method of making a hotbed with manure is to build it into a flat-topped heap and tread it down firmly. The manure used should, for preference, contain a fair amount of straw and the fresher it is the better. Throw it into a conical heap, wetting any portions that appear to be dry as this is done. After a few days the heap will generate a lot of heat and may then be turned, the inside portions being brought outside and the outside turned in. Again the heap will heat up and again it should be turned.

A few days later it should have become sufficiently decomposed to allow the hotbed to be built. It is usual to cover it with a frame or frames and the size will therefore be determined by the size of the frame or frames which are to be used. It should always be a little bigger than the frame so that it projects for 9 to 12 in. on every side.

A hotbed may be of any convenient depth, the point to be borne in mind being that the deeper it is the longer it will retain its heat and the greater the heat that will be generated. In general, a depth of about 2 ft. of trodden manure is adequate. The manure should be spread in a flat-topped heap which should be trodden firmly layer by layer. When the required depth of manure has been reached it should be covered with about 6 in. of good soil and a frame or frames placed in position on top of this with the frame lights in position.

After a few days, the manure will begin to generate a lot of heat. A soil thermometer should then be inserted well down into the heap through the soil in the centre of the frame. After a few days the first fierce heat will decline and when the temperature drops to about 24°C., seeds may be sown in the soil or plants placed in it according to requirements. The hotbed, if properly made, should continue to generate heat for eight to ten weeks, though the heat will steadily decline. The most suitable time for making

hotbeds is in early spring, because by the time they have lost their heat the sun will have gained in power sufficiently to warm the frame.

If hotbeds are to be formed with straw or chaff treated with a rotting agent, instructions supplied by the manufacturer of this rotting agent should be followed. As a rule it will be necessary to wet the straw or chaff and turn it several times after treatment before the bed is built.

If dead leaves are mixed with fresh horse manure to make it go further, the degree of heat generated will be rather less than if fresh manure alone is used, but the heat should be maintained for an even longer period. Mild hotbeds of this kind are often very serviceable for raising seedlings and other plants which do not like a lot of heat.

HOT WATER TREATMENT, see Eelworms

HOUSE PLANT Any plant that will live more or less indefinitely in a house as distinct from a greenhouse. Such plants must be able to grow in comparatively poor light and in a fairly dry atmosphere. Obviously the amount of light they will receive and the humidity of the air will differ greatly according to the nature of the building and the position in the room in which they are placed. The cultivation of house plants has increased greatly with the use of larger windows and better heating methods, and in some modern buildings conditions not very dissimilar from those in a greenhouse can be maintained.

House plant specialists often classify the plants according to the amount of light they require or the ease with which they may be grown under the most unfavourable conditions. Thus aspidistra, ficus (rubber plant), monstera, philodendron and sansevieria are all plants which will survive even with quite low illumination and so may be grown in poorly lighted rooms or passages.

Sponging the leaves of a rubber plant is a useful way of increasing local humidity as well as improving the plant's appearance

A great many house plants have little beauty in flower and are grown mainly for their foliage. Popular flowering plants such as cyclamen, Indian azalea and primulas are usually only happy in rooms for short periods or if near to a window.

Moisture in the atmosphere is often even more of a problem than light and various methods have been adopted to make a damper microclimate around the plants such as by standing them in containers filled with wet sphagnum moss or some other absorbent material. Syringing the leaves or sponging them with water are also methods of increasing local humidity.

HOVER FLIES, see Predators

HUMIDITY The amount of moisture in the atmosphere. This is expressed as a percentage of complete saturation but it should be borne in mind that the total amount of water that can be held in the air will vary according to the temperature of the air. The hotter it is the more water it can contain. Thus 100 per cent. humidity at a low temperature would represent a far lower water content than 100 per cent. humidity at a high temperature. One of the reasons for recommending fairly high temperatures for certain greenhouse plants, such as cucumbers and some tropical orchids, is that this allows the high degree of humidity to be maintained which these plants require.

Plants vary greatly in their reaction to differing degrees of humidity, some thriving in a comparatively dry atmosphere and others requiring one nearly saturated with moisture. Out of doors little can be done to control humidity and plants must be chosen to suit the natural humidity of the district. Under glass a considerable degree of humidity control can be exercised by opening or shutting ventilators; by using heat to circulate air drawing in drier air from outside and expelling damp air; by using heat to dry the air directly or to enable the air to absorb more moisture; by spraying water freely on plants, walls and paths, or by placing shallow vessels of water in the house so that water can evaporate from them. In living rooms extra humidity around house plants is sometimes attained by standing them in containers filled with wet sphagnum moss or some similarly absorbent material. Some insects are also much affected by humidity; red spider mites and thrips, for example, thrive in a dry atmosphere and die in a damp one.

Humidity is calculated as a percentage of complete saturation and can be measured by instruments known as hygrometers or by calculation from the temperatures of a wet and dry bulb thermometer. See Hygrometer, Ventilation.

HUMUS This name is given to the residue left when organic matter of any kind decays. It is a somewhat loose term as it is applied both to organic matter which is only partially decayed and may still contain considerable traces of its original structure, such as leaves, plant stems and animal refuse, and also to the end product of decay which will be a fine, dark brown or black sticky substance bearing no trace of its original source. In a strictly scientific sense the word humus should be confined to the latter product.

Organic matter at all stages of decay is of value in the soil because it improves its texture, giving it a spongy character which enables it to hold moisture without becoming waterlogged and also because it provides the most suitable medium for bacterial activity. It is upon the bacteria which multiply in humus that the soil depends for the breakdown into suitable plant foods of many of the complex chemicals which are contained in it. Soil which is deficient in humus will soon become infertile no matter how well it is supplied with chemicals, unless special measures are taken to ensure that these are available as plant foods and also to maintain the fertility of the medium by artificial means, as is done in those special methods of cultivation which come under the general term hydroponics or soilless culture.

The humus content of soil can be increased by applications of animal manure, leafmould, decayed vegetable refuse, peat, spent hops, seaweed, shoddy, straw, chaff, fish waste and offal. Smaller, but still useful, quantities of humus are also supplied by such organic fertilizers as hoof and horn meal and bonemeal and those also have a stimulating effect on bacterial activity.

All organic matter is gradually destroyed in the soil by the natural processes of decay and all measures of cultivation tend to hasten this natural rate of destruction. The more thorough and more frequent the cultivation, the more rapidly will the loss proceed and it is for this reason that soils which are intensively cultivated must be more heavily manured with humus-producing substances than those which are little disturbed. In a natural soil which is not cultivated, as for example, a meadow, a sufficient supply of humus is maintained by the decay of vegetation and the decaying bodies of worms and other creatures.

HYBRID To the geneticist any plant which is not true-breeding for all the genetical factors under consideration is regarded as a hybrid. In the garden the term is seldom used in this way, but is confined to the progeny of crosses between plants of different species or, at the very least, to crosses between plants of markedly different varieties of the same species. For the purpose of botanical nomenclature, the term is confined to the progeny of crosses between distinct species or genera.

Hybrid plants produced from the union of different parents will, as a rule, show some characteristics of both parents, though they may possibly resemble one parent far more than the other. Progeny of any primary hybrid, i.e. the progeny from a cross between two species, though differing in small degree one from another, will generally show a considerable amount of similarity. If each of the parent plants is completely homozygous, i.e. it is itself true-breeding, the progeny will also be extremely uniform and this is the basis of the F_1 hybrid technique (see F_1 Hybrid). Sometimes hybrid plants are themselves sterile, but when they are not their own progeny will usually show a much greater degree of variation than the original hybrid. This is due to the innumerable recombinations of genes which can occur in the second and succeeding generations. These facts are made use of by breeders, who often employ the primary or F_1 hybrid when they wish to produce a plant of known character, while they may exploit succeeding generations when in search of fresh possibilities.

Hybrid plants are often more vigorous than either of their parents, see Hybrid Vigour.

HYBRIDIZATION The art of making a cross between two plants with the object of producing a hybrid. For this purpose one plant will be selected as the seed, or female parent and the other as the pollen, or male parent. Ripe pollen is transferred from the anthers of the latter to the stigma, or stigmas of the former, this being done at a time when the flowers of the female parent are fully open and the stigma or stigmas are in a sticky and receptive condition. Frequently, though by no means invariably, the anthers of the flowers to be pollinated are removed a few days before the blooms begin to open; to achieve this, the blooms are forced open by hand, the object being to prevent fertilization with their own pollen. As a further precaution the prepared flowers may be covered with greaseproof paper or muslin bags, to prevent them being pollinated with pollen brought by insects.

As a result of the hand pollination, seed may be formed and if this is so it will be hybrid seed, carrying the genetical characters of both parents. When this seed has ripened it is harvested, cleaned and stored until the most favourable sowing time. If it then germinates satisfactorily it will produce hybrid plants which will carry genetical characteristics from both parents.

HYBRID VIGOUR The increased vigour or improved cropping capacity which is often possessed by hybrids in contrast to their parents. The reasons for hybrid vigour are somewhat obscure but its reality is well founded and has been put to practical use, for example, in the production of hybrid sweet corn which crops more reliably than ordinary sweet corn. The drawback of such methods of improving garden plants is that the increase in vigour is only fully developed in the first generation and tends to disappear in subsequent generations. In consequence the original cross must be remade each year with annual plants (or plants treated as annuals) such as sweet corn. See F_1 Hybrid page 298.

HYDROPONICS A name given to a particular form of soilless cultivation in which the roots of plants are allowed to grow in a tank containing a dilute solution of plant foods. The plants themselves may be supported on fine mesh wire netting stretched over the top of the tank or on glass wool or wood wool. This method of culture, which was used in early experimental work in soilless cultivation, has been almost entirely superseded for practical purposes by aggregate culture. See Soilless Cultivation.

HYGROMETER An instrument for measuring the humidity of the air. For most purposes relative humidity is calculated, i.e. the degree of moisture is shown as a percentage of the amount of moisture that would be necessary to secure saturation at that particular temperature. As hot air will absorb more moisture than cold air, it follows that any rise in temperature will be accompanied by a fall in relative humidity unless more moisture is taken up by the air as it becomes hotter.

Hygrometers are of three main types: wet and dry bulb thermometers, hair hygrometers, and electrolytic hygrometers. When wet and dry bulb thermometers are used, a reading must be taken from both columns of mercury and then a table is employed to calculate from the difference in the two readings the relative humidity of the air. The hair type of hygrometer has the advantage that it gives a direct reading on a dial, but it suffers from the disadvantage of not being very accurate. With good instruments readings accurate to about 3 per cent. can be expected. This is quite near enough for all normal purposes connected with the humidity control of greenhouses or store sheds.

The electrolytic instrument is extremely accurate and gives a direct reading like the hair hygrometer but is too expensive for ordinary garden use.

ICHNEUMON FLY, see Predators

IMBRICATE Overlapping; a botanical term used to describe leaves and bud scales which overlap one another like the tiles on a roof.

IMMORTELLE Everlasting, sometimes applied to flowers with a dry or chaffy texture that will retain their form and colour for many months or even years. See Everlasting.

IMMUNE Plants are sometimes described as being immune to this or that pest or disease, meaning that they are, by some peculiarity of their nature, protected from it. The term is frequently applied to certain varieties of potato, but in a restricted sense, meaning simply that they are immune to wart disease. In districts in which wart disease is prevalent, only immune varieties of potato should be planted.

Often plants which are regarded as immune to certain diseases, because they never show any symptoms of disease even when grown side-by-side with heavily infected plants of the same kind, are really infected with the disease but are more or less unaffected by it. Such plants should be classified as resistant to that particular disease. Though they can be of considerable use to the gardener they can be unsuspected carriers of disease, spreading it to susceptible varieties. Some dahlia and strawberry varieties are well-known virus carriers of this type.

INARCHING A special method of grafting, sometimes known as grafting by approach. See Grafting.

INCINERATOR Any apparatus designed for the efficient burning of rubbish. A well-made incinerator can be of great value in the garden though it should only be used for materials which are either too diseased or too woody to be placed with safety on the compost heap. Burning inevitably destroys all the organic matter in garden refuse and also much of its value as plant food, though wood ash contains an appreciable quantity of valuable potash.

A useful incinerator can be made from an old oil drum or similar container with the top removed and a number of holes punched in the bottom and sides. If this is placed on three or four bricks so that there is a free passage of air beneath it, a great deal of rubbish can be burned in it without difficulty.

Another useful type of incinerator can be made with loose bricks built in the form of a circle or rectangle with a small space left between each pair of bricks. A grid of iron bars should be placed inside this brick box

Imbricate

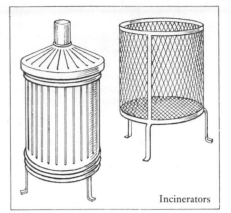
Incinerators

a few inches above ground level, supported on some more bricks or in any other convenient way. Such loose brick incinerators can be of any convenient size, one suitable for a small garden being 3 ft. square or in diameter.

In addition there are numerous manufactured incinerators on the market.

INCISED Cut or slashed; a botanical term usually applied to leaves which have rather deeply cut margins.

INCURVED, INCURVING Flowers with petals all or many of which curl inwards to form a ball-like bloom. It is used chiefly for chrysanthemums; incurved implying an almost perfectly ball-shaped flower, incurving a less globular flower in which some of the petals may not curl inwards. The opposite of recurved, reflexed (q.v.).

INDUMENTUM A dense covering of short hairs. A botanical term used to describe leaves or stems which have a covering of this character. In gardens it is frequently used in the description of certain species of rhododendron which have leaves heavily covered with short hairs on their under surface.

INFLORESCENCE The flowering part of a plant which may be composed of one or more flowers arranged in many different ways. See Panicle, Raceme, Head.

INFORMAL The opposite of formal – usually applied in gardening to those types of design in which an attempt is made to follow nature fairly closely and to avoid set lines and geometrical designs. Wild gardens, woodland gardens and rock gardens are typical examples of informal garden design but any design which is largely irregular may be so termed.

INJECTION Some chemicals used as soil sterilizers or to destroy nematodes or insects in the soil can be applied most safely or efficiently by injection and special apparatus has been developed for this purpose. Usually this takes the form of a kind of gigantic hypodermic syringe, the hollow spike of which is thrust into the soil so that the chemical can be forced through it by means of a simple plunge pump.

Injection of chemicals directly into the stems or branches of plants has also been used to counteract some mineral deficiencies which are due to peculiar soil conditions but this has been largely superseded by the use of chelated chemicals. See Sequestrol.

INK DISEASE A fungal disease attacking bulbous irises and producing black spots and blotches on leaves and bulbs, which may rot. All affected bulbs should be burned and others can be soaked for two hours in a 0.3 per cent. solution of formalin as a preventive measure.

INORGANIC The opposite of organic; in the strict interpretation any chemical compound not containing carbon. Inorganic chemicals, such as sulphate of ammonia, nitrate of soda, sulphate of potash, muriate of potash, sulphate of magnesium, play an important part in the feeding of garden plants and these or similar substances are frequently used to maintain fertility of the soil. Inorganic chemicals do not enrich the soil in humus and as a rule do little or nothing to improve its texture – in fact they may harm the texture of the soil. In consequence they have sometimes been condemned but, if properly used, they do no harm and a great deal of good. Inorganic forms of nitrogen are, in general, cheaper than organic forms and several of them, such as sulphate of ammonia and nitrate of soda, are quicker in action than any organic source such as hoof and horn meal or dried blood. Provided humus in sufficient quantity is applied in other forms (see Humus), correct feeding of the soil with inorganic foods can do nothing but good.

INSECT Strictly speaking this term applies only to a particular section of the animal kingdom, all members of which have six legs, and bodies composed of three distinct sections – a head, thorax and abdomen, as in butterflies, moths, bees, wasps, beetles and flies. Insects usually have a life cycle consisting of four distinct stages: first the egg, then the larva (popularly known as a grub, maggot or caterpillar), then the pupa or chrysalis and finally the perfect insect or imago which can be a bug, beetle or fly. The term insect is often loosely used in the garden for a great many small creatures which are not true insects at all e.g. spiders, centipedes, woodlice and even some worms.

INSECTICIDE Any substance which will destroy insects. Some insecticides are stomach poisons, some are contact poisons and some combine both properties. Stomach poisons must be eaten by the insects or other small creatures before they are effective in destroying them, whereas contact poisons have only to be brought into contact with the body of the insect to have their effect. Both types are of importance to the gardener, the stomach poison because it enables him either to prepare poisoned baits which are placed here and there for the insects to devour, or to use the plants themselves as baits, coating them with a thin film of the stomach poison so that the insect is poisoned by the first few bites it takes. Contact poisons provide an important means of destroying those insects which do not actually devour leaves or stems, but suck the juices from them by puncturing them with a proboscis or similar organ. Greenflies and other aphids are of this type and cannot be destroyed with stomach poisons unless these can be introduced to the sap of the plant (see Systemic).

A plant can be protected in advance of an attack by the use of stomach poisons; contact poisons, however, must generally be used at the first sign of attack, the spray, dust, smoke or vapour being applied in such a way that the insect is covered with poison. In a few instances it has been found possible to coat plants in advance with a poison which will act by contact through the feet or body.

Among the many insecticides used in the garden are azobenzene, BHC (lindane), calomel, carbaryl, chlordane, cresylic acid, demeton-s-methyl, derris, diazinon, dimethoate, DNC, formalin, formothion, malathion, menazon, naphthalene, nicotine, paradichlorbenzene, parathion, petroleum oil, pyrethrum, tar oil, tetrachlorethane, thiocyanate and trichlorphon. These will be found under their respective names.

Insecticides may be prepared in various ways (1) as liquids or as solids which can be dissolved in water and applied as sprays; (2) in the form of dusts which are applied dry as purchased. These usually contain quite a small proportion of the active ingredient the remainder being an inactive carrying agent; (3) combined with a pyrotechnic material so that, when ignited, smoke carries minute particles of the insecticide to any plants with which it comes in contact; (4) as liquids or solids which can be vaporized so that the vapour itself kills the insect; (5) prepared for discharge as aerosols or suspensions of extremely fine particles in air.

Smokes, vapours (or fumigants) and aerosols are primarily intended for use under glass, whereas sprays and dusts can be used anywhere. In the open, sprays appear to be rather more efficient, on the whole, than dusts, but dusts may well prove more economical to use, especially if water is not readily available.

INSECTIVOROUS Literally, insect eating. Horticulturally a term applied to plants which catch and destroy insects though it is not certain that all plants so described actually use the insects as food. Some plants

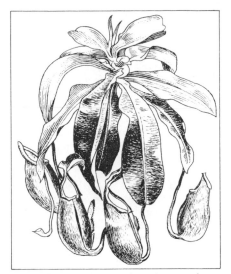
Nepenthes sanguinea, an insectivorous plant

have extremely ingenious devices for trapping insects; in the pitcher plants (nepenthes) some of the leaves are modified to form pitcher-like structures with a frill of down-pointing bristles round the inside of the mouth, rather in the manner of a lobster pot. The pitcher itself contains a small quantity of fluid which is attractive to insects. These enter the pitcher by the mouth but are unable to crawl out again because of the down-pointing bristles. In the Sundew, drosera, and Venus's Fly Trap, *Dionaea muscipula*, the leaves actually have the power of movement, being stimulated by a touch to fold inwards and grasp any object which may be lying on them.

INSECTS, FRIENDLY, see Predators

INTERCROP The practice of growing one crop between the rows of another crop, e.g. radishes are sometimes sown between rows of peas, or lettuces between rows of onions.

INTERNODE That portion of the stem of any plant situated between two joints or nodes.

INVOLUCRE The whorl of bracts which is to be found close beneath some flowers or

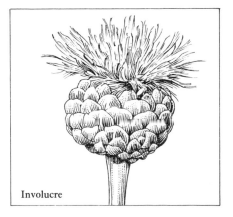
Involucre

flower clusters. An involucre is a prominent feature of all flowers of the daisy type.

IOXYNIL A selective weedkiller used to kill broad-leaved weeds, including chickweed, mayweed and other annuals in young seedling lawns. It is applied as a spray or from a sprinkle bar, 7 to 10 days after the grass seed germinates and when the seedling grass plants have two or more leaves each. Care should be taken not to let it drift on to plants that are not to be killed.

IRRIGATION The artificial application of water to land usually for the purpose of stimulating the growth of plants and so increasing the weight or quality of plants produced. In a really dry country irrigation can be an indispensable preliminary to any cultivation. In the British Isles the comparatively heavy rainfall somewhat obscures the value of irrigation. Nevertheless it has been proved time and again that droughts do occur sufficiently frequently and intensely to make irrigation a paying proposition, at any rate so far as the more valuable vegetable crops are concerned – lettuces, spring onions, early carrots, french beans and ridge cucumbers.

The most primitive form of irrigation consists in cutting channels across the ground and flooding these with water. This gives fairly good results but greater efficiency can be obtained by applying water overhead in the form of a fairly fine spray. A great deal of ingenious apparatus has been developed to spray water efficiently in this way. A simple and well-known type is the revolving lawn sprinkler in which two or three fine jets, mounted horizontally on a rotating axis, drive themselves round by the reflex force of the water passing through the jets. Impulse sprinklers are rotated by the jet of water striking and deflecting a spring-loaded hammer which knocks the spray nozzle around. Both these types water a circle,

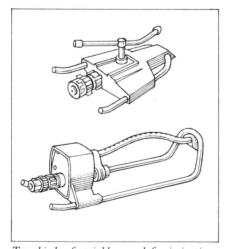

Two kinds of sprinklers used for irrigation: top, the two arm rotating type; bottom, the oscillating type

whereas oscillating sprinklers cover a rectangle and can be moved so that every portion of ground receives an approximately equal amount of water. Such sprinklers may be either quite small and suitable for home use, or they may be extensive line installations portable but intended primarily for commercial uses.

Pop-up sprinklers are designed for permanent installation on lawns. They are set in small holes just below the level of the turf so that the lawn mower can pass over them. They are connected to a mains or similar water supply and, when this is turned on, the pressure of water forces the head of each sprinkler upwards so that it sprays over the lawn.

The ideal irrigation plant should deliver water at a rate at which it can be easily absorbed by the soil without forming puddles on the surface.

A further development has been the introduction of apparatus which is capable of adding carefully graded quantities of fertilizer to the water so that the crops are fed at the same time as they are watered, see Dilutor.

JAPANESE DWARF TREES, see Bonsai

JOHN INNES COMPOSTS, see Compost

JOINT Where applied to plants this term is synonymous with node and indicates the point of junction between a leaf or leaf stalk and a stem. A plant is said to be short jointed when joints occur very frequently along the stems, the spaces between them being small, and long jointed when the joints are comparatively few in number and widely spaced. Plants tend to become abnormally long jointed when deprived of light or grown in too much heat.

JUNE DROP At about the time that apples and pears are forming their seeds, usually in the latter half of June, there is often a heavy natural fall of the partly formed fruits. For this reason final thinning is usually deferred until this June drop is complete.

JUVENILE Some conifers produce two quite distinct types of growth – one in the seedling state and while the plant is still young and another which gradually replaces it as the shrub or tree becomes mature. This distinctive type of early growth is frequently referred to as juvenile growth, in contrast to the later type which is referred to as adult. Some other non-coniferous trees and shrubs exhibit a similar difference between leaves on young and old plants, many species of eucalyptus being notable examples.

KAINIT A natural deposit which occurs in some parts of the world, notably in France and Germany, and which consists largely of

potash combined with common salt and Epsom salt. At one time it was largely used as a potassic fertilizer in gardens, but its place has been taken in a large measure by sulphate of potash and muriate of potash which have the merit of containing a considerably higher and constant percentage of potash, whereas in kainit the proportion of potash may vary from one sample to another. Moreover, the impurities in kainit, particularly the common salt, can sometimes cause serious damage to plants. Kainit is used principally as an autumn or winter dressing in orchards at rates varying from 2 to 4 oz. per sq. yd. An average sample of kainit will contain approximately 14 per cent of potash in the form of sulphate, 60 per cent. common salt and 20 per cent. sulphate of magnesium (Epsom salt).

KEEL The boat-shaped part of a leguminous flower such as a pea or lupin. The rest of the flower is composed of an erect petal, the standard, and two lateral petals, the wings.

Keel

KELP The ashes produced as the result of burning seaweed. Kelp itself is seldom used as a garden fertilizer though it does contain considerable quantities of potash. The name, however, is often applied to seaweed itself, which is a valuable and much-used manure. See Seaweed.

KNOT GARDEN A type of garden very popular in Britain in the 16th and 17th centuries, and now regaining popularity, in which patterns, often of a very elaborate nature, are made with plants, usually clipped evergreen plants such as the edging box, *Buxus sempervirens suffruticosa*. Such gardens were usually close to the home or adjacent to a raised terrace or walk so that they could be viewed from above and enjoyed as a more or less flat pattern on the ground.

LABEL, LABELLING If the correct names of plants are to be preserved in the garden some form of labelling often becomes essential. Its nature will depend very largely on the length of time it is expected to last and on the degree to which it must be

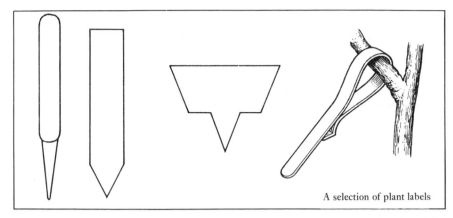

A selection of plant labels

hidden or made relatively inconspicuous. Thus for annuals and other temporary plants wooden labels may be entirely satisfactory even though they may not remain legible for more than a year. In nursery gardens and other purely utilitarian places very large wooden labels well painted or treated with preservative may provide cheap, satisfactory and quite long-lasting labels. But in the ornamental garden some more refined method of labelling must be found for permanent or semi-permanent plants. Many different materials have been used including plastics, lead strips or plates, anodized aluminium, or even sealed glass tubes containing names written on paper slips. Special inks have been developed which will bite into plastic and remain legible for years. Simple apparatus has been devised for stamping letters on lead. Precast metal labels bearing many of the more usual plant names can be purchased.

Lead labels are sometimes gnawed by rodents but are otherwise very satisfactory. Light plastic labels are frequently picked up by birds unless securely fastened or well pushed into the soil. If labels are attached to plants with string or wire care should be taken that this does not bite into the stems or branches as they grow. The ties may need to be replaced from time to time.

An alternative to placing the full names of plants on or beside them is to provide each plant with a number and record these, with the appropriate names, in a garden book. This has the merit that the label can be kept to minimal size and yet be made sufficiently substantial to last well.

LABELLUM The lip of a flower. A term frequently used in the description of the flowers of orchids.

LACEWING FLY, see Predators

LACINIATE Cut into narrow segments. A botanical term usually applied to leaves that are lobed in this fashion.

LACKEY MOTH The caterpillars of this moth protect themselves with silken webs similar to those produced by the caterpillars of the ermine moth (q.v.) and should be attacked in the same way. They are most likely to be found in the southern counties of England on apples, pears, plums, cherries, hawthorns, roses, oaks, willows, alders and elms.

LADYBIRD, see Predators

LANCEOLATE A botanical term meaning lance shaped and usually applied to leaves which are considerably longer than they are wide and taper at both ends.

LANDSCAPE GARDENING Strictly the art of laying out ornamental grounds so that they blend with the surrounding landscape. The 18th century was the great period of landscape gardening in Britain and its principal exponents were William Kent, Lancelot (Capability) Brown and Humphrey Repton. However, the concept has never been abandoned and many of the finest gardens of the 19th and 20th centuries have been designed as miniature landscapes in themselves or to form a part of the existing landscape.

The term has also been loosely applied to all forms of garden design and construction.

Landscape architect is similarly applied to almost any garden designer whether he is, in fact, working on schemes carried out on natural, or pseudo-natural lines, or engaged in the planning of small gardens without particular reference to their environment or to the creation of landscape effects.

LARVA The caterpillar, grub or maggot stage of an insect's life. It is one of the four stages in the usual life cycle and follows the egg. When fully grown the larva turns into a pupa or chrysalis.

LATERAL A side shoot or branch in contrast to a leading or terminal shoot found at the end of a branch. The term is frequently used in connection with the training and pruning of fruit trees.

LATEX The milky sap found in some plants e.g. poppies, dandelions and spurges (euphorbia).

LATTICE Another name for a trellis of wood, iron or any other material. Latticework is frequently used as a support for climbing plants and it may often be usefully employed to raise the height of a fence or wall without too drastic a reduction of light.

LAWN Any area of turf which is kept closely mown. Lawns are usually formed of grass but occasionally other herbage is used and at one time considerable interest was taken in the formation of chamomile lawns, which have the merit of withstanding drought better than grass lawns.

Ordinary grass lawns may be formed from seed, from imported turf, from tufts of creeping grass or from the natural turf of the site. If seed, turf or tufts are to be used, it is usual to prepare the site by thorough digging, followed by a period for weathering. The surface soil is then broken down finely with a rake or canterbury hoe and made firm but left with a crumbly surface.

Lawns from seed Spring and early autumn are the two best seasons for sowing seed. The rate of sowing may vary from $\frac{1}{2}$ to 2 oz. per sq. yd. The seed itself may be of one of the finer grasses such as Chewing's fescue, red fescue, browntop or velvet bent, or of coarser grasses such as rye grass and meadow grass, or of a mixture of all or some of these grasses.

It should be noted that the finer grasses in general take longer to germinate than those of a coarser nature and, being less vigorous in their early growth, are less able to compete with weeds. In consequence, if a lawn of fine grasses is required, it is desirable to take special pains to eliminate weeds before sowing, and this may be done by preparing the ground in spring or early summer and allowing it to lie fallow until the time for autumn sowing. During the intervening months successive crops of weeds will grow and should be destroyed at once by hoeing or other suitable cultivation.

Seedling grass should not be cut until it is at least 3 in. high and then only with a very sharp lawn mower set rather high, or with a sharp scythe. Frequent and close mowing should only be started when the grass is well established, which is likely to take several months, though the time will vary according to the season and weather and soil conditions.

Lawns from turf are usually made in autumn or early spring, though there is considerably more latitude than where seed is employed. The turf itself should be of good quality, containing a high proportion of the finer grasses and being reasonably free from weeds. It is usually cut in 3 ft. by 1 ft. rectangles which are then rolled up for easy transport. This is satisfactory for ordinary purposes but where very true lawns are

When making a lawn from turves lay them in straight lines with staggered joints

required, as for a tennis court, bowling green or putting green, it is desirable to cut the turf in one foot squares and not to roll them up. Whichever size of turf is used, it should be laid in straight rows on a perfectly even surface of finely broken soil, alternate rows being staggered so that the joints between the turves only meet in one direction. This helps the turves to knit together and so remain undisturbed while they are rooting into the foundation soil. The turves are usually settled in position by beating them gently but firmly with a special wooden turf beater or the back of a spade. Alternatively they can be rolled with a light roller.

Bowling greens, and some other lawns in which a very fine and true surface is required, are often made with what is termed sea-washed turf or Cumberland turf, because much of it comes from Cumberland. This is a particularly fine turf found in certain coastal districts and it owes its fineness to the fact that it is washed by salt water at high tides. Unfortunately such turf often proves troublesome in inland districts, dying out in patches after a few years no matter how carefully it is tended.

Lawns from tufts Creeping bent is the grass most commonly used for forming lawns from tufts. This grass roots freely from almost every joint and if tufts of it are planted a few inches apart on well-prepared ground they will quickly spread, rooting as they go and soon forming a continuous sward. But since many of the roots are formed on, or very close to, the surface, this grass will not survive constant close mowing. It is excellent for forming purely ornamental lawns cut to a height of between $\frac{3}{4}$ and 1 in.

Mowing of lawns that are newly established should never be done more severely than is necessary for the purpose for which the lawn is required. Sports greens will usually need to be mown more closely than those only required as a setting for plants. The very close shaving of lawns which is sometimes seen should be avoided whenever possible as it tends to weaken and even kill the grass.

Lawn grass, like any other herbage, requires feeding if it is to be maintained in good condition. For this purpose fertilizers containing a high percentage of nitrogen are usually employed in spring and early summer as these tend to encourage the finer grasses, whereas fertilizers containing phosphates may encourage the coarser grasses and clovers. However, after mid-August nitrogenous manures must not be used as they encourage disease in winter.

A fertilizer distributor; a useful tool for achieving an even application of fertilizer on lawns

In autumn a fertilizer mixture rich in phosphates and potash and with a low nitrogen content can be used. Fertilizer manufacturers prepare suitable mixtures for application to lawns in both spring and autumn.

Most weeds on established lawns can be killed with selective weedkillers such as 2,4-D, MCPA and mecoprop, the last of which kills clovers, which are largely unaffected by the first two. These weedkillers can be used at any time of the year but are most effective in spring and early summer when weeds are growing rapidly. A dressing of lawn fertilizer a few days before the application of the weedkiller makes the weeds more susceptible and helps the grass to overcome the slight check it receives from the weedkiller. The weedkiller can be applied as a spray or from a watering-can fitted with a wide sprinkle bar but great care should be taken to keep it off plants which may be severely injured or killed. Lawn sand (q.v.) is useful for killing some weeds that are resistant to these selective weed-killers. None of these weedkillers can be used with safety on young seedling grass but a special selective weedkiller containing ioxynil can be used on new lawns a week or so after germination. See also Mowing, Roller, Turf, Turf Beater, Turf Perforator.

LAWN SAND A mixture of sand and various chemicals used dry to kill weeds and moss on lawns. The usual formulation is 3 parts by weight sulphate of ammonia, 1 part sulphate of iron and 20 parts fine silver sand and this is applied at 4 oz. per sq. yd. in spring and summer. It is most effective in dry weather but may scorch grass temporarily. Mercuric compounds such as calomel are added to some commercial formulations to make the lawn sand even more effective against moss.

LAWN SWEEPER Various mechanical devices either power operated or hand propelled designed to pick up grass clippings, fallen leaves and other small litter.

LAYERING This is the name given to a particular method of propagation in which a shoot or stem is induced to form roots while still attached to the parent plant, after which it is severed and replanted to form a new plant. A layer is a shoot or stem so treated, and the name is applied equally to the shoot at the time at which it is selected and prepared, and to the same shoot when it has formed roots and been detached.

Layering is the usual method of propagation for border carnations and is also applied to many shrubs and some trees and climbing plants, including rhododendrons, magnolias, quinces and clematis. It is, in general, a somewhat slower method of increase than propagation by cuttings, but it has the merit of being considerably more foolproof, as the layer is supported by the parent plant until it has formed roots. A special form of layering is used in the propagation of such fruit stocks as the Paradise apple and quince.

There are two essentials in successful layering. First, the stem must be placed in close contact with the soil or, better still, lightly buried in it. Secondly, the flow of sap at the point of contact between stem and soil must be checked. This may be done either by slitting the stem or branch or by

Layering a rhododendron. 1. *A stem is slit on the underside*

2. *The wounded area may be treated with rooting powder and then pegged to the soil*

3. *The end of the branch is made secure by tying it to a cane*

4. *Finally, soil is placed over the wounded area. The layer is lifted when it is rooted*

twisting or bending it sharply. With border carnations the former method is usually adopted, a knife being inserted just below a joint which can be brought into contact with the soil, and then drawn up through the stem to form a tongue through the joint. A similar method is often employed with shrubs. An alternative is to remove a ring of bark about ¼ in. wide just below a joint which can be buried in the soil. Often, however, the incision is dispensed with and the stem is given a sharp twist and upward bend at the point of contact with the soil, so rupturing some of the tissues.

In all these instances the layer must be held down in the soil by some means. Frequently, forked wooden pegs are employed, driven firmly into the ground with one arm of the fork over the layered shoot. For small plants, such as border carnations, wire layering pins are often used. These are shaped rather like large hairpins and used in the same manner as the wooden pegs just described. Sometimes a large stone is used to hold a branch down.

If the natural soil round the plant is very close in texture it is wise to remove some of it where the layer will touch, and replace with a specially prepared mixture containing plenty of sand and peat or leafmould. The preparation of a gritty compost, in this

instance devoid of peat or leafmould, is particularly important with border carnations. The carnation layers must root fairly rapidly if they are to be successful and the soil should be kept well watered if the weather is dry.

With fruit stocks, such as Paradise apples and quince, the method commonly employed is to behead well-established plants in late winter, cutting them back to within a few inches of soil level. As a result numerous young shoots will be thrown up from the stumps. As these grow, soil is drawn up round them. No attempt is made to cut or bend the stems, as it is found that roots are formed readily into the mounded soil without any artificial stimulus.

For all layering it is preferable to rely on fairly young growths – current year's non-flowering shoots with the border carnations, and usually one-year-old stems for shrubs, trees and climbers. Older stems or branches can sometimes be treated successfully, but in general they are slower to make roots. The best time for layering trees, shrubs and climbers is usually in late spring, but work can be done at almost any time of the year. With plants of this type, roots are usually formed rather slowly, and it may be eighteen months before the layers are able to support themselves and can, therefore, be separated from the parent. With soft-wooded plants, such as border carnations, rooting is much more rapid. Border carnation layers are usually pegged down in July and, if all goes well, should be rooted and ready for transplanting in September or at latest early October. It is usually wise to sever the layers a short time before they are actually dug up and removed, as this lessens the shock of transplanting.

Sometimes it may be necessary to layer a shoot which cannot actually be bent down to soil level. This can be done by placing a pot or box filled with soil alongside the stem

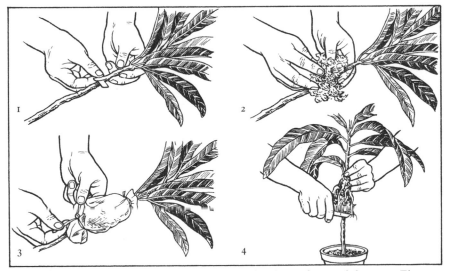

Air layering. 1. *The stem is slit and,* 2, *damp moss placed over the wounded area.* 3. *The moss is enclosed in polythene.* 4. *When roots appear the new plant is severed*

and layering it into this. The soil in this pot or box will have to be watered and must never be allowed to become dry. A further modification of this scheme, applicable to very stiff stems which cannot be bent at all, is to split a box or pot into two halves which can then be fitted together round the stem and bound in position with wire. The container so formed is then filled with soil and the layering continues in the ordinary way. This method, often referred to as Chinese layering or air layering, is sometimes used to reduce the height of leggy specimens of dracaena and the rubber plant (ficus), the stem being layered just below the tuft of leaves at the top. When rooted, the layer forms a new plant and the old leggy specimen below the point of layering can be discarded.

A further development relies on the properties of thin polythene films through which air can pass but which are impervious to moisture. This fact is of use in another method of air layering. A stem is wounded, either by ringing or slitting, and damp sphagnum moss is placed round the wounded area, which has first been dusted with hormone rooting powder. The whole is then covered with a sleeve of polythene film tied tightly around the stem. The moss will remain moist for months and roots will be formed into it, after which the rooted stem can be removed and planted.

LEACH A term used to describe the removal of soluble substances from a soil by water draining through it. In areas of heavy rainfall the loss of plant foods by this means may be considerable, especially of some of the very soluble nitrogenous salts. The winter leaching of such useful chemicals can sometimes be prevented by growing a green manure crop in the late summer and digging it in during the late autumn. By this means the plant foods are locked up temporarily in the green manure crop. By the time they have been liberated by decay the winter is over and more crops are ready to make use of them. See Green Manuring.

LEADER The shoot which terminates a branch and which, if left, will continue to extend it in the same general line of growth. The term can also be applied to a side growth or lateral from which it is intended to build up a main branch by allowing it to extend. A replacement leader is a side growth treated in this way with the intention of eventually cutting out the main branch beyond the point at which the replacement leader is growing. The replacement leader then takes the place of the branch.

LEAF BLISTER MITE An insect pest of pears which also occasionally attacks plums. The insects themselves are mites of such small size that they can only be seen with a lens. They enter the leaves and cause them

to develop yellowish green blisters. During the winter the mites live under the bud scales. The best method of control is to spray with a petroleum emulsion winter wash in winter and with 5 per cent. lime sulphur in March, just before the bud opens. Badly blistered leaves should be gathered when seen and burned.

LEAF CURL A disease of peaches, nectarines and almonds. It is caused by a fungus which attacks the young leaves, causing them first to turn yellowish and then very quickly to develop dark red patches which become thickened and distorted. The fungus may also attack twigs, which die back in consequence. Growth is weakened and in severe cases young trees may be killed outright. All infected leaves should be picked off and burned and twigs that are dying back should be removed and burned when pruning. Trees may be sprayed with Bordeaux mixture or a copper fungicide at the end of February or early in March just before the buds begin to swell.

Peach leaf curl

LEAF HOPPER Several distinct genera of small insects, not unlike the aphids or capsid bugs, are grouped under this popular name. Adult insects are pale yellow and have wings whereas the larvae, though of similar colour, have no wings. The larvae suck sap from the leaves in the same way as aphids or capsid bugs, but produce a characteristic white mottling quite distinct from the damage done by these other pests. Leaf hoppers often leave papery white cast-off skins on the undersides of the leaves and these, in conjunction with the white mottling, provide a method of diagnosis even when the insects themselves cannot

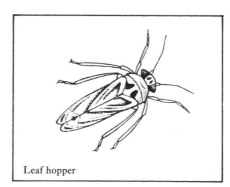
Leaf hopper

be found. Many kinds of plants are attacked, particularly under glass. Out of doors, roses are subject to attack by one particular kind of leaf hopper. The remedy, both indoors and out, is to spray with dimethoate, formothion, malathion, nicotine with a suitable wetter, derris or pyrethrum at the first sign of attack. Under glass, fumigation with nicotine may be carried out.

Leaf miner damage

LEAF MINER A general name given to the larvae of various kinds of fly all of which feed by tunnelling their way through the tissues of leaves without actually coming to the surface. In chrysanthemums, marguerites and cinerarias, snaky white lines are produced as a result of this tunnelling. In celery, lilacs and holly, blister-like patches appear. The presence of the larvae within the leaf can always be felt if the leaf is drawn between finger and thumb, and the larvae can usually be seen if the leaf is held up to a bright light. In mild attacks a sufficient control can be effected by stabbing the larvae within the leaf, using a penknife or pin for this purpose. In more severe cases badly attacked leaves should be removed and burned and the plants sprayed frequently with diazinon, nicotine, trichlorphon or lindane. Under glass a lindane aerosol may be used.

LEAFMOULD A term which is used for the dark brown powdery or flaky substance which results when leaves have been stacked and allowed to rot for a sufficiently long time.

As a rule leaves swept up and stacked one autumn will be converted into good leafmould by the normal processes of decay by the following autumn. Decay will go on more rapidly in warm, rather damp conditions than in dry, cold ones. In good leafmould it should not be possible to find whole leaves or even fragments of leaves recognizable as such, but only small flakes.

Leafmould is a valuable source of organic matter and humus and was at one time the main source of these in potting composts. It has been largely displaced by peat, partly because peat is free from weed seeds and the spores which spread disease, and partly because it decays more slowly and therefore retains its nature for a longer time in the compost than does leafmould. Nevertheless, leafmould is still preferred for some purposes.

The best forms of leafmould for seed and potting composts are those obtained from beech or oak leaves. Any leafmould may be used in the open garden either as a top-dressing to smother weeds and provide a mulch, or forked or dug into the soil as a substitute for manure. Leafmould is not as rich in plant foods as the best animal manures, such as those from horse, cow or pig, but it does contain some plant food and has a most important physical effect upon the soil and micro-organisms in it.

The usual rate of dressing for leafmould is 5 to 6 lb. per sq. yd. and in potting composts it will usually compose about one-third to one-fifth of the whole bulk.

Leafmould made from pine needles is not poisonous to plants, as is sometimes stated. However, it is highly acid and so is most suitable for plants that like acid soils, e.g. heathers, rhododendrons and azaleas, and for hydrangeas if blue or purple flowers are desired.

LEAF MOULD, TOMATO The name for a disease of tomatoes which attacks the leaves and causes them to develop spots or patches which are light in colour on the upper surface of the leaf and covered with a khaki felt on the lower surface. At first the leaves have a distinct mottled appearance but later they may wither completely. The disease is caused by a fungus which thrives under close and stuffy conditions. It is only likely to prove troublesome under glass. Preventives are to give plants plenty of space and to ventilate freely. If the disease appears despite precautions, plants should be sprayed with zineb or maneb. Some varieties of tomato are resistant to certain forms of this disease and these may be tried where the disease has proved troublesome.

LEAF ROLL In potatoes severe rolling of the leaves is sometimes a symptom of virus infection for which there is no cure. It may not affect the crop greatly but no planting sets (seed tubers) should be saved from infected plants. Longitudinal rolling of rose leaves is usually caused by the leaf-rolling sawfly (see Sawfly) but leaf rolling in many plants can occur purely as a physiological symptom of dryness, over-feeding or incorrect feeding.

LEAF SCORCH A physiological disorder which may affect many different kinds of plant but is particularly troublesome on apples and gooseberries. The characteristic symptom is browning and withering of the margin of each leaf. In severe attacks the whole leaf may eventually be affected or leaves may fall prematurely. With gooseberries the leaf margins assume an ashen grey colour which is very distinctive.

Leaf scorch is due to lack of potash and may be aggravated by the excessive use of nitrogenous fertilizers. The remedy is to give ample potash fertilizer which may be applied annually in autumn or spring in the form of sulphate or muriate of potash, at rates from $\frac{1}{2}$ to 2 oz. per sq. yd. according to requirements. Leaf scorch is liable to be most severe on soils that are badly drained. Leaf scorching of a different character may also be caused by dryness and high temperatures particularly under glass. See Scalding.

LEAF SPOT A general name given to many unrelated fungal diseases which produce more or less circular spots on the leaves of plants. Carnations and pinks are attacked by one kind of leaf spot in which the spots have a bleached appearance and the leaves eventually become pale yellow and curl lengthwise. Celery is attacked by a different kind of leaf spot. In this instance the spots are brown with minute black dots on them. Another fungus causes reddish spotting on strawberry leaves. Black currants are sometimes completely defoliated in late summer by a leaf spot disease peculiar to them. For this, bushes should be sprayed with zineb or thiram immediately after flowering and again in May, June and as soon as the fruit has been picked.

Badly affected leaves should always be removed and burned. Carnations and pinks can be sprayed frequently with zineb, maneb or captan, particularly before taking cuttings. Celery leaf spot is carried on the seeds and sterilization of the seeds may be advisable. This is effected by soaking the seeds for three hours in a solution of formalin, 1 teaspoonful to $\frac{1}{2}$ gallon of water or by placing the seeds in plain water at 50°C. for 25 minutes. If the disease appears plants can be sprayed with Bordeaux mixture, colloidal copper or zineb at fortnightly intervals until October. Strawberry leaf spot can be controlled by spraying with lime sulphur or dinocap in May, just before flowering, and repeating three or four times at fortnightly intervals after flowering. For other kinds of leaf spot, spraying with Bordeaux mixture, colloidal copper, colloidal sulphur, thiram or zineb may be tried.

LEAFY GALL A bacterial disease allied to crown gall (q.v.) and like it causing swellings on the stems of plants at or near ground level but differing in that many leaves or short shoots are produced from these growths. Many different kinds of plants are attacked including carnations, dahlias, chrysanthemums and pelargoniums. Infected plants should be destroyed and no cuttings or divisions taken from them.

LEATHER JACKETS The larvae of several species of crane fly or daddy-long-legs. Superficially these larvae look a little like dirty grey or blackish caterpillars, but closer examination will reveal that they have no legs. They have very tough skins, hence the name leather jackets. These larvae feed on grass roots and many other roots and are capable of causing a great deal of damage. On lawns they may kill the grass in small patches while in a herbaceous border or vegetable garden they are capable of checking or killing many kinds of plant. Damage from leather jackets is most likely to be severe on ground that has recently been broken up from pasture.

Finely powdered naphthalene dug or hoed in at 2 oz. per sq. yd. is of some value in controlling leather jackets. A more effective treatment is to fork in a soil insecticide containing lindane. Lawns may be cleared by watering them very heavily towards evening and then covering at night with wet sacks, tarpaulins or boards. This will exclude air and the leather jackets will come to the surface to breathe. If the covering is removed in the morning the leather jackets can be swept up. Potting soil which is believed to contain leather jackets should be sterilized or treated with lindane.

LEGUME Strictly speaking a botanical term used to describe the particular type of seed pod found in members of the pea family, but gardeners use the term more broadly to cover all plants of this family so 'to grow legumes' means to grow some member of the pea family. Such plants may be described as leguminous.

LENTICEL Breathing pores in the young bark which may be very clearly defined in some trees and shrubs as they are of a different colour and texture. By inexperienced gardeners these spots may be mistaken for disease.

LEPIDATE Covered with small, scurf-like scales. A botanical term used to describe the scale-like covering of some leaves and stems. In gardens it is most likely to be used in the description of certain species of rhododendron which have a scaly covering on the lower surface of the leaf in contrast to those which have a hairy covering or indumentum.

LEVELLING Much of the levelling of ground necessary in gardening can be done solely by eye, but where accuracy is essential, as in the formation of tennis courts or bowling greens, use must be made of a spirit level and boning rods. The latter are stakes each with a horizontal cross piece nailed at the top, rather like an elongated letter T. If several of these rods are driven into the soil in a row, it is possible to sight across them and obtain a true level or, if it is so desired, an even slope. Boning rods will only be needed when there is a great deal of variation in the existing levels of the ground and even then they will usually only be used to give a rough level, the final work being checked with a spirit level. Where the variation in levels is only slight, the work can be done with a spirit level only.

When working with boning rods, start at the lowest point of the ground and drive in one of the rods so that the cross member is at approximately eye level. Now drive in a second boning rod a few feet away in the direction of the highest ground. Place a straight-edged plank across the tops of these two posts and check for a true level with a spirit level. The second post can be driven in further or pulled out a little until a true level is obtained. Now drive in a third post at the topmost point of the slope in the line indicated by the first two. Sight across the first and second posts from time to time until the top of the third post is exactly in line with them. If the rise is very steep it may be necessary to open a trench between posts two and three in order to get a true level. If the ground rises in other directions, sights should be taken across these in exactly the same way, starting from the most convenient point along the first line. When all the boning rods required have been driven in, the differences in level between one part of the ground and another will be revealed, and a decision can be made whether to remove all the soil to the lowest level; to add more soil to build it all up to the highest level; or to strike some mean between these two extremes. In any case the exact point to which the soil should be brought can be marked on the boning rods, by measuring downwards from the top of the cross member an equal distance in each case.

When the soil has been roughly levelled to these marks on the boning rods, the final levelling should be done with pegs, planks and spirit level. The method here is to drive in a number of short pegs all over the ground and a few feet apart. As it will be necessary to place a straight-edged plank between each pair of posts, the exact dis-

When lifting plants for transplanting great care should be taken to retain a good ball of soil around the roots

tance apart for these pegs can be determined by the length of the plank that is to be used. Now starting from the post which seems to be nearest to the desired level, work on from post to post, first in one direction and then in another, using a mallet, the straight-edged plank and the spirit level to bring each post to a true level with post number one. The process is very similar to that used with the boning rods except that all the levelling is done with the spirit level and not by eye. When all the posts have been driven in to the correct degree, the soil should be levelled so that it is just flush with the top of each.

It is usually wise when levelling the ground, to keep the topsoil on top. If this is not done and instead much of the lower soil is exposed, this may prove to be relatively infertile. To avoid this danger it may be necessary to skim off all the topsoil first to a depth of about 10 in. and place it to one side. After this the lower soil is levelled and finally the topsoil is returned as an even topdressing all over the site. It is sometimes more convenient and less laborious to work in small sections, removing the topsoil from one part at a time, levelling the lower soil, returning the topsoil and then passing on to the next section.

LICHEN Lichens are primitive plants formed of a union between a fungus and an alga. They are capable of growing on rocks, the bark of trees, roofs and many other places where few, if any, other plants could survive and, since they are often beautifully coloured in greys, yellows and oranges, they may add considerably to the attractiveness of these objects. But on living plants they can be a nuisance, interfering with respiration and providing harbourage for insects and fungi. On trees they can be removed by spraying in winter with tar oil wash.

Lichens can also be troublesome on lawns, smothering the grass and eventually killing it. Aeration, good feeding and the use of mercurized lawn sand should eliminate them.

LIFTING This term is applied equally to the digging up of trees, shrubs and other plants that are to be moved from one place to another, and to the digging of potatoes and other root crops for storing. When any plants are lifted to be replanted elsewhere as much care as possible should be taken not to damage the roots unduly. With fairly large specimens of trees and shrubs this may necessitate a fairly extensive excavation. Certainly it can be expected that there will be many strong roots extending at least as far as the branch spread. Sometimes a tripod and tackle is used to lift such large specimens after they have been suitably undermined, and a low truck or trolley is then employed to transport them to their new site with as little disturbance as possible of whatever soil may remain clinging to the roots.

The best season for lifting deciduous trees and shrubs is usually the late autumn, though work can generally be continued during any fairly mild weather from mid-October to early April. This season is also suitable for most conifers, but broad-leaved evergreens usually lift more safely a little earlier in the autumn or later in the spring, early October and late April often proving particularly favourable times.

Herbaceous plants are usually lifted in March, April, September and October, but some have marked preferences for one season rather than another and some can be transplanted very successfully at other times even, in some instances, in mid-summer.

Bulbs are usually most safely lifted as soon as their foliage dies down and they start their normal resting period. Some bulbs benefit from fairly regular lifting each year and this is usually so with tulips and hyacinths, but others are much better left undisturbed until they become so over-crowded that there is a falling off in the number of flowers produced, and this is true of narcissi and crocuses.

The final stages of levelling can be carried out with the aid of a spirit level, straight-edged plank and pegs

The lifting of vegetable root crops is usually carried out in late summer or early autumn when they have completed their growth. Care should be taken to lift these crops without injury to roots or tubers, as bruises and cuts may cause premature decay in store. Some varieties of potato, such as Arran Banner, are particularly difficult to lift without some damage as they produce their tubers on long stolons well away from the centre of the plant. A fork should be used for all potato lifting and this should be thrust in well away from the plant and a good volume of soil lifted and then turned over and spread out with one movement so that all the tubers are exposed.

LIGHT This is essential for the healthy growth of all green plants since these trap the energy of sunlight and use it to convert simple chemicals containing carbon, oxygen, hydrogen and nitrogen, into complex carbohydrates and proteins. Light also has a second profound effect upon many plants by controlling the way in which their energies are directed either to the production of growth or of flowers. For a fuller account of this see day length. Artificial light is frequently used in greenhouses, either to supplement sunlight in the manufacture of plant foods or to control flower bud formation. Much greater illumination is required for the first purpose than for the second. Fluorescent and mercury vapour lamps are commonly used where high intensity lighting is required, and in many installations lights are arranged so that they can be brought close to the plants when in use and removed when not required so that they do not impede daylight. However, for some purposes, such as breaking the effect of long nights, ordinary tungsten lamps provide sufficient illumination.

LILY DISEASE A name sometimes given to a fungal disease caused by a species of botrytis which principally attacks the Madonna Lily, *Lilium candidum*, and nearly allied Nankeen Lily, *Lilium testaceum*. Brownish spots appear on the leaves, which later wither from the bottom of the plant upwards. The disease is likely to be most severe in late spring and early summer. Badly infected plants should be burned, others should be sprayed fairly frequently in spring and summer with Bordeaux mixture or colloidal copper.

LIME To the chemist, lime is the popular name for calcium oxide which the gardener knows as quicklime. In the garden the term lime is loosely employed for several different forms of calcium, but most commonly for calcium hydroxide, otherwise known as hydrated or slaked lime. Ground chalk and ground limestone may also come under this general term and are frequently used to 'lime' the soil.

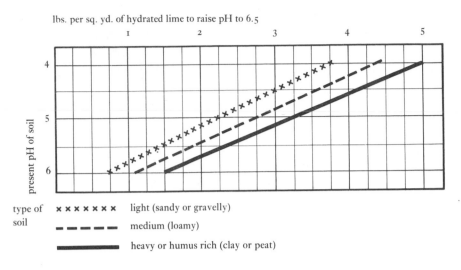

lbs. per sq. yd. of hydrated lime to raise pH to 6.5

type of soil

× × × × × × light (sandy or gravelly)

- - - - - - medium (loamy)

━━━━━━ heavy or humus rich (clay or peat)

Table of lime requirements

Calcium is a plant food and very occasionally it may become so deficient in the soil that lime in some form or other must be added to increase the calcium content. More frequently, however, lime is not required because calcium is deficient, but because it is an alkali which neutralizes acids in the soil, see Acid.

Lime in one of its forms is always used to correct excessive acidity. The more lime is applied the more will the soil be changed in the direction of alkalinity. No hard and fast rules can be given as to the amount of lime required to produce any given change as this will depend on the nature of the soil. Thus more lime is required to produce a given change on a soil that is heavily supplied with humus than on one that is markedly lacking in humus; in other words an acid sand can be corrected with a dressing of lime much smaller than that needed for an acid peat. The chart gives a general idea of appropriate rates of application for hydrated lime. Ground chalk and ground limestone will produce the same effect as hydrated lime but about twice the quantity will need to be applied. Chalk and limestone are slower in their action on the soil than hydrated lime or quicklime, although the rate increases the more finely the chalk or limestone is ground; in fact, if it were possible to grind them as finely as the powder which is naturally formed when quicklime is slaked, there would be little difference in their speed of action. Quicklime is quite as effective as hydrated lime at the same rates of application and also has marked insecticidal properties because of the heat generated as it slakes in the soil. It is, however, a very unpleasant material to handle as it tends to burn the skin and burst any bags in which it is stored. See Quicklime.

Lime tends to encourage some fungi which cause disease and discourage others, e.g. the fungus which causes club root disease of cabbage and other brassicas cannot thrive in a distinctly alkaline soil and is therefore checked by heavy applications of lime, whereas the fungus which causes common scab disease of potatoes thrives in an alkaline soil and is encouraged by heavy applications of lime.

In addition to these important functions, lime also has a marked physical effect on the texture of clay soils. This is due to the fact that lime will make the minute particles of such a soil cling together to form larger granules which make a soil more open in texture and less liable to bind or become waterlogged. This process is referred to as flocculation. Regular liming of clay soils is usually adopted as part of the cultural treatment to improve them, but it must be carried out in connection with acid–alkaline reaction tests and with reference to the type of plant to be grown upon them.

Lime can be applied at any time of the year but it is usually most economical to use it in the autumn or early winter on heavy soils, and in late winter or early spring on light soils. It is generally applied as a topdressing and then left to be washed down by rain, or it can be worked into the uppermost soil with rake or fork. Lime in any form should not be applied at the same time as animal manure, particularly fresh animal manure, as it reacts with this to liberate ammonia gas which escapes into the air and represents a heavy loss of nitrogen, one of the most important plant foods contained in dung. Usual policy is to apply lime to land that was manured a year previously but if this cannot be done the manure should be well dug in first and then the lime applied as a topdressing a few weeks later.

LIME-HATING PLANTS Some plants, notably rhododendrons and heathers, dislike free lime in the soil and grow best in soils that are moderately or even highly acid. See Calcifuge. Such plants are to be contrasted with others that either tolerate free lime, and are therefore known as lime-tolerant plants, or prefer soils that are chalky or limey in which case they are called calci-colous or calciphilous (q.v.).

LIME SULPHUR Proprietary fungicides made by combining sulphur and lime and largely used in the control of apple and pear scab. The strength of concentrated lime sulphur is estimated in terms of its specific gravity, a normal formulation having a specific gravity of 1.3. Lime sulphur of this strength is applied at four different dilu-tions. The weakest of these is usually known as summer strength and is made by adding 3 fl. oz. of the concentrated fluid to 2 gallons of water. This can be applied safely to most varieties of apple and pear after the blossom falls or at any time during the summer. It is useful not only to control apple and pear scab and other fungal dis-eases, but also to reduce infestations of red spider mites. The second strength is 6 fl. oz. of concentrated fluid to 2 gallons of water and this is used in spring and summer on strawberries, when the flowers first open, to control tarsonemid mite. The third strength, usually known as winter strength, is 11 fl. oz. of concentrated lime sulphur to 2 gallons of water. This is applied to apples and pears prior to blossom time and particularly at those stages of bud development known as green bud and pink bud (white bud of pears), see Bud Stages.

This stronger winter application should be used in conjunction with the summer strength application to control apple and pear scab. The fourth and strongest solution is 22 fl. oz. lime sulphur to 2 gallons of water. This is used in March to control cane spot of raspberries, blackberries and other bramble fruits, and also on black currants to control mites which cause big bud. For this last purpose it should be used when the most forward leaves are one inch in dia-meter.

LINDANE The standard popular name for a 99 per cent. (or better) extraction of the gamma isomer of benzene hexachloride, BHC (q.v.).

LINE Strong twine or thin nylon rope attached to two spikes, which can be thrust into the ground, is useful for marking out beds and borders, providing a straight edge for seed drills or when trimming lawn edges, and many similar purposes in the garden. One spike is often provided with a spool on which the line can be wound when not in use. Many modifications and improvements have been devised but the basic require-ments are always the same.

LINEAR Long and narrow; a botanical term used in the description of leaves which are of this shape.

LIP In some flowers all the petals or sepals are not of equal size, but one or more may

A miltonia is an example of an orchid with a decorative lip

be larger and so form a distinctive lobe or lip. In many orchids the lip is a highly developed and decorative feature of the flower. The Latin word for lip is *labellum* and the family of plants known as *Labiatae*, of which mint and salvia are familiar ex-amples, mostly have markedly lipped flowers. In antirrhinum the lip is expanded into a pouch.

LIVER OF SULPHUR, see Sulphide of Potassium

LIVERWORT The liverworts are primi-tive plants allied to the mosses but with pre-dominantly flat growth which can cover the ground, smothering grass and small plants in the process. Liverworts thrive in wet, badly aerated soils and rectification of these faults will go a long way towards eliminating them. They are also killed by applications of mercurized lawn sand.

LOAM A mixture of clay, sand and humus but the term is by no means a precise one and many different types of soil may be referred to as loam. The ideal loam sought after by experienced gardeners as a basis for potting composts, will contain enough sand

to keep the soil open and enough clay to prevent it drying out rapidly. Good loam always contains a considerable quantity of fibre provided by the dead and decaying roots of grasses and other small plants. This fibre helps to maintain the open texture of the loam and when loam is being prepared for potting composts great care should be taken not to remove all the fibre from it by sieving it too finely. Loam which differs considerably from this ideal, may be des-cribed by qualifying adjectives such as light loam, meaning one containing a high pro-portion of sand; heavy loam, containing a high proportion of clay, and fibrous loam, containing an unusual amount of fibre. The term chalky loam is sometimes employed, but this type of soil is more correctly re-ferred to as marl.

Loam is usually cut from the top spit of meadows. The turves should be stacked grass-side downwards in a heap and allowed to remain for at least twelve months, so that the grass may decay. Stacked loam will remain in good condition for a number of years, particularly if the stack is built with a ridged top to throw off rain.

LOGGIA A garden room attached to the house and usually forming an integral part of it. Generally loggias are open to the garden though they may be partly or com-pletely glazed.

LOP To remove large branches from a tree or to shorten branches drastically, as in the operations known as pollarding and heading back. Severe lopping almost invariably destroys the natural symmetry and habit of a tree and should, in consequence, only be practised when absolutely unavoidable.

MAGGOT The larva of a fly. Usually it is the maggot that does the damage in the case of flies regarded as garden pests, e.g. leaf miners, carrot fly, cabbage root fly and narcissus fly.

Loggia

MAGPIE MOTH The caterpillars of this moth, also known as the currant or gooseberry moth, do a great deal of damage to currants, gooseberries, apricots, plums, hazel, common laurel and evergreen euonymus. They are black, white and yellow and, though they hatch out in late summer, they do most damage the following spring, sometimes completely stripping bushes of their leaves. Spraying with BHC, carbaryl, derris or trichlorphon at the first sign of attack is the best remedy.

MAIDEN A tree or bush in its first year from grafting or budding. The term is principally applied to fruit trees, but it is also used for roses and occasionally for other trees and shrubs as well.

MALATHION An insecticide, allied to parathion but much less poisonous and therefore safer to use. It is particularly effective against all kinds of sucking pests, including aphids, leaf suckers, mealy bugs, scale insects, thrips and red spider mites. It can be used as an aerosol, dust or as an ordinary spray. Ferns, crassulas, antirrhinums, petunias, sweet peas and zinnias may be damaged by it.

MALE Flowering plants all make use of the functions of sex and have male and female organs, though the way in which these are disposed differs considerably from one kind of plant to another. The majority of flowers are monoecious, i.e. there are both male and female organs in the same flower. The male organs are known as stamens and consist of anthers attached to filaments. There are also types of plants in which the flowers are dioecious, i.e. some carry only male organs (stamens) and others carry only female organs (pistils). There is still further differentiation in certain plants in which all the flowers on one plant will be of one sex only. Examples are holly (ilex), Sea Buckthorn (hippophaë) and *Skimmia japonica*. In these the plants which produce nothing but male flowers are referred to as male plants and those with only female flowers as female plants.

MANEB A fungicide of the dithiocarbamate group which is very effective against downy mildews. It is practically non-poisonous but should not be inhaled. It is available as a wettable powder to be stirred into water as advised by the manufacturers and applied as a spray.

MANGOLD FLY, see Beet Fly

MANURE The derivation of this word is the same as that of manoeuvre and it is believed to have been applied originally to the general tillage of the soil rather than to its enrichment with any particular plant food or foods. However, with the passage of time, this meaning has been changed and nowadays manure always refers to the food itself or to the act of its application.

Manures are of vital importance to the gardener as without them it is impossible to maintain the fertility of the soil. They may be classified in several different ways, e.g. as organic or inorganic manures (see Fertilizer); as artificial or chemical manures – these terms being synonymous – in contrast to animal manures and those derived from garden waste, dead leaves, etc.

The term artificial manure is unfortunate, as it often gives the impression that this type of manure is inferior or in some way unnatural. It cannot be too clearly stated that chemicals are the natural food of plants and that, therefore, there is nothing unnatural in the application of chemical fertilizers to the soil. In nature these chemicals are added partly by the slow weathering of rock and partly by the breakdown of complicated organic substances into simple inorganic chemicals, this breakdown being produced by the natural process of decay caused by the activity of fungi, bacteria and many other microscopic soil organisms. Plants are as incapable of living on complex organic substances, such as proteins and carbohydrates, as animals are incapable of living on simple chemicals. Indeed the two kingdoms, animal and vegetable, are interdependent, the vegetables transforming the simple chemicals which are their food into more complex starches, sugars and proteins and the animals consuming these by eating either the vegetables themselves or other animals which have themselves consumed the vegetables. Both vegetables and animals die and their bodies are returned to the soil and become manure, which in time is broken down into simple chemicals once more. The same process is also applied to the dung of animals.

Nevertheless, though it is true that plants cannot make use of organic manure until it has been changed by decay into simple inorganic chemicals, organic substances, and particularly those of a very bulky nature such as dung and vegetable refuse, have certain notable advantages for soil feeding. Most important of these is that they almost always improve the texture of the soil, making it more open and yet more retentive of moisture in dry weather, and also easier to work at all times. Moreover, by stimulating the multiplication of micro-organisms in the soil they ensure an adequate population of these to bring about the necessary breakdown from complex to simple chemical forms. A third point is that the plant foods in organic substances are generally liberated steadily over a fairly long period, thus ensuring a regular supply of food without serious shortages or excesses. By contrast, some chemicals are available almost at once and if sufficient care in their application is not observed serious overdoses may result,

with consequent harm to the plants. A final advantage that may be observed is that most bulky manures contain many plant foods, including those such as manganese, magnesium, iron, boron, which are not present in the chemicals most commonly employed as fertilizers. Therefore there is less chance of minor chemical deficiencies occurring on soils that receive regular and adequate dressings of bulky organic manures than there is if chemical fertilizers only are used.

The practice of manuring is one that has engaged the attention of gardeners and scientists for a very long time, but there is still a great deal to be learned about it. Plants require a number of chemicals as food but, as a rule, only a few of these become exhausted so rapidly in the soil that they must be frequently renewed. The most important of these are nitrogen, phosphorus and potassium, and occasionally magnesium or iron may be required as well. Still less frequently deficiencies may occur of manganese, calcium or boron.

Food in the soil is lost by being washed away into the subsoil or into drains, ditches and streams, by being converted into gas and escaping into the atmosphere, by undergoing chemical or physical changes which make it insoluble or otherwise unavailable, and by being used by plants which are then removed from the land. Manuring is in part directed towards making good these losses and in part to altering the nature of the soil, making it richer than it was before, or producing a different ratio between one food and another.

This matter of ratio can be of great importance and is usually referred to as balance. If the balance of foods in the soil – that is to say the proportion of one in relation to another – becomes seriously wrong, growth of plants may be thrown out of gear. Thus too much nitrogen can produce an excessive growth of shoots and leaves, with a corresponding lack of roots and fruits. Too much phosphorus can produce an excessive growth of roots and too much potash excessive fruitfulness. These, it must be understood, are somewhat crude generalizations concerning effects which can have many subtle modifications. By contrast, lack of nitrogen may result in poor leaf development, and lack of phosphorus in weak roots and consequently general weakness into the bargain, while lack of potash may, in addition to causing poor production of fruit, also result in severe scorching of leaf margins. Lack of iron or lack of magnesium may result in severe yellowing of leaves, owing to a failure in the supply of chlorophyll, the green colouring matter of leaves. Many other symptoms are recognized as characteristic of various soil deficiencies.

The requirements of plants for different foods vary greatly, and the ideal would be, no doubt, to adopt a different manurial programme for each, according to its needs.

335

This usually proves impracticable except in a few instances, and an average of requirements must be arrived at which will suit a number of widely different plants. Fortunately, plants themselves have considerable powers of selection and are not entirely dependent upon the gardener to give them a properly balanced diet.

The practice of rotational cropping is partly intended to make the best use of manuring by following one type of crop with another in such a way that the residues left by one will be used up by another. For example, cabbages use a lot of nitrogen but relatively smaller quantities of phosphorus. Carrots, parsnips and beetroot, by contrast, need a lot of phosphorus in relation to nitrogen. It is only common sense therefore to follow one crop after the other, a usual sequence being cabbages first and carrots, parsnips or beetroot next. This matter is more fully discussed under rotation.

The best results can often be obtained by a combined use of both bulky organic and concentrated chemical fertilizers. The bulky manure ensures a suitable soil texture, a good population of micro-organisms and a steady supply of most of the necessary chemical foods. Then a few carefully chosen chemical fertilizers will alter the balance according to the known requirements of the crop – more nitrogen for leaf vegetables, more phosphates for root crops, more potash for fruits and so on. As a rule the bulky manures are best dug in during autumn or winter, while the chemical fertilizers are best applied as topdressings in late winter or spring, but inevitably these generalizations must be qualified by the special needs of particular plants.

As manures of any kind can only be used by plants when in solution, it is not surprising that gardeners have for long used manure in liquid form, particularly when they want a quick result. Nevertheless, though it is true that some chemicals in solution in water can be absorbed directly by plants this is not invariably true and others must undergo change in the soil before they become available as plant food. This is true of organic substances such as urine or the liquid made by steeping dung in water.

Liquid manure is much used for feeding pot plants during their season of growth. It should always be used very dilute and generally should be applied rather frequently. Quite commonly weak liquid manure may be used every week in place of ordinary water during the seasons of maximum growth and flower and fruit production.

Apparatus is available by which measured quantities of chemical fertilizers can be added to water as it flows along pipes to an irrigation apparatus such as an overhead sprinkler. By this means the physical labour of feeding can be greatly reduced and, incidentally, very great economy in the use of fertilizer is claimed for the method. See Dilutor.

MARCH MOTH One of the species collectively known as winter moths (q.v.).

MARL A natural type of soil in which clay is blended with chalk. Marl occurs in several parts of the British Isles, Nottingham marl being a favourite with gardeners. It has been much used as a topdressing for sports grounds, particularly for cricket pitches, as it helps to bind the surface together and prevent it from disintegrating under the heavy wear which occurs when a long match is in progress. For this purpose the marl is passed through a fine sieve and then applied as a topdressing not more than $\frac{1}{4}$ in. deep. Further small dressings may be given but not until the preceding dressing has disappeared, partly as a result of the growth of grass, and partly by being incorporated with the surface soil.

MASTIC The name sometimes applied to plastic substances used to cover grafting wounds, but grafting wax is the term more commonly used nowadays. These are proprietary substances purchased ready for use.

MATTOCK Tools with fairly broad heavy blades set at right angles to a handle similar to that used for a pickaxe. In an ordinary mattock, used mainly for breaking down hard clods of soil, there is one blade only but in a grubbing mattock, used for removing roots and tree stumps, there are two blades, one in the same plane as the handle, like an axe, the other transverse to it, like a heavy draw hoe.

MCPA An abbreviation used for 4-chloro-2-methylphenoxyacetic acid, a chemical which acts as a plant hormone and, in excess, is a useful selective weedkiller for the destruction of weeds on lawns. It is usually sold dry, or as a solution to be further diluted, and applied as a fine spray or from a watering-can fitted with a sprinkle bar. Manufacturers' instructions regarding rate of application should be followed.

MEALY BUG One of the most troublesome greenhouse pests. The insects are small and whitish, and they protect themselves with a white or greyish, waxy substance which at first sight looks like a little tuft of cotton-wool. The mealy bugs move about slowly on the stems and leaves of many greenhouse plants, including vines, and live by sucking sap from the plant. Growth may be greatly weakened as a result. Fumigation with nicotine is effective, while on a small scale mealy bug may be controlled by sponging the leaves and stems with derris insecticide. Spraying with derris, nicotine and soft soap, pyrethrum, diazinon, or with petroleum oil emulsion are other possible methods of keeping this pest in check. When vines are pruned in winter great care should be taken to remove loose strips of bark, particularly round the spurs, as mealy bugs may be concealed beneath these. After this treatment the vines should be painted with a suitable insecticide such as petroleum oil emulsion or nicotine and soft soap.

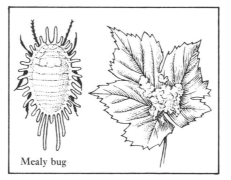

Mealy bug

MECOPROP A systemic selective herbicide chiefly used for the control of clover and other weeds on lawns. It is usually sold in combination with other herbicides and should be used according to label instructions.

MENAZON A systemic insecticide which kills aphids of all kinds. It is absorbed by the plant and so cannot be removed by rain or washing. It is of fairly low mammalian toxicity and is a relatively safe chemical to handle but crops should not be used within three weeks of application. Menazon is available as a liquid for further dilution or as a wettable powder. Manufacturers' instructions regarding strength should be followed.

MENDELISM Mendelism is the name given to the theories of inheritance propounded by Gregor Mendel, an Austrian monk, between the years 1860 and 1870. These theories were not taken up by other scientists at the time, but were rediscovered independently by three scientists around 1900 and have since formed the foundation of the modern science of genetics.

The basic assumption made by Mendel was that for the purposes of inheritance the characteristics of any living organism can be split up into many separate units, and that these units are passed on from generation to generation unchanged, though in many different combinations. Mendel further suggested that the presence of particular units in an individual might be masked by their coming into association with other units which were dominant to them.

One of Mendel's experiments which conveys this theory very clearly was carried out with dwarf and tall varieties of culinary peas. When a dwarf pea was crossed with a tall pea, all members of the next generation were tall, but Mendel found that if he fertilized these first generation hybrids with their own pollen in the next generation he obtained a proportion of dwarf plants again, in the approximate ratio of one dwarf to three talls. Further, if the tall plants from this second generation were themselves fertilized each with its own pollen, and the progeny of each was kept separate, it became apparent that, though all outwardly tall, they were not all genetically of the same character, as some of them produced nothing but talls, whereas some produced talls and dwarfs in the same proportions as the second generation hybrids, i.e. one dwarf to three talls.

To explain this hitherto unobserved fact, Mendel assumed that tallness and dwarfness can, for purposes of inheritance, be regarded as two contrasting units or factors, each distinct, indivisible and indestructible. These factors might be represented by the letter T for tallness and t for dwarfness. He further assumed that T was dominant to t, i.e. that if both T and t occurred in the same plant, the presence of t would be masked and the plant would appear tall. On this assumption, it will be seen that if a tall plant is regarded as having two doses of T, and a dwarf plant is regarded as having two doses of t, and if further it is assumed that the sex cells of these plants have only one dose of each of these characteristics, then when a tall plant is crossed with a dwarf plant the first will contribute one unit of tallness and the second one unit of dwarfness, with the result that all the progeny will be of the character Tt. When these same plants are bred together, the sex cells will be equally either of the character T or t, and if sufficient self-fertilized seeds are produced to allow the law of averages to work the possibilities of recombination will be as follows:

		Male Sex Cells	
		T	t
Female	T	TT	Tt
Sex			
Cells	t	Tt	tt

It will be seen from this that out of every four plants, one will be pure for the factor of tallness, one will be pure for the factor of dwarfness and two will be hybrid for these factors. But as we have already assumed that tallness is dominant to dwarfness, the two plants carrying the units Tt will be indistinguishable outwardly from the plant that is true for tallness. Therefore, in this generation we shall get three tall plants for every one dwarf plant. However, two out of every three tall plants will continue to breed as hybrids. The dwarf plants will all breed true for dwarfness because, as this character is recessive to tallness, it is only revealed when the plant is pure for it, i.e. has two units of it.

Mendel made no attempt to explain the physical basis of this behaviour. It was left to other scientists to prove that this physical basis resided in the minute chromosomes or threadlike bodies which exist in the nucleus of the living cell and can be detected at certain stages of its division. Moreover, it has been shown that the controlling units are, in fact, minute particles of matter or genes, distributed lengthwise along the chromosomes. Normally they are passed on from cell to cell and plant to plant as unchanged units, but occasionally they may be changed by radiation, chemical action or other causes. Such changes provide the physical explanation of the sports or mutations with which geneticists and gardeners are familiar.

MERCURIC CHLORIDE A highly poisonous chemical, also known as corrosive sublimate, which is sometimes used in the garden to prevent the spread of club root disease among cabbages and other brassicas. For this purpose 1 oz. of mercuric chloride is dissolved in 10 gallons of water and half a pint of this solution is poured into each hole prepared for a brassica seedling before it is planted out. The same solution is suggested as a remedy for gladiolus scab disease and in this case the corms are immersed in the solution for 5 to 10 minutes prior to planting. It has, however, been superseded to a considerable extent by safer chemicals such as calomel (q.v.).

MERCURY, see Calomel and Organo-mercury Compounds

METALDEHYDE Metaldehyde is a chemical which can be purchased in the form of bars and as a fine white powder. It is useful to the gardener as a slug poison. For this purpose it should be mixed with bran, oatmeal or some other attractive bait in the proportion of 1 oz. of metaldehyde to 3 lb. of bait. A little water may be added to make a crumbly but not wet mash. This poison bait should be placed in small heaps where slugs or snails are likely to feed, but out of reach of birds and domestic animals to which it is poisonous. When metaldehyde is purchased in bar form the bars should be well crushed before use. One bar is sufficient to make a $\frac{1}{4}$ lb. of poison bait. If purchased in powder form a heaped tablespoon is sufficient to make $1\frac{1}{2}$ lb. of poison bait.

Many proprietary slug killers are based on metaldehyde and should be used according to manufacturers' instructions. A liquid preparation containing metaldehyde can also be purchased and should be diluted with water according to manufacturers' instructions and applied from a watering-can to soil, plants and any places where slugs or snails are likely to be.

METHAM-SODIUM A soil sterilizer used to kill eelworms and the fungi causing some soil-borne diseases. It is highly damaging to plants so can only be employed on vacant land which is not to be used for growing plants for at least 10 weeks. It is a fluid which must be diluted with water according to manufacturers' instructions and watered on the soil, which should then be covered with wet sacks or tarpaulins for a few days after which the coverings should be removed to allow the fumes to disperse. Care should be taken to keep the chemical off the skin and out of the eyes.

METHIOCARB A chemical used to kill slugs and snails and said to be more effective than metaldehyde in damp conditions since it does not depend on dehydration to kill the slugs but is a direct poison. It is sold as granules to be sprinkled where slugs or snails are likely to feed.

MICE Great damage can be done to seeds and seedlings and to bulbs, corms and tubers of all kinds by mice. Crocus are particularly favoured and so are pea and bean seeds and those of marrows, cucumbers and melons. Mice may be killed with one of the many advertised mouse poisons. Under glass, trapping is often the most effective remedy with either break-back traps or cage traps baited with fat, nuts, chocolate, cheese or, probably best of all, cooked dried peas. Pea and bean seeds and small bulbs can be protected by rolling them in red lead prior to sowing. The seeds should first be moistened with either water or a very small quantity of paraffin.

MIDRIB The central vein of a leaf.

MILDEW A general name given to a number of diseases caused by various fungi which can be classified in two main groups: the powdery mildews, so called because they produce a powdery white or grey surface mould on leaves and stems, and the downy mildews which are deeper seated and may often produce a downy outgrowth particularly on the under surfaces of the leaves.

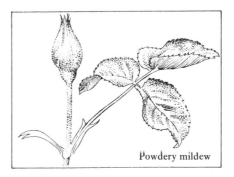

Powdery mildew

One kind of powdery mildew is to be found on peas, particularly those maturing rather late in the season. Another powdery mildew is common on chrysanthemums, and again is most noticeable in the autumn.

Two particularly troublesome powdery mildews attack gooseberries, and these are described under gooseberry mildew. The young growth of apples is liable to be attacked by the apple mildew, which is of the powdery type, and both vines and strawberries have powdery mildews of their own. Roses may be attacked by powdery or by downy mildew but the former is much more common. Plants commonly attacked by downy mildews are anemone, stocks, lettuce, onion, cabbage and spinach.

All these mildews thrive in damp, cool conditions. Under glass, ventilation and a rather dry atmosphere are means of keeping them at bay. Vines grown under glass should be well thinned so that all the leaves have ample light and air. Dusting with flowers of sulphur is a useful preventive for all kinds of powdery mildew, while with apples the routine lime sulphur spraying carried out against scab will also keep mildew away. Dinocap is a good specific against powdery mildew including the powdery rose mildew. For downy mildews zineb and copper fungicides such as Bordeaux mixture should be used. Several systemic fungicides, including benomyl, chloraniformethan and thiophanate-methyl also give good control of mildew.

MILLEPEDES Several different species of small soil pests are found under the general name millepedes. All have thin jointed bodies with hard coats and a great number of legs. Most are grey or blackish in colour, though a few are a dirty white or pink. The smallest are about ½ in. long while the largest may be well over an inch. Some kinds, when disturbed, curl themselves up like the hair spring of a watch. Millepedes are often confused with centipedes but may be distinguished from them by their rather slow movements, their greater number of legs and dull colour. Centipedes by contrast are active, have fewer legs and are bright yellow or orange yellow in colour.

Millepedes are to some extent scavengers, living on decaying matter in the soil, but they also attack the roots of plants and particularly roots that are already in an unhealthy condition. They may bore into soft roots or tubers such as those of the potato or carrot and in one way and another can cause such a lot of damage in the garden that they need to be controlled.

Finely powdered naphthalene forked or raked into vacant ground at 4 oz. per sq. yd. or round cultivated plants at 2 oz. per sq. yd. is a useful remedy. Many millepedes may also be trapped by burying sliced potatoes or carrots just beneath the surface of the soil. If each trap is first pierced with a wooden stick or skewer which is left sticking out of the ground, it will be a simple matter to collect the traps daily and empty them of their catch. Another remedy is to fork in a soil insecticide containing lindane.

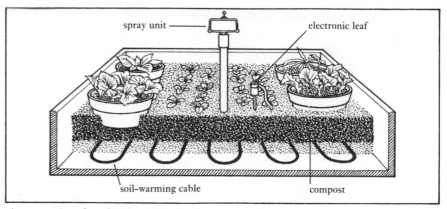

A cross section of an electric mist propagator

MIST PROPAGATION A method of rooting cuttings on an open bench in the greenhouse or in an open frame in contrast to the close, unventilated atmosphere once considered essential for cuttings of soft or half-ripe growth. To prevent the loss of moisture and consequent wilting and rapid death which would normally occur in such a freely circulating atmosphere, the cuttings are frequently moistened with a fine, mist-like spray of water. Various mechanical and electrical devices have been developed to control this spray automatically, some being operated purely on a time basis, some by the rate of evaporation, which will vary according to the weather and temperature. Provided the cuttings are kept constantly damp and yet the compost in which they are inserted never becomes waterlogged the actual quantity of water applied does not seem to be highly critical. As a rule very porous rooting composts are used, such as mixtures of sand and peat or even pure sand, vermiculite or perlite. Mist propagation is usually most effective when allied with soil warming and the use of root stimulating hormones. See Cuttings.

MITE A general term given to a class of small creatures which, though popularly regarded as insects, are not insects in the scientific sense. Several of these mites are serious garden pests, including the red spider mite, the big bud mite of black currants and the mushroom mite. These are all dealt with separately.

MOLES These familiar tunnelling creatures can be a great nuisance in the garden despite the fact that they do not eat plants of any kind but live entirely on insects and other small creatures, many of which are themselves plant pests. When dealing with moles the gardener has to balance the good they do in destroying soil pests against the harm they do in loosening the soil under seed beds and in throwing up mounds on lawns. Even quite large plants may be disturbed by their burrowing and seedlings often fail completely if moles tunnel beneath them and their roots dry out.

Moles can be destroyed by trapping, by poisoning and by gassing. Special steel traps are made for the first purpose, and these are set across the underground runs. A piece of turf or some soil should be removed to allow the trap to be placed in position, and should then be replaced round the trap in order to exclude light, to which moles are very sensitive. Gloves should always be worn when setting traps as moles have a keen sense of smell and will easily be scared by human scent. Traps are most likely to prove effective if set across main runs and particularly those leading towards water, as these are likely to be used frequently.

Poisoning may be effected by using worms as bait and placing strychnine on these. Calcium carbide, which is not poisonous, is sometimes recommended for gassing, and though the acetylene gas which it produces may drive moles away, it will not kill them. Special smoke generators, or fusees, are manufactured for killing or driving out moles. They are ignited and placed in the main runs.

A simple and effective method of keeping moles out of specific areas of land, e.g. preventing their access to a lawn, is to surround the area with naphthalene moth balls dropped into small holes about 3 in. deep and 3 to 4 in. apart.

MONOCARPIC The name given to a plant which dies after flowering but takes an indefinite period to attain flowering age.

MONOCOTYLEDON A plant which normally produces only one cotyledon or seed leaf. This may be contrasted with a dicotyledon which normally produces two seed leaves. The distinction is an important one to the systematic botanist as it serves to distinguish one great group of flowering plants from another. The lily family, *Liliaceae*, the amaryllis family, *Amaryllidaceae*, the iris family, *Iridaceae*, and the grasses are familiar examples of the great group of monocotyledons, whereas the cabbage family, *Cruciferae*, the buttercup family, *Ranunculaceae*, and the daisy family, *Compositae*, are examples of dicotyledons.

MONOECIOUS The name given to a plant which has flowers of two sexes, some with stamens or male organs only, and some with pistils or female organs only, but flowers of the two kinds are borne on the same plant. A familiar example is the common hazel, the male flowers of which form the familiar and showy catkins, while the female flowers are small, red, and held closely to the stems.

MORAINE The great accumulation of rocks, small stones and grit which occurs at the foot of, or beside, glaciers, and has been produced by the grinding effect of the ice on the surrounding rock. Scree is a term given to a similar kind of formation composed of rock debris that has accumulated at the foot of a cliff or mountain. Natural moraines or screes have their own characteristic vegetation, consisting of plants which are able to survive with a minimum amount of nourishment and are usually supplied with abundant moisture in spring and summer from melting snow and ice, combined with the freest possible drainage. Such plants are extremely difficult to cultivate in the garden unless they can be provided with similar conditions, and moraines or screes are a frequent adjunct to ordinary rock gardens for the purpose of growing these plants.

Though there is no real line of demarcation between the moraine and the scree in gardens, the former term is generally reserved for beds of small stones and grit which can be fed with water from below, whereas scree is used as a term for similar beds which are not watered from below. Any small stone chippings can be used as a basis for screes or moraines, but if lime-hating plants are to be grown, the chippings should be of lime-free rock such as sandstone or granite. The pieces may be graded from the size of coarse sand to fragments that will only just pass through a $\frac{1}{2}$-in. mesh sieve, and some larger rocks and stones may also be embedded in the scree or moraine. The bed should be at least 1 ft. and preferably 2 ft. deep, and should ideally be placed on a slight slope with an outlet for water at the bottom so that drainage may be really free at all times. Moraine and scree mixtures vary greatly according to the purpose for which they are required, but as a rule some soil is included. A good average mixture is 10 parts by bulk stone chippings, 1 part good loam, well broken up but not sieved, 1 part good horticultural peat, preferably sphagnum peat, 1 part coarse sand.

If the moraine is to be constructed so that it can be watered from below, this can be arranged by burying a length of water pipe at the highest point of the bed and about a foot below the surface. The pipe itself should be drilled with a few very small holes and connected with a water main. A tap should be provided so that the water can be turned on and off at will. It must be stressed that the holes should be few in number and small in size or the moraine will quickly be converted into a bubbling morass.

MOSAIC A general term used to describe certain forms of virus disease, all of which are alike in causing a pale green or yellowish mottling of the leaves of the plants attacked. One of the most familiar examples is the raspberry mosaic. In the early stages of attack the plants have quite an attractive appearance with leaves variegated with yellow and green, but later the growth is weakened, crops become light and leaves may wither completely. Another kind of mosaic disease attacks lilies, causing a pale green mottling of the leaves, which may also have dark coloured spots and streaks.

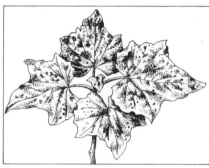

Mottled and speckled leaves indicate the presence of mosaic disease in cucumbers

Flower buds may fail to open or become badly distorted. As these and other mosaic diseases are caused by viruses present in the sap of the plant, exterior treatments with sprays and dusts prove ineffective. All affected plants should be removed and burned and care taken to obtain stock that is known to be free of virus infection. These virus infections are mainly spread by insects or on the blades of pruning knives and secateurs. They are not carried in the soil and so there is no danger in replanting on the same soil provided care has been taken to remove all the mosaic-infected plants including their roots.

MOSS The name for one of the great divisions of the vegetable kingdom. Mosses are of many different genera and species and in some conditions of soil and climate they provide the major vegetation of the land. For example, there are areas in Britain and even greater ones in Sweden almost completely covered by a dense growth of sphagnum moss and as the older plants die and decay, deposits of peat are formed which are known, because of their origin, as sphagnum peat. This moss peat is of particular value to the gardener as it is extremely absorbent of moisture and is of a fibrous or granulate nature, relatively free of dust, so that it does not tend to clog composts in which it is used.

Besides being of use to the gardener in the way just described, moss can also be a great nuisance and it may become a serious weed on lawns, entirely destroying the grass. Mosses are usually an indication of certain conditions of soil. They are most likely to be found abundantly where the soil is naturally rather poor and damp, with high acidity and bad aeration, though some mosses are adapted to grow in dry places and may be found covering the surface of stones. Mosses are also to be found abundantly in shady spots.

In consequence, when mosses behave as weeds in the garden, the first line of attack should be to rectify the conditions which may have encouraged them. Drainage may be improved, soil fed with fertilizer or suitable animal manures, and it may sometimes be possible to admit more light by cutting dense trees or lopping branches.

If none of these measures is possible, or having been tried, all fail to effect a sufficient improvement, the moss must be attacked directly. This may be done with various chemicals, particularly mercurial compounds such as calomel. Proprietary anti-moss dressings, which include these chemicals, are available and should be used as topdressings according to the manufacturers' instructions.

Permanganate of potash is a useful and safe chemical for killing moss, though not so effective as the mercurial compounds. It should be used at the rate of 1 oz. to a gallon of water – a gallon being sufficient to treat one square yard of moss.

Sulphate of iron is probably a more efficient moss-destroyer and also a cheaper one and this should be used at the rate of $\frac{1}{4}$ to $\frac{1}{2}$ oz. per sq. yd., preferably mixed with several times its own bulk of sand to act as a carrier and ensure even distribution, see Lawn Sand.

Hormone weedkillers do not destroy moss and may even indirectly encourage it by killing weeds which were previously in competition with the moss, and so leaving the moss a free hand.

MOTH Insects which are closely allied to butterflies, but may be immediately distinguished from them by the fact that the antennae of British butterflies are always clubbed at the end whereas those of moths are not clubbed though they may be feathery. Moths fly at night and many species are garden pests, not because the moths themselves do any damage to plants but because they lay eggs which then hatch out into caterpillars that feed on plants.

Familiar examples of moths which are troublesome in the garden are the cabbage moth, the caterpillars of which are green or reddish grey and feed on all kinds of brassica; the clearwing moth, the caterpillars of which attack currant bushes, boring their way into the pith of the stem and so causing the stem to wilt; the goat moth, the caterpillars of which are large and able to bore into quite large branches of trees, causing similar damage to that of the clearwing moth; the leopard moth, which attacks trees and shrubs in the same way as the goat moth; the pea moth, the whitish caterpillars of which are all too familiar in pea pods, and the so-called winter moths, including the March moth, the caterpillars of which feed on the young leaves of apple and other fruit trees in the spring. There are many others which may prove troublesome.

It is nearly always the caterpillars and eggs rather than the moths themselves that are most vulnerable. The caterpillars can usually be poisoned by spraying affected plants with insecticides such as BHC, carbaryl, derris or trichlorphon. The eggs may sometimes be killed by spraying with tar oil wash, DNC wash or similar preparations, but unfortunately these can only be used on hard-wooded plants while they are dormant in winter. They cannot be applied to plants in leaf or to soft-stemmed plants because of their caustic action on these. Female winter moths can be trapped on grease bands (q.v.).

MOULD This word is used in two distinct ways by gardeners as a synonym for soil and to describe the outgrowth caused by certain fungi. Thus leafmould may be the brown more or less granular 'soil' produced by the prolonged decay of leaves or it may also be a particular disease of tomatoes caused by the fungus *Cladosporium fulvum*.

MOUSE-EAR, see Bud Stages

MOWING The act of cutting grass, corn or any similar crop. In gardens the term is usually confined to the cutting of lawn grass, which nowadays is done almost entirely with mowing machines of one type or another. Nevertheless, it is still true that the first cutting of newly made lawns is best done with a very sharp scythe, provided this is used efficiently. Unfortunately few expert scythers remain and it is better to cut young grass with a really sharp mowing machine than to do the work clumsily with a scythe.

The constant mowing of lawns has a profound effect upon their composition, tending in time to destroy the coarser grasses and weeds and to encourage fine grasses and some creeping weeds, such as daisies, mouse-eared chickweed, yarrow and clover. The more closely and constantly a lawn is mown, the more this selective effect is observed. It has been said that the famous lawns of England have been produced by 200 years of continual mowing; though this is not always literally true, there is an element of truth in it.

Nevertheless, it is not desirable to mow all lawns very closely, it should only be done

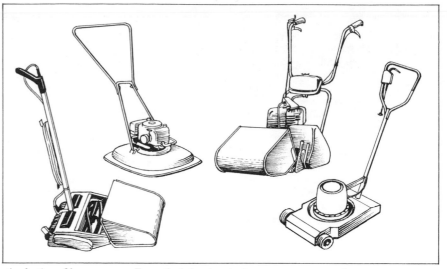

A selection of lawn mowers. From the left: electric, hover type, motor, and rotary

when it is essential for the purpose for which the lawn has been made, as, for example bowling greens or putting greens. Very few grasses can survive such extremely severe cutting and those that do remain are not, as a rule, the best kinds to withstand heavy wear. Lawns which are over-mown tend to develop bare patches, unless regularly fed and watered and carefully tended. For all ordinary purposes the blades of the lawn mower should be set to cut about ½ in. above the soil, and in autumn or early spring may be raised still further to allow about ¾ in. of growth of grass.

Some difference of opinion exists whether it is better to allow lawn mowings to fall on the turf and remain there, or to collect them in a grass box and remove them. If mowing is practised frequently during the spring and summer, there is much to be said in favour of allowing clippings to remain, though it tends to be unsightly for an hour or so. Longer clippings, which can result if lawns are cut rather infrequently, can smother the grass, causing bare patches. The advantage of leaving short clippings is that they act as a thin mulch, protecting the grass from sun scorching and also helping to feed the soil. If all the clippings are regularly removed, more feeding with chemical fertilizers or finely powdered animal manures and composts must be practised. See Lawn.

Cylinder mowing machines are of many different types and patterns ranging from the simple side-wheel lawn mower pushed by hand to the elaborate roller lawn mower driven by a powerful petrol engine. All types have their special uses and value. For hand work, side-wheel mowers are the easiest to use, but they do not give the striped finish of the roller machine nor can they be used to cut over the edge of a lawn. For rough cutting, the side-wheel machine should always be used. Sizes most serviceable for hand-propelled machines are 12, 14

and 16 inches. Above 16 inches the labour of pushing becomes too great.

Power-driven cylinder mowers may be propelled by petrol-driven motors and also by electric motors. Petrol-driven machines have the advantage that they can be used anywhere, whereas electrically-driven machines can only be used where electric current is available. If they are mains voltage machines they must be connected with the electric mains by means of a flexible cable, which to some extent limits the places into which the machine can be taken, but battery-operated machines can go anywhere and only have to be connected to a mains supply for re-charging. Electrical machines do not suffer from starting troubles, are cheaper to run and maintain than petrol-driven ones, are nearly noiseless and very simple to handle.

The smooth finish and lack of ribbing produced by cylinder mowers of all types depends on the number of cuts in relation to the forward movement of the machine. Rough cut machines may give only about 25 cuts per yd. whereas the very finest machines for use on bowling greens may give 130 cuts or more per yd. For ordinary use, hand-powered machines giving 40 to 50 cuts per yd. and power-driven machines giving 70 to 80 cuts per yd. are satisfactory.

An entirely different type of machine made possible by the use of motors, both petrol and electrical, is the rotary scythe in which a very rapidly revolving blade or blades cuts the grass off by the speed of its motion instead of by the scissor action of the ordinary cylinder or reel machine. Rotary grass cutters are usually mounted on wheels which are adjustable for height, but there is a type of machine which floats on a cushion of air like a hovercraft, and so can be moved in any direction. It is particularly serviceable for cutting banks.

Another application of mechanical power to grass cutting, is the motor scythe, usually with an oscillating blade of the same type as that used in farm hay cutters and reapers. Machines of this type can be employed to cut grasses and coarse weeds of almost any height. Yet a third type of grass cutter employs hinged metal flails mounted on a rotating drum.

MOWRAH MEAL An imported meal which is useful in the garden as a worm-killer. For this purpose the meal is sprinkled at the rate of 4 to 8 oz. per sq. yd. over the surface of the lawn or other place in which the worms are to be killed, and is then watered in very freely. As a result the worms will come to the surface and die. Mowrah meal is most effective if used in damp mild weather, particularly in spring and early autumn.

MUCRONATE Ending in a short, stiff point. A botanical term used in the description of leaves of this character.

MULCH Any fairly heavy topdressing applied to the soil. Mulches usually have a threefold purpose, partly to feed the soil and plants growing in it, partly to slow down surface evaporation and so conserve moisture in the soil and partly to check growth of annual weeds. Mulches generally consist of some fairly bulky organic material such as strawy manure, chopped straw, grass clippings or peat. They may be applied at any time of the year, though spring and early summer are probably the most favoured times. As a weed suppressor the mulch can be particularly useful in shrub borders in which fairly heavy dressings can be spread and renewed from time to time throughout the year, with the result that weeds are persistently smothered and little further cultivation is required.

It has been suggested that a good mulch of grass clippings of 1 in. or more in thickness applied to rose beds in early spring and maintained by occasional additions throughout the summer, will not only encourage more vigorous growth of roses, but also will check the spread of black spot disease. This it does by preventing spores of the fungus which causes the disease from being splashed or blown from the soil on to the stems or leaves of the roses.

The more loose and littery the material of which a mulch is composed, the better will be its capacity for preventing evaporation of moisture from the soil. Such mulches will also act as heat insulators, maintaining the soil at a more even temperature than would otherwise be the case. A drawback to mulches is that they are sometimes rather unsightly but this is not true of peat mulches which can have a very pleasant appearance.

MURIATE OF POTASH A chemical fertilizer which contains potash in combination with chlorine. Because of its chlorine content it is not so safe to use as sulphate of potash and may, in excess, even act as a plant killer. Nevertheless, used in the correct quantities, which should not exceed 1 oz. per sq. yd. at one application, muriate of potash is a good fertilizer, particularly for use on the more permanent subjects such as fruit trees. For potting and seed mixtures sulphate of potash is always to be preferred. Muriate of potash contains 50 per cent. potassium.

MUSHROOM FLY The tiny maggots of this fly sometimes attack mushrooms in great numbers, riddling them with small holes. Attacks are likely to be more severe in hot, dry weather. Lindane applied as a smoke or aerosol, malathion as a dust or aerosol, or diazinon as an aerosol will destroy the pest.

MUSHROOM MITE A small creature, often mistaken for an insect though not technically an insect, which attacks mushrooms, causing dark brown sunken wounds to appear on the caps. The mites may occur in great numbers. The pest also attacks shoot tips of cucumbers and french beans grown under glass. Remedies are to sprinkle finely powdered naphthalene, at the rate of 4 oz. per sq. yd., on the paths between the mushroom beds or to soak greenhouse borders with lindane or nicotine mixed with a wetter. This latter treatment is most effective if carried out towards evening.

MUSSEL SCALE One of the many scale insects which may attack fruit and other trees. The name refers to the shape and colour of the tiny scales which protect the insect when it is attached to the bark or stem. See Scale Insects.

MUTATION Any marked change in the character of a plant or animal due to an alteration in a gene (q.v.). Mutations affecting only a portion of a plant and appearing to have arisen from a single bud rather than from seed are often referred to as vegetative mutations or bud sports (see Sport). Mutations occur naturally but infrequently in all living things and provide the variations which have made evolution possible. They can be greatly speeded up by exposing plants and animals to radiation of various kinds and also by some chemicals. Most mutations are either of no benefit to the individual or are positively harmful and so in nature are eliminated by natural selection. Plant and animal breeders can preserve such mutant forms if they appear desirable for economic, decorative or other reasons by giving them a suitably protected environment.

MYCELIUM The thread-like growth of a fungus from which the spore-producing bodies arise.

MYCOGONE A fungal disease of mushrooms which causes white patches to appear on the gills. The whole mushroom may become distorted or produce warts. All diseased mushrooms, together with their stalks, should be removed and burned and the soil about them dusted with hydrated lime. The temperature of the mushroom house should be reduced below 10°C., water should be withheld temporarily and plenty of air admitted. When this disease has occurred the mushroom house may be disinfected with formalin solution after the mushrooms have been cleared. Between flushes of the crop spray or dust with zineb.

MYCOLOGY The name given to the scientific study of fungi. A person who practises this science is, therefore, known as a mycologist. As many plant diseases are

Herbaceous plants benefit from a mulch of garden compost or other organic matter. This should be spread around the plants in spring

caused by fungi, it is usually the case that a scientist who makes plant diseases his principal study is also a mycologist, but the name is not by any means confined to the study of harmful fungi.

NAPHTHALENE A chemical which is used as a soil and greenhouse fumigant (see Fumigation). For soil use, finely powdered naphthalene is generally employed, and this is applied at the rate of from 2 to 6 oz. per sq. yd. either dropped into holes about 9 in. deep and 9 in. apart, made with a stout dibber, or forked or dug into the soil in the ordinary course of autumn or spring cultivation. In either method fumes are slowly given off from the naphthalene, which is a volatile substance, and these penetrate the soil in all directions, either destroying insects or driving them out. Sometimes the second of these causes is at least as marked as the first, that is to say naphthalene is efficient as much because it drives pests into neighbouring ground as because it destroys them altogether. The effect on plants is not good at the highest rate of application, and this concentration should only be used on vacant ground, and then at least two months before it is to be cropped. Powdered naphthalene can, however, be used as a topdressing to plants in growth at the rate of 1 or, at most, 2 oz. per sq. yd. and may then be left to lie on the surface or be lightly hoed in. It is most valuable against wireworms and millepedes, and may have some effect on woodlice, slugs and snails.

NARCISSUS FLY The larvae of two species of fly attack narcissus (daffodil) bulbs, eating right into them and causing them to decay. The larvae are putty coloured and quite large. Beds of narcissi should be hoed or raked frequently during May and

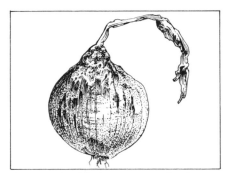

A bulb infected by narcissus fly larvae

June to fill crevices in which the flies might lay their eggs. Attacked bulbs should either be burned or else sterilized by being immersed for an hour in water at a temperature of 43°C. Alternatively, they may be soaked for three hours in a solution of BHC plus a wetter. BHC dust can be sprinkled around the necks of growing bulbs at fortnightly intervals from late April until the end of June.

NATURALIZE The practice of growing certain plants under as nearly natural conditions as possible. For example, daffodils are said to be naturalized when they are planted in grass and left to look after themselves. The term is also used to describe plants from foreign countries which have established themselves so well in the country into which they have been introduced that they behave like native plants and are able to maintain themselves without the aid of the gardener. When plants have been naturalized in this manner for a very long time it is often difficult to decide whether they are, in fact, foreign plants which are naturalized or are genuine natives. A case in point is the Stinking Hellebore, *Helleborus foetidus*, which is found growing, apparently wild, in many parts of Britain, but usually on or near the sites of Roman encampments. This lends colour to the belief that this is not really an indigenous British plant but one brought over by the Romans nearly 2,000 years ago.

NATURAL ORDER One of the major divisions used in the classification of plants. A natural order is composed of families which have many characters in common and are, in consequence, presumed to have a considerable degree of relationship. The term natural order is often erroneously used as synonymous with family. A family, in the botanical sense, is an aggregation of allied genera, and frequently a smaller aggregation than that represented by the natural order, which may contain several families, see Classification.

NECK ROT A disease of onions which may also attack shallots and garlic. It is caused by a fungus which infects the neck of the plant or the upper part of the bulb, causing this

to turn brown and become soft. A greyish mould may appear on the diseased parts. Sometimes the disease may not be observed until the onions have been placed in store. There is no satisfactory remedy. Very large onions or those with thick necks are most susceptible and good cultivation, resulting in medium-sized well-ripened bulbs, is the best means of prevention. Care should be taken to see that all onions are well dried

before they are stored and that they are stored in a really dry, well-ventilated place.

NECROSIS Literally death. Used in gardens to describe the small dead spots or patches found on the leaves of plants attacked by certain viruses and also the withering of the flower stalk in peonies and roses, sometimes referred to as pedicel necrosis. See Bud Disease.

NECTAR, NECTARY Nectar is the sweet liquid secreted by some flowers apparently with the function of attracting insects and so securing pollination, as the insects carry pollen from the anthers to the stigmas of the flowers. It is from the nectar of flowers that honey bees produce honey and from the pollen that they prepare the substance known to bee keepers as bee bread. This nectar is produced from glandular tissue which may be concentrated in one place which is then known as a nectary, e.g. the spur of a violet.

NEMATODE WORMS A group of worms mostly of small size, some microscopic, though a few are large, usually colourless and often, though by no means always, parasitic. The group is a very large one and includes many animal as well as vegetable parasites. The various eelworms which can be so troublesome in the garden belong here but in this book are dealt with separately under their own name. When the gardener speaks of nematode worms he usually means certain of the larger, free-living species that are frequently found in soil that is rather too freely supplied with partially decayed organic matter. Such nematode worms may be a quarter to half an inch in length, transparent, and pointed at each end and they usually lash about vigorously when disturbed. They are not parasitic and may be regarded as scavengers as they live on dead or decaying organic matter. Nevertheless, when they are present in great numbers they usually suggest a rather unhealthy soil condition and may indicate the need for liming, better cultivation and improved drainage.

NETTING The term is applied to the twine netting that is so frequently used by gardeners to protect fruit and other crops from birds, to the plastic-coated wire or steel netting often used to support plants, particularly those trained against walls, and to the galvanized wire netting which is mainly used in the garden to keep out pests such as rabbits. Old fish netting is frequently favoured for the first purpose. This has a diamond mesh and is usually sold by length, which is estimated when the netting is pulled out to its full extent lengthwise. When the netting is pulled out evenly in both directions for use as a cover, it will not be as long as stated by the salesman and this point must

An onion showing the symptoms of neck rot

Netting provides a good way of protecting strawberries and similar crops from the depredations of birds. Some method of support, such as stakes and wires, will be needed

be allowed for when estimating size; in fact, one third should be taken off the advertised length when estimating the actual coverage length. The advertised width will not be affected as this is correctly stated.

The size of the mesh of twine netting is a matter over which a certain amount of confusion can arise. The term one-inch mesh, for example, might mean a mesh of side one inch or of diagonal one inch, or it might mean a mesh that will only admit the passage of objects of diameter one inch or less (compare one-inch screen).

The constant dimension in a mesh is the length of one side, technically known as a bar. When ordering netting, therefore, the purchaser should follow the custom of the trade, and specify one-inch bar, three-inch bar, square, and so on. If, in addition, he states the length along the selvedge (the long side), which is usually mounted on a rope or otherwise strengthened, and the number of meshes in the width he requires, he will always know that he will get what he orders, without having to worry about losses of length when spread out. Netting, incidentally, is always assumed to be diamond mesh unless otherwise stated.

Nets should be cleaned, repaired and treated with preservative (there are several fluids sold for this purpose) before being stored for the winter.

Nowadays twine netting has largely been superseded by plastic netting which is much more durable and is made in many strengths and meshes, the stated sizes of which accurately indicate the covering capacity.

Galvanized wire netting used to keep out rabbits should not be more than one-inch mesh and preferably rather less. It should rise at least 3 ft. vertically out of the ground and be buried at least 9 in. in the ground. It is better that these measurements should be exceeded. If coarser mesh wire is used,

very young rabbits will get through, and eventually the ground inside the wiring may become as heavily stocked with rabbits as that outside.

NICKING, see Notching

NICOTINE A powerful alkaloid poison which is valuable to the gardener because of its insecticidal properties. It is particularly useful for destroying sap suckers such as greenfly and other forms of aphid, capsid bugs, thrips and leaf hoppers and it is also of use against sawfly larvae, including the destructive apple sawfly, and leaf-mining maggots. It can be used as a liquid spray, as a dust and as a fumigant, but it may be observed that, being a volatile substance, its efficiency as an insecticide is always, to some extent, bound up with the vapour which is produced from it. Because of this the liquid and powder forms are much more efficient in warm weather than in cold, in fact, at temperatures below 18°C. they lose a great deal of their value. This is a drawback as it means that nicotine cannot be used with full efficiency out of doors early in the year, unless the weather happens to be unusually mild. A second drawback is the fact that it is extremely poisonous to human beings and all warm-blooded animals. It is true that at the concentration at which it is usually employed as a spray its poisonous properties are greatly reduced and, further, that being so volatile the spray usually loses all poisonous properties within a few days. Nevertheless, this is an insecticide which must be used with due precautions.

As a liquid, nicotine can be purchased as a diluted solution with or without a spreading agent. Diluted proprietary brands of nicotine must always be used strictly in accordance with manufacturers' instruc-

tions and, if a spreading agent is already incorporated in the spray, no further addition need be made. Liquid nicotine should always be applied in the form of a heavy wetting spray; the more fully it can be brought into contact with the bodies of the insects to be destroyed, the more effective it will be.

Nicotine dust is sold ready mixed with a suitable carrying agent and has only to be scattered or blown over the plants to be protected. Nicotine is also prepared as shreds or in other forms which can be ignited and used for greenhouse fumigation.

NITRATE Any salt of nitric acid. In the garden the term is frequently used as an abbreviation for almost any concentrated nitrogenous fertilizer such as nitrate of soda, nitrate of potash, Chilean nitrate, etc.

NITRATE OF POTASH This is better known as saltpetre, the substance used for making touchpaper and an ingredient of old-fashioned gunpowder. It is too expensive for widespread use as a fertilizer, but as it contains both nitrogen and potash in readily available forms, it is a useful food for special purposes. It makes a first-rate liquid manure, used at the rate of ½ oz. per gallon. It can be applied dry at rates up to 2 oz. per sq. yd. The analysis is nitrogen 12.5 per cent., potash 40 per cent. It must not be confused with Chilean potash nitrate, which is quite a different substance with, on the average, a much lower potassic content.

NITRATE OF SODA A very quick-acting nitrogenous fertilizer which is useful to induce rapid growth, particularly of leaf and stem. It is highly soluble, and fairly easily washed out of the soil; in consequence, it is usually applied just before a crop is sown or planted, or while the crop is in growth. In excess, nitrate of soda can have a damaging effect on plants, scorching leaves and tender growth and even killing plants altogether. It is never wise to exceed a rate of application of 1 oz. per sq. yd. at a time, and no more should be given until this has been largely used up or washed out of the soil. The analysis of nitrate of soda shows 15.5 to 16 per cent. nitrogen. Nitrate of soda can also be used as a liquid manure at the rate of ¼ to ½ oz. per gallon of water.

NITROGEN An element which enters into the composition of plant growth and is an important plant food. Nitrogen itself is an inert gas and it forms four-fifths of the atmosphere of the world. It cannot, therefore, be applied to the soil, though organisms exist in the soil and in the roots of certain plants which are capable of converting the gaseous nitrogen of the air into salts of nitrogen, in which form they are available as plant food. The bacteria which form nodules on the roots of leguminous plants, such as peas and beans, are of this type. The gardener sometimes enriches the soil with nitrogen by sowing leguminous crops on the ground and then digging them in, but more frequently he makes use of animal manures or chemical fertilizers containing salts of nitric acid.

Most animal manures contain some nitrogen, but the quantity is liable to decrease the longer the manure is kept, partly by escape of nitrogen as ammonia gas to the atmosphere, and partly by soluble nitrogen salts being washed away by rain. Moreover, a great deal of the nitrogen in animal manure is in the liquid part of the manure and, unless steps are taken to preserve this, the quantity of nitrogen retained may be small. An average well-rotted sample of horse manure will contain 0.5 to 1 per cent. nitrogen.

The principal chemical fertilizers containing nitrogen are nitrate of soda, sulphate of ammonia, Chilean nitrate, Nitro-chalk, nitrate of lime, nitrate of potash and calcium cyanamide. Concentrated organic fertilizers which contain nitrogen are urea, dried blood and hoof and horn meal.

The most marked effect that nitrogen has upon plants is to increase the rate and vigour of their growth and to deepen the green colour of foliage. As it is one of the foods most readily washed out of the soil and most rapidly used by all plants, it is also one of those which the gardener has most need to apply.

NODE The joint of a stem at which point a leaf is borne or has been borne. Cuttings which are severed just below a joint are frequently described as nodal cuttings, whereas those which are severed midway

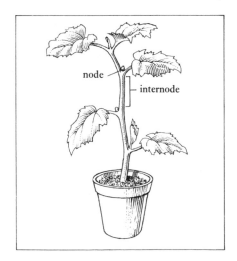

between joints are described as internodal cuttings. A growth bud or buds will be found at each node. The cambium layer at this point is usually more capable of producing adventitious roots or buds than the cambium in other parts of the stem. See Joint.

NODULE Small swellings will usually be found on the roots of leguminous plants such as peas, clovers and lupins. These nodules are caused by bacteria which are beneficial to the plant since they are able to fix nitrogen from the air and so make it available to the plant. Leguminous crops, such as vetches, are sometimes grown for digging in later as green manure because in this way the soil will actually be enriched in nitrogen.

NOTCHING AND NICKING The practice of making an incision above (notching) or below (nicking) a dormant growth bud, usually of a fruit tree. Nicking tends to check growth, notching (in which a small triangle or crescent of bark is sometimes removed) to encourage it. The operation is usually done in May.

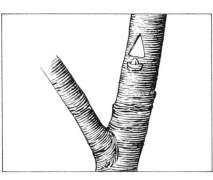

NUCLEUS The controlling part of a living cell. Cell division is preceded by division of the nucleus and the first indication of this is the appearance of chromosomes which ensure that the splitting of the nuclear material is exact, see Chromosome.

NURSERY That portion of the garden reserved for the rearing of young plants. The term is particularly applied to the beds in which plants are grown on after they leave the seed bed. Thus instructions to plant out in the nursery bed simply means to plant out in a piece of ground in which the plants can remain until they become large enough to go into their permanent quarters. Nursery beds are usually made in some out-of-the-way part of the garden as, for example, a plot in the vegetable garden. The ground should be well cultivated and thoroughly drained and, if possible, be provided with some means of applying extra water in dry weather, as the rate of growth of young plants is usually very adversely affected by drought. A nursery garden is a garden wholly devoted to the raising of young plants.

OBOVATE A term used to describe leaves that are oval in outline.

OBTUSE Blunt or rounded; a botanical term used in the description of leaves which are of this character.

OFFSET A young plant produced vegetatively alongside another plant and easily detached from it. The term is most commonly applied to bulbs and corms which usually produce offsets freely as a natural means of increase. The term, however, is also applied to fibrous-rooted plants, particularly to plants which form a number of separate crowns of shoots rather loosely connected together. Propagation by removal of offsets is really a form of propagation by division. Offsets, being vegetative in origin, almost invariably resemble the parent plant in every respect. See Vegetative Propagation.

ONION FLY The small white maggots of this fly attack young onions at, or just below, soil level, causing the foliage to flag. Planting sets may be soaked in lindane immediately before planting. Lindane dust should be sprinkled around seedlings when they are 1½ in. high and again a fortnight later.

OPPOSITE A botanical term describing a particular mode of producing leaves, in which the leaves appear in pairs on opposite sides of the stem. This may be contrasted with alternate, in which the leaves are produced singly and are usually arranged in a roughly spiral formation on the stem.

ORGANIC Any chemical compound of carbon. As a great many organic chemicals are derived from living organisms, the term is often loosely used to describe substances obtained from such organisms, in contrast to those obtained from non-living sources. For example, the terms organic gardening and organic manuring are frequently used to describe those systems of gardening and manuring which rely exclusively on bulky animal manures and vegetable composts and make no use of concentrated fertilizers. This, however, is really a misuse of the word, as there are many organic chemicals which are synthetically produced in the laboratory.

Plants are not designed by nature to make direct use of organic substances, their food being simple inorganic chemicals which they then synthesize, with the aid of sunlight, into the more complex organic substances, such as sugars, starches and proteins. The importance of organic substances in the soil lies in the effect which they have on soil texture and the micro-organisms which live in soil. Most organic substances undergo a process of decay in the soil and this decay is brought about largely by the activities of fungi, bacteria and other micro-organisms. In the absence of sufficient organic matter, these micro-organisms are reduced in numbers and, unless suitable inorganic foods are applied in carefully controlled quantities (as is done when using hydroponic and other soilless methods of cultivation), the soil quickly becomes unbalanced in food and the growth of plants is retarded or prevented. The presence of an abundant population of micro-organisms, particularly fungi, in the soil, improves its texture, helping drainage in wet weather and at the same time enabling the soil to absorb sufficient moisture to withstand reasonable periods of drought. It will be seen, therefore, that any wise system of gardening will take into account the value of both organic and of inorganic substances and will not rely on one to the exclusion of the other.

ORGANOMERCURY COMPOUNDS
A general name given to a number of chemicals, some of which are used as sprays to control diseases such as apple and pear scab, some as paints to control apple canker, and some as liquid or dust seed dressings to give protection against a wide variety of soilborne diseases. In all cases manufacturers' instructions regarding preparation and use must be followed.

OSMUNDA A brown fibrous material prepared from the roots of osmunda ferns and much used as an ingredient in orchid potting composts.

OVARY The seeds of a flowering plant develop from ovules that have been fertilized with pollen. That part of the plant which contains the ovules is known as the ovary.

OVATE In outline like an egg; a botanical term used in the description of leaves which are of this shape.

OVICIDE Any chemical which kills eggs. Winter washes are often applied to fruit trees to destroy the over-wintering eggs of red spider mites, aphids and other pests. In spring and summer other ovicides may be found useful particularly in the control of red spider mites (q.v.).

OXYDEMETON-METHYL An insecticide used primarily to kill aphids, red spider mites, leaf hoppers, apple and plum sawflies and pear suckers. It is highly poisonous to all mammals, including human beings, and ordinary formulations must be used with the greatest caution, protective clothing being worn, and so on. But a special aerosol formulation of this chemical in which the active chemical is already so dilute as to be relatively harmless to domestic animals and human beings, can be used without protective clothing and with only the normal precautions that apply to most toxic chemicals. It is ready for use and particularly effective in greenhouses.

OXYGEN An element which is a gas, and which forms one-fifth of the atmosphere of the earth. It is an essential plant food but is always present in sufficient quantity in any normal supply of air and need never be specially applied. Oxygen is required by the roots as well as by the leaves of plants, and this is one of the reasons for maintaining a good granular structure in the soil so that air may penetrate between the crumbs and reach the roots. If the soil becomes too consolidated or too waterlogged, air is driven out and the roots and beneficial soil bacteria die.

OYSTER SHELL Crushed oyster shell is sometimes used as a substitute for lime or sand. It is, however, too expensive for widespread use and has no special advantages over them except, perhaps, in bulb fibre (q.v.).

PALMATE Divided in the form of a hand; a botanical term used to describe leaves which are deeply divided into several lobes. The term digitate has a somewhat similar meaning but is usually reserved for leaves that are composed of several separate leaflets united to a common stalk at the base.

Palmate

PAN A term used to describe the hard layer of soil which may be formed through faulty methods of cultivation, and which, by becoming impermeable to moisture and air, may have a very adverse effect upon plant growth. In farm practice a pan often occurs a few inches beneath the surface as a result of constant ploughing to the same depth, the smooth base of the plough pressing the soil beneath the furrow into a hard cake. The same kind of effect can be produced when rotary hoeing is continued year after year to approximately the same depth on soils which are rather sticky; in fact panning is always more likely to be a trouble on clay soils than on those of a sandy nature. A natural pan unconnected with cultural practices often occurs on soils heavily supplied with iron. It may be necessary to break up such pans before satisfactory cultivation can be carried out.

Surface panning, i.e. the production of a smooth hard surface to the soil, is liable to occur after heavy rain on the heavier types of soil and may be aggravated by faulty treatment, such as walking on the soil while it is still wet, or rolling it before it has had time to dry out sufficiently.

Absence of sufficient humus and grit in the soil can aggravate panning and the addition of these materials will help to prevent panning.

When panning has occurred despite precautions, the layer of hard soil must be broken up by suitable cultivation, such as deep digging or trenching when the pan is several inches below the surface, or surface forking and hoeing for surface pans.

Pan is also used to describe shallow pots, usually of earthenware or plastic. They are useful for raising seedlings and other small plants which do not require much depth of soil. Such pans should be well supplied with drainage holes in the bottom.

PANICLE A particular kind of flower cluster consisting of several separate branches each of which carries numerous stalked flowers with the youngest at the top.

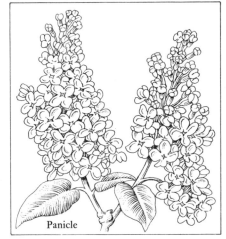
Panicle

PAPPUS The tuft of hairs or bristles found in the flowers of some members of the daisy family (*Compositae*) and which later enable the seeds to become airborne.

PARADICHLORBENZENE A strong-smelling chemical which is useful as a soil fumigant to kill or drive out wireworms, millepedes and cutworms. It is used at $\frac{1}{2}$ oz. per sq. yd. scattered over the surface and forked in or dropped into holes about 8 in. deep and 9 in. apart.

PARAQUAT A weedkiller of similar character to diquat (q.v.) and sometimes sold in mixtures with it. It operates through the leaves and green stems, severely damaging or killing most plants and particularly annuals and grasses. It is inactivated by the soil and so can be used selectively if it is applied only to the leaves and stems of the weeds that are to be killed. It can be purchased in crystal form or as a liquid to be dissolved in or diluted with water according to manufacturers' instructions and applied as a spray or by means of a sprinkle bar. Care should be taken to prevent drift onto plants that are not to be killed.

PARASITE Any living organism which lives upon another living organism, in contrast to a saprophyte which is a living organism which lives on a dead organism. Dodder is a plant parasite which lives on gorse and other heathland plants. It is entirely dependent upon the gorse or host plant for its nourishment and has neither roots nor leaves of its own. Mistletoe is mainly parasitic and has no roots, but it does possess some green leaves which are capable of manufacturing food and is, therefore, not a total parasite. Nevertheless it cannot live except in association with a suitable host plant. It is a semi-parasite.

PARATHION An organic phosphorus compound that is widely used as an insecticide in commercial establishments but is generally regarded as too dangerous for use by amateurs. It acts both as a stomach poison and as a contact insecticide and is effective against a wide range of pests including aphids, capsid bugs, caterpillars, flies, thrips and mites. It is largely because of its ability to kill red spider mite that it has become so popular in nurseries and in orchards. Unfortunately parathion is also very poisonous to all warm-blooded animals, including human beings, and may be absorbed through the skin or inhaled as well as being taken in through the digestive system. Protective rubber clothing, including rubber gloves, should be worn when it is applied and it is also recommended that a gas mask be used. Manufacturers' instructions should be followed, both with regard to any further safety precautions and to the strength of application.

PARTERRE A level area of any shape or size usually containing a design or pattern. Frequently the design was defined by formal edgings of clipped box or other shrubs. It was a form of gardening highly developed by French designers of the 17th century, and is now occasionally making a return on formal sites.

Parterres were intended to be seen as a pattern, for which reason they were often placed near a building or beside a raised terrace or partly surrounded by a raised walk from any of which vantage points they could be viewed from above. They varied greatly in their complexity from plain parterres of quite simple design and usually set in grass to parterres of embroidery in which the patterns might be exceedingly elaborate and carried out with the aid of coloured earth, gravel, sand, brick dust and other materials.

Parterres were usually further orna-

A traditional arrangement of parterres

mented with clipped evergreen shrubs and sometimes with vases, urns, statues, balustrades and other architectural objects.

PARTHENOCARPIC A term used to describe a fruit that has been produced without fertilization. Some kinds of plant produce parthenocarpic fruits of their own accord, e.g. greenhouse cucumbers. In other instances parthenocarpic fruits can be produced by applying very minute quantities of a suitable hormone to the flowers or the tiny fruits. This treatment has been used very successfully on tomatoes and also with fair success on strawberries, see Hormones.

PARTHENOGENESIS Reproduction without fertilization by a male. This is the normal method of producing young in the wingless stage of greenflies and other aphids.

PATHOLOGY The study of diseases.

PATHS Paths have been described as the backbone of the garden and this they very well may be. It is certain that well-made paths add greatly to the comfort of the garden and also, to some extent, when once made they dictate the rest of the design. This is not to say that the first thing to do, when developing any new ground, is to lay paths without thought of what is to follow. That was a policy too frequently adopted by the speculative builder of years ago and the result was almost invariably unhappy. The right course is to plan the whole garden from the start before the ground is even touched with the spade, let alone dealt with in any more permanent manner. In this original plan great thought should be given to the provision of paths, considering these not only as purely utility items, giving ready access to every part of the garden, but also as a part of the artistic scheme.

The width of paths will naturally vary

greatly according to the purpose which they have to serve. In the rock garden they may be reduced to tracks no more than a foot in width, whereas main drives may be 15 ft. or more wide. But taking an average throughout the garden, the ordinary paths for walking on should not, as a rule, be less than 2 ft. wide and from 3 to 4 ft. may be considered a more convenient width.

Many surfacing materials may be used and each has its own particular advantages and drawbacks. One feature is essential in all path making and that is a good foundation of some hard material such as brick ends or clinkers. This should be at least 6 in. thick, for the purpose is not only to provide a firm foundation for the surfacing material, but also to allow water to drain away freely. If water collects beneath the surface in winter and then freezes, it will exert a powerful pressure and in time will break up even the best-made paths.

Rectangular paving Genuine Yorkshire paving slabs or other stone slabs of the same character make a most dignified and satisfactory material for paths of all types except those in the wildest or most natural parts of the garden. These slabs can be purchased in a variety of sizes and almost always in squares or simple rectangles of some kind, and they can be laid in patterns if desired. Furthermore, they can be bedded in some loose material such as sand or sifted ashes or, for a more permanent result, they can be bedded in cement. The latter method suffers from the slight drawback that it is not so easy to establish plants in the crevices between the stones. This may or may not be considered a disadvantage according to the reaction of the gardener to plants in paths. However, it is possible to grow plants even in cement-bedded paths if some crevices are left open, no cement being placed either in or beneath them.

The concrete for this purpose should be made by mixing 2 parts by bulk of coarse aggregate, 1 part of builder's sand, 1 part of cement. Mix these ingredients thoroughly while dry, and then add water a little at a time until the whole can be worked quite freely and is about the consistency of rather stiff porridge. This concrete should then be spread to a depth of at least 2 in. on the hard core forming the foundation, and the paving slabs should be bedded down on it. Be very careful to keep the joints between one stone and another as level as possible, and do not make any attempt to fill the spaces between the slabs at this stage. This should be done a few days later when the base cement is already firm. Pointing should then be done with concrete made by mixing 3 parts of sand to 1 of cement, which may be coloured with a little yellow ochre, if desired, to get it exactly the same tone as that of the stones themselves. If paving slabs are laid in loose sand or ashes, they should be bedded down

There is a range of surfacing materials suitable for path making. Here, natural stone, pebbles, pre-cast slabs, and bricks are used in a variety of designs

with great care, keeping the edges quite level. Then, when all the slabs have been laid, some more sand should be scattered over the surface and brushed down into the crevices with a stiff broom.

Crazy paving This material is much favoured, particularly in the smaller or more informal gardens, and it has the merit of being cheaper in some districts than rectangular paving slabs. The price will vary a good deal, however, from place to place, as this is a heavy material and carriage charges can soon mount up.

Crazy paving is usually offered in several distinct thicknesses which vary from $\frac{3}{4}$ to $2\frac{1}{2}$ in. As a rule pieces ranging from $\frac{3}{4}$ to $1\frac{1}{2}$ in. thickness are graded together as thin crazy paving, and those from $1\frac{1}{2}$ to $2\frac{1}{2}$ in. in thickness are sold as thick crazy paving. When these gradings are adopted, it will be found that, on an average, thick crazy paving will cover about 9 sq. yd. per ton of material and thin paving about 14 sq. yd. per ton.

The same remarks regarding laying apply as with the rectangular paving slabs, i.e. crazy paving can be set in either a loose dry material such as sand or ashes, or in concrete, and with the same comparative advantages and drawbacks. Two differences to be observed are, first, that because of the irregular shape of the slabs, considerably more ingenuity will be required in fitting them together, so that there are no gaps between the adjacent slabs more than one inch or so in width, and secondly, as the slabs are likely to vary a little in thickness not only as between one slab and another but in different parts of the same slab, even more care will be needed to maintain a level surface. It will be necessary to scrape away the concrete, sand or ashes where the slabs are thick and add to the layer where they are thin, and for this purpose a builder's trowel should be kept at hand throughout the work of laying. As to the method of

fitting the slabs, each workman will probably have his own ideas, but one which proves serviceable is to place some of the larger slabs in position first, and then fill in the spaces between them with smaller pieces, much as one would do in fitting a jig-saw puzzle together. Pointing with either smooth cement for a concrete-bedded path, or with sand or ashes for a loose-bedded path, should be carried out in exactly the same manner as described for rectangular paving slabs.

Concrete Durable and clean paths can be formed of concrete alone. One drawback to this material is that it does not weather so readily or pleasantly as natural stone and, in consequence, never becomes quite as much a part of the garden. Nevertheless concrete has the great merit of being a comparatively cheap material and one which is fairly simple to use.

Concrete should be prepared as already described for the foundation of the stone

paved path. It should be spread on the hard rubble foundation, to a depth of at least 2 in. and should be made level with a piece of straight-edged wood. It will not be a drawback if some slight impressions of the edge of the wood are left on the concrete, giving it a fairly ribbed surface, as this will make it less slippery to walk on in wet weather.

If desired, concrete can be coloured in almost any manner, special colourants for this purpose being available from most builder's merchants. It is advisable to do a little experimenting with a small quantity of concrete before making the final mixing and to allow the samples to dry out thoroughly before pronouncing on the result, as the colour will change as the concrete becomes dry.

It is most important that concrete paths should not be allowed to dry too rapidly, nor under any circumstances must they be exposed to severe frost before they are completely set, though light ground frost may do them no harm. If paths have to be laid in warm weather, they should be covered with damp sacks and these should be kept moist for at least a week while the concrete is setting slowly beneath them. If concrete has to be made during winter or early spring, a sharp watch should be kept for frost, and at the least danger of this the concrete should be covered with dry sacks. This precaution should be observed for several days after the concrete has become firm on the surface, as there will still be a lot of moisture beneath.

If desired, concrete can be laid to imitate either rectangular paving slabs or crazy paving. If the former is decided upon, the simplest method is to mark out the position of the slab with smooth wooden laths, which should first be well greased. Then the concrete is spread level with the top edges of the laths, and when it is dry the laths should be carefully removed. An alternative is to pre-cast the slabs in shallow

Levelling a concrete path with a piece of wood. Note the hard rubble foundation

wooden moulds, and then lay them exactly as if they were natural paving slabs.

Imitation crazy paving can be made by either of these methods, but a simpler plan is to mark the crazy paving pattern on the surface of a plain concrete path with the point of a mason's trowel. This should be done when the concrete is partly set.

Ready mixed concrete is available in many localities and can be purchased in various mixes to suit the work to be done. This saves a lot of labour but since the concrete, once delivered, will immediately start the chemical processes which lead to setting in a few hours, it is important not to order more than can be handled conveniently in an hour or so and to make certain that it will be delivered at a convenient time when the necessary labour is available.

Pre-cast slabs These are available in a great many patterns and colours and should be laid just like natural stone slabs.

Bricks Bricks laid on edge make a very attractive and durable path, but they suffer from two drawbacks, first, that they are comparatively costly and secondly, that they become extremely slippery in wet weather, particularly if rubber-soled boots or shoes are worn. The bricks can be laid in a simple pattern or in herringbone formation. As with paving slabs, the most durable result is obtained by setting the bricks in concrete and the same method should be employed.

Asphalt At one time asphalt was an extremely popular paving material, but it is not seen so much nowadays, no doubt because it never looks very well in the garden. This is in part due to its black colour, and in part to the fact that the tar in it discourages the growth of all plants, even plants spreading from adjacent beds, and so the path never becomes assimilated with the garden. Nevertheless asphalt has the merits of being easily and quickly laid, and of making a very durable path which is quite pleasant to walk on. If used, the surface layer of asphalt should be about one inch in thickness.

Gravel Gravel is another material which has to some extent gone out of favour, having once been the most popular of all surfacing materials. No doubt a contributory cause to this is the labour involved in weeding, but this has now been removed by the introduction of improved weedkillers, particularly such substances as paraquat and simazine with which gravel paths can be kept quite clean with little labour and complete safety. Loose shingle is very cheap but never makes a really satisfactory surfacing material, as it is very tiring to walk on and must be frequently raked to keep it level. Gravel should contain sufficient sand and

clay to enable it to bind together into a smooth and firm surface. Once again it is necessary to insist on the importance of a good foundation layer of hard material. On this the gravel should be spread at least 3 in. thick, and for preference with a slight camber or fall towards the edges so that water runs off readily. Rake the gravel to a smooth, even surface and then roll it thoroughly, watering it occasionally while this is being done so that it becomes really compact and hard. A well-made gravel path should require little after-care beyond weeding. If it does become loose or worn the holes should be patched with more gravel, and rolling and watering repeated as in the first instance.

Pebbles and cobbles These set in concrete can look most attractive especially if they are placed to form patterns or if pebbles of different colours are used in patterns. But the rough surface is tiring to walk on and the principal use of these materials is in forming decorative panels in paths formed mainly of smoother material.

PCNB, see Quintozene

PEA AND BEAN BEETLE The small white grub of this beetle attacks the seeds of broad beans and peas, eating small holes in them. Most modern seed-cleaning stores are provided with ingenious machines for removing the seeds damaged by these beetles. Seeds may be dusted with lindane or thiram seed dressing before being sown.

PEACH LEAF CURL, see Leaf curl

PEAR MIDGE The small, yellowish white maggots of this insect enter the fruitlets of pears and feed within them; as a result the fruitlets become deformed, turn black and fall prematurely. The female midges lay their eggs in the flowers during the spring and the best remedy is to spray with nicotine when the blossom is fully open. Poultry penned beneath the trees from April to June will pick up many of the midges and their maggots.

PEAT Dead vegetation in an arrested state of decay. Peat is most likely to be formed from deposits of vegetation which has grown on heathland or in some boggy areas. Peat varies greatly in both its origin and its character, and while some peat is of great value to the gardener as a source of humus, other samples are of much less value being either too acid or of poor texture. Good grade peat has to a considerable extent replaced leafmould as a source of humus in potting composts, partly because it is relatively free of spores of fungi and of other organisms which may cause disease, and also of weed seeds, but even more because it decays more slowly than leafmould and

therefore retains its nature in the soil for a longer period. The best peat for this purpose is that derived from deposits of sphagnum moss, but any fibrous peat which is not too dusty in texture, and not too acid, may be used. In the well-known John Innes potting composts, horticultural grade peat is one of the recommended ingredients.

For outdoor use to improve soils lacking in humus, a wider range of peats can be used without harmful effects. However, it is wise to avoid those which are of a very dusty nature, as these will tend to clog up the soil rather than improve its texture. If peats of a very acid nature are used, it is often desirable to give a dressing of lime at the same time to counteract this acidity. For outdoor use, peat can be employed in the same way as leafmould at rates from 6 to 12 lb. per sq. yd. Finely-broken peat is also a useful topdressing for shrub borders, lawns and vegetable crops, to protect the surface soil from the heat of the sun and encourage the moist, cool conditions in which roots thrive.

Some plants, notably members of the heather family, *Ericaceae*, delight in peaty soils. When these are grown in places in which the soil is not naturally of this type, it may pay to import considerable quantities of peat, both for forking into the soil prior to planting and for use subsequently as topdressings. As these plants also like acid conditions, it will not, as a rule, matter if the peat is somewhat acid.

It is customary to dry peat thoroughly before it is made up in bales or bags for sale, as dry peat weighs considerably less than wet peat. In this condition, however, it is rather difficult to make it absorb moisture, so before dry peat is used, whether in potting composts or for digging into the soil, it should be thoroughly moistened. This may be done by spreading it out and soaking it or, if it is purchased in plastic bags, by opening these at one end, pouring in water and leaving it to soak in.

PEAT WALLS Peat cut in blocks, as it is for burning, can be used instead of stone to build low retaining walls or series of such walls in receding terraces rather like a rock garden. If the whole is then filled in with more peat or a very peaty mixture it will prove a suitable place in which to grow many peat-loving plants including certain kinds of primula and meconopsis as well as small rhododendrons, cassiopes, etc.

PEA WEEVIL This pest, also known as pea and bean weevil, attacks the leaves of peas and broad beans. It eats the margins of the leaves so that they have a scalloped appearance. Two separate species of weevil produce similar damage. Both are greyish in colour and about $\frac{1}{4}$ in. in length, but there is no need for the gardener to be able to distinguish between one and the other as

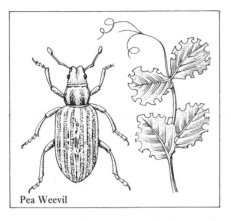

Pea Weevil

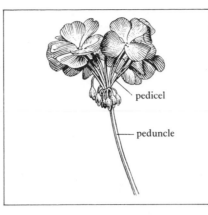

pedicel

peduncle

the remedy is the same for both. Damage is most likely to be severe in late spring and early summer. Control can be obtained by dusting or spraying the foliage with BHC, carbaryl or derris.

PEDICEL The stalk of a single flower.

PEDICEL NECROSIS A somewhat unwieldly name given to the trouble described under the heading bud disease.

PEDUNCLE Usually applied to the main stalk of a cluster of flowers, but can be used for the stalk of a single flower. See Pedicel.

PELTATE A botanical term used to describe leaves in which the stalk is attached within the leaf margin, as in the common nasturtium, *Tropaeolum majus*.

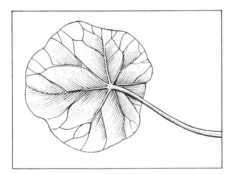

PEPPER DUST Ordinary pepper dust as used in the kitchen is useful in the garden as a deterrent to earwigs and cats. For either purpose the pepper dust should be sprinkled lightly over the leaves or flowers of plants that are liable to be damaged.

PERCH, see Rod

PERENNIAL Any plant that continues to live for an indefinite number of years and to flower time and again. Such a plant may be contrasted with an annual which completes the cycle of its growth in one year and dies after it has flowered and produced seed, a biennial which has a similar life cycle but takes two years to complete it, and a monocarpic plant which may live for several

years, but flowers only once and then seeds and dies. It is wrong to regard a perennial as a plant which goes on living for ever. There will come a time in the life of every plant when it will die of old age, but this period will not only vary greatly from one species of plant to another, but also from one individual to another within the same species. There are, for example, short-lived perennials such as lupins, which rarely live for more than five or six years, in contrast to long-lived perennials, such as peonies, which may continue in good health for a great many years. A tree or shrub is as much a perennial as a herbaceous plant in that it fulfils the qualifications in the first paragraph.

In show schedules the term perennial is sometimes wrongly used for herbaceous perennial. For example in a class for 'Six vases of perennials' an exhibitor would be quite justified in staging cut stems from trees and shrubs. If it is intended that such a class is to be confined to herbaceous perennials the qualification herbaceous must be used. Moreover, the term perennial refers to the natural character of the plant. A perennial from a tropical or sub-tropical habitat does not cease to be a perennial because, when grown in a colder climate, it is killed each winter. In this respect, also, show schedules are sometimes badly worded.

In a class for 'Six vases of herbaceous perennials' an exhibitor would be quite justified in including dahlias. If such half-hardy plants are to be excluded the word hardy should be used.

PERFOLIATE Penetrating the leaf; a botanical term applied to stems which are apparently completely encircled by the leaf, e.g. juvenile form of *Eucalyptus gunnii*.

PERGOLA A series of arches forming a covered walk. Pergolas are of many different kinds and can be made of many different materials. Simple pergolas are made of wood, either undressed poles such as those of larch or pine, or squared and treated timber. More elaborate constructions may have pillars of stone or brick with wooden cross-members. They can be of any dimensions, but if they are to be covered with climbing plants, care should be taken to see that there is enough head room to allow for the normal growth of plants and still leave room for a person of ordinary height to walk comfortably beneath. For example, wisterias are often planted to cover pergolas and look very beautiful when grown in this manner, but the builder must remember that when the wisteria is in flower, the trails of bloom will hang 2 ft. or more below the roof members of the pergola. In consequence, it will be necessary to build a pergola something like 8 ft. in height to accommodate in comfort plants of this type.

A bare pergola presents little resistance to wind, but when it is covered with plants the resistance will be greatly increased and, unless it is of substantial construction, it may easily be blown down. Wooden uprights should be of stout timbers, sunk 2 ft. or more into the ground, and brick or stone piers should be well cemented.

PERIANTH The name given to the outer parts of a flower which enclose the reproductive organs. Usually the perianth will

Pergola

comprise both sepals and petals but sometimes one or other may be missing or there may be no clear differentiation between them. In narcissi the term perianth segments is used for those parts which form the more or less flat part of the flower against which the trumpet or cup, known as the corona, is displayed.

PERMANGANATE OF POTASH The popular name for potassium permanganate, a chemical which is sometimes used by the gardener as an insecticide and fungicide and also as a moss killer. For the first two purposes it has been superseded, to a very large extent, by other more powerful chemicals. Nevertheless a ring of permanganate of potash closely placed round a choice plant will provide a very effective defence against slugs, and if it is believed that slugs are hiding under the carpet formed by spreading plants such as pinks and alpine phlox, it is quite safe to water these thoroughly with a deep pink solution of permanganate of potash, which will destroy the slugs or drive them away. A deep pink solution of permanganate of potash is also sometimes used to check damping-off disease in seedlings, though Cheshunt compound does this more effectively. It is, perhaps, as a moss killer that permanganate of potash is most serviceable to the gardener. For this purpose a stronger solution should be used – dark red rather than pink – and this should be applied freely to the patches of moss from an ordinary watering-can fitted with a fine rose. The remedy can be repeated several times at intervals of a week or so, if necessary, until the moss is completely destroyed. It can also be used to treat newly built concrete pools to remove unwanted chemicals, see Pool.

PERPETUAL This term is used to describe certain plants which continue to bloom more or less continually for a long period. Thus the perpetual flowering carnation can be had in bloom at almost any time of the year, provided an adequate temperature is maintained. Perpetual flowering races of pinks have been raised by crossing varieties of *Dianthus plumarius* with perpetual flowering carnations, and the race known as *allwoodii* is an example of this.

The hybrid perpetual race of roses was so named because it was more perpetual flowering than many varieties which had preceded it in the garden. However, this race is nothing like as perpetual flowering as some of the roses which have since been developed, for example the hybrid teas, and thus in this instance the word perpetual is somewhat misleading as most roses classed in this group only flower freely once each year and then produce a few later blooms.

PERUVIAN GUANO A natural deposit left by sea birds on some parts of the coast of Peru and other areas of South America. See Guano.

PEST A very loose term used in the garden to describe any member of the animal kingdom which may damage plants. Thus there are many insects which are garden pests and also many other small creatures which do not belong to the insect family as, for example, mites, woodlice, millepedes, slugs and snails. The term may also be used to cover mice, rats and even some destructive kinds of birds. It is often used in contrast to the word disease (q.v.).

PETAL One of the separate leaves of the corolla of a flower, usually coloured.

PETALOID Resembling a petal; a botanical term used to describe parts of a flower which though not true petals nevertheless resemble petals in many respects. For example, some peonies have small petal-like parts forming a boss in the centre of the flower. These are really modified stamens, not true petals, and such blooms are described as having a petaloid centre.

This peony has a petaloid centre formed from modified stamens

PETIOLE The botanical term for a leaf stalk.

PETROLEUM OIL (WHITE OIL) Proprietary insecticides made from petroleum oil. Some are for winter use only. Winter washes, sometimes containing other substances such as DNC (q.v.) or thiocyanate (q.v.), to make them more effective, are applied to fruit trees in late winter for the purpose of destroying insects and insect eggs. They are, therefore, comparable with tar oil washes which are used for a similar purpose, but petroleum oil winter washes differ from these in not controlling apple sucker and aphid though being more effective against the eggs of moths, and against capsid bugs and red spider mite. To be most effective these washes should be used as late as it is possible without causing injury to foliage or expanding flower buds, which may be up to the bud burst stage (page 270),

but not later. In the normal season in the southern half of England this will mean that spraying may be continued during March and the first week in April. Manufacturers' instructions regarding strength should always be followed where available, the usual recommendation being 3 pints of winter petroleum emulsion to 5 gallons of water. A fortnight should elapse before using a lime sulphur wash after petroleum oil or spray injury will result.

Other petroleum oil insecticides are made for summer use while plants are in leaf, and these are effective against capsid bugs and scale insects. Again manufacturers' instructions should be followed where available, the usual recommendation being 6 to 8 fl. oz. of summer petroleum emulsion to 5 gallons of water.

pH, see Acid

PHOSPHATE Any salt of phosphoric acid. It is in this form that phosphorus, an essential plant food, is applied in the garden. As phosphates are used in considerable quantity by plants, and in some instances are easily washed out of the soil, it is often necessary to give regular supplies. Natural manures, such as dung and compost, contain phosphates, but the percentage is always small and will differ considerably from one sample to another. The bones of animals are particularly rich in phosphates and provide a valuable source of this food if ground finely. Other sources of phosphate are basic slag, superphosphate of lime, and the natural deposits of mineral phosphate (or phosphate of lime) which occur in North Africa and some other places. All these are described more fully under their respective names.

PHOSPHATE OF LIME A term sometimes used for crude mineral phosphates, such as those obtained from natural deposits in North Africa, and sometimes incorrectly as a synonym for superphosphate of lime.

PHOSPHATE OF POTASH A chemical salt of phosphoric acid and potassium. It provides two necessary plant foods, phosphate and potash, but unfortunately it is too expensive for general garden use. It is, however, sometimes used for valuable pot plants, particularly where rapid stimulation is required. Phosphate of potash contains 51 per cent. phosphoric acid and 35 per cent. potash. It is usually applied as a liquid fertilizer at a rate of $\frac{1}{4}$ oz. to a gallon of water, given in moderate quantities in place of ordinary water and repeated, if necessary, every 10 to 14 days.

PHOTOPERIODISM The effect of light in controlling the flowering time of plants. Broadly speaking, plants may be classified in this respect under three headings, long-day plants, which will only flower when there are 14 hours or more of daylight each day; short-day plants, which will only flower when there are 10 hours or less of daylight each day; and indeterminate plants, the flowering of which is not affected by the day length. Many summer flowering annuals, such as stocks, clarkia and larkspur, are normally long-day plants and so are gladioli, fuchsias and strawberries. Chrysanthemums and dahlias are normally short-day plants. It is possible in some instances to break this natural habit by selective breeding, and plants may also be made to flower out of season, or be prevented from flowering in season, by artificial illumination or by the use of blackouts. See Day Length.

PHOTOSYNTHESIS The process whereby green plants make use of the energy of sunlight to convert simple chemicals into complex carbohydrates and proteins. Oxygen is formed as a waste product. Photosynthesis depends upon the green colouring matter or chlorophyll found in the leaves and often also in the younger stems.

PHYTOPHTHORA The name of a group of fungi one of which causes the familiar potato blight disease and another the damping-off that occurs in seedlings. See Blight and Damping-off.

PICK, PICKAXE Very similar tools used for breaking hard surfaces, but whereas the metal head of the pick is pointed at both ends that of the pickaxe is pointed at one end only, the other being flattened for cutting roots etc.

PICOTEE A particular type of carnation the flowers of which are white or yellow with a band of different colour around the edge of each petal. If this band is very narrow the variety may be described as wire-edge picotee. From this usage the term picotee or picotee flowered has been broadened to describe any flower in which petals of one colour are edged with another colour.

Examples of the picotee type of carnation. A wire-edge picotee, with its narrow band of second colour, is shown on the right

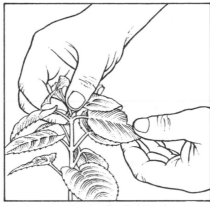

Pinching out the tip of a fuchsia plant to encourage the side shoots to grow

PIGEON MANURE Chemically this is one of the richest of all natural animal manures used by gardeners for plant feeding. Pigeon manure may be compared in manurial value with good Peruvian guano (see page 350). Because of its concentrated nature, it can easily cause scorching of roots and foliage if used in excess, and may be regarded as a concentrated fertilizer rather than as an ordinary animal manure. The usual method of use is to allow it to dry in an open shed or similar place and then to powder it and mix it with at least twice its own bulk of dry sand or soil. This mixture can then be applied as a light topdressing round plants in growth. Plain, dry pigeon manure should not be used at rates exceeding 6 oz. per sq. yd. at any one application.

PIG MANURE This is, as a rule, less rich in plant food than either horse or cow manure and it is also wetter and closer in texture than either of these. For the two last reasons it is less suitable for use in the heavier types of soil, but is more suitable for the improvement of very light, sandy soils. Pig manure appears to have got a bad name amongst many gardeners but there is no sound reason why this should be so if it is properly used. It can be applied at the rate of 10 to 15 lb. per sq. yd. at any time of the year and, like other animal manures, it is particularly suitable for autumn or late winter application. It is a valuable source of humus. Fresh pig manure should only be used on vacant ground that is not to be cropped for several months. Pig manure that is to be used as a mulch round growing crops, or is to be dug in on ground that is to be cropped at once must be well rotted.

PILL BUG, see Woodlice

PILOSE A botanical term used to describe leaves or stems which have long, soft hairs.

PINCHING A term used to describe the removal of the tips of growing shoots, see Stopping.

Taking a piping of a pink by pulling out a non-flowering shoot at a joint

PINK BUD, see Bud Stages

PINNATE Like a feather; a botanical term used to describe leaves which are composed of several leaflets attached on either side of a common stalk as in the rose.

PINNATIFID A botanical term used to describe leaves which are notched or cut in a pinnate manner, but are not actually composed of separate leaflets. Pinnatisect has the same meaning.

PIP The word is used by gardeners in two quite distinct ways, to describe the seeds of apples, pears and allied fruits and also for the individual flowers of auriculas and some other primulas, especially those highly developed for show purposes.

PIPING A particular kind of cutting which is sometimes used for propagating pinks and other members of the dianthus family. Pipings are obtained by pulling a young shoot out at one of the joints. No knife or other tool is used. The shoot is simply grasped between finger and thumb, just above a joint, while the stem below the joint is held firmly with the other hand. A steady pull will then bring the shoot cleanly away, and it is ready for insertion without any further preparation. Pipings are usually made from young non-flowering shoots and are taken in early summer. They are treated in exactly the same way as cuttings.

PISTILLATE Having pistils but no stamens. A botanical term applied to flowers which have the female organs only.

PIT An old name for a certain type of frame which has almost gone out of use. Pits were rather deep frames in which the floor was sunk below ground level and the frame light was at, or only just above, soil level. They were often used for forcing, the advantage of the pit construction being that warmth was more easily conserved, and the frame was less exposed to wind.

PIT ROT Another name for the dry rot disease of potatoes. See Dry Rot.

PLANTING The manner in which plants are placed in soil when they are shifted from one place to another can have a very important bearing upon their welfare. There are three vital points to observe in all planting. The first is to work only when the soil is in suitable physical condition, which means when it is neither too wet nor too dry; the second is to plant at the correct depth so that the roots are neither buried too deeply nor exposed on the surface of the soil; the third point is to plant firmly, and this applies to almost all types of plants though there are some variations in this respect, and a few plants, notably ferns, prefer a moderately loose soil.

The soil may be regarded as too wet for planting when it sticks freely to boots, spade or trowel. It is usually too dry if there is no sign of moisture in the top two or three inches. The ideal is that it should be just moist enough to cling together when squeezed in the palm of the hand, but dry enough for the ball so formed to fall apart freely when tossed back on to the ground. As the season for transplanting is often comparatively short, it may happen that work has to be continued under less favourable conditions than these, but the nearer one can get to the ideal the better. It is always better to wait a week or so than to plant in really unsuitable conditions.

With regard to the depth of planting, this will vary according to the nature of the plant under consideration. Some plants make most of their roots near the surface, e.g. tomatoes and privet (ligustrum); others plunge their roots much more deeply into the soil, e.g. roses worked on the canina stock, and lupins. The safest guide is to work out the depth to which the plant was growing before it was lifted. Frequently there is a soil mark on the stem of a shrub or tree, which will give this information

Planting a small plant with a trowel

Planting brassica seedlings with a dibber

quite accurately. With herbaceous plants one can usually be fairly certain that the crown, i.e. the point at which stems join roots, was level with the surface of the soil or at most only very slightly buried.

There is a frequent tendency to prepare holes which are too deep in proportion to their width. A few plants, such as lupins, sea hollies, globe thistles and hollyhocks, plunge their roots more or less perpendicularly into the soil, but most spread them out horizontally, or nearly so, and must be allowed to do the same when they are transplanted. This means that, in general, holes must be considerably wider than they are deep; even for a fruit tree three or four years of age a hole 1 ft. deep is usually adequate, though it may need to be 3 or 4 ft. in diameter. If narrow holes are prepared and the ends of roots are doubled up in order to accommodate them in these, it will often be found, if the plants are examined a few months later, that the root ends have died.

When plants are purchased in containers such as pots, tins or plastic bags they must be removed from these with as little injury

to the roots as possible. Pot-grown plants can usually be tapped out by turning them upside down and rapping the rim of the pot on something hard and firm such as the handle of a spade or fork thrust into the soil. Tins should be slit vertically and opened outwards so that the plants can be lifted out. Plastic bags can be slit and peeled off. If it is the normal planting season, the roots may be loosened a little from the tight ball in which they come out of the container but if planting is being done out of season, e.g. in late spring or summer, there should be no disturbance of soil, but the whole ball should be planted exactly as it comes out of the container. See Container-grown Plants.

The best tools for planting are the trowel and spade, the former for fairly small plants and the latter for those requiring a hole too large to be dug conveniently with a trowel. The dibber, though it enables work to be done very quickly, is not a satisfactory tool except for small seedlings and plants with tap roots, such as brassicas. The reasons for this are that the hole made by the dibber is too deep in proportion to its width, that the roots tend to be cramped or doubled up in consequence, and that the soil round the edge of the dibber hole tends to become too consolidated. Though roots need to be made firm, the soil should be evenly firm throughout and this is an aim not easy to attain when planting with a dibber.

When planting with a spade, it is an advantage if two persons can work together, one holding the plant in position in the centre of the prepared hole and the other returning the finer soil a little at a time. Meanwhile the plant should be gently jerked up and down so that the soil is settled thoroughly between and around the roots.

Firming of all except the smallest plants should be done with the foot, and can hardly be too thorough in the case of big plants, particularly shrubs and trees. Start to firm as soon as the topmost roots have been covered and then add some more soil, firm

When planting trees and shrubs it is important to make sure that the hole is wide enough to allow the roots to be fully extended

again, and finally give a scattering of loose soil on top to give a neat appearance and prevent puddling on the surface. Small plants can be firmed by pressing the knuckles of both hands on either side of the plant. When planting with a dibber, firming should be done by thrusting in the dibber a second time, an inch or so away from the first hole, and then levering it towards the plant.

Given sufficient care, there is practically no time of the year in which planting cannot be carried out and this is particularly so if plants are purchased well established in containers. Nevertheless there are some seasons when the risk is very much less than at others. In general it may be stated that herbaceous plants can be planted most satisfactorily in spring or early autumn; that deciduous trees and shrubs move best from mid-October to the end of March, a season which also suits evergreen conifers, but that some broad-leaved evergreens transplant more satisfactorily in early autumn or in spring. Bulbs are usually planted while dormant, which is generally in late summer or autumn.

PLEACH The practice of training the branches of trees in one plane to produce a narrow screen or hedge. Lime is commonly used because its flexible branches can easily be tied down to training wires or canes or can be intertwined (the word has the same origin as plait), but almost any tree can be pleached. Hornbeam and yew were at one time much used. Conveniently placed stems are trained as they grow and others are cut out.

PLENUS (A), PLENIFLORUS (A) With double flowers, see Flore pleno.

PLUMOSE Plumed or feathery; a botanical term used in the description of flower or seed parts which are of this form.

PLUMULE The young shoot in the seed.

PLUNGE BED A bed in which pot-grown plants are placed with the pots sunk to their rims to protect the soil and roots within from the ill effects of rapid drying out and sudden changes of temperature. Sharp, sifted boiler ashes, coarse sand and peat are the materials most commonly used for this purpose. Often the bed is made up above ground level with boards on edge around it to keep the plunging material in position. Where overhead protection is also required the plunge bed is made in a frame. A special use of the plunge bed is to allow bulbs intended for indoor cultivation to form plenty of roots before they are forced in any way. For this purpose the plunge bed is usually made in a shady place and the pots, bowls or boxes are completely covered to a depth of several inches. Bulbs in bowls

Making a plunge bed for newly potted bulbs

Hand pollinating peach blossom

without drainage must be protected from rain.

POLE, see Rod

POLLARD A name given to any tree which has been repeatedly pruned very severely, in other words has been polled or lopped. The term pollarding is used to describe the process of lopping such a tree. Pollarding is sometimes practised for purely utilitarian purposes, as with pollarded willows, which are cut back to encourage strong growth of young shoots or withies which are used for a variety of purposes, including basket-making. The usual result of any hard pruning is that strong young growth will be produced.

POLLEN The male sex cells of flowering plants are carried in dust-like particles known as pollen. To effect fertilization these must be transferred to the stigmas of the flowers where they germinate to form pollen tubes which grow down the style taking the male cell to the egg cells in the ovules.

POLLEN BEETLE A very small black beetle, not unlike the flea beetle, which lives on pollen and may be found on many different kinds of flower. As a rule pollen beetles do little damage from the gardener's point of view, but if a seed crop is being grown and the infestation of pollen beetles becomes too great, so much pollen may be destroyed that imperfect fertilization may result. The remedy for this beetle is to spray or dust occasionally with BHC or carbaryl as soon as the beetle is seen.

POLLINATION The act of transferring pollen from the anthers to the pistil of either the same flower or another flower with the object of causing fertilization (q.v.). Pollination may be encouraged by jarring plants while in bloom, by dusting their flowers lightly with a camel-hair brush or rabbit's tail tied to a stick, or sometimes syringing them with water.

POLYPETALOUS A term which describes petals that are separate, as in the rose. The opposite is sympetalous, meaning with joined petals, as in the campanula.

POLYPLOID A plant with more than the usual number of chromosomes characteristic of the species to which it belongs. Both triploids and tetraploids are particular types of polyploid, but the name is usually reserved for high multiplications of the basic chromosome number or for plants with odd numbers of chromosomes.

POME A botanical term used to describe the fruits of apples and pears.

POMPON A flower that is small and globular. It is used particularly for dahlias and chrysanthemums with flowers of this type but can be applied to other plants as well.

POOL A pool or pond can add greatly to the attraction of the garden and at the same time considerably widen the range of plants that can be grown. Water has the merits, from the garden designer's point of view, of providing a totally different type of surface from that of any other feature in the garden and of enabling the designer to exploit the artistic possibilities of reflections. A great deal of ingenuity can be displayed in using both these features of water to the best effect.

Pools and ponds may be either formal in character or informal. In the first instance the shape of the pool will usually be of some fairly simple geometrical form, such as a square, rectangle, circle or oval, though occasionally more elaborate designs are adopted. Informal pools, by contrast, will usually have an irregular outline and will be made to look as natural as possible – as if, in fact, the pool had formed part of the site before it was made into a garden.

Pools may be lined with concrete, or special plastic sheeting or they may be preformed in fibreglass and placed in a hole of roughly the same shape and size.

Concrete for pools should always contain some waterproofing substance. There are various proprietary preparations on the market for this purpose, some of them powders, some liquids, and any builder's merchant can supply them. These preparations should be used strictly in accordance with manufacturers' instructions and no general advice can be given on this matter, as this will vary from one brand to another. For the concrete itself, however, precise instructions can be given. The best ingredients are 3 parts by bulk coarse aggregate (ballast), 2 parts builder's sand and 1 part cement. These ingredients must be mixed thoroughly, which means that they must be turned several times on a hard floor. Then they should be turned again while water is added a little at a time, this process being continued until the whole mass becomes plastic and is of about the consistency of moderately stiff porridge. Meanwhile the waterproofing agent should have been added at the appropriate stage as indicated by the manufacturers.

This concrete should be spread to a depth of at least 3 in. over the bottom and sides of the pool. It is better if this thickness can be increased, as this will make the pool both more durable and more waterproof. As much as possible of the pool should be covered with concrete at one time, as there is always a certain danger that if the work has to be done by stages, leaks may develop where successive mixings of concrete join. If, however, it is impossible to complete the work at one time, one lot of concrete should be allowed to become firm before another is placed upon it. Moreover, before a further lot of concrete is put down, the edge of the preceding lot should be thoroughly moistened, as this will enable the new concrete to make a better join with it.

Concrete for pool making should always be allowed to dry very slowly and to ensure this it should be covered with damp sacks which may be left in place for a week or 10 days. In warm weather it will be desirable to wet these sacks at least once a day. In all except the smallest pools, it is also an advantage to reinforce the concrete by placing expanded metal, iron rods, or wire netting in it. This reinforcing material should be well embedded in the concrete, and no part of it should appear on the surface when the concreting is finished.

The overall dimensions of pools will, of course, vary greatly according to the requirements of the garden designer, but the best depth should be chosen to suit the plants that are to be grown in it. Few water lilies or other aquatics thrive in water deeper than 3 ft. and 2 ft. is adequate for most kinds. Many of the plants commonly found at the sides of streams and rivers do not like to be covered with more than 2 or 3 in. of water. Therefore it is a very general practice to make pools about 2 ft. deep in the centre and

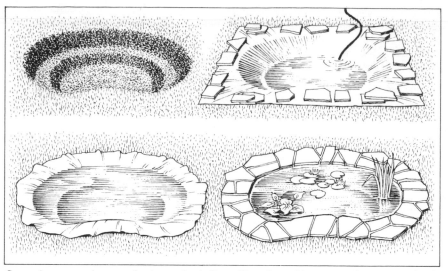

Stages in constructing a pool using a plastic liner. First the pool is excavated to give two levels which will allow for different planting depths. The liner is placed in position and the pool filled with water. The edges of the liner can then be trimmed and concealed by a surround of paving stones, as shown, or moisture loving plants

then either to build a shelf round the edge so that some plants can be accommodated in shallow water, or to slope the bottom upwards towards the sides. The top of the shelf should be about 9 in. to 1 ft. below the proposed water level of the finished pool so that 6 or 7 in. of soil may be spread on it, leaving a few inches of water above the crowns of the plants.

When pools are built with sloping sides, the concrete can be spread over these in the same way in which it is spread over the bottom, i.e. first roughly with a shovel and then firmed and smoothed down with a wooden block. When vertical or nearly vertical sides are adopted, shuttering must be used to hold the concrete in position while it is drying. This shuttering can be made of any boards nailed to a suitable framework. The interior faces of the boards should first be greased to prevent the concrete from sticking to them.

Plastic liners for pools should be purchased in a large enough size to cover the whole area including the sides. Suppliers will often weld two or more sheets together if necessary, or they can be joined on site with special adhesive strips. It is then only necessary to spread the sheet over the pool, anchoring it temporarily by placing stones or soil around the edge and to fill the pool with water, which will settle the flexible and slightly elastic plastic firmly into any inequalities. All large stones, sharp flints and debris must first have been removed as they might puncture the plastic; indeed, it is a good idea to cover the soil with a thin layer of sand before placing the sheet in position.

Formal pools are generally finished off with some kind of coping. This may be of stone paving slabs, crazy paving, concrete or brick. Whatever material is used it should

be firmly cemented in position, and as a rule it is allowed to overhang the edge of the pool by an inch or so. With informal pools grass may be brought right down to the water's edge or the soil suitably planted with moisture loving plants.

When pools are lined with concrete, it is necessary to treat them in some way before they are finally filled with water and stocked with plants and fish. This is because freshly made concrete contains certain chemicals which will be slowly dissolved by the water, and may prove harmful to plants and fish. One method is to paint the whole interior of the pool with one or other of the bituminous compounds advertised for the purpose. These have the effect of completely preventing the water from touching the concrete and, incidentally, they serve as a further waterproofing precaution, for they will fill up any small holes or imperfections left in the making.

Another method is to treat concrete chemically to remove unwanted elements. This can be done by filling with water and then adding permanganate of potash crystals until the water is coloured wine red. This should be left for a week, after which the water should be syphoned off and the pool can then be filled and stocked in the ordinary way.

The best time for planting pools is in spring, particularly in late April and early May. The best soil in which to grow aquatics is a rather stiff loam, and it is not desirable to add any dung or other manure to this, as it will only foul the water. The loam may be spread all over the bottom of the pool, and also on any ledges, to a depth of at least 6 in. or, if preferred, may be kept in small beds formed on the bottom of the pool by placing bricks on edge in the concrete while it is still moist. In either case it is desirable to cover the loam with a thin layer of clean, washed gravel, to prevent the water from becoming unduly muddy. Yet a third method is to plant the aquatics in wire or plastic baskets and confine the soil to these. The planting of aquatics is dealt with under the heading of Aquatics.

In winter small pools may become so thickly frozen that all plants and fish in them are killed. Even a comparatively thin covering of ice, if allowed to remain for many weeks, may result in the death of fish from suffocation. To prevent this danger, small pools should be covered with boards, sheets of corrugated asbestos or some similar material, whenever the weather threatens to be particularly cold, and sacks or straw should be thrown on top as an additional precaution. A small electric immersion heater of the type used to warm indoor aquariums may suffice to keep a small area free of ice but if, despite precautions, ice does form it should be broken carefully before it becomes thick. Heavy blows on thick ice may kill or cause injury to the fish in the pool.

POT Containers of many kinds and sizes in which to grow plants, either permanently or temporarily with the intention of planting them out at a later date. Traditionally clay was the material and the size of pots was often indicated by the number that could be made by the potter from one cast of clay. Thus pots of from 3 to $3\frac{1}{2}$ in. diameter were known as 60's, pots of 5 in. diameter as 48's and pots of 10 in. diameter as 12's. Nowadays size is usually indicated by diameter only. Plastic pots have become popular because they are stronger, cleaner and lighter, do not need crocking and take up water more readily than clay pots from capillary benches. Temporary pots may be made of compressed peat or sawdust or of specially treated paper and plants grown in these can usually be transplanted without removing the pot, though the material known as whalehide is tough and long lasting and is best removed. The same is true of the thin polythene bags often used by nurserymen and in garden centres as temporary containers for plants. If the polythene is not removed water will be unable to penetrate from the surrounding soil and roots may have great difficulty in growing out.

POTASH A term rather loosely applied by gardeners to indicate various substances containing potassium. The original application of the word seems to have been to carbonate of potassium, which is the salt of potassium formed when wood is burned, and it was named after the pot or vessels in which it was originally made. When the potash content of a manure or fertilizer is stated, it is always in terms of potassium oxide (K_2O). Manures and fertilizers containing potassium in some form are valuable because this is an essential plant food, and one which has considerable influence upon fruitfulness and maturity. In the absence of adequate potassium, plants may make excessively soft growth and fail to produce flowers or fruit. Severe scorching of leaves, particularly of leaf margins, is also a frequent result of potash deficiency in the soil.

The forms in which potash is most commonly applied to the soil are sulphate of potash (48 per cent. K_2O), muriate of potash (50 per cent. K_2O), various natural salts, of which the most familiar is known as kainit, and which may vary considerably in their K_2O contents from as little as 14 per cent. to as much as 20 per cent., and wood ashes containing varying percentages of potash from about 2 per cent. to 7 per cent. according to the kind of wood, rate of burning, and the way in which the ashes have been stored. There is also some potash (perhaps 0.25 to 1 per cent.) in most bulky organic manures, including dung. Seaweed is particularly rich, some samples containing as much as 1 per cent. of potash.

POTASSIUM NITRATE, see Nitrate of Potash

POTASSIUM PERMANGANATE, see Permanganate of Potash

POTATO CLAMP A method of storing potatoes by placing them in a heap and covering them with straw and soil, see Clamp.

POTTING The process of placing plants in pots or of removing them from one pot to another. Potting is a very important operation in the cultivation of almost all indoor plants, and also enters into the cultivation of some plants intended for growing out of

doors where these have to be raised in a greenhouse or frame. There are three vital things to know about the potting of any plant: when to do it; how to do it, and what compost to use. The first will naturally vary according to the nature of the plant and the time at which it makes its growth, though in general it may be said that most potting is done between February and May. It was once supposed that the third point would also vary greatly from one kind of plant to another and there are still many gardeners who prefer to make special compost mixtures for plants with different types of growth, e.g. one kind of mixture for hardwooded plants such as heaths, and another for vigorous plants of soft growth such as tomatoes, and yet others for plants differing in other characteristics. While there is nothing against this practice, it has been shown that one standard mixture with a few slight modifications can be made to serve for all, or practically all, plants, see Compost.

How to pot The technique of potting will vary somewhat according to the nature of the plant under consideration and also according to its age. It is a general rule that hardwooded plants should be potted more firmly than soft-wooded ones, and that old plants should be potted more firmly than young ones. However, like many other generalizations, this rule must be subject to certain exceptions, and when pure peat composts are used there should be very little firming at all, the compost simply being well worked in with the fingers and the pot given a couple of sharp raps on a firm surface such as a potting bench.

All pots should be clean. Cleanliness is important because, if the pot is dirty, roots will cling to it and it will be very difficult to remove the plant from the pot at a later date without injuring the roots. It should be possible to tap a plant from a clean pot with its ball of roots completely intact. Drainage is important because surplus water must not be permitted to collect in the pot or air will be driven out and, as a result, the soil will become sour. All pots are made with one or more drainage holes in the bottom and it was at one time considered essential to cover these holes with perforated zinc disks or pieces of broken earthenware pots, known as crocks. One fairly large piece was placed, convex side upwards, over the drainage hole and some smaller pieces of crock were scattered on top. If the pot was a large one, a handful of the rough rubble, left in the sieve after sieving the potting compost, was placed on top of the small crocks. This kind of crocking is still practised by some gardeners and it may be necessary with some types of seed and potting compost, but with porous composts, such as the John Innes mixes and also with most soilless composts based on peat, extra drainage

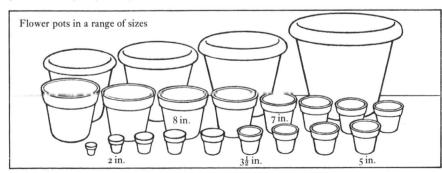

Flower pots in a range of sizes

8 in.   7 in.

2 in. $3\frac{1}{2}$ in.   5 in.

355

Potting on a plant. 1. *Some compost, such as John Innes or equivalent, is placed in the bottom of a pot*

2. *The plant is removed from its outgrown pot by knocking this against the edge of the bench*

3. *The plant is held in position in its new pot and compost is trickled in around the root ball and firmed*

material in the bottom of the pot is not essential.

Before putting in the plant, first place a little compost loosely in the bottom of the pot. Stand the plant on this and hold it in position with one hand, while, with the other, more compost is trickled round the roots. Fill the pot loosely in this way and slightly above its rim. Then, grasping the pot in both hands and placing the forefingers of each hand round the stem of the plant to hold it in position, give the plant two or three sharp raps on a firm wooden surface, such as a potting bench, to settle the compost down. Now press the compost further with the fingers, particularly round the edge of the pot, but this extra firming is not necessary with most peat-based mixtures. This will probably settle the compost something like an inch below the rim of the pot. Give a further scattering of loose compost on the surface to bring the level to between $\frac{1}{3}$ and $\frac{3}{4}$ in. from the rim, according to the size of the pot, and finish with one more sharp rap on the bench.

This technique will serve for most plants up to and including the 6-in. pot. Above the 6-in. size, particularly with plants which like very firm potting, such as heaths and

chrysanthemums, it may be necessary to make use of a potting stick in place of the fingers to firm the compost after the initial settling by rapping. This potting stick can be made out of any smooth wood. A piece of old broom handle is ideal. The bottom of the stick should be rounded, and it is used as a rammer in one hand to press the compost down round the edge of the pot. Again it should be noted that this extra firming is only necessary with soil composts not with those based solely or mainly on peat.

When potting plants such as ferns, which prefer a rather loose compost, no firming should be done with the fingers, but only by rapping the pot on the bench, even when soil-based composts are being used.

In all this potting it is important to have the compost at the right degree of moisture. If it is too wet it cannot be made sufficiently firm without danger of making it puddle or bake later on. If it is too dry it will be impossible to firm it sufficiently. The right degree of moderate moisture for soil composts can be gauged by taking a handful of the soil and squeezing it firmly in the palm. It should be sufficiently moist to bind together into a ball. Now toss this ball lightly back on the heap. It should be sufficiently

dry to fall immediately into separate crumbs. This test cannot be applied to peat composts which should be nicely moist throughout without being so wet that water can be squeezed out of them.

A different method of potting is necessary with many orchids grown not in soil or peat but in spongy mixtures of sphagnum moss and osmunda fibre. These mixtures are simply worked in around the roots with the fingers aided, where necessary, by a pointed stick. Care should be taken to pack in the compost evenly, leaving no hollow places, but no attempt should be made to firm it. Many orchids make aerial roots outside the compost and there is no need to cover these.

After potting, most plants will appreciate for a few days slightly moister and more shady conditions than those to which they have been accustomed just before. This will reduce the demand on their roots for moisture and will enable them to recover without undue check or flagging. As soon as the plants have resumed normal growth, the original amount of ventilation, shade and moisture should be resumed.

POTTING SHED A building in which the potting of plants, and also such operations as seed sowing, pricking out and the preparation of the potting and seed composts, are carried out. Very often the amateur has no room for a separate potting shed and must erect a temporary potting bench in the greenhouse itself. Sometimes it is convenient to combine a potting shed with a tool shed, and where greenhouses are heated by coal- or coke-burning boilers, it is often convenient to have a potting shed attached to one end of the greenhouse with the boiler inside the shed so that it is protected from draughts. The potting bench itself should be made of stout wood with boards on edge fixed along back and sides to form a rim which will hold the heap of potting soil. A firm, solidly constructed bench is essential so that pots may be rapped on it during potting to settle the soil in them.

When repotting chrysanthemums into large pots a potting stick is used as a rammer to press the compost firmly around the soil ball

Pricking out. 1. *The young seedlings are carefully lifted from the box in which they have germinated*

2. *Each seedling is replanted with the aid of a dibber. Take care to hold the seedling by its leaves and not the growing tip*

3. *The completed box is then watered to settle the soil. This should be done with a watering-can and fine rose*

POTTING SOIL The mixture of soil used for potting: generally termed a compost (q.v.).

POULTRY MANURE The droppings from poultry provide a rich animal manure which is considerably higher in its content of plant foods than horse, cow or pig manure, but is of a more pasty texture and is not very good for improving the texture of a heavy soil. Poultry manure in excess can cause severe scorching of stems and leaves. Fresh poultry manure is best applied to vacant ground at rates not exceeding 2 lb. per sq. yd. A better method of using poultry manure is to allow it to dry in a shed, then, if it is mixed with twice its own weight of dry soil or sand, it can be applied before planting or sowing, or to plants in growth, at rates not exceeding 1 lb. per sq. yd. The chemical analysis of poultry manure will vary greatly from one sample to another and also according to whether the droppings are fresh or dry. A good sample of wet droppings may contain as much as 2.5 per cent. nitrogen, 1.5 per cent. phosphoric acid, 1 per cent. potash, while a dry sample of the same manure may contain about three times as much of each plant food.

POWDERY MILDEW, see Mildew

PREDATORS Insects or other small creatures which attack plant pests and so benefit the gardener or farmer. Familiar examples are the ladybird and its larva, both of which feed on aphids; the lacewing fly and its larva and also the larvae of hover flies, all of which attack aphids; the ichneumon flies, the larvae of which live in or on certain caterpillars; the chalcid wasp, the larvae of which attack the scale stage of the white fly; and the black-kneed capsid which attacks red spider mites. Some of these insects are closely allied to plant pests; for example there are other species of capsid bug which do very serious damage to many plants. In consequence of this similarity in structure and habits, insecticides applied to plants to kill pests will often kill also the useful insects that prey on these foes. As a result there are occasions when the application of an insecticide may do more harm than good. Accurate timing will often kill the pest while sparing the friend and damage can also be avoided by using systemic insecticides, see Systemic.

In some instances a pest may be kept down by introducing a suitable parasite. This has been practised on a considerable scale with the chalcid wasp, which has been bred and distributed to greenhouse owners as a means of controlling white fly. In this instance the method of introduction is to hang up in the greenhouse tomato leaves bearing the scales of white fly already parasitized by the eggs of the chalcid wasp. In due course the eggs hatch out and the larvae develop into adult chalcid wasps which breed rapidly under favourable conditions, such as are found in a warm greenhouse well stocked with tomatoes which are themselves fairly heavily infested with white fly. The chalcid wasp is unable to survive low temperatures and so cannot be established out of doors in Britain.

PRICKING OUT The operation of transferring seedlings from the pots, pans, boxes, or beds in which they have been raised to other containers or beds in which they can be given more room. This is a task requiring great care, as in most cases seedlings will still be very small and tender when they are transplanted and it is easy to damage their roots severely or crush their leaves and tender shoots by undue pressure with the fingers. At one time it was recommended that pricking out should always be delayed until the seedlings had at least their first true leaves, as distinct from the seed leaves or cotyledons which are the first to appear. Investigation has shown, however, that less check is inflicted on growth and better plants result if the seedlings are pricked out while in the seed-leaf stage, and before they have any true leaves.

The compost for pricking out is usually the same as that in which the seeds were germinated, such as the John Innes seed compost or one of the peat-based seed composts. If the seedlings are to be pricked out in pots, pans, or boxes, these should be clean and filled with compost to within about half an inch from the rim and made level in the same way as recommended for seed sowing. If the seedlings are to be pricked out in a bed, the surface should be broken down as finely as possible and, if necessary, the soil should be enriched with a little well-rotted manure or compound fertilizer. The soil should always be just moist, as advised for potting.

The seedlings should be removed from the containers or beds with as little injury to the roots as possible. For this purpose a sharpened wooden label is often very serviceable as it can be used like a small trowel to lever the plants up. If the seedlings tend to be at all crowded in the seed beds, great care should be taken to separate them. Holes for them are made with a wooden dibber, the thickness of which will vary according to the size of the seedlings being handled, but will average about $\frac{5}{8}$ in. This dibber should have a rounded end. With one hand the hole is made in the prepared soil with the dibber, and with the other the seedling is carefully placed in position. The seedling should be held by its seed leaves. Make sure that the hole made is big enough to accommodate the roots without any unnatural doubling up or cramping, then press the soil round the roots with the rounded end of the dibber.

It is usually convenient to prick out the seedlings in straight rows, and to space them evenly in these rows, from $1\frac{1}{2}$ to 2 in. apart for most plants, though this will, of course, vary somewhat according to the nature of the plant under consideration and the rate at which it grows. When a box or a pot is completed, it should be watered thoroughly to settle the soil still further round the roots of the seedlings, and also to freshen them up after the move.

For a few days after pricking out it is wise to keep the seedlings in a slightly warmer and damper atmosphere than they have been accustomed to and with less ventilation and more shade from strong sunshine. As soon as they have become established in their new quarters, and begun to grow again freely, the original conditions should be restored.

For pricking out very small seedlings which it would not be possible to grasp at all easily, use may be made of a small, forked stick to lift the seedling and hold it in position while the hole is being prepared and the roots are being firmed in it.

PROLIFERATION The production of extra flowers or flower buds. The hen-and-chicken daisy in which a number of flowers surround the central flower is a fairly familiar example of proliferation.

PROPAGATING FRAME, see Frame

PROPAGATION The name given to the increase of plants by any means. Propagation is a very important part of the gardener's craft, most vital to nurserymen and others who are mainly concerned with producing large numbers of plants, though the amateur gardener is likely to need to master some part of it.

There are a great many methods by which plants may be increased, but these may all be grouped together under certain main headings, such as by seeds, cuttings, layers, division, grafting and budding, and it is under these headings that they are described in detail in this book.

It is important to distinguish between two main classes – seminal propagation, which means propagation by seed, and vegetative propagation, which means propagation by any other means. The importance of the distinction lies in the fact that every plant raised from seed is a completely new individual in every respect. It has resulted from the fusion of two cells, one male and the other female, each carrying a complete set of genes or units of inheritance. These two cells will carry genetical characters derived from the plant or plants from which they arose. The cells will be combined in the new individual which will, therefore, carry characters of both parents. Even if both the sex cells are derived from the same plant or from the same flower, the genetical characteristics which they carry may not be identical, especially if the parent plant is itself of hybrid origin. Because of these facts, seedlings nearly always differ in some characteristics from their parents and often in a very marked manner.

By contrast, plants propagated by any vegetative means are not new individuals in quite the same sense, as they do not contain any new combination of genes. They may, in fact, be considered almost as an extension of the original plant, an idea most readily grasped in the case of a division, which is simply a piece pulled from the parent plant complete with shoots and roots. Plants increased by vegetative means seldom differ in any marked respect from their parents, though there may be a modification in type of growth with a plant that is grafted, this being solely due to the influence of the root stock. All plants produced vegetatively from one original parent, no matter by how many removes, are said to constitute a clone. Thus all plants of the popular rambler rose American Pillar form a clone as they have all been produced by budding, layering, cuttings or other vegetative means from the original American Pillar or from a vegetatively produced descendant of it.

PROPHAM A selective residual herbicide used to prevent the emergence of weed seedlings among certain plants and vegetables. It is usually offered in combination with other herbicides as a liquid or wettable powder for application as a spray or sprinkle according to label instructions. It is less effective on peaty soils and is dangerous to fish.

PROTECTION In the garden protection is usually required for one of four reasons: to guard plants against injury caused by low temperatures; to protect them from injury caused by high winds; to shield them from excessive sunshine, and to shelter them from excessive rainfall. Naturally methods used for these four quite different objects will vary greatly and much ingenuity is sometimes displayed in providing protection of one kind or another.

The most obvious method of protection is that provided by glass in the form of a greenhouse, frame or cloche. Glass will give adequate protection against both wind and damp, and though by itself it will not be sufficient to keep out severe cold, particularly if prolonged for more than a few hours, it will give some measure of protection. It can also be used as a shield against strong sunshine if it is coated with limewash, one of the many advertised shading compounds, or something of that kind. A drawback to glass is its comparative costliness, its weight and its fragility.

Many substitutes for glass have been tried including various plastics. None of them appears to be quite as good as glass from the point of view of encouraging plant growth, but most of them give useful protection against winds and damp. Screens and shelters of various types can be easily made from some of them to stand round or over plants without disturbing them in any way.

Newly planted trees and shrubs, particularly evergreens, sometimes suffer severely during the first few months from the effects of wind. This is due more to the drying effect of the wind than to its chilling effect, and provided the plants can be sheltered in some way from the main blast, they usually pull through quite satisfactorily. For this kind of windbreak wattle hurdles are excellent. Hessian or sacks may also be used, nailed to strong wooden uprights. Yet another alternative is to use evergreen branches thrust into the soil like peasticks. All protection of this kind, applied for the purpose of keeping off wind, should be in the form of an open-topped screen, no attempt being made to cover the plant above as this would only cause it to make premature growth which would be more than ever susceptible to injury.

Slightly tender shrubs planted against walls can usually be protected from winter cold by placing one or two wattle hurdles in front of them, 6 or 7 in. away from the branches. If the weather should be very severe, the space between the hurdles and shrubs can be stuffed with clean (i.e. disease free) dry straw or bracken. Once again no attempt should be made to close in the top where there should be a free outlet for warm damp air.

Some herbaceous plants require a measure of protection from severe cold in winter.

A screen made from hessian or sacks acts as a windbreak for newly planted shrubs, particularly evergreens which are often difficult to establish

Two familiar examples are gunnera and eremurus. Both can be cut down to ground level in the autumn, and a simple method of protecting the crowns is to place a piece of wire netting over each, bent in the form of a low tent, and then to cover this with a good thick layer of straw or bracken with a further piece of netting pegged on top to prevent the whole from being blown away. The purpose of the lower piece of netting is to stop the covering material from pressing too closely on the crowns and possibly causing them to rot. Another method sometimes used, particularly with eremurus, is to cover the crown with a cone of sand or ashes which can be left in position until the shoots push through it in the spring.

Some perfectly hardy plants are very susceptible to excessive wet in winter, notable amongst these being many alpine plants from high altitudes, particularly those with rather woolly or hairy foliage. On their native mountains they are protected by a deep layer of frozen snow in winter and this keeps them perfectly dry. In our climate they are frequently wet and this tends to make them rot. The remedy is to support a pane of glass a few inches above each plant, but with the sides completely open, so that there is a free circulation of air. The piece of glass can be supported on sticks with notches cut in them, or on bent wires. Ordinary cloches are not suitable as they keep the plants too warm and encourage premature growth.

Alpine plants protected from winter rain with a pane of glass

Many plants suffer from the effects of strong sunshine in summer. This is particularly true in the greenhouse where the heat on a sunny day can become very intense, but it can also happen out of doors, especially with evergreen shrubs from countries in which the climate is very wet and the sky frequently covered with clouds. This is the case with many of the Asiatic rhododendrons, which in Britain often suffer more damage from hot sunshine than from frost. The remedy in this case is to

plant in the protection of trees or in a similar shady place. Under glass it is often very difficult to keep the temperature sufficiently low in summer, though shade can be provided by the means already described. Few small greenhouses have adequate provision for ventilation. There should be ventilators both in the sides and in the roof, so that a free circulation of air can be obtained when required.

PRUNING The act of cutting back a plant in any way, particularly applied to the cutting back of fruit and ornamental trees and bushes for the purpose of controlling their shape and regulating the crops of flowers and fruits which they produce. Pruning is one of the most difficult arts which the gardener has to master, and one upon which opinions vary greatly. With fruit trees alone there are a number of different systems of pruning, each with its own advocates, and each, no doubt, with some points in its favour.

There are four main purposes of pruning : (1) to form the specimen according to the requirements of the gardener; (2) to remove superfluous parts so that the energies of the plant can be concentrated upon what really matters; (3) to remove worn out, damaged or diseased parts, and (4) to control the quantity and quality of flowers and/or fruits produced. Different methods of pruning will be required for each different object.

Purpose No. 1 will be of greatest importance while the tree or shrub is still young and may become entirely unnecessary later on. This, however, is only likely to be fully true of comparatively informal shapes. The more artificial the shape, the more likely it is that some pruning will always be necessary to maintain it. Thus a standard apple tree will need little pruning for the purpose of keeping it in shape once its head of branches is well formed, whereas a cordon-trained apple tree will need to be pruned at least once annually, and possibly twice, as long as it is grown. If it is left unpruned for even a year or so it will lose its cordon character and develop into an untidy bush.

Pruning to remove superfluous parts (purpose No. 2) is immensely important with many fruit trees that are of bearing age and also with some ornamental trees and shrubs. Thus, with many flowering shrubs that produce their best blooms on young, or fairly young, wood, pruning is designed to get rid of as much as possible of the older wood without jeopardizing the production of young wood. Peach pruning is entirely of this character, and so is the routine pruning of raspberries and blackberries.

Pruning to remove damaged or diseased parts (purpose No. 3) is so much a matter of common sense that no more need be said about it.

Pruning to control the quantity and quality of the flowers and/or fruits produced (purpose No. 4) is closely linked with purpose No. 2. Some fruit trees tend to bear a crop one year and exhaust themselves so much in the process that they take the next year to recuperate. This is known as biennial bearing and it can be a great nuisance with certain varieties of apple. To prevent it, fruiting spurs are greatly reduced in size or number during the off year, i.e. the year when there is no crop. As a result less fruit than usual is produced during the following on year and the tree is able to produce a further lot of fruit buds to bear the next year.

Drastic thinning of fruiting spurs, fruiting wood or even the fruits themselves may also be used to increase the size of the individual fruits. This is because the flow of sap from the roots is not greatly checked by winter pruning though the number of fruits produced may be greatly reduced by the right kind of pruning. As a result each fruit gets a larger supply of sap and grows to a greater size. Pruning of this kind is used by rose growers who want blooms of the largest size. The branches are cut back really severely and, as a result, fewer shoots and fewer blooms are produced. But the root system remains as it was so that each new growth and the flowers it carries are able to develop more fully than on an unpruned or even on a lightly pruned tree.

The notes which follow are largely based on the pruning of apple and pear trees but many of the principles described can be applied to other trees and shrubs.

Pruning for shape Young plants, as they come from the nursery at the end of their first season of growth, are generally provided with one main shoot and a few subsidiary shoots; these are often known as feathers. This is the basic material upon which the gardener starts to work. If a single-stemmed cordon tree is to be formed, the side shoots are all cut back to within about half-an-inch of the main stem, but the main stem itself is left unpruned and is tied to a strong stake. This work is done in the autumn or winter with all deciduous trees or shrubs, including fruit trees, or in spring where evergreens are concerned. When growth restarts there will most likely be a strong shoot from the bud at the tip of last year's main stem. This should be tied to the stake and left to grow, while any side shoots which form below it may be shortened, and this is usually done in the middle of the summer. This process is continued for several years until the main stem has reached the required height, after which any further upward growing shoots are cut out each year, so that the whole strength of the tree is concentrated upon producing flowers and fruits on the side growths, which are themselves pruned back fairly severely to keep the distinctive and neat shape of the cordon. This is a popular form of training for some choice varieties of apples and pears, and also, to a lesser extent, for gooseberries and red and white currants.

A standard tree is formed in very much the same manner in the first two or three years, but then, when the main stem has reached a height of 5 or 6 ft. the top is shortened by a few inches in winter (or spring in the case of evergreens), so that it is forced to make several side growths at the top instead of one terminal growth. These side growths form the basis of the main branches which are to form the head of the standard. A year or so later, when the head itself is beginning to be well formed, all side growths on the main trunk are carefully removed close to the trunk. The standard head itself is formed in exactly the same way as a bush tree.

A bush tree consists of spreading branches radiating from a short main trunk or leg. It is formed in the first year by cutting back the main shoot of a young plant to within about 2 ft., or thereabouts, of soil level. As a result of this it will make several side growths, which will most likely be spaced fairly evenly all round the main stem. If they are not spaced evenly in this way, a dormant bud on the bare side of the tree must be encouraged to start into growth, and this can be done by removing a small, crescent-shaped piece of bark immediately above the bud, see Notching.

At the end of the first year's growth after pruning, the bush will have a short main stem with three or more side growths radiating from it. Each of these side growths is cut back to about a half its length, partly to stiffen it and partly to encourage further branching the following year. The point to bear in mind in this type of pruning is that any shoot left to itself will tend to grow without much branching, whereas a shoot that is shortened will tend to produce several branches just below the point of cutting. By altering the severity of the pruning the gardener can not only decide where the branches are to come but also, to some extent, control their vigour. It is a general rule with this type of pruning that the harder one cuts the stronger the growths will be the following season.

Where bush apple trees are concerned, it is desirable that the branches should be at least one foot apart, and so it will obviously be undesirable to prune any side growth back to a point at which it is nearer than one foot to its neighbour. Side growths which are not required to provide the basis of further branches are often shortened to a length of a few inches in the summer to prevent the tree from becoming overcrowded with weak or unwanted growth. In some instances it is better to cut some of these side shoots out altogether and retain others at full length but this will depend on

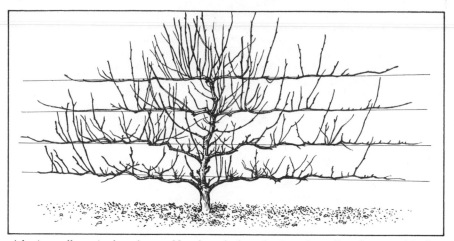

A horizontally-trained apple tree. Note how the branches have been allowed to extend in four pairs. To prune such a tree shorten or cut out the laterals

the nature of the tree or bush under consideration.

To form a fan-trained tree the young tree is cut back to within about 2 ft. of ground level, exactly as is done with a bush, but when growth starts in the spring only those shoots growing in one plane are retained; others which grow forward or backward are cut out at an early stage, unless they can be trained into the required plane. It is usually necessary to erect some kind of temporary framework of bamboos, or place the young trees against a trellis, so that slightly misplaced shoots can be trained into position. At the end of the first year, the side growths which are formed are themselves cut back by about half their length, as with a bush tree, the object being, as before, to make them branch. Once again only branches in the desired plane will be retained, all others being cut out. In this way a tree is built up in three or four years with main branches radiating rather like the ribs of a fan from one short main trunk. Such trees are very suitable for planting against walls. This is a popular form of training for plums, cherries, peaches, nectarines and apricots.

The horizontal-trained tree is slightly more complicated than the fan. It consists of one upright main trunk from which horizontal branches extend in pairs, and parallel to one another. The young tree is cut back to within about 18 in. of ground level, and the following spring only three shoots are retained – one to be trained upright, and the other two to be bent down gradually, one to the left and one to the right, and tied to a trellis or suitably placed bamboo canes. The second winter the upright shoot is cut back to within 15 to 18 in. of the first pair of horizontal branches, while the side shoots themselves are not pruned at all. As a result of this treatment each side growth will produce one main shoot the following summer, which should continue to be trained horizontally, while the upright shoot will produce several

branches of which only three should be retained; one to go upwards again, and two more to form the second pair of arms by being bent down to left and right. The third, fourth and any further pairs of arms can be added in the same way in successive years. When sufficient arms have been obtained, the central shoot is cut right out and thereafter no further growth is allowed in this direction. Similarly, the side arms are allowed to extend without pruning until they have filled their allotted space, after which the young terminal growth is cut out annually. This is a popular form of training for apples and pears.

The pyramid tree is something between the horizontal-trained tree and a bush, in fact it is very much like the Christmas tree of tradition. Many trees and shrubs, particularly conifers, have this habit quite naturally and no pruning whatever is required to impose it upon them. But with fruit trees it is not a natural habit, and careful pruning is required if a pyramid is to be formed. It consists of a main vertical stem with horizontal branches radiating from it in all directions, not just in one plane as with the horizontal-trained tree. The method of forming such a tree is rather similar to that of forming a horizontal-trained tree, i.e. the central growth is cut back each year to the point at which side growths are required. However, instead of only two side growths being allowed to form each summer, several are retained and no attempt is made to tie them down horizontally. They are permitted to take their natural course. One centre growth is retained each year and trained to grow as nearly upright as possible. Side growths are themselves shortened by about half their length each winter to encourage further branching.

Pruning of established trees and bushes
After a period of years, which will vary according to the rate of growth and character of the tree or bush in question, there will

be a gradual change in the pruning, less attention being paid to the formation of new branches and greater attention to the regulation of crops of flowers and/or fruits. Pruning is seldom solely directed towards attaining the maximum possible flower or fruit production in any one year. Probably the simplest way of doing that would be to leave the tree or bush completely unpruned, for, as it is the natural function of most trees and shrubs to produce flowers and fruits, they will certainly do so if left to their own devices. The trouble with this is that frequently the flowers or fruits are so numerous that they are of poor quality, and the tree or shrub may so exhaust itself one year that it takes a rest the next. The gardener's problem, therefore, is both to improve the size and quality of the produce, whether for utility or ornament, and to ensure that there are no blank years.

The method of pruning to be employed to produce these results will vary considerably according to the age of wood upon which the particular plant in question produces its best flowers and/or fruits. As an example, apple and pear trees flower and fruit most freely on shoots not less than one year, and up to four or five years old. They may continue to fruit on older wood than this, but the fruit will tend to be less abundant and of smaller size. By contrast, summer-fruiting raspberries produce all their crop on one-year-old canes which die after cropping, so making way for another lot of young canes to crop the following year. Less extreme than this is the behaviour of the Morello cherry, the peach, and the nectarine, which produce their best fruits on one-year-old shoots, though these shoots do not die after fruiting and may even bear some flowers and fruits in succeeding years. Obviously with apple and pear trees it would be a mistake to cut out all young growth after fruiting, whereas with raspberry canes this is essential, and with the Morello cherry, peach and nectarine it is desirable to remove quite a lot of the growth that has fruited.

A similar division, according to the method of bearing, can be made where trees and shrubs are grown solely for ornament. Brooms, for example, produce all their flowers on year-old stems, and the American Currant, *Ribes sanguineum*, also produces its best flowers on the shoots produced the preceding year. *Buddleia davidii* and *Leycesteria formosa* flower on the current year's growth. By contrast, ornamental crab apples and quinces (chaenomeles) flower freely on both year-old and older growths, and the same is true of pyracantha.

Regulation pruning Where both young and older growth is suitable for the gardener's purpose, several alternative systems of pruning may be adopted. The simplest of these is that known as regulation. This consists in a slight thinning out of the branches and stems each autumn or winter. The purpose of this is to remove any branches that are rubbing, or threatening to rub, other branches, or are so close to them that, when covered with leaves in the summer, they will cut off too much light and air. At the same time any diseased, worn out or damaged wood must be removed. When adopting this form of pruning, almost the only skill which the gardener has to exercise is that of deciding which of any two shoots is to be removed; he must always aim to cut out that which is older and less well provided with flower or fruit buds. This will involve a little study of the character of growth produced by the tree. Old wood is usually darker and harder looking than young wood, the bark is generally rougher and fruit or flower buds are usually more numerous than growth buds.

The aim in regulation pruning should always be to eliminate gradually the oldest wood, so making room for younger stems which are only just beginning to flower or fruit. If at times fairly large branches have to be removed because they have gradually sagged with the weight of former crops until they are dangerously near other branches, this should be done either right back to the main trunk, or to a suitably placed side branch. This latter process is known as dehorning. Even quite small pruning cuts should be made either to a bud or to a side shoot. If stumps of bare wood are left without buds or side growths, they will be unable to produce any leaves of their own and so will be deprived of a supply of sap and will in time die, causing decay which may spread into the remainder of the branch.

Regulation pruning is practicable with a great many ornamental trees and shrubs as well as fruiting trees, and is perhaps the most generally useful of all forms of pruning. The objects are always the same – to prevent overcrowding, to prevent branches from rubbing together and doing one another injury, and to get rid of the oldest stems or branches which may be presumed to be losing vigour. It is a system also applied to many roses, particularly rose species, vigorous roses of the hybrid musk and hybrid rugosa types, and also floribunda and shrub roses.

Renewal pruning A development of regulation pruning which is particularly applicable to apples and also to pear trees, is known as renewal pruning. The object of this is to regulate the growth of the tree in the manner already described and at the same time to ensure a succession of young shoots in the right places in order to replace older shoots as soon as they cease to be profitable. The method requires more skill and judgment than regulation pruning, but is not really difficult. Taking one typical branch of an apple tree as an example, this will be found on examination to have produced a number of side branches varying in length and age. The object is to cut back a proportion of these side shoots to stubs about 3 in. long, which will produce more young shoots the following season and so provide a succession of young growth. The remaining side shoots will be left unpruned so that they may produce flowers and fruits throughout their length. Where a variety of moderate vigour is making average new growth, two out of every three young (year-old) laterals can be cut back in this way, the third being left at full length, while of the two-year-old fruiting laterals, alternate ones may be shortened to about 8 or 9 in. to prevent overcrowding. Laterals that are three or more years old are always cut out as they are considered to be past their best. These older laterals are cut right out and not left with short stubs.

A young apple tree which has been pruned by the renewal system

Apple trees pruned in this manner tend to produce much longer fruiting branches than is normal with more severely pruned trees, and these may be weighed down by successive crops until they assume a semi-weeping habit. When this becomes too severe, so that the branches trail on the ground or interfere with other branches below them, they must be shortened to a strong side branch growing in a more erect position. With a little care replacement leaders, i.e. new stems which are to take the place of old branches, can be encouraged to form a year or so before they are actually required. This is done by selecting a suitably placed young side shoot and removing 4 or 5 in. from its tip in the autumn, which will encourage it to make one or two more strong shoots the following year. The less vigorous of these is left unpruned, or shortened to a 3-in. stub, while the more vigorous is shortened again by about 3 or 4 in. to encourage a further strong growth the next year. In this way, a sturdy replacement leader can be built up in three or four years and the original leader removed at the point at which this branch leader joins it.

The renewal system can be briefly described as one which aims at a suitable balance between growth of new wood and a supply of older wood to bear the crops. Cropping is encouraged by leaving some side growths unpruned, while new growth is encouraged by pruning some side growths fairly severely.

Spur pruning Renewal pruning is only suitable for trees of more or less informal shape, such as bushes and standards. It cannot be applied to cordons or other trained trees because these would quickly lose their distinctive shape. For these formal shapes, where trees that bear on fairly young and also on older growth are concerned, some variation of the system broadly known as

Spur pruning. The side growths are cut back in summer as shown on the left and cut back further in winter to two or three buds (right)

spur pruning must be adopted. A spur is the name given to the clusters of fruit buds which naturally tend to form on the older branches of trees such as apples and pears and others which have this manner of bearing. Some spurs will be produced quite automatically without any interference on the part of the gardener. Some may be induced by shortening the young side growths, particularly if this work is done in summer rather than in autumn.

One of the most satisfactory systems of spur pruning, so far as apples and pears are concerned, and one which can also be applied with slight modifications to many ornamental trees and shrubs, is to shorten all the thicker young (current year) side growths to a length of 5 or 6 leaves between the middle of July and the middle of August. This pruning causes considerable loss of leaf in the middle of the growing season, and consequently checks root growth and curbs excessive vigour. The following autumn the summer-pruned shoots are further cut back to a length of 2 or 3 buds.

Lorette pruning A special form of spur pruning named after a French fruit expert,

Monsieur Lorette, and applicable to apples and pears only. Side growths from the leaders are pruned during June, July and August as they reach pencil thickness at the base. They are cut back to a length of ¼ in., i.e. right into the basal rosette of leaves. At the last pruning in August side growths from other parts of the tree are also dealt with in a similar manner. Shoots which are not of pencil thickness by mid-August are tied downwards. Leaders are shortened by one third their length in late April. No winter pruning is done.

The object of Lorette pruning is to stimulate the stipulary buds at the base of each shoot and encourage them to develop into fruit buds.

Peach pruning This system of pruning, though it gets its name from the peach, can be applied to many other trees which produce the best fruits on young (year-old) stems, e.g. nectarine and Morello cherry. It is really a method of thinning and regulation with the intention of getting rid of as many as possible of the fruiting shoots after the crop has been gathered, and replacing them with at least an equal number of young shoots that will crop the following year. During the spring and summer most young side growths, besides producing some flowers and possibly fruits, will also produce some subsidiary side growths. Most of these are rubbed out at an early stage with finger and thumb, but about a third are retained; one situated at the tip of the shoot with the object of drawing sap through it, one or two midway up the shoot, and at least one as near its base as possible. In the autumn, when the fruit has been gathered, the original side shoot carrying both the young tip shoot and the midway shoots is cut out, but the basal young shoot is retained to take its place.

Remove unwanted side growths on wall-trained peaches during spring and summer

Currant and blackberry pruning A simplification of this form of pruning can be used when pruning black currants and

other bushes which bear their best crops of either flowers or fruits on year-old stems. Although, when in good health, these bushes usually make a sufficient quantity of replacement stems without any further help in the way of summer thinning. The method is to cut out the fruiting stems as soon as the crop has been gathered, removing them as far as the first sturdy young shoots which can replace them. Occasionally, when the plant loses vigour and refuses to make sufficient young replacement growth, a few or even all of the old branches must be cut hard back to within a few inches of the base, usually in autumn or winter, and the plant must be fed thoroughly to force vigorous new growths the following year. Red and white currants bear fruits on spurs and should be pruned like apples.

Raspberries, blackberries and loganberries are pruned on the same general principles, i.e. in the autumn the old canes that have already produced fruit are cut out and the young canes that have grown during the preceding summer, but have not yet produced any fruit, are retained to take their place. A variation is necessary, however, for autumn-fruiting raspberries in which all the old canes are cut back to within a few inches of ground level quite early in the year, fruit being produced on the young growth made later that year. Varieties of the *Jackmanii* class of clematis respond to this kind of pruning.

Many rambler roses need treatment similar to that suggested for blackberries and loganberries, the old stems that have just borne flowers being cut out in September, October or November, the young stems which have not yet had any flowers being retained.

Pruning of ornamental plants When dealing with shrubs or trees grown solely for their flowers, it is often advisable to complete pruning earlier than would be possible with trees or shrubs grown for fruit, e.g. with forsythia, which flowers in early spring mainly on the two-year-old wood, it is very desirable to cut this flowering wood out as soon as the flowers have faded, which may mean pruning in April. The flowering growths should be cut back as far as the first younger growths, which will replace them. This treatment prevents the bushes from becoming overcrowded and encourages the most vigorous production of young wood.

By contrast, there are a few flowering shrubs which carry their best flowers late in the summer or early in the autumn on young shoots produced that same year. This is notably so with *Buddleia davidii*, which can be pruned almost to ground level in spring and will, as a result, produce extremely strong young growths each terminated by a fine spike of flowers in August.

Buddleia davidii needs severe pruning in spring

Hybrid tea and floribunda roses also need a constant succession of young growth to keep them vigorous and free flowering. Pruning can be done at practically any time from November to late March. After removal of old, worn out and diseased wood the remaining young stems are shortened, by as much as two-thirds if the largest individual flowers are required, but by only one-third if larger bushes with more numerous but smaller flowers are preferred.

With many flowering shrubs, regular pruning in the accepted sense is hardly ever carried out, but faded flower heads may sometimes be removed to prevent the production of seed where this is not decorative, and would place an unnecessary strain on the plant. This is the treatment always advocated for rhododendrons; it is often known as dead-heading, and should be done as soon as the flowers have faded.

Pruning of climbing plants Climbing plants are as varied in their habits of growth

and of flower and/or fruit production as are trees and shrubs, but the same general principles of pruning apply.

With the grape vine, for example, pruning in the early years is largely intended to produce sturdy growth so that a strong main rod, or rods, may be produced in the shortest possible time. Therefore, the main young growth (each main growth of a vine that is intended to carry several rods) is shortened by a half or more every autumn so as to retain the sturdiest part of it and encourage this to throw out further strong shoots the following year. This pruning is done in winter when the vine is quite dormant. Once the main rods have been formed a kind of spur pruning is carried out each winter, every side growth from a main rod being cut hard back to one or at most two dormant growth buds. From these stumps new fruiting side growths are produced the following year, and these should be pinched before they get so long that they interfere with their neighbours or take too much light from the vinery.

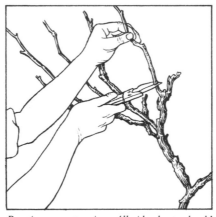

Pruning a grape vine. All side shoots should be cut back to one or two dormant growth buds

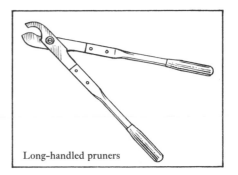

Long-handled pruners

Wisteria sometimes refuses to flower freely unless young side shoots are shortened to about five leaves in July and further cut back to two or three buds in autumn, much as a trained apple or pear might be pruned, see Spur pruning page 362.

Clematis must be pruned according to the character of the growth produced by the particular variety in question, which will depend to a considerable extent on the class to which the variety belongs. Thus varieties of the *Jackmanii* class can be pruned hard like autumn-fruiting raspberries, whereas *C. montana* and its varieties require practically no pruning.

Tools for pruning Probably the best pruning tool for cutting small stems is a sharp knife but clumsily used it can cause a great deal of damage and a sharp pair of secateurs is a better tool for the less expert person. In addition a sharp saw will be required for removing branches too large to be cut with secateurs or knife. A long-handled pruner will be found of great value in pruning standard trees and big bushes, the branches of which cannot readily be reached from ground level.

All cuts must be made cleanly. Saw cuts should be pared down with a sharp knife so that they are left as smooth as possible.

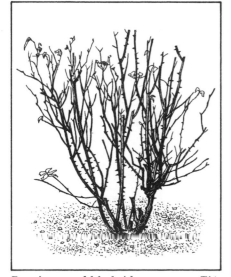

Pruning an old hybrid tea rose. 1. *This can be done at almost any time between late autumn and early spring*

2. *Thin weak shoots are removed and the main branches shortened by about two-thirds of their length*

3. *The cuts should always be made just above outward pointing buds so that the centre of the bush remains clear*

When branches or shoots are removed it should always be right back to the main branch or trunk from which they grow. When branches or shoots are shortened it should always be to a leaf or bud or to a side branch or side shoot. No snags of growth, unprovided with buds or shoots, must be left as they will die and the decay may spread to the main branch or stem.

Large wounds may be coated with warm grafting wax, white lead paint, Stockholm tar or one of the proprietary tree wound dressings, as a protection against infection by fungi. However, it should be observed that, as long as they do not become so infected, undressed wounds almost always heal more quickly.

PSEUDOBULB A bulb-like growth that is not a true bulb. The term is particularly used for the thickened stems of some species of orchid. These serve as storage organs for food and moisture while the orchid is at rest.

PUBESCENT Downy; a botanical term used to describe leaves or stems which are covered with soft but short hairs.

PUDDLING The practice of dipping the roots of plants into a thick mixture of water and soil, or some other substance, when they are transplanted. Puddling is practised for two main reasons, partly because it is supposed to protect the plants against the effects of drought immediately after planting, and partly because it is believed to be effective in protecting them against certain pests, notably cabbage root fly. It is, however, very doubtful whether puddling is of much practical value in either respect and this old-fashioned practice is dying out.

PUPA That stage in the life history of an insect in which it is encased in a hard covering or shell, e.g. chrysalis of a moth. It occurs immediately after the larval or grub stage and is followed by the adult flying stage. See also Chrysalis.

PYRAMID The name given to a form sometimes adopted in the shaping of fruit trees, particularly apples and pears. A pyramid tree consists of an upright central branch or trunk from which other branches radiate in all directions, in fact such a shape as one associates with the conventional Christmas tree. See Pruning.

PYRETHRUM An insecticide prepared from the flowers of the pyrethrum, *Chrysanthemum coccineum*. It can be purchased in the form of a powder mixed with a suitable carrier and ready for application as a liquid, and also as a liquid for dilution with water according to label instructions. In all forms it will kill or immobilize many insects, particularly greenflies and other species of aphid. It is especially valuable because of its quick knock-down effect, and is often included in domestic fly sprays for this reason. Manufacturers' instructions should always be followed with regard to mixing, as different brands may vary in strength. This is an insecticide which is virtually non-poisonous to warm-blooded animals, including human beings.

PYRIFORM Pear shaped; a botanical form used to describe fruits which are of this form.

QUASSIA The wood of a tropical tree which, when boiled in water, gives an extremely bitter extract which is obnoxious to many insects. At one time quassia was a favourite remedy in the garden, particularly for greenflies and other species of aphid. It has, however, little real insecticidal value and drives insects away rather than killing them. It has been almost entirely superseded by more effective insect poisons such as nicotine, lindane, derris, etc.

Quassia can be purchased in the form of chips which should be prepared by boiling for two hours in water, using 4 oz. of chips to 1 gallon of water, and, after boiling for 10 minutes, adding 1 teaspoonful of carbonate of soda. Strain off the chips after two hours and boil for a further hour in another gallon of water. Then strain again and add one lot of liquid to the other. Dissolve 8 oz. of soft soap in a further gallon of hot water and add this to the two gallons of quassia extract. Finally make up to 5 gallons with cold water, stir well and use in the form of a heavy spray.

QUICKLIME The popular name of oxide of lime, i.e. chalk or limestone which has been burnt in a lime kiln. Quicklime readily combines with water to produce hydrated lime, and in the process considerable heat is generated. Quicklime is sometimes known as lump lime. It can be used as a soil dressing but on vacant ground only, as it is extremely caustic to foliage and tender shoots. If the lumps are scattered over the surface of the soil, they will soon break down to a very fine white powder by combining with moisture in the atmosphere and surface soil, and this powder, which is hydrated lime, can then be spread more evenly and either be left to be washed in by rain, or mixed with the surface soil by digging or forking. Because of its caustic nature quicklime has some insecticidal value. It is, however, an unpleasant substance to handle as it burns the skin and clothes and tends to burst any bags in which it is stored. For the correction of soil acidity it is no more effective than hydrated lime, and as this is much easier to handle, it is the form of lime most commonly employed in the garden.

QUINTOZENE A fungicide used to control damping-off disease, wirestem, foot rot, root rot and other soil-borne diseases. It is supplied as a dust to be used according to manufacturers' instruction. Cucumbers, melons, gourds and other cucurbits and all members of the *Solanaceae*, except potatoes, should not be grown in soil treated with this chemical. It is also known as PCNB.

RABBITS These can be extremely troublesome pests in gardens in country districts. Most soft-stemmed plants are attacked and may be eaten to ground level, while many trees and shrubs may also be barked. If the bark is removed right round the main trunk or stem, the whole tree may be killed. Newly planted trees and shrubs are particularly likely to be attacked.

The only complete remedy against rabbits is to wire the whole garden, using for this purpose wire netting with a mesh not exceeding one inch. The wire should be buried to a depth of 1 ft. in the ground and should extend to a height of at least 3 ft. above ground level. Various substances have been recommended as having a deterrent effect upon rabbits. One of the best of these is foetid animal oil – an evil-smelling dark brown or blackish fluid which can be painted on the trunks or main stems of trees and shrubs likely to be attacked. Fish glue has also been recommended. There are various proprietary rabbit deterrents which can be used in much the same manner and it is also said that sacks soaked in creosote and placed on the ground will keep rabbits away. If, despite precautions, trees or shrubs are attacked and barked, they can be encouraged to heal if the wounded area is immediately painted with warm grafting wax. In very severe cases bridge grafting (see page 309) may be used to carry sap from the roots over the barked area to the branches above.

RACEME A botanical term used to describe elongated, unbranched flower clusters in which each flower is attached by a stalk to a

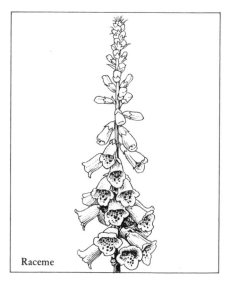

Raceme

main stem and in which the lower flowers open first. A hyacinth flower is of this type.

RADICAL Belonging to the root of a plant.

RADICLE The first root of a seedling.

RAFFIA A plant fibre used in gardens for tying material. It has to some extent been superseded by soft string of one kind or another, notably those types of string known as fillis and twist. Nevertheless, for many purposes, raffia is still unbeatable, as it is broad and pliable and does not tend to cut into tender growth as easily as string, however soft. The fibre is obtained from the leaves of an African palm known as *Raphia ruffia*.

RAKE Garden rakes are of several different kinds, according to the purpose for which they are required. The most familiar is no doubt the steel rake with rigidly fixed teeth an inch or so in length. Various sizes can be obtained, but for general purposes one about 12in. in width is most convenient. Its purpose is to complete the breaking down of soil when preparing seed beds, to remove stones and hard lumps of soil, to cover seeds, collect rubbish, smooth gravel paths. The very much larger wooden hay rakes are also sometimes employed in the garden, particularly for raking up dead leaves and other light refuse, and for levelling large areas of ground. Then there is the spring-tined rake in which the head is formed of a number of long springy tines sometimes made of steel, sometimes of split cane or other suitably resilient material, arranged in the form of a fan. Rakes of this type are used on lawns to remove refuse and drag out moss without injuring the grass itself. Rakes of various types are also available for attachment to mechanical cultivators or lawn mowers and wheel-borne rakes for hand use are also made.

The raking of soil, particularly in the preparation of seed beds, is a task calling for considerable judgment and skill. It should not be attempted when the surface of the soil is really wet and is most effective when it is drying out but not yet absolutely dry. In this condition the soil is most readily broken up and is unlikely to be unduly compacted. The rigid steel rake should always be used lightly and with long sweeping motions backwards and forwards. In the movement towards the body the rake is mainly effective in drawing stones and unbreakable lumps from the surface, whereas in the movement away from the body, the soil is broken down. When using a spring-tined rake, the teeth should only be kept in contact with the soil while being drawn towards the body. It is not possible to use this type of rake with the two-way action which can be achieved using a rake with rigidly mounted teeth.

Using a spring-tined rake on a lawn

If the ground is raked in one direction only, a number of tiny furrows will be left in the surface by the teeth of the rake. If seeds are then sown, many of them will fall into these furrows. Now if the ground is raked in the opposite direction, the furrows will be filled in and the seeds covered. This technique is often used for sowing and covering seeds which are to be distributed broadcast, e.g. grass seeds to form a lawn or seeds of hardy annuals to form informal groups of plants not regularly spaced.

RAPE DUST A waste product from oil mills, which contains 5 or 6 per cent. of nitrogen in organic form. Unfortunately this nitrogen is only very slowly liberated in the soil and rape dust is not of much value as a plant food, though it is often used to give bulk to more concentrated fertilizers. If used alone, applications should be at the rate of about 4 to 6oz. per sq. yd., at any time of the year.

RASPBERRY BEETLE This beetle is rather small and either greyish or golden brown in colour. It attacks the buds and flowers of raspberries sometimes causing a good deal of damage. Even more troublesome are the white maggots which emerge a few weeks later from the eggs laid by the beetles and at once eat into the ripening fruits so causing the familiar but objectionable maggoty raspberries. The remedy is to spray or dust with derris when the blossom is beginning to fall and again about a fortnight later or as the earliest fruits start to colour.

RATS These pests may cause damage to trees similar in character to that caused by rabbits though usually on a smaller scale. They will also eat bulbs, corms and tubers, both in store and in the ground. Potatoes and carrots in store are particularly liable

to be attacked. Rats can be poisoned with one of the many advertised poisons or viruses. Large nipper-type traps or cage traps may also be used to catch rats while yet another method is to coat pieces of board or stout cardboard with a sticky substance known as rat-sticker and place these where the rats are likely to run. If a bait is placed in the middle of the board it will attract rats on to it and they will be held firmly.

RAY FLORETS The outer florets of certain members of the daisy family in which the central disk of close packed florets (disk florets) is surrounded by other showier florets each with a strap-shaped corolla. See drawing on page 293.

REAP HOOK, see Sickle

RECEPTACLE The thickened end of a flower stalk from which the sepals, petals, stamens and pistils come. In some fruits, e.g. apple and strawberry, the receptacle becomes fleshy and edible.

RECURVED, REFLEXED Curved or bent downwards. A botanical term used in the description of leaves and petals which are formed in this way. It is also used by gardeners to describe a particular type of flower in which the petals curl outwards. Thus a reflexed chrysanthemum has mainly outward curling petals in contrast to an incurving chrysanthemum, or incurve, which has inward curling petals.

REDBERRY MITE A tiny mite which attacks the young fruits of blackberries, loganberries and other bramble fruits, causing them to ripen unevenly or to become malformed. The popular name refers to the fact that affected fruits are often partly black and partly red. The best remedy is to spray with lime sulphur at a strength of 1 part of the concentrated fluid to 40 parts of water, using this about three weeks before the blossom period.

RED LEAD The powder sold for the preparation of paint can be used to protect seeds from wireworms, mice and birds. The seeds are damped with paraffin then rolled in red lead. This substance is poisonous.

RED PLUM MAGGOT The name of this pest does not imply that it attacks red plums only, but that it is a red maggot which may attack any kind of plum. It is a small caterpillar which may be found in the fruits from mid-June onwards. Winter spraying with tar oil wash will do much to control it, but in troublesome cases trees should also be sprayed with derris towards the end of June.

RED SPIDER MITES The name of these familiar pests is rather misleading as they are neither spiders nor are they red. They

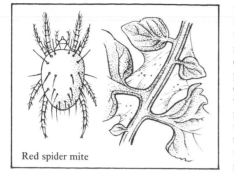

Red spider mite

belong to the family of mites and are brownish or at most reddish brown in colour. They are so small that they can only just be seen with the naked eye. A hand lens will reveal them as having roundish bodies and eight legs. They cluster on the undersides of leaves, chiefly in the angles of the veins, and they live by sucking sap. As a result the leaves develop a mottled appearance, usually greyish or bronzy in colour.

There are many different species of red spider mite which attack particular kinds of plants. Apples in the open, and peaches and nectarines under glass are particularly susceptible to attack, and so are vines, violets, cucumbers, melons and carnations.

Red spider mites thrive in a hot dry atmosphere and are discouraged by moisture and low temperatures. Under glass attacks can often be prevented by giving ample ventilation and maintaining a damp atmosphere by frequent syringing with clear water. Fumigation with azobenzene or the use of azobenzene aerosols will usually give complete control if an attack does occur. Parathion is also extremely effective but is such a poisonous chemical to use that it cannot be recommended for the amateur. Chlorbenside, derris, dimethoate, diazinon, dicofol and malathion are other chemicals that can be used to control red spider mites, and fruit trees can be sprayed in February with DNC or in early March and again after flowering with petroleum oil.

REFLEXED, see Recurved

RENIFORM Kidney-shaped; a botanical term used to describe leaves, etc. which are of this form.

RESTING Most plants have a period at which they make little or no growth, and are then said to be dormant or resting. In some plants, notably bulbs, this resting season is extremely marked and may continue for several months, whereas in other plants, particularly greenhouse evergreens, there is very little real resting period. The plants are in growth most of the time, though possibly more slowly at one period than another.

It is most important that plants should have their normal period of rest at the right

time of the year, and some cultural treatments are directed to this end. For example, with many greenhouse-grown bulbs it is necessary to reduce the water supply very considerably as the resting season approaches to encourage top growth to die down, and then to withhold water altogether while the bulbs are at rest. Most plants require less water and less warmth during the resting period than when in growth, though their requirements in both respects will differ tremendously according to their nature and the climatic conditions of their native habitat. Plants from tropical places, with a high or continuous rainfall, are likely

Hippeastrums placed under the greenhouse staging in autumn for their resting period. Water is withheld until early spring when they are started into growth again

to have a less marked resting period, whereas plants from cold areas, or from those in which there are long seasonal periods of drought, are likely to have a more clearly marked resting period.

RETARDING The practice of treating plants in such a way that they mature at a

later date than normal. This is usually done by low temperature treatment, but care must be exercised that the temperature is not sufficiently low to harm the tissues. Hyacinth bulbs are frequently retarded from one year until the next. Bulbs which would normally be starting into growth one autumn are kept so dry and cool that they are still dormant the following summer. If these bulbs are then planted and given normal treatment as regards moisture and temperature, they make extremely rapid growth. Retarded bulbs of this kind are used to obtain Christmas flowers.

It has also been found possible to retard development by application of certain chemicals, such as those known as hormones (q.v.). The growth of fruit trees has been retarded by spraying them in spring, just as they are about to start into growth, with a very weak solution of alpha-naphthalene-acetic acid. Potatoes sprayed with this solution in winter do not make their sprouts at the normal period and this technique has proved useful in storing potatoes for late spring and early summer use. Tecnazene, a chemical used to check dry rot disease in potatoes, also has a retarding effect on sprout development in the spring.

RETICULATE A term meaning netted and often applied to leaves with a netted pattern of veins or markings. However, petals may also be so marked and some bulbs are covered with a netted membrane e.g. *Iris reticulata.*

REVERSION This word is used by gardeners in two quite distinct ways. A hybrid plant or one that has been highly developed by years of selection may be said to revert if it changes to an earlier form. For example, polyantha pompon roses with orange or flame coloured flowers frequently produce red blooms. These orange varieties were

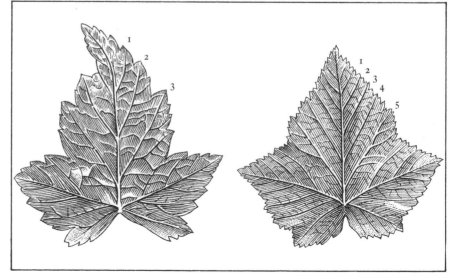

The effect of reversion on black currant leaves. On the left an infected leaf with only three pairs of veins can be compared with the normal leaf on the right

developed from red-flowered forms, so that the plant producing some orange and some red flowers may be said to be reverting to a prototype.

Reversion is also used as a name for a specific disease of currants. This disease is caused by a virus and the rather misleading name arose from the fact that, when first observed, it was not recognized as a disease but was believed to be a form of reversion similar to that described in the first paragraph. Black currants are most likely to be affected, and such bushes produce many leaves which are smaller, carry fewer lobes and have fewer veins branching from the main vein of each leaf than a normal plant. Moreover, the leaves at the ends of the branches tend to be crowded together, giving the plant a somewhat nettle-like appearance. One method of diagnosis is to count the veins on each side of the main vein. If fewer than five pairs of veins are found on all or most of the leaves in the height of summer, when they should be fully developed, the probability is that the bush is suffering from reversion.

The virus which causes this kind of reversion is carried from one bush to another by sucking insects and the mites which cause big bud. There is no remedy for reversion and affected bushes should be burned, but the disease can be kept down by taking measures against big bud mites, greenfly and other sucking insects. See Big Bud and Aphid.

RHIZOME An underground stem usually growing more or less horizontally and producing shoots at a distance from the parent plant. Common examples are the bearded or German iris and couch grass.

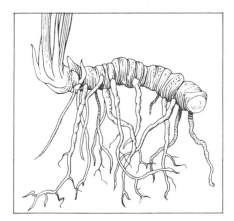

RHIZOME ROT The name used for soft rot when it attacks rhizomes of June flowering or bearded irises. Irises which are badly attacked by this disease should be lifted and burned, but milder cases can be treated by cutting out portions of rhizome which are found to be decaying and becoming watery, and lightly dusting the rhizomes with a copper dust fungicide and the soil around them with superphosphate of lime.

RHODODENDRON BUD BLAST, see Bud Blast

RHODODENDRON BUG A small bug, shiny black in colour with transparent wings, which attacks the undersides of the leaves of rhododendrons, sucking the sap from them and causing them to develop brown spots beneath, and a curious mottled or marbled effect on the upper surface. As a result of the brown spotting this damage is frequently referred to as rust, but in fact it is not caused by a fungus nor has it any connection with the true rust diseases. In June it is often possible to see clusters of the bugs on the rhododendron leaves and these can be gathered by hand and destroyed. In addition, the bushes should be sprayed with a nicotine and soft soap insecticide or with derris, lindane or malathion. As a rule two applications are necessary, one in mid-June and the second a fortnight or three weeks later. In severe cases all terminal growth should be removed and burned in March.

RHYNCHITES A name applied to the strawberry leaf weevil and strawberry blossom weevil, pests which are described under those names.

RIDDLE, see Sieve

RIDGING A method of cultivation by which the soil is thrown up into a number of steep ridges, so exposing a much greater surface to the beneficial action of wind and frost than would be the case if the surface were left flat. The usual method employed is to mark out the plot in strips $2\frac{1}{2}$ ft. wide. A start is made at one end of the first strip; a trench is opened across this, 1 ft. wide and

about 1 ft. deep and, of course, $2\frac{1}{2}$ ft. in length. The soil from this small trench is removed to the far corner of the plot. Now the gardener starts to dig down the strip, all the time turning the soil forward. The soil from the centre of the short trench is turned straight forward, whereas the soil on the left- and right-hand sides, is turned forward and towards the centre, so forming a ridge as the work proceeds. When the end

of the first strip is reached, the gardener turns round and works back along the length of the second strip and so on, until the whole plot has been ridged.

RINGING A method of preventing the return to the roots of trees of food or hormone elaborated in the leaves or terminal buds. As a result root growth is checked, and this in turn checks production of wood. Ringing is used as a means of checking excessive vigour and encouraging fruitfulness in apple and pear trees, but it is not a desirable practice with stone fruits as it is liable to cause gumming and other troubles. The method, in its simplest form, is to remove a ring of bark, $\frac{1}{4}$ in. wide, right round the main trunk of the tree and about 2 ft. from soil level. The bark should be removed right to the hard wood beneath. In this way the cambium layer is severed. If the work is done in late April or early May, a check is given to growth without injuring the tree permanently, for the ring will heal over during the course of the summer. Some gardeners prefer to give a less drastic check by removing the bark in the form of two semi-circles on opposite sides of the trunk,

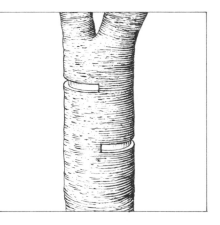

one 3 or 4 in. above the other, or to remove a spiral of bark. Yet another modification is to remove a ring of bark round part of the trunk only, stopping an inch or so short of a complete circle.

Knife-edge ringing is the name given to a less drastic method of checking the flow of sap by placing the blade of a knife against the bark and drawing it right round the stem or branch, so severing the bark to the hard wood beneath but not actually removing any bark. Knife-edge ringing is frequently used to encourage or check the growth of buds. If part of a stem of a fruit tree is bare, all the buds on it having remained dormant, knife-edge ringing carried out in late April or early May at the top of this bare section will usually induce many of the dormant buds to start into growth within a few weeks. By contrast, a knife-edge ring made at the bottom of a bare section will encourage the buds to remain dormant. These effects appear to be produced by interfering with the natural downward flow of hormones produced in the terminal buds or shoots.

RING SPOT A fungal disease of carnations and pinks causing grey spots surrounded by a ring of pustules to appear on the leaves. All such leaves should be removed and burned and the plants sprayed with Bordeaux mixture.

RIPE, RIPENING These terms are used by gardeners not only for the obvious purpose of describing the maturing of fruit and the conditions which promote it, but also the maturing and hardening of the young shoots of woody plants as winter approaches and the changes that take place in bulbs as they reach their resting period. Adequate supplies of potash in the soil appear to help in all these different kinds of ripening and so do adequate light and warmth.

Peaches and nectarines are often exposed to the sun by removing shading leaves and propping the maturing fruits forward with wooden labels, or something of the kind, so that they catch the direct sunlight. Properly timed summer pruning can assist the ripening of the shoots of many fruit trees and some ornamental plants, e.g. wisterias. With bulbs a reduction in the water supply coupled with a rise in temperature will promote thorough ripening but it is a mistake to dig bulbs up and expose them to the sun with the idea of ripening them. Some plants will only ripen properly if planted in very sunny, sheltered places such as the foot of a sunny wall.

ROCK GARDEN Any part of the garden reserved mainly or exclusively for the cultivation of mountain plants and those which naturally grow in very rocky places. The name rockery is really synonymous with this, though it is often reserved by gardeners to designate those constructions in which no attempt has been made to stimulate the natural placing of rocks as they would appear, for example, in an outcrop on a hillside. The term rock garden is reserved for those types of construction in which the natural principles of rock formation have been observed.

Rock gardens can be made in many different ways and of many different materials. The two most favoured types of stone are limestone and sandstone, but granite is also used and many other forms of rock. The best limestone for the purpose is probably that which is known as weather-worn limestone. It is obtained mainly from the surface in Westmorland and the Mendip Hills. It carries all the natural markings produced over the ages by the action of water and frost, and is often beautifully fretted and worn. By contrast, sandstone is usually quarried, and some years must elapse before it becomes fully weathered.

The site for a rock garden should always

A cross section through a rock garden showing the placement of rocks and plants

be as open a possible, as few genuine mountain plants like much shade and none appreciates the overhang of trees. The soil itself should be rather gritty and well drained but not dry. Usually the natural soil of the site can be used as a basis, with additions of coarse sand, stone chippings and peat to produce a suitable texture. The precise mixture used will vary greatly according to the type of plant to be grown and may be varied from one part of the rock garden to another.

If there is any doubt about the natural drainage of the site, some provision for artificial drainage should be made, either by laying land drains or by excavating all the soil over the site to a depth of about 18in. and placing a good layer of hard rubble in the bottom, after which the soil should be returned. As a rule the soil is thrown into a series of irregular mounds and valleys to simulate the irregularities characteristic of a hillside. However, it is quite possible to make an effective rock garden entirely on the flat, or a rock garden may be made on a plain bank without irregularities.

If the rock garden is to simulate a natural outcrop of rock, a study must be made of the appearance of the various rock strata when exposed by erosion and other natural influences. It will be observed that usually the rock crops out of the ground at an angle which is maintained throughout the whole of any one formation. Moreover, one layer or stratum of rock will overlie another like layers in a sandwich, and there will often be regular spacing between these successive layers.

When making rock gardens, the rocks should always be well bedded into the soil, so that they appear to form part of a larger formation below and do not merely look like stones dropped at random on the surface. Large pieces of rock will help to give an appearance of solidity and permanence, and often smaller pieces can be so cleverly built together that they appear to be part of the one large rock. In this way vertical crevices can be made, and, when packed with soil, many alpine plants will grow in them which would not thrive so well if planted on the flat.

Great care should always be taken to see that no empty spaces are left behind rocks, or any shallow pockets of soil formed which do not communicate with the greater bulk of soil behind or below. Rock plants, though often of small size, usually have extensive root systems which penetrate far and wide through fissures and crannies in the stones. For this reason they must be given an ample rooting medium and the soil in the rock garden should not anywhere be less than one foot in depth.

If choice is available, the best aspects for a rock garden are south-east or south-west. Gardens facing due south tend to get too hot in summer for many plants, while those facing north tend to be too shady and too cold. Nevertheless successful rock gardens can be made in every aspect, if care is taken in construction and the choice of plants.

No hard and fast rules can be given on the actual design to be followed – nature can be the only guide. A visit to a rocky hillside will prove far more instructive than any amount of verbal information. Faults to avoid are the rearing of rocks on end like tombstones, their haphazard arrangement, like currants in a bun, and the use of too many small pieces.

ROD A measure of length. A rod is $16\frac{1}{2}$ ft. and is synonymous with a pole and perch. Often these terms are used loosely for square rod, square pole or square perch. Thus if it is stated that an allotment is to be 10 rods in size, the meaning is that it is to be 10 square rods or $\frac{1}{16}$ of an acre.

ROGUE Any plant that is not true to the character or characters which it is supposed to possess, e.g. if a batch of pink antirrhinums is raised from seed and it turns out that a few of the plants are producing red flowers, these are termed rogues. It is an important part of the seed grower's technique to remove rogues from stock beds before they have a chance to ripen any pollen and possibly fertilize other plants, so causing them to produce some seed which will not breed true to type. Even plants which are propagated by some vegetative means, such as by cuttings, layers, or grafts, may occasionally differ from the type and must be removed. Another possibility is that rogues may be accidentally mixed with stock that is true, e.g. when seed potatoes are being sorted and graded in the warehouse it is not difficult for a few tubers of one variety to get mixed with the tubers of another variety and remain undetected. These tubers will, of course, produce rogue plants the following year.

ROLLER Rollers are made of cast iron, concrete, or wood, and vary greatly in size, shape and weight according to the purpose for which they are required. Heavy rollers, made of iron and weighted with water or sand, are only required on grassland used for sports which undergoes a lot of heavy wear. Even so, they should be used with discretion, as too much consolidation of the soil may kill the grass. Such heavy rollers should never be used when the surface is really wet, nor are they of much value when it is absolutely dry, the right time to use them being when it is just slightly moist. For use on pleasure lawns not intended for heavy sports, a roller of about 2 cwts. is most suitable. This can be used occasionally during spring and summer after mowing the grass. Lawns used for ornamental purposes only seldom require rolling, except in the very early stages when light rolling helps to settle down turves or produce a suitably firm soil for seedling grass.

Spiked rollers, i.e. rollers made of metal or wood with nail-like spikes projecting from them, are used to loosen and aerate turf that has become too consolidated by hard wear or repeated heavy rolling. The spikes should be designed to penetrate about 2 in. into the turf and puncture it without tearing it unnecessarily. Early autumn is the best time for the use of spiked rollers, and the benefit obtained is increased if an immediate topdressing of sharp sand or flint grit is given and brushed down into the perforations.

Light rollers are also sometimes used in the preparation of seed beds, particularly before the sowing of grass seed. However, when only comparatively small areas have to be considered, this work is more often done by treading the soil than by using a roller. Whichever method is adopted, great care should be taken to choose a suitable occasion when the soil is drying out on top and readily crumbles without becoming pasty.

ROLLING, see Roller

ROOT APHIDS These are grey lice-like insects, allied to greenflies, but infesting the roots of plants from which they suck the sap. As a result, the leaves may flag and, if the soil is dry, the plants may slowly die. Plants commonly infected include callistephus, auricula and lettuce. The roots can be washed with soapy water or BHC solution, or be treated with diazinon. Discarded plants should be burnt.

ROOT CUTTINGS Any cutting prepared from a root instead of a piece of stem, see page 286.

ROOT KNOT EELWORM, see Eelworm

ROOT MAGGOT A somewhat misleading name applied to a small yellowish white maggot which may be found in the roots or the stems of many different kinds of plant. Chrysanthemums are particularly liable to be attacked and so are lettuces. The maggot usually enters the plant by way of the roots or stem at about soil level and then tunnels up in the pith. As a result the leaves wither and the whole stem may die without apparent cause until it is split up and the maggot is found within. The maggot is the larva of a small fly, not unlike the carrot fly, which lays its eggs on the soil near to plants that may act as hosts. One preventive is to dust the surface soil occasionally with finely powdered naphthalene at about 2oz. per sq. yd. to prevent the flies from laying their eggs. Under glass the pest can be kept at bay by sterilizing the soil before use with steam, formalin or cresylic acid. Yet another possibility is to soak the soil, in April or immediately before planting, with lindane.

ROOT NODULES, see Nodules

ROOT PRUNING The shortening or removal of roots, usually with the intention of decreasing the vigour of a tree or shrub by depriving it of some of its supply of sap. At one time root pruning formed a regular part of the cultivation of fruit trees grown in restricted form as, for example, cordons, horizontally-trained trees and fan-trained trees. Nowadays, the introduction of dwarfing stocks for many of these trees has reduced the necessity for root pruning, but it is still sometimes required.

The best time to do the work is in autumn and the method is to open a trench $1\frac{1}{2}$ ft. in depth, and at a distance from the main stem or trunk to correspond with the ends of the outermost branches. Then the soil is removed on the inside of this trench with a fork, and the roots are exposed without being injured. Some of the thickest roots are then severed, either close to the tree or a foot or so away from it according to the severity of the check it is desired to give. Meanwhile the finer roots are carefully preserved and are eventually laid out once more in a natural manner and covered with soil, which is trodden firmly over them. Some gardeners prefer to root prune only one half of the roots at a time, opening a semi-circular trench one year, and then completing the operation the following year. By this means they reduce the shock to the tree.

Very much the same effect as that produced by root pruning can be obtained by ringing (q.v.).

ROOT ROT A number of unrelated diseases come under this general heading. All attack the roots of plants causing them to decay, as a result of which the plants themselves collapse and die. One of the commonest is caused by the honey fungus, *Armillaria mellea*. This gets its popular name from the honey coloured parasol-shaped toadstools which appear on the surface round affected plants. Below soil level the fungus appears as black threads not unlike bootlaces and these attach themselves to the roots of plants and slowly destroy them. Trees and shrubs are particularly liable to be attacked, and privet is a frequent victim, though the real cause of the trouble is often missed as the bushes above ground merely appear to be withering and dying as though from drought. There is no cure for affected plants and these should be burned, but the disease can be prevented from spreading by watering the soil round healthy trees or shrubs nearby with a solution of 4oz. of sulphate of iron per gallon of water. Good soil drainage will also help to keep the disease at bay. Soil from which infected trees have been removed should be sterilized with 2 per cent. formalin and left for several months before replanting.

Another kind of root rot, usually known as black root rot because it causes roots that are attacked to decay and turn black, is found most commonly on peas, violas and violets. With this, also, plants wither and die and the soil fungus is often not suspected. No remedy is known. Affected plants should be removed and burned and rotational cropping practised so that the same kind of plant is not grown year after year on the same ground. Soil can be sterilized with steam, 2 per cent. formalin or dazomet. Clovers and other trefoils may carry this disease and so should be removed.

A third kind of root rot is known as violet root rot because of the violet or purple coloured mould which appears on the surface of decayed roots. This disease is found on carrots, beetroot, potatoes, seakale, chicory and asparagus amongst others. Precautions are exactly the same as in the case of black root rot.

ROOTSTOCK A term sometimes used by gardeners for the stock as distinct from the scion in a grafted or budded plant. Thus an apple may be described as grafted upon Paradise rootstock. The word also has a botanical meaning and is used to describe rhizomes, particularly rather short or more or less erect rhizomes such as those found in many ferns.

ROSE COMB A curious disease of mushrooms which causes the caps to become deformed so that they have the appearance of a cock's comb. It is not due to any specific infection nor to attack by insects, but may be brought on by exposure to paraffin fumes. In consequence it is most likely to occur in mushroom houses that are warmed by paraffin stoves. If there is no other method of heating, great care should be taken to keep such stoves clean, the wicks well trimmed and to use only the highest grade paraffin. The disease can also be caused by spray fluids containing paraffin or petroleum oil and such sprays should never be used in the mushroom house.

ROSY RUSTIC MOTH The green caterpillars of this moth feed within the stems of certain plants, causing the leaves to wither and the stems to die. Potatoes are often attacked, and the caterpillars are also found frequently in dahlias and chrysanthemums. Sprays are useless as the caterpillars are completely protected within the stems. The only remedy is to cut off and burn all wilting shoots.

ROTATION The practice of varying the position of crops from one year to another so that the same crop does not occupy the same ground two years running. The purpose of rotation is twofold – partly to reduce the risk of damage by diseases or pests peculiar to one kind of plant, and partly to make the best possible use of the plant foods in the soil. This latter idea is based on the observation that plants differ in their food requirements, some needing more of one chemical and some of another. For example, most members of the cabbage family require heavy supplies of nitrogen, whereas root crops such as carrots, parsnips, turnips and beetroots do not require so much nitrogen but need considerable quantities of phosphate. If, therefore, a plot is prepared for brassicas with plenty of dung, which is rich in both nitrogen and phosphate, it is likely that, when the brassicas have been cut, considerable quantities of phosphate will remain in the soil, perhaps sufficient, with a little addition, to carry a crop of carrots, parsnips, turnips or beetroots.

A strict rotation, usually based on a three-year succession of crops, is frequently adopted by farmers, and a somewhat similar scheme has been suggested for vegetable gardens. However, it is seldom possible in the confined space of a vegetable garden to follow any regime of rotation rigidly, as there are other considerations such as the amount of ground to be devoted to each crop.

A simple three-year rotation for the vegetable garden can be devised by dividing the ground into three approximately equal parts and devoting one mainly to brassicas, one mainly to potatoes and one mainly to root crops. The brassica plot receives a heavy dressing of animal manure or compost and the crops, in addition, are fed with a nitrogenous fertilizer while in growth. The potato plot receives a smaller dressing of animal manure and also an artificial fertilizer containing nitrogen, phosphate and potash with the phosphate in greatest quantity. The root crop plot receives no animal manure or compost, but a fertilizer containing nitrogen, phosphate and potash with particular emphasis on the last two. The following year the brassicas are grown on what was formerly the potato plot; the potatoes are grown on what was formerly the root crop plot, and the root crops go to the former brassica plot. Each of these crops is manured and fed with fertilizer as previously described.

It will be observed that this skeleton scheme makes no provision for a number of crops such as peas, beans and onions, or lettuces, radishes and other small salads. These can be variously associated with the other crops according to the requirements of the household and other considerations, such as intercropping and catch cropping, e.g. some salads may be grown on the brassica plot before the brassicas are planted and some peas and beans may be grown on the root crop plot, but in special trenches to which manure has been added. Onions are frequently grown on the same ground year after year, which gives quite good results provided the ground is well manured and does not become infested with the fungus that causes the white rot disease of onions.

ROTENONE The active principle in derris and allied insecticides. See Derris.

ROUGH LEAVES A term sometimes used for the first leaves that appear on a seedling after the seed leaves or cotyledons (q.v.). Its point is that, whereas the seed leaves are always simple (i.e. with a smooth outline), the true leaves that follow are often indented, saw edged or otherwise diversified.

RUDIMENTARY Incomplete or imperfectly developed.

RUGOSE Wrinkled; a botanical term used mainly to describe leaves which have a wrinkled surface as in *Rosa rugosa*.

RUN A plant is said to have run to seed when it produces flowers (to be followed by seeds) prematurely. It is synonymous with bolt, see Bolting.

RUNNER A popular name for a stolon, i.e. a rooting stem produced at soil level. Some plants have the habit of producing runners freely and using them as a normal method of increase. A familiar example is the creeping buttercup, one plant of which is soon capable of throwing out sufficient runners to cover quite an extensive area of ground. Violets increase themselves in the same way, and so do most strawberries, though the alpine varieties do not produce runners.

The attitude of the gardener towards runners will depend upon the plant in question and the purpose for which he needs it. The buttercup runners are an unmitigated nuisance to him, and must be destroyed by every practicable means. The violet and strawberry runners provide a ready method of increasing stock, but if not needed for this purpose they should be removed at an early stage, as they tend to weaken the main plant and to overcrowd the bed.

Runners usually produce a succession of small plantlets along their length, each of

Propagating strawberries by pegging the runners into small pots sunk in the soil

which is capable of rooting and forming a new plant. When runners are used for propagation, it is generally advised that the number selected per plant should be strictly limited, usually to 5 or 6 per plant, and that only the first plantlet formed on each runner should be retained, the rest of the runner being removed. By this means really sturdy young plants are produced.

Runners are quite capable of rooting and making plants when left entirely to their own devices, but to make certain of it the gardener usually pegs the plantlets firmly to the soil, or holds them in position with a stone, making sure that they are well watered should the weather become dry. Sometimes the runners are pegged down into pots so that, when rooted, they can be transferred elsewhere with a minimum of root disturbance. This is a favourite method with strawberries, and the pots are usually sunk to their rims in the soil round the plant, so that they do not dry out too rapidly.

It is generally advisable to sever rooted runners from their parents a few days before it is intended to transplant them elsewhere. This minimizes the shock which otherwise might be inflicted by depriving a plant of the food supplies which it gets from its parent and also, at the same time, damaging some of its own roots.

Great care should be taken to select runners only from good, healthy plants. This is particularly important with strawberries, which often show a considerable variation from plant to plant, besides which some of the plants may be infected with virus disease which is passed on to the runners and the plants raised from them.

RUSSETING A brownish roughening of the skin of some fruits, notably apples and pears. It is a natural and admired feature of some varieties but it may also occur as a blemish due to the incorrect use of sprays or as a result of frost or attack by powdery mildew.

RUST A general term applied to a variety of diseases caused by different fungi which are alike mainly in the fact that they produce rusty coloured outgrowths on the leaves or stems of the plants attacked. These outgrowths may be in the form of rust coloured spots as with antirrhinum rust, carnation rust and chrysanthemum rust or larger rust coloured pustules as with hollyhock rust and mint rust. Rose rust has the appearance of rather bright orange spots or patches on the undersurface of the leaves. The so-called rust of rhododendrons is not caused by a fungus but by the attacks of rhododendron bug (q.v.).

Almost all the rust diseases are difficult to eliminate but frequent sprayings with thiram or zineb are likely to give a considerable measure of control. Treatment of this type should be supplemented by careful removal

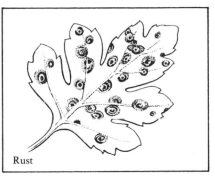

Rust

of all affected leaves or shoots which should be burned immediately. Rust-resistant varieties of antirrhinum have been produced and may be grown where the disease has proved particularly troublesome. Mint rust does not, as a rule, yield to any treatment and affected plants should be removed and burned.

SAGITTATE Arrow shaped; a botanical term used to describe pointed leaves which have two lobes projecting backwards giving them roughly the shape of an arrow-head.

SALT The term salt is applied to any combination of an acid with a base or a metal and in this sense most of the chemical fertilizers used in gardens are salts of one kind or another. Sulphate of ammonia is the salt of sulphuric acid and ammonium hydroxide; nitrate of soda is the salt of nitric acid and sodium; nitrate of potash is the salt of nitric acid and potassium or potassium hydroxide, and so on.

More popularly the term salt is used for common salt or sodium chloride. This is the ordinary salt of the kitchen and table. It is mainly used in the garden as a weedkiller, applied dry to the weeds, at the rate of from $\frac{1}{2}$ to 2 lb. per sq. yd. according to the type of weed to be destroyed, or the weeds are watered with a solution made by dissolving $\frac{1}{2}$ to 1 lb. of salt in each gallon of water. Salt has little or no selective action, i.e. it will kill all plant life, for which reason it cannot be used to destroy weeds on lawns or amongst growing plants.

Common salt is also occasionally used as an insecticide, particularly for destroying caterpillars on cabbages and other brassicas, for which purpose a solution of 2 oz. of salt per gallon of water is sprayed over the plants.

A few crops appreciate small dressings of salt as a fertilizer, notably those crops which by nature inhabit seaside districts, such as asparagus and seakale. For these a dressing of salt at the rate of 1 oz. per sq. yd. may be given in late winter or early spring. At this low rate the salt has no harmful effects on these particular crops.

SALTPETRE The popular name of potassium nitrate otherwise known as nitrate of potash (q.v.).

SAND This is chiefly of value for the cultivation of plants in greenhouses and frames, though occasionally it is used out of doors to lighten heavy soils. Sand usually has no manurial value, though in a few instances it may contain lime, usually in the form of crushed shells. It is, however, almost always used for its purely mechanical effect on the soil. It helps to keep the finer particles of soil apart and so improve drainage and aeration. For these purposes rather coarse and angular sand is to be preferred to sand that is fine and composed of smooth, round particles. The sand recommended for the John Innes seed and potting composts will grade from very tiny fragments up to pieces that only just pass through an $\frac{1}{8}$-in. mesh sieve. Such a sand may form up to a quarter of the bulk of a seed or potting compost. This proportion will vary according to the nature of the soil itself and the kind of plant which is to be grown in it.

Pure sand is also sometimes used as a rooting medium for cuttings. It has the merit of encouraging very rapid formation of roots, but it suffers from the drawbacks of containing no nutriment whatsoever, so that cuttings, if allowed to remain in it for any length of time after they have formed roots, will become starved, and also that it dries out rapidly so that frequent watering is essential in warm weather. This difficulty is overcome when automatic misting is installed, see Mist Propagation.

SANDSTONE One of the basic geological formations which occur in many parts of the country. Sandstone varies greatly in character, from soft sandstones which, when exposed to the weather, quickly break up into small fragments, to hard sandstones which will stand many years of exposure without appreciable effect except a gradual mellowing of colour. Hard sandstones of this type are particularly useful for the construction of rock gardens and garden walls. They have the merit of weathering in a pleasing manner, of being reasonably absorbent and, for this reason, of encouraging the growth of plants. Sandstone is entirely free of lime and can be used where lime-hating plants are to be grown, for which purpose limestone would be unsuitable. In colour, sandstone varies from a comparatively light yellow to a deep brick red.

SAPROPHYTE Any organism that lives on other organisms that have died, in contrast to parasites which live on organisms that are themselves alive. Saprophytic fungi are often very useful to the gardener as they initiate the decay of much dead matter. If a compost heap is opened at an early stage it will be found to contain plentiful quantities of the white, thread-like growths of saprophytic fungi. These are beneficial and do not harm living plants.

SAP-WOOD The outermost, and therefore youngest, wood of a tree immediately beneath the cambium. It is softer and contains more water than the heart-wood within.

SAW The only saw required for genuine horticultural operations is a pruning saw which is used to remove branches too thick to be cut off with knife or secateurs. Most pruning saws are made to cut in the reverse direction from an ordinary saw, i.e. when the blade is pulled towards the body and not when it is pushed away from the body. Frequently the blade is slightly curved. In all these saws the blade is comparatively narrow, and the whole saw is rather small, certainly not more than 2 ft. in length. The correct method of removing a branch of a tree with such a tool is first to make a small cut on the underside of the branch about 1 in. above the point at which it is to be removed and then to cut from the top of the branch downwards at the actual point of severance. When the two cuts are about level the branch will break off cleanly and the remaining small snag of wood, representing the difference between the level of the two cuts, can be removed without danger of the bark tearing. If a cut is made from the upper side of the bough without any preliminary cut below, the branch will start to sag and break before the saw cut can be completed, and it is almost inevitable that a strip of bark will be torn away as it falls.

It is advisable to trim down the surface of saw cuts with a sharp pruning knife, as a clean cut heals up much more quickly than a ragged one. Some gardeners like to cover wounds made by saw cuts with some protective substance such as white lead paint, Stockholm tar, warm grafting wax or a proprietary tree wound dressing. The object of this is to prevent infection of the wound by any fungus or other undesirable organism. A slight drawback to any of these measures is that they tend to slow down the rate at which a healing callus is formed over the wound.

SAWDUST This can be used at the rate of about 15 lb. per sq. yd. either as a soil dressing to be dug in like peat or leafmould, or as a mulch to be spread on the surface to suppress weeds and retain water. Undecomposed sawdust can produce a temporary lowering in soil fertility due to a withdrawal of nitrogen used by bacteria which attack the sawdust and cause it to rot. For this reason it is really better to allow sawdust to decay for a few months or to apply a soluble nitrogenous fertilizer such as sulphate of ammonia or Nitro-chalk at the same time as the sawdust.

SAWFLY A general name given to a number of fly-like insects. The larvae of several of these are troublesome in the

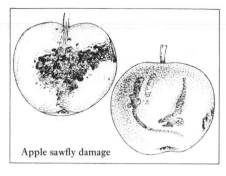

Apple sawfly damage

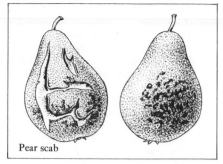

Pear scab

garden and are often mistaken for caterpillars, i.e. the larvae of moths or butterflies. One of the most familiar is the apple sawfly the white maggots of which tunnel into the tiny apple fruitlets in June and feed within them. As a result the fruits usually fall prematurely. Sometimes the maggots damage the skin of the tiny fruits without being able to penetrate to the flesh beneath. In such instances ribbon-like scars develop as the fruits swell. The damage caused by the apple sawfly maggot is often confused with that caused by the codling moth (q.v.). It is important to distinguish between these two pests as the remedy for each is quite different. The apple sawfly is best attacked with nicotine or lindane, applied about a week after the blossom falls, and again, if attacks have been serious in previous years, a week later. If poultry can be allowed to run under standard or half-standard trees in the summer they will pick up many of the grubs as they fall to the ground.

The maggot of another species of sawfly attacks roses, causing the leaf to roll up lengthwise into a tight coil. If the leaves are unrolled, a small greyish or green larva may be found within but the rolling actually starts directly the eggs are laid and before the larvae hatch out. Fortnightly spraying in May and June with BHC, derris, malathion or trichlorphon may also be tried. In hot weather nicotine dust can be effective but hand picking is usually necessary in addition to chemical treatment to destroy larvae which are already protected within the rolled leaves.

A small, creamy white sawfly maggot is sometimes found feeding in plum fruits. To prevent this spray with derris about a fortnight after the blossom falls. See also Slugworms.

SCAB A term which is applied to several quite distinct diseases. One of the most troublesome of these is the scab of apples and pears. It is caused by a fungus that attacks leaves, fruits, spurs and young shoots. Sooty blotches develop on the leaves, particularly from midsummer onwards, while black, sunken spots or patches occur on the fruits which, if severely attacked, may crack or remain small and misshapen. The bark of the young shoots and of spurs may become blistered. Several fungicides are

effective in controlling scab but several applications may be necessary in severe cases. If lime sulphur is used two applications at the full, or winter, strength (see page 334) are given before the blossom opens, the first at the green bud stage and the second at pink bud (in apples) or white bud (in pears). A third application at the reduced, or summer, strength is given when the blossom has fallen, and sometimes two or three further applications at summer strength may be necessary at intervals during the summer. The leaves of some varieties of apple are scorched by lime sulphur. In no case is severe scorching likely to result from pre-blossom application, but the post-blossom applications may have to be omitted in the case of Beauty of Bath, Belle de Boskoop, Lane's Prince Albert, Lord Derby, Newton Wonder, and Stirling Castle. Instead captan, colloidal sulphur or Bordeaux mixture can be used throughout or in the post-blossom period only. Captan is particularly satisfactory and is also much used for scab control in pears which are often damaged by lime sulphur. Bordeaux mixture is liable to damage the foliage of some apples including Beauty of Bath, Cox's Orange Pippin, Lane's Prince Albert and Lord Derby.

A totally different disease is potato scab. A fungus carried in the soil is responsible for this disease and it causes the skins of potatoes to develop rusty-looking patches or scabs. Only the skin is affected and the flesh is not attacked, so scabby potatoes, while unsightly, are usable. The disease is most likely to prove troublesome on soil that is markedly alkaline, and excessive applications of lime may encourage it. Potatoes should be grown in slightly acid soil and on soils in which the disease has occurred it is a good plan to dig in grass clippings liberally before planting and to surround the planting sets with plenty of peat or leafmould. Proprietary fungicides are advertised for treating the tubers prior to planting and these should be used according to manufacturers' instructions. It is wise to reject all planting sets which show scab damage.

Yet another disease known as scab attacks gladioli, producing brown spots on the foliage. These spots are particularly numerous around soil level. In severe cases the plants may rot right off at the neck so that the leaves collapse completely. Dark scabs with a gummy or varnished surface also appear on the corms but do not penetrate the flesh at all deeply. Corms that are badly affected should be discarded, while others less seriously injured may be dipped, prior to planting, for 5 to 10 minutes in captan or a solution made by stirring 1 oz. of calomel into a gallon of water. The liquid must be stirred constantly to keep the calomel in suspension.

SCALDING A physiological disorder of greenhouse plants which may affect leaves, young stems or fruits. It is due to rapid fluctuations in temperature, draughts, hot dry atmosphere and fumes, particularly the fumes of paraffin or coal gas. Symptoms are browning and withering of leaf edges, the appearance of brown or whitish spots more or less evenly distributed all over the surface of leaves, withering and browning of young shoots and shrivelling and browning of fruits. It is not always easy to determine from the damage which of the several possible causes of scalding is responsible though, in general, scalding from fumes tends to take the form of a more or less even spotting or blotching, whereas scalding from the sun or a hot dry atmosphere is more likely to affect the edges of the leaves. However, an examination of the surroundings of the plants and a consideration of the weather and atmospheric conditions during the preceding few days will usually resolve such doubts. The remedy is to avoid the cause of the scalding when the plants will, as a rule, grow out of the condition.

Scalding of grapes may sometimes be mistaken for shanking (q.v.). In both disorders the berries turn brown and collapse but in shanking a careful examination will

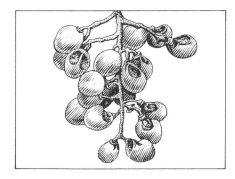

reveal that it is the stalk of the berry which has died first and that the collapse of the berry itself is due to the cutting off of its supply of sap. In scalding the stalk is, as a rule, unaffected and all the damage is on that side of the bunch which gets the most direct sunlight.

SCALE INSECTS A great many related insects pass under this general name. Their characteristic is that they are protected, at

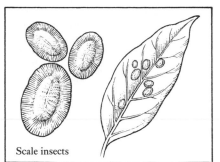

Scale insects

any rate during some part of their life cycle, by a scale. They attach themselves limpet-fashion to the branches, stems or leaves of the plants to be attacked and they then suck sap from them. The scales which cover them vary considerably in size, colour and shape. Brown scale, which is common on many greenhouse plants, is dome shaped, brown in colour and up to $\frac{1}{8}$ in. in diameter. Mussel scale, which is common on fruit trees, is oval in shape, not unlike the familiar mussel after which it is named but only about $\frac{1}{8}$ in. in length, and the colour is grey or blackish. One part of the life cycle of the familiar greenhouse white fly is in the form of a disk-like scale, about $\frac{1}{12}$ in. in diameter, attached to the underside of the leaf. Often leaves or stems which are attacked by scale insects become coated with a sticky substance, and sooty mould (q.v.) grows on this so that the shoots have a blackened appearance.

In the open, fruit trees, aucubas, rhododendrons, yews and beeches are particularly liable to be attacked, while under glass, orchids, ferns, palms, camellias and all kinds of foliage plants are favourite victims of the scale insects. Fruit trees can be cleared by spraying in winter with a tar oil winter wash when dormant or with DNC at bud burst. Under glass fumigation with nicotine will kill scale insects, or plants may be sprayed with nicotine and soft soap, petroleum emulsion insecticide, or treated with diazinon or malathion aerosols. In small attacks the scales can be removed one by one with the point of a knife, and the stems or leaves washed subsequently with soapy water.

SCALE LEAVES Rudimentary leaves such as those which envelop the growth buds of many plants or form the dry, membranous covering of some bulbs. Bulbs are themselves composed of fleshy scale leaves which in some species of lily can be detached and grown on in damp sand into complete bulbs.

In some plants green stems perform most of the normal functions of leaves and such leaves as remain are of a rudimentary nature and this is also true of some parasitic plants.

SCAPE A flower stem growing direct from the ground and bearing no leaves. The flower stems of hippeastrum, daffodil and dandelion are of this type.

SCHRADAN A systemic insecticide, particularly useful for the destruction of sucking insects such as aphids, capsid bugs, red spider mites and thrips. It is absorbed by plants and passes in their sap to all parts thus making them poisonous to certain insects. The chemical is also poisonous to human beings and other warm-blooded creatures, but it is decomposed a few weeks after being applied and so ceases to be toxic. It is sold under various trade names, and manufacturers' instructions regarding dose and method of application should be obtained. From April to July no crop should be used as food for human beings or animals within four weeks of being sprayed with schradan and during August and the first half of September this safety period should be extended to six weeks. Protective clothing should be worn by anyone using this chemical.

SCION Any shoot or bud separated from its parent plant and joined to another plant with the object of forming a union with it, as in grafting or budding. The scion is that part of the grafted or budded plant that provides the aerial shoots or branches, in contrast to the stock which is that part of the partnership which provides the roots.

SCISSORS There are several kinds of scissors made specially for various horticultural tasks. Of these perhaps the most important are vine scissors which resemble

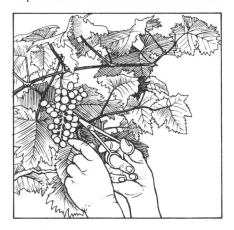

barber's scissors in having very tapering blades. The purpose of vine scissors is to thin out the tiny fruits in the young bunches of grapes and so prevent overcrowding. Special flower gathering scissors are also manufactured, some of which grip and hold the flower after it has been cut.

SCLEROTINIA ROT A name given to a series of diseases all caused by the same fungus, though the symptoms vary considerably according to the type and age of the plant attacked. For example, tomato plants when attacked by this fungus develop a decay of the main stem at or near soil level, a condition usually referred to as stem rot or collar rot. Roots in store decay completely to a wet slimy mass upon which a dense white mould appears. There is no remedy for this disease and affected plants or roots should be burned. As the disease is most likely to occur in wet or stuffy store houses, care should be taken to see that the conditions are both dry and airy. If the disease appears in tomato houses, the soil should either be removed after the crop has been gathered or should be sterilized with steam or formalin before it is used again. Watering the soil around healthy plants with Chestnut compound may check the spread of the collar rot forms of this disease.

SCORCHING, see Scalding

SCREE, see Moraine

SCRIM A fine cotton material sometimes used for shading plants in the greenhouse.

SCYTHE Many years ago the scythe was one of the most important tools of the garden for it was the only one available for the cutting of grass. Normal grass cutting is now done with one or other of the many types of lawn mower on the market, or with garden shears, but a really sharp scythe wielded by a skilled operator is still the best tool with which to make the first cutting of young grass raised from seed. The reason for this is that there is far less danger of dragging the grass out by the roots with a scythe than with a mowing machine. Once the grass has become established, its roothold is sufficiently secure to withstand the slight pulling effect of even the sharpest lawn mower.

Scythes vary considerably in design in different parts of the country. What is sometimes known as the bramble scythe has a comparatively short and stiff blade, whereas the mowing scythe has a longer and thinner blade. The bramble scythe, as its name implies, is used for cutting down rough weeds, brambles, etc., while the mowing scythe is used for grass. In both tools it is important that the scythe blade and the handles by which the scythe is held are set in the correct manner for the person who is to use it. Setting will differ according to the height of the person and should be such that the blade can be swung easily and freely with the arms extended and the blade just touching the soil and flat with it. Scything is not an easy art to acquire, and certainly not a task which the unskilled amateur should attempt without instruction. A very light type of scythe, and probably the easiest for an unskilled person to use, is known as the Turk scythe.

SEAKALE POT An earthenware pot used for forcing seakale. See Forcing.

SEAWEED This is valuable as a manure for the land and great quantities are gathered in many parts of the coast. The most suitable seaweeds for this purpose are the bladder wrack or fucus, which is also the commonest of all seaweeds on most of the coast of the British Isles, and the long, broad, ribbon-like seaweed known as laminaria. Such seaweeds can either be dug in wet, as gathered, at the rate of 10 to 20 lb. per sq. yd. or they may be spread out thinly in the sun to dry, and then be dug in at 2 to 3 lb. per sq. yd. Wet seaweed, if stacked, rots very quickly, and, though it is still suitable for use as a manure, the smell is most unpleasant. Dried seaweed, on the contrary, if built into cone-shaped or beehive-shaped stacks, can be stored for long periods without rotting and without an unpleasant smell.

Seaweeds vary considerably in their analysis, but an average wet sample may be expected to contain about 0.5 per cent. nitrogen, 0.1 per cent. phosphoric acid and 1 per cent. potash. It will be observed that the ratio of potash to nitrogen and phosphoric acid is unusually high for a bulky manure – certainly much higher than in any animal droppings.

Numerous proprietary fertilizers and liquid feeds are prepared from seaweed and these should be used according to manufacturers' instructions.

All forms of seaweed tend to improve the texture of the soil, sometimes to a degree which appears disproportionate to the quantity applied. These effects appear to be due to the humic and alginic acids which seaweed contains. These act as soil conditioners causing fine particles to aggregate into larger granules which provide more air space and better drainage.

SECATEURS These powerful scissor-like tools which are so frequently employed for pruning vary greatly in design. Some types have one cutting blade only, which presses down on an anvil made of soft metal or fibre, while some have two cutting blades each curved like a parrot's bill, or one sharp

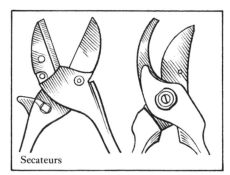

Secateurs

curved blade passing alongside another more obtuse-edged blade. There are also more elaborate types in which a cutting blade is drawn down and across the branch to be cut, with a guillotine action. All these different patterns have some points in their favour and the only real essentials are that the tool is capable of making a clean cut without bruising and is sturdy enough to sever a fairly stout branch, certainly one of finger thickness, without buckling or twisting in any way.

There is a tendency amongst expert gardeners to denigrate secateurs on the score that even the best of them are incapable of producing such clean cuts as those made with a sharp pruning knife expertly handled. This no doubt is true, but it is equally true that a good pair of secateurs is comparatively foolproof to use, whereas the best of knives is capable of working havoc in inexpert hands.

SEED Seeds provide the normal method of reproduction for most flowering plants. A seed results from the fertilization of an ovule (in the ovary) by the pollen, and contains an embryo which grows to form a new plant when the seed germinates. This new plant will have some of the characteristics of the pollen parent as well as some from the seed parent. Only in a very inbred race of plants will it appear identical with both parents. (As many flowering plants can be self-pollinated this does aid uniformity.) As the seed ripens the ovary wall becomes the fruit wall.

The seed often contains a store of concentrated food, e.g. starch or oil, either within the embryo or surrounding it, which is used during its early growth. The seed is prevented from drying by a thick coat or covering – the testa. In large seeds, such as sweet pea, this seed coat is often chipped by the gardener before sowing, in order to speed up the intake of water. Seeds do not usually carry any virus disease which may be present in the parent plant and are thus an important means of raising virus-free stock. But this is not always true of fungal diseases which may be seed borne, see celery leaf spot page 331.

The fruit wall may fuse with that of the seed, e.g. sunflower, or at least be shed with it and not split to let the seeds out while still on the plant, e.g. hazel nut.

SEED BED Any piece of ground specially prepared for the reception of seeds. This will usually imply that the surface soil has been broken down fairly finely and made level. If these precautions are not taken, it will be difficult to ensure that seeds are all covered to approximately the same depth, and, without this, irregular germination is almost certain to occur. See also Tilth.

SEED BOXES Any boxes in which seedlings are raised. As a general rule, seed boxes are rather shallow, a common measurement being 14 in. by 8½ in. by 2 in. The one essential is that there must be a ready outlet for surplus water in the bottom of each box. As a rule the bottoms of wooden seed boxes are made with two or more slats of wood, and there should be a small space between these

Preparing a seed bed for vegetables. After breaking down any large lumps of soil the ground should be firmed by treading. A dressing of fertilizer is applied and the surface raked to obtain a fine level tilth

slats through which moisture can escape. When preparing seed boxes for sowing, a row of broken pots (crocks) should be placed over the space or spaces, and these should be further covered with some of the rough rubble left in the sieve when preparing seed composts. These precautions are necessary to prevent fine soil from being washed down into the spaces and blocking them up.

If wooden seed boxes are not protected in some way, they will decay after a year or so. Creosote is not a suitable preservative for this purpose, as the fumes which it is liable to give off when warm are harmful to plants. The best chemical for preserving wooden seed boxes is copper naphthenate which is sold under proprietary names. This has no harmful effect on plant growth and is a more effective wood preservative than creosote. Many seed trays are now made of plastic and these need no preservative treatment and, as a rule, no drainage crocks.

SEED DISINFECTION Not many diseases are transmitted in the seed of the plant but a few are, a notable example being celery leaf spot. Then disinfection of the seed either chemically or by heat may be a useful method of controlling the disease. For celery leaf spot the seed may be steeped for three hours in a solution of one teaspoonful of formalin to half a gallon of water or it may be placed for 25 minutes in water at 50°C.

SEED DISPERSAL As seeds germinate to form new plants, elaborate methods are employed to remove them from the immediate neighbourhood of the parent plant. They may be so very small, e.g. orchids, that they are carried on the wind, or the fruits (dandelion) or seeds (willow) may be parachuted or assisted by hairs, or they may be winged,

e.g. gladiolus seeds or ash fruits. Seeds are often shot (broom) or swung (poppy) from the plant by uneven drying of the pods which may jerk them considerable distances. The fruits or seeds may be fleshy and attractive to animals which carry them away, either discarding or failing to digest the pips, e.g. plum. Other fruits stick to animals' coats, e.g. cleavers.

In order to collect seed it is often necessary to cut the fruits before they are ripe enough to disperse the seed, and keep them in paper bags until the seeds are shed. Paper is better than polythene which may become damp inside and encourage fungi.

SEED DRESSINGS Various chemicals are prepared specially for application to seeds to prevent attack by soil-borne fungi and insects and sometimes by diseases or pests in the early stages of growth. Principal among these chemicals are lindane, mainly against wireworm, calomel against onion fly and onion white rot, captan against damping-off, foot rot, etc., organomercury compounds against many soil-borne fungi, and thiram also against a number of soil-borne fungi. Usually these dressings are in the form of powders ready for mixing with the seeds as directed by the manufacturers but a few are prepared as liquids.

SEED DRILL The shallow furrows in which seeds are sown. The name is also applied to the machines developed for the purpose of sowing seeds in straight lines.

Seed drills in the garden are usually drawn with the corner of a draw hoe or of a dutch hoe though other tools are sometimes employed and for small drills a pointed stick may be used. A little skill is necessary in order to draw drills which are straight and of even depth throughout. A garden line or

the edge of a plank should be used to ensure straightness, while to keep a level depth it is necessary to hold the hoe firmly in both hands and use it with rather swift motions so overcoming any minor inequalities in the soil. Seed drills will vary in depth according to the nature of the seed to be sown in them, a rough guide being $\frac{1}{4}$ in. deep for the smallest seeds and 2 in. deep for the largest seeds such as beans, the average being $\frac{1}{2}$ in. deep. Seed drills are refilled after sowing with the soil removed from them, which may be done by gently drawing the back of a rake across them.

Mechanical seed drills, i.e. tools made to do the whole work of sowing and covering, vary greatly in design and usefulness. The simplest is the so-called brush drill in which a brush with stiff bristles revolves in a hopper containing the seeds, and pushes them through a small hole in the side or back of the hopper, from where they fall down a channel into a drill made by a suitably shaped share. More elaborate seed drills make use of holes which may be varied in size to suit the size of the seeds and the rate at which they are to be distributed, the seeds being agitated in some manner to prevent them blocking the hole. Models have even been developed which are capable of sowing seeds individually and spacing them as required.

SEED HARVESTING Many plants produce seeds freely and these can often be saved profitably and used to raise fresh stocks of plants. However, many highly developed garden plants do not reproduce entirely true to character from seed unless the plants are grown in isolation from other varieties of the same kind or are hand pollinated and suitably protected against fertilization by other, unwanted pollen.

Seed pods, fruits or heads should be gathered as they ripen but before they split open or otherwise discharge or disperse the seeds they carry or contain. This usually necessitates several harvestings over a period of some days or weeks so that the seeds can be gathered at the correct stage. They should then be laid in clean paper-lined trays or saucers in a dry, sunny place for a week or so to complete the ripening process, after which many can be shaken out of pods or seed heads or these can be rubbed off with the fingers. Seeds in fleshy fruits may need to be placed in moist sand out of doors for a winter so that the flesh can decay and the seeds be removed but often this can be done carefully by hand without this delay. It is desirable to remove dust and chaff from the seeds and this may be done by shaking them in a fine flour sieve, blowing gently across them or rolling them down a cloth or piece of blotting paper placed on an inclined board.

Seeds can usually be stored for a few months in a dry, cool place but some seeds lose their power to germinate rapidly and are best sown as soon as ripe.

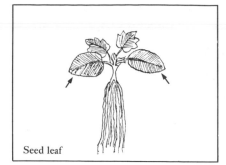

Seed leaf

SEED LEAF The first leaf or leaves produced in a seed. Seed leaves are also known as cotyledons (q.v.).

SEEDLING BLIGHT A fungal disease of zinnias which produces spots on the leaves and cankers on the stems. Badly attacked plants may die. Seed should be dressed with thiram seed dressing before sowing and plants sprayed with Bordeaux mixture or zineb.

SEEDLINGS A term rather loosely applied in gardens not only to very young plants which have been raised from seed, but also to much older plants which have been raised from seed, to distinguish them from other similar plants which have been raised by vegetative means. This can sometimes be of considerable importance, e.g. a seedling apple will always differ from its parent or parents and is, therefore, an entirely new individual, whereas an apple raised from a graft will resemble its parent in all essential details and is not in the same degree a new individual. The same thing applies to the seedlings of a great many other plants which have been highly developed, roses, for example, or chrysanthemums. The wider variation of the seedling often provides the plant breeder with valuable material for the selection and the building up of new types.

SEED PROTECTOR Any device for protecting seeds and seedlings, particularly from attacks by birds. The simplest of all seed protectors is black thread stretched, a few inches above the soil, between sticks thrust firmly into it. Birds seem incapable of distinguishing these threads clearly, and, flying into them, are frightened away. More permanent protectors can be formed of fine-mesh wire netting bent in the form of an inverted letter U and placed over the seed rows. String netting is also used for the same purpose, particularly diamond-mesh nets of the type used by fishermen; or fine mesh nylon netting which lasts longer. With these a large area of the ground can be covered very rapidly.

SEED SOWING The correct sowing of seed will have very great bearing on the degree of success obtained with it. Provided the seed itself is fertile, there are three essentials for good germination – moisture, warmth and air. With seed sown in the open ground, moisture will usually be provided by natural rainfall, though occasionally seed beds may have to be watered. Under glass, moisture will have to be given by the gardener and care should be exercised to provide enough but not too much, and also, when watering in, not to disturb the seed or tiny seedlings nor to beat the surface soil down too closely as this would deprive the seed of air. Out of doors, the gardener will be dependent on natural warmth provided by sunshine, though he may intensify and trap this by the use of cloches and portable frames. Under glass, warmth will be more under the gardener's control and again care should be taken to use enough but not too much. Excessive heat may prevent germination or cause weak growth. No general directions regarding ideal temperature can be given, as this will vary greatly from one plant to another. As some guide, however, few seeds will germinate in temperatures below 7°C. The seeds of many plants from temperate regions will germinate in a temperature of 10 to 16°C., but seeds of some plants from tropical regions may require a temperature of 24°C. or more.

A sufficient supply of air can only be ensured by using a suitable soil or peat mixture which will not pack down closely when watered. However, even the best of seed composts can be deprived of air if they are over-watered, as the water will fill up all the spaces between soil particles, and drive out air. Under these conditions seeds and seedlings will literally be drowned.

A suitable compost for use in pots and boxes for all kinds of seeds is that known as the John Innes seed compost and there are also numerous soilless composts based on peat, sand and vermiculite, see Compost.

Sowing seeds in boxes. 1. *The compost is firmed well with the fingers*

2. *Then a wooden presser is used to obtain an even surface*

3. *Water and leave for an hour or so to allow surplus moisture to drain away*

4. *The seeds are sown thinly over the surface of the compost*

5. *Lightly cover the seeds with a layer of sifted compost*

6. *Finally, a sheet of glass and piece of paper are placed over the box*

Out of doors, seed beds must be well broken down with fork and rake before sowing, and all large stones should be removed from the surface. This work should be done when the soil is reasonably dry on the surface. If it is too wet, it will be impossible to work on the bed without consolidating the surface too much and so depriving the seeds of air. Nevertheless, the seed bed must be fairly firm, and for this purpose it should be trodden carefully or rolled with a light roller.

There are two ways of sowing seeds, one broadcast and the other in drills (see Broadcast and Drill).

The correct depth of covering will vary according to the size of the seed. A general rule is to cover seeds with twice their own depth of soil, i.e. seeds which are $\frac{1}{8}$ in. in diameter will be covered with $\frac{1}{4}$ in. of soil. However, this depth may be a little exceeded when sowing very small seeds in the open ground, as it is practically impossible to draw drills less than a $\frac{1}{4}$ in. in depth.

Seeds should always be sown thinly, as overcrowding of seedlings will weaken them considerably. The larger seeds may even be spaced out separately $\frac{1}{2}$ in. or more apart, according to their size, and another method is to sow seeds in small pinches of 3 or 4 seeds every 2 or 3 in. in the drills. Then, if all the seeds germinate, the surplus can be removed and one seedling left standing at each station.

Whatever method of sowing is used, some thinning out is likely to be necessary in the early stages. Alternatively some or all of the seedlings will have to be pricked out to prevent overcrowding.

In a greenhouse it is a common practice to cover seedlings with a pane of glass and a sheet of paper – the former to check loss of moisture and the latter to keep the seeds dark and also to check evaporation. This is good policy provided the paper is removed at the first sign of germination. The seedlings must have light for them to be sturdy, and the pane of glass itself must be tilted a little at the first sign of germination, and removed entirely a few days later. Though the glass protection is beneficial to the seeds, it soon becomes harmful to the seedlings.

SEED TESTING Few seeds can be expected to germinate 100 per cent. and the viability of all seeds tends to diminish with the passage of time. A simple germination test can be carried out by placing a selected number of seeds on blotting paper or filter paper in a saucer containing a little water so that the paper is constantly moist. This is kept in a fairly warm place until the seeds germinate, when the number that grow and the number that fail can be counted and the percentage calculated. A more sophisticated version of this simple scheme is used by seed firms and those engaged in official seed testing, the degree of moisture and the temperature being accurately controlled in special incubators. The germination of certain seeds offered for sale is regulated under the Seeds Act 1920, and the purity of the seed (i.e. its freedom from contamination by seeds of other kinds or varieties) is also specified, but these regulations do not apply to flower seeds or those of ornamental plants. The prescribed declarable minimum percentages of germination and purity are as follows:

Kind of seed	Percentage Germination	Purity
Pea	80	99
Broad bean	80	99
Runner bean	70	99
French bean	80	99
Beetroot, not Cheltenham, germination of clusters	60	97
Beetroot, Cheltenham, germination of clusters	55	97
Spinach beet and chard	70	97
Carrot	60	93
Parsnip	60	97
Mustard	80	98
Cress	85	99
Rape	85	98
Swede	80	98
Turnip	80	98
Kohl rabi	75	98
Cabbage	70	98
Savoy	70	98
Kale and borecole	75	98
Cauliflower and broccoli	65	98
Sprouting broccoli	65	98
Brussels sprouts	79	98
Radish	75	98
Onion	65	98
Leek	55	98
Spinach	70	97
Vegetable marrow	75	—
Cucumber	85	—
Melon	85	—
Lettuce	75	98
Tomato	80	99
Celery	60	97
Celeriac	60	97
Parsley	65	97
Chicory	70	95
Sweet corn	75	99
Endive	70	95

SEED VERNALIZATION, see Vernalization

SELECTIVE WEEDKILLER A weedkiller which will kill certain kinds of plant but will leave other plants unharmed. Two popular hormone weedkillers of this type are 2,4-D and MCPA (q.v.). These kill many broad-leaved weeds but do not kill grass. By contrast, dalapon kills grass and monocotyledonous plants much more readily than it does dicotyledonous plants. Some weedkillers can be made selective by the manner in which they are applied e.g. paraquat kills plants if applied to their leaves or green stems but it is inactivated by the soil and so has no effect on roots. If, therefore, it is applied to the leaves of weeds but kept off the leaves of garden plants it will be selective in its action.

SELF This term is used by some specialist flower growers to describe flowers which are of one colour throughout in contrast to other varieties of the same kind of flower, which are of two or more colours. For example, self carnations are of this character in contrast to fancy carnations which have one ground colour with markings of a contrasting colour.

SELF-FERTILE Any plant which is capable of producing seeds when fertilized with its own pollen. In garden practice the term is most used in connection with fruit growing, and is of importance because so many varieties of fruit are not self-fertile, i.e. they will only produce seeds (and therefore only produce a crop of fruit) when fertilized with pollen from another variety of the same kind of fruit. This can be a drawback, particularly in small gardens in which it is not desired to grow several different varieties of the same kind of fruit.

SELF-POLLINATION The pollination of a plant with its own pollen or with the pollen of an identical plant.

SELF-STERILE, see Sterile

SEMI-DOUBLE A rather loosely defined term which may be applied to any flower which has more than the normal number of petals but has not had all or most of its stamens and pistils changed into petals as with a fully double flower.

SEMINAL By seed. Thus seminal propagation means propagation by seeds.

SEPAL One of the separate leaves forming the calyx of a flower.

SEQUESTROL A name for certain organic chemical complexes used for curing mineral deficiencies in soils. Iron and magnesium are the two chemicals usually offered as sequestrols in which form they remain available for some time as plant foods even in soils (mainly those that are markedly alkaline) in which, if applied as inorganic salts, e.g. sulphate of iron or sulphate of magnesium, they would rapidly undergo chemical changes which would render them insoluble and therefore unavailable. Sequestrated chemicals (also known as chelated chemicals) are available for dry or liquid application and should be used according to manufacturers' instructions.

SERRATE Saw edged; a term applied to leaves which have toothed margins of this type.

SESSILE Not stalked; a botanical term used in the description of leaves and flowers which have no stalks.

Daphne mezereum is an example of a shrub with sessile flowers

SET A term applied to certain tubers and corms used for planting. Thus potatoes which are to be planted are often referred to as sets, and so are shallot bulbs used for the same purpose.

Fruit blossom is said to be set when it has been fertilized and is starting to form fruit.

SEWAGE SLUDGE Wet sludge from sewage beds can be used as a substitute for farmyard manure at rates of 5 to 25lb. per sq. yd. It is, however, a rather unpleasant material to handle and should not be used for salad crops because of the danger of transmitting germs, intestinal worms etc. Many sewage works prepare dried sewage in various ways and this is a safer and more convenient way in which to use sewage in the garden. There are two basic types of treated sludge, what is known as digested sludge which may contain about 6 per cent. of nitrogen but very little phosphorus or potassium, and activated sludge with about 7 per cent. of nitrogen and 4 per cent. or more phosphoric acid. Such dried sludges may be applied at rates of from $1\frac{1}{2}$ to $2\frac{1}{2}$lb. per sq. yd.

SEX Flowering plants exhibit the characteristics of sex, i.e. they bear both male and female organs, the purpose of the female being to produce seeds, and of the male to fertilize the female egg cells or ovules. The essential male organs are known as stamens and consist of anthers and filaments, while the essential female organs are known as pistils and consist of stigmas, styles and the ovaries in which the seeds are developed. A great many plants produce flowers containing both male and female organs; these are known as hermaphrodite. But in some kinds of plants certain blooms have male organs only while others have female organs only. Such plants are known as monoecious. In other instances male and female flowers are borne on separate plants and plants of this character are termed dioecious. Those producing male flowers only are referred to as male plants, those with female flowers only as female plants.

SHADE Although light is essential to all plants with the exception of mushrooms and other fungi, plants vary greatly in their light requirements, and excessive light may damage them. In consequence the gardener must learn to distinguish those which require some degree of shade, either all the time or at certain stages of their development. This will apply to plants grown in the open and even more to plants grown under glass, where the effect of strong sunshine can be especially harmful. In fact, in the greenhouse some form of shading is almost always required in high summer, even for plants which normally like direct sunshine. This is because of the intense heat which can be developed under glass. Excessive shading, however, can do as much harm as excessive sunshine. The latter will result in scorched and yellowed foliage and stunted growth, whereas too much shade will result in attenuated, weak growth and pale green or yellowish foliage.

Methods of providing shade under glass are by coating the glass with a liquid such as whitewash, which will break the direct rays of the sun; by pinning up some thin material such as butter muslin inside the greenhouse; by using blinds, often made of thin plastic material, inside the house or by covering the glass outside the greenhouse with blinds made of hessian, canvas, or split bamboo cane. Temporary shade is sometimes provided by laying sheets of newspaper over individual plants, or boxes, pans and pots of seed. Whatever shading is used, it should be a kind which can easily be removed when the need has passed. Blinds should be mounted on rollers so that they may be quickly pulled down or wound up again. So-called permanent shade of the whitewash type should be prepared so that it can be readily washed off when no longer needed, though it must be sufficiently resistant to moisture to withstand the normal effect of rain for at least a few months. This apparent contradiction can be overcome by mixing a small quantity of white of egg or size with the whitewash, just sufficient to give it a slightly glue-like character. Special shading compounds are also manufactured for this purpose.

In the open garden, shade for plants that require it may be provided in a variety of ways: by erecting walls which will give almost full shade on their north face, and partial shade on east or west faces; by planting trees (though if this is done it must be observed that plants beneath the trees will have to compete for food and moisture with the tree roots), or by erecting tem-

Three methods of shading a greenhouse.
1. *Applying whitewash to the outside*

2. *Roller blinds fitted to the inside. These are made in various materials*

3. *Split cane or slatted wooden blinds attached to the outside*

porary or permanent screens with wattle hurdles, hessian, evergreen boughs and a variety of other materials.

Cuttings that have not yet formed roots will usually require greater shade than the plants from which they have been taken; the purpose of this being to reduce the evaporation of moisture from their leaves and stems while they are without roots. For shading cuttings in frames, a useful device is the lath light, i.e. a framework of wood, made to fit the frame, with ordinary builder's laths tacked across it, a small space being left between adjacent laths. These lath lights, placed over the cuttings in place of ordinary glass lights, will allow free circulation of air, but will break the force of direct sunshine. One of the advantages of mist propagation (q.v.) is that shading is not necessary and so the cuttings can have the benefit of all the sunlight there may be to help them to grow.

SHANKING A common disorder of grapes which affects the fruits as they approach the ripening period. The small stalks by which the berries are attached to the cluster wither and die. As a result the berries are deprived of sap and quickly wither and turn brown. This should not be confused with the damage caused by scalding (q.v.). Shanking is a physiological disorder which may occur when the soil in which the vines are growing becomes impoverished or waterlogged. Frequently it is necessary to remake the borders in order to get rid of the trouble. When this is done drainage should be attended to with care and the soil used for the border must be well supplied with humus and plant foods.

SHARPENING A sharp edge to some garden tools is very important if good work is to be done. This is most notably so with knives used for pruning, grafting, budding and the preparation of cuttings, the reason being that ragged cuts made with a blunt knife take much longer to heal than clean cuts made with a really sharp blade. In order to ensure an adequate degree of sharpness, two things are essential – first, a blade made of good, well-tempered steel, and secondly, correct sharpening. With knives, this sharpening can be done with a whetstone or an oilstone.

The art of using any type of stone correctly is one that some people do not find easy to master. The blade must be held at a slight angle to the stone; the angle must be neither too steep nor too flat. If it is the former, the blade will be given a bevelled edge similar to that of a chisel, and this will not make a sufficiently fine cut. If, on the contrary, the blade is held too flat, the edge will become too thin and weak, like that of a razor, and will not stand up to the comparatively hard task of cutting through wood. The second point is that as the blade is

pushed down the stone the angle must be maintained and not altered. The tendency is to sweep the blade along the stone in such a way that the further it gets away from the body, the steeper the angle becomes. This rocking motion, if continued, will give a rounded instead of a smoothly bevelled edge and will prevent anything approaching real keenness. The third point to be observed is that the stone must be sufficiently fine for the job. A coarse stone, such as that used for scythe sharpening, is no use, for example, on a pruning knife, which must be sufficiently smooth edged for such work as grafting and the preparation of cuttings. The fineness of the edge needed to give a really clean finish in some types of work is so important that occasionally an oilstone is used to give the final touches to knives required for grafting and the preparation of cuttings. The oilstone is used in the same way as the whetstone, with the difference that it is moistened with thin machine oil or soap and water.

The sharpening of scythes, sickles and hooks is always done with a whetstone, sometimes made of hard sandstone, but more commonly of carborundum. When using this it is the stone that is moved while the blade is held still. Once again it is important to hold the stone at the correct angle to the blade – neither too steep nor too flat – and to maintain this angle throughout the sweeping movement around the blade.

Some gardeners do not take much trouble over the sharpening of such tools as hoes and spades, but if these tools are kept reasonably sharp they do much better work and the labour of using them is considerably reduced. For all these purposes a file is the most suitable tool. Spades can be sharpened to a rather blunt edge like that of a chisel, as this will wear for a fairly long time, but with hoes it is better to give a more acute edge like that of a knife and to use an old, rather worn file for the purpose, so that the edge is fairly fine and not ragged. Moreover the file may with advantage be kept in the pocket while hoeing so that the edge can be touched up from time to time.

The sharpening of shears is also best done with a very fine file, and the blade should be fixed firmly in a vice or in some other convenient manner while the sharpening is being done. Stones with metal guides to maintain the correct angle are also available.

Axes and billhooks may also be sharpened with a fine file, though a much better job is done if they can be put on to a proper grindstone. The correct angle for grinding is rather more obtuse than that for a knife, but not so blunt as that for a spade.

Sharpening of cylinder lawn mowers is really a task for special machinery, as all the blades of the cylinder must be ground to exactly the same level and this cannot be conveniently done with either a file or a stone, but rotary mowers have detachable

blades or cutting bars which can be removed and sharpened with a file or on a grindstone.

SHEARS Large, scissor-like tools for trimming hedges and cutting lawns. Shears are of many different patterns including short-handled shears for hedge-trimming, long-handled for cutting the edges of lawns, and spring-handled shears, not unlike those used for shearing sheep, which can be operated with one hand.

Ordinary hedging shears are often made with a semi-circular indentation towards the base of the blades to facilitate the cutting of fairly stout stems. They are also always made with their handles cranked at a slight angle from the blades. When cutting the top of a hedge the shears should be held so that the handles slope downwards when the blades are horizontal. When cutting the sides of the hedge the handles should slope towards the user when the blades lie flush against the hedge.

SHELLS Crushed oyster or cockle shells are generally used to neutralize excessive acidity in the special bulb fibre intended for growing bulbs in bowls or other containers without drainage holes, see Bulb Fibre.

SHINGLE Any smoothly worn stone of small size may be given this name but the term is generally reserved for the water-worn stones found on sea beaches and at the margins of some rivers. Shingle is occasionally used in gardens as a surfacing material for paths, but is not very satisfactory as it cannot be compacted and, remaining loose, is exceedingly tiring to walk on.

SHODDY The refuse from a woollen factory. It may consist of anything from fragments of wool to small pieces of woollen fabric. Shoddy decays slowly in the soil, producing humus and at the same time liberating small quantities of nitrogen. It is, therefore, a slow-acting bulky manure and can be used in much the same way as animal manures, such as those from stable and farmyard. Unfortunately, it is not a material which is often available for the amateur, as supplies are limited and are usually contracted for by commercial growers and market gardeners. However, when shoddy can be obtained, it can be dug in at any time of the year at the rate of $\frac{1}{2}$ to 1 lb. per sq. yd. Analysis varies considerably and may be anything from 5 to 15 per cent. of nitrogen.

SHOT EYE A term applied, when propagating roses by budding, to those buds which do not remain dormant the first summer but produce shoots. As a rule such premature growth is not looked on with favour as the growing shoots are more liable to be killed by frost during the first winter than are the dormant buds.

SHOT-HOLE BORERS Certain species of small beetles and their larvae which tunnel into the bark and wood of many trees and shrubs and riddle them with small channels. Bad attacks may result in the death of a branch or even of a whole specimen. Weakly trees are most likely to be affected. There is no satisfactory method of attacking these beetles and their larvae with insecticide, but good cultivation, including proper drainage of the soil, will help to keep them at bay. All attacked branches should be removed and burned. Wounds made in pruning should be painted with stockholm tar or a proprietary wound dressing.

SHOT-HOLE DISEASE, see Bacterial Canker

SHOVEL Shovels are of several different patterns and are alike in having a large and comparatively light spade-like blade curved upwards at the edges. Some patterns have a blade which is rounded or pointed, and some a blade which is square ended, this last type of square-ended shovel is often known as the London shovel in contrast to the rounded or pointed shovel which is known as a navvy's shovel. Shovels of all types are used for scooping up loose material such as sand, gravel, stones, coke, coal or even the loose soil in the bottom of a trench when ground is being deeply dug.

SHOW BOARD (Show Box) Boards or boxes on which certain flowers are exhibited. At one time the show board and show box were very largely used, but they have gradually been superseded by more natural means of display, such as arrangement in vases or bowls. Nevertheless there are still classes at many shows for flowers shown on exhibition boards or in boxes, and rigid rules are laid down concerning the size and form of these boards or boxes. The principal flower concerned is the rose. See Exhibition Board.

SHRUB A term used for any plant with woody stems and branches, but without a tree-like trunk. It may be of any size from a few inches to several feet.

SHRUBBERY (Shrub Border) The term shrubbery was applied to any piece of ground mainly or entirely devoted to the cultivation of shrubs. It is a term which has acquired a bad connotation, because too often during the 19th century shrubberies were planted mainly with large-leaved evergreens, such as laurels and aucubas, and as a result became heavy and dull with little decorative merit. Because of this unfortunate association the term has tended to be dropped and replaced by shrub border, but the two terms are practically synonymous.

Shrub borders and shrubberies should be planned and planted with the same care and on somewhat similar principles as those employed when planning and planting borders of herbaceous perennials, i.e. each plant should be given room to develop in a natural manner and each should be placed so that it can contribute in the best way to the scheme as a whole. Consideration should be given to such matters as relative height and flowering time. Care must be taken not to plant tall-growing kinds in front of those of a dwarfer habit.

The border may be planned either for a concentrated colour display at one particular time, or for a successional display over a long period. In order to do all these things successfully, it is wise to prepare a planting plan drawn to scale with each shrub marked, together with its height, colour, flowering time and whether it is evergreen or deciduous. Bulbs can often be planted successfully under or in front of shrubs, and herbaceous plants, dahlias and bedding plants may also be associated with them to extend the flowering season.

SICKLE A tool primarily used for reaping, and also employed in the garden for cutting rough grass and weeds. Garden sickles are often known as reap hooks, grass hooks, bagging hooks or swap hooks. There are various patterns, each with some points of advantage, some having a fairly heavy blade curved almost in a semi-circle, others a lighter, less curved blade in shape more like that of a scythe. All are used with sweeping movements combined with a twist of the wrist, the blade being held close to the ground and parallel with it. When cutting rough grass or longer weeds, a hooked stick may be held in the other hand and used to left grass or weeds that have been trampled or beaten down. It is essential that the blade should be kept really sharp and for this purpose a scythe stone should be used.

SIDE SHOOT, see Lateral

SIEVE Sieves are made in a great many sizes and with meshes which may be as fine as a piece of butter muslin, or be coarse

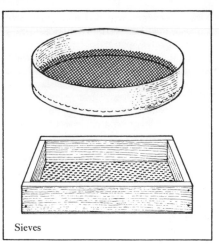
Sieves

enough to allow large stones to pass through. For ordinary garden purposes a sieve about 2 ft. in diameter and with a $\frac{1}{2}$-in. mesh will be found most useful, though it is desirable to have another smaller sieve with a mesh of $\frac{1}{4}$ in. for the purpose of preparing fine compost for seed pans and boxes and for covering seeds. In the garden, sieves are used mainly in the preparation of soil for potting and seed sowing, and in both instances the soil should be rubbed through the sieve, not merely shaken in it, the reason being that only by rubbing can the fibre from the soil be passed through, and this fibre is valuable in seed or potting composts. When potting soils are being prepared for fairly large plants, it is best to dispense with the sieve altogether, and simply break up the lumps of soil by hand, leaving the biggest pieces about the size of a hen's egg. Beginners usually err on the side of sieving soil too much and too finely, with the result that composts are too close in texture and tend after a time to become badly aerated, waterlogged and sour.

When large quantities of soil have to be sieved, it is a good plan to make a sieving bench, which should be done by fixing two pieces of wood about 15 in. apart, parallel with one another, on a framework which holds them about 2 ft. from the ground. The sieve can then be placed on these parallel bars and pushed backwards and forwards along them. The bars take all the weight of the soil, and the operator has only to provide the power to move the sieve.

Very fine sieves, of the type used in kitchens and generally known as flour sieves, are sometimes employed in the garden for cleaning fine seeds. Any dust harvested with the seeds will fall through the sieve but the seeds themselves will remain in it.

SILVER LEAF A disease which principally attacks plums, but may also occur on Portugal laurel, peaches, nectarines, apricots, almonds, cherries, apples and, less frequently, hawthorn, blackthorn and roses.

It is caused by a fungus which penetrates the wood and eventually kills the branches or even the whole tree. An early symptom is a change in the colour of the leaves which become silvery green instead of green. It should be observed that this silvering is not due to any outgrowth on the leaves, as with mildew, but is an actual change in the colour of the leaf. After the wood is dead the fungus develops its spore-bearing bodies on the outside of the wood in the form of flattish, or bracket-shaped outgrowths that are purplish mauve in colour. It is only at this stage that the disease can be passed on to other trees. In Britain it is an offence to allow wood that has been killed by silver leaf fungus to remain on the trees after July 15th. It is not necessary by law to remove branches which are alive but showing the characteristic silvering, but it is desirable to do so to prevent the disease from spreading to other parts of the tree. All wounds made in pruning should be painted with thick white lead paint, warm grafting wax, Stockholm tar or a proprietary wound dressing. It is wise not to prune plum trees in autumn or winter when the risk of infection with silver leaf is at its greatest, as infection may occur through pruning wounds.

SIMAZINE A weedkiller that is particularly effective in killing germinating weeds and so preventing fresh weed growth on ground that has already been cleaned by other means, e.g. digging, hoeing or the use of contact weedkillers such as paraquat or sodium chloride. It will also kill some established weeds but usually rather slowly. It is long lasting, is not easily carried about in the soil and is excellent for keeping drives and paths weed free. It can also be used around roses, bush and cane fruits, fruit trees etc. to prevent regrowth of weeds from seeds. It is a powder to be dissolved in water according to manufacturers' instructions and applied as a spray or from a sprinkle bar.

SINGLE A term used by gardeners in contrast to double, and meaning a flower with the normal number of petals.

SINGLING A term synonymous with thinning (q.v.).

SINKS, see Trough Gardens

SLASHER A type of sturdy, short-bladed billhook used for rough hedge trimming. It is a farm rather than a garden tool but may occasionally be required in large gardens where there are extensive hedges of hawthorn, beech, etc. Some slashers are made with short handles to be used in one hand only, and some with long handles so that the tool can be held with both hands.

SLEEPY DISEASE A name given to various forms of wilt disease. See Wilt.

SLIP A term synonymous with cutting, though it is generally used for that type termed a heel cutting. It is also applied to small pieces or single shoots which can be detached with some roots – these are really small divisions and are sometimes referred to as Irishman's cuttings. See Cutting.

SLUGS Many different species of slug may be found in the garden and not all are equally damaging. Slugs live on decaying vegetable matter as well as on living plants, and some species, particularly the very large slugs, appear to be more scavengers than pests. It is the small grey and black slugs that are most damaging. These eat leaves and stems and are quite capable of destroying small plants completely. The small black slug is particularly fond of fleshy roots, such as those of the potato, into which it will bore. Slugs feed at night and hide by day. In consequence they are often not noticed and the damage they cause is erroneously put down to other pests. They are most likely to be active in mild, damp weather. Slugs can be destroyed by hand picking after dark with the aid of an electric torch and by trapping in small heaps of vegetable refuse placed on the soil and turned over each morning so that any slugs that have hidden beneath can be collected and destroyed. The most effective method, however, is to poison them with a suitable poison bait such as bran and metaldehyde or to water soil and plants with a liquid slug killer based on metaldehyde (q.v.).

SLUGWORMS A general name applied to the caterpillar-like larvae of various species of sawfly. Slugworms have a slight resemblance to small slugs, but can be distinguished at once by the fact that they have legs. In colour they vary from yellow to black. They live on leaves and strip the surface from them, leaving the skeleton. This gives the leaves a very curious and distinctive appearance. Slugworms are most likely to be damaging to cherries, pears and roses, though other plants are attacked. The best remedy is to spray with BHC, derris, malathion, nicotine or trichlorphon directly an attack is observed.

SMOKES The most convenient way of distributing insecticides and fungicides in greenhouses is often as smoke which penetrates to all parts of the house and deposits the chemical as a fine covering on every aerial part of the plant. Several chemicals are available in pellets and canisters combined with a pyrotechnic ingredient which, when ignited, gives off a dense, heavy smoke. Manufacturers invariably give instructions as to the capacity of these pellets or containers, these being stated in terms of the cubic capacity of the house which they are capable of treating. Smokes can be applied without any special preparation, but the best results are obtained if the paths and walls of the house, but not the plants themselves, are first damped down, and if the temperature is allowed to rise a few degrees above the normal. See also Fumigation.

SMUT A name used in gardens for a fungal disease of onions and leeks which attacks the leaves, causing them to develop a black mould as though they had been sprinkled with soot. No reliable remedy is known and all infected plants must be burned. Seed pelleted with thiram may be used as a protection or the seed drills may be soaked with formalin solution, $1\frac{1}{4}$ fl. oz. per gallon, just prior to sowing. In Britain it is an offence to grow onions or leeks on infected land without a special licence from the Ministry of Agriculture, Fisheries & Food.

SNAG Any growth unprovided with leaves, buds or shoots to maintain a flow of sap through it. For example, when pruning cuts are not made just above a bud, leaf or shoot or right back to the main stem, branch or trunk from which the shoot grows, a snag will result and in time this will die. There is a danger that decay may then spread into living tissue below.

SNAILS The damage done by snails is very similar to that caused by slugs. Snails are most likely to be troublesome in greenhouses and near buildings. They are particularly fond of sheltering by day on walls or stones, particularly if they can find protection, as, for example, under ivy on a wall. Possible hiding places should be examined and snails collected. Snails can be killed with the same poison baits as slugs.

SOAP Soft soap is used as an insecticide, as a spreader to secure a more continuous and even distribution of sprays over the surface of plants, and, with washing soda, as a fungicide. As an insecticide it is principally used against aphids and red spider mites at the rate of 2 oz. per gallon of water but has been almost completely superseded by more efficient insecticides such as azobenzene, derris, dimethoate, malathion, diazinon or dicofol. As a spreader it is used at rates varying from $\frac{1}{2}$ to $1\frac{1}{2}$ oz. per gallon of wash according to the hardness of the water. It must not be used with any wash containing arsenate of lead as it causes this to curdle. As a fungicide it is principally used to control American and European gooseberry mildews, the recipe being 12 oz. washing soda and 8 oz. soft soap in 5 gallons of water. See Washing Soda.

SODA, see Washing Soda

SODIUM CHLORATE A white crystalline chemical used as a weedkiller. It is total in its effect, killing most plants and weeds, and acts through the leaves, stems and roots.

It can be carried a considerable distance in water moving through the soil. It is inflammable but commercial formulations for garden use usually include a fire-suppressant chemical to reduce this risk. Though often described as non-poisonous this is not strictly correct as moderate doses taken internally can be damaging, especially to children.

Sodium chlorate may be used dry, simply sprinkled over the weeds, or it can be dissolved in water at rates of from 2 to 4 oz. per gallon and applied as a spray or from a watering-can fitted with a sprinkle bar. Great care should be taken not to apply it in excess as it may be carried for some distance in the soil, and not to let it drift on to plants that are not to be killed. Pure sodium chlorate can be ignited by friction or a blow and clothes wetted with sodium chlorate will catch fire readily and burn fiercely.

It is unsafe to plant or sow on ground treated with sodium chlorate until it has all been washed out or broken down. This may be a matter of weeks or months according to the quantity of chemical applied, the amount of rainfall or water falling on the soil and the natural retentiveness of the soil.

SODIUM CHLORIDE, see Salt

SOFT ROT A disease caused by a bacterium which attacks the roots or stems of celery, carrots, cabbages, seakale, onions, and some ornamental plants including arum lilies and irises. As a result the centre of the plant or root becomes a wet, slimy mass of brown decay. The disease may occur in the ground, or, with carrots, while the roots are in store. The infection is likely to occur through wounds, so care should be taken to avoid damage to roots either by careless handling or by slugs. Soft rot of irises, often known as rhizome rot, can be checked by cutting off and burning affected portions of rhizome and dusting the soil around the plants with superphosphate of lime at 2 oz. per sq. yd. Affected portions of arum lily roots should be cut off in summer and the remainder of the root soaked for four hours in a 2 per cent. solution of formalin. Soil should be sterilized by steam or formalin before replanting or should be completely changed.

SOIL Soils may be broadly classified in several different ways, e.g. as light, medium or heavy, according to the proportion of sand or clay that they contain; as alkaline, neutral or acid according to their pH; as coarse or fine according to their texture; light or dark according to their colour, and mineral or organic according to the amount of humus contained. All these points are of importance to the gardener, and have some bearing both on the manner in which he will treat the soil in order to improve it for the cultivation of plants, and also on the kinds of plant which can be grown successfully in it.

For general garden purposes, the ideal soil will probably be a medium loam, fairly well supplied with humus, well drained, and with a pH of about 6.5. Soils which contain appreciable quantities of lime or chalk are almost always alkaline in reaction, and are consequently unsuitable for the cultivation of lime-hating plants such as heathers and rhododendrons. Soils with a very high percentage of humus are often acid in reaction and the same is true of many sandy heathland soils. When the pH reading is below 5.5 many cultural difficulties are experienced and numerous plants fail to thrive, but the acid-loving plants such as rhododendrons and some heathers delight in such conditions.

The colour of soil may be influenced by the amount of humus which it contains, and by other factors, including the use of soot. Dark soils absorb more sun warmth than light soils, and consequently tend to encourage the early growth of plants. Bad drainage has a retarding effect on growth, and by contrast well-drained soils are frequently early. Contrary to popular belief, plants cannot live on humus and humus-rich soils are not always highly fertile though they can usually be rendered fertile by suitable treatment, which will include thorough cultivation and, usually, heavy liming. The chief value of humus in the soil is the mechanical effect which it has on it, enabling it to absorb moisture readily and yet maintain a fairly open texture which allows air to penetrate and surplus water to drain away. Soils that are deficient in humus tend to dry out very rapidly in summer and, if they also contain clay, may set very hard after heavy rain or if they have been walked on. Humus-producing substances such as animal manure, decayed vegetable refuse and peat will tend to correct these faults.

Plants, in addition to requiring water in the soil and carbon dioxide and oxygen in the atmosphere, need as food a variety of chemical salts, all of which will be present in greater or lesser quantity in any fertile soil. It may well be, however, that the soil is deficient in one or more of these chemicals and that its fertility can, therefore, be increased by adding suitable chemicals to it. This is the justification and the basis for all feeding with chemical fertilizers.

In addition to containing minerals and decaying organic material, all natural soil contains a vast population of microscopic organisms including fungi and bacteria. Some of these are harmful to plant life, some neutral and some beneficial. In a fertile and healthy soil the beneficial micro-organisms will be in excess of the harmful ones, but the balance can be upset either by infection of healthy soil with disease-causing organisms, or by bad physical conditions, particularly lack of aeration and waterlogging. Under such conditions the healthy organisms tend to be destroyed and the harmful ones to be encouraged. Beneficial micro-organisms are useful for numerous reasons, including the physical effect which they exert in making the soil more granular in texture and, therefore, better drained and aerated, and for their chemical effect in breaking down organic matter into simple inorganic chemicals in which form they are available as plant food. Some harmful micro-organisms attack plants directly, living in their tissues and bringing about decay; some break down the chemicals the plants can absorb, releasing nitrogen and ammonia to the air; while others produce acids in the soil which are themselves harmful because they lower the pH of the soil and make it unsuitable for all but those plants which like extremely acid conditions. Soils in the open can usually be kept in healthy condition by regular and intelligent cultivation, including digging, forking, and the application of bulky organic and concentrated inorganic manures.

It may sometimes happen that the soil becomes so heavily infected with some disease-causing micro-organisms that remedial measures must be taken. Then it may well be necessary to sterilize the soil to get rid of these harmful organisms. It is not possible to sterilize in a completely selective manner, killing only the harmful organisms and sparing all those that are useful, but if the sterilization is carried out in one or other of the approved manners (see Sterilization) it will be found that, while the disease-causing organisms are destroyed, sufficient of the useful kind will remain to build up a thriving micro-population within a few weeks. This process will be encouraged if the soil contains an adequate amount of humus and of nitrogen.

Many cultural operations, including digging, forking and ploughing, are intended to improve the aeration of the soil and so encourage the multiplication of beneficial organisms, all of which require air for their existence. In contrast many harmful micro-organisms thrive in the absence of air, and it is for this reason that waterlogged or badly cultivated soils tend to become unhealthy.

Cultural operations such as digging and forking also tend to hasten liberation of plant foods locked up in the soil in chemical forms unsuitable for the use of plants. Cultivation of this kind is usually followed by an increase of fertility, but reserves of food in even the most fertile soil are not inexhaustible and if the cultivation is continued year after year without any other treatment, there will come a time when the fertility of the soil will begin to decline. After that, the more it is cultivated the more quickly will it lose fertility. This inevitable process can only be prevented by feeding soils which are under cultivation, and for this purpose both manures of a bulky organic character and concentrated fertilizer are useful.

Cultivation of the soil, by digging or the use of a rotary cultivator on larger areas, helps to improve aeration and encourages the multiplication of beneficial micro-organisms

Although plants require twelve or more different chemicals from the soil, and seem to derive some beneficial effect from several more, only five or six of them are likely to be readily exhausted. The three most often in short supply are nitrogen, phosphorus and potash, and after this iron, magnesium and calcium. Boron, manganese and molybdenum may occasionally be deficient for the needs of certain crops and zinc and copper are two other chemicals that may very occasionally have to be added.

Nitrogen, phosphorus, potash, magnesium and other useful chemicals are contained in bulky animal manures and in decaying vegetable refuse. They can also be applied in the form of chemical salts which are described under the headings, nitrogen, phosphorus, etc. Calcium is contained in many substances including wood ashes and organic matter. When lacking in the soil, it is usually applied in the form of lime, ground chalk or ground limestone.

A soil that is in natural condition and not cultivated tends to retain its chemical and physical balance as a result of the decay of vegetation and the death and decay of small creatures, including insects, in the soil, and also by droppings of animals. When cultivated, the balance of these natural processes is completely altered and fertility is impaired unless manuring is practised, as already outlined.

Bad drainage, in addition to resulting in bad aeration and the consequent increase in the population of undesirable micro-organisms, also tends to chill soils and make them late. It is often possible to hasten the growth of plants considerably by improving the drainage of a heavy wet soil.

SOIL BLOCKS Compressed blocks of soil which are used instead of pots for raising seedlings and growing on young plants. Numerous ingenious devices have been invented for making these blocks from ordinary potting compost, which should be slightly more moist than for normal potting. It is claimed for soil blocks that they save expense, and that plants when transplanted to their final quarters do not suffer any check to growth.

SOIL CONDITIONER Strictly any substance which improves the texture of soils. Animal manures, decayed vegetable refuse and peat are soil conditioners in this sense but the term is usually reserved for chemicals which have a marked effect on soil texture but are not themselves plant foods.

A range of chemicals derived from seaweeds and known as alginates are of this type. They include sodium alginate, calcium alginate, ammonium alginate and alginic acid but of these the first has been found most satisfactory. Alginates are colloidal in character and they cause the very fine particles found in clay soils to coagulate into larger granules which do not pack so closely and so leave larger spaces for air and the passage of water.

SOILLESS COMPOSTS Seed, cutting and potting composts based on peat, sand, vermiculite, etc. but excluding soil. See Compost.

SOILLESS CULTIVATION Any method of growing plants without soil. Probably the earliest example of soilless cultivation was in the mid-19th century when scientists began to investigate the way in which plants feed and the kind of foods they require. At this time soilless cultivation was entirely a laboratory process and it does not appear to have occurred to anyone that it had any wider value until about 1930. It was then discovered that some plants grew extremely well under certain forms of soilless cultivation, particularly when cultivated under glass or where there was a great deal of sunshine. Plants can be fed more intensively than is possible when they are grown in soil and as a result more plants can be grown in the same area and heavier crops can be obtained from them. This method of cultivation has proved particularly suitable for perpetual flowering carnations and for tomatoes, and has been highly developed on a commercial scale for both plants. It is also useful for many others, including some that are difficult under ordinary soil conditions, e.g. gerberas.

At first the method known as hydroponics was employed. In this the plants are supported on wire mesh, wood wool or glass wool, over a tank containing the nutrient solution into which their roots hang. This method has been almost entirely superseded by what is known as aggregate culture. In this the bed, tank, pot or box in which the plants are to grow is filled with some non-nutritive substance such as sand, gravel, washed breeze or vermiculite, which serves simply as a rooting medium. This aggregate is then flooded with nutrient solution.

Many different systems of feeding the plants have been tried with success. The simplest is to prepare the plant foods as a dry mixture of fertilizers, a measured quantity of which is sprinkled over the surface of the bed at stated intervals. Plain water is then used to wash these nutrients into the aggregate. A variation of this simple system is to prepare a nutrient solution with the chemicals and apply this to the sand in place of plain water.

A more complicated method of liquid feeding, which is used in many commercial installations, is that known as the sub-irrigation system. In this the aggregate is placed in a specially constructed tank or bed completely lined with concrete or some other impervious substance, but with suitable outlets for surplus moisture at the lowest points. The nutrient solution is prepared by dissolving the necessary chemicals in a large tank of water sunk below the level of the bed containing the aggregate. It is pumped up from this tank into the aggregate by means of an electric pump. When the aggregate is completely flooded with nutrient solution the pump is automatically cut off and the surplus solution slowly drains back into the storage tank. The pump is either switched on again by the gardener in charge or it may be switched on automatically by a time switch set to flood the bed at predetermined intervals. This system has the merit of reducing labour to a minimum but it suffers from the drawback that the strength of the solution gradually weakens and, even more serious, may change in the proportion of the nutrient elements one to another. In consequence frequent analysis of the contents of the storage tank must be carried out by a skilled chemist. Regular feeding with a nutrient solution applied from a watering-can seems to be the most practical method for the amateur.

The details of feeding and the frequency with which the feed is given will vary according to the type of plant being grown, the time of year and the amount of sunshine. Similarly the nutrient solution employed will vary according to the kind of plant being cultivated. Proprietary feeds specially blended for certain classes of plant can be purchased, and these should be used strictly in accordance with manufacturers' instructions. A good general solution for liquid feeding which will be found to give satisfactory results with the ordinary run of flowering plants, may be prepared as follows: nitrate of soda 14oz., sulphate of potash 2oz., superphosphate of lime 7¼oz., sulphate of magnesium (Epsom salts) 4½oz., water 50 gallons. A separate solution should be prepared by dissolving boric acid ¼oz., sulphate of manganese ¼oz., sulphate of iron 3oz., in 1 pint of water. Just before the main solution is used this subsidiary solution should be added to it, at the rate of 1 teaspoonful to 10 gallons.

When this kind of overhead feeding is adopted the aggregate should be of a kind that will not dry out too rapidly. Clean, sharp sand with medium-sized particles is ideal. It can be used in any kind of container with an outlet for surplus water, such as a flower pot, box, or bed lined round with boards or bricks. For sub-irrigation cultivation a much coarser aggregate must be used, such as gravel or broken clinker.

SOOT Ordinary domestic soot contains nitrogen in the form of sulphate of ammonia and is, therefore, a fertilizer. It is also of use because it darkens the soil and therefore enables it to absorb more heat from the sun. Fresh soot may contain quite a high percentage of sulphur and other chemicals, which, in excess, can be harmful to plants and so it is best to store it for three or four months before use. It can either be applied as a surface dressing round the plants in growth, or be hoed, raked, pricked or dug into vacant ground. The average rate of application is 6oz. per sq. yd. but this is only a rough guide as soot itself varies considerably in its nature, some samples containing far more nitrogen than others. If soot is exposed to rain, it quickly loses much of its value as a fertilizer as the sulphate of ammonia in it is soluble and easily washed out. Fresh soot has some insecticidal value and is occasionally used on vacant ground to kill or drive out wireworms, leather jackets and cockchafer larvae. Its value for this purpose is, however, not very great and it should be augmented by more efficient soil insecticides such as naphthalene and lindane.

SOOTY MOULD Sometimes leaves or stems of plants become covered with a black mould which can be removed quite easily if rubbed with a damp finger or cloth, leaving the leaf clean and unharmed. This is known as sooty mould, and the mould is, as a rule, growing on the deposits left on the leaves by various insects, particularly scale insects, white fly and aphids. Though the mould does not attack the leaf itself, it is detrimental as it blocks up the breathing pores of the leaf. It is also very unsightly. It can be removed by sponging with warm soapy water and steps should be taken to keep down insects by spraying with a suitable insecticide.

SOUR This term is often applied to soils which are in an unhealthy biological condition, i.e. with a preponderance of undesirable micro-organisms (see Soil). Such a condition is often due to waterlogging or to poor aeration caused by lack of cultivation and bad soil texture. Sour soils usually have a slightly unpleasant smell. All plants do badly in them and may even refuse to grow at all. The term should not be confused with acid, which refers to a physical not a biological condition of the soil. It is true that a soil which is sour is likely to become acid if the adverse conditions are allowed to continue, but it by no means follows that every sour soil is acid, and it is certainly not true that every acid soil is sour, using these terms in the sense in which they are employed in gardens. Moderate acidity is not in itself harmful and may even be beneficial to some plants, notably members of the heather family, whereas sourness is always bad and should be corrected as soon as noted. The remedy is to improve drainage, if this is at fault, and also to improve the texture of the soil, which may be done by thorough digging or forking, the incorporation of bulky organic substances such as compost and strawy manure, and also of coarse sand or stone chippings. Where heavy clay soils are concerned, liming may also help by flocculating the clay and so improving the drainage. See Lime.

SOWING, see Seed Sowing

SPADE The most important of the digging tools used in the garden, which will be required not only for ordinary digging but also for trenching and the planting of many large plants, including trees and shrubs. Spades do not vary greatly in pattern and for all ordinary purposes the standard pattern of short-handled spade with a slightly cranked shaft is recommended. It may have a D-shaped, T-shaped or Y-shaped handle, according to personal preference. The short-handled spade is usually made in three sizes known as full size, ladies (or boys) and border, for which the blade sizes are approximately 11½ × 7½in., 10 × 6½in. and 9 × 5½in. respectively. For all ordinary garden purposes a full size

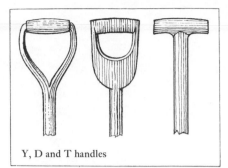

Y, D and T handles

spade will be satisfactory, and in many instances the ladies' or boys' spade will be found more convenient by the amateur who is inexperienced in doing heavy work. The border spade is useful for light work and for some kinds of planting.

Some spades have a tread on the top edge of the blade to lighten the wear on the boot when this is used for pressing the spade into the soil. This type of spade is often known as London-treaded and, for heavy digging, is to be preferred to the plain-topped blade. There is also some difference in the method of attaching the blade to the shaft. The usual garden type has a strapped socket with three rivets. For some very heavy work, such as the lifting of well-rooted plants in the nursery, spades with longer straps and 4 or 5 rivets are employed, but they are heavy and should only be used when the work really necessitates the increased strength. The alternative to the strapped socket is the tubular socket, but this is not recommended as it is much more likely to cause breakage at the point where the wooden handle enters the socket.

In addition to digging spades, there are special narrow, longer-bladed spades made for digging trenches for draining, etc. Those with rectangular blades are often known as grafting tools whereas those with slightly tapered blades are known as draining tools.

SPADIX A particular type of flower spike in which the stem is thick or fleshy and the insignificant flowers are more or less em-

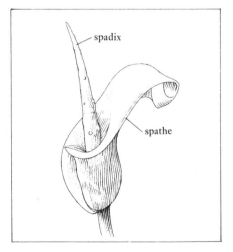

spadix

spathe

bedded in it. As a rule it is surrounded by a spathe as in the arum lily (zantedeschia) and anthurium.

SPATHE A special type of inflorescence, found in aroids and palms and well exemplified by the arum lily, in which one leaf or bract is folded around a central spadix consisting of a column-like spike of flowers.

SPAWN The term is used in several ways in gardening, but always to indicate some means by which a plant increases itself. Thus the spawn of a mushroom is the mycelium or thread-like growth of the mushroom. This is produced in a suitable medium, such as a sterilized culture in a bottle, or in a brick of suitable compost, which is then broken up into small pieces and placed in a mushroom bed where it proceeds to grow.

The small cormlets or tiny corms which form round the outside of gladiolus corms are also often known as spawn, and the name may be applied to other cormlets and bulbs forming around bulbous-rooted plants.

SPECIES, see Classification

SPECIMEN PLANT Any plant which is grown so that it can be viewed from all sides as distinct from being grouped with other plants.

SPHAGNUM A genus of mosses which are usually found in damp or boggy places. They make very dense growth which, because of its power to absorb moisture like a sponge, makes an excellent packing material for plants or for the stems of cut flowers. It is also extensively used in orchid potting compost, for which purpose it is chopped up finely. A wad of sphagnum moss is sometimes placed in the bottom of earthenware pots and pans in which seeds are to be germinated or cuttings struck, the idea being that it produces good drainage and yet holds sufficient moisture to keep the compost moist. Sphagnum moss is almost invariably used by florists as a basis for wreaths.

Decomposing sphagnum forms a particular kind of peat, usually known as sphagnum peat or moss peat. It is a suitable kind of peat for use in the garden, especially in seed and potting composts. Good sphagnum peat should be fibrous or granular in texture and should not contain a great deal of fine dust which would clog up the compost and impede drainage.

SPIKE A flower cluster very closely resembling a raceme (q.v.) but differing from it in having individual flowers which are stalkless or nearly so. The term is often loosely used by gardeners for any elongated flower cluster. For example, the flowers of delphiniums are often described as spikes though in fact many of them are racemes.

SPIT One spade's depth of soil. Obviously as spades vary in size so will spits vary in depth, but the convention is to regard a spit as between 10 and 12 in. Thus if a statement is made that ground is to be dug two spits deep, the intention is that it should be dug to a depth of 20 to 24 in. Top spit soil is the first 10 or 12 in. beneath the surface; second spit the next 10 or 12 in.; third spit soil the 10 or 12 in. below that, and so on.

SPORE The fine dust-like cells by which ferns and mosses distribute themselves. They may be compared with the seeds of flowering plants but the analogy, useful as it is in some respects, must not be carried too far as the spores are not themselves the product of union of the sex cells of the organisms but give rise to a prothallus which produces the sex cells. Therefore, if two ferns or mosses are to be hybridized together, all that the gardener can do is to take spores from both species or varieties, sow them together, and then hope that, when they produce their respective prothalli, nature will do the rest and cause hybridization between them.

The term is also used for the reproductive cells of fungi which are also dust like and produced in immense numbers but are otherwise entirely distinct in structure and function from those of ferns and mosses. The spores of fungi are produced from the fruiting 'pod', which may be a large object like a toadstool or mushroom, or quite tiny objects such as the conidia of a rust fungus on the back of hollyhock or rose leaves.

Spores of all kinds are freely distributed by wind because of their minute size and can be carried great distances by this means.

SPORT Strictly speaking any variation from the normal in the character of a plant may be termed a sport, but in garden practice the term is usually reserved for variations which occur apart from seed. For example, it will sometimes happen that some of the flowers on a chrysanthemum plant will be of a different colour from the other flowers on the same plant and this variation is termed a sport. The genetical term for such a variation is a mutation.

Sports occur spontaneously in many plants and some kinds of plants are particularly liable to produce sports. They are common, for example, in chrysanthemums and also in some varieties of polyantha pompon roses, particularly those with orange flowers which frequently sport to red. It must be clearly understood that sporting is by no means confined to a change in colour, but may affect any characteristic of the plant. In roses, bush varieties sometimes sport as vigorous climbing forms, and many of our best climbing roses have been obtained in this way.

Sporting is due to a change in the character of one or more genes carried in the chromosomes. If such a change occurs in the apical cell of a bud or growing shoot, the growth produced by that bud or shoot will be of a new type, though the remainder of the plant will remain unchanged. Such sports can only be perpetuated from material obtained from the sporting shoot or shoots. In the case of chrysanthemums, for example, if one shoot of a plant produces blooms of a different colour and it is desired to perpetuate this colour, cuttings must be obtained from this particular shoot and not from other shoots or from the base of the plant. This may necessitate using material which would normally be considered unsuitable for the purpose of making cuttings, but once plants of the new variety have been established, normal cutting material can be obtained.

SPOTTED WILT, see Wilt

SPRAING Sometimes potato tubers are discovered to have dark streaks in the flesh. This is known as spraing and is a physiological disorder, usually connected with rapid fluctuations in the water content of the soil. Improved drainage and good cultivation will generally prevent spraing from occurring.

SPRAYING Many chemicals used to destroy insects or fungi are most conveniently applied to plants in the form of a liquid spray. Many different types of apparatus have been produced for the purpose of applying such sprays, and these range from simple hand syringes, consisting of a plunger working inside a tube fitted with a fine nozzle, to complicated mechanically driven apparatus, capable of spraying liquid in a fine mist at considerable pressure over a large area. For many years the practice was to employ very dilute solutions and to distribute a comparatively heavy spray over the plants and this is still the usual custom in private gardens. For field crops and orchards much more concentrated solutions are often used in which far less liquid is atomized and distributed in the finest possible film over the plants. A development of this system is that known as the aerosol, produced by a cartridge of carbon dioxide under pressure, discharged into a small container filled with a spray fluid. The carbon dioxide not only blows the fluid at great pressure through a very fine hole, but also dissolves in the liquid and then discharges from it with the boiling action familiar in soda water. In consequence the liquid is broken up into a cloud-like mist of great penetrative power. Though aerosols have been used out of doors, they are on the whole more suitable for greenhouse use and for this purpose may be compared in efficiency and convenience with insecticidal and fungicidal-carrying smokes. See Smokes.

Normal spraying in the open garden is

usually done with some form of syringe or hand-operated pump, though in larger gardens small, mechanically-driven spray plants are employed, some operating from petrol and some from electric motors. The essential with all good spraying apparatus is that the liquid must be broken up into a fairly fine spray. Too coarse a spray may cause damage to the plants, as some insecticides and fungicides will scorch tender leaves, flowers and fruits, if applied too heavily. A second point of importance is that the spray must be produced with some force, so that it penetrates between the branches or leaves of the plant and covers all with equal efficacy. Weak spraying will result in partial coverage of the outer leaves, and pests and diseases will continue to thrive undisturbed in more out-of-the-way places. For the same reason it is often important to wet the undersides of the leaves of the plants as well as the upper surfaces. To enable this to be done conveniently it is an advantage to have the spray nozzle cranked at an angle to the lance or barrel of the spraying apparatus. Spraying apparatus which is to be used for fruit trees must be equipped with lances sufficiently long to enable the uppermost branches of the tree to be reached, or, failing this, the gardener must work from a ladder or steps.

Some spray fluids will corrode iron and certain other metals. For this reason most good spraying apparatus is made with working parts either of brass or plastic both of which have a high resistance to most of the fluids in common use. Even so it is highly desirable that all spraying apparatus should be thoroughly washed out with clear water after use.

It has been shown conclusively that some emulsified sprays, particularly those applied in winter to kill eggs of caterpillars and aphids (e.g. tar oil wash, petroleum oils and DNC) are more effective if applied at fairly high pressures, at least 200 lb. per sq. in. This appears to be due to the fact that such sprays are apt to remain in emulsion and so out of direct contact with the insects or eggs they are meant to destroy, unless they hit them with some force. Unfortunately it is seldom possible to obtain pressures of anything like this order with hand-operated

machines, though one or two ingenious devices have been produced for the purpose.

Wherever possible spraying should be done in dry, still weather. Most of the insecticides and fungicides in common use adhere firmly to the plants when dry, but if rain falls while they are being put on or within an hour or so of their application, they may be washed off or diluted to such an extent as to be ineffective. This difficulty does not occur with systemic chemicals which are actually absorbed by the plant, see Systemic. Spraying in windy weather is always a trying and wasteful operation. Unfortunately both these instructions are counsels of perfection which must often be ignored, as frequently the time margin for spraying is small, and it must be carried through almost irrespective of the weather. As an example, the use of lime sulphur to control scab of apples may be mentioned. One application should be given at the pink bud stage, and this stage normally lasts for only five or six days.

Sprays may be broadly considered under two headings, those which are preventive and those which are directly destructive. Examples of the former are most fungicides such as sulphur and copper compounds and also stomach poisons directed against biting insects such as caterpillars, e.g. carbaryl, BHC and derris. The intention with all these is to coat the entire plant with the finest possible film of the fungicide or insecticide before attack occurs, so that directly the spores of a fungus alight on leaf or stem and start to grow, they will be killed, or directly an insect bites stem or leaf it will at the same time obtain a fatal dose of poison. By contrast, the directly destructive sprays are used mainly against sucking insects such as aphids, red spider mites and thrips. Because of their method of feeding by inserting a thin proboscis like a needle into the cells of the plant and sucking the sap directly from them, these will escape the poisons spread on the surface of the plant. They must be attacked either with systemic insecticides or by being themselves coated with poison. When applying preventive sprays a fine covering is sufficient, and a fine, mist-producing nozzle can be used on the spraying apparatus, but for the directly

destructive or contact sprays a coarser nozzle and heavier, more wetting spray is to be preferred.

It is seldom wise to spray with insecticides while plants are in bloom, as at this time they are usually visited by many beneficial insects including honey bees, and the sprays which kill harmful insects are often fatal to useful insects as well. A further warning is that many of the sprays used against insects are also poisonous to warm-blooded animals including human beings, and kill some fish. All must be handled with care, and must be kept out of reach of children and unauthorized persons. Protective clothing is necessary when applying some dangerous chemicals and rubber gloves should always be worn when mixing them. All utensils and spraying apparatus should be thoroughly washed after use, and the containers carefully disposed of.

SPREADER Any substance added to another for the sole purpose of enabling it to be distributed more evenly. Thus chemicals that are to be used as dusts to destroy pests or diseases are usually mixed with an inactive substance which will give them bulk and enable them to be spread evenly over the plants to be protected. Similarly many concentrated fertilizers are mixed with sand or rape dust so that they can be properly distributed over the soil. Spreaders are also used in liquid sprays, not to add bulk but to lower surface tension so that the liquid spreads as a thin film instead of forming droplets. Soft soap may be used in this way but usually more concentrated substances, such as saponin, are employed.

SPRINGTAILS Very small white arthropods which are sometimes found in great numbers on the roots of various plants. The popular name refers to the habit of these insects of jumping when disturbed. This they accomplish by coiling and then rapidly uncoiling their bodies. Springtails feed on decayed vegetable matter and follow in the wake of other troubles, but it seems probable that, having started to feed on an unhealthy root, they may cause the decay to spread still further. Good cultivation and improved drainage will usually tend to reduce the number of springtails. Care should be taken to avoid an excess of half-rotted vegetable matter in the soil. Soil may be watered with BHC or be freely powdered with hydrated lime. Springtails can be cleared from mushroom compost by allowing it to heat up to 54 to 60°C. before use.

SPRINKLE BAR A perforated metal or plastic tube to be attached to a watering-can or similar container for the application of chemical solutions to soil, plants or grass. Sprinkle bars are excellent for the application of weedkillers since the fluid is delivered close to the soil or leaves with a minimum

A selection from the many kinds of spraying apparatus which are available for use in the garden and greenhouse

risk of drifting where it is not wanted. Sprinkle bars are manufactured in various widths, narrow ones being most suitable for applying chemicals between growing plants where considerable precision is required, wide ones for treating lawns and open, uncultivated ground. They are usually made either in the form of a capital T or inverted L.

SPRINKLER A name given to various types of apparatus for overhead irrigation. The most familiar type of sprinkler is the revolving water spray used for watering lawns. There are various patterns of this. Quite a different type of apparatus is the oscillating pipe-sprinkler in which jets are placed at intervals along a length of iron pipe, which itself rotates backwards and forwards through an angle of about 90 degrees, the power for this movement being provided by the water passing through a turbine on its way into the pipe. Small oscillating sprinklers are also made for watering lawns and flower borders and have the advantage over revolving sprinklers that they water a rectangle and not a circle. See Irrigation.

SPROUT Any young shoot and particularly the first shoot of a germinating seed. The young growths of potatoes are referred to as sprouts, and it is a common garden practice to place potato planting sets in boxes, in a light and cool but frostproof place so that they may form sturdy sprouts before they are planted in spring. This has two advantages: the sprouting potatoes are in a condition to grow very rapidly when soil conditions make it possible to plant, and the number of shoots produced per tuber can be artificially limited by rubbing out

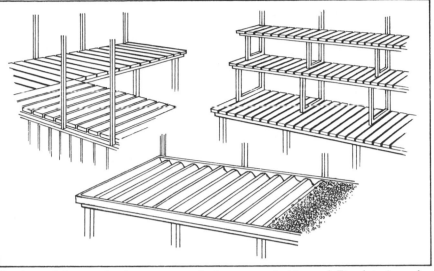

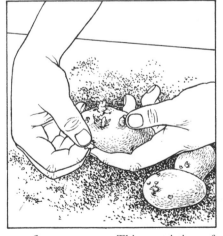

superfluous sprouts. This restriction of shoots is considered to be an advantage when potatoes are grown for exhibition, as with a small number of shoots, large tubers are more likely to be produced.

SPUD A very narrow-bladed hoe with either a long or short handle, used for

cutting out weeds without too much disturbance of the surrounding ground. Some spuds are made with a hook-like projection on one side of the blade with which the weed can be drawn out after it has been cut off.

SPUR This word is used in two quite distinct ways in the garden. Botanically a spur is a tube-like appendage to a flower in which nectar is produced to attract insects. A familiar example is the long, gracefully formed spur of aquilegia (columbine).

The word is also used by fruit growers to describe the rather complex clusters of fruit buds which occur on the older branches of certain kinds of fruit tree, notably apples and pears. Such spurs tend to branch and multiply so that, on an old tree, spurs of considerable size may occur, each carrying a large number of fruit buds. These big spurs are seldom satisfactory, as the fruit they carry tends to be overcrowded and small. The remedy is to reduce the size and number of spurs from time to time by drastic

Staging made from wooden slats or corrugated asbestos covered with gravel. Tiered staging makes the maximum use of greenhouse bench space

autumn or winter pruning, which may include the complete removal of some spurs and the reduction in size of others.

STAGE The tabling or shelving in a greenhouse on which the plants are arranged. Staging can be of many different kinds, ranging from open slat staging which is most suitable for those plants requiring a rather dry, airy atmosphere, to solid staging covered with gravel, peat or some aggregate, which is most suitable for those plants requiring a warm and moist atmosphere. Staging can be permanent or portable according to requirements. The term stage is also applied to the tables at flower shows and an exhibitor is said to stage his exhibit when he arranges it.

STAKING Many plants are sufficiently sturdy to support themselves without any artificial aid, but some require staking, and this is particularly true of highly developed garden forms that have very large flowers, for example the giant delphiniums and

When planting trees, the stake should be driven into the planting hole before the tree is placed in position

dahlias. Staking is also often necessary with young plants, particularly young trees and shrubs, until their roots have become sufficiently established in the soil to hold them firmly. Where possible stakes for trees should be put in position during planting so that the roots can be placed around the stake, rather than be damaged by it after they are covered with soil.

There are three points to be considered in all staking. First, the stake or stakes must be sufficiently strong for their purpose. Secondly, they must be of a type and size which will not damage the plant that they are meant to support and, thirdly, they must be as sightly and inconspicuous as possible.

Comparatively small or slender plants can be supported with bamboo canes, and, provided the canes are fairly stout, they will even be adequate for such things as delphiniums. When it comes to really heavy flowers, such as those of the giant decorative dahlias, bamboo canes are insufficiently sturdy. Instead 1 in. by 1 in. deal stakes may be used, or any other supports of comparable strength. For trees, 2-in. square stakes are the minimum that should be considered, or alternatively sturdy larch poles may be employed.

With regard to the second point, damage is most likely to occur if stakes are made of rough material, or are too long. For example, the stakes used for delphiniums should reach to the base of the flower spike but not beyond or it will be almost inevitable that, as the spikes sway in the wind, the lower flowers will be damaged by the stakes. Similarly, dahlia stakes should extend part of the way up the flower stems but not to the flowers themselves. Provided stakes are firmly fixed in the soil so that they cannot work themselves loose, it is not altogether a disadvantage if they are a little flexible. Thin steel stakes are excellent for delphiniums for this very reason, because they allow the long stems to give a little in a high wind, and this often results in less damage than would occur with a perfectly rigid support.

On the score of sightliness also it is important that stakes should not be too long. The ideal is that they should be completely covered by the growth of the plant. If this is to be achieved, they must be a little shorter than the eventual height of the plant, and should be inserted in the soil near to the plant's centre. With some plants it is an advantage to have three or more stakes pushed into the soil close to the plant but leaning a little outwards towards the top so that, when shoots are tied to the stakes, they are opened up a little in the form of a shuttlecock. This is very useful for tall plants with a lot of foliage such as delphiniums and Michaelmas daisies.

Many plants of weak or branching habit may be supported neatly by means of short bushy branches such as hazel. If two or three

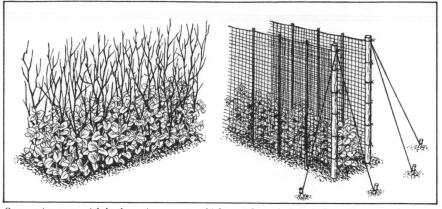

Supporting peas with bushy twigs, or nets which must be staked securely at the row ends

of these branches are thrust into the soil close to the plant quite early in the spring, the plant will grow up through the twigs, finding its own support in the process and at the same time completely hiding the twigs from view. This is very similar to the method of support commonly used in the vegetable garden for culinary peas, for which longer hazel branches are inserted on either side of the row to form a continuous support up which the plants can scramble.

Tomatoes need very strong stakes since, though the plants themselves are comparatively light, when laden with a crop of fruit the weight carried by the stake may be considerable.

Runner beans, though not particularly heavy, present an enormous area to the wind and for this reason require particularly secure staking. The usual method is to use long hazel rods or bamboo canes thrust firmly into the soil in a double row, spaced about 2ft. apart at the base and crossing near the top. Horizontal canes or rods are laid in the forks formed by the crossing uprights and are lashed to these with twine. This type of support is extremely strong and will stand up to quite high gales. An alternative method is to push the canes or rods in vertically and secure them at the top to horizontal wires strained between strong posts driven well into the soil and further strengthened by being joined by crossbars nailed to them. This kind of staking is often employed for sweet peas trained on the cordon system, one cane being placed for each plant.

In private gardens young fruit trees are usually supported with one strong stake driven in vertically close to the main trunk of the tree, but in commercial orchards a shorter stake driven in at an angle is more commonly employed. This method has the advantage of strength but is not as neat as the vertical stake and it does make it a little more difficult to cultivate the soil round the tree. The stake should be driven in on the side of the tree away from the prevailing wind (that is, usually on the north-east side of the tree in the British Isles), and should cross the main trunk 2½ to 3ft. above soil level. The trunks of trees should always be protected against chafing by the ties. Common practice is to wrap a piece of sacking

Stakes for runner beans should be strong and well secured at the top

round the trunk where the tie comes; alternatively a piece of old motor tyre inner tube may be used. Special rubber or plastic ties, which have the merit of being neat, strong and safe, are available for fruit trees.

When tying plants with string or raffia it is usually wise to make a double twist in the tie between the plant and the stake. This twist acts as a spring, allowing a certain amount of movement in windy weather and also room for further expansion of the shoot or branch.

Climbing and twining plants will need supports according to their habit of growth and the place in which they are planted. It is sometimes possible to use old tree trunks for the purpose or even to plant climbers such as clematis against living trees, which suffer little harm from their slender growth. When poles have to be provided, they should be made of some wood which will not rot easily, such as oak, teak or larch, but even then that part of the support which is to be put into the soil should first be treated with some preservative material such as copper naphthenate.

Plants growing against walls may be supported on wooden or plastic trellis-work. This is fastened to the wall with screws and plugs or by similar means, or wires may be strained against the wall, in which case the metal supports known as vine eyes will be found convenient to carry the wires a few inches away from the wall. It is seldom wise to fasten a plant direct to a wall with nails and string or by any other means, partly because a wall surface is likely to get too hot at times and partly because the wall is bound to become damaged by the frequent necessity of driving in fresh supports.

STAMEN The stamen is the male organ of the flower and it usually consists of two parts – a thin stalk or filament, and a head or anther. It is the latter which produces pollen with which egg cells in the ovary of the flower are fertilized. When hybridization is carried out ripe pollen is transferred from the male to the female parent, and where possible it is wise to remove all stamens from the flower which is to carry seed, so that there may be no chance of accidental self-pollination. This removal of stamens should be done quite early in the development of the flower before the anthers have become ripe and started to shed their pollen. It may be necessary to remove the petals of the expanding flower to get at the stamens so that they can be cut off with a small pair of pointed scissors.

Sometimes stamens become changed into petals and it is in this way that many semi-double and double flowers are produced. In the former instance only some of the stamens may be converted into petals, but in fully double flowers all or most will have been changed. Sometimes the stamen changes into a complete and fully-developed petal,

in other instances the petal is small and of a different character from the normal petal. It is in this latter manner that the petaloid flowers seen in some forms of peony and also in certain camellias are produced.

STANDARD A term with both a botanical and a horticultural application. Botanically a standard is the upper petal of a flower of the pea family, but gardeners also apply the term to the broad upright petals found in some irises including the so-called bearded irises. In pea flowers the standards are in contrast to the keel and wings; in irises the standards are in contrast to the falls.

Horticulturally the term standard is applied to any tree or shrub grown on a bare stem several feet in height. Most trees automatically assume a standard habit as they age, because the lower branches fall off leaving a bare trunk of varying height. Fruit trees are often trained by the gardener as standards from an early stage by removing all side growths and running up one central stem to a height of about 5 or 6 ft., after which the top of the stem is removed in order to force it to produce a head of branches at this height above ground level. Standard roses are usually produced by allowing a briar stem to grow to a height of $3\frac{1}{2}$ or 4 ft. and then inserting buds of the garden variety at this level, putting them either into the base of side shoots in stems of *Rosa canina* or direct into the main stem when using *R. rugosa*.

Sometimes quite small shrubs are trained as standards. Fuchsias and heliotropes are often grown in this way, both as specimens in the greenhouse and for summer bedding schemes. A strong main stem is first allowed to develop, and the plant is then beheaded at the required height in the manner already described for fruit trees. In the fuchsia the stems are rarely more than 3 ft. in height, and less for heliotrope.

Half-standard is a term applied to trees and bushes on a bare main stem considerably less than the length usual in standards. The precise height of the stem will, however, vary according to the nature of the plant under consideration. For example, half-standard roses are usually on stems $2\frac{1}{2}$ ft. in height, and half-standard fruit trees on stems 3 to 4 ft. in height.

STARTING This term is used in the garden for the process of bringing certain plants into growth after the dormant period. For example, begonia tubers, which are allowed to become dormant in the autumn and are kept quite dry until January or February, are later placed in damp peat, leafmould or some similar material in a warm greenhouse solely with the intention of starting them into growth. As there is little nourishment in the peat or leafmould to keep them growing they are transferred to a normal compost in which soil is included

To start tuberous begonias into growth, box them up and keep them in a warm place

as soon as shoots appear. A somewhat different application of the word is applied to greenhouse vines which are maintained in a dormant condition in winter by giving the fullest possible ventilation and withholding all artificial heat. These can then be started into growth, at the time chosen by the gardener, by the simple process of closing the ventilators and applying artificial heat to the vinery.

STEEPING Some seeds with hard coats germinate very slowly or irregularly unless steeped or soaked in water for a period before they are sown. The system is also often applied to the cormlets or tiny corms produced by gladioli, as these have extremely hard coats through which growth has difficulty in forcing its way. If, however, the cormlets are soaked in water for 24 hours before being planted, the hard coats are softened and growth is far more regular. Some gardeners use warm water for this purpose, but care must be taken with this as too much heat may kill the seed or corm.

STEM ROT A rather vague term used for various diseases that attack the stems of plants. Stem rot may be an alternative name for damping-off, foot rot, collar rot, various stem cankers, didymella, sclerotinia or botrytis.

STEPS Steps in the garden can be made in a variety of ways, from simple steps formed by cutting out the soil, to elaborate flights of brick or stone.

Much the same principles are applied to the making of steps in the garden as to steps in any other place, that is the riser or vertical part of each step should always be carefully proportioned to the tread or horizontal part. Very steep, narrow steps are uncomfortable and even dangerous to walk on, while steps which are very broad may be awkward to walk on unless the breadth is carefully proportioned to a normal stride, or strides. Shallow steps are also unsatisfactory as an average person walking without much concentration, will usually expect a step to be between 6 and 9 in. in height, and may easily move the feet accordingly, even when the step is only an inch or so high.

Work on the construction of steps should always start at the bottom and proceed upwards. If concrete is to be used as a surfacing material, 1-in. thick planks and pegs made from 2-in. square quartering should be used to form shuttering for the risers of each step. The step itself can be formed by floating the concrete level with it and smoothing with a builder's trowel. Curved steps in concrete can be made by using plywood in place of wood as the shuttering material, as it can be bent easily and evenly round stakes suitable driven in.

Brick used for step making should always be mortared and the same is true of paving slabs, but steps formed of flat-topped stones may go uncemented if well bedded down in sand or ashes. Such steps are often most suitable to use in the rock garden and other parts of the garden treated in a very natural manner.

Very good steps in a woodland setting can be formed by using untrimmed lengths of tree trunk as the risers, and beaten earth as the step itself. The trunks should be between 6 and 9 in. in diameter and as even as possible in size. They should be well bedded into the soil, and be still further secured by strong posts driven in firmly at each end in such a way as to hold the trunk back against the soil and prevent it from shifting forwards. The appearance of the steps can be greatly improved by suitable planting on each side and for this purpose ferns or shrubs of low-spreading habit, such as heathers, are often the most suitable.

STERILE A name given to any plant or flower which is incapable of producing seed or taking part in the production of seed. Thus the showy, bracted flowers of hydrangeas are sterile, producing neither ovules nor pollen. Some very double flowers are sterile because all the sex organs have been converted into additional petals.

There are certain plants which, though not sterile in this absolute sense, are only fully fertile in certain circumstances. For example, many of the sweet cherries, though they have flowers which appear normal in every respect and produce pollen-bearing anthers and pistils with ovules, are quite incapable of producing fruits when pollinated with their own pollen, and even fail when pollinated with pollen from certain other varieties of sweet cherry; yet with pollen from compatible varieties they prove completely fertile. This phenomenon is usually referred to as self-sterility. It is of great importance to the fruit grower, and much study has been devoted to it. In some fruit trees, notably apples and pears, there is a limited degree of fertility with some varieties when pollinated with their own pollen, but an increased degree of fertility when they are pollinated with pollen from

another variety of apple or pear, see Self-fertile.

Sterile is also sometimes used to describe soils of very low fertility and also to describe plant-growing media of various kinds, e.g. peat, sand and vermiculite, which are unlikely to contain any organisms harmful to plants.

STERILIZATION In gardens the term is frequently used to describe treatment applied to the soil, but in this connection it is a little misleading as complete sterilization is seldom carried out nor is it desirable. What is nearly always required is partial sterilization to destroy harmful organisms, including weed seeds, fungi and insects, but not carried so far as to rob the soil of all living organisms, particularly bacteria.

Broadly speaking, soil sterilization may be carried out in two distinct ways, by heat and by chemicals. In general, heat is more satisfactory as it is more universal in its application. Chemicals, by contrast, tend to be more selective. For example, two of the most popular chemicals used for soil sterilization are formalin and cresylic acid. Of these formalin is more effective against fungi in the concentrations normally used, whereas cresylic acid is more effective against insects. Heat, however, will destroy both fungi and insects with equal efficiency.

Sterilization by heat Soil can be heated by pouring hot water on it, by passing heated steam through it, by baking it in an oven or by passing an electric current through it. Of these the second and fourth are most satisfactory from the gardener's standpoint. Hot water is quickly cooled by contact with the soil and as a result sterilization obtained even by pouring boiling water on to the surface is extremely superficial. Steam, by contrast, penetrates to all parts of the soil and maintains its temperature far more effectively without making the soil sodden and so damaging its physical structure. Much elaborate apparatus is manufactured for the steam sterilization of soil on a large scale, but in the garden the work can be done quite efficiently by suspending a bag of soil in a boiler or other large vessel containing a few inches of water, bringing this to the boil, and placing a lid on top. The bag should be suspended just above the water so that the soil at no time becomes really wet, but is simply exposed to the steam. If the boiling is continued for approximately 20 minutes, the soil should be adequately sterilized. If larger quantities of soil or more elaborate apparatus are being dealt with, a soil thermometer may be used to check temperature. This should be plunged deeply into the soil and the temperature should be raised to about 93°C. and maintained at this for about 20 minutes. A considerably higher temperature or long treatment may result in too great a destruc-

tion of life, and make the soil sterile in the sense that it will no longer support plant life adequately.

Sterilization by baking is not very satisfactory as it is extremely difficult to avoid the charring of much useful organic matter.

Whenever soil is sterilized by heat, however carefully the work is done, it is found that there is a temporary falling off in the availability of certain plant foods, and this must be rectified by the addition of fertilizers. The various John Innes composts (see page 281) have been designed with this end in view.

Sterilization by chemicals Various proprietary chemicals are offered for the sterilization of soil and these should always be used strictly in accordance with the manufacturers' instructions. They will vary from one product to another. The four non-proprietary chemicals most commonly employed are cresylic acid, formalin, metham-sodium and dazomet. Cresylic acid can be purchased in varying strengths, that usually supplied for horticultural purposes being 97 to 99 per cent. of purity. This is diluted with 100 times its own volume of water, i.e. 1 pint of cresylic acid will need to be diluted with 100 pints (12½ gallons) of water. This is then applied to the soil from an ordinary watering-can fitted with a fine rose. The soil should be thoroughly soaked, which may mean applying 7 gallons of the solution to every square yard of soil. No plants or seed should be placed in the soil for at least a month after sterilization.

Formalin needs to be diluted with 49 times its own volume of water, i.e. 1 pint of formalin is diluted with 49 pints (approximately 6 gallons) of water. This is applied to the soil in the same manner as the diluted cresylic acid, with the difference that as soon as the soil has been soaked it should be covered with sacks or tarpaulins to trap the fumes given off by the formalin, as it is these fumes which are effective in producing sterilization. When comparatively small quantities of soil are to be dealt with, it is most convenient to spread the soil out thinly, water it with the diluted formalin, and then immediately throw it into a steep-sided heap and cover as described. The covering should be kept in position for at least 48 hours, after which it is removed and the soil which has been heaped should be spread out again so that the fumes can escape. Soil treated in this way should not be used for plants or seeds for at least three weeks, six weeks if it is heavy and so liable to hold the fumes.

Metham-sodium is used to kill eelworms and some soil-borne fungi. It is highly damaging to plants and so can only be used on vacant ground which should not be planted or sown for ten weeks after treatment. It is purchased as a fluid to be diluted according to instructions on the container and then watered on the soil until this is thoroughly wetted. Metham-sodium must not be allowed to get on the skin or into the eyes.

Dazomet is used for similar purposes and is purchased as a dust to be sprinkled on the soil and worked in to a depth of about one foot. Usual rate of application is 1lb. to 100 sq. ft. (or 7oz. per cu. yd. of soil) but instructions on the container should be followed. Treated soil should be covered with sacks or tarpaulins for three weeks, then uncovered and turned several times over a period of four or five weeks to allow fumes to escape before it is used.

Sterilization by electricity This method of sterilization is based on the fact that, if an electric current is passed through a substance which offers some resistance to it, heat will be generated. Soil offers such resistance and, moreover, the resistance of dry soil is considerably greater than that of wet soil. In consequence if two electrodes are separated by a volume of damp soil just sufficient to allow the current to pass through heat will be generated and the soil will gradually dry out. There will then come a stage at which the soil will be so dry that the resistance will be too great to allow current to pass any longer. The current will, in effect, be automatically switched off and no further heat will be generated. Most electrical soil sterilizers make use of these principles. They differ in detail, but essentially they consist of a box, made of some non-conducting material, with a plate electrode at each end. Damp soil is put in, the box is closed and current, usually at the normal domestic voltage of 250, is switched on. An ammeter on the box shows the flow of current and at first rises to the maximum figure at which the particular sterilizer is designed to work. Gradually the ampere reading drops and when it has fallen to zero sterilization is complete. The current supply is then disconnected and the box is opened and emptied.

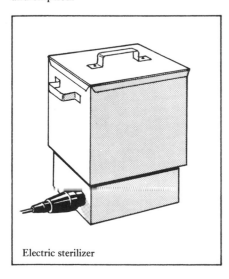

Electric sterilizer

STIGMA The end of the pistil, or female organ, of a flower on which pollen is retained. Usually the stigma becomes sticky when the flower is ready for pollination.

STIPE The leaf stalk of a fern.

STIPULE A leafy outgrowth at the base of the leaf stalk, sometimes with a small accessory bud in its axil, e.g. apple, oak.

STOCK A name given to that part of a grafted or budded plant which produces the roots, or to plants grown specifically for the purpose of providing roots for budding and grafting. Thus rose stocks are often seedlings of the common dog rose, *Rosa canina*, or rooted cuttings of *Rosa rugosa* or *Rosa polyantha*. Stocks for apple trees are nowadays generally of some form of Paradise apple, though at one time seedling crab apples were freely employed. Pears are frequently worked on stocks of quince or seedling pear. The wild gean (*Prunus avium*) is the common stock for cherries, while various plums, usually raised from layers or suckers, are used for stocks upon which to grow garden varieties of plums. Choice rhododendrons are often grafted on stocks of seedling *Rhododendron ponticum*. So the story might be continued for many other plants which are commonly increased by grafting or budding.

It is important to realize that though the tissues of stock and scion (that part of the graft or budded plant which produces the branches) normally remain entirely distinct, the stock can nevertheless influence the growth and behaviour of the scion in many ways. This is very clearly illustrated in the various Paradise stocks used for apples. Some of these tend to dwarf the varieties grown upon them, and to encourage very early maturity and heavy cropping. Others, by contrast, tend to produce much larger trees which reach maturity later in life, though they may continue to live longer than the dwarfed trees.

The influence of the stock on top growth is also clearly seen in roses. Varieties worked on *Rosa rugosa* tend to make a great deal of growth in the first few years, and to flower very freely, but the flowers are seldom of the same high quality, nor are the bushes, as a rule, as long lived as those on *Rosa canina*.

All these and many other matters must be considered when selecting stocks for any particular purpose. Sometimes it is not possible to get all varieties of one particular kind of plant to grow well on the same stock. A striking example of this is to be found with pears, some varieties of which will not make a proper union with the quince stock. This difficulty can be overcome by the process known as double-working, by which a variety that unites well with quince is first grafted to the stock and then the incompatible variety is grafted on to the compatible

one. The two operations can be carried out at the same time, and quite a short length of shoot of the compatible pear is sufficient.

It should be observed that all growths which emanate from the stock will be of the same character as the stock, even after this has been grafted or budded. It is, therefore, important to remove suckers from grafted plants, for if these are allowed to remain they may in time swamp the growth of the scion itself and leave the gardener with nothing but the stock, which is usually a wild form of inferior garden merit.

It may be asked why stocks should be employed at all. The answer is twofold, first, that there are some plants which it is difficult to propagate vegetatively by any means other than grafting or budding, and secondly, that the influence of the stock is often of real value to the gardener. This is certainly so with the dwarfing apple stocks to which reference has already been made, as, by using them, the gardener can produce small bushes or even single-stemmed cordon trees which will never make an excessive amount of growth, and will start to fruit in their second or third year in contrast to the twenty years which may be required by an unselected seedling. Such quick-fruiting dwarf trees have obvious uses in the garden.

STOCKHOLM TAR A special kind of tar obtained from pine trees which is of value as a dressing for wounds on trees and shrubs. Unlike ordinary tar it has no harmful effect on plant tissues. By sealing the wound completely it lessens the chance of infection by spores of harmful fungi or of attack by insects.

STOCK PLANTS Plants retained especially for the purpose of propagation. For example, in a nursery most of the plants will be for sale but some may be set aside as stock plants to provide seed, cuttings, layers, scions for grafting or budding or division. See Stool.

STOLON Any shoot which runs along the surface of the soil, forming roots as it goes. See Runner.

STOMATA The pores found on leaves, mainly on the under surface, which can open and close to control the amount of evaporation from the leaf.

STONE This word has two quite distinct uses in the garden. One is its purely literal meaning in connection with the stone used in building rock gardens, making dry walls, and paths and it is dealt with under these various headings in this book. But stone is also the name given to the seeds of some plants, notably fruits belonging to the prunus family such as plums, cherries, apricots, peaches and nectarines. Unless these seeds or stones are properly formed the fruits themselves do not come to perfection and so stoning, or the production of seeds, is an important feature of the development of these trees. Faulty stoning can be due to poor pollination of the blossom, lack of water in the soil, or to lack of mineral plant foods in the soil. At one time it was supposed that lime played a particularly important part in the production of the stones of these kinds of fruits but investigation has not substantiated this idea.

Although the seeds of grapes are not, strictly speaking, stones, the period in the development of the young grapes at which the seeds begin to harden is usually referred to as the stoning period, and again it is a time when careful management of the grape vines is essential. Lack of water, too low a temperature and insufficient ventilation can all cause trouble in stoning in greenhouse vines.

STONE CHIPPINGS Broken limestone, sandstone and occasionally granite are frequently used in the rock garden, either as topdressings or to mix with the soil, the object in both instances being to provide a greater degree of porosity for those plants that dislike having their roots or crowns wet. As a rule the chippings are of a size that would pass through a ½-in. mesh sieve, though occasionally larger chippings are used. They form an important ingredient of all scree and moraine mixtures (see Moraine). A surface layer of stone chippings not only improves drainage round the collar of the plant but also, paradoxically, keeps the soil beneath both cooler and moister than it would otherwise be. These twin factors will have the effect of encouraging root growth while discouraging decay around the crown.

Limestone chippings should only be used for those kinds of plants that tolerate free lime in the soil and they are unsuitable for lime-hating plants for which either sandstone or granite chippings should be used.

STOOL Any plant that is used solely or mainly for propagation. Thus the old roots

After flowering, chrysanthemum stools are boxed up to provide cuttings in late winter

of chrysanthemums after the blooms have been gathered are referred to as chrysanthemum stools, their main purpose then being to provide cuttings from which a stock of young plants can be produced for flowering the following year. A stool bed is a bed set apart for the growth of plants that are to be treated as stools, i.e. to provide cuttings or layers. Apple stocks are usually planted in stool beds with plenty of space between the rows, so that the young shoots can be pegged down to right and left and covered with soil so that they form roots. Such a bed of layered apple stocks is correctly referred to as a stool bed.

STOPPING The removal of the growing tip of a plant usually with the object of making it produce side branches, though sometimes the intention is quite literally to stop further growth of that shoot. Thus vine shoots are stopped a leaf or so beyond the point at which a cluster of flowers appears and any subsidiary growths that appear are stopped at the first or second leaf.

Stopping is applied to a great many plants, particularly those of a herbaceous character, but is of primary importance in the cultivation of chrysanthemums and perpetual flowering carnations. In both these

instances it is used partly to decide the time at which flowers shall be produced and partly to control their number. The first blooms of carnations are usually produced about six months after the last stopping, so that if young plants have their growing points removed in April and again towards the end of July, the first blossoms may be expected the following January or February, the precise date varying according to the amount of warmth given during the winter months.

Chrysanthemum varieties vary a good deal in their response to stopping, some varieties producing flower buds within eight or ten weeks of stopping and others taking considerably longer. By studying individual behaviour and by adjusting the stopping dates accordingly, the chrysanthemum grower can exercise a measure of control over the time at which his plants are in bloom, and this can be of great importance in the cultivation of chrysanthemums for exhibition.

By stopping a chrysanthemum or carnation several times it can be made to produce more branches than it would otherwise do and therefore makes a bushier plant carrying more flowers. Many seedling plants, such as wallflowers and antirrhinums, are stopped or pinched solely to make them branch quickly and form bushier plants.

Stopping, in the case of the chrysanthemum, has yet a fourth function: the control of the type of flower bud produced and consequently the number of petals and the character of the bloom. If a young plant is stopped once and then the first flower buds that appear, known as first crown buds, are allowed to develop, the resultant flowers will contain more petals than they would if the plants were stopped twice, when second crown buds would be produced. A third stopping would result in the formation of terminal buds with even fewer petals. Though frequently a large number of petals per bloom is desirable, this is not invariably so. There are some varieties which produce better-formed flowers when

1. *A young carnation plant is stopped when it has about eight pairs of leaves*

2. *This is done by carefully removing the growing tip*

3. *The removal of the tip encourages the growth of side shoots*

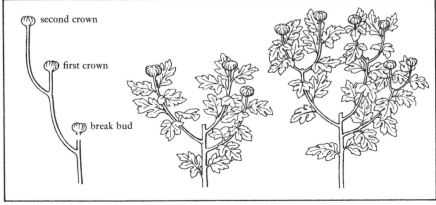

Stopping in chrysanthemums selects the type of flower bud. First crown buds appear after removal of the break bud, and second crown buds if first crown buds are removed

stopped twice and so forced to produce second crown buds.

Stopping is usually carried out by pinching out the tip of each stem between the first finger and thumb, although some gardeners prefer to use a knife, and, in carnations, stopping is effected by breaking the shoot off at a joint.

STORAGE ROTS Various diseases attack fruits or roots while they are in store and are therefore known as storage rots. Dry rot of potatoes is a familiar example. Careful selection of healthy roots or fruits, airy and hygienic conditions in the store shed and frequent inspection to remove infected specimens will help to keep down such troubles.

STORE Any shed, room, cellar etc. set apart as a place in which to keep fruits, vegetables, tubers or bulbous roots. In general such stores should be cool but frost-proof, dry but not drying. Ventilation is required, but it should not be too free, just a slow movement of air to prevent stagnation. In a heavy, damp atmosphere moulds or other fungi are likely to flourish on the stored fruits or roots. Many tubers are susceptible to frost damage in store, and this is true of potatoes, begonias, gloxinias and dahlias. Even a degree or so of frost penetrating to the roots for an hour or so may do them damage, while over-chilling without actual freezing may have an adverse effect on subsequent growth, though the tubers are not themselves obviously damaged by it.

Exception to the rule of a dry and reasonably airy store must be made for apples, which keep best in a rather damp atmosphere. The ideal for most fruits is a shed with a concrete, brick or wooden floor, but for an apple store a floor of beaten earth is to be preferred, as this will hold more moisture and so prevent fruits from shrivelling unduly. Where it is impossible to provide a store of this type, apples may be kept quite satisfactorily by packing them, about four

layers deep, in boxes and standing these one on top of the other so that circulation of air is reduced. The old-fashioned plan of storing apples in single layers on open slat shelves is convenient, but not really conducive to long keeping. This kind of airy storage is, however, ideal for pears.

The more equable the temperature within the store the better, and for this reason specially built store sheds are often provided with roofs of thick thatch. Failing this a lining of thick wallboard is useful in a store shed.

STOVEHOUSE Any greenhouse in which a fairly high temperature is maintained throughout the year. Though no arbitrary ruling can be given, it is usual for stovehouses to be maintained at a temperature of 21 to 27°C. in spring and summer, and a minimum of 18°C. in winter. Such houses are used for the cultivation of tropical plants.

STRAIN All plants that are raised from seed show a certain amount of variation and this is true even of so-called pure-breeding varieties, such as named varieties of sweet pea or onion. Unless special care is taken in

selection, this natural variation will tend to increase and the character of the original variety may deteriorate in consequence. As some seed producers will take more trouble than others in selecting their seed parents, or may pay greater attention to particular characteristics, small differences will appear in the same variety purchased from two or three different sources. These variations are known as strains. In consequence, Mr. A's strain of onion Ailsa Craig may be markedly different from Mr. B's strain of the same onion, and not infrequently one strain is to be preferred to another. The term is purely a horticultural one, and is not used by botanists or recognized in the international code of nomenclature. Even in vegetatively propagated plants small differences of character may creep in, owing to minor mutations or to the effect of disease and other outside causes. This can often be seen quite clearly in stocks of chrysanthemums. If plants of the same variety are obtained from two different sources, one batch may be considerably better than the other, and this superiority may be maintained even when the plants are grown under identical conditions for several years. It is legitimate to refer to this kind of variation as a difference in strain.

In order to keep a good strain in being it is essential to save seed or select cuttings only from those plants which conform in every detail to the best characteristics of the strain.

STRATIFICATION A term used by gardeners for the practice of exposing seeds to frost to hasten or improve germination. Some seeds germinate much better after a period of stratification than without it. This is true of hard-coated seeds of some hardy plants including numerous trees and shrubs. Seeds to be stratified are frequently placed in shallow pans or boxes and covered with sand, after which they are placed out of doors in a fairly exposed position and left there throughout the winter without any

If apples are to be stored for several months, each fruit may be wrapped in paper before it is placed in the box. This helps to prevent the spread of disease

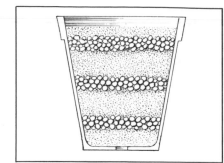

Stratification of seeds in sand

protection. The following spring the seeds are sown in the ordinary way, either out of doors or in boxes or pans of soil. When seeds are stratified in this way, it is often wise to protect the boxes or pans from the attacks of mice and this may be done by placing fine-mesh wire netting over them.

STRATUM A layer of rock. In many natural formations the rock is in superimposed layers referred to as strata. These layers usually follow the same plane which may be anything from horizontal to vertical according to the degree of subterranean pressure to which the rock has been subjected. Limestone and sandstone are typical stratified rocks and when they are used for rock garden construction it is desirable that the impression of stratification should be maintained by setting the rocks to simulate superimposed layers.

STRAW Wheat, oat or barley straw is useful to the gardener to improve drainage and aeration, to improve the texture of his soil, to add plant foods to it and also as a protective material. For the first purpose straw may be dug in exactly as it is obtained, or it may be inserted vertically in the soil. Vertical straw walls in the soil have been found particularly useful in the cultivation of tomatoes under glass. There are two ways of getting straw into the soil vertically; one to apply it during the ordinary process of digging or half-trenching, when a thick wall

of straw is laid as nearly vertical as possible against the face of each trench as it is completed, and then the soil from the next trench is thrown against it; the other is to make a V-shaped cut in the soil to the full depth of a spade, lay straw across this cut and push it in with a spade. Such walls have a marked effect on drainage and aeration if they are spaced not more than a yard apart.

When straw is dug directly into the ground, care should be taken to mix it with the soil as thoroughly as possible and not leave it in thick layers, as these may remain undecayed for a considerable period and actually hinder rather than help drainage. It is really best that the straw should be chopped before it is dug in. Fresh straw has little manurial effect – indeed it may actually depress the fertility of the soil for a time by lowering the amount of nitrogen available. This can be overcome by first composting the straw, either with green refuse and dung, or with chemicals. (See Compost.) Well-composted straw may have almost as high a manurial value as farmyard or stable manure and can be dug in in exactly the same way and at similar rates.

As a protective material straw may be used to keep out frost, as, for instance, in a potato clamp (see Clamp), to keep off rain when used as a thatch, or to prevent damage from bruising or splashing, by being spread beneath fruit trees or round strawberry plants. It often pays to place a thick layer of straw beneath varieties of apples, such as Beauty of Bath, which are prone to sudden heavy fruit drop before they are fully ripe, as the straw will prevent bruising and enable many of the windfalls to be picked up undamaged. Straw used for strawberry beds should be clean and fresh; old or damp straw may contain fungi which will prove harmful to the fruits.

STRAWBERRY BLOSSOM WEEVIL A small and active weevil very similar to the strawberry leaf weevil, which attacks the blossom stems, cutting them through and causing them to fall off. The remedy is to

A strig of black currants

dust with derris or carbaryl as soon as damage is observed.

STRAWBERRY LEAF WEEVIL This very small and active weevil chews the stems of both strawberry leaves and fruits, causing these to break as a result. It is often very difficult to discover the weevils themselves as they hide when disturbed, but the damage they cause is distinctive. The remedy is to dust with derris or carbaryl as soon as any damage is noted and to repeat every 10 days or so.

STRAW MATS Mats about a foot square with a central hole and used as protection for strawberry plants in place of the more conventional straw. One mat is placed round each plant. If removed as soon as the crop has been gathered and stored in a dry place the mats will last for several seasons.

STREAK A general name given to several diseases caused by viruses all of which produce sunken brown or blackish spots and streaks on stems, leaves and, in tomatoes, the fruits. Plants are weakened and may eventually be killed. Streak is common in tomatoes and sweet peas. It is spread by sucking insects such as greenfly and also on the blades of knives used for removing side shoots. Affected plants should be removed and burned. Sucking insects should be killed by spraying with effective insecticides such as lindane, malathion, menazon and dimethoate. Pruning knives should be sterilized with lysol. Plants which have an adequate supply of potash often escape injury, so it is desirable to give a dressing of potash fertilizer prior to planting tomatoes or sweet peas.

STRIG A complete cluster of fruits of a currant, whether black, red or white.

STRIKE A garden term used to denote the rooting of a cutting. Thus to strike a cutting is to treat it in such a way as to induce it to form roots, and a struck cutting is one that has formed roots. The term is also used for a

Straw used to protect strawberries from being splashed by rain and mud

dry measure; in this sense a strike is equal to two bushels.

STUB This term is not much used nowadays in gardening, but has survived in its adjectival form, stubbing. A stub is the stump of a tree left after felling, and a grubbing mattock is a tool used to grub out such stubs.

STUMP, see Stub

STYLE The stem of the pistil or female organ of a flower which joins the stigma to the ovary.

SUB-SHRUB, see Suffruticose

SUBSOIL That part of the soil which lies immediately beneath the surface soil. This is not a question of depth but of character, for there is always a marked difference in the appearance and the texture of the subsoil and that of the surface soil. Thus with soil on a chalk down there may be only two or three inches of surface soil, comparatively dark in colour and containing the roots of grasses and other herbs. Below this relatively fertile soil lies a solid bed of chalk. By contrast, in some river valleys where the soil is alluvial in character there may be several feet of surface soil of uniform texture before there is any marked change in character and the subsoil begins. The way to discover the depth, position and character of the subsoil is to dig a deep trench with at least one clean vertical face on which the character of the soil can be studied. The fertility of the surface soil may depend to a considerable extent on the character of the subsoil. Thus if the subsoil is stiff clay, drainage will be impeded and the surface soil will be liable to become cold, waterlogged and sour. By contrast a gravel subsoil will encourage quick drainage and a dry warm surface, but by allowing water to pass through so freely may cause considerable leaching of valuable plant food from the surface soil.

Subsoil is seldom as fertile as surface soil but its fertility can often be improved if it is broken up and manure or compost added to it. Part of the value of deep cultivation lies in the improvement of the subsoil in this manner.

SUBTROPICAL A term which has no precise definition but is used in gardens to describe those plants which come from regions near to the tropics of Cancer and Capricorn, and which in gardens require intermediate greenhouse rather than hot house treatment. Many subtropical plants can be placed out of doors for the summer months, but all are injured by more than a degree or so of frost.

SUCCULENT A term applied to all plants with thick, fleshy leaves or with thickened or fleshy stems which take the place of leaves. The cacti comprise one group of succulent plants characterized by certain botanical features which bring them within the family *Cactaceae*. Many succulent plants are found wild in regions which are subject to long periods of drought, and the succulent habit is of benefit to the plants by enabling them to withstand such periods without undue loss of moisture. It is not true, however, that succulents require to be kept comparatively dry all the year round, for they must have periods of fairly abundant moisture in which they can replenish their stores of sap. Very often in partly desert regions there is heavy rainfall for a time. In cultivation it is usually desirable to water succulents fairly freely while they make their growth and to give them some moisture even during the dormant season.

SUCKER Any growth which comes direct from the roots of a plant or from the stock of a grafted or budded plant may be called a sucker. Suckers on grafted and budded plants have a special importance as they will resemble the character of the rootstock and not of the scion which has been grafted or budded upon it. If such suckers are allowed to remain, the plant will have two distinct types of top growth, and as stocks are frequently more vigorous than the plants worked upon them, the suckers will in time tend to smother the scion growth and kill it altogether. Many bushes of *Rosa rugosa* to be seen in neglected gardens have arisen in this way, the garden rose having originally been budded on *rugosa* stock and the latter having been allowed to produce suckers indiscriminately until eventually the garden rose was destroyed, and only the suckers remained. Suckers from grafted or budded plants should, therefore, always be removed at the earliest possible opportunity. Care should be taken to cut them off cleanly, close to the roots from which they grow or to the stem of the rootstock if they grow from this on plants which have been grafted

If it is necessary to remove a sucker from a rose, draw away the soil and cut the sucker off at its point of origin

or budded above ground level. If any stumps are left, fresh suckers are likely to be produced from them. Frequently suckering is caused in the first instance by bruising the roots through careless soil cultivation. A callus forms over each wound and from this callus adventitious buds and eventually sucker growths are produced.

Suckers produced by plants which are growing on their own roots, as distinct from grafted or budded plants, are not harmful in the same way since they are of the same character as the rest of the plant and may serve to extend it. Such suckers are sometimes of value as a means of propagating the plant. The suckers can be detached with a few roots and planted on their own to form new specimens. This kind of propagation is commonly used for raspberries and also such ornamental shrubs as *Rhus typhina* and bamboos.

SUCKER, APPLE A small insect, closely allied to greenfly and not unlike it in appearance, which attacks the unopened or opening blossoms of apples. At first this insect is creamy white and wingless, but later it becomes green and develops a pair of transparent wings. It produces a whitish waxy substance in the form of globules or threads. This pest must not be confused with the maggots of the apple blossom weevil which also attack apple flowers, but in this instance cause them to become capped, i.e. covered by the brown unexpanded petals. Apple sucker is destroyed by spraying with tar oil in January or DNC in early March; and also by spraying with lindane, dimethoate or malathion and soft soap just before the blossom opens and again when it has fallen.

SUFFRUTICOSE A term used to describe perennial plants (sometimes known as sub-shrubs) in which the upper part is soft and herbaceous, but the lower part is woody. The wallflower is a familiar example.

SULPHATE OF AMMONIA A chemical fertilizer which supplies nitrogen to the soil. It is readily soluble, quick in action, and most suitable for application during the spring or summer months. An overdose can produce severe scorching of leaves and stems. In consequence, sulphate of ammonia is sometimes used as a weedkiller on lawns as it tends to slip off the erect and narrow blades of grass but to lie on the broader and flatter leaves of daisies, plantains, etc. and scorch them. For this purpose it is usually mixed with sand and sulphate of iron, the former ingredient to enable the sulphate of ammonia to be spread evenly and the latter to kill toadstools and other fungi. The proportions usually recommended for this purpose are: sulphate of ammonia 3 parts by weight, sulphate of iron 1 part by weight, fine silver sand 20 parts by weight. These ingredients should be mixed thoroughly, kept dry and used at the rate of 4oz. per sq. yd. during dry weather, in spring or summer. This mixture is usually referred to as lawn sand. Sulphate of ammonia as a fertilizer is used at rates from ½ to 1oz. per sq. yd. Sulphate of ammonia can be mixed with most other fertilizers except those containing lime. Analysis is 20.6 per cent. nitrogen.

SULPHATE OF COPPER, see Copper Sulphate

SULPHATE OF IRON

A chemical sometimes used as a fertilizer and sometimes as a fungicide. Iron is one of the essential plant foods but it is usually present in the soil in sufficient quantity for the needs of plants. When lacking there may be considerable yellowing of the foliage though similar symptoms are also caused by lack of magnesium. Iron deficiency is most likely to occur in soils that are heavily supplied with calcium carbonate. It is then not so much that there is actual shortage of iron, as that the iron is rendered unavailable by the presence of the calcium carbonate. When these conditions exist the application of sulphate of iron or other iron salt to the soil has little beneficial effect, as the fresh supplies are promptly locked up once more by the calcium carbonate. Some benefit may be obtained by spraying the foliage of the plants with a solution of sulphate of iron at the rate of ½ to 1oz. per gallon of water, but a more effective method is to make use of iron chelates or iron sequestrol (see Sequestrol). Even more lasting effects can be produced by correcting alkalinity of the soil due to excess of calcium carbonate.

As a fungicide, sulphate of iron is principally used for the destruction of toadstools and other fungi on lawns, for which purpose it is either mixed with sulphate of ammonia and sand (see Sulphate of Ammonia), or applied as a solution at the rate of 4oz. per gallon of water, the soil being freely wetted with this solution from an ordinary watering-can fitted with a fine rose.

SULPHATE OF MAGNESIUM (Epsom Salts)

Magnesium is one of the essential plant foods and is usually present in the soil in sufficient quantity for the needs of plants. Where it is lacking, considerable yellowing of the foliage may occur, particularly between veins of the leaves, but somewhat similar symptoms can be caused by iron deficiency. (See Sulphate of Iron.) When magnesium is in short supply the deficiency can be rectified either by dressing the soil with sulphate of magnesium or by spraying the foliage during the summer months with a solution of sulphate of magnesium. For the first purpose the chemical is used at the rate of 1oz. per sq. yd., for the latter it is dissolved in water at 2 to 3oz. per gallon and applied to the plants as a fine spray. Late

winter or early spring is the most suitable time for soil application; late spring or early summer for application as a spray.

SULPHATE OF POTASH

The most valuable potash fertilizer for use in the garden. Sulphate of potash contains 48 per cent. of potash and is used at rates varying from ½ to 1oz. per sq. yd. It can be mixed with most other fertilizers including sulphate of ammonia and superphosphate of lime. It is usually the best form in which to add potash to compound fertilizers. It dissolves readily in water and in this form can be used as liquid manure at the strength of ½ to 1oz. per gallon. It can be used at any time of the year.

SULPHUR

In one form or another sulphur is valuable as a fungicide for the control of plant diseases caused by fungi. It is also occasionally used to decrease the alkalinity of soils though this cannot be recommended when this is due to lime or chalk, as it usually is in the British Isles, since calcium sulphate may then be formed in the soil with possible damaging effects on plant growth. Various preparations of sulphur are used as fungicides, including lime sulphur (q.v.), colloidal sulphur and flowers of sulphur. The last named is employed as a dust (which can be obtained coloured green, so that it does not show too much on the leaves) without the addition of any carrying or spreading agent, and is particularly valuable for the control of mildew and similar diseases under glass. It can be dusted on foliage and even fruits without causing

Dusting a cyclamen with flowers of sulphur

injury. It has the added advantage that it does not affect the humidity of the greenhouse in which it is applied, as might occur if a spray were used. Sulphur has also some value as an insecticide, particularly against red spider and similar mites. See Fumigation.

SULPHUR-COPPER DUST

A mixture of sulphur and copper sometimes used as a

fungicide for dry application to the leaves or stems of plants. It is prepared by mixing 10 parts by bulk of hydrated lime, 3 parts of flowers of sulphur and 3 parts of finely powdered copper sulphate. This mixture has been recommended for use against foot rot disease of all kinds, for which purpose it is sprinkled on the lower part of the stems of plants liable to be attacked.

SUMMER PRUNING

Any pruning done during the months of June, July or August. The purpose of summer pruning is usually to check the vigour of trees and shrubs and to encourage the formation of flower buds. See Pruning.

SUN BLIND, see Blinds

SUNDIAL

Once the only reliable method of telling the time, the sundial has now become principally a decorative object in the garden. Nevertheless, even when used purely in this way, it is preferable that sundials should be properly constructed and set in the correct manner so that they do fulfil their purpose as time indicators. To do this the first thing is to discover the latitude of the district in which the garden is situated. For example, the latitude of London is 51½ and that of Paisley 55¾. Draw a vertical line down the centre of the sundial plate, from north to south. About two-thirds down this line draw another line across the plate at right angles, from west to east. Mark a spot on this line (x on the drawing) one-third of the distance between the left-hand side of the plate and the point where the two lines meet (o). From this spot draw a line in a north-easterly direction at an angle to the west–east line equal to the degrees of latitude (e.g. 51½ for London). This diagonal line should extend up to the north–south line (y). This diagonal should now be divided in half, and from the centre point (a) a line drawn at right angles to it in a south-easterly direction. This new line (ab) should be half the length of the diagonal (xy). Its extremity (b) should now be joined with the ends of the diagonal line, so forming two right-angle triangles (abx and aby) with one line (ab) common to each. Using this common line (ab) as a radius, draw an arc (cd) from bx to by and then divide this arc into five equal parts. Using a protractor with bx as the base line the angles will be 18°, 36°, 54° and 72°.

Lines drawn from the centre point (o) (where the north–south and west–east lines cross) through these division marks on the arc will give the 11, 10, 9 and 8 o'clock points on the edge of the plate. The 7 o'clock point is obtained by drawing a line through oc. The 6, 7, 8 and 9 o'clock marks on the east side of the plate are obtained by extending through o lines from the 7, 8, 9 and 10 o'clock marks already made on the west side. The remaining hour marks (3, 4,

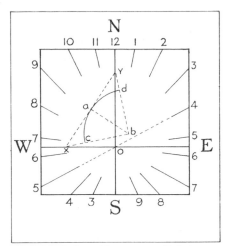

The method of marking out a sundial plate

5 and 6 o'clock) on the west side, are made by reproducing the spacing of the 6, 7, 8 and 9 o'clock marks on the east side. Lines drawn from the 3, 4, 5 and 6 o'clock marks on the west side through 0 will give the 2, 3, 4 and 5 marks on the east side. The 1 o'clock mark on the east side is obtained by measuring the space between 12 o'clock and 11 and reproducing this.

The gnomon or shadow caster should be about one third of the length of the north–south line and the angle it makes from the horizontal should be that of the latitude. It should be placed at right angles to the dial along the 12 (N) line.

Note that the west–east line is discarded after the hour marks have been made.

These instructions apply to the northern hemisphere only and must be reversed for the southern hemisphere.

SUPERPHOSPHATE OF LIME A phosphoric fertilizer which is of great value because of its ready solubility in water, and the speed with which it produces an effect on plants. It can be mixed with many other fertilizers and is the form of phosphate most commonly used in compound fertilizers. Despite its name it contains no free lime, and is valueless to improve the condition of soils which are too acid. Because of its ready solubility it is most suitable for application in spring or early summer. It is a fine greyish powder which is apt to clog and cake if it becomes damp. If scattered carelessly on young foliage it may cause some scorching. Superphosphate of lime varies considerably in analysis, the lowest grades containing about 13 per cent. of soluble phosphoric acid and the best grades 18 per cent. The analysis is sometimes quoted in terms of phosphate of lime which gives a figure 2.18 times greater than the quotation in terms of phosphoric acid. For instance, a sample of phosphoric acid described as containing 40 per cent. phosphate of lime is the equivalent of a sample described as containing 18 per cent. phosphoric acid. Super-

phosphate of lime is applied at rates varying from 1 to 3 oz. per sq. yd. or, if dissolved in water, at $\frac{1}{2}$ to 1 oz. per gallon.

SUSPENSIONS Some chemicals useful as insecticides or fungicides are not soluble in water but can be prepared as very fine powders which, when well stirred into water, remain for some time more or less evenly suspended in the water, in which condition they are known as suspensions and can be applied as sprays. It is necessary to keep such suspensions well agitated while they are being applied, otherwise there will be a tendency for the chemical to settle and form a sediment in the bottom of the container. See Wettable Powders.

SWAP HOOK, see Sickle

SYMBIOSIS The partnership of two living organisms for the benefit of both. Thus many orchids are dependent upon certain fungi for part of their food supply and the fungi in turn obtain some of their food from the orchids. A similar partnership may be observed between rhododendrons and soil fungi. The nodules found on the roots of many leguminous plants, such as beans, peas and clover, contain bacteria which are useful to the plants because they can fix nitrogen from the air. Sometimes the gardener can take active steps to promote such symbiotic association, either by introducing the necessary organism or by producing in the soil conditions which favour those organisms.

SYNONYM An alternative name. In botany many plants have at different times been known by different names and it is part of the systematic botanist's task to discover which is the correct name. Others may be listed as synonyms.

SYRINGE Syringes of various kinds are used both for the application of insecticides and fungicides and also for damping the foliage of plants and maintaining a moist

Spraying greenhouse plants to create a moist atmosphere

atmosphere in the greenhouse or frame. The syringe should be made of brass or plastic and be supplied with at least two alternative nozzles – one giving a fine mist-like spray, and the other a heavier and more wetting spray. A third nozzle, giving a solid jet is also useful.

Syringing can be an important item in the management of greenhouse plants, also of cuttings in the propagating frame. By keeping the foliage damp, loss of moisture by evaporation is cut down to a minimum, without wetting the soil heavily at the same time. This is often essential in the care of plants that like a moist atmosphere but do not appreciate a very wet soil. In some instances where it is not advisable to wet the foliage directly because this might cause decay or sun scalding, the syringe is used on the paths and stagings of the greenhouse to keep these thoroughly damp and so increase the humidity of the atmosphere. See Damping Down.

SYSTEMIC A term applied to certain chemicals which enter the sap of the plants to which they are applied instead of remaining on the outside. Some insecticides such as menazon, dimethoate, schradan and formothion are of this character and have several advantages over corresponding non-systemic insecticides. For one thing only those insects are destroyed which actually feed on the sap or tissues of the plant or are hit by the chemical when it is being applied. Useful insects are not at great risk. Another advantage of the systemic insecticide is that it is more readily spread all through the plants as it goes wherever the sap goes. However, there is considerable difference in the freedom of movement of different systemic chemicals and also, sometimes, of the same chemicals in different plants. External applications, by contrast, may miss many parts of the plant they are meant to protect. A third merit is that such insecticides cannot be washed off by rain, though as a rule they do disintegrate within the plant, some more rapidly than others.

A drawback of some systemic insecticides is that they are poisonous to warm-blooded animals (including human beings), as well as to insects. As they are within the plant it is impossible to get rid of them by wiping or washing and even cooking may not remove them.

There is also a range of systemic fungicides, including benomyl, chloraniformethan and thiophanate-methyl. These are especially useful against the fungal diseases black spot and powdery mildew.

Some weedkillers are systemic, notable examples being paraquat and diquat, both of which not only enter into the sap of the plant but also undergo chemical changes within the plant which bring about its death. Again they have the advantage of being unaffected by rain and of passing through the plant even when only applied to part of it.

2,4-D An abbreviation used for 2:4 dichlorophenoxyacetic acid, a chemical which acts as a plant hormone and, applied in excess, is a useful selective weedkiller to destroy weeds on lawns. It is obtainable in various commercial formulations which should be diluted with water according to manufacturers' instructions and applied as a spray or through a sprinkle bar.

2,4,5-T A selective weedkiller particularly useful for the destruction of woody plants such as brambles and scrub. It is also used as a nettle killer. 2,4,5-T is purchased as a liquid for dilution with water and application as a spray or from a watering-can fitted with a sprinkle bar. It is most effective if applied to the young growth. Manufacturers' instructions regarding dilution must be followed. It is often mixed with 2,4-D to give effective control of a wider range of weeds.

TAKE This term is used in two different senses. In one it is synonymous with strike or root, so that a cutting is said to have taken when it has formed roots. In the other sense it is used by chrysanthemum growers to describe the selection of buds which are to produce flowers. Those buds which are selected or retained are then said to have been taken, a somewhat confusing use of a word which might be supposed to mean that the buds have been removed.

TAP ROOT Strictly speaking the first root produced by a seedling which is usually undivided and which plunges straight down into the soil, but the term is also used more loosely to denote any strong root growing downwards. With some plants it is natural for the first root to continue its course unchecked, and occasionally, as in the carrot and parsnip, this is an important feature of the plant from the standpoint of its garden utility. In other instances it is natural for a root to branch after a time to

A typical tap root

produce further roots which spread horizontally in the soil. Occasionally it may be desirable to force this branching of the tap root before it would naturally occur. Many gardeners believe that this is so with most brassicas and allied plants such as wallflowers and they consider transplanting the seedlings of these plants as important, not only because seedlings are thereby given more space, but also because, in transplanting, the tap root is broken and the plant is forced to produce branch roots. It is widely believed that plants with tap roots tend to make coarser and more vigorous growth than those with roots of a more branching character, though it is by no means certain that this is true. Nevertheless, because of this belief it is often advised that, if fruit trees make gross shoots and refuse to fruit, the soil should be excavated round the trunk and any tap roots found should be severed, only the horizontal or nearly horizontal roots being retained.

TAR Coal tar is serviceable in the garden as a preservative for wood but it should not be brought into contact with living plants, though it is by no means so damaging to these as is its near ally creosote. See also Stockholm Tar.

TAR DISKS A device sometimes used to protect cabbage and allied plants from the cabbage root fly. The disks are circular pieces of tarred felt slit to a small hole in the centre so that each can be opened, slipped round the stem of a brassica seedling and then pressed firmly on the surface of the soil. Disks are usually about 3 in. in diameter and their value is due to the fact that they prevent the female flies from laying their eggs in the soil near the base of the plant.

TAR DISTILLATE A general term applied to various substances obtained by distilling tar, but in garden usage the term is generally applied to those distillates which are employed in the preparation of tar oil winter washes for fruit trees.

TAR OIL WASH A preparation of tar distillates which is valuable for application to fruit trees in winter, principally to kill the eggs of various insects particularly aphids, but also to destroy scale insects and hibernating caterpillars, and to rid the bark of algae, lichens and other unwanted growths. Tar oil winter washes are prepared both as oils which will mix with water and as emulsions, and with all these manufacturers' instructions regarding strength and mixing should be followed. The standard strength for fruit trees is usually $2\frac{1}{2}$ pints to 5 gallons of water. Tar oil washes are all very caustic to foliage and so can only be applied with safety while the trees are completely dormant. If used in orchards with a covering of grass they will usually cause con-

Spraying an apple tree with tar oil wash

siderable browning of the grass but it generally recovers quickly. It is desirable that tar oil washes should be applied in the form of a spray at considerable pressure, partly because the pressure will help to drive the spray into the crevices of the bark in which eggs are most likely to be, and partly because it helps to break the emulsion and so allow the tar oil to come into direct contact with the eggs or insects which are to be destroyed.

TARRED TWINE Twine that has been steeped in tar, or one of the tar distillates, to make it resistant to decay. Tarred twine can be purchased in various thicknesses and is a serviceable material for use where the ties must remain in good condition for a considerable period.

TARSONEMID MITES Several related pests are known by this general name, all similar to red spider mites in appearance and related to them. They attack many different kinds of plant including strawberries, begonias, cyclamen and fuchsias. The mites vary in colour from near white to light brown. They are found on the undersides of the leaves from which they suck the juice, causing them to curl up and become discoloured with purplish spots or blotches. Eventually the leaves become very brittle. Flower buds may be destroyed or become distorted. Tarsonemid mites can be destroyed by spraying with dicofol, or nicotine and soft soap, or by dusting with flowers of sulphur, or spraying with lime sulphur, though lime sulphur cannot be used with safety on greenhouse plants. With strawberries, plants may be sprayed with winter-strength lime sulphur in April, and young plants prior to planting may be immersed for 20 minutes in water at 43eC.

TAXONOMY The study of the classification of plants. See Botany and Classification.

TCNB, see Tecnazene

TECNAZENE (TCNB) A fungicide used to control dry rot in potatoes and botrytis on some greenhouse plants. For potatoes it is applied as a dust at ½lb. per cwt. when the tubers are stored. They must be covered at once with straw, sacks or tarpaulins. The treatment also retards the sprouting of the tubers. Under glass tecnazene is used as a smoke for tomatoes, lettuces, chrysanthemums and ornamental plants. Manufacturers' instructions regarding strength must be followed.

TEMPERATURE In the case of every seed or plant there is a minimum and maximum temperature below and above which it suffers injury; a minimum temperature below which growth ceases though the plant is not injured, and an optimum temperature at which growth is most rapid. Obviously it is an essential part of the gardener's art to know approximately what these temperatures are with respect to every plant which he proposes to cultivate. There are not many seeds which germinate at temperatures below 7°C., and the majority of seeds of greenhouse or half-hardy plants require temperatures between 13 and 21°C. to ensure germination. Most plants from temperate regions grow freely in temperatures between 10 and 21°C. Plants from tropical regions usually require temperatures between 18 and 27°C. for rapid growth. These are general figures to which many exceptions would have to be recorded.

Plants can become accustomed to temperatures considerably different from those to which they would normally be exposed, and, having become so accustomed, may be damaged by temperatures which they could normally have endured. It is for this reason that comparatively hardy plants which have been grown for a period in the greenhouse become more tender than they would normally be, and must be accustomed by gentle stages to ordinary outdoor conditions. By contrast, some plants which, when first introduced to this country appear to be too tender to be grown out of doors during the winter, gradually become acclimatized (probably by a process of selection of the hardier seedlings produced) and eventually can be left out of doors with safety, except during the most severe winters.

Exceptionally high temperatures can do quite as much damage as low ones, and one important item in the management of greenhouse plants in the summer is to prevent the temperature from reaching excessive heights during spells of very bright sunshine. Shading, ventilation and syringing all help to prevent these damaging temperatures being reached.

TENDER A rather vague term used in several different ways when applied to plants. Perhaps the best definition of a tender plant would be one that is injured by frost, but in many instances plants are said to be tender when they will not stand out of doors without protection in an ordinary winter. Such plants may be able to withstand a few degrees of frost, but will succumb when the temperature reaches those lower levels which are commonly experienced at some time during the winter in that place. Degree of susceptibility to frost may differ quite a lot according to the stage of growth and the conditions under which the plant has been grown. Thus young growth is usually more tender than old growth as a result of which spring frosts are usually more damaging than autumn or winter frosts. Also it is usually considered that shoots or leaves which are very full of moisture are more likely to be injured than those that are less turgid. In consequence, it is often advised that tender plants grown in poorly heated greenhouses should be kept rather dry during cold weather.

TENDRIL Thin, usually spiral, organs produced by some plants as an aid to climbing. Tendrils may be modified leaves or leaflets or modified leaf stalks or shoots. They are all very sensitive to contact, with the result that they twine round any suitable support. Familiar examples of plants which produce tendrils are peas, passion flowers and grape vines.

Tendril

TENT CATERPILLARS The caterpillars of some species of moth and sawfly live in colonies and protect themselves within tent-like webs of silken threads similar to those woven by spiders. Such caterpillars are usually vulnerable to the insecticides such as derris and trichlorphon which are used against caterpillars in general, but it is desirable to take steps to destroy the webs themselves either by removing them by hand or by burning them out with a blow-lamp. The lackey moth, the ermine moths and the social pear sawfly have web-forming caterpillars.

TEPAL The individual segment of any flower in which there is no clear distinction between sepals and petals. The term is most commonly used in describing the flowers of magnolias and of the amaryllis family *Amaryllidaceae*.

TERMINAL The end bud, shoot or flower, in contradistinction to lateral (side) or axillary (in the angle between a leaf and stem).

TERRACE Strictly speaking a raised but level place. In gardens the term is usually applied to level spaces created from naturally sloping ground. It is important when terracing is carried out, first to remove the surface soil and stack it in some convenient place, after which the necessary alterations in level can be made by moving the subsoil. When this has been completed the surface soil is returned and spread evenly over the terraced ground. If this precaution is not taken much of the topsoil may be buried far beneath the surface and infertile subsoil brought to the top. Terraces are usually retained by walls built either with or without cement. Well-proportioned terracing can add greatly to the architectural interest and beauty of gardens on sloping sites.

TESTA The skin or coat of a seed. Where this is very hard, e.g. sweet pea, it is wise to chip it and soak the seed in water before sowing.

TETRACHLORETHANE A highly volatile liquid used as a fumigant to kill white fly under glass. See Fumigation.

TETRAPLOID A plant with twice the normal number of chromosomes (i.e. four sets). Such plants are generally larger than the normal diploid ones, but unlike triploids (q.v.) are usually fertile.

THERMOMETER Instruments for measuring temperature are of great value to the gardener and particularly to the greenhouse

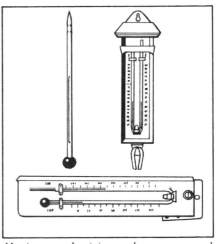
Maximum and minimum thermometers and (top left) a soil thermometer

owner. Several different scales are used, those most commonly employed for garden purposes being the Fahrenheit and centigrade. On the former, freezing point occurs at 32 degrees and boiling point 212 degrees. On the centigrade scale freezing point is at 0 degrees and boiling point 100 degrees. In order to convert Fahrenheit readings to centigrade readings, first subtract 32, then multiply the remainder by 5 and divide the product by 9. To convert centigrade readings to Fahrenheit, reverse this procedure, i.e. multiply by 9, divide by 5 and then add 32. In addition to the ordinary thermometer, it is possible to buy thermometers which automatically register the minimum temperature after being set, and others which will, in a similar manner, register both the maximum and minimum temperatures after being set. For greenhouse purposes maximum- and minimum-registering thermometers are very desirable as considerable fluctuations can occur while the gardener is away from the house. Many failures with greenhouse plants are due to low night temperatures which are unsuspected by the greenhouse owner, but which would be revealed by a minimum-registering thermometer. Special thermometers can be obtained for plunging into soil and registering the temperature of this. These are particularly useful in the formation of mushroom beds and compost heaps and when soil is sterilized by heat. Another type of thermometer is the wet bulb thermometer which can be used to estimate the humidity of the atmosphere, and also, from this information, to predict frost. See Hygrometer.

THINNING The process of reducing the number of plants in a bed or other place so that those which remain have more room to develop; of reducing the number of shoots or branches produced by any one plant; or of reducing the number of flowers or fruits it produces.

Thinning of plants may be applied at one extreme to seedlings in a seed bed, and at the other extreme to orchard or forest trees in a plantation. The thinning of seedlings is particularly important with those kinds of plant which are sown where they are to mature, e.g. many vegetable seedlings such as carrots, lettuces, turnips and beetroots, and the seeds of most hardy annuals such as calendulas, godetias, eschscholzias and cornflowers. The work should always be done as soon as the seedlings can be handled conveniently. Care should be taken not to disturb unduly those seedlings that are to remain. If the seedlings to be thinned are crowded together, it may be necessary to press two fingers down on to the soil, one on each side of the plant to be retained, so holding the plant in position while the surrounding seedlings are pulled out. It is often a good plan to spread thinning over two operations, in the first of which the plants

Thinning apples. The fruit in the centre of the cluster is usually the best one to remove

are left at least twice as thick as they will ultimately be required. This will allow for any casualties, and a final thinning can be carried out a few weeks later.

In orchards it is common practice to grow some of the trees on vigorous stocks which will eventually produce trees of considerable size but will be slow in bringing these into bearing, and to interplant these permanent trees with other temporary trees, often known as fillers, worked on dwarfing stocks which will keep them small and encourage them to fruit while still quite young. Then, after 10 or 12 years, the fillers are removed and the permanent trees permitted to occupy the whole of the space.

Reduction of the numbers of flowers or fruits produced by fruit trees may be necessary to prevent over-cropping, to encourage regular bearing, and to improve the quality of the fruit produced. If cooking apples of large size are required it is frequently necessary to reduce the number of fruits that set, and this should be done in two stages, first when the fruitlets are the size of small marbles and finally when they are as large as walnuts. Dessert apples of great size are not desirable and thinning of these is only necessary when very heavy crops are produced. Grapes almost always require thinning. This is done with pointed scissors specially manufactured for the purpose. It should be started about a fortnight after the berries begin to form, and should be continued a little at a time until the stoning period is completed. It is customary to begin thinning at the bottom of the bunch, and to thin this part of the bunch considerably more drastically than the top and shoulders.

Peaches and nectarines frequently require considerable thinning. If fruits of good quality are to be produced they should be spaced at least 9in. apart on the branches, though nectarines may be a little closer than peaches.

In all thinning care should be taken to remove fruits which are in any way damaged

or likely to be misshapen. In clusters of apples and pears the central fruit, sometimes known as the crown fruit, is often of poor shape. In consequence, exhibitors usually remove these crown fruits.

Thinning of branches is often desirable in trees, and particularly fruit trees, that have become overcrowded. The purpose here is to allow light and air to penetrate more freely to the leaves, and to encourage the production of new growth by concentrating sap on a reduced number of buds.

Thinning of shoots may be necessary for some herbaceous plants, particularly if flowers of large size are required. Thus, when delphiniums are grown for exhibition, the young shoots are usually reduced in number, not more than five being retained even on sturdy plants two or three years old. The quality of Michaelmas daisy flowers can be greatly improved by thinning the stems at an early stage, and large trusses of phlox can be obtained in the same way.

When roses, dahlias or chrysanthemums are grown for exhibition, considerable shoot-thinning is usually carried out. Exhibition sweet peas are produced on plants restricted to a single stem each – an extreme example of shoot-thinning. See also Disbudding.

THIOCYANATE Sometimes used with petroleum oil as a winter wash for application to fruit trees. This wash is particularly effective in the control of woolly aphid and red spider mite and has the merit that it can be applied in mid-March, later than most other winter washes. It must be purchased as a proprietary article and manufacturers' instructions regarding strength should be followed; as a rule from $1\frac{1}{2}$ to $2\frac{1}{4}$ pints of concentrated fluid to 5 gallons of water.

THIOPHANATE-METHYL A systemic fungicide for use against black spot and powdery mildew. It is a wettable powder which should be used at the rate of $\frac{1}{2}$oz. to 6 gallons of water and applied as a spray.

THIRAM A fungicide useful in the control of a wide range of plant diseases including botrytis, some rusts, apple and pear scab, black currant leaf spot and tulip fire. It is also used as a seed dressing to protect seeds and seedlings from soil-borne diseases. It should not be used on fruit intended for canning or deep freezing because of a tendency to taint and also to affect the lacquer within tins. It is not very poisonous to warm-blooded animals, including human beings, but can cause skin irritation. It is purchased as a dust for seed dressing and as a wettable powder to be well stirred into water as directed by the manufacturers and applied as a spray.

THRIPS A general name given to a number of related insects which attack a variety of plants, both out of doors and under glass.

They suck the sap from the leaves, stems and flowers, causing these to become distorted and to develop brown, silver, or white streaks and spots. Thrips are small, active and long in proportion to their width. They vary in colour from pale yellow to black. Flower buds that are badly attacked may turn brown and refuse to open. If the presence of thrips is suspected in flowers or buds, one of these should be tapped smartly over a sheet of white paper when many of the insects will fall out. Thrips are always most abundant in hot, dry weather. Therefore the first line of defence under glass is to give plenty of ventilation, to syringe foliage and damp down paths and stages frequently to maintain a damp atmosphere. Thrips may be destroyed under glass by fumigating with BHC or nicotine and out of doors by spraying with either of these insecticides or with malathion or diazinon.

THYRSE A botanical term used for a particular type of flower cluster which may be described as a compact and rather narrow panicle (q.v.).

TILL, TILLAGE The cultivation of soil by ploughing, digging, forking or any other method. The various operations of tillage are dealt with under digging and forking.

TILTH The crumbly soil texture produced by good tillage. Thus, when it is stated that a seed bed should have a good tilth, the meaning is that the surface soil should be broken down finely and should be in such a physical condition that it can be moved easily with rake or hoe. The provision of a good tilth is one of the most important objects of cultivation, particularly where crops are to be raised from seed or from small plants. Good tilth depends not only upon the way in which cultivation is carried out, but also upon the condition of the soil when this work is done. After winter digging, rough lumps of soil are most likely to break down to a fine tilth if they are forked after frost, but when the surface of the soil is fairly dry. The addition to the soil of bulky organic materials such as leafmould, peat and decayed manure also helps to produce a good tilth. On heavy clay soils tilth may be improved by adequate liming. See Flocculate.

TINE A name given to each individual prong of such tools as forks, cultivators, and some kinds of rakes.

TIP BEARER A fruit tree that produces many of its flowers, and consequently its fruits, at the end of shoots. The apple Worcester Pearmain is an example. Hard pruning can easily result in the removal of all fruit buds and therefore such varieties are more suitable for cultivation as bushes or standards than as trained specimens.

TOMENTOSE Covered with a close mat of hairs; a botanical term used in the description of leaves and stems which have a covering of this type. The covering itself is referred to as a tomentum.

TOPDRESSING A term used by gardeners to describe the application of some substance to the surface of the soil, in distinction to working something into the soil. Topdressings may consist of bulky substances such as dung or compost, though with these the process is more frequently referred to as mulching. More usually topdressings consist of artificial fertilizer, lime or some other fairly concentrated substance. Topdressings provide a convenient method of feeding plants while in growth. When soluble chemical fertilizers such as sulphate of ammonia, nitrate of soda, superphosphate of lime and sulphate of potash are applied, it is important not to exceed quantities recommended by experts, as otherwise there may be too great a concentration of the chemical in the surface soil with consequent injury to roots. It is also frequently important to keep topdressings to the soil only and not spread them over stems and leaves. Superphosphate of lime and sulphate of ammonia can both be very damaging to foliage and so can fresh soot. It is sometimes recommended that topdressings of fertilizers should be mixed with the surface soil by hoeing. This seems a matter to be dictated by tidiness rather than by utility.

Topdressing a wall-trained fruit tree with fertilizer

TOP FRUIT Fruits that grow on trees, e.g. apples, pears, plums and cherries, in contrast to bush fruits such as currants and gooseberries.

TOPIARY The art of clipping and training shrubs and trees to form patterns or artificial forms such as balls, cones, pyramids, peacocks and bears. The art was at its height in Britain during the 17th century and has declined during those periods in which the fashion has been for informal rather than formal gardening. The development of power-driven hedge trimmers has tended to bring topiary into favour again.

Yew and box are the two favourite plants of the topiary artist, though bay is used and also many other shrubs, including holly, privet, and *Lonicera nitida*. The shaping of the shrub is done partly with shears or secateurs and partly by tying young shoots to a wire frame shaped to the rough outline of the specimen. The frame remains as a permanent part of the specimen, but is eventually completely concealed by its growth. Frames are more necessary for the complex shapes than for those of comparatively simple outline. It is very desirable, though not absolutely essential, that the formation of the topiary specimen should be started while plants are still quite young. It may be necessary to tie and clip such specimens five or six times a year between early May and the end of September.

TOPPING A term which may be regarded as almost identical with stopping as it implies the removal of the growing point of a plant. If any distinction is to be made it may be on the grounds that whereas the purpose of stopping is usually to make plants produce side growths, that of topping is done for some other purpose. For example, in the case of broad beans the purpose of topping is to remove the soft growth which is most likely to attract black fly (aphid), a common pest of the broad bean in late spring and early summer.

TOXIC A word that is synonymous with poisonous.

TRACE ELEMENT The name given to certain elements which are required by plants in very minute quantities. Among the principal trace elements are iron, manganese, molybdenum, boron, copper and zinc.

TRAINING The art of inducing a plant to conform to a special shape or form which is required by the gardener. Thus trained fruit trees may be useful to plant against walls where the growth is to be confined to one plane only, or to produce trees of small dimensions as in the single-stemmed tree or cordon. Climbing plants are usually trained in some way. Occasionally climbing roses are grafted on the top of strong brier stems 5 to 7 ft. in height and are then trained downwards over umbrella-like wire frames to form specimens which are known as weeping standards.

With some plants training is merely a matter of tying growths to supports placed in convenient positions, but more often it involves some measure of pruning, including the removal of badly placed or superfluous shoots and the retention of those which can be trained most readily to the desired form. Pruning may also be used to induce growths to form in the right places. For example, in the formation of horizontally-trained fruit trees the central vertical shoot is cut back each year to a point a little above that at which the next pair of horizontal arms is required. Strong new shoots are generally produced just below the point of pruning and in this instance three of these shoots are retained, one being trained vertically and the other two bent down to left and right respectively to form the next pair of arms. In the same way pruning may be used to produce strong shoots in any part of a tree or shrub as required.

Growth can also be induced by notching, i.e. by the removal of a small triangle or crescent of bark just above a dormant growth bud. If this is done as growth starts in the spring, the result will often be that the bud immediately below the notch will start into growth. This technique can be used with advantage to fill in bare spaces of trained specimens. Where for one reason or another it is not practicable to notch, it is sometimes possible to graft a young shoot in the bare place and subsequently prune and train it to fill the position. See also Pruning.

TRANSPLANT This may be considered as a synonym for planting (q.v.). Alternatively, transplanting may be regarded as having particular application to the removal of plants from one place to another with the express purpose of either giving them more space to develop or checking their root growth. This kind of transplanting is common in the nursery garden where trees and shrubs are usually transplanted annually for both the purposes mentioned. The importance in this case of keeping roots in check is that, when the plant is eventually sold, it can be lifted with a compact ball of roots, as a result of which it will not suffer as much check as an untransplanted one which had sent its roots unchecked into a larger area. Young seedling plants of wall-flowers, brassicas, etc., are often trans-

planted from the seed bed to a nursery bed with the same object. The precautions to be observed in the methods adopted are in all instances those discussed under the heading Planting.

TRAYS Shallow boxes used for storing bulbs, potatoes and fruit. The term seed trays is also applied to shallow boxes used for the germination of seeds or the pricking out of seedlings. Trays for storage are frequently made with a wooden upright at each corner, projecting a couple of inches above the rim of the tray, so that one tray may be placed on top of another without pressing on whatever is in it. As a result, air can circulate freely between the trays, and light can also penetrate. Such trays are particularly useful for sprouting potato planting sets. Seed trays are manufactured in several sizes. Wooden seed trays will last much longer if treated with a suitable preservative but creosote should not be used because fumes from it can be deadly to plants. Copper naphthenate is harmless to plants and a better preservative than creosote.

TREAD, TREADING Seed beds are often trodden before being sown and when large plants, shrubs and trees are planted the soil is generally trodden firmly around the roots. The main purpose of treading seed beds is to provide a reasonably firm soil which will not subsequently subside unevenly. Moreover, moisture can rise from below by capillary attraction in such a soil and it will not dry out so rapidly as one that is left loose. Treading when planting has two objects, to get soil into close contact with the roots and to hold the plant securely in the ground until such time as it has made sufficient new roots to provide its own secure anchorage.

Where treading is to be carried out it is essential that the soil be in suitable condition, neither so wet that it sticks to the boots nor so dry that it is impossible to consolidate it by treading.

When planting a shrub it should be firmed in by treading

The term tread is also applied to that part of a spade or fork on which the foot is placed to drive it into the soil.

TREE Any woody plant with a distinct trunk or main stem. The expression may be used in distinction to shrub or bush, terms which are used for woody plants which begin to branch at or near soil level and consequently have no distinct main trunk.

TREE BANDING The practice of putting bands around trees to trap insects. These bands may be covered with some sticky substance (see Grease Band) or may be of hay or sacking under which some caterpillars may pupate or weevils hibernate. The bands can then be gathered up and destroyed, see Hay Band.

TREE GUARD Any device for protecting trees from the attacks of rabbits and cattle. Tree guards are often made of metal in the form of a number of upright bars curving outwards at the top and attached to two or three encircling bands which hold them in position round the trunk of the tree. Sometimes guards are made of wood, many patterns being adopted according to the type of material being used and the size of the tree to be protected. Wire netting may also be employed but if this is done care should be taken to see that it is strong enough to withstand the rubbing of cattle and that it is firmly fixed to suitable uprights well buried in the soil. Occasionally bundles of twigs are used as a temporary protection. They should be placed vertically all round the trunk and then tied securely in position. If a sufficiently thick layer of twigs or small branches is used in this way even small creatures such as rabbits will be unable to damage the trunks.

TREE PRUNERS Sometimes known as long-handled pruners, these are tools designed to enable the gardener to remove shoots or small branches from trees without

Transplanting. 1. *Lifting seedling leeks*

2. *Planting them in their cropping position*

climbing up into them. The commonest pattern has a fixed hooked head carrying a movable blade attached to a long wooden or hollow metal shaft, with a lever near the base by which the pruning blade can be operated. The length of this lever enables considerable force to be applied to the blade and in consequence such tools can be used to sever branches up to about half an inch in thickness. They can be used for the thinning of fruit trees, but should not be employed for spur pruning or other work involving considerable accuracy in cutting.

TREE SURGERY A term somewhat loosely used to cover the pruning of trees and the treatment of any wounds that may be caused during this work or which may develop through accident or the attacks of insects or fungi. Pruning is dealt with under that heading.

The treatment of pruning wounds is only likely to be necessary for fairly big wounds caused by the removal of large limbs. These may be coated with some dressing to prevent attack by fungi or other disease-causing organisms. It should be observed, however, that there are few, if any, wound dressings which do not actually delay the natural process of wound healing, so that their use cannot be considered wholly an advantage. One of the most satisfactory substances to use is grafting wax, warmed until it is sufficiently thin to be applied with a stiff paint brush. Stockholm tar is often recommended and has antiseptic qualities. There are also proprietary dressings on the market. Wounds caused by the breaking of branches, or superficial wounds caused by insects and disease, may be treated in the same way, but first the exposed surface should be pared down with a sharp knife so that a clean wound is made. Deep cracks or holes may need to be filled, and for this purpose concrete, made with 3 parts of builder's sand and 1 part of cement, is frequently used, or a polystyrene filling sealed with bitumen, which weighs much less.

TRELLIS Any erection made by fastening light wooden bars or laths together to form a cross-work pattern. This may take the form of plain square trellis, diamond pattern trellis or some more complex pattern for particular ornamental purposes. Trellis-work may be used as a support for climbing plants, to form a screen or barrier between one part of the garden and another, or to raise the height of existing fences or walls. Trellis-work is also hung on walls as a support for climbers and is particularly useful for this purpose as it obviates the necessity for driving nails into the wall at frequent points. Trellis is usually made of deal treated with a wood preservative such as creosote or copper naphthenate. If it is required to last for many years it should be made of teak or oak.

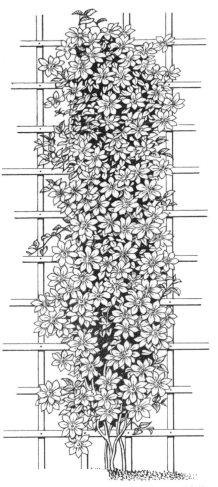

A square trellis used to support Clematis Nelly Moser

TRENCH It is sometimes advised that certain crops should be grown in trenches and this is the method occasionally recommended for sweet peas, runner beans, leeks and celery. The method will vary a little according to the crop to be grown. In general the idea is to cultivate, to a depth of 2 or 3 ft., a strip of soil no more than 1 to 2 ft. in width. The soil is first removed from this narrow strip to the desired depth and then it is replaced a little at a time, manure or compost being liberally added meanwhile. The method has the merit of concentrating plant food where it will convey the maximum benefit, but it suffers from the drawback that water tends to collect in the comparatively loose soil replaced in the trench, becomes stagnant and causes injury to roots. There is a good deal to be said in favour of trench cultivation on suitable soils, but it is open to criticism on heavy and wet soils.

The term trench or trenching is also used for a particular form of deep digging in which the soil is broken up to a depth of $2\frac{1}{2}$ to 3 ft. It is described under Digging.

TRICHLORPHON An insecticide used to control flies, fly larvae, leaf miners, caterpillars, cutworms, earwigs and ants. It is of fairly low mammalian toxicity but a period of two days should elapse between use and harvesting of any edible crops. It is applied as a spray according to manufacturers' instructions.

TRIPLOID A plant with three sets of chromosomes to each cell nucleus instead of the normal two. Such plants frequently have larger flowers or other parts than similar plants with two sets (diploids), but because of the impossibility of dividing three sets into two matching halves in the production of the sex cells (pollen grains and ovules) they are usually more or less sterile. See Polyploid.

TROUGH GARDENS Very attractive miniature gardens can be made in old stone drinking troughs and sinks. It is essential that they are provided with outlets for surplus water and these holes should themselves be covered with a few pebbles or broken pieces of earthenware to prevent soil washing down into them. The troughs should then be filled with good potting soil and a few small pieces of rock may be half buried on top to simulate a little rock garden. They

An old trough makes an attractive miniature garden for small-growing rock plants

A trowel is the ideal tool for planting small plants

can be planted with any small alpines such as saxifrages, thymes, sempervivums, sedums, moss phlox, etc. with perhaps one or two dwarf conifers such as *Juniperus communis compressa*. The soil should be kept well watered in spring and summer and just moist at other times. Such troughs make decorative objects for terraces, patios and paved gardens.

TROWEL Small planting tools made in two styles, one with a handle up to 15 in. in length, the other with a short handle 4 to 6 in. long. The latter is the more serviceable type and, though it may seem to involve more stooping, will in practice be found far less tiring to use. Trowels are made of steel, including stainless steel, or of aluminium alloy, the latter having the advantage of being non-rusting and light, though it is not as strong and durable as steel. A trowel should be used for the planting of all seedlings and small plants that are too big on the one hand to be transplanted with a small dibber, and too small on the other hand to be planted with a spade. It is to be preferred to the large dibber for almost all purposes with the possible exception of planting brassicas. The reason for this is that the large dibber tends to consolidate the soil unevenly and also to make a narrow deep hole in which roots are unnaturally cramped. Moreover, the hole may not be properly refilled with the result that the plant remains suspended with a hole beneath it in which water later collects. With the trowel a suitably wide and shallow hole can be scooped out to accommodate roots in a natural position and firming can be done according to the needs of the plants.

TRUE-BREEDING A plant is said to be true-breeding when its flowers, having been pollinated with their own pollen, produce seed which will give seedlings with all the essential characters of the parent. Thus with a variety of sweet pea, it can only be regarded as true-breeding if the seed saved

from it after self-pollination will produce plants bearing flowers of the same character and colour as those of the parent. It is important to observe that the term is relative and not absolute. No plant reproduces itself true in every minute detail. It is a question of what is important from the gardener's standpoint. The geneticist describes a true-breeding plant as homozygous, and one that is not true-breeding as heterozygous or hybrid.

TRUG A shallow oblong basket very useful in the garden for carrying small plants, tools, weeds etc. The original Sussex trug is made of thin overlapping boards, usually of chestnut, but trug baskets of other materials, mainly plastics, are now manufactured.

TRUMPET A term used to describe flowers that have the flaring shape of a trumpet. It is also used to describe the enlarged cup or corona of that class of narcissi known as trumpet daffodils.

The trumpet of a daffodil

TRUNCATE Cut off abruptly at the end; a botanical term applied to parts of plants which terminate in this manner.

TRUNK The woody main stem of a tree, covered with bark.

TRUSS A rather loose term for a cluster of flowers or fruits. Gardeners apply it quite arbitrarily to some clusters but not to others. Thus they speak of a truss of tomatoes but a bunch of grapes. The flower clusters of auriculas, polyanthus and some other primulas, calceolarias, pelargoniums, rhododendrons and verbenas are among those commonly referred to as trusses.

TUBER A thickened underground stem or root used for the storage of food, often in the form of starch. Familiar examples are the potato, a stem tuber, and the dahlia, a root tuber. The tuberous begonia may be contrasted with the crocus and its corm which resembles the tuber in some particulars, but is covered by a membranous coat. The difference between root and stem tubers can be determined by whether or not they produce eyes or buds. The stem tuber always has eyes, whereas the root tuber has not.

Potatoes are familiar examples of stem tubers

TUBERCLES, see Root Nodules

TUBS, PLANT Wooden tubs are frequently used as containers for ornamental plants, including shrubs, either grown naturally or clipped as topiary specimens, and also various bedding plants, bulbs etc. The tubs should be constructed of teak or some other durable hard wood and they must be provided with several holes in the base or low down in the sides to permit surplus water to drain away. Plants grown in tubs must be well watered and, once established, should be fed regularly in spring and summer as the soil soon becomes exhausted. Tubs containing hardy plants and shrubs can stand out of doors all the year but if half-hardy plants are grown in them the plants must either be removed to a frost-proof place in the autumn or the whole tub should be moved into such a place. Tubs can make very decorative features for terraces and paved gardens.

TUFA A name given to a type of limestone, frequently of a very porous texture. A particular type of hard tufa, found near Matlock in Derbyshire, has been used both for rock gardens and for miniature gardens in bowls and old sinks. Because of its porous nature it absorbs water freely and attracts roots. It quickly weathers and becomes covered with mosses, lichens and other pleasing growths.

TULIP FIRE, see Fire

TUNICATED A botanical term used to describe bulbs, such as the onion and narcissus, in which the scales are concentric, each being wrapped round that immediately beneath it.

TURF A term which may be applied to a surface covering of grass, clover or some other meadow forming plant, or to the complete surface layer of 2 or 3in. comprising both the covering herbage and the roots which it produces. Thus turfy loam may mean the first 3 or 4in. of grass and soil cut from a meadow or similar place, and turves for lawn making are usually cut with about a 1½in. thickness of soil. Good turf may be of natural formation or be produced by sowing seeds for the express purpose of producing a suitable herbage. For lawn making, natural turf, especially when cut from a site near to or of similar character to that on which the lawn is to be formed, has the merit that the grasses are likely to be of a character suitable for the soil and climate; but it suffers from the drawback that it is seldom free from weeds, including undesirable grasses. Weeds can usually be dealt with by cutting them out of the turves or by treating the lawn with a suitable weed-killer but undesirable species of grass are a much more difficult problem and can seldom be eradicated without injuring the useful species as well. The subject of lawn making both from seeds and from turves is dealt with under the heading Lawns.

Turves for the preparation of potting compost should be stacked, grass-side downwards, for a period of at least twelve months before use, so that the grass and some of the roots may rot. The stacks can be of any convenient size.

For compost making it is desirable that turves should be cut from a fairly rich meadow, one, for example, in which a considerable number of cattle have been allowed to graze. This kind of turf is seldom the most satisfactory for lawn making as it is apt to contain many coarse grasses, clovers, and weeds.

TURF BEATER A special tool, sometimes known as a turf beetle, which is used for settling turves that have been laid to form a lawn. Beaters are of various patterns, one of the most useful types being in the form of a smooth block of wood, 10 to 12in. in length and 4 to 6in. in width and depth, with one flat face and a shaped handle at one end. An alternative type has a handle 4 to 5ft. in length fixed at an angle on a flat block of wood, roughly 15in. by 12in. by 2in.

TURFING IRON A special implement for cutting and lifting turves required for lawn making. It has a double-edged blade set on a long handle at such an angle that it can be thrust in flat under the turf to cut it at an even thickness.

TURF PERFORATOR Tools of many different patterns are used to perforate turf which has become too consolidated by heavy wear and is consequently in need of aeration. An ordinary garden fork may be used for the purpose, pushed in at frequent intervals all over the surface of the turf to a depth of 2 to 3in. and then levered backward just sufficiently to raise and loosen the turf slightly. Special forks with hollow tines which remove narrow cores of soil from the turf are made and also various mechanical

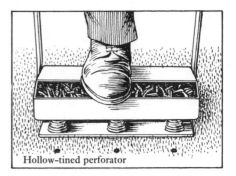
Hollow-tined perforator

devices employing hollow tines of this type. See also Roller.

TURF RACES Tools used for marking out turf before it is lifted for lawn making or for stacking. The usual type of race, or racer, has a long ash handle slightly curved at the base, with a sharp knife fastened almost at right angles near the bottom. The cutting edge of the knife is in reverse, so that if the tool is drawn towards the operator the knife will cut through the turf. More elaborate tools are made, some fitted with wheels and other devices to regulate the depth of cut.

TURNIP FLY, see Flea Beetle

TURNIP MOTH, see Cutworm

TWINER Used to describe climbing plants that obtain support by twisting themselves around other plants, posts, trellis or wires in contrast to those that produce special clinging tendrils, aerial roots or suction pads. Honeysuckles and runner beans are typical twiners.

TYING The tying of plants for support is included under the heading Staking. Here it may be observed that the choice of material for tying should be governed by the type of growth to be supported, the ultimate strain which the tie is likely to bear and the length of time that it will be required to last. Thus, for all those plants with soft or succulent growth, ties of very pliable material should be used, such as soft raffia, twist, fillis or twine, tarred or plain. Galvanized wire rings are often used for firm growths such as those of carnations, but should always be sufficiently loose to allow for expansion of growth. Ties of raffia, thin twist or fillis cannot be expected to last more than one year and often begin to deteriorate after a few months. This is sometimes an advantage, as with ties used for buds or grafts when budding and grafting. With these the tie has usually completed its purpose within five or six weeks, after which it is an advantage if it breaks easily so that the bark of the grafted plant may swell. Ties that are expected to remain for two or three years can be made of tarred twine, galvanized or plastic-coated wire, or some other durable material.

Good loam can be made by stacking turves grass side downwards for at least a year

It is often an advantage when tying plants, particularly those that are of soft growth which is likely to increase in girth rapidly, to make a double twist in the tying material between the stem and the stake or other support. This twist acts like a spring, allowing a reasonable degree of expansion, and yet holding the stem firm, even when the tie is first placed in position.

TYPE Botanically this term is used for that particular form of a species which has been described for the purpose of classification. Variations from this form, which are nevertheless not sufficiently distinct to justify classification as separate species, may be referred to as varieties or forms of the species and be given distinguishing names additional to the species name. It should be observed that it does not follow that the type form is the commonest form in nature, but merely that it is the first form to be described fully for the purpose of botanical classification. Thus, *Lilium brownii* was originally described in 1841 from plants which were descended from the bulbs introduced in England about 1835. No one seems to be quite clear as to the origin of these original bulbs, and no further plants of precisely this character have been found in the native habitat of *Lilium brownii*. At least two variants of the original *Lilium brownii* have since been introduced to cultivation, and these carry the distinguishing names of *Lilium brownii* var. *viridulum*, and *Lilium brownii* var. *australe*. The type itself may be distinguished, if desired, by a third name, though it is seldom used for any but botanical purposes. In the example chosen, the type plant may be distinguished as *Lilium brownii* var. *brownii*.

In gardens the term type plant is often used more loosely to distinguish the form commonly grown in gardens from other forms of the same plant of more unusual character. See Classification.

UMBEL A botanical term used to describe flower clusters in which the flower stalks or branches all arise from a common point at the top of the main flower stem. The flower head of a carrot is of this form.

Umbel

UNDULATE With wavy margins; a botanical term applied to leaves, etc. which are of this character.

UNISEXUAL Of one sex only. The term is used by botanists for flowers which produce stamens but no pistils, or pistils but no stamens. This is the opposite of hermaphrodite. The begonia provides a familiar example of a plant with unisexual flowers.

UREA A nitrogenous fertilizer that is very soluble in water and which produces a quick result when applied to growing plants. It contains 46 per cent. nitrogen and can be used at ½ to 1 oz. per sq. yd. or as a liquid fertilizer dissolved in water at 1 oz. to 7 gallons.

USEFUL INSECTS, see Predators

VARIABILITY When plants are raised from seed there is usually some variability in the seedlings and this is likely to be greater in hybrid plants than in natural species. Sometimes this variability is so great as to render seedlings useless for the particular purpose required, e.g. for planting apples or pears of a given variety, and then vegetative means of propagation such as cuttings, grafting, divisions or layers must be used. However, there may occasionally be slight variations even when such methods are used (see Sport). Natural variability can be of great value to the plant breeder, enabling him to develop new varieties with improved or different characteristics.

VARIEGATED Of two or more colours. As a rule the term is applied only to foliage and stems, but it may occasionally be used in connection with flowers that are blotched or marked with more than one colour. The commonest type of foliage variegation is due to lack of chlorophyll or green colouring matter in some parts. As a result patches of yellow or white appear and these may either be regularly disposed in bands or along the veins, or they may be irregularly disposed in spots or blotches all over the surface of the leaf. Variegation, especially of the spotted or blotchy type, is often a symptom of virus infection, and diseases known as mosaic show this symptom in a marked manner. Variegation can also be an inherited characteristic unconnected with any pathological condition. The handsome leaves of many kinds of maranta and the silver-variegated leaves of *Pilea cadierei* are of this kind. Variegations also arise as sports or mutations from normal unvariegated forms and usually in such cases the variegation occurs as a chimaera, i.e. tissues of two or more kinds occur, one often overlying the other like a glove but not covering the whole leaf or stem. As a result where both layers occur the normal colour is seen but where there is only one layer a different colour may appear.

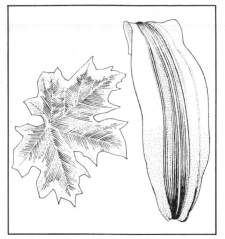

Two kinds of leaf variegation: left, a leaf from Acer platanoides drummondii; right, one from Dracaena fragrans

Variegated plants are often of great decorative merit. As a rule those that occur as chimaeras or as a result of virus infection can only be propagated true to type by vegetative means, i.e. by cuttings, grafts, or layers, but plants that are naturally variegated can usually be increased by seed. Variegated plants are often a little weaker in growth than their normal green counterparts, this being due to the lack of chlorophyll which is essential to the process of photosynthesis by which the plant manufactures its foodstuffs with the aid of energy obtained from sunlight. Often variegated forms tend to revert to normal forms. Branches or stems bearing normal green leaves must be cut out as soon as observed or, because of their greater vigour, they may soon crowd out the variegated parts of the plant.

VARIETY A division used in the classification of plants, see Classification.

VEGETABLE The term is used in two different ways, one scientific and the other horticultural. From a scientific standpoint a vegetable is any living organism that is not an animal. In the higher levels of life this is a distinction easily understood, as animals have the power of movement, often have a fairly highly developed nervous system, and live by breaking down complex organic substances. Vegetables, by contrast, are relatively motionless, have no obvious nervous system and build up their food from simple, inorganic compounds. In the lowest levels of life the distinction fades into obscurity and it becomes almost impossible to decide whether an organism is, in fact, a vegetable or animal.

Horticulturally a vegetable is an edible plant that is used primarily as a salad or as a complement to or in place of a meat course, in distinction to a fruit, which is used primarily for dessert. Thus at flower shows there are usually classes for vegetables and fruits and there is occasionally dispute whether certain things, tomatoes for example, should be shown in the one section or the other. To get this matter in clear perspective it must first be realized that the one term implies the other, i.e. a fruit is a part of a vegetable and is, therefore, vegetable in character. Botanically a tomato is a fruit but horticulturally it is shown in vegetable, and not in fruit classes, as a tomato is most frequently used in the manner defined for a garden vegetable.

VEGETATIVE PROPAGATION Any method of increasing a plant other than from seeds. Thus the term may include division in all its forms, taking of cuttings or the preparation of layers, grafts, buds, etc. An advantage of such methods of propagation over seed (seminal) propagation is that, as a rule, a plant produced in this way resembles its parent in every minute particular, whereas plants raised from seed always differ in some measure from their parents, though the difference may be so minute as to be unimportant. Nevertheless, many hybrid varieties will not breed anything like true to character from seed, but will show variations which will be serious from the standpoint of garden display. Most hybrid plants can only be reproduced true to type by vegetative propagation. All the plants vegetatively reproduced from one original parent constitute a clone and such groups of plants are sometimes designated by the letters cl. before or after their names to indicate their common origin.

A drawback of vegetative propagation is that often diseases or even pests occurring in the parent plant may be carried over to the offspring. This is particularly likely to happen with diseases and pests that are actually inside the plant, viruses, for example, and eelworms. Some diseases are seed borne but they are nothing like so numerous as those which may be spread by vegetative propagation.

Heat treatment of stock plants from which cuttings are to be taken or of the cuttings themselves, as well as the preparation of cuttings from very minute portions of the tips of growing stems, are devices by which it is sought to eliminate the danger of infection being passed on in this way.

VENATION The arrangement or pattern of the veins in a leaf.

VENTILATION Some circulation of air is necessary for most plants grown under glass, partly because without it temperatures will rise too high during sunny weather, partly because the moving air will help to keep the atmosphere from becoming too damp.

The degree of ventilation required for satisfactory growth will vary according to the time of year, the temperature out of

Greenhouses should be well provided with ridge ventilators

doors, the amount of wind and its direction, the amount of sunlight, the position of the greenhouse or frame and the character of the plants to be grown. In consequence, no general advice on this matter can be given except to remark that draughts should be avoided and that the change of air should take place as smoothly as possible without sharp currents occurring anywhere.

Greenhouses should have ventilators both at the ridge and at the sides, and in greenhouses provided with staging it is often an advantage to have some small ventilators in the walls below the level of the stages. In span-roofed or three-quarter span-roofed greenhouses, ventilators should be on both sides of the ridge so that, if necessary, air can be admitted only on the leeward side. This is essential in order to avoid sharp draughts and foliage scorching which may result from them. Top ventilation by itself can often be used with advantage to dry the atmosphere of a house which is too damp, without causing too great a drop in temperature. By contrast in hot sunny weather, both side and top ventilators should be used in conjunction, so that a steady flow of air occurs between them. Though very slight ventilation may be adequate much of the time, all greenhouses should be provided with sufficient ventilation space to allow a rapid exchange of air if necessary. Many small greenhouses fail in this respect. As a general rule the length of ridge ventilators in a span-roofed greenhouse should at least equal the whole length of the house, and the ideal for this type of house is that the total length of top ventilators should be double the length of the house, i.e. they should extend the full length of the house on each side of the ridge. Side ventilation in houses with vertical glass sides need not be on quite such a generous scale, but there should not be less than one 2ft. by 3ft. ventilator every 10ft., or the equivalent of this.

Various devices have been developed to make ventilation automatic. The simplest operate on much the same principle as a thermometer, i.e. a fluid in a closed cylinder expands when it becomes hotter and con-

Side ventilators are helpful in maintaining a good circulation of air

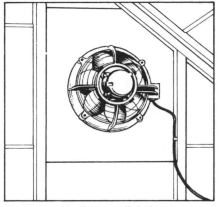

A thermostatically controlled electric extractor fan can be installed in the end of the greenhouse

tracts as it becomes cooler. This change in volume is used to operate a piston which itself opens or closes the ventilator by means of a crank. More elaborate apparatus makes use of an electric motor controlled by a thermostat to open or close ventilators, while another way to utilize electricity for automatic ventilation is to substitute electric extractor fans for normal hinged ventilators and operate these via a thermostat. Care should be taken to place the thermostat where it will register the average temperature of the house.

All plants that are reared under glass but are to be placed outside later on should have steadily increasing ventilation as the time for removal outdoors approaches. It is for this reason that frames are so valuable for hardening-off plants during the last few weeks, as in a frame the light can be entirely removed when weather conditions are favourable and the plants within fully exposed to the air. Even the best-ventilated greenhouse cannot give conditions comparable with this.

VERGE The edge of a lawn where it joins a path, bed or border. The term is also sometimes applied to a narrow strip of grass bordering a path, or bed, but the former meaning is more accurate.

VERMICULITE A natural substance, allied to mica, which, when subjected to intense heat, expands and forms granules that are full of air spaces. It is then extremely light in proportion to its bulk and very absorbent. Its principal use is in building, but it is also used in gardens, either by itself or in combination with sand or peat, as a medium in which to root cuttings or germinate seeds. For either purpose it is essential to obtain vermiculite that is not strongly alkaline. It has the merits of holding water without becoming waterlogged, of being entirely sterile, and of being so light that seedlings or rooted cuttings can be lifted from it without breaking even their finest roots. Its drawbacks are that it is rather expensive and completely devoid of plant food, so that plants left in it for long will starve. It is obtainable in various degrees of coarseness.

Vermiculite is recognized by the U.S. Customs as being sterile and so it need not be washed off the roots of plants sent to the U.S.A.

VERNALIZATION This name is given to various techniques by which seeds or plants can be made to pass through, at a greater rate than normal or at an unusual season of the year, those physical and chemical changes which would normally occur in winter. By this means seeds or plants may be brought into a condition in which they will start into growth rapidly directly they are subjected to sufficient light and warmth and given sufficient moisture. Techniques of this kind have been much used in the preparation of bulbs, such as narcissi, tulips, and hyacinths, for forcing. For this purpose the bulbs, when lifted in summer after having completed their normal growth, are placed in refrigerators or warm stores according to their respective requirements, at carefully controlled temperatures which will vary according to the nature of the plant under treatment. After remaining an appropriate number of weeks in these conditions, the bulbs are removed and stored normally. When potted or boxed and placed in a greenhouse with a suitable temperature, they grow very rapidly and produce flowers during the winter months.

Some seeds can be vernalized by exposing them for a while to low temperatures such as they would normally experience in winter, and some chemicals, such as gibberellic acid, have also been used to break dormancy in seeds and so enable them to be germinated.

Many seeds, particularly those of woody plants, respond to a period of cold, and the technique known as stratification (q.v.) is at least in part effective because it breaks the natural dormancy of the seeds exposed in this way. But more refined and controlled systems of vernalization have been developed and these sometimes necessitate alternate periods of warmth and cold. Though details of treatment necessarily differ from one species to another, in general a temperature of 4 to 5°C. maintained for two to four months seems to be adequate for cold treatment, and a temperature of 20 to 30°C. for four to six months for warm treatment. Seeds to be cold treated can be placed in moist sand or peat in polythene bags in an ordinary refrigerator. For warm treatment seeds are similarly packaged, the bags being carefully sealed to prevent evaporation, and kept in a warm room or cupboard. Some seeds are characterized by double dormancy, which means that under normal conditions outdoors they would not germinate until the second spring after ripening, by which time they would have passed through two winters and one summer. In such cases the warm treatment should precede the cold treatment, after which the seeds are sown immediately.

VINE SCISSORS, see Scissors

VIRUS There is considerable difference of opinion as to whether viruses are to be regarded as living organisms or merely as organic chemicals. They are extremely minute and exist in living organisms in which they often cause serious diseases. They are carried from one part of the plant to another in the sap. In consequence, exterior application of sprays, dusts or fumigants is ineffective. So far no satisfactory method has been discovered of curing virus diseases.

The symptoms caused by viruses in plants are very varied. They may produce yellow or white variegation of leaves, and symptoms in this category are often referred to as mosaic diseases. Alternatively, they may produce distortion of the young shoots of the plant, curling of the leaves, dwarfing of the whole plant, streaking, or small dry brown spots. The damage caused by viruses is often wrongly ascribed to weather or soil conditions.

Viruses are spread from one plant to another by transference of sap. The agents may be sucking insects, such as greenflies or thrips, or the sap may be carried on the blades of pruning tools or on the fingers of those working amongst the plants. One particularly troublesome virus, which attacks tobacco as well as many other plants, is often introduced to the garden on the fingers of smokers.

Methods of control include the rigorous removal and destruction of all plants that show virus symptoms, spraying, dusting, or fumigation to kill sucking insects, the disinfection of pruning tools by dipping them occasionally in strong disinfectant solution, and the production of virus-free plants in special nurseries or in districts in which virus infection is small. One of the advantages of purchasing seed potatoes from certain districts in Scotland and Ireland is that in these localities sucking insects seldom appear at all freely until late in the summer. Therefore, seed potatoes from these areas are usually virus-free. When these tubers are planted in more southerly districts where potato viruses are common, they will usually give a good crop the first season, because even if virus infection occurs it will not seriously affect growth the first year. It is a characteristic of many viruses that they weaken plants slowly and progressively over a period of years but do not kill them rapidly.

Some varieties of plants normally susceptible to virus diseases become infected but show no outward symptoms. Such plants are described as virus resistant and have obvious uses as well as less obvious drawbacks, the principal of which is that they often act as unsuspected carriers of virus.

VISTA A view which is confined on both sides by trees, hills or other objects. In gardens vistas are often carefully contrived by planting trees or hedges to confine the view and direct attention in a particular direction. An appearance of great depth can often be given to a comparatively small garden by a cleverly contrived vista.

VITICULTURE The art of growing grape vines.

VIVIPAROUS Producing live young as distinct from eggs. A term which strictly applies to the animal rather than the vegetable kingdom, but is used occasionally by botanists and gardeners for those plants that produce small bulbs or offsets that begin to grow while still attached to the parent. A familiar example is *Polystichum aculeatum angulare* which usually produces young plantlets along the midribs of its mature fronds.

VOLES Small rodents, usually found near water, which are vegetarian and may do considerable damage to bulbs, herbaceous plants and vegetables. They can be destroyed by any of the measures described for rats or mice (q.v.).

WALL Garden walls may be used for protection, to divide one part of the garden from another, or to retain soil that has been terraced. For the first purpose brickwork, stonework or ornamental cement blocks are almost always laid with cement to bind them together. Small dividing walls and also terrace walls are often made of loose stone and are known as dry walls in contradistinction to cemented or mortared walls. One of the merits of the dry wall is that it can be used as a home for many small plants, including alpines. These can be established successfully even in narrow crevices between the bricks or stones, and the plants often derive great benefit from the sharp drainage which they enjoy in such places.

No matter what system of building is adopted the bricks or stones should always be laid with some kind of bond, i.e. the bricks or stones in successive layers should be staggered so that they tie each other together. Dry walls are often built with a slight batter or backward slope as this gives them greater stability. When building dry walls, soil should be spread between each course of brick or stone and should also be rammed into crevices behind the bricks or stones. In this type of construction soil takes the place of cement and must be used to give every brick or stone a firm bed.

For high terrace walls which must hold back a considerable weight of soil dry wall construction is not, as a rule, satisfactory. Not only should the stones or bricks be set in cement but buttresses should be built every 15 or 20 ft. to give further support to the masonry. Holes should be left every few feet so that water collecting in the soil behind the wall may escape.

Walls for fruit trees should be at least 7 ft. and preferably 10 or 12 ft. in height. Low walls are not of much service for this purpose as the trees quickly grow above them and then part of the growth is protected and part exposed, which is not a happy combination. In the northern hemisphere walls facing south or west are satisfactory for many fruit trees, but it is also possible to clothe walls facing east or north. In particular many of the hardier plums will succeed in such places and so will the Morello cherry. Many slightly tender shrubs succeed better on walls facing north-west than they do in a southerly aspect, apparently because on south-facing walls they are often encouraged to make premature growth in early spring and this tender young growth may be cut by late spring frost. In the southern hemisphere all these aspects need to be reversed.

If plants are to be grown in a dry wall, it is a great advantage if they can be planted as the work of construction proceeds. It is possible to plant afterwards by scraping out soil from some of the crevices, pushing the roots of the plants carefully into the fissures made in this way, and then pressing more soil around them, but this is a laborious task compared with the comparative simplicity of planting as one builds.

Many ornamental plants may be grown against walls and some will derive benefit from the shelter, shade or extra warmth provided, dependant on the aspect of the wall. Some climbers cling naturally to walls, e.g. ivies, some species of ampelopsis and vitis, *Hydrangea petiolaris* and *Schizophragma hydrangioides*. There is a difference of opinion as to whether such climbers harm or benefit the walls on which they grow but much seems to depend on the nature of the mortar. Lime mortar may be gradually eaten away by the aerial roots of some of these plants but cement mortar is far more resistant and is unlikely to be damaged. On the contrary, such walls may derive benefit from the protection the climbers provide from rain and frost.

WALL NAIL Special nails with flexible metal attachments at the head used for fastening plants to walls. The nail itself is designed to be driven into the mortar or concrete between a course of brick or stone, and the flexible metal head can then be twisted round the shoot to be supported.

WARDIAN CASE A glass case with a close-fitting lid, used for the cultivation of certain rather difficult ferns and other greenhouse plants. The Wardian case is virtually a close frame in which the atmosphere can be kept very still and, if necessary, very damp. Since the case has glass sides the plants within can be seen readily and at one time Wardian cases were frequently used as objects of interest or ornament within the dwelling house, where they might be filled with filmy ferns or similar plants. The case was designed by

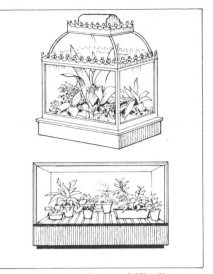

Top, the traditional type of Wardian case. Bottom, a modern version

Nathaniel Bankshaw Ward, 1791 to 1868. See also Bottle Garden.

WART DISEASE A fungal disease which is peculiar to potatoes. First symptom is the appearance of wart-like outgrowths on the young tubers. As the attack progresses the tubers may be almost completely destroyed, little being left but a small gnarled lump without much resemblance to a potato. Occasionally only part of a tuber will be

attacked, the rest continuing to grow normally.

This is a notifiable disease and no treatment should be attempted without guidance from the Ministry of Agriculture, Fisheries and Food.

Some varieties of potato are immune to wart disease. These are indicated in catalogues by the word immune, but it should be noted that the word only implies immunity to wart disease and not to other diseases.

WASHING SODA Common washing soda as used in the kitchen makes a useful fungicide either by itself or in combination with copper sulphate as in the formulation known as Burgundy mixture (q.v.). As a fungicide on its own, 12 oz. of washing soda and 8 oz. of soft soap are dissolved in 5 gallons of water. Dissolve the soft soap in a gallon of water, dissolve the washing soda in

Concrete screening blocks are available in a range of designs and make decorative walls for use where complete privacy is not required

another gallon and then mix the two solutions together. Make up the solution to 5 gallons, stir well and use at once. This spray is particularly useful to prevent the spread of gooseberry mildew.

WASPS These insects can be very troublesome to the fruit growers as fruit ripens. However, earlier in the summer they are useful to gardeners since they feed their young on insects and other protein foods. Nests are made in hedge banks, under eaves, etc. and should be destroyed by sprinkling BHC, carbaryl or derris dust in the entrance hole. Alternatively, they can be soaked in paraffin and burned. Individual fruits can be protected with paper or muslin bags and wasps can be kept out of greenhouses by covering the ventilators with muslin.

WATER This is an essential requirement for plants and, moreover, all the food absorbed by plants from the soil is in solution in water. An adequate supply of water is, therefore, of the first importance. Many plants have storage organs, e.g. bulbs, corms, tubers, rhizomes etc. to enable them to survive dry spells and some have protective devices, such as dense coverings of fine hairs or scales on the leaves, to reduce loss of water in hot dry weather. In herbaceous plants and the soft parts of other plants it is the water pressure within the tissues that supplies rigidity and when there is insufficient water the leaves and stems lose rigidity and wilt.

The chemical content of water may have a considerable effect on the growth and even the health of plants. Water containing a lot of calcium can be extremely harmful to lime-hating (calcifuge) plants. Excess of iron in water may present problems with some plants and chlorination can also be damaging. Gardeners often make provision to store rain water for their more delicate or difficult plants since this usually contains only a low level of chemicals of any kind and any additions necessary can be made at the gardener's discretion.

Dirty water may carry disease-causing organisms and storage tanks in greenhouses are particularly liable to become contaminated in this way, for which reason they should be cleaned out regularly.

When water freezes it expands and in soil this property can be valuable since it breaks down clods and produces a more crumbly, easily worked soil. In water pipes, pools etc. freezing water can cause a great deal of damage and in plants, too, ice crystals forming in the tissues can rupture cells and cause the death of leaves, shoots or complete plants.

WATER GARDEN In a narrow sense the term may be confined to lakes, pools and streams in which plants are cultivated, but it is usually extended to include planted bogs and damp ground surrounding such places. Even without the addition of plants, water can add greatly to the charm of a garden, by introducing a new and entirely different kind of surface in contrast with that made by plants or masonry, by the reflections which it makes possible, and by the pleasant sounds it may make. Nevertheless, it is in conjunction with good planting that water gardening can be exploited to the full.

Broadly speaking, water gardens can be divided into two classes, formal and informal. The former were brought to perfection by the Italian and French gardenmakers during the 16th and 17th centuries. They used water in a number of ingenious ways, not only in the form of pools, but also as canals, aqueducts and fountains. Though many formal water gardens are to be found in the British Isles, the tendency in this country has been rather towards the informal garden often produced by damming valleys to form lakes of extremely natural appearance. Many of the famous British landscape gardens of the 18th and early 19th centuries made use of water in this informal way. Small-scale informal water gardening has been associated particularly with rock gardens, in the form of pools and cascades. See also Pool and Bog Garden.

WATERING The correct application of water to plants, and particularly to plants grown under glass, is one of the most important parts of the gardener's art and one of the most difficult to master. Too much water may result in the soil becoming waterlogged, as a result of which air will be driven out of it and the roots of the plants will be suffocated. Moreover, over-watering results in chilled soil and retarded growth. On the other hand if insufficient water is applied growth may come to a standstill, for all the nourishment which plants take from the soil must be in solution.

The commonest fault is that of watering too frequently but in insufficient quantity. As a result the surface inch or so of soil is kept moist most of the time, but beneath this the soil becomes dry. As most of the plant's roots are well below the surface, it follows that growth under such conditions is poor. When watering pot plants it is necessary to give sufficient at each application to moisten the soil right to the bottom of the pot. As a guide to the quantity that will be required the novice should occasionally lift the pot after watering and watch for the first drips of water to appear at the drainage hole. However, this test is valueless if the soil has previously become very dry, because as a result of this the ball of soil in the pot will have shrunk and then water will run down the cavity between soil and pot and come straight out of the drainage hole. This test can only be applied with safety when plants have been potted in good compost and properly watered subsequently.

Various methods have been suggested for deciding whether a plant in a pot requires watering. One of these is to tap the pot with a cotton reel fastened to a short stick, with a small wooden hammer or the leg bone of a chicken. If the pot emits a ringing note, the soil within is dry, whereas if a dull thud is the result the soil is moist. This test can only be used with sound earthenware pots, for those which are cracked will always give a dull sound no matter how dry the soil and plastic pots are unaffected by the moisture of the soil within them. Another test is to lift the pot, for wet soil weighs much more than dry soil and this can be applied whatever the condition or nature of the pot. Various instruments have also been devised for gauging the moisture of the soil.

It is not so easy to advise methods of checking the moisture content of beds or borders. A soil-testing auger, a tool rather like an enormous gimlet which when thrust into the ground can be withdrawn carrying a core of soil, can be employed, but is usually possessed only by scientists and professional horticultural advisers. Experience is really the only sure guide, but the novice may be advised occasionally to excavate a hole to a depth of a foot or more and observe

A soil moisture meter or tensiometer shows at a glance the moisture content of the soil

Watering-cans are available in plastic or metal and various shapes and sizes. Roses should be used when watering seedlings and cuttings

the state of the soil at various depths. He may often be astonished by the result and will gain experience in correct watering.

In dealing with greenhouse borders used for vines, tomatoes, etc., it is, as a rule, only possible to replenish subsoil losses during the winter, so much water being required for this purpose that, if applied while plants are in growth, there will be serious danger of injury being done. In consequence it is good practice to run a hose on the border in January or February and give sufficient water to soak down to a depth of 18 in. or 2 ft. Failure to replenish subsoil supplies accounts for many mysterious troubles which occur later in the year, including blossom end rot in tomatoes and poor growth and small foliage in grapes.

The method of applying water must always be considered with care. Most watering-cans are fitted with roses, and often with roses of two different kinds, one fine the other coarse. Fine roses should only be used for sprinkling cuttings or other plants that need no more than an overhead damping. This method of watering gives a deceptive appearance of moisture on top. Small pools soon start to collect on the surface yet the soil beneath may be quite dry. Much inadequate watering is due to the frequent use of fine roses. Coarser roses are

better, but for all watering of well-established plants the water should be applied direct from the spout of the watering-can, held close to the soil to avoid disturbing the surface with a powerful jet of water. When watering out of doors no rose should be used except for very small plants. The best kind of watering in the open is with an irrigation plant of some kind which can be left to run for several hours and will give a rain-like spray. By this means the soil will be adequately moistened without being unduly beaten down. See Irrigation.

At one time it was supposed that the temperature of the water used for greenhouse plants was important, and that this must be at least equal to the air temperature of the house in which the plants are growing. Experiments have not confirmed this view and it does not seem that cold water gives plants any severe or prolonged check. Nevertheless, common sense would suggest that it is undesirable to use extremely cold water for plants that are growing in a warm atmosphere.

It is possible to feed plants as they are watered, in fact, water itself must be regarded as an important food element. Further plant foods can be added to it either in the form of chemicals, or by steeping bags of manure, soot, etc. in the water.

A trickle watering system which releases water through special nozzles. These may either be placed one in each pot or can rest on a bed of sand from which the plants draw water by capillary action. See also page 273

See also Capillary Watering, Manure, Irrigation and Dilutor.

WATER SHOOTS Strong shoots sprouting from the main branches or trunks of fruit trees. If left they will crowd the centres of the trees and so usually they should be cut right out leaving no stumps from which further shoots might grow. Water shoots are often the result of over-feeding especially with nitrogenous manures or fertilizers.

WATTLE Any structure made of interlaced pliable twigs or small branches, which may be either whole or split. Wattle hurdles, which are much used by farmers for penning sheep and other stock, are also sometimes used in the garden as temporary fences, as supports for plants or as screens for slightly tender plants.

WAX Many leaves have a natural covering of wax, e.g. cabbage and laurel, and water falling on them runs into drops. This makes spraying difficult unless a spreader is mixed with the water. The spreader may be soap or a detergent and its purpose is to lower surface tension and permit the water to spread out in an even film.

Paraffin wax or specially prepared waxes are frequently applied to the stems of roses and, less often, other plants lifted for sale. Here the object is to seal the stems and so prevent loss of water and withering while the plants are out of the ground. The waxy covering is harmless and there is no need to remove it.

Waxes of various kinds are used as wound dressings, especially for sealing the wounds made in grafting, see Grafting Wax.

WEB-MAKING CATERPILLARS, see Tent Caterpillars

WEED Any plant growing where it is not required. No hard and fast division can be made between weeds and cultivated plants. Thus grass is a weed in a bed or border or on a path but is a highly desirable plant in a lawn. Snow-in-summer, *Cerastium tomentosum*, can be attractive and useful if kept within bounds, but can become a troublesome weed if allowed to spread too freely.

Weeds can be killed mechanically by hoeing, hand weeding and digging, or they may be killed with various chemicals. When the true definition of a weed is grasped it will be realized how impossible it is to find any chemical which will kill all weeds and spare all cultivated plants.

It may sometimes occur that the removal of the weeds will do more harm than the weeds themselves. This is most likely to be the case if removal necessitates much disturbance of the soil with consequent injury to roots. It is often advised that a covering of weeds should be permitted to grow in orchards from about August to October as this will tend to improve the colour of the fruit and will then supply organic matter which can be dug or ploughed in. It is in any case generally conceded that weeds do most harm to young seedlings and unestablished or small plants and that they are far less damaging, if damaging at all, to larger and more firmly established plants, or to plants which are approaching maturity.

Weeds may be classified as annual and perennial, and, in general, the former are easier to destroy. If they can be prevented from ripening and distributing their seed all trouble will be at an end, provided that the soil is not already full of seeds from earlier crops which have not been controlled. Perennial weeds, by contrast, can continue to live and spread for years without ever producing a seed. Most are weakened and killed in time if they are repeatedly cut off at or just below soil level but some, such as ground elder, couch grass, bindweed and horsetail, show resistance even to this treatment. Some annuals will continue to develop and ripen their seeds even after they have been pulled up or cut down. Groundsel is particularly troublesome in this way and so should always be removed bodily if it is in flower at the time that it is attacked.

Most weeds can be placed on the compost heap to decay and make useful manure but exception should be made in the case of kinds that are known to have great powers of recuperation, for these may continue to grow even after having been in the compost heap for many months. Examples are sorrel, bindweed, docks, dandelions and oxalis. It is also unwise to place weeds that are seeding on the compost heap, since the seeds are unlikely to be destroyed and will be redistributed with the compost.

WEED FORK A small fork usually with two or, at most, three prongs and a cranked shaft, which may be used for grubbing out weeds on lawns or in beds.

WEEDKILLER Various chemicals can be used to kill weeds, but it may be observed that as a weed is simply a plant in the wrong place, all weedkillers are liable to damage some plants that are not regarded as weeds. For garden use weedkillers may be classified in three main groups: contact, selective and residual.

Contact weedkillers kill plants to which they are directly applied and some may remain for a time in the soil, killing or damaging the roots of plants. Sodium chlorate (q.v.) is of this latter kind and so it is usually unsafe to plant or sow anything for some weeks or even months after its application. By contrast, paraquat and diquat, which are also contact weedkillers, are inactivated by the soil and so have no effect on roots and do not damage plants put in or seeds sown after their application.

Selective weedkillers kill some types of

Painting weedkiller directly on to a weed in the lawn

plants but not others. Some, such as 2,4-D, MCPA, mecoprop and ioxynil, kill many broad-leaved herbaceous weeds such as plantains, daisies and buttercups, but are relatively harmless to grass, so they can be applied to lawns to kill the weeds in them. Lawn sand made with sulphate of ammonia and sulphate of iron is also selective on lawns since it lies on and scorches the comparatively broad leaves of weeds but slips off narrower, more vertical leaves of grass. 2,4,5-T kills shrubby plants and brambles, but does little damage to grass.

Residual weedkillers remain as a residue or film in the soil, checking the germination of seeds or killing seedlings and small plants as they attempt to emerge. Simazine and dichlobenil are two of the most valuable weedkillers of this type for garden use.

Some weedkillers, not naturally selective, can be made so by the manner of their application. Paraquat and diquat can be applied direct to the leaves of weeds amongst

growing plants, particularly shrubs, roses and fruit trees, provided they are kept off the leaves and soft stems of the garden plants or trees. They will not harm the roots of these plants since they are inactivated by the soil. Simazine and dichlobenil in moderate doses can be applied to soil beneath shrubs, roses and fruit trees since their roots are too far down to be harmed by them.

All apparatus used for the application of weedkillers should be thoroughly washed after use. If possible such apparatus should not be used for any other purpose, e.g. watering or spraying garden plants, as some weedkillers, especially the selective hormone weedkillers, are extremely persistent and can damage some plants even in minute quantities. Tomatoes are especially sensitive to some of these, such as 2,4-D and MCPA, and grass cuttings from lawns treated with these should not be used as a mulch or top-dressing around tomatoes.

Because of the danger of drift when fine sprays are applied it is usually safer to apply liquid weedkillers from a can or other container fitted with a sprinkle bar which can be held close to the ground or to the weeds to be destroyed, but this method does tend to use up rather more weedkiller than when it is sprayed through a fine nozzle.

WEEPING A term applied to the naturally pendulous habit of some trees and shrubs and also to the practice of training certain plants, including roses, in such a manner that they appear to have a pendulous habit. One of the most familiar examples of a natural weeping habit is to be found in the weeping willow, *Salix babylonica*. There are weeping forms of a great many other trees including the common birch, beech, ash, hornbeam and elm. Many conifers also have weeping forms, including *Chamaecyparis lawsoniana*, the common larch, yew

Selective weedkiller applied to a lawn with the aid of a sprinkle bar attachment on the watering-can. The watering-can should be kept for this purpose only or washed well after use

and *Picea omorika*. *Picea breweriana* is of naturally weeping habit.

WEEVILS A number of weevils attack plants and some are capable of causing serious damage. The adult insects are, in fact, beetles with a characteristically elongated snout. The larva or grub which precedes the adult weevil is often as damaging or even more so than the weevil itself.

One of the most universal and troublesome of these pests is the vine weevil. The creamy white or pale brown grub may be found in the soil feeding on various roots, tubers, corms and bulbs. It is particularly fond of begonias and cyclamen. The weevils themselves are black and they are leaf eaters, their characteristic irregular rather ragged-looking holes often being seen in the leaves of neglected vines.

Closely allied to this is the clay-coloured weevil, the whitish larvae of which are especially fond of the roots of roses though they will also attack many other plants. The weevils themselves are ashen grey.

The pea and bean weevil attacks both peas and broad beans and eats its way right round the edge of each leaf giving it a distinctive scalloped appearance. Seedlings are particularly likely to be attacked and may be weakened by the loss of leaf area.

Fruit growers are familiar with the apple blossom weevil. The adult is dark coloured with a grey V on the wing cases and it feeds on apple (occasionally pear) leaves. More serious damage is done by the small white grub which feeds within the blossom bud before it opens with the result that the bud turns brown and remains shut. Such blossoms are said to be capped and as they are completely destroyed no fruit can be obtained from them. In severe cases the whole of the blossom may be attacked in this way and the crop for that year completely lost.

All weevils are extremely vulnerable to carbaryl and this often provides the best remedy for them. It can be applied as a spray or as a dust. When dealing with apple blossom the period at which carbaryl can be used effectively is rather restricted, the best time usually being the first fortnight in March. In addition, trees may be sprayed with tar oil wash while dormant in winter and bands of hay or sacking may be placed around the trunks of the trees in early June so that weevils may hibernate beneath them and be readily collected and destroyed. For other weevils carbaryl should be applied as soon as an attack is seen to be developing. Derris may be preferred, especially for vegetables and fruits that are to be eaten. With those species which attack the roots of pot plants, repotting is generally the only remedy, coupled with a careful search for the larvae.

WETTABLE POWDERS Chemicals which are not soluble but are prepared as such fine powders that, when stirred vigorously in water, they remain in suspension for some time and can be applied as sprays. See Suspensions.

WETTING AGENT, see Spreader

WHEELBARROW The old-fashioned wooden wheelbarrow with its single wheel and two handles has to some extent been supplanted by modern developments, mostly in the form of metal or fibreglass wheelbarrows with rubber-tyred wheels. As a rule solid rubber tyres are employed, but occasionally the tyres are pneumatic. Other developments are barrows with twin wheels, which are easier to balance when filled with a heavy load but cannot be tipped so readily. Some models are fitted with a tipping body hinged to the main framework to overcome this difficulty.

WHETSTONE Any stone used for sharpening knives, scythes, sickles and similar cutting tools. See Sharpening.

WHIP GRAFT A particular kind of graft much used by fruit growers when working young stocks. See Graft.

WHITE BUD, see Bud Stages

WHITE FLY Tiny white winged insects which sometimes infest tomatoes in such numbers that, if disturbed, the flies appear in a dense white cloud. They are by no means confined to the tomato though they are particularly fond of this plant. Many greenhouse plants are attacked and there are allied white flies which attack plants out of doors, notably cabbages and other members of the brassica family.

In addition to the flies themselves damage is done by the scales which precede the adult stage and are attached like minute limpets to the lower surface of the leaves. Sap is sucked from the leaves and they are fouled with a sticky grey excrement which blocks up the breathing pores (stomata) in the leaves and prevents them from functioning properly. Though plants are seldom killed by white fly they are often severely weakened.

Under glass the most effective method of destroying white flies is by spraying or dusting with BHC, diazinon, malathion or carbaryl. An alternative is to fumigate with tetrachlorethane, an older method which has been largely superseded.

A small wasp-like insect, known as *Encarsia formosa*, preys upon the scales and, if introduced to a greenhouse in which there is a heavy infestation, will soon reduce it very considerably. Scales that have been attacked by this parasite have a distinctive dark appearance and contain the eggs of the parasite. If a leaf bearing scales of this kind is hung up in a greenhouse containing white fly, the parasite will be produced from the eggs and will multiply rapidly. This useful parasite is killed by fumigation with tetrachlorethane and also by cool temperatures so it cannot be over-wintered in an unheated greenhouse.

Out of doors fumigation is useless as a means of controlling white fly, but a fair measure of control can be obtained by occasionally spraying with BHC, carbaryl, diazinon or malathion.

WHITE ROT A disease of onions and allied plants including leeks, shallot and garlic. It is caused by a fungus which may be carried in the soil. Leaves of attacked plants become yellow and limp and roots die so that the whole plant can be pulled up very easily. Fluffy white tufts of mould appear on the bulbs and it is this feature which has occasioned the popular name. Where the disease has occurred it is advisable to give the ground a change of crop for a few years to starve the fungus out. The soil can be sterilized with formalin (see Sterilization) but this is usually too expensive a remedy to be practical in the open. In any case it can only be carried out when all plants have been removed from the ground. Some varieties of onion are much more resistant to the disease than others and it is desirable to grow these if the disease has proved troublesome. Among the resistant varieties are White Spanish, Improved Reading and Up-to-Date. Dressing the seed with 4 per cent. calomel dust will also help to control this disease.

WHITE RUST A disease of brassicas and certain allied plants including stocks, wallflowers and the common weed, shepherd's purse. It is caused by a fungus which produces dense white outgrowth, rather like felt in appearance, on the stems and leaves of attacked plants. Growth may be crippled as a result. Occasional spraying during the summer months with colloidal sulphur, Bordeaux mixture or thiram will prevent the spread of the disease but it is also very desirable to keep down all cruciferous weeds and particularly shepherd's purse.

WHORL A botanical term used to describe the arrangement of several leaves or flowers in the form of a circle at one joint or node on a stem. The flowers of *Primula japonica* are borne in whorls.

WILD GARDEN A term applied to certain kinds of planting in which an attempt is made to simulate nature. At its simplest a few ornamental trees or shrubs may be added to a natural woodland, or the ground beneath the trees may be planted with foxgloves or primroses in irregular drifts but frequently the whole wild garden is planted to a plan which makes it appear natural though it is, in fact, contrived. Great care must be taken to use only those kinds of plants which will be able to fend for themselves against considerable competition, for if too much cultivation is required to keep the plants alive, the natural effect is bound to be lost. As a rule the surface soil in a wild garden cannot be cultivated to any great extent, though it may be necessary to cut down grass and unwanted weeds from time to time with a scythe or rotary grass cutter and so prevent them from choking less vigorous plants which have been introduced by the gardener. A woodland garden may simply be regarded as a particular form of wild garden.

WILT The general name wilt is given to several quite unrelated diseases which are alike in causing a sudden flagging of the leaves of plants while they are in full growth. Of course wilting may also be caused by dryness or by loss of roots due to insect attack or other causes. Brassica plants which have been attacked by cabbage root fly usually wilt severely and this may be the first indication the gardener gets that something is wrong. Excessive watering or rainfall may also cause wilting by bringing about the death of roots by suffocation.

The four diseases that are usually known by the name of wilt are aster wilt, clematis wilt, sleepy disease and spotted wilt. Aster wilt is confined to annual asters (callistephus). It is caused by a fungus which attacks the stem near soil level causing it to decay and turn black. There is no cure, but resistant strains of aster have been raised. The fungus is carried in the soil but can be killed by soil sterilization with steam or formalin.

Clematis wilt is caused by a fungus, *Ascochyta clematidina*. Individual stems or whole plants suddenly wither and die when in full growth. Sometimes new growth appears from the base and occasionally this continues to grow healthily but usually it is soon infected and in turn collapses. Black or dark brown spots may be observed on the leaves and there is discolouration of the stem below the lowest pair of wilting leaves. The disease can be controlled by spraying with a copper fungicide every 14 days from mid- to late spring.

Sleepy disease or wilt is common in tomatoes and is also found in cucumbers, melons, potatoes, sweet peas, perennial asters, carnations and many other plants. It is caused by soil-borne fungi, either species of fusarium or *Verticillium albo-atrum*. Usually there is brown staining of the interior woody tissues of the stem. Little can be done to check the disease once it occurs and affected plants are best burned. Soil in which they have been growing should be sterilized with steam or formalin. Tomatoes can be grafted on a wilt-resistant stock. When wilt in a greenhouse crop is caused by *Verticillium albo-atrum* it may be

possible to check its spread by raising the temperature above 24°C. However, the opposite treatment is necessary to affect wilt caused by fusarium species which thrive in high temperatures (the optimum for them is around 27°C.) and they are checked or killed by lower temperatures.

Spotted wilt occurs in tomatoes and many other greenhouse plants including arum lilies, cinerarias and gloxinias. It is caused by a virus and a distinctive feature is the appearance on the leaves of tiny circular rings which rapidly increase in size. The growing tip of the plant often has a bronzed appearance, many leaves curve downwards and the plant becomes stunted and eventually dies. There is no cure and affected plants should be burned. As infection is spread by thrips and also on pruning knives the former should be destroyed by fumigation or spraying and the latter should be sterilized with a strong disinfectant such as lysol.

WIND Moving air can have a considerable influence upon the behaviour of plants, particularly if it is moving at such a velocity as to constitute a strong wind or gale. The influence may be in one of two ways, either direct disturbance of the plant, which, in severe form, may result in the roots of the plants being dragged bodily out of the soil, or an increase in the rate at which water is lost from the leaves by surface evaporation. The former needs little comment as the results are obvious, but damage of the latter kind may often be puzzling and be attributed to causes other than wind. Familiar symptoms are browning of leaf margins or a mottled browning of the whole leaf, and such markings may easily be mistaken for those caused by disease. Sharp draughts in greenhouses or frames will cause precisely the same symptoms, particularly on the tender young leaves of such plants as tomatoes or grape vines. Almost precisely similar damage can be caused under glass by sun scorch, and it is sometimes difficult to decide whether a particular outbreak of scorching is, in fact, due to strong sunshine or to draughts.

Out of doors, wind damage causing leaf scorching may be confused with damage caused by frost, and it is not possible to give any general rules by which one kind of damage may be distinguished from the other. The atmospheric conditions which have been prevailing during the few days before the damage is observed will usually give the clue. Some plants which are highly resistant to wind damage are extremely sensitive to frost damage and vice versa. A good example of the former can be found in *Senecio rotundifolius*, which in some very exposed gardens in Cornwall is used as an outer windbreak against Atlantic gales in positions in which few other evergreens would survive, yet is killed by temperatures

a few degrees below freezing point. See Protection.

WINDFALL Any fruit that falls by natural causes and is not picked. Such fruits are almost invariably bruised and, though they may be quite satisfactory for immediate use, no attempt should be made to store them as they will quickly decay.

WINDOW BOXES Boxes or containers specially made to be placed on window ledges, or to be suspended from such ledges, and to contain plants. It is obviously not as easy to devise a box for casement windows which must open outwards as for sash windows which are moved vertically. One way in which this difficulty can be overcome is by hanging the box a few inches below the level of the window ledge and by planting it entirely with trailing or low-growing plants. Window boxes can also be used in many places that could not be strictly described as windows, e.g. on the tops of porticos, on verandahs, balconies and in paved gardens.

Well-managed boxes can add greatly to the effectiveness of most buildings. They may be permanently planted with small evergreen shrubs and hardy perennials, or filled with temporary plants such as spring and summer bedding plants, including bulbs of many kinds. One very convenient method of ensuring a succession of flowers in window boxes is to prepare containers that will fit exactly in each box, and to have two or three containers for every box. These containers are filled with soil and suitable plants, and placed in a frame or greenhouse from which they can be removed to the window box when the plants are about to flower.

Whatever method is used, plants should be grown in a normal potting compost such as the John Innes compost or good soilless compost (see Compost). Window boxes and any containers made for them must be provided with holes through which surplus moisture can drain.

Choice of plants for window boxes must be conditioned to a large extent by the aspect of the box and the kind of atmosphere in which the plants will grow. Thus for a sunny window zonal pelargoniums, ivy-leaved pelargoniums, heliotropes, marguerites, lobelias, tropaeolums, gazanias, mesembryanthemums, stocks, zinnias, and sweet alyssum may be used for a summer display. Where there is little or no sunshine violas, pansies, bedding calceolarias, asters, begonias, and fuchsias will succeed; also the trailing *Campanula isophylla* and foliage plants such as *Glechoma hederacea variegata* and *Zebrina pendula*. For spring display daffodils, tulips (particularly the short-stemmed varieties), hyacinths, crocuses and other spring flowering bulbs may be used as well as wallflowers, primroses, polyanthus and double daisies, and these succeed quite well in all aspects, sunny and shaded.

Plants growing in potting compost in window boxes will need to be watered frequently, particularly during the summer months. During sunny weather it may even be necessary to water south-facing boxes twice a day.

WIND POLLINATION In many plants pollen is transferred from the anthers to the stigmas of the flowers by insects, but in some it is carried by wind, and such plants are said to be wind pollinated. Most of the catkin-bearing trees are of this type, for example, hazel and alder. It is probable that even with insect-pollinated flowers, such as those of fruit trees, wind is also an important agency for effecting pollination. Without pollination no fruit or seed can, as a rule, be produced.

WINDROCKING Disturbance of plants caused by wind. It is particularly likely to occur with recently planted trees and shrubs and can do a great deal of damage or even cause death. Roots may be broken or the constant movement may prevent new roots being formed. The main stem, where it enters the soil, may work itself a funnel-like hole in the soil in which water will collect, causing decay. Trees that have been badly windrocked in winter will often start into growth in the spring and then, after a week or so, all the leaves will wither and the trees will die. This is sometimes referred to as 'the death' and the explanation is that the roots or the main stem at, or just below, soil level are already dead, the leaves are produced from sap remaining in the stems and when this is exhausted the tree collapses. To prevent windrocking trees and shrubs must be firmly planted and securely staked.

WINDSCREEN Any protection provided specifically against wind. It may take the form of a wall, fence, hedge or belt of trees. See Wind and Protection.

WINTER GARDEN A large conservatory or greenhouse in which plants are grown in beds or borders with paths between, the effect being that of a garden under glass.

WINTER MOTHS Three species of moth, the winter moth, the mottled umber, and the March moth are known as winter moths because they lay their eggs in winter (March in the case of the March moth). The eggs are laid on fruit trees, principally apples, and the caterpillars hatch out just as the trees break into leaf in the spring. The result of a severe attack may be the complete loss of the leaves and this inflicts a very severe check on the trees.

There are three main ways of destroying these pests. First the moths themselves may be trapped by means of grease bands (q.v.).

The caterpillar of a winter moth and the damage it can cause to foliage

A second method is to spray the trees with tar oil winter wash or DNC, between December and early March, with the object of destroying the eggs. The later in the winter this can be applied the more likely it is to kill the eggs, but unfortunately the more likely it is to cause scorching of the fruit trees' buds and young growth. In general tar oil washes are applied in January and DNC washes the last week in February or first in March.

A third line of attack is to spray or dust with BHC, carbaryl or trichlorphon at the green bud and pink bud stages (about mid-April).

WINTER SPORES Many fungi, including a lot that cause plant diseases, produce spores in the autumn or early winter of a different character from those produced in spring or summer. These spores are able to resist cold or drought and to remain dormant for a considerable period, for which reason they are also known as resting spores. It is by these spores that the fungus is carried over from one year to another.

WINTER WASH Any insecticide or fungicide primarily intended to be applied during winter when plants are dormant. The name is particularly used for various insecticides derived from tar oil and petroleum and used mainly on fruit trees with the purpose of killing insects and insect eggs and cleaning from the bark lichen, algae and other unwanted growths. Winter washes of this kind form an important part of the spray routine in the fruit garden, for by their use trees can be given a comparatively clean start in spring. Tar oil and petroleum winter washes have little or no effect on fungi nor do they affect those pests which attack the trees during the spring and summer but are not on them in the winter. For further particulars regarding the application of these sprays, see Tar Oil Wash, Petroleum Oil DNC and Insecticides.

WIRESTEM A name applied to a particular type of foot rot or damping-off disease which attacks brassica seedlings and causes

the stems to shrivel and turn brown. Affected plants should be burned. As a preventive, seed can be dressed with captan or thiram before it is sown and quintozene can be raked into the soil before brassica seedlings are planted.

WIREWORMS The larvae of certain beetles found in the soil and popularly known as click beetles because some of them make a clicking noise with their wings. The beetles are brown, active and about half an inch in length. The wireworms are yellow, shiny and hard skinned, very slow in their movements, with segmented bodies and three pairs of legs near the head. They may be anything from a third of an inch to nearly an inch in length. Centipedes are sometimes mistaken for wireworms as they are also yellow, shiny and hard skinned, but they have a much greater number of legs and are very active.

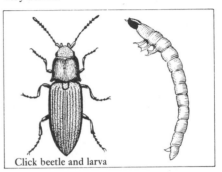

Click beetle and larva

Wireworms live in the soil and eat the roots of many different plants. They frequently bore into potatoes, making numerous narrow holes, and they may also attack fleshy seeds such as those of peas or beans. Attack is likely to be most severe on newly broken grassland and damage frequently reaches its climax the second year after the grass is turned in. As a rule wireworms tend to disappear with continued and thorough cultivation. Finely powdered naphthalene forked into vacant ground at 4 oz. per sq. yd. or round growing crops at 2 oz. per sq. yd. will lessen damage but will not entirely eliminate wireworms. This can be done by forking in lindane dust at 2 oz. per sq. yd., preferably in early autumn but this substance may sometimes impart a musty flavour to root crops, particularly if it is not very pure or is applied too close to planting time. Alternatives are naphthalene and paradichlorbenzene. Wireworms can also be trapped by burying sliced potatoes or carrots just below the surface of the soil. If these traps are impaled on sharp sticks which are left projecting from the soil it will be easy to collect them every day or so and destroy any wireworms they may have attracted to them.

WITCHES' BROOM Twiggy outgrowths sometimes found on trees and caused by a local irritation of the living tissue of the tree, which may be due to gall insects or to fungal infection. These curious growths are particularly common on birch trees though they may be found on all kinds of trees, including conifers. When the witches' broom is caused by fungal infection it will often be found that cuttings or grafts prepared from the affected shoots will continue to behave in the same curious manner and it is in this way that some of the dwarf or congested forms of familiar trees and conifers have been obtained.

WOOD ASH The ash obtained by burning wood is a valuable garden fertilizer because of the potash which it contains in the form of carbonate of potash. As this is a soluble chemical it will be washed out of the wood ashes fairly quickly if they are exposed to rain. For this reason wood ash should be stored in a dry place. It can be used at any time of the year either as a topdressing or worked into the soil at the rate of about 8 oz. per sq. yd. A good sample of wood ash may contain as much as 7 per cent. potash. The best quality wood ash is obtained from a rather slow-burning fire.

WOODLAND GARDEN A natural woodland has certain advantages as a site for a garden and also certain limitations. If carefully planted with suitable undergrowth, it may be made almost entirely self-supporting and require very little attention beyond the occasional cutting down of coarse growth and weeds. Nevertheless, because of the shade and the competition of tree roots, the range of plants that can be grown successfully is limited. Rhododendrons and azaleas thrive well under these conditions provided the shade is not too dense. Many other shrubs and shade-loving perennials can also be established successfully. Some examples are evening primrose, *Oenothera biennis*, common foxglove, *Digitalis purpurea*, verbascums, some of the taller campanulas and notably *Campanula lactiflora*, many lilies, the Willow Gentian, *Gentiana asclepiadea*, hellebores, including *Helleborus orientalis* and *Helleborus corsicus*, lily of the valley, polygonatum, trilliums, erythroniums, primroses, violets, periwinkles, wood anemones such as *Anemone nemorosa* and its varieties, hepaticas, heracleums, hostas, epimediums, lythrums, lysimachia and several of the hardy geraniums. Amongst shrubs, camellias are useful provided the shade is not too dense and many vacciniums and gaultherias can also be grown in non-calcareous soil. Many kinds of bulbs can also be planted including bluebells and daffodils. The planting of the woodland garden may be on natural lines with paths winding amongst irregular groups of shrubs and plants and some open glades; alternatively, wide, more or less straight paths, or

rides, may be cut through the wood to provide long vistas.

WOODLICE These familiar grey or blackish, hard-coated creatures, which roll themselves into a ball when disturbed, can be troublesome in the greenhouse, though they seldom do any serious damage out of doors. In the main they live on decaying wood and other refuse and may be regarded as scavengers but they are also quite capable of turning their attention to soft-stemmed plants and in particular to very small and tender seedlings, which they will sometimes mow off at soil level. Woodlice have various names in different parts of the country, slaters and pillbugs being two of the commonest. They may be trapped in flower pots stuffed with straw or hay and either inverted or laid on their sides, or in scooped-out potatoes placed on the soil. Decaying refuse should be burned or placed on the compost heap. Soil around seed boxes can be dusted or watered with BHC or carbaryl.

WOOD PRESERVATIVES Various substances can be used to preserve wood against decay caused by fungal infection. Tar and creosote are good preservatives but can be harmful to plants, creosote especially since fumes capable of scorching leaves can be given off months after application, particularly in hot weather. Copper napththenate is an even more efficient preservative and is harmless to plants. It is a liquid sold under various trade names ready for application with a brush, spray or by immersion.

WOOLLY APHID A species of aphid common on apple trees. It attacks the wood, often destroying buds in the process, causing gouty-looking swellings and cracks which may later develop canker. The most distinctive feature of the pest is the white, wool-like excretion with which it covers itself. A badly attacked tree may look as if it had been plastered with small wads of cotton wool. This covering acts as an efficient protection to the insect and unless sprays are applied with great force or insecticides are worked right into the woolly patches with a stiff brush, they may be quite ineffective. Tar oil wash may be applied in

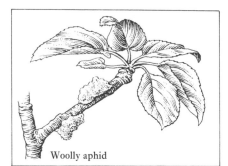
Woolly aphid

early January or nicotine at any time during the summer. An alternative is to spray heavily in early June with dimethoate or malathion and repeat a fortnight later. Methylated spirit or paraffin may be brushed directly into the woolly patches but care should be taken to keep these substances off the leaves. There is also a form of woolly aphid which lives on the roots of the trees, though this seldom, if ever, occurs in the British Isles. The fruit stocks known as Malling-Merton (MM) are resistant to this pest and should be used where it is troublesome. There are dwarfing, semi-dwarfing and vigorous varieties of these MM stocks.

WORKED A grafted or budded tree is said to be top worked when the scion or bud has been inserted high up on the stock, which thus provides all or most of the main trunk of the tree as well as its roots. It is said to be bottom worked when the scion or bud is inserted at or near soil level so that the stock provides little or no trunk but only roots.

WORMS, see Earthworms

WOUND DRESSINGS Stockholm tar, various bituminous products, white lead paint and grafting wax are used to seal large wounds made in pruning or when repairing storm damage to trees. The purpose is to exclude fungi and insects but it should be observed that most wound dressings slow down the rate of natural healing. It is only advisable to use them, therefore, for large wounds which might take months or even years to heal over completely and also for wounds made in removing diseased branches or when there is other strong reason to believe that infection is likely.

ZINC COLLARS Strips of zinc of any convenient length and about 2 in. in breadth, are sometimes placed in the form of collars round the bases of plants that are liable to be attacked by slugs, the idea being that these pests will not readily scale such barriers to reach the plants within. The base of each collar should be placed firmly on the soil and care should be taken to see that the two ends of the collar meet closely.

ZINEB A fungicide which gives effective control of many diseases including potato blight, tomato leaf mould, various mildews and rusts, black currant leaf spot and tulip fire. It has a low mammalian toxicity but should be kept off the skin and should not be inhaled. It is available as a dust for direct application, or as a wettable powder to be stirred into water as directed by the manufacturers and kept agitated while applied as a spray.

ZONING, see Hardy